I0820003

Wisdom of Ancient Sumer

WISDOM OF ANCIENT SUMER

Bendt Alster

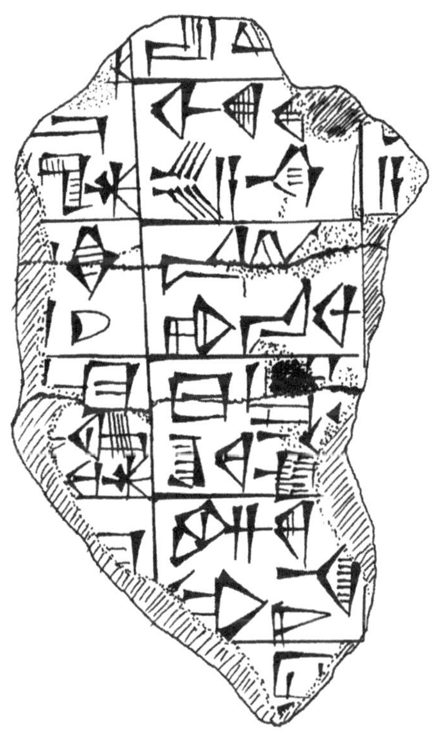

CDL Press
Bethesda, Maryland

LIBRARY OF CONGRESS CATALOGING-IN-PUBLICATION DATA

Alster, Bendt
Wisdom of ancient Sumer / Bendt Alster.
p. cm.
In English; Sumerian texts in transliteration and translation.
Includes bibliographical references and index.
ISBN 1-883053-92-7
1. Sumerian literature. I. Alster, Bendt. II. Title.

PJ4051.A45 2005
899'.9508—dc22 2005045764

Front page and cover illustration: Copy of an Adab tablet inscribed with *The Instructions of Šuruppak*, by Aage Westenholz.

Published by CDL Press, P.O. Box 34454, Bethesda, MD 20827;
E-Mail: cdlpress@erols.com; website: www.cdlpress.com; Fax: 253-484-5542

ISBN 1-883053-927

Preface

Already in 1944, in his pioneering book *Sumerian Mythology*, S.N. Kramer outlined the potential prospect of a full reconstruction of Sumerian literature, whose rediscovery, to a very large extent, was his own merit. But already in the second edition, from 1961, he realized that definitive editions of all the relevant texts "could not possibly be produced by one man." By that time, the first overviews of Sumerian wisdom literature had been made by J.J.A. van Dijk, in 1953, and Edmund I. Gordon, in 1960. The present work owes much to their pioneering efforts.

My own interest in the texts presented here started in 1971, when, at the suggestion of Prof. Å. Sjöberg, then curator of the tablet collection of the University Museum in Philadelphia, I made a first attempt to reconstruct *The Instructions of Šuruppak*. Since the appearance of the first edition, in 1974, new texts, thanks in large part to identifications made by W.G. Lambert and M. Civil, and numerous suggestions by various scholars have made a new revised edition mandatory. The present edition will seek to answer this demand, but it claims to be no more than another small step on a progressing scale of constant new discoveries and a growing degree of philological precision that enables us slowly to approach such difficult texts as would have been considered almost incomprehensible only fifty years ago.

An attempt is made to include some other Sumerian texts representing what may be considered Sumerian "wisdom literature." Although hardly speculative, some of them certainly represent a critical attitude toward existing values, which may be considered an unmistakable sign of ancient Near Eastern "wisdom" literature.

To thank individually and in detail all those scholars and institutions without whose help, hospitality, and assistance this work could not have been completed, a very long list would be needed indeed. The following names would be at the head of this list: Å.W. Sjöberg, the former curator of the Babylonian Section of the University Museum of the University of Pennsylvania, thanks to whose hospitality the tablet room became a true and inspiring center for Sumerological studies; W.G. Lambert, whose unequalled insight into the huge tablet collection of the British Museum led to the identification of the uniquely interesting Middle Babylonian version of *The Instructions of Šuruppak*. Since this was intended to be published in a second edition of *Babylonian Wisdom Literature*, I wish to express my gratitude for being allowed to include it here; M. Civil of the Oriental Institute of the University of Chicago has inspired every page of this work by his unique insight into Sumerian literature and lexicography; also my time at the Babylonian Collection of Yale University is remembered with gratitude, where, thanks to the hospitality of W.W. Hallo, the former curator of the Babylonian Collection of Yale University, I was able to search for duplicates in its tablet collections; and the staff of the Department of the Ancient Near East of the British Museum on innumerable occasions offered aid and assistance.

Special thanks are addressed to those who enabled me to study the Abū Ṣalābīkh sources in the Iraq Museum in 1990: Sabah Jasim, the former director of the Iraq Museum; Muajjed Damirji, the then Director-General of Antiquities and Heritage in Iraq; the British School of Archaeology in Iraq; Roger Matthews, the then director of the British Archaeological Expedition to Iraq; the then staff of the British Archaeological Expedition to Iraq in Baghdad.

A number of tablets from the British Museum are published here for the first time, with the permission of the Trustees of the British Museum.

The following scholars kindly provided unpublished material: the late Prof. I. Diakonoff and Dr. Irina Kaneva, in 1974, provided a transliteration of a tablet in the Hermitage in St. Petersburg—this was kindly collated by Th. Kämmerer, Talin, in 2002. A. Shaffer of the Hebrew University of Jerusalem provided copies of some tablets from Ur, which he had prepared in the British Museum.

Two tablets inscribed with proverbs in the Carl A. Kroch Library, Cornell University, are published here through the courtesy of David I. Owen, Curator of Tablet Collections, who supplied excellent digital photos and collations.

Martin Schøyen, the owner of the Schøyen Collection in Oslo, and his editorial staff headed by Prof. Jens Braarvig have kindly consented to the use of some cuneiform tablets owned by the Schøyen Collection.

Thanks are due to the following colleagues for providing photographs: D.I. Owen of Cornell University; Eleanor Robson of Oxford University, now Cambridge; R.D. Biggs for photographs reproduced here by courtesy of the Oriental Institute in Chicago; Renee Kovacs for photographs taken in the Schøyen Collection in Oslo; Bodil Bundgaard Rasmussen for photographs reproduced here by courtesy of the Antiquities Department of the National Museum in Copenhagen; Kevin Danti for photographs taken in the University Museum, Philadelphia; Jacob Dahl, p.t. Paris, for photographs taken in the Jena Collection; Peter Damerow of the Max Planck Institute for the History of Science in Berlin for photographs taken in the Schøyen Collection.

The following scholars helped with collations: M. Krebernik, Jena; Th. Kämmerer, Talin; Marie-Christine Ludwig, London; Jacob Dahl in the Louvre, Paris. M. Krebernik made an invaluable copy of a tablet in the Jena Collection published here for the first time.

The following colleagues have read parts of the manuscript in previous stages and have made invaluable suggestions and corrections: M.J. Geller, without whose constant encouragement over many years this manuscript would not have been completed; Laura Feldt and Dina Katz, for whose critical comments I am particularly thankful; Aa. Westenholz, G. Wilhelm, Jon Taylor, Thomas Kämmerer, and Helle Bak Rasmussen have read parts of the manuscript and made invaluable comments; the comments of Niek Veldhuis and J. Black have been indispensable for two chapters in this book; G. Wilhelm wrote the chapter included here on the Hurrian version of *The Instructions of Šuruppak*, a language into which I was totally uninitiated; M.J. Geller provided the copy of the Neo-Assyrian version of *The Ballade of Early Rulers*, identified by R. Borger and published here; Niels W. Bruun and Finn Gredal Jensen of the Søren Kierkegaard Institute of the University of Copenhagen provided useful comments and references regarding classical languages and medieval literature.

Among those scholars who allowed me to use studies before their publication, I wish to thank in particular M. Civil, J. Black, J. Klein, G. Selz, and P. Michalowski.

Among the many colleagues who over the years have contributed directly or indirectly by discussions or critical comments I want to thank in particular: W.G. Lambert, D.O. Edzard, A. Cavigneaux, H. Vanstiphout, Gonzalo Rubio, and J.M. Sasson.

Thanks are due to the Carlsberg Foundation, the Danish Research Council for the Humanities, the G.E.C. Gads Foundation, and the British School of Archaeology in Iraq for financial support.

In publishing this work I wish to acknowledge the great inspiration I have received from W.G. Lambert's work *Babylonian Wisdom Literature*, which since 1960 has become an inexhaustible source of inspiration for everyone interested in the literature of the ancient Near East.

This work was considered completed in the spring of 2004, but I have tried to incorporate what has appeared since then to the extent possible. I have tried, in all fairness, to take all important contributions into account, and I apologize for anything significant that I may have overlooked, as well as for all errors for which I am alone responsible. As everyone in this field knows, it may, I hope, be a consolation that no one has ever made progress in the field of Sumerology without occasionally stumbling over some of the many pitfalls that constantly lie in wait for us.

Bendt Alster
Helsingør, Denmark
February 2005

Table of Contents

Literature

T. Abusch (ed.), *Riches Hidden in Secret Places, Ancient Near Eastern Studies in Memory of Thorkild Jacobsen*. Eisenbrauns, Winona Lake, Ind., 2002.

B. Alster, *The Instructions of Suruppak*. Mesopotamia. Copenhagen Studies in Assyriology 2. Copenhagen, 1974.

———, *Studies in Sumerian Proverbs*. Mesopotamia. Copenhagen Studies in Assyriology 3. Copenhagen, 1975.

———, "Paradoxical Proverbs and Satire in Sumerian Literature," JCS 27 (1975) 210–230.

———, "Sumerian Proverb Collection xxiv," *Assyriological Miscellanies* 2 (1980) 33–50.

———, "Additional Fragments of The Instructions of Shuruppak," AuOr 5 (1987) 199–206.

———, "Shuruppak's Instructions—Additional Lines Identified in the Early Dynastic Version," ZA 80 (1990) 15–19.

———, "The Sumerian Poem of Early Rulers and Related Poems," in: OLP 21 (Leuven, 1990) 5–25.

———, "Sumerian Literary Dialogues and Debates and Their Place in Ancient Near Eastern Literature," in: *Living Waters—Scandinavian Orientalistic Studies presented to F. Løkkegaard*. Copenhagen, 1990, pp. 1–16.

———, "The Instructions of Ur-Ninurta and Related Poems," *Orientalia* 60 (1991) 1–17. Cf. "Corrections to The Instructions of Urninurta and Related Compositions," N.A.B.U. 83 (1991) 63.

———, "Väterliche Weisheit in Mesopotamien," in: Aleida Assmann (ed.), *Weisheit. Archäologie der literarischen Kommunikation III*, (Symposium: Urgeschichte der Weisheit. Werner-Reimer-Stiftung, 7–10. September 1987). Wilhelm Fink Verlag, München, 1991, pp. 103–115.

———, "OIP 99, 256: Collations to Šuruppak's Instruction, ED Version," pp. 32–34 + 51 in: "Early Dynastic Proverbs and Other Contributions to the Study of Literary Texts from Abū Ṣalābīkh," AfO 38–39 (1991–92) 1–51.

———, "An Akkadian Animal Proverb and the Assyrian Letter ABL 555," JCS 41 (1991) 187–193.

———, "Two Sumerian Short Tales Reconsidered," ZA 82 (1992) 186–201.

———, "The Sumerian Folktale of the Three Ox-Drivers from Adab," JCS 43–45 (1991–93) 27–38.

———, "Enmerkar, Lugalbanda, and Other Cunning Heroes," in: CANE IV, 2315–2326.

———, "Halt or Dwarf: The Meaning of ba-za = *pessû*," in: *von Soden AV*, 1–6.

———, "Literary Aspects of Sumerian and Akkadian Proverbs," in: *Mesopotamian Poetic Language: Sumerian and Akkadian*. Proceedings of the Groningen Symposium: The Study of Mesopotamian Literature, M.E. Vogelzang and H.L.J. Vanstiphout (eds.). Cuneiform Monographs 6. Styx Publications, Groningen, 1996, pp. 1–21.

———, *Proverbs of Ancient Sumer* I–II. CDL Press, Bethesda, Md., 1997.

———, "Updates to Šuruppak's Instructions, Proverbs of Ancient Sumer, and Ancient Rulers," *N.A.B.U.* 89 (1999) 88ff.

———, "*ilū awīlum: we-e i-la*, Punning and Reversal of Patterns in the Atrahasis Epic," in: *Jacobsen MV*, 35–40.

———, "Relative Construction and Case Relations in Sumerian," WZKM 92 (2002) 7–31.

———, "Why Wisdom Literature—or Why Not?" in: The Groningen Symposium 1995: *Genre*. Styx, Groningen: 2006 (forthcoming).

———, "Nanše and Her Fish," in: *Klein FS*, 1–18.

———, "Gudam and the Bull of Heaven," in: *Larsen AV*, 21–45.

———, "Text and Images on the Stele of the Vultures," AfO 50 (2005).

———, "Ninurta and the Turtle: On Parodia Sacra in Sumerian Literature," (forthcoming).

B. Alster and U. Jeyes, "A Sumerian Poem about Early Rulers," AcSum 8 (1986) 1–11.

B. Alster and H. Vanstiphout, "Lahar and Ashnan. Presentation and Analysis of a Sumerian Literary Dispute," AcSum 9 (1987) 1–43.

B. Alster and Aa. Westenholz, "The Barton Cylin-

der," AcSum 16 (1994) 15–46.
D. Arnaud, *Emar VI/4: Textes de la bibliothèque: transcriptions et traductions*. Missions Archaéologique de Meskéné-Emar, Recherches au pays d'Aštata, 1987.
A. and J. Assmann, *Weisheit. Archäologie der literarischen Kommmunikation*, Bd. 3. Wilhelm Fink Verlag, München, 1991.
P. Attinger, "L'Hymne à Nungal," in: *Wilcke FS*, 15–34.
———, "Les préfixes absolutifs de la première et de la deuxième personne dans les formes marû ergatives," ZA 75 (1985) 161–178.
———, *Eléments de linguistique sumérienne. La construction de* du_{11}*/e/di «dire»* (OBO, Sonderband). Fribourg Suisse & Ruprecht Göttingen: Editions Universitaires/Vandenhoeck, 1993.
J. Bauer, *Altsumerische Wirtschaftstexte aus Lagasch*. Würzburg, 1967.
G. Beckman, "Proverbs and Proverbial Allusions in Hittite," JNES 45 (1986) 19–30.
R.D. Biggs, "The Abū Ṣalābīkh Tablets. A Preliminary Report," JCS 20 (1966) 73–88.
———, "An Archaic Sumerian Version of the Kesh Temple Hymn from Tell Abū Ṣalābīkh," ZA 61 (1971) 193–207.
———, *Inscriptions from Tell Abū Ṣalābīkh*, OIP 99. Chicago, 1974.
———, "The Semitic Personal Names from Abū Ṣalābīkh and the Personal Names from Ebla," in: *Eblaite Personal Names*, 1988, pp. 89–117.
J.A. Black, *Sumerian Grammar in Babylonian Theory*, Studia Pohl, Ser. Maior 12. Rome, 1984.
———, "A Note on Genre and Translation," in *The Groningen Workshop on Genre* 1995. Forthcoming 2006(?).
———, *Reading Sumerian Poetry*. Cornell University Press, Ithaca, 1998.
J. Bottéro and S.N. Kramer, *Losque les dieux faisaient l'homme: mythologie mésopotamienne*. Éditions Gallimard, 1989.
S. Brock, "The Dispute Poem: From Sumer to Syriac," in: *Bayn al-Nahrayn (Mosul)*, Vol. 7 (28) (1974) 426–417.
G. Buccellati, "Tre saggi sulla sapienza mesopotamica," OA 11 (1972) 1–178.
———, "Wisdom and Not: The Case of Mesopotamia," in *JAOS* 101 (1981) 35–47.
J.L. Burckard, *Arabische Sprüchwörter oder die Sitten und Gebräuche der neueren Aegyptier*. Weimer, 1834.
A. Cavigneaux, in: *Bagdader Mitteilungen* 13 (1982) 22 + 24 (copy of W 20248,5).
———, "Notes Sumérologiques," AcSum 9 (1987) 45–66.
———, "Miette de l'Eduba," in: *Limet FS*, 11–26.
———, "Fragments littéraires susiens," in: *Wilcke FS*, 53–62.
A. Cavigneaux and Farouk N.H. Al-Rawi, "New Sumerian Literary Texts from Tell Haddad (Ancient Meturan): A First Survey," *Iraq* 55 (1993) 91–106.
———, *Gilgamesh et la Mort*. Texts de Tell Haddad VI, avec un appendice sur les textes funéraires sumériens. Cuneiform Monographs, 19. Styx, Groningen, 2000.
D. Charpin, *Le clergé d'Ur au siècle d'Hammurapi (XIX–XVIIIe siècle av. J.C.)*, Hautes études orientales, 22. Genève, Paris, 1986.
M. Civil, "Notes on Sumerian Lexicography, I," JCS 20 (1966) 119–121.
———, "Supplement to the Introduction to ISET I," *Orientalia* 41 (1972) 83–90.
———, "Enlil and Namzitarra," AfO 25 (1974/75) 65–71.
———, "Notes on the Instructions of Šuruppak," JNES 43 (1984) 281–298.
———, "Bilingualism in Logographically Written Languages: Sumerian in Ebla," in: L. Cagni (ed.), *Il Bilinguismo a Ebla*. Istituto Universitario orientale, Dipt. di studi asiatici, Series Minor xxii. Napoli, 1984, pp. 75–97.
———, "Feeding Dumuzi's Sheep: The Lexicon as a Source of Literary Inspiration," in: *American Oriental Series* 67 (E. Reiner vol.; 1987) 37–55.
———, "Sur les 'livres d'écolier' à l'époque paléo-babylonienne," in: *Birot FS*, 67–78.
———, "More Additional Fragments of the Instructions of Shuruppak," AuOr 5 (1987) 207–210.
———, "Sumerian Riddles: A Corpus," in AuOr 5 (1987) 17–37.
———, "The Texts from Meskéné-Emar," AuOr 7 (1989) 5–25.
———, "On Mesopotamian Jails and Their Lady Warren," in: *Hallo FS*, 1993, pp. 72–78.
———, *The Farmer's Instructions. A Sumerian Agricultural Manual*. AuOr Supplementa 5. Sabadell, AUSA, 1994.
———, "The Instructions of King Ur-Ninurta: A New Fragment," AuOr 15 (1997) 43–53.
———, "Bilingual Teaching," in: *Borger FS*, 1–7.
———, "Modal Prefixes," AcSum 22 (2000).

———, "The Forerunners of *Marû* and *Ḫamṭu* in Old Babylonian," in: *Jacobsen MV*, 63–71.
———, "Reading Gilgameš II," *Wilcke FS*, 77–86.
———, "Misogynic Themes in Sumerian Literature," paper read at the 47th RAI, Helsinki, 2001 (forthcoming).
M. Civil and R.D. Biggs, "Notes sur des textes sumériens archaïques," RA 60 (1966) 1–16.
M.E. Cohen, *The Canonical Lamentations of Ancient Mesopotamia*, CDL Press, Bethesda, Md., 1988.
F.C. Conybeare, J. Rendel Harris and A.S. Lewis, *The Story of Aḥikar*. London, 1898.
J.S. Cooper, "Bilinguals from Boghazköi. I," ZA 61 (1971) 1–22.
———, "Bilinguals from Boghazköi. II," ZA 62 (1972) 62–81.
———, "Bilingual Babel: Cuneiform Texts in Two or More Languages from Ancient Mesopotamia and Beyond," *Visible Language* 27 (1993) 68–96.
———, "Sumerian and Semitic Writing in Most Ancient Syro-Mesopotamia," in: RAI 42 = OLA 96 (1999) 61–77.
J.L. Crenshaw, "The Contemplative Life in the Ancient Near East," in: CANE, 2445–2457.
M. Dietrich, "Die akkadischen Texte der Archiven und Bibliotheken von Emar," UF 22 (1990) 25–48.
———, "Dialogue zwischen Šūpê-amēli und seinem 'Vater'," UF 23 (1991) 38–65.
———, "«Ein Leben ohne Freude». Studie über eine Weisheitskomposition aus dem Gelehrtenbibliotheken von Emar und Ugarit," UF 24 (1992) 9–29.
J.J.A. van Dijk, *La sagesse suméro-accadiens: Recherches sur des genres littéraires des texte sapientiaux avec choix de textes*. Leiden, 1953.
———, *LUGAL UD ME-LÁM-bi NIR-GÁL, Texte, Tradution et Introduction*. Brill, Leiden, 1983.
———, "«Inanna raubt den großen Himmel.» Ein Mythos," in: *Borger FS*, 9–38.
J.J.A. van Dijk and M.J. Geller, *Ur-III Incantations, Texte und Materialien aus der Hilprecht Sammlung*. Jena 6. Harrassowitz, Wiesbaden, 2003.
Disticha Catonis, conveniently available in *Minor Latin Poets*, in The Loeb Classical Library.
E. Ebeling, "Dei babylonische Fabel und ihre Bedeutung für die Literaurgeschichte," in: *Mitteilungen der Altorientalischen Gesellschaft*, 2. Band Heft 3. Leipzig, 1927.
———, *Tod und Leben nach der Vorstellung der Babylonier*. Berlin/Leipzig, 1931.
D.O. Edzard, "Sumerische Komposita mit dem «nominalpräfix» nu," ZA 55 (1963) 91–112.
———, "Fara und Abū Ṣalābīkh. Die «Wirtschafttexte»," ZA 66 (1977) 156–195.
———, *Sumerian Grammar*, Handbook of Oriental Studies, Section One, The Near and Middle East, vol. 27. Brill, Leiden, 2003.
———, "Das sumerische Verbalmorphem /ed/ in den alt- und neusumerischen Texten," in: HSAO, 29–62.
ETCSL, Oxford Electronic Text Corpus of Sumerian Literature: http://www-etcsl.orient.ox.ac.uk/catalogue/, by J.A. Black, E. Robson, G. Cunningham, G. Zólyomi. (Sub 6: many valuable observations on Sumerian proverbs by Jon Taylor, 2003).
A. Falkenstein, "Das Potentialis- und Irrealissuffix -e-še des Sumerischen," in: *Indogermanische Forschungen* 60. Berlin, 1952, pp. 113–130.
———, "Sumerische religiöse Texte" 1–3, ZA 50 (1952) 61–91; 55 (1963) 11–67; 56 (1964) 44–129.
R.S. Falkowitz, "Discrimination and Condensation of Sacred Categories: The Fable in Early Mesopotamian Literature," in: *Entretients sur l'antiquité classique*, Tome xxv. Fondations Hardt, Vandœvres-Genève, 1984, pp. 1–32.
A. Finet, "Citations littéraires dans la correspondance de Mari," RA 68 (1974) 35–47.
I.L. Finkel, "Bilingual Proverbs: An Unexpected Join," *N.A.B.U.* (1993) 15, p. 11. (BM 38297+ joins BWL 267–269 = pl. 69).
E. Fischer-Jørgensen, *Almen fonetik*, 3rd ed. Copenhagen, 1974.
E. Flückiger-Hawker, "Urnammu of Ur in Sumerian Literary Tradition," OBO 166 (1999) 93–182.
B. R. Foster, "Humor and Cuneiform Literature," *Journal of the Ancient Near Eastern Society of Columbia University* 6 (1974) 69–85.
———, *Before the Muses. An Anthology of Akkadian Literature*, 3rd ed. CDL Press, Bethesda, 2005.
J.L. Foster, "Texts of the Egyptian Composition «The Instruction of a Man for His Son» in the Oriental Institute Museum," JNES 45 (1986) 197–211.
D. A. Foxwog, Review of Alster 1974, *Orientalia* 45 (1976) 371–374.
J. Friberg, "Mathematics at Ur in the Old Babylonian Period," RA 94 (2000) 98–188.
M. Fritz, *«... und weinten um Tammuz» Die Götter Dumuzi-Ama'ušumgal'anna und Damu*, AOAT 307. Ugarit-Verlag, 2003.

H. Galter, "Die Wörter für «Weisheit» im Akkadischen," in: I. Seybold (ed.): *Meqor Ḥajjim, Festschrift für Georg Molin zu seinem 75. Geburtstag.* Graz 1983, pp. 89–105.

J.G. Gammie and L.G. Perdue (eds.), *The Sage in Israel and the Ancient Near East.* Eisenbrauns, Winona Lake, Ind., 1990.

M.J. Geller, "The Landscape of the «Netherworld»," in: *Landscapes, Frontiers and Horizons in the Ancient Near East.* xliv Rencontre Assyriologique Internationale, 1997, L. Milano et al. (eds.). History of the Ancient Near East, Monographs iii, 3. Padova, 1999.

S.R.K. Glanville, *The Instructions of 'Onchsheshonqy, Catalogue of the Demotic Papyri in the British Museum,* Vol. II. London, 1955.

Jean-Jacques Glassner, *Écriture à Sumer. L'invention du cunéiforme,* Paris, Editions du Seuil, 2000.

W.W. Goodwin, *A Greek Grammar.* Macmillan, London, 2nd ed. 1894 (numerous reprints).

E.I. Gordon, *Sumerian Proverbs. Glimpses of Everyday Life in Ancient Mesopotamia.* University Museum Monographs. Philadelphia, 1956 (repr. 1968).

———, "Sumerian Animal Proverbs and Fables: «Collection Five»," JCS 12 (1958) 1–21, 43–75.

———, "A New Look at the Wisdom of Sumer and Akkad," BiOr 17 (1960) 122–152.

G.B. Gragg, "The Syntax of the Copula in Sumerian," in: *The Verb "Be" and Its Synonyms,* 3: Philosophical and Grammatical Studies, Foundations of Language, Supplementary Series, vol. 8, ed. J.W.M. Verhaar, Dordrecht, 1968, pp. 86–109.

———, "The Fable of the Heron and the Turtle," AfO 24 (1973) 51–72.

———, *Sumerian Dimensional Infixes,* AOAT 5, 1973.

J.C. Greenfield, "Two Proverbs of Aḥiqar," in: *Studies Moran,* 195–201.

———, "The Wisdom of Ahiqar," in *Studies Emerton,* 43–52.

R. Haase, *Keilschriftliche Marginalien nebst einem bibliographischen Anhang.* Leonberg, 1996(a).

———, "Über allgemeine Rechtsregeln in den keilschriftlichen Rechtscorpora," *Zeitschrift für Altorientalische und Biblische Rechtsgeschichte* 3 (1996(b)) 131–134.

W.W. Hallo, "Individual Prayer in Sumerian: The Continuity of a Tradition," JAOS 88 (1968) 71–89.

———, "Proverbs Quoted in Epic," in: *Studies Moran,* 203–217.

———, "Nippur Originals," in: *Sjöberg FS,* 237–247.

———, *Origins. The Near Eastern Background of some Modern Western Institutions.* Leiden, New York, Köln, 1996.

W.W. Hallo (ed.), *The Context of Scripture.* E.J. Brill, 1997.

J. Hertel, *The Hitopadeśa.* Leipzig, 1894.

Hesiod, *Works and Days,* in: The Loeb Classical Library: Hugh G. Evelyn-White: *Hesiod, The Homeric Hymns and Homerica.* Cambridge, 1914 (repr.), pp. 1–65.

B. Holbek and I. Kjær, *Ordsprog i Danmark.* Copenhagen, 1969 (later eds.).

Th. Jacobsen, *The Sumerian King List,* AS 11. Chicago, 1939.

———, "The Sumerian Verbal Core," ZA 78 (1988) 161–220.

T.R. Kämmerer, *šimâ milka. Induktion und Reception der mittelbabylonischen Dichtung von Ugarit, Emār und Tell el-'Amārna.* AOAT 251. Münster, 1998.

D. Katz, *The Image of the Netherworld in the Sumerian Sources.* CDL Press, Bethesda, Md., 2003.

J. Klein, "Personal God and Individual Prayer in Sumerian Religion," in: CR 28[e] RAI, AfO Beiheft, 1982, pp. 293–306.

———, "The 'Bane' of Humanity: A Lifespan of One Hundred Twenty Years," AcSum 12 (1990) 57–70.

———, "«The Ballade about Early Rulers» in Eastern and Western Tradition," in: OLA: *Languages and Cultures in Contact,* 2000, pp. 203–216.

———, "An Old Babylonian Edition of an Early Dynastic Collection of Insults (BT 9)," in: *Wilcke FS,* 135–149.

S.N. Kramer, *Sumerian Mythology,* The American Philosophical Society. Philadelphia, 1944. Rev. ed. Harper Torchbook, 1961.

———, *The Sumerians. Their History, Culture, and Character.* University of Chicago Press, 1963.

M. Krebernik, "Fragment einer Bilingue," ZA 86 (1996) 170–176.

———, "Die Texte aus Fāra und Tell Abū Ṣalābīḫ," in: *Mesopotamien; Späturuk und Frühdynastische Zeit. Annäherungen* 1, P. Attinger und M. Wäfler (eds.), OBO 160/1. Freiburg Schweiz und Göttingen, 1998.

J. Krecher, "Das sumerische Phonem g̃," in: *Matouš FS,* 7–73.

———, "Sumerische und nichtsumerische Schicht," in: L. Cagni (ed.), *Il Bilinguismo a Ebla.* Istituto Universitario orientale, Dipt. di studi asiatici, Series Minor xxii. Napoli, 1984, pp. 139–166.

———, "Die *marû*-Formen des sumerischen Verbums," in: *von Soden AV*, 141–200.

K. Krumbacher, *Mittelgriechische Sprichwörter*, Sitzungsberichte der Phil.-hist. Classe der könig. Bayerischen Akademie der Wissenschaften, 1893, Bd. II; repr. Hildesheim, 1969.

W.G. Lambert, "Ancestors, Authors and Canonicity," JCS 12 (1958) 1–14.

———, *Babylonian Wisdom Literature*. Oxford, 1960.

———, "Enmeduranki and Related Matters," JCS 21 (1967) 126–138.

———, "The Theology of Death," in: *Death in Mesopotamia*, B. Alster (ed.), Mesopotamia 8, 1980, pp. 53–58.

———, "A New Interpretation of Enlil and Namzitarra," *Orientalia* 58 (1989) 508–509.

———, "Some New Babylonian Literature," in: *Studies Emerton*, 30–42.

———, "A Note on the Three Ox-Drivers from Adab," *N.A.B.U.* 1995/1, no. 2, pp. 1–2.

W.G. Lambert and A.R. Millard, *Atra-Ḫasīs. The Babylonian Story of the Flood*. Oxford, 1969.

M. Lewin, *Aramäische Sprichwörter und Volkssprüche*. Berlin, 1895.

M. Lichtheim, *Ancient Egyptian Literature. Volume I: The Old and Middle Kingdom*. Berkeley, University of California Press, 1973; *Volume II: The New Kingdom*, 1976.

———, *Late Egyptian Wisdom Literature in the International Context: A Study of Demotic Instructions* (OBO 52). Vandenhoeck & Ruprecht, Göttingen, 1983.

H. Limet, "La pensée religieuse des Sumériens et le Livre de *Job*," in: *Recherches pluridisciplinaires sur une province de l'empire archémenide*, Transeuphratène 22, 2001, Gabalda, 115–127.

———, "Les jeux dans les mythes et dans les rituels de Mésopotame," in: *L'autre, l'étranger, sports et loisirs, J. Duchesne-Guillemin in honoram*, AcOrB 16. Bruxelles, 2002, pp. 95–114.

———, "Le bestiaire des proverbes sumériens," in: *L'animal dans les civilisations orientales*, AcOrB 14. Bruxelles, 2002, pp. 29–43.

J.M. Lindenberger, *Proverbs of Ahiqar*. The Johns Hopkins University Press. Baltimore and London, 1983.

E. Lipiński, "The King's Arbitration in Ancient Near Eastern Folk-Tale," in: K. Hecker and W. Sommerfeld, (eds.), *Keilschriftliche Literaturen*, Berliner Beiträge zum Vorderen Orient 8, Berlin, 1985, pp. 137–141.

W. McKane, *Proverbs. A New Approach*, The Old Testament Library. London, 1970.

P. Martin, *Studien auf dem Gebiete des griechischen Sprichwortes*. Plauen i. V., 1889.

W. Mieder, "Proverbs," in: J.H. Brunvand (ed.), *American Folklore: An Encyclopedia*. Garland Publishing, New York, 1996, pp. 597–601.

W. Mieder (ed.), *Wise Words. Essays on the Proverb*. Garland Publishing, New York & London, 1994.

M. Van De Mieroop, *The Ancient Mesopotamian City*. Oxford, 1997.

B. Mogensen, *Israelitiske leveregler og deres begrundelse*. G.E.C. Gad, Copenhagen, 1982.

H.-P. Müller, "Keilschriftliche Parallelen zum biblichen Hiobbuch. Möglichkeit und Grenzen des Vergleichs," *Orientalia* 47 (1978) 360–375.

F. Nau, *Histoire et sagesse d'Ahiqar. Trad. des versions syriaques avec les principales différences des versions arabes, arménienne, grecque, néo-syriaque, slave et roumaine*. Paris, 1909.

S. Noegel (ed.), *Puns and Pundits. Word Play in the Hebrew Bible and Near Eastern Literature*. CDL Press, Bethesda, Md., 2000.

J. Nougayrol, "Sagesse," in: *Mission de Ras Shamra*, Tome XVI = *Ugaritica* V. Paris 1968, pp. 273–300.

A. Otto, *Die Sprichwörter und sprichwörtlichen Redensarten der Römer*. Leipzig, 1890.

———, Nachträge zu A. Otto, *Die Sprichwörter und sprichwörtlichen Redensarten der Römer*, R. Häussler (ed.). Hildesheim, 1968.

S. Parpola, *Letters from Assyrian Scholars* (= AOAT 5).

N.J. Postgate, *Ancient Mesopotamia*. Routledge, London, 1992.

M.A. Powell, "Ukubi to Mother ...," ZA 67 (1977) 163–195.

J.D. Ray, "Egyptian Wisdom Literature," in: *Studies Emerton*, 17–29.

Herr von Reinsberg-Düringsfeld und Ida von Reinsberg-Düringfeld, *Die Sprichwörter der germanischen und romanischen Sprachen vergleichend zusammengestellt* i–iii. Leipzig, 1872–75.

E. Robson, *Mesopotamian Mathematics 2100–1600 B.C.: Technical Constants in Bureaucracy and Education*. Oxford, 1998.

W.H.Ph. Römer, "Miscellanea Sumerologica V. Bittbrief einer Gelähmten um Genesung an die Göttin Nintinugga," in: *Wilcke FS*, 237–249.

———, "Rat des Schuruppag," 48–67 in: W.H.Ph. Römer and W. von Soden: *Weisheits-*

texte, Myten und Epen, Texte aus der Umwelt des Alten Testaments, Band III: Weisheitstexte I. Gütersloher, 1990.

M. Roth, "The Slave and the Scoundrel," JAOS 103 (1983) 275–282.

G. Rubio, "On the Alleged «Pre-Sumerian Substratum»," JCS 51 (1999) 1–16.

H.H. Schmid, "*Wesen und Geschichte der Weisheit. Eine Untersuchung zur altorientalischen und israelitischen Weisheitsliteratur,*" (BZAW 101). Töpelmann, Berlin, 1966.

K.M. Schretter, *Emesal-Studien: sprach- und literaturgeschichtliche Untersuchungen zur sogenannten Frauensprache des Sumerischen.* Innsbrucker Beiträge zur Kulturwissenschaft. Sonderheft, 69. Verlag des Instituts für Sprachwissenschaft der Universität Innsbruck, Innsbruck, 1990.

M. Schul, *Sentence et proverbes du Talmud et du Midrasch, suivi du Traité d'Aboth*, Paris. 1878.

R.B.Y. Scott, *Proverbs and Ecclesiastes.* The Anchor Bible, 1973.

Y. Sefati, *Love Songs in Sumerian Literature.* Bar-Ilan University Press, 1988.

G.J. Selz, "Bemerkungen zum sumerischen Genitiv nebst einigen Beobachtungen zur sumerischen Wortbildung," WZKM 92 (2002(a)) 129–153.

———, "«Streit herrscht, Gewalt droht»—Zu Konflitregelung und Recht in der frühdynastischen und altakkadischen Zeit," WZKM 92 (2002(b)) 155–203.

———, "«Babilismus» und die Gottheit «^{d}Nindagar»," in: *Dietrich FS*, 647–684.

S. Seminara, *La versione accadica del Lugal-e*, MVS 8. Roma, 2001.

A. Shaffer, *Sumerian Sources of Tablet xii of the Epic of Gilgameš*, Ph.D. diss. University of Pennsylvania, 1963.

M. Sigrist, *Drehem.* CDL Press, Bethesda, Md., 1992.

———, *Neo-Sumerian Texts from the Royal Ontario Museum* II, CDL Press, Bethesda, Md., 2004.

Å.W. Sjöberg, "«He is a Good Seed of a Dog» and «Engardu, the Fool»," *JCS* 24 (1971–72) 107–129.

———, "Der Vater und sein missratener Sohn," JCS 25 (1973) 105–169.

———, "The Praise of Scribal Art," JCS 24 (1974) 126–131.

———, "The Old Babylonian Edubba," in: *Jacobsen FS*, 19–48.

———, "Der Examenstext A," ZA 64 (1975) 137–167.

———, "Miscellaneous Sumerian Texts I," *Orientalia Suecana* 23–24 (1976) 159–181.

———, "Notes on Selected Entries from the Ebla Vocabulary eš$_2$-bar-kin$_5$," in: *Wilcke FS*, 251–266.

Å.W. Sjöberg, E. Bergmann, and G. Gragg, *The Collection of the Sumerian Temple Hymns.* Texts from Cuneiform Sources, III. J.J. Augustin, Locust Valley, N.Y., 1969.

W.H. van Soldt, "Babylonian Lexical, Religious and Literary Texts and Scribal Education at Ugarit," in: M. Dietrich and O. Loretz (eds.), *Ugarit, Ein ostmediterranes Kulturzentrum im Alten Orient*, Band 1: *Ugarit und seine altorientalische Umwelt.* Ugarit-Verla, Münster, 1995, pp. 171–212.

———, "The Written Sources," in: W. Watson and N. Wyatt (eds.), *Handbook of Ugaritic Studies.* Brill, Leiden, 1999, pp. 28–45.

P. Steinkeller, "Early Political Development in Mesopotamia and the Origins of the Sargonic Empire," in *Akkad*, 107–129.

———, "An Ur III Manuscript of the Sumerian King List," in: *Wilcke FS*, 267–292.

F.A. Stenzler, *Elementarbuch der Sanskritsprache*, 4. Auf., Berlin, 1960.

M. Stol, "Biblical Idiom in Akkadian," in: *Hallo FS*, 246–249.

A. Taylor, *The Proverb.* Harvard University Press, 1931; *An Index to "The Proverb,"* Folklore Fellows Communications No. 113. Helsinki, 1934. Both reprinted with a foreword by Archer Taylor, Hatboro, Pa., and Copenhagen, 1962. Also reprinted with an introduction and bibliography by Wolfgang Mieder, *Sprichwörterforschung*, Band 6. Bern, 1985.

M.-L. Thomsen, *The Sumerian Language*, Mesopotamia 10. Akademisk Forlag, Copenhagen, 1984 (repr. 2000).

H. Vanstiphout, "Some Thoughts on Genre in Mesopotamian Literature," in RAI 32, pp. 1–11.

———, "The Importance of the Tale of the Fox," AcSum 10 (1988) 191–227.

N. Veldhuis, "Kassite Exercises: Literary and Lexical Texts," JCS 52 (2000) 67–94.

———, *Elementary Education at Nippur: The Lists of Trees and Wooden Objects*, Ph.D. diss., Groningen, 1997.

———, "Sumerian Proverbs in Their Curricular Context," in JAOS 120 (2000) 383–399.

P. Veyne, *Les Grecs ont-ils cru à leurs mythes?*, éd. du Seuil (Essais). Paris, 1983. Eng. translation by

Paula Wissing, *Did the Greeks Believe in Their Myths?: An Essay on the Constitutive Imagination.*

C.-L. Vincente, "The Tell Leilan Recension of the Sumerian King List," ZA 85 (1995) 234–270.

M. Vogelzang and H. Vanstiphout (eds.), *Mesopotamian Poetic Language: Sumerian and Akkadian.* Styx, Groningen, 1996.

K. Volk, *Inanna und Šukalletuda*, SANTAK 3. Harrassowitz, Wiesbaden, 1995.

———, "Edubba'a und Edubba'a-Literatur," ZA 90 (2000) 1–30.

H. Waetzoldt, "Der Schreiber als Lehrer in Mesopotamien," in: J.G. Prinz von Hohenzollern and M. Liedtke (eds.), *Schreiber, Magister, Lehrer. Zur Geschichte und Funktion eines Berufstandes.* Bad Heilbrunn, 1989, pp. 33–50.

N. Wasserman, *Style and Form in Old-Babylonian Literary Texts*, Cuneiform Monographs 27. Brill (Styx), 2003.

Cl. Wilcke, *Das Lugalbandaepos.* Wiesbaden, 1969.

———, *Kollationen zu den sumerischen literarischen Texten aus Nippur in der Hilprecht-Sammlung Jena*, Abh. der Säch. Akad. der Wissenschaften zu Jena, phil.-hist. Klasse Bd. 65, Hf. 4. Berlin, 1976.

———, "Philologische Bemerkungen zum Rat des Šuruppag," ZA 68 (1978) 202–232.

———, "Die Sumerische Königsliste und erzählte Vergangenheit," in: J. von Ungern-Sternberg and H. Reinau (eds.), *Vergangenheit in mündlicher Überlieferung* (Colloquium Rauricum Band 1). Stuttgart, 1988, pp. 113–40.

———, "Der Kodex Urnamma (CU)," in: *Jacobsen MV*, 291–333.

———, "König Šulgis Himmelfahrt," in: *Festschrift László Vajda.* Münchener Beiträge zur Volkerkunde, Bd. I, 245–255.

J.V. Kinnier Wilson, *The Legend of Etana. A New Edition.* Warminster, 1985.

A. Zgoll, *Der Rechtsfall der Enḫedu-Ana im Lied nin-me-šara.* Ugarit-Verlag, Münster, 1977.

Abbreviations

Common abbreviations are listed in W. von Soden, *Akkadisches Handwörterbuch* (AHw) and *The Assyrian Dictionary of the Oriental Institute of the University of Chicago* (CAD).

AcOrB: *Acta Orientalia Belgica.*

AcSum: *Acta Sumerologica.*

AfO: *Archiv für Orientforschung.*

Akkad: M. Liverani (ed.) *Akkad—The First World Empire: Structure, Ideology, and Traditions.* Padua, 1993.

ANET: J. Pritchard (ed.): *Ancient Near Eastern Texts Relating to the Old Testament*, 2nd ed. Princeton, N.J., 1969.

AnSt: *Anatolian Studies.*

AOAT: *Alter Orient und Altes Testament.*

AS: *Assyriological Studies.*

AuOr: *Aula Orientalis.*

AWL: J. Bauer: *Altsumerische Wirtschaftstexte aus Lagasch.*

Bilinguismo a Ebla: L. Cagni (ed.), *Il Bilinguismo a Ebla.* Istituto Universitario orientale, Dipt. di studi asiatici, Series Minor xxii. Napoli, 1984.

BiOr: *Bibliotheca Orientalis.*

Birot FS: *Miscellanea Babylonica.* Paris, 1985.

Borger FS: S.M. Maul (ed.), *Festschrift für Rylke Borger zu seinem 65. Geburtstag: tikip santakki mala bashmu*, Cuneiform Monographs 10. Styx, Groningen, 1998.

BWL: W.G. Lambert: *Babylonian Wisdom Literature.*

CAH: *Cambridge Ancient History.*

CANE: J.A. Sasson et al. (eds.), *Civilizations of the Ancient Near East*, 1–4. Charles Scribner's Sons, New York, 1995.

CM: Cuneiform Monographs, Styx, Groningen.

CRRAI: *Compte rendu du rencontre assyriologique internationale.*

Dietrich FS: O. Loretz et al. (eds.), *Ex Mesopotamia et Syria Lux. Festschrift für Manfred Dietrich.* Ugarit-Verlag, Münster, 2002.

Düringfeld: See Reinsberg-Düringsfeld.

ED: Early Dynastic Period.

ELS: P. Attinger, *Eléments de linguistique sumérienne. La construction de du$_{11}$/e/di «dire».*

ETCSL: Oxford Electronic Text Corpus of Sumerian Literature: http://www-etcsl.orient.ox.ac.uk/catalogue.

GGL: A. Falkenstein, *Grammatik des Gudea von Lagaš*, Analecta Orientalia 28–29. Rome, 1949–1950.

Hallo FS: *The Tablet and the Scroll. Near Eastern Studies in Honor of William W. Hallo*, M.E. Cohen et al. (eds.). CDL Press, Bethesda, Md., 1993.

HSAO: *Heidelberger Studien zum Alten Orient* 1. Harrassowitz, Wiesbaden, 1967.

Jacobsen FS: *Sumerological Studies in Honor of Thorkild Jacobsen on His Seventieth Birthday, June 7, 1974*, AS 20. Chicago and London, 1974.

Jacobsen MV: T. Abusch (ed.), *Riches Hidden in Secret Places, Ancient Near Eastern Studies in Memory of Thorkild Jacobsen.* Eisenbrauns, Winona Lake, Ind., 2002.

JAOS: *Journal of the American Oriental Society.*

JCS: *Journal of Cuneiform Studies.*

JNES: *Journal of Near Eastern Studies.*

Klein FS: Y. Sefati et al. (eds.), *An Experienced Scribe who Neglects Nothing, Ancient Near Eastern Studies in Honor of Jacob Klein.* CDL Press, Bethesda, Md., 2005.

Lambert FS: A.R. George and I.L. Finkel (eds.), *Wisdom, Gods and Literature, Studies in Assyriology in Honour of W.G. Lambert.* Eisenbrauns, Winona Lake, Ind., 2000.

Larsen AV: J.G. Dercksen (ed.), *Assyria and Beyond, Studies Presented to Mogens Trolle Larsen.* Netherlands Instituut vor het Nabije Osten, Leiden, 2004.

LAS: Late Assyrian Scholars: S. Parpola: *Letters from Assyrian Scholars* (= AOAT 5).

Limet FS: Ö. Tunca and D. Deheselle (eds.), *Tablettes et images aux pays de Sumer et d'Akkad*, Mélanges offerts à Monsieur H. Limet, Association pour la Promotion de l'Histoire et de l'archéologie Orientales, Mémoires no. 1. Liège, 1996.

Matouš FS: B. Hruška und G. Komoróczy (eds.), *Festschrift Lubor Matouš*, *Assyriologia* V. As Eötvös Loránd Tudományegyetem, Budapest, 1978.
MEE 3(–4): G. Pettinato et al., *Testi lessicali monolingui della Biblioteca L.2796*. Materiali epigrafici di Ebla 3 (–4). Napoli, 1981 (4: ditto, 1982).
MVS: Materiali per il Vocabolario Sumerico.
N.A.B.U.: *Nouvelles Assyriologiques Brèves et Utilitaires*.
NG: A. Falkenstein: *Neusumerische Gerichtsurkunden*.
OA: *Oriens Antiquus*.
OBO: *Orbis Biblicus et Orientalis*.
ODEP: *The Oxford Dictionary of English Proverbs*, Compiled by W.G. Smith with an introduction by J. Wilson, 3rd ed. Oxford University Press, 1970.
OIP: Oriental Institute Publications.
OLA: *Orientalia Lovaniensia Analecta*.
OLP: *Orientalia Lovaniensia Periodica*.
OLZ: *Orientalische Literaturzeitung*.
OrNS: *Orientalia* Nova Series.
Proverbs: Alster, *Proverbs of Ancient Sumer* I–II.
RA: *Revue d'Assyriologie*.
RlA: *Reallexikon der Assyriologie und Vorderasiatischen Archäologie*.
Sagesse: J. van Dijk: *La sagesse suméro-accadiens*.
SANTAK: *Arbeiten und Untersuchungen zur Keilschriftkunde*, Wiesbaden: Harrassowitz.
Sjöberg FS: H. Behrens et al. (eds.), *Dumu-e$_2$-dub-ba-a. Studies in Honor of Åke W. Sjöberg*, Occasional Publications of the Samuel Noah Kramer Fund, 11. Philadelphia, 1989.
SP: (1) used for Sumerian Proverb Collection as numbered in Alster: *Proverbs* I–II; (2) for E.I. Gordon: *Sumerian Proverbs*. University Museum Monographs. Philadelphia, 1956 (repr. 1968).
SS: standard Sumerian.
Studies Emerton: J. Day, R.P. Gordon and H.G.M. Williamson (eds.), *Wisdom in Ancient Israel: Essays in Honour of J.A. Emerton*. Cambridge, 1995.
Studies Moran: T. Abusch et al. (eds.), *Lingering over Words: Studies in Ancient Near Eastern Literature in Honor of William L. Moran*. Harvard Semitic Studies 35. Scholars Press, Atlanta, 1990.
TCS: *Texts from Cuneiform Sources*. J.J. Augustin: Locust Valley, N.Y.
TUAT: *Texte aus der Umwelt des Alten Testaments*. Gütersloher.
Ugaritica 5: *Mission de Ras Shamra*, Tome XVI = *Ugaritica* 5. Paris 1968.
Visible Language: 15/4 (ed. M. Powell). Cleveland, 1981.
von Soden AV: AOAT, Band 240. Neukirchen-Vluyn, 1995
Wilcke FS: *Literatur, Politik und Recht in Mesopotamien. Festschrift für Claus Wilcke*, her. von W. Sallaberger u.al., Orientalia Biblica et Christiana 14. Harrassowitz, Wiesbaden, 2003.
WZKM: *Wiener Zeitschrift für die Kunde des Morgenlandes*.
YNER: *Yale Near Eastern Researches*.
ZA: *Zeitschrift für Assyriologie*.

Introduction

Previous Attempts to Define Mesopotamian Wisdom Literature

In 1960, when W.G. Lambert published his monumental work *Babylonian Wisdom Literature*, he started with the following cautious remark: "«Wisdom» is strictly a misnomer as applied to Babylonian literature" (p. 1).

Our knowledge of Sumerian literature has increased enormously in the decades following the publication of Lambert's work, so it would be a very challenging task to seek to write a Sumerian counterpart to *Babylonian Wisdom Literature*. Actually, this would not be possible for two basic reasons. First, the Sumerian material would require not just one, but a number of books to match the contents of *Babylonian Wisdom Literature*. In particular, the proverbs, the dialogues, and the debate poems would each require more than one book. Second, although Sumerian literature certainly had a strong influence on the later development of Babylonian and Assyrian literature, it would be appropriate to question whether "wisdom" is to be understood in the same way for early Mesopotamian literature as for the later periods, with implications that might lead to the inclusion of a different choice of texts.

In earlier treatments of Mesopotamian literature, "wisdom" was used with a wide variety of texts, as will appear from the following brief survey of the definitions of some leading scholars, among which Lambert's from 1960 is by far the most important.

Of the others, that of G. Buccellati from 1981 stands apart as the most theoretical approach so far: "Wisdom should be viewed as an intellectual phenomenon in itself. It is the second degree reflective function as it begins to emerge in human culture; ... it provided the mental categories for a conscious abstract confrontation with reality, from common sense correlations to higher level theory."[1] Wisdom is thus typically seen as a cultural phenomenon already on its way to a higher and more abstract level of reflection. Yet, when we go back in time to what is normally considered the earliest "wisdom" texts known in history, these may not conform to the definition, although what the Mesopotamians understood by "wisdom" may have covered many complex notions.[2]

Lambert's Definition of Wisdom

Lambert, in 1960, was fully aware that he used a term that had been "retained as a convenient short description" (p. 1). The criterion for inclusion is, according to Lambert's introduction, that "the sphere of these texts is what has been called philosophy since Greek times." Among the relevant themes he found (1) ethics (practical advice on living); (2) "intellectual problems inherent in the then current outlook on life"; and (3) fables, popular sayings, and proverbs.

Lambert's categories comprise:[3] (1) The Poem of the Righteous Sufferer (*Ludlul bēl nēmeqi*); (2) *The Babylonian Theodicy*; (3) precepts and admonitions; (4) preceptive hymns (in particular the Šamaš hymn); (5)

1. Cf. G. Buccellati, JAOS 101 (1981) 44. Cf. "Tre saggi sulla sapienza mesopotamica," in: OA 11 (1972) 1–178.
2. A good overview of the complexity of the native Akkadian terms is H. Galter, "Die Wörter für «Weisheit» im Akkadischen," in: I. Seybold (ed.), *Meqor Ḥajjim, Festschrift für Georg Molin zu seinem 75. Geburtstag* (Graz, 1983) 89–105.
3. Cf. the introduction to Lambert, BWL, 1. Folktales were not included—the most remarkable example in Akkadian literature, *The Poor Man of Nippur*, was unknown at the time of BWL's publication.

The Dialogue of Pessimism; (6) fables or contest literature; (7) popular sayings; and (8) proverbs.

In 1995, Lambert updated his views and added two more text categories to Mesopotamian wisdom literature, thereby suggesting new ways for the study of Mesopotamian wisdom.[4] An attempt to proceed further along these lines is made in the present volume. The new categories are: (9) The vanity theme of Qoheleth, recognizable in the Babylonian *Dialogue of Pessimism*, and reflected as the *carpe diem* theme of the Akkadian *Gilgameš Epic*; (10) *Ubi sunt*-poems ("Where are ...?"),[5] reflected in the *Ballade of Early Rulers*, which goes back to Sumerian times and was transmitted in the Syro-Mesopotamian Akkadian literature of Ugarit and Emar of the second millennium B.C.[6] The two latter categories are particularly interesting from the point of view of Sumerian literature, and will be discussed further in *Chap. 3: The Vanity Theme and the Syro-Mesopotamian Literary Tradition.*

What is more important, however, is that, in 1995, Lambert recognized a singular example of the use of the Babylonian term *nēmequ*, "wisdom," as a "way of life," an existential attitude, a "philosophy of life," similar to the Hebrew *ḥokmā*.[7] This is reflected in the well-known advice given by the barmaiden Siduri to Gilgameš, who, when searching for eternal life, is given the advice to be satisfied with enjoying the pleasures of the present day instead. It is obvious, therefore, that it would be worth basing a study of Mesopotamian "wisdom" on native terms. The problem remains, however, that there is no frequent and easily recognizable term, such as Akkadian *nēmequ* or Sumerian nam-kù-zu, that is frequent enough to be the sole criterion for inclusion. So the study must necessarily take more elusive criteria into account.

Obviously the texts or text types mentioned above do not form a uniform group. The unifying term "philosophy" is interesting in this context, because it calls to mind an old concept that regarded the biblical book of Proverbs as an early stage of philosophy,[8] although one must take into consideration that "philosophy" was then also understood more as an existential attitude than as speculative thinking. Yet, if we stick to the speculative approach, is it fair to say that "wisdom literature" is merely a convenient label under which to bring together under a common heading a number of very different text types thought to represent a rational approach regarded as an early stage of philosophy? Is such a rational approach really common to these texts? *Ludlul bēl nēmeqi* and the *Babylonian Theodicy* indeed display a high degree of complex thinking that is miles apart from the practical advice characteristic of the Mesopotamian precept compositions of the early second millennium B.C. and earlier. Yet *Ludlul bēl nēmeqi* could be read, primarily, as a personal lamentation praising Marduk as the "Lord of Wisdom."[9] Marduk's wisdom is foremost his expertise in magic, and this was not meant as wisdom in any philosophical or theological sense.

Further, why include hymns under the heading wisdom? Lambert explains this by referring to the highly ethical contents of those particular hymns that were accepted under this heading. Yet, since moral issues were hardly a concern of the texts included under the label Babylonian wisdom, why include the Šamaš hymn precisely because it deals with ethics? Instead, one might argue that the hymns of Asal-

4. "Some New Babylonian Wisdom Literature," *Studies Emerton*, 30–42.
5. Cf. Chap. 3.3, where the *Ballade of Early Rulers*, exemplifying the *ubi sunt* theme, is treated. For the *carpe diem* theme, see also Chap. 3.1–2, where *Níŋ-nam nu-kal zi-ku$_7$-ku$_7$-da* ("Nothing is of value, but life should be sweet-tasting") is treated, also relating to the vanity theme.
6. Particularly interesting is the small sententious addition to the *Ballade of Early Rulers*, for which a poorly preserved Sumerian forerunner has now been found (edited below, in Chap. 3.4).
7. Lambert, 1965, 30–32, referring to Šurpu II 173: ^{d}*ši-du-ri* ... ^{d}*ištar né-me-qí*, "Šiduri ... goddess of wisdom."
8. So in Johann Friedrich Bruchs book, *Weisheitslehre der Hebräer*, with the subtitle: *Ein Beitrag zur Geschichte der Philosophie* (1851).
9. For *Ludlul bēl nēmeqi*, see H.P. Müller, "Keilschriftliche Parallelen zum biblichen Hiobbuch. Möglichkeit und grenzen des Vergleichs," *Orientalia* 47 (1978) 360–375. There is now an outstanding new discussion of *Ludlul* by Lambert, 1995, 32–36. Cf also H. Spieckermann: "Ludlul bēl nēmeqi und die Frage nach der Gerechtigkeit Gottes," *Borger FS*, 329–41.

luhi-Enki and Marduk, god of wisdom *par excellence*, indeed belong to the wisdom category, not because of their ethical contents, but because, from the point of view of Mesopotamian culture, these undoubtedly exemplify what the Mesopotamians understood by wisdom.[10] Further, since the Babylonian concept of wisdom included insight into cult, magic, and divination, why not include magical texts, and why not divination texts, such as omens, under the heading wisdom?[11] All this is covered by Marduk's wisdom (*nēmequ*), rather than being a forerunner of rational philosophy.

Lambert did, indeed, discuss the possibility of including the Babylonian epics in the wisdom category, but chose not to do so, because these do not live up to the "more openly rational attitude." Yet, one could argue that not only the Akkadian epics of Gilgameš and Atrahasis, but the Sumerian epics of Gilgameš and Huwawa, as well as the Enmerkar and Lugalbanda epics, could with equal right be regarded as manifestations of Mesopotamian wisdom.[12] The fact that Gilgameš learned by practical experience, and not by intellectual insight, would be a good point rather than a relevant objection.

Attempts at Defining Sumerian Wisdom Literature

The most important contribution of J. van Dijk's book, *La sagesse suméro-akkadienne* (1953), was its description of the Sumerian school, the *edubba*, in which van Dijk found the first example of the mentality of true humanism (nam-lú-ùlu ak, "to perform humanism"). E.I. Gordon's review of van Dijk's book (Gordon, 1960)[13] became a milestone in the study of Sumerian literature.

Gordon established a long list of categories of what he considered to be wisdom literature, and he was the first to bring order to a large number of hitherto little-known Sumerian texts. According to Gordon "wisdom literature" is "all literary writings ... whose content is concerned in one way or another with life and nature, and man's evaluation of them based either upon his direct observation or insight. Among the subjects treated are such everyday practical matters as the economy and social behavior, as well as the ethical values and aesthetic appreciations of society and of the individual." Gordon's categories included:[14] (1) Proverbs; (2) Fables and Parables; (3) Folktales; (4) Miniature "Essays"; (5) Riddles; (6) Edubba Compositions; (7) Wisdom disputations or "Tensions"; (8) Satirical Dialogues; (9) Practical Instructions; (10) Precepts; (11) Righteous Sufferer Poems. In Gordon's classification of wisdom literature there is no discussion of a philosophical outlook or a rational attitude thought to anticipate philosophy, so the criterion for inclusion basically seems to be that anything not pertaining to the usual categories of hymns, myths, epics, and so forth, could be relevant.[15]

Newer Attempts at Classification

An example of a more cautious attempt is that of D.O. Edzard in his lexicon contribution "Literatur."[16] He makes a much narrower selection and includes only fables (but not as a separate genre), riddles, proverb collections, narrative didactic literature, and satirical school compositions, under the heading "wisdom literature." By "proverbs" he understands certain types of phrases rather than proverbs in the strict sense. Under this heading he also includes fables appearing in the so-called "Proverb Collections" and riddles.

The groups are thus put together according to

10. In some cultures, hymns, such as the Vedas, would be regarded as wisdom literature.
11. Cf. already F.R. Kraus: "Ein Sittenkanon in Omenform," in: ZA 43 (1936) 77–113.
12. Cf. Alster: "Enmerkar, Lugalbanda, and Other Cunning Heroes," in: CANE, 2315–2326. These texts should, of course, be classified as epics, should there be any meaning in making distinctions from the point of view of genre. Enmerkar, Lugalbanda, and Gilgameš are presented as memorable ancient sages. Cf. also Vanstiphout, "Sanctus Lugalbanda," in *Jacobsen MV*, 259–289.
13. E.I. Gordon, "A New Look at the Wisdom of Sumer and Akkad," in: BiOr 17 (1960) 122–152.
14. Gordon, p. 124.
15. Some of Gordon's groups, such as his "miniature essays," are now outdated in view of the present state of Sumerological research.
16. RlA, 7, 35–66.

subject matter. Strict formal criteria, which would be needed for a detailed discussion of genres, might suggest other categories, especially since the group "narrative didactic literature" is said to include texts as dissimilar as *The Praise of Scribal Art* and *The Instructions of Šuruppak*, which can hardly be regarded as a uniform group.[17]

In the *Oxford Electronic Text Corpus of Sumerian Literature* wisdom literature is a subgroup of "Scribal Training Literature," which, to date, comprises only three texts: *The Instructions of Šuruppak*, *The Farmer's Instructions*, and *The Three Ox-Drivers from Adab*. Although one may argue over this classification,[18] it should be recognized as an attempt to limit the "wisdom" genre to clearly defined texts, and to acknowledge the great influence of the Sumerian scribal school in the transmission of these texts.

Assmann's Four Types of Wisdom

In J. Assmann's comprehensive studies of wisdom, he distinguishes four fundamental types:[19]

1. *Salomo:* the wisdom of the ruler and judge.
2. *Prospero:* magical wisdom.
3. *Jacques:* critical wisdom.
4. *Polonius:* the wisdom of the fathers.[20]

Based on these premises, the Mesopotamian outlook would have to be revised as follows:

1. *Law and wisdom:* Hammurapi's law, and the wisdom of the king as judge.
2. *Magic and wisdom:* The magical wisdom of Marduk, the "Lord of Wisdom"; the "wisdom" of incantations and divination as well.
3. *The wisdom of the scribal schools:* The humorous critical wisdom embedded in the Sumerian dialogues and school compositions.[21]
4. *The wisdom of the ancient sages:* The wisdom of Atrahasis, Gilgameš, Adapa, Šuruppak, Aḫiqar, and the ancient sages.

In conclusion: Wisdom is a term that covers a number of existential or intellectual attitudes. Or, rather, wisdom is not only an attitude, but a number of very different attitudes that may come to light in literary works belonging to various text types, or genres. But "wisdom" as the traditional genre designation does not do justice to the subtleties of the ancient cultures. Nobody would classify Shakespeare's comedy *As You Like It* or *Hamlet*, a drama, as a "wisdom" composition. Yet, some of the main characters have become emblematic of certain types of wisdom. We might, therefore, consider to abandon the generic term "wisdom literature," but this does not in any way mean that wisdom becomes an obsolete concept. Assmann's approach may be taken as a fruitful starting point for a revaluation of the Sumerian texts that may or may not be regarded as representative of Early Mesopotamian "wisdom" compositions.

17. Praise of Scribal Art: Sjöberg, JCS 24 (1974) 126–131, dupl. CT 58, no. 66. Note, however, that proverb collections are wisely regarded as a genre, but not proverbs as such; cf. the discussion below.
18. Especially because a folktale, such as *The Three Ox-Drivers from Adab*, is placed together with father-and-son didactic compositions. The categories reflect mainly what is available on the ETCSL-site, where a number of rarely attested texts, such as *The Instructions of Ur-Ninurta*, *The Fields of Ninurta*, and the folktale *The Old Man and the Young Girl* (poorly preserved; only edition: Alster, 1975, 90–94; now re-edited in Chap. 5) have not yet been included.
19. A. and J. Assmann, *Weisheit. Archäologie der literarischen Kommmunikation*, Bd. 3 (München: Wilhelm Fink Verlag, 1991).
20. The rationale behind Assmann's categories is that wisdom is, after all, what everyone seeks to have in common with all human beings, dead or alive. Wisdom is the human quality that makes life attractive, a quality without which all philosophy, all religions, all scholarship, and all sciences may end up in the fanaticism of dry, uninspiring professional knowledge.
21. It is the merit, in particular, of Vanstiphout to have called attention to this aspect of Sumerian literature; cf. Vanstiphout, "On the Sumerian Disputation between the Hoe and the Plough," in: AuOr 2 (1984) 239–251, and later publications by Vanstiphout, cf., e.g., his contribution to Hallo (ed.): *The Context of Scripture* (E.J. Brill, 1997), 575–593. Also: Alster and Vanstiphout: "Lahar and Ashnan. Presentation and Analysis of a Sumerian Literary Dispute," in: AcSum 9 (1987) 1–43.

Sumerian Text Types Relating to "Wisdom"

The label "wisdom" used of early Mesopotamian literature is certainly as much alive in recent works as ever.[22] So the following short list may—or may not—with some right be regarded as wisdom literature in Sumerian:

Father-and-son instructions and similar didactic precept compilations:[23] These are certainly the text type that best deserves the designation "wisdom literature." Yet, in the early literature of Mesopotamia, these represent one particular type of wisdom, the wisdom of the fathers (the wisdom of Polonius, cf. above), but not in any way an intellectual forerunner of philosophy.

Practical instructions:[24] There would be a point in arguing that a composition such as *The Farmer's Instructions* is a type of wisdom composition, since it conveys an attitude of life, by admonishing the farmer to be modest, patient, and so forth. Without these extra qualifications, these should not be included under the heading "wisdom literature." They are relevant only in so far as they convey an aspect of existential wisdom. Professional skills as such are not necessarily "wisdom."

Dialogues and disputations: These may be classified as a subgroup under "wisdom literature," as representatives of one particular type of wisdom, that is, the humor, wit, and irony of Jacque, cf. above.[25]

School compositions:[26] The refreshing self irony of the Sumerian scribes belongs to the same type of wisdom as that of the dialogues and disputations.

Proverb collections:[27] These certainly form a remarkable group of Sumerian literature, but is there any need to put them as a subgroup under "wisdom literature"? A point sometimes overlooked is that while "proverb collections" may be a literary genre, "proverbs" as such are not. Cf. the discussion in *Chap. 1.1: Proverbs and School Education.*

Riddle collections (rare):[28] These may have been collected simply for enjoyment and intellectual pleasure, and possibly even for their usefulness in scribal education. It is remarkable that riddle solving belongs to the traditional features of wisdom. Riddles are represented also among other early literatures, such as Anglo-Saxon and Old Norse.

Short tales, morality tales, and humorous tales (rare): The term "*exempla,*"[29] used in Medieval literary scholarship, would cover a number of somewhat artificial subgroups.

22. Cf., e.g., the series *Texte aus dem Umwelt des Alten Testaments.* Wisdom is considered one of the traditional genres in Egyptian literature, but in Egyptology the term is restricted mainly to didactic precept compilations, which make its use really meaningful.
23. The central subject of this book (Chap. 1).
24. The best-known text is *The Farmer's Instructions,* edited by Civil, 1994. It is obvious that some of the texts associated with *The Instructions of Ur-Ninurta* could be considered relevant for similar reasons, cf. Chap. 2. It is noteworthy that some classical works, such as Hesiod's *Works and Days,* likewise combine practical advice with moral instruction.
25. Cf. the literature mentioned in n. 21 above.
26. An up-to-date edition of *Schooldays* is regrettably not yet available. Cf. Kramer, *Schooldays,* University Museum Monographs, 1949.
27. Cf. the introduction to *Proverbs* I, xiii–xxxvi. Cf. further the discussion below under Chap. 1.1.1.
28. A Sumerian collection of riddles was published by M. Civil, "Sumerian Riddles: A Corpus," in: AuOr 5 (1987) 17–37. To these can be added CBS 2149, published by Cavigneaux, 1996, 12 and 15. Riddles belong to the corpus of the Exeter book, cf. F. Tylor, *The Riddles of the Exeter Book* (Boston, 1910), and A.J. Wyatt, *Old English Riddles* (Boston, 1912). An old Norse collection was *Heidreksgaaderne,* see *Den ældre Edda og Eddica Minora,* I, trans. by Martin Larsen (Copenhagen 1943), 191–201. The riddle-like plot of the Sumerian epic *Enmerkar and the Lord of Aratta* is comparable to an episode in *Ragnar Lodbrobrokar's Saga* in which Kraka is told to appear before Ragnar Lodbrog without being dressed, and not having eaten, yet, not being hungry, not alone, but not accompanied by someone. She appears dressed in her long hair, having tasted an onion, and accompanied by her dog. Cf. *Völsunga Saga* ... ed. Magnus Olsen (Copenhagen 1906–8), 124. There are comparable episodes in the Talmud and in the Aramaic Aḥiqar story, and so forth. Cf. Galit Hasan-Rock, "Riddle and Proverb. The Relationship Exemplified by an Aramaic Proverb," in: *Proverbium* 24 (Helsinki, 1974) 936–940. The Sumerian epic is thus the first example of a plot-type reflected in Shakespeare's *Macbeth.* Cf. in general Jan de Vries, *Die Märchen von den klugen Rätsellösern,* FF Communications No 73, Helsinki, 1928. Cf. also the riddles proposed by the queen of Saba to King Solomon, in 1Kings 10:1–3; further, the literature cited by Limet, AcOrB 16 (2002) 106, n. 30.
29. The use of this term was suggested by Vanstiphout.

Fables: Gordon regarded these as a separate Sumerian wisdom genre, although some of the relevant texts actually appear in the proverb collections. There would be good reasons to regard fables of the *Aesopian* type, the earliest examples of which occur in Sumerian texts, as a type of wisdom literature. Cf. the discussion in Chap. 4.

Folktales (rare): These certainly make up a distinct genre, but in other linguistic areas folktales are not generally classified as wisdom literature. In a folktale there is often a "problem solver," and it is typically a person of the lower social strata who prevails over his superiors because he is cleverer than they. The two folktales included here (Chap. 5) are, however, mainly burlesque parodies of legal proceedings. They illustrate how a group of "wise women" may have functioned as counsellors to the king in actual life, using proverbs in a way that illustrates proverbial wisdom in an uniquely interesting way.

Satires (rare): These also form a separate genre whose importance has often been overlooked.[30] Their instruction does not assume the form of a direct message, but instead they use humor, wit, and irony to reveal "folly" and so make the pupil learn by an indirect message.

The notion that there may have been a specific genre of Sumerian texts related to the biblical righteous sufferer problem was almost entirely abandoned long ago. Yet, since the notion of a relenting angry deity seems to go back to Sumerian times and there is a rare number of Sumerian personal laments, in which the speaker's undeserved disaster is described, followed by his subsequent recovery, it is possible to see them as models for the framing story of the book of Job, although on a much less elaborate scale.[31]

Does the so-called *Early Dynastic Proverb Collection*[32] represent an early type of wisdom literature? Civil has now thrown new light on this question, showing that it basically consists of deprecatory "misogynic" sayings about women,[33] or as Klein puts it, a collection of proverbial insults.[34] Copies were made in the Isin-Larsa period and even later,[35] when the original meaning of some of the sayings was no longer understood. Apparently the later scribes had great difficulty interpreting the Early Dynastic sources, which implies that later Akkadian translations of such sayings cannot always be trusted. The insults are similar to those frequently quoted in the female dialogues, where some of the same say-

The short text *Níŋ-nam nu-kal* (Nothing is of value) treated in Chap. 3.1–2 could perhaps best be considered to belong to this group.

30. The satire was, after all, one of the important genres of classical literature and education. A few Sumerian examples are known. Two texts were published by Å.W. Sjöberg, "«He is a Good Seed of a Dog» and «Engardu, the Fool»," in: JCS 24 (1972) 107–119. A third example is *Dím-ma-ni ús-a-ni*, which approximately means "His plan is what comes after him." D.T. Potts: "Sumerian Literature and a Farsi Insult," in: N.A.B.U. 1995/2, no. 43, points out that Sum. a-dùg-ga-ur-ra, "good seed of a dog," corresponds to Farsi *tokhm-e sag* "a real bastard." This is similar to the paradoxical expressions exemplified by sophomore, "a wise fool." Cf. also Alster: "Two Sumerian Short Tales Reconsidered," in: ZA 82 (1992) 186–201 and the discussion of the meaning of níŋ-nam nu-kal zi ku_7-ku_7-da, "nothing is of value, (but) life should be sweet tasting," in *Chap. 3.3: Attempt at a New Interpretation* Cf. also n. 31 below.

31. Lambert, 1995, 30, rejects the idea, but, on p. 32, nevertheless points to a Sumerian personal name Mir-šà-kúšu, "Savage-relenting," attested in many Ur III sources. This is much older than the relevant texts, but cannot be disregarded, because, as Lambert points out, the goddess can hardly be both at the same time. The relevant Sumerian text, *A Man and His God*, was first published by Kramer in 1955 and immediately declared a Sumerian forerunner of the book of Job. Cf. already Gordon, 1960. Also translated by Klein, in Hallo (ed.), *The Context of Scripture*, 573–575.

32. Edited by Alster, 1991–92.

33. Cf. M. Civil: "Misogynic Themes in Sumerian Literature," paper read at the 47th RAI, Helsinki, 2001 (forthcoming). To these should be added BT 9, see the following note.

34. J. Klein, "An Old Babylonian Edition of an Early Dynastic Collection of Insults (BT 9)," in: *Wilcke FS*, 135–149.

35. Known SS texts are WB 169 = OECT I 13; UM 29-15-174 (bilingual with glosses in phonetic Sumerian), cf. M. Civil and R.D. Biggs, RA 60 (1966); UET 6/2 197, cf. Alster, 1991–92, 2. To these should be added BT 9, published by Klein, 2003, and the texts mentioned by Civil (not yet available). A partial published duplicate is the Crozer Theological Seminary tablet no. 199, now seemingly lost, but fortunately published by Goetze, JCS 4 (1950) 137, dupl. CBS 13872; cf. PSD B, 150 sub bi_7, where two lines are cited.

ings are cited, undoubtedly with the purpose of arousing laughter among the audience.[36] If such collections of insults are to be regarded as "wisdom" literature in any serious sense, it would blatantly betray the term as very hollow indeed.

In conclusion, it is not possible to identify precisely those texts that deserve the designation "wisdom literature" in Sumerian. The choice depends on the criteria chosen at the outset, such as the above-described categories suggested by Assmann. Throughout this work, the term "wisdom literature" will be restricted to father-and-son didactic compositions, as well as to a few short texts that deal explicitly with the understanding of the conditions of human life, exemplifying the *vanity* theme, the *carpe diem* theme, the *ubi sunt* theme, as well as some *fables,* particularly those of the Aesopian type, and some folktales. Fundamentally, wisdom is here considered an existential attitude rather than a genre designation.[37]

Sumerian Wisdom Literature: The Scope of the Present Work

It stands to reason that the only major viable criterion for selecting the compositions that may be assumed to be representative of Sumerian wisdom is that these are written in the Sumerian language. As such it is highly possible that they originated in the atmosphere of the Sumerian scribal schools, the *edubba* of the early second millennium B.C., which undoubtedly left lasting marks in the literary creativity of the following centuries, even far outside the original Mesopotamian arena. However, it should always be kept in mind that by the time when the *edubba* was flourishing, in the first part of the second millennium B.C., Sumerian had become a "dead" language, kept alive mainly in academic scribal circles.

The aim of the present work is not to revive an outdated concept of "wisdom literature," but, on the contrary, the aim is to redefine "wisdom" as an existential attitude permeating certain texts, limiting it to the relatively few texts that may properly be regarded as "wisdom" literature in a strict sense, but keeping the choice open for new text types to be included.

In this study, "wisdom" is not in itself considered a usable genre designation, but "wisdom" is retained as a useful label that may be used to characterize a number of text types. "Cleverness" and insight into the conditions of human life are here considered decisive features. Humor, wit, and satire, difficult as these may be to recover from a language long since extinct, are frequent and common features in these texts. The focus will be on wisdom as a means with which to make the best out of life, from the point of view presented in the texts themselves, rather than "wisdom" as a philosophical, speculative, or theoretical perspective of the existing world.

The following section is an overview of all the text groups included in the present volume. These are as follows:

1. Father-and-son didactic instruction compositions, represented by *The Instructions of Šuruppak.*

36. Cf. previously Alster, "Sumerian Literary Dialogues and Debates and Their Place in Ancient Near Eastern Literature," in: *Living Waters. Studies … Løkkegaard* (Copenhagen, 1990), 1–16. Cf. Klein in the study mentioned in n. 34, above. More details in Civil's forthcoming study of the text.

37. Other texts that have been considered wisdom compositions are TCL 15, 58, (Pl. CXIX AO 6719) mentioned by van Dijk, *Sagesse,* 5, who lists TCL 15, 37; 46; 56 and 57 as "sapientielle" or "des lamentations individuelles?" TCL 15, 58 is duplicated by u17818A, to be published in the forthcoming UET 6/3 volume as no. 428. The new duplicate offers a much improved reconstruction of the text. These texts belong to the circle of Larsa, for which see W.W. Hallo: "The Royal Correspondence of Larsa: I. The Appeal to Utu," in *Kraus FS,* 95–109.

2. Other didactic compositions: *The Instructions of Ur-Ninurta* and *Counsels of Wisdom.*
3. Texts relating to the vanity theme, represented in particular by *The Ballade of Early Rulers, Níŋ-nam nu-kal* ("*Nothing is of value, but life should be sweet-tasting*") versions A–D, and *Enlil and Namzitarra.*
4. Animal fables and short stories not involving humans, including the Aesopian type of fable and some so-called morality tales.
5. Folktales, represented by only two texts: *The Three Ox-Drivers from Adab* and *The Old Man and the Young Girl.*
6. Some examples of so-called proverb collections used as source books for scribal education.

It may not be immediately apparent why these text groups should be grouped together under a common heading "wisdom literature." It must be admitted that "wisdom" can be regarded as a relic from the early days of oriental scholarship, when the wisdom of Zarathustra had already become a common cliché. "Wisdom," indeed, was one of the literary topics that first aroused interest when Babylonian and Assyrian literature started to become available to scholarship around the turn of the twentieth century. Today, using the designation "wisdom" would make sense only if this is redefined and restricted to a much narrower group of texts.

As expected, Babylonian and Sumerian wisdom has been understood as testifying as to how the Mesopotamians understood the world, whether from a social, ethical, existential, or speculative point of view, or even as an early type of philosophy. Here I would simply initially confine myself to stating that in the texts selected, two contrasting underlying existential attitudes come to light. These are a conservative, traditional outlook versus a critical approach. I find these to be existential attitudes, rather than strict formal criteria, decisive for inclusion under the heading "wisdom literature."

A Traditional, Conservative Outlook versus a Critical Approach

A traditional, conservative outlook is typically represented by father-and-son instructions. Their aim is clearly to transmit the wisdom of wise old men to future generations, in other words, to put forward the past as a model for future generations, with no fundamental changes in the existing social order intended.

The key text, *The Instructions of Šuruppak*, goes back to Early Dynastic IIIa, that is, around 2600 B.C. It became the classic expression of this conservative type of wisdom. Also texts edited in Chap. 2 (*The Instructions of Ur-Ninurta* and *Counsels of Wisdom*) belong to this category.

On the other hand, some texts express a critical attitude toward existing values. These texts are often satirical or ironical in tone, but one cannot state categorically that they represent a speculative attitude. These texts are included under the heading "The Vanity Theme" (no. 3 above), and appear to be forerunners of the critical wisdom that has become emblematic through the biblical book of Ecclesiastes. So, although such Sumerian texts are rarely attested and very difficult to interpret, they are invaluable as sources for the history of thought and ideas in the ancient Near East.

A closer look at the critical attitude embedded in some fables (4) and folktales (5) will justify the inclusion of these under the heading "wisdom literature." Among the fables incorporated into the Sumerian proverb collections are the first examples of what may be termed the Aesopian type of fable. In these an argument may be turned upside-down in an unexpected way, which forces one to reconsider existing values generally taken for granted. A closer examination of the two so-called folktales I have included reveals that by no means is the aim of these tales to collect "folklore" in any modern sense. On the contrary, the intent is to present a traditional scene, the king's judgment, in a burlesque way that reveals a satirical and critical attitude questioning existing institutions.

Some examples of proverb collections (6) used as source books for scribal education are also included. The proverb collections were used as a kind of source book from which the students could learn how to use apt rhetorical phrases. Thus, the proverb collections were, by no means, recordings of living proverbs in the sense of a modern proverb collection, but, rather, examples of scribal wit. Whether scribal wit was always wisdom can be disputed, but, at least, we are very lucky to know some of the source books.

Chap. 1: The Instructions of Šuruppak

The text is said to be addressed by "the man from Šuruppak" to his son Ziusudra, that is, to be handed down from a ruler of what was considered the last of the antediluvian cities, to his son Ziusudra, who, like the biblical Noah, was the only one among mortals to gain eternal life. One might assume that the advice given to Ziusudra would be intended specifically to teach him how to become a good leader of his people. Yet, in the instructions themselves, there is nothing that points toward an origin at a royal court. The impression is rather that the bulk of the precepts have their origin in an agricultural setting. The ethical attitude can best be described as "modest egoism," that is, don't do anything to others that may provoke them to retaliate against you.

Some early Egyptian precept compilations are the only ones known that may date approximately as early as this one. Unlike those, our text does not expressly state in what existential situation the father is handing down his advice to his son, though typically it occurs when the father's death is imminent.

Chap. 2: The Instructions of Ur-Ninurta and Related Compositions, Counsels of Wisdom

The Instructions of Ur-Ninurta is a relatively little known and rarely attested text. The text consists of three parts, of which the first is *The Instructions of King Ur-Ninurta* proper. This contains a clear statement of the "classic" wisdom concept: a just man is expected to be rewarded with happiness in his own lifetime and will enjoy a long life for himself and his successors. A righteous man is here clearly understood to be one who serves the gods with regular offerings, in other words, more a cultic than an ethical quality. All this is phrased in a literary style that imitates the classic Sumerian high style known from epics and myths. The whole composition is clearly intended as praise of King Ur-Ninurta of Isin (1923–1896 B.C.) as the righteous ruler of Nippur.

The second part is written syllabically, which makes its meaning almost impenetrable, but it is clear that it concerns animal husbandry, field work, and irrigation. The main objective is to teach the subjects of Ur-Ninurta to be diligent and work hard on their canals and fields.

The third part, consisting of only seven lines, is a short treatise punning on various expressions of humbleness and physical submission. The purpose seems to be to teach the subjects of Ur-Ninurta to work hard and to obey those who put them to work early in the morning!

The title *Counsels of Wisdom* perhaps covers two separate compositions, of which the first is too poorly preserved to make a detailed description possible. From the preserved portions, it appears to deal with the king as judge. The following, much longer section of *Counsels of Wisdom* is much less well preserved than the *Instructions of Šuruppak*. The preserved parts yield some glimpses of religious duties, social relations, and so forth.

The compositions in Chap. 2 were traditionally written on the same *Sammeltafel*, indicating that already in antiquity they were thought of as somehow related.

Chap. 3: Critical Wisdom

Under the heading "The Vanity Theme" have been grouped a number of short compositions that present a critical view, as opposed to the traditional attitude of the father-and-son didactic compositions.

First of these is a short composition that exists in at least four versions, all of which share the same two opening lines. These are here titled, in agreement with ancient archival tradition (according to the first line) *Níŋ-nam nu-kal (Nothing is of value)*, versions A, B, C, and D. This very phrase is quoted as line 253 of *The Instructions of Šuruppak*: "Nothing is of (lasting) value (so therefore) life should be sweet-tasting." This can thus be proved to be a notion genuinely at home in Sumerian wisdom tradition. It expresses the concept that, since no material things are of lasting value, the best one can do is to enjoy the present life as much as one can, in other words, this is an expression of the *carpe diem* theme.

Obviously, the traditional opinion, according to which a righteous man is rewarded in his own lifetime, had to confront reality. There can be no doubt that thoughts about what must have been felt as undeserved disasters had long been versed in Sumerian thinking. These are reflected in a lament that mourns the untimely death of King Ur-Namma (2112–2095 B.C.) of the Third Dynasty of Ur. Also the untimely deaths of young warriors were bewailed, and the shepherd-god Dumuzi became emblematic of the youth who had died before ever having been married. This resulted in a contradiction, the traditional answer to which was that no one can understand the dispositions of the gods; the best one can do is to make the most of his present life, serve the gods, and hope not to arouse divine anger unintentionally.

In Mesopotamian literature, the *carpe diem* theme is generally thought to be first expressed in the Old Babylonian version of the Akkadian *Gilgameš Epic* (first part of second millennium B.C.), in which the barmaid Siduri advises Gilgameš to forget about seeking eternal life and instead be satisfied with enjoying his present life, his wife, and children. The texts presented here can, however, be taken as evidence of the presence of the *carpe diem* theme much earlier in Sumerian sources. To the Mesopotamians, very unlike the Egyptians, there was no prospect of a happy life after death, so in itself the presence of the *carpe diem* way of thinking should not come as a great surprise.

The texts clearly inform us that whatever goods a man can gather to secure his future can be lost in no time at all. The most elaborate version of *Níŋ-nam nu-kal,* version D, seems to go one step further by questioning the value of smoke offerings, since not even smoke, the most elusive of all substances, can reach the gods in the sky. This leads to an agnostic, but not pessimistic, attitude, anticipating the wisdom of Qohelet (Ecclesiastes) in the Hebrew Bible.

The so-called *Fable of Enlil and Namzitarra* provides a slightly different answer. Namzitarra, realizing that material wealth, including gold, is not of lasting value, is rewarded by Enlil with a lasting office in Enlil's temple for himself and his successors. The text was copied by later scribes, and exists in a version from Emar in Syria in which the theme of the length of the human lifetime is elaborated upon.

The *Ballade of Early Rulers* is a short, but remarkable, text of only twenty-two lines. It is also attested in a Sumero-Akkadian bilingual version from the Syro-Mesopotamian area from about 1300 B.C. The text is a characteristic creation of literate men, who were able to rework quotations from earlier works in a new light. After a brief prologue, stating that the rules for human kind were instituted by the gods, comes a theme familiar to everyone: since time immemorial it has been claimed that things are not what they used to be, everything has deteriorated. The expression used in line 3: "Since time immemorial there has been wind!"[38] anticipates a classic expression of vanity of the biblical Qohelet, probably dating from the second half of the first millennium B.C. It has now been commonly recognized that the biblical book was not influenced by Greek philosophy as much as had previously been thought. Instead, current scholarship suggests that Qohelet has drawn upon a number of Near Eastern sources, including Egyptian; but that such ideas are related to Sumerian sources from the beginning of the second millennium B.C. comes as a great surprise.

The early rulers are said to have had incredibly long lives, up to 36,000 years, somewhat like the patriarchs of Genesis, but they are all said now to be in their everlasting houses, that is, they are all dead. To enjoy the descriptions fully, one has to be familiar with the many allusions that must have been evident in the contemporary academic circles to which the text belonged. Yet, the conclusion is unambiguous. Since no one, not even Ziusudra, the only mortal to be granted eternal life, can match the achievements of those bygone rulers, the best one can do in the here and now is to enjoy a happy life with wine and good food! Only the Syro-Mesopotamian version spells the drinking aspect out so clearly, but the point was certainly similar in the original Sumerian version. In other words, this is a clear statement of the *carpe diem* theme, presumably intended to be enjoyed at some banquet celebrating the highest wisdom in a joyous symposium.

38. A Neo-Assyrian fragment relating to the same text uses a different Sumerian word for "wind," but the idea seems to be essentially the same.

The *Ballade of Early Rulers* in its Syro-Mesopotamian version is known also from a bilingual tablet from Ugarit in which it is connected with a short sequence of bilingual proverbs, at least one of which is known from older Sumerian sources.

The essential message is that, since no one can understand the dispositions of the gods, no one should look down upon those struck by misfortune or disease, for he may well be in the same situation tomorrow. This is, thus, an expression, not of ethics in any strictly Christian or modern sense, but a type of social understanding that accords well with a similar idea expressed in the Egyptian *Instructions of Amen-em-ope*, dating to the second half of the first millennium B.C. This shows that such ideas may have been common in "wisdom" circles in wide areas of the ancient Near East in the second and first millennia B.C.

A bilingual Assyrian fragment of *The Ballade of Early Rulers* from the library of King Assurbanipal (668–627 B.C.) at Nineveh, dating ca. 650 B.C., testifies to the persistence and further development of the ideas associated with the *Ballade*. The preserved parts do not genuinely duplicate the *Ballade* itself, but contain a short sequence of proverbial sayings, similar to those from Ugarit. Like those, these share the short prologue also known from the *Ballade*. It is thus highly likely that these were derived from a Sumerian collection of sayings exemplifying the conditions of human life, including the vanity and *carpe diem* themes. The preserved Neo-Assyrian fragment questions any attempt to climb higher up the social ladder, since not even a female weaver can be expected to stay (in marriage) with a hired worker. It also questions the value of academic knowledge, since it provides no lasting joy to the scholar's student, who is destined to die anyway!

A more radical solution to the question of life and death may appear in the six concluding lines of the Sumerian epic text *Gilgameš, Enkidu, and the Netherworld*, later incorporated into the Akkadian *Gilgameš Epic* as its twelfth tablet. This contains the oldest example of a journey to the underworld. Enkidu reports to Gilgameš of what he has seen in the realm of the dead. The individual descriptions are somewhat ironic or morbid in character and, in fact, seem more a description of conditions among the living than among the dead. Yet, the final six lines permit an interpretation that has unusual consequences for understanding the way in which life and death were regarded by the Mesopotamians.

If we read the sequence as a progressing scale of relative success or lack of success in the hereafter, we note that the stillborn children (l. 298), playing at a table of gold and silver (l. 299), were much better off than the average inhabitants of the netherworld. Yet, those who were actually born, but died at an early age (l. 300), were even better off, since they lie on the bed of the gods (l. 301). In other words, one is entitled to see here an idea similar to that expressed by Herodotus, that the best thing that can happen for those living is to die young, "that it is better for a man to die than to live." To draw the conclusion that such ideas were common among the Mesopotamians would certainly be to go much too far, since numerous dedicatory inscriptions and hymns aim at providing a long life for the donor or for those rulers for whose benefit the hymns were composed. Besides, life in the hereafter was never considered attractive, but, on the contrary, rather dull. Nevertheless, one must keep the possibility in mind that such an idea may be intended here as a critical alternative to commonly held views.

The intent of the very last line of *Gilgameš, Enkidu, and the Netherworld* (l. 303) is, however, unambiguous: the man who was set on fire does not exist even in the underworld, since both his body and his "soul" were completely destroyed by the fire. This is the reason for the ban against cremation known in many religions of the world. It accords well with the way in which abstract concepts are generally bound to physical reality in Mesopotamian thinking.

Chap. 4: Animal Fables and Short Stories

That animal tales and fables were included in the Sumerian proverb collections became clear when Gordon published *Proverb Collection Five* in 1958. Since then these have played an ever greater role in the study of the history of the fable as a literary type.

Animal tales may, of course, have been invented spontaneously and independently in many places in the world, but the answer to the origin of the fable as a literary type may not be so simple. The European tradition of fables depends heavily on the classical tradition, so it is obviously of interest to know that the Greek fables were preceded by much older Sumerian ones. A number of classical Greek and Latin authors cite fables, and at least some of them ascribed to Aesop must have been known in Athens from the fifth century B.C. onward. A very limited number of fables are known from Egyptian and Babylonian sources. Numerous fables are known from Indian sources, but these, although very difficult to date, are mostly considered less ancient than the Greek examples. Reminiscences of fables occasionally come to light in the Hebrew Bible.

The fables included in this volume consist of four groups:

(1) Three fragments included in Chap. 4.2 may have belonged to a larger series in which the fox played a major role. Already in BWL, Lambert discussed how a number of Akkadian fragments dealing with the deeds of a fox may be combined into a larger series. In 1988, the subject was taken up by H. Vanstiphout, who tried to reconstruct a connected sequence by means of European medieval texts, in particular, the "beast epic" *Roman de Renart.* The three fragments included here: *The Fox and Enlil as Merchant, A Fable of a Fox and a Dog*, and *A Fragment Involving a Hyena and a Dog* cannot yet be connected to a single text, but for the time being it is safe to say that these may be regarded as belonging to a common set of animal tales.

(2) *The Goose and the Raven*, edited in Chap. 4.3, is an example of a relatively long "literary" fable that has many affinities to the so-called contest literature: each of two antagonists competes to be acknowledged as superior.

(3) Some short animal tales of the Aesopian type are included in Chap. 4.4.

(4) Chap. 4.5 includes a few short stories not involving animals: *The Adulterer, The Lazy Slave Girl*, and *The Fowler and His Wife.* In the latter, the point is humorous and anything but moral, relating to the fowler's potency problems. So if these are labelled morality tales, this should be understood *cum grano salis. The Adulterer* exemplifies an ethical attitude not primarily resting on religious, modern or Christian, considerations: the reason for warning against sleeping with another man's wife is simply that it isolates the offender socially.

The fables treated here do not exhaust the complete number of Sumerian fables, since some are included as episodes in larger contests or in mythological texts.

Chap. 5: Folktales:
The Three Ox-Drivers from Adab and
The Old Man and the Young Girl

The two Sumerian folktales presented here give the impression that there was a group of wise men or, perhaps, women whom the kings used to consult in difficult cases. Such cases were clearly seen as similar to judicial court decisions, but were obviously independent of them, more depending on the counsellor's ability to find a clever solution, like Solomon's judgment.

The most remarkable feature of *The Three Ox-Drivers from Adab* is that, although it has so far been described as a "folktale," it seems to be quite the opposite, almost an "anti-folktale." It is characteristic of a folktale that a "small" man prevails over his superiors, proving in the end to be more successful than they. In this text, however, none of the main characters seems to end up being successful. Rather, the point is that the three men cannot solve their problem themselves, thereby creating an opportunity to present a solution carrying the marks of sophisticated literature. Although the text is far from fully understood, it is clear that the solution is expressed through puns and allusions, even to legal procedures. This may have been a main reason why it was written down and incorporated into the scribal curriculum. Furthermore, the message seems to have been very different from one expected from a folktale problem-solver, proposing a solution to the benefit of those seeking his advice. The important lesson, "nothing ventured, nothing gained," is phrased in a way that may have been very characteristic of wisdom circles. The outcome seems rather to have been to the benefit of the king, and the whole setting is more like a parody of a legal case. The pompous way in which a god acts as a clerk in this trivial case, where a calf is said to be engendered and born in an unrealistically short period of time, confirms the satirical nature of the whole text.

The Old Man and the Young Girl contains the oldest known example of a theme well attested in world literature (see Chap. 5.2 for details). The story as presented here is surprisingly brief and is partly phrased in detailed circumlocutions, quoting a sequence of proverbs that obviously were popular in scribal circles, since some of the same phrases occur in proverb collections with the same implications. It is thus justified to assume that the entire story was meant as an occasion to present just that section as an example of scribal wit, rather than as testimony to the king's judicial wisdom. Add to this the realization that the solution suggested by the wise women—to give the old man a young girl in marriage—does not require any exceptional degree of ingenuity. The text is, therefore, best described as a burlesque invention of the scribal schools, similar to *The Three Ox-Drivers from Adab*.

Chap. 6: Examples of Proverb Collections Used as Literary Source Books

The rediscovery of Sumerian literature is an ongoing process, as two tablets presented to the Cornell University Library in 2000 illustrate. One of these covers some lacunae in *Sumerian Proverb Collection* 1, which had obstinately resisted recovery, although the latest edition, by Alster, *Proverbs*, from 1997, utilizes no less than close to a hundred sources for that collection alone. Although the findspot is unknown, like a number of tablets inscribed with proverb collections, one of the two Cornell University tablets is a characteristic product of the scribal schools, in which the teachers were used to making their own specific choice of lines to be included from proverb collections and other literary sources, reflecting the needs that may have arisen during the teacher's confrontation with the pupil's varying degree of competence. This meant that not only proverbs in the strict sense, but also sententious sayings from literary compositions were sometimes included. This procedure can be seen as reflecting the way in which written texts were accompanied by oral comments in the Sumerian schools, which affected the texts both ways, and, ultimately, makes the traditional dichotomy between "written" and "oral" literature seem obsolete.

Conclusion

The traditional type of wisdom is represented mainly by the father-and-son didactic compositions, and their wisdom is mostly proverbial, often bound to the traditional wisdom concept: a good man is recompensed by the gods in his own lifetime.

The critical type of wisdom is mostly represented by compositions characterized by scribal wit.

Both types of wisdom draw heavily upon proverbial wisdom, but the critical type of wisdom is characterized by the sophisticated use of literary and proverbial references in new and unexpected contexts.

Full editions of the Sumerian school compositions and the Sumerian debates and dialogues would be needed to complete the picture. This also implies that the specific school compositions are not included here. These, for the first time, express the professional pride of the Sumerian scribes, who saw scribal education as a means to avoid hard physical labor, most clearly expressed in *Father and Son*.[39]

In order to appreciate the literary merits of the Sumerian schools, the *edubba*, one must bear in mind that although the education of scribes undoubtedly served other, distinctly practical purposes, such as accounting, land measurement, and so forth, the literature of the *edubba* was completely self-contained, being addressed solely to a closed circle of "academics."

39. Sjöberg, JCS 25 (1973) 105–179. Cf. also Addendum p. 403.

CHAPTER 1

The Instructions of Šuruppak

1.1 Introduction

1.1.1 Early Mesopotamian "Wisdom Literature"

The Instructions of Šuruppak shares a number of features with some of the vast number of literary sources that can be adduced for comparison from other linguistic areas.

First, it is generally recognized that proverbs often played a major role in the formation of early "wisdom literature."

Second, there is no attempt at understanding the world in a new way, not in order to promote a specific social class, or to introduce a new type of conduct, or to promulgate a new type of religion as a basis for that. The values of the existing world are taken for granted. What matters is instruction on how best to live in the given world order under the given circumstances. Since the outlook of proverbs is usually very conservative, they were suitable for this kind of instruction.

Third, there appears to be a common setting for these compositions, or at least some similarities, in that the counsels are usually transmitted by a father to his son in an existentially crucial situation, in particular, when the death of the father is imminent.

It is remarkable that this early Sumerian example of a father-and-son didactic composition is phrased in a secular way. There are very few passages mentioning the gods, and the question of divine retaliation does not openly play a role. Yet, it would be a mistake to understand this as a secular way of thinking in opposition to religious thought. On the contrary, in the texts of the third and early second millennia B.C., religious precautions are thought of just like any other type of practical advice regarding human behavior. The motivation for not doing harm to one's neighbor is in no way specifically religious, but simply that it would not be clever from a social point of view. It can best be described as "modest egoism."[1] So, for the early periods, one must appreciate a type of wisdom that is secular, practical, and not speculative in nature, in other words, no early philosophy.[2]

The frequent use of motivation clauses[3] in *The Instructions of Šuruppak* can be understood as reminiscent of an old traditional type of oral instruction. Cf. line 14: dùr gù-di na-ab-sa$_{10}$-sa$_{10}$-an érin-zu ša-ra-ab-si-il-le, "do not buy an ass that brays (too much); it will tear your yoke apart"; or line 17: gán-zu-àm pú na-an-ni-dù-e-en ùŋ-e ša-re-eb-ḫul-ḫul, "Don't place a well in your own field; the people will do harm to you" (scl. when they come to fetch water). The plain, literal, meaning of these phrases is all there is to them. There is no attempt to add a generalizing, metaphorical, meaning. Yet, this should not mislead us to believe that abstract thinking did not occur. The very development of cuneiform writing, as well

1. I have borrowed the expression "modest egoism" from B. Mogensen, *Israelske visdomsregler*, 1982.
2. One could argue that a true aspect of ethics in early Mesopotamian history becomes apparent in the royal hymns and law codes that emphasize the king's role as protector of the poor. But, on the other hand, this reflects the notion that it serves the king's honor if his subjects are treated well.
3. Motivation clauses are frequent in the Hebrew Bible. A first mention of them in a Mesopotamian context was made in Alster, AuOr 5 (1987) 199–206, esp. 204–205, where some literature is mentioned. Cf. further below: *Legal Aspects of Proverbs*.

as the puns associated with it, are very much the results of abstractions, although very different from modern approaches.[4]

Šuruppak's Family Relations and the Implications of the Flood

As interpreted here, the *The Instructions of Šuruppak* are said to come from a father, who was the son of Ubar-Tutu, otherwise known as the only ruler of the dynasty of Šuruppak. The name Ubar-Tutu can be understood as "Foreigner of Tutu," that is, a foreigner protected by *Tutu*, in which Tutu may be the name of an Akkadian god. According to the *Sumerian King List*, 33, Ubar-Tutu ruled for 18,600 years and was the last Sumerian ruler who reigned before the Flood. The name of his son (= the father of Ziusudra) is remarkably nowhere expressly mentioned, but instead a telling epithet is given: "The man from Šuruppak." The significance of this is underscored through an unusually long list of epithets (ll. 4–7) stressing his ability as giver of wise counsel and, most of all, his connection with the city Šuruppak.[5]

In the Standard Sumerian version, the name of the son is given as Ziusudra. This person is known from other sources: the Sumerian flood story and the Akkadian epics of *Atrahasis* and *Gilgameš*,[6] in which his Akkadian name is Utnapishtim, "he of long life," which is a direct translation of the Sumerian name (or vice versa). This name does not occur in the Early Dynastic versions of *The Instructions of Šuruppak*, but the Adab version includes what seems to be another name, or an epithet of the son, ÚR.AŠ, which presumably means "father-in-law." If that is the case, it would make good sense as an epithet of someone thought to be the "father-in-law" of all living generations.[7]

This interpretation suggests that the mythological connotations associated with the Flood, as an all devouring disaster that separates the antediluvian times from the postdiluvian period, went back in time at least to ED III, ca. 2400 B.C.[8] The absence of the name zi-u_4-sud-rá in the Early Dynastic period seems, however, to indicate that the specific role he plays later, as the only mortal who was transferred to Dilmun to live happily there forever, was a later mythological elaboration, dating probably from the Isin-Larsa period.[9]

4. Cf. Cavigneaux: "Aux sources du Midrash: l'herméneutique babylonienne," in: AuOr 5 (1987) 243–255, who, like previously Lambert, AfO 17 (1956) 311, points out that certain techniques used in some Babylonian commentaries resemble the rabbinic exegetic techniques characteristic of the Midrash. The kind of thinking involved is very different from the notion of scientifically valid etymologies, the point being that puns were seen as constituting reality; cf. Alster, *Jacobsen MV*, 35–40. For the development of early cuneiform writing, cf. the innovative approach by Glassner, *Écriture à Sumer. L'invention du cunéiforme*, 2000, and now Selz, "«Babilismus» und die Gottheit «dNindagar»," in: *Dietrich FS*, 647–684.
5. Cf. the discussion in Chap. 1.4, comments to lines 4–5 and 5–7 with notes, where the basic discussions by Jacobsen and Wilcke are mentioned.
6. Also alluded to in *The Ballade of Early Rulers* 13, cf. Chap. 3.3.
7. The evidence has hitherto mostly been understood as follows: In the Early Dynastic Sumerian version, the father was given an epithet, ÚR.AŠ, which seems to mean "father-in-law," here understood as a name or epithet of the son. The father, himself being named Šuruppak, was said to be the son of Ubar-Tutu. This is here understood as "the man from Šuruppak," "the Šuruppak'ean," as indicated by *Gilg.* XI 23: lú *šu-ri-ip-pa-ku-ú* dumu mubar-tu-tu, "the man from Šuruppak, son of Ubar-tutu."

   Since Šuruppak, as a name of the father, would be an unusual personal name, being identical to the name of the city itself, this information has usually been understood as reflecting an existing generation: Ubar-Tutu, Šuruppak, Ziusudra, in which the name of the father is secondary, being on old misunderstanding of *dumu Šuruppak, meaning "the man from Šuruppak," "the Šuruppak'ean," later misunderstood as "the son of Šuruppak," i.e., a personal name. He was then taken as the father of Ziusudra.
8. The name Ziusudra may even owe its existence to influence from the same sources as became manifest in the Akkadian epics of *Gilgameš* and *Atrahasis*. In other words, Utnapištim may have been primary, and Ziusudra secondary. The specific details of the mythology connected with the Flood story as we know them were probably relatively late phenomena in Sumerian literature, presumably not older than the Isin-Larsa period.
9. The *Sumerian Flood Story* was edited by Civil, in Lambert and Millard, *Atra-ḫasīs*, pp. 138–145 and 167–

The Existential Situation: To Whom Was the Text Addressed?

Many of the phrases are expressed generally in the third person, "one should not ...," but a several are addressed in the second person, "you should not ..."[10] Since many of these statements are of a proverbial character, they may have existed before their occurrence in *The Instructions of Šuruppak*, in which case they were, of course, not originally intended to be addressed to Ziusudra.[11]

Although *The Instructions of Šuruppak* in the Standard Sumerian version is said to be addressed to the son of a ruler of the antediluvian city of Šuruppak—and thus a potential ruler himself—there is remarkably nothing in the advice given to him that explicitly seems to prepare him for that role. On the contrary, it would be ludicrous or even quite insulting that such advice as "don't steal anything" (l. 28) were to be understood as seriously addressed to a future king. Rather, the main focus is on exactly the kind of advice that would have been useful for any owner of a household.[12]

The Instructions of Šuruppak differs from some early Egyptian didactic wisdom compositions that pretend to be addressed specifically to the son of a ruler. These texts provide specific advice on assuming one's future duties as a dynastic ruler. *The Instructions of Šuruppak* also differs by not specifying any details surrounding the situation in which the counsels are being handed over from father to son, typically just before the imminent death of the father.

These observations are in keeping with the general character of the counsels given in the text. These are practically oriented counsels intended to prepare any man to live a prudent life in society, in particular, preparing him to take control of his own household,[13] not specifically the royal throne.

In sum, the sayings included are traditional rules for prudent social behavior, sometimes close to the earliest law codes or possibly reflecting orally transmitted traditional sayings related to legal proceedings. It is remarkable that occasionally a critical attitude toward those in power, even toward the royal palace, comes to light.[14]

172. The general impression, based on the late grammar of the Sumerian text, apparently influenced by Akkadian, is that the main source, PBS 5, no.1 = CBS 10673, is late Isin-Larsa (cf. the discussion by Civil, op. cit., 139). Since then only a single duplicate has turned up, Schøyen MS 2026. The flood story seems to be much more at home in the *Atrahasis Epic* than in Sumerian mythology, and the concept in the *Sumerian Flood Story* that Ziusudra was transferred to Dilmun as a sort of Paradise certainly makes best sense in the Isin-Larsa period, when trade with Dilmun flourished. If the notion of an all-destructive flood had been known much earlier, it would be remarkable that it was not incorporated into *Inanna and Šukalletuda*, in which all the "plagues" traditionally associated with Inanna were included; cf. Volk: *Inanna und Šukalletuda*, SANTAK 3 (Wiesbaden: Harrassowitz, 1995). Volk suggests a pre-Ur III date for the original composition, but this can be contested. The presence of the city name Šuruppak in the Early Dynastic version of *The Instructions of Šuruppak* is, however, best understood as a hint that at least similar ideas existed in the middle of the third millennium B.C., although they may not at that time have been associated with the specific details of the Flood story as we know it.

10. For the form "one should not ...," cf. Taylor, *The Proverb*, 150–152, often considered to be characteristic of Germanic proverbs.

11. There are a number of variants that show that the text sometimes vacillates between the second and the third person, e.g., lines 109; 129; cf. *Chap. 1.10: The Second Person versus the Third Person* for more examples.

12. Examples of counsels not primarily relating to the duties of a future ruler: Drinking (l. 67); boasting (l. 37; 67); quarreling (ll. 24ff.; 35; 36); slandering (l. 65); rape (l. 49); theft (l. 28); burglary (l. 29); murder (l. 31); loans, lending money, guaranteeing (ll. 19ff.; 53); positioning of a house or field (ll. 15–18; cf. ll. 271–273); purchase of animals (ll. 14; 214, etc.); purchase of slaves and slave girls (ll. 154–163); irrigation (ll. 51; 158); trade (l. 68(?)); relations between neighbors (l. 54). It is worthy of mention that none of these is seen specifically from the point of view of scribal education, nor from the vantage of the profession of scribes. Lines 284ff., however, connect the entire collection of counsels with the benefit of the palace; cf. the comments to line 284. Yet, some sayings are directly critical toward those in power; cf. below.

13. Advice concerning the management of a good household frequently appears in the book of Proverbs. Cf., e.g., "The good wife," Prov 31:10–31.

14. Esp. lines 104; 110; cf. also lines 207; possibly 157; 258; 261. The ultimate loyalty rests with the nearest family members (ll. 172–174; 202–203; 265–270), but good

How Much Context Is There Attached to the Sayings?

It is difficult to determine the extent to which an individual saying should be understood within the context of the other sayings surrounding it. On the one hand, many sayings seem detached, devoid of context, but, on the other hand, the sequence of sayings frequently offers important hints about the interpretation. There is always a risk of depending too greatly on one or the other point of view. Generally, for an interpretation to be successful, it should be able to explain a given line as an independent saying and, at the same time, as belonging within a specific context.[15]

Theoretical Outlook on Proverbs

The notion that proverbs represent the wisdom of "wise old men" has been common since ideas expressed in Aristotle's *Poetics* became highly influential.[16] It was not until 1931, when Archer Taylor in his book *The Proverb* (p. 3) first described the proverb as a "saying current among the folk" that this opinion was finally challenged. The belief that proverbs represent the "wisdom" of wise old men went so far that the biblical book of *Proverbs* became regarded as an early type of philosophy.[17] Yet, in origin, most proverbs belong to the world of daily discourse; they become repeated, often as apt humorous, satirical, or sarcastic remarks. Thus, proverbs do not represent a systematic attempt at expressing a coherent view of the world. Therefore, proverbs that contradict each other may well exist side by side.[18]

Proverbs and School Education

Sumerian proverbs, like many other ancient proverbs, carry indicators of their being considered literature. Many ancient proverbs are, in fact, known only through literature, are spread through literature, are revived though literature, and are translated as part of literary works. Countless proverbs have

relations to the nearest neighborhood, mainly of farmers, is always seen as important (cf., e.g., l. 153). What matters is to have a good household with a reliable wife (ll. 185; 215), and no quarrels within the household (cf. ll. 154–157). Society is viewed as a group whose members all contribute something of value (ll. 181–182; 271), so that everyone should be satisfied with the lot he has received (cf. ll. 272–273). Diligence and hard work at the time of the harvest is almost a motto for prudent behavior (cf. ll. 131–133), whereas laziness and drinking stands for the opposite (cf. l. 221). Travelling and trade were obviously within the normal sphere of life (cf. l. 166). Destiny is seen as something unpredictable (cf. l. 170), and its consequences are unavoidable (cf. l. 118). The value of material wealth is clearly recognized, but one should not let oneself become dependent on it (l. 253).

15. For some examples, see below p. 42, *Context-Related Expansion of the Strophic Pattern*.
16. Aristotle is known to have made a collection of proverbs, now regrettably lost. His ideas about proverbs: περί ὧν 'Αριστοτέλης φησίν ὅτι παλαιᾶς εἴσι φιλοσοφίας ἐν ταῖς μεγίσταις ἀνθρώπων φθοραῖς ἀπολομένης ἐγκαταλείμματα, περισωθέντα διὰ συντομίαν καὶ δεξιότητα. Παροιμία δὴ καὶ τοῦτο καὶ λόγος ἔχων ἀξίωμα τῆς ὅθεν κατηνέχθη φιλοσοφίας τὴν ἀρχαιότητα, ὥστε βόειον ἐπιβλέπειν αὐτῇ. Πάμπολυ γὰρ οἱ πάλαι τῶν νῦν εἴς ἀλήθειαν εὐστοχώτεροι, "about which Aristotle says that they are remains of very old philosophies that have been destroyed in enormous catastrophes caused by humans, and that they have been saved because of their conciseness and cleverness. Accordingly a proverb is both this and a spoken message worthy of the philosophy from which it derives, so that an ignorant one can consider it closely. In fact, the ancients to a very high degree hit the truth and were more acute than those living now" (I am indebted to Finn Gredal Jensen for the Greek translation). See Synesius Cyrenensis, *Encomium Calvit.*, p. 85 B; cited in Leutsch and Schneidewin, *Paroemiographi Graeci*, Praefatio I f. As a late classical text, it is to be read *cum grano salis* if taken as a genuine quotation of Aristotle. The word βόειον, here translated "ignorant one," is apparently derived from βῶς, "ox," and strongly suggests an ironic attitude.
17. Cf. *Introduction*, p. 19, n. 8 above, referring to Johann Friedrich Bruchs book, *Weisheitslehre der Hebräer*, with the subtitle: *Ein Beitrag zur Geschichte der Philosophie* (1851).
18. For contradictory proverbs, cf. W. Mieder: "Proverbs," in: J.H. Brunvand (ed.), *American Folklore: An Encyclopedia* (New York: Garland Publishing, 1966), 597–601, quoted in Alster, *Proverbs of Ancient Sumer* I, p. xiii, n. 2. The more advanced literary compositions, such as Ecclesiastes, take advantage of this feature by discussing the validity of some proverbs by quoting contradictory ones.

been used for didactic purposes in school education. The Sumerian proverbs are no exception. Thus, the study of Sumerian proverbs must take into account the constant tension between what may have been a living tradition of proverbs and their use in the school curriculum, as well as in the literary tradition on a larger scale.[19] Oral comments may undoubtedly have accompanied the written sources in the schools, but are rarely reflected in the written sources.[20]

Negative and Positive Types of Advice in the Instructions of Šuruppak

The Instructions of Šuruppak, even in its earliest versions, consists mainly of two types of sayings: (1) those expressing an imperative, mostly in the form of an explicit prohibition: "Don't ..."; (2) sententious sayings that are plain indicatives or wishes not explicitly expressing an imperative.

The presence of the negative imperatives is immediately explicable given the nature of the text. The remaining large group of sayings consists mainly of short statements, often humorous, setting things "right" by revealing "folly," i.e., the kind of indirect message that would be expected in the Sumerian dialogues, satires, and satirical school compositions.[21]

The Development of the Instructions of Šuruppak

The Abū Ṣalābīkh version seems to have contained the same types of saying as the Standard Sumerian one, and approximately in the same order. Already in the earliest version, there are traces of the slight humor—sometimes even morbid—that characterizes the later versions (cf., e.g., line 31). The later additions thus appear to have stayed true to the original pattern and attitude. The enjoyment of wit, humor,

19. In the case of Sumerian, there has been a frequent tendency simply to regard the proverbs as creations of the scribal schools, in whose curriculum they were used. Most recently Veldhuis: "Sumerian Proverbs in Their Curricular Context," in: JAOS 120 (2000) 383–399, has argued that the notion that the Sumerian proverbs are genuine proverbs that originated in daily life situations is "romantic" (p. 383). His main argument is that the Sumerian proverbs appear in proverb collections that were composed for the instruction of Sumerian lexicography. They reflect a graduating scale of linguistic competence, preparing the students for the study of Sumerian literary compositions.

    There are a number of reasons to reconsider the argument. First, the Sumerian proverbs in many cases present lexical problems not typical of the known literary corpus. Although there are many links between the proverb collections and the literary corpus, the study of "artificial proverbs" would have been a superfluous and unnecessarily difficult step to undertake if the sole purpose had been to prepare the pupils for reading literary texts, in which many of the lexical peculiarities typical of the proverbs do not occur. So the most likely conclusion is that the proverbs were considered worthy of study for their own sake, whether or not that use was identical to their original linguistic setting. Cf. also *Addendum,* p. 45.

    Second, as pointed out by Limet: "Le bestiaire des proverbes sumériens," in: *L'animal dans les civilisations orientales,* AcOrB 14 (Bruxelles, 2002) 29–43, the Sumerian proverbs typically preserve sets of images that are often left behind from earlier cultural states in which these images were easily understandable. This, in particular, was the case with proverbs dealing with animals, but it is a universal and well-known phenomenon. Cf., e.g., "Shoemaker, stick to thy last"; "The blind man eats many a fly" (revealing an unpleasant side of Elizabethan English culinary manners), etc.; cf. Taylor, *The Proverb,* 76–82 for this phenomenon, esp. p. 76: "... proverbs may become old-fashioned and pass out of use" and p. 77: "A systematic examination of obsolete proverbs might yield interesting results."

    Third, a number of female proverbs in *emesal* seem to reflect the daily use of certain proverbs in domestic settings. No complete list of such proverbs exists as yet, but cf. preliminarily Alster, "Literary Aspects of Sumerian and Akkadian Proverbs," in: *Mesopotamian Poetic Language: Sumerian and Akkadian.* Cuneiform Monographs 6 (Groningen: Styx Publications, 1996), 1–21. An example: 3N-T 731: "Thus speaks a widow after her husband's death: «There is any number of widows, but there is no husband (to marry)!" (Alster, *Proverbs of Ancient Sumer,* I, 305). In contrast to what has sometimes been asserted, there are no *emesal*-sayings in our text, however; cf. the comments to line 54.
20. Cf. *Chap. 6: Introduction: Proverbs ... as Literary Source Books,* and the literature there mentioned.
21. Examples: lines 97–100 (97: "If you say, I'll give you a piece of bread ..., etc."); 111–114; 115–117 (117: "How wonderful I am"); 119–123, etc.

irony, sarcasm, and satire seems to have played an important role in the later development of the composition.

In *The Instructions of Šuruppak*, the negative counsels are expressed usually in the 2nd person, with a prohibitive na- preformative, followed by an imperfective (*marû*) verb and a form of the 2nd person absolute marker -en, "you should not …." There are few direct imperatives (e.g., line 27), but quite a number of sayings are straightforward statements, "maxims," or "apophthegms" (e.g., line 30) that do not express any explicit imperative.

Inclusion of Proverbial Sayings

It is occasionally possible to discern the inclusion of proverbial sayings, apparently quoted as they may have existed beforehand without regard to their causing minor incongruities in the context. The criteria for recognizing a proverb in such a text have been concisely summarized by Hallo, 1990, 212–213: "first, and most subjectively, the apparent incongruity of the epigrammatic saying in its narrative context, second and more objectively, as an explicit statement that «people are always saying this» or, thirdly, and ideally, as the recurrence of the saying (more or less verbatim) in one of the Sumerian proverb collections. The final ground is the recurrence of the saying outside Sumerian wisdom literature."

An example is lines 172–173, in which the advice to pay attention to an older brother—already in the Adab version (ED_2 Fr. 8 ii 1–2)—is evidently not to be taken seriously as being addressed to Ziusudra. In such cases, the address is to the "pupil" listening to the advice. Similar examples occur in lines 153 and 167.

Another example is line 140: inim-šèd-dè-ŋu$_{10}$ ḫé-ŋál-la-àm, "My words of prayer mean abundance." Use of the 1st person suffix seems out of place within the context.[22] This is hardly meant to indicate that the "man from Šuruppak" is the speaker, but presumably this simply reveals the form in which the saying was generally quoted.

Occasionally sayings, apart from the negative imperatives, are quoted as explicitly referring to a second person, e.g., line 191: "After a man has dwelled with the 'big men' of your city, …." Other sayings include direct quotations, e.g., lines 113–114; 260–261.

International-Type Parallels

Many of the sayings included deal with themes well known from proverbial wisdom, and ancient Near Eastern didactic literature in particular. This should not be mistaken to mean that proverbs necessarily teach a moral lesson, since it is well known that many proverbs are without moral implications.[23] Yet, obviously those sayings that appear in the ancient didactic compositions tend to have moral or social implications. A few examples are listed here:

Line 28: níŋ nam-mu-zuḫ-z[uḫ] ní-zu nam-mu-úš-e, "Don't steal anything; don't kill yourself!" for the double negative imperative, cf. κόπτε χρέος, κόπτε λύπας, "verringere Schulden, verringere Sorgen!" (Krumbacher, 1887, p. 78, no. 16).

Line 39: lú-da níŋ-zuḫ-a nam-mu-da-gu$_7$-e, "Don't eat something stolen with a *thief" (cf. the comments to l. 39 for variants) belongs to a widespread warning against becoming an accomplice by receiving stolen goods; cf. "Si tu veux être sage, refuse ta bouche au mensonge et ta main au vol, et tu seras sage" (*Aḫiqar* III 87); Eccl 5:17; and Düringsfeldt I 698: "Der Hehler ist so gut wie der Stehler" "The concealer (receiver) is as bad as the thief"; Autant vaut recéler que voler; *Utrique sunt fures et qui accipit et qui furatur, Agens et consentiens pari poena digni.*

Line 67: lú-lul-la-ka é-kaš-ka KA nam-tar-tar-re inim-zu ŋar-ra-[àm], "Don't boast in the way of a liar in an ale house; your word stands forever (lit., your word is placed)." The last section occurs also in line 37: inim-zu ŋar-ra; cf. "The spoken word can

22. Cf. the comments on line 140 for an alternative.

23. Veldhuis, 2000, p. 385, correctly states "Many proverbs do not seem to have a moral implication at all." Cf. Alster, "Literary Aspects of Sumerian and Akkadian Proverbs," CM 6, 1996, 3: "The widespread notion that proverbs are expressions of «wisdom» is not a criterion for the identification of proverbs … collectors of all periods have had difficulties in harmonizing the occasionally unpolished vocabulary and unmistakenly cynical attitude of some proverbs with that befitting sagacious wisdom."

never be recalled"; "Det talte ord står ikke til at ændre" (Danish).

Line 106: ka-tuku ^{kuš}lu-úb-a-ni sá im-dug$_4$, "The boaster reached (out for) his (empty) leather bag"; cf. "Det duer ikke at lyve i sin egen pung" "It's no use to lye into one's own purse" (Danish) (Holbek and Kjær No. 2843).

Line 128: an sù-ud-dam ki kal-kal-la-àm, "Heaven is far away, (and/but) earth is precious"; cf. τὰ μικρὰ (read μακρά?) και θαυμαστὰ τὰ κοντὰ τε καὶ ἐπίκερδα, "Das Ferne ist auch bewunderbswert, das Nahe aber auch nützlich" (Krumbacher, 1893, p. 126, no. 99); *Aḫiqar* III 68: "Une chèvre proche vaut mieux qu'un taureaux qui est loin, et un passereaux que tu tiens dans ta main l'emporte sur cent qui volent dans l'air." This is the prototype of a very common proverb in many languages, e.g., "Der Sperling in der Hand ist besser als die Taube auf dem Dach."[24]

Lines 131–133: u$_4$-buru$_{14}$-šè u$_4$ kal-kal-la-šè géme-gim ri-ga-ab eŋi-gim gu$_7$-a dumu-ŋu$_{10}$ géme-gim ri eŋi-gim gu$_7$-a ur$_5$ ḫé-en-na-nam-ma-àm, "At the time of the harvest, at the most priceless time, glean like a slave girl, eat like a queen; my son, glean like a slave girl, but eat like a queen, that is how it should be indeed!" There are two proverbial points here: (1) cf. "He who gleans in summer shows insight, but he who sleeps during the harvest is a disgrace" (Prov 10:5); "but let it be your care to order your work properly, that in the right season your barns may be full of victuals" (Hesiod, *Works and Days,* 305–306); "Make hay while the sun shines" (ODEP, p. 501); "Den der sover i høsten skal hungre i vinteren" "He who sleeps during the harvest will have to starve in winter" (Danish) (Holbek and Kjær, no. 3177). (2) Cf. the antithetical pair in SP. 2.137: [en]-gim dù saŋ-gim du; [sa]ŋ-gim dù en-gim du, "build like a lord, walk like a slave; build like a slave, walk like a lord"; cf. also "Drik som en gæst og æd som hjemme er van" "Drink like a guest and eat as you are used to at home" (Holbek and Kjær, no. 738).

Line 153: dumu eŋar-ra-ra níŋ nam-mu- ra-ra-an e-pa$_5$-zu šè-im-ra, "Don't beat a farmer's son; he will «beat» your irrigation canal." Although the meaning is disputed,[25] it is worth mentioning some sayings that may express similar ideas: "In den Brunnen, aus welchem du getrunken hast, wirf keinen Stein" (Lewin, *Aram. Sprichwörter*, p. 29); "Wirf keinen Stein in die Quelle, von welcher du trinkest. Bete nicht um die Zerstörung des Hauses, vom dem du issest. Dem Ochsen, welcher pflügt, muß man nicht das Maul verbinden" (Burchardt, nos. 150–151; 172); cf. also Deut 25:4.

Lines 154–157, warning against acquiring certain types of slaves, is reminiscent of *Aḫiqar* III 35: "Mon fils, n'acquiers pas un eslave querelleurs ni une servante voleuse, car ils perdront tout ce qui sera confié à leur mains."

Line 166: dili-zu-ne kaskal na-an-ni-du-un, "Don't travel alone"; cf. "Mon fils, ne te mets pas en route sans glaive et ne cesse pas de faire mémoire de Dieu dans ton cœur" (*Aḫiqar* III 38); *eko na gacchedadhvānam*, "one should not walk on a road alone" (Stenzler, *Elementarbuch der Sanskrit Sprache* Š 333). Cf. further the comments to line 166 for Akkadian parallels.

Line 169: kur-ra kur na-an-na-dub-bé, "Don't pile up a mountain among the mountains!" For parallels to this paradoxical type, see the comments to line 169. Cf. also "Nach den Orte, wo [viel] Gemüse ist, dort trage Gemüse hin" (Lewin, *Aram. Sprichwörter*, p. 50); "To carry coals to Newcastle." Cf. also βώλοις 'άρουραν (scl. ἄυξανεις), "to add lumps of earth to the earth" (Martin, *Studien*, p. 11).[26]

Lines 187–188: é gul-gul-lu-dè é ša-ba-da-an-gul-e lú zi-zi-i-dè lú ša-ba-da-an-zi-zi-i, "He who is about to destroy houses will destroy (any) house with them. He who is about to stir up men will stir up (any) man with them"; cf. ARM 10, 150: 9–10: *šu-up-pa-am i-ša-tum i-ka-al-ma ù ta-ap-pa-ta-ša i-qú-ul-la*, "When a reed is devoured by fire, its «girl-friend» is attentive."[27] Cf. also *nam tua res agitur, paries cum proximus ardet*, "It's your safety that is at stake when your neighbor's wall is in flames" (Horats,

24. Cf. Taylor, *The Proverb*, 22–24.25.
25. Cf. the comments on the line and *Chap. 1.9: Aspect- or Tense-Related Verbal System?*
26. This is not the same type as the "rope of sand" (cf. Conybeare, 1898, p. 78) that plays a role in the Aḫiqar story, but rather brings to mind the riddle-like difficult tasks in *Enmerkar and the Lord of Aratta.*
27. Cf. A. Finet, RA 68 (1974) 35–47.

Epist. I 18:84); "Når der er ild i en nabos væg, da må enhver ræddes for sin egen" "When a neighbor's wall has caught fire, everyone must be afraid of his own" (Holbek and Kjær, no. 1310).

Lines 191–192: lú-gu-la ere-za-ka ba-e-zal-ta dumu-ŋu$_{10}$ za-a ur$_5$-re ḫé-em-me-re-a-e$_{11}$-dè, "When you have passed alongside a «big man» of your city, my son, this will make you ascend!" If the translation is reliable, it is remarkable that in this case the outcome of associating with mighty men is seen as something positive. But, perhaps, it is to be said with an ironic wink of the eye. Warning against associating with the mighty otherwise belongs to the standard repertoire of proverbial wisdom. Cf., e.g., ἄλευ' ἀπὸ μείζονος ἀνδρός, "Keep away from the mightier one!" (Diogenes II 56); "Ne recherche point la faveur des grandes; Fuis les honneurs" (*Pirqe Aboth* I 10); "L'amour des dignités devient le tombeau de celui qui les recherche" (Schul, no. 28); "Få ord med store herrer" "Little talk with big lords" (Holbek and Kjær, no. 3518).

Lines 193–194: géme-⌜zu⌝ ḫur(?)-saŋ-ta ši-im-ta-an-tùm sa$_6$-ga ši-in-ga-àn-tùm ḫul ši-in-ga-àm-ta-an-tùm, "Your(?) slave girl, whom you bring down from the mountains, she will bring good, (but) she will also bring evil." Cf. *Post gaudia luctus*; Nach Freude folgt Leid; Jede Freud' hat ein Leid auf dem Rücken" (Düringsfeldt I 493); "Vil man have det søde, må man tage det sure med" "If you want something sweet, you must take the sour with it" (Holbek and Kjær, no 431).

Line 195: sa$_6$-ga šu-àm ḫul šà an-ga-àm, "The good is a hand, but the evil is also a heart"; cf. "Süßigkeit steht auf der Zunge, Todesgift im Herzen" (*Hitopadeśa* I 77).

Lines 202–203: šà ki-áŋ níŋ é dù-dù-ù-dam šà-ḫul-gig níŋ é gul-gul-lu-dam, "A loving heart is something that builds houses, (but) a hateful heart is something that destroys houses"; cf. "Hatred provokes animosity, but love covers up all crimes" (Prov 10:12); "Hade, det kan mangen mand skade; Moderens velsingelser bygger børnenes huse, men faderens forbandelse river dem ned igen" "Hatred can be harmful to many men; the blessing of a mother builds the houses of the children, but the cursing of a father tears them down again" (Holbek and Kjær, no. 3560).

Line 204: nir-ŋál-e níŋ-du$_{12}$-du$_{12}$ gaba-ŋál me nam-nun-na, "To an authority, riches and a stout appearance are princely charismatic powers"; cf. αἰδὼς τοι πρὸς ἀνολβίῃ, θάρσος δε πρὸς ὄλβῳ, "Shame is with poverty, but confidence with wealth" (Hesiodos, *Erga* 319); "Auf jedem Orte und zu jeder Zeit ist der Reiche mächtig auf der Welt. Auch die Macht der Könige gründet sich auf Reichtum. Durch Reichtum wird jeder stark, wegen seines Reichtums wird er geehrt" (*Hitopadeśa* I 115–116).

Line 208: ezem-ma-kam dam na-an-du$_{12}$-du$_{12}$-e, "Don't choose a wife during a festival"; cf. "Eile einen Acker zu kaufen, sei gelassen, willst du eine Gattin heimführen" (Lewin, *Aram. Sprichwörter*, p. 60); "En mand skal ses ved sit arbejde, en kvinde i et dejtrug, og ikke i en springdans" "A man should be seen at his work, a woman at a dough-trough, and not in a leaping dance" (Holbek and Kjær, no. 3547).

Lines 209–211: šà-ga ḫuŋ-ŋá-àm bar-ra ḫuŋ-ŋá-àm kù ḫuŋ-ŋá-àm za-gìn ḫuŋ-ŋá-àm túg(?) ḫuŋ-ŋá-àm gada(?) ḫuŋ-ŋá-àm, "Inside it is (all) borrowed; outside it is (all) borrowed: the silver is borrowed; the lapis lazuli is borrowed; the dress(?) is borrowed; the linen(?) is borrowed"; cf. "Mon fils, ne t'approche pas de la femme querelleuse et à la voix altière, ne désire pas la beauté de la femme bavarde (et impure), car la beauté de la femme est (cause de) sa honte, et ce n'est rien que l'éclat de son vêtement et la beauté extérieure avec lesquels elle te captive et te trompe" (*Aḫiqar* III 26).

Line 261: lú-gu-la á-diš-e ga-na-gam-me-en-dè-en, "The «big man», let us make him bow down with «one arm»"; cf. *Concordia res parvae crescunt; discordia res magnae dilabunt*; Union is strength; Eintracht bringt Macht (Düringsfeldt, I 404).

Line 264: ummeda ga-arḫuš-a-ke$_4$ lugal-bi-ir nam ši-im-mi-ib-tar-re, "The wet-nurses of the milk of mercy decide the destinies for their lords." Cf. the comments to line 264, where alternative translations are suggested. If "milk of mercy" is justified, it is reminiscent of "the milk of human kindness" (*Macbeth* I 5); cf. further "Den hånd der rører vuggen, styrer verden" "The hand that touches the cradle governs the world" (Holbek and Kjær, no. 527).

Line 271: é ere-bar-ra-ke$_4$ ere šà-ga ši-dù-dù-e, "The houses on the outskirts of a city maintain the houses inside the city." This is a formal parallel to "Den ene hånd vasker den anden" "The one hand washes the other" (Düringsfeldt I 375).

Legal Aspects of Proverbs

It is well established that in illiterate societies proverbs tend to be used as decisive arguments in lawsuits. The same phenomenon is sometimes reflected in literary sources.[28] Such an example occurs in the *Disputation between Lahar and Ašnan* ("ewe and grain"), in which the final verdict depends on the apt quotation of a frequently repeated proverb favoring grain over sheep.[29]

As noted by Selz, 2003,[30] a number of sayings in *The Instructions of Šuruppak* are thematically linked to provisions that occur in the oldest known law code, the *Codex Urnamma.*[31] This should not be surprising in view of the fact that gnomic sayings relating to legal proceedings play an obvious role in the early Greek comparable sources by Solon. The themes, such as false accusations and false testimony, are very much alike. Previously (Alster, 1974, 19) I had pointed out that the Abū Ṣalābīkh sequence iii 5; iii 7; iv2 = SS 30; 31; 33 is paralleled in a sequence in ED lú E 152–154; 157 (MSL 12, 19), which seems to suggest that already in Early Dynastic times such sequences were traditional.

This leads to the further conclusion that the characteristic form in which many of the sayings of *The Instructions of Šuruppak* appears, with a protasis followed by an apodosis (here a motivation clause, cf. below), may reflect legally valid provisions, possibly going back in time to an illiterate society. The apodosis often assumes the character of a motivation clause, stating the consequences of disregarding a warning. In this way, the motivation clauses can be seen from a much larger perspective, since similar considerations apply to the motivation clauses of the Hebrew Bible, esp. Deuteronomy.[32]

Selz lists the following sayings (quoted here with the line count used in the present edition, with his translations, but without the Early Dynastic parallels):

Line 19: šu-du$_8$-a nu-e-tùm lú-bi ša-ba-e-dab$_5$-bé, "Don't act as a guarantor; that man will have a hold on you." This is comparable to *Codex Ešnunna* (CE) Š 18.

Line 21: lú-ra igi-du$_8$-a na-an-ak-e úru-bi ša-re-e[b]-su-su, "Don't testify against a man; you will be submerged by a flood (arising) from it!" This is comparable to *Codex Urnamma* (CU) ŠŠ 28–29.[33]

Line 27: du$_{14}$ bar-bar-ta gub-gub-[ba] in-nu-uš sila-kúr-ra níŋin-na-ma-a[n], "Stand aside from quarrels; when facing an insult go around it on another road!" (Selz: "Im Streit nimm' die andere Straße, vom Hohn nimm Abstand").

Line 28: níŋ nam-mu-zuḫ-zuḫ ní-zu nam-mu-úš-e, "Don't steal anything; don't kill yourself!" (Selz: "Stehle nichts, gib dich nicht selbst auf [od. wirft Dich nicht selbst weg] [aB bring dich nicht selbst um]"). Cf. CE ŠŠ 12–13.

28. Cf. Taylor, *The Proverb*, 86–97. A classic example is "First come, first served." Legal proverbs have been extensively studied, in particular in German, in which Graf and Dietherr, *Deutsche Rechtsprichwörter*, 1864, has become a classic.
29. Cf. Alster and Vanstiphout, 1987, 189–190; Alster, 1996, 14, referring to UET 6/2 263 and 266 (Alster, *Proverbs*, I, p. 311). The same saying is alluded to in *Enlil and Namzitarra* 19 (Chap. 3.5).
30. "«Streit herrscht, Gewalt droht» - Zu Konflitregelung und Recht in der frühdynastischen und altakkadischen Zeit," in: WZKM 92 (2002(b)) 155–203, esp. pp. 173–178, in what follows cited as Selz, 2002, with the line counting used in the present edition.
31. Now best available in the reconstruction by Wilcke, *Jacobsen MV*, 291–333.
32. Cf. the introduction above, p. 11: *Early Mesopotamian «Wisdom Literature»*, and Alster, AuOr 5 (1987) 199–206, esp. pp. 204–205, referring to W. Baumgartner, "Die literarischen Gattungen des Jesus Sirach," ZAW 34 (1914) 161–199; B. Gemser, "The Importance of the Motive Clause in Old Testament Law," *Suppl. Vetus Testamentum* I (Leiden, 1953), 50–66; W. Richter, *Recht und Ethos. Versuch einer Ordnng des Weisheitlichen Mahnspruches* (Munich, 1966); and newer literature not listed here.
33. Cf. the comments to line 21 with alternative suggestions. Cf. further Selz, 2002, 175, referring to *Codex Lipitištar* — 33;*Codex Ešnunna* — 17; Selz comments "vermutlich ist gemeint, daß der Zeuge die Ganze Stadt gegen sich hat," which is convincing, although the translation was based on a slightly older text reconstruction than presented here. Cf. further Haase 1996a: 32.

Line 29: é na-a-an-ni-bùr-e-en mi-si-saḫar-ra al nam-me, "Don't break into a house; don't demand the money chest!" (Selz: "Brich nicht in ein Haus ein[, frag'/verlang' keinen *Transportbehalter*(?)]").

Line 30: ní-zuḫ piriŋ na-nam ul-dab$_5$ saŋ na-nam, "The thief is indeed a lion; when he has been caught, he is indeed a slave!" (ED version not quoted; Selz: "Der Dieb ist fürwahr ein Drache [aB Löwe], gepackt ist er in der Tat eine Sklavin [aB Sklave]"). Cf. CE Š 50.

Line 31: dumu-ŋu$_{10}$ sa-gaz nam-mu-ak-e ní-zu àga-àm nam-bí-ib-bar-re-e, "My son, don't commit murder; don't let yourself be mutilated with an axe!" (Selz: "Begeh' keinen Mord. [Spalte dich nicht selbst mit einer Axt]"). Cf. CU Š 1: "Wenn ein Mann einen Mord/Totschlag begeht, soll dieser getötet werden."

Line 32: ninta niŋir-si na-an-ak ní-zu na-an-⌜x⌝-⌜x⌝, "Don't make a (young) man best man; don't [humiliate(?)] yourself!" (Selz: "Nimm keinen Mann als Brautführer, [betrüge dich nicht selbst]").[34]

Line 33: ki-sikil dam tuku-d[a] e-⌜ne⌝ nam-mu-un-KA-e inim-sig-bi ma[ḫ-àm], "Don't laugh with a girl if she is married; the slander (arising from it) is strong!" (Selz: "Spricht nicht mit einem Mädchen [das einen Gemahl nehmen will(?)], die Verleumdung ist riesengroß").[35]

Lines 42–43: ù-nu-ŋar-ra na-ab-bé-⌜e⌝ eŋir-bi-šè ŋiš-pàr-gim ši-i-ši-íb-lá-e, "Don't speak fraudulently; in the end it will bind you like a trap!" (Selz: "Sprich nichts Haltloses, später [ist es] eine Fälle").

Line 49: géme-zu-úr ŋìš na-an-dù zu-úr šu-m[u]-ri-in-sa$_4$, "Don't have sexual intercourse with your slave girl; she will neglect you." (Selz: "Hab' keinen Geschlechtsverkehr mit deiner Sklavin; sie wird dich ... nennen").[36]

Line 62: dumu lú-ra ŋìš á-zi na-an-ne-en kisal-e bí-zu-zu, "Don't rape a man's daughter; the courtyard will find out about you!" (Selz: "Vergewaltige keines Mannes Tochter, der 'Hof' wird es wissen [bzw im 'Hof'] wird sie dich(?) bekannt machen"). Cf. CU Š 8: "Wenn einer Sklavin, die nicht defloriert ist, ein (anderer) Mann Gewalt antut und sie defloriert, soll er 5 Scheqel Silber zahlen."

Selz further mentions lines 53; 124–125; 132;135 as examples of didactic saying in the SS version possibly reflecting rules of social behavior.

The Relations between Proverbs and Sententious Sayings

Sometimes *The Instructions of Šuruppak* includes sententious sayings that occur also in the Sumerian proverb collections. Thus, it is clear that these sayings were thought of as belonging to the same category, and, obviously, whether or not these were genuine proverbs in origin was not an issue.

The situation is similar to that found, for example, in the Anglo-Saxon *Proverbs of Alfred*, in which quoted proverbs are intermingled with sententious sayings, coined in the same pattern as already existing ones to such an extent that it would be futile to try to sort out which is which. The literary merits lay just here, that is, the ability to express advice through phrases that sound as if they are supported by the authority of old proverbial wisdom, although some of them may have been coined by a literate author, who thus, to some extent, became a compiler as well. The use of proverbs by those who are literate sometimes furthered what may have become the beginning of literary analysis, by causing an awareness of the problems of metaphorical speech and double meaning. Since we are dealing with some of the oldest known literary sources in the world, the details escape us forever, but the later development of the genre of didactic precept compilation in the ancient Near East illustrates some of the same characteristics.

The Direct Address "My son"

The direct address "my son" occurs in all versions of the text, but not in quite the same way.

In the Abū Ṣalābīkh version there seems to be no clear pattern as to where it is repeated. It occurs in:

34. Cf. the comments to line 32.
35. Selz's translation is based on the 1974 edition; my translation "Don't laugh with a girl, etc.," is based on the Akkadian translation, then unknown. Cf. the comments to line 33.
36. Cf. the comments to line 49, where the reasons for an improved understanding are stated.

ED_I obv. i 7 = SS 9 (= introd. form.); ED_I obv. iv 7 (= introd. form.); ED_I rev. v 7 (introd. form.). The ED_I forms of SS 31 = ED_I obv. iii 7; SS 62 = ED_I obv. vi 8+; SS 207 = ED_I rev. iv 10; and SS 272 = ED_I rev. vi 4 do not include dumu-ŋu$_{10}$.

In the Adab version it seems to be repeated more frequently, but the text is too poorly preserved to yield a precise picture. It occurs in Adab 8 f (restored) = introd. form.; cf. further Alster, 1974, 21–22: II 8 = 31(?) (restored) = introd. form. and further fragments that indicate more repetitions. (For details, cf. Chap. 1.6).

In the SS version it occurs in lines (9); 31; 34 (restored); 61; (79); 133; (149); 160; 165; 192; 207; 219; 236; 254; 272 (those in parenthesis form part of the introductory sequence).

There seems to be a tendency to include "my son" in the very last entry of a larger sequence, obviously to give it greater emphasis, something which occasionally may help in recognizing larger patterns of sayings; cf. lines 133; 160; 192; 207; 219; but not 165 and 264, however.

Context-Related Expansion of the Strophic Pattern

A visible principle that led to the expansion of the text comes to light when a contrast embedded in a single line was followed by the addition of parallel lines that "spell" out the contrast embedded in the preceding line. An example occurs in lines 129–130, which elaborate on the contrast embedded in line 128. Cf. also lines 172–174; apparently also 195–197; 208–211. Sayings were generally included by way of contrast or association, which means that they are not totally devoid of context. The context should not be pressed too hard to obtain a connected meaning in each case, however; cf., e.g., the comments on line 198, and many more examples, especially in the comments on Wilcke's translations. Notable examples are lines 65–66; 124–125; 128–130.

A similar principle of expansion frequently comes to light in *Counsels for Šūpē-amēli* (cf. below).

Other Didactic Wisdom Compositions from Later Mesopotamian Sources

In Sumerian literature the major comparable text is *The Instructions of Ur-Ninurta*, possibly associated with the Sumerian text titled (*Sum.*) *Counsels of Wisdom* (these are both treated in Chap. 2). The text is regrettably very imperfectly preserved.[37] The religious outlook is, at least in large sections, more pronounced. The composition is centered more on religious duties and offerings, which presumably reflects the attitude of the early second millennium B.C., during which it apparently came into being.[38]

In Babylonian literature, the so-called *Counsels of Wisdom* goes back to Middle Babylonian times (the middle of the second millennium B.C.).[39] It differs from *The Instructions of Šuruppak* in having a decisively more "literary" character, and it can perhaps be ascribed to a specific author. This text probably became a prototype of the Aramaic version of the sayings of Aḥiqar.[40] Some compositions related to Sumerian wisdom were transmitted throughout the later Syro-Mesopotamian area, undoubtedly through sources that came from Babylonia proper.[41]

The most interesting and best-preserved comparable Akkadian text from the Syro-Mesopotamian area is that which may be named *Counsels for Šūpē-amēli*.[42] Attention should be paid in Dietrich's careful edition to the detailed strophic pattern in which it is phrased. Apparently its author or redactor was a very deliberate, methodical scholar. Perhaps he was familiar with *The Instructions of Šuruppak* and used it for inspiration. The possibility is certainly worth

37. In order not to mistake this for the Akkadian composition of the same title, I suggest simply calling them *Sum. Counsels of Wisdom*, and *Akk. Counsels of Wisdom*, respectively.
38. Cf. the discussion in Chap. 2, p. 222. Cf. Lambert, BWL, 96–107, and the comments below, p. 43, nn. 50–55, for details.
40. Cf. *Chap. 1.1.2: The Sayings of Aḥiqar*, for bibliographical details.
41. Cf. the discussion under *Chap. 3.3: The Ballade of Early Rulers* and *Chap. 3.5: Enlil and Namzitarra*. See now also Cavigneaux, in *Wilcke FS*, 60.
42. Cf. Dietrich: "Dialogue zwischen Šūpê-amēli und seinem 'Vater'," in: UF 23 (1991) 38–65; Kämmerer, 1998, pp. 176–207. Also Foster, *Before the Muses*, 3rd ed. (Bethesda, 2005), 416–421.

considering, because, although the text undoubtedly came from Babylonia, changes are likely to have been made in the Syro-Mesopotamian area, where a fragment from a contemporary Akkado-Hurrian version of *The Instructions of Šuruppak* has now been found, probably from the same area and period as that from which *Counsels for Šūpē-amēli* is known. There are at least two passages in *The Instructions of Šuruppak* that suggest this.[43] It is more likely, however, that contact occurred much earlier, when the *Counsels for Šūpē-amēli* was originally composed in Babylonia proper. That text differs from *The Instructions of Šuruppak* in being constructed much more as a dialogue between teacher and pupil.[44]

Another father-and-son fragment from the Syrian area is written on the same tablet, Emar 771, as the Emar version of the fable *Enlil and Namzitarra* (for which see Chap. 3.5). It appears only in Akkadian and has no Sumerian version. It has been treated by Klein, 1990, p. 67, and Kämmere, 1998, pp. 225–227.

1.1.2 Father-and-Son Compositions from Other Linguistic Areas

The father-and-son aspect of *The Instructions of Šuruppak* invites comparison with other ancient literature, since (1) father-and-son didactic compositions tend to belong to the oldest attested genres; and (2) proverbs or sententious sayings tend to occur in the oldest text types and are frequently attested in father-and-son didactic text compilations.

Both in regard to age and geographical proximity, Egyptian literature is obviously source for comparison with the Sumerian material.

Egyptian Precept Compositions

Didactic precept compositions belong to the earliest genres attested in Egyptian literature. These were ascribed to authors who were kings or individuals holding important offices. A book of wisdom is reported to have been composed by Imhotep under the third dynasty (ca. 2613–2494 B.C.), which is not preserved. A small fragment remains of the instructions of Djed-ef-Hor of the fourth dynasty. Better preserved are the instructions of Kagemi from approximately the same time. The instructions of Ptahhotep from the fifth dynasty (ca. 2494–2345 B.C.) are well preserved. Later examples include the *Instructions for King Merikare*, approximately 2100 B.C.[45]

A hieratic wisdom text dating between the tenth and the sixth centuries B.C. is *The Instructions of Emenem-opet*. This text includes a section that has been considered to be a model for biblical Proverbs 22:17–23:11.[46] This is particularly interesting because of some similarities to sources from Ugarit, which may go back to Sumerian forerunners.[47]

A Demotic text, *The Instructions of ᶜOnchsheshongy*, from the fifth century B.C., is introduced by a framing story according to which the text was composed by a father, who was a priest.[47] *The Instructions of ᶜOnchsheshongy* is a highly interesting literary work

43. *Instructions of Šuruppak* 17 and 208–212.
44. The pupil's final answer, starting in Spruch IV.ii, ending in IV.vi, in Dietrich's edition, quoted in Kämmerer, 1998, 200–203, is, in fact, rather impertinent.
45. The dates are those of W. Stevenson Smith, in "The Old Kingdom of Egypt," in: CAH, 1962. Helck's dates, in *Geschichte des Alten Ägypten* (Leiden, 1968) are slightly different: fourth dynasty ca. 2578–2463; fifth dynasty ca. 2463–2322 B.C.
46. Among the vast literature on Egyptian precept compilations, a few basic works are mentioned here: Miriam Lichtheim, *Ancient Egyptian Literature* (Berkeley, 1976), Vol. II, 61–80: The Instructions of Ptahhotep; 97–109: The Instructions Addressed to King Merikare; 135–146: The Instructions of Any; 146–163: The Instructions of Amenope. Also W.K. Simpson (ed.), *An Anthology of Stories, Instructions and Poetry* (New Haven, 1972; 2nd ed. 1973), 159–176; Merikare 180–192; Amenope 241–265. Further: W. Helck: *Die Lehre für Merikare*, Kleine ägyptische Texte herausgegeben von Wolfgang Helck (Wiesbaden, 1977).
47. The basic edition is H.O. Lange, *Das Weisheitsbuch des Amenemope* (Copenhagen, 1925). Cf. *Chap. 3.4: Proverbs from Ugarit* for details.

from our perspective. On pp. xiii–xv of Glanville's edition it is briefly characterized as: (1) an insistence on a certain moral standard in dealing with men; (2) insistence on the superiority of the "wise man" (... and, as a corollary, on the disastrous state of the "fool"); and (3) insistence on man's dependence on God. These are common "essentials of all Near Eastern Wisdom Literature." In the specific work, there is no logical principle in the organization of the sayings. It is said to be written by an imprisoned author, somewhat similar to the Aḥiqar story, but the circumstances behind his imprisonment are not described.[49] The contents are close to the practical instructions of Anii, with no similarity to the religious instructions of Amenemope. They are not addressed to a man of the court, "a man ... in the council chamber," but the author is a "priest" addressing "the peasant farmer, living in the country, or in a village or small town in Egypt." What matters is "man's relations with his family, with his friends and neighbors, and with his landlord, and the management of his small affairs, with only an occasional reference sprinkling of moral commonplaces. The wise man and the fool, the good and bad influences in a man's life who appear so frequently in the texts are to be thought of against that background."

Aramaic and Syriac: The Sayings of Aḥiqar

The Aramaic *Sayings of Aḥiqar* exists in a number of languages and versions, and may go back to a Babylonian prototype, the Middle Babylonian text known as *Counsels of Wisdom*. This has become clear since 1962, when van Dijk discovered that the name Aḥiqar occurs in a Late Babylonian tablet from Uruk, dating to the 147th year of the Seleucid era (165 B.C.).[50] The document is a list of antediluvian kings and their sages (*apkallū*), followed by some postdiluvian kings and their scholars (*ummânū*). According to the document, one of these, Aba-[d]ninnu-dari, was a "scholar" (*ummânu*) living in the time of King Esarhaddon of Assyria (680–669 B.C.), whom "the Aḫlamû (i.e., Arameans) call Aḫu-ʾaqari," that is, Aḥiqar.[51] Aḥiqar the sage thus goes back to a Babylonian archetype. The Uruk document is "fictitious," however, since Parpola has pointed out that Aba-[d]ninnu-dari was the name of scholar already in the Middle Babylonian period, and possibly the author of the Babylonian *Counsels of Wisdom*.[52] This may thus have been a "Babylonian archetype of the Sayings of Aḥiqar." A few parallels in the Babylonian text seem to suggest this.[53]

The story of Aḥiqar is known from the Aramaic version found at Elephantine,[54] the book of Tobit, and the later Aḥiqar tradition, which is attested in Syriac, Greek, Armenian, Arabic, as well as Slavic versions.[55]

Although Aramaic texts undoubtedly formed a bridge between Babylonian tradition and later literature, Šuruppak, the Sumerian sage, was far over-

48. S.R.K. Glanville, *The Instructions of ʿOnchsheshonqy*, Catalogue of the Demotic Papyri in the British Museum, Vol. II (London, 1955). Cf. M. Lichtheim, *Late Egyptian Literature in the International Context. A Study of Demotic Instructions*. Orbis Biblicus et Orientalis (Freiburg/ Göttingen, 1983); A. Volten, *Kopenhagener Texte zum Demotischen Weisheitsbuch*, Analecta Aegyptiaca (Copenhagen, 1940).
49. It is tempting to suggest that the story of the imprisoned scribe or sage goes back to a Sumerian prototype; cf. Civil's interpretation of the *Nungal Hymn*: "On Mesopotamian Jails and Their Lady Warren," in: *Hallo FS*, 72–78, suggesting that the *Nungal Hymn* was composed by an imprisoned scribe sentenced to death, but then released.
50. UVB 18 (1962), 45, 11:19–20.
51. J.C. Greenfield: "Two Proverbs of Aḥiqar," in: *Studies Moran*, 195–201, esp. p. 195, nn. 1–5, referring to studies by Parpola, LAS, p. 270, and W.G. Lambert, JCS 11 (1957) 1–14. Cf. also J.C. Greenfield, "The Wisdom of Ahiqar," in *Studies Emerton*, 43–52.
52. Lambert, BWL, 96–107.
53. Already Lambert pointed out that lines 31–36 occur in the Arabic *Aḥiqar* (cf. BWL, p. 281). Greenfield, 1990, p. 195, n. 5, points out that the proverb quoted in ABL 403, obv. 4–7, occurs in the Syriac and Arabic *Aḥiqar*. These are missing in the Aramaic *Aḥiqar*, however.
54. The Elephantine version is now available in full publication by M. Lindenberger, *The Aramaic Proverbs of Ahiqar*, The Johns Hopkins Near Eastern Studies 14 (Baltimore, 1983).
55. The later *Aḥiqar* versions are collected in F. Nau, *Histoire et sagesse d'Ahiqar. Trad. des versions syriaques avec les principales différences des versions arabes, arménienne, greques, néo-syriaque, slave et roumaine* (Paris, 1909); also in F.C. Conybeare, J.R. Harris, A.F. Lewis, *The Story of Ahiqar, from the Syriac, Arabic, Armenian, Ethiopic, Greek and Slavonic Versions* (London, 1898).

shadowed in the post-Babylonian tradition by Aḫiqar the sage.[56] Neither did the counsels addressed to *Šūpē-amēli* in the Syro-Mesopotamian area become comparably renowned.[57]

Biblical and Rabbinic Sources

In the biblical books Proverbs,[58] Ecclesiastes,[59] and Jesus Sirach,[60] a teaching setting is occasionally reflected. So, too, the following passages in the Hebrew Bible reflect such didactic compositions: Proverbs 1:8ff.; 4:1ff.; 7:1ff.; 22:17ff.; and the testaments of Jacob (Gen 49), Moses (Deut 33:1ff.), and David (1Kings 2:1ff.).

Occasionally New Testament proverbial sayings are reflected in older Western Asiatic sources.[61] These may well stem from a widespread common fund of sententious sayings in Aramaic. Didactic compositions are known from rabbinic literature as well, especially *Pirqê Abôth*.[62]

Arabic Sources

In Arabic, father-and-son didactic compositions are reflected in the Quran, Sura 31 (*Luqman*).[63]

Classical, Medieval and Other European Sources

Didactic father-and-son compositions are known from many other areas, among these:

Hesiod's *Works and Days* is one of the most obvious sources for comparison.[64]

The *Distics of Cato* became a highly influential source in Medieval scribal education.[65] The genre may be vaguely echoed in somewhat similar medieval European collections of instructions, some of which are addressed by a father to his son, using proverbs and brief tales, such as Peter Alfonsi's *Disciplina Clericalis*.[66] Its author was a Spanish Jew who had converted to Christianity and claims to have used Arabic sources, such as philosophical sentences, verses, and fables.

56. One may guess that it was the realistic features attached to the framing story that played a decisive role in this development, but, of course, the content matter was important, characterized by poignant sayings easy to remember.
57. These were not originally composed in Syria. Cf. p. 288, n. 1; cf. also *Chap. 3.5: Enlil and Namzitarra: Introduction to the Emar Version*, p. 331.
58. Of the vast quantity of literature that exists on biblical proverbs and wisdom, only a few titles of special interest for Mesopotamian studies are mentioned here. A thorough study of the relations between the biblical proverbs and other Near Eastern wisdom compositions is William McKane, *Proverbs. A New Approach*, The Old Testament Library (London, 1970). A good general introduction is *Proverbs and Ecclesiastes*, trans. with an introduction and notes by R.B.Y. Schott, The Anchor Bible (1973). A good overview is Carole R. Fontaine, "Proverb Performance in the Hebrew Bible," in: *Journal for the Study of the Old Testament* 32 (1985) 87–103, repr. in W. Mieder (ed.), *Wise Words. Essays on the Proverb* (New York and London: Garland Publishing, 1994), 393–413.
59. Cf. Jean de Savignac, "La sagesse du Qôhéléth et l'épopée de Gilgamesh," in: *Vetus Testamentum* 38 (1978) 318–323. Cf. further the literature mentioned on p. 296, n. 43.
60. A good discussion of the *Sitz im Leben* of wise men teaching wisdom in the book of Proverbs and Jesus Sirach is Bernhard Lang, "Klugheit als Ethos und Weisheit an der Wand. Zur Lebenslehre im Alten Testament." Cf. also Karl Loening (Hrsg.), *Rettendes Wissen. Studien zum Fortgang weisheitlichen Denkens im Frühjudentum und im frühen Christentum*, AOAT 300 (Münster, 2002).
61. Cf. W.G.E. Watson: "Antecedents of a New Testament Proverbs," in: *Vetus Testamentum* 20 (1970) 368–370, pointing to a substratum of sententious sayings that may have been widely spread. Cf. also M. Stol, "Biblical Idiom in Akkadian," in: *Hallo FS*, 246–249.
62. Moïse Schul, *Sentences et proverbes du Talmud et du Midrasch, suivis du traité d'Aboth* (Paris, 1878). Also, *The Mishnah*, translated by Herbert Danby, D.D. (Oxford University Press, 1938), 446–461: "Aboth" ("The Fathers").
63. Cf. Th. Noeldeke: *Delectus veterum carminum araborum*, 1933 (repr. Wiesbaden, 1961), 1–4.
64. Conveniently available in The Loeb Classical Library: Hugh G. Evelyn-White, *Hesiod, The Homeric Hymns and Homerica* (Cambridge, 1914 (repr.)), 1–65.
65. *Distícha Catonis*, conveniently available in *Minor Latin Poets*, in The Loeb Classical Library; for a detailed edition see Wayland Johnson Chase, *The Distichs of Cato*, University of Wisconsin Studies in the Social Sciences and History 7 (Madison, 1922), 1–43.
66. Alfons Hilka and Werner Söderhjelm (eds.), *Peter Alfonsi Disciplina Clericalis*, Acta Societatis Scientiarum Fennicae 38, nos. 4–5, I Lateinischer Text, II Französischer Prosatext (Helsinfors, 1911–12). Brief edition: A. Hilka und W. Söderhjelm, *Die Discplina Clericalis*

In Anglo-Saxon literature, the *Proverbs of Alfred* is among the best-known works.[67]

The genre had a long history in English literature. Polonius's advice to Laertes in Shakespeare's *Hamlet* (1.3) has became part of world literature:

And these few precepts in thy memory
See thou character. Give thy thoughts no tongue,
Nor any unproportioned thought his act.
Be thou familiar, but by no means vulgar …

There are many lesser-known predecessors in Elizabethan English literature and earlier.[68]

The genre was also known in Celtic (*Instructions of King Cormac*)[69] and Old Norse (*Havamál; Loddfáfnismál*)[70] literature.

Sanskrit

Sanskrit literature is interesting from the point of view of Mesopotamian wisdom literature, not so much because of the huge collections of sententious sayings that exist, but rather because of the numerous animal tales and fables that may have had an impact on European examples. Whether some of these could ultimately go back to Mesopotamian sources is doubtful, however.[71]

Addendum

As to the discussion on the nature of the Sumerian proverbs—whether they are genuine proverbs or simply scribal inventions made for didactic purposes, as reported on pp. 34–35—K. Volk, ZA 90 (2000) 14, makes some very pertinent remarks with which I fully agree. According to Volk, the scribal education of the *edubba*-schools was primarily meant for pupils whose native language was not Sumerian, with the objective of enabling them to master conversation in Sumerian. From this perspective, the proverbs served as "Fragmente von Umgangssprachen" and the dialogues as training in "Alltagskonversation." A nice example illustrating this occurs in a lexical text from Nippur recently published by M. Krebernik, ZA 94 (2004) 226–249, in which some lexical terms prompted the inclusion of two proverbs illustrating the use of those terms. Cf. my forthcoming study "Groats Dropping on the Widow: HS 1461," *Kaskal* 2 (2006).

des Petrus Alfonsi, Sammlung mittellateinischer Texte 1 (Heidelberg, 1911).

67. O.S.A. Arngart (ed.), *The Proverbs of Alfred*, Skrifter utgivna av kungliga Humanistiska Vetenskapssamfundet i Lund 32 (1942–55) 2 vols. For *Faether Larcwidas*, see: Krapp-Dobbei (ed.), *The Exeter Book*, The Anglo-Saxon Poetic Records III (New York, 1936), 140–143.
68. F.J. Furnivall (ed.), *How the Wise Man Taught His Son*, Early English Text Society, Original Series, 32 (Oxford, 1868). T.F. Mustanoja (ed.), *The Good Wife Taught Her Daughter*, Annales Academiae Scientiarum Fennicae B, 61, 2 (Helsinki, 1948). Charlotte d'Evelyn (ed.), *Peter Idley's Instructions to His Son* (Boston, 1935). A much later reflection occurs in Francis Poulenc's opera *Dialogue des Carmilites*, Act I/4 (1952), based on a novel by Gertrud von Les Forts (1876–1971).
69. Kuno Meyer (ed.), *Instructions of King Cormac*, Todd Lecture Series 15, Royal Irish Academy (Dublin, 1909).
70. Victor Nilsson, *Loddfáfnismál* (University of Minnesota, 1898). Hans Kuhn: *Edda, die Lieder des Codex Regius* (Heidelberg, 1962).
71. Cf. the discussion under fables in Chap. 4.1. The huge collection by Böhtlingk, *Indische Sprüche. Sanskrit und Deutsch* (2. Aufl. 1870–73 [1. Aufl. 1863–1865], St. Petersburg), does not offer much guidance for those who want to sort out proverbs of popular origin. Rather, it is a collection of sententious sayings based on literary sources. The translation of *The Hitopadeśa* by J. Hertel (Leipzig, 1894) is, however, very helpful. A number of interesting Sanskrit proverbs are quoted in A.F. Stenzler, *Elementarbuch der Sanskritsprache* (4. Auf. Berlin, 1960), quoted without references to the sources from which they come, but undoubtedly genuine.

1.2 Survey of Texts Included

1.2.1 Publication History

The first to recognize the existence of *The Instructions of Šuruppak* was S.N. Kramer, in the late 1940s.[72] He left a handwritten manuscript in the University Museum, which was helpful in the initial stage of the preparation of my first full edition of 1974.[73] M. Civil, in collaboration with R.D. Biggs, 1966, was the first to treat sections of the text with quotations large enough to give the first glimpses of its contents. Also in 1966, Biggs announced the discovery of the Early Dynastic version from Tell Abū Ṣalābīkh, just unearthed by Donald Hansen's expedition. This discovery came as a great surprise, since no one had expected such "wisdom" texts to go as far back in time as the middle of the third millennium B.C. This subsequently led to a complete revision of the oldest literary history of Mesopotamia. A copy of the text was published in 1974 by Biggs in his complete edition of the Abū Ṣalābīkh tablets (Biggs, 1974). It included a preliminary attempt to treat some lines of the Early Dynastic version.

When the first attempt to edit the whole text, including the two Early Dynastic versions, was published in Alster, 1974, the main sources had been studied and copied in the University Museum, Philadelphia, and collations of the Ur texts had been made in the British Museum. An important tablet in the Hermitage, St. Petersburg, was incorporated by the courtesy of I.M. Diakonoff and I. Kaneva. Some additions were made in Alster, 1975.

Further additions were made in Civil, 1984, where Civil identified and edited an additional fragment of the Abū Ṣalābīkh tablet, published a tablet in the Abbey of Montserrat, Barcelona, and identified some highly interesting school tablets from Susa.

Around 1980, W.G. Lambert identified the uniquely interesting Middle Babylonian tablet in the British Museum, which contains an Akkadian translation of the first third of the text. The tablet was in several pieces and additions were made over time.

Minor additions were made in Alster, 1987, and Civil, 1987. In 1999, Civil identified a fragment published in 1966 by Krebernik from a private collection in Munich, as an Akkado-Hurrian bilingual translation, probably from Emar (cf. Alster, 1999). The Hurrian version is treated here by G. Wilhelm, in Chap. 1.7, pp. 204ff. Krebernik was the first to suggest that it is a bilingual, including a Hurrian column.[74]

The full revised edition, which is finally presented here, was started in 1989, when I prepared a completely new transliteration of the text from the Nippur sources in the University Museum, Philadelphia. I collated the Ur texts in the British Museum again in the following years. The Abū Ṣalābīkh tablet was collated in the Iraq Museum, Baghdad, in 1990 (cf. Alster, 1991–92).

Complete translations have been provided in Wilcke, 1978, and Römer, 1990. Parts of the text were translated in Civil, 1984. The edition that

72. See S.N. Kramer, JCS 1 (1947) 33, n. 208, and the two photographs published in *From the Tablets of Sumer* (1956), 138. In 1963, Kramer described the text as "interesting because of its stylistic device of ascribing whole wisdom collections to presumably very wise rulers of the distant past," comparable to the biblical book of Proverbs. He translated the initial phrases, dating the text to around 2000 B.C., although it is ascribed to "King Shuruppak, who was the father of Ziusudra, the Sumerian Noah, a suitable candidate for the position of sage par excellence" (cf. Kramer, 1963, p. 224).

73. Kramer's manuscript was undated, but it is earlier than 1960, when Lambert mentioned it in BWL, 93–94. In 1961, Civil made a handwritten addition to it, in which he identified the Montserrat and the Copenhagen duplicates as well as some other Philadelphia sources.

74. The fragment was recognized independently by A. Cavigneaux.

appeared on the ETCSL web-site in 1999 does not belong, strictly speaking, to the printed sources, but it is worthy of mention because the site marks a breakthrough in Sumerology, making a large number of texts easily accessible to anyone interested. Although the ETCSL editions are not to be considered finally published sources, they are widely based on critical evaluation of manuscripts prepared by leading scholars. These might otherwise not have become available to the public for some time, and so the ETCSL site has become a highly useful tool for both laymen and scholars. The ETCSL translation of *The Instructions of Šuruppak* was prepared by Gabor Zólyomi, using a previous version of the manuscript published here.

In the present edition, I have tried to find a reasonable compromise between quoting too little and too much of what has already been written about the translation of each individual line. Both for those who may think I have quoted too much and for those who may think the opposite, it may be consoling to see that, although the interpretation of unilingual Sumerian texts is still hampered by countless difficulties, it is by now evident that the contributions and discussions of scholars generally point toward similar conclusions.

1.2.2 *Sources*[75]

Early Dynastic Sources

Abū Ṣalābīkh

ED_1 = AbS-T 323 (OIP 99, 323), joins AbS-T 393 (OIP 99, 256). The photographs shown on pls. 26–27 were made before the publication of OIP 99, 323, and do not include the join. A new copy of the joined tablets by Biggs, JNES 43 (1984) 282–283.

I collated the tablets in the Iraq Museum, Baghdad, 1990, where they could not be physically joined owing to a layer of gypsum used to hold them together. The results of the collations were published in AfO 38–39 (1991–92) 32–34.

Adab

ED_2 = A 649 and 645. Provenience: Adab (Bismaya). Copy: OIP 14, nos. 55 (fragments 1–9) and 56 (the main fragment consists of four joined fragments). Photograph: Oriental Institute 56573, reproduced in OIP 99, p. 58; repeated here, pl. 29. The photograph shows the relative position of the three fragments of OIP 14, 55 that can be joined or placed in relation to the obverse of the main piece, OIP 14, 56 (cf. OIP 99, 57, n. 4). The other fragments, OIP 14, 55, probably belong to the reverse. The thickness along a preserved part of the edge is 3.3 cm.

The fragments are here numbered clockwise from left to right, starting with the upper left corner of OIP 14, 55. Edges are not always indicated on the copy, but have been checked on photographs. The total number of columns on the obverse was at least 6 (cf. fragment 1), but may have been much higher. The columns on the reverse ran from right to left, and ended with at least one blank column, probably more (cf. fragment 6).

The main fragment
i = 10?; 14; 15; approximately 17.
ii = # 6; 28; 30; 29.
iii = (joins Fr. 3) 62 cont'd.; 38; similar to 64? (not 49, but cf. ED_1 v 1?); similar to 214 (cf. ED_1 v 2).
iv = One unidentified line (cf. ED_1 obv. vi 1 and 45?); 47. (Joins Fr. 1 i: 48.)

Fr. 1 Fragment from the obverse, from cols. iv and v, as shown on the photograph in OIP 99, p. 58, here pl. 28.
iv = SS 48;
v = SS 58–59.

75. The siglas used in the 1974 edition are given in parentheses whenever different from those used here.

The photograph leaves some doubt as to the precise position. In col. iv, the sequence SS 47 on the main piece, followed by SS 48 on Fr. 1, seems reasonably certain. Yet, Fr. 1 cannot join exactly as shown. Presumably Fr. 1 barely touches the main fragment, and probably should be placed nearly 5 mm farther to the right, yet in the same columns, and the right side should be turned a bit upward to line up with the column lines. Alternatively, Fr. 1 must be placed somewhat lower, with room for some lines between this and the main piece. The consequence would be that the sequence SS 47–48 was separated by some entries in this version. There are remains of cols. iii and vi, with no signs preserved. No edges preserved.

Fr. 2 Belongs to the top of main piece, cols. i–ii, but does not join. The position shown on the photograph is slightly misleading in that the top piece does not physically join the main piece, and should have been placed somewhat higher up in the same columns; cf. the attempted reconstruction in Alster, 1974, 21–25. Cf. OIP 99, p. 57, n. 4.
i = SS 4–5.
ii = SS 21; 19; 20; two signs from an unidentified line.

Fr. 3 Joins the main piece, col. iii. = SS 35–36; 62.

Fr. 4 Two cols., probably from the reverse, including a repetition of the opening lines and three unidentified lines. Probably no edges preserved.
Left col. = Three unidentified fragmentary lines; # to SS 5 or similar.
Right col. = One fragment. line; # to SS 5–6.

Fr. 5 Fragment, presumably from the reverse, with the right and bottom edges preserved (checked on photographs). Including a parallel to SS opening line 6 or 8, and two unidentified lines.

Fr. 6 Fragment from the reverse, apparently with the top edge preserved. The first column has two unidentified lines reminiscent of ED_I rev. iv 17–18. The second column is blank, and shows that this was near the end of the composition.

Fr. 7 Fragment, either from the obverse or, more probably, reverse, with both the upper and right edges preserved. Two columns, of which the right included remains of one unidentified line, apparently followed by a parallel to line 6. The left col. has affinities with ED_I rev. vi 7.

Fr. 8 Fragment of two columns, of which the right included SS 172. The left column has remains of one sign, like DILI.

Fr. 9 Fragment, either from the obverse or reverse with the right edge preserved. The line shown on the bottom of the copy probably does not coincide with the bottom edge. Probably SS 187–188.

Monolingual Akkadian Translations

From Aššur

Akk_I = VAT 10151, published as KAR 27, republished by Lambert in BWL, pl. 30. Obv. = 7–23, rev. = traces of one unidentified line; 58–72 (61 omitted). Monolingual Akkadian.

The Lambert Akkadian translation

Akk_2 = BM 50522 + 52767 + 52946 + 77468 + ? Published here in copy by Lambert pls. 13–15. Identified by W.G. Lambert in the British Museum, probably Middle Babylonian, = 27–88; 149–152 (or parallels). Cf., p. 207, *Chap. 1.8: The Akkadian Versions.*

Akkado-Hurrian translation

Akk_3 = Krebernik, ZA 86 (1996) 170–176. Akkado-Hurrian bilingual. The Akkadian translation is in the left column, the Hurrian translation in the right column on each side. Unnumbered tablet in private possession in Munich. Provenience: probably Emar. Obv. i a = 9–17 (10 missing); obv. i b = corresponding Hurrian column. Rev. i a = variant of 55 (cf. 49); 60, (61 omitted), 62, 63, 65, 66, 67, 64, 67a(?) or 68(?); rev. i b = corresponding Hurrian column; treated here by G. Wilhelm, pp. 204ff.

Copy by Krebernik, ZA 86 (1996) 172, repeated here pl. 71.

Standard Sumerian Tablets

From Nippur

UM_1 UM 29-16-9, copy pls. 1–2 (cf. Alster, 1974, pls. iii–iv.); photographs pls. 17–18. Obv. = 117–150, rev. = 151–178.

UM_2 UM 29-13-326, copy pls. 3–4 (cf. Alster, 1974, pls. v–vi); photographs pls. 19–20. This is the larger top fragment of the same tablet as UM 29-16-240. Two-column tablet. Obv. i = 153–164; obv. ii = 184–201; rev. i = 250–265; rev. ii = 286–290. (U_1).

UM_2 UM 29-16-240, copy and photograph: same as preceding (cf. Alster, 1974, pls. v–vi). This is the smaller bottom fragment of the same tablet as UM 29-13-326. Obv. i = 179–183; obv. ii = 213–219; rev. i = 220–230; rev. ii = 266–274(?). (U_2).

UM_3 UM 55-21-345 = 3N-T 549. Copy: pl. 5 (cf. Alster, 1974, pl. vii); photograph pl. 22. Obv. = 91–103, rev. = 104–115. (U_3).

UM_4 UM 55-21-334 = 3N-T 515. Copy: pl. 5 (cf. Alster, 1974, pl. viii). Obv. = 123–134, rev. = 141–153. (U_4).

C_1 CBS 4611. Copy: Langdon, PBS 10/1 4. Photograph pl. 22. Obv. = 149–153, rev. 155–170.

C_2 CBS 13107. Joins CBS 2203. Copy of the joined tablet pl. 5 (cf. Alster, 1974, pl. ix); photograph pl. 23. Obv. = 213–225, rev. = 250–252.

C_2 CBS 2203. Copies and photographs: same as preceding. Previous copy: Chiera, STVC 126.

C_3 CBS 8001. Copy: pl. 6 (cf. Alster, 1974, pl. x); photograph pl. 23. Obv. = 253–264, rev. = 273–287.

C_4 CBS 10320. Transliteration by Civil, 1987, 210. Obv. i = 1–4, rev., last column = 286–290. Checked and transliterated March 1989.

I_1 Ni 4271. Copy: ISET I 138. Obv.(?) = 30–34. Rev.(?) destroyed. Probably joins I_2.

I_2 Ni 4152. Copy: ISET I 134. Obv.(?) 31–35. Probably joins I_1, although the sign nam in line 5 cannot be placed in line 33.

I_3 Ni 9820. Copy: ISET I 188 (also copied by Kramer as Ni 3820, ISET II 34). Obv. = 35–41, rev. = 42–48.

I_4 Ni 9559. Copy: ISET I 187. Obv. = 58–70, rev. = 111–117 (end of excerpt).

I_5 Ni 4001. Copy: ISET II 92. Obv. destroyed, rev. = 72–80.

I_6 Ni 9612. Copy: ISET II 92. Obv. destroyed, rev. i = 72–76, ii = 117–122. Two-column tablet. (Therefore cannot join I_9?)

I_7 Ni 4543. Copy: ISET I 125. = 78–84.

I_8 Ni 9928. Copy: ISET I 203. = 91–97.

I_9 Ni 9731. Copy: ISET I 181. Obv. = 93–99, rev. 114–121 (end of excerpt).

I_{10} Ni 9884. Copy: ISET I 193. Two-column tablet. Rev.(?) i = 4 + unidentified lines; ii = 93–98.

I_{11} Ni 9917. Copy: ISET I 201. Obv. = 125–132; Rev. = 177–182. Might join I_{13}.

I_{12} Ni 9778. Copy: ISET I 183. = 130–133.

I_{13} Ni 9989. Copy: ISET I 202. = 170–177. Might join I_{11}.

I_{14} Ni 9793. Copy: ISET II 55. Obv(!) = 179–184, rev. = 223(?)–228. Top edge preserved. Original length of excerpt: 179–228.

I_{15} Ni 9558 (courtesy Kramer). Obv. = 8–16, rev. = 49–52.

N_1 N 901. Copy: pl. 8 (Alster, 1974, pl. xv). Obv. = 116–125, rev. = 132–140.

N_2 N 3774. Copy: pl. 8 (cf. Alster, 1974, pl. xv) = 124–129.

N_3 N 3708. Copy: pl. 8 (cf. Alster, 1974, pl. xv). Fragment from a two-column tablet. i = unidentified traces; ii = 143–150. May belong to the same tablet as N_{11}. In this case it belonged to a large fragment that included the end of the composition.

N_4 N 3432. Copy: pl. 9 (cf. Alster, 1974, pl. xvii). Obv. = 187–195.

N_5 N 3298. Copy: pl. 9 (cf. Alster, 1974, pl. xvi). Photograph of rev. in Kramer, FTS p. 138, Fig. 61. Obv. = 197–204, rev. = 205–213. Lower edge preserved.

N_6 N 3757. Copy: pl. 10 (cf. Alster, 1974, pl. xvii). Photograph of rev. in Kramer, FTS p. 138, Fig. 62. Obv. = 254–263, rev. = 283–288 (285 A-B omitted).

N_7 N 3260. Transliteration: Civil, 1987, 208.

Checked and transliterated from the original tablet March 1988: GA in Civil's line 186 (here 181) is amar. Civil's x following zag in line 195 (here 191) is zu. Obv. = 183–191, rev. = 225–228. Upper and right edges preserved. Beginning of excerpt: 183. End of excerpt: 232.

N_8 N 7047. Transliteration: Civil, 1987, 210. Very small fragment of obv. or rev. No edges preserved. Checked March 1988. = 259–261.

N_9 N 4148. Copy pl. 10 (cf. Alster 1975, p. 139). Obv.(?) = 262–269, rev. destr. No edges preserved.

N_{10} N 3643. Transliteration: Civil, 1987, 210. Obv.(?) destr., rev.(?) = 272–277. Bottom(?) and left edges preserved. Checked and transliterated March 1988. Civil's line 268: x é (here line 275) are urudu (almost certainly) gín.

N_{11} N 3707. Variants to 287–290 given by Civil, 1987, 210. May belong to the same tablet as N_3 = N 3708. Obv. destr., rev. = 287–290. Lower and left edges preserved. End of excerpt: 282. Transliterated and checked March 1988.

N_{12} N 2715 = 253–260.

T_1 3N-T 917,397. Copy: pl. 6 (cf. Alster, 1974, pl. xi); photograph pl. 21; Obv. = 12–23, rev. = 26–33.

T_2 3N-T 904,152. Copy: SLFN 65. Change sides. Same tablet as T_5 (cf. Civil, 1984, 287). Obv. = 118–126, rev. = 143– ca. 153 (149–152 omitted). Bottom edge preserved. Beginning of excerpt: 118; end: around 153.

T_3 3N-T 917,379. Copy: SLFN 65. Obv. = 78–81, rev. = 113–117. Top and bottom preserved. Beginning of excerpt: 78 or the line before? End: 117.

T_4 3N-T 917,371. Copy: SLFN 66. Obv. = 113–118, rev. destroyed. Beginning of excerpt: 113.

T_5 3N-T 537. Copy: pl. 7 (cf. Alster, 1974, pl. xii), (from a cast in the University Museum; original in Baghdad). Obv. = 116–128, rev. = 139–153. Same tablet as T_2 (cf. Civil, 1984, 287).

T_6 3N-T 722. Copy: pl. 7 (cf. Alster, 1974, pls. xiii–xiv), (from a cast in the University Museum; original in Chicago). Obv. = 130–145, rev. = 146–153 (end of excerpt). Bottom edge preserved.

T_7 3N-T 917,398. Copy: SLFN 65. Obv. = 153–160, rev. = 194–189. Beginning of excerpt: 153; end: 189.

T_8 3N-T 543. Copy: pl. 6 (cf. Alster, 1974, pl. xi), (from a cast in the University Museum; original in Chicago) = 153–160.

T_9 3N-T 917,367. Copy: SLTF 66. = 153–154.

T_{10} 3N-T 460. Copy: pl. 8 (Cf. Alster, 1974, pls. xiii–xiv), (from a cast in the University Museum; original in Chicago). Obv. = 163–171, rev. = 172–179. Bottom edge preserved.

T_{11} 3N-T 906,255. Copy: SLTF 66. Fragment from a four-column tablet. Obv. i = 164–171, ii = 200–207. Rev. destroyed.

T_{12} 3N-T 905,186. Copy: SLTF 65. Obv. = 199–205. Top edge preserved. Rev. two unidentified lines. Could belong to 221–222, or around 240? Beginning of excerpt: 199; end depending on the identification of rev.

T_{13} 3N-T 904,162. Copy: SLFN 64. Obv. = 219–224, rev. 5 unidentified lines belonging after 240 or toward the end of the composition?

T_{14} 3N-T 123 (= IM 58342). Copy: Civil, 1987, p. 207. Obv. = 46–51, rev. = 52–54. Lower and left edges preserved.

T_{15} 3N-T 756 (IM 58682). Transliteration by Civil, 1984, 287–291. Obv. = 107–119, rev. = 122–135. Right and lower edges preserved.

T_{16} 3N-T 907,264, pl. 66. Obv. = 109–110, rev. = 111–114. Lower and right edges preserved.

T_{17} 3N-T 917,382. Copy: SLFN pl. 66. Obv. = 133–138, rev. = 139–145. (See Civil, 1984, 291–292.) Right and apparently lower edges preserved.

T_{18} 3N-T 919,485. Copy SLFN 64 (change sides). Obv. = 168–173, rev. = 174–181. Lower edge preserved.

T_{19} 10N-T 21 (= A 33687). Copy of obv. missing, apparently by mistake. Copy of rev. and left edge by Civil, 1987, 208. Obv. = 196–205, rev. = 229–238. Left edge: one unidentified line, probably close to line 240. Left edge preserved. Close to upper left corner.

T_{20} 3N-T 916,335. Copy: SLFN 64. Findspot:

TA 191 X 4. Transliteration by Civil, 1987, 209. Obv. = 215–226, rev. destr. Right edge and apparently lower edge preserved.

T_{21} 3N-T 911p (= UM 55-21-407). Findspot: TA 205 XI 2. Fragment from a multicolumn tablet. Transliteration: Civil, 1987, 209. Rev. i' = 257–260, rev. ii': traces of a colophon? Checked Oct. 1989. There are two fragments with this number; the other, larger, fragment is a lexical text. There are traces of a third su at the end of Civil's line 225 = here 221. There is an erased LU between TUR and ÉŠ in Civil's line 226 (here l. 222).

T_{22} 2N-T 534 (= IM 58969). Findspot: TB 121 II/2. Upper half of a one-column tablet, obverse only. Transliteration: Civil, 1987, 209. Obv. = 259–267, rev. uninscribed?

T_{23} 3N-T 918,422. Copy: pl. 10 (cf. Alster, 1975, p. 139). Also SLFN 64. Obv. = 267–274, rev. = 275–281. Lower and left edges preserved. A join with T_{24} should be an obvious possibility, but not checked, Oct. 2003.

T_{24} 3N-T 907,282 (SLFN pl. 86). Rev. = 277–281, obv. destr. Left edge preserved. Identified May 1992. A join with T_{23} should be an obvious possibility, but not checked, Oct. 2003.

Non-Nippur Sources

From Ur

Ur_1 UET 6/2 169. Collated and transliterated from the original tablet in the British Museum, Feb. 1990. Obv. = 1–32, rev. = 33–66. A set of excellent British Museum photographs have not been reproduced here: BM neg. nos. 163047; 165946.

Ur_2 UET 6/2 170. Collated and transliterated from the original tablet in the British Museum, Feb. 1990. Obv. = 26–41, rev. = 44–69, left edge: 70–72. BM neg. nos. 166018; 166020.

Ur_3 UET 6/2 171. Collated and transliterated from the original tablet in the British Museum, Feb. 1990. Obv. = 53–76 (77–78 omitted), rev. = 79–102. Ur_3 subscript: 47 (scl. lines). BM neg. nos. 166036; 166037.

Ur_4 Copy: A. Shaffer, forthcoming, Preliminary publ. no. UET 6/3 227, with joins added to previous Ur_4. Transliterated from the original tablet in the British Museum. The joined fragments contain: obv. = 143–159 (l. order: 143, 144, 145, 149, (150 om.), 151, 152, 152 a, 154, 155, 156, 157, 158, 159), rev. 172–191. The new fragment adds to lines 172–191, and includes lines 182–191, not on the first fragments.

Ur_5 Copy: A. Shaffer, forthcoming. Preliminary publ. no. UET 6/3 59. Transliterated from the original tablet in the British Museum. Obv. = 197–203, rev. = 205–212. Bottom edge preserved.

Ur_6 UET 6/3 429. U. 7827 y. A transliteration from the original tablet, 1993, and my own copy, published here pls. 11–12, have been used. Fragment of a six- or eight-column tablet originally inscribed with the entire composition. The thickest part of the tablet is just above the preserved part of the inscription, indicating that there may have been slightly more lines in the missing part. There were 11 missing lines at the beginning of obv. i, and approximately 18 lines in each column. The bottom edge is partly preserved. Calculating 18 lines per column, and eight columns on each side, the total number of lines may have been close to 290. Obv. i = 12–18, obv. ii = 30–32, rev. i' not placed (8 entries are undoubtedly to be placed approximately after line 240, in which case the connection between 240 and what follows [here = 251] is doubtful); rev. ii' = 269–279.

Findspot: No. 7 Quiet Street.

From Kiš

K_1 Ashmolean Museum No. 1932.156 b, findspot: Ingharra C.15. Copy: O.I. Gurney, OECT 5, 33. Obv. i = 49–70 (end of column), obv. ii + edge = 123–145 (141–145 written on the edge), rev. i (beginning with top edge) = 151 (om. 152–153), 154–168, rev. ii = 218–240. Collated by Jon Taylor, 2003.

Since there were two columns on each side, there may have been approximately 50 lines missing at the top of the tablet. So approximately 50 lines are missing after 240, and the total number of lines may have to be increased by about 10, compared to the previous edition, ending close to 285. Approximately 10 lines should then be inserted after 240, in part covered by U_6.

For details about the findspot and other tablets found at the same place, see Zólyomi, ZA 93 (2003) 80–81 and the literature there cited.

K_2 PRAK II B 20. Copy by de Genouillac. Obv. = 131–138, rev. = 193–203.

From Susa

S_1 MDP 27, 260 = 135–136; rev. dodges and crosshatchings, see Civil, 1984, 291.

S_2 Sb 12355 = obv. = 198–199; 39–41. Small oblong tablet in syllabic orthography. See Civil, 1984, 297–298.

S_3 MDP 27, 186 = 172. See Civil, 1984, 298.

S_4 MDP 27, 109 = 10 and parallel lines. See Civil, 1984, 298. But this could also be, e.g., *Incantation to Utu*, line 104.

Tablets of Unknown Provenience, Possibly from Ur, Sippar, or Babylon

British Museum Tablets

BM_1 K 13942. Copy: Geller in Alster, 1987, 201. Identified by Civil. Obv. i = 8–24, obv. ii = 78–87. Fragment from a multicolumn tablet. No edges preserved. In spite of the number this is not a Kuyunjik tablet. The most likely source of origin is Ur (cf. Alster, 1987, 201, n. 5). A join to Ur_6 is excluded, in particular in view of the shorter lines in Ur_6.

BM_2 BM 82952. Copy: Alster, 1987, 200. Obv. = 17–28, rev. = 252–264. Fragment from a multicolumn tablet originally inscribed with the entire composition. There were apparently 10 line marks in the column separators. A join to BM_1 has not been confirmed by Geller, cf. Alster, 1987, 202, n. 5. According to him, there is too much clay between the two fragments to allow for a join. Nevertheless, I still consider a join to be an obvious possibility, in particular since both fragments are from rare multicolumn tablets, and the break along the same line would be a very unusual coincidence. A join to Ur_6 is excluded in view of the overlapping signs in line 17.

Tablets in Other Collections

TCL AO 8899, Louvre. Copy: de Genouillac, TCL 16, no. 93 (pl. clxiv). Findspot unknown. Obv. = 172–183, rev. = 201–211. Beginning of excerpt: 172; end: 211. Collated by J. Dahl.

Cop Copenhagen National Museum, Antiksamlingen A 10054. Copy: Th. Jacobsen, JCS 8 (1954) 85 (collated). Change sides. Obv. = 90–103, rev. = 104–118. Beginning and end of excerpt 90–118, or slightly before and later respectively. Acquired by Th. Jacobsen from the antiquities market in Iraq, ca. 1930; findspot unknown. Photographs: pls. 24–25.

MM MM 477 (collection of the Abbey of Montserrat, Barcelona), copy by Civil, 1984, 288. Obv. 100–115, rev. 128–143. Two-column tablet. Right, left, and lower edges preserved. End of excerpt: 143.

P GE 45445, The Hermitage, St. Petersburg. Cited from a transliteration prepared in 1974 by I. Kaneva and I.M. Diakonoff. Collated by Th. Kämmerer, Nov. 2002. Obv. = 1–26, rev. = 44–69. (L). Number according to Natalya Koslova, Nov. 2002: 15339.

The Schøyen Sources

The following sources, of unknown provenience, are included by courtesy of the Schøyen Collection in Oslo. For further details, see pp. 101–103, *Chap. 1.3x: The Schøyen Sources.* MS 3396 has also been reported as a possible additional duplicate, but has not been checked.

Sch_1 MS 2788. Obv. = 1–25; lower edge = 26–27; rev. = 28–48. Photographs, by courtesy of the Schøyen Collection, pls. 61–61.

Sch_2 MS 3352. Obv. = 1–14; rev. = 15–18 plus ca. 3 unidentified lines. Photographs, by courtesy of the Schøyen Collection, pls. 62–63.

Sch_3 MS 3366. Obv. = 123–152; rev. = 153–181. Photographs, by Renee Kovacs, pls. 64–67.

Sch_4 MS 2291. Obv. = ca. 81; 84?; maybe about three lines belonging to the poorly preserved lines after 84; rev. 1–3 = not clearly identified; 4 = 127; 5 = 128; 6 = 129; 7 = 130. Photographs, by courtesy of the Schøyen Collection, pl. 68.

Sch_5 MS 2040 = ca. 203–ca. 212. Photographs, by courtesy of the Schøyen Collection, pl. 69.

Identifications and First Publications

Additions to the 1974 edition:

Alster, 1975, 137–139: N_9; T_{23}.

Heimerdinger, SLFN: T_{18}; (T_{23}); T_2 (see Civil, 1984, 291–292); T_{16}.

Alster, RA 77 (1982) 191: T_{24}.

Civil, 1984, 281–298: ED_1 (join): AbS-T 323 (OIP 99,323), join to OIP 99, 256. New copy by Biggs JNES 43 (1984) 282–283; T_{15}; MM 477; T_{17} (SLFN, pl. 66); S_1; S_2; S_3.

Alster, 1987, 199–206: BM_1; BM_2.

Civil, 1987, 207–210: T_{14}; N_7; T_{19}; T_{21}; T_{22}; N_{10}; N_{11}; C_4; N_8. Ur_4; Sch_{1-5}.

Join added by Aaron Shaffer to the previously known part of Ur_4.

First edition of particular sources:

Alster in N.A.B.U. 1999: Ur_6.

Krebernik, 1996, 170–176: Akk_3, copy p. 172 (first identified by Civil, private communication, May 1999; to the best of my knowledge seen independently by A. Cavigneaux).

W.G. Lambert identified and copied BM 50522 + 52767 + 52946 + 77468 + ? Published here for the first time.

Published here for the first time: I_{15}; N 2715.

Collations:

Collations to ED_1 (AbS-T 393 = OIP 256) + (AbS-T 305 = OIP 323) in Baghdad 1990: Published by Alster in AfO 38–39 (1991–92) 32–34.

1.2.3 On the Transliterations and Translations

In this volume I have not adopted the practice of using g̃ (g-tilde) or g-circumflex for the Sumerian nasalized phoneme, whose precise nature is much debated (cf. Krecher, 1978; Black, RA 84 [1990] 108ff.), but instead have used ŋ. g̃ has become a widely accepted solution by Sumerologists in recent decades, but I prefer ŋ (the prolonged n) used by Civil, 1994, because a modified form of g conveys the notion of a stop, whereas a modified form of n conveys a form of a nasal, which seems more correct.[76]

The use of a special sign for this phoneme, which does not occur in Akkadian, has many advantages, but unfortunately it also entails some disadvantages. In particular, it would have been highly desirable had such a new sign value been immediately "translatable" from the old system, which goes back to Thureau-Dangin and has become the basis for the sign-lists of Labat and Borger. If a sign has, e.g., index number 1 (= nothing) the same index number should preferably be assigned to the new sign value. Therefore, if a sign is read un in the old system, the corresponding value in the new system should ideally be ug̃ or uŋ, rather than ùg̃ (used by Krecher, 1995, 146, n. 7) or ùŋ.[77]

I have not, however, used a special sign, e.g., r̂, for the d^r phoneme, for which see Edzard, *Sum.*

76. In the *International Phonetic Alphabet* (IPA), ŋ designates a velar nasal, whereas the same sign with the left vertical stroke prolonged instead: ɲ denotes a palatal nasal. This might actually have been worth considering in some cases, cf. *Chap. 1.9: Modal verbal Prefixes.* The tilde (~) is used to express nasality. g-tilde (g̃) would thus denote a nasalized velar stop, whereas ŋ denotes a velar nasal and thus perhaps the most acceptable solution, whereas I consider the g-circumflex (g+^), less fortunate. The present work was in an advanced stage of preparation when Edzard's *Sum. Grammar,* 2003, appeared. The phoneme in question is there, pp. 16–17, described as possibly a palatal nasal, somewhat different from my own suggestion on pp. 211ff., *Chap. 1.9: The Grammatical and Graphical Elements.*

77. This plays a role, e.g., in 211, where the phonetic variant -un, for ḫun, must be transliterated ùg̃ in Krecher's system, although ug̃ would have been the straightforward solution. Cf. also, e.g., line 19, where it makes a difference whether UN, especially in the ED version, is understood as -un or as ùg̃.

Grammar, p. 18, and the literature there cited.[78]

The reason for using traditional accents for index number 2, 3 (and 4) in this volume is purely aesthetic, making the text more pleasant from a graphic point of view. One may object that, say, a_2 is as easy to read as á, or a_3 as easy to read as à, but many subscript numbers undoubtedly make the text more cluttered and less pleasant to read and are, therefore, graphically less satisfactory. Yet, when a sign has two or more syllables, subscript numbers are ideally to be preferred, because this is the best way to avoid the ambiguities embedded in Thureau-Dangin's system, as later amended by Borger, compared to Deimel's *Šumerisches Lexikon* in various editions. Even in Civil, 1994, the problem becomes apparent.[79]

I have reluctantly updated my transliterations from *Proverbs of Ancient Sumer* when it seems most needed, to make them conform to those preferred in recent studies. Ideally all transliterations should conform to a common standard, preferably based on the best lexical information of Old Babylonian Nippur *ProtoEa* (cf. Krecher, 1995, 146, n. 7). Yet, some conservatism would undoubtedly be welcomed by those who think of transliterations first of all as a working tool, to be kept as simple as possible.

Users of *Proverbs of Ancient Sumer* will notice the following changes in this volume: -mu as the 1st person suffix has been replaced by $ŋu_{10}$; uru by ere; sum by šúm; nitaḫ by ninta. I have tried to keep such changes to a minimum, however, for the reasons just stated. The transliteration aims at a sign by sign rendering, as far as possible unambiguous, of the text on a purely morphological level. No attempt has been made to express phonological details, which are considered irrelevant on the transliteration level.

When columns are counted consecutively from the obverse to the reverse, the columns on the reverse are introduced by the initial mark (rev.) in parenthesis. When bilingual sources contain the same line in two languages or versions, such as syllabic Sumerian beside ordinary orthography, either arranged vertically or horizontally, the line counting has been retained as identical for both versions (cf. *Chap. 3.3: The Ballade of Early Rulers*; *Chap. 3.5: Enlil and Namzitarra*).

On the Translations

Words in parentheses are not in the original text, but have been added for the sake of clarity. Identification of speakers is added in parentheses, and, if not explicit in the original text, is the translator's suggestion. These are not indicated in the original text.

For readers unfamiliar with cuneiform literature: signs broken in the original text are placed between brackets [ ], and words only partly broken are placed between half brackets: ⸢ ⸣. This applies both to the transliterated text and its translation. This causes an inevitable contradiction, because the grammatical structure of the two languages differs so much that, say, substituting a grammatical ending to an English word does not necessarily cover a precise rendering of the possibilities that can be suggested for the corresponding Sumerian word. So far no good alternative solution has been proposed.

Readers should be aware of a minor discrepancy, in that some of the authors quoted use italics to indicate uncertain translations, whereas I have exclusively used a question mark to indicate the same, reserving italics for emphasis only. In such cases, I have included the quoted passages exactly as taken from the publications in which they appear.

78. In the *International Phonetic Alphabet* (IPA), ɾ, that is, r with a rounded top, denotes a flapped dental and alveolar r, which I consider the most likely approximation and suggest should be preferred if needed. This could be considered relevant in view of such variants as na-di/ri, line 137. Cf., however, the critical remarks in the comments on bad-rá, p. 108, n. 1, suggesting that perhaps this is no separate phoneme in Sumerian, but a free pronouncing variant.

79. In Thureau-Dangin's system, polysyllabic signs carry the accent corresponding to index no. 2 on the last syllable, unless the sign value is a long variant of a monosyllabic value, etc. Borger, however, chose to avoid this ambiguity by consistently placing accent = 2 on the first syllable. This is followed in the present volume. Civil chose to place accent 2 on the last syllable, etc.

Special Symbols

\# (1) in the transliteration of signs: indicates that two signs are written above one another as one single sign;
(2) in the left columns of the reconstructed texts: indicates that the line is found in parallel repetitions of the same line (mainly used in *Chap. 1.6: The Adab Version*).

| indicates the start of a new line (also mainly used in *Chap. 1.6: The Adab Version*).

/ indicates an indented line (only used where significant).

: in the transliteration of ED sources: indicates that the signs are transliterated in the order in which they are written, irrespective of the order in which they are to be read. In the SS sources: reverse order.

1.3 Transliteration and Translation

1 u$_4$ ri-a u$_4$ sud-rá ri-a

C$_4$: [...] u$_4$ sud-rá r[i-]; Ur$_{I}$: [...] u$_4$ sud-rá ri-a; P: [u$_4$] ri-a u$_4$ sud-rá ri: Sch$_{I}$: u$_4$ ri-a u$_4$ s[ud]-rá ri-a; Sch$_{I}$: u$_4$ ri-a u$_4$ s[ud]-rá ri-a; Sch$_2$: u$_4$ ri-a u$_4$-sud-{bad}-rá ⸢ri-a⸣

(1) In those days, in those far remote days;

2 ŋi$_6$ ri-a ŋi$_6$ bad-rá ri-a

C$_4$: [...]-⸢a⸣ ŋi$_6$ bad-rá [...]; Ur$_{I}$: [...] ŋi$_6$ bad-rá ri-a; P: [ŋ]i$_6$ ri-a ŋi$_6$ bad-rá ri; Sch$_{I}$: ŋi$_6$ ri-a ŋi$_6$ ⸢bad-rá⸣ ri-a; Sch$_2$: ŋi$_6$ ri-a ŋi$_6$ bad-⸢rá ri-a⸣

(2) in those nights, in those faraway nights;

3 mu ri-a mu sud-rá ri-a

C$_4$: [...] mu sud-r[á]; Ur$_{I}$: [...]-⸢ri⸣-⸢a⸣ mu sud-rá ri-a; P: [mu] ri-a mu sud-rá ri; Sch$_{I}$: mu ri-a mu sud-rá ri-a; Sch$_2$: mu ri-a mu su[d-r]á r[i-a]

(3) in those years, in those far remote years;

4 u$_4$-ba ŋéštu-tuku inim-galam inim-zu-a kalam-ma ti-la-a

ED$_{I}$ o. i 1–2 ŋéštu inim-zu | [ka]lam [t]i-la

ED$_2$ o. i 1–2 = Fr. 2 i 1–2 [ŋéštu-tuku inim-galam inim-zu-a]m$_6$ [kalam-m]a [ti]-la-am$_6$

C$_4$: [... tu]ku ⸢inim⸣(?) [...]; Ur$_{I}$: [ ]-ba ŋéštu-tuku inim-galam inim-zu-a kalam-ma til-la-àm; P: u$_4$-ba ŋéštu-tuku inim-galam inim-zu-a kalam-ma ti-la-a: Sch$_{I}$: u$_4$-ba ú-KAM(? hardly ÚḪ?) inim zu-a kalam-ma(?) ti-la-àm; Sch$_2$: u$_4$-ba ŋéšt[u (GIŠ.TÚG.P[I])-[ga(?)-k]am

(4) in those days, the intelligent one, the one of elaborate words, the wise one, who lived in the country;

5 šuruppak[ki] ŋéštu-tuku inim-galam inim-zu-a kalam-ma ti-la-a

ED$_{I}$ o. i 3–5 [šuruppak Ú]R.[A]Š | [ŋéš]tu inim-zu | kalam ti-la

ED$_2$ i 3–5 = Fr. 2 i 3–5 [šurupp]ak[ki] [Ú]R.AŠ | [ŋéš]tu-[tu]ku inim-[galam inim]-zu-am$_6$ | [kalam-m]a [ti-la-am$_6$]

Ur$_{I}$: šuruppak[ki]-e ŋéštu-tuku inim-galam inim-zu-a kalam-ma til-la-àm; P: šuruppak[ki] ŋéštu-tuku inim-galam inim-zu-a kalam-ma ti-la-a; Sch$_{I}$: šuruppak[ki] ŋéštu ú-KAM(? hardly ÚḪ?) inim-zu-a kalam-ma ti-la-àm; Sch$_2$: inim-ma(sic!)-zu kalam-ma ti-la

(5) the man from Šuruppak, the intelligent one, the one of elaborate words, the wise one, who lived in the country;

6 šuruppak^{ki}-e dumu-ni-ra na na-mu-un-ri-ri

ED$_1$ o. i 6 — šuruppak dumu na [n]a-mu-ri
ED$_2$? Fr. 4 ii 2–3 & Fr. 10 ii 1–2 — [šuruppak^{ki}] ÚR.AŠ | dumu-ni-ra na na-ri-ri

Ur$_1$: šuruppak^{ki}-e dumu-ni-ra na na-mu-un-ri-ga-àm; P: šuruppak^{ki}-ké(GI) dumu-ni-ra na na-mu-un-ri-ri; Sch$_1$: šuruppak^{ki} dumu-ni-ra na na-mu-un-ri-ri; Sch$_2$: ⸢SAḪAR⸣ ⸢šuruppak⸣^{ki} ŋéštu-<ga(?)>-kam

(6) the man from Šuruppak, gave instructions to his son
(ED translation: See commentary)

7 šuruppak^{ki} dumu ubar-tu-tu-ke$_4$

Akk$_1$ — ^{m}*šu-ru-u[p-pa-ak …]*

Ur$_1$: šuruppak^{ki} dumu ubar-tu-tu-ke$_4$; P: šuruppak^{ki} dumu [ub]ar-tu-tu-ke$_4$; Sch$_1$: šuruppak^{ki} dumu ubar-tu-tu-ke$_4$; Sch$_2$: SAḪAR šuruppak^{ki} ⸢A.AN⸣ (or, hardly, ⸢a⸣-⸢maš⸣)-ḪAR-tu-tu-ke$_4$

(7) - the man from Šuruppak, the son of Ubartutu -

8 zi-u$_4$-sud-rá dumu-ni-ra na na-mu-un-ri-ri

Akk$_1$ — ^{m}*ut-na-p[u-uš-te …]*

I$_{15}$: (traces); Ur$_1$: zi-u$_4$-sud-rá dumu-ni-ra na na-mu-un-ri-ri; BM$_1$: [… -u]n-ri; P: zi-u$_4$-sud-rá dumu-ni-ra na [na-m]u-u[n]-r[i]-r[i]; Sch$_1$: zi-u$_4$-sud-rá dumu-⸢ni⸣-ra na na-mu-un-ri-ri; Sch$_2$: zi-u$_4$-sud-rá dumu-ni-ra na na-mu-un-ri-ri

(8) gave instructions to his son Ziusudra:

9 dumu-ŋu$_{10}$ na ga-ri na-ri-ŋu$_{10}$ ḫé-dab$_5$

ED$_1$ o. i 7 — dumu-ŋu$_{10}$ na ga-ri
ED$_2$ — [dumu-ŋu$_{10}$ na ga-ri]
Akk$_1$ — *ma-ri l[u(?)-šu-ur-ka …]*
Akk$_3$ o. i 1–2 — *[ma-ri lu-šu-ur-ka / a-ši]-ir-ti ṣa-bat*

I$_{15}$: dumu-ŋu$_{10}$ … ; Ur$_1$: dumu-ŋu$_{10}$ na ga-ri na-ri-ŋu$_{10}$ ḫé-dab$_5$; BM$_1$: [… ḫ]é-dab$_5$; P: dumu-ŋu$_{10}$ na ge-ri na-ri-ŋu$_{10}$ ḫé-dab$_5$; Sch$_1$: dumu-mu na-ri-ge(sic!) ⸢na⸣-ri-⸢ŋu$_{10}$⸣ ḫé-dab$_5$; Sch$_2$: dumu-ŋu$_{10}$ na ge(sic!)-ri na-ri (no ŋu$_{10}$) ḫé-⸢dab$_5$⸣

(9) "My son, let me give instructions; let my instructions be taken!

10 zi-u$_4$-sud-rá inim ga-ra-ab-d[ug$_4$] ŋizzal ḫé-em-ši-ak

ED$_1$ o. i 8 — GIŠ.PI.[TÚG] ḫé-m[a]-ak
ED$_2$ Fr. 10 i 1' — [ŋizz]al ḫé-⸢x-x⸣ (= -⸢ma-ak⸣?)
Akk$_1$ — ^{m}*ut-na-pu-u[š-te …]*
Akk$_3$ o. i 3–4 — broken

I$_{15}$: zi-u$_4$-sud-[…]; Ur$_1$: omits line; BM$_1$: [… ŋiz]zal ḫé-em-<ši>-ak; P: zi-u$_4$-sud-rá inim ga-ra-ab-d[ug$_4$] ŋizzal(?) ḫé-em-ši-ak; Sch$_1$: zi-u$_4$-sud-rá inim ŋizzal ḫé-em-ši-ak; Sch$_2$: zi-u$_4$-sud-rá inim ga-ra-ab-dug$_4$ ŋizzal(written nearly as ŋéštu) ḫé-em-ši-a

(10) Ziusudra, let me speak a word to you; let attention be paid to them!

11	na-ri-ga-ŋu$_{10}$ šu nam-bí-bar-re	*(11)* Don't neglect my instructions!
Akk$_1$	*a-šèr-ti* [...]	
Akk$_3$ o. i	*[a-ši-ir-]x(?)-šu i-šar / [la-a ta-...-t]a-AK*	
+ Hurr. o. ii 5–6	ir-[...] / az-k[i-ir ...]	
	I$_{15}$: na-ri-ga [...]; Ur$_1$: na-ri-ga-ŋu$_{10}$ šu nam-bí-bar-ra (sic!); BM$_1$ [...]-bar-re; P: na-ri-ga-ŋu$_{10}$ šu nam-bí-bar-re; Sch$_1$: na-ri-ga-ŋu$_{10}$ šu nam-bí-bar-re-en; Sch$_2$: na-ri-ga-ŋu$_{10}$ šu nam-bí-bar-re	
12	inim dug$_4$-ga-ŋu$_{10}$ na-ab-ta-bal-e-dè	*(12)* Don't transgress the words I speak!
Akk$_1$	*a-mat a[q-bu ...]*	
Akk$_3$ o. i 7	*[a-mat aq-bu la]-a te-ti-iq*	
+ Hurr. o. ii 7	a-ri-BA(?) [...]	
	I$_{15}$: inim dug$_4$- ... ; T$_1$: [... -t]a-b[al- ...]; Ur$_1$: inim dug$_4$-ga-ŋu$_{10}$ na-ab-ta-bal-e; Ur$_6$: inim dug$_4$-ga [...] / na-ab-te-bal-[... -e]n; BM$_1$: [... -b]al-e-dè; P: inim dug$_4$-ga-ŋu$_{10}$ na-ab-ta-bal-e-dè; Sch$_1$: inim dug$_4$-ga-ŋu$_{10}$ na-a[b-t]a-bal-e-dè; Sch$_2$: <inim> dug$_4$-ga-ŋu$_{10}$ na-[a]b-ta-bal-e-⸢dè⸣	
13	na-ri ab-ba níŋ-kal-la-àm gú-zu ḫé-em-ši-ak	*(13)* The instructions of an old man are precious; you should comply with them! (Akk$_3$:) they should be believed!
Akk$_3$ o. i 4	*[a-ši-ir-ti ...] x šu-qa-ri it-ta-qí-ip*	
+ Hurr. o. i 8	az-ki-ir [...]	
	Akk$_1$, I$_{15}$, and T$_1$ omit line. Ur$_1$: [n]a-ri ab-ba níŋ-kal-la gú-zu ḫé-em-ši-ak-e (coll. Alster 1974, pl. I); Ur$_6$: na-ri ab-ba níŋ-k[al]-la-àm / gú-zu ḫé-em-ši-ŋál; BM$_1$: [... -e]m-ši-ŋál; P: na-ri ab-ba níŋ-kal-la-àm; Sch$_1$: na-ri ab-ba-šè níŋ-kal-la-a gú-zu ḫé-em-ši-ŋál; Sch$_2$: na-ri ad-da n[íŋ-kal-l]a-àm gú-zu ḫé-em-ši-ŋál gú-zi(sic!) ḫé-m[e]-⸢x⸣-⸢x⸣ (may be ŋ[á-ŋá?])	
14	dùr.⸢ùr⸣ gù-di na-ab-sa$_{10}$-sa$_{10}$ érin-zu ša-ra-ab-si-il-le	*(14)* Don't buy an ass that brays; it will split your yoke!
ED$_2$ Fr. 10 i 2–3	ANŠE [K]A gù-di nàb(AN+AN)-| sa$_{10}$-sa$_{10}$ [...] na-e	
Akk$_1$	*mu-ú-ra na-[gi-ga la tu-ša-am ...]*	
Akk$_3$ o. i 9	*[... l]a-a tu-ša-am / [...]x-ta-ak ú-sà-pa-ḫa*	
+ Hurr. o. i 9	zu-ḫi-ra x [...] / ḫa-i-x [...]	
	I$_{15}$: ANŠE ... ; T$_1$: [... e]ŋir(?)-zu ša-[...]; Ur$_1$: dùr.⸢ùr⸣ gù-di na-ab-s[a$_{10}$-s]a$_{10}$ érin-zu ša-ra-ab-si-il; Ur$_6$: dùr gù-di na-ab-sa$_{10}$-sa$_{10}$-an / érin(?)-zu(!) (copy ba) ša-ra-si-il-le; BM$_1$: [... ér]in-zu ša-ra-si-il; P: dùr.⸢ùr⸣ gù-di na-[a]b-sa$_{10}$-s[a$_{10}$ (x)] eŋir(?) ša-ra-ab-si-il(?); Sch$_1$: dùr.⸢ùr⸣ gù-di na-ab-sa$_{10}$-sa$_{10}$ érin-zu ša-re-eb-si-i[l(?)]; Sch$_2$: ⸢ANŠE⸣ ⸢na⸣(sic!)-⸢di⸣ e na-ab-sa$_{10}$-sa$_{10}$-⸢an⸣(?) ⸢érin⸣-zu-šè(sic!) a-ra-si-le	

15 gán kaskal-la nam-bí-íb-ŋá-ŋá nam-silig gum-ŋá-àm

ED$_1$ o. i 9 gán-zu [kaskal na-ŋá-ŋá]
ED$_2$ i 12–13 gán kaskal na-ŋá-ŋá | nam-[silig] ⌜x⌝ [x]
Akk$_1$ *me-re-ša i-na ḫ[ar(!)-ra-ni la te-re-eš ...]*
Akk$_3$ o. i 10 *[me-re-ša i-na ḫar-ra-n]i la te-ri-iš GU-la / -lu*
+ Hurr. o. i 10 e-ba [...]

I$_{15}$: gam(sic!) ... ; T$_1$: [... n]am-silig gú-ŋá-[...]; Ur$_1$: gán kaskal-[la] nam-bí-íb-ŋá-ŋá [na]m-silig ga-ŋá-àm; Ur$_6$: gán kaskal na-bi-ŋá-ŋá-an / nam-silig gum-àm; BM$_1$: [... -si]lig gú-ŋá-à[m]; P (inverts 15 and 16): gán [...] nam-ba-[e]-ŋá-ŋ[á] nam-silig [...]; Sch$_1$: gán kaskal-la nam-ba-e-ŋá-ŋá nam-silig gum-ŋá-àm; Sch$_2$: gán [kaskal-l]a [nam-b]i-⌜ŋá⌝-ŋá nam-⌜silig⌝ [...]-ŋá-àm

(15) Don't cultivate a field on a road; the decimation will be crushing(?).

(15, Akk$_3$, second part:) "(it means) discrediting."

16 a-šà ka-ŋìri-ka nam-ba-e-ur$_{11}$-ru zi bulug-ga-àm

Akk$_1$ *e-qe-el-ka [i-na ... la te-...]*
Akk$_3$ o. i 11 *[e-qe-el-ka i-na ... l]a-a te-ri-iš pu-ku / nu-qù-ur*
+ Hurr. o. i 11 e x [...]

I$_{15}$: a-... ; T$_1$: [...]-e-ur$_{11}$(APIN)-ru zi bulug-àm; Ur$_1$: a-šà kaskal [k]a(? vertical only)-ŋìri-ka nam-ba-e-[u]r$_{11}$-⌜re⌝ zé-bulug-ga-àm (coll. Alster 1974, pl. I); Ur$_6$: a-šà ka(not saŋ)-ŋìri-ka / na-bi-ur$_{11}$-en / zag-e bulug gu$_7$-a; BM$_1$: [...] ⌜ù⌝-bulug-gu$_7$; P (inverts 15 and 16): a-šà ⌜x⌝ ŋìri-ka(?) nam-ba-e(?)-úr-ru ⌜x⌝ [...]; Sch$_1$: a-šà ka-ŋìri-ka nam-ba-⌜e(?)⌝-⌜ùr(?)⌝-ru a zu(hardly zé) IGI(?) (or ši-i[m(?)-) bulug NE; Sch$_2$: a-šà k[a ŋìri-ka nam-ba-e-ùr]-⌜e⌝ KA-a ⌜x⌝ [...]

(16) Don't plow a field on a pathway; (the result is) the tearing out of(?) boundary stones.

(16, Akk$_3$, second part, with a slight emendation:) "the *boundary stones (will be) torn out."

Sch$_2$ 27–28 unidentified:
27 cf. SS 18? a-SI ⌜sila⌝ [daŋal]-[...]
28 = unidentified a-šà ki nu-zuḫ(KA)-⌜un⌝(?) (...)

17 gán-zu-àm pú na-an-ni-dù-e-en ùŋ-e ša-re-eb-ḫul-ḫul

ED$_1$ o. ii 4 gán-za pú na-⌜dù⌝ ⌜ùŋ⌝ ⌜šè⌝-⌜mu⌝-ra-⌜ḫul⌝
ED$_2$ Fr. 10 i 6–7 [... náb]-⌜du⌝ [x]-e | [...]-LU
Akk$_1$ *ina me-re-ši-ka ⌜x⌝ [...]*
Akk$_3$ o. i *[ina me-re-ši-ka burtu] la-a ti-ḫé-ri / [... ù-n]a-kar-ka*

T$_1$: [...]-dù a ùŋ-e ša-ra-eb-ḫ[ul- ...]; Ur$_1$: gán [x (x)]-àm pú na-an-dù-[x (x)]-⌜e⌝ ša-ra-eb-ḫul-ḫul (coll. Alster 1974, pl. I); Ur$_6$: gán-zu-àm(?) pú na-ni-[...] / ùŋ-e ši-re-eb-ḫ[ul-ḫul]; BM$_1$: [...]-ḫul; BM$_2$: [...]-an-ni-dù-e-en ùŋ-⌜e⌝ ⌜ša-re(?)-x⌝-[...]; P: ere(?) šà(!)-[ba(?)]? pú na(!)-[an(?)]-⌜x⌝(or: nam)-zal-e-en ùŋ-e ša-[re-eb-...] (coll. Th. Kämmerer); Sch$_1$: gán-zu-a pú na-an-dù ⌜ùŋ(?)⌝-⌜e⌝ ... [ ]-eb-ḫul(?)-⌜x⌝; Sch$_1$: gán-zu-a pú na-an-dù ⌜ùŋ(?)⌝-⌜e⌝ ... [ ]-eb-ḫul(?)-⌜x⌝; Sch$_2$: gán-zu ⌜pú⌝ na-⌜A⌝(?) [(x)] ⌜x⌝ [... (traces of two more signs) ...]

(17) Don't place a well in your own field; the people will turn hostile against you.

18 é sila-daŋal-la nam-bí-ib-lá-e KÉŠ-da ŋál-la-àm

ED$_1$ o. ii 1–2 é sila(!)-daŋal na-dù(text: NI) x-sír LAK 218 ŋál-am$_6$

Akk$_1$ *bīt-ka a-na re-[bi-ti ...]*

T$_1$: [... -b]í-ib-lá-e KÉŠ-da ŋál-la-àm; Ur$_1$: é [x x]-la nam-bí-íb-lá-e ⸢KÉŠ⸣-⸢da⸣ ŋál-la-àm; Ur$_6$: ⸢é⸣ sila-⸢daŋal⸣-⸢la⸣ n[a- ...]; BM$_1$: [... -à]m; BM$_2$: [...] nam-bí-íb-lá-e KÉŠ-da ŋál-l[a- x]; P: é(?) sila x (x) daŋal nam-bi-ib-lá-e-en KÉŠ(!) (post OB sign form)-d[a]-[...] (coll. P. Kämmerer); Sch$_1$: é sila-daŋal-la-ta nam-bí-⸢íb⸣-⸢lá⸣-⸢e⸣-⸢en⸣ kéš-da ⸢ŋál⸣-la-àm; Sch$_2$ (l. 31): ⸢é⸣(?) sila x(= IGI?) B[I [... (½ line)] (l. 32): kéšda [...] ⸢x⸣ ⸢x⸣ [...]

(18) Don't extend a house too close to a public square; it will cause obstruction.

19 šu-du$_8$-a nu-e-tùm lú-bi ša-ba-e-dab$_5$-bé

ED$_1$ o. ii 7–8 šu-dù na-túm lú | šè-ba-dab$_5$

ED$_2$ Fr. 2 ii 2–4 ⸢šu⸣-du$_8$-a na-| túm lú-bi ša$_4$-ba-| dab$_5$

Akk$_1$ *qa-ta-te la te-l[e-eq-qe ...]*

T$_1$: [...]-tùm lú-bé še-ba-e-dab$_5$-bé; Ur$_1$: šu-⸢dù⸣-⸢a⸣ ⸢nu⸣-mu-un-ti l[lú-b]é ša-ba-e-dab$_5$-bé; BM$_1$: [... -b]é; BM$_2$: [... -m]u(?)-te-ŋá-e lú-bé ša-ba-e-⸢x⸣ [x]; P: šu-du$_8$-a nu-e(?)-tùm lú-bé ša-b[a- x x (x x)] (coll. Th. Kämmerer); Sch$_1$: šu-du$_8$-a nu-un-tùm ⸢(traces compatible with lú-bi ša)⸣-[ba]-e-dab$_5$-bé-en; Sch$_2$ (l. 30): A[N [(x)] ⸢ME⸣(= igi?) SI-e ⸢x⸣ [... (½ line)] (belongs here?)

(19) Don't act as a guarantor; that man will have a hold on you;

So the oldest texts; later: "Don't accept a pledge, etc."

20 za-e šu-du$_8$-a nam-mu-ak-e

(addition, Ur$_1$: [l]ú saŋ bí-íb-sal-la-e-a)

cf. ED$_1$ o. ii 9: šà šu-bad na-ak [me]-zu a[k]

cf. ED$_2$ Fr. 2 ii 4–5 ur šu-ba na-ak | ní-zu na-du$_7$-né

Akk$_1$ *ù at-ta qa-t[a-te la te-...]*

T$_1$: [...]-mu-e-⸢x⸣-⸢x⸣ (end of line); Ur$_1$: za-[e šu]-dù-a nam-mu-e-[x l]ú saŋ bí-íb-sal-la-e-a (coll. Alster 1974, pl. I); BM$_1$: [...]-e; BM$_2$: [...]-igi-du$_8$-a nam-mu-ak-[x (x)]; P: za-e šu-du$_8$-a(!) nam(!)-mu-a[k] (!) [x x (x x)] (coll. Th. Kämmerer); Sch$_1$: za-e šu-du$_8$-a nam-mu-ak-en; Sch$_2$ (not identified)

(20) and *you*, don't accept a pledge; (that man will be discredited).

(20) The second part is an addition in Ur$_1$ only; the ED texts mean, lit., "Do not make an 'open hand'; don't make yourself ...(= Don't humiliate yourself?)." Cf. perhaps line 35.

21 lú-ra igi-du$_8$-a na-an-ak-e úru-bi ša-re-e[b]-su-su

ED$_1$ o. ii 5–6 [i]gi-du na-⸢x⸣-⸢ba⸣ | lú uru$_5$ ši-sù x x

ED$_2$ ii = Fr. 2 ii 1–2 [...] URU×A l[ú (x = small sign or nothing)] ši-su-su

Akk$_1$ *a-na a-me-li mu-u[m-ma la ...]*

T$_1$: [... d]u$_8$ na-an-ak úru-bi ša-[...]; Ur$_1$: lú-[ra] igi-du$_8$-a na-an-[x x]-bi ša-⸢re⸣-⸢eb⸣-s[u-s]u; BM$_1$: [...]-su-su; BM$_2$: [...] igi-du$_8$ na-an-ak-e úru-bi ša-re-e[b- x x]; P: lú-ra igi-du$_8$ na-an-⸢ak⸣-e dè/úru(?)-bi-[...] (coll.

(21) Don't testify against a man; the city(?) will repay you! (or: you will be submerged by a flood [arising] from it!)

Pun, may also mean: "you will be repaid for it by a flood!"

Th. Kämmerer); Sch$_1$: lú-ra igi-du$_8$-a na-an-ak-en ⸢úru⸣-bi ša-ba(! looks like ma)-re-eb-su-su; Sch$_2$ (l. 34) [(x)] ⸢x⸣(like ga)-bi š[u(?) ...] ⸢x⸣ ⸢NE⸣

22 ki du$_{14}$-da-ka nam-ba-e-gub-bu-dè-en

Akk$_1$ *a-šar ṣa-al-[te ...]*

T$_1$: [...] nam-bi-DU-[...]; Ur$_1$: ki d[u$_{14}$-d]a-ka n[am-b]í-D[U-(x)-d]è; BM$_1$: [...]-⸢x⸣-dè; BM$_2$: [x x -d]a-ka nam-bí-DU-[x (x)]; P: ki du$_{14}$-ka nam-b[i]-[...] (coll. Th. Kämmerer); Sch$_1$: ki du$_{14}$-da-ka nam-ba-e-gub-bu-dè-en

(22) Don't loiter about where there is a quarrel!

23 du$_{14}$-dè lú ki-inim-ma-šè nam-ba-e-ku$_4$-ku$_4$-un

Akk$_1$ *ṣa-al-tu a-na ⸢x⸣* [...]

T$_1$: [x -d]è ⸢ki⸣-inim-bi ⸢x⸣ [...]; Ur$_1$: du$_{14}$-dè lú [...]-ku$_4$ (collated); BM$_1$: [...]-ku$_4$-ku$_4$; BM$_2$: [x x] lú ki-inim-ma nam-ba-e-[x x]; P: du$_{14}$ lú ki-inim-BA(!) [...] (coll. Th. Kämmerer); Sch$_1$: du$_{14}$-dè lú ki-inim-ma-šè na-an-ku$_4$-ku$_4$-un

(23) Don't let yourself be made a witness in the quarrel!

24 du$_{14}$-dè ní-zu nam-⸢mu⸣-*e(?)-da-zu-zu-un

Akk$_1$ *[ṣa-a]l-tu ⸢x⸣*[...]

Ur$_1$: [d]u$_{14}$-dè ní-[...] (collated); BM$_1$ (traces); BM$_2$: [x x] ní-zu nam-b[a- ...]; P: du$_{14}$ ní-BA(!) [...] (coll. Th. Kämmerer); Sch$_1$: du$_{14}$-dè ní-zu a-na(?) ⸢nam(?)⸣-⸢mu⸣ -⸢ŋá⸣(could be ⸢e⸣?)-da-zu-zu-un

(24) Don't [let] yourself become known as an accomplice in the quarrel!

25 du$_{14}$ n[am-a]k-dè-en ⸢x⸣ ...

Ur$_1$: (illegible traces); BM$_2$: [x x -a]k-dè-en ⸢x⸣ [...]; P: du$_{14}$ n[am-a]k-dè-en [...]; Sch$_1$: [(x)]-⸢x⸣(may be d]u$_{14}$) nam-x x(like da) KA nam-ùr(?)-[ùr(?)-re(?)]

(25) Don't cause a quarrel; don't [...]!

26 [x (x) k]á é-gal-la-ka bí-in-gub-[x-(x)]

T$_1$: [...]-⸢ra⸣-si-⸢ga⸣; Ur$_1$: [...]-⸢x⸣ ba-sig; Ur$_2$: [x] ⸢x⸣-ka é-⸢x⸣-la-⸢ka⸣ / šèg ba-ra-si-g[a]; BM$_2$: [... k]á é-gal-la [...]; Sch$_1$: [(x)] ⸢x⸣ é-gal-ka bí-in-gub-[x-(x)]

(26) ... on [him who stands] in the gate of the palace ...

27 du$_{14}$ bar-bar-ta gub-gub-[ba] in-nu-uš sila-kúr-ra níŋin-na-ma-a[n ...]

ED$_1$ o. iii 1–2 du$_7$ sila-kúr ⸢x⸣-ma | NI.LAK 134 bar-tar-ta gub-ma

Akk$_2$ [... *nu*]-*uk*-[*kir* ...]

T$_1$: [... -r]a(?) na-mu-DAGAL(? too long for ma)-NE; Ur$_1$: [... -r]a(?) ⸢nam(or, rather = è, or gub?)⸣-⸢ma⸣-ni-ib (copy correct; nothing missing after ib); Ur$_2$: du$_{14}$-dè bar-bar-ta gub-gub-[ba] / in-nu-uš sila-kúr-⸢x-ra(?)⸣ ⸢nam⸣-⸢ma⸣-è(?); BM$_2$: [...] bar-bar-ta [/ ... si]la kúr-ra [...]; Sch$_1$: du$_{14}$-ta bar-ta gub-gub-[x-(x)] ⸢ì(?)⸣-ni-⸢ta⸣(?) sila-kúr-ra níŋin-na-ma-a[n-x (x)]

(27) Stand aside from quarrels; when facing an insult, go around it on another road!

28 nín nam-mu-zuḫ-zuḫ ní-zu nam-mu-úš-e

ED$_1$ o. iii 4 nín na-mu-zuḫ-zuḫ me-zu na-MUNŠUB
ED$_2$ Fr. 10 ii 4–5 nín nám-zuḫ-zuḫ ní-zu | nàb(AN+AN)-MUNŠUB
Akk$_2$ *[m]i-i[m(?)-ma la ta-šar-raq ra-man-k]a*(?) *la*(?) [...]

T$_1$: [... n]í-zu nam-mu-úš-e; Ur$_1$: [...] ní-zu na-an-úš-e (collated); Ur$_2$: nín nam-mu-⸢zuḫ⸣-⸢zuḫ⸣ / ní-zu nam-úš-⸢e⸣-⸢en⸣; BM$_2$: [...]-zuḫ-z[uḫ ...]; Sch$_1$: nín-nam nu-zuḫ-zuḫ ní-zuḫ ⸢nu(?)⸣-uš-⸢en⸣ (room for two more signs?)

(28) Don't steal anything; don't kill yourself!

29 é na-a-an-ni-bùr-e-en mi-si-saḫar-ra al nam-me

ED$_1$ o. iii 6 é na-[bùr] ⸢x⸣ [x x]
ED$_2$ Fr. 10 ii 7 é nam-m[u]-⸢bùr⸣ [...]
Akk$_2$ *bī[ta la ta]-p[al-la]-áš* NI T[A(?) ...] *l[a ...]*

T$_1$: [...] mi-si-saḫar-ra nam-[...]; Ur$_1$: [...] ⸢x⸣ mi-si-saḫar al nam-me; Ur$_2$: é na-a-an-ni-bùr-e-en / mi-si-saḫar al <nam>-me-en; Sch$_1$: é nam-mu-bùru-dè-en ⸢mi(?)⸣-(⸢x⸣)-si(?)-saḫar al ⸢nam⸣-[me]:

(29) Don't break into a house; don't demand the money chest!

30 ní-zuḫ pirin na-nam ul-dab$_5$ san na-nam

ED$_1$ o. iii 5 nu-zuḫ ušum na-nam ul-dab$_5$ géme na-nam
ED$_2$ Fr. 10 ii 5–6 nu-zuḫ | [p]irin na-nám ù-| dab$_5$ géme na-nám
Akk$_2$ *šar-ra-qu ne-e-šu* [...] *x* [...]

I$_1$: [... -z]u pirin na-n[am ...]; T$_1$: [... -d]ab$_5$ san na-n[am]; Ur$_1$: [... n]a-⸢nam⸣ ul-dab$_5$ san na-nam (coll. Alster 1974, pl. I); Ur$_2$: ní-zu ⸢pirin⸣ ⸢na⸣-na-àm ul-dab$_5$ san na-na-àm; Ur$_6$: [...] ul-[...]; Sch$_1$: ní-zu(sic!) san(sic!) ⸢na⸣-nam ul-GAN(?) na-nam

(30) The thief is indeed a lion; when he has been caught, he is indeed a slave!

ED$_1$: "The thief is indeed a dragon, after he has been caught, he is indeed a slave girl"; ED$_2$ same, but "... lion ... and slave girl."

31 dumu-nu$_{10}$ sa-gaz nam-mu-ak-e ní-zu àga-àm nam-bí-ib-bar-re-e
(var. 2nd part: [(...) š]e(?)-búr(?)-re nam-bí-bar-[re])

ED$_1$ o. iii 7 [x]-gaz na-ak ⸢x⸣ sír(?) [na]-⸢bar⸣(?)
Akk$_2$ *ma-ri ḫab-ba-tu-tam la te-p[u-uš ra-m]an-ka RU x* [...]

I$_1$ + I$_2$: [dumu-n]u$_{10}$ sa-gaz n[a]m-m[u- ...] / [... š]e(?)-sír-re-eš ⸢x⸣ + [n]am-bi-[...]; T$_1$: [...] nam-m[u- ...] / [... b]í-bar-[re]; Ur$_1$: [x x x g]az nam-mu-ù-ak-e / [...] ⸢x⸣(not še) ⸢búr(?)⸣-re nam-bí-ib-bar-ra (coll. Alster 1974 pl. I); Ur$_2$: dumu-nu$_{10}$ sa-gaz na-àm-ma-[ak]-e / ní-zu àga-àm na-àm-bí-[íb-bar-r]e-e (coll. Alster 1974, pl. II); Ur$_6$: dumu-n[u$_{10}$ ...] na-bi-[...] ní-zu àg[a ...] na-bi-b[ar- ...]; Sch$_1$: dumu-nu$_{10}$ ⸢sa-gaz nam-mu-ak⸣-en ní-zu ⸢x⸣(like mu)-⸢x⸣(like še)-⸢x⸣-⸢x⸣(like ke$_4$) ⸢x⸣(may be nam)-⸢bar⸣-re

(31) My son, don't commit murder; don't let yourself be mutilated with an axe!

Variant, second part: "Don't [let yourself] be split with ..." (a tool to chop grain):

32 ninta niŋir-si na-an-ak ní-zu na-an-⸢x⸣-⸢x⸣

ED_1 iii 8 ninta$_x$(SAL+NITAḪ) mi-si ⸢na⸣-⸢x⸣(=ḪI×DIŠ+GIŠ?) [m]e-zu [x] x

Akk_2 *su-sa-pi-in-nu-tam la te-ep-p[u-uš ra-ma]n-ka l[a ...]*

I_1 + I_2: [... n]a-an-[... + ... n]í-zu nam-⸢x⸣-[...]; T_1: [...] nam-m[u ...]; Ur_1: [... n]a-an-ak ní-zu na-an-[x x]; Ur_2: ninta-niŋir-si na-[...] ⸢x⸣ / ní-zu na-àm-⸢x⸣-⸢x⸣ (could be gíd?-e); Ur_6: é niŋir-[...] ní [...]; Sch_1: ninta ⸢niŋir⸣(?)-⸢si⸣(? looks rather like ra) na-⸢an⸣-...(traces of ca. 8 signs)-en

(32) Don't make a (young) man best man; don't [humiliate(?)] yourself!

33 ki-sikil dam tuku-d[a] e-⸢ne⸣ nam-mu-un-KA-e inim-sig-bi ma[ḫ-àm]

ED_1 o. iv 1 [si]kil-da [(x)] [n]e na-da-⸢e⸣
(o. iv 2) inim-sig [m]áḫ(AL)
Akk_2 *it-ti ár-da-ti šá mu-ti aḫ-z[u la t]e-ṣe-eḫ kar-ṣ[u ...]*

I_1 + I_2: [...] nam-[(belongs where? perhaps = nam-[dam-tuku?]) + ... n]e(?) nam-mu-u[n- ... / ...]-bi maḫ(!)-[x]; T_1: [... na]m-[...]; Ur_1: [ki-sikil dam tu]ku-d[a x x] nam-mu-un-KA(the sign is not NE)-e inim-sig-⸢ga (rather than bi)⸣ ma[ḫ-àm]; Ur_2: ki-sikil dam tuku-⸢da⸣ e-⸢ne⸣ [...] inim si-bi(bi rather than ga) ma[ḫ-àm]; Sch_1: ⸢ki⸣-⸢sikil⸣ ...

(33) Don't laugh with a girl if she is married; the slander (arising from it) is strong!

34 dumu-[ŋu$_{10}$] *daggan-na lú dam tu[ku-d]a dúr nam-⸢bí⸣-e-ŋá-ŋá

Akk_2 *i-na da-ak-ka-ni it-ti aš-t[i] a-mi-li la tu-[uš-ša-ab]*

I_1 + I_2: [...] dag [... + ...] ⸢x⸣ nam-bí-[...]; Ur_1: [x x x x] lú dam tu[ku-d]a dúr nam-⸢bí⸣-e-ŋá-ŋá (collation Alster 1974, pl. I; there is space for dumu-ŋu$_{10}$ daggan-na); Ur_2: dumu-[ŋu$_{10}$] ⸢x⸣-na lú [...] / dúr [na]m-bí-[...]; Sch_1: ka ... (traces of ca. 6 mostly illegible signs) -ŋá-ŋá

(34) My son, don't sit in a chamber with someone who is married!

Sum., "with someone who has a spouse," (neutral gender), but Akk. "with a man's wife," clearly referring to a married woman.

35 du$_{14}$ nam-[mú-m]ú-dè ní-zu na-an-[pe]-el-lá

ED_1 o. iv 4 du$_7$ na-mú-mú níŋ-z[u na-š]ub
Akk_2 *la mu-uṣ-ṣa-la-ta ra-man-ka la tu-[qal-lil(?)]*

I_2: [...]-nam-[...]; I_3: [d]u$_{14}$ n[am- ...] / [n]í-z[u ...]; Ur_1: [x x x-m]ú-dè ní zu na-an-[pe]-el-lá; Ur_2: du$_{14}$ [...]; Sch_1: du$_{14}$ nam-...(almost destroyed)-en

(35) Don't be quarrelsome; don't disgrace yourself!

36 lul nam-gur$_5$-gur$_5$ saŋ gú-⸢sal-sal⸣-la

ED_1 o. iv 5 l[ul na- x x] ⸢ra⸣ [x x] x-sal-sal ⸢x x⸣ su
ED_2 Fr. iii 1–2 [lu]l [na]-gur$_5$-gur$_5$ | [s]aŋ sal-sal-[a]m$_6$
Akk_2 *a-na <ṣa>-al-ti la tu-uk-tap-pa-ad qá-qá-du qa-l[a-...]*

I_3: lul na[m]-gu[r$_5$- ...] / s[aŋ] kù [...]; Ur_1: [x x -gu]r$_5$-gur$_5$ saŋ gú ⸢sal-sal⸣-la; Ur_2: [...] / saŋ KU [x x (x)] ⸢x⸣-àm; Sch_1: lul nam-... (almost destroyed)

(36) Don't plan lies; it is discrediting.

37 KA nam-tar-tar-re-⸢e⸣-en inim-zu ŋar-ra-àm

ED$_{I}$ o. iv 3 KA na-tar me(?)-⸢zu⸣ ŋar-ra

Akk$_2$ *la mu-uš-ta-la-ta a-ma-tu-ka* ⸢*šá*⸣*-a*[*k-na*]

I$_3$: KA(!) nam-tar-tar-r[e- ...]; Ur$_{I}$: [x x ta]r-re inim-zu ŋar-⸢ra-àm⸣; Ur$_2$: KA nam-tar-[tar-re]-⸢e⸣-en / inim-zu ŋar-ra-àm; Sch$_{I}$: ⸢ka⸣ ⸢tar⸣(?) (almost destroyed)

(37) Don't be (exaggeratedly) advising; your word stands forever!

38 ⸢ad⸣ nam-gi$_4$-gi$_4$ igi-dugud nu-mu-un-da-íl(-e-en)

ED$_{I}$ o. viii 10–11 [a]d gi$_4$-gi$_4$ [...]-šè NE [...]

ED$_2$ Fr. 10 o. iii 3–4 ad nà[b(A[N]-A[N])-gi$_4$-gi$_4$] | igi ⸢x⸣ (= [du]gud?]) nàb(AN-AN)-íl

Akk$_2$ *la tam-ta-na-al-lik pa-ni kab-tu-ti ul ta-na-áš-*[*ši*]

I$_3$: [a]d nam-g[i$_4$- ...] / ig[i ...]; Ur$_{I}$: [na]m-gi$_4$-gi$_4$ igi-dugud nu-mu-un-da-íl; Ur$_2$: ⸢ad⸣(? certainly not KA) na-àm-gi$_4$-gi$_4$-e igi-dugud nu-mu-u[n- x x]-⸢e⸣-en

(38) Don't make (bad) plans, a «heavy eye» is unbearable to you.

39 lú-da níŋ-zuḫ-a nam-mu-da-gu$_7$-e

ED$_{I}$ o. v 6–7 [...] | [níŋ]-zuḫ na-gu$_7$

Akk$_2$ *it-ti šar-ra-qa šur-qa la tak-kal*

I$_3$: lú-da [...]; Ur$_{I}$: l[ú-da] ⸢níŋ⸣-zuḫ-a nam-mu-da-gu$_7$-e (collated); Ur$_2$: lú-da níŋ gu$_7$-[a] na-m[u-d]a-gu$_7$-e (collated); Sch$_{I}$: na- ...; S$_2$: 5: lú-⸢zuḫ⸣-a níŋ-zuḫ-a na-[...] (JNES 43 [1984] 297)

(39) Don't eat something stolen with a *thief!

40 šu-zu úš-àm na-di-ni-ib-su-su

ED$_{I}$ o. v 8 ⸢šu⸣ ⸢x⸣⸢x⸣ DU

Akk$_2$ *qa-at-ka ru-šá-a la ta-bal-*⸢*lal*⸣

I$_3$: šu-zu ⸢x⸣ [...]; Ur$_{I}$: š[u-zu úš-à]m na-di-ni-ib-su-su; Ur$_2$: šu-zu úš-àm [... -s]u-⸢su⸣ (collated); Sch$_{I}$: na-...; S$_2$: 6: šu-zu ⸢mud⸣(?) na-bí-íb-s[á(?) ...] (JNES 43 [1984] 297: reading mud is suggested here instead of gi)

(40) Don't mix (drugs) with your hands being filthy!"

41 ŋìri ur$_5$-re gud ša-ba-re-eb-su-su udu ša-ba-re-eb-su-su

ED$_{I}$ o. v 9 anše (or: ŋìri) ur$_5$ gud sa$_{10}$

Akk$_2$ *e-ṣe-em-*⸢*tam*⸣ *ina e-se-qí-ka* GUD *uš-rab-bu-ka* UDU.NITAḪ *uš-rab-bu-ka*

I$_3$: ⸢x⸣ ur$_5$(!)-⸢re⸣ [...] / udu ša-[...]; Ur$_{I}$: ŋì[ri u]r$_5$-re gud ša-b[a-re]-eb-su-su udu ša-ba-re-eb-su-su; Ur$_2$: [x] ur$_5$-e [...]; Sch$_{I}$: ŋìri ⸢ur$_5$⸣(?)-⸢re⸣(?) ⸢x⸣-ab-⸢x⸣ ... (illegible traces); S$_2$: 7: ŋìri ur$_5$-re gud ša-ba-re-[...] udu ša-bi-ri-ib-TÚG-[...]

(41) When you draw a bone as a lot (scl. to select an offering animal), it makes the ox tremble, it makes the sheep tremble! (So according to Akk$_2$, cf. comm.).

ED perhaps: "(If you) hire a donkey for rent, (you will have to) pay for an ox!"

42 ù-nu-ŋar-ra na-ab-bé-⸢e⸣

ED$_{I}$ o. v 10 ù-nu-ŋar na-dug$_{4}$
Akk$_{2}$ *ù nu-ul-la-a-ti la ta-ta-a-mi*

I$_{3}$: ù-nu-ŋar-ra [...]; Ur$_{I}$: ù-nu-ŋar-ra na-ab-bé-⸢e⸣; Sch$_{I}$: omits

(42) Don't speak fraudulently;

43 eŋir-bi-šè ŋiš-pàr-gim ši-i-ši-íb-lá-e

ED$_{I}$ o. v 11 [e]ŋir ŋiš-búr
ED$_{2}$ Fr. 10 iv [0]–1? [...] | b[úr(?) x (x)] ši-[...]
Akk$_{2}$ *ár-kat-si-na ki-ma giš-par-ru ib-ba-lak-ki-ta-a-ka*

I$_{3}$: eŋir-bi-šè ŋiš-[...] / ši-me-š[i- ...]; Ur$_{I}$: eŋir-bi ŋiš-pàr-gim ⸢ši-i⸣-ši-íb-lá-e (collated); Sch$_{I}$: eŋir-bi-šè ⸢x⸣ (like še) ⸢x⸣(like ur$_{5}$)-gim IGI ⸢x⸣ ⸢x⸣ ... (½ line destroyed)

(43) in the end it will bind you like a trap.

44 ú nu-kiŋ-ŋá-šè udu-zu [s]ág nam-me

ED$_{I}$ o. v 12 ú nu-kiŋ$_{x}$(ḪUL) udu sá.ság na-dug$_{4}$
Akk$_{2}$ *ana šam-mi la ši-te-ú-ti bu-ul-ka la ta-na-as-saḫ*

I$_{3}$: ú nu-kiŋ-ŋ[á- ...]; Ur$_{I}$: ú nu-kiŋ-ŋá-šè udu-zu [s]ág nam-me; Ur$_{2}$: [... -ŋ]á-šè udu-z[u ...]; P: ú nu-[...]; Sch$_{I}$: ú nu(?)-kiŋ(?)-kiŋ(?)-⸢ŋá⸣(?)-šè udu .... (almost destroyed)

(44) Don't transfer your sheep into uninvestigated grazing grounds!

45 uš nu-sì-ga-šè ⸢gud⸣-lú na-ḫuŋ-e

ED$_{I}$ o. vi 1 gud ŋi$_{6}$ [x x]
Akk$_{2}$ *a-na šid-di la búr-ru-tú a-lap* LÚ *la ta-ag-gar*

I$_{3}$: uš nu-sì-ga [...]; Ur$_{I}$: uš nu-sì-ga-šè [...]-⸢x⸣-e; Ur$_{2}$: [x x -s]ì-ga-šè ⸢gud⸣-lú na-ḫuŋ-[x]; Sch$_{I}$: uš nu-sì-⸢ga⸣-šè

(45) Don't hire a man's ox for an edge (of a field) not well placed.

46 uš sì-ga kaskal sì-ga-àm

ED$_{I}$ v l. edge u[š] é
\+ vi top edge uš dim$_{4}$
Akk$_{2}$ *[ši]d-⸢di⸣ dam-qu ḫar-ra-nu da-mi-iq-tú*

I$_{3}$: uš sì-ga [...]; I$_{15}$: (traces); T$_{14}$: uš sì-g[a ...]; Ur$_{I}$: uš sì-ga [...]-àm; Ur$_{2}$: [x] sì-ga kaskal sì-ga-àm; P: uš sì-ga [...]; Sch$_{I}$: uš sì-ga kaskal ... ⸢x⸣-⸢àm⸣

(46) A placed boundary is a placed road.

(Or translate like Akk$_{2}$: "A good borderline is a good road.")

47 kaskal ŋi$_{6}$ na-an-du šà-bi sa$_{6}$ ḫul-a

ED$_{I}$ o. vi 2–3 kaskal ŋi$_{6}$ na | šà ⸢sá⸣(?) ḫul
ED$_{2}$ Fr. 10 iv 2 kaskal ⸢x⸣ x -d[u ...]
Akk$_{2}$ *[ḫar-r]a-nu i-na mu-ši la tal-lak lìb-ba-šá da-me-eq u le-mun*

I$_{3}$: kaskal ŋi$_{6}$ na-a[n- ...] / šà-bi sa$_{6}$ [x x]; I$_{15}$: kaskal ŋi$_{6}$ ... ; T$_{14}$: kaskal ŋi$_{6}$ na-⸢du⸣ [...]; Ur$_{I}$: kaskal ŋi$_{6}$ <na>-an-du-u[n x x x ḫ]ul-a; Ur$_{2}$: kaskal ŋi$_{6}$ nu-du šà-bi sa$_{6}$ ḫul-a; P: kaskal ŋi$_{6}$ na-an-du [...]; Sch$_{I}$: ⸢kaskal⸣ ... -⸢àm⸣

(47) Don't walk on a road at night; its interior is both good and bad.

48	anše-edin-na na-ab-sa$_{10}$-s[a$_{10}$] u$_4$ da-bé-eš ì-za-al	*(48)* Don't buy a "steppe-ass" (i.e., an onager); you will (have to) spend (the whole) day at its side(?).
ED$_1$ o. vi 4–5	edin na-sa$_{10}$ u$_5$-šè sa$_{10}$	(Akk$_3$: "walk (imp.) ... at its side(?)" (or: "go ... at its full working time").
ED$_2$ Segm. 4.3 = Fr. 1.1–2	anše-edin | nàb(AN+AN)-sa$_{10}$-[x]	
Akk$_2$	[ANŠE *ṣ*]*e-ri la tu-šam ši-tam-ma a-na a-di-šu a-lik*	
	I$_3$: anše-edin-na [...] / ú(? text: PA)-da-bi-[...]; I$_{15}$: anše-edin-na ...; T$_{14}$: anše-edin-na [...]; Ur$_1$: anše-edin-na na-a[b- ...]-e-zal; Ur$_2$: anše-edin-na na-ab-sa$_{10}$-s[a$_{10}$-(x)] u$_4$ da-bi-eš ì-za-al; P: anše-edin-na na-ab-s[a$_{10}$- ...]; Sch$_1$: ⸢anše⸣ ... (traces) -ak-⸢x⸣	
49	géme-zu-úr ŋìš na-an-dù zu-úr šu-m[u]-ri-in-sa$_4$	*(49)* Don't have sexual intercourse with your slave girl; she will neglect you.
ED$_1$ o. vi 6–7 + 323 i 1	géme-zu$_5$ ŋìš$_x$(SAL+NITAḪ) na-e | zú-ur$_5$ šè-mu-š[a$_4$(DU)]	
ED$_2$ Fr. 10 iii 5	ŋiš(sic!) n[a]-e šu-[mu- ...]	
Akk$_2$	[*a-ma-at-k*]*a it-ti-ka la it-tal i-še-el-le-e-ka*	
Cf. 55: Akk$_3$ r. i 1?		
	I$_{15}$: géme-zu-úr ...; T$_{14}$: géme-zu-úr gì[š ...]; Ur$_1$: géme-zu ŋìš na-an-[...]-in-sa$_4$ (collated); Ur$_2$: géme-zu-úr ŋìš na-a-dù zu-úr šu-m[u]-ri-in-šà (collated); K$_1$: géme-zu-ú[r ...]; P: géme-zu-úr ŋìš na-an-d[ù ...]	
50	áš á-zi na-ab-bal-e šu-uš im-ši-niŋin	*(50)* Don't curse with violent intent; it will turn back on you!
Akk$_2$	[*ar-rat ša*]*g-gaš-ti la tar-ra-ar i-saḫ-ḫu-rak-ka*	
	I$_{15}$: áš (!) á ... ; T$_{14}$: omits line; Ur$_1$: ú(sic! cannot be áš) á-zi-⸢da⸣ [... -n]iŋin; Ur$_2$: áš á-zi nu-bal-e šu-uš ⸢im⸣-ši-niŋin; K$_1$: áš á-zu na-ab-[...]; P: ás á-zi na-ab-bal-e š[u- ...] (coll. Th. Kämmerer)	
51	a šu nu-gíd-i na-an-è-dè / á-sig šu-mu-⸢e⸣-ra-ŋál	*(51)* Don't descend to unchecked water; weak (or, perhaps: paralyzed) arms will confound you. (cf. comm.).
Akk$_2$	[*a-na mê la l*]*a-at-ku-ti la tur-rad i-da-a-ti* <?> *i-šu-ka*	
	I$_{15}$: a šu-nu ... ; T$_{14}$: a šu nu-gíd-i na-a[n- ...] / á ša(?)-[...]; Ur$_1$: a šu nu-gíd-⸢dè⸣ [...]-ra-ŋál(collated); Ur$_2$: a šu nu-du$_8$ na-[a]n-né-de-de / á-sig šu-mu-⸢e⸣-ra-ŋál; K$_1$: a šu nu-gíd-dè na-an-è-dè á š[a(?)- ...] (coll. J. Taylor); P: a šu nu-gíd(!)-dè na-an-e$_{11}$-dè-dè-[(en)] (coll. Th. Kämmerer)	
52	maḫ-bi níŋ-gíd-i (x) ba-an-šub-bé níŋ-e b[a(?)-x]-šub-bé	*(52)* Whatever «long thing» you(?) throw with violence(?), the thing will throw (back)(?) ....
Akk$_2$	[*x x x*] *mim-mi-ka* ⸢*x*⸣ *ka-la nam-di mim-ma-šú-u in-nam-di-ka*	(Akk$_2$: "Whatever of yours is thrown, something he has will be thrown at you(?)").
	I$_{15}$: maḫ ...; T$_{14}$: maḫ-bi níŋ-gíd-i ⸢x⸣ [...] / níŋ-⸢x⸣ [...]; Ur$_1$: maḫ-b[i ... (traces) ...]- šub-bé; Ur$_2$: omits line; K$_1$: maḫ-bi níŋ x ba-an-šub-bé níŋ-e b[a(?)- ...]; P: maḫ-bi x ḪUŠ x na-an-dab$_5$-bé-en; coll. Th. Kämmerer: maḫ-bi níŋ(?)-gíd(?) (Wagerechter Keil wirklich doppelt oder nur Bruchstelle?) x na-an-dab$_5$-bé-en; Ur$_1$ places lines 63 and 64 after line 52	

53	ur$_5$-tuku na-an-bad-e lú-bi ša-ba-e-⸢x⸣-⸢x⸣-kúr	*(53)* Don't drive away a debtor; that man may turn hostile toward you.
Akk$_2$	*[be-el ḫu-bul-l]i-ka l[a] ⸢tu⸣-raq-qú amêlu šu-ú i-na-ki-ir-k[a]*	
	T$_{14}$: ur$_5$-tuku na-an-bad-⸢x⸣ [...]; Ur$_1$: [x x] na-an-bad-e lú-bi ša-ba-e-⸢x⸣-⸢x⸣-kúr (collated, -re-eb- possible, but can be anything); Ur$_2$: omits line; Ur$_3$: ur$_5$-tuku na-an-bad-e lú-bi ša-ba-e-[...]; K$_1$: ur$_5$-tuku na-an-bad-e lú-ba ša-ba-[...]; P: ur$_5$-tuku na-an-bad-e-en lú-bi-š[a] [...]	
54	sun$_7$-na-da aša$_5$(GÁN) na-an-da-ŋá-ŋá-a[n]	*(54)* Don't cultivate a field alongside a quarrelsome person;
Akk$_2$	[...] *x* A.ŠÀ *la ter-r[eš] ina mi-iṣ-ri iz-zi-ba-ak-ka*	Akk$_2$ adds to line 54: "he will leave (it to?) you at the borderline."
	T$_{14}$: (traces); Ur$_1$; [...] aša$_5$(GÁN) nam-ba-e-ŋá-[ŋá-(an)]; Ur$_2$: á(sic!) - (traces of three unidentifiable signs) - an-ŋá-ŋá; Ur$_3$: sun$_7$-na-da aša$_5$ na-an-da-ŋá-ŋá-a[n]; K$_1$: sun$_7$-na-da [... -ŋ]á; P: sun$_7$-na x-tuk-dè-en [...]	
55	gi$_4$-in-šè du-dè ši-me-ši-ib-šub-šub	*(55)* he will leave it to you to walk in the way of a slave girl.
Akk$_2$	*(omits)*	(Using an *emesal*, i.e., female, word for "slave girl.")
Akk$_3$ r. i 1 = 49? + Hurr. r. i 1	*[... -t]a ta-[aṣ(?)]-ṣe-el / [... t]a(?) la tu-ma-sa-ra* (broken)	
	Ur$_1$: [... -d]è ši-mu-en-ši-ib-šub-šub; Ur$_2$: gi-i[n-š]è du-[...]-ši-ib-šub-šub (collated); Ur$_3$: gi$_4$-in-šè du-dè ši-me-ši-íb-š[ub- x]; K$_1$: gi$_4$-in-na du-dè ⸢x⸣[... -d]è, coll. Taylor; P: gi$_4$-in-šè du-dè ši-me-ši-ib-[...]	
56	ere lú-ka na-ab-ta-bal-e-dè-en	*(56)* Don't trespass a man's home; (Vars. "a man's city, the city where he lives, a man's house")
Akk$_2$	omits	
Akk$_3$	*[la ib]-ba-lak-kat-ka* (something missing?)	
	Ur$_1$: ⸢ere⸣⸢ki⸣(?) ⸢lú⸣-ka na-ab-ta-bal-e; Ur$_2$: ki-tuš lú-ka [na-a]b-bal-e-dè; Ur$_3$: ere-tuš lú-ka na-ab-ta-bal-[e-d]è-en; K$_1$: ere l[ú-k]a [... n]a-ab-ta-an-bal-e-dè; P: é lú-ka na-ab-ta-ba[l- ...]	
57	igi du-un igi du-un ši-mu-e-ši-ib-e-ne	*(57)* "Go away! Go away!" they will say to you. (Or: "Go in front!")
Akk$_1$ r. 1	*(illegible traces)*	
Akk$_2$	*ina* IGI *[a]l-ka ina* IGI *<al>-ka i-qab-bu-ka*	
	Ur$_1$: i[gi] du-un [igi d]u-un ši-m[u-u]n-ši-íb-bé-e-ne; Ur$_2$: igi ì-du igi ì-[du ši-me]- ši-ib-e-ne; Ur$_3$: i[gi d]u-un igi du-un ši-me-ši-íb-b[é]-en; K$_1$: igi d[u- ...] ⸢x⸣ ši-⸢x⸣-⸢x⸣-[...]-e-ne	
58	gi-sig-ga ŋiškiri$_6$-ka da-ga nam-bí-du$_8$-e-en	*(58)* Don't undo the knots of a fence of an orchard;
ED$_2$ Adab Segm. 5.1 = Fr. 1 ii 1–2	[ki]ri$_6$-k[a da]g-ga nám- | bí-du$_8$-e	
Akk$_1$ r. 2	*ki-iṣ-ri ⸢ki⸣(?)-[...]*	
Akk$_2$	*[ina(?) k]i-ri-i ri-ki-is-⸢su⸣ la ta-paṭ-ṭar*	
	I$_4$: gi-s[ig- ...]; Ur$_1$: gi-⸢sig⸣(?)-⸢ga⸣(?) ŋiš⸢kiri$_6$⸣-ka da-[x]	

nam-bí-du$_8$-e; Ur$_2$: gi-sì(sic!)-ga ${}^{\text{ŋiš}}$kiri$_6$-k[a] ⌜nam⌝-⌜bí-du$_8$⌝-⌜e⌝; Ur$_3$: g[i]-sig-ga ${}^{\text{ŋiš}}$kiri$_6$-ka da-ga(cannot be -bi on this tablet) nam-bi(sic!)-du$_8$-e-en (-en is visible on the following line; collated); K$_1$: g[i- ...] nam-ba-du$_8$-e; P: gi-sig(?) ${}^{\text{ŋiš}}$kiri$_6$-ka da-bi (so Diakonoff, read ga?) nam-[...]

59 su-ga-ab su-ga-ab ši-me-ši-íb-bé-e-ne

ED$_2$ Adab Segm. 5.2
= Fr. 1 ii 2 su-a su-a | [...]
Akk$_1$ r. 3 *ri-i-ib r[i-i-ib ...]*
Akk$_2$ *ri-bi-am ri-bi-am i-qab-bu-ka*

I$_4$: su-ga-a[b ...]; Ur$_1$: sù-ga-a[b s]ù-ga-ab ši-mu-un-ši-íb-bé-e-ne; Ur$_2$: su-ga-ab su-ga-ab ši-⌜x⌝-[...]; Ur$_3$: su-g[a-a]b su-ga-ab ši-me-ši-íb-bé-ne; K$_1$: [...]-⌜sù⌝-ga ši-me-ši-íb-e-ne, cf. coll. J. Taylor; P: su-g[a]-ab su-ga-ab ši-me-ši-ib-bé-e-e[n]

(59) "Restore them! Restore them!" they will say to you.

60 ur nam-mu-un-gu$_7$-en du$_{14}$ nam-ùr-ùr-re

Akk$_1$ r. 4 *a-ḫe-e la tu-uš-[ta-kal ṣa-al-ta la ta-...]*
Akk$_2$ *[a-ḫe-e la tu-uš-t]a-kal ṣa-⌜al-ta⌝ la ta-šak-kan*
Akk$_3$ r. i 2 *[a-ḫe-e la tu-uš-ta-ka]l ṣa-al-ta la tu-([x])-ma-ša-ra*
+ Hurr. r. i 2 (traces of two signs)

I$_4$: ur nam-mu-[...]; Ur$_1$: ur nam-m[u-u]n-gu$_7$-en LÚ(sic!) nam-ùr-ùr-re; Ur$_2$: ur nam-<mu>-ni-gu$_7$-e-[en] / du$_{14}$ nam-úr-úr-àm; Ur$_3$: ur ⌜nam⌝(?)-mu-⌜gu$_7$⌝-e du$_{14}$ mu-ùr-ùr-re (coll. Alster 1974, pl. II); K$_1$: [x n]am-mu-un-<gu$_7$>-e LÚ (so copy; coll. J. Taylor) bí-ùr-ùr-re; P: ur nam-mu-un-gu$_7$-e-en du$_{14}$ nam-ùr-ùr-re-en

(60) Don't feed a "foreigner"; don't "wipe out" a quarrel!

(or: "don't resolve a dispute," meaning, perhaps, "don't underestimate (the causes that may lead to) quarrels"; Akk$_2$: "don't cause a quarrel.")

61 dumu-ŋu$_{10}$ nam-silig nam-mu-ak-en lú ki nam-ús-e-en

Akk$_1$ *omits line*
Akk$_2$ *[ša-ga-p]u-ru-ta la te-⌜ep⌝-p[u-u]š uq-qú-rak ma-tum ma-ʾ-da*
Akk$_3$ *omits line*

I$_4$: dumu-ŋu$_{10}$ nam-[...]; Ur$_1$: [x -ŋ]u$_{10}$ [x x (x)]-mu-gu$_7$-me-en lú ki nam-ús-sa; Ur$_2$: dumu-ŋu$_{10}$ na-silig na-àm-ak-e lú ki na-àm-ús-àm; Ur$_3$: dumu-ŋ[u$_{10}$ na]m-silig nam-mu-ak-en lú ki ús-en (collated); K$_1$: [x]-ŋu$_{10}$ nam-silig nam-mu-ke$_4$ lú ki na-ús-sa; P: dumu-ŋu$_{10}$ nam-silig nam-mu-e-ak-en lú ki nam-ús-e-en

(61) My son, don't cause (financial) ruin; don't leave a man prostrated on the ground.

(Akk$_2$ has instead of the second part of the line: "the whole country holding you in esteem matters much." Cf. the commentary.)

62	dumu lú-ra ŋìš á-zi na-an-ne-en kisal-e bí-zu-zu	*(62)* Don't rape a man's daughter; the courtyard will find out about you.
ED$_1$ o. vi 8 + 323 i 2	lú-ra [x] ⌜na⌝-dug$_4$ [x x x] ⌜SAL⌝	
ED$_2$ Fr. 3 iii 2 +10 iii	dumu lú- | ra ŋì[š] á-zi na-e kisal na-zu-zu	
Akk$_1$ r. 5	*ma-ar-ti a-me-l[i ina ...]*	
Akk$_2$	*[marti] a-mi-li ina š[a-ga-aš-ti] la ta-na-qí-ip pu-uḫ-ri i-lam-mad-ka*	
Akk$_3$ r. i 3	*[marti a-me-li ina š]a-ga-aš-ti la-a ta / -[na-qí-ip pu-uḫ-ru la]-a(?) i-la-ma-ad-ka*	
+ Hurr. r. i 3	ta-x [...] / ḫi ra [...]	
	I$_4$: dumu lú-ra [...]; Ur$_1$: [... gì]š á-zi na-an-è kisal-e ba-e-su-su (collated); Ur$_2$: dumu lú-ra ŋìš á-zi na-né-e / kisal-e bí-zu-zu; Ur$_3$: dumu [lú-r]a ŋìš á-zi na-an-ne-en kisal-e bí-zu-zu (collated); K$_1$: dumu lú-ra áš-zu na-an-è gis-sal-šè(?) bi-zu-zu; P: dumu lú-ra ŋìš á-zi na-an-ne-en kisal-e ba-e-zu-zu-e	
63	á-tuku na-an-úš-e-en bàd-šul-ḫi na-an-gul-e-en	*(63)* Don't kill a strong man; don't destroy your outer wall.
Akk$_1$ r. 5	*bêl e-mu-qi la [tu-uš-...]*	
Akk$_2$	*bé-[el] ⌜e⌝-mu-qí la tuš-ma-a[t] šul-ḫa-a la tab-bat*	
Akk$_3$ r. i 4+5	*[...] x eṭ-la la tu-ḫal-la-aq* | *[... sa]k*(SAG)*-kul-šu la tu-qa-ba-ar*	
+ Hurr. r. i 4+5	ta-aḫ a-KU [...] | uš-da-na x [...] at-ki x [...]	
	In Ur$_1$ lines 63 and 64 follow line 52. I$_4$: á-tuku [...]; Ur$_1$: á-tuku na-an-úš-e [šu]l-ḫi na-[an-gul]-e (collated, no room for bàd); Ur$_2$: á-tuku na-àm-úš-e-en / bàd-šul-ḫi na-àm-gul-e-en; Ur$_3$: [...]-an-úš-en bàd-sìl na-an-gul-e; K$_1$: usu-tuku na-an-úš-e bàd-šul(?) na-an-gul-e; P: á-tuku na-an-úš-en bàd-sìl-ḫi ...	
64	ŋuruš na-an-úš-e-en ere-ta na-an-gur-re-e[n]	*(64)* Don't kill a young man; don't turn him away from the city.
Akk$_1$ r. 7	*eṭ-la la tu-uš-[...]*	
Akk$_2$	*eṭ-la la tuš-ma-at u[l-tu âli] la tu-pa-ḫar*	
Akk$_3$ r. i 9	*[eṭ-la l]a tu-uš-mit* / + r. i 10? traces of one sign	
+ Hurr. r. i 9	tu x [...] // + r. i 10? traces of one sign	
	I$_4$: ŋuruš-e [...]; Ur$_1$: [...] na-an-úš-e [er]e-ta na-an-gur-[r]e; Ur$_2$: ŋuruš na-àm-úš-e-en ere^{ki}-šè mu-ra-ab-gur-re-e[n] (illegible sign above gur) (coll. Alster 1974, pl. II); Ur$_3$: [...]-en ere-šè na-an-gur-ru-un; K$_1$: ŋuruš-e na-an-úš-e [éri]n-šè(?) na-gur-en; P: [... n]a-an-úš-e-en ere-šè na-an-gur-re-e[n]	
65	lú eme-sig-ga-ke$_4$ igi ^{ŋiš}bala-gim ši-sir$_5$-sir$_5$	*(65)* The slanderer moves his eyes (quickly) like a spindle.
Akk$_1$ r. 8	*a-kíl kar-ṣi [...]*	
Akk$_2$	*a-kil kar-ṣi i-na-šu ki-ma* ^{ŋiš}BALA *i-na-am-[maš]*	
Akk$_3$ r. i 6	*[...] x ki-ma pí-li-ik-ki i-te-ru*	
+ Hurr.r. i 6	pu-ta-ni-ia-aš [...] / ti-ir-ḫa [...]	

I$_4$: lú e[me ...]; Ur$_1$: [½ line] ⌜x⌝(?) ⌜sig⌝(?)-ga(cannot be bal)-⌜a⌝ ši-sir$_5$-r[e] (collated); Ur$_2$: lú inim(probably eme!)-sì-ga-gim igi ^{ŋiš}bala-ke$_4$ (rather than gim) ši-in-sir$_5$-[sir$_5$] (collated); Ur$_3$: l[ú ...]-ke$_4$ igi ^{ŋiš}bala-gim ši-sir$_5$-sir$_5$ (collated); K$_1$: lú eme-sig-ga-ke$_4$ igi bala-ke$_4$ ši-sir$_5$-sir$_5$; P: lú eme-sig gu$_7$-a-gim(? probably -ke$_4$) igi ^{ŋiš}bala-gim ši-sir$_5$-sir$_5$

66 igi-a nam-ba-e-gub-gub-bu-dè-en šà-ge bí-kúr-kúr

(66) Don't stand in front; (your) heart (may be forced to) change (its mind)!

Akk$_1$ r. 9 *i-na pa-ni la ta-[za-az ...]*

Akk$_2$ *[i-n]a pa-ni la ta-az-za-az lìb-ba-šu tu-šá-an-na*

Akk$_3$ r. i 7 *[i-na pa-ni la-a ta]-az-za-az* ŠÀ *la-a / ([...]) ú-ša-ni-ku*

+ Hurr. r. i 7 ta-ag-ga ba [...] / pu-ri-ga [...]

I$_4$: igi-a; Ur$_1$: [...] šà-ge nu-mu-e-kár-[kár]; Ur$_2$: igi-àm na-àm-ba-gub-gub-bu-dè šà-ge me-kúr-kúr; Ur$_3$: igi-šè [...]-en šà-ge bí-kúr-kúr; K$_1$: igi-a nam-bi-du-dè šà ab-kúr-kúr; P: igi-a nam-ba-e-gub-gub-bu-dè-en šà-ge na-mu-un-kúr-kúr

67 lú-lul-la-ka é-kaš-ka KA nam-tar-tar-re

(67) Don't boast in the way of a liar in an alehouse.

Addition in Ur$_2$: "Your word stands forever." Cf. line 37.

Ur$_2$ addition inim-zu ŋar-ra-[àm]

ED$_1$ o. vii 3' ka nam-tar ŋar

Akk$_1$ r. 10 *ki-ma sa-ar-ri [...]*

Akk$_2$ *ki-ma sà-ar i-na bīt šikâri la tuš-tar-ra-aḫ*

Akk$_3$ o. i 8 *[ki-ma sà-ar] a-na* É*-ti ši-kà-/[ri la-a tuš-tar]-ra-aḫ*

I$_4$: lú-l[ul ...]; Ur$_2$: lú-lul-la-ka é-kaš-ka KA nam-tar-tar-re inim-zu ŋar-ra-[àm] (collated); Ur$_3$: lú-lul-l[a]-ka KA nam-tar-tar-re (collated); K$_1$: lú-lul-la-gé é-kaš-kam KA nam-tar-tar-re; P: lú-lul-la-gim é-lunga-ka KA nam-tar-tar-re

67 A

Akk$_1$ r. 11 *ki-ma ser-ri i-[...]*

Akk$_3$ r. i 10 *traces of one sign*

+ Hurr. r. i 10 *traces of one sign*

68 ki nam-ninta$_x$(NITAḪ)-ka um-me-te šu nam-gu$_4$-gu$_4$-dè

(68) When you approach the battlefield, don't conclude a sale!

Akk$_2$ *a-[šar zi-k]a-ri ina ṭe-ḫe-ka la mu-up-pi-ša-a-ta*

I$_4$: ki nam-[...]; Ur$_2$: igi(? rather than ki) nam-ninta$_x$-ka um-me-te [š]u na-ku$_5$-ku$_5$-dè-[en] (collated); Ur$_3$: k[i nam]-ninta$_x$-ka um-ma-te [...] na-an-gu$_4$-gu$_4$-dè (collated); K$_1$: ki nam-ninta$_x$-ke$_4$ um-ma-ta ⌜šu⌝ nam-ku$_4$-ku$_4$-dè; P: ki nam-ninta$_x$-a-ka um-ma-te-en šu nam-gu$_4$(?)-x-dè(?)

69 ur-saŋ dili na-nam dili-ni lú šár-ra-àm

Akk$_{1}$ r. 12 *[x] ⸢x⸣ qar-ra-di [...]*

Akk$_{2}$ *[qar-r]a-du e-diš-šu-ma e-diš-ši-šú ki-ma [š]á-ar*

I$_{4}$: ur-[...]; Ur$_{2}$: [...] na-na-àm dili-ni ⸢lú⸣ ⸢šár⸣-ra-à[m]; Ur$_{3}$: ur-⸢saŋ⸣ ⸢dili⸣ na-nam dili-⸢ni⸣(rather than dù) l[ú] šár-r[a-à]m; K$_{1}$: ur-saŋ dili na-nam dili-dù(read ni?) nu šár-ra; P: ur-saŋ dili na-nam dili-ni lú šár-ra-àm

(69) A warrior is alone; when alone, he is (like) many!

70 ^{d}utu dili na-nam dili-ni lú šár-ra-àm

Akk$_{1}$ r. 13 *[x x] ^{d}šá-maš i-[diš-ši-šu ...]*

Akk$_{2}$ *[^{d}šamaš] ⸢e⸣-diš-ši-šú-ma ⸢e⸣-diš-ši-šú k[i]-ma [šá]-ar*

I$_{4}$: ^{d}[...]; Ur$_{2}$: [...] ⸢dili⸣ na-na-àm [dili]-⸢ni⸣ lú šár-ra-àm (written on the left edge); Ur$_{3}$: ^{d}[u]tu ⸢x⸣ ⸢x⸣-nam dili-ni lú [šár]-ra; K$_{1}$: ⸢^{d}utu⸣ dili na-nam dili-ni (copy dù) nu-šár-ra

(70) Utu (i.e., the sun-god) is alone; when alone, he is (like) many!

71 ur-saŋ-da gub-bu-dè zi-zu ḫé-en-da-ŋál

Akk$_{1}$ r. 14 *[a-na qar]-ra-di [...]*

Akk$_{2}$ *[a-na qar-r]a-du i-ziz-ma na-piš-ta-...*

Ur$_{2}$: ur-saŋ-da gub-bu-[d]è zi-zu ḫé-en-da-ŋál; Ur$_{3}$: [...] su$_{8}$-bu-da zi-zu [ḫé-e]n-da-an-ŋál (coll. Alster 1974, pl. II)

(71) Standing with the "hero," your breath will stay with you!

(The "hero" is Utu, the sun god).

Akk: "stand with the hero."

72 ^{d}utu-da gub-bu-dè zi-zu ḫé-en-da-ŋál

Akk$_{1}$ r. 15 *[a-na] ^{d}[šá-maš ...]*

Akk$_{2}$ *⸢a⸣-na ^{d}šamaš i-ziz-ma ...*

I$_{5}$: (traces); I$_{6}$: ^{d}utu [...]; Ur$_{2}$: ^{d}utu-da [gu]b-bu-dè zi-zu ḫ[é-e]n-da-ŋál; Ur$_{3}$: [su$_{8}$-bu]-da zi-zu ḫ[é-e]n-da-an-ŋál

(72) Standing with Utu, your breath will stay with you! (I.e., rising early, or: "standing with Utu," (= with Utu's emblem in the battlefield.) Akk: "stand with the hero").

73 šuruppak^{ki}-e dumu-ni-ra na-šè mu-un-ni-in-ri

Akk$_{2}$ *šu-ri-ip-pa-ku-ú ...*

I$_{5}$: [šurup]pak^{ki}-e dumu-ni-ra na n[a- ...]; I$_{6}$: šuruppak^{ki} du[mu ...]; Ur$_{3}$: [...] na-šè mu-un-ni-in-ri

(73) The man from Šuruppak gave instructions to his son

74 šuruppak^{ki} dumu ubar-tu-tu-[ke$_{4}$]

Akk$_{2}$ *šu-ri-ip-pa-ku- ...*

I$_{5}$: [šurup]pak^{ki} dumu ubar-tu-tu-[...]; I$_{6}$: šuruppak^{ki} dumu ubar-tu-tu-[...]; Ur$_{3}$: omits line

(74) - the man from Šuruppak, the son of Ubartutu,

75 zi-u$_{4}$-sud-rá dumu-ni-ra na na-mu-un-ri-ri

Akk$_{2}$ *ú-t[a-na-pi]š-ta ma-ra-šu iš-[šar]*

I$_{5}$: zi-u$_{4}$-sud-rá dumu-ni-ra na šè-m[u-un]-ni-in-ri-[ri]; I$_{6}$: zi-u$_{4}$-sud-rá dumu-ni-ra na / [na]-mu-un-ni-in-r[i-ri] (NB the two na's are separated by the indented line); Ur$_{3}$: [...-r]á dumu-ni-ra [na] / na-mu-un-ri-ri

(75) gave instructions to his son Ziusudra.

76 min-kam-ma-šè šuruppak^{ki}-e dumu-ni-ra na na-mu-un-ri-ri

Akk$_2$ *omits line*

I_5: [x]-kam-ma-šè šuruppak^{ki}-e dumu-ni-ra na na-mu-un-ri-ri; I_6: min-kam-ma-šè šuruppak^{ki} [...]; Ur$_3$: [... du]mu-ni-ra [... -u]n-ri

(76) For a second time the man from Šuruppak gave instructions to his son

77 š[urupp]ak^{ki} dumu ubar-tu-tu-ke$_4$

Akk$_2$ *omits line*

I_5: [šurupp]ak^{ki} dumu ubar-tu-tu-ke$_4$; T_3: š[urupp]ak^{ki} dumu [...]; Ur$_3$: omits line

(77) - the man from Šuruppak, the son of Ubartutu -

78 zi-u$_4$-sud-rá dumu-ni-ra na na-mu-[un-ri-ri]

Akk$_2$ *omits line*

I_5: [...]-sud-rá dumu-ni-ra na na-mu-[...]; I_7: [...] na [...]; T_3: zi-u$_4$-sud-ra(sic!) [...]; Ur$_3$: omits line; BM$_I$: ⌈zi-u$_4$⌉-[...]

(78) gave instructions to his son Ziusudra:

79 dumu-ŋu$_{10}$ na ge-ri na-ri-mu ḫé-d[ab$_5$]

Akk$_2$ *[ma-ri] áš-šar-ka a-še[r-ti ṣa-bat]*

I_5: [... g]a-ri n[a- ...]; I_7: [... -r]i-ŋu$_{10}$ ḫé-da[b$_5$]; T_3: dumu-ŋu$_{10}$ na ri ga ⌈x⌉ [...]; Ur$_3$: dumu-ŋu$_{10}$ na ge-ri na-ri-ŋu$_{10}$ ḫé-d[ab$_5$]; BM$_I$: dumu-ŋ[u$_{10}$ ...]

(79) "My son, let me give you instructions; let my instructions be taken!

80 zi-u$_4$-sud-rá inim ga-ra-ab-dug$_4$ ŋiz[zal] ḫé-em-ši-ak

Akk$_2$ ⌈*ú*⌉*-[ta-na-piš-ta a-ma-tim (luqbîka)]*

I_5: (traces); I_7: g]a-ra-ab-dug$_4$ [gizzal ḫ]é-em-ši-ia-ak; T_3: zi-u$_4$-sud-ra(sic!) inim [...]; Ur$_3$: zi-u$_4$-sud-rá.ra inim [ga-r]a-ab-dug$_4$ giz[zal] ḫé-em-ši-[...]; BM: zi-sud-⌈x⌉-[...]

(80) Ziusudra, let me speak a word to you; may attention be paid to them!

81 na-ri-ga-ŋu$_{10}$ šu [nam]-bí-bar-re-en

Akk$_2$ ⌈*a*⌉*-šer-ta la ta/tu-[...]*

I_7: [...]-bí-bar-re-en; T_3: na-ri-ga-ŋu$_{10}$ šu [...]; Ur$_3$: na-ri-ga-ŋá [nam]-bí-bar-[re- ...]; BM$_I$: na-ri-ga-[...]

(81) Don't neglect my instructions!

82 inim dug$_4$-ga-ŋá [na-a]b-te-bal-e-d[è]-en

Akk$_2$ *[qí-bi-t]i-ia la te-et-[ti-iq]*

I_7: [... -a]b-te(sic!)-bal-e-d[è]; Ur$_3$: inim dug$_4$-ga-ŋá [na-ab-t]a-bal-[e-d]è-en; BM$_I$: inim dug$_4$-ga [...]

(82) Don't transgress my spoken words!

82 A na-ri ab-b[a níŋ-kal-la-àm gú-zu ḫé-em-ši-ak]

BM$_I$: na-ri ab-b[a ...]

(82A) The instructions of on old man [are precious, you should comply with them!]

83 ka kaš naŋ-a [...] ⌜x⌝-kam

Akk$_2$ (broken)

I$_7$: [...] ⌜x⌝-kam [...]; Ur$_3$: ka kaš naŋ-a [...] (coll. Alster 1974, pl. II); BM$_1$: ka kaš naŋ-[...]

(83) A mouth drinking beer is the ... of a ...

84 dumu-ŋu$_{10}$ [...] lú ⌜x⌝ [...]

Akk$_2$ [... *a-me-l*]*i ma-ri a-me-l*[*i* ...]

I$_7$: (traces); Ur$_3$: lú-tur [...] lú ⌜x⌝ [...] (coll. Alster 1974, pl. II); Ur$_5$: dumu-ŋ[u$_{10}$ ...]; BM$_1$: lú-tur-ŋu$_{10}$ [...]

(84) My son, a man's son ...

85 ka kaš na[ŋ-a ...] ⌜x⌝

ED$_1$ r. ii 2–3 ⌜x⌝ [x k]a ⌜kaš⌝ x | x x LUL šè

Akk$_2$ [... *š*]*i-ka-ri šá-tu-ú* [...] ⌜*x*⌝ *ú-da* [...]

Ur$_3$: ka kaš [...] ⌜x⌝; Ur$_5$: ka(?) na-x [...]; Ur$_6$: cf. 84; BM$_1$: ka kaš na[ŋ-a ...]

(85) A mouth drinking beer ...

86 ^{d}nin-ka-si [...]

ED$_1$ r. ii 4 nin-kaš-si ⌜x⌝ ⌜x⌝ ùr(?)

Akk$_2$ [...] *x x x* [...]

Ur$_3$: ⌜^{d}nin⌝-⌜ka⌝-s[i ...] (cf. coll. Alster 1974, pl. II); BM$_1$: ^{d}nin-ka-[si ...]

(86) Ninkasi ...

87 [...] K[A] ⌜x⌝ ùr x [x]-em

Akk$_2$ [...] *x* [...]

Ur$_3$: [...] K[A] ⌜x⌝ ùr ⌜x⌝ [x]-em; Ur$_6$: ŋiš(?)-ḫur(?) [...]; BM$_1$: (traces)

(87) *(No translation)*

88 [...]-ùr-ùr-re

Akk$_2$ [...] *x la ta-k*[*al* ...]

Ur$_3$: [...]-ùr-ùr-re

On Akk$_2$ some signs remain from a later repetition, probably: 147–152, after which they are transliterated below.

(88) *(Too poorly preserved for translation)*

89 ⌜x⌝ ⌜x⌝ a mu-u[n]-ni-[íl]-íl

ED$_1$ r. ii 5 lú x é IGI.DU KA šè-íl

Ur$_3$: [...] ⌜x⌝ a mu-u[n]-ni-íb-[íl]-íl; Ur$_5$: ⌜x⌝ [...]

(89) ... carried

90 [... i]m-sar-re

Ur$_3$: [...] ⌜x⌝ im-sar-re; Cop: [... i]m-sar-re-em

(90) ... drives away ...

91 KA ⌜x⌝ saŋ im-ta-ab-dúr(?)-dúr(?)-re

UM$_3$: KA ⌜x⌝ [...]; I$_8$: (traces); Ur$_3$: [... s]ag im-ta-ab-dúr-dúr-re (rather than gur$_4$-gur$_4$); Cop: [...] s[aŋ i]m-ta-ab-gur$_4$-gur$_4$-re

(91) *(No translation)*

92 lú ní-zu-a-ke$_4$ nu-e-ši-su-su

UM$_3$: lú ní-z[u …]; I$_8$: […] na(?)-e-ši-su(?)-s[u]; Ur$_3$: […]-za-ke$_4$ nu-e-ši-su-su; Cop: [… -z]u-a-ke$_4$ na(?)-[š]i-su-su-un

(92) Your own man will not repay you.

93 ŋiš-gi máš-ú na-nam šà-bi inim-sig-ga-àm

ED$_I$ r. ii 9 ŋiš-gi šà sig

UM$_3$: ŋiš-gi máš-ú n[a- …]; I$_8$: […]-ú na-nam šà-bi (? - copy ga) inim-s[ig-x]; I$_9$: ŋiš-gi máš (! copy gi) […]; I$_{10}$: ŋiš-gi ⸢máš⸣-[…]; Ur$_3$: g[iš-gi m]áš-ú na-nam šà-bi inim-sig-ga-àm (collated); Cop: […] máš-ú na-nam šà-bi inim-sig-ga

(93) The canebrake is a grass-fed goat; its heart is slanderous.

94 é-gal íd maḫ-àm šà-bi gud du$_7$-du$_7$-dam

ED$_I$ r. ii 10 é-gal A-máḫ šà-bi gud [d]u$_7$

UM$_3$: é-gal íd maḫ-àm šà-bi g[ud …]; I$_8$: [… m]aḫ-a šà-bi gud du$_7$-d[u$_7$- x]; I$_9$: é-gal íd maḫ-àm […]; I$_{10}$: é-gal id(!) […]; Ur$_3$: é-gal íd-da maḫ-e šà-bi gud du$_7$-du$_7$-dam; Cop: [… í]d maḫ-a šà-bi gud du$_7$-dam

(94) The palace is a huge river; its interior is a goring bull.

95 níŋ-ku$_4$-ku$_4$ níŋ sá nu-di-dam

ED$_I$ r. ii 6 ši-kù

UM$_3$: níŋ-ku$_4$-ku$_4$ níŋ sá nu-di-dam; I$_8$: […] níŋ sá nu-di-dam; I$_9$: níŋ-ku$_4$-ku$_4$ níŋ sá […]; I$_{10}$: níŋ-ku$_4$-ku$_4$ […]; Ur$_3$: […]-ku$_4$-ku$_4$ [níŋ] sá nu-di-dam; Cop: […] níŋ sá nu-di-dam; MM: […] níŋ sá n[u- …]

(95) The income is unrivalled;

96 níŋ-è níŋ nu-silig-ge-dam

ED$_I$ r. ii 6 níŋ-silig

UM$_3$: níŋ-è níŋ nu-silig-ge-dam; I$_8$: [… n]íŋ nu-silig-⸢x⸣ […]; I$_9$: níŋ-è níŋ nu-sili[g- …]; I$_{10}$: níŋ-è […]; Ur$_3$: [x]-è-e níŋ nu-silig-ge-dè; Cop: n[íŋ]-⸢è⸣-⸢a⸣ níŋ nu-silig-ge-dam; MM: […] níŋ nu-si[lig- …]

(96) (but) the expenditure is endless.

97 ninda lú-ka ga-ra-ab-šúm-bi ku-nu-a

ED$_I$ r. ii 11 ninda lú BU ga-šúm-š[úm]

UM$_3$: ninda lú-⸢ka⸣ ga-ra-ab-⸢šúm⸣-bi ku-nu-a; I$_8$: [… -r]a-ab-š[úm …]; I$_9$: ninda lú-ka ga-ra-ab-šúm(!)-b[i …]; I$_{10}$; ninda lú-k[a …]; Ur$_3$: ninda lú-ka ga-ra-ab-šúm-bi ku-nu-a; Cop: ninda lú-ù gu$_7$ ga-ra-ab-šúm-bi gùn-a; MM: […] ga-ra-ab-šúm-bi ku-nu-a

(97) (To say) of a man's bread, "I'll give it to you" (is easy enough);

98 šúm-mu-da-bi an bad-rá-àm

ED$_I$ r. ii 12 šúm-da-bi ⸢x⸣

UM$_3$: […] bad-rá-àm; I$_9$: [… -m]u-da-bi an […]; I$_{10}$: […]-m[u …]; Ur$_3$: šúm-mu-da-bi an bad-rá-àm; Cop: šúm-mu-da-bi an bad-rá-àm; MM: […]-bi an bad-rá-àm

(98) (but) when one has to give it, it's far away!

99 ga-ra-ab-šúm-bi lú-ra ga-ni-in-ús

In Cop line 100 comes before line 99. UM$_3$: g[a(!)-r]a-ab-šúm-bi lú-ra ga-ni-in-ús; I$_9$: [... -a]b-šúm-⸢mu⸣ lú-ra [...]; Ur$_3$: ga-⸢ra⸣-ab-šúm-bi lú-ra ga-<ni>-in-ús; Cop: ga-ra-ab-šúm-bi lú-ra ga-ni-in-ús; MM: ga-[ra-ab-šú]m-mu lú-ra ga-ni-in-ús

(99) "Let me hold onto the man (who says) this: «Let me give it to you."

100 nu-ra-ab-šúm-mu ninda igi-bi-šè til-la-àm

In Cop line 100 comes before line 99; UM$_3$: nu-ra-ab-šúm-mu ninda igi-bi-šè til-la-àm; Ur$_3$: nu-ra-ab-šúm-mu ninda igi-bi-šè ti-la-àm; Cop: nu-ra-ab-šúm-mu ninda igi-bi-šè til-àm; MM: nu-r[a-ab]-šúm ninda igi-bi-šè til-la

(100) (means:) "I'll not give it to you" - when faced with it, the bread is finished.

(99–100) Or: "(When I say:) «Let me be near to the man who says this: let me give it to you», *(100:)* (then he will say) «I will not give it to you» - when faced with it, the bread is finished."

101 níŋ-ú-rum níŋ á-sì-ga-a-da

ED$_1$ r. ii 13 níŋ-ú-g[u x] níŋ ⸢x⸣ [x x]

UM$_3$: níŋ-ú-rum níŋ á-sì-ga-ta; Ur$_3$: [x] ú-rum níŋ á-sì-ga-a-da; Cop: níŋ-ú-rum níŋ á-sì-ga-a-ta (collated); MM: níŋ-⸢ú⸣-[x] níŋ-á-sì-ga-ta

(101) To things that have been set aside(?),

102 lú-tur-ŋu$_{10}$ níŋ nu-mu-um-da-sá

ED$_1$ r. ii 14 [dumu-ŋ]u$_{10}$ [níŋ nu-da-sá]

UM$_3$: lú-tur-ŋu$_{10}$ níŋ nu-um-da-sá; T$_{15}$: [...]-⸢e⸣(?); Ur$_3$: lú-tur-ŋu$_{10}$ níŋ nu-um-da-sá; Cop: lú-tur-ŋu$_{10}$ níŋ nu-un-da-sá; MM: lú-[x x] níŋ nu-mu-un-da-sá

(102) my little one, nothing is comparable.

103 ka-sa$_6$-sa$_6$-ge inim ì-šid-e

UM$_3$: ka-sa$_6$-sa$_6$-ge inim ì-šid-e; T$_{15}$: [... ini]m(?) ì-šid-e; Cop: ka-sa$_6$-sa$_6$-ge inim ⸢ì-šid⸣-⸢e⸣; MM: ka sa$_6$-sa$_6$ inim ì-šid-e

(103) He whose mouth (speaks) pleasant (words) recites words well,

104 ka-dù-dù-e kišib ì-íl-íl

UM$_3$: ka dù-dù-e kišib ì-í[l-íl]; T$_{15}$: [...] kišib i-il-il; T$_{16}$: [... -d]ù-e kišib ì-íl-íl; Cop: ka ⸢x⸣ ⸢x⸣ kišib e-íl-íl; MM: ka dù-dù-e kišib ì-íl-íl

(104) (but) he who has a harsh mouth carries a (litigation) document.

105 ka-làl-e ú-làl ì-bu-re

UM$_3$: ka-làl-e ú-làl e-bu-re; T$_{15}$: [...] ⸢ú⸣-làl e-bu-re; T$_{16}$: [...]-e ú-làl ì-bu-re; Cop: [x là]l-e ú-làl e-búr-re; MM: ka-làl-e ú-làl e-bu-re

(105) The "honey-mouth" gathers sweet herbs.

106 ka-tuku ^{kuš}lu-úb-a-ni sá im-dug$_4$

UM$_3$: ka-tuku ^{kuš}lu-úb-ni sá im-KA×U; T$_{15}$: [...]-úb-a-ni sá im-du; T$_{16}$: [x x] ^{kuš}lu-úb-a-ni sá im-dug$_4$; Cop: lul ^{kuš}lu-úb-a-ni sá im-du (collated); MM: ⸢ka⸣ ⸢x⸣ [...]-úb-a-ni sá im-[x]

(106) The boaster reached (out for) his (empty) leather bag.

107 gal-gal-di ^{kuš}lu-úb sù-ga ša-mu-un-túm

UM$_3$: gal-gal-di ^{kuš}lu-úb sù-ga ša-mu-un-túm; T$_{15}$: [... k]uš-ni šè-ba-du(sic!)-e; T$_{16}$: [...]-e kuš-ni šè-ba-dù-en; Cop: kuš-dù-dù-e kuš ní še-ba-NI-e (collated): MM: [...] kuš-ni [...]

(107) The haughty one brought an empty bag,

108 silim-dug$_4$ ka-sù-ga ša-ba-ni-ib-ŋar

UM$_2$: silim-dug$_4$ ka sù-ga ša-ba-ni-ni-ib-ŋar; T$_{15}$: [... -g]a ša-ba-ni-ib-ŋar; T$_{16}$: [...]-dug$_4$ ka su(sic!)-ga ša-ba-ni-ŋál; Cop: silim-di ka sù-ga ša-ba-ni-in-ŋar (collated); MM: [...] ša-ba-[...]

(108) (and) the false accuser put emptiness in it.

109 kuš-dù-dù-e kuš-ni šè-ba-e-dù-e

UM$_2$: kuš-kuš-dù-e kuš-ni šè-ba-e-dù-e; T$_{15}$: [... k]uš-ni šè-ba-du(sic!)-e; T$_{16}$: [...]-e kuš-ni šè-ba-dù-en; Cop. kuš-dù-dù-e ní še-ba-NI-e (collated); MM: [...] kuš-ni [...]

(109) The leatherworker will work his own leather.

110 usu-tuku šu lú-ta ša-ba-ra-an-tùm

UM$_3$: usu-tuku šu lú-ta [š]a-ba-ra-an-tùm; T$_{15}$: [...]-ta ša-ba-ra-an-túm; T$_{16}$: [...] ⸢ša⸣-[...]; Cop: usu-tuku šu lú-ta ša-ba-ra-an-tùm (collated); MM: [... š]a-ba-ra-a[n- ...]

(110) The strong one takes away from a man's hand.

111 lú-lil-e níŋ ú-gu ì-ib-dé-e

UM$_3$: lú-lil-e níŋ ú-gu ì-ib-dé-e; I$_4$: l[ú ...]; T$_{15}$: [...] ú-gu ì-ib-dé-e

(111) The fool loses something.

112 ⸢ù⸣-sá lú-lil-e níŋ ú-gu ì-dé-e

UM$_3$: ⸢ù⸣-sá lú-lil-e níŋ ú-gu ì-dé-e; I$_4$: ⸢x⸣ [...]; T$_{15}$: [...]-⸢x⸣ ú-gu ì-ib-dé-e; Cop: u$_6$-di lú-lil-e níŋ ú-gu ì-dé-e

(112) Sleeping, the fool loses something.

113 na-an-šèr-šèr-re-dè kiri$_4$ šu àm-mi-in-ŋál

UM$_3$: na-an-šèr-šèr-re-dè kiri$_4$ šu àm-mi-in-ŋál; I$_4$: na-a[n- ...]; T$_3$: na-[an-š]èr-šèr-re-d[è ...]; T$_4$: [... -šè]r-re-dè kiri$_4$ šu àm-[...]; T$_{15}$: [...] kiri$_4$ šu àm-mi-ib-ŋál; Cop: [... n]a-an-šèr-šèr-re-dè

(113) "Don't tie me up!" (is what) the one who prays (is willing to say).

114 ga-ti-la kiri$_4$ šu àm-mi-in-ŋál

UM$_3$: ga-ti-la k[iri$_4$] šu àm-mi-in-ŋál; I$_4$: ga-ti-[...]; I$_9$: [g]a-[ti-l]a ki[ri$_4$] š[u ...]; T$_3$: ga-ti-la kiri$_4$ àm-[...]; T$_4$: [...] kiri$_4$ šu àm-[...]; Cop: [... -t]i-e kù-šè(sic! written over an erasure) àm-mi-ni-in-{in}-ŋál

(114) (I will give) an offering for life (lit., «a let-me-live») (is what) the one who prays (is willing to promise).

115 saŋ-du nu-tuku nam ši-ib-tar-re

UM$_3$: saŋ-du nu-tuku ⸢nam ši⸣-[...]; I$_4$: saŋ-du nu-[...]; I$_9$: saŋ-du nu-tuku na[m ...]; T$_3$: saŋ-du nu-tuku nam ši-im-[...]; T$_4$: [... -tu]ku nam ši-ib-tar-[...]; Cop: [...]-tuku nam ši-ib-tar-re

(115) The unwise decide the fate.

116 téš nu-tuku lú úr-šè mu-un-dé-e

I$_4$: téš nu-tuku [...]; I$_9$: téš nu-tuku l[ú ...]; T$_3$: téš nu-zu lú úr-šè m[u- ...]; T$_4$: [...] lú úr-šè m[u- [...]; T$_5$: [...]-e; N$_1$: téš [...]; Cop: [...] lú úr-šè mu-un-dé-e

(116) The shameless one piles up in another man's lap:

117 ŋá-e na-nam u$_6$-e ba-gub

UM$_{I}$: ŋá-e na-[...]; I$_4$: ŋá-e na-[...]; I$_6$: [... -g]ub; I$_9$: ŋá(!)-e {na} na-nam u$_6$-e [...]; T$_3$: ŋá-e na-nam u$_6$-e [...]; T$_4$: [... -n]am ...]; T$_5$: [...] ba-gub; T$_{15}$: [... -g]ub; N$_{I}$: ŋá-e [...]; Cop: [... b]a-gub

(117) "I, indeed, am to be admired!"

118 dam ⸢dìm⸣-e [na]m(?) tar-re ba-dab$_5$-dab$_5$(KU-KU)

UM$_{I}$: dam ⸢dìm⸣-⸢e⸣ [...]; I$_6$: [... -r]e ba-KU-KU; I$_9$: dam dìm(!)(copy ŠEŠ)-e ⸢x⸣ [...]; T$_2$: d[am [...]; T$_4$: (traces); T$_5$: [...] ⸢x⸣ tar-re KU; T$_{15}$: [... -K]U-KU; N$_{I}$: dam ⸢x⸣ [...]; Cop: [...] ⸢x⸣ ba-KU

(118) A week wife is always caught by fate.

119 lú-ḫuŋ-ŋá-zu [^{kuš}]lu-úb ši-me-da-ba-e

UM$_{I}$: lú-ḫuŋ-ŋá-zu [...]; I$_6$: [... š]i-me-da-ba-e; I$_9$: lú-ḫuŋ-ŋá-zu lu(!)-úb [...]; T$_2$: lú-ḫuŋ-[...]; T$_5$: [...] ši-me-da-ba-e; T$_{15}$: [...]-da-ba-e; N$_{I}$: lú-ḫuŋ-⸢x⸣-[...]

(119) Your hired worker will share his leather bag with you.

120 ^{kuš}lu-úb ši-mu-e-da-gu$_7$-e

UM$_{I}$: ^{kuš}[lu-ú]b ši-mu-e-da-g[u$_7$- ...]; I$_6$: [...]-me-da-gu$_7$-e; I$_9$: ^{kuš}lu-úb ša-mu-da-[...]; T$_2$: ^{kuš}lu-úb [...]; T$_5$: [...]-gu$_7$-e; T$_{15}$: omits line; N$_{I}$: ^{kuš}lu-[...]

(120) He will eat his leather bag with you.

121 ^{kuš}lu-úb š[i-me-d]a-til-e

UM$_{I}$: omits line; I$_6$: [... -d]a-til-e; I$_9$: (traces); T$_2$: ^{kuš}lu-úb š[i- ...]; T$_5$: [...]-til-en; T$_{15}$: [...]-la; N$_{I}$: ^{kuš}[...]

(121) He will finish his leather bag with you,

122 ŋá-la ši-m[e]-da-dag-ge

UM$_{I}$: omits line; I$_6$: [... -d]ag-ge; T$_2$: ŋá-la ši-m[e- ...]; T$_5$: [...]-da-dag-ge; T$_{15}$: [...]-dag-ge; N$_{I}$: ŋá-[...]

(122) (and then) he will stop working with you,

123 ga-ba-ra-gu$_7$ é-gal-la ba-gub

UM$_{I}$: g[a-b]a-ra-gu$_7$ [...]; UM$_4$: ga-ba-ra-gu$_7$ é-gal-la ba-g[ub]; I$_6$: [...]-gub; T$_2$: ga-ba-ra-g[u$_7$ ...]; T$_5$: [... -g]u$_7$ é-gal-la ba-gub; T$_{15}$: [... -ga]l-la ba-gub; N$_{I}$: ga-b[a- ...]; K$_{I}$: [... -r]a-gu$_7$ é-gal-l[a ...]; MM: [...]-⸢la ba⸣-[...]; Sch$_3$: ga-ba-ra-gu$_7$ ⸢x⸣ [... b]a(?)-⸢an⸣(?)-gub

(123) (and saying): "Let me have something to eat from it" he stands (ready to serve) at the palace.

124 dumu-ninta(NITAḪ)-zu é-zu-šè im-me

UM$_{I}$: dumu-ninta-zu é-zu-[...]; UM$_4$: dumu-ninta-zu é-zu-šè im-me; T$_2$: dumu-ninta-zu [...]; T$_5$: [...] é-zu-šè im-me; T$_{15}$: [... -š]è im-me; N$_{I}$: dumu-ninta-[...]; N$_2$: [... -z]u é-zu-šè i[m- ...]; K$_{I}$: [... -z]u é-zu-šè i[m- ...]; MM: [...] ⸢é⸣-zu-⸢šè⸣ [...]; Sch$_3$: dumu-ninta-zu [... š]i-im-me; Sch$_4$: [dumu]-⸢ninta⸣-zu ⸢é-ni-šè ši-im-me⸣ (nearly illegible)

(124) Your son will speak for *your* house,

125 dumu-munus-zu ama$_5$-ni-šè im-me

ED$_1$ r. i 8' dumu-mun[us x]-šè du[g$_4$]

UM$_1$: dumu-munus-zu ama$_5$-ni-š[è ...]; UM$_4$: [du]mu-munus-zu ama$_5$-ni-šè im-me; I$_{11}$: [du]mu-mun[us- ...]; T$_2$: dumu-munus-zu [...]; T$_5$: [...] ama$_5$-ni-šè im-me; T$_{15}$: [... -i]m-me; N$_1$: dumu-[...]; N$_2$: [...] ama$_5$-ni-šè im-[...]; K$_1$: dumu-munus-mu ama$_5$-zu-{na}-šè im-me; MM: [...] ama$_5$-⸢x⸣-⸢šè⸣ [...]; Sch$_3$: dumu-munus-zu [... š]i-im-me; Sch$_4$: dumu(?)-munus-zu ⸢ama$_5$⸣(?)-⸢bi⸣(or ta?) ši-im-me

(125) (but) you daughter will speak for *her* women's quarters.

126 kaš naŋ-a-zu-ne di na-an-ne-e

ED$_1$ o. vii 1' ka[š x -z]u$_5$ ⸢DI⸣ na-⸢x⸣-[dug$_4$]

UM$_1$: kaš naŋ-a-zu-ne di na-an-ne-e; UM$_4$: [k]aš naŋ-a-zu-ne di na-an-ne-e; I$_{11}$: kaš naŋ-a-zu-[...]; T$_2$: ⸢kaš naŋ⸣-[...]; T$_5$: [...] di na-an-[n]e; T$_{15}$: [...]-ne; N$_2$: [... -z]u-ni di na-an-ne-[...]; K$_1$: kaš naŋ-zu-ne di na-an-è; MM: ⸢kaš⸣ [...] di na-[...]; Sch$_3$: kaš naŋ-a-z[u]-⸢ne⸣ [...]-⸢x⸣-⸢x⸣-⸢x⸣ (looks like x-na-ni); Sch$_4$: GA(?)-zu(?) é-ta KA šu ⸢x⸣ AN (unidentified line or variant?) | kaš naŋ-ŋá-zu / ⸢šà/di?⸣ ... (illegible traces)

(126) When you drink beer, don't pass judgment!

127 é-ta è šà-zu na-an-gu$_7$-e

ED$_1$ o. vii 2' + 323 ii 1 ⸢x⸣-ta ù SAR-zu$_5$ gu$_7$

UM$_1$: é-ta è šà-zu <na>-an-[...]; UM$_4$: ⸢é⸣-ta è šà-zu na-an-gu$_7$-e; I$_{11}$: é-ta è š[à- ...]; T$_5$: [...]-zu na-a[n-g]u$_7$-e; T$_{15}$: [...]-⸢an⸣-gu$_7$-e; N$_2$: [... -t]a è šà-zu na-an-[...]; K$_1$:è-a šà-zu na-an-KA-⸢e⸣, cf. coll. Taylor; MM: e(sic!)-ta [x x] ⸢šà-zu na⸣-[...]-⸢x⸣; Ur$_5$: cf. rev. ii 3: e-ta(? copy bi SILA$_3$) e [...]; Sch$_3$: kaš naŋ-a-z[u]-⸢ne⸣ [...]-⸢x⸣-⸢x⸣-⸢x⸣ (looks like x-na-ni); Sch$_4$: / é(! looks like bi)-ta è(!) šà-zu ⸢na⸣-⸢gu$_7$⸣-e

(127) On leaving (your) house, don't be troubled!

128 an sù-ud-dam ki kal-kal-la-àm

UM$_1$: an sù-ud-dam ki kal-ka[l- ...]; UM$_4$: [...] sù-dam ki kal-kal-la-àm; I$_{11}$: an sù-ud-dam k[i ...]; T$_5$: [...] ki kal-[ka]l-la-àm; T$_{15}$: [...]-kal-kal-la; T$_{17}$: [...]-kal-la; N$_2$: [...]-dam kal-kal-la-[...]; K$_1$: an sù-da ki kal-kal-la; MM: an [...] ki kal-kal-la-àm; Sch$_3$: omitted?; Sch$_4$: an sù-da-⸢àm⸣ ⸢ki⸣ ⸢kal-kal⸣-la-àm

(128) Heaven is far away, (and) earth is precious;

129 an-da níŋ im-da-lu-lu-un

UM$_1$: an-da níŋ [i]m-da-lu-lu-[...]; UM$_4$: [...]-da níŋ im-da-lu-lu-un; I$_{11}$: an-da níŋ i[m- ...]; T$_{15}$: (traces); T$_{17}$: [...]-lu-lu-un; N$_2$: [...] im-da-lu-[...]; K$_1$: ⸢an⸣-da ⸢x⸣ ⸢x⸣ -da-lu-lu-un, cf. coll. Taylor; MM: an-[x] níŋ ⸢im-da⸣-lu-lu; Sch$_3$: an-d[a ...]-lu; Sch$_4$: an-da níŋ im-da-lu-lu-àm

(129) but it is it with heaven that you multiply (your) goods,

130 kur-kur-re zi ši-im-da-pa-an-pa-an

UM$_1$: kur-kur-re zi ši-im-da-pa-an-p[a-an]; UM$_4$: [... -k]ur-re zi ši-im-da-pa-an-pa; I$_{11}$: [...]-re zi ˹x˺ [...]; I$_{12}$: [...] zi ši-im-da-[...]; T$_6$: [...] zi š[i- ...]; T$_{15}$: [...]-pa-an-pa-[...]; T$_{17}$: [...]-˹im-da-pa˺-an-mul; N$_2$: [...] z[i ...]; K$_1$: kur-kur-re zi ši-in-pa-an-pa-an; MM: kur-kur-[...] zi š[i]-˹x˺-[x]-an-pa; Sch$_3$: kur-kur-re [... -a]n-˹pa˺(?); Sch$_4$: (about 3 signs erased) kur-kur-re zi im-(traces)

(130) (and) all the mountains breathe with it.

131 u$_4$-buru$_{14}$-šè u$_4$ kal-kal-la-šè

UM$_1$: u$_4$-buru$_{14}$-šè u$_4$ kal-k[al- ...]; UM$_4$: [... -bu]ru$_{14}$-šè u$_4$ (erasure) kal-kal-la-šè; I$_{11}$: [... -bu]ru$_{14}$-šè u$_4$ k[a(sic!) ...]; I$_{12}$: [... -bu]ru$_{14}$-šè u$_4$ kal-kal-la-[...]; T$_6$: [...]-buru$_{14}$-šè u$_4$ kal-[...]; T$_{17}$: [...] u$_4$ kal-kal-la-šè; K$_1$: u$_4$-buru$_{14}$-šè u$_4$ kal-kal-la-šè; K$_2$: u$_4$-buru$_{14}$-šè [...]; MM: u$_4$-bu[ru$_{14}$- x] u$_4$(copy ki) kal-kal-la-àm; Ur$_5$: Cf. rev. II 7: u$_4$-buru$_{14}$-šè (... traces ...); Sch$_3$: u$_4$-buru$_{14}$-... (traces)

(131) At the time of the harvest, at the most priceless time,

132 géme-gim ri-ga-ab eŋi-gim gu$_7$-a

UM$_1$: géme-gim ri-ga-ab eŋi-gim [...]; UM$_4$: [... -g]im ri-ga-ab eŋi-gim gu$_7$-a; I$_{11}$: [... -gi]m ri-ri-g[a ...]; I$_{12}$: [... -gi]m ri-ga-ab eŋi-gim g[u$_7$- ...]; T$_6$: [...]-gim ri-ga-ab e[ŋi- ...]; T$_{17}$: [... -g]a-ab eŋi-gim gu$_7$-a; N$_1$: géme-gi[m ...]; K$_1$: géme-gim KU-ga-ab eŋi-gim gu$_7$(!)-a; K$_2$: géme-gim ri-ga-ab [...]; MM: géme-[... r]i-ga-˹ab˺ eŋi-gim gu$_7$-a; Ur$_5$: cf. rev. I 6: ˹x˺(= ri?)-˹ga-ab˺ [...]; Sch$_3$: ˹géme-gim˺ [... -a]b [... (½ line)

(132) glean like a slave girl, eat like a queen,

133 dumu-ŋu$_{10}$ géme-gim ri eŋi-gim gu$_7$-a ur$_5$ ḫé-en-na-nam-ma-àm

UM$_1$: dumu-ŋu$_{10}$ géme-gim ri eŋi gim gu$_7$ a ur$_5$ ḫ[é àm]; UM$_4$: [... -ŋ]u$_{10}$ géme-gim ri eŋi-gim ku ur$_5$ ḫé-en-na-nam-ma-àm; I$_{12}$: [... gé]me-gim ri eŋi-gim g[u$_7$ ...]-en-na-nam-[...]; T$_6$: ˹dumu˺-ŋu$_{10}$ [gé]me-gim ri eŋi-[...]; T$_{17}$: [...] ri eŋi-gim gu$_7$-a [...]-nam-ma-àm; N$_1$: dumu-ŋu$_{10}$ géme-g[im ...]; K$_1$: dumu-ŋu$_{10}$ géme-gim ÉŠ-ga-ab eŋi-gim KA-a ur$_5$ <ḫé>-in-a[n-n]a-me-en; K$_2$: dumu-ŋu$_{10}$ géme-gim ri eŋi-gim k[u ...]; MM: [...]-gim ri eŋi-gim ku ur$_5$ ḫé-en-n[a- ...]; Ur$_5$: du$_5$ x x géme-gim ˹x˺ [...]; Sch$_3$: (... traces of two signs, a bit short for first part of 133) ˹ur$_5$˺ ḫé-(traces ...)

(133) my son, glean like a slave girl, but eat like a queen, that is how it should be indeed!

134 áš dug$_4$-dug$_4$-ge bar ši-in-dar

ED$_1$ o. viii 8'–9' áš dug$_4$-d[ug$_4$] | bar šè-dar

UM$_1$: áš dug$_4$-dug$_4$-ge bar ši-in-[...]; UM$_4$: [... d]ug$_4$-g[e] ba[r ... -i]n-[...]; T$_6$: áš du[g$_4$-dug$_4$-g]e bar ši-[...]; T$_{17}$: [...]-dar; N$_1$: áš dug$_4$ dug$_4$-[...]; K$_1$: áš tuk$_5$(tag)-tuk$_5$(tag)-ge bar ši-in-dar; K$_2$: áš dug$_4$-dug$_4$-ge b[ar(!) ...]; MM: [... -d]ug$_4$-ge bar šè-im-⸢dar⸣; Sch$_3$: áš [dug$_4$-dug$_4$, but perhaps not space enough for two signs]-ge bar(? looks like pa$_5$)-ra(rather than šè-, hardly a gloss) dar(hardly x-bar) [... room for 3 to 4 signs]

(134) An insult breaks only the skin,

135 igi-tùm-lá saŋ ŋiš im-ra-ra

UM$_1$: igi-tùm-lá saŋ ŋiš im-ra-r[a]; T$_6$: igi-tùm-[... sa]ŋ ŋiš im-ra-r[a]; T$_{17}$: [...]-ra; N$_1$: igi-tùm-lá [...]; K$_1$: igi-tùm-lá saŋ ŋiš íb-ra-ra; K$_2$: ⸢igi-tùm⸣-lá s[aŋ ...]; MM: [...] saŋ ŋiš ra-ra; S$_1$: i-gi-tu-ul-la saŋ ŋiš im-ra-ra; Sch$_3$: ⸢igi-tùm-lá⸣ ⸢saŋ⸣ ŋi[š ...]

(135) but envy kills.

136 gù-mur-re lú-lul-e túg ši-bir$_7$-bir$_7$-e

UM$_1$: gù-mur-re lú-lul-e túg ši-bir$_7$-bir$_7$-e; T$_6$: gù-mur-[r]e lú-lul-e túg ši-[...]; T$_{17}$: [...]-bir$_7$-re; N$_1$: gù-mur-re; K$_1$: gù-mur-ra lú-lul-la túg(!)(text: ÉŠ) bir$_7$-bir$_7$-ra; K$_2$: [...] lú-lul-la túg [...]; MM: [... l]ú-lul-la túg šè-bir$_7$-bir$_7$-re; S$_1$: gu-mu-ru *lu-ru-la zu-uš ši-bi-ir-bi-re; Sch$_3$: ⸢gù mur-re⸣(?) lul-e ⸢túg⸣ [...]

(136) Shouting, the liar tears up garments.

137 áš-di níŋ-érim-e na-ri šè-íl-íl

UM$_1$: áš-di níŋ-NE-e na-di šè-íl-íl; T$_6$: áš-di níŋ-érim-e na-ri šè-í[l- ...]; T$_{17}$: [...]-íl; N$_1$: áš-di níŋ-NE-[...]; K$_1$: áš-dè níŋ-érim-e na-ri(= de$_5$) šè-íl-íl; K$_2$: [...] ⸢x⸣-e [...]; MM: [... -é]rim-e na-di šè-íl-íl; Sch$_3$: ⸢x⸣ ⸢x⸣ (= áš-di?) ⸢x⸣ ⸢x⸣ ⸢x⸣ ⸢x⸣ na-ri ⸢x⸣

(137) Insults encourage malice.

138 inim-diri ù-bu-bu-ul ú-libiš-gig-ga-àm

UM$_1$: inim-diri ù-bu-bu-ul ú-libiš-gig-ga; T$_6$: inim-diri ù-bu-bu-ul-la-àm ú-libiš-gig-ga-àm; T$_{17}$: [...] ⸢ú⸣-libiš-gig-ga; N$_1$: inim-diri ⸢x⸣ [...]; K$_1$: inim-diri ⸢ú⸣-⸢bu⸣-⸢bu⸣-⸢ul⸣(!) ú-libiš-gig-KA-a, cf. coll. Taylor; K$_2$: [...] ù-[...]; MM: [... -b]u-bu-ul-àm ú-libiš-gig-ga-àm; Sch$_3$: [...] ⸢ù⸣-bu-bu-ul ⸢x⸣ [...]

(138) To speak arrogantly is like fire, a herb that makes the stomach sick.

139 mu gùn-gùn-da ga-mu-e-da-zala-ge

UM$_1$: mu gùn-gùn-da ga-mu-e-da-zala-ge; T$_5$: [...]-ab-zala-ge; T$_6$: mu [x x]-gùn-da ga-mu-e-da-ab-[...]; N$_1$: mu gùn-gùn-[...]; K$_1$: mu ⸢gùn-gùn⸣-dè ga-mu-ra-ab-za-az-ge; Sch$_3$: ⸢mu-gùn⸣-[gùn]-dè ⸢ga-mu⸣-(traces of one sign)

(139) With a multicolored name let me make you happy!

140 inim-šèd-dè mu ḫé-ŋál-la-àm

UM$_1$: inim-šèd-dè-ŋu$_{10}$ ḫé-ŋál-la-àm; T$_5$: [... -ŋ]ál-la-àm; T$_6$: inim-[šè]d-da-ŋu$_{10}$ ḫé-ŋál-la-à[m]; N$_1$: inim-š[èd- ...]; K$_1$: inim-šèd(!)(text: KA)-dè-ŋu$_{10}$ ḫé-ŋá[l-l]a-à[m]; Sch$_3$: ⸢inim-šèd⸣-[d]a (long blank space) ⸢mu⸣ [... (traces of 1 sign)]

(140) Words of prayer are an abundant year.

(or, reading ŋu$_{10}$ instead of mu: My words of prayer mean abundance.)

141 a-ra-zu a-šed$_4$-da šà-ge im-šed$_4$-e

UM$_1$: a-ra-zu a-š[e]d$_4$ šà-ge im-šed$_4$-e; UM$_4$: [...] a-šed$_4$-da šà-g[e ...]; T$_5$: [... -g]e im-[š]ed$_4$-e; T$_6$: a-[ra-z]u a-š[ed$_4$-d]a šà-ge im-š[ed$_4$]-e; K$_1$: a-ra-zu ⸢šed$_4$⸣ ⸢šà⸣-g[e ...]; Sch$_3$: a-ra-zu [a]-⸢x⸣.⸢DI⸣-dè ⸢šà⸣-[...]

(141) A prayer is cool water that soothes the hearth;

142 áš-ḪAR na-ŋá-aḫ di-da ŋizzal kalam-ma-ke$_4$

UM$_1$: [áš x x -ŋ]á-aḫ di-da ŋizzal kalam-ma-ke$_4$; UM$_4$: omits line; T$_5$: [... -d]a ŋizzal kalam-ma-kam; T$_6$: áš di(miscopy for ḪAR?) na-ŋá ⸢x⸣(copy like NE⸣-da ŋizzal kalam-ma-ke$_4$; K$_1$: áš(?) di(?) na-ŋá(?)-DU d[ug$_4$ ...] (coll. Taylor); Sch$_3$: áš-ḪAR na-[x]-⸢x⸣ ⸢x⸣(may be ḪAR, but ending in a vertical) ŋi[zzal ...]

(142) (but) uttering(?) curses and stupid speech is (what) the attentive(?) of the country (should avoid(?)).

143 šuruppak^{ki}-e dumu-ni-ra na na-mu-un-ri-ri

UM$_1$: [...]^{ki}-e dumu-ni-ra na na-mu-un-ri-ri; UM$_4$: [...]-e dumu-ni-ra na-šè mu-ni-in-ri; N$_3$: [...] na na-mu-un-ri-r[i]; T$_2$: šuruppak [...] + T$_5$: [... -r]a na-šè mu-ni-in-ri; T$_6$: šuruppak-e dumu-ni-ra na na-mu-un-ri-ri; Ur$_4$: [... -r]i-ri; K$_1$: šuruppak DU dumu-ni-r[a ...]; Sch$_3$: šuruppak-e ⸢dumu-ni-ra⸣ na [...]

(143) The man from Šuruppak gave instructions to his son;

144 šuruppak^{ki} dumu ubar-tu-tu-ke$_4$

UM$_1$: [šurupp]ak^{ki} dumu ubar-tu-tu-ke$_4$; UM$_4$: [...]-⸢e⸣ dumu ubar-tu-tu-ke$_4$; N$_3$: [...] šuruppak^{ki} dumu ubar-tu-tu-[...]; T$_2$: šuruppak^{ki} [...] + T$_5$: [... uba]r tu-tu-ke$_4$; T$_6$: šuruppak dumu ubar-tu-tu-ke$_4$; Ur$_4$: [... -t]u-tu-ke$_4$; K$_1$: SU.KUR.(traces) [...]; Sch$_3$: šuruppak ⸢x⸣ [...]

(144) the man from Šuruppak, the son of Ubartutu,

145 zi-u$_4$-sud-rá dumu-ni-ra na na-mu-un-ri-ri

UM$_1$: [x]-u$_4$-sud-rá dumu-ni-ra na na-mu-un-ri-ri; UM$_4$: [x x -s]ud-rá dumu-ni-ra na-šè mu-ni-in-ri; N$_3$: zi-u$_4$-sud-rá dumu-ni-ra na [na] mu-un-ri-⸢ri⸣; T$_2$: zi-u$_4$-sud-[...] + T$_5$: [...]-ra na-šè mu-ni-in-ri; T$_6$: zi-u$_4$-sud-rá dumu-ni-ra na na-mu-un-ri-[...]; Ur$_4$: [... -m]u-un-ri-ri; K$_1$: zi-u$_4$-sud-rá dumu-ni-r[a ...]; Sch$_3$: ⸢zi-u$_4$⸣-s[ud]-ra [dum]u-ni-r[a ...]

(145) gave instructions to his son Ziusudra.

146 èš-kam-ma-šè šuruppak^{ki} dumu-ni-ra na na-mu-un-ri-r[i]

UM$_1$, UM$_4$, and (probably) N$_3$ and Ur$_2$ omit line; T$_2$: min-kam-ma-šè [...] + T$_5$: [... šu]ruppak-e dumu-ni-ra [na šè]-mu-ni-in-ri; T$_6$: [x x]-ma-šè šuruppak-e dumu-ni-r[a] na na-mu-un-ri-[...]; K$_1$: eš-kam-ma-šè šuruppak^{ki} dumu-[...]; Sch$_3$: èš-⸢kam⸣- ... (traces) [...]

(146) For a third time, Šuruppak gave instructions to his son;

147 [šuruppak^{ki} dumu ubar]-tu-tu-ke$_4$

UM$_1$, UM$_4$, T$_6$, K$_1$ and (probably) N$_3$ and Ur$_4$ omit line. T$_2$: (traces) + T$_5$: [...]-tu-tu-ke$_4$; Sch$_3$: (traces)

(147) [The man from Šuruppak, son of Ubar]tutu,

148 [zi-u$_4$-sud]-ra na-šè mu-ni-in-ri

UM$_1$, UM$_4$, T$_6$, K$_1$, and (probably) N$_3$ and Ur$_4$ omit line. T$_2$: (traces) + T$_5$: [...]-ra na-šè mu-ni-in-ri; Sch$_3$: ⸢zi-u$_4$⸣- ... (traces)

(148) gave instructions to his son [Ziusudra]:

149 dumu-ŋu$_{10}$ na ga-ri na-ri-ŋu$_{10}$ ḫé-dab$_5$

UM$_1$: [x] na ga-ri na-ri-ŋu$_{10}$ ḫé-dab$_5$; UM$_2$: [...] ga-ri na-ri-ŋu$_{10}$ ḫé-dab$_5$; C$_1$: [...] na ge-ri na-ri-[...]; T$_2$: + T$_5$: omit line; T$_6$: dumu-ŋu$_{10}$ na ga-ri na-ri-ŋu$_{10}$ ḫé-dab$_5$; N$_3$: [...] dumu-ŋu$_{10}$ na ge-ri na-r[i...]; Ur$_4$: [... -r]i-ŋu$_{10}$ ḫé-dab$_5$; K$_1$: dumu-ŋu$_{10}$ na-ri-⸢ga⸣(?) na-[...]; Sch$_3$: dumu-ŋu$_{10}$ ... (traces)

(149) My son, let my give you instructions; let my instructions be taken!

150 zi-u$_4$-sud-rá inim ga-ra-ab-dug$_4$ ŋizzal ḫé-em-ši-ak

UM$_1$: [x x -s]ud-rá inim ga-ra-ab-dug$_4$ ŋizzal ḫé-em-ši-ak; UM$_4$: [x x -s]ud-rá inim ga-ra-ab-dug$_4$ ŋizzal ḫé-em-ši-ak; C$_1$: zi-u$_4$-sud-rá inim ga-ra-ab-du[g$_4$ ...]; T$_2$ + T$_5$: omit line; T$_6$: zi-u$_4$-sud-rá inim ga-ra-ab-dug$_4$ ŋizzal ḫé-em-ši-ak; N$_3$: [z]i-u$_4$-sud-rá inim g[a- ...] giz[zal ...]; Ur$_4$: omits line; K$_1$: zi-u$_4$-sud-rá inim ga-ra-ab-dug$_4$ ŋizzal [...]; Sch$_3$: zi-u$_4$-sud- ... (traces)

(150) My son, let me speak a word to you; let attention be paid to them!

151 na-ri-ga-ŋu$_{10}$ šu nam-bí-bar-re

UM$_1$: [...] šu nam-bí-bar-re; UM$_2$: [...]-ga-ŋu$_{10}$ šu nam-bí-bar-re; C$_1$: na-ri-ga-ŋu$_{10}$ šu nam-bí-[...]; T$_2$ + T$_5$ and T$_6$ omit line; N$_3$: (traces of one sign); Ur$_4$: [x]-ri-[...] šu nam-bí-íb-bar-re; K$_1$: na-ri-ga-ŋu$_{10}$ šu <nam>-bí-bar-[...]; Sch$_3$: [n]a-⸢ri-ga⸣-[...]

(151) Don't neglect my instructions,

152 inim dug$_4$-ga-ŋu$_{10}$ na-ab-ta-bal-e-dè

UM$_1$: [... n]a-ab-ta-bal-e-dè; UM$_4$: [... -g]a-ŋu$_{10}$ na-ab(!)-ta-ab-bal-e-dè; C$_1$: inim dug$_4$-ga-ŋu$_{10}$ na-ab-ta-b[al- ...]; T$_5$ and T$_6$ omits line; Ur$_4$: (traces) ⸢ta⸣-bal-e; K$_1$: inim dug$_4$-ga-ŋu$_{10}$ na-ab-ta-bal-e-[...]; Sch$_3$: ⸢inim⸣-⸢dug$_4$⸣-⸢ga⸣-[...]

(152) Don't transgress the words I spoke!

From Akk$_2$ some signs remain, probably belonging to line 147ff.:

147 = 7 = 82 *šuruppakû*
148 = 8 = 83 *utnapištu* [
149 = 9 = 84 *mâri lu*-[
150 = 10 = 85 *utnapištu* [
151 = 11 = 86 *aširti*-[
152 = 12 = 87 *amât a*[*qbû*

152 A na-ri ab-ba níŋ kal-la-àm gú-zu ḫé-em-ši-ak

Ur$_4$: na-ri [ab-ba … g]ú-zu ḫé-em-ši-ak; K$_1$: na-ri ab-ba níŋ kal-la-àm ⌜x⌝ ⌊x⌋ ⌜x⌝(lá), coll. Taylor; (cf. line 13); Sch$_3$: omits

(152a) The instructions of a father are precious, you should comply with them!

153 dumu eŋar-ra-ra níŋ nam-mu-ra-ra-an e-pa$_5$-zu šè-im-ra

ED$_1$ o. 10–11 dumu eŋar níŋ na-ra e-pa$_5$-zu$_5$ šè-ra

UM$_1$: […]-mu-ra-ra e-pa$_5$-zu šè-im-ra; UM$_2$: [… e]ŋar-ra-ra níŋ nam-mu-ra-ra-an e-pa$_5$-zu ši-im-ra; UM$_4$: [… n]íŋ nam-mu-ra-[… -p]a$_5$-zu ši-im-[…]; C$_1$: dumu ⌜x⌝ […]; T$_1$: traces + T$_5$: […]-zu ši-im-ra; T$_6$: dumu eŋar-ra-[…] nam-mu-ra-ra-an e-[p]a$_5$-zu šè-im-ra; T$_7$: [… n]íŋ nam-mu-ra-ra-a[n] (nothing missing); T$_8$: […]-mu-ra-ra-an e-pa$_5$-zu […]; T$_9$: [… e]ŋar-ra-ra níŋ nam-mu-ra-ra-an e-pa$_5$-zu šè-im-ra; Ur$_4$: [… -r]a-ra e-pa$_5$-zu im-ra-⌜an⌝(?); K$_1$: dumu eŋar-ra níŋ nam-mu-ra-ra e-pa$_5$ šè-i[m]-⌜x⌝; Sch$_3$: […] níŋ n[am- …]-ra-ra-an e-pa$_5$-zu š[è- …]

ED$_1$ o. vii 3' níŋ-nam-tar dug$_4$: to be placed where?

(153) Don't beat a farmer's son; he will(?) "beat" your irrigation canal.

154 [kar-k]id na-an-sa$_{10}$-sa$_{10}$-an ka u$_4$-sar-ra-kam

ED$_1$ o. ii 3 géme kar-kíd na-an-sa$_{10}$ ka ù-sar-kam$_4$

UM$_1$: […]-sa$_{10}$ ka u$_4$-sar-ra-ka; UM$_2$: [… -k]id na-an-sa$_{10}$-sa$_{10}$-an ka u$_4$-sar-ra-kam; T$_7$: [… -s]a$_{10}$ ka u$_4$.Ù.sa[r …]; T$_8$: […] ka u$_4$-sar-ra-ka; T$_9$: [… -s]a$_{10}$-sa$_{10}$-an ka u$_4$-sar-ra-⌜kam⌝; Ur$_4$: [… -s]a$_{10}$ ka ù-sar-ra-ka; K$_1$: šà im (coll. J. Taylor) na-sa$_{10}$-sa$_{10}$ ka u$_4$-sar-r[a- x]; Ur$_5$: Cf. rev. I' 11: sar-ra-kam; Sch$_3$: ⌜kar-kíd⌝ [na-an⌝-⌜sa$_{10}$⌝-[…] ka ⌜x⌝(might be ù over an erasure?) sar-ra-k[a]

(154) Don't buy a prostitute; she is a mouth with sharpened teeth!

155 émedu(AMA.A.TU) na-an-sa$_{10}$-sa$_{10}$-an ú-libiš-gig-ga-àm

ED$_1$ o. vi 12–13 ḪAR-tu na-sa$_{10}$ ú-libiš-gig

UM$_1$: […]-sa$_{10}$ ú-libiš-gig-ga-àm; UM$_2$: [x].A.TU na-an-sa$_{10}$-sa$_{10}$-an ú-libiš-gig-ga-àm; C$_1$: […].TU na-an-sa$_{10}$-s[a$_{10}$] ú-li[biš …]; T$_7$: […]-sa$_{10}$-A.AN ú-libiš-g[ig …]; T$_8$: […] ú-libiš-gig-ga-àm; Ur$_4$: […].TU [… -s]a$_{10}$ ú-libiš-gig-ga-àm; K$_1$: AMA.A.TU na-ab-sa$_{10}$-sa$_{10}$ u$_4$-libiš-gi[g]; Ur$_5$: Cf. perhaps rev. i' 11, 2nd part - ii 12: ⌜x⌝ a ⌜x⌝ NI nam-sa$_{10}$-sa$_{10}$-an (NI may belong to a previous

(155) Don't buy a home-borne slave; he is a herb that causes stomach aches!

column); Sch$_3$: AMA.A.TU na-an-[sa$_{10}$-sa$_{10}$-a]n ú-libiš-gig-g[a-àm]

156 dumu-gi$_7$ na-an-sa$_{10}$-sa$_{10}$-an zag é-ŋar$_8$-e ús-sa-àm

UM$_1$: dum[u ...]-sa$_{10}$ zag é-ŋar$_8$-e ús-sa; UM$_2$: [x -g]i$_7$ na-an-sa$_{10}$-sa$_{10}$-an zag é-ŋar$_8$-e ús-sa-àm; C$_1$: [x -g]i$_7$ na-an-sa$_{10}$-sa$_{10}$ zag é-ŋar$_8$-e [...]; T$_7$: [... z]ag é-ŋar(sic!)-e ús-[...]; T$_8$: [...]-an zag é-ŋar$_8$-e ús-sa; Ur$_4$: [x] ⸢x⸣ [...] ⸢x⸣ zag é-ŋar$_8$-e in-ús; K$_1$: dumu-gi$_7$ na-ab-sa$_{10}$-sa$_{10}$ zag ŋar(sic!)-re ús-s[a ...]; Sch$_3$: dumu-gi$_7$ na-an-sa$_{10}$-sa$_{10}$-an(sic!) z[ag] ⸢x⸣(like šu) ⸢x⸣(like KA) ⸢x⸣(like sìla) gar$_8$-⸢e⸣ ú[s(-sa)]

(156) Don't buy a free man; he leans (his) side towards a wall.

157 géme é-gal-la na-an-sa$_{10}$-sa$_{10}$ ŋìri dúr-bi-šè é ŋál-ŋál-la-àm

UM$_1$: géme [... -s]a$_{10}$ ŋìri dúr-bi-šè(! text: KU) é ŋál-ŋál-la-àm; UM$_2$: géme é-gal-la na-an-sa$_{10}$-sa$_{10}$-an ŋìri dúr-bi é ŋál-ŋál-la-àm; C$_1$: ⸢géme⸣ é-gal na-an-sa$_{10}$-sa$_{10}$ ŋì[ri x]-bi-šè é ŋ[ál-...]; T$_7$: [...]-sa$_{10}$-A-[AN] ⸢é⸣ ŋál-ŋál-[...]; T$_8$: [...]-sa$_{10}$-an ŋìri dúr-bi-šè ŋál-ŋál-la; Ur$_4$: [...] ⸢dúr⸣-bi-šè ⸢é⸣ ŋál-ŋál-la-àm; K$_1$: géme é-gal-la na-ab-sa$_{10}$-sa$_{10}$ ŋìri dúr-bi-šè ⸢ŋál(?)⸣-ŋ[ál-lá-à]m; Sch$_3$: ⸢géme⸣ ⸢é⸣(?)-<gal>-⸢a⸣(?) na-sa$_{10}$-⸢sa$_{10}$⸣-⸢en⸣(sic!) ⸢ŋìri⸣ ⸢dúr-bi-šè⸣ é-ŋál-ŋál-l[a]

(157) Don't but a slave girl from the palace; the whole house will always get the worst of it.

158 saŋ-kur-ra kur-bi-ta um-ta-a-e$_{11}$

UM$_1$: saŋ-k[ur- ...]-ta-e-e$_{11}$; UM$_2$: saŋ-kur-ra kur-bi um-ta-a-e$_{11}$; T$_7$: [...]-ta-a-e$_{11}$; T$_8$: [... -t]a-⸢e$_{11}$⸣-e$_{11}$; C$_1$: saŋ-kur-ra kur-bi um-ta-e-⸢e$_{11}$⸣; Ur$_4$: [...]-e$_{11}$; K$_1$: ⸢saŋ-kur⸣-ra kur-bí(sic!) im-ta-a-⸢x⸣-[x]; Sch$_3$: saŋ-⸢kur-ra⸣ kur-bi um-ta-ab-⸢è⸣-e[n](sic?)

(158) Once you have brought a slave down from the mountains,

159 lú ki-nu-zu-a-ni-ta ù-mu-e-túm

UM$_1$: [...]-ta ù-mu-e-túm; UM$_2$: lú ki-nu-zu-a-ni-ta ù-me-túm; T$_7$: [...]-mu-e-[...]; T$_8$: [...]-ta ù-mu-túm; C$_1$: lú ki-nu-zu-a-ni-ta ù-um-[...]; Ur$_4$: [...]-túm; K$_1$: [... -t]a ù-mu-[...]; Sch$_3$: lú ki-nu-zu-ni-ta ù-⸢mu⸣(? looks like en)-tùm

(159) once you have brought a man from his unknown place,

160 dumu-ŋu$_{10}$ ki ^{d}utu-è-a-aš

UM$_1$: dumu-ŋu$_{10}$ ki ^{d}utu-è-a-aš; UM$_2$: dumu-ŋu$_{10}$ ki ^{d}utu-è-a-šè; T$_7$: [...]-⸢è⸣-a-[...]; T$_8$: [...]-è-a-aš; C$_1$: dumu-ŋu$_{10}$ ki ^{d}utu-è-a-[x]; K$_1$: [...] ^{d}u[tu]-⸢è⸣-⸢a⸣(?)-⸢aš⸣(?); Sch$_3$: dumu-ŋu$_{10}$ ki ^{d}utu è-a-šè

(160) my son, toward the place where the sun rises,

161 a ḫu-mu-ra-an-dé-e igi-zu-šè ḫé-du

UM$_1$: a ḫu-mu-ra-an-dé-e igi-zu-šè ḫé-du; UM$_2$: a ḫu-mu-ra-an-dé-e igi-zu-šè ḫé-du; C$_1$: a ḫu-mu-ra-an-dé-e igi-zu-šè ḫé-d[u]; K$_1$: a ḫu-[...] ⸢x⸣ igi-zu-šè ḫé-⸢x⸣-in-du; Sch$_3$: a ḫu-mu-ra-an-dé-e igi-zu-šè ḫé-du

(161) he will walk in front of you, libating water for you;

162 é nu-tuku é-a-ni-šè la-ba-du

UM$_1$: é nu-tuku é-a-ni la-ba-du; UM$_2$: é nu-un-tuku é-a-ni-šè la-ba-du; C$_1$: é nu-tuku é-a-ni-šè la-ba-d[u …]; K$_1$: é nu-tu[ku] é-a-ni-šè la-ba-du; Sch$_3$: é ⸢nu⸣-tuku é-a-ni-šè ⸢la⸣-ba-du

(162) Since he does not have a house, he does not go to his house;

163 ere nu-tuku ere-ni-šè la-ba-du

UM$_1$: ere nu-tuku ere-ni-šè la-ba-du; UM$_2$: ere nu-un-tuku ere-ni-šè la-ba-du; C$_1$: ere nu-tuku ere-ni-šè la-ba-[…]; T$_{10}$: [… -tu]ku ere-a-ni-š[è …]; K$_1$: ere nu-tu[ku er]e-ni-šè la-ba-dù; Sch$_3$: ere nu-tuku ere-ni-šè la-ba-du

(163) since he does not have a city, he does not go to his city.

163 A
K$_1$ only: ^{ŋiš}ig k[ur- … š]u ba-an-da-ús-sa

(163a) Knocking at the door of the nether[world],

163 B
K$_1$ only: ⸢UD⸣ [x x]-⸢ šè⸣ la-ba-an-da-ku$_4$-ku$_4$

(163b) he does not enter […].

164 la-ba-da-ḫi-li-e la-ba-e-da-sun$_7$-e

UM$_1$: la-ba-da-ḫi-li-e la-ba-da-[…]; UM$_2$: [l]a-ba-e-da-ḫi-li la-ba-e-da-sun$_7$-e; C$_1$: la-ba-da-ḫi-li-e la-[…]; T$_{10}$: la-ba-e-da-ḫi-li l[a- …]; T$_{11}$: [… -su]n$_7$-e; K$_1$: […]-ḫi-li la-ba-an-da-sun$_7$-na; Sch$_3$: la-ba-e-da-ḫi-li-e ⸢la⸣-⸢ba⸣-⸢e⸣-da-sun$_7$-e

(164) He does not estimate it higher than you, he does not quarrel with you.

165 dumu-ŋu$_{10}$ ki ^{d}utu-è-a-aš

UM$_1$: dumu-ŋu$_{10}$ ki ^{d}utu-è-a-aš; C$_1$: […]-ŋu$_{10}$ ki ^{d}utu-è-[…]; T$_{10}$: [… du]mu-ŋu$_{10}$ ki(! text: di) ^{d}utu-[…]; T$_{11}$: […]-aš; K$_1$: […] k[i] ^{d}utu-è-a; Sch$_3$: dumu-ŋu$_{10}$ ki ^{d}utu-⸢è⸣-a-⸢šè⸣

(165) My son, toward the place where the sun rises,

166 dili-zu-ne kaskal na-an-ni-du-un

UM$_1$: dili-zu-ne kaskal n[a]-a[n- …]-⸢un⸣; C$_1$: […] na-an-ni-[…]; T$_{10}$: dili-dù-zu-ne kaskal na-[…]; T$_{11}$: [… -d]u-un; K$_1$: [… kas]kal(?)-šè na-an-ni-du; Sch$_3$: dili-zu-ne kaskal na-an-ni-du-un

(166) don't travel alone!

167 nu-zu-a-zu saŋ šu-bal ⸢ì⸣-ak-e

UM$_1$: nu-zu-a-zu s[aŋ …]-a-⸢x⸣; C$_1$: […] ba-⸢ra⸣-⸢ak⸣-⸢x⸣-[…] (ak on a detached fragment); T$_{10}$: lú-zu-a-zu saŋ-šu-UD(?)-ba (miscopy for saŋ-šu-bal?) ⸢x⸣-[…]; T$_{11}$: […]-⸢ak⸣-e; K$_1$: […]-⸢x⸣-⸢x⸣-ak-ke$_4$; Sch$_3$: lú ⸢nu⸣-⸢zu(?)-a⸣(?)-zu-um saŋ šu-bal ⸢ì⸣-[(x)]-ak-e

(167) Someone whom you don't know will trade you as a slave.

168 mu-mu-a sì-ga saŋ-du lú-ù-ra im-ma(?)-⌜ak(?)⌝-e

ED$_1$ r. iv 15 mu-mu sì-ga ⌜x⌝ | lú na[m] šè

UM$_1$: mu-mu-a sì-ga s[aŋ ...] im-ma(?)-⌜x⌝-e (x like búr; maybe ⌜gíd⌝); C$_1$: [...] lú/-ù-ra i[m- ...] (lú no longer visible; ù-ra i[m on a detached fragment); T$_{10}$: mu-mu-a sì-ga saŋ-du lú-[...]; T$_{11}$: [...] lú-ra [...]-⌜x⌝-e (x is ak rather than gíd); T$_{18}$: (traces); K$_1$: [...]-⌜x⌝ (perhaps e or ke$_4$); Sch$_3$: mu-mu-a sì-ga saŋ-du lú-ra im-da(?)-na-an-ak-⌜e⌝

(168) When at home(?) (lit., placed among (familiar names) one can ... the head toward someone.

169 kur-ra kur na-an-na-dub-bé

UM$_1$: kur-ra k[ur ...]-bé; C$_1$: [... -n]a-dub-b[é] (on a separate fragment); T$_{10}$: kur-ra kur na-an-na-dub-bé; T$_{11}$: [... -d]ub-bé; T$_{18}$: [...]-an-[...]; Sch$_3$: ⌜x⌝(could be kur)-ra kur(?) na(?)-an(?)-dub-bé-en

(169) Don't pile up a mountain among the mountains!

169 A Sch$_3$ only: ⌜x⌝(could be kur)-ra KAM(?) na lú ab-bé-en

170 nam-tar peš$_{10}$ dur$_5$-ra-àm

UM$_1$: nam-tar [... -à]m; C$_1$: [...]-àm (on a separate fragment); I$_{13}$: n[am- ...]; T$_{10}$: nam-tar peš$_{10}$ dur$_5$-ra-àm; T$_{11}$: [...]-àm; T$_{18}$: [...]-dur$_5$-[...]; Sch$_3$: nam-tar peš$_{10}$(KI.A) x(like si)-dur$_5$-ru-⌜àm⌝

(170) Destiny is a wet bank

171 lú-da ŋìri-ni im-ma-da-an-zé-er

UM$_1$: lú-da ŋìri-[...]; I$_{13}$: lú-[...]; T$_{10}$: lú-da ŋìri-ni im-ma-da-an-zé-[er]; T$_{11}$: [... -a]n-zé-er; T$_{18}$: [... -ŋì]ri-ni im-ma-[...]; Sch$_3$: (5 signs erased) lú-da ŋìri-ni im-ma-da-an-z[é-er]

(171) that makes a man's feet slip away from him!

172 šeš-gal a-a na-nam nin$_9$-gal ama na-nam

ED$_2$ fr. 8 i 1–2 šeš-[gal a-a] na-nám <[nin$_9$-gal]> ama na-[nám ...]

UM$_1$: šeš-[gal] a-a na-nam [...]; T$_{10}$: šeš-gal a-a na-nam nin-gal ama na-[...]; I$_{13}$: šeš-gal a-[...]; T$_{18}$: [... n]a-nam nin$_9$-gal [...]; Ur$_4$: [...]-a na-nam [...]; TCL: šeš-gal a-a na-nam nin$_9$-gal ama na-nam; S$_3$: šeš-gal é na-na nin$_9$-gal ama(?) na-na; reverse of S$_3$, syllabic version: šeš-eš-gal é an-na-[na] ni-in-gal ⌜x⌝ dam é [...]; Sch$_3$: šeš-gal a-a na-nam nin$_9$-gal ama na-nam

(172) An older brother is indeed a father; an older sister is indeed a mother!

173 šeš-gal-zu-úr ŋizzal ḫé-em-ši(!)-ak

UM$_1$: šeš-gal-zu-úr [...]; T$_{10}$: šeš-gal-zu-úr ŋizzal ḫé-em-[...]; I$_{13}$: šeš-gal-zu-⌜x⌝ [...]; T$_{18}$: [...] ŋizzal [...]; Ur$_4$: [... -z]u-šè ŋizzal [...]; TCL: šeš-gal-zu-úr(!) ŋizzal ḫé-en(?)-ši(!)-ak; Sch$_3$: šeš-gal-zu-úr ŋizzal ḫé-em-ši-⌜x⌝-(⌜x⌝)(?)

(173) You should pay attention to your older brother;

174 nin$_{9}$-gal ama-zu-gim šu ḫé-en-NE-ŋál-le

UM$_{1}$: nin$_{9}$-gal ama-zu-g[im ...]; I$_{13}$: nin$_{9}$-gal ama-[...]; T$_{10}$: nin-gal ama-zu-gim šu ḫé-en-NE-[...]; T$_{18}$: [... -gi]m šu ḫe-e[n- ...]; Ur$_{4}$: [...]-gal ama(!)-zu-šè gú ḫé-em-ši-[...]; TCL: nin$_{9}$-gal ama-zu-gim šu ḫé-en-⸢x⸣-⸢ŋál⸣; Sch$_{3}$: nin$_{9}$-gal ama-zu-gim šu ḫé-en-NE-ŋál-le

(174) you should be supportive(?) of an older sister like your mother.

175 za-e igi-zu-ta kiŋ na-an-ak-[e]

ED$_{1}$ o. vii 4' [i]gi-zu$_{5}$-ta kiŋ$_{x}$(ḪUL) na-ak x (like TAB)

UM$_{1}$: za-e igi-zu-ta [...]; T$_{10}$: za-e igi-zu-ta kiŋ na-an-ak-[...]; I$_{13}$: za-e igi-zu-ta [...]; T$_{18}$: [...] kiŋ na-an-[...]; Ur$_{4}$: [...]-e igi-zu-ta kiŋ na-an-[...]; TCL: za-e igi-zu-ta kiŋ na-an-na-⸢ak⸣-e (coll. Dahl); Sch$_{3}$: za-e igi-zu-ta kiŋ na-an-na-ni-ak-en

(175) *You* should not work with your eyes (alone).

176 ka-zu-ta níŋ-nam nu-lu-lu-un

ED$_{1}$ r. vii 5' ka-zu$_{5}$-ta níŋ na-lu-lu

UM$_{1}$: ka-zu-ta [...]; T$_{10}$: ka-zu-ta níŋ-nam nu-⸢lu-lu⸣-[...]; I$_{13}$: ka-zu-ta n[íŋ ...]; T$_{18}$: [... n]íŋ-nam nu-lu-[...]; Ur$_{4}$: ka-zu-ta níŋ nam-mu-un-⸢x⸣-lu(!); TCL: ka-zu-ta níŋ im-lu-lu-⸢un⸣; Sch$_{3}$: ka-zu-ta níŋ nam-lu-lu-un

(176) You will not multiply anything with your mouth (alone).

177 ŋá-la dag-ge é dúr-bi-šè mu-un-du

ED$_{1}$ r. vii 6' ŋá-la d[ag] é dúr-šè [(x)] ⸢du⸣

UM$_{1}$: ŋá-la dag-ge ⸢é⸣ [...]; I$_{11}$: (traces); I$_{13}$: ŋá-la d[ag- ...]; T$_{10}$: ŋá-la d[ag]-ge é dúr-[...]; T$_{18}$: [...] é dúr-bi m[u- ...]; Ur$_{4}$: ŋá-la nu-dag-ge é dúr-[x x x -u]n-du; TCL: ŋá-la dag-ge é dúr-bi-šè mu-⸢un-du⸣ (coll. Dahl); Sch$_{3}$: ŋá-la-dag-ge é dúr-bi mu-un-du

(177) A lazy one makes a house go "down to the bottom."

178 ninda-e lú-kur-ra bí-in-e$_{11}$-dè

UM$_{1}$: ninda-e lú [...]; I$_{11}$: [...] lú kur-ra b[í- ...]; N$_{7}$: [... ku]r-ra bí-in-e$_{11}$-dè; T$_{10}$: [...] lú kur-ra bí-i[n- ...]; T$_{18}$: [...]-ra bí-i[n- ...]; Ur$_{4}$: ninda-e lú kur-ra bí-[...]; TCL: ninda-e lú kur-ra bí-in-e$_{11}$-dè; Sch$_{3}$: ninda-e lú-kur-ra bí-in-e$_{11}$-dè

(178) (The need for) bread makes those who live in the mountains descend;

179 lú-lul lú-bar-ra bí-in-túm-mu

UM$_{2}$: (traces); I$_{11}$: lú-lul lú-bar-ra b[í(!)- ...]; I$_{14}$: lú-lul lú-bar-ra bí-in-túm; N$_{7}$: [...] lú-bar-ra bí-in-túm-mu; T$_{10}$: [...]-e lú-[...]; T$_{18}$: [...]-ra bí-i[n- ...]; Ur$_{4}$: [x]-e lú-bar-ra bí-in-[tú]m-mu; TCL: lul-e lú-bar-ra bí-in-túm-mu; Sch$_{3}$: lul-e lú-bar-ra bí-in-tùm-mu

(179) it brings liars and strangers along;

180 ninda-e lú kur-ta im-ma-da-ra-an-e_{11}-dè

UM_2: [...]-ra-an-e_{11}-dè; I_{11}: ninda-e lú kur-ta im-ma(!)-[...]; I_{14}: [x]-e lú ⸢kur⸣-ta im-ma-da-ra-an-e_{11}-dè; N_7: [... -t]a im-ma-da-ra-an-e_{11}-dè; T_{14}: [...]-e lú kur-ta im-ma-da-ra-an-e_{11}-dè; T_{18}: [...]-ma-da-[...]; Ur_4: [x]-⸢e⸣ lú kur-ra im-ma-⸢da⸣-ab-e_{11}-dè; TCL: ninda-e lú kur-ta im-ma-da-ra-an-e_{11}-dè; Sch_3: ninda-e lú kur-ta (im, erased) im-da(? or perhaps ta)-ra-an-e_{11}-dè

(180) (The need for) bread makes people descend from the mountains.

181 úru tur-re lugal-bi-ir amar ši-in-ga-an-ù-tu

ED_I r. iii 2 é ⸢x⸣ amar ⸢x⸣ ⸢x⸣

UM_2: [... š]i-in-na-ù-tu; I_{11}: úru ⸢tur⸣-⸢re⸣ lugal-bi-ir a[mar ...]; I_{14}: [...]-ra lugal-bi-ir ⸢amar⸣ ši-in-ga-an-⸢ù-tu⸣; N_7: [...]-bi-⸢ir⸣ amar (sure!) ši-in-na-ù-tu; T_{18}: [...] amar ši-[...]; Ur_4: [...]-re lugal-bi-[x x] ši-in-ga-ù-tu; TCL: uru(coll. Dahl) tur-re lugal-bi-⸢ir⸣ gud (coll. Dahl) ši-in-na-ù-tu; Sch_3: ere-tur-re lugal-bi-ir amar ši-in-na-an-ù-tu

(181) A small town also creates calves for its lord;

182 úru maḫ-e é-dù-a ši-ḫur-re

ED_I r. iii 1 x (= e/ere?) máḫ é dù ⸢x⸣ ḫur

UM_2: [... -š]i-ḫur-e; I_{11}: (traces); I_{14}: [... -r]e é-dù-a ši-ḫur-re; N_7: [...] ⸢é⸣-dù-a ši-ḫur-re; Ur_4: [...]-dù-a ši-ḫur(!)-re; TCL: uru(coll. Dahl) maḫ-e é-dù-a ši-ḫur-re

(182) (but) the huge city designs house buildings.

183 [...]-⸢x⸣-ke_4 á šu im-du_7-du_7

UM_2: [...] im-du_7-du ⸢x⸣; I_{14}: [... i]m-du_7-du_7; N_7: [...] á šu im-du_7-du_7; Ur_4: [...]-du_7-du_7; TCL: [x]-⸢x⸣-ke_4 á šu im-du_7-du_7

(183) [...] is well equipped;

184 lú níŋ tuku lú níŋ nu-tuku gig-šè im-ŋar

ED_I r. iii 7–8 lú níŋ tuku lú níŋ nu-tuku | áš-gig-šè ŋar

UM_2: lú níŋ-tuku lú níŋ nu-tuku ⸢gig⸣-⸢šè⸣ i[m- ...]; I_{14}: [...]-ŋál; N_7: [...] lú níŋ nu-tuku gig-šè ì-ŋál (šè looks like LAGAB); Ur_4: [...] gig-šè im-ŋar; TCL: [... ní]ŋ nu-tuku gig-šè im-ŋar

(184) A poor man inflicts all kinds of illnesses on a wealthy man.

185 lú dam tuku á šu im-du_7-du_7

ED_I r. iii 11 dam tuku šè-du_7

UM_2: lú dam tuku šu im-du_7-du_7; N_7: [...] á šu im-du_7-du_7; Ur_4: [...]-⸢du_7⸣; TCL: [x x x] ⸢šu⸣ im-du_7-du_7

(185) A married man is well equipped;

186 dam nu-un-tuku še-er-tab-ba mu-un-ná

ED_I r. iii 12 dam nu-tuku šér-díb DU

UM_2: dam nu-un-tuku še-er-tab-ba mu-un-ná; N_7: [... š]e-er-tab-ba mu-un-ná; Ur_4: [...] še-er-tab-ba-aš(or: dili) mu-un-ná

(186) (but) an unmarried man sleeps in a haystack.

187 — é gul-gul-lu-dè é ša-ba-da-an-gul-e

ED$_1$ r. iii 14 — é gul é šè-da-[(x)]

ED$_2$ Fr. 9.1 — [...] ⸢AN⸣(? perhaps = [nà]b?)-gul-gul (text like gir$_4$-gir$_4$)

UM$_2$: é gul-gul-lu-dè é ša-ba-da-an-gul-e; N$_4$: [... -d]è é ša-ba-da-a[n- ...]; N$_7$: [... -d]è é ša-ba-an-da-ná-e; Ur$_4$: [...] é ša-ba-ra-an-[z]é-e

(187) He who is about to destroy houses will destroy (any) house with them.

188 — lú zi-zi-i-dè lú ša-ba-da-an-zi-zi-i

ED$_1$ r. iii 13 — [l]ú zi lú šè-da-[z]i

ED$_2$ Fr. 9 ii — [lú(?)] zi AN.[x (= n[àb?)]-⸢x⸣(like ka, not zi)-e

UM$_2$: lú zi-zi-i-dè lú ša-ba-da-an-zi-zi-i; N$_4$: [... -d]è lú ša-ba-da-a[n- ...]; N$_7$: [... -d]è lú ša-ba-da-zi-zi-i (no an!); Ur$_4$: [...] lú ša-ba-ra-an-zi-zi

(188) He who is about to stir up men will stir up (any) man with them.

189 — gud maḫ-a gú-bi lú a-ba-an-dab$_5$

UM$_2$: gud maḫ-a gú-bi lú a-ba-an-dab$_5$; N$_4$: [...]-bi lú ba-an-d[ab$_5$]; N$_7$: [...] gú-bi lú ba-an-dab$_5$; Ur$_4$: [...] lú ba-an-dab$_5$

(189) After he has held onto the neck of a huge bull,

190 — lú íd-dè ba-ra-an-bal-e

UM$_2$: lú íd-dè ba-ra-an-bal-e; N$_4$: [...]-ra-bal-e; N$_7$: [... -d]a ba-ra-bal-e; Ur$_4$: [... -d]a ba-[x]-bal-e; N$_4$ places line 261 after 190: [lú-gu-la á-diš]-e ga-na-gam(!)-en-dè-[en]

(190) a man can cross a river.

191 — lú-gu-la ere-za-ka ba-e-zal-ta

UM$_2$: lú-gu-la ere-za-ka zag-ba ù-ba-e-zal-ta (ta is written with a very small sign between the signs on the end of lines 253 and 254 on UM 29-13-326 = rev. i 15–16); N$_4$: omits line (cf. above, line 190); N$_7$: [... -k]a zag-zu ba-e-zal-ta (sic!); Ur$_4$: [...]-ti

(191) When you have passed alongside a "big man" of your city,

192 — dumu-ŋu$_{10}$ za-a ur$_5$-re ḫé-em-me-re-a-e$_{11}$-dè

UM$_2$: dumu-ŋu$_{10}$ za-a ur$_5$-re ḫé-em-me-re-a-e$_{11}$-dè; N$_4$: [...] ḫé-em-mu-re-e$_{11}$-d[è]; N$_7$: [...]-⸢an⸣-[...]

(192) my son, this will make you ascend!

193 — géme-⸢zu⸣ ḫur(?)-saŋ-ta ši-im-ta-an-tùm sa$_6$-ga ši-im-ta-an-túm

Cf. ED$_1$ r. vi 3 — še mar ama lú-ra níŋ-sa$_6$-ga nu-túm

UM$_2$: géme-⸢zu⸣ ḫur(?)-saŋ-ta ši-im-ta-an-tùm sa$_6$-ga ši-im-ta-an-túm; N$_4$: [...]-in-da-tùm sa$_6$-ga šà š[i- ...]; K$_2$: (traces)

(193) ⸢Your⸣(?) slave girl, whom you bring down from the mountains, she will bring good;

194 — ḫul ši-in-ga-àm-ta-an-tùm

UM$_2$: ḫul ši-in-ga-àm-ta-an-tùm; N$_4$: [... -a]n-da-tùm; T$_7$: [...] ⸢x⸣-an-[...]; K$_2$: [... ḫu]l ši-in-[...]

(194) (but) she will also bring evil.

195 sa$_6$-ga šu-àm ḫul šà an-ga-àm

UM$_2$: sa$_6$-ga šu-àm ḫul šà an-ga-àm; N$_4$: [... š]à àm-ga-àm; T$_7$: [...] ⸢šu(?)⸣ an-ga-[...]; K$_2$: sa$_6$-ga šu-àm ḫul [...]; cf. SP 22 ii 15–16: sa$_6$-ga šu-àm ḫul šu(sic!) an-ga-àm

(195) The good is a hand, but the evil is also a heart!

196 sa$_6$-ga šà-ge šu nu-bar-re

ED$_I$ r. iii 15 sa[ŋ] ⸢x⸣ ⸢x⸣ nu-BAD

UM$_2$: sa$_6$-ga šà-ge šu nu-bar-re; T$_7$: [...] šu nu-bar-[...]; T$_{19}$: [s]a$_6$- [...]; K$_2$: sa$_6$-ga šà-ge šu nu-b[a- ...]; cf. SP 22 ii 17–19: [sa$_6$-ga] šà-ge [šu nu-bar]-re

(196) The heart cannot let go of the good;

197 ḫul šà-ge šu nu-di-ni-bar-re

ED$_I$ r. iv 1 ḫul šà nu(sic!)-bar(?) TUR

UM$_2$: ḫul šà-ge šu nu-di-ni-bar-re; N$_5$: [...] ⸢x⸣ [...] (x perhaps da); T$_7$: [...] nu-di-ni(!)-bar; T$_{19}$: ḫul šà-g[a ...] (not -ge); Ur$_5$: [...]-ni-ba-[r]e; K$_2$: ḫul šà-ge šu nu-d[a-...]

(197) (but) the heart cannot let go of the evil either.

198 sa$_6$-ga ki-dur$_5$-ru-àm šà-ge nu-tag$_4$-tag$_4$

UM$_2$: sa$_6$-ga ki-dur$_5$-ru-àm šà-ge nu-tag$_4$-tag$_4$; N$_5$: [... -à]m šà-ge nu-tag$_4$-tag$_4$; T$_7$: [... š]à-ge nu-tag$_4$-[tag$_4$]; T$_{19}$: sa$_6$-ga k[i ...]; Ur$_5$: [...] ki-dur$_5$-⸢x⸣-àm šà-ga n[u-t]ag$_4$-tag$_4$; K$_2$: šag$_5$-ga ki-dur$_5$-àm šà(!) [...]; S$_2$: sa$_6$-ga ki-dur$_5$-àm šà-ge nu-tak$_4$-[...]

(198) The good is a watery place that the hearth cannot leave.

199 ḫul é-níŋ-gur$_{11}$-ra ur$_5$-e la-ba-an-gu$_7$-e

UM$_2$: ḫul é-níŋ-< gur$_{11}$>-ra ur$_5$-e la-ba-an-gu$_7$-e; N$_5$: [... g]ur$_{11}$(?)-ra ur$_5$-re la-ba-an-gu$_7$-e; T$_{12}$: [... g]ur$_{11}$-ra ur$_5$-re la-b[a- ...]; T$_{19}$: ḫul é-níŋ-[...]; Ur$_5$: [...]-níŋ-gur$_{11}$-ra ḪAR.ḪAR la-ba-gu$_7$; K$_2$: ḫul é níŋ-gur$_{11}$-ra [...]; S$_2$: ḫul é níŋ-gur$_{11}$-ra ur$_5$ nu-te-e[n(?) ...]; cf. SP 22 ii 23-24: ... [ḫul] é-[gur$_{11}$-ra ur$_5$-e] [la-b]a-an-g[u$_7$-e]

(199) The evil is a storeroom that the interests cannot consume (alt. that does not yield(?) by interest, or: does not consume/feed by interest).

In S$_2$ lines 39–41 follow 199 + a–b

199 A S$_2$ mu-un-sa$_6$ mu-[un]-s[a$_6$]

(199a) She(?) was good, she(?) was good;

199 B S$_2$ ka-ni mu-[un]-ta[g-tag]

(199b) It does not ... her(?) mouth.

200 ḫul-da íd-da má ḫé-en-da-su

ED$_I$ r. iv 2 ḫul-da ⸢A⸣ ⸢má⸣(? doubtful) su

UM$_2$: ⸢ḫul⸣ ⸢x⸣ [...]; N$_5$: [...] íd-da ⸢má⸣(?) ḫé-en-da-su; T$_{11}$: ḫ[ul- ...]; T$_{12}$: [...] íd-da ⸢má⸣(?) ⸢ḫe⸣-⸢en⸣-da-[...]; T$_{19}$: ḫul-da íd-[...]; Ur$_5$: [...] íd-da má(?) ḫé-da-BAD; K$_2$: ḫul-da íd-da [...]; cf. SP 22 ii 25–26: ḫul-da íd-da má ḫé-en-da-su

(200) Let the boat sink in the river with the evil one;

201 an-edin-na ^{kuš}ùmmu ḫé-en-da-dar

ED$_{\text{I}}$ r. iv 3 edin ^{kuš}A.EDIN dar

UM$_2$: (traces); N$_5$: [x]-edin-na ^{kuš}ùmmu(A.EDIN.LÁ) ḫé-en-da-dar; T$_{11}$: an-[...]; T$_{19}$: an-edin-na ^{kuš}[...]; Ur$_5$: [... -n]a ^{kuš}ùmmu ḫé-dar-dar; K$_2$: an-edin-na [...]; TCL: an-ed[in- ...]; cf SP 22 ii 27–28: an-edin-na ^{kuš}ùmmu [ḫé]-dar-dar

(201) let the water skin be split on the high plain with him.

202 šà ki-áŋ níŋ é dù-dù-ù-dam

ED$_{\text{I}}$ r. iv 4 šà ki-áŋ níŋ é dù-dù

N$_5$: [...] ki-áŋ níŋ é dù-dù-ù-dam; T$_{11}$: šà k[i- ...]; T$_{12}$: [...] níŋ é dù-d[ù- ...]; T$_{19}$: šà ki-áŋ n[íŋ ...]; Ur$_5$: [...] ⌜x⌝ níŋ é dù(!)-dù-e; K$_2$: šà ki-áŋ [...]; TCL: šà ki-áŋ [...] é dù-dù-dè

(202) A loving heart is edifying (lit., something that builds houses);

203 šà ḫul-gig níŋ é gul-gul-lu-dam

ED$_{\text{I}}$ r. iv 5 šà ḫu(!) (text: RI)-gig níŋ é gul-gul

N$_5$: [...] ḫul-gig níŋ é gul-gul-lu-dam; T$_{11}$: šà ḫ[ul ...]; T$_{12}$: [...] níŋ é g[ul- ...]; T$_{19}$: šà ḫul gi$_4$(sic!) n[íŋ ...]; Ur$_5$: [... ní]ŋ é gul-gul-e; K$_2$: [...] ḫul-gig [...]; TCL: šà ḫul-gig [...]-gul-lu-dè; cf SP 11.148: šà ḫul-gig níŋ é gul-gul-lu-dam; Sch$_5$: (obv. 3 preceded by traces of two lines not identified) [...] ⌜x⌝(not ḫul)-gig ⌜x⌝(like ga) (traces of 3 more signs)

(203) (but) a hateful heart destroys houses (lit., is something that destroys houses).

204 nir-ŋál-e níŋ-du$_{12}$-du$_{12}$ gaba-ŋál me nam-nun-na

ED$_{\text{I}}$ r. iv 6–7 nir-ŋál níŋ du$_{10}$-du$_{10}$ gaba-ŋál me nam-nun-kam$_4$

N$_5$: [...]-ŋál-e níŋ-du$_{12}$-du$_{12}$ gaba-ŋál me nam-nun(!)-na; T$_{11}$: nir-ŋál [...]; T$_{12}$: [... -d]ug$_4$(?) gaba ⌜ŋál⌝ [...]; T$_{19}$: nir-ŋál níŋ-tu[ku ...]; Ur$_5$: [... -d]u$_8$-du$_8$ gaba-ŋál me nam-nun-na-k[a](?); TCL: nir-ŋál níŋ-du$_{12}$-du$_{12}$ (coll. Dahl) gaba(!)-ŋ[ál me] nam-nun-na; Sch$_5$: [...] (omitted?)

(204) To an authority, riches and a stout appearance are princely charismatic powers.

205 nir-ŋál-ra gú ḫé-en-ne-ni-ŋál

ED$_{\text{I}}$ r. iv 8 gaba-ŋál gú ḫé-ŋál

N$_5$: [... ni]r-ŋál-ra gú ḫé-en-ne-ni-ŋál; T$_{11}$: nir-ŋál [...]; T$_{12}$: (traces); Ur$_5$: [... g]ú ḫé-ne-ni-⌜x⌝; TCL: nir-ŋál-ra gú ḫé-en-ne-ni-⌜ŋál⌝(copy misleading); Sch$_5$: [...] (traces, may not belong here)

(205) The neck should be bent to the respected;

206 á-tuku ní-zu ḫé-en-ne-ši-lá

ED$_{\text{I}}$ r. iv 9 á-tuku KA-zu$_5$ ḫé-lá

N$_5$: á-tuku ní-zu ḫé-en-ne-ši-lá; T$_{11}$: á-tu[ku ...]; Ur$_5$: [... n]í-zu ḫé:ni:ne-lá; TCL: á tuku ní-zu ḫé-en-ne-al-al (copy correct, coll. Dahl); Sch$_5$: [...] ⌜x⌝ ní-zu ḫé-ga(? hardly bi)-ni(?)-lá(?)

(206) yourself should be prostrated before the powerful,

207 dumu-ŋu$_{10}$ lú-ḫul-ŋál ḫé-en-ne-ši-ŋál-le

ED_I r. iv 10 lú-ḫul-ŋál ḫé-⸢x⸣

N_5: dumu-ŋu$_{10}$ lú-ḫul-ŋál-ra ḫé-en-ne-ši-ŋál-le; T_{11}: dumu-m[u ...]; Ur_5: [...]-ḫul-úr ḫé-en-ši-ŋál; TCL: dumu(coll.)-ŋu$_{10}$ lú-ḫul-la-ra ḫé-en-ne-ši-⸢x⸣ (coll.); Sch_5: [... ŋá]l-la-ra ⸢ḫé-em⸣-ši-ŋ[ál-l]e

(207) My son, (then) you will stand up against the evil ones.

208 ezem-ma-ka dam na-an-du$_{12}$-du$_{12}$-e

N_5: ezem-⸢ma⸣-ka dam na-an-dù-dù-e; Ur_5: [... -k]a dam na-ba-du$_{12}$-du$_{12}$; TCL: ezem-ma-kam dam(coll.) na-an-du$_{12}$-du$_{12}$; Sch_5: (obv. 6): ⸢ezem⸣-ma-ka dam na-⸢x⸣(looks like UD)-⸢x⸣(looks like en, but too long); cf. SP 11.150: ezem-ma-kam dam na-an-du$_{12}$-du$_{12}$-un-e-še

(208) Don't choose a wife during a festival.

209 šà-ga ḫuŋ-ŋá-àm bar-ra ḫuŋ-ŋá-àm

N_5: [... ḫu]n-ŋá-àm bar-ra ḫuŋ-ŋá-àm; Ur_5: [... b]ar-ra ḫuŋ-ŋá-àm; TCL: šà-ga ḫuŋ-ŋá-àm bar-ra ḫuŋ-ŋá-àm; Sch_5 (obv. 8–9): [š]à-ga ḫuŋ-ŋá-àm ⸢bar⸣(?)-ra ⸢ḫuŋ⸣-ŋá-àm; cf SP 4.18: [túg ḫuŋ-ŋ]á-àm gada ḫuŋ-ŋá-àm za ḫuŋ-ŋ[á-à]m šu ḫé-ma-ŋál

(209) inside it is (all) borrowed, outside it is (all) borrowed:

210 kù ḫuŋ-ŋá-àm za-gìn ḫuŋ-ŋá-àm

N_5: [kù-à]m za ḫuŋ-ŋá-àm za ḫuŋ-ŋá-àm(sic!); Ur_5: [...] ⸢x⸣ DUB ḫuŋ-ŋá-àm (Wilcke: na$_4$.n]ír!); TCL: kù ḫuŋ-ŋá-àm za-gìn ḫuŋ-ŋá-àm; Sch_5 (obv. 10–11): ([x]) kù ⸢huŋ⸣(?)-ŋá-àm ([...]?) ⸢za⸣(?)-gìn huŋ-ŋá-àm

(210) the silver is borrowed; the lapis lazuli is borrowed;

211 *túg(?) ḫuŋ-ŋá-àm gada(?) ḫuŋ-ŋá-àm

N_5: [...]-ùŋ(?)-ŋá-àm; Ur_5: [... z]a-gìn ḫuŋ-ŋá-àm; TCL: *túg(text: NÍGIN?, copy correct) ḫuŋ-ŋá-àm gada(possible, coll.; copy: PA) ḫuŋ-ŋá-àm; Sch_5 (obv. 11): túg(?)] huŋ-ŋá-àm (nothing missing)

(211) the dress(?) is borrowed; the linen(?) is borrowed;

212 [...] mu-un-da-sá

N_5: [... -a]n-da(?)-sá; Ur_5: [...]-mu-un-da-sá-a; Sch_5 (rev. 1): [...] ⸢lú⸣ ta ⸢mu⸣(?)-⸢x⸣(looks like ra)-sá(looks like ki) (or may not belong here?)

(212) [she(?) is] comparable [to ...].

213 gud [...(?)] ní-ŋ[ál na]-⸢an⸣-ni-sa$_{10}$-sa$_{10}$

ED_I o. v 1 ⸢gud⸣ na-MUNŠUB ⸢gud⸣ e-KAL

UM_2: (traces); C_2: gud [...] ní-ŋ[ál]; N_5: [... na]-⸢an⸣-ni-sa$_{10}$-sa$_{10}$

(213) Don't buy an ox that spreads terror;

214 gud-l[ul-l]a na-[s]a$_{10}$-sa$_{10}$ é-tùr gul(?)-l[a-àm]

ED_I o. v 2 gud-lul na-ḫuŋ(ŠÈ)-ḫuŋ(ŠÈ) KA LUM GABA-kam$_4$

UM_2: [...]-la na-ab-s[a$_{10}$- ...] é-tùr gul(?)-l[a-àm]; C_2: gud-l[ul-l]a na-[s]a$_{10}$-sa$_{10}$ é [...]

(214) Don't buy a vicious bull, (it means) a destroyed cattle pen.

215 munus-zi gán-zi-šè lú ši-i[n-ŋá-ŋá]

ED$_1$ o. v 5 munus-z[i (x)] gán ⌜x⌝

UM$_2$: munus-zi gán-zi-šè lú š[i- ...]; C$_2$: munus-zi gán zi-šè lú ši-i[n- ...]; T$_{20}$: [...] lú ⌜x⌝ [...]

(215) A man [installs] a good woman as a fertile field.

216 u$_4$-buru$_{14}$-ka anše na-an-sa$_{10}$-sa$_{10}$

UM$_2$: u$_4$-buru$_{14}$-ka an e na-an-[...]; C$_2$: u$_4$-buru$_{14}$-ka anše n[a]-a[n]-[...]; T$_{20}$: [...] na-[a]b-sa$_{10}$-sa$_{10}$

(216) At the time of the harvest don't buy a donkey;

217 anše LA gu$_7$ anše-da im-[...]

UM$_2$: anše LA KA anše-da i[m- ...]; C$_2$: anše LA gu$_7$ anše-da im-[...]; T$_{20}$: [...]-da ⌜im⌝-[...]

(217) A donkey that eats ... will ... with a donkey.

218 anše-lul-la gú-tar im-lá

UM$_2$: anše-lul-la gú-tar im-lá; C$_2$: anše-lul-la gú-tar im-[lá]; T$_{20}$: [...]-tar im-lá; K$_1$: [x x]-⌜la⌝ gú-ta[r i]m-lá

(218) A vicious donkey hangs with the neck;

219 dumu-ŋu$_{10}$ lú-lul-e zag-si mu-un-sa$_6$-sa$_6$

UM$_2$: dumu-ŋu$_{10}$ lú-lul-e zag-si mu-un-sa$_6$-sa$_6$; C$_2$: dumu-ŋu$_{10}$ lú-lul-la zag-si mu-un-s[a$_6$- ...]; T$_{13}$: dumu-ŋu$_{10}$ lú-[...]; T$_{20}$: [...] še-si mu-un-sa$_6$-[...]; K$_1$: dumu-ŋu$_{10}$ lú-lul-la zag-si mu-un-sa$_6$-sa$_6$

(219) (but) my son, a liar makes (his) shoulders(?) pleasant (to look at).

220 munus-bar-šu-ŋál-e é dúr-bi-šè mu-un-du

ED$_1$ r. iv 11–12 munus-bar-[š]u šè-ŋál | [x x x]-šè du

UM$_2$: munus-bar-šu-ŋál-e é dúr-bi-šè mu-un-du; C$_2$: [mu]nus-bar-šu-ŋál-e é dúr-bi-šè mu-un-[...]; T$_{13}$: munus-bar-šu-ŋál-[...]; T$_{20}$: [...] é dúr-bi mu-un-[x]; K$_1$: munus-bar-šu-ŋál-la [... d]úr-bi-šè mu-un-du$_8$

(220) A woman who has a fortune ruins a house.

221 KAŠ kúrun naŋ-naŋ-e buru$_{14}$ im-su-su-su

ED$_1$ r. iv 13 [x kú]run naŋ-naŋ gu[ru$_7$] šè-LAGAB-LAGAB

UM$_2$: KAŠ kúrun naŋ-naŋ-e buru$_{14}$ im-su-su-su; C$_2$: [...] naŋ-naŋ-e buru$_{14}$ im-su-su-[...]; T$_{13}$: KAŠ kúrun naŋ-naŋ-[...]; T$_{20}$: [... bu]ru$_{14}$ im-su-[s]u-s[u]; K$_1$: [...] kú[run n]a-an-na-ak-⌜ak⌝ [... i]m-su-su

(221) A drunkard drowns the harvest.

222 munus-šu-ḫa ^{ŋiš}kun$_5$ lú min-e da nu-sá

UM$_2$: munus-šu-ḫa ^{ŋiš}kun$_5$ lú min-e da nu-sá; C$_2$: [...] ^{ŋiš}kun$_5$ [l]ú min-e da nu-[...]; T$_{13}$: munus-šu-ḫa ^{ŋiš}k[un$_5$ ...]; T$_{20}$: [...] TUR-(LU erased)-ÉŠ [... d]a nu-sá; K$_1$: [...] ⌜x⌝ lú [...]

(222) A fisherwoman (is like?) a ladder that (not even) a couple of men can make stand upright(?):

223 é-a nim-gim mi-ni-ib-dal-dal-en

UM$_2$: é-a nim-gim mi-ni-ib-dal-dal-en; C$_2$: [... ni]m-gim mi-ni-íb-dal-[...]; T$_{13}$: é-a nim-g[im ...]; T$_{20}$: [...]-ni-ib-dal-dal-e; I$_{14}$: [... -r]a(?) (apparently does not belong here); K$_1$: [...] mi-ni-ib-dal-dal

(223) "like a fly, you make it fly into all houses";

224 ème sila-a inim ì-šid-e

UM$_{2}$: ème(SAL.ANŠE) sila-a inim ì-šid-e; C$_{2}$: [...]-a inim ì-š[id- ...]; T$_{13}$: e[me$_{3}$ ...]; T$_{20}$: [... in]im ì-šid-e; I$_{14}$: [... -r]a(?)-šid(? or: gù ì-r]a-ra); K$_{1}$: [...] in[im ì]-šid-e

(224) A she-donkey recites words in the street.

225 SAL.ŠAḪ sila-a dumu-ni-ra ga mu-ni-ib-gu$_{7}$-e

UM$_{2}$: SAL.ŠAḪ sila-a dumu-ni-ra ga mu-ni-ib-gu$_{7}$-e; C$_{2}$: [...] ⸢x⸣ dumu-ni-r[a] g[a ...]; N$_{7}$: [...]-e; T$_{20}$: [... -n]i-ra ga mu-[...]; I$_{14}$: [...] dumu-ni-ra ⸢x⸣ mu-ni-ib-gu$_{7}$-e; K$_{1}$: [... -r]a ga mu-[ni-í]b-gu$_{7}$-e

(225) A sow suckles her young in the streets.

226 munus-zú-ur$_{5}$-ak KA×LI gi$_{4}$-gi$_{4}$-dam

UM$_{2}$: munus-zú-ur$_{5}$-ak KA×LI gi$_{4}$-gi$_{4}$-dam; I$_{14}$: [...]-ak gi$_{4}$-gi$_{4}$-gi$_{4}$-da; N$_{7}$: [...]-⸢gi$_{4}$-gi$_{4}$⸣-da; T$_{20}$: [... -g]i$_{4}$-g[i$_{4}$ ...]; K$_{1}$: ⸢x⸣ [...] KA-x [... -g]i$_{4}$-dè (coll. Taylor)

(226) A woman who prickles herself will be screaming;

227 ^{ŋiš}bala ur$_{5}$-ra šu-na na-mu-un-ŋál

UM$_{2}$: ^{ŋiš}bala ur$_{5}$-ra šu-na na-mu-un-[...]; I$_{14}$: [... b]ala zú-ur$_{5}$-ra šu-na na-mu-un-ŋál; N$_{7}$: [...] na-mu-un-ŋál; K$_{1}$: bala ⸢x⸣ (= gim?) ur$_{5}$-ra šu bí-ŋál (coll. Taylor)

(227) she holds the spindle on which she was hurt(?) in her hand;

228 é-é-a i-in-ku$_{4}$-ku$_{4}$-ku$_{4}$

UM$_{2}$: é-é-a i-in-ku$_{4}$-ku$_{4}$-k[u$_{4}$ ...]; I$_{14}$: [...] é-a i-ni-in-ku$_{4}$-ku$_{4}$; N$_{7}$: [...]-ni-in-ku$_{4}$-ku$_{4}$; K$_{1}$: é-é-a i-ni-ku$_{4}$-[ku$_{4}$]-ku$_{4}$

(228) she enters all houses;

229 e-sír e-sír-ra gú mu-un-gi-gi-dè

UM$_{2}$: e-sír e-sír-ra gú mu-un-⸢x⸣-[...]; T$_{19}$: [e]-sír [...]; K$_{1}$: e-sír e-sír-ra gú mu-un-⸢gi⸣-gi-dè

(229) she peers into all streets;

230 ⸢da⸣ ⸢ùr⸣(?)-ra im-me im-me è-è

UM$_{2}$: [...] ⸢x⸣ i(?)-im(?)-me im-d[ug$_{4}$ ...]; T$_{19}$: á(or: da) ùr-ra [...]; K$_{1}$: ⸢da⸣(?) ⸢ùr⸣(?)-ra im-me im-me è-è (coll. Taylor)

(230) and keeps saying from the roofs(?): "Get out!"

231 bàd-si bàd-si-a igi mu-ši-⸢x⸣-íl-íl(?)-e

T$_{19}$: bàd-si b[àd- ...]; K$_{1}$: bàd-si bàd-si-a igi mu-ši-⸢x⸣-íl-íl(?)-e (Taylor: si correct in both cases)

(231) she keeps watching from all parapets;

232 ki du$_{14}$-dè ŋál-la-šè zi im- ...

T$_{19}$: ki du$_{14}$-d[a(?) ...]; K$_{1}$: ki du$_{14}$-dè ŋál-la-šè zi im-x-[x(-x)]-RI (coll. Taylor)

(232) she(?) pants(?) toward a place where there is a quarrel,

233 ki mu-[š]ub-ba á-za [x x] ⸢x⸣ im-[x]

T$_{19}$: ki mu-šub-[...]; K$_{1}$: ki mu [š]ub-ba á-za [x x] ⸢x⸣ im-[x] (coll. Taylor)

(233–234) (*Too poorly preserved for translation*)

234 zi ⸢x⸣-ge$_{4}$-eš mu-un-ne(?)-pà ši-mi-ni-dug$_{4}$

T$_{19}$: KA ere [...]; K$_{1}$: zi ⸢x⸣-ge$_{4}$-eš mu-un-ne(?)-pà ši-mi-ni-dug$_{4}$

235 *[inim-di]ri(?) šà-ḫul-gig ˹du$_{12}$˺-˹du$_{12}$˺

Cf. ED$_{I}$ r. v 3 inim-diri bu-bu$_{7}$(KU) šà ḫu-gig šè-du$_{8}$-du$_{8}$

T$_{19}$: bar-sud [...]; K$_{I}$: [x x]-ke$_{4}$(erased) šà-ḫul-gig ˹du$_{12}$˺-˹du$_{12}$˺ (coll. Taylor)

(235) *[A word of arrogance] entails(?) a hateful heart.

236 dumu-ŋu$_{10}$ [x x] lum-lam$_{x}$(LUM) mi-ni-ib-za

K$_{I}$: [x x x] ˹x˺ lum-lam$_{x}$(LUM) mi-ni-ib-za; T$_{19}$: ˹dumu-ŋu$_{10}$˺ [...]; Ur$_{6}$: lum-lum ḫé-ni-[...] (rev. I' 2, assigned line number 242 below, belongs here?)

(236) My son ...

237 ...

T$_{19}$: ˹ki(?)/šà(?)˺ [...]; K$_{I}$: [...] a ˹x˺ ˹x˺ in-TAR; Ur$_{6}$: ki-a naŋ-e [...] (rev. I' 1, assigned to line number 241 below, belongs here?)

(237–240) (Too poorly preserved for translation)

238 ...

T$_{19}$: ˹x˺ [...]; K$_{I}$: [...] ˹x˺ ˹x˺ [...]-tùm

239 ...

K$_{I}$: [...]-ná

240 ...

UM$_{2}$: (traces); C$_{2}$: (traces); K$_{I}$: [...]-DU

Unplaceable: T$_{19}$ left edge:

a-ba ì-lá a-gim ši-in-TAR (or: a-ba-ni-lá 2-gim, etc.).

T$_{12}$ = 3N-T 905,186 rev.:

1–2 illegible traces
3 [...] ši(?) lú [...]
4 [...] ˹x˺(like ki) [...]
5 [...] ˹e$_{11}$˺-na-ka š[u- (or similar)...]

(line 5 as read from my own transliteration; the copy shows:
DU e na-ka n[u ...])
Double line = end of excerpt.

T$_{13}$, rev.
1 ˹a˺-b[a (or similar) ...]
2 níŋ ˹x˺ [...]
3 UD ˹x˺ [...]
4 ur(?) ˹x˺ [...]
5 ^{kuš}lu-úb-[...]
(traces)

The following section of Ur$_{6}$ rev. i' cannot be placed with certainty, but must belong after 240. It is tentatively numbered 241–248.

241 = 1' ki-a naŋ-e [...] (cf. 237)

242 = 2 lum-lum ḫé-ni-[...] (cf. 236)

(241–245) (No translation attempted)

243 = 3 e gú dù lá-e [?]
in-šè ŋál(?) [...]
addir(NÍG.A.BI.GIŠ.NÍG.UD)
x(like im or nam?) ga-ab-[...]

244 = 4 u$_4$-min-šè x [...] / (erasure) x x [...]

245 = du$_5$(?) x (like TUM) géme-gim ⸢igi+X⸣? [...]
im-da šà(?) lá TÚG UD šà
/ gal-KU-NI in-lá

246 = 6 tu-ra dùg-ga-a-ni [x?]

(246) A sick man's recovery [...].

247 = 7 nam-⸢gig-ga⸣-àm ⸢im⸣-[x]
du$_{14}$ nam-mú-m[ú-dè] / NI IM ni [...]

248 = 8 ⸢x⸣ in [...]

(247) [When affected(?) by] disease [...] don't make a quarrel [...].

Connection Uncertain

(Connection uncertain)

250

C$_2$: ⸢x⸣ (like in, or similar) [...]; UM$_2$: ⸢x⸣ (dam/mi, or similar) [x (x)] ⸢x⸣ (like lugal) [... ½ line ...]

251 šà-ḫúl-la i-im-diri-g[e ...]

UM$_2$: šà-ḫúl-la i-im-diri-g[e ...]; C$_2$: šà- [...] ⸢x⸣ [...]

(251) A heart overflowing with joy [...].

252 níŋ-nam nu-kal zi ku$_7$-ku$_7$-da

UM$_2$: níŋ-nam nu-kal zi ku$_7$-ku$_7$-da; C$_2$: níŋ-nam nu-kal ⸢x⸣ [...]; BM$_2$: (traces of one sign)

(252) Nothing at all is of value, but life should be sweet tasting.

253 níŋ nam-kal-kal-en níŋ-e me-kal-kal

UM$_2$: níŋ nam-kal-kal-en níŋ-e me-kal-kal; C$_3$: [...] níŋ-e mu-e-[...]; BM$_2$: [...] níŋ [...]; N 2715: [...]-⸢kal-en⸣ níŋ-⸢e⸣ m[u- ...]

(253) Don't appreciate things (too much); (because then) things will evaluate you (i.e., you will become dependent on their evaluation).

254 dumu-ŋu$_{10}$ gùn-gim igi gùn-gùn

UM$_2$: dumu-ŋu$_{10}$ gùn-gim igi-gùn-gùn; C$_3$: [...] gùn-gim igi gùn-g[ùn]; N$_6$: (traces); T$_{21}$: dumu-ŋ[u$_{10}$ ...]; BM$_2$: (traces of one sign); N 2715: [...] ⸢ḪU⸣-ḪU-gim [...]

(254) My son, there will be eyes of as many colors as there are colors (lit. eyes will be as multicolored as multicolors).

255 ^{d}ašnan-ra na-an-šèr-šèr-re-dè-en ŋiš-á-bi ì-šár

UM$_2$: ^{d}ašnan-ra na-an-šèr-šèr-re-dè-en ŋiš-á-bi ì-šár; C$_3$: [... -r]a na-an-šèr-šèr-r[e- ...^{ŋiš}á-b]i ì-[šár]; N$_6$: [^{d}aš]nan-r[a ...]; T$_{21}$: ^{d}ašnan-ra [...]; BM$_2$: [...]-an-šèr-šèr-r[e- ...]; N 2715: [... -a]n-šèr-šèr-re-d[a- ...]

(255) (Don't say) to the grain "Don't bind me!"; its branches are many!

256 kir$_{11}$-e áš nam-en dumu-munus in-ù-tu-un

UM$_2$: kir$_{11}$-e áš nam-en dumu-munus in-ù-tu-un; C$_3$: [...] ⸢x⸣ dumu-munus in-ù-t[u ...]; N$_6$: kir$_{11}$ áš nam-[...]; T$_{21}$: ⸢kir$_{11}$⸣-re áš n[am- ...]; BM$_2$: [...]-me(?)-en dumu-mu[nus ...]; N 2715 [... na]m-me dumu-munus i[n- ...]

(256) Don't abuse(? lit., curse) a ewe; (then) you will give birth to a daughter!

257 mi-si-saḫar-a lag nam-bí-šub-bé-en dumu-ninta in-ù-tu-un

UM$_2$: mi-si-saḫar-a lag nam-bí-šub-bé-en dumu-ninta in-ù-tu-un; C$_3$: [...]-ra lag nam-ba-e-šub-b[é- ...] in-ù-tu-[...]; N$_6$: ^{ŋiš}mi-si-sa[ḫa]r-r[a ...] dumu-ninta i[n- ...]; T$_{21}$: ^{ŋiš}mi-si-saḫar-ra [...]; BM$_2$: [...]-ra ⸢lag⸣ na-bí-íb-šub-bé-[...]; N 2715: [...]-ra lag nam-bi(sic!)-š[ub- ...]

(257) Don't throw a lump (of clay) into a money chest; (then) you will give birth to a son!

258 dam nam-mu-un-kar-re-en gú KA na-an-ŋá-ŋá

UM$_2$: dam nam-mu-un-kar-re-en gú KA na-an-ŋá-ŋá; C$_3$: [... -k]ar-re gù KA na-an-ŋá-ŋá; N$_6$: dam mu-kar-re gù K[A ...]; T$_{21}$: omits line; BM$_2$: omits line; N 2715: [...]-kar-re gù KA [...]

(258) Don't abduct a wife; don't raise an outcry!

259 ki dam kar-re nam-silig gum-ŋá-àm

UM$_2$: ki dam kar-re nam-silig gum-ŋá-àm; C$_3$: [...] nam-silig gum-ŋá-àm; N$_8$: [x] dam kar-⸢re⸣ [...]; N$_6$: ki dam kar nam-silig gum-ŋá-[...]; T$_{21}$: ki dam kar-re [...]; T$_{22}$: ki dam kar-re nam-silig gum-ŋá-àm; BM$_2$: [...] nam-sil[ig ...]; N 2715: [... na]m-silig gum-ŋ[á- ...]

(259) At a place where a wife has been abducted, the decimation is crushing!

260 a ŋìri a gú níŋin-na ga-àm-me-re$_7$-dè-en

UM$_2$: a ŋìri a gú níŋin-na ga-àm-me-re$_7$-dè-en; C$_3$: [... n]a ga-àm-[m]a-re$_7$-en-dè-en; N$_6$: a ŋìri gú níŋin-na ga-àm-m[a- ...]; N$_8$: [x] ŋìri a gú níŋin-na [...]; T$_{21}$: [a] ŋìri a g[ú ...]; T$_{22}$: a ŋìri a gú-níŋin-na ga-àm-me-DU-x-dè-en; BM$_2$: [...] ga-an-ši-re$_7$-e[n- ...]; N 2715: (traces of one sign)

(260) (Saying) "Oh (my) foot; oh (my) neck," let us go round in circles.

261 lú-gu-la á-diš-e ga-na-gam-me-en-dè-en

UM$_2$: lú-gu-la á-diš-e ga-na-gam-me-en-dè; C$_3$: [... di]š-e ga-na-gam(!)-en-dè-en; N$_4$: (following line 190); N$_6$: lú-gu-la á-diš-e ga-n[a- ...]; N$_8$: [x] gu-⸢la⸣ ⸢á⸣ [...]; T$_{22}$: lú-gu-la á diš-e ga-na-gam-e-dè-en; BM$_2$: [...]-⸢diš⸣-e ga-na-gam-e-[...]

(261) The «big man», let us make him bow down with «one arm» (i.e., with united forces).

262 galam-ma na-an-ug$_5$-ge-en dumu in-sù-ge tu-da

UM$_2$: galam-ma na-an-ug$_5$-ge-en dumu in-sù-ge tu-da; C$_3$: [... -g]e-[...] dumu in-sù-ge tu-ud-da; N$_6$: galam-ma na-an-ug$_5$-ge-e[n ...]; N$_9$: (traces); T$_{22}$: galam-ma na-an-⸢x⸣-ge-en dumu ⸢x sù-ge⸣ tu-da; BM$_2$: [... -u]g$_5$-ge dumu in-sù-g[e ...]

(262) Don't kill an "artful one" (lit., elaborate one); the child is born in vain(?) (lit., emptiness?);

263 en-ra BAD-a-gim ^{d}nanna-ug$_5$-ge-en šu na-an-dù-dù-en

UM$_2$: en-ra BAD-a-gim ^{d}nanna-ug$_5$-ge-en šu na-an-dù-dù-en; C$_3$: [... ^{d}nan]na-ug$_5$-ge-e[n ...]-dù-e; N$_6$: [...]-a-gim ^{d}nan[na ...]; N$_9$: [...] šu na-an-dù-d[ù- ...]; T$_{22}$: ⸢en-ra(?)⸣ BAD(?)-a-gim ^{d}nanna ge ⸢ŋá⸣ šu na-an-dù-dù-en; BM$_2$: [...] ^{d}nanna-ug$_5$-{ga}-ge-⸢en⸣ ⸢x⸣ [...]

(263) Don't kill (him?) like a ... before a lord; don't bind him.

264 ummeda ga-arḫuš-a-ke$_4$ lugal-bi-ir nam ši-im-mi-ib-tar-re

UM$_2$: ummeda ga-arḫuš-a-ke$_4$ lugal-bi-ir nam ši-im-mi-ib-tar-re; C$_3$: [...]-bi-ir na[m ...]; N$_9$: [...] ga-lá-arḫuš-a-ke$_4$ lugal-bi-ir [...]; T$_{22}$: ⸢ummeda-ga x-a-ke$_4$ lugal-bi⸣-ir ⸢nam ši-im-mi-ib⸣-tar-re; BM$_2$: [... -k]e$_4$ lugal-bi-⸢x⸣ [...]

(264) The wet-nurses of the milk of mercy decide the destinies for their lords.

(alt.: The wet-nurses of the women's quarters decide the destiny for their lords.)

265 ama-zu-úr inim-diri nam-ba-na-ab-bé-en ḫul ša-ba-ra-gig-ga-àm

UM$_2$: ama-zu-úr inim-diri nam-ba-na-[...] ḫul ša-ba-ra-gig-ga-à[m]; N$_9$: ama-zu inim-diri nam-ba-na-a[b- ...]; T$_{22}$: [ama-z]u-úr ⸢inim diri nam⸣-ba-an-na-ab-bé-en

(265) Don't speak an arrogant word to your mother; there will be hatred caused against you.

266 inim ama-za inim diŋir-za ka-šè nam-bí-ib-díb-bé-en

ED$_I$ r. vii 7–8 [inim a-a-za inim-diŋir-za]-gim | GIŠ.[TÚG.PI] [ḫ]é-ak

UM$_2$: [...] ⸢x⸣-šè nam-bí-ib-díb-bé-en; N$_9$: inim ama-za inim diŋir-za ka-šè n[am- ...]; T$_{22}$: [...]-bí-ib-dab$_5$-bé-en

(266) Your mother's words (and) the words of your god, don't take them to (your) mouth!

267 ama ^{d}utu-à[m] lú mu-un-ù-tu

UM$_2$: [...] mu-un-ù-tu; N$_9$: [a]ma ^{d}utu-à[m] lú mu-u[n- ...]; T$_{22}$: [...] ⸢ù⸣-tu; T$_{23}$: [...] ^{d}utu-à[m ...]

(267) A mother is (like) Utu who gives birth (i.e., life) to man(kind);

268 ab-ba diŋir-ra-à[m (x)] mu-un-zala-zala-ge

UM$_2$: [...] mu-un-zala-zala-ge; N$_9$: [a]b-ba diŋir-à[m x] mu-[...]; T$_{23}$: ab-ba diŋir-ra [...]

(268) a father is (like a personal) god who makes [a name(?)] shine.

269 ab-ba diŋir-àm [i]nim-ma-ni zi-da

UM$_2$: [... i]nim-ma-ni zi-da; N$_8$: [a]b-ba diŋ[ir ...]; T$_{23}$: ab-ba diŋir-àm; Ur$_6$: ⸢ab⸣-[ba ...] / zi-[...]

(269) A father is like a (personal) god; his words are just;

270 na-ri ab-ba-šè ŋizzal ḫé-em-ši-ia-ak

UM$_2$: [...] ŋizzal [ḫé-e]m-ši-ia-ak; T$_{23}$: na-ri ab-ba-šè giz[zal ...]; Ur$_6$: na(!)-ri ab-ba ŋizzal ḫé-em-ši-ŋál

(270) you should pay attention to the instructions of a father!

271 é ere-bar-ra-ke$_4$ ere šà-ga ši-dù-dù-e

ED$_I$ r. vi 2 é šà ere šà šè-dù-dù

UM$_2$: [... -k]e$_4$ ere šà-ga ši-dù-dù-e; T$_{23}$: é ere-bar-ra-ke$_4$ e[re ...]; Ur$_6$: é ere bar-ra-ke$_4$ ere šà-ga / ši-dù-dù-e

(271) The houses on the outskirts of a city maintain the houses inside the city.

272 dumu-ŋu$_{10}$ gán e dúr-bi-šè ŋ[ál-la]

ED$_I$ r. vi 4 gán dur$_5$ dúr-šè ŋál

UM$_2$: [... -b]i-šè ŋál-la; N$_{10}$: dumu-ŋu$_{10}$ gán ⸢e⸣ [...]; T$_{23}$: dumu-ŋu$_{10}$ gán e dúr-bi-šè ŋ[ál- ...]; Ur$_6$ (4): dumu-ŋu$_{10}$ gán(? rather than é) tùr-šè ŋál-⸢la⸣

(272) My son, a field placed in the bottommost position (in relation to) a ditch,

273 al-dur$_5$ kur$_6$-ra-àm al-ḫád kur$_6$-ra-àm

ED$_I$ r. vi 4 an-dur$_5$ kur$_6$(!)-rum an-ḫád(UD) kur$_6$(!)-rum

UM$_2$: [... a]l-ḫád kur$_6$-ra-àm / [al-dur$_5$ k]ur$_6$-ra-àm; C$_3$: traces; N$_{10}$: al-dur$_5$ ku[r$_6$- ...]; T$_{23}$: al-dur$_5$ kur$_6$-ra-àm al-UD k[ur$_6$- ...]; Ur$_6$ (5): al-<ḫád> kur$_6$-àm al-dur$_5$-⸢ra⸣

(273) whether it is wet, it is a field that provides a source of income, or whether it is dry, it is nevertheless a field that provides a source of income.

274 níŋ ú-gu dé-a níŋ-me-ŋar-ra

ED$_I$ r. vi 8 níŋ u$_4$-[g]u-dé níŋ-mud$_5$

C$_3$: [...] ú-g[u- ...]; UM$_2$: [...]-⸢íb⸣-⸢sì⸣; N$_{10}$: níŋ ú-gu dé-[...]; T$_{23}$: níŋ ú-gu dé-a níŋ-me-ŋar-⸢x⸣ lá (NB like šè) [...]; Ur$_6$ (6): níŋ ⸢gu-dé⸣ níŋ-me-ŋar-ra

(274) To lose something is awful.

275 gín-dilmun^{ki}-na sa$_{10}$-šè *sù(? copy TE)-ga

ED$_I$ r. vi 9 [x (x)] ⸢x⸣ gín [x (x)] an [x x] ki ta TAR x

C$_3$: [... g]ín-dilm[un ...]; N$_{10}$: urudu(?)-gín-dilmun [...]; T$_{23}$: ⸢gín⸣-dilmun^{ki}-na-sa$_{10}$-šè í[l(?)- ...]; Ur$_6$ (7): ⸢x⸣ [x x]-⸢na⸣ sa$_{10}$-šè TE(hardly šà-ga)

(275) To buy at the (standard of the) Dilmun shekel is *a sure loss(?).

276 ur nu-zu ḫul-àm lú nu-zu ḫuš-àm

ED$_I$ r. vi 6 ⸢x⸣ GÍR ur nu-zu ḫuš

C$_3$: [...]-⸢àm⸣ lú ⸢nu⸣-[...]; N$_{10}$: ur nu-zu ḫ[ul- ...]; T$_{23}$: ur nu-zu ḫul-àm lú nu-z[u ...]; Ur$_6$ (8): ki nu-⸢zu⸣ ḫuš-àm / ur nu-zu téš-àm

(276) A unknown dog is evil; an unknown man [is horrible].

277 kaskal nu-zu gaba kur-ra-ka

C$_3$: [... ga]ba-kur-ra [...] ⸢x⸣; N$_{10}$: [x n]u-⸢zu⸣ [...]; T$_{23}$: kaskal nu-zu gaba kur-r[a-ka]; T$_{24}$: kaskal nu-[zu ...]; Ur$_6$ (9): [...] nu-zu gaba kur-ra-ka

(277) On an unknown road at the edge of the mountains,

278 diŋir-kur-ra lú gu$_7$-gu$_7$-ù-[me]-eš

C$_3$: [...]-gu$_7$-gu$_7$-ù-[me]-eš; N$_{10}$: diŋir-kur-ra lú gu$_7$-[gu$_7$-ù-me-eš]; T$_{24}$: diŋir-kur-ra [...]; Ur$_6$ (10): [x] kur-ra lú gu$_7$-gu$_7$-/u(sic!?)-me-eš

(278) the gods of the mountains are man-eaters;

279 é lú-gim nu-dù ere lú-gim nu-dù

C$_3$: [x x -gi]m nu-dù ere lú-gim nu-dù; T$_{23}$: é lú-gim nu-dù ere lú-[gim nu-dù]; T$_{24}$: é lú [...]; Ur$_6$ (11): [... -g]im nu-dù [...]-⸢dù⸣

(279) they do not build houses like men; they do not build cities like men;

280 ki-<nu>-zu-a lú-ka lú ša-ba-ra-an-è-dè

C$_3$: [...]-ka lú ša-ba-ra-an-è-dè; T$_{23}$: ⸢x⸣ ⸢x⸣-a lú-ka lú ša-ba-[ra-an-è-dè]; T$_{24}$: ki-zu-a [...]

(280) it is characteristic of men from *[un]known(?) places that they descend (scl., from the mountains);

281 sipa-⸢ra(?)⸣ ⸢ú⸣(?) kiŋ-kiŋ mu-na-til udu gi$_4$-gi$_4$ mu-na-til

C$_3$: [...] kiŋ-kiŋ mu-na-til udu gi$_4$-gi$_4$ [...]; T$_{23}$: (traces, maybe [x x] ⸢x⸣ ⸢ú⸣ [x x] ⸢gi$_4$⸣ [x]); T$_{24}$: sipa ⸢x⸣ [...] (⸢x⸣ like r[a)

(281) (with the result that) work on the pastures is brought to an end for the shepherd; his bringing back the sheep is brought to an end;

282	[eŋa]r-ra a-šà ur_{11}-ru mu-na-til	*(282)* the farmer's plowing his field is brought to an end.
	C_3: [x] ⸢x⸣-ra a-šà ur_{11}-ru mu-na-til	
283	. . .	*(283)* (*Too poorly preserved for translation*)
	C_3: [. . .] ⸢x⸣-gi_4 mu-[n]a(?)-KU-e[n](?); N_6: [. . .]-la [. . .] ú ri-g[e . . .]	
284	kadra inim-ma-bi níŋ šà-te-na m[u(?)- . . .]	*(284)* A gift of words [brings(?)] something soothing to the heart;
Cf. ED_I r. vii 4'	[x] ⸢ŠU⸣ a(?) me kadra	
	C_3: [. . . ini]m-ma-bi níŋ šà-te-na m[u(?)- . . .]; N_6: kadra i[nim- . . .]	
285	é-ga[l-la k]u_4-ra-bi níŋ-šà-te-na [. . .]	*(285)* when it enters the palace, it [brings] something soothing to the heart.
	C_3: [. . . -k]u_4-ra-bi níŋ-šà-te-n[a . . .]; N_6: é-ga[l-. . .]	
285 a	[ka]dra inim-inim-ma mu[l-an . . .]	*(285a)* (For this) gift of many words, [like] the stars of heaven,
	UM_2: (omits line); C_3: [ka]dra inim-inim-ma mu[l . . .]; N_6: (omits line)	
285 b	[šuruppak^{ki} du]mu ubar-ubar-tu-[tu-ke_4]	*(285b)* (which are instructions that) [the man from Šuruppak], the son of Ubartutu (gave as instructions),
	UM_2: (omits line); C_3: [šuruppak^{ki} du]mu ubar-ubar-tu-[tu-ke_4]; N_6: (omits line)	
286	[ka]dra inim-inim-ma mu[l an . . .]	*(286)* - (this) gift of many words, [like] the stars [of heaven],
ED_I cf. r. vii 5'	[i]nim AN.[A]N [. . .]	
	UM_2: [. . .] mu[l . . .]; C_3: [ka]dra inim-inim-ma mu[l . . .]; C_4: [(x)] ⸢kadra⸣ [. . .]; N_6: ka[dra . . .] mu[l . . .]	
287	na-ri šuruppak^{ki} dumu ubar-tu-tu-ke_4 na ri-ga	*(287)* is instructions that the man from Šuruppak, son of Ubartutu, gave as instructions;
ED_I cf. r. viii 8	šuruppak Ú[R].A[Š](?) dumu na ⸢ri⸣-ri-ga	
	UM_2: na-ri šuruppak^{ki} dumu ubar-tu-tu-ke_4 na ri-ga; C_3: [. . . uba]r-tu-[. . .]; C_4: [. . . šu]ruppak^{ki} dumu ubar-t[u- . . .]; N_6: na-ri šuruppak du[mu . . .]; N_{11}: [. . .] ubar-tu-tu-ke_4	
288	šuruppak^{ki} dumu ubar-tu-tu-ke_4 na ri-ga	*(288)* (that) the man from Šuruppak, son of Ubartutu, gave as instructions,
	UM_2: šuruppak^{ki} dumu ubar-tu-tu-ke_4 na ri-ga; C_4: [x x -s]ud-rá dumu-ni-r[a . . .]; N_6: šu[rupp]ak du[mu . . .]; N_{11}: [. . .] ri-ga	
289	nin dub gal-gal-la šu du_7-a	*(289–290)* praise be to Nisaba, the maiden who perfects the big tablets!
	UM_2: nin dub gal-gal-la šu du_7-a; C_4: ⸢dub⸣ gal-gal-e šu du_7-⸢a⸣; N_{11}: [. . . g]al-gal-e šu du_7-e	
290	ki-sikil ^{d}nisaba zà-mí	
	UM_2: ki-sikil ^{d}nisaba zà-mí; C_4: [x x] ⸢x⸣ zà-mí [(x)]; N_{11}: [. . .] ^{d}nisaba zà-mí	

The Schøyen Sources of the Instructions of Šuruppak

The Schøyen duplicates are included thanks to the courtesy of the owner of the Schøyen collection and Jens Braarvig, leader of the editorial committee of the Schøyen collection. Although the provenience is unknown, at least Sch_1 and Sch_2 seem related in that they share some variants not found elsewhere. For the sake of greater clarity, Sch_4 and Sch_5, which present particular problems, are completely transliterated below; transliterations and comments on these, as well as the others, are incorporated into the main text (*Chaps. 1.3 and 1.4*).

Sch_1: 2.2788

One-column tablet, with 25 lines on the obv., 3 lines on the lower edge, and 25 lines on the rev. Obv. = *Instr. Šur.* 1–25; lower edge = 26-27; rev. = 28–48.

Photographs, by courtesy of the Schøyen Collection, on pls. 60–61.

Sch_2: 9.3352

One-column tablet, 22 lines on the obv.; 13 inscribed lines on the rev., followed by a ruler and a blank space. Obv. = *Instr. Šur.* 1–14; rev. = 15–18 plus ca. 3 unidentified lines.

Photograph, by courtesy of the Schøyen collection pls. 62–63.

Sch_3: 3366

One-column tablet, 30 lines on the obverse, and 28 lines on the reverse, followed by a double separating line and a blanks space with room for two to three lines. The obverse is mostly badly destroyed, but the reverse is well preserved. Obv. = *Instr. Šur.* 123–152; rev. = 153–181.

Photographs, by Renee Kovacs, pls. 64–67.

Sch_4: 0.2291

Nearly square tablet, perhaps Kassite or later. Obv. has seven lines apparently with some erased lines left, and three lines running over from the reverse. The reverse has seven lines. Obv. may belong after ca. line 81ff., but not identified with certainty, or, perhaps, an extract from a different text. Obv. = ca. 81; 84; and maybe about three lines belonging to the poorly preserved lines after 84; rev. 1–2 = 124–125; 3 not clearly identified; 4–8 = 126–130.

Photographs, by courtesy of the Schøyen Collection, pl. 68.

Obv.

1 = SS ca. 81	[x (x)] KUR^{ki}-ke$_4$ ⸢ki⸣(?) x(like šu) búr-r[a]
2 = SS …	[l]ú-tur-ŋu$_{10}$ lú IGI … (traces of ca. 5 signs)
	⸢x⸣(like mu?) KA GIŠ GAR da[m] ⸢x⸣ x(like KU)-un
3 = SS …	zi TUR-bi(or ga) zu šà-bi-a ⸢kal⸣-bi
	KA KA nun(?) da(?) bi
4 = SS …	[x (x)] ⸢x⸣ ⸢KA⸣ im(?) ⸢ud⸣ ŋá me-en(?)
	[(…)] ⸢x⸣ ⸢x⸣ ⸢x⸣ IGI(?)-ŋá me-en(?)

The remainder of obv. = 3 illegible lines seem to be from an erased earlier inscription. The lower edge is not inscribed.

Rev.

1 = SS 124	[dumu]-⸢ninta$_x$⸣-zu ⸢é-ni-šè ši-im-me⸣ (nearly illegible)
2 = SS 125	dumu(?)-munus-zu ⸢ama$_5$⸣(?)-⸢bi⸣(or ta?) ši-im-me
3 = unidentified	GA(?)-zu(?) é-ta KA šu ⸢x⸣ AN
4 = SS 126	kaš naŋ-ŋá-zu ⸢šà⸣- … (illegible traces)
5 = SS 127	é(! looks like bi)-ta è(!) šà-zu ⸢na⸣-⸢gu$_7$⸣-e
6 = SS 128	an sù-da-⸢àm⸣ ⸢ki⸣ ⸢kal-kal⸣-la-àm
7 = SS 129	an-da níŋ im-da-lu-lu-àm
8 = SS 130	(about 3 signs erased) kur-kur-re zi im-(traces)

Line; bottom edge not inscribed.

Sch$_5$: 0.2040

One-column tablet with ca. 11 inscribed lines on the obv.; only one line followed by a ruler and blank space on the rev. = *Instr. Šur* ca. 203–ca. 212. The traces on the left side of the obv. may belong to a different column. Photographs, by courtesy of the Schøyen Collection, pl. 69.

Obv.

1 = SS ??	(traces, not identified)
2 = SS ca. 203?	[…] é(?) ⸢x⸣(like gul?)
3 = SS 203	[…] ⸢x⸣(not ḫul)-gig ⸢x⸣(like ga) (traces of 3 more signs)
4 = SS 205	[…] (traces, may not belong here)
5 = SS 206	[…] ⸢x⸣ ní-zu ḫé-ga(? hardly bi)-ni(?)-lá(?)
6 = SS 207	[… ŋá]l-la-ra ⸢ḫé-em-ši⸣-ŋ[ál-l]e
7 = SS 208	⸢ezem⸣-ma-ka dam na-⸢x⸣(looks like UD)-⸢x⸣(looks like en, but too long)
8 = SS 209	[š]à-ga ḫuŋ-ŋá-àm
9 = SS 209f	⸢bar⸣(?)-ra ⸢ḫuŋ⸣-ŋá-àm
10 = SS 210	([x]) kù ⸢huŋ⸣(?)-ŋá-àm
11 = SS 210f	([…]?) ⸢za⸣(?)-gìn huŋ-ŋá-àm
12 = SS 211?	[túg(?)] huŋ-ŋá-àm

Rev.

1 = SS 212?	[…] ⸢lú⸣ ta ⸢mu⸣(?)-⸢x⸣(looks like ra)-sá(looks like ki)

Separating line. Nothing more inscribed on the tablet.

1.4 Comments on Individual Lines

Lines 1–3: Variants: Ur_1: u_4 sud-rá ri-a; P: u_4 sud-rá ri.

The introductory lines are identical to the first three lines of *Gilgameš, Enkidu, and the Netherworld*: u_4 ri-a u_4 sud-rá ri-a, ŋi$_6$ ri-a ŋi$_6$ bad-rá ri-a, mu ri-a mu sud-rá ri-a. u_4 ri-a alone is listed in the literary catalogues from Nippur and the Louvre, edited by Kramer, BASOR 88 (1942) 10–19; also in TMHNF 3, 54, line 5. Apart from our composition, u_4 ri-a alone occurs in the incipits of *Enki and Ninmah*, *Enki's Journey to Nippur*, and *Gilgameš, Enkidu, and the Netherworld*. The *Second Ur Catalogue*, UET 6/1 123, line 29, edited by Kramer, RA 55 (1961) 169–176, lists: u_4 ri-a u_4 sud$_4$-ta ri(!)-a, which, thus, may represent either our composition or *Gilgameš, Enkidu, and the Netherworld*. The Andrews University catalogue, published by M. E. Cohen, RA 70 (1976) 129–144, line 19, lists [u_4] ri-a šuruppak[ki]. This is likely to be a variant of the incipit to our composition, especially since the two compositions listed in what follows are related: *The Instructions of Ur-Ninurta* (cf. *Chap. 2.2*) and *The Farmer's Instructions*.

The reading of sud-DU and bad-DU is almost unanimously taken as sud-rá and bad-rá, suggesting a d^r phoneme. Some unexpected variants do not support that reading, however; cf. PRAK II D 42 ii 1: an-ša-né kur bad-tu-bi, "in the faraway mountains of Anšan."[1–3]

The introductory formula of *The Instructions of Ur-Ninurta* is somewhat similar: u_4-ul-li-a-ta u_4-ub-ba til-la-[a-ta], gig-ri bi-ri gi$_6$ ba-sù-[da-a-ta], mu-sù-da mu ba-ši-[sù-da-a-ta], cf. *Chap. 2.1*.

Line 4: ED_1: ŋéštu inim-zu | [ka]lam [t]i-la; ED_2: [ŋéštu-tuku inim-galam inim-zu-a]m$_6$ [kalam-m]a [ti]-la-am$_6$.

SS Variants: Ur_1: kalam-ma til-la-àm, til phonetic for ti(-l) = tìl; P: kalam-ma ti-la-a. Sch_1: ti-la-àm. Sch_2: u_4 sud-{bad}-rá ⸢ri-a⸣ is an obvious mistake.

Lines 4–5: Sch_1: In neither case is there a tuku after ŋéštu. This is in accordance with Sch_2, which has ŋéštu-[<ga>(?)]-kam, but no tuku. The sign following ú looks like KAM or ÚTUL, rather than galam. It is too long for ÚḪ or ḪAR. Yet, it may be the same sign as is meant in line 142, UM_2: ⸢ú⸣-ḪAR. Although it is tempting to connect this to ú-UG, or ú-ḪÚB; the meaning "deaf" (cf. AHw 1055, *sukkuku*, "taub") would not fit, unless this also had a positive meaning (*bona parte*), which is unlikely. The only reference known to me that might point to a different meaning is UET 6/2 339 ii 4 (Alster, *Proverbs* I, 322): ú-ḫúb ti-la-š[è ..., but the context is too damaged to warrant any conclusion. If, in fact, galam is meant, it would be difficult to explain ú as a variant of inim. Sch_2, however, has: perhaps ú-ḪAR in the beginning of line 7, apparently as an epithet of the father, and perhaps related to our line. It is tempting to suggest that this is a writing for ubara, normally written EZEN×KASKAL, but an explanation of the writing found here has so far not been found.

kalam-ma ti-la-a, "who lived in the land," is a honorific reference to the very ancient times when the father lived in Šuruppak. The same expression is used of the goddess Nanše in *Nanše Hymn* 60. Here the point is to connect the father from whom the counsels were transmitted, with Šuruppak, the last mentioned of the antediluvian cities in *The Sumerian King List*.

inim-galam occurs also in the conclusion of *The Three Ox-Drivers from Adab* 92–93, in which the solution to the problem presented in the plot is summarized as inim galam-galam-ma, "the elaborate words," of a wise "woman" of high rank.[4]

Line 5: ED_1: [šuruppak Ú]R.[A]Š | [ŋéš]tu inim-zu | kalam ti-la. ED_2: [šurupp]ak[ki] [Ú]R.AŠ | [ŋéš]tu-[tu]ku inim-[galam inim]-zu-am$_6$ | [kalam-m]a [ti-la-am$_6$].

Lines 5–6: ÚR.AŠ in the ED sources was previ-

1–3. *Edin-na ú-saŋ-ŋá-ke$_4$*-litany, describing where Ibbisin lies buried after his capture; belongs approximately to VS 2, 26 vii 15: [...] ⸢x⸣ ki-sud-rá-ka; cf. Katz, *Image*, 310, n. 4.

4. Cf. p. 381, *Chap. 5.1: Three Ox-Drivers*, and p. 389, *Chap. 5.2:* Comments on *The Old Man* 13.

ously understood by Alster, 1974, as an honorific epithet of Šuruppak with no counterpart in the SS version, but it is, in fact, an ED name for the son called Ziusudra in the SS version, as pointed out below. The precise meaning of ÚR.AŠ cannot be pinpointed, but it can hardly be separated from ÚR×Ú-AŠ = ùšbar or ur_9. In later orthography, ÚR became replaced by NÍNDA, and NÍNDA×Ú-AŠ became the normal writing for $ušbar_6$ or $muru_{11}$, *emu rabû*, "father-in-law," although the reading $urum_x$ would be expected, i.e., $ÚR^{ú-rum}$. That this is indeed intended in the ED sources is the position of Wilcke, 1978, 202. Yet, since it is now clear that it refers to the son, it must be the son, from Old Babylonian times called Ziusudra, who is said to be the "father-in-law," presumably of all coming generations.

In Sch_2, SAḪAR = *kizû* is an epithet of the father that does not occur in any of the other sources. It is possibly to be read šùš, which denotes a high official in charge of animals, approximately "knight" or similar. The reading šùš was proposed by R.H. Beal, in *N.A.B.U.* 1992/2 no. 48 (pp. 38–39), who understands it as a "chariot-fighter" in Hittite sources. It is very common in Ur III sources, in which it denotes a high official in charge of donkeys, etc. The reading was contested by Cavigneaux, *N.A.B.U.* 1992/4 no. 104 (p. 77–78), who defends the reading ku-uš, rather than su!-uš in Proto-Ea. The reading šùš or sùš, however, seems justified on the basis of *Incantation to Utu* 92 (Alster, AcSum 13 [1991] 52), where it is written phonetically su-sa(-zu) and su-úš-a-(zu), as well as other texts cited by Beal. Since $kuš_7$ obviously is related to *kizû*, it seems that a Sumerian term yielded to an Akkadian loanword, or that they are both related by an as yet unexplained sound shift.

Sch_2 has ŋéštu-<ga(?)>-kam instead of ŋéštu-tuku, and inim-ma(sic!) zu instead of inim-galam inim-zu-a, most likely scribal errors.

For inim-galam inim-zu-a, the following explanations can be suggested: (1) two parallel nouns or noun phrases, inim-galam and inim, are dependent on a common verb, zu, as direct objects. Yet, it would be strange that the first noun, inim-galam, is more specific than the second, which consists of inim alone; (2) inim-galam is a separate *bahuvrihi*-like construction, "the one of artistic words"; or (3) inim-galam depends on inim – zu as a composite verb, approximately meaning "with a deep understanding of artistic words." Although the latter is attractive, it would undoubtedly have required a dimensional case marker following inim-galam. Therefore, the second possibility is the more likely solution.

Lines 5–7: In these lines, as well as in the parallel lines 73–75+76–78; 143–145+146–147, šuruppak(ki) is to be understood as "the man from Šuruppak,"[5–7a] which accords with the Akkadian translation *šurippakû*, preserved in line 73, where Akk_2 has: *šu-ri-ip-pa-ku*, as well as the detached fragment of the same text that probably corresponds to line 147 (= 7 = 82): *šurippakû*. This is confirmed by *Gilg.* XI 23: LÚ *šu-ri-ip-pa-ku-ú* DUMU ^{m}ubar-tu-tu, "the man from Šuruppak, son of Ubar-tutu."

In the SS version, the antediluvian city of Šuruppak, for which the father was named, is most often written with the ki-determinative. ED_1 writes it without the determinative, whereas ED_2 includes it. A real name for the father is nowhere given, but his designation as "the man from Šuruppak" makes good sense in the context. It fits well with the great emphasis attached to the information that he "lived in the country," undoubtedly referring to the primordial times when the wisdom of the ancient sages was handed over through the ancient city of Šuruppak, a theme alluded to also in *Gilg.* XI.

The recognition of the characteristic anticipating type of adding parallelism is decisive for a correct translation here. There is a caesura following line 6, implying that line 7: "the man from Šuruppak, the son of Ubartutu" merely recapitulates line 5: "the man from Šuruppak" without the appositions. Likewise, the parallel Early Dynastic source ED_2: [šurupp]ak^{ki} [Ú]R.AŠ | [ŋéš]tu-[tu]ku inim-[galam inim]-zu-am_6 | [kalam-m]a [ti-la-am_6], [šuruppak^{ki}] ÚR.AŠ | dumu-ni-ra na na-ri-ri (see *Chap.1.6*), means: "Šuruppak (to) ÚR.AŠ—the intelligent one (= Šuruppak), the one of artistic words, the wise

5–7a. I am grateful to M.J. Geller, whose insistence on translating "the Šuruppakean" led me to reconsider the question and to the conclusions reached here.

one—Šuruppak gave instructions to ÚR.AŠ, his son," which is a caesura following the first ÚR.AŠ. This means that the first ÚR.AŠ is a *casus pendens*, recapitulated in the following dative: ÚR.AŠ | dumu-ni-ra. The conclusion is that ÚR.AŠ is, in fact, the name of the son in at least one of the Early Dynastic versions (ED_2), possibly also in the Abū Ṣalābīkh version (ED_1), although it is not preserved there.[5–7b] Adding parallelism occurs also in lines 69–72; 209–211.

Th. Jacobsen, in *The Sumerian King List*, p. 74, line 32: šuruppak[ki] ubar-tu-tu, understood šuruppak[ki] as the name of the city, and ubar-tu-tu as the name of the ruler. On pp. 75–76, n. 32, Jacobsen (and Landsberger) explained the later development of the name of the ruler Šuruppak as a misunderstanding of the city name, "Ziusudra, the son of Šuruppak," instead of "Ziusudra, the man from Šuruppak." The fragment published ibid., p. 60, n. 113: zi-u_4-sud-ra dumu u[bar-tu-tu], "Ziusudra, the son of Ubartutu," differs from our text in not including a generation between Ziusudra and Ubartutu. Yet, already in our ED sources there was a step between them: "the man from Šuruppak," otherwise unnamed. In our ED sources it is hardly necessary to postulate a form like *dumu Šuruppak([ki]) to explain this, since apparently Šuruppak alone was understood as "the man from Šuruppak." If this were to be understood as a mistaken "genuine" personal name, the mistake must go back in time to the third millennium B.C. The presence of the ki-determinative in ED_2 does not support that solution, however.[5–7c]

Jacobsen, in *The Sumerian King List* (W-B 62:10), cf. his n. 107, p. 58, explained the -gi/-ge (= kí) following SU.KUR.LAM as a "thoughtless rendering of dictated(!) -ke_4." I agree with this explanation, and do not consider the reading *Šuruppag compulsory, unless one wants generally to question the reading of the Sumerian genitive suffix /-ak/. Wilcke, 1978, 202, however, advocates the reading Šuruppag, referring to two variants in *Nanna's Journey to Nippur* line 231, text O, and 242, text S, both of which indicate šuruppag[ki]-ga, as variants of ditto-a. The reason for hesitating to accept the -g ending is that I consider the name SU.KUR.LAM([ki]) = šuruppak([ki]) a normal genitive compound, which exceptionally may have had a variant reading ending in -g.[5–7d]

The only clue as to the k/g-ending in our text is a variant in line 6, text P: šuruppak[ki]-ké(GI), = var. of ditto-e, where the reading -ge would be the straightforward choice, cf. Wilcke, 1978, 202. Since the name Šuruppak lacks a clear etymology, it may not have been Sumerian in origin and, therefore, it is far from certain that it actually contained the Sumerian genitive ending. Yet, the most likely explanation is that the name was, indeed, Sumerian, and that it belonged to the rare category of genitive compounds that were formed so early that they were no longer treated as living genitives,[5–7e] similar to the city name larak/g[ki], for which similar considerations apply.[5–7f,g]

5–7b. This is contrary to the conclusion of Alster, 1974, 25, followed by Wilcke, 1978, 202, who took ÚR.AŠ as an epithet of the father, owing to its position in the Adab version. Civil, 1966, 2, and Biggs, 1966, 78, were right in taking it as the name of the son. Krebernik, 1998, 319, with n. 779, referring to p. 241, n. 45, however, takes ÚR×AŠ as an epithet of Šuruppak, following Steinkeller; cf. also Selz, WZKM 92 (2002) 173, n. 35.

5–7c. There would then have been a link through *dumu šuruppak[ki], meaning "the man from Šuruppak." Wilcke, 1978, 202, like Jacobsen, proposed that an original epithet dumu šuruppag-ga meant "(Ziusudra) der Mann von Š.," then later taken as a personal name. This is certainly possible, being analogous to dumu ŋír-su[ki], "the man from Girsu." There is, in fact, no *dumu šuruppak attested in our text. That there was a generation between Ubar-tutu and Ziusudra is clear from line 7, where the father is = "the man from Šuruppak," compared to line 8, where Ziusudra is said to be his son, i.e., son of "the man from Šuruppak."

5–7d. Jacobsen, JNES 32 (1973) 165, points to such names as [d]*nin-kar-ra-ak*, [d]*in-šu-si-na-ak*, and *aš-nun-na-ak*, in which the Sumerian genitive was visibly preserved in loanwords. I would class the city name Šuruppak among these.

5–7e. Cf. the discussion of the type saŋa, from saŋ-ak, but no longer treated as a genitive, by Selz, 2003, WZKM 92 (2002) 131–132. I would even class the name Enki, i.e., */[d]en-ki(-k)/ to this group. This becomes [d]en-ki-ga-ke_4 in context, but the possibility, of course, exists that the etymology was different from *[d]en-ki-ak. Cf. however, the Ur III spelling [d]en-ki-ka-ke_4, van Dijk/Geller, *Ur III Incantations*, 77, no. 5, line 13, which simply suggests that [d]en-ki-ga is caused by dissimilation of [d]en-ki-ka.

5–7f. In line 143, T_6 has the variant šuruppak-e, also line 146, T_2+T_5, T_6, whereas Ur_1, lines 5, 6, 73 (also I_5), as well as I_5, line 76, have šuruppak[ki]-e, with the deter-

Line 6: ED_1: šuruppak dumu na [n]a-ri; ED_2: [šuruppak^ki^] ÚR.AŠ | dumu-ni-ra na na-ri-ri.

SS variants: Ur_1: šuruppak^ki^-e. P: šuruppak^ki^-ké(GI); Ur_1: na na-mu-un-ri-ga-àm; P: na na-mu-un-ri-ri. Note also the following variants, line 73, Ur_3: na-šè mu-un-ni-in-ri; line 75, I_6: zi-u_4-sud-rá na / [na]-mu-un-ni-in-r[i-ri], where the two na's are separated by the indented line. Cf. also the variants line 143, T_5: na-šè mu-ni-in-ri, and line 145, N_3: na [na] / mu-un-ri-⌜ri⌝, which, however, has both na's before the indented line, either as a minor scribal error or because the second -na actually represents the 3rd person suffix in the locative, > /na-ani-a/, "into his instruction." Cf. also the comments on line 143.

na-ri (= na-de_5) = *ašāru* is the traditional expression for giving an instruction. I line 80, UM_1, and MM have the variant na-di, pointing to a d^r phoneme; cf. the variant of Ziusudra's name mentioned in the comments to line 8. The variant na-šè, apparently meaning "as instruction," quoted above, indicates that na was a noun that could be used in the terminative, possibly from na = na_4, a common phonetic writing for "stone." Whether na ri(-g) developed the meaning "to instruct" from "throwing stones" is doubtful, however. Alternatively na can be explained as = *awīlum*, *zikarum*, "Menchen führen," or similar; cf. Selz, AcSum 17 (1996) 261f., with n. 51, with references to earlier literature.

Lines 6–13: Cf. lines 73–75+76–82; 143–152; and 287–288.

Line 7: Jacobsen comments on Ubar-tu-tu, later read ubur-tu-tu, in *The Sumerian King List*, 75f. ubar contains the Akkadian term *ubāru* (*wabrum*); cf. AHw 1399, "Ortsfremder," "Schutzbürger." Tutu is an Akkadian divine name. It occurs in the month name ezem ^d^tu-tu an-nu-ni-tum, in PDT 430 = Š 45; cf. Sigrist, *Drehem*, CDL Press, 1992, 166.

Wilcke, 1978, 202, discusses earlier theories by Jacobsen and Landsberger, concluding that presumably "die Herrscher – Familie *Ubār-Tutu* – Šuruppag – Ziusudra ursprünglich nichts mit dem seinem Kind und Schwiegerkind ratende Šuruppag zu tun hat und diese Namen erst später wegen der Namengleichheit mit dem 'König' Šuruppag eindrangen." In my opinion, this generation exists only in connection with the legendary rulers.

Line 8: There are no variants.

zi-u_4-sud-rá: Only the SS version gives the name of the son, which coincides with the name of the hero of the Sumerian flood story. In line 80 it occurs in the form zi-u_4-sud-rá-ra, in which ra seems to be a phonetic indicator for DU = rá.[8] Cf. the comments on sud-DU above, lines 1–3, and p. 309.

Line 9: Cf. lines 79 and 149. Variants: Ur_1: na ga-ri; P: na ge-ri.

The Sumerian precative ḫé-dab_5 is translated in Akk_3: *ṣa-bat* by an imperative. Cf. line 13 and *Chap. 1.9: On the Akk. translations of Sum. gram. forms.*

Line 10: ED_1: GIŠ.PI.[TÚG] ḫé-m[a]-ak; ED_2: [ŋizz]al ḫé-⌜x-x⌝ (= -⌜ma-ak⌝?). SS Variants: Ur_1: omits the line altogether; BM_1: ŋiz]zal ḫé-em-<ši>-ak; P: ŋizzal(?) ḫé-em-ši-ak. Cf. further lines 80 and 150.

minative. Had a non-genitival noun ending in -g been intended, one might expect *šuruppag^ki^-ge in most cases, as, in fact, P line 6 has it. For a summary of the theories that Šuruppak and other names may have been non-Sumerian in origin, see Rubio, 1999, 6, who challenged Landsberger's frequently and often uncritically repeated proto-Sumerian substrate theories. Previously, Steinkeller, in: M. Liverani (ed.), *Early Political Development in Mesopotamia* (Padua: Sargon, 1993), 111, considered some geographical names ending in -k to be Sumerian in origin and including the genitive suffix. I fully agree with this opinion.

5–7g. The reading ke_4 was introduced by Kramer in 1936 (AS 8, 8 with n. 95), and confirmed by such phonetic renderings as -ke, cf. Jacobsen, JNES 32 (1973) 161, n. 3, to which more can be added, i.e., *Incantation to Utu* 4: ^d^utu lugal an-ki-ke, var. -ke_4 (Alster, AcSum 13 [1991] 38; also line 235: lugal an-ki-ke(sic!) ^d^utu). -ke_4 has been widely accepted and rarely questioned. The reading gé would also be worth considering and was long maintained by Thureau-Dangin. Cf. now also Edzard, *Sum. Grammar*, 36, who points out that ke_4 is not attested in Proto-Ea, cf. MSL 14, 41, lines 241–254.

8. Jacobsen, *The Sumerian King List*, 76–77, n. 34, argues for Zi-u-sud-ra (with u representing u_4 for typographical reason) as the form most likely to be correct. *Gilgameš's Death*, Meturan version has 17: zi-ud-sù-ta(!)-aš ki-tuš-bi-a. Cf. also *Chap. 3.3: Ballade of Early Rulers* 11 with p. 296, *Attempt at a new interpretation.*

ŋizzal is normally written GIŠ.TÚG.PI.ŠIR (vertical ŠIR, crossed with ŠIR).SÌLA, but in Sch_2, lines 10f., the last part simply seems to be a normal PI with some extra strokes in its left side. The corresponding part is destroyed in line 4. Note the variant -a for -ak in Sch_2.

Line 11: Ur_1: šu nam-bí-bar-ra (sic!); BM_1:]-bar-re, agrees with P and Sch_2: šu nam-bí-bar-re. Only Sch_1 has nam-bí-bar-re-en.

The translation of Akk_3: [*a-ši-ir-*]*x*(?)*-šu i-šar* / [*la-a ta-...-t*]*a-AK*, is probably best explained as a mistaken 3rd person form, "his(?) (*-šu*) instructions, (which(?)) he gives" (*iššar*), instead of the expected 2nd person. There can be no doubt that the verb is *ašāru*, cf. CAD A/2, 420: *ašāru* A, "to muster, control, instruct"; it is unlikely that another verb, such as *ašāru* C, CAD A/2, 422: "to release," is involved.

Line 12: Ur_1: na-ab-ta-bal-e; Ur_6: na-ab-te-bal-[... -e]n; BM_1: -b]al-e-dè, agrees with P and Sch_1: na-ab-ta-bal-e-dè. Only Ur_6 has -te-bal-. The translation of Akk_1: ... na-ab-ta-bal-e-dè = [*a-mat aq-bu la*]*-a te-ti-iq*, "don't trespass," is precise. With the ablative verbal infix, bal means "transgress, overstep." Here bal is equated with *etēqu*, but in line 56 with *nabalkutum*.[12] Cf. the discussion in the commentary to line 180.

Line 13: This line is omitted in the Nippur sources, I_{15}, and T_1, as well as Akk_1. It is paralleled in lines 82A and 152A, also omitted in the Nippur sources. It is here included in Ur_1, Ur_6, P, Sch_1, Sch_2, as well as Akk_3. Ur_1: [n]a-ri ab-ba níŋ-kal-la gú-zu ḫé-em-ši-ak-e; Ur_6, níŋ-k[al]-la-àm; P: na-ri ab-ba níŋ-kal-la-àm gú-zu ḫé-em-ši-ŋál; Ur_6: gú-zu ḫé-em-ši-ŋál, agrees with BM_1: -e]m-ši-ŋál; For P: gú-zu ḫé-em-ši-ŋál, cf. the variant in line 270, Ur_6: ŋizzal ḫé-em-ši-ŋál, in which ŋál likewise replaces ak. It, thus, seems that Akk_1 and Akk_3 do not depend on the same Sumerian source, and that the later mainstream of transmission was closer to the Ur sources than those from Nippur, possibly through a Sippar or Babylon link close to P.

Sch_1: Note the variant ad-da for ab-ba. Both denote a father, but ad-da is restricted to a father in direct relationship, whereas ab-ba can be used honorific. Note also the variant gú-zi ḫé-m[e ..., apparently misunderstood from SS 13: gú-zu – ŋál. Cf. also the comments on SS 205.

The Sum. verb gú – ak occurs also as a variant of šu – ak in line 174. It is here translated by Akk_3: *it-ta-qí-ip*, best explained as a rare Ntn imp. of *qâpu*, "to be believed," although not previously attested; cf. CAD Q, 97, *qâpu* A, "to be believed."[13] It cannot be a precise translation of the Sum. precative gú-zu ḫé-em-ši-ak, with var. ŋál; cf. a similar example in line 9. For the variant gú – ŋál, cf. lines 174 and 205 with comments. Since gú – ak occurs also in the parallel line 152A, it is taken as primary here.

Line 14: ED_2: ANŠE [K]A gù-di nàb(AN+AN)-| sa_{10}-sa_{10} [...] na-e.

Variants in the SS text: Both Ur_1 and P have dùr.⌜ùr⌝; Ur_6: dùr. T_1: e]ŋir(?)-zu ša-[, and P: eŋir(?) ša-ra-ab-si-il(?), seem to support the reading eŋir, "your after," but Ur_6: érin(?)-zu(!) (copy ba) ša-ra-si-il-le, and BM_1: ér]in-zu ša-ra-si-il, suggest the reconstruction érin-zu ša-ra-ab-si-il-le. Sch_2: The sign following ANŠE is not gù, but probably na (hardly something like làl). If the reading na-di is justified, this may be either a scribal error for gù-di or related to the special use of the modal preformative na- characteristic of the Adab source (cf. *Chaps. 1.6* and *1.9*).

The two Akkadian texts can here be harmonized as *mu-ú-ra na-*[*gi-ga l*]*a tu-ša-am* .... The end of the line remains doubtful, however. If Akk_3: [...]*x-ta-ak ú-sà-pa-ḫa*: "they will scatter your ..." is a translation of érin-zu ša-ra-ab-si-il-le, it approximately covers the probable meaning, although it is not a normal equivalent of si-il. Cf. CAD S, 151, s.v. *sapāḫu*, lex., which lists bir and ság – dug_4 = *sapāḫu*. si-il = *salātu*, "to cut off," occurs, e.g., in saŋ-kul – si-il, "to remove the bolt." *-ta-ak* is the 2nd pers. masc. abbreviated suffix pronoun *-ka* following the fem. *-t*,

12. The translation given in PSD B, 54, s.v. bal D: "Do not change the words I speak," is unjustified. In addition to the examples cited by PSD, cf. also *Incantation to Utu* 162: zà diŋir-re-e-ne-ke_4 a-ba-da-⌜ab⌝-bal, "who overstepped the border of the gods."

13. Krebernik, 1996, 173, suggests among other possibilities: *qí-ip* "vertraue (an)!" or *it-ta-ki-ip*, "stoße (immer wieder)!" Cf. AHw 718, "vorstoßen." Cf. ABL 555: *ina muḫḫi kaspē pí-túq*, "He always pays attention to silver," probably a Dt or Dtn-Stative from *puqqum*, although not listed by the dictionaries; cf. Alster, JCS 41 (1989) 190.

probably from an accusative form, possibly corresponding to érin-zu.

"An ass that brays" can perhaps be understood as «brays more than normal for an ass», implying that everyone will want to flee from there, taking érin as "folk." Geller, however, suggests taking érin as *ṣimittu*, "yoke," which I have accepted; cf. CAD Ṣ, 198: *ṣimittu* (= ŋiš/níŋ-érin), "crosspiece of a yoke."

Line 15: ED_1 obv. i 6: gán-zu [kaskal na-ŋá-ŋá]; ED_2: gán kaskal na-ŋá-ŋá | nam-[silig] ⸢x⸣ [x].

Akk_1: *la te-re-eš*; Akk_3: *te-ri-iš*. The end of the line is preserved only in Akk_3: *GU-la-lu*, cf. below.

SS variants are: T_1 and BM_1: gú-ŋá-à[m; Ur_1: ga-ŋá-àm. The same expression occurs also in line 259: nam-silig gum-ŋá-àm, which here agrees with Sch_1; nam-silig alone occurs in line 61.

The ED reading of GÁN may be $aša_5$, but juxtaposition of the two signs GÁN and a-šà, in lines 15–16 and elsewhere, seems to indicate that the two terms are not simple synonyms, so the traditional reading gán is preserved here. Cf. p. 189, the comments on the Abū Ṣalābīkh version 6 and the literature cited there.

I have accepted a suggestion by Foxvog, 1976, 372, who takes nam-silig from the verb silig, "to come/bring to an end," which occurs in line 96; therefore, "annihilation, decimation, ruin"; he compares it to CAD *agasalakku* (an ax). This probably contains the same word silig. Cf. the discussion of silig in the comments to line 96. He understands gú-ga-àm (with variants) either as a pure sound-based verb displaying the well-known idiomatic u/a vowel alliteration pattern (cf. Civil, JCS 20 [1966] 120f.; Black, *Wilcke FS*, 45–46) or from the reduplicated verb ŋum, "to crush," with the same vowel alternation; therefore, "the decimation will be crushing(?)."

In Akk_3: *GU-la* / [...]-*lu*, there is probably nothing missing between *-la* and *-lu*; Krebernik, 1996, 174, suggests *GU-la-lu,* "Geringschätzung," from *qulālu*, cf. CAD s.v. *qulālu*, discredit," cf. also *qalālu*, "to become thin, weak, light," etc. This would be the first attested equivalent of Sum. nam-silig gú-ŋá-àm, yet it is unclear how the two precisely relate to one another. Apparently the Akkadian text did not translate every word, but chose a single word to cover the essential meaning, or it was made from a tablet in which one side of a column was imperfectly preserved (cf. line 16 below).[15]

Line 16: SS variants: T_1:]-e-ur_{11}(APIN)-ru zi bulug-àm; Ur_1: a-šà kaskal [k]a(?)-ŋìri-ka nam-ba-e-[u]r_{11}-⸢re⸣ zé-bulug-ga-àm; Ur_6: a-šà ka-ŋìri-ka / na-bi-ur_{11}-en / zag-e bulug gu_7-a; BM_1:] ⸢ù⸣-bulug-gu_7; P (inverts 15 and 16): a-šà ⸢x⸣ ŋìri-ka(?) nam-ba-e(?)-úr-ru ⸢x⸣ [...], úr phonetic for ur_{11}. Sch_1: supports a-šà ka ŋìri-ka; ùr, phonetic for ur_{11}, and bulug.

Akk_3: [*e-qe-el-ka i-na* ... *l*]*a-a te-ri-iš pu-ku* / *nu-qù-ur*, cf. below.

Only Ur_1 seems to have kaskal [k]a-ŋìri-ka. kaskal is not clearly written as a gloss, but is best explained as such. The other sources support the reconstruction ka-ŋìri-ka without kaskal, probably a superfluous addition explaining ka-ŋìri-ka, in itself a path or road.

Of the variants in the second part of the line: I_{15}: zi bulug-àm; Ur_1: zé-bulug-ga-àm; BM_1: ⸢ù⸣-bulug-gu_7; Ur_6: zag-e bulug gu_7-a, Ur_6 might mean "the boundary stones will be 'eaten' by the sides (of your fields)," i.e., the road will slowly move into the arable land and, thus, devour it. If this was, indeed, the intended meaning, it seems inexplicable why it is not simply written zag-ge, instead of zag-e. Yet, there can be no doubt that bulug, a boundary stone, belongs to the original expression. Maybe gu_7, "to eat," belonged to the original text as well, but was confused with ga, which in Ur_1 occurs as a complement to bulug. It is much more likely, however, that the variants zé and zi are verbal nouns from zi(-r) or zé(-r), "to tear out," i.e., "tearing out the boundary stones."

Akk_3 has the Akkadian translation *pu-qá nu-ku-ur*, for which Krebernik, 1996, 174, suggests the D-stative from *nukkur*, "ist verändert," or (more likely) *nuqqur*, "ist abgerissen/zerstört." For *pu-KU* he considers, i.a., *pukku*, "Trommel," *pūqu*, "Spalt, Gesäß," or *pūgu*, "Netz." Yet, it is much more likely to be an

15. It is not possible to derive *GU-la-lu* from *gullulu*, "to act in a hostile way," or from *gullultum*, "hostile act," denom. from *gillatu*, "sin," unless some scribal error is involved. Wilcke, 1978, 203 suggests: "*Es bedeutet ein Ende durch Trampeln*(?)!" (italicized to indicate uncertain translation).

abbreviated writing of *pu-<lu-uk>ku* = *pulukku*, "boundary stone." It would fit the readings of I_{15} and Ur_1: zé bulug-ga-àm, "tearing out the boundary stone." In this case, bulug is constructed as the direct object of the verb, not as a genitive, *bulug-ga-kam.

Line 17: ED_1: gán-za pú na-⌜dù⌝ ⌜ùŋ⌝ ⌜šè⌝-⌜mu⌝-ra-⌜ḫul⌝. According to collation by Alster, 1991–92, 32: za, ⌜dù⌝, and ⌜ùŋ⌝ are reasonably certain. The last sign is clearly ḫul. ED_2: [... náb]-⌜du⌝ [x]-e | [...]-LU cannot be fully harmonized with ED_1. In na-⌜dù⌝ ⌜UN⌝, the sign un means "people" = ùŋ, since here it can hardly be a grammatical element = the 2nd person verbal suffix /-en/, which would not normally be included in the writing of an ED text. ED_2 seems to have had: [ùŋ]-e.

Akk_3: [*ina me-re-ši-ka burtu*] *la-a ti-ḫé-ri* / [... *ù-n*]*a-kar-ka*.

Ur_6 and BM_2 have: ùŋ-e with no a; P alone, possibly by mistake, has: dù ùŋ a-e, "the people will do damage to the water for you."[17a] It is most likely that it is the people coming to fetch water that will do damage to the field by trampling down the seed, rather than the water being considered harmful in itself, or that damage is done to the water. The existence of wells for drinking water, not only irrigation, is, in fact, attested, both in textual records and in some archaeological finds, cf. M. de Mieroop, *The Ancient Mesopotamian City*, 158–161 and the literature there cited; cf. also *Gilgameš and Agga* 11–13, and p. 370, *Chap. 4.5: The Lazy Slavegirl* 5. This interpretation is corroborated by a passage from *Counsels for Šūpē-amēli*: Spruch III.iii:[17b]

U r a 5	*ina rēš eqlī-*[*k*]*a burta lā* ⌜*te-ḫe-ru*⌝
B v i 7	[*ina*] *rēš eqlī*[*-ka b*]*u-ur-tá la-a tá-a-ḫar-ri*
U r a 6	*ina rēš eqlī-ka burta* ⌜*te*⌝*-ḫe-ru-ma t*[*u*]*-ta-*⌜*šar*⌝
B v i 7	[*ina*] *rēš eqlī*[*-ka b*]*u-u-ur-tá tá-ḫar-ri*
U r a 7	*šepī*(GÌR.ME.DIDLI)*-ka* [*na*]*-ak-ra-*⌜*ti*⌝ *ina eqlī-ka*
B v i 8	*bašû-ma šepī-*[*ka na-ak*]*-ru-ti a-na eqlī-ka*
U r a 8	*ka-tá i-ṣ*[*u-t*]*u_4 šu-ru-*⌜*bá*⌝*-ku ḫu*(!)*-mu-ṭe_4-ti*
B v 9	[*ka-tá i-ṣu-tu$_4$ š*]*u-ul-pí-ka* ⌜*ḫu*⌝*-u-mu-ṭa-a-ti*
U r a 9	*ù a-ka-š*[*a*] ⌜*ú*⌝*-še-ṣu-*⌜*ú*⌝ *ina mamīti*
B v i 10	[*ù a-ka-ša i-š*]*a-dá-du-ka* ⌜*a-na*⌝ *ma-a-mi-ti*

"Am Anfang deines Ackers darfst du keinen Brunnen graben!
Wenn du (doch) am Anfang deines Ackers einen Brunnen gräbst, (dann) wirst du vertrieben, deine Füße werden fremd auf deinem (eigenen) Acker).
Sobald dann wenige eiligst bei dir eingedrungen sind, werden sie dich unter Eid ausweisen."[17c]

Line 18: ED_1: é sila(!)-daŋal na-dù(text: NI) x-sír LAK 218 ŋál-am$_6$: sila is clear from collation; the x in front of BU/sír looks similar to dumu on Biggs' copy. It is hardly e or i; cf. collation by Alster, 1991–92, 32.

Akk_1: *bīt-ka a-na re-*[*bi-ti* translates é sila-daŋal-la, but with no corresponding -zu, "your," in the Sumerian text.

SS variants: T_1: -b]í-ib-lá-e KÉŠ-da ŋál-la-àm; Ur_1: é [x x]-la nam-bí-íb-lá-e ⌜KÉŠ⌝-⌜da⌝ ŋál-la-àm; Ur_6: ⌜é⌝ sila-⌜daŋal⌝-⌜la⌝ n[a-; BM_1: [... -à]m; BM_2:] nam-bí-íb-lá-e KÉŠ-da ŋál-l[a-x]; P: é ⌜x x x⌝ nam-bi-ib-lá-e KÉŠ-d]a ŋál-la-àm; Sch_1 alone has é-sila daŋal-la-ta.

The reading sèr-da in SS KÉŠ-da ŋál-la-àm may be suggested on the basis of ED_1 by x-sír, where the sign x is not e, thus, excluding *e-sír. Yet, it is uncer-

17a. Wilcke, 1978, 203, translates: "Das Volk wird dir (das Wasser) vernichten!"

17b. Quoted here from Kämmerer, 1998, 190, using Dietrich's strophic divisions (UF 23, 50f.). Previous edition: Nougayrol, *Ugaritica* 5, 279 iii 5–6 (cf. the comments on p. 288). Nougayrol's text is quoted as source U, with a duplicate from Emar, quoted as source B. Cf. also Foster, *Before the Muses*, 420–421.

17c. One is tempted to see this advice as so general that it suggests no connection with our text. Yet, it is, indeed, possible that our line was known and served as inspiration for the author of *Counsels for Šūpē-amēli*. If that were the case, he very deliberately expanded the one-line plain statement into a four-line unit exemplifying the same pattern as appears elsewhere in the text. An elaborate strophic pattern was worked out by Dietrich in his edition of the text (UF 23 [1991] 38–65). A similar case is our lines 198–212, which also seem to be echoed in *Counsels for Šūpē-amēli*. Cf. p. 41, *Chap. 1.1: Context related expansion of the strophic pattern*.

18a. Wilcke, 1978, 213, suggests that LAK 218 might be zukum, "to trample." Alster, 1990, 18, tried to connect sír-da with Akkadian *si/erdû*, but this is hardly relevant.

tain how to harmonize the two sources, and the reading kéš-da ŋál-àm cannot be excluded.[18a] The reading of LAK 218 has been discussed by Pomponio, *Orientalia* 53 (1984) 10–18, who suggests lum$_{x}$, which can denote a plant; cf. Civil, *Bilinguismo a Ebla*, 91, n. 23. Whether the whole expression is covered by ED$_{I}$: LAK 218 ŋál-am$_{6}$ is uncertain. x-sír might even look like a gloss in the ED$_{I}$ text itself.[18b] Perhaps it indicates the reading of LAK 218 as ★sirda, but I know of no other reference that could confirm that reading of the sign. Edzard suggests "dort ist doch der dichteste Verkehr"; cf. Wilcke, 1978, 213, who suggests "Gedränge." Foxvog, 1976, 372, suggests: "Do not let a house extend out onto a public square—it will cause obstruction," which I have accepted as the most convincing solution so far.

Line 19: ED$_{I}$: šu-dù na-túm lú | šè-ba-dab$_{5}$; ED$_{2}$: ⸢šu⸣-du$_{8}$-a na-| túm lú-bi ša$_{4}$-ba-| dab$_{5}$: note that in the Adab source the line separation does not follow the logical segmentation.[19a]

SS variants: T$_{I}$:]-tùm lú-bé še-ba-e-dab$_{5}$-bé; Ur$_{I}$: šu-⸢dù⸣-⸢a⸣ ⸢nu⸣-mu-un-ti l[ú-b]é ša-ba-e-dab$_{5}$-bé; BM$_{I}$: -b]é; BM$_{2}$: -m]u(?)-te-ŋá-e lú-bé ša-ba-e-⸢x⸣ [x] (or more precisely: -te-ŋe$_{26}$-e; cf. p. 237, *Instr. Ur-Ninurta* 32 and the literature there cited); P: šu-du$_{8}$-a nu-e-tùm lú-bé ša-b[a-...]; Sch$_{I}$: šu-du$_{8}$-a nu-un-tùm ⸢(traces compatible with lú-bi ša)-[ba]-e-dab$_{5}$-bé-en. There is, thus, considerable discrepancy between T$_{I}$: tùm, Ur$_{I}$: ti, and BM$_{2}$: te-ŋá; cf. the comments below.

ED$_{I}$ writes šu-dù DU, whereas ED$_{2}$ as expected has šu-du$_{8}$-a DU (= de$_{6}$/túm), "to put oneself under the obligation of a pledge," "to act as a guarantor." In ED$_{2}$ the expression is šu-du$_{8}$-a DU, but in the SS sources tùm is used for the *marû* form: šu-du$_{8}$-a tùm. ED$_{I}$ and ED$_{2}$ consistently use the spelling túm where the SS version uses tùm, cf. *Chap. 1.9: Ḫamṭu-marû verbal distinctions*. The -a following šu-du$_{8}$ indicates a nominalized construction, lit., "a released hand."[19b]

The later scribes seem to have understood the Sumerian differently from the older sources. It is translated in Akk$_{I}$ by *qatāte leqû*, to accept a pledge, i.e., to accept someone's providing a pledge, whereas originally it seems to have meant the opposite, i.e., one's own providing a pledge; cf. the comments on line 20 below. Wilcke, 1978, 214, cf. pp. 203 and 213, accordingly translates the whole line "Du sollst keinen Bürgen bringen! Der Mann wird dich packen!" and understands the term as "sich verbürgen," explaining the Sumerian text of Ur$_{I}$: -ti, as a "Lehnübers. aus dem Akkadischen und die Akkad. Version." I understand Ur$_{I}$ as ★<šu> – ti, lit., "to receive," reflected in Akk$_{I}$: *qa-ta-te la te-l[e-eq-qe]*, whereas T$_{I}$ and P preserve the original meaning, lit., "to bring a pledge." BM$_{2}$: -m]u(?)-te-ŋá(= ŋe$_{26}$)-e is also based on ★šu ti/te(-ŋ).

For the negative indicative verbal form in P: nu-e-tùm, cf. Ur$_{I}$: ⸢nu⸣-mu-un-ti, and Sch$_{I}$: šu-du$_{8}$-a nu-un-tùm. For the -e- in ša-ba-e-dab$_{5}$-bé, cf. p. 211, *Chap. 1.9: Second person "object" element in preradical position*: cf. also lines 23; 53; 54 (var.); 66 (var. P); 253. Sch$_{I}$: (ša)-[ba]-dab$_{5}$-bé-en, makes the discussion somewhat dubious.

The ED sources have the expected prohibitive form: na-túm. For the ED writing of the so-called affirmative preformative /ša/ as šè and ša$_{4}$, see pp. 211–216, *Chap. 1.9: ED and SS ... /ša/, šè-, ši-, šu-*.

Line 20: cf. ED$_{I}$: šà šu-bad na-ak [me]-zu a[k]; ED$_{2}$: ur šu-ba na-ak | ní-zu na-du$_{7}$-né.

Akk$_{I}$: *ù at-ta qa-t[a-te la te-le-eq-qe]*, cf. below.

SS variants: T$_{I}$: nam]-mu-e-⸢x⸣-⸢x⸣ (no more missing before the end of line);[20] Ur$_{I}$: za-[e šu]-dù-a nam-mu-e-[x l]ú saŋ bí-íb-sal-la-e-a; BM$_{I}$:]-e; BM$_{2}$:]-igi-du$_{8}$-a nam-mu-ak-[x (x)]; P: za-e šu-du$_{8}$-[a] nam-mu-ak-[(en) ... ?]; Sch$_{I}$: za-e šu-du$_{8}$-a nam-mu-ak-en.

18b. Cf. line 44, ED$_{I}$: sá.sáŋ = ^{sá}sáŋ.

19a. Cf. p. 195, introduction to *Chap. 6: The Adab Version*, and previously Alster, 1974, 24.

19b. The term was read as šu-du$_{8}$-a gub by Falkenstein, NG 3 s.v., which makes sense as "to stand under the obligation of a pledge" ("sich verbürgen"), but see now, i.a., J. Marzahn and H. Neumann, AoF 22 (1995) 115 ad ii 1'. The expected sing. *ḫamṭu*-base is de$_{6}$ and the corresponding *marû*-base is túm or tùm. H. Sauren, ZA 60 (1970) 70ff., read šu-du$_{8}$-a-túm, but this was rejected by Wilcke, 1978, 213, n. 12. He considers the ED forms túm "unorthographic" (p. 214, n. 12) writings for tùm = "die finite *marû*-Basis." Cf. line 193 for an occurrence of both túm and tùm in the same SS line. Cf., p. 211, *Chap. 1.9: Ḫamṭu-marû alternation in ED.*

20. Nothing is, in fact, missing in T$_{I}$ after mu-e-⸢x⸣-⸢x⸣, although Wilcke, 1978, 214, erroneously indicates that at least two signs are missing.

It is uncertain how ED_I: šà šu-bad, and ED_2: ur šu-ba relate to the SS text: za-e šu du_8-a. These may, in fact, be two independent lines (so Wilcke, 1978, 214). Cf., however, line 196, where ED_I BAD corresponds to SS bar. I know of no other instances of ED šà representing za-e. ur might possibly represent an indefinite personal pronoun, like "one," but šà looks like an error. ED šu-bad and šu-ba, lit., "an open hand," may mean the same as šu du_8-a in the SS version, since du_8 is also "to open." In the SS version, P has: šu-du_8-[a]; Ur_I: šu]-dù-a; but BM_2: igi-du_8-a. The evidence is, thus, not uniform, and an old misunderstanding may be involved. Both lines 19 and 20 are translated by Akk_I as *qatāte lā teleqqe*, but this does not necessarily mean that it was a precise rendering of the original text, which might literally have meant "do not make an 'open hand'," i.e., perhaps, "do not be exaggeratedly generous." šu – ba/bad might then later have been confused with the term šu-du_8-a, "pledge." For *qatāte* cf. CAD Q, 168, s.v. *qatāte*, "to guarantee"; AHw 120, *bēl qatāte*, "Bürge"; AHw 910, *qātu* D, "Sicherheit, Bürge," mostly plural.

For the -e in front of -ak (partly broken), which occurs in two sources, T_I and Ur_I, cf. p. 211, *Chap. 1.9: Second person element* .... Cf. also lines 66; 257, var. C_3: nam-ba-e-šub-bé, var. of -bí-.

For the writing of ní-zu in ED_I: me-zu, cf. *Chap. 1.9: Use of special ED signs*.

The motivation clause [l]ú saŋ bí-íb-sal-la-e-a is included in Ur_I only. It seems related to the second part of line 36. Cf. the comments on that line. The ending (-l)a–e–a seems to render a gliding a-e vowel, separating a nominalized verbal clause, ending in -/a/, from a following -àm intensifier. The e then functions as a *hiatus tilger*: /-a-y-àm/. The result seems to be great emphasis, like "the situation being: a discredited man." This may be seen in the light of Krecher's "Isolierende Postpositionen," in ZA 57 (1965) 28–29; cf. Geller in *Jacobsen MV*, 93, and Sjöberg, JCS 40 (1988) 165, n. 2, referring to the repeated ending -/a-e/ in the Ur 3 *Inanna Prism*, i 4–8. It is similar to the ia-glide that appears, e.g., in line 80: I_5: [ŋizzal ḫ]é-em-ši-ia-ak; also in line 270: UM_2.

In ED_2: ní-zu na-du_7-né: the reading du_7 is not beyond doubt; du_7(UL), with a different reading, might reflect a form of (pe-el-)lá or similar. Yet, one can hardly read UL-lí/lé.

Line 21: ED_I: [i]gi-du na-⌜x⌝-⌜ba⌝ | lú uru_5 ši-sù x x; ED_2: [...] URU×A l[ú (x = small sign or nothing)] ši-su-su.[21a]

Akk_I; *a-na a-me-li mu-u[m-...]*. Cf. below.

SS variants: T_I: d]u_8 na-an-ak úru-bi ša-[; Ur_I: lú-[ra] igi-du_8-a na-an-[x x]-bi ša-⌜re⌝-⌜eb⌝-s[u-s]u; BM_I:]-su-su; BM_2:] igi-du_8 na-an-ak-e úru-bi ša-re-e[b-x x]; P: lú-ra igi-du_8 na-a[n]-ak-e-dè(?) [; Sch_I: lú-ra igi-du_8-a na-an-ak-en ⌜úru⌝-bi ša-ba(! looks like ma)-re-eb-su-su.

igi-du_8 was understood as *tāmartu*, a gift, by Wilcke, 1978, 214 (cf. p. 203: "Du sollst niemandem ein Begrüßungsgeschenk machen!"). If this is correct, the implication would rather be "Don't be exaggeratedly generous when spending such gifts," which, however, seems less convincing. For Akk_I: *mu-u[m-...* Geller suggests *mu-u[m-ma la-a ...*, "upon no one." The context suggests that igi-du_8-a might literally mean "looking" or "spying," or, probably more convincing, with Selz, WZKM 92, 175, "evidence" ("Zeugnis"). The ETCSL translates "don't make an 'inspection'," presumably with the purpose of obtaining a bribe. PSD A/3, 88, translates "you shall not keep a check on a person." Cf. *Counsels of Wisdom* 191: igi-du_8-du_8-meš.

úru (uru_2) = URU×UD. Apparently the ED sources have URU×A = uru_x (ED_2) and uru_5 (ED_I), probably = *abūbu*, "flood," or similar.[21b]

Note, however, that Sch_3 in line 181 uses úru where simply uru/úru is expected. I, therefore, do not in this case consider úru *emesal*, but a writing for úru = *abūbu*, "flood," if it is not simply an irregular writing for uru/ere.

su-su can be "submerge" (*ṭubbû*) or "restore" (*riābu*). A double entendre may well be intended, "you will be repaid with a flood" or "a flood will

21a. Details: ED_I first part: [I]GI:na:ba:DU:x. Cf. the copy of the two signs following na:ba in Alster, 1991–92, 51 "Obv. ii 5": look like é:IGI:UR, doubtful; second part: lú: uru_5:IGI:sù:x:x. Cf. the copy of the two last signs in Alster, 1991–92, 51 "Obv. ii 6": look like ⌜PA.NAM⌝) = [i]gi-du na-ba x / lú uru_5 ši-sù x x.

21b. The sign following lú in the ED sources is not ta (as read by Wilcke, 1978, 214), but probably uru_5 (cf. Alster, 1991–92, 32). It is broken in ED_2.

submerge you." Cf. lines 39–41. ED$_I$ apparently has sù instead of su-su.[21c] Cf. the collation in Alster, 1991–92, 32 with copy p. 51.

Line 22: SS variants: T$_I$:] nam-bi-DU-[; Ur$_I$: ki d[u$_{14}$-d]a-ka n[am-b]í-D[U-(x)-d]è; BM$_I$:]-⸢x⸣-dè; BM$_2$: -d]a-ka nam-bí-DU-[x (x)]; P: ki du$_{14}$-da-ka nam-[. Sch$_I$: ki du$_{14}$-da-ka nam-ba-e-gub-bu-dè-en, only source that preserves the entire line. T$_I$ has a rare example of bi used for the verbal prefix /bi/, usually written bí-; cf. vars. lines 16; 31; 58; 66.

Line 23: SS variants: BM$_2$ and apparently P: lú ki-inim-ma; T$_I$ has ki-inim-bi. Sch$_I$: du$_{14}$-dè lú ki-inim-ma-šè na-an-ku$_4$-ku$_4$-un, only source that has -šè. For nam-ba-e-ku$_4$-ku$_4$, cf. the comments on line 19 and p. 211, *Chap. 1.9: Second person ... element.*

Line 24: SS variants: Ur$_I$: [d]u$_{14}$-dè ní-[; BM$_2$:] ní-zu nam-b[a-; P: du$_{14}$-dè ní-ba (read zu?) [. Sch$_I$: du$_{14}$-dè ní-zu a-na(?) ⸢nam(?)⸣-⸢mu⸣-ŋá (could be ⸢e?⸣)-da-zu-un, a-na unexplained, epigraphically uncertain.

Line 25: BM$_2$: -a]k-dè-en ⸢x⸣, agrees with P: du$_{14}$ n[am-a]k-dè-en [; Sch$_I$: [(x)]-⸢x⸣(may be d]u$_{14}$) nam-x x(like da) KA nam-ùr(?)-ùr(?)-re(?)]. It is tempting to restore something like *du$_{14}$ – ùr-ùr, from line 60, but it is difficult to see why almost the same line should occur more than once within the same composition.

Line 26: SS variants: T$_I$:]-⸢ra⸣-si-⸢ga⸣; Ur$_I$:]-⸢x⸣ ba-sig; Ur$_2$: [x] ⸢x⸣-ka é-⸢x⸣-la-⸢ka⸣ / šèŋ ba-ra-si-g[a]; BM$_2$: k]á é-gal-la [.

The reading šèŋ (A.AN), "rain," is based on Ur$_2$: šèŋ ba-ra-si-g[a], where it seems fairly certain. -àm would hardly be possible here. In T$_I$: ...-si-⸢ga⸣; Ur$_I$: ba-sig, and Ur$_2$: ba-ra-si-g[a], a common verb, like /si-g/, "to come down," may be intended. Yet, Sch$_I$ does not support that interpretation, and the expected expression, said of rain, might rather have been *im ba-ra-šèŋ = *zanānu*, cf. e.g., SP 3.149, so no attempt is made here to reconstruct the line fully. It is uncertain whether one or two signs are missing in front of k]á é-gal-la-⸢ka⸣. A vague pronoun, such as lú, "he who sits (under the protection) of the gate of the royal palace," may be missing.

Line 27: ED$_I$: du$_7$ sila-kúr ⸢x⸣-ma | NI.LAK 134 bar-tar-ta gub-ma.

Akk$_2$: [... *nu*]-*uk*-[*kir* ...]. Probably from *nu*]-*uk-kir*, D "verändern," imp.; hardly read *nu*]-*uq-qir*, D from *naqāru*, "niderreißen."

SS variants: T$_I$: [... -r]a(?) na-mu-DAGAL(? too long for ma)-NE; Ur$_I$: [... -r]a(?) ⸢nam(or, rather = è, or gub?)⸣-⸢ma⸣-ni-ib (nothing missing after ib); Ur$_2$: du$_{14}$-dè bar-bar-ta gub-gub-[ba] / in-nu-uš sila-kúr-⸢x-ra(?)⸣ ⸢nam⸣-⸢ma⸣-è(?); BM$_2$: [...] bar-bar-ta [/ ... si]la kúr-ra [...]; Sch$_I$: du$_{14}$-ta bar-ta gub-gub-[x-(x)] ì(?)-ni-ta(?) sila-kúr-ra níŋin-na-ma-a[n-x (x)].

In ED$_I$, a verb corresponding to SS gub-gub-[ba] is expected, but what is left is an illegible sign followed by ma. The illegible sign in the upper right corner has a short upper horizontal and cannot be gub (cf. collation by Alster, 1991–92, 32).

SS in-nu-uš: probably in-nu, "insult" + šè; cf. UET 6/2 286 (Alster, *Proverbs* II, 314). The parallelism suggests a term nearly synonymous with du$_{14}$, "quarrel." The two parts of the line are reversed in ED$_I$, but with the verbs in the same order as the SS version. du$_7$, thus, represents du$_{14}$, and NI. LAK 134 corresponds to in-nu-uš.[27a]

In Ur$_I$, there is no missing verb following -ib at the end of the sentence, so the form must be understood as an imperative, parallel to gub-gub-ba.[27b] Ur$_I$ does allow a reading such as ⸢gub⸣-⸢ma⸣-ni-ib, or similar. Ur$_2$ seems to have ⸢nam⸣-⸢ma⸣-è(?), which may be an ill understood attempt to interpret an imperative as a prohibitive verb. This may have been caused by attraction from the many such forms in the text, which, however, did not affect gub-gub-[ba] in the first half of the line. The second SS verb can unfortunately not be restored from ED$_I$, where it corresponds to the first illegible verb: ⸢x⸣-ma. A verb like gub or dab$_5$, "take another road," might fit. I cannot explain T$_I$: -r]a(?) na-mu-DAGAL(?)-NE,

21c. The ED$_I$ text is "ohne *marû*-Redupl." as noted by Wilcke, ZA 68 (1978) 214. This is normal for ED texts. Cf. p. 212, *Chap. 1.9: Ḫamṭu-marû-reduplication in ED?*

27a. Wilcke, 1978, 214 (ad 31), however, suggests [... -r]a nam-ma-ni-ib-<DU>, but nam is not so certain.

27b. The ED sign is NI.LAK 134, as intended by Alster, 1974, 11, where iii 2: i(LAK).ni is a misprint for i(LAK 134).ni. It is strictly speaking not NI.I as transliterated by Wilcke, 1978, 214 (l. 31), but it is, of course, a reasonable assumption that LAK 134 represents an early form of i, from which it differs only by having six horizontals instead of five.

which, however, points to a variant reading with a prohibitive verbal form. If the reconstruction of Akk$_2$: *nu]-uk-[kir* as a D-imperative is justified, it would confirm the understanding of at least the first of the Sum. verbs as an imperative. Sch$_I$: sila-kúr-ra níŋin-na(-)ma-a[n-x (x)] may be a hybrid form of the verb níŋin, "to walk in a circle"; cf. *Instr. Šuruppak* 260: níŋin-na ga-àm-me-re$_7$-dè-en, "Let us go round in circles."

The most likely solution is to see the phraseology as similar to the examples quoted by Alster, 1974, 82, from *Enmerkar and Ensuhkešdanna* 209–210: ... ŋìr-kúr ba-ra-an-dab$_5$ ... sila-kúr ba-ra-an-dab$_5$, "took another way ... took another road"; *Emeš and Enten* 111: nu-érim-gim bar-ta im-da-gub da-bi nu-mu-un-tag-ge, which the ETCSL translates "turned away as from an enemy and would not draw near."

Line 28: ED$_I$: níŋ na-mu-zuḫ-zuḫ me-zu na-MUNŠUB; ED$_2$: níŋ nám-zuḫ-zuḫ ní-zu | nàb(AN+AN)-MUNŠUB.

Akk$_2$: *[m]i-i[m(?)-ma la ta-šar-raq ra-man-k]a(?) la*(?) [...].

SS variants: T$_I$: n]í-zu nam-mu-úš-e; Ur$_I$:] ní-zu na-an-úš-e; Ur$_2$: níŋ nam-mu-⌜zuḫ⌝-⌜zuḫ⌝ / ní-zu nam-úš-⌜e⌝-⌜en⌝; BM$_2$:]-zuḫ-z[uḫ; Sch$_I$: níŋ-nam nu-zuḫ-zuḫ ní-zuḫ ⌜nu(?)⌝-uš-⌜en⌝ (room for two more signs?).

For the ED$_I$ writing of the negative prohibitive preformative as na-, and ED$_2$ as na-, but also nam, nám, and nàb(AN+AN), cf. pp. 212–216, *Chap. 1.9: Modal verbal prefixes*.

Both ED texts have MUNŠUB = LAK 672, for which see Civil, RA 61 (1967) 63ff., = sumur, designating a cover of reed or similar, protecting the center of a boat against the sun. The sign seems to have wider uses in the ED sources, so it is not impossible that here it represents the same verb as SS bad. The reading of BAD as úš, "to kill," is not beyond doubt, however; apparently BAD represents a different verb here from line 53, where it is bad = *rêqu*, "to remove far away." Cf. also line 63, where Akk$_3$ has *la tu-ḫal-la-aq* (= úš?), but Akk$_2$ *la tuš-ma-at.*[28]

ní-zu, "yourself," in the SS version is a pun on ní-zuḫ, "thief." The pun would not be recognizable in the ED versions; cf. the comments on line 30 below, and *Chap. 1.9: Use of special ED signs: me, ní.*

The text here makes use of a characteristic stylistic feature, a motivation clause that expresses the retaliation of a crime in terms of an exaggerated consequence of the crime: by stealing something, one does not necessarily kill oneself with an ax, but eventually this may lead to one's own mutilation, or even cause one's own death. This gives such motivation clauses a sense of morbid humor characteristic of proverbial wisdom. Cf. the comments, p. 214, under *Chap. 1.9: ED na- versus ša-.*

Line 29: ED$_I$: é na-[bùr] ⌜x⌝ [x x]; ED$_2$: é nam-m[u]-⌜bùr⌝ [...].

Akk$_2$: *bī[ta la ta]-p[al-la]-áš* NI T[A(?) ...] *l*[*a* ...].

SS variants: T$_I$:] mi-si-saḫar-ra nam-[; Ur$_I$:] ⌜x⌝ mi-si-saḫar al nam-me; Ur$_2$: é na-a-an-ni-bùr-e-en / mi-si-saḫar al <nam>-me-en; the writing na-a-ni- is unexplained; Sch$_I$: é nam-mu-bùru-dè-en ⌜mí(?)⌝-(⌜x⌝)-si(?)-saḫar al nam-[me]. There is, thus, one text that has mi-si-saḫar-ra and one that omits -ra. Cf. line 257, where one text has mi-si-saḫar-a (locative), whereas two texts include -ra. It is there further written with the ŋiš-determinative in one source. It is equated with *nēpištu*, cf. AHw s.v. *nēpeštum*, referring to MSL 9, 100 and 94, 77. This occurs also in *Curse of Agade* 236, where a container of wood or leather to transport precious metals such as gold is clearly intended.

Line 30: ED$_I$: nu-zuḫ ušum na-nam ul-dab$_5$ géme na-nam; ED$_2$: nu-zuḫ | [p]iriŋ na-nám ù-|dab$_5$ géme na-nám.

Akk$_2$: *šar-ra-qu ne-e-šu* [...] *x* [...].

SS variants: I$_I$: -z]u piriŋ na-n[am; T$_I$: -d]ab$_5$ saŋ na-n[am]; Ur$_I$: n]a-⌜nam⌝ ul-dab$_5$ saŋ na-nam; Ur$_2$: ní-zu ⌜piriŋ⌝ ⌜na⌝-na-àm ul-dab$_5$ saŋ na-na-àm (cf. line 69); Ur$_6$:] ul-[; Sch$_I$: ní-zu saŋ(sic!) ⌜na⌝-nam ul-GAN(?) na-nam: ul-GAN(?) is unexplained; the variant saŋ, slave," for piriŋ, "lion," may simply be a scribal error, but perhaps rather a reflection of a variant form of the saying.

For the well-known ní-zuḫ, *šarrāqu*, "thief," the ED sources write nu-zuḫ, but Ur$_2$ phonetically ní-zu. Cf. pp. 217ff., *Use of special ED signs: me, ní.*

28. Cf. the comments on line 63 below. In view of the ED texts, sumun might be considered, cf. Wilcke, 1978, 214, but the meaning would be obscure.

For the SS version as well as ED$_2$: piriŋ, "lion," ED$_1$ has ušum, usually understood as a mythological animal, like a "dragon," but cf. Sjöberg, *Wilcke FS*, 265–266 for other possibilities, among these an ED profession.

For the affirmative na-nam, ED$_1$ uses na-nam, but ED$_2$ na-nám; elsewhere in ED$_2$ na-, and nàb- are used, cf. p. 214, *Chap. 1.9: ED prohib. na-/nám-*. The verbal prefix in ul-dab$_5$ is best taken as the prospective ù, "after he has been caught," following the ETCSL edition. The line was previously understood as "The thief is indeed a lion, the receiver(?) is indeed a slave" (Alster, 1974, 37, line 34). There is no unambiguous attestation of a word ul-dab$_5$ meaning "receiver," although it might well have been a frozen verbal form meaning just that.[30] It is remarkable that the SS version preserves the rare (or unique?) spelling ul-dab$_5$ from ED$_1$, whereas ED$_2$ has ù-dab$_5$, which later would have been the normal standard writing. The ED sources have géme, "slave girl," instead of saŋ, "slave."

Line 31: ED$_1$: [x]-gaz na-ak ⸢x⸣ sír(?) [na]-⸢bar⸣(?); Akk$_2$: *ma-ri ḫab-ba-tu-tam la te-p[u-uš ra-m]an-ka RU x* [...]. Cf. CAD *ḫabbātum*: "robber," but *ḫabbatūtam*, "robbery," has not previously been attested.

SS variants: I$_1$ + I$_2$: [dumu sa-gaz n[a]m-m[u-...] / [š]e(?)-sír-re-eš ⸢x⸣ [n]am-bi-[...]; T$_1$:] nam-m[u-...] / [... b]í-bar-[re] ; Ur$_1$: [x x x g]az nam-mu-ù-ak-e / [...] ⸢x⸣(not še) ⸢búr(?)⸣-re nam-bí-ib-bar-ra; Ur$_2$: dumu-mu sa-gaz na-àm-ma-[ak]-e / ní-zu àga-àm na-àm-bí-[íb-bar-r]e-e; Ur$_6$: dumu-ŋ[u$_{10}$ ...] na-bi-[...] ní-zu àg[a ...] na-bi-b[ar-...]; for -bi-, cf. the comments on line 22. Sch$_1$: dumu-ŋu$_{10}$ ⸢sa-gaz nam-mu-ak⸣-en ní-zu ⸢x⸣(like mu)-⸢x⸣ (like šè)-⸢x⸣-⸢x⸣(like ke$_4$) ⸢x⸣(may be nam)-⸢bar⸣-re.

àga – bar, "to cut with an ax," (previously read tùn) is well attested, cf. PSD A/3, 40, s.v. aga B, which quotes ample evidence, yet without committing itself to a translation, arguing, p. 40, that "Gudea Cyl. A xv 22–25 shows that àga bar is a procedure that takes place after the cutting down (ku$_5$) of a tree; similarly, Gudea Cyl. A vii 15–18, «dress (a tree)» would fit all the passages." On p. 40, our line is quoted, as well as OIP 99, 213 ii(?) 7': igi-a bur àga nám-bar-bar, but no translation is ventured.[31] Even if the translation "to dress" a tree, in the sense "to smooth it by ribbing it of superfluous branches," etc., is justified in most cases, this cannot be meant in our text, unless some very morbid sense of humor was intended. There is no reason for not considering the plain translation, "to cut (lit. "split") with a ax," but maybe more precisely "Don't let yourself be mutilated with an ax."

The second part of the line had a variant form in I$_{1+2}$: š]e(?)-sír-re-eš ⸢x⸣ [n]am-bi-[...; and Ur$_1$: ⸢x⸣(not še) ⸢búr(?)⸣-re nam-bí-ib-bar-ra, perhaps also in Sch$_1$. A separate term for an ax or a similar tool may have been involved. Foxvog, 1976, 272, suggests the reading [še](!?)-zur-re in Ur$_1$. This may be correct, although my collation shows "⸢x⸣(apparently ŋot še) ⸢búr(?)⸣-re." He correctly connects it with I$_{1-2}$, which he reads še-sír-re-eš, comparing it to CAD *ṣīru* C: a copper tool with a wooden handle. This is attested in Ḫḫ VII A 167f. as giš-zé-ir, etc. The writing še(-)sír-re-eš, cf. ED$_1$: ⸢x⸣(= še?) sír(?) [na]-⸢bar⸣(?), suggests a tool with which to chop grain, or similar. This variant seems to have been close to ED$_1$: ⸢x⸣ sír(?) [na]-⸢bar⸣(?).

Line 32: ED$_1$: ninta$_x$(SAL+NINTA) mi-si ⸢na⸣-⸢x⸣(= ḪI×DIŠ+GIŠ?) [m]e-zu [x] x. Cf. collation Alster, 1991–92, 32: ED$_1$, read sign by sign: MI.SI SAL+NINTA ⸢na⸣-'NE'. The fourth sign is neither me (as the copy shows) nor [a]k, but can safely be read ⸢na⸣. The sign tentatively read 'NE' looks rather like ḪI×DIŠ+GIŠ. It can be neither na nor ak.

Akk$_2$: *su-sa-pi-in-nu-tam la te-ep-p[u-uš ra-ma]n-ka l[a ...]*.

SS variants: I$_1$ + I$_2$: [... n]a-an-[... n]í-zu nam-⸢x⸣-[...]; T$_1$:] nam-m[u-...]; Ur$_1$: [... n]a-an-ak ní-zu na-an-[x x]; Ur$_2$: ninta-niŋir-si na-[...] ⸢x⸣ / ní-zu na-àm-⸢x⸣-⸢x⸣ (could be gíd?-e); Ur$_6$: é niŋir-[...]

30. Yet, see perhaps SP 2.82, now Alster, *Proverbs* I, 62: ul-tuš, "after he had been waiting." Other readings are, of course, possible.

31. I suspect that the translation of PSD "to dress (a tree)," is borrowed from Jacobsen's Gudea translation, *Harps*, 397. The *Oxford Advanced Learner's Dictionary of Current English*, s.v. dress (verb) recognizes sub 6, "make ready to use, prepare," said, e.g., of leather, a salad, etc., and 7: "brush and comb." If àga – bar denoted the action that could be used to "dress a tree," there must, of course, have been a more precise technical meaning behind it.

ní [...] (é unexplained); Sch_1: ninta ⌜niŋir⌝(?)-⌜si⌝(? looks rather like ra) na-⌜an⌝ ... (traces of ca. 8 signs).

For the ED sign $ninta_x$(SAL+NINTA), cf. the comments on line 49, below. Some further qualification to ninta is expected, not just any man. ED_1 mi-si seems to represent SS niŋir-si = *susapinnu*, "best man."

The missing verb might have been similar to that of line 35. Ur_2 might be read àm-⌜gíd⌝-⌜e⌝, but this is very uncertain.

Line 33: ED_1: [si]kil-da [(x)] [n]e na-da-⌜e⌝ inim-sig [m]áḫ(AL).

Akk_2: *it-it ár-da-ti šá mu-ti aḫ-z[u la t]e-ṣe-eḫ kar-ṣ[u ...].*

SS variants: I_1 + I_2: [...] nam-(perhaps = nam-[dam-tuku?]) ... n]e(?) nam-mu-u[n-... / ...]-bi maḫ(!)-[; T_1: na]m-[...]; Ur_1: [ki-sikil dam tu]ku-d[a x x] nam-mu-un-KA(the sign is not NE)-e inim-sig-⌜ga⌝(rather than bi) ma[ḫ-àm]: Ur_2: ki-sikil dam tuku-⌜da⌝ e-⌜ne⌝ [...] inim si-bi(bi rather than ga) ma[ḫ-àm]; Sch_1: ⌜ki⌝-⌜sikil⌝ ....

ED_1 seemingly writes ki-sikil without the ki-sign. The use of AL with the reading máḫ in ED_1 is normal for ED texts.

The verb is [n]e na-da-⌜e⌝ in ED_1, which suggests a *marû*-form of *e-ne dug_4,[33a] but it is doubtful how to interpret the SS verb of which only e-⌜ne⌝ remains in Ur_2, and nam-mu-un-KA-e in Ur_1. Since here either *ne-e or *-dug_4-ge would have been expected if the base of the compound verb had been *e-ne dug_4, it is tempting to suggest that another term is involved, and that the sign KA has been copied from a misunderstood NE, obviously representing *zú – li_9(-r)(NE) = *ṣiaḫum*, "to laugh," as Akk_3 has it.[33b] I understand the -da following dam tuku as the comitative, but the verbal -/ed-a/ cannot be completely ruled out; cf. Selz, WZKM 92 (2002) 173–178 "Spricht nicht mit einem Mädchen (das einen Gemahl nehmen will(?)), die Verleumdung ist riesengroß."

inim-sig occurs also in line 93, where Ur_1 seems to have inim-sig-ga (rather than -bi), whereas I_{1-2} has:]-bi, and Ur_3: si-bi(rather than ga). The expected expression is rather *eme-sig-bi, "its slander," i.e., the slander arising from it, but apparently eme-sig is restricted to the term eme-sig gu_7 = *ākil karṣi*. *Dialogue* 5, 58: e-ne-èŋ sig gu_7-gu_7, however, shows that KA-sig can be read inim-sig; cf. Alster, 1974, 84, with p. 128, note 39, also referring to MSL 13, 249, n. 5. Cf. also Sjöberg, *Kienast FS*, 542, n. 26.

Line 34: Akk_2: *i-na da-ak-ka-ni it-ti aš-t[i] a-mi-li la tu-[uš-ša-ab]*. The initial dumu-[$ŋu_{10}$], "my son," is, thus, omitted in Akk_2.

SS variants: I_1 + I_2: [...] dag [...] ⌜x⌝ nam-bí-[...]; Ur_1: [x x x x] lú dam tu[ku-d]a dúr nam-⌜bí⌝-e-ŋá-ŋá (collation Alster, 1974, pl. I; there is room for dumu-$ŋu_{10}$ daggan-na); Ur_2: dumu-[$ŋu_{10}$] ⌜x⌝-na lú [...] / dúr [na]m-bí-[...]; Sch_1: ka ... (traces of ca. 6 mostly illegible signs) -ŋá-ŋá.

Alster, 1974, 36 (l. 39) restored dumu-[$ŋu_{10}$ daggan]-na, on the basis of OECT VI pl. XXIV, K. 5158, rev. 8–9: [da]ggan lú dam-tuku-a dúr nam-bi-ŋá-ŋá = *ina takkanni itti alti amēli la tuššab*, "do not sit (alone) in a chamber with a man's wife" (cited p. 84). daggan = KI+GIŠGAL. I_{1+2} has simply dag-[, probably = dag-[ga-na]. U_2: an illegible sign followed by -na. Alster, 1974, 37 (l. 39), translated "My son, do not sit (alone) in a [chamber] with someone's wife." The Akkadian translation *it-ti aš-t[i] a-mi-li*, "with a man's wife," confirms that lú in lú dam tuku-da is a genderless reference to a woman, "someone who has a spouse" = "is married."[34]

33a. The ED writing E may represent both a *ḫamṭu* and a *marû*-form, cf. p. 211, *Chap. 1.9: Ḫamṭu-marû distinctions*.

33b. Wilcke 1968, 215 (l. 38), suggests that a euphemism "für verfänlichere [that is, delicate] Situationen" is involved, tentatively reading Ur_1: [ki-sikil-dam]-⌜tuku⌝ mí-[zi(?) n]am-mu-un-dè(!)-e, and e-ne-e, partly following Foxvog 1976, 374, who, however, reads: Ur_1: [ki-sikil dam (du_{12}-)]du_{12}-d[am n]am-, and Ur_2: ki-sikil dam du_{12}-[du_{12}]-e-dè ..., which is more convincing.

34. Wilcke, 1978, 204, however, translates "niemals sollst du dich bei einem verheirateten Manne niederlassen!" arguing, p. 215, that there is no room for *daggan-na, and suggesting m[e]-na instead (meaning "niemals"?). Yet, there is room for *daggan-na, even if written with a relatively large sign for daggan, or as dag-[ga-na, as I_{1-2} seems to have had. Besides, dumu-$ŋu_{10}$ might have been omitted, as in Akk_2. Wilcke denies that lú could be used with reference to a woman, but the Akkadian text is unequivocal and cannot possibly be mistaken at this point. The line cannot have been addressed to a girl, since it starts with the address

Line 35: ED_1: du_7 na-mú-mú níŋ-z[u na-š]ub. ED_1: níŋ-z[u seems to be an unexpected writing for the SS version ní-zu.[35] ED_1 has du_7 instead of the SS version du_{14}.

Akk_2: *la mu-uṣ-ṣa-la-ta ra-man-ka la tu-[qal-lil(?)]*. For du_{14} – mú-mú Akk_2 gives *lā muṣṣalāta*, from *muṣṣālu* (Gt from *ṣâ/êlu*); cf. AHw 679, "streitsüchtig." Cf. line 54 below.

SS variants: I_2:]-nam-[; I_3: [d]u_{14} n[am-...] / [n]í-z[u; Ur_1: [x x x-m]ú-dè ní zu na-an-[pe]-el-lá; Ur_2: du_{14} [; Sch_1: du_{14} nam-... (almost destroyed)-en.

The second verb may have been similar to that of line 32. The SS version must have had na-an-[pe]-el-lá, but ED_1, according to the copy, has na-š]ub, perhaps "Don't cast down yourself," but very uncertain.

Line 36: ED_1: l[ul na-x x] ⌜ra⌝ [x x] x-sal-sal ⌜x x⌝ su, perhaps = *l[ul na-gur_5-gur_5]-ra? but the rest cannot be fully harmonized with ED_2: [lu]l [na]-gur_5-gur_5 / [s]aŋ sal-sal-[a]m_6.

Akk_2: *a-na <ṣa>-al-ti la tu-uk-tap-pa-ad qá-qá-du qa-l[a-...]*, "Don't ponder over quarrels." The first part of the Akkadian text apparently translates an unknown variant of the first part of the Sumerian text, like *du_{14} na[m]-gur_5-gur_5. The possibility, of course, exists that an underlying du_{14} had mistakenly been repeated from the preceding line and caused confusion or a damaged sign lul may mistakenly have been read as du_{14}. Even then, gur_5 = *kapādu*, "to plot, to plan," is very different from what has hitherto been expected; cf. below. The normal equivalent would have been ir-pak – ak.

SS variants: I_3: lul na[m]-gu[r_5-...] / s[aŋ] kù [...]; Ur_1: [x x-gu]r_5-gur_5 saŋ gú ⌜sal-sal⌝-la; Ur_2: [...] / saŋ KU [x x (x)] ⌜x⌝-àm; Sch_1: lul nam-... (almost destroyed).

lul gur_5-gur_5 has previously been understood as "to spit out lies," but if the Akkadian translation above is reliable, it means "to plan, to plot lies." The expression is known from *Dím-ma-ni ús-a-ni* 5 (TMHNF 3, 42 viii 28): šà-ta [nu]-mu-un-sa_9 lul gú-gur_5-àm, "from birth he is not good, he plots lies" (cf. Alster, 1974, 84).

Geller in van Dijk/Geller, *Ur III Incantations*, p. 53, ad no. 14, line 7, compares nar-kur-ku_5, which he tentatively interprets as "onomatopoeia for the sounds made by birds whose voice has been altered by the demons," but alternatively considers a translation in line with "do not belch forth lies," suggested by Alster, 1974, 84.

The second part of the line is partly parallel to the addition in the second part of line 20: [l]ú saŋ bí-íb-sal-la-e-a. Ur_1 has saŋ gú ⌜sal-sal⌝-la, in which the meaning of gú remains doubtful. It may reflect an ancient scribal error, since Ur_2: saŋ KU, and I_3: s[aŋ] kù, both seem to reflect attempts at rendering a text that was not fully understood. Cf. *qaqqadu qalālu*, "to become discredited," CAD s.v. *qalālu* 2 b; cf. also *qullulu*, "to discredit," 3.b) with *qaqqadu*, "to discredit."

Line 37: ED_1: KA na-tar me(?)-⌜zu⌝ ŋar-ra; Akk_2: *la mu-uš-ta-la-ta a-ma-tu-ka ⌜šá⌝-a[k-na]*.

SS variants: I_3: KA(!) nam-tar-tar-r[e-; Ur_1: [x x ta]r-re inim-zu ŋar-⌜ra-àm⌝; Ur_2: KA nam-tar-[tar-re]-⌜e⌝-en / inim-zu ŋar-ra-àm; Sch_1: ⌜ka⌝ ⌜tar⌝(?) (almost destroyed). Cf. line 67.

ED_1 seems to have me(?)-⌜zu⌝ instead of inim-zu, apparently with me representing inim or me, cf. p. 217, *Chap. 1.9: Use of special ED signs.*

For KA nam-tar-tar-re-⌜e⌝-en, Akk_2 gives KA – tar = *lā muštalāta*. Cf. AHw 685, *muštālu*, "der sich berät, umsichtig," and CAD M/2, 283 "judicious, thoughtful, full of concern," which, however, normally corresponds to za-ra-KA-KA. Apparently this, as well as the corresponding verb in line 38, was meant negatively (*mala parte*). It may simply be the Sum. za-ra dug_4-dug_4, "(she) keeps speaking to you," indicating that she is so busy giving advice to everyone that it causes irritation everywhere, which became a frozen verbal phrase. It hardly came from a different word, cf. CAD s.v. *muštālu*, p. 284: from *šâlu*, "to attack." Cf. comments on line 113 below, referring to SP 3.41.

dumu-$ŋu_{10}$, "my son!" That the advice should have been addressed to the son warning him "vor den folgen des Wohnens im Hause eines verheirateten Mannes" has not been confirmed by Akk_2; the most likely possibility is to accept lú dam tu[ku-d]a as a genderless reference to a woman, "someone who is married."

35. The second part of ED_1 is, however, very difficult to read and uncertain at this point. The photograph does not help here.

Our KA – tar is probably not related to ka-tar si-il = *da/ilīlu dalālu*, "to praise." Cf. CAD s.v. *dalīlu*, "fame, praise, glory" = ka-tar. Proto Sag Text A ix (MSL SS 1, 18): 12'–21': ka-tar-re-a, ka-téš-a-sì-ga, ka-bal-bal-la, ka sag_9-sag_9-ge, ka-ta-du_{11}-ga, ka-ta-kar-ra, ka-ta-ḫé-gál, ka-búr-ra, ka-sun_7-na, ka dun_5-na. Proto Sag Text A x (MSL SS 1, 19): 18'–19': ka-ka-tar, ka-tar-si-il. Sag A iii 14 (MSL SS 1, 21): ka-tar-ri-a = *pu-ú wa-at-rum*; alpha 11: ka-tar-si-il = *di-li-lu da-la-lu*. Sag A iii (MSL SS 1, 22), after 48, alpha 12: ka-tar-zi = *qú-ur-du*. Cf. also lú-ka(?)-⌜tar⌝ in UET VII, 73 iv 11, treated by Sjöberg, *Limet FS*, 120 and 135f.

In line 67 it is equated with *šarāḫum* Dt, cf. AHw 1183, "sich rühmen"

inim-zu ŋar-ra-àm means literally, "your word is placed," i.e., "will stand forever." Cf. the addition to line 67 in Ur_2.

Line 38: ED_1: [a]d gi_4-gi_4 [...]-ŠÈ NE [...]. I cannot offer anything constructive to the reconstruction of ED_1:]-ŠÈ NE [. ED_2: ad nà[b(A[N]-A[N])-gi_4-gi_4] igi ⌜x⌝ (= [du]gud?]) nàb(AN-AN)-íl.

Akk_2: *la tam-ta-na-al-lik pa-ni kab-tu-ti ul ta-na-áš-[ši]*.

SS variants: I_3: [a]d nam-g[i_4-...] / ig[i ...]; Ur_1: [na]m-gi_4-gi_4 igi-dugud nu-mu-un-da-íl; Ur_2: ⌜ad⌝(? certainly not KA) na-àm-gi_4-gi_4-e igi-dugud nu-mu-u[n-x x]-⌜e⌝-en; Sch_1: ⌜ad⌝ nam ....[38a]

For ad gi_4-gi_4 Akk_2 gives = *lā tamtanallik*: cf. AHw 593, *malāku*: Gtn only rarely attested, and only about Gods, but Gt "sich betaten" is common. CAD lists *mitluku*, "to deliberate." AHw Gtn lists *im-ta-lik*. Here the meaning seems to be "Don't devise bad plans (with others)" in a negative sense (*mala parte*); it would be difficult to understand ad = "advice" in a positive sense (*bona parte*) here.[38b]

The motivation clause in the SS version is phrased as a simple indicative, nu-..., "you cannot bear," but in ED_2 it is phrased as a second prohibitive clause, igi ⌜x⌝ (= [du]gud?]) nàb(AN-AN)-íl, which presumably means "Don't cause a heavy eye to be raised upon yourself." I take the comitative infix in nu-mu-un-da-íl(-e-en) as "you cannot bear," lit., "it is not with you to bear."

igi-dugud: No parallels seem to be known, but dugud, lit., "heavy," is well attested in the sense "honorable," or similar. Here igi-dugud, rather, seems to mean, lit., "a reproachful eye," or, following a suggestion by Geller, you cannot make a "pompous impression" (lit., raise an important face). Cf. also *Chap. 2.3: Counsels of Wisdom*, 161–162.

Line 39: ED_1: [... níŋ]-zuḫ na-gu_7; Akk_2: *it-ti šar-ra-qa šur-qa la tak-kal*.

SS variants: I_3: lú-da [; Ur_1: l[ú-da] ⌜níŋ⌝-zuḫ-a nam-mu-da-gu_7-e; Ur_2: lú-da níŋ gu_7-[a] na-m[u-d]a-gu_7-e; S_2: 5: lú-⌜zuḫ⌝-a níŋ-zuḫ-a na-[...].

As it stands the sentence means "Do not eat something stolen with a man." Yet, what is intended is perhaps rather "Do not eat stolen things with a thief," implying that the thief is the same person as the one with whom the stolen items are eaten.[39] This is what is intended in S_2: 5: lú-⌜zuḫ⌝-a níŋ-zuḫ-a na-[...] (cf. Civil, 1984, 297), which, thus, surprisingly seems to preserve the better text in this case, although it is a Susa text of a type that may be expected to contain errors.

Line 40: ED_1: ⌜šu⌝ ⌜x⌝⌜x⌝ DU. Akk_2: *qa-at-ka ru-šá-a la ta-bal-⌜lal⌝*.

Geller points out that *ru-šá-a* is not "red," but, rather, *rušû*, "filthy," translating, "Don't mix (drugs) with your hand being filthy." *ruššû* is normally equated with ḫuš; cf. AHw 996, *ruššû* I = "rot," but note also *ruššû* II D: "rücksichtslos behandeln." It could be the contamination with red, the color of blood, that creates the association with crime. su is here equated with *balālu*, "to mix."

SS variants: I_3: šu-zu ⌜x⌝ [...]; Ur_1: š[u-zu úš-à]m na-di-ni-ib-su-su; Ur_2: šu-zu úš-àm [... -s]u-⌜su⌝; S_2: 6: šu-zu ⌜mud⌝(?) na-bí-íb-s[á(?) ...] (cf. below); Sch_1: na-....

38a. Alster, 1974, 36 (l. 43), cf. p. 54, read inim nam-gi_4-gi_4, but the first sign is clearly [a]d in I_3, and ⌜ad⌝ in Ur_2, with no KA in any source, which accords with the ED texts, where, both in ED_1 (viii 10, cf. Civil 1984, 282), and ED_2, ad is clear.

38b. Wilcke, 1978, 204 (l. 43), translates "Du sollst keine rat spenden! Du sollst keine schweren Blicke auf dich lenken!" He comments, p. 215 (l. 43), on the 2nd pers. comitative: "Du sollst nicht verursachen, daß bei dir ...; wohl ungebetener Rat gemeint."

39. Cf. already Foxvog, 1976, 372, who suggested: "Do not eat stolen food with the person (who stole it)."

In this case line 40 seems to contain the motivation clause belonging to line 39. úš is here probably *da-mu*, "blood." S_2: 6 again has an interesting variant: šu-zu ⌜mud⌝(?) na-bí-íb-s[á(?) ...] (where the reading mud is suggested here instead of gi, as read in by Civil, 1984, 297). mud = *damu*, "blood," would make good sense as a variant of úš, and the copy might—with a minute emendation—favor mud rather than gi, which hardly makes sense in the context. The verb na-di-ni-ib-su-su is rendered in ED_I as DU, cf. p. 190. Cf. also Addendum p. 403.

Line 41: ED_I: ŋìr ur_5 gud sa_{10}; Akk_2: *e-ṣe-em-⌜tam⌝ ina e-se-qí-ka* GUD *uš-rab-bu-ka* UDU.NINTA *uš-rab-bu-ka*: *esēqu* = "to draw a lot." *ušrabbūka*: The same form of the verb *râbu* is quoted in CAD R, 57: "to shake, tremble." The meaning seems to be that when one draws a bone as a lot, it makes the ox and sheep tremble (with fear), because they know they will be slaughtered (suggested by Geller). This strangely would interrupt the sequence of practical advice, which supports the impression that this is a later re-interpretation of the line; cf. below.

SS variants: I_3: ⌜x⌝ ur_5(!)-⌜re⌝ [...] / udu ša-[...]; Ur_I: ŋì[r u]r_5-re gud ša-b[a-re]-eb-su-su udu ša-ba-re-eb-su-su; Ur_2: [x] ur_5-e [...]; S_2: 7: ŋìr ur_5-re gud ša-ba-re-[...] udu ša-bi-ri-ib-TÚG-[...]; Sch_I: ŋìri ⌜ur_5⌝(?)-⌜re⌝ ⌜x⌝-ab-⌜x⌝ ... (illegible traces).

In ED_I, the first sign can be ANŠE or GÌR; the upper left wedges are broken, so the precise identification of the sign is uncertain. In Ur_I, the sign looks like GÌR rather than ANŠE. In S_2 it looks rather as GÌR.[41a] ED_I ŋìr might be a short writing for GÌR.PAD.DU, "bones." If the reading ŋìr ur_5-re in ED_I is justified, ur_5 is a verb both in ED_I and the SS text. GÌR would then have been left unaltered since ED_I, without being "updated" to GÌR.PAD.DU.

The verb can be read as an abbreviated form of zú-ur_5 = *esēqu*, "to incise, to cut," although with a different meaning, "to draw a lot"; cf. the comments on line 49, below. Cf. also lines 226–227, on zú-ur_5 – ak, and *Chap. 3.3: Ballade of Early Rulers* 3: sur.

If ED_I is read anše, a meaning like "renting an ass for rent —you will pay for an ox" must be considered (similar to the suggestions by Wilcke, 1978, 215).[41b] If that is the case, the SS version represents a deviation and reinterpretation of the ED text. The parallelism with gud, "ox," in ED_I supports this solution. At least ED_I: sa_{10}, can hardly be understood in the same way as the SS text. Cf. p. 190, *Chap. 1.5: Comments on AbSt 36*.

Line 41 seems to be connected with line 39 as an additional motivation clause linked together with line 40 by the common verb su-su, which may be meant as a double entendre: su is here = *râbu*, Š, "to make tremble," but the meaning *riābu*, "to restore, repay," is within view, cf. lines 21 and 92; in line 40, it is equated with *balālu*, otherwise = *ṭubbû*, "to submerge," or similar. ED_I has sa_{10}, instead of SS su-su, which I cannot explain. It may simply be meant as a phonetic writing for /su/.

Line 42: ED_I: ù-nu-ŋar na-dug_4; Akk_2: *ù nu-ul-la-a-ti la ta-ta-a-mi*: *nullâtu*, "improper matters, maliciousness, treacherous talk." *ta-ta-a-mi*: *atwû*, Gt. *ù* is an incorrect translation of ù-nu-ŋar-ra.

SS variants: I_3: ù-nu-ŋar-ra [...]; Ur_I: ù-nu-ŋar-ra na-ab-bé-⌜e⌝. Sch_I omits the entire line. ù-nu-ŋar-ra[42] is attested in ED Lú E 196 (MSL 12, 19) and in the list of crimes in *Enlil Hymn* 21: inim kúr níŋ-kúr ù-nu-ŋar-ra, meaning approximately "hostility" or "fraud." The SS text has the expected *marû*-form of the verb /e/: na-ab-bé-⌜e⌝, but in ED_I it is written with the *ḫamṭu*-form dug_4. Cf. pp. 211–212, *Chap. 1.9: Ḫamṭu-marû verbal distinctions*.

Line 43: ED_I: [e]ŋir ŋiš-búr; ED_2: [...] | b[úr(?) x (x)] ši-[...]. Akk_2: *ár-kat-si-na ki-ma giš-par-ru ib-ba-lak-ki-ta-a-ka*.

SS variants: I_3: eŋir-bi-šè ŋiš-[...] / ši-me-š[i-

41a. Civil, 1984, 297 does not commit himself to either GÌR or anše (his "gír" in the reconstructed text of line 46 is a misprint for gìr). Wilcke, 1978, 204 (l. 46), with p. 215, categorically states "eindeutig ANŠE," and translates "Ein Esel gegen Zins (verliehen)—man wird dir einen Stier zurückerstatten (oder) man wird dir ein Schaf zurückerstatten." For the difference between anše and ŋìr, cf., e.g., line 48, where Ur_I writes anše with a sign that does not differ from GÌR. This is exactly the sign we have in line 41.

41b. The ETCSL translates "when you cut the bones, they will make you restore the ox, they will make you restore the sheep," which goes back to an earlier tentative translation in my own manuscript.

42. ù-nu-ŋar-ra = inim-nu-ŋar-ra, possibly through i_5-nu-ŋar-ra, shortened form of inim, with regressive vowel assimilation or, less likely, through níŋ-nu-ŋar-ra, to be explained similarly.

...]; Ur_I: eŋir-bi ŋiš-pàr-gim ⌜ši-i⌝-ši-íb-lá-e; Sch_I: eŋir-bi-šè ⌜x⌝(like še) ⌜x⌝(like ur_5)-gim IGI ⌜x⌝ ⌜x⌝ ... (½ line destroyed).

I_3 has eŋir-bi-šè, "in the end it will bind (something) like a trap ...," but Ur_I omits -šè, which actually gives a simpler text, "the end will bind like ...,"[43] ED_I has ŋiš-búr, whereas the SS version has the expected writing.

ŋiš-pàr = *gišparru*, "net," which is normal in OB and older writing.

Line 44: ED_I: ú nu-$kiŋ_x$(ḪUL) udu sá.ság na-dug_4.[44a] Akk_2: *ana šam-mi la ši-te-ú-ti bu-ul-ka la ta-na-as-saḫ*: kiŋ(-ŋá) = *ši-te-ú-ti*, from *še'û*, cf. AHw 1222f., "suchen," Gtn.[44b] sáŋ – dug_4 is here equated with *nasāḫu*, "to tear out," here: "to transfer (cattle)"; cf. CAD N/2, 102.

SS variants: I_3: ú nu-kiŋ-ŋ[á-...]; Ur_I: ú nu-kiŋ-ŋá-šè udu-zu [s]ág nam-me; Ur_2: [... -ŋ]á-šè udu-z[u ...]; P: ú nu-[...]; Sch_I: ú nu(?)-kiŋ(?)-kiŋ(?)-⌜ŋá⌝-šè udu ... (almost destroyed).

For ú nu-kiŋ-ŋá-šè, ED_I has ú nu-$kiŋ_x$(ḪUL). There can, thus, be no doubt that in this case ED ḪUL represents SS $kiŋ_x$(KIN). This occurs also in line 175, but I know of no other attestations of that sign value. In ED_I: sá.ság, sá is an unusual phonetic indicator to ság. For the ED_I writing na-dug_4, cf. line 42.[44c]

Line 45: ED_I: gud $ŋi_6$ [x x], cf. below. Akk_2: *a-na šid-di la búr-ru-tú a-lap* LÚ *la ta-ag-gar*, cf. below. *búr-ru-tú*: probably from *bâru*, but no satisfactory explanation has as yet been found.[45a]

SS variants: I_3: uš nu-sì-ga [...]; Ur_I: uš nu-sì-ga-šè [...]-⌜x⌝-e; Ur_2: [x x-s]ì-ga-šè ⌜gud⌝-lú na-ḫuŋ-[x].

J. Taylor suggests "a man should not hire an ox for a boundary that has not been placed," i.e., "Don't put the cart before the horse."

Line 46: ED_I: uš sì-ga kaskal sì-ga-àm; the edges have: perhaps: u[š] é; uš dim_4. Akk_2: [*ši*]*d-*⌜*di*⌝ *dam-qu ḫar-ra-nu da-mi-iq-tú*. SS variants: I_3: uš sì-ga [...]; I_{15}: (traces); T_{14}: uš sì-g[a ...]; Ur_I: uš sì-ga [...]-àm; Ur_2: [x] sì-ga kaskal sì-ga-àm; P: uš sì-ga [...]; Sch_I: uš sì-ga kaskal ... ⌜x⌝-⌜àm⌝.

The meaning "a placed boundary is a placed road," i.e., what's done is done, was suggested by J. Taylor.

Lines 45–46: The ED_I text: gud $ŋi_6$ [x x], "an ox ... at night ...," seems to belong elsewhere, or to represent an unexplained variant of line 45, possibly by confusion with line 47.

For uš = *šiddu*, cf. AHw 1230, "Seite, Längseite, Bereich"; it is also the edge of a field. If the signs u[š] é uš dim_4, in ED_I, on the lower edge of v and the top edge of vi, do, in fact, belong here this seems to mean, "the foundation of a house (is) well tested," yielding a text along the same lines.

⌜gud⌝-lú is a genitive compound, "a man's ox."[45–46a] In line 46, sì-ga might be phonetic for sa_6(-g), *damqu*?[45–46b] Or, more likely, sì(-g) is the verb = *šakānu*, attested in connection with kaskal in

43. Wilcke, 1987, 215 (l. 48), comments: "Die von Alster, I 54, notierte Koll. von Ur_I 44 findet sich nicht auf Taf. I," but the relevant signs are copied as giš.pàr-gim on p. 137, pl. I under "Line 48 (rev. 44)" (cf. Foxvog, 1976, 374). On p. 215, he understands the verbal form as "reflexiv: «es wird sich ... » oder ... Akkusativ «es wird dir etwas wie ein Fangnetz(?) spannen»."

44a. The last sign in ED_I is clearly dug_4, not saŋ, collated.

44b. Cf. kin-kin-na = *ašri ši-te-'e-e*, ... 22,80, 65, quoted by AHw 1223, sv. *še'û(m)* Gtn 2.

44c. Cf. perhaps line 18, ED_I: x-sír LAK 218, in which x-sír might be a phonetic indicator to LAK 218.

45a. Cf. CAD B, 115: *barû* A, "to look upon, to inspect"; cf. AHw 108, *bâru* III "deutlich machen." Also D. Hardly from *bêru*, AHw 122, "auswählen," but rather from *bâru*, which is related to *bārûtu*, "divination"; cf. also AHw 141, *būrtum* III, "Beweis"; cf. perhaps also AHw 96, *ba''erūtu*, "Beweisaufnahme?"

45–46a. As indicated by Akk_2: *a-lap awīlim*. Wilcke 1978, 215 (l. 50), however, suggests reading Ur_2 rev. 2 as gud(?) kin(?) na-⌜x⌝[...], rather than ⌜gud⌝ lú. This is very unlikely and has not been confirmed by the Akkadian translation.

45–46b. As suggested by Akk_2: *damqu*; *damiqtu*; or sig_7. Also PBS 12 52 rev. ii 10 might, therefore, be translated: "May your god make the road good for you!" but the context suggests that it means to prepare, level the road. The ETCSL translates "May your god pave the road for you, may he level the hills and depths for you!" Cf. also the parallel from the same text quoted under line 71, as well as rev. 11: íl-lá du_5-lá ḫa-ra-ab-di-di, "(may your god) level the hills and the depths for you" (Alster, 1974, 93: dusu-lá TÙN-lá should be corrected to íl-lá du_5(TÙN)-lá = *mūlâ u mušpāla*). Cf. *Lugal-e* 85: du_6-du_6 túl-lá-a mu-un-si-ge_4 = *mūlâ u mušpāla uštamaḫḫar*, "he levels the hills and

Inanna and Dumuzi Y (PBS 12, 52 rev. ii 10): diŋir-zu kaskal ḫa-ra-ab-sì-ge, "May your god prepare the road for you!" (cf. Alster, 1974, 67, 130 n. 56 [p. 130]).

Line 47: ED$_{I}$: kaskal ŋi$_{6}$ na | šà ⌜sá⌝(?) ḫul; ED$_{2}$: kaskal ⌜x⌝ x-d[u ...]. Akk$_{2}$: [*ḫar-r*]*a-nu i-na mu-ši la tal-lak lìb-ba-šá da-me-eq u le-mun.*

SS variants: I$_{3}$: kaskal ŋi$_{6}$ na-a[n-...] / šà-bi sa$_{6}$ [x x]; I$_{15}$: kaskal ŋi$_{6}$ ... ; T$_{14}$: kaskal ŋi$_{6}$ na-⌜du⌝ [...]; Ur$_{I}$: kaskal ŋi$_{6}$ <na>-an-du-u[n x x x ḫ]ul-a; Ur$_{2}$: kaskal ŋi$_{6}$ nu-du šà-bi sa$_{6}$ ḫul-a; P: kaskal ŋi$_{6}$ na-an-du [...]; Sch$_{I}$: ⌜kaskal⌝ ... -⌜àm⌝.

ED$_{I}$ has ŋi$_{6}$ na, remarkably with the verb omitted. ED$_{I}$ ⌜sá⌝? is apparently phonetic for sa$_{6}$-(g).

sa$_{6}$ and ḫul occur also elsewhere as a proverbial pair, cf. lines 193–194; 195; 196–197.

Line 48: ED$_{I}$: edin na-sa$_{10}$ u$_{5}$-šè sa$_{10}$; ED$_{2}$: anše-edin | nàb(AN+AN)-sa$_{10}$-[. Akk$_{2}$: [ANŠE *ṣ*]*e-ri la tu-šam ši-tam-ma a-na a-di-šu a-lik*, cf. below.

SS variants: I$_{3}$: anše-edin-na [...] / ú(? text: PA)-da-bi-[...]; I$_{15}$: anše-edin-na ...; T$_{14}$: anše-edin-na [...]; Ur$_{I}$: anše-edin-na na-a[b-...]-e-zal; Ur$_{2}$: anše-edin-na na-ab-sa$_{10}$-s[a$_{10}$-(x)] u$_{4}$ da-bi-eš ì-za-al; P: anše-edin-na na-ab-s[a$_{10}$-...]; Sch$_{I}$: ⌜anše⌝ ... (traces)-ak-⌜x⌝.

The imperative *alik*, of Akk$_{2}$ "walk," is at best a free rendering of the Sum. text, which is regrettably very uncertain here. For *a-di-šu*, cf. AHw 13, *adīšu*, "bis dahin,"[48a] etc. *šitamma*: hardly from AHw 1252, *šittu* II, "Übriggelassenes, Rest," but cf. perhaps AHw 1253, *šītu* ? II etwa "Zügel"? based on MSL 7, 150, 166f.: ^{kuš}kir$_{4}$-tab-ba-anše = ... *ši-i-t*[*im*!?[48b] anše-edin-na, equated with *imēr ṣēri*, lit., "a steppe ass," occurs also in the proverb tablet N 3395 (probably Kassite), rev. 4: [anše-edin-n]a = *i-me-er ṣe-ri*, cf. Alster, *Proverbs* I, 189, in a poorly understood context.[48c] This is likely to have been a designation of an onager, an equid whose behavior was too violent to make full domestication possible, although it could be useful for dragging heavy loads.

The ED$_{I}$ writing edin = SS anše-edin-na, is abbreviated beyond recognition.

ED$_{I}$: edin na-sa$_{10}$ u$_{5}$-šè sa$_{10}$ is problematic in itself. Apparently ED u$_{5}$ here represents u$_{4}$, "day," and sa$_{10}$ means "to buy," but this is somewhat doubtful, since unexpected uses of the same sign occur elsewhere in ED$_{I}$. Cf. line 41, ED$_{I}$ sa$_{10}$ = SS su-su; cf. also p. 211, *Chap. 1.9: Ḫamṭu-marû reduplication in ED.*

The SS texts have: I$_{3}$: ú(! text: PA)-da-bi-[...]; Ur$_{I}$:]-e-zal; Ur$_{2}$: u$_{4}$ da-bi-eš ì-za-al. EŠ can be interpreted in two ways, either as the numeral 30 or as the terminative marker /šè/. I$_{3}$: ú (copied or misunderstood as PA) might also represent u$_{4}$; Ur$_{2}$: za-al is phonetic for (u$_{4}$) – zal, "to let the day pass." Ur$_{2}$: u$_{4}$ da-bi-eš, understood as /ud da-bi-šè – zal/, might mean "(it will last only) to the day's end," in which case da can possibly be explained as the regens of an indefinite genitive,[48d] lit., "the day—to its side," i.e., "it will spend the day to its end (scl. in idleness)," in other words, an anticipatory genitive with no genitive marking /-ak/ following the u$_{4}$ as rectum. Yet, the agent is rather the 2nd person (cf. below), "you will spend the day at its (the ass's) side." -da cannot simply be explained as a double writing of u$_{4}$(-d). Further, -da cannot represent an anticipatory genitive resumed in eš, "30," because then we would have expected: /ud-ak eš-bi ì-zal/ > u$_{4}$-da eš-bi, etc., "the thirty days."[48e] So the most likely solution is that eš represents the terminative, although it is

the depths" (vars. not quoted). Cf. references in Sefati, *Love Songs*, 279–280, referring to Sjöberg, ZA 65 (1975) 237, etc. Sefati, 279, gives for sì-g = *šutamḫuru*, and translates "to level the road."

48a. *a-di-šu*: from *adû*, "Arbeitspensum," but this would correspond to Sum. á-dù; could there be a mistake in the transmission here? A simple writing error for *i-di-šu*? is perhaps the most likely solution. For *adû*, cf. p. 324, *Chap. 3.4: Proverbs from Ugarit*, U$_{5}$ 28'–29': a-dù nam-lú-u$_{18}$-lu-ke$_{4}$ = *a-da a-wi-lu-ti*, with comments.

48b. No satisfactory explanation of *šitamma* found as yet.

48c. Cf. CAD S, 318 s.v., *sirrimu*, lex., and the refs. quoted there.

48d. In the Sum. indefinite genitive construction (the *Sumer Bankası construction*), there is no genitive /ak/-marker following the rectum, which indicates an indefinite non-possessive genitive relationship between the two, cf. Alster, "Relative Construction and Case Relations in Sumerian," WZKM 92 (2002) 24–25, and Selz in the same volume, pp. 129–153.

48e. Wilcke, 1987, 215–216 (l. 53), argues the other way round, considering u$_{4}$(!?)-da-bé-eš and PA(= ú(!))-da-bé-[... "unorth. Schreibungen für *u$_{5}$-da-bé-eš." He translates, p. 204, "Du sollst keinen Steppenesel kaufen! Vor den Tagen (des Monats) laßt er dreißig verstreichen(?)" He, thus, takes eš as 30. The full text

remarkable that no duplicate simply has *u_4 da-bi-šè, or similar. An alternative would be to read á(!), "its term," etc., but this would make no difference from a grammatical point of view.

I have, therefore, accepted a suggestion by Foxvog, 1976, 372, as the simplest and most convincing solution: "Do not buy a «steppe-ass»—you will spend (all of your time) by its side." The agent is then the 2nd person, as indicated by Ur_1: (-)e-zal; u_4 is the direct object of a transitive verb in the perfective; da-bi-eš is the terminative relating to the side of the animal = *da-bi-šè. The problem remains, though, that an imperfective verb would have been more likely, but this can perhaps be seen in the light of the examples, p. 209, *Chap. 1.9: Tense or aspect related verbal system.*

Line 49: ED_1: géme-zu_5 ŋiš$_x$(SAL+NINTA) na-e | zú-ur_5 šè-mu-š[a_4]. ED_2: ŋiš(sic!) n[a]-e šu-[mu-...]. Akk_2: *[a-ma-at-k]a it-ti-ka la it-tal i-še-el-le-e-ka.*

SS variants: I_{15}: géme-zu-úr ...; T_{14}: géme-zu-úr gì[š ...]; Ur_1: géme-zu ŋìš na-an-[...]-in-sa_4; Ur_2: géme-zu-úr ŋìš na-a-dù zu-úr šu-m[u]-ri-in-šà; K_1: géme-zu-ú[r ...]; P: géme-zu-úr ŋìš na-an-d[ù ...].

In ED_1: ŋiš$_x$(SAL+NINTA), ŋìš is written as a combination with SAL, which can be observed also in line 32, where the reading of SAL+NINTA is evidently ninta_x = ninta (nitaḫ). For the ED examples of zu_5(AZU), cf. p. 217, *Chap. 1.9: Use of special ED signs.* The ED writings na-e are remarkable, because ED_1 has na-dug_4 in the parallel expression in line 62. Cf. p. 211, *Chap. 1.9: ḫamṭu-marû-alternation in ED*; cf. further lines 21 and 42.

In Ur_2 ŋìš – dù is a phonetic writing for *ŋìš – dug_4, cf. line 62: ŋiš á-zi na-an-ne-en. In ED_2, šu is the verbal preformative */šè/ša/ with vowel harmony > šu. Since this is rarely used in SS orthography, it might suggest that Ur_2: šu-m[u]-ri-in-šà was directly dependent on an ED forerunner; cf. also line 51, Ur_2: šu-mu-⌜e⌝-ra-ŋál.

The reading zú-ur_5 of KA-ḪAR and $ša_4$ of DU in ED_1 is certain in view Ur_2: zu-úr šu-m[u]-ri-in-šà. This was probably meant to form a pun with géme-zu-úr in the beginning of the line. The meaning seems to be, approximately, "Do not give cause for yourself to be despised," lit., be "called *zur.*"

Civil, 1984, 295–296, discusses various meanings of KA.ḪAR. The equivalents mentioned by Civil, p. 295, sub 3, based on VE 0151 f; VE 208–209, are: a) *esēqu*, "to incise, to cut,"[49a] b-c) *šebēru*, "to cut into pieces," d) "to tear or grind with the teeth." On the strength of the latter, Civil translates our line 49 "Do not have sex with a slave of yours, she will 'chew you up'."[49b] There can be no doubt that this achieves the approximate intent of the saying, but the Akkadian equivalent of KA-ḪAR is in this case given as *šelû*, "to neglect"; cf. AHw 1211, *šelû* IV: "vernachlässig sein," which perhaps gives a more precise translation.[49c] Alternatively $ša_4$ can be taken as a form of the verb /ak/, meaning "to do/ make *zur*" = perform neglect, be negligent.[49d]

Line 50: Akk_2: *[ar-rat ša]g-gaš-ti la tar-ra-ar i-saḫ-ḫu-rak-ka.*

SS variants: I_{15}: áš (!) á ... ; T_{14}: omits line; Ur_1: ú(sic! cannot be áš) á-zi-⌜da⌝ [... -n]iŋin; Ur_2: áš á-zi nu-bal-e šu-uš ⌜im⌝-ši-niŋin; K_1: áš á-zu na-ab-[...]; P: ás á-zi na-ab-bal-e [...].

might then have been */ud itid-ak(-ak) eš-bi / > u_4 <iti->da(-ka) eš-bi ... zal, "30 days of (the month)," but the absence of a -bi or -àm following eš makes it doubtful. Yet, "dreißig" is contradicted by the transliteration da-bé-eš, which would have required da-bi eš. Wilcke's suggestion that the ED_1 text "für sich genommen ... am einfachsten als Imperativ zu verstehen [ist]: ... «Kaufe (einen Esel) zum Fahren»" is hardly convincing, because in this case ED_2 has a full verbal form: nàb(AN+AN)-sa_{10}-[x], so the absence of verbal prefixes in ED_1 is here best explained as a mere Early Dynastic graphic convention.

49a. Cf. SAG A 24+: zú-ur_5 = *e-sé-qú* (MSL SS 1, 23).

49b. Foxvog, 1976, 372, translates "She will call you *harlot,*" referring to munus-KA-ḪAR-ak in line 226, which he understands as a prostitute. A male counterpart of a harlot, a Sumerian Don Giovanni, would be more appropriate, but is it likely in this cultural environment? For KA.ḪAR – ak = zú-ur_5 – ak, "durchboren mit einer Spindel," see the comments on line 226.

49c. It is not related to ù-sar ak = *šêlu*, "to sharpen," for which see the comments on line 154.

49d. There is no doubt that AK can be read $ša_5$; cf. Cavigneaux, AcSum 9 (1987) 49–51; further PRAK II D 41 ii 29: úru-ta ka-a-e-ni-im-ša ŋuruš ta im-ša, with the duplicate VS II 27 iii 10: úru-ta ga-e-ni-in-ša ŋuruš ta im-ša, which is clearly = ta im-AK, "what has been done?"; cf. Alster/Jacobsen in *Lambert FS*, 330, n. 30.

In áš á-zi na-ab-bal-e, á-zi is used as an adverbial expression "violently, with violent intent"; cf. the similar use of á-zi in line 62: ŋìš á-zi na-an-ne-en.[50a] In this case it is tempting to suggest that áš á-zi bal refers to the use of black magic. In Ur_1, the variants ú(sic!) á-zi-⸢da⸣ seem to be scribal errors. -da is the result of confusion with the common á-zi-da, "right arm," cf. Alster, *Proverbs* I, 310, UET 6/2 259: [áš á]-zi-da bal-e, in which á-zi-da likewise replaces á-zi-ga, cf. the parallel text SP 26 obv i 4 (p. 278): áš á-zi-ga bal-e-di.[50b] šu-uš = *šu-šè. K_1: á-zu seems to be a scribal error.

Line 51: Akk_2: *[a-na mê la l]a-at-ku-ti la tur-rad i-da-a-ti* < ? > *i-šu-ka*: *latku*, "ausprobiert." Cf. further below.

SS variants: I_{15}: a šu-nu ... ; T_{14}: a šu nu-gíd-i na-a[n-...] / á ša(?)-[...]; Ur_1: a šu nu-gíd-⸢dè⸣ [...]-ra-ŋál; Ur_2: a šu nu-du_8 na-[a]n-né-de-de / á-sig šu-mu-⸢e⸣-ra-ŋál; K_1: a šu nu-gíd-dè na-an-è-dè á š[a(?)-...] (coll. J. Taylor); P: a šu nu-gíd-dè na-an-e_{11}-dè-[dè-(en)].

There seems to have been a missing adjective "<weak/paralyzed> arms" following *i-da-a-ti*, corresponding to Sum. sig. For *i-šu-ka*, cf. CAD E, 378, s.v. *ešû*, "to confound," rather than *išû*, "to have," which, however, would suit the Sum. verb ŋál with the dative infix -ra-(e-ra-ŋál). The meaning could be that one will suffer from paralysis if one drinks unexamined water (suggested by Geller, who refers to the Talmud, which warns against leaving water out over night, because it may be bewitched). Alternatively, the Akkadian translation suggests that šu in the Sum. á-sig šu-mu-⸢e⸣-ra-ŋál should be understood as "wages," but I do not know other examples of that use. The Akkadian translation *i-da-a-ti* < ? > *i-šu-ka* might then contain the rare *idū* fem. pl.; cf. CAD I, *idū*, "hires, wages," p. 20: "the rare form *idāti* refers to rent on more than one object or for more than one object at a time."

a šu nu-gíd-i na-an-e_{11}-dè, lit., "water that your hands cannot reach (or: hold)." The variant in Ur_2: a šu nu-du_8 na-[a]n-né-de-de is from */-e_{11}d.ed-en/ > e_{11}-dè-dè, "water that you cannot hold in your hands."

á-sig šu-mu-⸢e⸣-ra-ŋál may mean, lit., "there will be weak/paralyzed arms for you," i.e., "your arms will be too weak"(?) scl., to control the water, unless Geller's suggestion above is accepted. šu-mu- is a case of vowel harmony, cf. line 49.

Line 52: Akk_2: *[x x x] mim-mi-ka ⸢x⸣ ka-la nam-di mim-ma-šú-u in-nam-di-ka.*

SS variants: I_{15}: maḫ ... ; T_{14}: maḫ-bi níŋ-gíd-i ⸢x⸣ [...] / níŋ-⸢x⸣ [...]; Ur_1: maḫ-b[i ... (traces) ...]-šub-bé; Ur_2: omits line; K_1: maḫ-bi níŋ x ba-an-šub-bé níŋ-e b[a(?)-...], coll. Taylor; P: maḫ-bi x ḪUŠ x na-an-dab_5-bé-en (Diakonoff: "the sign before ḪUŠ looks like AŠ or BU, the sign after it like one or two Winkelhaken. May be one sign, all of it"). Ur_1 places lines 63 and 64 after line 52, attracted by the common verb BAD in line 53. Cf. the comments on line 53.

Line 52 has not yet been satisfactorily explained.[52] maḫ-bi is the adverbial use of -bi, "violently." níŋ-gíd-i seems simply to mean "something long" or "something stretching out," but the precise implication escapes me. A kind of boomerang might fit, contrasting nu-gíd-dè in line 51. The -e following níŋ-e seems to be a mistake, whether interpreted as a loc.-term. or an ergative marker. At least, the literal translation, "whatever 'long thing' is thrown with violence (toward you?), you(?) will throw it back to the thing" or "(ditto) the thing will throw it back to you" does not seem to make sense. In front of the first verb, a preformative such as *ša-ba-an-šub-bé might be intended. Maybe níŋ – šub means "to neglect," cf. Alster, 1974, 88, who quotes an Ur variant in *The Farmer's Instructions* 22: kiŋ-zu níŋ nam-mu-un-šub-bé-en, "Don't neglect anything relating to your work"; cf. Bauer, *Orientalia* 67 (1998) 121.

Line 53: Akk_2: *[be-el ḫu-bul-l]i-ka l[a] ⸢tu⸣-raq-qú amêlu šu-ú i-na-ki-ir-k[a].*

SS variants: T_{14}: ur_5-tuku na-an-bad-⸢x⸣ [...]; Ur_1: [x x] na-an-bad-e lú-bi ša-ba-e-⸢x⸣-⸢x⸣-kúr; Ur_2: omits line; Ur_3: ur_5-tuku na-an-bad-e lú-bi ša-ba-e-[...]; K_1: ur_5-tuku na-an-bad-e lú-ba ša-ba-

50a. The translation given in PSD B, 55, 2.2, for áš bal: "to desire," "to need," is in my opinion unjustified. The ETCSL translates á-zi-ga "cursing violently" and á-zi-da "cursing with the right hand."

50b. The same proverb is reflected in *Incantation to Utu* 148 (AcSum 13 [1991] 27–91): ... áš á zi-ga nu-búr-ru-d[a] with an illegible variant ⸢á⸣-zi-x (perhaps = da).

52. Th. Kämmerer's collation of P was inconclusive.

[...]; P: ur$_5$-tuku na-an-bad-e-en lú-bi š[a-...]. Ur$_2$ omits the line. In K$_1$ and P the signs following ša-(ba) are broken. For the verbal infixes in ša-ba-e-⌜x⌝-⌜x⌝-kúr, cf. *Chap. 1.9: Second person element ....*

Akk$_2$: *l[a]* ⌜*tu*⌝*-raq-qú*: from *rêqu*, cf. AHw 970, "sich entfernen"; cf. CAD R, 174f. "to remove"; Cf. the comments on line 63 below.

The Akkadian translation *i-na-ki-ir-k[a]* shows that ša-ba-e-⌜x⌝-⌜x⌝-kúr does not denote an action in the past tense.[53a]

All sources agree on ur$_5$-tuku na-an-bad-e; only P has ditto -bad-e-en. In Ur$_1$, lines 63 and 64 have been placed after line 53, undoubtedly attracted by the common verb BAD. Yet, in line 53 BAD is bad = *rêqu*, "to drive away," whereas in lines 63 and 64 it is úš = *šumūtu*.[53b] Cf. the commentary on line 63 below.

ur$_5$-tuku = *bēl ḫubulli* seems here to be the debtor, although the normal meaning would have been "creditor"; cf. AHw 351, *ḫubullu* 2 a) *bēl ḫ.*, "Gläubiger." Yet, also in *Chap. 2.3: Counsels of Wisdom* 170 (VS 204, 10 vi 3, with dupl., cf. the comments on line 61 below), ur$_5$-tuku seems to denote a debtor. In both cases it refers to the weaker part, who is most likely to incur debt.

Line 54: Akk$_2$: [...] *x* A.ŠÀ *la ter-r[eš] ina mi-iṣ-ri iz-zi-ba-ak-ka*, "Don't plow a field in ..., he will leave (it to?) you at the borderline(?)." *miṣru*, "border, border line, territory."

SS variants: T$_{14}$: (traces); Ur$_1$; [...] aša$_5$(GÁN) nam-ba-e-ŋá-[ŋá-(an)], -e-mistaken?; Ur$_2$: á(sic!) - (traces of three unidentifiable signs) -an-ŋá-ŋá; Ur$_3$: sun$_7$-na-da aša$_5$ na-an-da-ŋá-ŋá-a[n]; K$_1$: sun$_7$-na-da [... -ŋ]á, coll. J. Taylor; P: sun$_7$-na-da aša$_5$ na-an-d[a-...], "Don't place a field with a quarrelsome one."

SS sun$_7$-na = *ṣaltu*, cf. also line 164, where the reading sun$_7$-e can be established through K$_1$: sun$_7$-na.

All sources have aša$_5$(GÁN), not é as read by Alster, 1974, 37 (l. 59), with the only exception of Ur$_2$: á, which might be explained as a phonetic writing for é. This indicates that the text may have been understood differently in some later sources, dealing with the founding of a household rather than that of a field.[54]

Akk$_2$ does not seem to translate the Sum. text or, at least, it was a variant that differed considerably from it, adding a second part to line 54: "he(?) will leave (it to?) you at the borderline(?)." This would then be a warning against causing quarrels among neighbors over the rights of using land for cultivation, but apparently the text was later understood as a warning against founding a household with a quarrelsome person, cf. above.

Line 55: Akk$_2$ omits the line. Akk$_3$: [... *-t]a ta-*

53a. Wilcke, 1978, 205, however, translates "Der Mann hat es für dich geändert!" and states categorically, p. 216 (l. 53): "2. Zeilenhälfte präterial: Der Gläubiger hat eine Wende (zum Guten) gemacht." This would imply that the intent is to make the creditor consider some beneficial act shown by the debtor in the past, but such a notion would be alien to the text, where the only concern is that of the one to whom the advice is addressed. A similarly case occurs in line 153, where a reference to a former beneficial act done by the victim is likewise unlikely. Cf. the discussion under the comments on line 153, and p. 209, *Chap. 1.9: Tense or aspect related verbal system.* If kúr in line 53 and ra in line 153 are *ḫamṭu* forms, they apparently both denote non-preterite aspectual actions. In line 66, however, Wilcke, p. 205 (l. 71), translates "Du sollst ihn stets im Blick haben; sonst wird er dem/im Herzen (das Urteil) ändern!" That a non-preterite form is intended in line 53 is recognized by PSD B, 36: "Do not drive away a debtor; that man will (thereafter) be hostile towards you," and Römer, 1990, 54, (l. 54): "Ein Schuldner sollst du nicht fortschicken: Es wird der betreffene Mann dir (nachher) feindlich gesinnt sein."

53b. As already suggested by Wilcke, 1978, 216 (l. 58): "úš «sterben (lassen)»."

54. Wilcke, 1978, 216 (l. 59), states categorically, "Der mit dieser Zeile beginnende Abschnit (bis Z. 62? [i.e., 57]) richtet sich an eine Frau; Sprecher(in) ist ebenfalls eine Frau; s. das eindeutige *Emesal* in Z. 60 [i.e., 55]!" This was accepted by Römer, 1990, 54 (n. 55 b: "In 55–58 spricht sicher eine Frau"). Yet, the relevant lines are not in *emesal*. The occurrence of a single *emesal*-form, like gi$_4$-in, in standard orthography is not unique, and, in the present case, a number of words could have been used in *emesal*-forms had the difference been significant, e.g., 54: *-ma-ma-an instead of ŋá-ŋá-an; 56: úru instead of ere. Since most ancient precept compilations are father-and-son instructions addressed to men, with some rare examples of mother-daughter instructions, e.g., in Elizabethan English literature (cf. T.F. Mustanoja (ed.): *The Good Wife Taught Her Daughter.* Annales Academiae Scientiarum Fennicae

[*aṣ*(?)]-*ṣe-el* / [... *t*]a(?) *la tu-ma-sa-ra*, cf. the comments below.

SS variants: Ur_1: [... -d]è ši-mu-en-ši-ib-šub-šub; Ur_2: gi-i[n-š]è du-[...]-ši-ib-šub-šub; Ur_3: gi_4-in-šè du-dè ši-me-ši-íb-š[ub-x]; K_1: gi_4-in-na du-dè ⌜x⌝[... -d]è, coll. Taylor ; P: gi_4-in-šè du-dè ši-me-ši-ib-[...].

gi_4-in has so far been understood as *emesal* for géme, "slave girl," and no serious alternative has as yet been suggested, although an *emesal*-form is suspicious in this context. Cf. line 49, which has géme. If, in fact, it means "slave girl" here, this is not a sufficient reason to draw the conclusion that this line or even more were spoken by, or addressed to, a woman.[55a] It is much more likely that the original text was addressed to a man and dealt with field work. This fits the continuation well, warning against trespassing the boundaries of the property belonging to others, which would be sensible if addressed to anyone, and especially to a male owner of a household. The reason for the presence of an occasional *emesal*-form might rather be a tendency to preserve certain traditional expressions customarily used in *emesal*. This is probable in view of the proverbial character of many of the phrases involved.[55b] Or, rather, maybe the ultimate reason is that such an *emesal*-form was meant as a deliberate and strongly depreciatory insult when said of a man. The meaning might then be "he will leave it to you to walk in the way of a slave girl," in which case -šè is used, not in a spacial sense, "in the direction toward a slave girl," but nearly like -gim, "as"; cf. line 215.[55c] Another possibility would, of course, be that gi_4-in might mean something entirely different here.

Akk_3: [... -*t*]*a ta*-[*aṣ*(?)]-*ṣe-el* / [... *t*]*a*(?) *la tu-ma-sa-ra*: this was explained by Krebernik, 1996, 174, as a Gt-form *taṣṣêl* from *ṣâ/êlu*, "streiten." Since *tumassara* is inexplicable from any known Akkadian root, he suggests reading **lā tubassara*, "... sollst du nicht benachrichten!" from *ba*(!)-ditto, or possibly a scribal error influenced by *tu-ma-ša-ra*, which occurs in the following line of Akk_3. Yet, it remains doubtful whether this is a translation of line 55, or of an entirely different line. Since this line in Akk_3 (Seite B I = 55) is followed by line 60, Akk_3 B I need not be a translation of line 55. Yet, it is, of course, tempting to connect 55: ši-me-ši-ib-šub-šub with *tu-ma-sa-ra*, but the preceding part of the line, esp. *ta*-[*aṣ*(?)]-*ṣe-el*, does not seem to confirm it. The phraseology is somewhat reminiscent of lines 22–25, which deal with quarrels (*ṣaltu* = du_{14}), and use a related terminology. This seems to have been a different line, possibly meaning "Don't quarrel [with a slave girl], she will throw it back to you!" Could the Sum. gi_4-in-šè DU-dè possibly mean "When you oppose a slave girl, she will throw it back to you!"? DU might then be gub, but we would have expected gub-bu-dè. The suspicion is, however, that the line was already misunderstood when the translation of Akk_3 was made.

Line 56: Akk_2: omits the line. Akk_3: [*la ib*]-*ba-lak-kat-ka* (the second part seems to be missing). bal is here equated with *nabalkutum*, but in line 12 with *etēqu*. Cf. also line 190: lú íd-dè ba-ra-an-bal-e.

SS variants: Ur_1: ⌜ere⌝⌜ki⌝(?) ⌜lú⌝-ka na-ab-ta-bal-e; Ur_2: ki-tuš lú-ka [na-a]b-bal-e-dè; Ur_3: ere-tuš lú-ka na-ab-ta-bal-[e-d]è-en; K_1: ere l[ú-k]a [... n]a-ab-ta-an-bal-e-dè; P: é lú-ka na-ab-ta-ba[l-...].

Ur_1: ⌜ere⌝⌜ki⌝(?), "city," and K_1: ere are mere graphic variants, but the other sources differ: Ur_2: ki-tuš, "dwelling place"; Ur_3: ere-tuš, "the city (in which) someone lives"; P: é, "house."

B, LXI, 2 [Helsinki, 1948]), it would be very interesting, but unlikely, if such texts could be found in early Mesopotamian literature. These might then be reflected as *emesal* quotations in "male compositions," but in the present case the evidence is much too elusive.

55a. Cf. the preceding note (l. 54).

55b. This would imply, admittedly, that some proverbial phrases incorporated were used originally in a female setting, but were included later in a "male" context. This is not unlikely in view of the many *emesal* proverbs that exist in the Sumerian proverb collections. Cf. Alster, 1997, xiv. The use of *emesal* expressions was not a purely neutral linguistic phenomenon, but was loaded with connotations from the social context where they originally belonged.

55c. Wilcke, 1978, 205 (ll. 59–60) translates: "Zusammen mit einem hoffartigen Menschen sollst du nicht Wohnung nehmen! Er(/Sie?) wird es dir zufallen lassen, als Sklavin zu gehen!"

Line 57: Akk_2: *ina* IGI [*a*]*l-ka ina* IGI <*al*>*-ka i-qab-bu-ka.*

SS variant: Ur_1: I[GI] du-un [IGI d]u-un ši-m[u-u]n-ši-íb-bé-e-ne; Ur_2: IGI ì-du IGI ì-[du ši-me]-ši-ib-e-ne; Ur_3: I[GI d]u-un IGI du-un ši-me-ši-íb-b[é]-en; K_1: IGI d[u-...] ⌜me⌝ -ši-⌜ib⌝-b[é]-e-ne.

IGI can be read either as the verbal preformative ši-, or as a noun, igi, "in front." This applies to: Ur_1: I[GI] du-un [IGI d]u-un IGI m[u-u]n-ši-íb-bé-e-ne; Ur_3: I[GI d]u-un IGI du-un IGI me-ši-íb-b[é]-en and K_1: IGI d[u-un ...] ⌜x⌝ IGI ⌜me⌝-⌜ši⌝-⌜ib⌝-b[é]-e-ne. In all these, both igi and ši- are possible, but the third IGI is more likely to be ši-; Ur_2: IGI ì-du IGI ì-[du ... can alternatively, but less convincingly, be read ši-ì-du, etc. The presence of a ši- preformative followed by an ì-prefix would be unusual in the first two verbal forms. The possibility exists that an original ši-sign, rendering a grammatical element, was later understood as a noun, igi, but this is less likely. Cf. pp. 212ff., *Chap. 1.9: Modal verbal profixes.* If read igi, it could mean either "in front" or maybe just "forward" (= /igi-a/). If read ši-, the verb phrase might mean either "go forward" or, perhaps, "There you go!" as the ETCSL translates, indicating the irritation or wrath of the neighbors. Yet, it is remarkable that the text does not simply have an imperative, as suggested by the Akkadian translation; cf. p. 217, *Chap. 1.9: On the Akk. trans. of Sum. gram. forms.*[57]

Line 58: ED_2: [ki]ri₆-k[a da]g-ga nám-bí-du₈-e. Akk_1: *ki-iṣ-ri* ⌜*ki*⌝(?)-[. Akk_2: [*ina*(?) *k*]*i-ri-i ri-ki-is-*⌜*su*⌝ *la ta-paṭ-ṭar*, cf. the comments below.

SS variants: I_4: gi-s[ig-...]; Ur_1: gi-⌜sig⌝(?)-⌜ga⌝(?) ^{ŋiš}⌜kiri$_6$⌝-ka da-[x] nam-bí-du$_8$-e; Ur_2: gi-sì(sic!)-ga ^{ŋiš}kiri$_6$-k[a] ⌜nam⌝-⌜bí-du$_8$⌝-⌜e⌝; Ur_3: g[i]-sig-ga ^{ŋiš}kiri$_6$-ka da-ga(cannot be -bi on this tablet) nam-bi(sic!)-du$_8$-e-en (-en is visible on the following line); K_1: g[i-...] nam-ba-du$_8$-e; P: gi-sig(?) ^{ŋiš}kiri$_6$-ka da-bi (so Diakonoff, read ga?) nam-[...].

For the ED_2 use of nám = SS nam, cf. p. 214, *Chap. 1.9: ED prohibitive na- / nám-.*

The reading of SS gi-sig-ga is certain in view of the Ur_2 variant: gi-sì-ga. gi-sig = *kikkišu* (AHw: "Rohrzaun"). The ED signs are not preserved at this point. Ur_3 certainly has -ga, not -bi; Ur_2 omits the two signs altogether, apparently by mistake; in Ur_1 the second sign is destroyed, whereas P, according to Diakonoff's transliteration, has da-bi. The latter is attractive, because it would make it possible to explain the entire construction as an anticipatory genitive, "the sides of the reed-fence of the gardens"; the reading da-ga seems reasonably certain, however, in view of ED_2 da]g-ga. In this case, da-ga is a separate noun, and ^{ŋiš}kiri$_6$-ka must be the locative: /gi-sig-ga ^{ŋiš}kiri$_6$-ak-a/, "on the reed-fence of the gardens," leaving da-ga as the direct object of the sentence. If so, the noun is /daga/, not just da(-g).[58a]

The context might suggest that, in our case, da-ga denotes the joints where the parts of the fence are connected. Wilcke, 1978, 216 (ad line 63), suggests reading ⌜*ki*⌝-[*iṣ-ri* in Akk_1, and equal to da-ga, which would fit the idea nicely. Cf. AHw 488, *kiṣru* = kéš-da, "knoten, Zusammenfügung"; CAD "knot," etc., but no da-ga = *kiṣru* is as yet attested. Akk_2: [*ina*(?) *k*]*i-ri-i ri-ki-is-*⌜*su*⌝ *la ta-paṭ-ṭar*, however, suggests that da-ga corresponds to *riksu* or *rikis/štu*, cf. AHw 984–985, "Vertrag." In this case du$_8$ = *paṭāru* refers to the breach of an agreement concerning the boundary between two gardens. Cf. also AHw 986, *riksu* C "Vertrag" 3) with *paṭāru* (j/spB). The equation da(-g) = *riksu* seems to be new.

It, therefore, remains doubtful whether our da-ga is related to the word da(-g), which Krecher, AcSum 9 (1987) 88, n. 39 considers a separate word to be distinguished from both da, "side," and dag =

57. Wilcke's understanding of lines 54ff. as a united *emesal* group is the reason for his connecting them in his translation: "An einer menschlichen Behausung kannst du (dann) nicht vorbeigehen, (ohne daß) sie dir nachrufen: «Du läufst! Die ... eines Gartenzaumes sollst du nicht lösen! «Ersetze es! Ersetze es! wird man zu dir sagen!»" This was followed by Römer, 1990, 54, and the ETCSL: "You should not establish a home with an arrogant man: he will make your life like that of a slave girl. You will not be able to travel through any human dwelling without being shouted at: «There you go! There you go!»" This reaction would be a normal response if addressed to anyone trespassing the property of others or destroying their fence, but it would not be typical specifically of a woman married to an arrogant husband.

58a. The ETCSL: "You should not undo the ...... of the garden's reed fence; 'Restore it! Restore it!' they will say to you."

šubtu. He interprets it as the close vicinity of someone. It occurs in the term da-ga-na (cf. refs. below), which he translates "quite near to her." The word is reflected in the Akkadian translation *ana idīšu*, "at his side." da-ga-na has usually been interpreted as a syllabic writing of *daggan-na, "in the (bed-)chamber." It occurs, in connection with witnesses, in TMHNF 1/2 259 = NG 212, obv. 4: da-ga-na ì-gub, where "bedchamber" is excluded. Cf. also Steinkeller, FAOS 17 (1989) 198.

Surprisingly, although Krecher denies this etymology, our source ED_2, writing da]g-ga, could be taken as a confirmation of it. It is probably the same word as occurs in NBC 11108 (Ur 3 lit.), edited by van Dijk, AOAT 25, 129, line 8: an-né ⌜da⌝-ga-an-na-ka-ni ⌜nu(?!)⌝-mu-ni-íb-$guru_{17}$ (so read by Sjöberg, *Jacobsen MV*, 240). Sjöberg interprets it as dag-an(-na), from dag = *šubtu*, comparing JCS 40 (1988) 168 (Ur III *Inanna Prism*): ii 8–9: dag-da[g]-ga ti-la-mu-ne dag-a[n]-⌜na-ka⌝ ti-la-mu-ne, "when I (Inanna) was living in (my) dwelling places, when I was living in the heavenly dwelling ...," interpreting dag-an-na as *šubat šamê* (read by Geller slightly differently in the same volume, p. 90).

The following references are perhaps related to our da-ga: SP 1.19: da-ga nam-kù-zu ^{d}lama á bí-ib-ŋar; cf. Alster, *Proverbs* I, 10, who translates "Good Fortune reinforces organization and wisdom," following Civil; cf. Alster, *Proverbs* II, 343, where further examples are quoted, including Civil's translation "l'organization." In *Gilgameš and Huwawa* 149: ní-te-a-ni 7-kam-ma mu-un-na-til-la-ta da-ga-na ba-te, da-ga has mostly been understood as a dwelling place, equal to dag = *šubtu*, but Krecher, loc. cit., "approached him closely";[58b] Edzard, ZA 80 (1990) 189: "unmittelbar vor seiner Behausung"; *Inanna-Ninegalla Hymn* 55: ur KA da-ga-na-ke_4 has been understood as an imprecisely defined part of a building, relating to the lions with which Inanna is represented in glyptic art; *Inanna and Ebih* 83: muš-saŋ-KAL kur-bi-ta e_{11}-da-gim da-ga ḫu-mu-da-DU, has generally been understood as a "den."[58c] Attinger, ZA 88 (1998) 187, however, tentatively accepts Krecher's interpretation (p. 175: "*dans le voisinage*") and hesitates to accept Civil's "l'organization."[58d]

The most likely preliminary conclusion seems to be that our da-ga means "agreement" or the like = *riksu*/*rikištu*, and that it is different from Krecher's da(-g), but probably related to Civil's suggestion, the reasons for which are unknown to me.

Line 59: ED_2: su-a su-a | [...].Akk_1: *ri-i-ib r[i-i-ib ...]*; Akk_2: *ri-bi-am ri-bi-am i-qab-bu-ka*. Note that the two Akkadian translations do not depend on one another.

SS variants: I_4: su-ga-a[b ...]; Ur_1: sù-ga-a[b s]ù-ga-ab ši-mu-un-ši-íb-bé-e-ne; Ur_2: su-ga-ab su-ga-ab ši-⌜x⌝-[...]; Ur_3: su-g[a-a]b su-ga-ab ši-me-ši-íb-bé-ne; K_1: [...]-⌜sù⌝-ga ši-me-ši-íb-e-ne; P: su-g[a]-ab su-ga-ab ši-me-ši-ib-bé-e-e[n].

ED_2: su-a = SS su-ga-ab is interesting as a rare example of an imperative in ED orthography. Cf. lines 21–22 and 40–41 for the sign su. Ur_1 has sù-ga-ab instead of su-ga-ab.

Line 60: Akk_1: *a-ḫe-e la tu-uš-[ta-kal ṣa-al-ta la ta-...]*; Akk_2: *[a-ḫe-e la tu-uš-t]a-kal ṣa-⌜al-ta⌝ la ta-šak-kan*; Akk_3: *[a-ḫe-e la tu-uš-ta-ka]l ṣa-al-ta la tu-([x])-ma-ša-ra*. The Akkadian of Akk_2: *la ta-šak-kan*, "don't establish," cannot be a literal translation of nam-ùr-ùr-re; cf. the comments below. The Akkadian St-form *tu-uš-[ta-kal* of *akālu* is mainly attested in mathematical context, cf. AHw 27; CAD A/1, 258, *šutākulu*, "to multiply, to square"; cf. *šutakūlu*, "to make hold," from *kullum*.

SS variants: I_4: ur nam-mu-[...]; Ur_1: ur nam-m[u-u]n-gu_7-en LÚ(sic!) nam-ùr-ùr-re; Ur_2: ur nam-<mu>-ni-gu_7-e-[en] du_{14} nam-úr-úr-àm; Ur_3: ur ⌜nam⌝(?)-mu-⌜gu_7⌝-e du_{14} mu-ùr-ùr-re; K_1: [x] n]am-mu-un-<gu_7>-e LÚ(so copy) bí-ùr-ùr-re; P: ur nam-mu-un-gu_7-e-en du_{14} nam-ùr-ùr-re-en.

Discussion of variants: I_4, Ur_1, Ur_3, K_1, and P all agree on: nam-mu; only Ur_2 has nam-<mu>-ni-gu_7-. Ur_1 alone has -u]n-gu_7-en; Ur_2: gu_7-e-[en];

58b. The ETCSL translates "When Huwawa had finally handed over to him his seventh terror." Is "finally" meant as a serious attempt to translate da-ga or is it just a rudiment of -til-?

58c. Civil, "Like *sagkal*-snakes coming down from the mountains let (my) organized (forces) come ..." The ETCSL translates differently "May he make them slither (i.e., = da-ga ... DU?) around like a *sa*ŋ*-kal* snake coming down from a mountain."

58d. "Came very close to him" would make better sense.

Ur$_3$: ⸢gu$_7$⸣-e; K$_I$: n]am-mu-un-<gu$_7$>-e; only P has: -un-gu$_7$-e-en; only Ur$_I$ and apparently K$_I$ have LÚ; Ur$_2$, Ur$_3$, and P: du$_{14}$; Ur$_I$: nam-ùr-ùr-re; Ur$_2$, phonetic: nam-úr-úr-àm (for the intensifying -àm, cf. line 61); these agree with P: nam-ùr-ùr-re-en on a negative verbal form; Ur$_3$: mu-ùr-ùr-re, agrees with K$_I$: bí-ùr-ùr-re on a positive verbal form.

In Ur$_I$ and K$_I$, LÚ is an abbreviated writing for du$_{14}$ = LÚ×NE, as elsewhere. The verb ùr-ùr-re is probably meant as a pun on ur, which is translated in Akk$_I$ by *aḫû*, "foreigner," (or: "stranger"?). In Ur$_2$, the verb is written phonetically nam-úr-úr-àm, which indicates poor understanding on the part of the scribe. I know of no other occurrence of du$_{14}$ with ùr. Cf. du$_{14}$ – mu$_4$(-r), "to pick a quarrel," which occurs in lines 35 and 247. ùr is translated in Akk$_3$ by *tu-ma-ša-ra*, which can be interpreted as "Don't release a quarrel" (from *wuššuru*); this undoubtedly makes sense, but the normal Sum. equivalent of *wuššuru* is šu bar. Therefore, an alternative suggestion by Krebernik, 1996, 175, is worth considering. Besides "du wirst den Streit senden/aufgeben," he suggests also *ṣālta tupaššara* (*ma* may represent *ba*(!) or *pá*(!)), "don't dissolve." The latter is perhaps the more likely solution. Possibly the implication is that by inviting a foreigner "for dinner" one runs the risk of overlooking an old cause of a quarrel.[60a] Cf. also ùr in lines 86–88 (broken context).[60b] A meaning like "Don't get involved, because when trying to do things right, one may suffer adverse effects" was suggested by J. Taylor.

Line 61: Akk$_2$: [*ša-ga-p*]*u-ru-ta la te-*⸢*ep*⸣*-p*[*u-u*]*š uq-qú-rak ma-tum ma-ʾ-da. uq-qú-rak*: from *waqāru*: "Don't act pompously (lit. majestically), the country's holding you in esteem matters much" (suggested by Geller). The Akkadian text of Akk$_2$ is not a verbatim translation of the Sumerian, however. Both Akk$_I$ and Akk$_3$ omit the line. AHw 1126, *šagapūru* = šilig/silig?, "überaus kraftvoll." The equation nam-silig – ak = *šagapurūta epēšu* occurs here for the first time.

SS variants: I$_4$: dumu-ŋu$_{10}$ nam-[…]; Ur$_I$: [x] -ŋ]u$_{10}$ [x x (x)]-mu-gu$_7$-me-en lú ki nam-ús-sa; Ur$_2$: dumu-ŋu$_{10}$ na-silig na-àm-ak-e lú ki na-àm-ús-àm[61a]; Ur$_3$: dumu-ŋ[u$_{10}$ na]m-silig nam-mu-ak-en lú ki ús-en; K$_I$: [x]-ŋu$_{10}$ nam-silig nam-mu-ke$_4$ lú ki na-ús-sa; P: dumu-ŋu$_{10}$ nam-silig nam-mu-e-ak-en lú ki nam-ús-e-en.

dumu-ŋu$_{10}$, "my son" is the address of the father to the son, as in lines 62; 79; 133; 149; 160; 165; 192; 207; 219; 236; 254; 272. Cf. lú-tur-ŋu$_{10}$, "my little one," line 84, where the variant dumu-ŋu$_{10}$ in Ur$_5$ indicates that this was, in fact, meant as an address to the son; also 102 (ED$_I$: probably [dumu-ŋ]u$_{10}$, broken).

The variant in K$_I$: nam-mu-ke$_4$(= kid) instead of nam-mu-ak-en shows the same form of the verb /ak/ as kar-ke$_4$/kid, from */kar-ak-ed/?, "she who works the quay," i.e., "a prostitute." Cf. the commentary on line 154 below.

nam-silig nam-mu-ak might be related to line 259: ki dam kar-re nam-silig gum-ŋá-àm; cf. also line 15: nam-silig gú-ŋá-àm, and the commentary on line 15.

In the end of the line, Ur$_I$ has: nam-ús-sa; Ur$_2$: na-àm-ús-àm; Ur$_3$: ús-en (with no verbal prefixes); K$_I$: na-ús-sa; P: nam-ús-e-en. The 2nd person imperfective was clearly intended, and it is not clear why it was replaced by a nominalizing /a/, or an intensifying -àm in three sources. Apparently two constructions were confused, "Do not prostrate a man" = lú ki nam-ús-e-en, and "it would mean the prostration of the man" = lú ki ús-àm. Alster, 1974, 39 (l. 66) translates: "Do not use violence, do not

60a. Along these lines, Alster, 1974, 39 (l. 65) translated: "Do not wipe out a quarrel," assuming, p. 88, that ùr is *pašāṭu* (= šu – ùr). Apparently this was accepted by the ETCSL: "You should not provide a stranger (?) with food; you should not wipe out (?) a quarrel."

60b. Wilcke, 1978, 205 (l. 65), translates "Du sollst einem Fremden(?) nichts zu essen geben! Du sollst einen Streit nicht schlichten(?)!" Römer, 1990, 54 (l. 61) suggests: "Du sollst (*streitende*) nicht in *Kampf gegen aneinander geraten lassen*, (aber auch) sollst du einen Streit nicht *immer* schlichten!" comparing M.W. Green, JCS 30 (1978) 153ff., who discusses ur – gu$_7$ and related forms, such as ur-bi ì-gu$_7$-e = *mitḫāriš ītakkalū*, "devours altogether," or "instantly," where she prefers the reading ur to téš, relating it to the well-known UR#UR or LÚ#LÚ. In view of the Akkadian translation *a-ḫe-e*, this does not seem to be relevant in our text.

61a. For the intensifying -àm, cf. line 60, Ur$_2$: nam-úr-úr-àm.

throw down a man."[61b]

I have accepted an interpretation suggested by Foxvog, 1976, 372, "My son, do not cause (financial) ruin, do not prostrate anyone," referring to line 15 and the use of silig in *Counsels of Wisdom* 170 (VS 204, 10 vi 3) (cited by Alster, 1974, 88, to line 58): ur_5-tuku-zu-šè nam-ba-silig-ge níŋ ba-an-tur-re (var. VS 10, 205 iii 5: ur_5-tuku-zu-àm nam-ba-ši-li_9-ki bi-tur-tur-[re]; here included p. 252, *Chap. 2.3*). Following Foxvog's suggestion, this might mean "Don't cause financial ruin to a debtor; (then) he will have even less!" with the result that the creditor has less chance of retrieving anything.[61c] Cf. also the discussion of silig in the commentary to line 96 and the comments on line 53 above.

lú ki – ús, "to put a man down on the ground" is similar to the English idiom "to bite the dust," (from the Greek "to bite the grass"). It is not quite the same as, e.g., *Gilgameš and Huwawa* 158: ki-za nam-ba-an-tùm, "prostrated himself before him," which indicates submission. Cf. *The Ballade of Early Rulers* 12. The translation of Akk_2: *uq-qú-rak ma-tum ma-ʾ-da*, "the country's holding you in esteem matters much," does not render the same expression verbatim; the alliteration pattern might suggest that a proverbial phrase from a living Akkadian dialect was quoted. Something similar may have happened in Akk_3 in the translation of line 63, cf. below.

Line 62: ED_I: lú-ra [x] ⌜na⌝-dug_4 [x x x] ⌜SAL⌝; ED_2: dumu lú-ra ŋì[š] á-zi na-e kisal na-zu-zu.

Akk_I: *ma-ar-ti a-me-l[i ina ...]*; Akk_2: *[marti] a-mi-li ina š[a-ga-aš-ti] la ta-na-qí-ip pu-uh-ri i-lam-mad-ka*; Akk_3: *[marti a-me-li ina š]a-ga-aš-ti la-a ta-[na-qí-ip pu-uh-ru la]-a(?) i-la-ma-ad-ka*.

SS Variants: I_4: dumu lú-ra [...]; Ur_I: [... ŋì]š á-zi na-an-è kisal-e ba-e-su-su (su-su mistaken for -zu-zu); Ur_2: dumu lú-ra ŋìš á-zi na-né-e / kisal-e bí-zu-zu; Ur_3: dumu [lú-r]a ŋìš á-zi na-an-ne-en kisal-e bí-zu-zu; K_I: dumu lú-ra áš-zu na-an-è gis-sal-šè(?) bi-zu-zu (here è is an unusual phonetic writing for e; gis-sal-šè is apparently phonetic for kisal; the expression ŋìš á-zi – e was misunderstood as áš-šu – e); P: dumu lú-ra ŋìš á-zi na-an-ne-en kisal-e ba-e-zu-zu-e.

Line 62 was first translated by Civil and Biggs, 1966, 3.

ED_I has ⌜na⌝-dug_4, but ED_2: na-e. This indicates that *hamṭu-marû* distinctions began to be reflected at least in the later ED sources. Cf. p. 211, *Chap. 1.9: Marû-hamṭu reduplication in ED.*

ED_2 has the verbal prefix na-zu-zu, instead of bí- (with variants). I take this as a humorously exaggerated negative statement, "Do not (give the courtyard occasion) to be informed"; cf. a similar case in line 28.[62] Cf. p. 214, *Chap. 1.9: ED na- versus ša-: Prohib. or affirm?*

For ŋìš á-zi – e, cf. line 50: áš á-zi na-ab-bal-e. In Akk_3 this is equated with *ina š]a-ga-aš-ti la-a ta-[na-qí-ip*, from *naqāpu*, "deflorieren."

The reconstruction in Akk_3 r. i 3: [... *la*]-*a*(?) *i-la-ma-ad-ka* is offered with reservation, since the negation seems to be included by mistake here, attracted from the many lines with that construction. The writing *la-a* would, however, be characteristic of Akk_3, cf. lines 17; 62; and 66.

kisal is hardly used here in relation to official

61b. Tentatively accepted by the ETCSL: "My son, you should not use violence (?)," leaving the second part of the line untranslated.

61c. Wilcke's translation, 1987, 205 (l. 66): "du sollst keinen Ruin(?) verursachen! Du sollst keinen Grund für einen Streit geben" needs Foxvog's interpretation to make sense. The emendation of lú to du_{14} is, however, unjustified. On p. 216 Wilcke states "In der 2. Zeilenhälfte unsicher, ob lú oder du_{14} vorliegt." Yet, there is no reason to question the reading lú, which is clear in all duplicates: Ur_I, Ur_2, Ur_3, K_I, and P, with no attestation of du_{14}. *du_{14} ki nam-ús-e-en, lit., "Don't put a quarrel down to the ground," would not be idiomatically plausible. That it is reminiscent of the German "keinen Grund" is mere coincidence. LÚ is admittedly used as a short writing of du_{14} in two duplicates of line 60: Ur_I and K_I, but since three texts, Ur_2, Ur_3 and P have du_{14} in line 60, it would be difficult to explain why the same writing does not occur also in line 61 had that been the intended meaning. Römer, 1990, 54 (l. 62) translates: "du sollst *keine übertriebene Kraftscheierei* anstellen, du sollst *niemanden (dadurch)* auf der Erde *liegen* lassen!" on the basis of AHw 1126, *šagapūru(m)* LL.

62. The role of the assembly in court proceedings is well attested, cf., i.a., van Mieroop, "Urban Government," *The Mesopotamian City State* (Oxford, 1997), 118–141, with bibliography. There seems to be no reason to assume that in our case lú, "man," denotes a special group of "free men," like *awīlu* in Hammurapi's law.

legal proceedings. What is meant in this case is probably that one should avoid arousing gossip in one's own circle, because it would be inconvenient, and not that the outcome would be an actual court investigation. If that were the case, the older term unken might have been used, whether or nor replaced in the later sources by *puḫrum*, which became a commonly used loanword in Sumerian already in the third millennium B.C.[62]

Line 63: Akk_1: *bêl e-mu-qi la* [*tu-uš-*...]. Akk_2: *bé-*[*el*] ⌜*e*⌝*-mu-qí la tuš-ma-a*[*t*] *šul-ḫa-a la tab-bat*. Akk_3: [...] *x eṭ-la la tu-ḫal-la-aq* // [... *sa*]*k*(SAG)*-kul-šu la tu-qa-ba-ar*.

SS variants: I_4: á-tuku [...]; Ur_1: á-tuku na-an-úš-e [šu]l-ḫi na-[an-gul]-e (no room for bàd); Ur_2: á-tuku na-àm-úš-e-en / bàd-šul-ḫi na-àm-gul-e-en; Ur_3: [...]-an-úš-en bàd-sìl na-an-gul-e; K_1: usu-tuku na-an-úš-e bàd-šul(?) na-an-gul-e, only text that has usu-tuku, all others have á-tuku; P: á-tuku na-an-úš-en bàd-sìl-ḫi. There are, thus, three variants of bàd-šul-ḫi: Ur_1: [šu]l-ḫi; Ur_3: bàd-sìl; P: bàd-sìl-ḫi.

Does BAD represent the same verb in all three lines, 63, 64, and 53, or is the similarity graphic only? In line 63, Akk_3 has the unexpected translation *la tu-ḫal-la-aq*, "don't destroy," but in line 64, the same text has *l*]*a tu-uš-mit*, "don't kill," and these may be considered reliable translations of both lines (apart from the form *tu-uš-mit* (pret.), for which Akk_2 has *tuš-ma-at*, which is better). Yet, in line 53, "killing" may be too drastic a measure to be convincing if used as an ordinary retaliation against a debtor, and the Akkadian translation points to bad = *rêqu*, "to remove," so it seems that they represent different Sum. verbs.

bàd-šul-ḫi = *šulḫû*, is the outer city wall, cf. AHw 1147, s.v. *ša/ulḫu(m)*. Killing the strong men of a city is like destroying one's own best protection.

For na-an-gul-e-en, Akk_3 has [... *a*]*k-kul-šu la tu-qa-ba-ar*. Among other possibilities is *sakkulšu lā tuqabber*, "Seine [Ke]ule(?) sollst du nicht begraben!" from Sum. saŋ-gul, "the head smasher," which suits the context best.[63] The question remains, however, how this relates to the Sumerian text. The second part of this line would fit nicely as the second half of line 60, but it is more likely that Akk_3 here incorporates what may have been a genuine Akkadian proverbial expression not present in the Sumerian text. A similar case occurs in Akk_2, line 61: *uq-qú-rak ma-tum ma-ʾ-da*, discussed above.

Line 64: Akk_1: *eṭ-la la tu-uš-*[...]; Akk_2: *eṭ-la la tuš-ma-at u*[*l-tu âli*] *la tu-pa-ḫar*; Akk_3: [*eṭ-la l*]*a tu-uš-mit* // + r. i 10? traces of one sign; *tu-uš-mit* preterite, unexplained.

SS variants: I_4: ŋuruš-e [...], -e erroneous?; Ur_1: [...] na-an-úš-e [er]e-ta na-an-gur-[r]e; Ur_2: ŋuruš na-àm-úš-e-en ere^ki^-šè mu-ra-ab-gur-re-e[n] (illegible sign above gur); Ur_3: [...]-en ere-šè na-an-gur-ru-un; K_1: ŋuruš-e na-an-úš-e [éri]n-šè(?) na-gur-en; P: [... n]a-an-úš-e-en ere-šè na-an-gur-re-e[n].

ŋuruš is here the class of workers that could easily be moved from place to place according to where they were needed. Ur_1: [er]e-ta na-an-gur-[r]e, "Don't turn him away from the city," is definitely the better text, although it is only supported by a single source, versus Ur_2, etc.: ere^ki^-šè; Ur_3: mu-ra-ab-gur-re-e[n] (only source that has -b- and -en); P: ere-šè, "Don't let them return to the city." K_1: [éri]n-šè(?) na-gur-en is too uncertain for comments.[64] For úš = BAD, cf. the comments on lines 63 and 53.

63. Suggested by Krebernik, 1996, 175, who considers various other possibilities: *akkullu*, "Dechsel"; alternatively: *kakkullu* I "Maischbottich," II "Frühtekorb," *šakkullu*, "eine Weidenart," or *sakkullu*, "Kopfschmetterer." The verb is likely to be *qebēru*. He also does not exclude *gapāru* D, "gewaltig machen(?)," and *kabāru* D, "(kultisch) reinigen." The English expression "to bury the hatchet" is of late origin, relating to the American Indians.

64. Wilcke, p. 205, line 69, translates "Du sollst einen (arbeitsfähigen) Mann nicht fortschicken(?)! Du sollst ihn zur Stadt nicht zurückkehren lassen!"; "Fortschicken" is now to be revised in view of the Akkadian translation, and Ur_1: -ta, "from the city," makes better sense. Theoretically the ghost of those killed could return and become a nuisance to a city, but this is far from the most obvious intent of the text. On p. 215 (ll. 68–69) Wilcke understands Ur_2: mu-ra-ab-gur-re-e[n] as including "einen Akkus. der Sachkl.: «du wirst (sonst) die Stadt sich gegen dich wenden lassen»." I regard the relevant -b- as a collective plural marker, which implies that the reference is to several young men expelled from the city. Wilcke's interpretation is, in fact, contradictory, since the text includes ere-šè,

Line 65: Akk_1: *a-kíl kar-ṣi* [...]; Akk_2: *a-kil kar-ṣi i-na-šu ki-ma* ŋišBALA *i-na-am-[maš]*, "his eyes move like a spindle"; Akk_3: [...] *x ki-ma pí-li-ik-ki i-te-ru*, "... turn like spindle." Neither *namāšu* nor *târu* is a normal equivalent of sir_5, but both cover the intended meaning with ad hoc translations. This indicates that Akk_2 and Akk_3 were two independent translations made from the Sumerian text without a common Akkadian base.

SS variants: I_4: lú e[me ...]; Ur_1: [1/2 line] ⌜x⌝(?) ⌜sig⌝(?)-ga(cannot be bal)-⌜a⌝ ši-sir_5-r[e]; Ur_2: lú inim(probably eme!)-sì-ga-gim igi ŋišbala-ke_4/gé ši-in-sir_5-[sir_5]; Ur_3: l[ú ...]-ke_4 igi ŋišbala-gim ši-sir_5-sir_5; K_1: lú eme-sig-ga-ke_4/gé igi bala-ke_4 ši-sir_5-sir_5; P: lú eme-sig gu_7-a-gim(? probably -ke_4/gé) igi ŋišbala-gim ši-sir_5-sir_5.

After Ur_1: ...⌜x⌝(?) ⌜sig⌝(?)-ga-⌜a⌝ follows ši-sir_5-r[e], so apparently igi ŋišbala-gim was omitted by mistake; Ur_2: inim-sì-ga, instead of eme-sig-ga, possibly with inim as a mistake for eme. eme is clear in K_1 and P, but inim-sig should be possible in view of lines 33 and 93. Provided that the transliteration is reliable, only P has eme-sig gu_7-a-gim, with -gim as a mistake for ke_4.[65a] Similarly Ur_2: igi ŋišbala-ke_4, and K_1: bala-ke_4/gé, for gim. Only K has bala without the determinative. Five texts have ši- as a verbal preformative; cf. pp. 212ff., *Chap. 1.9: Modal verbal prefixes.*

Alster, 1974, 38, translated, "The slanderer turns like a «turncoat»," in an attempt to render an implicit pun, commenting, p. 90, that two notions may have been contaminated: ŋišbala-gim sir_5: "to spin (or turn) like a spindle," and *igi – bal, "to turn the eyes," meaning, "to changes one's face," i.e., to be unreliable.[65b] bala sir_5, "spinning," and the connotations attached to that notion are well known from many linguistic areas and mythologies, and there is ample Sumerian evidence for them, cf., e.g., the references quoted by Alster, 1974, 89–90: *Enki and the World Order* 438, etc. igi – bal is also well attested, cf. OB Lú A 287–288 (MSL 12, 166): lú-igi-bal = *e-et-*[*x*]*-ru*, lú-igi-bal = *mu-*[*te-er i-nim*]; *Two Scribes* (*Dialogue* 2) 122 A: ka-sìg igi-bal ú(?)-nu-ŋar-ra, "who insults, changes his face, deceitful person(?)." Cf. also Sjöberg, JCS 24 (1972) 113, n. 9, etc.[65c]

Wilcke, 1978, 205 and 217 (ll. 70–71), however, connects line 65 with line 66, and translates 65: "Der Verleumder umspinnt die Augen wie mit einer Spindel," paraphrasing "Ein Verleumder trübt den klaren Blick," and comparing *semper aliquid haeret.* The Akkadian translation, Akk_3: *ki-ma pí-li-ik-ki i-te-ru* ..., "turns like a spindle," does not confirm "umspinnt die Augen"; cf. also the slightly different translation of Akk_2: *ki-ma* ŋišBALA *i-na-am-[maš]*, "moves like a spindle." Neither *târu* nor *namāšu* is a normal equivalent of sir_5,[65d] and the Akkadian translations clearly attempted to describe the movement of eyes rather than that of a spindle, yet compare it to a spindle. I have, therefore, not adopted Wilcke's interpretation of line 65. Neither have I accepted the connection with line 66. Cf. the comments below.[65e]

Line 66: Akk_1: *i-na pa-ni la ta-[za-az ...]*; Akk_2:

"Do not turn it (= the city) toward the city(sic!) for your sake." Only Ur_2 has -b- instead of -n-, and even if we accept bad instead of úš, it would sound like the revolt against a city ruler, which is most unlikely to be the intent here. There are two solutions: either that -šè is an error for -ta or, more likely, that we should read <nu>-mu-ra-ab-gur-re-en, "you will not make them return to the city for your own sake." Perhaps an expression such as *Lugal-e* 33: lugal-$ŋu_{10}$ lú ere-ni-šè gur-ra ama-ni-šè ak-a is reflected here.

65a. Wilcke, 1978, 216 (l. 70): "Trifft die Lesung gim(?) in [P] zu, so zieht dieser Text noch die Zeile zur vorherigen; Subject kann nur ŋuruš aus Z [64] sein." There can be no doubt that lines 64 and 65 are not connected in this way.

65b. The Akkadian translation, "turns (or: moves) the eyes like a spindle," shows that the interpretation was relevant, although Wilcke, 1978, 217, found "keine Anzeichen."

65c. Cf. also igi an-kúr-kúr 5 ì-lul = *mu-te-ra-at i-[nim] ki-ma ḫa-mi-iš sà-ra-at*, "she changes her eyes/face, she tells a lie five times," Alster, 1991–92, 10, line 5.

65d. *i-te-ru*: Krebernik, ZA 86 (1996) 175 (ad B6) took it as a form of *watāru*, "[der(?)] wie eine Spindel ... hervorragt(e)," but it must be *itarrū* (from *târu*): "turns like a spindle."

65e. PSD B, 64, suggests another solution, apparently taking igi-ŋišbala-gim/ke_4 as a genitival compound, indicated by the hyphen, but ventures no translation. It would mean, lit., "(turns like) the eye of a spindle," versus "turns the eye like a spindle." The sole explanation given is a reference to Wilcke, who, however, did not consider that solution. It is worth taking into account, however, although Akk_3: *ki-ma pí-li-ik-ki* [*i-n*]*a pa-ni la ta-az-za-az lìb-ba-šu tu-šá-an-na*, cf. below; Akk$_3$: [*i-na pa-ni la-a ta*]*-az-za-az* ŠÀ *la-a* / ([ ]) *ú-ša-ni-ku*.

SS variants: I$_4$: igi-a; Ur$_1$: [...] šà-ge nu-mu-e-kár-[kár]; Ur$_2$: igi-àm na-àm-ba-gub-gub-bu-dè šà-ge me-kúr-kúr; Ur$_3$: igi-šè [...]-en šà-ge bí-kúr-kúr; K$_1$: igi-a nam-bi-du-dè šà ab-kúr-kúr; P: igi-a nam-ba-e-gub-gub-bu-dè-en šà-ge na-mu-un-kúr-kúr.

Discussion of variants: I$_4$, K$_1$, and P: igi-a; Ur$_2$: igi-àm; Ur$_3$: igi-šè; Ur$_2$: na-àm-ba-gub-gub-bu-dè; K$_1$: nam-bi-du-dè, bi = bí, cf. com. line 22; du-dè is probably a mistake for gub-gub-bu-dè; Ur$_1$: šà-ge ... kár-[kár]: (only text that has kár) is probably influenced by šà-ge – KÁR (= guru$_7$), "to wish"; Ur$_2$: šà-ge me-kúr-kúr; Ur$_3$: šà-ge bí-kúr-kúr; K$_1$: šà ab-kúr-kúr; P: šà-ge na-mu-un-kúr-kúr. Four sources agree on šà-ge, only K$_1$ has šà alone. It is difficult to find the most reliable text for the second verb phrase. For P: -ba-e-, cf. the comments on line 19. Only P has the negative na-, but cf. Ur$_1$: nu-mu-e-kár-[kár]. Ur$_2$: me-, Ur$_3$: bí-, as well as K$_1$: ab- agree on a positive verbal form. I have chosen bí- because Ur$_3$ is generally more reliable than Ur$_2$. Yet, both a negative and a positive verb makes sense, cf. below.

Wilcke, 1978, 205 and 217 (ll. 70–71), connects line 66 with line 65, translating 66: "Du sollst ihn nicht stets im Augen haben; sonst wird er dem/im Herzen (das Urteil) ändern." Römer, 1990, 54, translates: "Der Verleumder umspinnt die Augen wie (mit) eine(r) Spindel, vor Augen sollst du (ihn dir) nicht stets stellen: Dem Herzen hat er immer wieder das Urteil geändert!" referring to PSD B, 64. The ETCSL translates: "The eyes of the slanderer always move around as shiftly as a spindle. You should never remain in his presence; his intentions(?) should not be allowed to have an effect(?) on you." The fact that line 66 can be seen as a motivation clause to line 65 speaks in favor of seeing the two as connected.[66a] Yet, if that is the case, why does the text not simply start with line 66 before line 65, like "Do not stay in the presence of a man who moves his eyes like a spindle; he will change his mind, ..."?

Although there, thus, seems to be almost unanimous agreement about the connection of lines 65 and 66, there are still reasons to consider the older solution by Alster, 1974, 39 (l. 71), who took line 66 as a separate entry standing alone: "Do not stand in front, you will change your mind." These are:

First: line 66 is not formed as a "normal" motivation clause consisting of a single phrase stating what may be the consequences of a "protasis," i.e., line 65. Here, line 65 is not phrased as a precept at all, but is just a single positive statement, whereas line 66 consists of two parts, which look like a "protasis" and a motivation clause in itself. To make the connection plausible, Wilcke adds "ihn" and "sonst" to his translation of line 66: "Du sollst ihn nicht stets im Augen haben; sonst ..." He takes the /e/ in šà-ge as the loc.-term., "dem/im Herzem (das Urteil) ändern," and states, p. 217: "Wegen des Lok.-Term. in šà-ge ist seine Überz. «do not change your mind» ausgeschlossen."[66b] Yet, why add "Urteil"?

I prefer to try first to see if the phrases make sense when taken as separate statements, which, of course, does not preclude the possibility that secondary implications may have been added to them when they were incorporated into a precept compilation. There is no reason to add "Urteil," when the changing of the heart is sufficiently clear in itself. It is, of course, the common word igi in lines 65 and 66 that attracted the second line to the first. Therefore, the most likely solution is, in fact, to understand šà-ge as the ergative. This results in a rare, but not unique, construction in Sumerian: a transitive verb with ellipsis of the object; cf. lines 139; 153. The reason is that the full object would have repeated the subject,

does not support it; cf. Alster, 1974, 90: "not surprisingly two variants have igi-^{giš}bala-gim." Wilcke's additional note, p. 232, on "durchboren mit einer Spindel," referring to line 227: ^{giš}bala, is hardly relevant here.

66a. Note that the presence of motivation clauses is not obligatory (cf. line 44). Obviously, the text incorporated some traditional sayings that did not conform to the pattern.

66b. Yet, it conforms well to the Akkadian translation of Akk$_3$: ŠÀ *la-a ú-ša-ni-ku*. "The heart will not change for you." A number of unnecessary assumptions had, in fact, to be made in order to understand the statement as suggested by Wilcke, p. 217: "Ich vermute, daß der Verleumder von Z. 70 Objekt des ersten Satzes ist und Subjekt des zweiten, in dem etwa «deine Meinung» «dein Urteil» als Objekt zu subintelligieren wäre."

or vice versa, like a *figura etymologica*, "the heart will change its heart," i.e., it will change its own mind, or, maybe, in other words, an impersonal expression for: "you will change your mind."

Second: There are now three Akkadian translations that unequivocally show: *ina pāni la tazzāz*, "don't stand in front."[66c] In this case the Akkadian expression—and even the Sumerian one—corresponds precisely to the English "in front," as well as to the German "vor Augen," by not having a pronominal suffix or a determiner attached to "eye" or its equivalent. "In front of him" or "in front of yourself" would have required a pronominal suffix. Cf. the similar use of igi-a in *Counsels of Wisdom* 182: igi-a nam-ba-e-gub-bu, "let him not stand outside" (cf. *Chap. 2.3*). The translation "vor Augen" shows an awareness of the problem, so why not draw the pertinent conclusion, that the reference is general, "in front," not "in front of anyone particular," in other words, don't put yourself in the frontline where you are most exposed to danger. The image obviously comes from the battlefield. Cf. line 68.

Third: For the second part of the line, Akk$_3$ has: ŠÀ(= *libbu*) *la-a ú-ša-ni-ku*, "(the) heart will not change for you," implying, probably, "you cannot change your mind." This makes good sense, but, unquestionably, in view of the Sum. text, the negation might be secondary, so that the original intent may have been "(you may regret this, because, remember,) you may (have to) change your mind (later)." Akk$_2$: *lìb-ba-šu tu-šá-an-na*, "you will change his mind," seems to be erroneous.

Line 67: ED$_1$ o. vii 3': ka nam-tar ŋar (cf. Alster, 1991–92, 33).

Akk$_1$: *ki-ma sa-ar-ri* [...]; Akk$_2$: *ki-ma sà-ar i-na bīt šikâri la tuš-tar-ra-aḫ*: Akk$_3$: [*ki-ma sà-ar*] *a-na* É-*ti ši-kà-/*[*ri la-a tuš-tar*]*-ra-aḫ*. *tuš-tar*]*-ra-aḫ* from *šarāḫu* AHw 1183, Dt, "sich rühmen"; cf. MSL 13, 199: 304 and our line 37.

SS variants: I$_4$: lú-l[ul ...]; Ur$_2$: lú-lul-la-ka é-kaš-ka KA nam-tar-tar-re inim-zu ŋar-ra-[àm]; Ur$_3$: lú-lul-l[a]-ka KA nam-tar-tar-re; K$_1$: lú-lul-la-gé é-kaš-kam KA nam-tar-tar-re; P: lú-lul-la-gim é-lun-ga-ka KA nam-tar-tar-re.

Discussion of variants: Only P has: lú-lul-la-gim; Ur$_2$ and Ur$_3$: lú-lul-la-ka; K$_1$: lú-lul-la-gé; Ur$_2$: é-kaš-ka; Ur$_3$: omits é-kaš-ka, but adds inim-zu ŋar-ra-[àm] as a second part of the line (this is included in Ur$_2$ only, and has been added from line 37, where it genuinely belongs; yet, if the identification of the second part of ED$_1$: ŋar = SS inim-zu ŋar-ra-[àm] is correct, it shows that the second part genuinely belongs to the text). P: é-lunga(=BAPPIR)-ka instead of é-kaš-ka; K$_1$ alone has: é-kaš-kam.[67a]

Why -ka instead of -gim or -gé? The fact that only two texts, and even less reliable ones, have -gim or -gé, suggests that -ka is primary and does not simply replace the equative.[67b] gim can be explained as an attempt to simplify a less common construction, the *genitive of characteristics*, that is, in this case, a double genitive, of which the second lacks its regens, denoting what is characteristic of the rectum > lú-lul-ak-ak: "in a way that is characteristic of a man of lies."[67c] There is regrettably no Nippur source preserved here, so the readings of the two Ur texts, Ur$_2$ and Ur$_3$: lú-lul-la-ka represent the best available evi-

66c. On p. 217 (l. 71) Wilcke states that the restoration of Akk$_1$ to *ta-*[*za-az* ...] is "nicht zwingend," but it has now been confirmed by Akk$_2$: *ta-az-za-az*, and Akk$_3$: *ta*]*-az-za-az*. Otherwise a Š-form, *tu-*[*uš-*, would have been required.

67a. The variant K$_1$: é-kaš-kam, is a genitive intensified by -àm, which as any such construction can represent any case, almost in the way of a split sentence construction, "it is in a beer-house that you should not ...." Cf. p. 210, *Chap. 1.9: Split sentence construction.*

67b. Cf. Wilcke, 1987, 205 (l. 72): "Wie ein falscher Kerl sollst du im Wirtshaus keine Lobrede halten! (Dein wort ist (dadurch) festgelegt!)." Wilcke, 1987, 217 (l. 72), explains -ka in lú-lul-la-ka as derived from <*kam. This again would create a split sentence construction: "It is a man of lies (like) whom you should not boast"; with the equative this is less convincing, although not impossible. Cf. p. 210, *Chap. 1.9: Genitive of characteristics.*

67c. This construction, which is well known in Latin as the *genitivus proprietatis*, does, in fact, occur in Sumerian, as a variant of the so-called "regensloser Genitive." Cf. p. 210, *Chap. 1.9: The Genitive of Characteristics.* Cf. SP 3.147: al-ur$_4$-ur$_4$-na-ka-nam al-ri-ri-e-na-ka-nam ba-an-gin ba-an-gin mu-ni-ib-bé-ne, "It is characteristic of your harvesting, it is characteristic of your gleaning, that they say, «he is gone, he is gone»," from /ur$_4$-ur$_4$-en-a-ak-nam/ -nam is difficult to explain. It is probably an intensifier, based on -àm(-kam), but may be confused with the 2nd person suffix -en here

dence and should be taken as the primary text.

Line 67 A: It is doubtful where Akk_1: *ki-ma ser-ri i-*[belongs. In Akk_3 there are only traces of one sign, so it is uncertain whether it was the same line.

Line 68: Akk_2: *a-*[*šar zi-k*]*a-ri ina ṭe-ḫe-ka la mu-up-pi-ša-a-ta*; cf. below.

SS variants: I_4: ki nam-[...]; Ur_2: igi(? rather than ki) nam-ninta-ka um-me-te [š]u na-ku_5-ku_5-dè-[en], igi uncertain; Ur_3: k[i nam]-ninta-ka um-ma-te [...] na-an-gu_4-gu_4-dè; K_1: ki nam-ninta-ke_4 um-ma-ta ⸢šu⸣ nam-ku_4-ku_4-dè, coll. J. Taylor; P: ki nam-ninta-a-ka um-ma-te-en šu nam-gu_4(?)-x-dè(?).

Discussion of variants: Ur_2 (probably), and Ur_3: ki nam-ninta-ka; P: ki nam-ninta-a-ka; K_1: ki nam-ninta-ke_4; Ur_2: um-me-te; Ur_3: um-ma-te; K_1: um-ma-ta (probably by mistake or miscopy for -te); P: um-ma-te-en; Ur_2: [š]u na-ku_5-ku_5-dè-[en] (phonetic for gu_4-gu_4-dè); Ur_3: na-an-gu_4-gu_4-dè; K_1: ⸢šu⸣ nam-ku_4-ku_4-dè (Wilcke, 1987, 217 suggests: kur(!)-ku_4-dè, but see the collation above); P: šu nam-gu_4(?)-x-dè(?) (unexplained).

ki-nam-ninta, lit., "the place of manhood," is attested in *Gilgameš, Enkidu and the Netherworld* 229–237, where it is equated with *ašar taḫāz zikāri*, "the battlefield" (quoted by Alster, 1974, 92); further in the *Barton Cylinder* MBI 1, xx 9: ki-nam-ninta-ni, regrettably in a difficult context, probably in connection with a description of Ninurta's heroic victory in a mythological battle (cf. Alster and Westenholz: AcSum 16 [1994] 15–46). Cf. also ki-nam-munus, OSP I 1 iii' 4'.[68]

gu_4-ud-gu_4-ud in itself is *šaḫāṭu*, which can describe spasmodic movements in a patient's body; cf. van Dijk/Geller, *Ur III Incantations*, p. 13, ad no. 1, line 7: gú-sa gi-a šè-mu-gu_4-gu_4, "whose diseased neck twitches." Cf. further CAD Š/1, 88. The verb occurs in *Lugal-e* 587: ḫé-em(-ta)-gu_4-ud-e = *šitaḫḫuṭu*, "to leap up and down."

The verb šu gu_4-ud is attested elsewhere: SP 9 Sec. A 13 and parallels: ^{šáḫ}zé-eḫ-tur-e šu al-gu_4-gu_4-ud. Alster, *Proverbs* I, 179–180, translates "The small pig roots ..."; cf. Alster, *Proverbs* II, 419, where a variant omitting šu is mentioned, suggesting gu_4-ud = *šitaḫḫuṭu*, probably meant as a description of a pig searching for food.[68] An example of gu_4-ud, denoting a reed swaying from side to side, is quoted by Alster, 1974, 93: *Dialogue 4*: gi al-gu_4-ud-da-gim ì-gu_4-ud-[dè]-en kiŋ-ŋá bí-in-sì-ge, "I set to work swaying like a swaying reed." Here, as in many languages, the swaying reed is proverbial for instability. Alster, 1974, 39 (l. 72), translates "When you approach the battlefield, do not wave your hands," which is still worth considering, that is, one should avoid drawing unnecessary attention to oneself in dangerous situations. The Akkadian translation *lā muppišāta*, however, points in a very different direction: "Don't conclude a sale when you approach the battlefield," i.e., under pressed situations, from *muppišu*, (from *epēšu*, D), cf. CAD E, 191; 231–231: *epēšu* 4: *uppušu*: "to conclude a sales agreement"; in other words, "don't be a salesman" or "don't conclude a sale" or try to do business under adverse or hostile conditions (suggested by Geller). How exactly it came to mean that is uncertain, but it certainly seems to be derived from a meaning similar to Alster's earlier proposal, cited above.

Line 69: Akk_1: [x] ⸢x⸣ *qar-ra-di* [...]; Akk_2: [*qar-r*]*a-du e-diš-šu-ma e-diš-ši-šú ki-ma* [*š*]*á-ar.*

SS variants: I_4: ur-[...]; Ur_2: [...] na-na-àm dili-ni ⸢lú⸣ ⸢šár⸣-ra-à[m]; Ur_3: ur-⸢saŋ⸣ ⸢dili⸣ na-nam dili-⸢ni⸣(rather than dù) l[ú] šár-r[a-à]m; K_1: ur-saŋ dili na-nam dili-dù(read ni?) nu šár-ra; P: ur-saŋ dili na-nam dili-ni lú šár-ra-àm.

Discussion of variants: Ur_2: na-na-àm (occurs elsewhere in Ur_2, cf. line 30; all others: na-nam); Ur_3: ⸢dili⸣ na-nam dili-⸢ni⸣; so all others except K_1, which has dili dù (probably to be read ni(!), but possibly influenced by dili-dù, cf. *Dumuzi's Dream* 28, etc.), and nu šár-ra instead of lú šár-ra. The variant nu for lú occurs also in line 167: nu-zu-a-zu versus lú-zu-a-zu, and is an example of the well-known /n:l/ variation, e.g., nu-bànda = *laputtum*, etc.; cf. generally Edzard, 1962, and Edzard, *Sum. Grammar*, p. 18.

following the verb itself or with the well-known nam-verbal preformative. Cf. also line 280.

68. Wilcke, 1987, 205 (l. 72) translates: "Wenn du zum Ort des Mannestums kommst, sollst du (die Hand(?)) nicht ...!" which I find unnecessarily vague. What the "Ort des Mannestums" refers to is sufficiently clear in view of *Gilgameš, Enkidu and the Netherworld* 229–237.

69–72. Variant forms play a decisive role in lines 5–7 and

Wilcke, 1978, 217 (l. 74) compares: "Der starke ist am mächtigsten allein."

Lines 69–72: These form a well-known pattern of parallelism, the adding parallelism, that rarely occurs in *The Instructions of Šuruppak.*[69–72] The subject of the first couplet is an anticipating epithet, which is replaced by a specifying reference when the first line is repeated in the second. Therefore, the "warrior" in line 69 refers to Utu, and the reference in 71: ur-saŋ, "the hero," is also to Utu, although 69 and 71 could be taken alone and would make perfectly clear sense as such.

Line 70: Akk$_1$: [x x] ^{d}*šá-maš i-[diš-ši-šu* ...]; Akk$_2$: [^{d}*šamaš*] ⸢*e*⸣*-diš-ši-šú-ma* ⸢*e*⸣*-diš-ši-šú k*[*i*]*-ma* [*šá*]*-ar.*

SS variants: I$_4$: ^{d}[...]; Ur$_2$: [...] ⸢dili⸣ na-na-àm [dili]-⸢ni⸣ lú šár-ra-àm (written on the left edge); Ur$_3$: ^{d}[u]tu ⸢x⸣ ⸢x⸣-nam dili-ni lú [šár]-ra; K$_1$: ⸢^{d}utu⸣ dili na-nam dili-ni (copy dù) nu-šár-ra. Discussion of variants: cf. line 69.

There is a remarkable allusion to the same saying in Schøyen MS 2108 rev. 11: ^{d}utu nun na-na dili-⸢ni(?)⸣ lú šár-a ušum ur-saŋ dili na-na dili-ni lú šar-àm, "the sun god is «prince», when alone he is a multitude of men; a dragon(?) is a lone hero, when alone he is a multitude of men"; for ušum, cf. line 30, var. with comments.

Line 71: Akk$_1$: [*a-na qar*]*-ra-di* [...]; Akk$_2$: [*a-na qar-r*]*a-du i-ziz-ma na-piš-ta-*..., "stand with the «hero», and breath [will stay with you?]": *i-ziz-ma* imperative.

SS variants: Ur$_2$: ur-saŋ-da gub-bu-[d]è zi-zu ḫé-en-da-ŋál; Ur$_3$: [...] su$_8$-bu-da zi-zu [ḫé-e]n-da-an-ŋál.

Discussion of variants: Only Ur$_2$: has gub-bu-[d]è; Ur$_3$: su$_8$-bu-da; su$_8$(-b) is the *marû* plural form of DU, "to go." It seems to be used here by mistake, because zi-zu, "your life," is clearly singular. Yet, maybe the plural here indicates a repeated action?

The line was translated "When you stay with the «hero», your life will last," by Alster, 1974, 39 (l. 76), and this seems to be approximately the best solution so far.[71a] Utu is the god of justice, whose connection with long life is evident. Cf. Alster, 1990, 9, where Borger, *Contribution*, No. 107:21 (OB letter): *šamaš šû balāṭka liq*[*bi*], "may he, Šamaš, command good health for you," is cited. I understand zi as "breath," that is, the mere physical aspects of breathing. "Good health" would rather have required *balāṭka.*

ur-saŋ/^{d}utu gub-bu-dè can be understood in two ways: either as an image from a battlefield, in which Utu's emblem may have been carried in front of an army, or, perhaps more likely, as meaning "rising with the sun," i.e., "getting up early."[71b] The latter possibility appears from the parallels cited by

parallels, though, and in line 209–211; cf. also Chap. 3.3: *The Ballade of Early Rulers* 5.

71a. Alster, 1975, 141 (l. 76), however, translated "in order to stay with the «hero», let your life be with him." This was an attempt to answer the criticism that the difference between -dè and -da had been overlooked. In such cases it is justified to look for a simpler solution, that both -dè and -da may be mere graphic variants for a single /ed-a/ morpheme, in which the vowels of -/ed-e/ are colored by the preceding /u/. There admittedly seems to be a clear pattern in most cases, but it cannot be trusted in all periods and texts of mixed origin. Cf. p. 216, *Chap. 1.9: Verbal extension suffixes.* The Akkadian translations of Akk$_2$: [*a-na qar-r*]*a-du i-ziz-ma*, "stand with the «hero»," and 72: ⸢*a*⸣*-na* ^{d}*šamaš i-ziz-ma*, confirm that an *infinitivus finalis* was not intended. Yet, on the other hand, the imperative cannot be a verbatim translation of the Sum. gub-bu-dè.

71b. Wilcke, 1978, 205 (l. 76), translates: "Bei dem(= wie ein?) Krieger zu stehen, das sei dein Streben!" and line 72 (77): "Bei Utu (= wie Utu?) zu stehen, das sei dein Streben!" In both cases "wie" is a misleading paraphrase. da means exactly "with," i.e., either getting up "with" the sun, or standing "with" (the support of) the sun-god, perhaps in the form of a standard carried in front on a battlefield and, thereby, increasing one's chances of survival in the battle. Römer, 1990, 55 (ll. 72–73) translates "möge dein Leben bei ihm sein," referring to AHw 738, *napištu(m)* B and CAD N, 296ff. He acknowledges Wilcke's translation "Streben" as "freier." A third possibility is mentioned by Sefati, *Love Songs*, 279, n. 24, who translates "Staying with the hero/Utu, may always be your *endeavor,*" commenting "'Staying with Utu' probably has a broader meaning here, namely: to walk in the ways of the Sun-god and to keep his commandments, or to be like him." The gist ("commandments") here sounds more biblical than necessary, and why translate "endeavor" when the plain translation "life" or, rather, "breath" makes perfectly good sense? The most important objection is, however, that concrete images take precedence over abstract formulation in proverbial wisdom, and the translations should reflect this, whenever possible.

Alster, 1974, 93:[71c] *Inanna and Bilulu* 86–87: ᵈutu-da gub-bu-da silim-ŋá en(-nu-ùŋ-ba me-gub), "rising with the sun I kept watch over you ...," and the love song *Inanna and Dumuzi Y* (PBS 12, 52 rev. ii 8–11): ŋi$_6$-a ŋá-nu ŋi$_6$-a gub-ba ᵈutu-da ŋá-nu ᵈutu-da gub-ba, "come at night, stay at night, come with the Sun, stay with the sun."[71d]

Line 72: Akk$_1$: *[a-na]* ᵈ*[šá-maš* ...]; Akk$_2$: ⸢*a*⸣*-na* ᵈ*šamaš i-ziz-ma* ....

SS variants: I$_5$: (traces); I$_6$: ᵈutu [...]; Ur$_2$: ᵈutu-da [gu]b-bu-dè zi-zu ḫ[é-e]n-da-ŋál; Ur$_3$: [su$_8$-bu]-da zi-zu ḫ[é-e]n-da-an-ŋál. Cf. line 71.

Lines 73–75+76–82: Cf. lines 6–13; 143–152; 287–288.

Line 73: Akk$_2$: *šu-ri-ip-pa-ku-*..., "the man from Šuruppak," cf. the comments on lines 5–7 above.

SS variants: I$_5$: [šurup]pakᵏⁱ-e dumu-ni-ra na n[a-...]; I$_6$: šuruppakᵏⁱ du[mu ...]; Ur$_3$: [...] na-šè mu-un-ni-in-ri, "gave as an instruction"; cf. the comments on line 6.

Line 74: Akk$_2$: *šu-ri-ip-pa-ku-*.... SS variants: I$_5$: [šurup]pakᵏⁱ dumu ubar-tu-tu-[...]; I$_6$: šuruppakᵏⁱ dumu ubar-tu-tu-[...]; Ur$_3$: omits the line.

Line 75: Akk$_2$: *ú-t[a-na-pi]š-ta ma-ra-šu iš-[šar]*. SS variants: I$_5$: zi-u$_4$-sud-rá dumu-ni-ra na šè-m[u-un]-ni-in-ri-[ri]; I$_6$: zi-u$_4$-sud-rá dumu-ni-ra na / [na]-mu-un-ni-in-r[i-ri]; Ur$_3$: [...-r]á dumu-ni-ra [na] / na-mu-un-ri-ri. The two na's are separated by the indented lines in two duplicates; cf. the comments on line 6.

Line 76: Akk$_2$ omits the line altogether. SS variants: I$_5$: [x]-kam-ma-šè šuruppakᵏⁱ-e dumu-ni-ra na na-mu-un-ri-ri; I$_6$: min-kam-ma-šè šuruppakᵏⁱ [...]; Ur$_3$: [... du]mu-ni-ra [... -u]n-ri.

Line 77: Akk$_2$ omits the line altogether. SS variants: I$_5$: [šurupp]akᵏⁱ dumu ubar-tu-tu-ke$_4$; T$_3$: š[urupp]akᵏⁱ dumu [...]; Ur$_3$: omits line.

Line 78: Akk$_2$ omits the line altogether. SS variants: I$_5$: [...]-sud-rá dumu-ni-ra na na-mu-[...]; I$_7$: [...] na [...]; T$_3$: zi-u$_4$-sud-ra (sic!) [...]; Ur$_3$: omits line; BM$_1$: ⸢zi-u$_4$⸣-[...].

Line 79: Cf. lines 9 and 149. Akk$_2$: *[ma-ri] áš-šar-ka a-še[r-ti ṣa-bat]*, cf. Akk$_3$ line 9. SS variants: I$_5$: [... g]a-ri n[a-...]; I$_7$: [... -r]i-ŋu$_{10}$ ḫé-da[b$_5$]; T$_3$: dumu-ŋu$_{10}$ na ri ga ⸢x⸣ [...], ga ri mistakenly inverted; Ur$_3$: dumu-ŋu$_{10}$ na ge-ri na-ri-ŋu$_{10}$ ḫé-d[ab$_5$]; BM$_1$: dumu-ŋ[u$_{10}$ ...]. Note Ur$_3$: na ge-ri = na ga-e-ri.

Line 80: Cf. lines 10 and 150. Akk$_2$: ⸢*ú*⸣*-[ta-na-piš-ta a-ma-tim (luqbíka)]*. SS variants: I$_5$: (traces); I$_7$: g]a-ra-ab-dug$_4$ [ŋizzal ḫ]é-em-ši-ia-ak; T$_3$: zi-u$_4$-sud-ra(sic!) inim [...]; Ur$_3$: zi-u$_4$-sud-rá.ra inim [ga-r]a-ab-dug$_4$ ŋiz[zal] ḫé-em-ši-[...]; BM$_1$: zi-sud-⸢x⸣-[...]. Note Ur$_3$: zi-u$_4$-sud-rá.ra: ra is here a phonetic indicator for DU = rá, unless it is the dative element that has come into the text by mistake. Note, however, that T$_3$ has zi-u$_4$-sud-ra. I$_7$: ḫ]é-em-ši-ia-ak; same variant in UM$_2$, line 270.

Lines 81ff.: Sch$_4$ obv. perhaps belongs here, but in view of the poor state of preservation this is not included in the composite text reconstruction. A separate transliteration is provided pp. 102ff., *Chap. 1.3x: The Schøyen sources: Sch$_4$.*

Line 81: Akk$_2$: ⸢*a*⸣*-šer-ta la ta/tu-*[...]. SS variants: I$_7$: [...]-bí-bar-re-en; T$_3$: na-ri-ga-ŋu$_{10}$ šu [...]; Ur$_3$: na-ri-ga-ŋá [nam]-bí-bar-[re-...]; BM$_1$: na-ri-ga-[...].

Line 82A: Only BM$_1$. Cf. line 13.

Line 83: SS variants: I$_7$: [...] ⸢x⸣-kam [...]; Ur$_3$: ka kaš naŋ-a [...] (coll. Alster, 1974, pl. II); BM$_1$: ka kaš naŋ-[...]. "A mouth drinking beer is a ... of a ...."

Line 84: Akk$_2$: [... *a-me-l*]*i ma-ri a-me-l*[*i* ...]. SS variants: I$_7$: (traces); Ur$_3$: lú-tur [...] lú ⸢x⸣ [...]; Ur$_5$: dumu-ŋ[u$_{10}$ ...]; BM$_1$: lú-tur-ŋu$_{10}$ [...].

lú-tur-ŋu$_{10}$, "my little one": This is almost certainly a variant of the common address by the father to Ziusudra: dumu-ŋu$_{10}$; this is clear from the variant in Ur$_5$: dumu-ŋu$_{10}$. Cf. the comments on line 61.

Line 85: ED$_1$: ⸢x⸣ [x] k]a ⸢kaš⸣ x | x x LUL šè. Akk$_2$: [... *š*]*i-ka-ri šá-tu-ú* [...] ⸢*x*⸣ *ú-da* [...].

ED$_1$: LUL(-)šè, might indicate that the line was similar to line 67, etc.

Line 86: ED$_1$: nin-kaš-si ⸢x⸣ ⸢x⸣ ùr(?).

Ninkasi is the well-known beer-goddess, whose name probably means, lit., "The lady who fills beer."

71c. Considered by neither Wilcke, 1978, 217, nor Römer, 1990, 55 (ll. 72–73): "mit Utu zusammenstehen": "Was heißt das genau?"

71d. Cf. "Early to bed and early to rise, makes a man healthy, wealthy, and wise," ODEP, p. 211; "Morgenstund hat gold im Mund."

Cf. Alster, 1990, 16 with n. 6, and the references quoted there. The last sign in ED$_I$ is that treated by Biggs, OIP, p. 54, ad lines 104–107, copy p. 112. The reading "ùr" was established by Alster, 1991–92, 24: comment on *ED Proverbs* line 60. It is simply an early form of ùr.

ùr in itself means "to sweep," typically used in šu – ùr, "to rub" (the body ritually); cf. CAD M/1 351, *mašādu*; cf. Geller in van Dijk/Geller, *Ur III Incantations*, p. 45, who relates it to the symptoms of palsy.

Line 87: SS variants: Ur$_3$: [...] K[A] ⸢x⸣ ùr ⸢x⸣ [x]-em (cf. line 90); Ur$_6$: ŋiš(?)-ḫur(?) [...]; BM$_I$: (traces). Too poorly preserved for comments.

Line 88: Only text: Ur$_3$: [...]-ùr-ùr-re. Too poorly preserved for comments.

Line 89: For ED$_I$, see Alster, 1990, 16: In ED$_I$, the sign is strictly speaking not íl, but the "unfinished"-íl (íl-*nutillû*), which occurs also in ED$_2$, cf. line 38: nàb-íl.

Line 90: Ur$_3$: [...] ⸢x⸣ im-sar-re; Cop: [... i]m-sar-re-em; -em looks suspicious, but seems to be from -àm; cf. line 87.

Line 91: Variants: Ur$_3$: s]aŋ im-ta-ab-dúr-dúr-re (rather than gur$_4$-gur$_4$); Cop: s[aŋ i]m-ta-ab-gur$_4$-gur$_4$-re. What saŋ – dúr would mean is doubtful.

Line 92: Variants: UM$_3$: lú ní-z[u ...]; I$_8$: [...] na(?)-e-ši-su(?)-s[u]: Ur$_3$: [...]-za-ke$_4$ nu-e-ši-su-su; Cop: [... -z]u-a-ke$_4$ na(?)-[š]i-su-su-un.

Wilcke, 1987, 217 (97) (p. 206), convincingly explains lú ní-zu-ke$_4$ as /lú-ní-zu-ak-e/, "your own man."[92] The grammatically better text is Ur$_3$: -za-ke$_4$, whereas Cop (and apparently UM$_3$, partly broken) has zu-a-ke$_4$. Whether or not line 92 is to be closely connected with line 91 cannot be decided as long as that line is imperfectly preserved, but line 92 does, in fact, make sense when taken alone, implying: "Don't expect gratitude from your own people."

Line 93: ED$_I$: ŋiš-gi šà sig, includes only a few key words to cover the entire sentence. SS variants: UM$_3$: ŋiš-gi máš-ú n[a-...]; I$_8$: [...]-ú na-nam šà-bi (? - copy ga) inim-s[ig-x]; I$_9$: ŋiš-gi máš (! copy gi) [...]; I$_{10}$: ŋiš-gi ⸢máš⸣-[...]; Ur$_3$: ŋ[iš-gi m]áš-ú na-nam šà-bi inim-sig-ga-àm; Cop: [...] máš-ú na-nam šà-bi inim-sig-ga.

Selz, WZKM 92 (2002) 174, points out that line 93 expresses a critical view toward those in power ("Herrschaftskritisch"), whereas he understands line 94 as a riddle.

Line 94: ED$_I$: A-maḫ, writes simply A for íd, that is, only the first component of the composite sign. SS variants: UM$_3$: é-gal íd maḫ-àm šà-bi g[ud ...]; I$_8$: [... m]aḫ-a šà-bi gud du$_7$-d[u$_7$-x]; I$_9$: é-gal íd maḫ-àm [...]; I$_{10}$: é-gal íd(!) [...]; Ur$_3$: é-gal íd-da maḫ-e šà-bi gud du$_7$-du$_7$-dam; Cop: [... í]d maḫ-a šà-bi gud du$_7$-dam. Variants: UM$_3$ and I$_9$ agree on maḫ-àm; I$_8$: maḫ-a; Ur$_3$: maḫ-e. Ur$_3$: gud du$_7$-du$_7$-dam; Cop: gud du$_7$-dam.

Cf. SP 6.2: é-gal íd-maḫ-[àm] šà-bi [gud] ⸢du$_7$-du$_7$⸣-[dam].[94]

Line 95: ED$_I$: ši-kù; cf. Alster, 1990, 16. In ED$_I$, ši seems to be used as a verbal preformative; cf. pp. 212–216, *Chap. 1.9: Modal verbal prefixes*. There are no variants in the SS text.

Lines 95–138 have been treated in detail by Civil, 1984, 287–296 (ll. 100–143).

Lines 95–96: Foxvog, 1976, 372, translates: "Things are always going in, but they never 'arrive'," i.e., there is no end to the process of entering. Civil, 1984, 292 (ll. 100–101), translates "Income should never reach an end, expenditures should never stop," commenting, p. 293, that "the lines are a wish for unlimited income that will allow unlimited giving." The verb is clearly sá dug$_4$/di/e with no infix -da-.[95–96a] Alster, 1990, 16, translates "Its income is something that never reaches (its aim), expenditure is something that never stops," com-

92. "Dein eigener Mann wird es dir(?) nicht zurückerstatten(?)!" This was accepted by the ETCSL: "Your own man will not repay (?) it for you." Alster, 1974, 39 (l. 97), translated "The thief(?) does not restore to you," assuming that lú ní-zu-a-ke$_4$ means "the man of theft," i.e., "a thief," referring to line 30, where ní-zuḫ alone means "thief."

94. SP 6 has now by Veldhuis, 2002, 389–391, been combined with SP 2 as already predicted by Gordon, cf. Alster, *Proverbs* I, 145. The missing link is provided by CBS 6832 (Alster, *Proverbs* I, 287).

95–96a. Wilcke, 1978, 206 (ll. 100–101) translated "Was hineingeht ist ohnegleichen, Was herauskommt, ist ohne Ende." This translation does not take the DI before the verb in line 95 into account.

menting, n. 9, that Civil's translation as a wish would better fit a verbal form with a ḫé- prefix. What is intended by the gerund /ed-am/ > -dam suffix is, however, more precisely "the income is never to reach an end, the expenditure is never to cease." The intent, thus, seems to be that no matter how much income there is, it will never be enough to match expenditures. The saying seems slightly ambiguous, so that in itself it does not provide an answer as to what it refers to, almost like a riddle-proverb (cf. below).

There is unanimous agreement on the translation of silig as "to stop, cease," although the lexical evidence is meager. Basic is MSL 2 (*Ur-E-a = nâqu*) 145: 30–33: si-li-ig = *x-ul-ḫu-um; ša-pa-a-tum; ka-a-du-um, pe-tu-ú-um*. For *šapātum* AHw 1172, tentatively accepts "aufhören," but quotes no other evidence. For *pe-tu-ú-um*, Sjöberg, TCS 3, 64, n. 21, alternatively suggests *wa-tu-ú-um*.

silig occurs in Ḫḫ vi 229–230 (MSL 6, 73); Ḫḫ IX 372–373 (MSL 7, 143): ^ŋiš/urudu^aga-šilig/silig = *agasilikku; kalmakru*, a battle ax; cf. the comments on line 15: nam-silig (also in ll. 259) and 61: nam-silig-ak = *šagapurūtam epēšum*. The question of silig versus šilig is unresolved, but silig is favored by the lexical attestations quoted below. The variant quoted in the commentary on line 61: nam-ba-ši-li$_9$-ki, from VS 10, 205 iii 5, however, suggests šilig; cf. p. 252, *Chap. 2.3: Counsels of Wisdom* 170 (cf. also 97). silig alone occurs in Sb Voc. II 166 (MSL 3, 146) = *šagapūru; līšu*, "dough," etc. (hardly relevant here) and as a verb in Níg-ga B 3 (MSL 2,145) (quoted below), where Sjöberg, TCS 3, 31, restores *i-k[a-ad*, from *kâdum*, "wachen," whereas AHw 420 translates "festhalten." Lambert, BWL, 275, however, restores: *ka-[la*, "and not cease," from *kalû*, "to withhold." It frequently occurs in expressions such as Gudea Cylinder A 29, 6: é-gudu$_4$ kù a nu-silig$_5$-ge-dam, "The holy house of the *gudu*-priests from which water never ceases," which justify the translation "(not) to cease."

Parallels to lines 95–96 are quoted by Alster, 1974, 94–95: Níg-ga B 3–4 (MSL 13, 115): an-ku$_4$-ku$_4$ nu-si-si ab-ta-è-a nu-silig-ge = *i-ru-um-ma ú-ul i-m[a-al-li] ú-ṣí-ma ú-ul i-k[a-ad(?)]*; this is preceded in line 2 by níŋ-gur$_{11}$ lugal = *ma-ak-ku-ur šar-r[i-im]*, "the kings property."

This is quoted in the *edubba*-composition UET 6/2 165, lines 59–60 with duplicates: um(?)-ku$_4$-ku$_4$ nu-si-si ní-á nu-silig(!)-ge$_4$ níŋ-gur$_{11}$ lugal-(la-)kam;[95–96b] A duplicate is KBo 57, see Civil, *N.A.B.U.* 1987, 25–27, no. 47. The text there reads (rev.! 2–4): níŋ-gur$_{11}$ ku$_4$-ku$_4$ [nu-si-sá] / íb-ta-è-a nu-si[lig-ga] / níŋ-gur$_{11}$ lugal-ak-ke$_4$. These examples show a tendency to replace níŋ sá-nu-di-dam with nu-si-si, "does not fill," i.e., are unlimited or never enough.[95–96c]

Other parallels are *Temple Hymns* 95–96: níŋ ku$_4$-ku$_4$ níŋ sá nu-di-dam níŋ è níŋ nu-silig-ge-dam, said of Ningirsu's temple Eninnu in Girsu; SP 26 obv. I 3: an-ku$_4$-ku$_4$ [níŋ-sá nu-di-dam] / íb-ta-è nu-silig-ge-[dam] (Alster, *Proverbs* I, 278); SP 25.12: an-ku$_4$-ku$_4$ nu-si-si / nu-silig-ge // níŋ-gur$_{11}$ lugal-la-ke$_4$ /igi-zu na-an-íl-en (Alster, *Proverbs* I, 277). The latter agrees with the lexical attestation found in Níg-ga in explaining the reference as "royal property," but it is the only text that adds the warning, "Don't raise your eyes toward it."[95–96d] Since this is a saying that could be applied to the property of a temple as well, as it mostly stands alone, without any explanation, it has the character of a riddle proverb, to which "royal property" is one among other possible answers.[95–96e] The expansion in SP 25.12 is a rare glimpse of the use of proverbs in the scribal schools, where oral explanations undoubtedly accompanied the lexical lists and proverb collections to

95–96b. Note ní-á = níŋ-è.

95–96c. For the expression níŋ-DI nu-di-dam, Sjöberg, TCS 3, 31, suggested "is unequalled."

95–96d. Cf. Hallo, 1990, 210, who translates "It enters and does not fill up, it leaves but does not diminish—(what is it?)—royal property!" Cf. also Alster, 1991, 1–17, commenting on *Instr. Ur-Ninurta* 25, now read níŋ-ugu-<dé>-a-ni níŋ-ab-si-e, which perhaps is an allusion to the same saying in difficult phonetic writing; cf. p. 237, *Chap. 2.2*, comments on line 25.

95–96e. Although Wilcke, 1978, 218, comments "will nicht recht einleuchten, denn in Níg-ga stünde die Lösung vor dem Rätsel." The various attestations show that the saying was only exceptionally quoted with the explanation found in Níg-ga.

a much higher degree than appears from the written sources.

Line 96: ED_I: níŋ-silig, cf. Alster, 1990, 16.

SS variants: UM_3, I_9, I_{10}, and apparently Cop agree on níŋ-è; only Ur_3 has níŋ-è-e. UM_3 and Cop agree on -silig-ge-dam; only Ur_3 has -silig-ge-dè.

Line 97: ED_I: ninda lú BU ga-šúm-š[úm]; the verb is reduplicated, which is rare for this ED source. Is BU a scribal error for $-kam_4$? *Cf. Chap. 1.5: Comments on AbSt Vers. 110.*

SS variants: UM_3: ninda lú-⌜ka⌝ ga-ra-ab-⌜šúm⌝-bi ku-nu-a; I_8: [... -r]a-ab-š[úm ...]; I_9: ninda lú-ka ga-ra-ab-šúm(!)-b[i ...]; I_{10}: ninda lú-k[a ...]; Ur_3: ninda lú-ka ga-ra-ab-šúm-bi ku-nu-a; Cop: ninda lú-ù gu_7 ga-ra-ab-šúm-bi gùn-a; MM: [...] ga-ra-ab-šúm-bi ku-nu-a. Ur_3 and MM, thus, agree on ku-nu-a, but Cop has gùn-a, phonetic for ku-nu-a. ku-nu = *qerēbu*, "to be near."

All texts seem to agree on ninda lú-ka ga-ra-ab-šúm-bi, i.e., a double anticipatory genitive, which makes the entire line a noun phrase < ninda lú-ak-ak ga-ra-ab-šúm-bi, "the {of a man's bread, its «let me give it to you»}." Cf. the similar -bi in line 99.

Lines 97–99: For ED_I, cf. Alster, 1990, 16. As to the reason for reading -bi instead of kaš here as well as in lines 98–99, cf. Wilcke, 1978, 218, who points out that níŋ connects lines 97 with 96 through a common sign, which would have formed a graphic similarity only if read ninda. Alternatively the reading ninda might apply in both cases, but ninda is hardly possible in line 96. It is doubtful, however, if the reading níŋ would apply in lines 97 and 100, although Civil, 1984, 293, considers it "equally possible." Civil points out that the lines are divided with a break after -bi, before the indented lines start, indicating that -bi belongs to the preceding noun phrase, rather than to the verb as an object, or similar. There are two variants that read -mu instead of -bi in line 99, which point in the same direction.

Lines 97–100: The meaning was clarified by Civil, loc. cit., who translates (p. 292): "(To say) «I will give it to you» about someone's bread is near. (but) giving it is as far away as the sky. I will go after the man (who says) «I will give it to you». (but he will say:) «I cannot give it to you! The bread was finished up (just) before (now)». The ETCSL translates: "When it is about someone else's bread, it is easy to say «I will give it to you», but the time of actual giving can be as far away as the sky. If you go after the man who said «I will give it to you», he will say «I cannot give it to you—the bread has just been finished up»."

Line 98: ED_I rev. ii 12, probably: šúm-da-bi ⌜an⌝ [x]. There are no variants in the SS text. an is likely to be a noun, "the sky," and not a verbal prefix.

Civil, 1984, 293, explains the contrast between "near/far" as that between "easy/difficult" in more idiomatic English. The second part of line 98 literally means "the sky is far away," as a comment on the situation, implying "(but the time of actual giving can be as far away as) the sky is far away." Cf. line 128 with commentary.

Line 99: In Cop, line 100 comes before line 99, which is less meaningful. SS variants: UM_3: g[a(!)-r]a-ab-šúm-bi lú-ra ga-ni-in-ús; I_9: [... -a]b-šúm-⌜mu⌝ lú-ra [...]; Ur_3: ga-⌜ra⌝-ab-šúm-bi lú-ra ga-<ni>-in-ús; Cop: ga-ra-ab-šúm-bi lú-ra ga-ni-in-ús; MM: ga-[ra-ab-šú]m-mu lú-ra ga-ni-in-ús. UM_3, Ur_3, Cop, thus, agree on -šúm-bi; I_9, and MM agree on -šúm-mu. All texts agree on lú-ra ga-ni-in-ús, except Ur_3, which omits -ni- by mistake.

The -bi following the verb phrase in three sources functions almost as a determiner or demonstrative particle: "This: «let me give it to you»," slightly different from line 97.

Line 100: In Cop, line 100 comes before line 99.

SS variants: UM_3, Ur_3, and Cop agree on: nu-ra-ab-šúm-mu; UM_3 Cop and MM agree on til-àm; only Ur_3 has ti-la-àm.

I understand igi-bi-šè as "when faced with it," lit., "in front of it."

Lines 101–102: ED_I seems to have níŋ-ú-g[u for níŋ-ú-rum, perhaps a scribal error. Ur_3 alone has níŋ á-sì-ga-a-da; UM_3 and MM: níŋ á-sì-ga-ta; Cop: níŋ á-sì-ga-a-ta.

níŋ á-sì-ga-a-da is problematic. Wilcke, 1978, 206, translates, "Mit dem Eigentum, auf das man Mühe verwandt hat, mein Kind, kann sich nichts messen!" Civil, 1984, 292, translates, "Property is something to be expanded(?), (but) nothing can equal my little ones," commenting, p. 293, that "á – sì is still unclear, but may be explained by a gloss sum to á-SUM = *išdiḫu* in BRM 4, 33 8'; or, alternatively, that it is = *šapāku*." Alster, 1974, 41: "With well-established property, My little one, nothing is comparable," guessing from the context. Römer, 1990, 56, however, translates lines 102–103 "Eigentum (*ist*) eine Sache, *um Kraft anzuwenden*, (doch) kann sich mit meinen Kleinen nichts messen!" commenting (n. 102 a) that the comitative verbal infix mu-da- points to the personal class. The evidence is not compelling, however, no texts have simply mu-da; UM_3, which is the better text, agrees with Ur_3 on nu-um-da-sá, whereas only the weaker sources Cop and MM have mu-un-da.

Selz, WZKM 92 (2002) 174, translates 101–102: "Mit Eigentum (auf) die Seite gesetzt, mein Kind, ist nichts vergleichbar," which I have accepted as convincing.

Line 102: ED_1 seems to have had [dumu-ŋ]u_{10} (with only room for one sign in front of ŋ]u_{10}). UM_3 and Ur_3 agree on nu-um-da-sá; Cop and MM: nu-un-da-sá.

There are two ways to interpret lú-tur-ŋu_{10}: (1) it is an address by the father to the son; or (2) it belongs to the advice itself. This latter is the solution of Civil, 1984, 292, and Wilcke, both quoted above under lines 101–102. In that case, it is the entire contents of line 101, that is, material wealth, that is compared to the speaker's children. Although this makes good sense, I prefer the first solution for two reasons. First, lú-tur-ŋu_{10}, is used elsewhere as a variant of the common dumu-ŋu_{10}; cf. the comments on lines 61 and 84, where Ur_5: lú-tur-ŋu_{10} is a variant of dumu-ŋu_{10}. Second, the 1st person suffix (-ŋu_{10}) following "little ones" would be awkward, since otherwise the sayings are not explicitly related to a first person.

Line 103: UM_3 and Cop agree on ka-sa_6-sa_6-ge; MM: ka sa_6-sa_6.

For ka-sa_6-sa_6-ge, Alster, 1974, 96, provides the following references: *Dialogue* 5, 249: ka ma-ab-sa_6-sa_6, "her mouth has become friendly with me"; *Lullaby* 61: ka-sa_6-sa_6-ge [d]lama tuku ḫé-me-en, "may you be one who has a pleasantly speaking mouth as a guardian angle"; UET 6/2 167, rev. 33 with duplicates (*edubba*-composition): um-mi-a-ŋu_{10} ka-sa_6-sa_6-ge dùg-UD ak; TCL 16, 56, obv. 10: ka-sa_6-sa_6-ge-ŋu_{10} maḫ(-àm) (now *Siniddinam to Utu* 33, for which see the ETCSL edition, translating "my fervent entreaties are sublime"). While the *edubba* reference may conform to Civil's translation "artistic mouth" (quoted below), the other references, incl. *Lullaby*, suggest a more general meaning, like "a mouth speaking kindly," "kindness."

Civil, 1984, 292, translates "The artistic mouth recites words (well)." Wilcke, 1978, 206: "Wer stets freundlich spricht ...." Like Wilcke, 1978, 218, I understand KA-sa_6-sa_6-ge as a contrast to ka-dù-dù-e in line 104. Therefore, "flattering mouth" (Alster, 1974, 41), or maybe just "a flatterer," may fit better here than "artistic mouth." Falkenstein, SGL 1, 136, understood KA sa_6-sa_6 as "beten," which may simply be another aspect of the same meaning.

The reading inim – šid was provided by Civil, 1984, 293. Although this is likely to be a term referring to the recital of scribal exercise texts, this is not supported by line 224, in which the same expression occurs, said of a female donkey: ème sila-a inim ì-šid-e. The literal translation "a she-donkey recites words well in the streets" can apply there only if irony is intended, which actually seems to be the case. The reference seems ultimately to be to a woman behaving like a donkey, so something like "screams/ recites loudly" would fit. In line 103 I suggest "He whose mouth (speaks) pleasant (words) recites words well," implying, probably, that he knows how to formulate his petitions well or, generally, that he whose speech is friendly has success when articulating his speech.

Line 104: UM_3, T_{15}, T_{16}, and MM agree on ì-íl-íl; only Cop has e-íl-íl.

Civil, 1984, 292, translates "the harsh mouth brings (litigation) documents," which I have followed. References for ka-dù-dù = *pûm wa-aš-DU-um*, are given by Alster, 1974, 96; cf. MSL 13, 244: *Ká-gal D*, Sec. 3, 4, and CAD A/2, 475 s.v. *ašṭu*, "fierce mouth." Wilcke, 1978, 218, sees ka-dù-dù as possibly related to KA-šu-dù-dù = *munaggirum*, "Verleumderer."

Line 105: UM_3, T_{15}, and MM agree on e-bu-re; T_{16}: ì-bu-re; Cop: e-búr-re.

Civil, 1984, 293, n. 17, explains the verb -bu-re, written phonetically búr-re in Cop, as *nasāḫu*, "to pull out," commonly used of plants and weeds, translating "the sweet mouth gathers sweet herbs."

For ka-làl, lit., "honey mouth," see Alster, 1974, 96, referring to Hallo/van Dijk, YNER 3, 80; also Sefati, *Love Songs*, 82, n. 127 and the literature there cited, and esp. pp. 128–131: DI B (SRT 31, 3ff.).

ú-làl, lit., "honey plants," occurs in *The Home of the Fish* as a sweet water plant; cf. the references mentioned by Civil, *Iraq* 23 (1961) 170; also Gragg, AfO 24 (1973) 69; VS 17, no. 33, lines 5–6, cf. Th. Jacobsen, *Orientalia* 42 (1973) 279–280. Wilcke, 1978, 206, translates "Der Honingmund reißt das Honigkraut aus!" thus, preserving the pun undoubtedly intended by the Sum. text, and convincingly paraphrasing "mit Freundlichkeit hat man die besten Erfolge."

Line 106: UM_3 has a clear KA-tuku, but Cop has lul instead of the two signs, apparently by mistake. UM_3, (T_{15}), T_{16}, Cop and MM agree on ^{kuš}lu-úb-ni. UM_3: sá im-KA×U; only T_{16} has sá im-dug_4; Cop: sá im-du. Following Civil, 1984, 293, the final verb is best taken as a form of sá – dug_4/di/e, confirmed by the phonetic variant du in Cop.

KA-tuku occurs also in SP 3.97; SP 3.101; UET 6/2 281 (Alster, *Proverbs* I, 314). Civil's translation "garrulous" may hit the mark better than "boaster."

Civil translates "The garrulous sends(?) his leather bag." The verb would then be a causative form of sá – dug_4 = *kašādu*. I rather suggest that the meaning is that he reaches out for an (empty) leather bag, despite his boasting of possessing a (full) bag. Römer, 1990, 56, translates "Der *Geschwätzige* hat seinen (Nahrungs-)Beutel *herangebracht*," referring to possibly *ḫabābum* AHw 301, G 4 and Š 3.

For ^{kuš}lú-úb in lines 106–107 and 120–121, Wilcke's translation "Brotbeutel" seems justified in the context, where a bag containing food is clearly meant. This is clearly confirmed by line 120. Cf. Alster, 1974, 97, who refers to *The Farmer's Song* 16; 24; 31 (now Civil, AOAT 25 [1976], 85–95). Cf. also CT 58, 21, line 26, quoted in the commentary on line 201. Civil translates "leather bag," which, of course, may have been used by those working in the fields for that purpose.

Line 107: UM_3 and T_{16} agree on: (gal-gal-di) ^{kuš}lu-úb sù-ga; UM_3: ša-mu-un-túm; T_{15}:]-úb sù-ga-a mu-un-túm; only MM has: ...]-⌜sù⌝-ga-aš-ŋ[u_{10}, with a ligature of*sù-ga and ša-mu-. Cop alone for the entire line has: lul ^{kuš}lu-úb-a-ni sá im-du, which seems to be a different line, unless di/sá simply was mistakenly repeated from the preceding line.

Römer, 1990, 56, refers to CAD M/2, 181 *mukabbiru* lex., and translates "der Prahler."

Line 108: UM_3, and apparently T_{16} agree on: silim-dug_4 ka sù-ga; T_{16} has the phonetic variant su-ga for sù-ga. UM_3 and T_{15} agree on: ša-ba-ni-ib-ŋar; T_{16}: ša-ba-ni-ŋál. Cop has for the entire line: silim-di ka sù-ga ša-ba-ni-in-ŋar, with DI-di as an alternating *marû*-form of DI-dug_4, cf. Wilcke, 1978, 218, who comments: "der Großsprecher hat nichts zu essen und muß sich an seiner Prahlerei sättigen."

For silim-di, cf. Alster, 1974, 98, referring to Lú = ša iv 241 (MSL 12, 136): SILIM dug_4-dug_4 = *muštarriḫu*. Römer, 1990, 56, convincingly translates "der Angeber," referring to CAD M/2, 287 lex. This occurs also in *Dialogue 2*, 121.

Civil, 1984, 292 connects lines 107–108, and translates: "the haughty one brings an empty bag, (and) the braggart puts emptiness in it," reading the line: silim-di dug_4 sù-ga ša-ba-ni-ib-gar. I consider this less likely, because UM_3, which is the most reliable source available, has silim-dug_4 KA, where the reading dug_4-dug_4 is unlikely, although not impossible. Since here KA can hardly be an auxiliary verb to silim-dug_4, and only Cop, a less reliable source, has silim-di KA, I prefer to understand ka sù-ga as "an empty mouth," but possibly meaning "emptiness." Cf. Izi F vi 317: ka sù-ga = *ri-qa-tu*. Römer, 1990, 56, accordingly translates "inthaltslose Sachen," referring to possibly AHw 988, *rīqum* I LL. The verbal chain ša-ba-ni-ib-ŋar supports this interpretation. I tentatively translate "the false accuser put emptiness in it," although an ergative suffix is expected following silim-dug_4. Cf. also lines 262 and 275.

Line 109: UM_3, T_{15} and T_{16} agree on kuš-ni; only Cop has kuš ní, "his own." UM_3: šè-ba-e-dù-e; T_{15}: šè-ba-du(sic!)-e; T_{16}: šè-ba-dù-en (for the 2nd person verbal form, cf. p. 219, *Chap. 1.10: The second person versus the third person*); Cop: še-ba-NI-e (probably misunderstanding of še-ba-dù-e).

Civil, 1984, 289, translates "The one who works with leather will work with his own leather," but what is the point? Perhaps "Shoemaker, stick to your last" (suggested by Alster, AfO 38–39 [1991–92] 30), which is also the opinion of Römer, 1990, 57: "Wer Leder *bearbeitet*, wird sein (*eigenes*) Leder bearbeiten!" commenting, n. 110c: "Etwa «*sutor ne supra crepidam*»" (from Plinius maior 35, 85, "the shoemaker should not [express his opinion about anything] beyond a sandal"). Alster, 1974, 41, translated

"The leather-dresser—his own skin will be dressed," which may seem too drastic, but nevertheless seems to point in the right direction. Wilcke's comparison, 1978, 218, with the expression "sich ins eigene Fleisch schneiden" seems justified. Wilcke, however prefers the reading su instead of kuš, in view of the writing KUŠ-ni, not *kuš-a-ni. The reason for preferring kuš here is that this seems more likely to be referring to a professional class of workers.

Line 110: UM_3 and Cop agree on ša-ba-ra-an-tùm, but T_{15} has the variant túm for tùm; cf. the comments on lines 19 and 193.

Civil, 1984, 292, translates "the strong one takes away from anyone's hand," which is more convincing than Wilcke's suggestion "Der starke kann sich aus eines Mannes Hand erretten!"

Line 111: There are no variants.

lú-lil is equated with *lil-li-du* in Lú = *ša*, Frag. iv 8 (MSL 12, 142), which, according to Civil, MSL 12, p. 147, is a error for *lillu*, "fool."

Line 112: UM_3: and Cop have ì-dé-e; T_{15} has: ì-ib-dé-e. Civil, 1984, 293: both UM_3 and Cop seem to have ù-sá rather than u_6-di, although my collation of Cop favors u_6-di; cf. photographs pls. 24–25. I have followed Civil in preferring ù-sá, "sleeping." Civil, 1984, 292, translates "The fool loses things, sleeping the fool loses things."

Line 113: UM_3: šu àm-mi-in-ŋál; T_{15}: šu àm-mi-ib-ŋál.

Civil, 1984, 292, translates "One takes a supplicating position not to get tied up, (and) one takes a supplicating position for an offering for his life," explaining, p. 294, ga-ti-la literally as an «I want to live», that is, "a wish for a very definite purpose," whereas he considers ex-voto a misleading translation, since it "designates an offering in fulfillment of a promise, regardless of its contents or purpose." Wilcke, 1978, 206: "«Mögest du nicht binden!» fleht er, mit einem Exvoto fleht er." In the present case, I consider the literal meaning of the term ga-ti-la, "a «let me live»" (a frozen verbal form) to be still active. This is suggested by the parallelism with na-an-šèr-šèr-re-dè in line 113. Alternatively, Wilcke, p. 219, comments "Der Verlust des Tölpers wird ironisch als Exvoto bezeichnet"; but there is hardly any need to read the same subject as in lines 111–112.

In both lines 113 and 114, the expressions are somewhat ironically put into the mouth of someone who prays in the characteristic Sumerian supplicating position with a hand raised toward his nose. Cf. also p. 240, comments to *Instr. Ur-Ninurta* 67. Römer, 1990, 57, strikes the tone well: "«Er soll mich nicht fesseln!» (flehte er, indem) er sich niederwarf, indem er sich mit einem Weihgeschenk niederwarf!"

The line should be compared to SP 3.37 (2–3): géme é-gal-la za-ra dug_4-dug_4 arad é-gal-la ga-ti-ba gu_7-gu_7, which Alster, *Proverbs* I, 87, translates "A slave girl from the palace is inconsiderate(?). A slave from the palace devours its goodwill"; cf. ibid., II, 380–381: za-ra dug_4-dug_4 = *muštālu*, the Akk. of which also occurs in *Instr. Šuruppak* 37. The ETCSL translates SP 3.41: "The slave girl from the palace offers advice(?) continually. The slave from the palace eats the ex-voto offering (perhaps an idiom)."

Line 114: UM_3, (I_4), I_9, and T_3 agree on ga-ti-la; only Cop has -t]i-e. UM_3: šu àm-mi-in-ŋál; T_3 omits šu by mistake. Cop: kù-šè(sic! written over an erasure) àm-mi-ni-in-{in}-ŋál, which evidently shows that the scribe had difficulties with the line.

Line 115: Variants: T_3: nam ši-im-[...]; T_4: nam ši-ib-tar-[; Cop: nam ši-ib-tar-re.

Civil, 1984, 292, translates "The unwise decrees the fates." Wilcke, 1978, 206: "Ein Dümmling entscheidet das Schicksal." nam – tar can, in fact, mean something less general than to decree the fates; cf. Alster, 1974, 41: "The idiot takes decisions." Cf. lines 118 and 170 with comments.

Line 116: All texts seem to agree on lú úr-šè, with no variants *lú-ra ša/ši-etc., which would have been expected if */lú-ra ša-mu-un-dé-e, or similar, had been intended. I have, therefore, accepted Civil's interpretation (Civil, 1984, 290 and 292): "the shameless one piles up things in another's lap."

Civil comments that sag-du is likely to represent sag-dù; cf. JCS 28, 78, n. 22; that dé is *šapāku*; and that the line uses "an idiomatic expression for ... impoliteness ..., lit. «piling up (burdens) on other people's laps»." Since there is no visible object, like níŋ, I suggest that it is the saying quoted in the following line that he piles up, that is, he repeats it endlessly.

Line 117: Only I_9 has {na} na-nam, by scribal error.

Literal translation: "I, indeed, he stands to admiration." It is remarkable that the verb is not in the 1st person: *ba-gub-bé-en, "I stand," etc., but apparently this is abbreviated from something like "he stands to be admired (saying) I, indeed (am admirable)."

Line 118: UM_1: dam ⌜dìm⌝-⌜e⌝; I_9: dam dìm(!) (copy ŠEŠ)-e. The sign read [na]m(?) is only preserved in T_5: ⌜x⌝ tar-re KU; T_{15}: -K]U-KU; I_6: [... -r]e ba-KU-KU; Cop: ⌜x⌝ ba-KU.

Civil, 1984, 294, explains, dìm as (1) "pole, post" = *makūtu*; (2) "weak, fragile, delicate" = *dunnamu, šerru, ulālu*; (3) "corpse"; and, possibly (4) "figurine." Of these meanings no. 2 fits best here. He translates "A weak wife is always seized(?) by fate." dìm in Ur III can also denote (5) a ghost, i.e., (gi)dim and *eṭimmu*; cf. van Dijk/Geller, *Ur III Incantations*, p. 45, referring to Wilcke, 1988, 246, who cites SBH 44: 31: [ninda-d]ìm // *a-kal e-ṭi-im-mi*, and MSL 11, 88: 60–61 (Hargud B vi): ninda-dìm = *pannigu* = *akal eṭimmi*.

The verb may well be dab_5, with reduplication indicating repetition.

Line 119: I_9: lu(!)-úb without the determinative; it may have been included in the now broken part of UM_1, cf. line 120. For (kuš)lu-úb, cf. lines 106–107.

Line 120: UM_1: kuš[lu-ú]b ši-mu-e-da-g[u_7-e]; I_6: [ši]-me-da-gu_7-e; I_9: ša-mu-da-[gu_7-e]; T_5:]-gu_7-e; T_{15} omits the entire line.

Line 121: UM_1: omits the entire line. I_6: -d]a-til-e; T_5: [...]-til-en; T_{15}: [...]-la.

Line 122: UM_1 omits the line.

Line 123: There are no variants.

The verbal form ga-ba-ra-gu_7 perhaps is the 2nd person dative, "let me give you (something) to eat." In that case it is uttered by the one to whom the advice is addressed. Alternatively, -ra- is here an ablative infix, cf. line 180 and the literature there cited. So Wilcke, 1978, 219, who, asserts: "Die Präfixkette ba-ra- enthält in keinem mir bekannten Beleg einen Dativ." It gives a different separation of the roles of speakers, with a shift of speech to the hired worker: "*(122)* Dann wird er die Arbeit bei dir verlassen (und) *(124)* (mit den Worten) «Ich möchte daraus etwas zu essen haben» im Palast stehen." Whichever translation is preferred, the role of the palace is clear: it was the place from which hired workers could expect to find seasonal employment easily. To understand it as "eine Wohlfahrtsorganisation" (p. 219) in this case would be to miss the point; and so would the alternative interpretation, according to which the ablative should refer to the "Brotbeutel," since the whole point rests on the fact that he has just finished it up (l. 121).

The ETCSL translates (122–123) "Then he will quit working with you and, saying, «I have to live on something», he will serve at the palace." This may be approximately correct, but the translation of ga-ba, "I have to," is dubious.

Line 124–125: In Sch_3 and Sch_4: ⌜é-ni-šè ši-im-me⌝, etc., ši is used as a writing of the verbal *šè; cf. pp. 212–216, *Chap. 1.9: Modal Verbal Prefixes*.

Civil, 1984, 292, translates lines 124–125: "You tell your son (to come) home, you tell your daughter (to go) to her woman's quarters." Wilcke, 1978, 294: "«Dein Sohn zu seinem Haus!» sagt er; «Deine Tochter zu ihrem Frauengemach!» sagt er." Who is the speaker? Civil's 2nd person is problematic. Wilcke, p. 219, sees these lines as belonging "zum Abschnitt über den -mietarbeiter und seine Verpflegung. Will er die Kinder seines Arbeitsgebers nicht an der Mahlzeit teilhaben lassen?" which hardly is convincing. In my opinion lines 124–125 should be taken as meaningful units standing alone, with the son and the daughter in each line as subjects. So already Foxvog, 1976, 372: "your heir will speak on behalf of your house. Your daughter will speak on behalf of her (future) women's quarter." A hint might be given by the position of the lines in the Abū Ṣalābīkh version, ED_1 rev. i 8', where, as far as can be judged from the preserved parts, it is not preceded by any section corresponding to lines 119–123. The point, thus, seems to be that a son's loyalties are likely to be toward the father's household, whereas a daughter stays loyal to her female companions.

Line 125: ED_1: du[g_4] instead of im-me (*ḫamṭu* instead of *marû*), cf. pp. 211ff., *Chap. 1.9: Ḫamṭu-marû verbal distinctions*. K_1 alone has: dumu-munus-$ŋu_{10}$ ama_5-zu-{na}-šè, "my daughter speaks for your women's house," or "for her women's house."

Sch_4 seems to use ama_5-bi instead of ama_5-ni, a typical grammatical feature of late texts, possibly of Kassite date.

For ama_5, cf. also line 264.

Line 126: ED_1: ka[š x-z]u_5 ⌜DI⌝ na-⌜x⌝-[dug_4].

For zu$_5$ and [dug$_4$], cf. p. 218, *Chap. 1.9: Use of special ED signs;* and *Ḫamṭu-marû verbal distinctions.* N$_2$ has an interesting variant: [... -z]u-ni for -zu-NE, which points to the reading -zu-ne, rather than -zu-dè (unless one wants to read NI = dik/di$_x$). Cf. p. 217, *Chap. 1.9: -NI : -NE variation*, and the literature cited there. UM$_1$: di na-an-ne-e; T$_5$: di na-an-[n]e; T$_{15}$:]-ne; K$_1$ alone has: kaš naŋ-zu-ne di na-an-è, with no a following naŋ, and è phonetic for e.

Wilcke, 1978, 220 (with lit.), insists on translating di – dug$_4$/e "einen Proßen führen," rather than "to render a verdict."

Line 127: ED$_1$: ⌜x⌝-ta ù SAR-zu$_5$ gu$_7$ has been discussed by Civil, 1984, 282, and Alster, 1990, 18, where possible ways to harmonize this with the SS text are discussed (note that in Alster, loc. cit., "might be ⌜è⌝" is a misprint for ditto ⌜é⌝).

UM$_1$: é-ta è šà-zu <na>-an-[(omits na by mistake); K$_1$: è-a šà-zu na-an-KA-⌜e⌝ (only text that has è-a, and KA apparently as a mistake for gu$_7$, cf. K$_1$ line 133); MM: e(sic!)-ta (e, phonetic for é); Ur$_5$: cf. rev. ii 3: e-ta(? copy bi SÌLA) e [...] (first e phonetic for é; second e phonetic for è).

é-ta è is identical to the first part of SP 3.42 with parr. (Alster, *Proverbs* I, 88): é-ta è sila-ta ku$_4$-ra gi$_4$-in-e ga-ša-an-na-ni ŋisbuN-ma bí-in-tuš, "After (the lady) had left the house ...." Cf. also the additional Cornell Univ. Prov Tabl. 2, no. 17, edited in *Chap. 6.2*, where an alternative translation is considered on the basis of the var. ka-ša-an-na-na, "the lady of heaven." It is there likely to refer to a person who leaves the house and then enters (ku$_4$-ra). I, therefore, translate line 127: "On leaving (your) house"; Wilcke, 1978, 207, however, translates: "Wer das Haus verläßt, soll deinem Herzen nicht weh tun!" which I consider less likely. Since a header that could make such grammatical constructions less ambiguous is absent, this, in fact, is as open to various interpretations as the English construction "On leaving." I would consider é-ta è a personal construction. Had it been non-personal, *níŋ é-ta è-a would be more likely in this case. This is clear from comparison with lines 95–96: niŋ-ku$_4$-ku$_4$ versus níŋ-è, and agrees with Civil's translation (Civil, 1984, 292) "Do not eat too much(?) away from home." Ultimately é-ta-è is not a participle, but a segment on the word-formation level, exempt from concrete references to time, lit., "house-leaver," which may well be translated "when leaving (your) house" in a given context; cf. Selz, WZKM 92 (2002) 140–141. Only K$_1$, a less reliable source, has è-a, whereas three good Nippur sources simply have è. The ETCSL, however, translates "You should not worry unduly about what leaves the house."

I consider it most likely that šà-zu na-an-gu$_7$-e, lit., "Don't eat your heart," is an idiom similar to such as occur in a number of languages: Spenser, *Fairy Queen* I ii 6: "He could not rest, but did his stout heart eat"; French: "se ronger le cœur"; Hesiod, *Erga* 717 (cf. 789): θυμοφθόρον; contemporary Danish: "lad ikke sorg fortære dit hjerte," ("Don't let grief devour your heart"), already reflected in *Loddfafnismál* 121: "Sorg æder hjertet, naar sige du kan til ingen din hele hu" ("grief eats your hear when you cannot tell anybody all that which is on your mind"). Cf. also *Nin-me-šar-ra* 105: zi-ŋu$_{10}$ um-mi-gu$_7$, "my life is consumed," as an expression of utter despair (Hallo, van Dijk, YNER 3, 28 and 95). Cf. Alster, 1974, 41: "Don't worry!(?)"

Line 128: Variants: UM$_1$: sù-ud-dam agrees with UM$_4$:]-sù-dam, I$_{11}$: sù-ud-dam, and N$_2$: [...]-dam; UM$_4$: ki kal-kal-la-àm agrees with T$_5$: ki kal-[ka]l-la-àm, and MM on ki kal-kal-la-àm; K$_1$: sù-da ki kal-kal-la.

Civil, 1984, 292: "Heaven is far, earth is most precious"; cf. line 98 with commentary. Wilcke, 1978, 207, however, translates: "Der Himmel ist weit—die Erde ist sehr kostbar," commenting, p. 220, that [129–130] are "ironisch gemeint und finden ihr (ernst gemeintes) Gegenstück in Z. [131–133]," which I consider unlikely, for the reasons below.

The intent is that all living beings depend on Heaven, and the point in contrasting Heaven and Earth is that this applies although Heaven is much wider than earth and not to a similar degree within reach, in other words, a reminder that things can be viewed in a larger perspective. I do not see any ironic attitude in this (Wilcke: "Wunchträume"). Neither do I understand this as an expression of any specifically religious attitude. Lines 129–130 merely spell out in an expanded couplet the contrast embedded in line 128, and what follows is best to be understood as further exemplifications of the same attitude (as implied in Civil's translation). Cf. the similar stylistic feature in lines 172–174; cf. also 195–197 and 208–211.

The line forms an interesting contrast to *The Ballade of Early Rulers* 16–17: [an sù-ud-da-gi]m šu-ŋu$_{10}$ sá bí-in-dug$_4$-ga [ki bùru-da-gim] na-me nu-mu-un-zu-a, "like the remote heaven, my hand cannot reach them; like the deep earth (= underworld) nobody understands them." Cf. the parallels cited under p. 296, n. 43, *Chap. 3.3: Attempt at a new interpretation* .... In that couplet, the point is the inaccessibility of both Heaven and Earth (i.e., the underworld), whereas in our line 128 it is positively meant.

Line 129: UM$_4$:]-da níŋ im-da-lu-lu-un agrees with T$_{17}$:]-lu-lu-un and K$_1$: ⸢an⸣-da ⸢x⸣ ⸢x⸣-da-lu-lu-un; MM: ⸢im-da⸣-lu-lu agrees with Sch$_3$ -lu, which may be a defective writing for the 2nd person, or understood as the 3rd person, in not explicitly having the 2nd person -un; only the late Sch$_4$ (Kassite?) clearly has the 3rd person im-da-lu-lu-àm; cf. *Chap. 1.10: The second person versus the third person.*

Civil, 1984, 292: "(but it is) with Heaven that you multiply your goods" (connecting this with line 130); Wilcke, 1978, 207: "Mit dem, was dem Himmel angeht, wirst du viel erreichen"; why "was ... angeht"?

Line 130: UM$_1$: ši-im-da-pa-an-p[a-an] probably agrees with K$_1$: ši-in-pa-an-pa-an on -an; UM$_4$: ši-im-da-pa-an-pa agrees with MM on not having the final -an; T$_{17}$: [ši]-⸢im-da-pa⸣-an-mul is the only text that has -mul, probably a scribal error, a confusion with an.

Civil, 1984, 292, translates "(and) the mountains can breathe"; here apparently "can" renders the -da-infix. It can, of course, be taken as resuming the comitative -da following an in line 129. Wilcke, 1978, 207: "alle Fremdländer atmen unter ihm."

Line 131: I$_{11}$ is the only text that has: u$_4$ k[a(sic!)-al(?)-ka-al(?) ...], phonetic for kal-kal-.... MM alone has ki, probably a mistake for u$_4$. It is uncertain how this line relates to Ur$_5$: rev. ii 7: u$_4$-buru$_{14}$-šè (... traces ...).

For u$_4$-buru$_{14}$-šè, cf. *Chap. 2.2: Instr. Ur-Ninurta* 52: u-buru$_{14}$ ezen-gal ^{d}en-líl-lá-ka. The line here refers to collecting the harvest at the time when it is possible, without connecting it to any particular god. Wilcke, 1978, 220, without further argument, categorically states that the terminative following u$_4$-buru$_{14}$ means "was anbelangt," "hinsichtlich," but there is no need not to see the two terminatives as exactly parallel; cf., however, line 216: u$_4$-buru$_{14}$-ka. Civil, 1984, 292, translates "At harvest time, at the most precious time."

Line 132: Only K$_1$ has KU-ga-ab, cf. line 133: K$_1$: ÉŠ-ga-ab. UM$_4$: gu$_7$-a agrees with T$_{17}$: gu$_7$-a, K$_1$: gu$_7$(!)-a, and MM: gu$_7$-a, apparently with no variants in the missing parts. It is uncertain how this line relates to Ur$_5$: rev. i 6: ⸢x⸣(= ri?)-⸢ga-ab⸣ [...].

Wilcke, 1978, 220, insists that lines 132–133 are addressed to a woman, but this is clearly contradicted by dumu-ŋu$_{10}$, "my son," not dumu-munus-ŋu$_{10}$ in line 133. The comparison with line 34 does not prove the point; cf. the comments on that line above.

Line 133: Variants: K$_1$ is the only text that has: ÉŠ-ga-ab, for ri, attracted from line 132, and KA-a, with KA for gu$_7$, cf. K$_1$, line 127; UM$_4$ agrees with K$_2$, and MM on ku, phonetic for gu$_7$(-a). UM$_1$ is the only text that has the short text: ur$_5$ ḫ[é-àm]; UM$_4$: ur$_5$ ḫé-en-na-nam-ma-àm; T$_{17}$:]-nam-ma-àm; K$_1$: ur$_5$ <ḫé>-in-a[n-n]a-me-en; MM: ur$_5$ ḫé-en-n[a-me-en]. Only Ur$_5$ has the unexplained variant: du$_5$ x x géme-gim ⸢x⸣ [...].

Of the two verbs ri and gu$_7$-a, the first can best be understood as an abbreviated imperative repeating the parallel ri-ga-ab in the preceding line. Or perhaps ri is simply an undeclined verb, corresponding to an "infinitive"; cf. Civil's translation, 292: "to glean like a slave girl, to live like a queen, this is how it should be."

Line 134: ED$_1$: áš dug$_4$-d[ug$_4$] / bar šè-dar, with reduplication of dug$_4$, cf. p. 211, *Chap. 1.9: Ḫamṭu-marû-reduplication in ED.*

UM$_1$: áš dug$_4$-dug$_4$-ge; agrees with UM$_4$: [... d]ug$_4$-g[e] and T$_6$: áš du[g$_4$-dug$_4$-g]e; agrees with N$_1$: áš dug$_4$ dug$_4$-[ge] and K$_2$: áš dug$_4$-dug$_4$-ge; MM: -d]ug$_4$-ge; only K$_1$ has: áš tuk$_5$-tuk$_5$-ge (or read simply tag-tag?), with an interesting phonetic writing for dug$_4$; cf. p. 239, *Instr. Ur-Ninurta* 60 with comments, and Civil, 1984, 294. UM$_1$: bar ši-in-[dar], agrees with UM$_4$: ba[r ši-i]n-[dar], and K$_1$: bar ši-in-dar; only MM has: bar šè-im-⸢dar⸣. Sch$_3$ is epigraphically uncertain.

ETCSL, combining lines 134 and 135, translates: "Who insults can hurt only the skin; greedy eyes(?), however, can kill." Nothing prevents us from seeing the two lines as a contrasting pair, but, nevertheless, it is worth noting that in ED_1 o. viii 8'–9', line 134 is not followed by something corresponding to line 135, cf. p. 181.

For áš-dug_4, cf. SP 1.79 and the comments on line 256.

AHw 269, *ezēru* G "beschimpfen" = áš; AHw 340, *ḫepû* II G = gaz/tar ([dar]), "zerschlagen"; AHw 836, *pāru* II, "Haut" = [bar].

Line 135: Only S_1 has i-gi-tu-ul-la, phonetic for igi-tùm-lá. UM_1: saŋ ŋiš im-ra-r[a], agrees with T_6: sa]ŋ ŋiš im-ra-r[a] and S_1: saŋ ŋiš im-ra-ra; K_1: saŋ ŋiš íb-ra-ra; MM: saŋ ŋiš ra-ra.

igi-tùm-lá has been discussed by Wilcke, 1978, 220–222, with references to earlier literature, who suggests "Almosen"; and Civil, 1984, 294, suggests "to spy, look with envy." I agree with the latter, since a meaning like "envy," greediness," "coveting," or similar, would fit in most places, whereas I consider "Almosen" misleading. This is corroborated by the following examples: SP 3.175, var. KK: igi-tùm-lá igi-du_8 níŋ-gig ^{d}nin-urta-kam, "coveting and spying" (CBS 8065 obv. 2), where the main text reads: igi-tùm-lá gíd-i-da níŋ-gig-^{d}nin-urta-ke_4, "coveting and reaching out (in greediness) are abominations to Ninurta" (Alster, *Proverbs* I, 109; II, 394). Further references in PSD A/3, 88, venturing no translation.

M. Powell, 1977, 194, arrived at the translation "I'm fed on looks alone," in line 7 of the *Monkey Letter*: igi-tùm-lá mu-gu_7-en, seeing this as the monkey being "fed" solely on being looked at, but it could perhaps better be taken actively as a desire for something it cannot obtain, like "I'm fed on having to be on the look-out."

Cf. further Jacobsen and Alster, in: *Lambert FS*, 343, *Ningizzida Boatride* 82: E: ama $gudu_4$(!)-zu ug_5-ga igi-tùm-lá é lugal-la-ke_4 / bí-in-du_8-e ... (the line occurs only in E; B differs); on p. 328, this is tentatively translated "For the mother of the slain anointed one, at whom the king's house looked askance ...," etc., with the following references: M. Stol, BiOr 29 (1972) 276–277 ("Drohung/drohen"); AHw 1172, *šapāṭ/tum* II, "etwa (be)drohen"; this is evidently a line that came from a different context, influenced by Akkadian syntax, cf. p. 328: "possibly it is a matter of his trying to avoid military service for himself or others."

Charpin, in: *Nippur at the Centennial*, Philadelphia, 1992, in A.1258, rev. 7 (p. 13) provides an interesting equation: igi-bu_4(TÚL)-lá = *im-ru-um ša ṭup-šar-ru-tim uš-tam-ri-ṣa-an-ni*, "j'ai été affligé de la maladie des yeux propre aux scribes"; Charpin, in the comments on p. 17 alternatively considers the reading igi-túl-lá, and comments that "*imrum* désigne ici une maladie" (contra CAD I/J, 138a "observation post), "sans doute ... une affection des glandes lacrymales." This recalls a remark by Civil, 1984, 294: "Curiously, no connection has so far been suggested between igi-tùm-lá and igi-túl-la – (ak)." Civil translates the latter "to look with anger." Cf. PSD A/3, 88 (8.98): igi-túl(-lá) – ak, "to look with anger." igi-tùm-lá may further be related to Gudea Statue I iv 3–4: igi-x-la-ak, which Yoshikawa, AcSum 6 (1984) 141f., translates "Do not watch maliciously the house of my god," reading igi-tul_x-la. In conclusion, igi-tùm-lá seems to denote "spying" or "looking with envy" in a way that may result in physical violence. This fits well in line 135, where the second part of the line: saŋ ŋiš im-ra-ra, "kills," confirms just that.

Selz, WZKM 92 (2002) 178, translates "ein Neider, ist einer der mordet," with which I agree.

Line 136: The reading UM_1: gù-mur-re lú-lul-e túg ši-bir_7-bir_7-re is provided by S_1: gu-mu-ru *lu-ru-la zu-uš ši-bi-ir-bi-re (Civil, 1984, 294: ku-ru-la). It agrees with N_1: gù-mur-re [, and T_6: gù-mur-[r]e lú-lul-e túg ši-[; K_1: gù-mur-ra lú-lul-la túg(!) (text: ÉŠ) bir_7-bir_7-ra, agrees with K_2: lú-lul-la [, and MM: l]ú-lul-la túg šè-bir_7-bir_7-re; Sch_3: lul-e, is the only source that omits lú.

For bir_7 = *šarāṭu*, cf. PSD B, 160, and *Chap. 4.3: Comments on Goose and Raven* 8.

gù-mur-re was interpreted as a participial construction, "shouting," by Civil, 1984, 294, with n. 21, on the basis of *qardu*, which he interprets as "one who shouts, is noisy" (erroneously placed under *gardu* in CAD G, 50a), different from the common *qardu*, "heroic," suggesting that *qarādu* A may be related to our *qardu*, since a meaning "to urge (by shouting)" seems to fit its occurrences; see CAD Q, 126a s.v.). Civil quotes further examples of gù-mur-ak.

No completely convincing explanation of our

line has, however, as yet been put forth. Why would it be said that a liar, shouting, tears up garments? The impression is that maybe gù-mur-re, after all, has a more specific implication or, are the two nouns ending in -e really exactly parallel? Perhaps gù-mur-re is the ergative and lú-lul-e the loc.-terminative? Since the reading is confirmed by S_1: gu-mu-ru, other readings of KA-ḪAR are excluded. Tearing up garments would be normal behavior in connection with mourning rites, which might also be true of noisy behavior. Our line might then refer to a hypocrite who displays signs of grief while not seriously mourning at all. The word "liar" seems strange if used in such a meaning, which may sound a bit anachronistic, although it might fit in the context of the whole line sequence 134–137. Cf. line 219, where lú-lul-e likewise occurs. The context of both lines may favor a translation such as "hypocrite," rather than "liar."

Line 137: The reading of UM_1: áš-di is provided by K_1: áš-dè; it agrees with T_6, N_1, and Sch_3(?): áš-di. Only UM_1 has níŋ-NE-e, mistake for NE.RU-e = érim-e; T_6: níŋ-érim-e na-ri šè-í[l-...], agrees with N_1: níŋ-NE.[RU...]; UM_1: na-di šè-íl-íl, is phonetic for na-ri(= de_5) šè-íl-íl, cf. T_6: na-ri šè-í[l-, and K_1: na-ri šè-íl-íl. It agrees with MM: na-di šè-íl-íl.

Civil, 1984, 293, translates "Insult brings advice to the evil ones." Yet, there are reasons to consider the alternative interpretation na-ri-šè íl-íl, "A curse is raised to malice as an instruction," because otherwise it is difficult to explain why all sources agree on šè- as a verbal prefix, since ši- is used in lines 115, 119–122, 130, 134, 136, etc. But what would it mean?

Line 138: inim-diri: also in line. ED_1 rev. v 3: inim-diri bu-bu_7(KU) šà ḫu-gig šè-dug_8-dug_8 quoted under line 235; line 265: ama-zu-úr inim-diri nam-ba-na-ab-bé-en, "Don't speak arrogantly to your mother"; cf. the references quoted by Alster, 1974, 101; Falkenstein, NG III, 136, cf. also NG II, 137 ad 13: "Großsprecher, Lügner." This was tentatively explained as "Aufschneiderei" by Römer, 1990, 59, who refers to AHw 1493, *watrûm*; Civil: "to speak too much"; Wilcke, 1978, 207: "Großsprecherei"; Alster, 1974: "Arrogance." I still consider the comparison with Enmetena CIRPL 28 I 13–17 valid: nam-inim-ma diri-diri-šè e-ak, "acted in an unspeakable way," lit., "in a way too big for wording." Decisive is also *Lugal-e* 389: diŋir-maḫ inim-diri-ge ḫul gig, "the supreme goddess who hates arrogance." *Dialogue* 5 (*Two Women*) 132: e-ne-èm diri ka bal-e nu-sa_6 ...; SP 4.62: gu-du-⸢e⸣(?) $še_{10}$-dúr-e dug_4-ge in[im-di]ri-ge àm-ta-ab-tùm; bil. vers. ditto, but diri-ga = *[qin-na]-tum ṣú-ru-tam pu-ú ba-ba-nu-tam ub-lam*, "the anus emitted flatus, and talking (Akk: the mouth) (emitted) excessive words" (Alster, *Proverbs* I, 117–118). These confirm that "excessive talking, arrogance" or, perhaps, rather, "hybris" are valid translations.

UM_1: ù-bu-bu-ul; agrees with K_1: ⸢ú⸣-⸢bu⸣-⸢bu⸣-⸢ul⸣(!); T_6: ù-bu-bu-ul-la-àm; MM: [... -b]u-bu-ul-àm; UM_1: ú-libiš-gig-ga, agrees with T_{17}: ⸢ú⸣-libiš-gig-ga; T_6: ú-libiš-gig-ga-àm, agrees with MM: ú-libiš-gig-ga-àm; K_1: ú-libiš-gig-KA-a.

ù-bu-bu-ul = *nablu*, "fire," or, alternatively, *bubūtu*, "inflammation in the skin"; cf. the discussion by Civil, 1984, 296, who translates: "To speak too much is like fire, food that makes the stomach sick." The first occurs in the expression ù-bu-bu-ul – šub, "to hurl fire," in *Lament Destr. of Ur* 260; the second in *Lugal-e* 261, both cited by Alster, 1974, 101. Wilcke, 1978, 222, here prefers "Entzündung," but cf. Civil: "The second meaning is, of course, derived from the first." The ETCSL translates "To speak arrogantly is like an abscess: a herb that makes the stomach sick."

The association of (angry) speech with fire is well attested in proverbial context; cf. Alster, RA 85 (1991) 1–11 (no. 3), who cites the following parallels: *Bird and Fish* 92: si-ga kalag-ga-ŋá nu-mu-e-dè-zu inim ù-bu-bu-ul ì-bal, "You cannot comprehend my weakness and my strength; yet you spoke inflammatory words" (Civil, 1985, 296, 27, however, takes this from bu-bu-ul-(ak), "to search"); *Couns. Wisdom* 94: du_{14}-da izi-gim lú ba-an-gu_7-e te-en-te-en-bi ḫé-en-zu, "men feed a quarrel like fire; but you should know how to extinguish it" (so C = VS X 204 V 18; cf. p. 247, *Chap. 2.2* incl. the variant J: *ṣa-al-tum* GIM ⸢*i*⸣-*ša-t*[*i*]; *Good Seed of a Dog* 20 (JCS 24 [1972] 107): du_{14} izi-a ba-ra-an-si-ig, "who does not how know to calm down a heated quarrel." An Egyptian example is *Die Prophezeiung des Neferti* (W. Helck, *Kleine ägyptische Texte*, pp. 42, XI a + 45; cf., e.g., Dietrich et al. [eds.], *Texte aus der Umwelt des*

Alten Testaments, II [Gütersloher, 1968], 108): "Eine Rede (wirkt) auf das Herz wie Feuer."

ú-libiš-gig-ga-àm: Civil explains this as "food that makes the stomach sick," commenting that "the second genitive here and in line [155] [indicates] the effects caused by the plants rather than the disease for which it is a cure." Note, however, that in the present context it is constructed as a non-genitival compound, which seems to cause a difference of meaning; cf. below. Civil quotes further evidence from incantations: Ebla (quoted below), with dupls. WVDOG 43, 26 iii, 6N-T 1014, and 1002 (Ur–3). The unidentified text Ni 9764, obv. 1–2 (ISET I, 124), cited by Alster, 1974, 102, is to be read ú šà gig kur-ra ma-ab-è ù libi[š] gig kur-ra ma-ab-è, which Civil translates "he/she has made grow for me the mountain herb of (= that cures) bellyache"; these may be partly phonetic variants of the same line—for the second line note ù for ú, and šà gig for LIBI[Š] gig. This might confirm the reading $ša_x$(ÀB-ŠÀ)-ge in *Enmetena Cone A* end, suggested by Civil, loc. cit., and may even suggest the reading $ša_x$-gig-ga in our text. Yet, the reading libiš is confirmed by an ED spelling li-bi-$iš_{11}$ gi(!) (= libiš gig), in an incantation from Ebla published by Pettinato, *Oriens Antiquus* 18 (1979) 346 ii 2; cf. Civil, loc. cit., p. 296. This also occurs in *Instr. Šuruppak* ED_1 obv. vi 12–13: ḪAR-tu $na-sa_{10}$ ú-libiš-gig = SS 155: émedu na-an-sa_{10}-sa_{10}-an ú-libiš-gig-ga-àm, "Don't buy a home-borne slave; he is a herb that causes stomach ache!" Here, as in our line, the compound is non-genitival, since otherwise *-gig-ga-kam would have been required, or even -ga-ka-kam, if two genitives had been intended. This suggests that there were two different meanings: (1) with the genitive: "a herb that cures stomach ache," which is normal for ú followed by a genitive; cf. Civil, who refers to Ḫḫ XVII 209ff.; and (2) non-genitival: "a herb that causes stomach ache." This would apply to our text lines 138 and 155.

Line 139: UM_1: mu gùn-gùn-da, agrees with T_6: mu [x x]-gùn-da and N_1: mu gùn-gùn-[; K_1: mu ⌜gùn-gùn⌝-dè; only Sch_3 has ...-gùn]-dè. UM_1: ga-mu-e-da-zala-ge agrees with the preserved parts of T_5:]-ab-zala-ge and T_6: ga-mu-e-da-ab-[; K_1: ga-mu-ra-ab-za-az-ge, has an interesting phonetic writing for, probably, zala-zala-ge; cf. Edzard, *Sum. Grammar*, 80–81, where this example is worth adding.

gùn (MUŠEN-*gunû*), lex. attested as gùn-gùn = *burrumu*, "to be multicolored," is sometimes difficult to distinguish from dar (= su_4 = SI-*gunû*); cf. CAD B, 332, but seems certain here.

gùn occurs also in line 254; cf. the comments on line 254. For zalag, comparison with line 268: ab-ba diŋir-ra-à[m (x)] mu-un-zala-zala-ge also seems relevant.

The -e-da- included in the verb phrase is the comitative suffix with the 2nd person personal element, whereas the -da following gùn is the verbal extension suffix /eda/. A possible meaning is that a name chosen for a child may be decisive for its future, in other words, *Nomen sit omen*, a notion that plays an essential role in *Enlil and Namzitarra*; cf. *Chap. 3.5*. Both verbs gùn and *zalag may seem surprising in such a context, but seem paralleled in line 268, where the restoration [mu] mu-un-zala-zala-ge is tempting. Wilcke, 1978, 292, combining lines 139–140, translates: "Um den Namen(?) 'bunt' zu machen (sagt er): «Ich will dir leuchten lassen! Meine Worte des Gebets bedeuten Überfluß»." Cf. p. 310.

Line 140: UM_1: inim-šèd-dè, agrees with K_1: inim-šèd(!)(text: KA)-dè; T_6: inim-[šè]d-da. UM_1: ḫé-ŋál-la-àm, agrees with T_6: ḫé-ŋál-la-à[m] and K_1: ḫé-ŋál-[l]a-à[m], with no variants.

Wilcke's translates "Meine Worte des Gebetes bedeuten Überfluß," stating that the translation of Alster, 1974, 43: "A word of prayer is a year of abundance," would have required a genitive construction, *mu ḫé-ŋál-la-kam, not -la-àm. This is contradicted by the spacing of Sch_3, which clearly separates MU from ḫé-ŋál-la. Besides the form šèd-dè, attested first of all in a main source, UM_1, would be suspicious; why not simply šèd-da-$ŋu_{10}$? Furthermore, taking MU as the personal suffix is problematic, because who is the speaker? A guess would be that both lines 139 and 140 quote already existing proverbial phrases in the 1st person, rather than that it is "the man from Šuruppak" who speaks in such cases (cf. Römer, 1990, 59, 141b: "Meint hier der Vater seine eigene Gebete?"). The most likely solution seems to be that ḫé-ŋál(-la) is here used in a non-genitival attributive construction, "an abundant year." A comparable example occurs in Urninurta E 24: mu ḫé-ŋál bala u_4 sud-da (Römer, *Königshymnen*, 15–17; 61–62). Yet, in view of the 1st person speaker in line 139, the decision remains doubtful.

Line 141: UM_1: a-š[e]d$_4$; K_1: ⌜šed$_4$⌝; UM_4: a-šed$_4$-da; Sch_3: [a]-⌜x⌝.⌜DI⌝-dè ⌜šà⌝-[.

Cf. *Couns. Wisdom* 47: kadra-ŋar-ra-bi kadra a-šed$_{10}$(MÙŠ-DI)-[da(?)].

I translate "I prayer is cool water that soothes the heart," comparable to a split sentence construction in European languages; cf. p. 210, *Chap. 1.9: Split sentence* .... Wilcke, 1978, 222, however, translates: "das Gebet kühlt eiskaltes Wasser für den Sinn."

Line 142: UM_4: omits the entire line; UM_1: [áš x x-ŋ]á-aḫ di-da ŋizzal kalam-ma-ke$_4$; partly agrees with T_6: áš di(?) na-ŋá du(?)-da ŋizzal kalam-ma-ke$_4$ (Wilcke, 1978, 222: áš(?)-⌜di(?)⌝ na-ŋá-x ⌜di⌝-da); T_5: [... -d]a ŋizzal kalam-ma-kam; K_1: áš(?) di(?) na-ŋá-du d[ug$_{11}$ ...] (collation Taylor: DU copy correct; Wilcke: áš(!)-di(!) na-ŋá(!) DU.K[A ...]); Sch_3 has almost certainly áš-ḪAR for the first signs, but the continuation is epigraphically uncertain. The reconstruction of the first part of the line, thus, remains highly uncertain. The first signs are also preserved in T_6, in which the second sign may look like a slightly miscopied ḪAR, rather than di, or similar. In K_1, áš(?) di(?), di may similarly represent a slightly misread ḪAR. For the continuation, UM_1 clearly has -ŋ]á-aḫ di-da; the copy of T_6 has na-ŋá-⌜x⌝(like NE)-da.

Wilcke, 1978, 207, translates: "(aber) Fluchen und tölpenhaft zu reden—dem gilt die Aufmerksamkeit des Landes." Since Sch_3 now clearly has áš-ḪAR for the first signs, it is tempting to suggest that the reading áš-di rests on a misreading of ḪAR. What is expected would rather be something like "to turn away curses and ignorant speech," etc.; ŋizzal kalam-ma-ke$_4$/kam, clearly anticipates ŋizzal ḫé-em-ši-ak in line 150, which makes the sense "dem gilt die Aufmerksamkeit des Landes" suspicious. Similarly the ETCSL: "Only (?) insults and stupid speaking receive the attention of the Land," which gives the line an ironic twist that hardly is convincing. One could also question the reading of DI-da, which might be sá-da, but the meaning would remain doubtful.

Lines 143–152a: These are the third repetition of lines 6–13; 73–82; cf. also lines 287–288.

Line 143: UM_1: [šuruppak]^{ki}-e agrees with T_6: šuruppak-e; K_1: šuruppak DU stands apart as unexplained, perhaps DU = GUB, gu$_x$? Sch_3 omits the determinative, as in line 144. UM_1: na na-mu-un-ri-ri agrees with N_3: na na-mu-un-ri-r[i], T_6: na na-mu-un-ri-ri and Ur_4: -r]i-ri; UM_4: na-šè mu-ni-in-ri agrees with agrees with (T_2 +) T_5: na-šè mu-ni-in-ri. There were, thus, two main streams of tradition: (1) na na-mu-un-ri-ri; (2) na-šè mu-ni-in-ri. Cf. line 145 and the comments on line 6.

Line 144: UM_1: [šurupp]ak^{ki} agrees with N_3: [...] šuruppak^{ki} and T_2(+ T_5): šuruppak^{ki}; only UM_4 has [šuruppak^{ki}]-⌜e⌝ by mistake. T_6 and Sch_3: šuruppak without the determinative.

Line 145: UM_1: na na-mu-un-ri-ri agrees with N_3: zi-u$_4$-sud-rá dumu-ni-ra na [na] mu-un-ri-⌜ri⌝, but the latter remarkably has both na's before the indented line; cf. the comments on line 6; further with T_6: zi-u$_4$-sud-rá dumu-ni-ra na na-mu-un-ri-[and Ur_4: -m]u-un-ri-ri. For (T_2): + T_5: na-šè mu-ni-in-ri: cf. line 143.

Line 146: Line omitted in UM_1, UM_4, (probably) N_3, and Ur_2. T_2+ T_5: min-kam-ma-šè [šu]ruppak-e dumu-ni-ra [na šè]-mu-ni-in-ri, "a second time"; cf. lines 143 and 145; T_6: [x x]-ma-šè šuruppak-e dumu-ni-r[a] na na-mu-un-ri-[ri]. K_1: èš-kam-ma-šè, "a third time," which is as expected and agrees with Sch_3.

Line 147: Cf. line 144.

Line 148: UM_1, UM_4, T_6, K_1, and (probably) N_3 and Ur_4 omit the line. It is only included in (T_2) + T_5. Cf. line 145.

Line 149: Cf. lines 9 and 79. All texts agree on na ga-ri, except N_3, which has na ge-ri, and K_1, which has na-ri-⌜ga⌝(?), possibly influenced by the end formula, cf. line 288.

Line 150: Cf. lines 10 and 80. T_2 + T_5 and Ur_4 omit the entire line. There are no variants.

Line 151: Cf. line 11 and 81. T_2 + T_5 and T_6 omit the entire line; K_1: <nam>-bí-bar-[, nam omitted by mistake. There are no variants.

Line 152: T_5 and T_6 omits the entire line; UM_1: n]a-ab-ta-bal-e-dè, agrees with Ur_4: (traces)-⌜ta⌝-bal-e, and K_1: na-ab-ta-bal-e-[; UM_4: na-ab(!)-ta-ab-bal-e-dè.

Line 152A: Cf. line 13. This line is included in Ur_4, where the second part reads: g]ú-zu ḫé-em-ši-ak, and K_1, where the second part is uncertain: ⌜x⌝(like dumu) [x] ⌜x⌝(like me). The line is omitted in all the other sources.

Line 153: ED_I: dumu eŋar níŋ na-ra e-pa_5-zu_5 šè-ra, with no genitive marking, and the verbal prefixes condensed to a minimum. UM_2: e]ŋar-ra-ra, agrees with T_6: dumu eŋar-ra-[ra], and T_9: e]ŋar-ra-ra; K_I: dumu eŋar-ra. UM_I:]-mu-ra-ra agrees with Ur_4: -r]a-ra and K_I: níŋ nam-mu-ra-ra. UM_2: níŋ nam-mu-ra-ra-an, agrees with T_6: nam-mu-ra-ra-an, T_7: n]íŋ nam-mu-ra-ra-a[n] (with the rest of the line omitted), T_8:]-mu-ra-ra-an, and T_9: níŋ nam-mu-ra-ra-an, and Sch_3. UM_I: šè-im-ra; UM_2: ši-im-ra, agrees with UM_4: ši-im-[, and T_I + T_5: ši-im-ra; T_6 and T_9: šè-im-ra; Sch_3: š[è-; (these variants exclude the possibility of reading -šè in UM_I as the terminative suffix); Ur_4: im-ra-⌜an⌝(?); K_I: šè-i[m]-⌜x⌝.

For the extra line in ED_I o. vii 3': níŋ-nam-tar dug_4, see Civil, 1984, 284, and p. 181/191, *Chap. 1.5: The Abū Ṣalābīkh Version*, where the line alternatively, but tentatively, is interpreted as an ED version of line 127 instead of 153.

For the translation of the verb form šè-im-ra cf. p. 209, *Chap. 1.9: Tense or aspect related verbal system?* where it is argued that the verbal system was primarily aspect related, rather than tense related. In this case, the alliteration pattern -ra-ra ... nam-mu-ra-ra-an e-pa_5-zu šè-im-ra, with -ra repeated graphically no less than five times, may also have influenced the phraseology in terms of a pun or alliteration pattern, since "to beat (ra) an irrigation canal" may not have been a usual idiom. I consider it unlikely that is should mean "Er hat deine (Bewässerungs-)Kanäle *angelegt!*" (Römer, 1990, 59), for the following reasons; (1) those stated above; (2) such a meaning of ra is otherwise unattested; and (3) the establishing of irrigation canals was hard physical work unlikely to have been done by the "son of a farmer" alone. In the first part of our line, ra = *ramû* occurs as a compound verb: níŋ – ra, lit., "to throw things, to beat"; it is more likely that the second part of the line repeats the same expression with ellipsis of níŋ, than that ra is used with an entirely different meaning; cf. the comments of line 66. It would not help here to read éš – ra, "to throw a measuring cord," first, because the variant ši- shows that šè- is a verbal profix; and second, because canals were undoubtedly dug without any surveyor's tools on a local level.

Lines 154–163: Cf. *Akk. Counsels of Wisdom*, 72 (Lambert, BWL, 172–173, also Foster, *Before the Muses*, 413), which warns against marrying a prostitute.

Line 154: ED_I: géme kar-kíd na-an-sa_{10} ka ù-sar-kam_4.

The beginning of the line seems to be different in K_I: šà im na-sa_{10}-sa_{10}; perhaps, but very tentatively, read: šà im as ḫar(!)-tum_9, cf. the ED_I variant of line 155: ḪAR.TU. [kar-k]id is not fully preserved in any source, but reasonably certain in UM_2, where only the left vertical stroke is missing, and Sch_3, which seems to have ⌜kar-kíd⌝ for the first signs, but is otherwise epigraphically uncertain. UM_I:]-sa_{10}, agrees with T_7 and Ur_4: -s]a_{10}; K_I: na-sa_{10}-sa_{10}; UM_2: na-an-sa_{10}-sa_{10}-an, agrees with T_9: [... -s]a_{10}-sa_{10}-an. UM_I: ka u_4-sar-ra-ka, agrees with T_8: ka u_4-sar-ra-ka; Ur_4: ka ù-sar-ra-ka; UM_2: ka u_4-sar-ra-kam, agrees with T_9: ka u_4-sar-ra-⌜kam⌝; Ur_5: cf. rev. I' 11: sar-ra-kam. T_7: ka u_4.Ù.sa[r ...], stands apart, with Ù as a phonetic complement to u_4.

kar-kid/kíd was explained as = kar-ak, "she who makes the quay," i.e., a prostitute, by Civil, RA 70 (1976) 189–190. In view of ED_I: kar-ak (= kíd) the most likely explanation is that this is from /kar-ak-ed/ > *kar-ked; cf. Selz, WZKM 92 (2003) 147. A text published by J. Taylor, *Orientalia* 70 (2001) 209ff., esp. pp. 227–228, however, does not seem to confirm this etymology, since it has a variant kar-e-kid, suggesting kar-a-[kid] in Proto-Lu 717.

ka, followed by ù-sar-kam, var. u_4 for ù, was understood by Alster, 1974, 102 as zú, "tooth," which may be better than ka, "mouth."

Civil, 1984, 284, explains ù-sar from the Ebla equations MME 4, p. 322: VE 1134: ù-sar = *za-la-sa*; 1135: *sa-ʾà-lum*, *sa-ʾà-a-um*, of which the first corresponds to Arabic *ḍaraṣa* and the second to Semitic / *šaḥālu*/, Akk. *šêlu*, "to sharpen," cf. Arabic *ṣaḥala*. ù-sar – ak was first correctly explained by Cooper, *Curse of Agade*, pp. 245f. as = *šêlu*, "to sharpen," different from Arabic *šahr*, "new moon" (proposed as an etymology by Krebernik; see Civil, nn. 5–6). Civil translates "... she is a mouth that bites (lit., a mouth of bite)." In spite of some graphic confusion (cf. not least our T_7: u_4.Ù.sa[r), the two terms are separate, corresponding to ù-sar – ak, "to sharpen," and u_4-sákar, "moon crescent," respectively (for the latter, cf. Civil, RA 60 [1960] 92). Cf. now also

Sjöberg, *Wilcke FS*, 261–266.

Line 155: ED$_1$: ḪAR-tu na-sa$_{10}$ ú-libiš-gig; ḪAR-tu is, thus, the ED equivalent of émedu (AMA.A.TU). This is fully preserved in K$_1$ and Sch$_3$: AMA.A.TU; cf. UM$_2$:].A.TU, C$_1$ and Ur$_4$: [...]-TU. UM$_1$:]-sa$_{10}$, agrees with C$_1$: na-an-sa$_{10}$-s[a$_{10}$], and Ur$_4$: s]a$_{10}$; K$_1$: na-ab-sa$_{10}$-sa$_{10}$; UM$_2$: na-an-sa$_{10}$-sa$_{10}$-an; T$_7$: [...]-sa$_{10}$-A.AN, cf. line 157. UM$_1$: [...]-sa$_{10}$ ú-libiš-gig-ga-àm, agrees with Sch$_3$; Ur$_5$: Cf. perhaps rev. i' 11, 2nd part ii 12: ⸢x⸣ a ⸢x⸣ NI nam-sa$_{10}$-sa$_{10}$-an (NI may belong to a previous column).

For émedu(AMA.A.TU), cf. CAD s.v. *dušmû*; PSD A/3, 206–207: ama-a-tu, "(house-born) slave (servant)"; further *Instr. Ur-Ninurta* 14; *Couns. Wisdom* 102; 155 with comments to 156; SP 1.47: UET 6/279 (Alster, *Proverbs* I, 313). Further references cited by Alster, 1974, 103: Letter from *Šulgi to Irmu*; JCS 8 (1954) 86, A 10099, obv. 5, dupl. VS 2 47 obv. (incantation, cf. Lambert, "Dingir.šà.dib.ba Incantations," JNES 33 [1974] 267–322, esp. 291–292). Note that our ED$_1$ has ḪAR.TU, apparently an ED spelling of AMA.A.TU. For references to ED ḪAR-tu, see Bauer, AWL, p. 95: "Hausdiener." Note also the variant ŠÀ-IM (tentatively read ḪAR(!)-tum$_9$?) in K$_1$, line 154, cf. Addendum, p. 175. ED list E 175 (MSL 12, 19), however, has the entry ama-tu. It is clear from these occurrences that a home-born slave could be expected to be treated at least a bit better than other slaves, which is why he might cause trouble ("stomach-ache") if bought by another household.

For ú-libiš-gig-ga-àm, see the comments on line 138, where a similar expression occurs said about arrogant speech.

Line 156: UM$_1$:]-sa$_{10}$, agrees with C$_1$: na-an-sa$_{10}$-sa$_{10}$; UM$_2$: na-an-sa$_{10}$-sa$_{10}$-an, agrees with T$_8$: [...]-an, and Sch$_3$; K$_1$: na-ab-sa$_{10}$-sa$_{10}$. UM$_1$: zag é-ŋar$_8$-e ús-sa, agrees with T$_8$: zag é-ŋar$_8$-e ús-sa; UM$_2$: zag é-ŋar$_8$-e ús-sa-àm; Ur$_4$: zag é-ŋar$_8$-e in-ús; only T$_7$ has: z]ag é-ŋar(sic!)-e ús-[, which confirms the reading gar$_8$ of SIG$_4$; similarly K$_1$: zag ŋar(sic!)-re ús-s[a; Sch$_3$ is epigraphically uncertain.

For dumu-gi$_7$, here translated "free man," cf. F.R. Kraus, *Sumerer und Akkader* (Amsterdam, 1970) 53–60, who accepts "Sumerer" as "eigentliche Bedeutung" (p. 58), but "Freier/ Freie" as a legal term since Ur III times. Further discussion in Alster, 1974, 104; Steinkeller: "Early Political Development in Mesopotamia and the Origins of the Sargonic Empire," in: M. Liverani (ed.), *Akkad*, 110–111, n. 9, suggests "native."

For zag é-ŋar$_8$-e ús-sa-àm, lit., "leaning the side against a wall," cf. Alster, 1974, 104, comparing it to *Enmerkar and the Lord of Aratta* 373–374, and *Urnamma's Death* 187, where this expression denotes despair or grief. In the present context, the reason why a free man would lean against a wall is that he would be spoiled or lazy, as first suggested by Edzard in Alster, 1975, 142. Cf. also *Lugal-e* 32: zag-ŋu$_{10}$ ga-bí-íb-ús-e, which, however, points toward a meaning such as "to avoid" (Jacobsen: "to jostle").

Line 157: UM$_1$: -s]a$_{10}$, agrees with C$_1$: na-an-sa$_{10}$-sa$_{10}$; T$_7$:]-sa$_{10}$-A-[AN], cf. line 155; UM$_2$: na-an-sa$_{10}$-sa$_{10}$-an, agrees with T$_8$:]-sa$_{10}$-an; K$_1$: na-ab-sa$_{10}$-sa$_{10}$. UM$_1$: ŋìri dúr-bi-šè(! text: KU) é ŋál-ŋál-la-àm, agrees with C$_1$: ŋì[ri x]-bi-šè é ŋ[ál-, T$_7$:] ⸢é⸣ ŋál-ŋál-[...]; UM$_2$: ŋìri dúr-bi é ŋál-ŋál-la-àm; Ur$_4$: ⸢dúr⸣-bi-šè ⸢é⸣ ŋál-ŋál-la-àm; K$_1$: ŋìri dúr-bi-šè ⸢ŋál?⸣-ŋ[ál-lá-à]m; coll. Taylor; Sch$_3$: ⸢géme⸣ ⸢é⸣(?)-<gal>-⸢a⸣(?) na-sa$_{10}$-⸢sa$_{10}$⸣-⸢en⸣(sic!) ⸢ŋìri⸣ ⸢dúr-bi-šè⸣ é-ŋál-ŋál-l[a]. The only source that omits é is, thus, T$_8$: ŋìri dúr-bi-šè ŋál-ŋál-la, while it is attested in six sources. Cf. line 177, where a similar expression occurs.

The reading of KU as dúr is confirmed by the phonetic variant gán tùr-šè ŋál-la in Ur$_6$, line 272. The meaning of dúr(KU)-bi-šè has been discussed by Civil, 1984, 285–286, who translates "Do not buy a palace slave girl, she will always be at the end of the road," commenting that "the palace sells only its decrepit, useless slaves," and, n. 13, that gìr, "road," is taken in the sense of "sequence," as qualitive ranking; further, that the end of the road must not be understood in its idiomatic sense, but as "the last choice," like "the bottom of the barrel." Wilcke, 1978, 208, translates "sie hat Plattfüßen!" Wilcke (pp. 222–223) overlooks the well-attested é, cf. Alster, 1991–92, 33, with n. 17, who translates "Do not buy a palace slave girl, the whole house will always be «at the end of the road»" (i.e., get the worst of it). "Always" seeks to render the rarely reduplicated ŋál, cf. Civil, 1984, 286, n. 13. The omission of é was repeated by Civil, loc. cit., Römer, 1990, 61, and the ETCSL: "she will always be the bottom of the barrel (?)." There can be no doubt that é is a significant part of a proverbial expression, since it occurs in parallel expressions in lines 177: ŋá-la dag-ge é dúr-bi-šè mu-un-du, "A lazy one makes a house go «down to the bottom»"; 220: munus-bar-šu-ŋál-e é-dúr-bi-šè mu-un-du, "a woman who has a fortune ruins a house"; cf. the comments on those lines. In line 157, it is not the slave girl who suffers from the encounter with the palace, but the whole household that acquires her.

The sign DÚR is a square KU, which in origin is a picture of the buttocks; "Plattfüßen" seems less convincing.

Line 158: K$_1$: kur-bí(sic!), the only text that has the rare phonetic reading bí for bi. UM$_1$:]-ta-e-e$_{11}$; T$_7$:]-ta-a-e$_{11}$; T$_8$: -t]a-⸢e$_{11}$⸣-e$_{11}$; C$_1$: um-ta-e-⸢e$_{11}$⸣; Ur$_4$: [...]-e$_{11}$; K$_1$: im-ta-a-⸢x⸣-[x]; Sch$_3$: kur-bi um-ta-ab-⸢è⸣-e[n](sic?), only source that has the explicit 2nd person suffix. For the verbal prefixes -a-e$_{11}$, cf. line 192.

Line 159: UM$_1$: ù-mu-e-túm; T$_8$: ù-mu-túm; C$_1$: ù-um-[; Sch$_3$: ù-⸢mu⸣(? looks like en)-tùm.

I understand ki-nu-zu-a-ni-ta as "from his unknown place," that is, one does not know where he comes from. Slightly differently the ETCSL: "from a place where he is alien." Wilcke, 1978, 225: "kann heißen «von einem Ort, den er nicht kennt» oder «von seinem (dir) unbekannten Ort»." Cf. also the comments on line 276: ur/lú nu-zu, "an unknown dog/man," for which "(whose whereabouts) are unknown" has been suggested, and line 280, where the reading ki-<nu>-zu-a is suggested.

Line 160: UM$_1$: ki ^{d}utu-è-a-aš, agrees with T$_8$:]-è-a-aš; UM$_2$: ki ^{d}utu-è-a-šè, agrees with Sch$_3$; K$_1$:] ^{d}u[tu]-⸢è⸣-⸢a⸣(?)-⸢aš⸣(?) (coll. J. Taylor).

ki ^{d}utu-è-a-aš occurs also in line 165. This can be understood as the place where the sun rises, or simply "the East," but here, of course, not too concretely of a specific place.

Line 161: There are no variants, except K$_1$, which seems to have a sign between ḫé- and -in-du (coll. J. Taylor).

Libating water seems here to be used of a way in which servants were used to making life easier and more pleasant for their masters. Römer, 1990, 60, considers it as possibly "eine rituelle Handlung." Cf., however, pp. 229ff., *Instr. Ur-Ninurta* 29 and 35, which may very well suit the situation described here.

Line 162: UM$_1$: é nu-tuku, agrees with C$_1$: é nu-tuku, and Sch$_3$; UM$_2$: é nu-un-tuku; UM$_1$: é-a-ni, only text that omits -šè; the others have é-a-ni-šè.

The concept of the nomads (Martu) having no houses and cities is well known in Sumerian literature; cf. *Enki and the World Order*, 131; 248: ere nu-tuku(-ra) é nu-tuku-ra; *Martu's Marriage*, 137: u$_4$ tìl-la-na é nu-tuku-a, "who, as long as he lives, has no house"; cf. also the remarkable parallel in our text lines 276–282, esp. 279.

Line 163: UM$_1$: ere nu-tuku, agrees with C$_1$: ere nu-tuku, K$_1$: ere nu-tu[ku, and Sch$_3$; UM$_2$: ere nu-un-tuku.

Lines 163 A-B: These are included in K$_1$ only. Cf. Alster, 1974, 105–106 (ll. 168 a-b), who compares it to the Damu-text MAH 16016, now published by Cavigneaux, "Fragment d'élégie," RA 94 (2000) 11–15, obv. 13–rev. 1:

^{ŋiš}ig-kur-ra gù ba-an-dé-e ki-ba ba-da-gur
^{ŋiš}ig-kur-ra šu ba-da-an-ús ki-ba ba-[da]-gur
nin$_9$-e ^{ŋiš}ig kur-ra šu ba-da-an-ús ki-ba ba(!)-da-gur

She shouted at the door of the netherworld, but was turned back;
she knocked at the door of the netherworld, but was turned back;
the sister knocked at the door of the netherworld, but was turned back.

This is similar to *Inanna's Descent* 74–75: ^{ŋiš}ig-kur-ra-ka šu ḫul ba-an-ús; abul$_x$(KÁ.GAL)-kur-ra-ka gù ḫul ba-an-ús. Cf. also CT 58, 3, BM 79510, obv. 14–15, cf. Description p. 9. These refer to a mythological scene in which a deity arrives at the gates of the netherworld and tries to enter. It was apparently the mention of those who have no houses and cities that gave the association to knocking the door (of the netherworld) and caused the lines to be inserted here, although they are out of place. Cf. p. 219, *Chap. 1.10: Other school versions?*

Line 164: UM$_1$: la-ba-da-ḫi-li-e la-ba-da-[sun$_7$-e], agrees with C$_1$: la-ba-da-ḫi-li-e la-[. K$_1$: [...]-ḫi-li la-ba-an-da-sun$_7$-na; only K$_1$ has sun$_7$-na; UM$_2$: [l]a-ba-e-da-ḫi-li la-ba-e-da-sun$_7$-e, agrees with T$_{10}$: la-ba-e-da-ḫi-li l[a-, and Sch$_3$; T$_{11}$: -su]n$_7$-e.

ḫi-li is here used as a verb; cf. *Inanna-Ninegalla Hymn* 99, and the love song edited by Sefati, *Love*

Songs, 353–359, as *Šusin B*, 2; 4; 12; 15; cf. also MSL 12, 179, OB Lu B II 46: lú-al-⌜ḫi-li-a⌝ = [*m*]*u-ma-nu-*⌜*ú-úm*⌝, "flatterer," cited by Wilcke, 1978, 225, also referring to Civil, ibid., p. 188: *Dialogue* 5 12.

sun_7(KAL) = *ṣaltu*, "quarrelsome" (Wilcke: "stoltz, anmaßend sein") occurs also in line 54. Cf. CAD Ṣ, 86 *ṣaltu*, "quarrel, disagreement, fight."

Line 165: UM_I: ki ᵈutu-è-a-aš, agrees with T_{II}:]-aš; K_I: k[i] ᵈutu-è-a; Sch_3: ki ᵈutu-⌜è⌝-a-⌜šè⌝.

Line 166: UM_I: kaskal agrees with T_{10};]-⌜un⌝, agrees with T_{II}: -d]u-un, and Sch_3; only K_I has kas]kal(?)-šè and na-an-ni-du.

The warning against travelling alone belongs to the standard repertoire of wisdom literature; cf. *Šūpē-amēli* 9–16, esp. 13 (Spruch I.ii in Dietrich's strophic pattern, cf. Kämmerer, 1998, 178–179).

Line 167: UM_I: nu-zu-a-zu s[aŋ ...]-a-⌜x⌝; C_I:] ba-⌜ra⌝-⌜ak⌝-⌜x⌝-[(ak on a detached fragment); T_{10}: lú-zu-a-zu saŋ-šu-UD(?) ba-⌜x⌝-[; T_{II}:]-⌜ak⌝-e; K_I:]-⌜x⌝-⌜x⌝-ak-ke_4; Sch_3: lú ⌜nu⌝-⌜zu(?)-a⌝(?)-zu-um saŋ šu-bal ⌜ì⌝-[(x)]-ak-e. T_{10}: lú-zu-a-zu is best explained as an error omitting nu, cf. below. The sign following bal in Sch_3 has the outer shape of NI, but seems to lack the two verticals characteristic of NI in lines 39–40 above. T_{10} (cf. pl. 8), hitherto read saŋ šu-UD(?) ba-⌜x⌝-..., is probably a slight miscopy for saŋ šu-bal (...). C_I (cf. pl. 22) has the remains of two signs, probably -z]u s[aŋ. In Sch_3 it is unlikely that there is a missing sign between this and ak, so the reconstruction saŋ šu-bal ì-ak-e is reasonably certain.

Sch_3 shows that nu-zu-a-zu stands for lú nu-zu-a-zu, "your (man) who doesn't know you." Otherwise, it would be highly likely that the variant nu-zu-a stands for lú-zu-a, in view of the well-known nu : lú correspondence; cf. the comments on line 69–70, where nu šár-ra has a variant lú šár-ra.

For šu-bal – ak, here understood as "to exchange in trade," cf. PSD B, 72, bala – a_5, "to transport for trade," etc.; *Lugalbanda in Hurrumkurra* 114: ḫur-saŋ-$ŋi_6$-ta šu-a bal-a (= ak?), "(iron) imported from the black mountain." Cf. also kù-bala in *Níŋ-nam* B 8 (p. 272, *Chap. 3.1*).

Line 168: ED_I: mu-mu sì-ga ⌜x⌝ / lú na[m] šè.

UM_I: mu-mu-a sì-ga s[aŋ ...] im-ma(?)-⌜x⌝-e (x like búr; maybe ⌜gíd⌝); C_I:] lú/-ù-ra i[m-; T_{10}: mu-mu-a sì-ga saŋ-du lú-[; T_{II}:] lú-ra [...]-⌜x⌝-e (x is ak rather than gíd); K_I: [...]-⌜x⌝ (perhaps e or ke_4); Sch_3: mu-mu-a sì-ga saŋ-du lú-ra im-da(?)-na-an-ak-⌜e⌝; the sign tentatively read da can perhaps be ta, but hardly ma. The most likely restoration is, thus, im-ma-...-ak-e, with some uncertainty as to the signs following -ma, maybe with some variant in UM_I.

Civil, 1984, 297, suggests that ED_I iv rev. 15–16: "mu mu sì ga is to be understood as mu-sì-ga mu-sì-ga, with sì-g for sag_9" (= sa_6-g). Yet, it may be relevant to connect it with OB Proto-lú 516 (MSL 12, 51): mu-mu-a, for which the same interpretation would then also have to apply. Alster, 1974, 45, guessing from the context, suggests, "when you are among known persons, you can rely on(?) a man" (lit., "among all names"). The ETCSL translates "a name placed on another one ...," which is hardly convincing. I tentatively suggest "when placed among (familiar) names," implying "at home."

Line 169: There are no variants, but Sch_3 is epigraphically uncertain.

Paradoxical proverbs are well known in many languages. For some examples in Greek; cf. P. Martin, *Studien auf dem Gebiete des Griechische Sprichwortes*, 11, mentioning among others: γλαῦκα Ἀθήναζε, "(to bring) an owl to Athens," (futile, since the owl is the symbol of Athene); ἄστρα τοξεύειν, "to shoot arrows toward the stars"; εἰς ὕδωρ γράφειν, "to write in water," Αἰθίοπα λευκαίνειν, "to wash an Ethiopian white"; cf. also "Sand in Sahara verkaufen," etc.

SS 169 A: This line is an addition that does not occur in the other sources. If the reading kur-ra is justified, it would line up with the preceding entries, meaning, approximately, "In the mountains a man does not say ..." Alternatively, the first signs might be ur_5-ra, "someone who is in debt." The sign tentatively read KAM can hardly be BIR, but perhaps límmu-*tenû*, or a variant of ad_4, cf. SP 1.66 and 2.119. This suggests that KAM here represents a verb in the imperative, ending in -n. This is perhaps vaguely related to SP 27.9: ere[ki] ere[ki] silim nu-ub-dug_4 lú lú-a silim(?) ab-bé, but very uncertain.

Line 170: There are no variants, apart from Sch_3: nam-tar $peš_{10}$(KI.A) x(like si)-dur_5-ru-⌜àm⌝, which is epigraphically uncertain. The sign SI following KI.A in Sch_3 is perhaps best to be explained as inadvertently influenced by the common sign combination

SI.A, since the following sign is indeed A, yet here to be read dur$_5$.

For nam – tar and the notion of Fate or Destiny in proverbial context, cf. lines 115 and 118, and, in particular, SP 2.2–6; 2.9–13 (Alster, *Proverbs* I, 46–48); cf. also SP 1.26; 1.67; 1.80; SP 3.83; 3.176; SP 14.45; SP 2.64: níŋ-nam-tar-ra, "the things of fate." These yield a rather sinister picture, although far from devoid of humor. In SP 2.4, Fate is said to be floating past in a river; in 2.10 it is said to be like a sickness demon; in 2.11 it is compared to a dog that bites, clinging to its victim like an old rag; in 2.13 it is compared to a storm befalling the country; in SP 2.14 nam-tar is a variant of du-lum, "labor." Cf. also nam-tar-eŋir-ra, "the future state of things," in *Chap. 4.5: The Lazy Slave Girl* 15 (p. 371).

Line 171: There are no variants.

For ŋìri zé-er = *neḫelṣû*, cf. Hallo and van Dijk, YNER 3, 75; CAD N, 149f. *neḫelṣû* lex.; 2.

Wilcke, 1978, 225, with a categorical statement: "das Verbum in Z. [171] ist präterial," touches upon an essential problem without discussing it. Cf. the discussion p. 209, *Chap. 1.9: Tense or aspect related verbal system*. An argument is there made for seeing such statements as ex-temporal, timeless, generalizations, rather corresponding to the Akkadian stative. This is in agreement with the ETCSL, translating lines 170–171 with a present verb: "Fate is a wet bank; it can make one slip." Wilcke, 1978, 208, however, translates: "Das Schicksal ist (wie) ein feuchtes Ufer; es hat (schon) Menschen ausgleiten lassen." Römer, 1990, 60, translates similarly: "Beim Menschen hat es (schon) den Fuß zum Ausgleiten gebracht." By inserting (schon) both clearly illustrate the difficulty in pressing a tempus system onto a language in which it is alien. Cf. also the comments on lines 193.

I translate "Fate is a slippery bank that makes a man's feet slip away," for the reasons stated on p. 210, *Chap. 1.9: Split sentence construction*.

Line 172: ED$_2$ fr. 8: šeš-[gal a-a] na-nám [nin$_9$-gal] ama na-[nám ...]. nám for nam is typical of ED$_2$, cf. p. 217, *Chap. 1.9: Use of special ED signs*.

All texts have na-nam, except S$_3$, which has šeš-gal é na-na nin$_9$-gal ama(?) na-na; and the reverse of S$_3$, which is a syllabic version of the same: šeš-eš-gal é an-na-[na] ni-in-gal ⸢x⸣ dam é [...]. Civil, 1984, 298, suggests that this might be a joke on the part of a scribe intending to write éš-dam: "your big brother, your big sister, a brothel." In Civil's transliteration of the Adab source, ED$_2$ (Ad), Civil, 1984, 298, na-nam is a misprint for na-nám.

Respecting family members is a well-known sapiential theme; cf., e.g., *Counsels of Wisdom* 76–77; 80–83.

Line 173: UM$_1$: šeš-gal-zu-úr [, agrees with T$_{10}$: šeš-gal-zu-úr, and (probably) I$_{13}$, TCL: šeš-gal-zu-úr(!), and Sch$_3$. T$_{10}$: ŋizzal ḫé-em-[; TCL: ŋizzal ḫé-en(?)-ši(!)-ak; Sch$_3$: šeš-gal-zu-úr ŋizzal ḫé-em-ši-⸢x⸣-(⸢x⸣)(?); the traces ḫé-em-ši-⸢x⸣-(⸢x⸣) do not seem to confirm the expected reading ...-ak(-e).

Line 173 evidently quotes an already existing proverbial phrase, not specifically addressed to Ziusudra, who hardly would be expected to have an older brother. Cf. p. 36, *Chap. 1: Inclusion of proverbial sayings*.

Römer, 1990, 61, translates "Deinem älteren Bruder mögest du darauf achten," which seems to be an attempt to render the -ši- term. infix, which, however, is standard with ŋizzal – ak, as appears from line 10 and parallels.

Line 174: UM$_1$: ama-zu-g[im, agrees with T$_{10}$: ama-zu-gim; only Ur$_4$ has ama(!)-zu-šè; T$_{10}$: šu ḫé-en-NE-[; only Ur$_4$ has gú ḫé-em-ši-[; TCL: šu ḫé-en-⸢x⸣-⸢x⸣-ŋál(?). The best Nippur reading is, thus, šu ḫé-en-[NE-gál], possibly with a sign missing between NE and ŋál. In Ur$_4$ this was confused with the common expression gú ŋál, with a terminative ši verbal infix, which occurs in line 13; cf. the comments on that line.

Of the verbal phrase šu ḫé-en-NE-[?]-ŋál, šu (– ŋál) is supported by a Nippur source and has, therefore, been taken as primary here. The last signs are only extant in TCL, but poorly preserved, which makes it difficult to judge whether NE is a plural dative infix or should be read -dè-. Wilcke, 1978, 208, translates: "Der älteren Schwester soll du wie deiner Mutter behilflich sein!" which may sound too influenced by modern social expectations, yet may be approximately right. The precise implication of the verb šu – ŋál may be some kind of support or obedience. Römer, 1990, 61, takes the variant gú – ŋál as primary, and translates: "der älteren Schwester mögest du dich wie einer Mutter deswegen den Nacken beugen!" referring to PSD A/3, 141. The

ETCSL: "You should be obedient to your elder sister as if she were your mother" also translates gú – ŋál. The variant may have been influenced by line 13, however, where gú – ŋál occurs as a variant of gú – ak = *qâpu Ntn? Cf. the comments on that line. The parallel line 152a has gú – ak, which seems to be primary.

Line 175: ED_I: [i]gi-zu_5-ta $kiŋ_x$(ḪUL) na-ak x (like TAB, copy like zur, incorrect). For zu_5 and ḪUL, here read $kiŋ_x$, cf. p. 217, *Chap. 1.9: Unusual sign values in the ED texts*, and Civil, 1984, 285. Civil, however, considers the SS text a result of a replacement with a change of meaning: "OB adds za-e and replaces ⸢x⸣-ḫul – ak by kin – ak with a change of meaning, unless one assumes that kin – ak is here a euphemism to avoid mentioning the effects of the 'evil eye'." The reason why I hesitate to accept this is that in ED_I, line 54, ḪUL likewise seems to have a reading $kiŋ_x$. For kiŋ – ak, cf. *Instr. Ur-Ninurta* 46: kiŋ – $ša_4$, which makes it tempting to suggest the reading kiŋ – $ša_5$ for AK; cf. note on line 49.

There are otherwise no variants. Cf. the comments on line 176 for the interpretation.

Line 176: ED_I: ka-zu_5-ta níŋ na-lu-lu. T_{10}: ka-zu-ta níŋ-nam nu-⸢lu-lu⸣-[un], agrees with T_{18}: n]íŋ-nam nu-lu-[lu-un], and Sch_3; Ur_4: ka-zu-ta níŋ nam-mu-un-⸢x⸣-lu(!); TCL: ka-zu-ta níŋ im-lu-lu-un, "with your words you make things multiply," the only text that has a positive verbal form, apparently by mistake. In Sch_3 there is no nu. It is, thus, possible to combine either níŋ-nam or nam-lu-lu-un, of which I have chosen the latter as the more plausible construction, "you shall not multiply things," similar to Ur_4: níŋ nam-mu-, etc.

Since za-e, "you," strictly speaking is superfluous, it may have been included for greater emphasis or to suit a rhythmical pattern.

Cf. Civil, 1984, 285: "The idea is that only hard work, not words or incantations, make business prosper." Reading inim, "word" is perhaps more likely than ka, "mouth."

Line 177: ED_I: ŋá-la d[ag] é dúr-šè [(x)] ⸢du⸣; cf. Civil, 1984, 285. UM_I: ⸢é⸣ [; T_{10}: é dúr-[; T_{18}: é dúr-bi m[u-, agrees with Sch_3; note that Sch_3 has no šè following dúr-bi; Ur_4: é dúr-[x x x-u]n-du. TCL: é dúr-bi-šè mu-un-[. Six sources, thus, include é. Cf. the comments on line 157, where a parallel expression occurs.

For ŋá-la dag-ge = *naparkû*, "to stop working," cf. line 122, and, e.g., *Dialogue 4*, 34: a-na-aš-àm lú ŋá-la-dag-ga-gim ŋiš ma-ab-ḫur-re, "Why do you instruct me as if I were a lazy person."

Lines 178–180: Wilcke, 1978, 225, categorically understands kur-ra e_{11} in line 178 as "ins Bergland hinaufsteigen," contrasting kur-ta e_{11} in line 180, "aus dem Bergland herabsteigen," and translates: "*(178)* (Der Wunsch nach) Broot läßt jemanden ins Gebirge hinaufsteigen, *(179)* (aber) ein Falscher wird den Mann fehlleiten(?). *(180)* (Dann) läßt (der Wunsch nach) Broot den Mann vom Gebirge wieder herabsteigen." The verbal prefixes bí-in- versus im-ma-da-ra-an- might point in that direction. Yet, if correct, it could not possibly be "bread" that causes "men," that is, the Mesopotamians, to ascend to the mountains, but, rather, such material goods as were difficult to obtain on the Mesopotamian alluvial plain, such as stones, timber, and metals. This would leave line 179, lú-lul lú-bar-ra bí-in-túm-mu, unexplained in the context. Wilcke translates lú(-) kur-ra "jemanden ins Gebirge," but cf. the comments on line 179 below. I understand both the verbs e_{11} in lines 178–180 as "to descend." In my opinion, line 180 summarizes the two preceding lines with a more explicit wording, possibly reflecting already existing sayings, perhaps only slightly modified. There can be no doubt that line 280 expresses a related idea.

Römer, 1990, 61, translates: "*(178)* Das (Bedürfnis nach) Brot läßt die Gebirgler heruntersteigen, *(179)* es bringt Falsche (und) Fremde (heran), *(180)* das (Bedürfnis nach) Brot läßt die Leute aus dem Bergland heruntersteigen!" with which I basically agree.

Line 178: There are no variants.

GAR, here and in line 180, can be read níŋ, "things," or alternatively ninda, "bread." ninda is preferred here for the reasons stated above, under the comments to lines 178–180. Already van Dijk, 1953, 110, commenting on *Counsels of Wisdom* 174, convincingly translated "descendre *pour* du pain." Cf. also the comments on line 179 below.

In line 178, lú-kur-ra is a genitival compound, "the men of the mountains," parallel to lú-bar-ra in line 179, and different from line 180, where kur-ta is independent in the ablative. Wilcke's translation, quoted above, understands this differently.

Line 179: I_{11}: lú-lul lú-bar-ra, agrees with I_{14}: lú-lul lú-bar-ra; Ur_4: [lul]-e, apparently agrees with TCL: lul-e and Sch_3, which, however, has -tùm-mu instead of túm-mu; this gives a slightly different text: "Liars bring strangers along"; cf. p. 212, *Chap. 1.9: SS Verbal Alternation: túm:tùm.*

The line is easiest to understand if referring to strangers *descending* from the mountains together with others, possibly nomads, who seek food on the alluvial plain, since this is a classic situation in Mesopotamian culture. It would be too far-fetched to understand the reverse, as the Mesopotamians ascending to the mountains in connection with foreign trade, implying that, thereby, the quest for foreign goods entails the arrival of foreigners.

Wilcke's translation (1978, 208), separating lú and bar, "(aber) ein Falscher wird dir fehlleiten(?)" fails to carry conviction, because lú-bar-ra occurs as a term for "foreigner," e.g., in *Curse of Agade* 18, in which lú-zu-ù-ne is parallel to lú-bar-ra, "foreigner." Cf. also the comments on line 167, and OB Lú 149 (MSL 12, 162): lú-[zu-a] = [*mu-du*]-*ú-um*. PSD B, 106, translates "bread causes the mountaineers to come down, it brings traitors and foreigners," with further examples of lú-bar-ra, "foreigner, stranger," among these *The Fowler and His Wife* 4, edited p. 372, *Chap. 4.5*.

Line 180: I_{14}: im-ma-da-ra-an-e_{11}-dè, agrees with UM_2:]-ra-an-e_{11}-dè; N_7: im-ma-da-ra-an-e_{11}-dè; T_{14}: im-ma-da-ra-an-e_{11}-dè; T_{18}:]-ma-da-[; TCL: im-ma-da-ra-an-e_{11}-dè; only Ur_4 has: im-ma-⌜da⌝-ab-e_{11}-dè; Sch_3 seems to have im-da(?)-ra-an-e_{11}-dè.

The verbal prefixes -da-ra- can be taken either as a frozen pleonastic use of two variants of the ablative /ta/ or, perhaps better, the first can be the comitative, "with them/him/it?" Cf. the similar verbal form in line 192: ḫé-em-me-re-a-e_{11}-dè. Cf. also Gragg, AOAT 5, 99ff. and Edzard, *Sum. Grammar*, 108. Cf. lines 12 and 55.

I here understand lú, "man," as a grammatical singular expressing a collective plural, like the English "people," or occasionally Akk. *awīlum*; cf. Moran, *Reiner FS*, 247, n. 7; Alster, *Jacobsen MV*, 37. This also occurs in line 280.

Lines 180–181: It is remarkable that in ED_I, line 181 comes before line 180, because this, in fact, makes better sense. This is clear in view of the verb in line 180, in which ši-in-ga-an-ù-tu, "also creates ..." obviously relates to line 181, although it would be expected to follow it. The reason that the line order became reversed in the SS version is not clear.

Line 181: ED_I: é ⌜x⌝ amar ⌜x⌝ ⌜x⌝.

I_{11}: úru ⌜tur⌝-⌜re⌝, agrees with Ur_4: [tur]-re, and TCL: uru tur-re (NB uru, according to J. Dahl's collation), "creates oxen for its lord"; I_{14}: tur]-ra. UM_2: š]i-in-na-ù-tu; I_{14}: ši-in-ga-an-⌜ù-tu⌝; T_{18}: ši-[; Ur_4: ši-in-ga-ù-tu; TCL: ši-in-na-ù-tu. TCL: gud is correct, according to J. Dahl's collation. Cf. Alster, 1990, 15, n. 3. Two texts, thus, agree on ši-in-ga-, while two, including UM_2, a main source, have ši-in-na-, which agrees with Sch_3: ere-tur-re lugal-bi-ir amar ši-in-na-an-ù-tu. Note that TCL and Sch_3 use ere(URU) where the other sources have úru, which confirms the impression that the latter is sometimes simply used for ere, "city"; cf. the comments on line 21.

The verb ù-tu, "to give birth to," seems here to be used in the sense "to provide/create." This is similar to the well-known use of tu in the sense "to create," said of a statue.

Line 182: ED_I: x (= e/ere?) máḫ é dù ⌜x⌝ ḫur.

I_{14}: [... -r]e, is the only text that has -re in front of é-dù-a, perhaps the rest of ma]ḫ. TCL: uru(coll.) maḫ-e é-dù-a ši-ḫur-re is the only text that preserves the two first signs of the line; maḫ seems certain in view of ED_I: máḫ.

Unlike Wilcke, 1978, 225, "eine kleine Stadt bringt ihrem König/Herrn ein bescheidenes, aber nützliches Erzeugnis hervor, aber eine große nur Planungen: ein Paradox," I do not see the emphasis as resting on a paradox, but simply on the fact that both contribute something useful, especially since, as stated above, comments on lines 180–181, the two lines are ideally best to be read in reverse order. In line 181, lugal may, of course, be translated "king," but it may also simply mean "lord," as often, so there is no need to stress the role of the king as a political power here. The ETCSL: "A small city provides (?) its king with a calf; a huge city digs(?) a house plot(?)."

Line 183: TCL: [...] ⌜x⌝-ke_4, is the only text that preserves the beginning of the line. The two first signs are, thus, uncertain. The verb was certainly similar to that of line 185.

á-šu – du_7 is to be connected with á-$šita_4$ = *ḫišiḫtu*, "need, lack, necessities." The variant á-šu-du_7 for á-$šita_4$ occurs in *Curse of Agade* 90 and *Enki and the World Order* 321; cf. Civil, JAOS 88 (1968) 7, where more references can be found.

Line 184: ED_I: lú níŋ tuku lú níŋ nu-tuku / áš-gig-šè ŋar. None of the SS texts includes áš. UM_2: ⸢gig⸣-⸢šè⸣ i[m-, agrees with Ur_4: gig-šè im-ŋar; N_7: gig-šè ì-ŋál, agrees with I_{14}: [...]-ŋál.

Whether šè should be read as the terminative to be combined with the preceding gig or as a verbal profix can perhaps be decided from the variant in N_7: gig-šè ì-ŋál, which favors the first possibility.

In ED_I rev. iii 7–8, the second part is read áš-gig-šè ŋar, because Steinkeller, RA 74 (1980) 178–179, has shown that ZÍZ and ÁŠ are distinguishable in the Fara and Abū Ṣalābīkh texts, although this does not apply from the Pre-Sargonic period onward. Our source ED_I shows ÁŠ (it has an unbroken vertical through the sign, whereas ZÍZ has a broken vertical). Therefore, Wilcke's interpretation "bitterer Kompensationsleistung" (Wilcke, 1978, 226; cf. also RA 73 [1979] 95–96) has not been accepted here. Wilcke's translation (1978, 209) of the SS version, "Der Besitzende hat dem Armen Bitteres auferlegt" has not been confirmed by the bilingual parallel cited below. The possibility that the line may have been understood differently in the later sources, in which áš was omitted, may, however, have to be taken into consideration. áš might simply mean "curse" in the ED version, unless some unknown meaning is involved.

The same saying is cited in TIM 9, 19 (rev.) 12 (Alster, *Proverbs* I, 299): lú níŋ-tuku lú níŋ nu-tuku gig-šè in-[ŋar] = UET 6/2 367 (Alster, *Proverbs* II, 324): lú níŋ-tuku lú níŋ nu-tuku gig-šè im-ŋar, glossed *la-ap-nu a-na šar-r*[*i*]-⸢*im*⸣ *mim-ma ur-ṣí-im ša-ki-in-šu*, "a poor man inflicts all kinds of illnesses on a wealthy man."

If the Akkadian translation is trustworthy, it is remarkable that the saying is seen from the point of view of a wealthy man, who is said to suffer from the encounter with the poor. This is the opposite view of the Mesopotamian law codes and royal hymns, in which the mighty rulers claim to protect the poor. The intent may be a warning against employing poor people in a household, where they may cause contagious diseases to spread, or similar.

The parallel from the *Barton Cylinder* (MBI 1), cited by Alster, 1974, 107, has now been edited by Alster and Westenholz, AcSum 16 (1994) 15–46; cf. also PSD A/2, 185; Wilcke, 1978, 226, and Black, *Jacobsen MV*, 44–45. It is questionable whether it contributes to the understanding of our line.

For the extra lines elaborating further on the contrasting pair níŋ-tuku : níŋ nu-tuku in ED_I iii 9–10, see p. 192, *Chap. 1.5*, comment on *AbSt 121–122*, and p. 219, *Chap. 1.10*: *The AbSt version* ....

Line 185: ED_I: dam tuku šè-du_7. The ED text, thus, has a šè- verbal prefix, cf. p. 212, *Chap. 1.9: Modal Verbal Prefixes*. There are otherwise no variants. Cf. line 183.

Line 186: ED_I: dam nu-tuku šér-dib DU. Only Ur_4 has še-er-tab-ba-aš(or: dili) mu-un-ná, presumably influenced by the expression dili ná, "to sleep alone." There are otherwise no variants.

še-er-tab-ba = *kurullu*, "corn stack." The line was first commented upon by Civil and Biggs, RA 60 (1966) 4, and subsequently by Civil, JCS 20 (1966) 124, n. 17. Further references in Alster, 1974, 108.

Line 187: ED_I: é gul é šè-da-[(x)]; ED_2: [...] ⸢an⸣(? perhaps = [nà]b?)-gul-gul (text like gir_4-gir_4). The variant in Ur_4: ša-ba-ra-an-[z]é-e makes good sense, "tears out" instead of "destroys," or maybe it is only a scribal error. There are otherwise no variants.

I understand lines 187–188 as "He who is about to destroy houses will destroy (any) house with them; he who is about to stir up men will stir up (any) man with them"; cf. the comments in Alster, 1975, 143, who compares to SP 2.135 (and parr.), here cited from SP 19 Sec. B 4 (cf. Alster, *Proverbs* I, 70): é gul-gul-e kù ì-gul-e é gul-e kù-sig_{17} ì-gul-e, "he who destroys houses destroys silver; he who destroys a house, destroys gold," i.e., *commune naufragium dulce est*; cf. Alster, *Proverbs* II, 374. This is formally parallel to lines 187–188, although the intent is different: two entries are juxtaposed, of which the second is less comprehensive than the first, but included in it. I, therefore, translate "will destroy (any) house with them," and "will stir up (any) man with them." I understand the verbs as extended by -ed-e. Wilcke, 1978, 209, translates 192–193: "Wer dabei ist, Häuser zu zerstören, den wird ein Haus dabei zerstören; Wer dabei ist, Menschen hochzuschrecken(?), den werden Menschen hochschrecken(?)." The ETCSL: "He who wishes to destroy a house will go ahead and destroy the house; he who wishes to raise up will go ahead and raise up." Here lú in line 188 is apparently taken as the head of the whole sentence, "he who," whereas line 187 clearly shows that such a head is not needed; this is, therefore, less convincing. In my opinion it misses the point, that is, what applies to a whole group will also apply to each individual within the group.

Line 188: ED_1: [l]ú zi lú šè-da-[z]i; ED_2: [lú(?)] zi AN.[x (= n[àb?)]-⌜x⌝(like ka, not zi)-e.

UM_2: lú ša-ba-da-an-zi-zi-i, agrees with N_4: -d]è lú ša-ba-da-a[n-; Ur_4: lú ša-ba-ra-an-zi-zi.

Line 189: UM_2: lú a-ba-an-dab$_5$; N_4: lú ba-an-d[ab$_5$]; N_7: lú ba-an-dab$_5$; Ur_4: lú ba-an-dab$_5$. The prospective a > ù- is, thus, included in UM_2 only.

Line 190: UM_2: lú íd-dè; Ur_4: [... -d]a. UM_2: ba-ra-an-bal-e; N_4:]-ra-bal-e; Ur_4: ba-[x]-bal-e, can agree with both.

The ETCSL translates lines 189–190: "By grasping the neck of a huge ox, you can cross the river." Wilcke, 1978, 209: "Wenn jemand den Hals eines sehr großen Stieres festhält, dann wird ihn der Fluß nicht *fortspülen*!" taking íd-dè as the subject and lú as the object; in view of the frequent use of bal with the ablative verbal prefix in the sense "to cross a river," this is less likely. Cf. PSD B, 52, which lists many references for bal meaning "to cross a river," typically with íd, in the locative or loc.-term., and the verb with -da-, -ra-, or even with -ra-ta- in the prefix chain. I prefer to understand íd-dè as the loc.-term., resumed by the ablative in the verbal prefixes. Römer, 1990, 61–62: "Nachdem jemand den Nacken eines übergroßen Stieres ergriffen hat, wird er den Menschen den Fluß (so) überqueren lassen." Lines 189–190 can, of course, be understood as proverbial expressions exemplified in lines 191–192, but they can, with equal right, be understood as separate sayings, possibly already existing before they were included here, attracted by the similarity of their intents. Yet, Wilcke, 1978, 226, categorically states that lines 189–190 are related to lines 191–192, in that the former are "sprichwortartiger bildhafter Ausdruck für die konkrete Aussage von Z. [191–192]."

Line 191: N_4: omits line altogether and instead places line 261 after line 190: [lú-gu-la á-diš]-e ga-na-gam(!)-en-dè-[en], evidently attracted by the common word lú-gu-la in both lines. UM_2: zag-ba ù-ba-e-zal-ta, N_2: zag-zu ba-e-zal-ta. Ur_4:]-ri, variant of -ta?.

For lú-gu-la, cf. Lú = *ša* I 132 b (MSL 12, 97) = *rabû*. This also occurs in CIRPL Ukg. 4 xi 1–18. Cf. also line 261.

Alster, 1974, 45, translates line 191: "After you have dwelt side by side with the mighty men of your city"; Civil, AfO 25 (1974/77) 69, comments on the line in connection with *Enlil and Namzitarra* 1 (cf. *Chap. 3.5*) and translates "when you have passed by the side of the notables of your town," which I have accepted, although I see no need to take lú-gu-la as plural. This is also the opinion of Römer, 1990, 62, who translates lines 191–192: "Nachdem du dich *an* einen Großen deiner Stadt *angesch<loßen>* hast, wird dich, mein Sohn, *dieses* hochkommen lassen!"; the ETCSL translates 191–192: "By moving along (?) at the side of the mighty men of your city, my son, you will certainly ascend (?)."

Line 192: UM_2: ur$_5$-re ḫé-em-me-re-a-e$_{11}$-dè: N_4: ḫé-em-mu-re-e$_{11}$-d[è]; N_7: -ra(?)]-⌜an⌝-[e$_{11}$(?)].

For the verbal prefixes -a-e$_{11}$, cf. line 158, where a similar form occurs. For the prefix chain, cf. further Wilcke, 1978, 226, referring to forms similar to ḫé-em-me-re-a-e$_{11}$-. Cf. also Edzard, *Sum. Grammar*, 106; 108; 109. Cf. also the comments on line 20: sal-la-e-a and the literature there cited.

Note that the text has za-a, not za-e. Could this indicate a locative, replacing a dative (-ra): "thus (= in a corresponding manner) will he ascend (or: descend) to you"? Cf. the similar verbs in lines 178 and 180. The verbal prefixes could then indicate the matching 2nd person dative, in spite of Wilcke's reference to similar forms in *Das Lugalbandaepos*, p. 163f. with n. 432, where ablatives are involved. Wilcke translates "mein Kind, so wirst du gewiß von dort aus nach oben kommen!"

ur$_5$-re can be understood adverbially = *kiam*, as in line 133: ur$_5$; cf. line 199, where ur$_5$-e is *ḫubullu*, "interest"; cf. also line 53; different lines 41; 227; cf. also the comments on *Instr. Ur-Ninurta* 53. Here it might mean "in a matching manner," that is, on the same social level. Wilcke's statement, 1978, 225, "ur_5-re adverbial 'so' oder Agentiv 'dieses'...?" is worth considering: ur_5 as a demonstrative non-personal pronoun occurs with case endings; cf. Edzard, *Sum. Grammar*, 55 and 57. This would then yield the alternative translation "this will make you ascend." The interpretation is not beyond doubt, however, since ur_5-e – e_{11} may be related to *Death of Dumuzi* 40–41, cf. Katz, *Image*, 100: ... ur_5 nu-mu-un-da-⌜e_{11}⌝, which presumably means "does absolutely not let me ascend from there."

Line 193: UM_2: géme-⌜zu⌝ ḫur(?)-saŋ-ta ši-im-ta-an-tùm sa_6-ga ši-im-ta-an-túm; N_4: ši]-in-da-tùm sa_6-ga šà š[i-. The first five signs are preserved in UM_2 only. The sign read -⌜zu⌝ is not entirely certain. It is preserved only in U_2 and may be zu written over an erasure. There are some doubts about the sign read ḫur. The line is similar, but not identical, to ED_I rev. vi 3: še mar ama lú-ra níŋ-sa_6-ga nu-túm.

Lines 193–194 have the sequence tùm : de_6(DU) : tùm, corresponding to the *ḫamṭu, marû, ḫamṭu*-forms of tùm. Only in line 110 does túm occur as a variant of tùm, but note that here the ED_I parallel seems to use túm where tùm would be expected; cf. p. 212, *Chap. 1.9: SS verbal alternation túm : tùm*; cf. also the comments on line 19. Some caution seems to be warranted in overemphasizing the significance of the difference, especially since, in the present case, a difference, whether temporal of aspectual, between the verbs used in 193 and 194 seems unlikely. This is in agreement with the ETCSL, which translates: "When you bring a slave girl from the hills, she brings both good and evil with her." A similar opposition is embedded in line 47: šà-bi sa_6 ḫul-a = *lìb-ba-šá da-me-eq u le-mun*, "its interior is both good and bad." Wilcke, 1978, 209, translates "Du bringst eine ... Sklavin vom Gebirge her – Gutes hat sie von dort gebracht, aber Schlimmes hat sie dabei von dort gebracht."

Line 194: UM_2: ši-in-ga-àm-ta-an-tùm; N_4: -a]n-da-tùm; K_2: ḫu]l ši-in-[.

For ḫul here, and in lines 195; 197; and 199, the reading $ḫulu_x$ is suggested by the variant ḫul-úr in line 207; cf. Wilcke, 1978, 226, with further literature. This makes it possible to understand ḫul as the loc.-term, which is relevant in line 197. In view of the parallelism with sa_6-ga, it is most likely that here ḫul is to be understood as non-personal, "the evil," but it is remarkable that it is not *níŋ-ḫul, or similar. It seems, however, that a personification of the notion "evil" is meant, at least in line 200; cf. the comments on that line below.

Line 195: This is paralleled by SP 22 ii 17–19: [sa_6-ga] šà-ge [šu nu-bar]-re; apparently the whole line sequence 195–201 was quoted there; cf. Alster, *Proverbs* I, 262.

Alster, 1974, "Pleasure is a hand, but wickedness is also a heart." Wilcke, 1978, "Das Gute sind die Hände, das Schlimme aber ist das Herz." The ETCSL translates "The good is in the hands; the evil is in the heart," which should be *šu-a and šà-ga to justify the translation. The crucial an-ga-àm, "also," has not been taken into account, thereby missing the point that the evil is present, but better concealed than the good.

There are many international parallels, e.g., *Macbeth* I.1: "look like the innocent flower, but be the serpent under't"; German: "Rosen haben Dornen"; *Hitopadeśa* I 77: "Süßigkeit steht auf der Zunge, Todesgift im Herzen"; cf. further p. 38, *Chap. 1: Some international type parallels*.

Line 196: ED_I: sa[ŋ] ⌜x⌝ ⌜x⌝ nu-BAD. Note SS has šu bar. There are otherwise no variants.

Wilcke, 1978, 226, understands šu – bar as "nicht hemmen"; similarly line 197, "freilassen, weglaufen lassen"; cf. lines 198–199.

Line 197: ED_I: ḫul šà nu(sic!)-bar(?) TUR. UM_2: ḫul šà-ge, agrees with K_2: ḫul šà-ge; T_{19}: ḫul šà-g[a. UM_2: šu nu-di-ni-bar-re, agrees with Ur_5: -di]-ni-ba-[r]e; N_5: perhaps]-⌜da⌝-[; T_7:] nu-di-⌜ni(!)⌝-bar; K_2: šu nu-d[a-...].

Line 198: UM_2: ki-dur_5-ru-àm, seems to agree with Ur_5:] ki-dur_5-⌜x(= ru?)⌝-àm. UM_2: šà-ge nu-tag_4-tag_4, agrees with N_5: šà-ge nu-tag_4-tag_4; T_7: š]à-ge nu-tag_4-[tag_4]; S_2: šà-ge nu-tak_4-[; Ur_5: šà-ga n[u-t]ag_4-tag_4; K_2: šà(!) [.

tag_4-tag_4 = *ezēbu*, "to leave."

For ki-dur_5 = *ruṭibtu*, see AHw 997, "Feuchtichkeit"; cf. Civil, 1984, 285: dur_5 wet from natural sources, not irrigation. Cf. also Alster, 1974, 108, where this is seen as having positive connotations. dur_5 occurs in line 272, where gán-dur_5 denotes a place of unlimited resources. It is, therefore, surprising that Wilcke, 1978, 227, asks: "Meint ki-dur_5-ru hier «Morast»?" The ETCSL translates "As if it were a watery place, the heart does not abandon the good." Cf., p. 210, *Chap. 1.9: Split sentence ....*

Römer, 1990, 62, n. 198a, comments: "Ist etwa gemeint, daß die Sklavin sich durch ihre Gefühle für ihre Arbeit nicht voll einsetzen kann, aber auch nicht die Möglichkeit hat, sich auszusprechen?" I, however, see lines 198–199 as expansions elaborating upon the contrast embedded in line 195, but not specifically referring to the slave girl mentioned in line 193, whose presence there, on the other hand, was caused by association with the verb in line 192. If Römer's suggestion is justified, it would be difficult to explain that a parallel sequence occurs in SP 22 ii 15–28 (Alster, *Proverbs* I, 262), without being connected to a slave girl. Cf. p. 41, *Chap. 1.1: Expansion of the strophic pattern.*

Line 199: UM_2: é-níŋ-<gur_{11}>-ra; N_5: g]ur_{11}(?)-ra, agrees with T_{12}: g]ur_{11}-ra; UM_2: ur_5-e; N_5 and T_{12}: ur_5-re; Ur_5: ur_5-ur_5 (plural redupl.). UM_2: la-ba-an-gu_7-e, agrees with N_5: la-ba-an-gu_7-e, T_{12}: la-b[a-; Ur_5: la-ba-gu_7; S_2: ur_5 nu-te-e[n(?), probably a misunderstanding. The line is cited as SP 22 ii 23–24: ... [ḫul] é-[gur_{11}-ra ur_5-e] [la-b]a-an-g[u_7-e].

ur_5-e is here = *ḫubullu*, "interest," in contrast to line 192; cf. the comments on that line.

I understand the sentence as a split sentence construction: ḫul é-níŋ-gur_{11}-ra = *-ra-àm; é-níŋ-gur_{11}-ra is not a genitive composite, lit., "house in which things have been stored." This makes it possible to understand the whole initial part, ending in *-àm as a virtual object of la-ba-an-gu_7-e, "evil is a storeroom that interests do not consume" or, perhaps better, as a virtual ergative subject of gu_7: "wickedness is a storeroom that does not feed by interest," perhaps implying "does not yield interest." Cf. the comments on the similar syntax, p. 210, *Chap. 1.9: Split sentence construction.* Wilcke, 1978, 209, translates "Das Schlimme ist (wie) eine Vorratskammer, die die Zinsen nicht aufzehren können"; cf. the comments on line 171.

Line 199 A and 199 B: These are included in S_2 only. Cf. p. 219, *Chap. 10: The Susa Sources.*

It was undoubtedly the common verb sa_6 in lines 199 A and in 198 that caused the lines to be included by association, but, since the Susa fragment contains only lines 198–199 + 199a-b, it is not possible to see exactly how they were meant in the context. The impression is, however, that these lines were meant as quotations not belonging to a particular context. It is difficult to explain tag in line 199 B. It could be a phonetic writing for dug_4; cf. the comments on line 134.

Line 200: ED_I: ḫul-da ⌜A⌝ ⌜má⌝(? doubtful) su; cf. Alster, 1991–92, 34 with n. 20. N_5: ḫé-en-da-su, agrees with: T_{12}: ⌜ḫe⌝-⌜en⌝-da-[; Ur_5: ḫé-da-BAD. Apart from the ED_I sign tentatively read má, má is (partly) preserved in N_5 and T_{12}. It can now safely be read má, as predicted by Wilcke, 1978, 227, in view of SP 22 ii 25–26: ḫul-da íd-da má ḫé-en-da-su (Alster, *Proverbs* I, 262), where this line is quoted.

Lines 200–201 seem to quote from a magical incantation ritual in which a visible representation of the evil is sunk on a boat, and a waterskin is split in the desert with a similar purpose in mind. It is of considerable interest that both lines occur in ED_I.

Wilcke, 1978, 209, translates: "Dem Schlimmen soll auf dem Fluß das Schiff sinken!"

Line 201: ED_I: edin ^{kuš}A.EDIN dar. N_5:]-edin-na ^{kuš}ùmmu(A.EDIN.LÁ) ḫé-en-da-dar; Ur_5: -n]a ^{kuš}ùmmu ḫé-dar-dar. Cf. SP 22 ii 27–28: an-edin-na ^{kuš}ùmmu [ḫé]-dar-dar, where this line is quoted.

PSD A/1, 64–66, discusses the reading and meaning of A.EDIN.LÁ, and denies that A belongs to the logogram. The ED writing of A.EDIN.LÁ here appears as A.EDIN alone, but in my opinion there is no reason to question the reading of A.EDIN.LÁ as ùmmu(-d). That there is a graphic pun on an-edin-na in the ED_I version of this line (see PSD A/1, 66) does not indicate that the reading of the logogram is not ùmmu, because such texts abound in graphic puns, whether or not audible in pronunciation. To the evidence for the reading ùmmu can be added CT 58, 21: BM 23111, rev. 9: a $^{kuš\ um\text{-}mi}$ùmmu sír-ra dè-ma-an-dé.

Lines 201–202: The same set of phrases is quoted in SP 11.147–148 (Alster, *Proverbs* I, 197), quoted below. There are allusions to this proverb in a lexical list from Ebla, MEE 4, no. 78, quoted below under line 203. Cf. p. 246, also *Chap. 2.3: Couns. Wisdom*, 83: šeš šeš-za [dugud(?)-d]a(?)-bi hé-en-zu níŋ é-dù-ù-dè, "You should know how to honor your brother, it is something that builds houses"; further p. 232,

Instr. Ur-Ninurta 51.

Line 202: ED_I: šà ki-áŋ níŋ é dù-dù. N_5: níŋ é dù-dù-ù-dam; T_{12}: níŋ é dù-d[ù-; Ur_5: níŋ é dù(!)-dù-e; TCL:] é dù-dù-dè. Cf. SP 11.147: šà ki-áŋ níŋ dù-dù-dam (Alster, *Proverbs* I, 196); note -dam. Cf. also Krecher, quoted in the commentary on line 203 below.

Line 203: ED_I: šà ḫu(!)(text: RI)-gig níŋ é gul-gul. N_5: ḫul-gig, agrees with T_{11}: ḫ[ul, K_2: ḫul-gig, and TCL: šà ḫul-gig; T_{19}: šà ḫul gi_4(sic!), is the only text that writes gig phonetically; N_5: níŋ é gul-gul-lu-dam; T_{12}: níŋ é g[ul-; Ur_5: ní]ŋ é gul-gul-e; TCL:]-gul-lu-dè; Sch_5: epigraphically uncertain. Cf. SP 11.148: šà ḫul-gig níŋ é gul-gul-lu-dam (Alster, *Proverbs* I, 198).

An observation by Krecher, *Il Bilinguismo a Ebla* (Napoli, 1984), 162, is of considerable interest. He points to MEE 4, no. 78, which has ŠÀ.ḪUL and NÍG.É.GUL.GUL, with Eblaitic equivalents, of which the second includes a gloss, ŠÀ.ḪUL : *za-a-rúm /zaʾr-um/*, equivalent of Akk. *zêru*, "to hate"; NÍG.É GUL.GUL, is glossed NÍG É.GUL-*lum* : *ʾà-na*-LUM. Krecher sees these as "eine Replik der zweiten Hälfte eines sumerischen Sprichwörtes," i.e., our text lines 202–203, which, thus, seem to have been known in the school curriculum of Ebla in the middle of the third millennium B.C., albeit only indirectly attested.

Line 204: ED_I: nir-ŋál níŋ du_{10}-du_{10} gaba-ŋál me nam-nun-kam_4. N_5: nir-ŋál-e; T_{19} and TCL omit -e; T_{11}: nir-ŋál [can be both. N_5: níŋ-du_{12}(TUKU)-du_{12}, agrees with T_{19}: níŋ-TU[KU; T_{12}: -d]ug_4(?), or: du_{11}, phonetic for TUKU; Ur_5: -d]u_8-du_8, also phonetic for TUKU, but reduplicated = du_{12}-du_{12}, as also indicated by ED_I: du_{10}-du_{10}. N_5: gaba-ŋál me nam-nun(!)-na, agrees with TCL: gaba(!)-ŋ[ál me] nam-nun-na; Ur_5: gaba-ŋál me nam-nun-na-k[a](?), similar to ED_I: nam-nun-na-kam_4; Sch_5 seems to omit the line.

I tentatively understand the -e following nir-ŋál as a loc.-term. indicator, although -ra would be expected of a person, as in line 205. The use of the loc.-term. -e in connection with a noun of the personal class is rare or dubious; Edzard, *Sum. Grammar*, 44, provides a rare example, Gudea Cylinder A xiv 3: dumu-ni, which I do not acknowledge as a loc.-term., as it can simply be understood as a normal dative: < /dumu-ni-ra/ > dumu-ni(-ir). When used as here of a person, like saŋa-e, I suggest that it might rather point to the institution that he represents, somewhat on the verge of a non-personal construction, in our case: "to an authority." The parallel in SP 9 Sec. A 1–2 and parallels, both of which are introduced by nir-ŋál-e, is hardly coincidental: nir-ŋál-e a-na bí-in-dug_4 nu-sa_6, "as to an authority, whatever he spoke, it was not pleasant," etc.

Selz, WZKM 92 (2002) 174, translates "Autorität (NIR-ŋál), Besitz (níŋ-du_{10}-du_{10}// níŋ-tuk-tuk) und Stärke sind (nur AS) die Wesenseigenschaften der Aristokratie (me-nam-nun-kam_4)." The ETCSL translates, perhaps with a similar intent: "To have authority." Wilcke, 1978, 227, however, considers the -e "wohl eine -ed-Erweiterung," but this seems to be contradicted by his translation, quoted below. The -e is omitted in at least one Nippur source, T_{19}, besides TCL. Since it is attested only in N_5, it might be erroneous, but that would not make the line easier to translate.

níŋ-du_{12}-du_{12} is remarkably written phonetically as níŋ-du_{10}-du_{10}, in ED_I. Since this would be an unexpected example of *marû*-reduplication in ED_I, cf. *Chap. 1.9: Ḫamṭu-marû reduplication in ED*, and, since the writing with du_{10}(DÙG) is exceptional, I hesitate to follow Wilcke, 1978, 227, in assigning an infinite *marû*-form to the ED verb, but rather understand the reduplication as a plural indicator, "possessing many things," that is, "great riches"; this also applies to the SS verb. Line 208: dam na-an-du_{12}-du_{12}-e, however, represents the *marû* reduplication of TUKU, since the meaning clearly is "Don't choose a wife," not "many wives."

For gaba-ŋál me nam-nun-na, a parallel occurs in *Išmedagan and Enlil's Chariot* 34, edited by Civil, JAOS 88 (1968) 3–14, cf. also Klein, AcSum 11 (1989) 27–67: ⌜gaba⌝-ŋál-zu me maḫ nam-⌜nun⌝-[na-kam] gal-bi kíŋ-kíŋ-⌜ŋá⌝-[me-en], which the ETCSL translates "Your farings are the exalted princely divine powers sought out with great care." This indicates that gaba-ŋál is used in line 204 as a figurative image, taken from the context of a battle chariot, in which gaba-ŋál is seen as "powers" (*me*), whether visible or not, protecting the warrior leading the battle from his chariot.

The term me, which occurs in me-nam-nun-na,

is usually rendered with the untranslated Sumerian word *me* (then best in English as a collective plural in the singular) or it is translated "divine powers," following Falkenstein's "Göttliche Kräfte"; cf. Farber-Flügge, RlA 7, 607–613; Cavigneaux, JCS 30 (1978) 177–185, who stresses the relation to ní, "self"; cf. p. 375, n. 15, *Chap. 6.1: Three Ox-Drivers: Introd.* and comments on lines 90–92; Glassner, "Inanna et les me," in: M. de J. Ellis (ed.), *Nippur at the Centennial* (Philadelphia, 1992), 55–86; Selz, WZKM 92 (2002) 161, stresses that the list of the *me* includes deified offices and cultural functions ("vergöttliche Berufe"), such as deciding what is right and wrong; Lambert's remarks, "something like the Platonic ideas" (*Studies Emerton*, 35), are crucial, because he clearly envisioned a situation in which doubt is cast "on whether the gods do maintain justice in the universe" (p. 36). So the traditional rendering seems to fit well here. Yet, strictly speaking, "divine powers" is an unfortunate translation of a term that, ultimately, denotes something beyond the powers of the gods. "Supernatural" would be more fitting. Although it is a common opinion, *me* was not created by the gods; cf., e.g., Katz, *Image*, p. 177: "the *me*, created by the gods, are the source of all the properties of civilization and especially of the socio-political order." I rather see *me* as a kind of "raw material" of which the gods could avail themselves, to the extent they were able to acquire and handle it, mainly by means of magic. Apart from the ritual aspects, *me* often has two indistinguishable sides, both of which play a role in line 204: (1) a person's or a deity's "charisma" and (2) the visible aspect through which it becomes manifest, like the emblems, garments, or jewelry of a goddess.

In particular, the symbols of power, such as the "tablet of destinies," can be designated *me*; cf. Alster, "Ninurta and the Turtle: On Parodia Sacra in Sumerian Literature," forthcoming. In our line 205, the protruding protective shield that appears in front of a ruler leading his army into the battlefield from a chariot is a particularly suitable symbol of power, and me-nam-nun-na is perhaps best understood as "princely charismatic powers (or: insignia)." The protective shield can be seen on the representation of Ningirsu's battle chariot, and possibly that of Eannatum as well, although imperfectly preserved, on the *Stele of the Vultures*; cf. the large scale drawings in Alster: "Images and Text on the *Stele of the Vultures*," AfO 50 (2005, forthcoming). In line 204, however, gaba-ŋál refers to the persons who possess the qualities of such a shield, meaning "stout," or the like. It is undoubtedly the same meaning that appears in the name Lugal-gaba-ŋál, the singer of Gudam (cf. Alster, "Gudam," *Larsen AV*, 30, referring to line 13) and Gilgameš (cf. Cavigneaux and al-Rawi, RA 87 [1993], 118).

me-nam-nun-na, "the *me* of lordship" occurs, e.g., in *Enmerkar and the Lord of Aratta* 142: kur-gal me-nam-nun-na-ka; and 340: gidru-ŋá úr-bi me nam-nun-na-ka. In both cases a translation like "princely charismatic powers/insignia" would fit. nam-nun-na is probably meant as the kind of authority that stems from the leader's personal authority, his "charisma."

That me nam-nun-na in line 204 is a genitive construction appears from the ED_1 var.: -kam_4. This shows that such an ending may, in fact, disappear in the writing of SS texts, not least in recurring standardized expressions, but note that the genitive /-ak/ seems to be present in Ur_5: -ka. It is less likely that gaba-ŋál-me-nam-nun-na in this case should be regarded as a non-genitival "Bahuvrihi-Konstruktion: «Eine Brustwehr, die die me der Fürstlichkeit besitzt»" (so Wilcke, 1978, 227).

Wilcke, 1978, 209, translates: "Der Erwerb von Ansehen und Eigentum bedeutet eine Brustwehr für die *me* des Fürstentums," followed by Römer, 1990, 62: "Ansehen (und) Besitz zu erwerben, (ist) eine Brustwehr der «göttlichen Kräften» *de*[*s*] Fürstentums." In both cases du_{12}-du_{12} seems to have been understood as a verbal noun, "erwerben," with both nir-ŋál and níŋ as common objects. This makes good sense, but it contradicts the interpretation of the -e following nir-ŋál as /ed/ mentioned above. The ETCSL: "To have authority, to have possessions and to be steadfast are princely divine powers" avoids this difficulty, taking gaba-ŋál is as an undeclined compound verbal noun, "steadfast," lit., "(for whom) a breast is present." This may hit the mark well, although it does not openly reflect the *Išme-Dagan* parallel cited above. A pun on both possibilities may well be intended; cf. the similarly ambiguous gú – lá in line 205.

Line 205: ED_I: gaba-ŋál gú ḫé-ŋál. N_5: ni]r-ŋál-ra gú ḫé-en-ne-ni-ŋál, agrees with TCL: nir-ŋál-ra gú ḫé-en-ne-ni-ŋál(!); Ur_5: g]ú ḫé-ne-ni-⸢x⸣; Sch_5 is epigraphically uncertain. Cf. also Addendum p. 403.

The ED_I variant gaba-ŋál for nir-ŋál is best explained as a scribal error, caused by the presence of the same signs in the preceding line. Cf. ED_I, lines 206, where KA likewise seems to be a scribal error, and 271: one šà erroneously copied as a dittography of the other.

The verbal prefix chain -en-ne- indicates a personal plural dative. gú – ŋál can be understood as a compound verb, meaning "to submit," which occurs as a variant of gú – ak in line 13. Here the literal meaning of gú – lá, "to bend the neck" (scl. in submission to someone)," comes to light, exemplifying a pattern of ambiguity often embedded in Sumerian compound verbs, which for the same reason at times can be very difficult to translate. Wilcke, 1978, 209, translates "Den Angesehenen sei der Nacken geboten!"

Line 206: ED_I: á-tuku KA-zu_5 ḫé-lá. N_5: ní-zu ḫé-en-ne-ši-lá, with -ši- probably attracted from line 207; Ur_5: n]í-zu ḫé:ni:ne-lá, with ni and ne reversed by scribal error; in TCL: ní-zu ḫé-en-ne-al(?)-al, the copy is correct according to J. Dahl's collation. Wilcke, 1978, 227, suggests: "silbische Aussprengung von *ḫennealal, i.e., ḫé-en-ne(-a)-lal"; Sch_5: [...] ⸢x⸣ ní-zu ḫé-ga(? hardly bi)-ni(?)-lá(?) is epigraphically uncertain, but it is noteworthy that the reading of TCL may have been similar.

Like in line 205, á-tuku is a collective personal plural, but with the verb governing the terminative. I, therefore, translate ní-zu, as the subject of lá, "yourself should be prostrated." This is different from ní-zu ... [pe]-el-lá, which occurs in line 35. Alternatively lá is = *maṭû*, "don't diminish yourself."

It is remarkable that ED_I has KA-zu_5 instead of ní-zu, but I do not accept Wilcke's interpretation "«deine Worte» (oder «dein Mund») für «du selbst»." I rather suggest that KA, in fact, is an early phonetic writing or a mistake for ní, perhaps through (i)ni(m). Cf. the unusual ED_I writing níŋ-zu, for ní-zu in line 35. Cf. p. 217, *Chap. 1.9: Use of special ED signs*. It is, in fact, not unlikely that a scribal error has occurred in ED_I, cf. the comments on line 205.

Römer, 1990, 63, 207a, comments that ní-zu – lá might stand for ní ki-šè lá, cf. CAD Q, 44, *qadādu*, but there is no need not to take the text as it stands in this case.

Line 207: ED_I: lú-ḫul-ŋál ḫé-⸢x⸣. N_5: dumu-$ŋu_{10}$, agrees with T_{11}: dumu-ŋ[u_{10}; TCL: dumu (not lugal!)-$ŋu_{10}$, collated by J. Dahl. N_5: lú-ḫul-ŋál-ra, agrees with Sch_5: ŋá]l-la-ra and TCL: lú-ḫul-la-ra, = ḫul-<ŋál>-la-ra, or miscopy for ŋál(!)-ra; Ur_5:]-ḫul-úr; suggesting $ḫulu_x$-úr; cf. the comments on line 194. N_5: ḫé-en-ne-ši-ŋál-le; Ur_5: ḫé-en-ši-ŋál; TCL: ḫé-en-ne-ši-⸢x⸣ (coll. Dahl); Sch_5: ⸢ḫé-em⸣-ši-ŋ[ál-l]e. This source remarkably in part shares the variant [lú-ḫul-ŋá]l-la-ra with TCL.

Also here lú-ḫul-ŋál is a collective plural, lit., "you will be present against the evil ones." Wilcke, 1978, 209, translates "Mein Kind, dann wirst du gegenüber bösen Menschen bestehen!" ETCSL: "My son, you will then survive (?) against the wicked."

Lines 208–211: This sequence has an interesting parallel in *Instructions of Šūpē-amēli*, Spruch III.iv in Dietrich's edition, UF 23 (1991) 38–65, here quoted from Kämmerer, 1998, 192–193 (U = Ugarit source; B and E = Emar sources, cf. ibid., p. 177, n. 444):

U r a 10	*e ta-šá-am alpa* [*ša*] ⸢*di-ša-ti*⸣
B v i 12	[*e ta-ša-am*] *alpa* [*š*]*a dì-i-ša-a*-⸢*ti*⸣
U r a	*e ta-ḫu-uz*[11] *ardata ina* ⸢*i*(?)⸣-[*še-en-ni*]
B v 13	[*a ta-ḫu-uz*] *ardata i-na i*-[*še*]-*en-ni*
E	[...] *idammiq*(SIG_5)
U r a	*alpu*(?) [*šu-ú*(?)] *idammiq*(SIG_5) *i*(!)-*na*(!) *ši-i-ma-ni*
B v i 14	[...] ⸢*i*⸣-*da-mì-i*[*q*][15] [*i-na*] *Simāni*(ITI. SI]G_5(!?))
E f 69	*ardata*([MÍ.K]I.SIKIL!) [*ši*(?)-*i la-ba-ab-ša-at-ma*][70] *lu-ba-r*[*a*] *s*[*i-i*]*m*-[*te-ma*]
E c 2	[...] ⸢*x*⸣ *x*
U r a 12	*ardata*(MÍ.KI.⸢SIKIL⸣) ⸢*ši*(?)⸣-[*i*] [*la-ab-ša-at*]-⸢*ma*⸣ [*lu-ba*]-⸢*ar-tá*⸣ *si-im-te-ma*
B v i 16	*ardata* ([MÍ.KI.SIK]IL.[L]A) [*ši*(?)]-*i la-ab-ša-at-ma lu-ba-ra*
17	[*si-im-te-ma*]
E f	[*qe-re-eb ša-at-t*]*i šamnū*(Ì.ḪI.A)[71] [*a-ia ṣ*]*u-up-pu-ú*
E c	[*qe-re-eb ša-at-ti*] *šamnū*(Ì.ḪI.A)
E g	⸢*x*⸣-[...]
U r a 13	*qe-r*[*e-e*]*b* [*ša-at-t*]*i šamnū*(Ì) *ṭābū*(DÙG. ⸢GA⸣) *ḫubuttati*(EŠ.DÉ.A)
14	⸢*a*⸣-*i*[*a*] *ṣu-p*[*u*]-⸢*ú*⸣

B vi [*qe-re-eb ša-at-ti*] *ša-am-n*[*u*] *ṭābū*(DUG.GA(?)) [*ḫu-bu*]*-u-tá-tù*
18 *e*(?) [*ṣ*]*u*(!)*-i-pu*

"Kaufe nicht ein Rind (in der Zeit) des Frühlingsgraswuchses, nimm kein 'spätes Mädchen' in der Festzeit!
[(Denn) jenes Rind] ist gut (bei der Sache) im Frühlingsmonat, jenes 'spätes Mädchen' ist mit einem festtaggemäßen Prachtgewand bekleidet!
Mitten im Jahr(?) ist gewiß kein gutes Öl (erworben) aus einem zinslosen Darlehen mehr aufgetragen!"

It is tempting to suggest that the sequence was composed with *The Instructions of Šuruppak* in mind, especially since line 17 contains a similar parallel. Cf. the comments on line 17, p. 41, *Chap. 1.1: Other didactic wisdom compositions from later Mesop. sources.*

Line 208: N_5: ezem-⌜ma⌝-ka dam na-an-dù-dù-e, dù-dù phonetic for du_{12}-du_{12}; Ur_5: -k]a dam na-ba-du_{12}-du_{12}; TCL: ezem-ma-kam dam(!) na-an-du_{12}-du_{12}; Sch_5: ⌜ezem⌝-ma-ka dam na-⌜x⌝(looks like UD)-⌜x⌝(looks like en, but too long).

Line 208 is paralleled in SP 11.150: ezem-ma-kam dam na-an-du_{12}-du_{12}-e-še (Alster, *Proverbs* I, 196); only SP 11.150 has the -e-še addition, which shows that this was considered a quotation (scl. of a proverb). For the *marû* or plural reduplication of TUKU, cf. line 204: na-an-du_{12}-du_{12}-e. I understand du_{12}-e as the 2nd person <...-dù-en. ezem-ma-ka(m) is a free genitive without a regens, lit., "it is (characteristic) of a festival (that) ...." Cf. the comments on p. 210, *The genitive of characteristics.*

Line 209: The verb ḫuŋ(-ŋá) in lines 209–211 was first correctly explained by Wilcke, 1978, 227–228, as a *ḫamṭu*-participle with -àm, corresponding to *agāru*, "to hire." šà-ga and bar-ra are both in the locative, which excludes the well-known šà/bar ḫuŋ = *nâḫu*, "calm down." Strictly speaking, ḫuŋ-ŋá means "hired" here, but I allow myself to translate "borrowed," which provides a nice parallel to the well-known proverbial expression "to stunt in borrowed plumes" (from Aesop: the *Fable of the Jackdaw*) and conforms nicely to the *Šūpē-amēli* parallel cited under lines 208–211 above. PSD B, 107, however, translates "(with) a quiet hearth, a quiet mood," etc., following Alster, 1974.

I understand the locatives šà-ga and bar-ra in line 209 slightly differently from Wilcke. Although šà-ga and bar-ra are both in the locative and the verbs are without any apparent subject, there is no need to assume a change of subject from the girl to her clothes, etc., in lines 210–211. The subject rather stays the same in the whole sequence, but line 209 can be understood as an exemplification of a frequent Sumerian stylistic feature, that is, the adding parallelism, which also occurs in lines 5–7 (and parallels), as well as in lines 69–72. This implies that the subject is not mentioned in the first line of the sequence, but has to be understood from its more complete occurrences in the following lines. We can, thus, safely translate: "Inwardly it is (all, scl. her clothes and jewelry) borrowed, outwardly it is (all) borrowed." Wilcke, 1978, 209, however, translates lines 209–211 "Innen ist sie geliehen; außen ist sie geliehen. Das Silberschmuck ist geliehen; die Edelsteine sind geliehen; das Wollkleid ist geliehen; das Leinengewand ist geliehen," commenting "Das Innere entspricht das Äußeren." The ETCSL translates "Her inside is illusory(?); her outside is illusory," which is unnecessarily inaccurate, since the following verbs are translated "borrowed."

Line 210: N_5: [kù-à]m za ḫuŋ-ŋá-ám za ḫuŋ-ŋá-àm(sic!), by error caused by dittography; Ur_5: [...] ⌜x⌝ DUB ḫuŋ-ŋá-àm (Wilcke: na_4.n]ír!, i.e., ZA+G]UL); TCL: kù ḫuŋ-ŋá-àm za-gìn ḫuŋ-ŋá-àm. Sch_5: ([x]) kù ⌜huŋ⌝(?)-ŋá-àm ([...]?) ⌜za⌝(?)-gìn huŋ-ŋá-àm seems to confirm the reconstruction of the main text, but the variant of Ur_5 cannot be fully reconstructed.

A parallel in SP 4.18: [túg ḫuŋ-ŋ]á-àm gada ḫuŋ-ŋá-àm za ḫuŋ-ŋá-à]m šu ḫé-ma-ŋál, "Let there be borrowed [clothes], borrowed lines, and borrowed precious stones in my hand," indicates that a proverbial expression is, indeed, involved. This would fit as a satirical utterance of a woman who "stunts in borrowed clothes."

Line 211: N_5:]-un(?)-ŋá-àm, a phonetic writing for ḫuŋ-ŋá-àm, but note un = ùŋ, for */ḫuŋ/; Ur_5: z]a-gìn ḫuŋ-ŋá-àm; TCL: NÍGIN (so apparently according to J. Dahl's collation; read *túg(?)) ḫuŋ-ŋá-àm gada(possible according to J. Dahl's collation; copy: PA) ḫuŋ-ŋá-àm. The reconstruction túg(?) ḫuŋ-ŋá-àm gada(?) ḫuŋ-ŋá-àm is, thus, not beyond doubt.

At least Ur$_5$ had a different text, and there may have been other variants caused by inversion of the lines. Sch$_5$ seems to have omitted the second part of the line.

Line 212: N$_5$: -a]n-da(?)-sá; Ur$_5$:]-mu-un-da-sá-a; Sch$_5$ (rev. 1): [...] ⸢lú⸣ ta ⸢mu⸣(?)-⸢x⸣(looks like ra)-sá, seems to belong here, but remains uncertain. The beginning of the line is not preserved, but it is tempting to restore dumu-ŋu$_{10}$ from line 102: lú-tur-ŋu$_{10}$ níŋ nu-mu-um-da-sá. Regrettably not enough of the text is preserved to suggest a restoration based on the *Šūpē-amēli* parallel cited above. This might have been crucial in showing a closer relationship between the two texts.

Line 213: ED$_I$: ⸢gud⸣ na-MUNŠUB ⸢gud⸣ e-KAL, seems related, but is not an exact parallel to line 213. The SS textual evidence is weak: UM$_2$: (traces); C$_2$: gud [...] ní-ŋ[ál], perhaps with some missing sign following gud; N$_5$: [... na]-⸢an⸣-ni-sa$_{10}$-sa$_{10}$.

ní-ŋál is "frightening, awe-inspiring," as in *Gilgameš and Huwawa* 118: ní ì-ŋál ní ì-ŋál gi$_4$-a, "There will be terror, turn back!"

Line 214: ED$_I$: gud-lul na-ŠÈ-ŠÈ KA LUM GABA-kam$_4$, may not belong here, but is at least related. The SS textual evidence is weak: UM$_2$: [gud-lul]-la na-ab-s[a$_{10}$-...]; C$_2$: gud-l[ul-l]a na-[s]a$_{10}$-sa$_{10}$ é [.

PSD B, 202, translates "Do not buy a ferocious bull—breaking (a hole) in the stall, it ...," understanding bùr as a verb, "to make a hole."

The second part of the line, é-tùr gul(?)-l[a-àm], means with a reasonable degree of certainty "(it would mean) a destroyed pen," or similar; cf. the similar construction in lines 15–16; 18.

ED$_I$ na-ŠÈ-ŠÈ may be na-ḫuŋ-ḫuŋ, from *agāru*, "don't hire," with plural reduplication; cf. the comments on line 209. The second part of the line in ED$_I$ contains a genitive, but the implication remains obscure.

Line 215: ED$_I$: munus-z[i (x)] gán ⸢x⸣, clearly has gán, not é. The end of the line is not preserved in any SS source. Of the only two available sources, UM$_2$, and C$_2$, both clearly seem to have gán, not é. Cf. the copies in pl. 3: UM 29-13-326 ii 4, gán, clearly distinguishable from é in the preceding line; pl. 5: CBS 13107 obv. 3: probably gán, rather than é. Cf. the photographs on pls. 19 and 23.

A probable reconstruction, lú ši-i[n-ŋá-ŋá], is based on *Nanše Hymn* 62–63, cf. Heimpel, JCS 33 (1981) 84: munus-zi gán-zi-šè lú ši-in-ŋá-ŋá; munus-zi gán-zi-šè lú mu-un-ŋar-ra-ta, which Wilcke, 1978, 228, translates "Sie (= Nanše) läßt den Mann eine tüchtige Frau als fruchtbares Feld anlegen; nachdem der Mann eine tüchtige Frau als fruchtbares Feld angelegt hat, ..." The ETCSL, however, reads é instead of gán, and translates: "(The lady = Nanše) acting as a good woman for a good household, is to make the appointments; after she, acting as a good woman for a good household, has made the appointments"; cf. the similar -šè in line 55. It is, of course, tempting to read gán in both texts.

Like Wilcke, 1978, 228, I now take gán as primary both in ED$_I$ and SS, meaning "a man [installs] a good woman for a good field (or: as a good field)."

Römer, 1990, 63, partly following Wilcke, translates "Eine zuverlässige Frau [wird] einen Mann als wohlbestelltes *Feld* [anlegen]," commenting (n. 216 a) that line 215 still belongs to the preceding sequence, lines 208–212, "die noch zum Abschnitt über das Heiraten ... zu gehören scheint." Note, however, that the man (lú) is not the subject in Wilcke's translation.

It is regrettably not possible to restore the two entries that precede SS 215 in ED$_I$ (obv v 3–4), but the whole sequence seems not to pertain directly to the theme of SS lines 208–212. The essential theme that links these lines together is not marriage, but avoiding acquiring animals at a time when they look better than they really are. This is then linked to choosing a wife under similar circumstances. At least two preceding entries in ED$_I$ (obv. v 1–2) deal with animals; cf. the full reconstruction p. 179.

Line 216: UM$_2$: na-an-[, agrees with C$_2$: n[a]-a[n]-[; T$_{20}$: na-[a]b-sa$_{10}$-sa$_{10}$.

For u$_4$-buru$_{14}$-ka, cf. line 131: u$_4$-buru$_{14}$-šè.

Line 217: UM$_2$: anše LA KA anše-da i[m-, KA for gu$_7$; C$_2$: anše LA gu$_7$ anše-da im-[; T$_{20}$:]-da ⸢im⸣-[. The end of the line is not preserved in any duplicate.

No translation of our LA has so far been suggested. LA can be šika, "potsherd," which occurs in SP 1.166; SP 2.101: ur šika-da ra, "a dog chased away with potsherds." This also occurs in *Lament. Destr. Ur* 192: šika bar$_7$-bar$_7$-re-da saḫar im-da-tab-tab ùŋ-e še àm-ša$_4$, which the ETCSL translates: "The scorching potsherds made the dust glow (?)—the people groan"; also line 210; this would hardly help here, where šika must be something that can be eaten, at least by an animal. The context suggests that it is something that affects the temper or sexual behavior of the animal. Or, maybe, after all, šika here denotes the poorest kind of food, like "refuse," to which an animal could be exposed? The ETCSL translates "A donkey that eats ... will ... with another donkey."

Line 218: There are no variants.

For references for gú-tar – lá, see Sjöberg, TCS 3, 111. In *Inanna's Descent* 320 it is "hairdresser," or similar, with lá meaning "to bind," but here lá obviously means to "hang the head." gú-tar is *kutallu*, for which see CAD K, 603, "back of the head."

Line 218, in which a vicious donkey openly shows hostility by hanging its head, is contrasted by line 219, according to which a liar conceals his intent in a less conspicuous way.

Line 219: UM_2: lú-lul-e; C_2: lú-lul-la, agrees with K_I: lú-lul-la. UM_2: zag-si, agrees with C_2: zag-si, and K_I: zag-si; T_{20}: še-si, is either a phonetic writing for zag-si or a mistake.

lú-lul-e likewise occurs in lines 67 and 136. The context of both lines 136 and 219 may favor a translation such as hypocrite, rather than liar.

References for zag-si, a part of the body, can be found in Sjöberg, *Orientalia* 39 (1970) 94. As pointed out by Römer, 1990, 66, zag-si in line 219 may well be meant as a contrast to gú-tar, "Rücken, Hinterkopf," in line 218; cf. his n. 220 on p. 64, who refers to Edzard, AfO 19 (1959–60) 20 with n. 53.

Line 220: ED_I: munus-bar-[š]u šè-ŋál / [x x x]-šè du. In this case the ED version differs from the SS version, which has no verbal prefix in front of ŋál. UM_2: é dúr-bi-šè, agrees with C_2: é dúr-bi-šè, and K_I: d]úr-bi-šè; T_{20}: é dúr-bi is the only text that omits -šè.

(munus) bar-šu-ŋál = *sikiltu*, "possession, acquisition." PSD B, 129–130, understands bar-šu-ŋál as a person who "performed services connected with barbering or cosmetic procedures, childbirth, and funerary functions."

The implication has been dealt with in detail by Wilcke: "Vom Verhätnis der Geschlechter im Alten Mesopotamien: «Eine Frau mit Vermögen richtet das Haus zugrunde»," in: I. Nagelschmidt (ed.), *Frauenforscherinnen stellen sich vor, Leipziger Studien zur Frauen- und Geschlechtsforschung* (Leipzig, 2000), 351–383.

Line 221: ED_I: [x] kú]run naŋ-naŋ gu[ru_7] šè-LAGAB-LAGAB: unusual ED phonetic writing for su-su. UM_2: naŋ-naŋ-e, agrees with C_2:] naŋ-naŋ-e, and T_{13}: naŋ-naŋ-[; only K_I: n]a-an-ak-ak, has what seems to be a phonetic or misunderstood unexpected writing for naŋ-naŋ-e. UM_2: im-su-su-su, with unusual triplication of su, seems to agree with C_2, and T_{20}; K_I: i]m-su-su. For the triplication of verbs, cf. lines 226: 228; Edzard, *Sum. Grammar*, p. 81.

The /guru/ : /buru/ variation in ED_I: gu[ru_7] versus SS: $buru_{14}$ is an example of the labiovelar gb, or similar, treated by Civil, JNES 32 (1973) 57–61: "From Enki's Headaches to Phonology"; Edzard, *Sum. Grammar*, 14–21, does not include this type in his list of Sum. consonants, but it is well attested, and at least deserves to be considered as more than free variants. That in this case the ED source has a velar, but the SS text a labial consonantal stop might suggest a historical development in which the velar type gradually was replaced by a labial type, but it is too early to draw any conclusions from this case alone.

Line 222: UM_2: munus-šu-ḫa $^{ŋiš}kun_5$ lú min-e da nu-sá, agrees with C_2:] $^{ŋiš}kun_5$ [l]ú min-e da nu-[, and T_{13}: munus-šu-ḫa ^{ŋiš}k[un_5; T_{20}:] TUR-(LU erased)-ÉŠ (correction for intended kun_5) [... d]a nu-sá. kun_5 = TUR.ŠÈ. Note that the indented line starts before da both in UM_2 and T_{20}.

I tentatively understand the verb as an unknown compound da – sá, tentatively meaning "to lean the side (in order to align)." This may be compared to Gudea *Cylinder B* iii 11–12: é-ninnu ^{d}suen ù-tu-da saŋ im-ma-da-ab-sá, "Eninnu «aligned the top» with the new-born Suen." In contrast to previous attempts, I now prefer to base this on the literal translation, "two men do not lean(? da – sá?) a side toward(? = *-e/-da or similar)," scl. the ladder. The two men are the subject of a relative construction in which kun_5 is a virtual dimensional object; cf. below.

Why not lú min-ne-ne? I understand lú min-e as a collective plural in the singular, meaning "a couple of men"; cf. the singular use of lú, "man/men," mentioned in the commentary to line 180. Cf. also lines 205–206.

The construction of line 222 is best explained as a subject, munus-šu-ḫa, followed by a predicate, consisting of a relative sentence construction headed by $\star^{\eta i \check{s}}$kun$_5$(-àm); cf. *Chap. 1.9: Split sentence construction.* This is then followed by an attributive verbal sentence construction, which explains why there is no dimensional marker following $^{\eta i \check{s}}$kun$_5$. The disappearance of an -⋆àm following kun$_5$ can otherwise be explained by assuming that kun$_5$ had a long reading ending in a vowel, like ⋆/kunu/(-um). For $^{\eta i \check{s}}$kun$_5$ (= TUR.ŠÈ) = *simmiltu*, "ladder, stair, stair of a house, stepladder," see CAD S, 273–275.

The intent seems to be that a fisherwoman is so busy meddling into everyone's affairs, that she is compared to a ladder that not even a couple of men can make stand upright. This seems to fit the continuation in the following line.

Otherwise ladders occur as tools used to break into houses, e.g., *Curse of Agade* 106; cf. Falkenstein, ZA 57 (1965) 95. The only text that seems to connect a fisherwoman with a ladder is *Dialogue* 5 (*Two Women*) 31–33, quoted by Alster, 1974, 110, and Wilcke, 1978, 229, but inconclusive.

Line 223: UM$_2$: é-a nim-gim mi-ni-ib-dal-dal-en, is the only preserved text that has -en; C$_2$: ni]m-gim mi-ni-íb-dal-[; T$_{20}$:]-ni-ib-dal-dal-e; K$_I$:] mi-ni-ib-dal-dal; I$_{14}$: -r]a(?) (apparently does not belong here).

The 2nd person -en, which occurs only in UM$_2$, might reflect either that a saying in the 2nd person is quoted, which is likely in view of the parallel quoted below (cf. lines 129; 176) or that the recital of the text in the 2nd person before a "pupil" may occasionally have influenced the sources. Cf. p. 291, *Chap. 1.10: The second person....* A third possibility is to understand line 223 as indicating that "you" make it, that is, the fisherwoman's ladder (l. 222), fly like a fly. Since the verb is transitive and requires an object, this is the solution I tentatively prefer.

Flying like a fly into all houses is a well-attested image. The basic image occurs in *Inanna's Descent* 394–403 and the *Eršemma* CT 19, no. 19; CT 58, no. 11 (BM 109167); it is used to describe busy behavior in *Inanna-Ninegalla Hymn* 199–200: [é]-⌜e⌝-a in-ku$_4$-ku$_4$-dè-en [e-sír]-e-sír-ra gú mu-un-gíd-gíd-dè-en; *Lugalbanda in Hurrumkurra* 412–413.

Line 224: UM$_2$: ème(SAL.ANŠE) sila-a inim ì-šid-e, agrees with the preserved parts of C$_2$, T$_{13}$: è[me, and K$_I$; I$_{14}$: -r]a(?)-šid(? or: gù ì-r]a)-ra), seems to have had a different text.

inim šid occurs also in line 103, for which see the comments on line 103. It seems, in fact, to be meant ironically here, "the female ass recites words (well)," where, ultimately, a braying ass stands for bad female behavior. Cf. the comments on line 225.

Line 225: UM$_2$: SAL.ŠAḪ sila-a dumu-ni-ra ga mu-ni-ib-gu$_7$-e, agrees with the preserved parts of C$_2$, N$_7$, T$_{20}$, and I$_{14}$; only K$_I$ has ...-í]b-gu$_7$-e.

The personal suffix, dumu-ni-ra, "her young," not ⋆-bi-ra/e, shows that the line, although describing an animal, is intended as a description of a woman who behaves like that animal; cf. the comments on line 224.

Line 226: UM$_2$: munus-KA-ḪAR-ak KA×LI gi$_4$-gi$_4$-dam; N$_7$:]-⌜gi$_4$-gi$_4$⌝-da; T$_{20}$: -g]i$_4$-g[i$_4$; I$_{14}$ is the only preserved text that has the triple reduplication gi$_4$-gi$_4$-gi$_4$-da; K$_I$: ...-g]i$_4$-dè, is the only text that has -dè. For the triple reduplication of the verb, cf. lines 221; 228, and the literature quoted in the commentary on line 221.

The meaning of lines 226–227 has basically been clarified by Wilcke, 1978, 232, in his additional note, who suggests that here KA.ḪAR – ak is "durchboren mit einer Spindel" (zú-ur$_5$ – ak); cf. AHw 832, *parāṣu* I. Cf. further the discussion of KA.ḪAR in the commentary on line 49.

Line 227: There are no variants.

ur$_5$-ra, here translated "on which she was hurt," seems to be elliptical for zú-ur$_5$ – ak, which occurs in the preceding line.

Line 228: UM$_2$: i-in-ku$_4$-ku$_4$-k[u$_4$; I$_{14}$: i-ni-in-ku$_4$-ku$_4$, agrees with N$_7$:]-ni-in-ku$_4$-ku$_4$; K$_I$: i-ni-ku$_4$-[ku$_4$]-ku$_4$. Cf. the parallel quoted under line 223.

Line 229: UM$_2$: gú mu-un-⌜x⌝-[...]; K$_I$: gú mu-un-⌜gi⌝-gi-dè, clearly phonetic for gíd-gíd(-i)-dè, which, however, is not preserved in any source. Cf. the parallel quoted under line 223.

For gú – gíd cf. AHw 1130, *šaḫāṭu* I, Gtn *šitaḫḫuṭu* = gu$_4$(-ud)-gu$_4$-ud, "herumspringen."

Lines 230–240: The available sources are too imperfectly preserved for a complete reconstruction of the text. The comments are kept to a minimum.

Line 230: UM$_2$: [...] ⌜x⌝ i(?)-im(?)-me im-d[ug$_4$

...]; T_{19}: á(or: da) ùr-ra [...]; K_1: ⸢da⸣ ⸢ùr⸣(?)-ra im-me im-me è-è; coll. Taylor: the first sign is da, followed probably by ùr; the last sign is dè/bí. These are presumably phonetic writings for é-ùr-ra, "roof." Cf. AHw 1434, *ūru* = (^{ĝiš})ùr, "Dach."

Römer, 1990, 64, translates "[*ne*]*ben dem Dache* ruft sie, ruft: «Ziehe sie heraus!»," commenting (n. 231 a) "Was besagt das genau?" I understand this simply as the woman calling from the roofs of the houses, where people were used to sleeping in the hot season. Römer further comments "auf die Spindel zu beziehen, die eine normal reagierende Frau selbst herauszogen hätte."

Line 231: T_{19}: bàd-si b[àd-; K_1: bàd-si(! text: ni) bàd-si-a igi mu-ši-⸢x⸣-íl-íl(?)-e.

Line 232: T_{19}: ki du_{14}-d[a(?); K_1: ki du_{14}-dè ŋál-la-šè zi im-x-[x(-x)]-RI, coll. Taylor.

"Pants," lit. translation: "She breathes," suggested restoration from zi – pa-an, which occurs in line 130, but not confirmed by Taylor's collation.

Line 233: T_{19}: ki mu-šub-[; K_1: ki mu ⸢x⸣ [š]ub-ba á-za [x x] ⸢x⸣ im-[x].

Line 234: T_{19}: KA ere [...]; K_1: zi ⸢x⸣-ge_4-eš mu-un-ne(?)-pà ši-mi-ni-dug_4.

Line 235: The reconstruction *[inim-di]ri(? text: ...-k]e_4) šà-ḫul-gig ⸢du_{12}⸣-⸢du_{12}⸣, is based on ED_1 rev. v 3: inim-diri bu-bu_7(KU) šà ḫu-gig šè-du_8-du_8. The first part of the line is preserved in T_{19}, which has bar-sud. This cannot be harmonized with the proposed reconstruction. If the reconstruction based on ED_1 is justified, the missing signs before šà might be the rest of [inim-diri] (according to J. Taylor's collation, the ke_4 in K_1 is an erasure), whereas T_{19} would belong to a different line. Already Wilcke, 1978, 230, connected ED_1 rev. v 3 with line 138: inim-diri ù-bu-bu-ul ú-libiš-gig-ga-àm, suggesting the reading bu-bul_x for BU.DÚR in ED_1; cf. the comments on lines 138 and 265.

If taken as the primary verb, du_{12}-du_{12} seems to be a reduplicated form of TUKU or, if dug_8-dug_8 is taken as primary, it may be the same verb as occurs in the expression ḫi-li – du_8-du_8, "full of allure," for which see Sefati, *Love Songs*, 175, and the references mentioned there.

Line 236: K_1: [x x x] ⸢x⸣ lum-lam_x(LUM) mi-ni-ib-za; T_{19}: ⸢dumu-$ŋu_{10}$⸣ [...]; Ur_6: lum-lum ḫé-ni-[...] (rev. i' 2 has been assigned line number 242 below, but may belongs here?).

lum-lam_x (LUM) mi-ni-ib-za apparently belongs to the alternating verb of the u-a types last treated by Black, *Wilcke FS*, 35–52.

Line 238: T_{19}: ⸢ki(?)/šà(?)⸣ [...]; K_1: [...] a ⸢x⸣ ⸢x⸣ in-TAR; Ur_6: ki-a naŋ-e [...] (rev. i' 1, has been assigned line number 241 below, but may belong here?).

Line 239: Only fragment: K_1: [...]-ná.

Line 240: The reconstruction depends on whether two fragments can correctly be connected: UM_2: (traces); C_2: (traces); K_1: [...]-DU. In what follows two fragments may be placed: T_{19}, left edge; T_{13}, rev.

Line 241–248: It is assumed that Ur_6 rev. i' belongs here, cf. Alster, *N.A.B.U.* 1999, 88D (p. 89). If this is not the case, it seems impossible to place it in the existing text reconstruction, but Ur_6 may represent a version that differed considerably from the known text.

Line 243: in-šè is reminiscent of the phraseology of the disputations.

Line 244: u_4-min-šè, "for a second day."

Line 246: tu-ra dùg-ga-a-ni [x?], "the ill (person), his recovery ..." seems to link with line 247: nam-⸢gig⸣-ga, "disease." There are not many proverbs dealing with diseases, but cf. SP 27.1: šà níŋ-tuku tu-ra-àm an-t[u(?) x (x)] / šà diri tu-ra-àm an-t[u x (x)], "a pregnant(?) womb(?) that is ill, [is] ill (indeed). An exceedingly (pregnant) womb is (exceedingly) ill [indeed]" (Alster, *Proverbs* I, 282).

Line 247: nam-⸢gig-ga⸣-àm ⸢im⸣-[x] / du_{14} nam-mú-m[ú-dè] / NI IM ni [...], seems related to line 35: du_{14} nam-[mú-m]ú-dè ní-zu na-an-[pe]-el-lá, but the sentence structure is different in that here the second part is not a motivation clause.

Lines 250ff.: It is not possible to establish a link between line 248 = the end of Ur_6 rev. i', and 250 = UM_2: rev. i beginning. There may have been a limited number of missing lines between them.

Line 250: The first sign in C_2: ⸢x⸣ looks like in, or similar; in UM_2 the beginning reads: ⸢x⸣ (dam, or mi, or similar) [x (x)] ⸢x⸣ (like lugal) [, followed by space for a half broken line.

Line 251: UM_2: šà-ḫúl-la i-im-diri-g[e, agrees with C_2: šà-[...] ⸢x⸣ [.

Line 252: UM_2: níŋ-nam nu-kal zi ku_7-ku_7-da, agrees with; C_2: níŋ-nam nu-kal ⸢x⸣ [; BM_2: (traces of one sign).

This is the opening line of the composition *Nothing Is of Value*, which occurs in at least four versions, treated in *Chap. 3.1–2*. For the interpretation and implication of the line, see further p. 295, *Chap. 3.3: Attempt at a new interpretation of The Ballade of Early Rulers.*

Line 253: UM_2: níŋ nam-kal-kal-en níŋ-e me-kal-kal; the first part agrees with N 2715: [...]-⌜kal-en⌝ (not preserved in the other duplicates), but N 2715 continues: níŋ-⌜e⌝ m[u-; this agrees with C_3: níŋ-e mu-e-[. This line does not occur in any of the known fragments of *Nothing Is Precious.*

The apparent 2nd person verbal form me-kal-kal can be explained by means of an observation by Attinger, 1993, 163–167; also ZA 75 (1995) 161–178; now also Edzard, *Sum. Grammar*, p. 85. Attinger has shown that the absolute 1st and 2nd personal element -en can occur before the root in *marû* transitive verbs. me-kal-kal can, therefore, be understood as including a 2nd person element -en-, indicating the "object" of kal-kal. I assume that this has become abbreviated to e (or lengthened? to *ē?) in front of the consonant /k/. The full form might then have been *mu-en-kal-kal. Note that kal-kal is not followed by an *-e. The variants in C_3: mu-e-[, and N 2715: m[u-, indicate that a mu- prefix was, indeed, involved and the assumption that it was followed by an -en- element can explain why it was contracted to me in UM_2. Cf. lines 19; 23; 53; 54; and, less likely, 66.

The meaning may be "Don't evaluate things; (because then) things will evaluate you," the intent being, probably, that you will make yourself dependent on material goods.

The ETCSL translates: "You should not serve things; things should serve you"; why "serve"? kal is *waqāru*, "to be precious."

Line 254: UM_2: dumu-ŋu$_{10}$ gùn-gim igi-gùn-gùn agrees with the preserved parts of C_3, etc. The only variant is N 2715:] ⌜ḪU⌝-ḪU-gim [, probably a mistake for gùn-gùn-gim, but no sources have the reduplicated form *gùn-gùn-gim.

gùn-gim seems here to be used as an unusual undeclined verbal noun, lit., "like multi-color." igi gùn-gùn is then best taken as "eyes (will be) multi-colored," that is, there are as many eye colors as there are colors. This is interesting, because the preserved statues of humans do not give any precise details as to what was considered normal eye colors, although inlaid eyes of lapis lazuli may give a hint.

In line 139, mu, gùn, and zalag seem to have related connotations; cf. further line 268, where zalag, "to shine," seems to be said of a name (mu, restored) with similar intent.

Line 255: UM_2: ^{d}ašnan-ra na-an-šèr-šèr-re-dè-en ŋiš-á-bi ì-šèr, agrees with the preserved parts of C_3: -r]a na-an-šèr-šèr-r[e-...^{ŋiš}á-b]i ì-[šár], etc.; N 2715: -a]n-šèr-šèr-re-d[a-.

The saying is an example of the paradoxical type warning against doing the impossible; cf. line 169.

Since no speaker is mentioned, an already existing saying was undoubtedly included here.

Line 256: UM_2: kir$_{11}$-e áš nam-en dumu-munus in-ù-tu-un, agrees with the preserved parts of C_3; N_6: kir$_{11}$; T_{21}: ⌜kir$_{11}$⌝-re; N 2715: na]m-me instead of nam-en; BM_2 seems to have]-me(?)-en instead.

The ETCSL translates (l. 246) "You should not abuse a ewe; otherwise you will give birth to a daughter." I do not know the justification for áš – dug$_4$ meaning "to abuse," which is otherwise = *arāru*, "to curse," but it certainly makes good sense here. Maybe áš – dug$_4$ was used as a kind of euphemism. áš – dug$_4$ occurs also in line 134: áš dug$_4$-dug$_4$-ge bar ši-in-dar. Cf. also lines 137: áš-di; 142 (doubtful); cf. further lines 50: áš-zi – bal; 62: ŋiš á-zi – e; 184, ED_1: áš-gig-šè ŋar; *Couns. Wisdom* 82: áš-dug$_4$ – gi$_4$; 153 (cf commentary: áš(?) = CAD Ṣ, 167: *ṣibûtu* A "need, want, request"; doubtful). In my opinion lines 256–257 do not primarily reflect magic, but are simply logical puns on the actions involved; for different opinions, see Wilcke, 1978, 229, and Römer, 1990, 65: "Die ... angeredete Frau ... soll offenbar (aus magischen Gründen) nicht in der genannten Weisen verfahren."

Line 257: UM_2: mi-si-saḫar-a: C_3:]-ra; N_6: ^{ŋiš}mi-si-sa[ḫa]r-r[a, agrees with T_{21}: ^{ŋiš}mi-si-saḫar-ra, N 2715:]-ra, and BM_2:]-ra. UM_2: lag nam-bí-šub-bé-en; C_3: lag nam-ba-e-šub-b[é-; N 2715: lag nam-bi(sic!)-š[ub.

For the verbal prefixes nam-ba-e-, cf., e.g., line 20, vars. nam-mu-e-(ak-e).

For mi-saḫar(-ra), = *nēpeštu*, cf. the comments

on line 29, where it is translated "money chest"; cf. also Wilcke, 1978, 229.

I simply see throwing a lump of clay into a money chest as symbolic of a son dispersing a fortune, and not as indicative of magic. Cf. however, the comments on line 256 for different opinions.

Line 258: UM_2: dam nam-mu-un-kar-re-en; C_3: -k]ar-re, agrees with N_6: mu-kar-re, and N 2715:]-kar-re; UM_2: gú KA; C_3: gù KA, agrees with N_6: gù K[A, and N 2715: gù KA. T_{21} and BM_2 omit the line altogether.

The reading of the first KA is definitely gù, in view of the phonetic variant gú in UM_2. It is tempting to suggest that the second KA is also gù.

For kar = *ekēmu*, cf. Wilcke, 1978, 230, referring to CAD E, 67, *ekēmu* d: *mutam ekēmu*, "to snatch away a spouse, to kidnap."

Who is the speaker? Probably the abducted wife, but cf. the comments on line 260. Cf. Römer, 1990, 65 (n. 249 a), who translates "*Geschrei* sollst du ihn nicht *erheben* lassen," understanding this as referring to the husband, who has suffered a loss, which perhaps is more convincing.

The ETCSL translates lines 258–260: "You should not abduct a wife; you should not make her cry(?). The place where the wife is abducted to ...."

Line 259: There are no variants.

For nam-silig gum-ŋá-àm, see the comments on line 15, where a variant of the same expression occurs.

Line 260: UM_2 is the only text that has ga-àm-me-re$_7$-dè-en, which seems partly to agree with T_{22}: ga-àm-me-DU-x-dè-en; C_3: ga-àm-[m]a-re$_7$-en-dè-en, agrees with the preserved parts of N_6: ga-àm-m[a-; BM_2: ga-an-ši-re$_7$-e[n. There are otherwise no variants.

The reading follows Wilcke, 1978, 230, who translates (p. 211): "(Man wird sagen:) Wir wollen im Kreis herum laufen, (während er ruft:) «Weh, der Fuß, weh, der Nacken!»."

Who is the speaker? Probably the people of a household that has been deprived of the wife, and who, therefore, are considered to have suffered a loss (l. 259). This may belong to the following line 261, where a "revolt" against a powerful man (lú-gu-la) seems to be intended. The ETCSL translates lines 260–261: "Let us go round in circles (?), saying: «Oh, my foot, oh, my neck!». Let us with united forces (?) make the mighty bow!"

Line 261: UM_2: ga-na-gam-me-en-dè, is the only text that has -gam-me-en-dè; C_3: -gam(!)-en-dè-en; T_{22}: ga-na-gam-e-dè-en; BM_2: -gam-e-[.

lú-gu-la occurs also in line 191: cf. the comments on line 191. Whereas there it seems to be used of a mighty man whose status is considered worth attaining, it here denotes a person who abuses his powers.

á-diš-e, Wilcke, 1978, 230: "Mit vereinigten Kräften," lit., "die Kräfte zu einem." Cf. lines 69–70 for a proverbial saying expressing a similar notion.

Line 262: UM_2: na-an-ug$_5$-ge-en, agrees with N_6: na-an-ug$_5$-ge-e[n, and probably T_{22}: na-an-⌜x⌝-ge-en. UM_2: dumu in-sù-ge tu-da, agrees with C_3: in-sù-ge tu-ud-da, BM_2: in-sù-g[e, and apparently T_{22}: ⌜x sù-ge⌝ tu-da.

For galam, cf. lines 4ff: inim-galam. Cf. also CAD N/1, 187f. *naklu*, "ingenious, clever, artistic, artful, sophisticated, complicated." Possibly related parallels to galam-ma are quoted by Alster, 1974, 113, who compares the expression galam(-ma) ḫu-ru, already understood as "clever fool" by C.J. Gadd, *Teachers and Schools of the Oldest Schools* (London, 1956) 34. Gadd compared it to *exymore* and *sophomore*. Cf. further to *Bird and Fish* 124: galam-ma ḫu-ru ú-ḫúb ŋalga sùḫ, "clever fool, deaf one, nitwit"; *Dialogue 3*, 66: galam ḫu-ru ŋéštu šú-a-ab šú-a-ab, "Clever fool, stop, stop your ears"; *Dialogue 4*, 74: galam ḫu-ru-um eme zag-ga bar-bar, "clever fool, who stammers." There is, thus, good evidence for galam used in an ironic context. Here galam-ma seems to denote a person similar to lú-gu-la; maybe a kind of supervisor would fit, but I can offer no other parallels. The impression is that galam-ma is here used as a colloquial expression or a euphemism for something like "supervisor" (lú-banda = *laputtum*) who acted on behalf of a "lord" (en-ra), and whom his subjects were tempted to kill, somehow similar to the classic situation that opens the *Atrahasis Epic*. Regrettably, the meaning of BAD in line 263, which might have confirmed this, is not clear; cf. the comments below.

No convincing translation has as yet been suggested for dumu in-sù-ge tu-da. Wilcke, 1978, 230, takes the -/e/ following in-sù-(g) as an ergative marker, but I rather suggests that it indicates the loc.-term., lit., "the child is born by ...." Alster, 1974, 113, understood sù(-g) as = *erû*, *urrû*, "to be naked," referring to Wilcke, *Lugalbandaepos*, pp. 168–170. I cannot suggest a good explanation for what the in- could be here; it seems to be a frozen verbal form. What this could possibly mean is perhaps to be guessed from line 108, where sù(-g) conveys the notion of "emptiness" (*riqātu*), or similar; it perhaps occurs also in line 275 (with a slight emendation). Here it could perhaps mean "the child is born to be barren" or similar. Whose child is meant? It seems to refer to galam-ma, which might then denote something like "artful," which in English covers the notions "cunning, deceitful." This might then be a sarcastic remark that all his cunning is in vain.

Römer, 1990, 65, translates "Einen *Kunstvollen* (Menschen) sollst du nicht töten, einen Sohn, den ... geboren hat"; similarly Wilcke, 1978, 211. The ETCSL translates lines 262–263: "You should not kill a ..., he is born by .... You should not kill ... like ...; you should not bind him."

Line 263: UM_2: en-ra BAD-a-gim, seems to agree with T_{22}: ⌜en-ra(?) BAD(?)-a-gim; the initial signs are not preserved in the other sources; UM_2: ᵈnanna-ug_5-ge-en, agrees with C_3: ᵈnan]na-ug_5-ge-e[n, N_6: ᵈnan[na ...], T_{22}: ᵈnanna ge ⌜ŋá⌝ (unexplained); BM_2: ᵈnanna-ug_5-{ga}-ge-⌜en⌝; UM_2: šu na-an-dù-dù-en, agrees with T_{22}: šu na-an-dù-dù-en. Alster, 1974, 120, compares this to the "scribal whimsies" discussed by Civil, JAOS 92 (1972) 271, and suggests that ᵈnanna is written as a scribal pun on the prefix na-an(-na-). If this is justified, then it is remarkable that it occurs in no less than five sources, including the BM_2 sources of unknown origin. These must all depend on a common source, since the variants are unlikely to have come into being spontaneously in independent sources. Cf. p. 220, *Chap. 1.10: Textual history*.

For BAD (clear in UM_2; less clear in T_{22}), readings like úš or til would hardly make sense with the known meanings. Context suggests a meaning such as subject or slave of the lower classes, or an outcast or outlaw whom anyone could kill without provoking retaliation against himself. Or, perhaps, en-ra, "for the lord," indicates that he was owned by a "lord," but considered easy to punish or kill without causing too much trouble. The ETCSL translation is quoted under line 262.

Line 264: UM_2: ummeda ga arḫuš/ama_5-a-ke_4, probably agrees with T_{22}: ⌜ummeda ga x-a-ke_4⌝, and BM_2: -k]e_4; N_9: [ummeda] ga-lá arḫuš/ama_5-a-ke_4. Only N_9 has ga-lá. There are otherwise no variants.

Wilcke, 1978, 230, categorically rejects the reading arḫuš, whereas Alster, 1974, 49, reads arḫuš, translating "the milk of mercy." Wilcke's argument for rejecting this is that "Bei einer Lesung arḫuš ist kein Beziehungswort der Sachklasse für das Suffix -bi vorhanden," and so he reads ama_5, "women's quarter," followed by all commentators so far. For ama_5 cf. line 125. There is no difficulty in taking the -bi-ir following lugal as a collective plural of the personal class, however. The genitive in ama_5-a-ke_4 can be understood as a locative genitive, "the wet-nurses in the women's quarters." Wilcke, 1978, 230, however, translates "die Amme, die in das Frauenhaus gehört, bestimmt diesem für dessen Eigentümer das Schicksal." The ETCSL, less artificial, translates "The wet-nurses in the women's quarters determine the fate of their lords," which sounds more natural. The reading arḫuš, "mercy," should not, however, be totally excluded. In its favor definitely speaks the fact that three sources have -a-ke_4, with no variant -ke_4 alone, which would have been expected after a vowel, whereas ama_5-a-ke_4 seems difficult to justify. Reading arḫuš would provide a fine parallel to a proverbial expression in *Macbeth* I 5: "Yet, do I fear thy nature; it is too full o'the milk of human kindness to catch the nearest way. Come to my husband's breasts and take my milk for gall, you murderous ministers." In this case, the -bi refers to the nurses as a collective plural in the singular, and ga-(lá)-arhuš is a non-genitival compound, "the mercy-milk of," although /ummeda ga(-lá) arḫuš-ak-ak-e/ > *ummeda ga(-lá) arhuš(-a)-ka-ke_4 might have been expected.

For the idea, cf. SP 3.2 (Alster, *Proverbs* I, 78): ⌜um⌝(?)-me(?)-da dumu-lugal-la-gim bàd-si-a igi al-bar-bar-re "you look from the parapet, like that nurse of the prince," which Civil explains as an allusion to *Lullaby* 39ff.

Line 265: UM_2: ama-zu-úr; agrees with T_{22}: [ama-z]u-úr; N_9: ama-zu. UM_2: nam-ba-na-[...], probably agrees with N_9: nam-ba-na-a[b-, and T_{22}: nam⌝-ba-an-na-ab-bé-en. UM_2: ḫul ša-ba-ra-gig-ga-à[m].

For inim-diri, cf. the comments on line 138. ḫul – gig occurs also in line 235. It is written phonetically ḫu-gig in ED_I rev. v 3.

Line 266: There are no variants.

Line 266 corresponds roughly to ED_I rev. 7–8: [inim a-a-za inim-diŋir-za]-gim | GIŠ.[TÚG.PI] [ḫ]é-ak, which was the last line before the end formula, corresponding to SS 287. The section incorporated in between them in the SS version is a uniquely interesting description of the barbaric customs of the mountaineers, as opposed to the civilized life of Sumer. This was an essential theme, elaborating on the conditions that made it possible to comply with the counsels contained in the composition. Therefore, Wilcke's statement, 1978, 231, "warum an diesen organischen Schluß weitere Ratschläge angefügt sind, die z.T. an anderer Stelle erscheinen, muß unklar bleiben" seems unwarranted.

I translate "Your mother's words (and) the words of your god, don't take them to (your) mouth!" probably meaning "don't abuse them," somewhat similar to *Instr. Ur-Ninurta* 22–23 (p. 228): *mu diŋir-ra-na mu-un-na-kal-la *(23)* nam-érim ku_5-ru-da-bi im-ma-da-ab-te-ŋá-a "to whom the name of his god is dear; who keeps away from swearing," cf. lines 32a; 32. Although the expressions used are not identical in the two texts, the intent may well be related, in particular because not only the mother's words, but also those of a personal god are involved.

Wilcke, 1978, 211, however, translates "Die Worte deiner Mutter (und) die Worte deines (Schutz)gottes sollst du nicht *diskutieren*!" commenting, p. 230, that the translation of KA-šè dab_5 "ist geraten," and referring to Falkenstein, SGL 1, 144: KA-ge dib. The ETCSL translates "You should not question the words of your mother and your personal god." I see no justification for either "diskutieren" or "question." Römer, 1990, 66, translates "Die Worte deiner Mutter (und) die Worte deines (persönlichen) Gottes sollst du nicht in den Mund *nehmen*!" with which I agree, but not to the comment "wohl um sie zu diskutieren?" as it would be improper in the cultural context to "discuss" the words of a god. Alster, 1975, 137, translated "The word ... do not ignore it," lit., "Do not let it pass (past your) mouth."If that is justified, the reading of KA may be questioned, but I now prefer to take it literally, "to take to mouth." *Counsels of Wisdom* 78: á-tuku-zu-šè nam-ba-e-dib-bé, "Do not infringe on (the rights of) him who is stronger than you," does not seem to help. Cf. also Cavigneaux, ZA 85 (1995) 33, who translates inim da-ab (= dab_5) "fait passer (?) une parole," in magical context.

Line 267: There are no variants. For the construction, cf. p. 210, *Chap. 1.9*. Since here the verb ù-tu is an obvious pun on the god Utu, and refers to both the mother and to Utu, it is best taken as "gives life to," rather than "gives birth to." ù-tu occurs in a variety of usages, such as revitalizing someone who has been imprisoned (*Nungal Hymn*) and fashioning a divine statue. lú is here clearly used in the collective sense, "humankind," cf. lines 180; 222.

Line 268: N_9: [a]b-ba diŋir-à[m x] mu-[; T_{23}: ab-ba diŋir-ra [; there may be room for a missing sign or two between diŋir-ra/àm and mu-.

For zala(-g), cf. the similar use in line 139. The missing sign might then well be mu, "name." mu in connection with gùn occurs in line 254; in line 139, mu occurs with both gùn and zalag. The intent seems to be similar in lines 139 and 268, that is, the name predicts the destiny of its bearer; *nomen sit omen*. Cf. also the comments on line 254.

For lines 268ff., cf. p. 248, *Counsels of Wisdom* 76–77; 80–83.

Line 269: There are no variants.

ab-ba diŋir-àm introduces a relative sentence of the same type as those mentioned in *Chap. 1.9: Split sentence construction*, but it differs in that the possessive -/ani/ in inim-ma-ni, "his word," probably is meant primarily as referring to the personal god. There is some ambiguity here, since translating "whose word is just" would also be possible, but it would miss the explicit reference embedded in the possessive suffix.

Line 270: UM_2: ŋizzal [ḫé-e]m-ši-ia-ak, cf. variant in I_7; Ur_6, line 80: Ur_6: na(!)-ri ab-ba ŋizzal ḫé-em-ši-ŋál; T_{23}: probably ŋiz[zal ḫé-em-ši-ak].

Line 271: ED_I: é šà ere šà šè-dù-dù. In ED_I, the first šà is an obvious error for bar, caused by dittography of the second šà. Cf. the comments on line 205, where a similar error occurs. There are no variants in the SS version.

The contrast between ere-šà and ere-bar occurs

also in *Lament Destruction of Ur* 261–262: úru bar-ra úru-bar ḫu-mu-da-an-gul ... (262) úru šà-ba úru-šà-ab ḫu-mu-da-an-gul ..., "(261) Outside the city, the outer city was destroyed before me .... (262) Inside the city, the inner city was destroyed before me ...." Lines 163–264 repeat this with é úru-bar-ra-ŋu$_{10}$ é-ŋu$_{10}$ ... (264) é úru šà-ba-ŋu$_{10}$, etc., "my houses in the outer city ... my houses in the inner city, etc."; -ŋá would be expected instead of the first -ŋu$_{10}$.

I translate ši-dù-dù-e as the houses of the outskirts maintaining or supporting the houses of the inner city, but it can, of course, also be taken quite literally, as building them. Cf. Römer, 1990, 66, n. 262a, who translates "Die Häuser der Außenstadt *bauen* die Innenstadt." Wilcke, 1978, 211 (l. 264), translates "Die Häuser der Außenstadt bauen (= schaffen) die Innenstadt." The ETCSL translates "without suburbs a city has no center either," which renders the meaning, but not verbatim correctly.

Line 272: ED$_{I}$: gán dur$_{5}$ dúr-šè ŋál. dumu-ŋu$_{10}$ is omitted in ED$_{I}$. T$_{23}$: gán e dúr-bi-šè ŋ[ál-...], seems to agree with N$_{10}$: gán ⸢e⸣ [; Ur$_{6}$ (4): gán(? rather than é) tùr-šè ŋál-⸢la⸣; tùr is phonetic for dúr and confirms the reading, but was obviously poorly understood.

Wilcke, 1978, 223, established the reading AN-duru$_{5}$ kur$_{6}$(!)-AŠ AN-UD kur$_{6}$-AŠ, "... ist er feucht so ist es das Versorgungsfeld, ist er trocken, so ist es auch das Versorgungsfeld," commenting "ein Versorgungsfeld muß man nehmen wie es ist." AŠ can safely be read rum: an-duru$_{5}$ kur$_{6}$-rum an-ḫád(UD) kur$_{6}$-rum, as the SS version shows: al-dur$_{5}$ kur$_{6}$-ra-àm al-ḫád kur$_{6}$-ra-àm; cf. Alster, 1990, 15–19. This is of considerable interest because it shows that in ED the enclitic copula /am/ (= -àm) was exposed to vowel harmony to a higher extent than expected. Cf. Alster, WZKM 92 (2002) 12.

dur$_{5}$ = *ruṭibtu*, denotes a place wet from natural sources, not irrigation, cf. the literature quoted under line 198.

For dúr-bi-šè ŋál, see the comments on line 157, and the literature there quoted. The connection with e, "dike" occurs also in the final lines of the *Gudam Tale* 43 (PBS 5, 26: 34): a-šà zabalam[ki]-a dúr-ŋar bí-e-ŋar-ra e dúr-bi-šè ná-ba, "having established a throne on field Zabala, lie there at the bottommost ditch!" The following line, 44, with collations by Cavigneaux, reads: ama-zu(! text: ba) anše ḫa-ra-ab-ḫuŋ-e *bára al ḫu-mu-ra-ab-bé "Let your mother hire a donkey for you, let her demand a sack for you!" This shows that the doxology is ironically meant, Gudam being reduced to a donkey driver or peddler. Cf. Alster, "Gudam and the Bull of Heaven," *Larsen AV*, 30. For a previous interpretation of the line, see Wilcke, 1978, 224, who reads bí-e-gar-ra-e dúr-bí-šè nú-ba, and translates "Auf(?) dem Feld, auf dem ich den Tron in Zabala aufgestellt habe, liege du unter ihm (/als sein Fundament)," not recognizing e as a noun here; cf. further Civil, 1984, 286, who comments that "Gudam is made to sleep «at the bottom» (dúr-bi-šè) of the fields of Zabalam, i.e., far at the end of the cultivated land."

The ETCSL translates lines 272–273: "My son, a field situated at the bottom of the embankments, be it wet or dry, is nevertheless a source of income." This displays the alternative understanding of e(-g) = *iku* as a dike, rather than a ditch. I my opinion both translations are possible and are reflected in the full expression e-pa$_{5}$ = *iku palgu*, "dike-ditch," stemming from the fact that in Iraq, any ditch is accompanied by a matching dike, just as the two English words "dike" and "ditch" are etymologically related. Cf. Alster, "Images on the Stele of the Vultures," AfO 50 (2005, forthcoming) n. 29, referring to earlier opinions of Civil and Thureau-Dangin, esp. Civil, *The Farmer's Instructions* 109–135.

Line 273: ED$_{I}$: an-dur$_{5}$ kur$_{6}$(!)-rum an-ḫád(UD) kur$_{6}$(!)-rum. The reading -rum for ED$_{I}$: AŠ appears from the SS version; cf. the comments on line 272. T$_{23}$: al-dur$_{5}$ kur$_{6}$-ra-àm al-ḫád k[ur$_{6}$-, agrees with UM$_{2}$: a]l-ḫád kur$_{6}$-ra-àm / [al-dur$_{5}$ k]ur$_{6}$-ra-àm; Ur$_{6}$ (5): al-<ḫád> kur$_{6}$-àm al-dur$_{5}$-⸢ra⸣.

I tentatively read UD as ḫád = *abālu*; cf. CAD A/1, 29 *abālu* B, "to dry up," and AHw 3, "(aus)trocken" D "trocknen, trockenlagen," typically said of sun-dried fruits, etc.; cf. also CAD Ṣ, 150–152, *ṣētu* (UD-da), said of the shining appearance of the sun and the sultry weather arising from it.

Line 274: ED$_{I}$: níŋ u$_{4}$-[g]u-dé níŋ-mud$_{5}$. The main text: níŋ-me-ŋar-ra, is based on Ur$_{6}$. UM$_{2}$: [...]-⸢íb⸣-⸢sì⸣, seems to have had a text different from the others; T$_{23}$: níŋ ú-gu dé-a níŋ-me-ŋar-⸢x⸣ lá (x like šè) [...], seems to have had an unexplained addition; Ur$_{6}$ (6): níŋ ⸢gu-dé⸣ níŋ-me-ŋar-ra.

For the identification of the line with its ED parallel see Alster, 1990, 15–19. The writing u_4 for ú in the ED version differs from the writing used in the same text rev. ii 13: níŋ ú-g[u x] níŋ ⌜x⌝ [x x], which corresponds to OB 101: níŋ-ú-rum níŋ á-sì-ga-a-da. The ED variant mud_5 may be seen in the light of the fact that both níŋ-me-ŋar and mud_5-me-ŋar are equated with *qūlu*, "calm, silence, stupor," in Erimhuš iv 86 (MSL 17, 61): mud_5-me-gar = *ri-ša-a-tu*. Cf. also Recip. Ea F 10'f.: [m]u-ud ŠIM = *ri-šá-a-tum*, *qu-lu*, quoted in CAD Q, 303 s.v. *qûlu*, "calm, silence, stupor" = ME, $^{mu-ud}$ŠIM, [níŋ-m]e-ŋar.

For me ŋar, *Lament Destr. Ur* 199: u_4 kalam til-til-e úru-a me bí-ib-ŋar, "the storm that destroyed the country put total silence into the city." The ETCSL translates "The storm that annihilates the Land set up its powers in the city." The meaning of me – ŋar, as the spreading of total silence or stupor is well attested, however. See in particular Kramer: "BM 96679: A New Inanna Iršemma," in: *Sachs FS*, 243–250, where lines 5; 10–14; 16–17 repeat me-me im-ma-an-mar, which Kramer translates "(Enlil) has struck it dumb for me." Here the meaning rather seems to be that the loss of something is considered an ominous sign. The ETCSL translates our line 274: "It is inconceivable (?) that something is lost forever," which hardly is more than a guess from context and difficult to justify. Wilcke, 1978, 211, translates "Das Verlorene ist etwas, worüber man fassungslos staunt."

The line should undoubtedly be seen in connection with *Instr. Ur-Ninurta* 25, according to which the gods will restore to a pious man what he has lost.

Line 275: ED_I: [x (x)] ⌜x⌝ gín [x (x)] an [x x] ki ta TAR x. The SS text cannot be fully reconstructed from the available fragments. N_{10}: urudu(?)-gín-dilmun [; T_{23}: ⌜gín⌝-dilmun^{ki}-na-sa_{10}-šè í[l(?)-, seems to agree with C_3: g]ín-dilm[un. The end of the line is preserved only in Ur_6 (7): dilmun]-⌜na⌝ sa_{10}-šè TE, which hardly can be a misreading of šà-ga; but perhaps of *sù-ga, i.e., "emptiness," that is, buying at the Dilmun rate would be a sure loss. This might fit as the continuation of line 274. If the reading *sù-ga is justified, it can be compared to lines 108 and 262.

Line 276: ED_I: ⌜x⌝ GÍR ur nu-zu ḫuš; GÍR unexplained. Cf. Alster, 1990, 15–19. T_{23}: ur nu-zu ḫul-àm lú nu-z[u ...], seems to agree with the remains of C_3:]-⌜àm⌝, and N_{10}: ur nu-zu ḫ[ul-; Ur_6 (8) differs: ki nu-⌜zu⌝ ḫuš-àm / ur nu-zu téš-àm; if correct, this seems to be elliptical for *lú ki nu-zu, etc., which would support the interpretation of nu-zu given below. The rest would mean "for a dog to get lost is shameful," probably meant as shameful to its owner. Civil, AuOr 5 (1987) 208, takes téš nu-zu, "who knows no shame," as the primary reading, rather than ur, "dog."

Line 276 quotes the same saying as *Lugalbanda in Hurrumkurra*, 162–165; these were edited by Wilcke, *Das Lugalbandaepos*, p. 79; but are quoted here from the more recent ETCSL edition: ur nu-zu ḫul-a lú nu-zu ḫuš-àm *(163)* kaskal nu-zu gaba kur-ra-ka, *(164)* ^{d}utu lú nu-zu lú ḫul rib-ba-àm *(165)* a-gin_7 ki-lul-la nam-ma-e, "A lost dog is bad; a lost man is terrible. On the unknown way at the edge of the mountains, Utu, is a lost man, a man in an even more terrible situation." The ETCSL accordingly translates our lines 276–278 "to get lost is bad for a dog, but terrible for a man. On the edge of the mountains, the gods are man-eaters," translating the variant as "An unknown place is terrible; to get lost is shameful (?) for a dog."

I understand nu-zu in the straightforward way as "unknown." The ETCSL, however, understands nu-zu, lit., "not known," as "lost," that is, presumably, an elliptical construction for "(someone) to whom (his whereabouts = *ki nu-zu-a) are unknown." Black, *Reading Sumerian Poetry*, 179, translates similarly. Cf. the comments on line 159: ki-nu-zu-a-ni-ta.

Line 277: There are no variants. The final a in kur-ra-ka indicates that -/ak-a/ marks the locative after a genitive. -ka is preserved only in Ur_6.

For the construction representing the *genitive of characteristics*, cf. p. 210, *Chap.1.9*.

A parallel is quoted under line 276 above.

Line 278: The beginning of the line is preserved in T_{24}: diŋir-kur-ra [, and N_{10}: diŋir-kur-ra. C_3:]-gu_7-gu_7-ù-[me]-eš, probably agrees with N_{10}: gu_7-[gu_7-ù-me-eš]; Ur_6 (10): lú gu_7-gu_7-/u(sic!?)-me-eš.

diŋir-kur-ra, meaning "the gods of the netherworld," occurs in *Two Elegies* 98; cf. Katz, *Image*, 375.

The statement that the gods of mountains "eat men" is unique in Sumerian literature. Cf. Katz,

Image, 73. That lú-gu_7-gu_7, "man-eater," occurs as an attribute of the river of the netherworld in *Enlil and Ninlil* 93–95; 98–99, does not provide a real parallel; cf. Katz, *Image*, 73.

The ETCSL translation is quoted under line 276.

Line 279: There are no variants.

A parallel is quoted under line 276.

Line 280: C_3: [ki-zu-a]-ka lú, apparently with -ka misplaced before lú instead of after lú. The -ka occurs after lú in T_{23}, where it is well motivated; cf. the comments below. Only T_{24} preserves the initial signs: ki-zu-a [, probably from the same tablet as T_{23}. I suggest that this may be a mistake for *ki-nu-zu-a, since this is similar to line 159: lú ki-nu-zu-a-ni-ta, and otherwise the sense would be obscure. There are no other variants. Römer, 1990, 67, however, takes the text without emendation, "an den *bekannten Orten* der Menschen kommt man heraus," commenting (n. 271 a) "ob damit etwa offene Höhlen, in denen primitiven Gebirgler wohnen, gemeint sein könnten?" which hardly is convincing.

The second genitive in the double genitive -ka is an example of the "free genitive," or, more precisely, cf. p. 210, *Chap. 1.9: The genitive of characteristics*. The underlying construction was */ki-nu-zu-a-lú-ak-ak/, "it is characteristic of men of places that are unknown that ...."

The verbal form -è-dè is the *marû*-root è(-d) = expanded by -/ed/: /-ed-ed > è-dè. Cf. Edzard, *Sum. Grammar*, 75.

There can be little doubt that this line expresses an idea similar to lines 178–180; cf. the comments to those lines. Also in line 180, lú occurs as collective plural in the singular.

Line 281: The reconstructed text is basically that of C_3:] kiŋ-kiŋ mu-na-til udu gi_4-gi_4 [, with the first two signs provided by T_{24}: sipa ⸢x⸣(= ra?).

kiŋ-kiŋ is the subject for mu-na-til, "work stops for him," (scl. the shepherd); similarly line 282.

The ETCSL translates lines 281–282: "For the shepherd, he stopped searching, he stopped bringing back the sheep. For the farmer(?), he stopped ploughing the field," without explaining who is meant by "he." I disagree with the translation for the reasons stated above.

Line 282: The only source is C_3: [x] ⸢x⸣-ra a-šà ur_{11}-ru mu-na-til. The reconstructed eŋar is an obvious guess suggested by the parallelism with sipa in line 281. There may be a missing sign in front.

Line 283: The three existing duplicates: C_3:] ⸢x⸣-gi_4 mu-[n]a(?)-KU-e[n](?); N_6:]-la [...] ú ri-g[e ...], do not suffice for a complete reconstruction of the line.

Line 284: ED_I: [x] ⸢ŠU⸣ a(?) me kadra. This seems to be the same line as SS C_3: [... ini]m-ma-bi níŋ šà-te-na m[u(?)-...], and N_6: kadra i[nim-...]. Cf. *Counsels of Wisdom* 47: kadra-ŋar-ra-bi kadra a-$šed_{10}$, "The gifts provided there [are a] gift of cool soothing water."

The -bi following inim-ma refers to the counsels of the entire composition; so Wilcke, 1978, 231, who understands the reduplicated inim-inim-ma in line 286 as "viele einzelne «Worte», d.h. Ratschläge." That the instructions are said to be something that soothes the heart is to be seen as an expression of the common sapiential wisdom that a well-tempered mind is needed in order to act wisely. This is nicely expressed in *Couns. Wisdom* 92. Wilcke, 1978, 231, comments "Auch die öffentliche Verwaltung, den Palast, sind die gegebenen Ratschläge von Vorteil."

The ETCSL translates lines 284–286: "The gift of words is something that soothes the mind ...; when it enters the palace, it soothes the mind .... The gift of many words ... stars."

Line 285: Sources: C_3: [... -k]u_4-ra-bi níŋ-šà-te-n[a ...] and N_6: é-ga[l-...] suffice to suggest é-ga[l-la k]u_4-ra-bi níŋ-šà-te-na [, perhaps with a missing -[kam], or similar, at the end.

Line 285a: Only included in C_3: [ka]dra inim-inim-ma mu[l-an. This may have been followed by -na-kam, or similar. The line is omitted in UM_2 and N_6, which seems better.

Line 285b: Included only in C_3: [šuruppak[ki]] du[mu ubar-ubar-tu-[tu-ke_4]; UM_2 and N_6 omit the line, which seems better.

Line 286: ED_I: [i]nim AN.[A]N [...]. There are no variants in the SS text, but the end is missing.

For the reduplicated inim-inim-ma, see the comments on line 284

Lines 287–288: Cf. lines 6–13; 73–82; and 143–152.

Line 287: ED_I cf. rev. viii 8: šuruppak Ú[R].A[Š](?) dumu na ⸢ri⸣-ri-ga. This is unusual for two reason: (1) the reduplication; and (2) the final nominalization -/a/ in an ED text. There are no variants in the SS text.

Lines 287–290 are reminiscent of the final doxology in *The Farmer's Almanac* 110–111: na ri-ga ^{d}nin-urta dumu ^{d}en-líl-lá-ke_4; ^{d}nin-urta eŋar-zi ^{d}en-líl-lá zà-mí-zu dùg-ga-àm, edited by Civil, 1994.

Line 288: C_4: [zi-u_4-s]ud-rá dumu-ni-r[a, includes the name of the son in the end formula, (287:) "(these are instructions that the man from Šuruppak) (288:) gave as instructions to his son Ziusudra." UM_2: šuruppak^{ki} dumu ubar-tu-tu-ke_4, agrees with N_6: šu[rupp]ak du[mu ..., "The man from Šuruppak, son (of Ubartutu)," in only naming the father here. Cf. the comments on lines 5–7.

Line 289: UM_2: nin dub gal-gal-la; C_4: ⌜dub⌝ gal-gal-e, agrees with N_{11}: g]al-gal-e. UM_2: šu du_7-a, agrees with C_4: šu du_7-⌜a⌝; N_{11}: šu du_7-e.

Line 290: There are no variants.

Addendum

Line 154: The var. K_1: ŠÀ.IM, can now be explained by means of the Assyrian Collection of Proverbs iii 13 (Lambert, BWL 228), for which see CAD E, 313, s.v. *eršu* A, referring to *nu'u*, ŠÀM.IM, "a lout" (a low status person), cf. KAR 4 rev. 19. This is undoubtedly identical to our ŠÀ.IM.

1.5 The Abū Ṣalābīkh Version

All lines that could be identified as parallels to the SS version are transliterated under the main SS text in *Chap. 1.3*. Details pertaining to the interpretation of the main SS text are discussed in the commentary in *Chap. 1.4*. For the sake of clarity a separate complete transliteration of the Abū Ṣalābīkh version (AbSt) is included here. Comments pertaining only to the Abū Ṣalābīkh version are added to this chapter. To make comparisons easier, the corresponding SS lines are repeated here (without variants) under the relevant lines of the Abū Ṣalābīkh text. For the Adab text nearly the same procedure is followed in the reconstruction attempted in *Chap. 1.6*.

The obverse had nine (hardly more) columns. The reverse had seven columns. These were divided into cases of uneven size, varying between 8 and 17, with an average of ca. 12 to 14 cases, corresponding to the same number of lines, which means that it is impossible to calculate the original number of lines with precision. A running numeration of the lines of the Abū Ṣalābīkh version is, nevertheless, attempted below, counting approximately 85 cases on each side. This is considered a reasonable compromise, because, by and large, the only major damage applies to the right edge of the tablet. The resulting line numbers should, of course, be taken as no more than a tentative guideline. Since large parts of the tablet are preserved with no major breaks, this is thought to be reasonably accurate.

The Abū Ṣalābīkh text largely follows the organization of the SS version, yet with a number of remarkable differences.

The Adab version also seems to have followed a roughly similar pattern, but apparently included some lines not present in the AbSt version, and thus seems a bit closer to the SS version. Cf. *Chap. 1.6* for details. The number of lines that were specific to the AbSt version seems to have been limited, cf. AbSt lines 21–22, etc.

For a copy by Biggs of the joined Abū Ṣalābīkh tablets, OIP 99, 256+323, see Civil, JNES 43 (1984) 282–283. For a transliteration and edition of the new piece, OIP 99, 323, see Civil, ibid., 281–286. The join was first recognized by Civil, 1984, but in 1990, when I tried to confirm it on the original tablets in Baghdad, the exact position of the two parts could not be physically verified owing to the layer of gypsum applied to reinforce them; cf. Alster, 1991–92, 32.

Transliteration

AbSt 1		
ED$_{I}$ obv. i 1–2	ŋéštu inim-zu | [ka]lam [t]i-la	*(AbSt 1)* The intelligent one, the wise one, who lived in the country,
= SS 4	u$_{4}$-ba ŋéštu-tuku inim-galam inim-zu-a kalam-ma ti-la-a	
AbSt 2		
ED$_{I}$ obv. i 3–5	[šuruppak Ú]R.[A]Š | [ŋéš]tu inim-zu | kalam ti-la	*(AbSt 2)* the Man from Šuruppak, to "Father-in-Law"—the intelligent one, the wise one, who lived in the country,
= SS 5	šuruppak^{ki} ŋéštu-tuku inim-galam inim-zu-a kalam-ma ti-la-a	
AbSt 3		
ED$_{I}$ obv. i 6	šuruppak dumu na [n]a-mu-ri	(*AbSt 3*) the Man from Šuruppak gave instructions to his son:
= SS 6	šuruppak^{ki}-e dumu-ni-ra na na-mu-un-ri-ri	

AbSt 4		
ED$_{I}$ obv. i 7	dumu-ŋu$_{10}$ na ga-ri	(*AbSt 4*) "My son, let me give you instructions,
= SS 9	dumu-ŋu$_{10}$ na ga-ri na-ri-ŋu$_{10}$ ḫé-dab$_{5}$	
AbSt 5		
ED$_{I}$ obv. i 8	GIŠ.PI.[TÚG] ḫé-m[a]-ak	(*AbSt 5*) let attention be paid to them!
= SS 10	zi-u$_{4}$-sud-rá inim ga-ra-ab-d[ug$_{4}$] ŋizzal ḫé-em-ši-ak	
AbSt 6		
ED$_{I}$ obv. i 9	gán-zu [kaskal na-ŋá-ŋá]	(*AbSt 6*) Don't [place] your field [on a road; the decimation is crushing!]
= SS 15	gán kaskal-[la] nam-bí-íb-ŋá-ŋá nam silig gú ŋá àm	
AbSt 7'	*One line missing at the end of col. i. Probably = SS 14.*	(*AbSt 7*) [*Missing*]
AbSt 8'		
ED$_{I}$ obv. ii 1–2	é sila(!)-daŋal na-dù(text: NI) x-sír LAK 218 ŋál-am$_{6}$	(*AbSt 8*) Don't extend a house too close to a public square; it will cause obstruction(?)!
= SS 18	é sila-daŋal-la nam-bí-ib-lá-e KÉŠ-da ŋál-la-àm	
AbSt 9'		
ED$_{I}$ obv. ii 3	géme kar-kíd(AK) na-an-sa$_{10}$ ka ù-sar-kam$_{4}$	(*AbSt 9*) Don't buy a prostitute; she is a mouth with a sharpened tooth!
= SS 154	[kar-k]id na-an-sa$_{10}$-sa$_{10}$-an ka u$_{4}$-sar-ra-kam	
AbSt 10'		
ED$_{I}$ obv. ii 4	gán-za pú na-⸢dù⸣ ⸢ùŋ⸣ ⸢šè⸣-⸢mu⸣-ra-⸢ḫul⸣	(*AbSt 10*) Don't place a well in your field; the people will do damage to you!
= SS 17	gán-zu-àm pú na-an-ni-dù-e-en ùŋ-e ša-re-eb-ḫul-ḫul	
AbSt 11'		
ED$_{I}$ obv. ii 5–6	[i]gi-du na-⸢x⸣-⸢ba⸣ | lú uru$_{5}$ ši-sù x x	(*AbSt 11*) Don't give evidence against a man; the flood (arising from it) will submerge you!
= SS 21	lú-ra igi-du$_{8}$ na-an-ak-e úru-bi ša-re-e[b]-su-su	
AbSt 12'		
ED$_{I}$ obv. ii 7–8	šu-dù na-túm lú | šè-ba-dab$_{5}$	(*AbSt 12*) Don't guarantee for a man; that man will have a hold on you!
= SS 19	šu-du$_{8}$-a nu-e-tùm lú-bi ša-ba-e-dab$_{5}$-bé	
AbSt 13'		
cf. ED$_{I}$ obv. ii 9	šà šu-bad na-ak [me]-zu a[k]	(*AbSt 13*) Don't make a pledge(?); … [your]self!
= SS 20	za-e šu-du$_{8}$-a nam-mu-ak-e	
AbSt 14':	*One or no blank line at the end of obv. ii?*	
AbSt 15'		
ED$_{I}$ obv. iii 1–2	du$_{7}$ sila-kúr ⸢x⸣-ma | NI.I(LAK134) bar-tar-ta gub-ma	(*Abst 15*) When encountering a quarrel, take another road; when facing an insult, stand aside from it!"
= SS 27	du$_{14}$ bar-bar-ta gub-gub-[ba] in-nu-uš sila-kúr-ra níŋin-na-ma-a[n …]	

AbSt 16'		
ED$_{\text{I}}$ obv. iii 3	šuruppak dumu na na-mu-ri	(*Abst 16*) The Man from Šuruppak gave instructions to his son:
AbSt 17'		
ED$_{\text{I}}$ obv. iii 4	níŋ na-mu-zuḫ-zuḫ me-zu na-MUNŠUB	(*Abst 17*) "Don't steal anything; don't kill yourself!
= SS 28	níŋ nam-mu-zuḫ-z[uḫ] ní-zu nam-mu-úš-e	
AbSt 18'		
ED$_{\text{I}}$ obv. iii 5	nu-zuḫ ušum na-nam ul-dab$_5$ géme na-nam	(*Abst 18*) The thief is indeed a dragon; when caught he is indeed a slave girl!
= SS 30	ní-zuḫ piriŋ na-nam ul-dab$_5$ saŋ na-nam	
AbSt 19'		
ED$_{\text{I}}$ obv. iii 6	é na-[bùr] ⸢x⸣ [x x]	(*Abst 19*) Don't break into a house; [don't demand the money chest!]
= SS 29	é na-a-an-ni-bùr-e-en mi-si-saḫar-ra al nam-me	
AbSt 20'		
ED$_{\text{I}}$ obv. iii 7	[x]-gaz na-ak ⸢x⸣ sír(?) [na]-⸢bar⸣(?)	(*Abst 20*) Don't commit murder; [don't] ⸢mutilate⸣ yourself [with an] ax(?)!
= SS 31	dumu-ŋu$_{10}$ sa-gaz nam-mu-ak-e ní-zu + (var. 2nd part: [(...) š]e(?)-búr(?)-re nam-bí-bar-[re])	
AbSt 21'		
ED$_{\text{I}}$ obv. iii 8	ninta$_x$(SAL+NITAḪ) mi-si ⸢na⸣-⸢x⸣(=ḪI×DIŠ+GIŠ?) [m]e-zu [x] x	(*Abst 21*) Don't [make] a young man best man; don't [humiliate] yourself!
= SS 32	nitaḫ niŋir-si na-an-ak ní-zu na-an-⸢x⸣-⸢x⸣	
AbSt 22'		
ED$_{\text{I}}$ obv. iv 1–2	[si]kil-da [(x)] [n]e na-da-⸢e⸣ | inim-sig [m]áḫ(AL)	(*Abst 22*) Don't laugh with a girl [who has a husband]; the slander is strong!
= SS 33	ki-sikil dam tuku-d[a] e-⸢ne⸣ nam-mu-un-KA-e inim-sig-⸢ga⸣ ma[ḫ-àm]	
AbSt 23'		
ED$_{\text{I}}$ obv. iv 3	KA na-tar me(?)-⸢zu⸣ ŋar-ra	(*Abst 23*) Don't boast; your *word(?) stands forever (lit. is placed)!
Cf. AbSt 55	ka nam-tar ŋar	
= SS 37	KA nam-tar-tar-re-⸢e⸣-en inim-zu ŋar-ra-àm	
AbSt 24'		
ED$_{\text{I}}$ obv. iv 4	du$_7$ na-mú-mú níŋ-z[u$_{(5)}$ na-š]ub	(*Abst 24*) Don't be quarrelsome; don't cast down(?) yourself(?)!
= SS 35	du$_{14}$ nam-[mú-m]ú-dè ní-zu na-an-[pe]-el-lá	
AbSt 25'		
ED$_{\text{I}}$ obv. iv 5	l[ul na- x x] ⸢ra⸣ [x x] x-sal-sal ⸢x x⸣ su	(*Abst 25*) Don't [plan] lies; it is [dis]crediting!"
= SS 36	lul na[m]-gur$_5$-gur$_5$ saŋ gú-⸢sal-sal⸣-la	
AbSt 26'		
ED$_{\text{I}}$ obv. iv 6	šuruppak dumu na na-mu-ri	(*Abst 26*) The Man from Šuruppak gave instructions to his son:

AbSt 27'		
ED$_{I}$ obv. iv 7	dumu-ŋu$_{10}$ na ga-ri	(*Abst 27*) "My son, let me give you instructions;
AbSt 28'		
ED$_{I}$ obv. iv 8	ŋéštu ḫé-ma-ak	(*Abst 28*) let attention be paid to them!
AbSt 29'		
ED$_{I}$ obv. v 1	⸢gud⸣ na-MUNŠUB ⸢gud⸣ e-KAL	(*Abst 29*) Don't … an ⸢ox⸣; the ⸢ox⸣ …
= SS 213	gud [… na]-⸢an⸣-ni-sa$_{10}$-sa$_{10}$	
AbSt 30'		
ED$_{I}$ obv. v 2	gud-lul na-ḫuŋ(ŠÈ)-ḫuŋ(ŠÈ) KA LUM GABA-kam$_{4}$	(*Abst 30*) Don't hire malicious oxen …
cf. SS 214	gud-l[ul-l]a na-[s]a$_{10}$-sa$_{10}$ é-tùr gu[l(?)-la-kam]	
AbSt 31'		
ED$_{I}$ obv. v 3	[x LAG]AB DU [x N]I	(*Abst 31*) …
AbSt 32'		
ED$_{I}$ obv. v 4	[x x] na-[x x]	(*Abst 32*) Don't …
AbSt 33'		
ED$_{I}$ obv. v 5	munus-z[i (x)] gán ⸢x⸣	(*Abst 33*) A man installs a good woman as a good field.
= SS 215	munus-zi gán-zi-šè lú ši-i[n- …]	
AbSt 34'		
ED$_{I}$ obv. v 6–7	[…] | [níŋ]-zuḫ na-gu$_{7}$	(*Abst 34*) Don't eat something stolen [with a man]!
= SS 39	lú-da níŋ-zuḫ-a nam-mu-da-gu$_{7}$-e	
AbSt 35'		
ED$_{I}$ obv. v 8	⸢šu⸣ ⸢x⸣ ⸢x⸣ DU	(*Abst 35*) Don't [sprinkle your] hands [with blood]!
= SS 40	šu-zu úš-àm na-di-ni-ib-su-su	
AbSt 36'		
ED$_{I}$ obv. v 9	anše (or: ŋìr) ur$_{5}$ gud sa$_{10}$	(*Abst 36*) (If you hire(?)) a donkey for rent, (you will have to(?)) pay for an ox!
= SS 41	ŋìr ur$_{5}$-re gud ša-ba-re-eb-su-su udu ša-ba-re-eb-su-su	
AbSt 37'		
ED$_{I}$ obv. v 10	ù-nu-ŋar na-dug$_{4}$	(*Abst 37*) Don't speak something unreliable;
= SS 42	ù-nu-ŋar-ra na-ab-bé-⸢e⸣	
AbSt 38'		
ED$_{I}$ obv. v 11	[e]ŋir ŋiš-búr	(*Abst 38*) in the end it will bind you like a trap!
= SS 43	eŋir-bi-šè ŋiš-pàr-gim ši-i-ši-íb-lá-e	
AbSt 39'		
ED$_{I}$ obv. v 12	ú nu-kiŋ$_{x}$(ḪUL) udu sá.ság na-dug$_{4}$	(*Abst 39*) Don't transfer your sheep to uninvestigated grazing grounds!
= SS 44	ú nu-kiŋ-ŋá-šè udu-zu [s]ág nam-me	

AbSt 40'		
ED_{I} v l. edge	u[š] é	(*Abst 40*) A foundation of a house
+ vi top edge	uš dim$_4$	is a tested foundation.
Cf. SS 46	uš sì-ga kaskal sì-ga-àm	
AbSt 41'		
ED_{I} obv. vi 1	gud ŋi$_6$ [x x]	(*Abst 41*) A black ox ... (ox error?)
= SS 45	uš nu-sì-ga-šè ⸢gud⸣ lú na-ḫuŋ-e	
AbSt 42'		
ED_{I} obv. vi 2–3	kaskal ŋi$_6$ na | šà ⸢sá⸣(?) ḫul	(*Abst 42*) Don't (walk on) a road at night; its interior is (both) good(?) and bad!
= SS 47	kaskal ŋi$_6$ na-an-du šà-bi sa$_6$ ḫul-a	
AbSt 43'		
ED_{I} obv. vi 4–5	edin na-sa$_{10}$ u$_5$-šè sa$_{10}$	(*Abst 43*) Don't buy a steppe-ass (i.e., an onager); you will buy for the day(?)!
= SS 48	anše-edin-na na-ab-sa$_{10}$-s[a$_{10}$] u$_4$ da-bé-eš ì-za-al	
AbSt 44'		
ED_{I} obv. vi 6–7	géme-zu$_5$ ŋiš$_x$(SAL+NINTA) na-e |	(*Abst 44*) Don't have sexual intercourse with your slave girl; she will neglect you!
+ 323 i 1	zú-ur$_5$ šè-mu-sa$_4$	
= SS 49	géme-zu-úr ŋiš na-an-dù zu-úr šu-m[u]-ri-in-sa$_4$	
AbSt 45'		
ED_{I} obv. vi 8	lú-ra [x] ⸢na⸣-dug$_4$ [x x x] ⸢SAL⸣	(*Abst 45*) Don't rape a man's daughter; ..."
+ 323 i 2		
= SS 62	dumu lú-ra ŋiš á-zi na-an-ne-en kisal-e bí-zu-zu	
AbSt 46'		
ED_{I} obv. vi 9	[šurup]pak dumu na na-mu-ri	(*Abst 46*) The Man from Šuruppak gave instructions to his son:
AbSt 47'		
ED_{I} obv. vi 10–11	dumu-eŋar níŋ na-ra | e-pa$_5$-zu$_5$ šè-ra	(*Abst 47*) "Don't beat a farmer's son; he will(?) 'beat' your irrigation canal.
= SS 153	dumu eŋar-ra-ra níŋ nam-mu-ra-ra-an e-pa$_5$-zu šè-im-ra	
AbSt 48'		
ED_{I} obv. vi 12–13	ḪAR-tu na-sa$_{10}$ | ú-libiš-gig	(*Abst 48*) Don't buy a home-born(?) slave; he is an herb that causes a stomachache!
= SS 155	ama-a-tu na-an-sa$_{10}$-sa$_{10}$-an ú-libiš-gig-ga-àm	
AbSt 49'		
ED_{I} obv. vi 14	KASKAL KA SILA x(= LAGAB or similar)	(*AbSt 49*) ...
AbSt 50' - 51':	*Approximately two or three lines missing at the beginning of obv. vii.*	(*AbSt 50ff.*) (missing)
AbSt 53'		
ED_{I} obv. vii 1'	ka[š x -z]u$_5$ ⸢DI⸣ na-⸢x⸣-[dug$_4$]	(*AbSt 53*) When you [drink] beer, don't [pass] judgment!
= SS 126	kaš nag-a-zu-ne di na-an-ne-e	

AbSt 54'		
ED_I obv. vii 2' + 323 ii 1	⸢é⸣-ta ù SAR-zu_5 gu_7	(*AbSt 54*) When (you) leave(?) (your) house, (don't) be troubled(?)!
= SS 127	é-ta è šà-zu na-an-gu_7-e	
AbSt 55'		
ED_I obv. vii 3'	ka nam-tar ŋar	(*AbSt 55*) Don't boast! (Your *word(?)) stands forever (lit. is fixed)!
Cf. AbSt 23	ka na-tar me(?)-⸢zu⸣ ŋar-ra	
= SS 37	KA nam-tar-tar-re-⸢e⸣-en inim-zu ŋar-ra-àm	
= 67, Ur_2 addition:	inim-zu ŋar-ra-[àm]	
AbSt 56'		
ED_I obv. vii 4'	[i]gi-zu_5-ta $kiŋ_x$(ḪUL) na-ak x (like TAB)	(*AbSt 56*) Don't work with your eyes (alone)!
= SS 175	za-e igi-zu-ta kiŋ na-an-ak-[e]	
AbSt 57'		
ED_I obv. vii 5'	ka-zu_5-ta níŋ na-lu-lu	(*AbSt 57*) Don't multiply things with your mouth (alone!)
= SS 176	ka-zu-ta níŋ-nam nu-lu-lu-un	
AbSt 58'		
ED_I obv. vii 6'	ŋá-la d[ag] é dúr-šè [(x)] ⸢du⸣	(*AbSt 58*) A lazy one makes a house go 'down to the bottom'.
= SS 177	ŋá-la dag-ge é dúr-bi-šè mu-un-du	
AbSt 59'		
ED_I obv. vii 7'	ka[š ...].	(*AbSt 59*) Beer ...
AbSt 60'–61':	*Approx. two lines missing at the bottom of obv. vii.*	(*AbSt 60–66: destroyed*)
AbSt 62'–65':	*Approx. four lines missing at the beginning of obv. viii.*	
AbSt 66'		
ED_I obv. viii 2'	[...] še ŠE+x [x]	
AbSt 67'		
ED_I obv. viii 3'	PAP ḪI×x AŠ+ŋiš dalla(?) [x]	(*AbSt 67*) ...
AbSt 68'		
ED_I obv. viii 4'	⸢ḪI⸣ DUB [x] ⸢EN⸣ [x x]	(*AbSt 68*) ...
AbSt 69'–71':	*Approx. 3 lines missing*	(*AbSt 69–71: Destroyed*)
AbSt 72'		
ED_I obv. viii 8'–9'	áš dug_4-d[ug_4] | bar šè-dar	(*AbSt 72*) An insult breaks only the skin.
= SS 134	áš dug_4-dug_4-ge bar ši-in-dar	
AbSt 73'		
ED_Iobv. viii 10'–11'	[a]d gi_4-gi_4 | [...] ŠÈ NE [...]	(*AbSt 73*) (Don't make) (bad) plans; ...
= SS 38	⸢ad⸣ nam-gi_4-gi_4 igi-dugud nu-mu-un-da-íl	

AbSt 74'–85':	*Of obv. col. ix only traces of a single sign remains, total approx. 12 lines.*	(*AbSt 74–91: Destroyed*)
AbSt 86' ED_I rev. i 1'	 ⸢x⸣ níŋ [x x]	
AbSt 87' ED_I rev. i 2'	 PA[D x x] ḪI(?) [x x]	
AbSt 88' ED_I rev. i 3'	 za [x x] ⸢x⸣ [x x]	
AbSt 89'-ca. 91	*Approx. 3 lines missing*	
AbSt 92' ED_I rev. i 7' = **SS 124**	 *Traces of one sign* dumu-ninta-zu é-zu-šè im-me	 (*AbSt 92*) [Your son will speak for your house;]
AbSt 93' ED_I rev. i 8' = **SS 125**	 dumu-mun[us x]-šè du[g_4] dumu-munus-zu ama_5-ni-šè im-me	 (*AbSt 93*) Your daughter will speak for [her woman's quarters].
AbSt 94' ED_I rev. i 9'	 *Traces of one sign*	 (*AbSt 94–100: Destroyed*)
AbSt 95'–100'	*Approx 5 lines missing at the bottom of rev. i; one line destroyed at the beginning of rev. ii.*	
AbSt 101' ED_I rev. ii 2–3 = **SS 85**	 ⸢x⸣ [x] k]a ⸢kaš⸣ x | x x LUL šè ka kaš na[ŋ-a …] ⸢x⸣	 (*AbSt 101*) A mouth [drinking] beer …
AbSt 102' ED_I rev. ii 4 = **SS 86**	 nin-kaš-si ⸢x⸣ ⸢x⸣ ùr(?) ^{d}nin-ka-si […]	 (*AbSt 102*) Ninkasi …
AbSt 103' ED_I rev. ii 5 = **SS 89**	 lú KALAM(?) é IGI.DU KA šè-íl ⸢x⸣ ⸢x⸣ a mu-un-ni-íl-íl	 (*AbSt 103*) …
AbSt 104' ED_I rev. ii 6 = **SS 95**	 ši-kù níŋ-ku_4-ku_4 níŋ sá nu-di-dam	 (*AbSt 104*) What enters (is unrivalled);
AbSt 105' ED_I rev. ii 6 = **SS 96**	 níŋ-silig níŋ-è níŋ nu-silig-ge-dam	 (*AbSt 105*) (but) [what comes out] is endless.
AbSt 106' ED_I rev. ii 7	 k[a(?) x x] ⸢x⸣(= like LAGAB)	 (*AbSt 106: Destroyed*)

AbSt 107'
ED_I rev. ii 8 — *(Traces. Perhaps two lines)*

(AbSt 107: Destroyed)

AbSt 108'
ED_I rev. ii 9 — ŋiš-gi šà sig
= SS 93 — ŋiš-gi máš-ú na-nam šà-bi inim-sig-ga-àm

(*AbSt 108*) The canebrake (is a grass-fed goat); (its) interior is slander(ous).

AbSt 109'
ED_I rev. ii 10 — é-gal A-máḫ šà-bi gud [d]u_7
= SS 94 — é-gal íd maḫ-àm šà-bi gud du_7-du_7-dam

(*AbSt 109*) The palace is a huge river; its interior is a goring ox.

AbSt 110'
ED_I rev. ii 11 — ninda lú BU ga-šúm-š[úm]
= SS 97 — ninda lú-ka ga-ra-ab-šúm-bi ku-nu-a

(*AbSt 110*) (If you say) of a man's bread: «let me give it!»

AbSt 111'
ED_I rev. ii 12 — šúm-da-bi ⸢x⸣
= SS 98 — šúm-mu-da-bi an bad-rá-àm

(*AbSt 111*) (when you actually have to give it), the giving [is far away]!

AbSt 112'
ED_I rev. ii 13 — níŋ-ú:d[ù]g:rum níŋ ⸢x⸣ [x]
= SS 101 — níŋ-ú-rum níŋ á-sì-ga-a-da

(*AbSt 112*) To property that [has been set aside(?)],

AbSt 113'
ED_I rev. ii 14 — [dumu-ŋ]u_{10} [níŋ nu-da-sá]
= SS 102 — lú-tur-ŋu_{10} níŋ nu-mu-un-da-sá

(*AbSt 113*) M[y son, nothing is comparable!]

AbSt 114'
ED_I rev. iii 1 — x (= e/ere?) máḫ é dù ⸢šè⸣-ḫur
= SS 182 — úru maḫ-e é-dù-a ši-ḫur-re

(*AbSt 114*) A huge ⸢city⸣ designs house buildings;

AbSt 115'
ED_I rev. iii 2 — é ⸢x(= tur?)⸣ amar ⸢x⸣ ⸢x⸣
= SS 181 — úru tur-re lugal-bi-ir amar ši-in-ga-an-ù-tu

(*AbSt 115*) (but) a ⸢small⸣(?) *town (text: house) [creates] calves (for its master).

AbSt 116'
ED_I rev. iii 3 — ⸢GI⸣(?) MUL LUL

(*AbSt 116*) …

AbSt 117'
ED_I rev. iii 4 — saŋ ŠID šè-ŠID

(*AbSt 117*) …

AbSt 118'
ED_I rev. iii 5 — ur-saŋ TA-*gunû* ŋál

(*AbSt 118*) …

AbSt 119'
ED_I rev. iii 6 — šu-šè x x

(*AbSt 119*) …

AbSt 120'
ED_I rev. iii 7–8 — lú níŋ tuku lú níŋ nu-tuku | áš-gig šè-ŋar
= SS 184 — lú níŋ tuku lú níŋ nu-tuku gig-šè ŋar

(*AbSt 120*) A poor man inflicts (all kinds of) curses and diseases on a wealthy man.

AbSt 121'		
ED$_{I}$ rev. iii 9	níŋ-tuku saŋ me-te-ŋál	(*AbSt 121*) To have possessions (means) to be well esteemed.
AbSt 122'		
ED$_{I}$ rev. iii 10	níŋ nu-tuku saŋ <nu>(?)-è-a$_{x}$(GI)	(*AbSt 122*) Not to have possessions (means) *<not>(?) to prevail(?).
AbSt 123'		
ED$_{I}$ rev. iii 11	dam tuku šè-du$_{7}$	(*AbSt 123*) A married man is well equipped;
= SS 185	lú dam tuku á šu im-du$_{7}$-du$_{7}$	
AbSt 124'		
ED$_{I}$ rev. iii 12	dam nu-tuku šér-díb DU	(*AbSt 124*) (but) an unmarried man sleeps in a haystack.
= SS 186	dam nu-un-tuku še-er-tab-ba mu-un-ná	
AbSt 125'		
ED$_{I}$ rev. iii 13	[l]ú zi lú šè-da-[z]i	(*AbSt 125*) He who is about to stir men will stir (any) man with them.
= SS 188	lú zi-zi-i-dè lú ša-ba-da-an-zi-zi-i	
AbSt 126'		
ED$_{I}$ rev. iii 14	é gul é šè-da-[(x)]	(*AbSt 126*) He who is about to destroy houses will [destroy] (any) house with them.
= SS 187	é gul-gul-lu-dè é ša-ba-da-an-gul-e	
AbSt 127'		
ED$_{I}$ rev. iii 15	sa[ŋ] ⌜x⌝ ⌜x⌝ [(x)] nu-bad	(*AbSt 127*) The *heart(?) (text: head) cannot let go [of the good];
= SS 196	sa$_{6}$-ga šà-ge šu nu-bar-re	
AbSt 128'		
ED$_{I}$ rev. iv 1	dumu ḫul šà nu-bar	(*AbSt 128*) <My> son(?), but the heart cannot let go of the evil either.
= SS 197	ḫul šà-ge šu nu-di-ni-bar-re	
AbSt 129'		
ED$_{I}$ rev. iv 2	ḫul-da ⌜A⌝ zág(PA, probably read má!) su	(*AbSt 129*) Let the *boat sink in the river with the evil one;
= SS 200	ḫul-da íd-da má ḫé-en-da-su	
AbSt 130'		
ED$_{I}$ rev. iv 3	edin ^{kuš}A.EDIN dar	(*AbSt 130*) let the waterskin be split on the high plain with him.
= SS 201	an-edin-na ^{kuš}ùmmu ḫé-en-da-dar	
AbSt 131'		
ED$_{I}$ rev. iv 4	šà ki-áŋ níŋ é dù-dù	(*AbSt 131*) A loving heart is something that builds houses;
= SS 202	šà ki-áŋ níŋ é dù-dù-ù-dam	
AbSt 132'		
ED$_{I}$ rev. iv 5	šà ḫu(!)(text: RI)-gig níŋ é gul-gul	(*AbSt 132*) (but) a heart of hatred is something that destroys houses.
= SS 203	šà ḫul-gig níŋ é gul-gul-lu-dam	
AbSt 133'		
ED$_{I}$ rev. iv 6–7	nir-ŋál níŋ-du$_{10}$-du$_{10}$ gaba-ŋál me nam-nun-kam$_{4}$	(*AbSt 133*) To have authority and to acquire riches are the faring (Brustwahr) of the aristocracy.
= SS 204	nir-ŋál-e níŋ-du$_{12}$-du$_{12}$ gaba-ŋál me nam-nun-na	

AbSt 134'
ED$_{I}$ rev. iv 8 gaba-ŋál gú ḫé-ŋál
= SS 205 nir-ŋál-ra gú ḫé-en-ne-ni-ŋál

(*AbSt 134*) The neck should be bent to the stout one (error for: the respected one?);

AbSt 135'
ED$_{I}$ rev. iv 9 á-tuku KA-zu$_{5}$ ḫé-lá
= SS 206 á-tuku ní-zu ḫé-en-ne-ši-lá

(*AbSt 135*) your mouth (error for yourself?) should be prostrated before the powerful;

AbSt 136'
ED$_{I}$ rev. iv 10 lú-ḫul-ŋál ḫé-⌜x⌝
= SS 207 dumu-ŋu$_{10}$ lú-ḫul-ŋál ḫé-en-ne-ši-ŋál-le

(*AbSt 136*) (then) you will [stand up against] the evil ones.

AbSt 137'
ED$_{I}$ rev. iv 11–12 munus-bar-[š]u šè-ŋál | [x x x]-šè du
= SS 220 munus-bar-šu-ŋál-e é dúr-bi-šè mu-un-du

(*AbSt 137*) A wife who has a fortune ruins [a house].

AbSt 138'
ED$_{I}$ rev. iv 13–14 [x kú]run naŋ-naŋ | gu[ru$_{7}$] šè-LAGAB-LAGAB
= SS 221 KAŠ kúrun naŋ-naŋ-e buru$_{14}$ im-su-su-su

(*AbSt 138*) A drunkard drowns the harvest.

AbSt 139'
ED$_{I}$ rev. iv 15–16 mu-mu sì-ga ⌜x⌝ | lú na[m] ŠÈ
= SS 168 mu-mu-a sì-ga saŋ-du lú-ù-ra im-ma(?)-⌜ak(?)⌝-e

(*AbSt 139*) When at home(?) (lit., placed among (known) names), a man …

AbSt 140'
ED$_{I}$ rev. iv 17 ki áš dug$_{4}$-ga SU ⌜x⌝ ⌜x⌝

(*AbSt 140*) …

AbSt 141'
ED$_{I}$ rev. iv 18 KA SI kalam ma

(*AbSt 141*) …

AbSt 142'
ED$_{I}$ rev. v 1 SUD [L]U[L] PA x mu

(*AbSt 142*) …

AbSt 143'
ED$_{I}$ rev. v 2 á-zi šè-sa$_{4}$

(*AbSt 143*) …

AbSt 144'
ED$_{I}$ rev. v 3 inim-diri bu-bu$_{7}$(KU) šà ḫu-gig šè-du$_{8}$-du$_{8}$
Cf. = SS 235 *[inim-di]ri(text:-ke$_{4}$) šà-ḫul-gig ⌜du$_{12}$⌝-⌜du$_{12}$⌝

(*AbSt 144*) A word of arrogance (is) a flame that provides(?) a heart of hatred.

AbSt 145'
ED$_{I}$ rev. v 4 ù ŋá NI rum A SI ŠÈ DÍM NI

(*AbSt 145*) …"

AbSt 146'
ED$_{I}$ rev. v 5 šuruppak du[mu]

(*AbSt 146*) The man from Šuruppak

AbSt 147'
ED$_{I}$ rev. v 6 na na-mu-ri

(*AbSt 147*) gave instructions to his son:

AbSt 148' ED$_{I}$ rev. v 7	dumu-ŋu$_{10}$ na ga-ri	(*AbSt 148*) "My son, let me give you instructions:
AbSt 149' ED$_{I}$ rev. v 8	ŋi$_{6}$ á-áŋ šè-⸢x⸣	(*AbSt 149*) At night, an instruction…
AbSt 150' ED$_{I}$ rev. v 9	u$_{4}$ éš-bar-kiŋ š[è]-TU	(*AbSt 150*) by day a decision …
AbSt 151' ED$_{I}$ rev. v 10	… x DÙG nam x gig	(*AbSt 151*) …
AbSt 152' ED$_{I}$ rev. v 11	níŋ LUL LUL x kúr-kúr(?)	(*AbSt 152*) …
AbSt 153' ED$_{I}$ rev. vi 1	mu ri ri ŠÈ	(*AbSt 153*) …
AbSt 154' ED$_{I}$ rev. vi 2 = SS 271	é šà ere šà šè-dù-dù é ere-bar-ra-ke$_{4}$ ere šà-ga ši-dù-dù-e	(*AbSt 154*) The houses on the *outskirts of a city (text: inside) maintain the (houses) inside the city.
AbSt 155' ED$_{I}$ rev. vi 3	še mar ama lú-ra níŋ sa$_{6}$-ga nu-túm	(*AbSt 155*) …
AbSt 156' ED$_{I}$ rev. vi 4 = SS 272	gán A(= dur$_{5}$?) dúr-šè ŋál dumu-ŋu$_{10}$ gán e dúr-bi-šè ŋ[ál-la]	(*AbSt 156*) A field placed in the bottommost position (in relation to) a *dike(? text water(?)),
AbSt 156f.' ED$_{I}$ rev. vi 4 = SS 273	an-dur$_{5}$ kur$_{6}$(!)-rum an-ḫád kur$_{6}$(!)-rum al-dur$_{5}$ kur$_{6}$-ra-àm al-ḫád kur$_{6}$-ra-àm	(*AbSt 156f.*) whether it is wet, it is a field (that provides) a source of income; or whether it is dry, it is nevertheless a field (that provides) a source of income.
AbSt 157' ED$_{I}$ rev. vi 5 Cf. SS 102	sa$_{10}$ DUL(?) ⸢x⸣ dumu mu-da-sá lú-tur-ŋu$_{10}$ níŋ nu-mu-un-da-sá	(*AbSt 157*) … (my) son, nothing compares (with it).
AbSt 158' ED$_{I}$ rev. vi 6 SS 276	⸢ki⸣ nu-zu GÍR ur ḫuš ur nu-zu ḫul-àm lú nu-z[u ḫuš-àm]	(*AbSt 158*) An unknown ⸢place⸣ (mistake for dog?) is a knife(?, mistake for evil?); (even) the dogs are ferocious.
AbSt 159' ED$_{I}$ rev. vi 7	šà diri níŋ KIN ḫé AN ⸢ḪUB⸣(?)	(*AbSt 159*) …
AbSt 160' ED$_{I}$ rev. vi 8 = SS 274	níŋ u$_{4}$-[g]u-dé níŋ-mud$_{5}$ níŋ ú-gu dé-a níŋ-me-ŋar-ra	(*AbSt 160*) To lose something is awful.

AbSt 161' ED$_{I}$ rev. vi 9 = SS 275	 [x (x)] ⸢x⸣ gín [x (x)] an [x x] ki ta TAR x gín-dilmun^{ki}-na sa$_{10}$-šè *sù(? text: TE)-ga	 (*AbSt 161*) … (at the standard of the Dilmun)-shekel …
AbSt 162'	*One lines missing at the beginning of rev. vii.*	(*AbSt 162–165: Destroyed*)
AbSt 163' ED$_{I}$ rev. vii 1	 […] na?	
AbSt 164' ED$_{I}$ rev. vii 2	 [x] ⸢x⸣ gi(?) ⸢x⸣	
AbSt 165' ED$_{I}$ rev. vii 3	 [x] ḫul ⸢é⸣ AN NAM	
AbSt 166' ED$_{I}$ rev. vii 4' Cf. SS 284	 [x] ⸢ŠU⸣ me(?) NÍG.ŠÀ.A(?)(= kadra) kadra inim-ma-bi níŋ šà-te-na m[u(?)- …]	 (*AbSt 166*) (this) gift …,
AbSt 167' ED$_{I}$ rev. vii 5' = SS 286	 [i]nim AN.[A]N […] [ka]dra inim-inim-ma mu[l an …]	 (*AbSt 167*) of (many) words (is) [like] the stars [of heaven] …
AbSt 168' ED$_{I}$ rev. vii 6'	 *(destroyed)*	 (*AbSt 168–169: Destroyed*)
AbSt 169' ED$_{I}$ rev. vii 7'	 DÍM […]	
AbSt 170' ED$_{I}$ rev. vii 8' (cf. line 6:	 [GIŠ.PI.TÚG ḫ]é-[m]a-ak GIŠ.PI.[TÚG] ḫé-m[a]-ak)	 (*AbSt 170*) let attention be paid!
AbSt 171' ED$_{I}$ cf. rev. vii 8 = SS 287	 šuruppak Ú[R].A[Š](?) dumu na ⸢ri⸣-ri-ga na-ri šuruppak^{ki} dumu ubar-tu-tu-ke$_{4}$ na ri-ga	 (*AbSt 171*) (These are instructions which) the Man from Šuruppak gave as instructions to "Father-in-Law," his son.

End sign in ED$_{I}$.

General Remarks on the Abū Ṣalābīkh Version

The following instances represent types of phonetic writing that could be expected in syllabically written Sumerian texts of the Isin-Larsa period, but for the Early Dynastic period this is a novelty in unilingual Sumerian texts: AbSt 15: du_7 = SS 27 du_{14} (also in AbSt 24 = SS 35); AbSt 42: ⸢sá⸣(?) = SS sa_6; AbSt 43: u_5, if correctly interpreted as phonetic for SS 48: u_4, "day"; AbSt 104: kù = SS 95: ku_4-ku_4; apparently also in AbSt 54: ù = SS 127: è; AbSt 133: níŋ-du_{10}-du_{10} = SS 204: níŋ-du_{12}-du_{12}; AbSt 132: *ḫu(written RI)-gig = SS 203 ḫul-gig; AbSt 144: ḫu-gig = ḫul-gig (cf. SS 235); ibid. dug_8-dug_8 = SS 235: du_{12}-du_{12}; AbSt 160: u_4-gu-dé, for SS 274: ú-gu-dé-a. In view of the fact that such phonetic "spellings" played an important role at Ebla in the same period, and obviously were important factors in the development of cuneiform writing as a tool adaptable for both Semitic and Sumerian, this may, after all, not come as a very great surprise.[1]

In most cases of textual history, misunderstandings or misinterpretations of early sources are likely to occur in the later ones; cf. *Chap. 3.3: The Ballade of Early Rulers* for some obvious examples. Yet, in this specific case, the development remarkably seems occasionally to have worked the other way: At least in the following instances, the Abū Ṣalābīkh source seems to display scribal errors that have been "corrected" in the later sources: AbSt 13: šà is incomprehensible (perhaps an error for za-e?); AbSt 15: gub-ma error for gub-ba? = SS 27; AbSt 23, apparently, but unintentionally(?), duplicates AbSt 55 (cf. SS 37 and 67); in AbSt 134: gaba is an obvious error for SS 205: nir, caused by dittography; in AbSt 154: one šà is an obvious error for SS 271: bar, also caused by dittography. Also AbSt 40–41 give the impression of corrupted versions of SS 47 and 45. In AbSt 110, BU might be a corrupt form of -kam_4 = SS 97: -ka. In AbSt 132, RI-gig is an error for ḫu-gig (= SS 203: ḫul-gig). In AbSt 135: there is a strong suspicion that KA-zu_5 is a mistake for ní-$zu_{(5)}$, "yourself," or similar (cf. SS 206: ní-zu). In AbSt 158, GÍR seems suspicious (does it stand for SS 276: ḫul, or lú?). Also, in AbSt 158: ⸢ki⸣ nu-zu GÍR ur ḫuš, ki, and perhaps also ur are suspicious, cf. SS 276. Finally, the sign PA in AbSt 129, representing SS 200: má, may be a simple scribal error. Even if some of these cases should turn out to find good orthographic explanations, those that unquestionably will remain lead to the inevitable conclusion that the Abū Ṣalābīkh tablet was a copy from a more correctly written Early Dynastic tablet, now lost, and that the main stream of transmission did not depend on the Abū Ṣalābīkh source known to us. These features fit the impression of the Abū Ṣalābīkh tablet as a "pupil's" copy of minor importance, not provided with a detailed colophon listing the scribes, whereas the Adab tablet evidently was a fine piece of scribal work.

The interpretation of the Abū Ṣalābīkh source is hampered by the many omissions characteristic of the orthography of the ED period, in particular in that most grammatical elements are unexpressed in writing. Another problem is that sign combinations can be expressed through a single sign representing a whole complex. Add to these difficulties the fact that the signs need not be written in the order in which they are to be read within their cases. It stands to reason that such writings make the interpretation hazardous unless a duplicate or parallel text in ordinary SS orthography is available.

1. Cf. Cooper, 1999, 71: "The new paradigm has it that Sumerian literature was first written down in ED IIIa as a response to the possibilities, and perhaps the challenges, arising from the development of Semitic writing." This reverses the roles traditionally assigned to early Sumerian and Semitic writing.

Synopsis of Lines Included in Both ED Versions

The following lines, apart from the introductory lines, occur in both the Abū Ṣalābīkh version and that from Adab.

AbSt 6 = Adab Segm. 1.11 = SS 15.
AbSt 10 = Adab Segm. 1.12 = SS 17.
AbSt 11 = Adab Segm. 2.1 = SS 21.
AbSt 12 = Adab Segm. 2.2f = SS 19.
AbSt 13 = Adab Segm. 2.3 = SS 20.
AbSt 17 = Adab Segm. 2.10 = SS 28.
AbSt 18 = Adab Segm. 2.11 = SS 30.
AbSt 19 = Adab Segm. 2.12 = SS 29.
AbSt 25 = Adab Segm. 3.1 = SS 36.
AbSt 29 = Adab Segm. 3.4 (cf. SS 213).
AbSt 38, cf. Adab Segm. 4.1? = SS 43.
AbSt 43 = Adab Segm. 4.3 = SS 48.
AbSt 125–126 = Adab Fr. 9 = SS 187–188.

Note that Adab Segm. 1.10 = SS 14 does not occur in AbSt, at least as far as can be judged from the preserved parts, although this might have been expected. Yet, it might have been in the destroyed AbSt 7.

The sequences are, thus, roughly the same in the three versions. A remarkable case of reorganization occurs, however, in AbSt 9 (obv. ii 3), which in the SS version has been removed to a context similar to SS 154, where it fits into the sequence concerning acquiring slaves.

Comments on Individual Lines

AbSt 1 *= SS 4, etc:* ŋéštu for ŋéštu-tuku.

AbSt 5 *= obv. i 8 = SS 10:* GIŠ.PI.[TÚG] probably for ŋizzal.

AbSt 6 *= obv. i 9 = Adab Segm. 1.11 = SS 15, etc.:* The AbSt source in this case has gán-zu, "your field," whereas Adab and SS have simply gán without the possessive suffix. In view of the use of a-šà = *eqel-ka* in SS 16, versus gán = *me-re-ša* in SS 15 (cf. also SS 17), it clearly seems that the two terms are distinguished, a-šà meaning "field," whereas gán means "area," although the latter is also used for aša$_5$, in particular in Nippur and Adab. Cf. the comments on SS 15, and Civil, JCS 25 (1973) 171–172. Cf. p. 232, *Instr. Ur-Ninurta* 46–47.

AbSt 8 *= obv. ii 1–2 = SS 18:* Cf. the comments on SS 18 for the sign LAK 218. It is doubtful whether this, together with ŋál-am$_6$, represents SS KÉŠ-da ŋál-la-àm or whether it is the signs x-sír alone that represent SS KÉŠ-da.

AbSt 9 *= obv. ii 3 = SS 154:* Cf. the comments on SS 154, where the reading and etymology of kar-kíd(AK) is discussed.

AbSt 10 *= obv. ii 4 = Adab Segm. 1.12 = SS 17:* Cf. the comments on SS 17.

AbSt 11 *= obv. ii 5–6 = Adab Segm. 2.1 = SS 21:* igi-du here represents SS igi-du$_8$; cf. comments on SS 21.

AbSt 12 *= obv. ii 7–8 = Adab Segm. 2.2 = SS 19:* šu-dù represents ED$_2$ and SS šu-du$_8$-a. Cf. the comments on SS 19.

AbSt 13 *= obv. ii 9 = SS 20; cf. Adab Segm. 2.3:* The initial šà, for which the parallels have ur and za-e, looks very much like a scribal error. šu-bad = ED$_2$ šu-ba; SS: šu-du$_8$-a; cf. the comments on SS 20. [me]-zu, if correctly restored, may be a phonetic rendering of ní-zu, "yourself"; cf. AbSt 23 and 24, however. The restoration [ak] is based on the SS version, but doubtful.

AbSt 15 *= obv. iii 1–2 = SS 27:* du$_7$ = SS du$_{14}$; also in AbSt 24. NI.I(= LAK 134) = in(-nu); cf. the comments on SS 27. Although there is no -ba preserved in any of the SS sources, the AbSt form gub-ma is suspicious, and perhaps best to be explained as an error for gub-*ba.

AbSt 17 = *obv. iii 4* = *Adab Segm. 2.10* = *SS 28:* me-zu = Adab and SS ní-zu, "yourself," punning on ní-zuḫ, "thief." MUNŠUB(= LAK 672), here apparently = úš, "to kill"; cf. the comments on Adab vers. 2.10, and p. 217, *Special ED signs.*

AbSt 18 = *obv. iii 5* = *Adab Segm. 2.11* = *SS 30:* Cf. the comments on Adab vers. 2.11 and SS 30.

AbSt 19 = *obv. iii 6* = *Adab Segm. 2.12* = *SS 29.* Cf. the comments on SS 29.

AbSt 20 = *obv. iii 7* = *SS 31:* For the variant ⌜x⌝ sír(?), cf. the comments on SS 31.

AbSt 21 = *obv. iii 8* = *SS 32:* Cf. the comments on SS 32.

AbSt 22 = *SS 33:* [si]kil = ki-sikil. The possibility that NE here represents a form of (zú –) li_9(-r), *ṣiāḫu*, "to laugh," should also be taken into account, suggested by Akk_2: [*la t*]*e-ṣe-eḫ*, "don't laugh." Cf. the comments on SS 33.

AbSt 23 = *obv. iv 3* = *SS 37; cf. AbSt 55:* If me(?)-⌜zu⌝ ŋar-ra, represents SS 37: inim-zu ŋar-ra-àm, this seems to be a variant of an expression that occurs also in AbSt 55 = ED_I obv. vii 3: ka nam-tar ŋar, in which the second part is simply abbreviated to ŋar. Cf. the comments above, p. 188, *General Remarks.* Since this would be the only case where this source "duplicates" itself (apart from the introductory formula, etc.), it is, of course, also possible that these are entirely different lines; yet, there is a strong impression that one of these lines entered the text by mistake.

AbSt 24 = *obv. iv 4* = *SS 35:* For du_7, cf. AbSt 15. níŋ-z[$u_{(5)}$ na-š]ub: apparently níŋ-zu represents me-zu = ní-zu, "yourself," but Westenholz alternatively suggests "don't drop your own," i.e., "mind your own business."

AbSt 25 = *obv. iv 5* = *Adab Segm. 3.1* = *SS 36:* Cf. the comments on SS 36.

AbSt 29 = *obv. v 1; cf. Adab Segm. 3.4; cf. SS 213:* This cannot be the same as SS 213, but they may be related. For MUNŠUB, cf. the comments on AbSt 17. Here it can hardly mean "to kill."

AbSt 30 = *obv. v 2; cf. 214:* This cannot be the same as SS 214, but they seem related. If the translation "don't hire oxen" for na-ḫuŋ-ḫuŋ is justified, it would be a rare ED case of reduplication indicating a non-personal plural object.

AbSt 33 = *obv. v 5* = *SS 215:* Cf. the comments on SS 215.

AbSt 34 *obv. v 6–7* = *SS 39:* Implying "with the man (who has stolen it)"; cf. the comments on SS 39.

AbSt 35 = *obv. v 8* = *SS 40:* Tentatively, perhaps the Akkadian translation represents a deviation and re-interpretation from the ED text. I, therefore, take úš as "blood" and su-su as "to sprinkle" (with blood). The connection between blood and hands is attested in *The Good Seed of a Dog* 11 (Sjöberg, JCS 24 [1972] 107), quoted by Alster, 1974, 86, who reads: l[ú-l]a-ga é si-ga šu úš-a-kam a, "robber, when the house is quiet, he acts(?) with bloody hands." For the Akkadian version of SS 40–41, cf. the comments on SS 40.

AbSt 36 = *obv. v 9* = *SS 41:* The most likely reading in ED_I is anše, rather than ŋìr, in particular since the second part of the line has gud, "ox." If this is correct, then also in this case the SS version represents a deviation and reinterpretation from the ED version. Cf. the comments on SS 41.

AbSt 37 = *obv. v 10* = *SS 42:* Cf. the comments on SS 42.

AbSt 38 = *obv. v 11* = *SS 43; perhaps* = *Adab Segm. 4.1:* Cf. the comments on SS 43.

AbSt 39 = *obv. v 12* = *SS 44:* For ḪUL, apparently read $kiŋ_x$, cf. AbSt 56 and p. 217, *Special ED signs.* sá is a phonetic indicator to ság; cf. SS 44: [sá]g.

AbSt 40 = *v left edge and vi top edge* = *47:* It is uncertain whether this can be connected to SS 47; perhaps dim_4 means "tested," somewhat like uš sì-ga, "a (well-)placed foundation." It would be remarkable, however, that é would correspond to SS uš.

AbSt 41 = *obv. vi 1* = *SS 45:* gud does not correspond to SS 45: uš, so the assignment of the line to SS 45 remains uncertain. As in the preceding line, a mistake may be involved. Maybe $ŋi_6$ was erroneously repeated from the following line by dittography.

AbSt 42 = *obv. vi 2–3* = *SS 47:* In the second part sá seems to be phonetic for SS 47 sa_6(-g).

AbSt 43 = *obv. vi 4–5* = *Adab Segm. 4.3* = *SS 48:* u_5 is very tentatively interpreted as phonetic for u_4, although this seems unexpected. Cf. the comments on SS 48.

AbSt 44 = *obv. vi 6–7* = *SS 49:* Cf. the comments on SS 49 and Adab Segm. 3.3.

AbSt 45 = *obv. vi 8* = *SS 62:* Cf. the comments on 62 and Adab Segm. 3.2.

AbSt 47 = *obv. vi 10–11* = *SS 153:* Cf. the comments on SS 153 and p. 209, *Chap. 1.9: Tense or Aspect Related Verbal System?*

AbSt 48 *= obv. vi 12–13 = SS 155:* For the ED writing ḪAR-tu, apparently representing SS ama-a-tu (= émedu), cf. the comments on SS 155 and the literature there cited.

AbSt 49 *= obv. vi 14:* Cf. the collation by Alster, 1991–92, 33: "KASKAL KA SILA x(= like LAGAB). ... clearly KA, not SAG."

AbSt 53 *= obv. vii 1 = SS 126:* For di – e /dug_4, cf. the comments on SS 126.

AbSt 54–55 *= obv. vii 2–3+ = SS 127; cf. SS 37 and 67:* Alster, 1990, 18 (l. 132) suggests that this is SS 127, with ⌜x⌝ representing é, reading ⌜é⌝-ta ù $šà_x$(SAR)-zu_5 <na>-gu_7. In this case ù is phonetic for è, and SAR is apparently mistaken for SS šà. Both are without parallels and, therefore, problematic. Civil, 1984, 282 reads: ù-sar-zu_5-ta ⌜x⌝ gu_7 | níg-nam sag-ku_5, "With your bite, eating ... you slaughter(?) everything," connecting this with ù-sar–ak = *šêlu*, "to sharpen." He sees this as perhaps related to SS 127 ("OB 132?"). Cf. the comments on SS 127.

AbSt 55 *= obv. vii 3 = SS 37 and SS 67, addition.* Cf. AbSt 23, ED_I obv. iv 3: KA na-tar me(?)-⌜zu⌝ ŋar-ra, in which the second part apparently is a variant of the same expression as the second part of SS 37. This is the only instance where ED_I seems to quote the same expression twice.

AbSt 56 *= obv. vii 4 = SS 175:* Cf. the comments on SS 175, and for ḪUL, possibly = $kiŋ_x$, cf. AbSt 39.

AbSt 57 *= obv. vii 5 SS = 176:* Cf. the comments on SS 176.

AbSt 58 *= obv. vii 6 = SS 177:* Cf. collation by Alster, 1991–92, 33 ("Obv. vii 5'"): "gá-la d[ag] é dúr-šè [(x)] ⌜du⌝." The reading du is confirmed by a variant in SS 220, K_I: du_8, cf. ibid., p. 33, nn. 15–17, and comments on SS lines 177 and 220.

AbSt 59 *= obv. vii 7:* Alster, 1991–92, 33: "Obv. vii 6," reading ka[š ...], should be corrected to "Obv. vii 7"; this also applies to the copy p. 51.

AbSt 68 *= obv. viii 4:* Cf. comments in Alster, 1991–92, 33, with copy p. 51: "The sign in front of dub is ⌜HI⌝ (or similar), ... not IGI." Civil, 1984, 283, reads: I[GI].DUB ⌜su⌝ [...].

AbSt 93 *= rev. i 7 = SS 125:* Cf. the comments on SS 125. The parallelism suggests that AbSt 92 should be restored in accordance with SS 124.

AbSt 101 *= rev. ii 4 = SS 85:* Cf. the comments on SS 85.

AbSt 102 *= rev. ii 4; cf. SS 86:* The last sign is that shown by Biggs, OIP 99, p. 99, ad lines 104–107, with a copy p. 112. It is similar to $sila_4$, or ùr, depending on the identification of our line as SS 86; it, thus, is very likely to be an ED variant of ùr; cf. Alster, 1991–92, 25 ad line 60.

AbSt 103 *= rev. ii 5 = SS 89:* Cf. collation by Alster, 1991–92, 33: "The sign in the upper right corner (after lú) could be KALAM."

AbSt 104 *= rev. ii 6 = SS 95:* If the assigment of the line to SS 95 is justified, ši-kù is phonetic for *šè-ku_4-ku_4 (SS níŋ-ku_4-ku_4), but it is remarkable that the SS níŋ-clause is here introduced by a verbal "contrapunctic" clause. Cf. the comments on SS 95–96, and Alster, ZA 80 (1990) 15–19. Westenholz, however, alternatively suggests reading ši as igi, translating "a bright eye is a powerful thing" (silig = *šagapūru*, relating to spiritual power), which I hesitate to accept, because, since it was the recognition of similarity with SS 95 that led to the identification of the line, it is unlikely that the meaning was completely different in the ED and the SS versions. The issue remains, of course, that so much meaning has to be supplied from the SS version that the ED text would make sense only if understood as mnemotechnical aid for someone who had the complete wording in mind. Since the SS text can, indeed, be understood as an expansion of the ED text, remaining within approximately the same range of meaning, I consider this to be the most likely solution and, in fact, to have been a general characteristic of a larger number of ED IIIa tablets. This is in line with the general impression from some other grave omissions, cf., e.g., AbSt 108.

AbSt 105 *= rev. ii 6 = SS 96:* níŋ-silig seems to represent SS 96 níŋ nu-silig-ge-dam, but again, if justified, it is remarkable that the meaning of the ED sentence largely has to be supplied from the SS text, like AbSt 104.

AbSt 108 *= rev. ii 9 = SS 93:* This is a much abbreviated form of SS 93, with máš-ú omitted.

AbSt 109 *= rev. ii 10 = SS 94:* A represents SS íd. The -bi following šà is written here, although it is omitted in the preceding line. The short writing A for íd occurs also in AbSt 129.

AbSt 110 = *rev. ii 11* = *SS 97:* BU remains unexplained, but it might be a corrupt form of -kam$_4$, marking the genitive, like SS -ka. The reduplication of šúm is remarkable; it apparently denotes the plural, "several loaves." The second part of SS 97 does not appear here.

AbSt 111 = *rev. ii 12* = *SS 98:* The -da is a rare rudiment of a grammatical element, the gerund -/eda/, in ED; cf. SS 98: šúm-mu-da-bi.

AbSt 112 = *rev. ii 13* = *SS 101:* Cf. the collation by Alster, 1991–92, 34: "níŋ-ú:d[ù]g:rum níŋ ⌜x⌝ [x]." I cannot explain the meaning of d[ù]g here. For the second part, cf. the comments on SS 101. I have adopted the translation "things set aside" from Selz, 2002(b), 174.

AbSt 113 = *rev. ii 14* = *SS 102:* Partly repeated as AbSt 157 below.

AbSt 114 = *rev. iii 1* = *SS 182:* Cf. the collation by Alster, 1991–92, 34: "máḫ e é dù ⌜x⌝ ḫur. ... x can be šè ..." = e/ere(?) máḫ é dù ⌜šè⌝-ḫur, "The huge city builds houses and digs canals." For the interpretation, cf. the comments on SS 181–182, where it is pointed out that the sequence of the ED version makes better sense than that of the SS version.

AbSt 115 = *rev. iii 2* = *SS 181:* Cf. collation by Alster, 1991–92: "é x (= GAR) amar ⌜x⌝ ⌜x⌝."

AbSt 116–118 = *rev. iii 3–6:* This section, which I cannot translate, seems to have dropped out of the SS version. Cf. the comments in Alster, 1991–92, 34 and the copy ibid., p. 51. MUL is clear on the tablet. MUL might be a form of /nab/, written nàb(= AN+AN) in ED$_2$. This would be the only place, however, where ED$_I$ does not simply write the verbal preformative /na/ as na-.

AbSt 118 = *rev. iii:* Cf. the collation by Alster, 1991–92, 34: "The third sign is certainly ta-*gunû*."

AbSt 120 = *rev. iii 7–8* = *SS 184:* The first sign is ÁŠ (one unbroken vertical), rather than ZÍZ (broken vertical). According Steinkeller: "(z)a-áš-da = *kiššātum*," RA 74 (1980) 178–179, this distinction can clearly be made in texts from Fara and Abū Ṣalābīkh. For the interpretation, cf. the comments on SS 184. I here tentatively take áš as "curse," strangely not included in the SS version.

AbSt 121–122 = *rev. iii 9–10:* Alster, 1991–92, 34, suggests "The one who possesses something is an adorned person, he surpasses the one who has nothing." This would fit as the continuation of AbSt 118 = SS 184, so it is remarkable that the lines have dropped out of the tradition. Cf. below for a slightly different interpretation.

AbSt 122 = *rev. iii 10:* The reading of GI seems to be a$_x$, cf. Alster, 1991–92, 23, ad line 27; and p. 23 ad line 27. This would give saŋ è-a$_x$. For the reading a$_x$ for GI, cf. Biggs, JCS 20 (1966) 80, n. 48, who suggested reading A as gi$_{23}$, whereas Postgate, AfO 24 (1973) 77, correctly suggested reading GI as aš$_x$, when it occurs as a variant of A (before š). In view of the parallelism, there can hardly be any doubt that a negation, like nu-, has to be understood before the verb. Westenholz, however, points out the presence of a grammatical element, such as /a/, is unlikely in an ED IIIa text and contests the reading a$_x$.

AbSt 123 = *rev. iii 11* = *SS 185:* Cf. the comments on SS 185.

AbSt 124 = *rev. iii 12* = *SS 186:* Cf. the comments on SS 186. šér-díb represents SS še-er-tab-ba; DU seemingly represents SS ná, not unlikely in view of the many readings attached to DU, but I have no further evidence for this.

AbSt 125–126 = *rev. iii 13–14* = *Adab Fr. 9* = *SS 188; 187:* Cf. the collation by Alster, 1991–92, 34: "The sign copied ... as TAR is the rest of zi." For the interpretation, cf. the comments on SS 187–188, but note that the line order is reversed here. Note also the grammatical elements -da- and šè-, for which see pp. 212–216, *Chap. 1.9: ED Modal verbal prefixes: ED examples of ša-/ši-šu-*.

AbSt 127 = *rev. iii 15* = *SS 196:* Cf. the collation by Alster, 1991–92, 34: "sa[g] ⌜x⌝ ⌜x⌝ [(x)] nu-bad." bad strangely represents SS bar here; cf. AbSt 13: šu-bad = Adab Segm. 2.3: šu-ba (but SS 20: šu-du$_8$-a).

AbSt 128 = *rev. iv 1* = *SS 197:* Cf. the collation by Alster, 1991–92, 34: "dumu ḫul ⌜šà⌝ nu-bar. I clearly see nu and bar (rather than me)." Cf. the comments on SS 197. If the reading dumu is justified, it seems to represent the address dumu-ŋu$_{10}$, "my son," which, however, seems rather unmotivated here.

AbSt 129 = *rev. iv 2* = *SS 200:* Cf. the collation by Alster, 1991–92, 34: "ḫul-da A zág(PA) su." Wilcke, 1978, 227, was undoubtedly right in explaining PA as a writing for má(!), as appears from the parallel SP 22 ii 25–26: ḫul-da íd-da má ḫé-en-da-su (Alster, *Proverbs* I, 262), in spite of the doubts expressed by Alster,

1991–92, 34, n. 20. The short writing A = íd occurs also in AbSt 109.

AbSt 130 = *rev. iv 2* = *SS 201:* ùmmu is here written ^{kuš}A.EDIN; later it is written ^{kuš}A.EDIN.LÁ, cf. the discussion in the commentary to SS 201, where PSD A/I, 64–66, is quoted for a critical view on the reading ùmmu(-d) for A.EDIN.LÁ.

AbSt 131–132 = *rev. iv 3–4* = *SS 202–203:* These lines are reflected in an ED lexical list from Ebla, quoted in the comments on SS 202–203. RI-gig is an obvious error for ḫu-gig, phonetic for ḫul-gig.

AbSt 133 = *rev. iv 6–7* = *SS 204:* -kam$_4$ shows that also SS 204: me nam-nun-na was meant as a genitive; níŋ-du$_{10}$-du$_{10}$ is phonetic for níŋ-du$_{12}$-du$_{12}$; cf. the comments on SS 204.

AbSt 134 = *rev. iv 8* = *SS 205:* gaba-ŋál certainly looks as caused by dittography for SS 205: nir-ŋál. Cf. the comments on SS 205.

AbSt 135 = *rev. iv 9* = *SS 206:* KA-zu$_5$ is hardly "your mouth" or "your word," but might be a scribal error for *me-zu$_5$, = ní-zu, "yourself," perhaps through inim-zu or *eme-zu; cf. the comments on SS 206.

AbSt 136 = *rev. iv 10* = *SS 207:* Cf. the comments on SS 207.

AbSt 137 = *rev. iv 11–12* = *SS 220:* munus-bar-[š]u šè-ŋál is written without the verbal preformative šè- in SS 220. Cf. the comments on SS 220.

AbSt 138 = *rev. iv 13–14* = *SS 221:* It is remarkable that the ED source has a velar stop in gu[ru$_7$, for which the SS form indicates a labial stop in buru$_{14}$; perhaps they both reflect a double articulation, like /g^b/; cf. the comments on SS 221 and the literature there cited. I cannot explain the use of LAGAB-LAGAB for SS su-su-su.

AbSt 139 = *rev. iv 15–16:* Civil, 1984, 297, considers the possibility that "mu mu sì ga is to be understood as mu-sì-ga mu-sì-ga, with sì-g for sag$_9$" (= sa$_6$-g). I suggest that mu-mu-a sì-ga means "placed among (known) names," i.e., among friendly people, which suits the context of the SS version. Cf. the comments on SS 168, where OB Proto-lú 516: mu-mu-a, is cited. I cannot suggest anything for lú na[m] ŠÈ and its SS correspondence.

AbSt 140 = *rev. iv 17:* Collation by Alster, 1991–92, 34: "ki áš dug$_4$-ga su-lu-⌜x⌝ ⌜x⌝"; copy p. 51. It is tempting to connect this with ^{kuš}lu-úb, in SS lines 106–107; 119–121, but the traces do not fit the second part of any of those lines.

AbSt 141–142 = *rev. iv 18 rev. v 2:* These so far remain unidentified.

AbSt 143 = *rev. iv 18:* The expression á-zi is reminiscent of SS 50 and 62 (= AbSt 45), but there seems be no further connection between the lines.

AbSt 144 = *rev. v 3; cf. SS 235:* bu-bu$_7$(KU) can perhaps be explained as a phonetic indicator: ^{bu}bu$_7$(KU), cf. AbSt 39 = SS 44: ^{sá}ság; or perhaps, rather, as bu-bul$_x$, phonetic for SS ù-bu-bu-ul. "flame." Cf. the comments on SS lines 138; 235; and 265. ḫu-gig is phonetic for ḫul-gig; cf. the similar writing in AbSt 132. du$_8$-du$_8$ is phonetic for du$_{12}$-du$_{12}$.

AbSt 145 = *rev. v 4:* I cannot offer anything constructive for this line.

AbSt 146–148 = *rev. v 5–7:* A three-line repetition of the introductory phrases.

AbSt 149–153 = *rev. v 8 - vi 1:* So far these have not been identified. AbSt 149-150: Reading according to Sjöberg, *Kienast FS*, 527, cf. also PSD A/2, 32, a$_2$-aga$_2$.

AbSt 154 = *rev. vi 2* = *SS 271:* One of the two šà signs is an obvious mistake for bar. Cf. the comments on SS 271.

AbSt 155 = *rev. vi 3:* This is reminiscent of SS 193ff., but is no clear duplicate.

AbSt 156 = *rev. vi 4* = *SS 272:* A seems to stand for e(-g), "dike/ditch," perhaps best to be explained as a dittography of the following sign A, to be read dur$_5$, *ruṭibtu*, "wet." Cf. the comments on SS 272 for details.

AbSt 157 = *rev. vi 5; cf. 102:* I cannot make sense out of the first three signs; the rest is almost certainly the same phrase as AbSt 113 = ED$_I$ rev. ii 14: [dumu-ŋ]u$_{10}$ [níŋ nu-da-sá] = SS 102: lú-tur-ŋu$_{10}$ níŋ nu-mu-un-da-sá, which, thus, may have been a kind of refrain; cf. the comments on SS 102.

AbSt 158 = *rev. vi 6* = *SS 276:* The first part, ⌜ki⌝ nu-zu, seems to represent ur nu-zu, either with ki as an error for ur or perhaps for ur ki nu-zu, "a dog whose place is unknown"; cf. the comments on SS 276. GÍR looks like an error for ḫul or ḫuš, which is strange, because the sign ḫuš occurs at the end of the line. Or, maybe either GÍR or ur is a scribal error for lú, which is expected in the second part. Perhaps the explanation is simply that the signs have to be read in a different order. A. Westenholz alternatively suggests taking this literally as it stands, "an unknown place is a knife, (even) the dogs are ferocious." If justified, it would be one of the relatively few cases of a proverbial expression having changed considerably from ED to SS Sumerian, in which the saying occurs elsewhere similar to our SS 280 (see the comments on SS 280).

AbSt 159 = *rev. vi 8* = *SS 274:* u_4-gu-dé is phonetic for ú-gu-dé-a. níŋ-mud_5 is replaced by níŋ-me-ŋar-ra is the SS version. Cf. the comments on SS 274 for the interpretation.

AbSt 160 = *rev. vi 9; cf. SS 274:* Only the sign gín indicates that this equals SS 275, but unfortunately it is not possible to retrieve it in detail.

AbSt 163–165 = *rev. vii 1–3:* These have not yet been identified.

AbSt 166–167 = *rev. vii 4–5; cf. SS 284:* These seem related to SS 284ff., but are too poorly preserved to show how far the parallel goes.

1.6 The Adab Version

All lines that could be identified as parallels to the SS version are transliterated under the main SS text in *Chap. 1.3*. Details pertaining to the interpretation of the main SS text are discussed in the commentary in *Chap. 1.4*. For the sake of clarity a separate complete transliteration of the Adab version (here ED_2) is included below. To make comparisons easier the corresponding lines in the Abū Ṣalābīkh version (ED_1), as well as those of the SS version, are repeated here (without variants) under the relevant lines of the Adab text. Nearly the same procedure is followed for the Abū Ṣalābīkh text in the reconstruction attempted in *Chap. 1.5*.

For a detailed list of the Adab sources used, see pp. 47–48, *Chap. 1.2: Sources*. Copies of the fragments by D. Luckenbill are published in OIP 14, pls. 55–56; a photograph is shown in OIP 99, p. 58.[1] The obverse had at least six columns, probably more. The reverse probably had the same number of columns as the obverse, or less, if it was not fully inscribed, as Fragments 1 and 6 suggest.

A. Westenholz dates the text as late as perhaps Early Sargonic. The level of scribal ambition is much higher than that of the Abū Ṣalābīkh source, which does not even have a colophon.

Biggs, OIP 14, 57, n. 4, noted the epigraphical similarity with the Barton Cylinder, MBI, no. 1, found at Nippur.[2]

The Segmentation of the "Lines"

The vertical columns were divided horizontally into cases of equal size,[3] which implies that the grammatical line breaks in many cases do not coincide with the case divisions, but frequently are interrupted by the automatic segmentation of the cases. As a result it is impossible to calculate the original number of "lines" corresponding to the "verses"[4] of the SS version.[5] This principle occurs in some rare later instances, in particular some Ur III literary tablets. Cf. also Alster, 1975, 144, who points to the same phenomenon in the Kurigalzu inscription published by T. Baqir and S.N. Kramer, *Sumer* 4 (1948) 1–29. Similar examples are mentioned by Sjöberg, *Jacobsen MV*, 242, n. 26.

A running enumeration of the lines of the Adab version is only attempted for the first part, owing to the fragmentary state of preservation of the rest.

The Relations to the Other Versions

The Adab version largely follows the organization of the SS version, yet with a number of remarkable differences, and apparently had a few more lines in common with the SS version than the Abū Ṣalābīkh version. The line sequences of the Adab version seem to have followed a pattern roughly similar to that of the AbSt and the SS versions, but apparently it included some lines not present in the AbSt version and, thus, seems a bit closer to the SS version. Also from an epigraphical point of view, the Adab version is less "archaic" than the Abū Salābīkh version, with decisively fewer examples of defective writings. Cf. *Chaps. 1.5* and *1.9: The Grammatical and Graphical Elements* for details. The Adab version seems not to have included lines not incorporated into the other

1. Here pl. 28. Note that the alignment of the upper fragment is not quite correctly shown on the photograph, in that the upper fragment should have been placed somewhat higher up; cf. Alster, 1974, 25, confirmed on the original fragments by Biggs.
2. Cf. the detailed information provided by A. Westenholz, in Alster and Westenholz, AcSum 16 (1994) 15–17.
3. The columns are here described as "vertical" following common consensus, although I consider the tablets to have been written in vertical alignment on columns running horizontally from top to bottom, with the case boxes running from right to left (on the obverse); cf. the brief discussion by Alster, "Text and Images on the Stele of the Vultures," AfO 50 (2005, forthcoming), with references to the basic discussions by S. Picchioni.
4. Cf. previously Alster, 1974, 24.
5. In this edition theses are called "lines," although in this special case, the designation "verses" would admittedly have been better.

versions, but this is uncertain in view of the fragmentary state of preservation of the text.

For a previous attempt to reconstruct the Adab version, see Alster, 1974, 21–25, who assigned 19 "lines," that is, cases of equal size, to each column. This seems to be approximately right and is also the basis for the present attempt. The introductory lines seem to have been repeated a number of times, so the repeated occurrences of those lines have been used to restore the imperfectly preserved occurrences.

Transliteration

Adab Segm. 1.1–2

ED$_2$ obv. i 1–2		
= Fr. 2 i 1–2	[ŋéštu-tuku inim-galam inim-zu-a]m$_6$ | [kalam-m]a [ti]-la-am$_6$	*(Segm. 1.1–2)* The intelligent one, the one of artistic words, the wise one, who lived in the country;
= ED$_I$ obv. i 1–2	ŋéštu inim-zu | [ka]lam [t]i-la	
= SS 4	u$_4$-ba ŋéštu-tuku inim-galam inim-zu-a kalam-ma ti-la-a	

Adab Segm. 1.3–5

ED$_2$ = Fr. 2 i 3–5	[šurupp]ak^{ki} [Ú]R.AŠ | [ŋéš]tu-[tu]ku inim-[galam inim]-zu-am$_6$ | [kalam-m]a [ti-la-am$_6$]	*(Segm. 1.3–5)* the Man from Šuruppak, to "Father-in-Law"—the intelligent one, the one of artistic words, the wise one, who lived in the country,
= ED$_I$ obv. i 3–5	[šuruppak Ú]R.[A]Š | [ŋéš]tu inim-zu | kalam ti-la	
= SS 5	šuruppak^{ki} ŋéštu-tuku inim-galam inim-zu-a kalam-ma ti-la-a	

Adab Segm. 1.6–7

ED$_2$ # Fr. 4 ii 2–3		
& 10 ii 1–2	[šuruppak^{ki}] ÚR.AŠ | dumu-ni-ra na na-ri-ri	*(Segm. 1.6–7)* the Man from Šuruppak gave instructions to "Father-in-Law," his son:
ED$_I$ obv. i 6	šuruppak dumu na [n]a-mu-ri	
= SS 6	šuruppak^{ki}-e dumu-ni-ra na na-mu-un-ri-ri	

Adab Segm. 1.8

ED$_2$	[dumu-ŋu$_{10}$ na ga-ri]	*(Segm. 1.8)* ["My son, let me give you instructions,]
ED$_I$ obv. i 7	dumu-ŋu$_{10}$ na ga-ri	
= SS 9	dumu-ŋu$_{10}$ na ga-ri na-ri-ŋu$_{10}$ ḫé-dab$_5$	

Adab Segm. 1.9

ED$_2$ Fr. 10 i 1'	GIŠ.PI.[TÚG] ḫé-m[a]-ak	*(Segm. 1.9 = SS 10)* Let attention be paid to them!
ED$_2$ i 9	[ŋizz]al ḫé-⌜x-x⌝ (= -⌜ma-ak⌝?)	
= SS 10	zi-u$_4$-sud-rá inim ga-ra-ab-d[ug$_4$] ŋizzal ḫé-em-ši-ak	

Adab Segm. 1.10

ED$_2$ Fr. 10 i 2–3	ANŠE [K]A gù-di nàb(AN+AN)- | sa$_{10}$-sa$_{10}$ [...] na-e	*(Segm. 1.10 = SS 14)* Don't buy an ass that brays; don't [...]
= SS 14	dùr.⌜ùr⌝ gù-di na-ab-sa$_{10}$-sa$_{10}$ érin-zu ša-ra-ab-si-il-le	

Adab Segm. 1.11 (- 12?)

ED$_2$ Fr. 10 i 4–5 gán kaskal na-ŋá-ŋá | nam-[silig] ⌜x⌝ [x gán-za]
ED$_1$ obv. i 6 gán-zu [kaskal na-ŋá-ŋá]
= SS 15 gán kaskal-[la] nam-bí-íb-ŋá-ŋá nam-silig gú-ŋá-àm

(*Segm. 1.11 = SS 15*) Don't place a field on a road, the [decimation is crushing(?)].

Adab Segm. 1.12 (f.)

ED$_2$ Fr. 10 i 6–7 [pú náb]-⌜du⌝ [ùŋ]-e | [...]-LU
ED$_1$ obv. ii 4 gán-za pú na-⌜dù⌝ ⌜ùŋ⌝ ⌜šè⌝-⌜mu⌝-ra-⌜ḫul⌝
= SS 17 gán-zu-àm pú na-an-ni-dù-e-en ùŋ-e ša-re-eb-ḫul-ḫul

(*Segm. 1.12 = SS 17*) [Don't] place [a well in your field; the people will ...]

Adab Segm. 1 ca. 13–14: *x number of lines missing, perhaps corresponding to:*

ED$_1$: obv. ii 1–2: é sila(!)-daŋal na-dù(text: NI) x-sír LAK 218 ŋál-am$_6$
= SS 18: é sila-daŋal-la nam-bí-ib-lá-e KÉŠ-da ŋál-la-àm
ED$_1$ obv. ii 3: géme kar-kíd(ak) na-an-sa$_{10}$ ka ù-sar-kam$_4$
= SS 154 [kar-k]id na-an-sa$_{10}$-sa$_{10}$-an ka u$_4$-sar-ra-kam

Adab Segment 2.1'

ED$_2$ ii = Fr. 2 ii 1–2 [...] URU×A l[ú (x = small sign or nothing, hardly uru$_5$?)] | ši-su-su
ED$_1$ obv. ii 5–6 [i]gi-du na-⌜x⌝-⌜ba⌝ | lú uru$_5$ ši-sù x x
= SS 21 lú-ra igi-du$_8$ na-an-ak-e úru-bi ša-re-e[b]-su-su

(*Segm. 2.1 = SS 21*) Don't give evidence against a [man(?); the [city(?)] will repay you! (Altern. translation: A flood (arising from it) will submerge you!

Adab Segm. 2.2' + 2.3a

ED$_2$ Fr. 2 ii 2–4 ⌜šu⌝-du$_8$-a na- | túm lú-bi ša$_4$-ba- | dab$_5$
= ED$_1$ obv. ii 7–8 šu-dù na-túm lú | šè-ba-dab$_5$
= SS 19 šu-du$_8$-a nu-e-tùm lú-bi ša-ba-e-dab$_5$-bé

(*Segm. 2.2 = SS 19*) Don't guarantee for a man; that man will have a hold on you!

Adab Segm. 2.3 cont. + 2.4

ED$_2$ Fr. 2 ii 4–5 ur šu-ba na-ak | ní-zu na-du$_7$-né
ED$_1$ obv. ii 9: šà šu-bad na-ak [me]-zu a[k]
Cf. SS 20 za-e šu-du$_8$-a nam-mu-ak-e
(addition, Ur$_1$: [l]ú saŋ bí-íb-sal-la-e-a)

(*Segm. 2.3; cf. SS 20*) Don't make a pledge(?) for someone(?); don't humiliate yourself!

Adab Segm. 2.5

ED$_2$ Fr. 2 ii 6 [x] ⌜x⌝ G[Á] (or similar) [...]

Adab Segm. 2.6 *Probably one line missing =*

ED$_1$ obv. iii 1–2 du$_7$ sila-kúr ⌜x⌝-ma | NI.LAK 134 bar-tar-ta gub-ma
= SS 27 du$_{14}$ bar-bar-ta gub-gub-[ba] in-nu-uš sila-kúr-ra níŋin-na-ma-a[n ...]

(*Perhaps:*) [Take another road when encountering quarrels; stand aside when facing an insult!]

Adab Segm 2.7

ED$_2$ Fr. 10 ii 1 ⌜šuruppak⌝[ki]

(*Segm. 2.7–9*) The Man from Šuruppak gave instructions to "Father-in-Law," his son:

Adab Segm 2.8

ED_2 Fr. 10 ii 2	ÚR.AŠ dumu-ni-ra	

Adab Segm 2.9

ED_2 Fr. 10 ii 3	na na-mu-ri-ri	

Adab Segm. 2.10

ED_2 Fr. 10 ii 4–5	níŋ nám-zuḫ-zuḫ ní-zu | nàb(AN+AN)-MUNŠUB	(*Segm. 2.10 = SS 28*) Don't steal anything; don't kill yourself!
ED_1 obv. iii 4	níŋ na-mu-zuḫ-zuḫ me-zu na-MUNŠUB	
= SS 28	níŋ nam-mu-zuḫ-z[uḫ] ní-zu nam-mu-úš-e	

Adab Segm. 2.11

ED_2 Fr. 10 ii 5–6	nu-zuḫ | [p]iriŋ na-nám ù- | dab$_5$ géme na-nám	(*Segm. 2.11 = SS 30*) The thief is indeed a lion; when caught he is indeed a slave girl!
ED_1 obv. iii 5	nu-zuḫ ušum na-nam ul-dab$_5$ géme na-nam	
= SS 30	ní-zuḫ piriŋ na-nam ul-dab$_5$ saŋ na-nam	

Adab Segm. 2.12

ED_2 Fr. 10 ii 7	é nam-m[u]-⸢bùr⸣ [...]	(*Segm. 2.12 = SS 29*) Don't break into a house; [don't demand the money chest!]
ED_1 obv. iii 6	é na-[bùr] ⸢x⸣ [x x]	
= SS 29	é na-a-an-ni-bùr-e-en mi-si-saḫar-ra al nam-me	

Adab Segm. 2.13ff. x number of lines missing at the end of obv. ii

For the following section, no connected reconstruction is attempted, but cf. Alster, 1974, 22, assigning approximately 10 lines to the break, of which only part of iii 2 remains:

ED_2 Fr. 2 iii 1	x [...] ⸢x⸣ [x]	

Adab Segm. 3.1'–2

Fr. 3 iii 1	[lu]l [na]-gur$_5$-gur$_5$ |	(*Segm. 3.1'f. + Fr. 10 iii 1–2 = SS 36 + 62*) Don't plan lies! It is degrading(?). Don't rape a man's daughter; don't let it be known in the courtyard!
Fr. 3 iii 2	[s]aŋ sal-sal-[a]m$_6$ / dumu-lú- |	
Fr. 10 iii 1	ra ⸢ŋìš⸣	
Fr. 10 iii f	á-zi na-e	
Fr. 10 iii 2	kisal na-zu-zu |	
= SS 36	lul na[m]-gur$_5$-gur$_5$ saŋ-gú ⸢sal-sal⸣-la	
= SS 62	dumu lú-ra ŋiš á-zi na-an-ne-en kisal-e bí-zu-zu	
Fr. 10 iii 3	ad nà[b(A[N]-A[N])-gi$_4$-gi$_4$] |	(*Segm. 3.2 Fr. iii 3–4 = SS 38*) Don't be exaggeratedly advising; don't (let them) lift a [reproachful] eye (towards yourself!)
Fr. 10 iii 4	igi ⸢x⸣ (= [du]gud?]) nàb(AN-AN)-íl [géme]	
= SS 38	⸢ad⸣ nam-gi$_4$-gi$_4$ igi-dugud nu-mu-un-da-íl(-e-en)	

Adab Segm. 3.3

Fr. 10 iii 5	ŋiš (sic! not ŋìš) n[a]-e š[u- x]	(*Segm. 3.3 = SS 49*) Don't have sexual intercourse with your slave girl; don't ...
= SS 49?	géme-zu-úr ŋiš na-an-dù zu-úr šu-m[u]-ri-in-sa$_4$	

Adab Segm. 3.4

Fr. 10 iii 6 [g]ud-l[ul(?)] nà[b-[x] |
ED$_2$ obv. v 2 ⸢gud⸣ na-MUNŠUB ⸢gud⸣ e-KAL
Cf. SS 213 gud [...(?)] ní-ŋ[ál na]-⸢an⸣-ni-sa$_{10}$-sa$_{10}$

The continuation of Fr. 10 iii missing.

Adab Segm. 4

Fr. 10: an unknown number of cases missing at the beginning of obv. iv (cf. Alster, 1974, 22: tentatively estimated to 13 cases between iii 6 and iv 9).

Adab Segm. 4.1'

Fr. 10 iv 1' gu[d x] igi [x]
Cf. ED$_1$ obv. vi 1? gud ŋi$_6$ [x x]
Cf. SS 45? uš nu-sì-ga-šè ⸢gud⸣-lú na-ḫuŋ-e

Adab Segm 4.2

Fr. 10 iv 2 kaskal ⸢x⸣(hardly ŋi$_6$) [na-]
Fr. 10 iv 2f d[u (x) x]
Cf. ED$_1$ obv. vi 1 kaskal ŋi$_6$ na | šà ⸢sá⸣(?) ḫul
Cf. SS 47 kaskal ŋi$_6$ na-an-du šà-bi sa$_6$ ḫul-a

(*Segm. 4.2 = SS 47*) Don't walk on a road *at night(?); [...]

Adab Segm. 4.3

Fr. 1 i 1' [x x]
Fr. 1 i 1' f anše-edin
Fr. 1 i 2' nàb-sa$_{10}$-
Fr. 1 i 2' f ⸢sa$_{10}$⸣ [x]
ED$_1$ obv. vi 4–5 edin na-sa$_{10}$ u$_5$-šè sa$_{10}$
SS 48 anše-edin-na na-ab-sa$_{10}$-s[a$_{10}$] u$_4$ da-bé-eš ì-za-al

(*Segm. 4.3 = SS 48*) Don't buy a "steppe-ass" (i.e., an onager); [...]

Lacuna (by Alster, 1974, 22, estimated to approximately 17 cases)

Adab Segm. 5.1 (obv. v)

Fr. 1 ii 2' [ki]ri$_6$-k[a]
Fr. 1 ii f [d]ag-ga nám-
Fr. 1 ii 3' bí-du$_8$-
Fr. 1 ii 3' f e su-a su-a
(Continuation missing)
SS 58 gi-sig-ga ^{ŋiš}kiri$_6$-ka da-ga nam-bí-du$_8$-e-en
SS 59 su-ga-ab su-ga-ab ši-me-ši-íb-bé-e-ne

(*Segm. 5.1 = SS 58–59*) Don't break [the reeds regarding] an agreement of a garden; Restore them! restore them! [they will say to you]

An unknown number of cases missing (by Alster, 1974, 22 estimated to approximately 13 cases, corresponding to AbSt v 1 and 3–12 = SS 213; 214; ?; 215; 39; 40; 41; 42; 43; 44. It is at least very likely that the two sequences were nearly identical in the two ED sources).

The photograph shows a small part of Fr. 1 iii, with no signs preserved, indicating that the obverse had at least 6 columns.

The following fragments seem to be from the reverse:

Fr. 5 has the right edge preserved, and seems therefore to be from the first column on the reverse:

Fr. 5.1	[x] ⸢x⸣
Fr. 5.1 con't	[x r]i-ri (introd. lines)
Fr. 5.2	[x u]r
Fr. 5.2 con't	[(x)] ⸢x⸣ LUL

(Lower edge preserved)

Fr. 6 is a fragment with only the right column inscribed, apparently with a part of the top edge preserved. Since the left column is uninscribed, it seems to belong to the top of the last column of the reverse, toward the very end of the composition:

Fr. 6 i 1	ki [x x]
	AN [x x]
	KA×X(like ZÍD) ⸢x⸣(like the beginning of b[al]
	⸢šà⸣ ⸢x⸣
Fr. 6 i 2	SI UNKEN GÁ
	⸢x⸣ [x x]
Cf. ED$_I$ rev. iv 17–18	ki áš dug$_4$-ga SU ⸢x⸣ ⸢x⸣
	KA SI kalam ma

Fr. 7 is a top piece with the right edge and parts of two columns preserved; it seems to be from the beginning of cols. i–ii on the reverse:

Fr. 7 i' 1	á ⸢x⸣
	šuruppak (= introd. form)
(Cf. perhaps ED$_I$ iii 11 ff.)	
(Cf. SS 187?)	lú dam tuku á šu im-du$_7$-du$_7$
Fr. 7 i' 2	[x] ⸢x⸣
Fr. 7 ii 1	[x] ⸢x⸣(vertical) SI
	[x] ⸢x⸣

(cf. perhaps ED$_I$ rev. vi 7, or SS 219)

Fr. 8 is a middle fragment with parts of two columns preserved.

Fr. 8 i' 1'	šeš-[gal a-a] na-nám
Fr. 8 i' 2'	ama na-[nám]
	[x] KA×A
Cf. SS 172	šeš-gal a-a na-nam nin$_9$-gal ama na-nam

(*Fr. 8 = SS 172*) A [older] brother is indeed [a father; <an older sister> is] indeed a mother!

NB no space for nin$_9$-gal in the Adab version.

Of Fr. 8 ii only a long horizontal line remains.

Fr. 9 is a fragment apparently from the reverse with the right edge preserved. A part of the bottom edge is shown on Luckenbill's copy, but this is hardly correct.

Fr. 9.1'	⌜x⌝ gul(?)-gul(?)	(*Segm. 9 = SS 187–188*) [He who is about to destroy houses] will destroy houses; he who is about to stir up men will not [...]
Fr. 9.2'	[lú(?)] zi AN.[x (= n[àb?)]-⌜x⌝(like ka, not zi)-e	

There can hardly be any doubt that this is related to SS 187–188:

SS 187	é gul-gul-lu-dè é ša-ba-da-an-gul-e
SS 188	lú zi-zi-i-dè lú ša-ba-da-an-zi-zi-i

Comments on Individual Lines

***Adab Segm. 1.3–5**, Fr. 2 i 3–5, etc.:* ÚR.AŠ is here understood as a name or an epithet of the son named Ziusudra in the SS version. Cf. the discussion in the comments on SS lines 5–7, esp. 5–6. I understand Šuruppak^{ki} as an epithet of the father of the first generation, that is, the Šuruppak'ean, and posit an anacoluth after the first occurrence of ÚR.AŠ, as explained in the discussion loc. cit.

***Adab Segm. 1.10**, Fr. 10 i 2 = SS 14:* ANŠE [K]A here corresponds to SS 14 dùr.⌜ùr⌝. Note the negative motivation clause introduced by na-; cf. the comments on Adab Segm. 2.3 = SS 20.

***Adab Segm. 1.11**, Fr. 10 i 4–5:* gán is here written without the possessive suffix -zu, and kaskal without the locative marking.

***Adab Segm. 1.12**, Fr. i 6–7:* The assignment of this line to SS 17 is not quite certain, since it would imply that ⌜du⌝ is written phonetically for dù, and in the second part of the line LU is difficult to harmonize with SS 17.

***Adab Segm. 2.1'**, Fr. 2 ii 1–2 = SS 21:* URU×A here corresponds to ED_2 uru_5, and SS úru. The beginning of the line probably had igi-du_8, here understood as "testifying"; cf. the comments on SS 21.

***Adab Segm. 2.2' + 2.3a**, Fr. 2 ii 2–4 = SS 19:* ⌜šu⌝-du_8-a na-túm is here understood as "Don't act as a guarantor"; cf. the comments on SS 21. In the verbal form $ša_4$-ba-dab_5, if correctly read, DU = $ša_4$ is used as a verbal profix = šè. This has no further parallels in the sources presented here, but ši- occurs in Adab Segm 2.1 = SS 21, etc. and the Abū Ṣalābīkh examples listed pp. 212–216: *Modal Verbal Prefixes: ED Examples of /ša/ ... ša, šè, ši.* The verb itself is without the imperfective (*marû*) marker /e/.

***Adab Segm. 2.3 cont. + 2.4**, Fr. 2 ii 4–5 = SS 20:* For a discussion of the relation to SS 20, see the comments on that line. Since Ed_1: šu-ba, Ed_2: šu-bad, and SS 20: šu-du_8-a, all include a verb that can mean to "open," or similar; it is likely that all three lines have approximately the same meaning. The SS version za-e šu-du_8-a nam-mu-ak-e is best understood as "and *you*, don't make a pledge," but it is questionable whether this was understood in the same way as the ED versions. It is likely that the ED texts are to be understood as "don't make a pledge," or similar. Instead of SS 20: za-e, ED_2 has ur, which perhaps can be understood as an obsolete personal(?) pronoun, "someone." For this possibility, cf. Attinger, 1993, 171, referring to Edzard, BiOr 28 (1983) 165ff. (p. 166 "ein pronominales Element ...ur ... - zur Personenklasse gehörig - im Genus ursprünglich indifferent"). ED_1 has šà, which looks erroneous; cf. p. 188.

The second part of the line: ní-zu na-du_7-né, cannot be harmonized with the other versions, but probably means "don't humilate yourself," perhaps for sun_5(-na) = *wašru*, "demütig"; cf. AHw 1488. It represents a motivation clause including a second negative imperative. This is a feature particular to the Adab version; cf. p. 214, *Modal Verbal Prefixes: ED Ex. ... of /ša/ ... ša, šè, ši.* Apart from our line, Adab Segm. 2.3 (cf. SS 20), this phenomenon occurs in

Adab Segm. 1.10 = SS 14; Adab Segm. 2.10 = SS 28; Adab Segm. 3.2 = SS 62; Adab Fr. 10 iii 4 = SS 38; Adab Segm 3.3 = SS 49. The use of this negative motivation clause is not automatic, because positive motivation clauses occur in Adab Segm. 2.1 (ši-) = SS 21; Adab Segm. 2.2 ($ša_4$-) = SS 19.

Here the negative motivation clause, of course, reflects the heavy punishments prevailing in early Mesopotamian society, but it can be understood also as a morbid humorous overstatement; cf. p. 39, *Introd. to Instr. Šuruppak: Legal Aspects* ..., and the literature there cited.

***Adab Segm. 2.1'**, Fr. 2 ii 1–2= SS 21:* ši- is here unambiguously used as a verbal prefix; cf. the comments on Segm. 2.10 = SS 28, etc.

***Adab Segm. 2.10**, Fr. 2.10 ii 4–5 = SS 28:* The sign MUNŠUB here seems to be used for úš, "to kill." Cf. p. 217, *Special ED Signs: LAK 672.*

For the motivation claused phrased as a second negative imperative, cf. the comments on Adab Segm. 2.3 (cf. SS 20) above.

***Adab Segm. 2.11**, Fr. 10 ii 5–6 = SS 30:* Note nu-zuḫ punning on ní-zu, "yourself"; nu is an old form for lú; cf. p. 217, *nu : lú.* Note further the variants ED_2 and SS: piriŋ for ED_I: ušum; ED_2 and ED_I: géme for saŋ. This suggests that different orally existing sayings influenced the transmission in this case. It is remarkable that ED_2: ù-dab_5 has the expected prospective ù profix, whereas ED_I is closer to the SS sources, reading ul-dab_5. This could perhaps be from ù + al > ul, written defectively ù in Adab? (oral suggestion by A. Westenholz).

***Adab Segm. 3.1'–2**, Fr. 10 iii 1–2 = SS 36:* Cf. the comments on SS 36, where the meaning of lul – gur_5 is discussed. The possibility that the Akkadian translation *la tu-uk-tap-pa-ad*, "don't devise lies," may be a later development should, of course, be taken into account. The meaning may have been "do not spit out lies," or similar. The second part of the line, [s]aŋ sal-sal-[a]m_6, is remarkable in that there is no gú following saŋ, as in the SS version. It is likely to denote a more serious consequence than "it is silly(?)," tentatively suggested by Alster, 1974, 23, rather "it is degrading."

***Adab Segm. 3.1'–2**, Fr. 3 iii 2 – Fr. 10 iii 1–2 = SS 62:* For the second part: kisal na-zu-zu, "don't inform the courtyard," which is a motivation clause including a second negative, cf. the comments on Adab Segm. 2.10 = SS 20 above. It does not occur in this form in SS 62, which has a positive verbal form. Cf. the detailed discussion in *Chap. 1.4: Comments on line 62.*

***Adab Segm. 3.1'–2**, Fr. 10 iii 3–4 = SS 38:* PSD A/3, 4, lists Adab version iii 11–12 (here Fr. 10 iii 3–4) and its duplicates, but note that there is no variant inim for ad in SS 38.

I cannot harmonize the second part of SS 38: igi-dugud, with Fr. 10 iii 4, where the sign following igi does not seem to be dugud.

***Adab Segm. 3.3**, Fr. 10 iii 5 = SS 49:* ŋiš is undoubtedly phonetic for ŋiš, which strangely occurs just above in Fr. 10 iii 1 = SS 62. The second part, n[a]-e š[u- x], also displays a negative motivation clause, and cannot be harmonized with the second part of SS 49: zu-úr – sa_4, which I understand as phonetic for zú-ur_5 – $ša_5$(AK), translated *i-še-el-le-e-ka*, "she will neglect you"; cf. the comments on SS 49.

***Adab Segm. 3.1'–2**, Fr. 10 iii 6:* May be related to SS 213, but difficult to harmonize.

***Adab Segm. 4.1**, Fr. 10 iv –1 = SS 45?:* By Alster, 1974, 22 (iv 9) tentatively taken as SS 45, but it could perhaps rather be = SS 43, in which case the first sign might be a form of búr, instead of gud, while IGI would be the verbal preformative ši-. This is rare but not unique in ED, cf. pp. 214ff., *Modal Verbal Prefixes: ED Ex. ... of /ša/ ... ša, še, ši.* In any case, the sources are difficult to harmonize.

***Adab Segm. 4.2**, Fr. 10 iv 2 = SS 47?:* The sign following kaskal does not look like $ŋi_6$, but starts with a vertical.

***Adab Segm. 4.3**, Fr. 1 i 1' = SS 48:* Cf. the comments on SS 48. The line may have been understood differently in the later sources.

***Adab Segm. 5.1**, Fr. 1 ii 2'f = SS 58–59:* For dag-ga, cf. the comments on SS 58–59.

***Fr. 6**:* Seems related to ED_I rev. iv 17–18, but difficult to harmonize.

***Fr. 8 i' 1'–2'** = SS 172:* nin_9-gal seems to have been omitted by scribal error in the Adab version, which has no room for it. KA×X may belong to one of the following SS lines, maybe a variant of SS 174.

***Fr. 9.1** = SS 187–188:* The two signs read gul look like LAK 179 or gir_4. It has too many horizontals to be a traditional gul, but there can be no doubt that gul is intended and that these are SS 187–188. It seems, however, that the preserved part of 9.1 represents the second part of SS 187, in which case the second occurrence of gul was reduplicated, contrary to the SS version.

1.7 The Hurrian Version
by Gernot Wilhelm

The bilingual fragment of unknown origin published by M. Krebernik, *ZA* 86 (1996) 170–176, has been identified by M. Civil as a part of the Sumerian composition *The Instructions of Šuruppak*. The reconstruction of this text by B. Alster seems to confirm Krebernik's hesitant suggestion that the right columns on both sides of the fragment might contain a Hurrian translation of the Akkadian text in the left columns. The present edition shows that Krebernik's "Seite A" belongs to the obverse, "Seite B" to the reverse of the tablet. The preserved text on the right column of the obverse corresponds to lines 11–16, that on the reverse to lines 60–67.

The syllabary used in the right columns does not display the traits typical for Hurrian. It uses TA and DA without applying the Hurrian rules of positional distribution of voiced and unvoiced stops (TA: initial [line 63], [line 66], intervocalic non-double [line 65], DA in contact with Š [line 63]).

The Obverse

Lines 11, 13: *az-k*[*i-ir*(-), *az-ki-ir*[(-): Lines 11 and 13 have the noun na-ri = *as̆ertu* "instruction" in common. Consequently, *azkir*(...) is likely to be its equivalent, though in line 11 it belongs to the second part of the line, whereas *as̆ertu* is the first word of the Akkadian line. No Hurrian word meaning "instruction" is known, nor is a root *ask*-; a root that comes close to this is *as̆k*- "to demand compensation," often used with *verba dicendi*. In derivations whose meaning remains unknown, *as̆k*- is followed by -*ir*-.[1] It can be neither excluded nor proven that *azkir*(...) is to be derived from this Hurrian root.

Line 14: *zu-ḫi-ra and ḫa-i-...*: In consideration of the normal position of the Hurrian verb (non-initial; initial only when topicalized) and the Hurrian adjective (following its head), it is likelier that this word is the rendering of ANŠE, dùr = *mūru* "donkey foal" than that of gù-di = *nāgigu* "braying" or a form of sa_{10} = *s̆âmu* "to buy." The word should thus be identified with Hurr.[2] *suġe/iri* "donkey/horse foal" as attested in the Hurrian plural *sú-ḫé-er-ra*^{meš} (*suġer*(*i*) =*ra* < ...=*na*) AdŠ 119:9 (= HSS 13.323). AdŠ 98:2 (= *HSS* 13.382) refers to *murū* instead.[3] AHw 1054b is certainly correct in calling Akk. *suḫīru* (attested in Nuzi, Alalaḫ and, seldom, in Middle and Neo-Assyrian) a Hurrian loanword.

The ending in -*a* is difficult to explain. Since the Sum. and Akk. show a singular form, a Hurr. plural as in the Nuzi passage quoted above is out of the question. We might, however, be dealing with the essive ending -*a*, which encodes the goal of an action in the so-called "absolutive-essive-construction."[4]

The second preserved word of the double line, *ḫa-i-x*[ ], seems to be the equivalent of Akk. *ú-sà-pa-ḫa* "it will scatter." Hurrian has a well-attested root *ḫa*- "to take away"[5] (followed by the vowel -*i*- indicating transitivity). The meanings do not match perfectly; whether or not *ḫa*- "to take away" is applicable here, depends on the sense of the passage, which remains doubtful.

1. G. Wilhelm, "A Hurrian Letter from Tell Brak," *Iraq* 53 (1991) 164f.
2. A Hurrian root with the meaning "buy" is *alad*-; see G. Wilhelm, "*aladumma epēšu* «begleichen; kaufen»," SCCNH 8 (1996) 361–364.
3. See commentary on the last passage in: G. Wilhelm, *Das Archiv des Šilwa-teššup*, Heft 3 (Wiesbaden, 1985), 69.
4. For this construction, see G. Wilhelm, "Die Absolutiv-Essiv-Konstruktion des Hurritischen," in: Y. Nishina (Hg.), *Europa et Asia Polyglotta — Sprachen und Kulturen: Festschrift für Robert Schmitt-Brandt zum 70. Geburtstag* (Dettelbach, 2000), 199–208.
5. Established by E. Laroche, "Études de linguistique anatolienne III," RHA 28 (1970) 63 on the basis of the bilingual ritual passage KBo 19.145 iii/iv 45 (~Hitt. *da*- "take (away)") and confirmed by E. Neu, "Hurritische Verbalformen auf -*ai* aus der hurritisch-hethitischen Bilingue," in: P. Kosta (ed.), *Studia indogermanica et slavica. Festgabe für Werner Thomas zum 65. Geburtstage,* Specimina philologiae slavicae Suppl. 26 (München, 1988), 508 with n. 22.

Line 15: *e-ba-*[...]; *Line 16: e-x*[...]: Both lines begin with words for "field" (gán = *mērešu*, a-šà = *eqlu*) followed by words for "road," "passway" (kaskal = *ḫarrānu*, ka-ŋìr [= *padānu*]?). The well-attested Hurrian word for "field" is *avari*. There is a noun *ebāni* (ChS I/1 6 [KBo 20.126] iii 40', plural *eban(i)=n(a)=až =a-*: ChS I/1 65 "Vs. ii?" [KBo 33.8 iii] 8')[6] whose meaning cannot yet be determined from context; hence, it is unclear whether it is connected to Urart. *ebani* "land, country."

Line 62: *ta-ḫ*[*é*?(...)], *ḫi-ra*[(...)]: The Akkadian version starts with *mārti amēli* "the daughter of a man," which should be rendered in Hurrian as **taḫḫe/taġe=ne=ve šala*. This matches the preserved part of the Hurrian version satisfactorily, because the horizontal wedges following TA might well be the first part of a ḪÉ (the ḪÉ is used in the Akkadian column obv. 12a [= line 17]).

The word *ḫi-ra*[(...)] could correspond to any of the last words of the Akkadian version. The Hurrian equivalents to *naqāpu* "rape," *puḫru* (gathering [of judges], i.e., court), and *lamādu* "learn" have not yet been found.

Line 63: *ta-aḫ-a:* As Krebernik already noticed, *ta-aḫ-a* could well be equivalent to Akk. *eṭlu* "young man." The "broken spelling" *-aḫ-a* is well attested in Hurrian, especially in Mari, Alalaḫ and ūattuša, [7] and usually represents a double consonant as in Old Akkadian.[8] The spelling *da/ta-aḫ-e* is attested at ūattuša. [9]

The final *-a* might be explained as an essive in an absolutive-essive-construction or as the stem-ending of a variant *a*-stem.[10] The following sign *ma-* (or BA?; not KU, based on the form of KU in the Akk. column obv. 11b [= line 16]) perhaps belongs to an adjective qualifying *taḫḫe*. The rest of line 63 cannot be connected to the Sumerian or Akkadian text; *ušt-* is a root with the meaning "to go out (for battle)" (hence *uštanni* "warrior, hero"). If, indeed, the Akk. text has [*sa*]*kkul-šu* "his club" in the second half of the line, there is a remote possibility that Hurr. *atki* is a variant of *itki*, a noun that is attested in the quadrilingual S^a Vocabulary from Ugarit as equivalent to Akk. *urṣu* "mortar" and that is based on the root *id-* "to beat."[11]

Line 65: *pu-ta-ni-ia-aš*[(...)], *ti-ir-ḫa*[...]: The first noun should be the (otherwise unattested) equivalent to Akk. *ākil karṣi* "slanderer." It seems to be a *nomen agentis* like *ašḫ=i=a=šše* "sacrificer," *tad=i=a=šše* "lover" or *pin=i=a=šše* "s.o. who raises (a child)"[12] (ergative verbal form 3rd person sing. with nominalizer in *-šše*). The root *pud-* or *putt-*

6. The word *e-ba-ni-we-* quoted by E. Laroche, *Glossaire de la langue hourrite* (Paris, 1980), 72, from a Hurrian text from Mari (Mari hurr. 6+7:15, see M. Salvini, "Un texte hourrite nommant Zimrilim," RA 82 [1988] 59–69) is doubtful, because the second sign could be MA as well.
7. G. Wilhelm, ZA 77 (1987) 233; SCCNH 8 (1996) 339 n. 26. *AoF* 24 (1997) 283 n. 34. Mari: *Ḫa-wa-al-e*, *Ḫa-wa-al-im*[ki] ON, 11405:78, 99. Alalaḫ: *eġelli*: *e-ḫé-el-e* Al.T. 133:37 (cf. *e-ḫe-el-li Al.T.* 211:47), Pl. *e-ḫé-el-e-na Al.T.* 129:44; *Am-ma-ri-ik-e* ON *Al.T.* 189:52 (cf. *Am-ma-ri-ik-ki Al.T.* 35:13). Ḫattuša: *I-ki-in-kal-iš-* KBo 32.19 iii 1; *ku-la-aḫ-e-na* (also *ku-la-aḫ-ḫe-na*) "the aforementioned"; *za-a-an-a* KBo 32.223 iii 7', *am-me-e-et-a* ~ 8'; AḪ-*(a-)aš-te-tap* KUB 47.93 Vs. 2, 6, AḪ-*a-aš-te-et-u* ~ 5, *ki-ip-e* ~ 9, *ma-aḫ-a-ar-(r)a* ~ Rs. 6', 7', *ú-bi-e-et-a* ~ 8', *ki-iḫ-e-né-eš* ~ 11', *ḫa-at-ḫé-e-et-a* ~ 12'.
8. I.J. Gelb, *Old Akkadian Writing and Grammar*, MAD 2 (Chicago, ³1973), 42.
9. *ta-aḫ-e* ChS I/5, 138 (= KBo 33.148) r. Kol. 13', *ta-aḫ-i* ChS I/5, 41 (= KBo 11.19+) Rs. 18, *da-aḫ-e* ChS I/5, 40 Rs. 43' (// LÚ). A form with double *ḫ* is attested at Ḫattuša (*ta-aḫ-ḫé-né-e* ChS I/5, 2 Vs. 36', transliteration corrected according to KBo 23.23 Vs. 18') and as a personal name at Nuzi (Taḫḫe NPN s.v.). There is, however, a spelling at Ugarit that suggests a glottal stop instead: LÚ = *amīlu* = *ta-a-e* RS 94–2939 v 5', ed. B. André Salvini / M. Salvini, "Un nouveau vocabulaire trilingue sumérien-akkadien-hourrite de Ras Shamra," SCCNH 9 (1998) 7, 17f. Again, an even better-attested personal name at Nuzi can be adduced: Ta-e (s. NPN s.v.).
10. Perhaps it is an older form that by addition of the honorific *-i* led to *taḫḫe* via **taḫḫai* like in Šimiga => Šimigai => Šimige.
11. J. Huehnergard, *Ugaritic Vocabulary in Syllabic Transcription*, HSS 32 (Atlanta, 1987), 24f.
12. G. Wilhelm apud I. Röseler "Hurritologische Miszellen," SCCNH 10 (1999) 398 n. 20. Cf. also G. Wilhelm, "Die Könige von Ebla nach der hurritisch-hethitischen Serie «Freilassung»," *AoF* 24 (1997) 280 with n. 13 for *ḫam(a)z=i=a=šše* "oppressor"(?) KBo 32.15 i 19'.

apparently is not the same as in *futt=ož =a* "he begot him," *put=ki* "son" etc. For a homonymic root *fud-* in *fud=ar=i=nni* "fuller, washman" see KBo 32.15 i 28'.

The second word is completely broken; according to the Akk. text it should be a form of *ši, šini* "eye."[13]

The last preserved word *ti-ir-ḫa*[...] reminds one of *ti-ir-ḫa-aḫ-e-na* ChS I/5, 66 (= KUB 47.51) iv 6' of unknown meaning, but apparently not "spindle," as Sum. ᵍⁱšbala-gim and Akk. *kīma pilikki* suggest. The Hurr. equivalent of bal and *pilakku* in the quadrilingual Sª Vocabulary is *tiyari*,[14] which might be connected to *ti-ir-ḫa*.

The Reverse

For most of the remaining words of the rev. right column (*ta-ag-ga(-)ba*[ ], *pu-ri-ga*? [rev. ii 7, l. 66] and *zi-im-*x[ ] [rev. ii 8, l. 67]) no plausible analyses and meanings can be offered. igi-a // *ina pāni* "in front of" normally would be rendered by *av/b(i)=ī=da* in Hurrian. But if *pu-ri-ga*? can be read as *pu-ri-t*[*a*], it might be analyzed as *p/fur(i)=i=da* "to his eye,"[15] though this meaning would remain without a parallel; *fur(i)=ī=da* in the Mittani Letter is a postposition meaning "with regard to."

Rev. ii 9, line 64: *tu-*x[ ] seems to be the equivalent of Akk. *eṭlu*, which, however, is rendered by *taġe* in line 63 and presumably also in line 62. There is an adjective *tur=o=ḫḫe* "male" whose basis **turi* is not attested.

13. M. Giorgieri, "Die hurritischen Kasusendungen," SCCNH 10 (1999), 238f. n. 60 with previous literature.
14. Huehnergard, loc. cit. 38f. For further attestations cf. Laroche, GLH, 265f.
15. For *p/furi* "eye," cf. IGI // ⌜*e*⌝*-nu* // ⌜*wu*⌝*-ri* RS 94-2939 ii 1; B. André-Salvini and M. Salvini, SCCNH 9 (1998) 5.

1.8 The Akkadian and Hurrian Versions

Akk_1 is a unilingual Akkadian fragment from Assur, dating from the Middle Assyrian period; Akk_2 is a unilingual Akkadian tablet, probably Middle Babylonian; and Akk_3 is a bilingual that includes the Hurrian fragment edited in *Chap. 1.7*. For further details, see below: *The Akkado-Hurrian Fragment.*

Typical post-OB grammatical forms in Akk_2 are /m/ instead of OB /w/, e.g., line 62, Akk_1: *a-me-l[i*; Akk_2: *a-mi-li*; Akk_3: *a-me-li*. Akk_2 has the typical MB assimilation of /dd/ to /md/ in line 52: *nam-di ... in-nam-di-ka*.

The three Akkadian versions overlap only in a few cases, but enough to reveal that they were made independently of each other. In line 65 Akk_2 translates the Sum. sir_5-sir_5 by *i-na-am-[maš]*, "the spindle moves," whereas Akk_3 translates by *i-te-ru*, "turns"; cf. the comments on line 65 for details. Also line 59, where Akk_1 has *ri-i-ib*, but Akk_2: *ri-bi-am*, "restore!" seems to show that these were made independently as well.

As to the reliability of the three Akkadian translations, in line 11: *i-šar*, "[the instructions that] I/he speak(s)" Akk_3 obviously had problems with the 1st person and mistook it for the 3rd person.

More serious doubts on the correctness of the Akkadian translation are cast by lines 40–41, where the later sources seem to have interpreted the ED sign anše, "donkey," as ĝìr, "foot," which was then understood as a short form of GÌR.PAD.DU, "bone." This resulted in a completely different meaning, referring to the behavior of sacrificial animals. Cf. the comments on lines 40–41 for details; further *Chap. 1.5: Comments on AbSt 36 = SS 41.*

To understand how the three Akkadian versions came into being, issues similar to those relating to the two Akkadian versions—Middle Assyrian and Neo-Babylonian—of *Lugal-e* have to be considered. These have recently been discussed in detail by Seminara.[1] He refers to the period of Tiglat-Pilesar I (1115–1077) as the time when interest in Babylonian literature is most likely to have played a major role in Middle Assyrian Assur, since that ruler is known to have brought Babylonian tablets to Assur as booty,[2] resulting in the existence of a library of Babylonian tablets in Assur.[3] As a result, some important literary works, such as *Lugal-e*, were transmitted in Assur as Sumero-Akkadian bilinguals.

It is remarkable, therefore, that *The Instructions of Šuruppak* was known in Assur in a unilingual fragment, without a corresponding Sumerian version, and likewise that the Akkado-Hurrian fragment, probably of Syrian origin, has no Sumerian version. Seminara deals with the problem of the survival of the Sumerian language in later Akkadian-spoken periods by describing it as a language of prestige.[4] This would conform to the situation resulting in the

1. S. Seminara: *La versione accadica del Lugal-e*, MVS 8 (Roma, 2001), esp. p. 40.
2. Cf. Lambert, BWL, 118, and the literature cited there. The time of Tukulti-Ninurta I (1244–1208) would be a less likely date for the Middle-Assyrian Babylonian literary tablets.
3. Cf. van Dijk, *Sagesse*, 114–118; Lambert, BWL, 118–120; Lambert in *Iraq* 38 (1976) 85–94, n. 2.
4. Seminara, 2001, 524–525: "Lingua di prestigio." He summarizes four theories that have been proposed to explain the survival of the Sumerian language in the scribal curriculum: (1) the translation of Sumerian texts served to initiate the pupils into the system of cuneiform writing, as well as into the Sumerian language itself; this practice is well attested in the *edubba*-literature (so Cooper, 1993, etc.; Hallo, 1966); (2) the preservation of Sumerian texts together with their Akkadian versions served as guaranteeing their authenticity (so von Soden, *Zweisprachigkeit* [Wien, 1960], 12); (3) the transmission of bilingual or multilingual inscriptions often motivated political and ideological changes (so E. Reiner, in: *Storia della Linguistica*, 107–108); (4) the preservation, or often, in an ambitious (quasi-bilingual) cultural environment (Seminara: "in ambito culturale"), the creation of artificial versions of assumed Sumerian originals served to convey the text with greater authenticity ("a dare al testo una patente di autenticità"). Of these, Seminara considers the last by far the most important one. Cf. further Seminara, p. 525: "Tanto più plausibile è l'ipotesi dell'impiego del sumerico come «lingua di prestigio» nei casi in cui al testo è stata creata un'artificosa «preistoria» tradizionale in lingua sumerica mediante la «retro-traduzione» del testo originale in sumerico." For this phenomenon, see now also Cavigneaux, in *Wilcke FS*, 54, who points out that some literary works, such as

transmission of Babylonian bilinguals, such as *The Ballade of Ancient Rulers*, in the Syro-Mesopotamian area, as discussed in *Chap. 3.3*. These considerations, however, do not provide an answer to the existence of unilingual versions, or even an Akkado-Hurrian one, of *The Instructions of Šuruppak*. In such a case, it was presumably interest in the literary composition as such that warranted its inclusion in the scribal curriculum, whereas interest in the Sumerian versions as such was of minor importance, or maybe the Sumerian language was then considered too remote or difficult to be a relevant object of study for the average scribe.

The Akkado-Hurrian Fragment

This is similar to those bilinguals from Emar and Ugarit that have the Sumerian text in left columns and the Akkadian translation in the right ones. In this case the left columns contain the Akkadian text and the right ones the corresponding Hurrian translation. It contains no Sumerian version.

Addition to Akkado-Hurrian Fragment by Gernot Wilhelm

This is the normal format of Hattian-Hittite[5] and Hurro-Hittite[6] bilingual texts at ūattuša. Sumero-Akkadian bilingual or trilingual texts from Hittite archives may be written in the same format,[7] but the Babylonian interlinear format[8] was also known. The only Akkado-Hurrian bilingual attested otherwise is a short wisdom composition found at Ugarit.[9]

the disputation between *The Date Palm and the Tamarisk*, known from the Syro-Mesopotamian area, apparently existed in Akkadian before a Sumerian version was added. The situation was thus very different from that leading to the survival of Sumerian compositions originally composed in Sumerian. Of the compositions treated in this volume there is hardly any that is likely to have existed in Akkadian before it was translated "backward" into Sumerian, perhaps with the sole exception of the Emar version of *Enlil and Namzitarra* (cf. *Chap. 3.5*) (but hardly in connection with the proverbs added to *The Ballade of Early Rulers*; cf. *Chap. 3.4: Proverbs from Ugarit* and *3.3c: The Neo-Assyrian Version*).

5. H.-S. Schuster, *Die ḫattisch-hethitischen Bilinguen*, I. *Einleitung, Texte und Kommentar*, Teil 1, DMOA 17 (Leiden, 1974); II. *Textbearbeitungen*, Teil 2 und 3, DMOA 17/2 (Leiden, 2002).
6. E. Neu, *Das hurritische Epos der Freilassung. Untersuchungen zu einem hurritisch-hethitischen Textensemble aus Ḫattuša*, StBoT 32 (Wiesbaden, 1996). Cf. also KBo 19.145, edited by V. Haas and I. Wegner, *Die Rituale der Beschwörerinnen* SALŠU.GI, Teil 1 (Die Texte), (ChS I/5) (Rome, 1988), 209–215, with commentaries by M. Giorgieri, "Die erste Beschwörung der 8. Tafel des Šalašu-Rituals," SCCNH 9 (1998) 71–86, and I. Röseler, "Hurritologische Miszellen," SCCNH 10 (1999) 393–400.
7. E.g., KUB 4.16 (udug.ḫul.a.meš; only Akkadian preserved but the horizontal lines crossing the column divider prove that the tablet was bilingual); KUB 57.126 (Edubba), see M. Civil, "An Edubba Text from Boghazköy," *N.A.B.U.* 2 (1987) 25–27, no. 47; KUB 37.100a+ (incantations), see J. Cooper, "Bilinguals from Boghazköi," ZA 61 (1971) 1–22 with corrections in KBo 36, p. IV no. 11; for a trilingual hymn, see E. Laroche, "Un hymne trilingue à Iškur-Adad," RA 58 (1964) 69–78.
8. E.g., KUB 4.11 (hymn to Utu-Šamaš); KBo 36.12, 17, 21.
9. See G. Wilhelm, "Bemerkungen zu der akkadisch-hurritischen Bilingue aus Ugarit," in: *Wilcke FS*, 341–345 with previous literature.

1.9 Comments on the Grammatical and Graphic Elements

Tense of Aspect-Related Verbal System?

I prefer to use the terms *perfective* versus *imperfective* of the Sumerian verbal forms, although this may only be a preliminary solution.[1]

The issue is best illustrated by lines 170–171: nam-tar peš$_{10}$ dur$_5$-ra-àm lú-da im-ma-da-an-zé-er, "Fate is a wet bank that made a man's feet slip away from him." The verb translated "made slip" in traditional terminology is considered the past tense. There are two ways in which this can be explained: (1) the line quotes an already existing saying with a verb in the past tense, in which the full context has not be included in the quotation; (2) the Sumerian verbal system was not primarily tempus related in the same way as, say, modern German. Since the first solution is unlikely in the present case, where a general characterization of "fate" is certainly meant, the second is more likely. I tentatively prefer the designations *perfective* versus *imperfective* for the Sumerian verbs, first used by Steinkeller in *Orientalia* 48 (1979) 54–67, although other possibilities would be worth considering, especially *punctual* versus *durative*, which might be more precise.

Perfective verbs, traditionally described as preterite, in fact tend to occur in Sumerian proverbs[2] where, from the point of view of most European languages, we would expect present forms. I would, therefore, draw attention to the fact that the Sumerian use of such forms is comparable to the classical Greek so-called *gnomic aorist*.[3] This implies that general statements tend to occur with verbs in the aorist, which in such cases is tenseless, ex-temporal. This seems exactly to be the case in line 171, where a general characterization of "fate" is undoubtedly intended. Had the verb been in the imperfective form, it would probably have meant "Fate is a wet bank that makes a man's feet slip away from him," scl., in a concrete situation, whereas the form used indicates a general statement exempt from references to time. This leads to the conclusion that "perfective" forms simply, in some cases, represent the "unmarked" neutral tenseless verbal form in Sumerian, somewhat like the Greek aorist, which is ex-temporal when it occurs in forms other than the plain indicative. It is likely, therefore, that the terms perfective versus imperfective could ideally be replaced by a more precise aspectual distinction in Sumerian.

The translations of lines 170–171 by Wilcke, 1978, 208: "Das Schicksal ist (wie) ein feuchtes Ufer; es hat (schon) Menschen ausgleiten lassen" and Römer, 1990, 60: "Beim Menschen hat es (schon) den Fuß zum Ausgleiten gebracht" clearly illustrate the difficulty in pressing a tempus system onto a language in which it is alien. Why should it be neces-

1. Edzard, *Sum. Grammar*, 73–74, deals with the problem by stating that the so-called *ḫamṭu-marû* forms correspond to the Akkadian preterite and present verbal forms, such as *iprus* versus *iparras*, and does not discuss the problem in detail, yet gives a useful list of references to previous studies. There is now an important addition to be made: Civil, in *Jacobsen MV*, 69–70, explains the difference between *ḫamṭu* and *marû* simply as that between a "short" basic declension versus a more elaborate "expanded" one, in other words, in practice corresponding to what already Poebel in 1923 described as the preterite versus the present-future declension. This is the point of view that I have adopted in this study. Cf. Black, *Sumerian Grammar in Babylonian Theory* (1984), 102–134 for an older informative discussion. It should also be taken into account that *ḫamṭu*-forms may represent the Akkadian stative. Cf. UET 6/367: lú níŋ-tuku lú níŋ nu-tuku gig-šè im-ŋar, glossed *la-ap-nu a-na ša-r*[*i*]-⌜*im*⌝ *mim-ma mu-ur-ṣi-im ša-ki-in-šu-um*, "a poor man inflicts all kinds of diseases on a wealthy man" (Alster, *Proverbs* I, 324).
2. Cf., e.g., SP 1.10; 1.21, and many more examples. Until greater consensus has been reached, I consider it advisable to translate by a past tense, however.
3. W.W. Goodwin, *A Greek Grammar*, 271 —1268: "The gnomic aorist is a primary tense, as it refers to the present time"; p. 276 ——1291–1292: "The present is the tense commonly used ... to denote a general truth or an habitual action. ... In animated language the aorist is used in this sense. This is called the gnomic aorist, and is generally translated by the English present."

saries to insert "schon" in such a general statement?

A similar case occurs in line 153: dumu-eŋar-ra-ra níŋ nam-mu-ra-ra-an e-pa$_5$-zu šè-im-ra, "Don't beat a farmer's son; he will «beat» your irrigation canal," where it seems that a tempus system can only be applied by pressing it onto the text by resorting to unlikely lexical meanings, as the translation by Römer illustrates: "Er hat deine (Bewässerungs-) Kanäle *angelegt!*" (Römer, 1990, 59). Cf. the comments on line 153.

Cf. also the comments on lines 53 and 193, in which likewise a plain tempus distinction would seem artificial.

Split Sentence Construction

In this construction, a nominalized sentence ending in the enclitic copula, -a-àm, "being the fact that," can be translated by a split sentence construction in most European languages. Such constructions occur in lines 141; 170–171; 198; 199; 222 (without a visible -àm, cf. commentary), and are frequent in Sumerian generally.[4]

The phrase marked with -àm corresponds exactly to a split sentence construction in most European languages, where a variety of possibilities are open, e.g., "it is he who/ to whom/ from whom/ whose," etc.; the only difference being that Sumerian does not need—and does not possess—a primary relative pronoun heading the relative clause.[5] I, therefore, translate, e.g., line 198 "the good is a watery place that the heart cannot leave." My position is a restatement of Falkenstein's basic observation, that an -àm can represent any case in Sumerian, substantiated in GSGL II, pp. 32–35, with a list of examples from the inscriptions of Gudea. By using a term, such as a "split sentence," open to many variations and not bound to any rigorous pattern, in no way do I wish to disregard the merits of the detailed study by Gragg: "The syntax of the copula in Sumerian and its subdivisions."[6] However, as an initial position, I wish to start with an open category that has a chance of becoming widely accepted, instead of a category with many subgroups, some of which are likely to be considered less evident than others, thereby detracting attention from the essential point: any part of a sentence can be brought into focus by being marked with the enclitic copula (-àm), which can represent any virtual case relation, just as the most important part of a sentence can be emphasized by means of a split sentence construction in European languages. This was an important way to create emphasis and variation in Sumerian, in much the same way as *-ma* in Akkadian.

The Genitive of Characteristics

This is a rephrasing of a term well known from classical grammar, the *genitivus proprietatis*. In Sumerian grammar it is a special case of the so-called free genitive, that is, a genitive without a regens. It denotes what is characteristic of its possessor, or what is to be expected of him or it. Notable examples occur in lines 67: lú-lul-la-ka é-kaš-ka KA nam-tar-tar-re, "Don't boast in an alehouse in the way characteristic of a liar"; 208: ezem-ma-kam dam na-an-du$_{12}$-du$_{12}$-

4. A correct translation of lines 170–171 was mistakenly criticized by Foxvog, 1976, 371.
5. Cf. Alster, "Relative Clauses and Case Relations in Sumerian," WZKM 92 (2002) 7–31, esp. pp. 8–11 with n. 4; p. 15, n. 12. In principle I stand by the opinion expressed there, that there need not be any relative pronoun in Sumerian, which was the position of Poebel, 1923, but I admit that there are some rare examples where lú, in fact, may best be understood as a relative pronoun. I do not include among them the example cited by Edzard, *Sum. Grammar*, 155, from *Lament Sumer and Ur* 165: ^{d}en-líl lú (= *lú-ra/lú-úr?) nam-tar-tar-re-dè, which, in my opinion, means "Enlil, who decides the fates for man/men," with lú used as a collective plural in the singular, as elsewhere; cf. the comments on *Instr. Šuruppak* 180 and 222; 267. It is not necessary to postulate that this could have been expressed only through nam-lú-ù-lu$_{18}$, "humankind." If lú, indeed, functioned as a relative here, it would exemplify the construction that I consider unlikely to exist, *lugal lú, "the king who" (op. cit., p. 8). lú can, however, be used genderless; cf. *Instr. Šuruppak* line 34, where lú dam tu[ku-d]a, "with someone who has a spouse," is translated into Akkadian by *aš̆ti amīli*, "a man's wife." This might, of course, be a good starting point for lú becoming a general relativizer.
6. In: *Foundations of Language*, Supp. Ser. 8 (Dordrecht, 1968), 86–106; cf. also the remarks by Vanstiphout, RA 74 (1980) 67–71.

e, "It is characteristic of a festival that you shouldn't choose a wife"; 280: ki-<nu>-zu-a lú-ka lú ša-ba-ra-an-è-dè, lit., "It is characteristic of people's *<un>known places that people come down (scl., from there, i.e., the mountains)"; cf. the comments on the line.

Second Person "Object" Element in Pre-radical Position

That the 2nd person absolute element -en can occur as an object marker following a transitive perfective verb is well known. The same element can occur in pre-radical position before an imperfective transitive verb. In *Instr. Šuruppak* there is at least a single case, line 253, in which this -en- appears abbreviated to -e-. Less certain examples occur in lines 19, 23, 53, and 54; cf. the examples below. For a discussion with references to previous literature, in particular by Attinger, see the comments on line 253. Cf. also the variant in line 66.

EXAMPLES

Line 19: šu-du$_8$-a nu-e-tùm lú-bi ša-ba-e-dab$_5$-bé, "Don't(?) act as a guarantor; that man will have a hold on you." The second verb seems to include the pre-radical 2nd person element -*en-, abbreviated to -e-. Sch$_1$, although poorly legible, however, seems to have -ba]-e-dab$_5$-bé-en, in which the final -en casts doubt on the argument.

Line 23: du$_{14}$-dè lú ki-inim-ma nam-ba-e-ku$_4$-ku$_4$, lit., "Don't let them make you enter as a witness in the quarrel." In this case, Sch$_1$ has na-an-ku$_4$-ku$_4$-un, which similarly makes the argument somewhat dubious.

Line 253: níŋ nam-kal-kal-en níŋ-e me-kal-kal, "Don't evaluate things; things will evaluate you," i.e., you will become dependent upon things evaluating you. Note that here the reduplicated imperfective verb has no visible *marû*-ending, like -e.[7]

Ḫamṭu-marû Verbal Distinctions

Ḫamṭu-marû ALTERNATION IN ED: KA, DUG$_4$, DI, E, ETC.

At least in ED$_1$, the oldest ED source, KA was used invariably irrespective of whether the SS texts require a *marû*-form: e, or a *ḫamṭu*-form: dug$_4$.[8] Therefore, it seems that, in ED$_1$, KA can represent both dug$_4$ and e, and hypothetically even di. The distinction was active in ED$_2$, however. Cf. the following examples:

SS 42: ù-nu-ŋar-ra na-ab-bé-⌜e⌝, versus ED$_1$: ù-nu-ŋar na-dug$_4$ (written KA); ED$_2$, line 14: ANŠE [K]A gù-di. The latter shows that, at least in ED$_2$, the dug$_4$: di: e alternation was active; cf. also line 62, where ED$_1$ has KA, but ED$_2$: e, and SS: /e/ (written -ne-en).

The ED$_1$ writing dug$_4$ (or, rather KA) for */e/ occurs also in line 44. Rather than arguing whether KA has a hypothetical value e_x in such cases, or whether the *ḫamṭu-marû* variation was not yet fully developed, the ideal solution would be to use an "indifferent" sign value for the logogram "to speak," transliterating, e.g., na-[SPEAK], or similar, in such cases. This would cover both the *ḫamṭu* and the *marû* sign values.[9] In other words, the ED writing may simply be construed as a logogrammatic writing convention, not attempting to render the actually spoken sign value, and not intending to reveal its phonetic and grammatical realization. Otherwise the logical solution would be to postulate an ED sign value $*e_x$ in such cases.[10]

7. In line 54, the form [...] aša$_5$ nam-ba-e-ŋá-[ŋá-an], which occurs Ur$_1$, as a variant of na-an-da-ŋá-ŋá-a[n], is probably erroneous. For an unambiguous example of the pre-radical -en-, see *Šusin Lovesong B*, line 5: en-dab$_5$-en, "you keep me captivated" (Sefati, *Love Songs*, 353).
8. Cf. Wilcke, ZA 68 (1978) 215, ad line 47: "Liegt ... ein Fehler vor, oder konnte man damals (noch?) die Basen du$_{11}$ und e mit einem Zeichen KA schreiben?"
9. The discussion by Diakonoff, AS 20 (1974) 99–121, is basic to the understanding of this phenomenon. We usually think in terms of transliterations of single signs, but the writing system was originally constructed as a set of logograms, and this continued to be the case even long after the ED period. The gradual addition of more grammatical elements continued through the Isin-Larsa period.
10. In order not to complicate things further, I continue to use a conventional sign value, such as KA, in such cases, however. Cf. Edzard, *Sum. Grammar*, 77, and the literature there cited, which, however, does not discuss the impact of the original logogrammatic character of cuneiform writing.

Similarly, the ED sources seem to use the (sing.) *ḫamṭu* verbal root túm (de_6) indiscriminately from the (sing.) *marû*-root tùm (tùmu). Cf. line 19: ED_1 and ED_2 na-túm versus SS nu-e-tùm.[11]

FURTHER ED EXAMPLES

Line 33: ED_1: [n]e na-da-⌜e⌝ = SS e-⌜ne⌝ nam-mu-un-KA-e (doubtful).

Line 44: ED_1: sá.ság na-KA = SS [s]ág nam-me.

Line 62: ED_1 has ⌜na⌝-KA, but ED_2: na-e; (discussed above).

Line 125: ED_1: KA(du[g_4]) instead of im-me = /i-b-e/, (not = the verbal prefix im-mi-).

Line 126: ED_1: ⌜DI⌝ na-⌜x⌝-[KA(dug_4)] = im-me (probably).

Ḫamṭu-marû REDUPLICATION IN ED?

Reduplication occasionally occurs in ED_1 where it might not have been expected:

Line 134: ED_1: áš dug_4-d[ug_4] = SS áš dug_4-dug_4-ge, indicates plural?

Line 21: The ED_1 text: lú uru_5 ši-sù x x, seems to be without *marû*-reduplication.[12] This is normal for ED texts. Cf. line 21: SS úru-bi ša-re-e[b]-su-su.

Line 204: ED_1 has the reduplicated form níŋ-du_{10}-du_{10}, indicating a plural object; cf. the comments on line 204. The SS text has níŋ-du_{12}-du_{12}.

SS VERBAL ALTERNATION: TÚM/TÙM

Line 110: T_{15} has the variant túm for tùm. Cf. line 19, where the ED texts have túm = SS tùm.

Line 179: Sch_3 has bí-in-tùm-mu as a variant of bí-in-túm-mu. Cf. further line 193, where ED_1 has túm (de_6) = SS tùm (tùmu), but perhaps rather = SS túm. Depending on the interpretation, such cases confirm the suspicion that the graphic significance of the túm/tùm alternation tends to be overrated in SS texts.

Grammatical Elements in the Standard Sumerian Text with ED Correspondences

Modal Verbal Prefixes

na- and *ša-* are both modal prefixes. *ša-* was labelled "contrapunctive" by Jacobsen, AS 16, 75. Other discussions are: Falkenstein, ZA 48 (1944) 69–118 (on ša-) (cf. his study of na- in ZA 47 [1942] 181–223); see now Edzard, *Sum. Grammar*, 119: affirm. 2 = na; p. 120: affirm. 3 = ša.[13] The description there conforms to the conclusions below, reached independently. I tentatively accept Jacobsen's terminology.

The relatively rare attestation in SS texts compared to the relatively frequent occurrence in ED Sumerian texts poses special problems. In particular, some of the SS cases may represent obsolete survivals of a grammatical element directly influenced by ED forerunners. This applies in particular to ši-, which is rarely used in the function of a verbal prefix in SS texts.[14]

11. Cf. now Edzard, *Sum. Grammar*, 78, where the relevant forms, singular and plural, of DU = *ḫamṭu* de_6, *marû* tùmu, are listed. Krecher, 1995, 177, n. 81, lists TUM_3, or, rather *$tumu_3$, as the *marû*-form of de_6. Wilcke, 1978, 213, n. 12, considers the ED forms "unorthographisch" (p. 214. n. 12) writings for tùm = "die finite *marû*-Basis." I do not use the term "unorthographic" in this connection. Since Early Dynastic orthography does not reflect *ḫamṭu-marû* distinctions in the same way as do SS sources, it seems too early to judge what are correct and incorrect ED spelling conventions. Wilcke, 1978, 215, ad line 47, was aware of the problem, cf. note 8 above. Yet, even in SS sources some sound skepticism is warranted, not least in view of Diakonoff's remarks, cf. note 9 above.
12. As noted by Wilcke, ZA 68 (1978) 214.
13. Other studies: Michalowski: *Sumerian*, in: R. Woodard, ed., *The Cambridge Encyclopedia of Ancient Languages* (Cambridge, 2004); Civil, "Modal Prefixes," in *Acta Sumerologica* 22, in press (not seen, 2005), and Alster, "Nanše and Her Fish," in: *Klein FS*, 1–18, commentary on obv. 11–14, with notes 15–16. Further opinions of Civil (apud Heimpel, *The Structure of the Sumerian Prefix Chain*, unpubl. ms.), and A. Ganter (Zgoll) (: na- "effective"; ši: "resultative") are reported by Edzard, in: *Wilcke FS*, 95, n. 17. Edzard, *Sum. Grammar*, 120, cites Civil's opinion as follows: "ša «main event precedes». na stresses the importance of something in the past, still meaningful for the future."
14. Some SS references may hitherto have been misread as igi, however.

The /ša/ range denotes one single type of verbal prefix, whereas the /na/ range covers two types of modal prefix that behave slightly differently:[15] (1) the so-called affirmative na-, which combines with a *ḫamṭu*-form of the verb; and (2) the prohibitive na, which combines with a *marû*-form of the verb. It is the first of these two that can be termed "contrapunctive" in Jacobsen's terminology.

The following questions may be raised:

(1) How do SS ša- and na- relate to each other?

(2) Do SS ša-/šè-/ši- (and even, but rare, šu-) go back to a common ED grammatical element, possibly the ED sign ŠÈ, which later, in SS, when NÁM was only exceptionally used, was mistaken for NÁM and read as šè-?[16]

(3) How do ED nám-/na-/nam- relate to ED šè-/ša-/ši-? If these represent different ways of rendering a common morpheme /na-/ = /ša-/, the SS examples of na- and ša- might also represent reflections of a common phoneme, possibly a palatal nasal */nš/ (= ɲ), no longer in use in Standard Sumerian.[17]

It is basic to the discussion that ED writing distinguishes more signs than later: ED NÁM is twice as tall as it is wide, with two inner horizontals; ED TÚG also has two inner horizontals, but is square; ŠÈ has the same outer form as NÁM, but has six or seven inner horizontals.[18]

The following list of references from *The Instructions of Šuruppak* does not confirm any of the theories mentioned under (2)–(3), but rather disproves them:

The SS references cannot simply be explained as reflections of ED ŠÈ (or later misinterpretations of NÁM as the same sign), for there are already examples of the use of ši- in the same function in ED texts,[19] and even the sign nam is occasionally used for NÁM in ED.

Since there was already what seems to be a distinct verbal prefix range šè-, including šè-, ša-, ši- variants, versus a na- range, including na-, nám-, and even nam- variants, in ED Sumerian, the SS forms ša- and na- can hardly be explained as developments from a single ED phoneme. If that were the case, the development would probably have taken place even earlier than ED iii, with little hope of ever finding any written attestation.[20]

15. I continue to use the traditional terms "affirmative" and prohibitive. Civil, 1994, has advocated a different view, using the terms deontic and epistemic of modality; cf. F.R. Palmer: *Mood and Modality* (Cambridge University Press, 1986).
16. This seems to be the opinion of Civil, in a detailed study in the forthcoming Yoshikawa Anniversary volume (AcSum 22) (mentioned above, n. 13), known to me only through a brief summary by Michalowski (2004, also mentioned above).
17. As suggested by Alster, "Nanše and Her Fish," in: *Klein FS*, 1–18, commentary on obv. 11–14, with notes 15–16. This is even more likely in view of the fact that ŠA is also na_5. Further that, e.g., na – ri(-g) is šà – ri(-g) in *emesal*. For a full study of these phenomena it would be necessary to include more examples of the use of š for n in *emesal*, as well as the UD.GAL.NUN orthography, also sometimes using ša for na. For a detailed description taking most of these into account, see Schretter, *Emesal-Studien*, 1990.
18. I am grateful to A. Westenholz for critical comments and for details regarding the ED sign forms. The distinctions are valid everywhere up to the first part of the Old Akkadian period except in Lagaš, where TÚG and NÁM are identical.
19. In ED_I rev. ii 6–7: ši-kù níŋ-silig seems to represent SS 95–96: níŋ-ku_4-ku_4 níŋ sá nu-di-dam | níŋ-è níŋ nu-silig-ge-dam, that is, ED ši-kù = *ši-ku_4-ku_4? Similarly SS line 21: ED_I: uru_5 ši-sù-x-x; ED_2: URU×A ši-su-su = SS úru ša-re-e[b]-su-su.
20. The very limited number of ED III sources available for comparison must, of course, also be taken into account. Only two texts, *The Instructions of Šuruppak*, and *The Keš Temple Hymn* (Biggs, 1971), are known to have survived in SS versions. Other ED sources may be reflected in SS texts, foremost *The Collection of the Sumerian Temple Hymns* (Sjöberg, 1969), of which a forerunner is often supposed to go back to the time of Enheduanna, the daughter of King Sargon of Agade, ca. 2300 B.C., although this is far from certain. Yet, even if these should display a particular archaic verbal prefix pattern, with relatively many examples of ša- and na- prefixes compared to other SS texts, before drawing any conclusions, I would take into consideration that hardly any other comparable sources of the same type, even from the time of SS, are at present known. This may be the main reason why a relatively high number of ša-/ šè-/ ši-/ šu- prefixes occurs in the SS version of *The Instructions of Šuruppak*. It is worth noting that ša- does not occur in *Counsels of Wisdom* (*Chap. 2.3*), which probably was of much more recent origin. A relatively high number of ša-/na- prefixes occurs, however, in *Lugalbanda in Hurrumkurra*. That the šè- prefix was genuinely present in Ur III appears

Apparently both na- and ša- connect a verb with what precedes it or what is expected to follow, with a preference for na- as the first part of a sequence, and ša- in the second part. An example is ED_I obv. i 6: šuruppak dumu na [n]a-mu-ri (and parallels).[21] The na-prefix seems to inform that more is to follow, "Šuruppak gave instructions to his son, as follows ...." ša-, however, seems mainly to come in the second place.

In conclusion: The ED texts seem generally to differentiate a /na/ and a /ša/ range. Jacobsen's designation "contrapunctive" seems justified.

ED and SS Examples of /na/ versus /ša/ (ša/šè/ši/še/ šu)

ED PROHIBITIVE NA- / NÁM-

ED_I writes the negative prohibitive preformative as na- (e.g., ll. 28, 29, 31, 32, 33, 35, 39, 42, 44, 45, 47, 48, 49, etc.); ED_2, however, uses na- (l. 62 bis), but also, in a single case nam (l. 29), and nám (ll. 28, 58); also nàb(AN+AN) (ll. 14, 28).

ED NA VERSUS ŠA: PROHIBITIVE OR AFFIRMATIVE?

In a few cases ED_2 has na- (or similar) where the SS texts have ša- (or similar):

Line 62: ED_2 has the verbal prefix na-zu-zu, where the SS sources have bí- (with variants). I take this as a humorously exaggerated prohibition, "Do not let the courtyard (find reason to) investigate you(r case)"; cf. a similar case in line 28: níŋ nam-mu-zuḫ-z[uḫ] ní-zu nam-mu-úš-e; ED_I: níŋ na-mu-zuḫ-zuḫ me-zu na-MUNŠUB; ED_2: níŋ nám-zuḫ-zuḫ ní-zu / nàb-MUNŠUB, "Don't steal anything, don't kill yourself!" Another explanation would be possible, admittedly, i.e., that in line 62 the second na- in ED_2 is an ED variant of the affirmative ša-, possibly developed from the same ED phoneme, */nš/, which in SS may have been split up into ša- and na-; cf. the discussion above.

In line 28, however, both ED sources have na- in the second part of the saying, and so do the SS sources. Therefore, the most likely solution is that na- should be interpreted as a prohibitive verbal prefix in all sayings following the same pattern, including all ED variants.

ŠA/ŠÈ/ŠI/

Even in the ED versions ši is sometimes used for šè, e.g., line 21: ED_I and ED_2 ši-sù; ši-su-su = SS ša-re-eb-su-su, making it unlikely that SS ša-/ši- owes its existence to a graphic misunderstanding of ED sources, interpreting NÁM as šè.

EXAMPLES OF ED ŠI-:

Line 21: ED_I: [i]gi-du na-⌜x⌝-⌜ba⌝ / lú uru_5 ši-sù x x; ED_2: [...] URU×A l[ú (x)] ši-su-su; SS: lú-ra igi-du_8 na-an-ak-e úru-bi ša-re-e[b]-su-su.

Line 43: ED_2: [...] / b[úr(?) x (x)] ši-[...]; SS: eŋir-bi-šè ŋiš-pàr-gim ši-i-ši-íb-lá-e.

Lines 96–97: ED_I: ši-kù níŋ-silig; SS: níŋ-ku_4-ku_4 níŋ sá nu-di-dam; cf. Alster, 1991, 16–17.

Line 134, however, has ED_I: bar šè-dar, but SS: bar ši-in-dar.

EXAMPLES OF ED ŠÈ-

Line 17: ED_I: šè-mu-ra-ḫul; SS: un-e ša-re-eb-ḫul-ḫul; var. ši-.

Line 153: ED_I: dumu eŋar níŋ na-ra e-pa_5-zu_5 šè-ra, cf. below on SS 153.

Line 185: ED_I: dam tuku šè-du_7; SS differs: lú dam tuku á šu im-du_7-du_7.

Line 187: ED_I: é gul é šè-da-[(x)]; cf. SS 187: é gul-gul-le-dè é ša-ba-da-an-gul-e.

Line 188: ED_I: [l]ú zi lú šè-da-[z]i; cf. SS 188: lú zi-zi-i-dè lú ša-ba-da-an-zi-zi-i.

Line 220: ED_I: munus-bar-[š]u šè-ŋál / [x x x]-šè du. SS differs by not having any prefix at all: munus-bar-šu-ŋál-e é dúr-bi-šè mu-un-du.

Line 221: ED_I: [x kú]run naŋ-naŋ gu[ru_7] šè-LAGAB-LAGAB. SS differs: KAŠ kúrun naŋ-naŋ-e $buru_{14}$ im-su-su-su.

Line 235: ED_I: inim-diri bu-bu_7(KU) šà ḫu-gig šè-du_8-du_8. Cf. SS: bar-sud [...]-ke_4 šà-ḫul-gig ⌜du_{12}⌝-⌜du_{12}⌝ (uncertain meaning).

from van Dijk/Geller, *Ur III Incantations*, 11, no. 1, line 2: ... šè-mu-ŋá-ŋá, "is directed toward the man." The variant šu mu-ŋá-ŋá may either be a miscopy or indicates that already the OB copyist had problems in coping with an obsolete grammatical form.

21. In view of SS 6: šuruppak[ki]-e dumu-ni-ra na na-mu-un-ri-ri, etc., one would hardly prefer the reading na mu-na-ri.

/ŠA/, ŠÈ , ŠI-, ŠU-

Lines 19ff.: ED$_1$ writes the so-called affirmative preformative /ša/ as šè (ll. 19, 49, 89, 134, 153, 185, 187, 188, ED var. of line 214, 220(?), 221, ED var. of ll. 235(?), 271). The standard version uses ša-, šè-, ši-, or (rarely) šu-, following the principles of vowel harmony. It is of considerable interest to note that, in a number of cases, the standard version uses the sign ši- for this grammatical element. The use of ši- as a verbal preformative is relatively rare in SS orthography, but there are relatively many examples in *The Instructions of Šuruppak.* A few of these are ambiguous, however, so that alternative readings are possible. The use of šè- in this function is also relatively rare in the Isin-Larsa period. Note also that ED$_2$ once uses the writing ša$_4$(DU), in line 19.

Note in particular the following passages: lines 115; 119–122 (in line 120 I$_9$ has the variant ša for ši).

EXAMPLES OF SS ŠA-, ŠÈ-, ŠI- WITH SOME ED PARALLELS

Line 14: dùr.⌜ùr⌝ gù-di na-ab-sa$_{10}$-sa$_{10}$ érin-zu ša-ra-ab-si-il-le. ED$_2$: ANŠE [K]A gù-di nàb(AN+AN)-/sa$_{10}$-sa$_{10}$ [...] na-e.

Line 17: gán-zu-àm pú na-an-ni-dù-e-en ùŋ-e ša-re-eb-ḫul-ḫul. ED$_1$: gán-za pú na-⌜dù⌝ ⌜ùŋ⌝ ⌜šè⌝-⌜mu⌝-ra-⌜ḫul⌝; ED$_2$: not preserved.

Line 19: šu-du$_8$-a nu-e-tùm lú-bi ša-ba-e-dab$_5$-bé. ED$_1$: šu-dù na-túm lú / šè-ba-dab$_5$; ED$_2$: ⌜šu⌝-du$_8$-a na-/túm lú-bi ša$_4$-ba-/dab$_5$.

Line 21: lú-ra igi-du$_8$ na-an-ak-e úru-bi ša-re-e[b]-su-su. ED$_1$: ... lú uru$_5$ ši-sù x x; ED$_2$: [...] URU×A l[ú (x)] ši-su-su.

Line 41: ŋìr ur$_5$-re gud ša-ba-re-eb-su-su udu ša-ba-re-eb-su-su.

Line 43: eŋir-bi-šè ŋiš-pàr-gim ši-i-ši-íb-lá-e.

Line 49, Ur$_2$: géme-zu-úr ŋìš na-an-dù zu-úr šu-m[u]-ri-in-šà: šu- is a rare case of vowel harmony in a SS Sumerian text = *ša-mu-; similarly line 51,

Line 51: Ur$_2$: a šu nu-gíd-i na-an-e$_{11}$-dè / šu-mu-⌜e⌝-ra-ŋál.

Line 53: ur$_5$ tuku na-an-bad-e lú-bi ša-ba-e-⌜x⌝-⌜x⌝-kúr.

Line 55: gi$_4$-in-šè du-dè ši-me-ši-ib-šub-šub.

Line 57: Ur$_1$: i[gi] du-un [igi d]u-un ši-m[u-u]n-ši-íb-bé-e-ne; Ur$_3$: i[gi d]u-un igi du-un ši-me-ši-íb-b[é]-en and K$_1$: igi d[u-un ...] ⌜x⌝ ši-⌜me⌝-⌜ši⌝-⌜ib⌝-b[é]-e-ne can all be both, but the third IGI is more likely to be ši-; Ur$_2$: igi ì-du igi ì-[du ... can alternatively, but less convincing, be read ši-ì-du. Akk$_2$: *ina pānī alka* definitely suggests igi.

Line 59: su-ga-ab su-ga-ab ši-me-ši-íb-bé-e-ne.

Line 65: lú eme-sig-ga-ke$_4$ igi ^{ŋiš}bala-gim ši-sir$_5$-sir$_5$.

Line 107: gal-gal di ^{kuš}lu-úb sù-ga ša-mu-un-túm. Var. MM: (-ga-)aš-m[u-.

Line 108: silim-dug$_4$ ka sù-ga ša-ba-ni-ib-ŋar.

Line 109: kuš dù-dù-e kuš-ni šè-ba-e-dù-e, might be -šè? If it is šè-, it must be caused by regressive vowel harmony by the following ba-e-.

Line 110: usu-tuku šu lú-ta ša-ba-ra-an-tùm.

Line 115: saŋ-du nu-tuku nam ši-ib-tar-re.

Lines 119–122: 119: ši-me-da-ba-e; 120: ši-mu-e-da-gu$_7$-e; 121: š[i-me-d]a-til-e; 122: ši-m[e]-da-dag-ge. Of these I$_9$ has the variant ša-mu-da-[in line 120.

Line 130: kur-kur-re zi ši-im-da-pa-an-pa.

Line 134: áš dug$_4$-dug$_4$-ge bar ši-in-dar, var. MM: šè-im-dar. NB ED$_1$: áš dug$_4$-d[ug$_4$] / bar šè-dar.

Line 136: gù-mur-re lú-lul-e túg ši-bir$_7$-bir$_7$-re.

Line 137: áš-di níŋ-érim-e na-ri šè-íl-íl; one may here alternatively propose the transliteration na-ri-šè íl-íl, but meaning?

Line 153: ED$_1$: dumu eŋar níŋ na-ra e-pa$_5$-zu$_5$ šè-ra; SS: dumu eŋar-ra-ra níŋ nam-mu-ra-ra-an e-pa$_5$-zu šè-im-ra, var. ši-im-ra. This is a rare example of both variants šè- and ši- being present.

Line 181: amar ši-in-ga-an-ù-tu. Variant ši-in-na-.

Line 182: úru maḫ-e é-dù-a ši-ḫur-re; ED$_1$: x (= e/ere?) máḫ é dù ⌜šè⌝-ḫur.

Line 184: lú níŋ tuku lú níŋ nu-tuku gig šè-ŋar; or: gig-šè ŋar; ED$_1$: lú níŋ tuku lú níŋ nu-tuku áš-gig šè-ŋar.

(*Line 185:* ED$_1$: dam tuku šè-du$_7$ dam tuku šè-du$_7$. SS lú dam tuku á šu im-du$_7$-du$_7$).

Line 187: é gul-gul-lu-dè é ša-ba-da-an-gul-e; cf. ED$_1$: é gul é šè-da-[(x)].

Line 188: lú zi-zi-i-dè lú ša-ba-da-an-zi-zi-i; cf. ED$_1$: [l]ú zi lú šè-da-[z]i.

Line 193: géme-⌜zu⌝ ḫur(?)-saŋ-ta ši-im-ta-an-tùm sa$_6$-ga ši-im-ta-an-túm.

Line 194: ḫul ši-in-ga-àm-ta-an-tùm.

Line 215: munus zi é zi-šè lú ši-i[n- ...].

Line 234: zi ⌜x⌝-ge_4-eš mu-un-ne(?)-pà ši-mi-ni-dug_4 (uncertain).

Line 240: Unplaceable after line 240: a-ba ì-lá a-gim ši-in-TAR (uncertain).

Line 264: ummeda-ga arḫus-a-ke_4 lugal-bi-ir nam ši-im-mi-ib-tar-re.

Line 265: ama-zu-úr inim-diri nam-ba-na-ab-bé-en ḫul ša-ba-ra-gig-ga-àm.

Line 271: é ere-bar-ra-ke_4 ere šà-ga ši-dù-dù-e. Cf. ED_1: é šà ere šà šè-dù-dù.

Line 280: ki-zu-a lú-ka lú ša-ba-ra-an-è-dè.

IN-GA- PREFIXES

Line 181: amar ši-in-ga-an-ù-tu. Variant ši-in-na-.

Sentence Determiners in ED

ED_1 occasionally includes the nominalization suffix /a/ or the enclitic copula /am/, corresponding to -am_6 in ED_2, and -a or -àm in SS.

EXAMPLES

Line 4: ED_1: ŋéštu inim-zu / [ka]lam [t]i-la; ED_2: [ŋéštu-tuku inim-galam inim-zu-a]m_6 [kalam-m]a [ti]-la-am_6; SS: u_4-ba ŋéštu-tuku inim-galam inim-zu-a kalam-ma ti-la-a.

Line 287: ED_1: šuruppak Ú[R].A[Š](?) dumu na ⌜ri⌝-ri-ga; SS: na-ri šuruppak^{ki} dumu ubar-tu-tu-ke_4 na ri-ga.

Verbal Extension Suffixes, /ed/, -(e)-da, -(e)-dam, -(e)-dè

Edzard, *Sum. Grammar*, 130–137, states, p. 136, that the subject implied in -/eda/ and the subject of the following verb are different, but acknowledges that loss of the distinction may have occurred in OB literary texts; cf. also Attinger, 1993, 307. On p. 135, bottom, Edzard mentions a long sequence of -/ede/ forms with no -/eda/ variants.

Although there is, thus, every reason to be on the lookout for a distinction between the forms -(e)-dè, -(e)-da, and -(e)-dam, at least in a well-defined corpus from a limited period, the fact that all these may occur as variants of each other in the same lines indicates that great caution is needed if "overinterpretation" is to be avoided.

EXAMPLES

Line 12: inim dug_4-ga-$ŋu_{10}$ na-ab-ta-bal-e-dè; so BM_1 and P; vars. omit -dè = line 152: inim dug_4-ga-$ŋu_{10}$ na-ab-ta-bal-e-dè; Ur_4 omits -dè.

Line 22: ki du_{14}-da-ka nam-bí-gub-[bu]-dè.

Line 35: du_{14} nam-[mú-m]ú-dè ní-zu na-an-[pe]-el-lá.

Line 55: gi_4-in-šè du-dè ši-me-ši-ib-šub-šub.

Line 66: igi-a nam-ba-e-gub-gub-bu-dè-en šà-ge bí-kúr-kúr, var. omits -en.

Lines 71 (and 72): ur-saŋ-da gub-bu-dè zi-zu ḫé-en-da-ŋál, "standing with the hero, let your life stay with you (text: him)"; so Ur_2; variant Ur_3: su_8-bu-da; the Akkadian translation [*a-na qar-r*]*a-du i-ziz-ma*, "stand by the hero," shows that -dè is not to be taken as an *infinitivus finalis*, and does not differ in meaning from -da, cf. the comments on line 71.

Line 94: é-gal íd maḫ-àm šà-bi gud du_7-du_7-dam; no variants.

Line 95: níŋ-ku_4-ku_4 níŋ sá nu-di-dam; no variants.

Line 96: níŋ-è níŋ nu-silig-ge-dam; var. Ur_3: -dè.

Line 113: na-an-šèr-šèr-re-dè $kiri_4$ šu àm-mi-in-ŋál.

Line 126: kaš naŋ-a-zu-ne di na-an-ne-e.

Line 128: an sù-ud-dam ki kal-kal-la-àm; var. K_1: an sù-da.

Line 139: mu gùn-gùn-da ga-mu-da-zala-ge, var. K_1: mu ⌜gùn-gùn⌝-dè.

Line 142: áš-ḪAR na-ŋá-aḫ DI-da ŋizzal kalam-ma-ke_4 (variants not clear).

Line 166: dili-zu-ne kaskal na-an-ni-du-un.

Line 187: é gul-gul-lu-dè é ša-ba-da-an-gul-e.

Line 188: lú zi-zi-i-dè lú ša-ba-da-an-zi-zi-i.

Line 202: šà ki-áŋ níŋ é dù-dù-ù-dam; var. TCL: -dè.

Line 203: šà ḫul-gig níŋ é gul-gul-lu-dam; var. Ur_5: gul-gul-e, probably mistake; TCL:]-gul-lu-dè.

Line 226: UM_2: munus-KA-ḪAR-ak KA×LI gi_4-gi_4-dam. Of the duplicates, one Nippur source, N_7, has -da, and the major Kish text, K_1, has -dè. In this case, at least the variants -da and -dam seem to be used with no major difference of meaning.

-NI : NE (-NE/DÈ) VARIATION EXAMPLES

Line 126: The variant N_2: naŋ-z]u-ni for naŋ-zu-NE is one of more examples that suggest the reading -ne instead of dè (unless one wants to read NI = dik/di_x) for the 1st and 2nd person verbal suffix. If the reading ne is justified, one would have to dissociate this from the verbal extension morpheme /ed-a/ > (e)-da and /ed-àm/ > (e)-dam, but regard it as a morpheme of unknown origin. There is, however, good evidence for the reading -ne for the 1st and 2nd person suffix, cf. Attinger, ZA 75 (1985) 161–178; Alster, AcSum 13 (1991) 93; *The Goose and the Raven* 4, var. in F 3: daŋal-la-zu-NI, for -zu-NE (*Chap. 4.3*), and now Edzard, *Sum. Grammar*, 137.

Akkadian Translations of Sumerian Grammatical Forms

The Akkadian translation tends to use the imperative where the Sumerian text has a modal ḫé- prefix, usually considered a modest, polite way to express an imperative.

EXAMPLES

Line 9: The Sumerian precative ḫé-dab_5 is translated in Akk_3: *ṣa-bat* by an imperative.

Line 13: Akk_3: *it-ta-qí-ip*, "let it be believed," apparently translates gú-zu ḫé-em-ši-ak (var. ŋál), cf. the comments on line 13.

Line 48: Akk_2: *a-na a-di-šu a-lik*, "walk," does not directly translate the Sumerian text: u_4 da-bé-eš ì-za-al (with variants), cf. the comments on line 48.

Line 57: Akk_2: *ina* IGI *[a]l-ka*: "go forward"; translates ig[i] (or: š[i]-)du-un (with variants), cf. above *Modal verbal prefixes.*

Emesal?

The Ur duplicate Ur_2 shows a clear tendency toward *emesal*-like verbal prefixes, such as na-àm- (not genuinely *emesal* na-áŋ-, though) instead of na-an-, cf. lines 31; 32; 38; 61; 63; 64; 66, and other *emesal*-like forms occur, such as na-na-àm = na-nam, e.g., lines 30; 31; 69; 70. Since there are many unusual variant readings in Ur_2, it is tempting to suggest that it was copied from an older source in which obsolete uses of the sign nám occurred. If so, in these cases na-àm- does not indicate *emesal*.

The only example of *emesal* is otherwise gi_4-in in line 55: gi_4-in-šè du-dè ši-me-ši-ib-šub-šub = Akk_2: [... *-t*]*a ta-*[*aṣ*(?)]*-ṣe-el* / [... *t*]a(?) *la tu-ma-sa-ra*; cf. the comments on line 55.

A few signs may indicate *emesal*: SS line 21: úru; 181, also ED_I: úru-tur; 182, but they rather seem to be relics from earlier writing conventions.

Use of Special ED Signs

LAK 134: Apparently used for i in line 27. Cf. the comments on that line. The sign may well represent an early form of i, from which it differs only by having six horizontals instead of five.

LAK 218: The sign is ZU#ZU+SAR. See the comments on line 18.

LAK 672: = MUNŠUB, sumur, etc., cf. Civil, RA (1967) 63ff., designating a cover of reed or similar protecting the center of a boat against the sun. The use of the sign seems wider in ED sources, cf. line 28, ED_I: me-zu na-MUNŠUB; ED_2: ní-zu nàb(AN+AN)-MUNŠUB; SS: ní-zu nam-mu-úš-e; line 213: ED_I: ⸢gud⸣ na-MUNŠUB; SS: gud [... na]-⸢an⸣-ni-sa_{10}-sa_{10}.

ÍL-*nutillû*: Cf. the comments on lines 38; 89.

me, ní: *Line 20:* ní-zu is rendered in ED_I as me-zu, cf. line 28, but in ED_2 as ní-zu. This is the reason for believing that an ED spelling convention is reflected in such names as en-mete-na, written EN.TE+ME-na (cf. Alster, JCS 26 [1974] 178–180). On the use of the sign zu/zu_5, cf. the comments below.

Line 28ff.: ní-zu, "yourself," in the Standard version seems to be a pun on ní-zuḫ, "thief" (or lú-zuḫ, lú-níŋ-zu/zuḫ), but apparently the pun would be less evident in ED_I, in which "yourself" is written me-zu; cf. the comments on SS 30. Cf. also the comments under *nu / lú* below.

Line 206: KA in ED_I seems to be used as a phonetic writing for ní-zu, unless it is a scribal error; cf. the comments on the line.

nám, nam, nàb: The forms are listed under *ED prohibitive na- /nam-* above; for details, see *Chap. 1.5: The Abū Ṣalābīkh Version*; and *Chap. 1.6: The Adab Version.*

nu / lú: *Line 30:* For ní-zuḫ, *šarrāqu*, "thief," the

ED sources write nu-zuḫ. The ED form is in agreement with the well-known /nu/ as a writing for /lú/, e.g., nu-kiri$_6$, nu-bànda, etc. Cf. the nu/lú variation in SS line 167: nu-zu-a-zu, where a variant lú-zu-a-zu occurs (T$_{10}$), although nu-zu there means "not." More examples are listed by Edzard, 1962, 91ff. The SS equivalent ní-zuḫ would be much easier to explain if derived from */lú-zuḫ/, "man who steals."

"ùr": Cf. the comments on line 86.

u$_5$, phonetic for u$_4$?: Cf. the comments on line 48.

zu / zu$_5$ (AZU): ED examples of zu$_5$(AZU), used for the possessive /zu/, are ED$_I$, lines 49, 126, 127, 153, 175, 176, 206. ED examples of simple zu used for the verb /zu/ are: ED$_I$, lines 4–5; ED$_2$, lines 62 and 276, and ED$_2$, line 5. There seems to be no consistent ED pattern, though, for apparently the simple zu represents the possessive /zu/ both in ED$_I$ and ED$_2$, lines 20, 28, 32(?): me-zu / ní-zu (cf. perhaps also ED$_I$ 35: níŋ-z[u).

Unusual Sign Values in the ED Texts

ḪUL = kiŋ$_x$: In line 44, for ú nu-kiŋ-ŋá-šè, ED$_I$ has ú nu-kiŋ$_x$(ḪUL). There can thus be no doubt that in this case ED ḪUL represents SS kiŋ$_x$(KIN).

Another case occurs in line 175: ED$_I$: [i]gi-zu$_5$-ta kiŋ$_x$(ḪUL) na-ak = SS: za-e igi-zu-ta kiŋ na-an-ak-[e]. I know of no other attestations of that sign value. Civil, 1984, 285, however, understands this differently: "OB ... replaces [hul] ... by kin – ak with a change of meaning"; cf. the comments on line 175.

Phonetic Complements in the ED Texts

In ED$_I$, sá.ság, sá is an unusual phonetic indicator to ság. Cf. perhaps also ED$_I$ rev. ii 5: bu-bu$_7$(KU) (= SS 235), or read bul$_x$? Cf. the comments on line 235. For bu$_7$^{bu}, cf. Civil, AuOr 7 (1989) 147; cf. also the Ur III spelling lú ḫu-bu$_7$^{bu}-me (part of a common year name).

1.10 Textual History

The Relations between the ED Sources and the SS Version

In many cases the sequences of the Abū Ṣalābīkh version are reflected in the SS version, but with some remarkable exceptions. These are:

(1) Lines occurring in different contexts in the two versions, e.g., line 158.

(2) Lines not included in the SS version, although they might have been expected to be included there, e.g., AbSt 155 (= rev. vi 3).

(3) Larger sequences in the AbSt version seemingly not reflected in the SS version, e.g., AbSt 116–119 (= ED_I rev. iii 3–5); AbSt 140–143 (= ED_I rev. iv 17–v 5); AbSt 149–153 (= ED_I rev. v 8–vi 1).

An ED Version from Ebla?

Since a sign list from Ebla, MEE 4, no. 78: šà-ḫul níg-é-gul-gul, seems to contain allusions to SS lines 202–203, it is tempting to suggest that an early version of the composition was incorporated into the scribal curriculum at Ebla, but so far no further evidence has been found; cf. the comments on lines 202–203.

The Susa Sources

It is to the merit of Civil, 1984, 297, to have shown that *The Instructions of Šuruppak* was known at Susa, from where he identified MDP 27, 260 (here S_1 = 135–136); Sb 12355 (here = S_2 = 39–41; 198–199); MDP 27, 186 (here = S_3 = 172). Another Susa tablet, MDP 27, 109 (here S_4), has a line that is reminiscent of line 10 and its repetitions, but it may belong to other texts as well. Of these tablets, S_2 preserves enough of the text to show that *The Instructions of Šuruppak* may have existed in a version different from the SS text, since it has two lines in another order and includes two lines not present in the SS version. Cavigneaux, "Fragments littéraires susiens," in: *Wilcke FS*, 53–62, gives examples of texts included in the Susa scribal tradition. These include *Chap. 4.2: The Fable of a Fox and a Dog*, which shows that many irregular variants may be expected, so it would be premature to draw far-reaching conclusions.

Other School Versions?

Another example that may give the impression of other independent versions occurs is the Kiš source K_1, which adds two lines after line 163. These are here numbered as 163a and 163b and read: ^{ŋiš}ig k[ur- ... š]u ba-an-da-ús-sa; ⸢x⸣ [x x]-⸢ šè⸣ la-ba-an-da-ku_4-ku_4. However, I understand these as a quotation from another text, apparently alluding to an episode in *Inanna's Descent* 74–75, or a related composition, so the most likely conclusion is that a scribe added these lines simply because he associated them with what preceded them.

Quotations in Proverb Collections

Proverb Collection 22, of unknown provenience, includes a sequence quoting lines 195–201 of the *Instructions of Šuruppak*; cf. Alster, *Proverbs* I, 262 and II, 445.

Can the Nippur Sources Be Grouped?
Second Person Address?

Many of the variants occurring in the Nippur sources are such common minor variations that they can hardly be used for the construction of a significant stemma. Nevertheless, a few significant cases are worth mentioning.

The 2nd person verbal suffix -en indicates that the text may occasionally have been recited in the scribal schools to a pupil in the 2nd person, creating the illusion that the whole text is addressed to Ziusudra. Examples occur in lines 109: T_{16}: šè-ba-dù-en; 129: níŋ im-da-lu-lu-un, in three sources against MM; 130: ši-in-pa-an-pa-an in at least two sources against MM; 176, TCL: im-lu-lu-un, versus nu-lu-lu([-un]); 166, T_{11}: -d]u-un; 223: UM_2: é-a nim-gim mi-ni-ib-dal-dal-en.[1] Cf. the discussion on p. 34, *Introd. to Instr. Šuruppak*: *To whom was the text addressed?*

The occurrence of the same scribal pun in a number of sources, UM_2, C_3, N_6, T_{22}, and BM_2, in line 263: ^{d}nanna-ug_5-ge-en = *na-an-na-ug_5-ge-en, "don't kill," of which the BM source is non-Nippurian, indicates that these go back to a common source. Note that the same pun does not occur in the preceding line.

Reflections of Older ED Sources?

Ur_2 displays a number of peculiarities. In particular, one may see the frequent na-àm as an attempt to "modernize" an ED text using the sign NÁM, which later became obsolete, rather than a sign of *emesal* writing, which otherwise does not occur in the text (apart perhaps from gi_4-in-šè in line 55).[2] The na-àm writing occurs in Ur_2, lines 31; 32; 38; 61; 63; 64; 66; 69; 70.

This raises the question as to how the three major Ur sources, Ur_1, Ur_2, and Ur_3, relate to each other. Of these, Ur_2 certainly is the weakest source, displaying a number of irregularities, so it would be remarkable if that text alone was derived from an ED original.

Nevertheless, there is at least one more detail that may suggest that Ur_2 is closer to the ED sources than the Nippur string of textual evidence. In line 67, only Ur_2 includes an extra second part: inim-zu ŋar-ra-[àm], which surprisingly seems to go back to ED_1: ŋar, albeit condensed almost to unrecognizability.

1. Lines 253: UM_2: níŋ nam-kal-kal-en níŋ-e me-kal-kal; 255: UM_2: ^{d}ašnan-ra na-an-šèr-šèr-re-dè-en; 256: UM_2: kir_{11}-e áš nam-en dumu-munus in-ù-tu-un; 258: UM_2: dam nam-mu-un-kar-re-en are hardly relevant here.

2. The "correct" *emesal* form of nam would have been na-áŋ.

CHAPTER 2

The Instructions of Ur-Ninurta and Counsels of Wisdom

2.1 Introduction

Publication History

The main sources of the compositions to be edited below were first edited by M. Witzel, "Ein Stück sumerischer «Weisheit»," *Orientalia* 17 (1948) 1–16. While this is since long outdated, an attempt by van Dijk, *Sagesse*, 102–111, meant considerable progress and has been quoted extensively in the second part of the edition below.[1]

The first to attempt a description of the compositions inscribed on VS 10, 204 and duplicates was Civil, *Orientalia* 41 (1972) 88–89. The complete tablet had three columns on each side. Civil assigned approximately 84 lines to each column, and pointed out that a number of compositions were involved, leaving the question open as to whether some of them could, in fact, be combined into larger compositions. Cols. i–ii had already then been identified as *The Disputation of the Bird and the Fish*,[2] yet with an unknown composition preceding it in the now missing part of col. i. The remaining four columns were roughly identified by Civil as compositions C_1 (37 lines), C_2 (27 lines), and C_3 (7 lines) respectively. These are edited below as *The Instructions of Ur-Ninurta*; C_{1-3} are followed by a lengthy composition D, possibly to be divided into D_1 and D_2, edited below as *Counsels of Wisdom*. If D_1 and D_2 were, in fact, two separate compositions, the point of transition between them must have been in the now missing part of col. iv (= rev. i), i.e., between lines 64 and 73 in the edition below.

C_1–C_3 were edited by Alster, "The Instructions of Urninurta and Related Compositions," *Orientalia* 60 (1991) 141–157, with some corrections in *N.A.B.U.* 1992, no. 83. Cavigneaux, "Miette de l'Eduba," in: *Limet FS*, 11–26, esp. 18–21, published a bilingual duplicate: CBS 11945, with copy (p. 18). Civil: "The Instructions of King Ur-Ninurta: A New Fragment," *Aula Orientalis* 15 (1997) 43–53, published two duplicates: UM 29-13-419A (photographs p. 53; the reverse was published only in this photograph) and MM 487b (with a photograph p. 53), which meant considerable progress.

In 1976 Sjöberg among his "Miscellaneous Sumerian Texts I," *Orientalia Suecana* 23–24 (1976) 166–167, with a description p. 160, published a duplicate then identified as closely related to the Nungal hymn.[3] It was then unknown that it would

1. TRS 93, treated pp. 104–105; 106–107, belongs to *Instr. Šuruppak*.
2. Translation: Vanstiphout, in: Hallo (ed.), *Context of Scripture*, 581–584; now also available on the ETCSL-site. The text mentions King Šulgi (CT 58, no. 62, rev. 20) in a section that can be regarded as praising Šulgi's ability as judge. Although there is no specific reason to connect it with Ur-Ninurta's court, one may surmise that this was the reason why it appears on a *Sammeltafel* with other texts that may have served a similar purpose. Cf. the discussion on p. 223.
3. Å. Sjöberg, AfO 24 (1973) 19–50. The decisive point is that Nungal's "temple" é-kur was a prison. This appears from the designation é-éš, in line 118, lit. "rope-house," clear in BM 108866 = CT 58, no. 27, cf. Alster and Walker in *Sjöberg FS*, 7–10. Civil: "On Mesopotamian Jails and Their Lady Warren," in: *Hallo FS*, 72–78, suggests a detailed reinterpretation of the text, according to which it was composed by a scribe sentenced to death and then saved by the compassionate goddess. The most recent edition is by Attinger, "L'Hymne à Nungal," in: *Wilcke FS*, 15–34. Cf. also Civil, *Wilcke FS*, 85. Cf. already G. Komoroczy: "Lobpreis auf das Gefängnis in Sumer," *Acta*

turn out to belong to this unexpected context, and crucial to the reconstruction of D_1.[4]

Civil's compositions C_1–C_3 are marked in at least one manuscript as follows: C_1: á-áŋ-ŋá, "precepts," of a god (l. 37), and C_2: "precepts" of a farmer (l. 64).[5] For the last lines of C_3 (ll. 65–71), Civil tentatively suggests the translation "the one who gives orders, at the gate(?) (or inside?), of the palace, should know how «to wake up» (people)," but this belongs to the main text itself, rather than to a subscript of C_3.

The Contents of C_{2-3}: The Instructions of Ur-Ninurta

C_3 (lines 65–71) is a short didactic composition advising an unknown person (perhaps any man, or specifically the subjects of the king?)[6] to whom it is addressed to observe the worship of the gods. The exact implication of the composition remains uncertain, but cf. the suggestions below under *The ideological contents of C.*

C_2 is vaguely related in phraseology and contents to *The Instructions of Śuruppak* and *The Farmer's Instructions*,[7] but it does not belong explicitly to the father-and-son instructions, and rather represents a less ancient wisdom tradition, one in which religious worship, rather than practical consideration, forms the basic motivation for moral instruction, and one in which a "literary" type of maxim takes preponderance over the oral diction of proverbs.[8]

Thus, in C_2, the argument for advising one to be prepared to work at the time of the harvest is not only that this is necessary to secure a good income (l. 62), but also that the harvest is a religious feast of Enlil and other gods (ll. 53–54ff.). In *Instr. Śuruppak* the argument for working hard at harvest time is simply that this will be to one's own benefit, cf. lines 136–137: u_4-$buru_{14}$-šè u_4 kal-kal-la-àm / géme-gim ri-ga-ab eŋi-gim gu_7-a, "at the time of the harvest when days are precious, collect like a slave girl, eat like a lady!" etc.

Our text leaves us with the impression of a social environment in which the person addressed has the staff or workers needed to carry out the practical work of agriculture, irrigation, and animal husbandry for himself. In his capacity as master of his household, he is expected to be personally in charge of the practical decisions of household management.

Comparing our text with *Instr. Šuruppak*, one gets the impression that the casuistic type of motivation clause of the latter has here been replaced by a more generalizing, and less humorous, type of intellectual argumentation. Cf. *Instr. Śuruppak* 14: $dùr^{ùr}$ gù-di na-ab-sa_{10}-sa_{10} érin-zu ša-ra-ab-si-il, "Do not buy an ass that brays, it will split your yoke apart," compared to our line 48, where the intent simply seems to be that one should keep one's eyes open and be prepared for the expenses when buying an ox.

Themes common to our text, to *Instr. Śuruppak*, and to later Mesopotamian father-and-son instructions are the acquisition of domestic animals and counsels concerning fields. Compare, e.g., our line 40 with *Instr. Śuruppak* 17: gán-zu-àm pú na-an-ni-dù-e-en ùŋ-e ša-re-eb-ḫul-ḫul, "Do not place a well in your field, the people will cause damage to you," and *Ugaritica* 5, 279 iii 5–8, dupl. KUB 4, no. 3 obv. i 6–9, cited in the commentary on *Instr. Śuruppak* line 17.

Ant. Scient. Hungaricae, 23/3–4 (1976) 173–174, who interprets Nungal's temple primarily as a place where those accused of crimes are taken into custody before trial. Cf. also Hallo, JCS 39 (1979) 161–166, who correctly interprets Nungal's "big house" (é-gal) in SP 6.3 as a prison.

4. It was already included in Civil's description of 1972, though.
5. Alster, 1991, 149, read: a-⌜šà⌝-da apin x x; Civil, obviously correctly, must have read this as phonetic for *á-áŋ-ŋá eŋar.
6. Alster, 1991, 149, line 65, cf. pp. 151 and 156, read either [lu]gal, following Civil, 1972, 88, or l[ú], cf. p. 156. The latter has turned out to be correct. As a consequence this may be considered addressed to "any man," rather than to a king (cf. p. 143). The obvious conclusion is that a reference to the subjects of Ur-Ninurta is intended, although the ruler's name is explicitly mentioned only in the beginning of C_1.
7. Edited by Civil: *The Farmer's Instructions. A Sumerian Agricultural Manual.* Aula Orientalis Supplementa 5 (Sabadell: AUSA, 1994).
8. As is also the case with *Counsels of Wisdom* (D_2), cf. below.

The Ideological Contents of C

It is possible to suggest a coherent ideological line of progression in the three initial compositions: Ur-Ninurta, king of Isin approximately 1923–1896 B.C., is established as the righteous ruler of Nippur. Then follows, as a continuation within the same text (C_1), a religious sequence describing the pious man who fears his god, as opposed to the one who does not. There then follows a section describing the daily routines of agricultural work, field work, and irrigation (C_2). This concludes in C_3: a short section presumably advising "men," i.e., apparently, the subjects of Ur-Ninurta, to be extremely humble and submissive (i.e., by performing the religious duties and the field work as described in C_2).

One may further suggest that D_1 is a logical continuation of C, reminding the subjects that trials and serious retaliation, even prison, face those who do not comply. It is less likely that D_2 originally belonged to the same sequence, though.

The Contents of D_{1-2}: Counsels of Wisdom

In D_1 "the text speaks of a king building a palace, and his administration of justice, in terms reminiscent of the hymn to Nungal, the Lady-Warren of the Mesopotamian jails" (so Civil, 1997, 50).[9] After a missing passage follows D_2, which includes precepts concerning religious duties, similar in tone to the second part of part C_1, but also precepts concerning social behavior are included. The overall impression is, however, that if the text had been more completely preserved, these may have played a more dominating role.

The large final part, D_2: the composition *Counsels of Wisdom* proper, hardly owes its existence to the royal court of Ur-Ninurta. Rather, this seems to be a text that may have incorporated a number of preexisting precept compilations. From what is preserved, it is remarkable that at least one theme recurs more than once: the treatment of domestic slaves or servants (ll. 101–103, which seems to be resumed in ll. 155–160). Only two major parts of the text are sufficiently well preserved to yield a reasonably meaningful connected translation (ll. 76–ca. 100 and 150–192). These are of unique interest, however, for the glimpses they give into what was considered prudent social manners, religious services, and, not least, the social obligations and precautions between relatively wealthy people and their neighbors of the Isin-Larsa or early Old Babylonian periods, when private economic enterprises and trade obviously came to play an increasing role compared to what may have been the case earlier.

The Contents of the Collected Sammeltafel

Some of the compositions C_{1-3} and D_{1-2} may have been originally independent compositions that existed before they were combined into the presently known form, presumably with the specific purpose of glorifying King Ur-Ninurta. It is tempting to see at least D_2 as an originally independent precept compilation that became associated with King Ur-Ninurta when the combined texts were written down on a *Sammeltafel*, presumably in connection with a major event in the king's reign. This may have been his coronation or an annually repeated judgment scene in which the king acted as judge at the river of ordeal. Strictly speaking, since the name of King Ur-Ninurta is neither mentioned in the preserved parts of D_1 nor in D_2, it is, however, far from certain that these were, in fact, ever associated with that king.

Not enough of D_1 is preserved to decide whether the building of a palace (é-gal) refers to a royal palace or perhaps to a temple for the goddess Nungal, "the Lady-Warren of the Mesopotamian jails," whose presence in this context would then find an obvious explanation. This could have been meant as a warning to Ur-Ninurta's subjects, reminding them that the prison was a physical reality for those who might not be willing to comply with the king's orders. Yet, it must be admitted that the presence of D_1 in this context remains somewhat of a mystery as long as so little of it is preserved. The overall impression is that the text refers to the building of a royal

9. Cf. the literature on *The Nungal Hymn* mentioned above *Publication history*, n. 3.

palace from which the king could administer his duties as a judge.

The texts included under C: *The Instructions of Ur-Ninurta* have a much more openly religious character than *The Instructions of Šuruppak*, and are better designed to teach the subjects to obey their sovereign. Religious submissiveness was obviously seen as serving the interests of the ruler. So, whether or not the two parts included under D: *Counsels of Wisdom* were, in fact, to be seen as related to King Ur-Ninurta, the Sumerian scribal schools must, at some point, have served the glorification of the king to a very high degree. This may explain why the first two columns of VS 10, 204 are inscribed with *The Disputation of the Bird and the Fish.* One reason may be that the conclusion of that text describes King Šulgi of the Ur III dynasty acting as arbiter in a dispute between two combatants. Although the scene is set in terms of an animal tale, some of its features are highly realistic. King Šulgi was the Sumerian ruler *par excellence*, whom the rulers of the Isin dynasty may naturally have chosen as their favorite model.

The particular selection of our compositions may be seen as a mere result of the practice of the scribal schools to collect a number of composition on *Sammeltafel* for the sake of purely scribal exercises. It seems, however, that this specific selection reflects the ambitions of the royal court of King Ur-Ninurta. The bombastic introduction to *The Instructions of Ur-Ninurta*, reflecting the literary phraseology of epics and myths, and perhaps even deliberately alluding to *The Instructions of Šuruppak*,[10] the relatively low number of duplicates from the "orthodox" scribal school of Nippur, the existence of a phonetically written source from Tell Ḫarmal, apparently from the hand of a scribe to whom the Sumerian text seems mostly to have meant unintelligible sounds, as well as the late Sumerian grammar, including forms that hardly would have passed in the good Nippur tradition, all these features point to a relatively late Isin-Larsa date of origin for the text. A typically late grammatical feature is the use of the ablative -ta for the locative; cf. the comments on *Instr. Ur-Ninurta* 16; 24.

It is highly likely that it is the attitude that comes to light in *Counsels of Wisdom*, 47: kadra-ŋar-ra-bi kadra a-šed$_{10}$-[da(?)], "The gifts provided there [are?] gifts of cool soothing water," reminiscent of *Instr. Šuruppak* 284, that prompted D_1 to be associated with the wisdom literature in the first place.

Reconstruction of the Compositions

Civil's compositions C_{1-3} are included under the title *The Instructions of Ur-Ninurta* (*Chap. 2.2*); D_1 and D_2 are here treated as one single text, with the common title *Counsels of Wisdom*,[11] with a continuous running line count starting at line 71 with D_1, where C_3 ends. This was thought to be a reasonable compromise, because that title had already been used by van Dijk in his edition of sections of the Sumerian text, and because the point that may have separated D_1 from D_2 is not preserved. As stated above, D_2 may have been an independent precept compilation not originally associated with King Ur-Ninurta. The only feature that may have to be changed should new duplicates be found showing that D_1 and D_2 should better be taken as separate compositions is the line count of D_2.

Below follows a list of all the sources used to reconstruct Civil's compositions C_{1-3} and D_{1-2}. Remarkably there seems to be no separating line in C marking the transition between C and D, so that it is, in fact, difficult to decide to which of the two C iv 7 belongs. Civil, 1997, 44, gave a complete listing of all the sources A–J with a common running line numbering for all the compositions included on the relevant *Sammeltafel*, which gives a good overview.

In order to avoid unnecessary confusion the line numbering and the siglas proposed by Civil are given in parenthesis.

10. Cf. Civil, 1997, 49.

11. To avoid confusion with the Babylonian text of the same title, the titles *Sum. Counsels of Wisdom* and *Akk. Counsels of Wisdom* (= BWL 96–107; cf. p. 41) may be used for the two compositions respectively.

Sources

A: TIM 9, 1 = IM 55403.
= *The Instructions of Ur-Ninurta*, lines 1–71.
First publ. by J. van Dijk, *Sumer* (1955) 11, pl. XIII, no. 9. Revised copy by van Dijk TIM 9 (1976) no. 1. Provenance: Tell Ḫarmal. Collated in Baghdad by Alster, 1990, cf. *Orientalia* 60, 157.
See *Chap. 2.2: The Instruction of Ur-Ninurta.*

B: SLTNi 137 (Ni 4035), obv. = *The Instructions of Ur-Ninurta*, lines 17–32, incl. 29a–c; rev. = lines 44–61.
Provenance: Nippur.
See *Chap. 2.2: The Instruction of Ur-Ninurta.*

C: VAT 6977+ 6978, VS 10, 204.
Six-column tablet. Length of columns: About 84 lines, according to Civil, *Orientalia* 41 (1972) 88–89. This should give a total of approximately 245 lines to *Counsels of Wisdom* (less if the end of col. vi was not fully inscribed).
iii 1' – iv 7 = *The Instruction of Ur-Ninurta*, lines 24–71 (om. 26–28). (Obv. iii = 24–63, iv 1' – 7 = 65–71).
iv 8ff. = *Counsels of Wisdom* 1–194.
iv 8 (or 7?)–32= 1–26; v 1–41 = 77–117; vi 1–26 = 168–194.
[In Civil's reconstruction = 29a?–62, 65–93, 147–186, 231–257].
Provenance unknown, possibly Sippar. Photograph of rev.: VS 10, pl. I.
See *Chap. 2.2: The Instruction of Ur-Ninurta* and *Chap. 2.3: Counsels of Wisdom.*

D: UM 29-13-419A.
Obv. i = *The Instructions of Ur-Ninurta.*
(Obv. i = 23–37, incl. 29a–c.)
Obv. ii and rev. i'–ii' = *Counsels of Wisdom.*
(Obv. ii = 1–11; rev. i': beginnings of three unidentified lines; rev. ii' = ca. 204'–225'.) There may be remains of the right side of rev. iii, with no signs preserved (difficult to judge from the photograph). If so, there are no missing signs in the left side of rev. ii'.
[In Civil's reconstruction = obv. i = 23–37, obv. ii = 70–79, rev. = 274'–296'.]
Fragment from the left side of a six-column tablet with 40–50 lines per column, cf. Civil, 1997, 44. Middle Babylonian or late Old Babylonian. Provenance: Nippur. Published by Civil, AuOr 15 (1997) 43–53, photograph p. 53, bottom right, which is the only available photograph.
See *Chapter 2.2: The Instruction of Ur-Ninurta* and *Chap. 2.3: Counsels of Wisdom.*

E: MM 487b. 4 cols. (Montserrat Museum, Barcelona).
Obv. = *The Instruction of Ur-Ninurta* lines 20–33; 56–68. (Obv. i = 20–33; ii = 56–68).
Published by Civil, AuOr 15 (1997) 43–53, photograph p. 53. Provenance: possibly Babylon. Middle Babylonian. Only a part of the obverse is preserved. The reverse is completely destroyed. Civil, pp. 43–44, calculates that the tablet probably had a total of four columns originally containing "something like 148 (= 37×4) lines." Based on this calculation, the tablet is, thus, likely to have continued with *Counsels of Wisdom,* and to have ended approximately where the hypothetical composition D_2 starts, around the still missing line 70. If so, it would be the only tablet so far that separates D_1 from D_2. I consider it more likely, however, that the tablet, in fact, had six or even eight columns, with a total of ca. 8×40 = 320 lines, which would fit the total length of all the compositions, although the format of the tablet would have been somewhat unusual (cf. Civil's description, 1997, 43).
See *Chap. 2.2: The Instruction of Ur-Ninurta.*

F: UM 29-15-979.
= *Counsels of Wisdom* lines 16–52. (Obv. = 16–33, rev. 36–52; there is a small lacuna between 33 and 36.)
Published by Sjöberg, *Orientalia Suecana* 23–24 (1974–75) 159–181, transliteration pp. 166–167, (no translation), comments pp. 175–176, photographs p. 180. Provenance: Nippur. One-column tablet. The top is missing, but a part of the bottom edge seems to be preserved. This is the only tablet inscribed with D_1 alone.
See *Chap. 2.3: Counsels of Wisdom.*

G: Ni 4193 (ISET I 78).
= *Counsels of Wisdom* lines 73–82; 145–156.
(Obv. = 73–82; rev. 145–156.) There is a small gap before 145.
Fragment from the right edge of a one-column tablet. This seems to be an excerpt that ended with line 156, marked with a double line.
See *Chap. 2.3: Counsels of Wisdom.*

H: VAT 6448 (+) 6479 + 6503 (VS 10, 205).
= *Counsels of Wisdom* lines 85–111; 148–185; 227–247.
(Obv. i = ca. 85–111; obv. ii = 148–165, rev. i = 166–185; rev. ii = ca. 227–247.)
Two joined fragments from a four-column tablet with ca. 45–50 lines per column. The bottom edge is preserved. This apparently contained the entire D_{1-2}, with nothing of D_1 preserved.
[In Civil's reconstruction = 154–178, 212–247, ?, 280'–299'].
See *Chap. 2.3: Counsels of Wisdom.*

I: VAT 6464 + 6604*. VS 10, 206.
= *Counsels of Wisdom* lines 24–27; 50–64.
(Rev. i = 24–27; ii = 50–64.)
Small center fragment from a four-column tablet. The remains of the right column on the copy duplicates F obv. 8–11; the conclusion is that this must be a fragment from the reverse, as suggested by Alster, 1991, 142, n. 5.
[In Civil's reconstruction = 117–130, ii unplaced].
See Chap. 2.3: *Counsels of Wisdom.*

J: CBS 11945.
= *Counsels of Wisdom*, lines 146; 146a; 150–161.
(Obv. = 146; 146a [obv. 1–9 too poorly preserved for reconstruction; belongs before 146]; rev. 10–18 = ca. 146–161.)
[In Civil's reconstruction = 156–165, 210–224].
One-column tablet, bilingual. Published by Cavigneaux, *Limet FS*, 18 (copy), 19–21 (transliteration and translation). Neo-Babylonian or, according to Civil, 1997, 43, rather Middle Babylonian, which is the more likely possibility. The Sumerian column is to the left, the Akkadian translation to the right. The vertical line shown on the copy of the rev. is not a column divider.
See *Chap. 2.3: Counsels of Wisdom.*

Excursus on Sammeltafel

A number of compositions in the present volume occurs on *Sammeltafel*. The more obvious examples are:

Chap. 2.2–3: The Instructions of Ur-Ninurta and related compositions; *Counsels of Wisdom*, including a beginning reminiscent of *Hymn to Nungal.*
Chap. 3.1–2: Níŋ-nam nu-kal (Nothing Is of Value) versions A–D, and related compositions.
Chap. 3.3(a): The Ballade of Early Rulers.
Chap. 3.5: Enlil and Namzitarra.
Chap. 4.3: The Fable of the Goose and the Raven.
Chap. 5.2: The Folktale of the Old Man and the Young Girl.

There seems to be some rationale behind the way in which the compositions are grouped together. However, this should not be thought of in terms of modern groupings according to library definitions, literary genres, or similar. Association seems to have played a great role.[12]

12. A telling example is VS 10, 198, (cf. Alster, "Nanše and Her Fish," in: *Klein FS*, 1–18), in which a hymn to Inanna is combined with one to Nanše, seemingly because they are said to have one unusual feature in common: Inanna carries the sky as a tiara on her head and the earth as a sandal on her feet; likewise, in the hymn *Nanše and Her Fish*, the goddess is said to wear a fish as a tiara on her head, and a fish as a sandal on her feet. In other words, the connection seems to be this unusual verbal association, which is far from immediately intelligible to us.

2.2 *The Instructions of Ur-Ninurta*
Text Reconstruction, Translation, and Comments

* following the line number indicates a reconstructed text not necessarily based on any single source.

Line	Source	Text	Translation
1	A	u$_{4}$-ul-li-a-ta u$_{4}$-ub-ba til-la-[a-ta]	*(1)* When the days of yore had come to an end,
2	A	gig-ri bi-ri ŋi$_{6}$ ba-sù-[da-a-ta]	*(2)* after nights had been become far remote from those distant nights,
3	A	mu-sù-da mu ba-ši-[sù-da-a-ta]	*(3)* after years had become remote from remote years,
4	A	eŋir a-ma-ru ba-ŋar-ra-[a-ta]	*(4)* after the flood had swept (the land),
5	A	ŋéštu šúm-ma ^{d}en-ki-[ga-ta]	*(5)* the one given wisdom by Enki,
6	A	KA-KA ^{d}nisaba-[(x)-t]a	*(6)* the one … by Nisaba,
7	A	ša-ak-šu ^{d}⸢x⸣ ⸢x⸣-inanna-ta	*(7)* the one who takes counsel with … Inanna,
8	A	ŋiš-ḫur kalam-ma-ke$_{4}$ si-sá-e-si	*(8)*—in order to organize the plans of Šumer,
9	A	níŋ-érim ḫa-la-mi-it-te níŋ-gi-na gin-te	*(9)* — in order to abolish wickedness, to implement righteousness,
10	A	ùŋ-e dúr-bi ki-bi gi$_{4}$-gi$_{4}$-te	*(10)* — in order to let the people return to their dwelling places,
11	A	[nam]-sipa ur-^{d}nin-urta suhuš-bi gi-ne-te	*(11)* — in order to consolidate the foundation of Ur-Ninurta's shepherd[ship],
12	A	⸢u$_{4}$⸣-⸢ba⸣ [(x)]-⸢x⸣-la lugal é-šu-me-ša$_{4}$ ⸢ù⸣-tu-da nibru^{ki}	*(12)* — [on that day, (Ninurta),] the lord of Ešumeša, (installed the one) born in Nippur (= Ur-Ninurta),
13	A	šà x [x EN?].ZU-⸢na⸣-ka	*(13)* [the one chosen in his] heart [by] Suen,

14		
A	émedu(ama-a-˹tu˺) [(x)]-^{d}nin-urta-ka	*(14)* the "home-born slave" of [(...(?))] Ninurta,
15		
A	u$_4$-sù-šè ba-˹an˺-[(x)-s]ì-˹ga˺-te	*(15+17)* — in order (for him, i.e., Ninurta) to install (him, i.e., Ur-Ninurta) for long days
16		
A	nibru^{ki} ere ki-[á]ŋ-ŋá-ta	*(16)* in Nippur, his beloved city)-
B obv. 2	[nibru^{ki}] ere ˹ul-la mu-un˺(?)-[...]	(Var. B: in Nippur, the very old city ...)
17		
A	u$_4$-sù-šè da-ru-[šè ...]-ŋar	*(17)* he installed him for long days to last,
B obv. 3	˹x˺ da-rí ùŋ-ŋá ˹x˺ [...]	(B: eternally among the people ...)
18		
A	˹x˺ kalam-ma-ke$_4$ ˹u$_4$˺ nu-˹da˺-˹x˺-[(x)]-te	*(18)*— in order not to [terminate(?) his sovereignty(?)] of the land.
B obv. 4	[...]-˹ni˺ DÉ(?) ˹x˺ [...] (may not belong here?)	(B: uncertain variant).
19 # 30		
A	lú-lú níŋ-diŋir-ra-ka ˹ní˺-[it]-˹te˺-èn-bi mu-u[n-zu(-a)]	*(19)* He who knows how to respect religious affairs,
B obv. 5/1	[...] diŋir-ra-ni-šè	
20 # 30A	*ní-te-a-ni diŋir-ra mu-un-da-[ab-sá-(a)]	*(20)* who voluntarily [pleases his god],
A	ní-˹ta˺-a-ni <diŋir> mu(?)-un-da-[ab-zu(?)-a]-˹ra˺ im-mi-e-[(x)]	
B obv. 5 cont.	ní [...]	
E	[...] *im-ḫu-˹x˺* mu-un-da-[ab-sá-(a)]	
21		
A	(traces of two signs)-˹ta(?)˺ KA AN NE(?) ˹siskur˺-re im-ma-ŋá-ŋá-[a]	*(21)* who performs the rites,
B obv. 6	[...] siskur-ra im-m[a- ...]	
E	[x x x] *šá* | s[is]kur *i-na-aq-qú-ú* im-ma-an-ŋ[á-ŋá-a]	
22 # 32a	*mu diŋir-ra-na mu-un-na-kal-la	*(22)* to whom the name of his god is dear,
A	˹mu˺ diŋir-ra mu-un-na-ka[l(?)]-la	
B obv. 7	[...] mu-un-˹x˺ [...]	
E	[...-r]a-na *šu-qú-ru-šu* mu-un-na-kal-[la]	
23 # 32	* nam-érim ku$_5$-ru-da-bi im-ma-da-ab-te-ŋá-a	*(23)* who keeps away from swearing,
A	nam-érim x(nearly uš(?))-a-ni ib-bi-da-˹x˺-e	
B omits		
D obv. 1	[...-d]è im-ma-[...]	
E	[-ér]im-da ku$_5$-ru-da *dup-ru* im-ma-da-ab-te-ŋá-a	

24		
A	ki diŋir-ra-ta si-sá-bi i-da-bé	*(24)* he goes straight to the place of worship,
B obv. 8	[...] si-sá-bi ì-[...]	
C iii 1	ki(?)-[...]	
D obv. i 2	[...] si-sá-bi [...]	
E	[...-r]a-ni-ta si-sá-bi ì-dib-bé.	
25		
A	níŋ-ugu-<dé>-a-ni níŋ ab-si-si(!)(text: e)	*(25)* what he has lost is restored (to him).
B obv. 9	[...]-⸢in⸣-na-⸢ab⸣-[...]	
C iii 2	níŋ-⸢ú(!)⸣-[gu ...]	
D obv. i 3	[...] in-na-a[b(!)-...]	
E	[níŋ-ug]u-dé-a-ni im-ma-ab-su-su	
26		
A	⸢u_4⸣-da-a-ni u_4 mu-un-daḫ	*(26)* Days will be added to his days.
B obv. 10	[...] mu-da-an-[...]	
C *om.*		
D obv. i 4	[...] u_4 mu-da-⸢an-daḫ⸣-[(e)]	
E	[...-n]i-šè ana $^{u_4\text{-}mi\text{-}šu}$ u_4 mu-un-da-an-daḫ-e	
27		
A	⸢mu⸣ ⸢tuku⸣-a-ni mu im-ma-(ni erasure)-⸢si(?)⸣	*(27)* Years will be plenty in addition to the years he (already) has.
B obv. 11	[...] ⸢mu⸣ mu íb-[...]	
C *om.*		
D obv. i 5	[...-n]i ⸢mu⸣(?) mu-a íb-diri-diri	
E	[...-r]a-na $^{šá\text{-}na\text{-}a\text{-}tim}$ mu bí-íb-diri-diri-ge	
28 # 34; # 35a		
A	eŋir-a-ni šu <mu>-un-di-ib-gi_4-gi_4	*(28)* His descendants will experience good health.
B obv. 11–12	eŋi[r- .../ ...šu]-gi_4-a ⸢bí⸣-[...]	
C *om.*		
D obv. i 6	[...-n]i šu-gi_4 bí-íb-sù-sù	
E	[eŋir-r]a-na $^{ú\text{-}šá\text{-}al(!)\text{-}la\text{-}am}$ šu mu-ub-gi_4-gi_4	
29 # 36		
A	ibila-a-ni a mu-un-na-de-(de erased)-⸢e⸣	*(29)* His heir will pour water libations for him.
B obv. 13	[...] a mu-un-na-d[é-e] /	
C obv. iii 3	ibi[la ...]	
D obv. i 7	[...-n]i a mu-na-⸢dé(!)⸣-e	
E	[...]-⸢a⸣-ni a mu-na-an-dé-e	

29a–29c: Included only in B and D.

29a		
B obv. 13 cont.	[diŋir-ra]-ni igi ba-an-[ši-bar-re]	*(29a)* [His god] will look (favorably) upon him.
D obv. i 8	[diŋir]-ra(?)-ni igi mu-un-ši-bar-re	

29b		
B obv. 14	[...ŋé]štu ḫé-em-˹x˺-[...]	*(29b)* [He will pay attention to him] ...
C obv. iii 4	ŋéšt[u ...]	
D i 9	[(x) x] ŋéštu ḫé-bí-ib-gub-b[é] DI-e-dè(?)	
	═══ (double line in D)	
29c		
B obv. 15	igi ba-an-[...]	*(29c)* His is chosen in his eyes.
D obv. i 10	[...]-˹ni˺(?) igi ba-ni-in-suḫ-a	
30 # 19		
A	lú-˹lú˺ níŋ-diŋir-ka ní-it-te-˹èn˺-bi nu-mu-un-˹zu˺	*(30)* But the man who does not fear the affairs of (his) god,
D obv. i 11	[l]ú ní-te-ŋá nu-mu-un-zu-a	
30a # 20		
E i 12	[ní-te-a-ni diŋir] nu-mu-un-da-ab-sá-e-a	*(30a)* [who does not voluntarily] please [(his) god],
31		
A	šu˺-ub-la-bi nu-mu-na-[ab]-kal-la	*(31)* to whom prayers are not dear,
B obv. 16	[...] nu-mu-un-na-[...]	
C iii 4	šu-we-e[l ...]	
D obv. i 12	[...]-bi nu-mu-na-kal-le	
32 # 23	*nam-érim ku$_{5}$-ru-da nu-mu-un-na-gig-ga	*(32)* to whom swearing is not abominable,
A	nam-érim un-˹ni˺-ib-bé nu-˹mu˺-un-na-te-ŋi$_{6}$-e	*(var. A:* who does not keep away from swearing)
B obv. 17	[...] nu-mu-u[n- ...]	
C iii 5	nam-ér[im ...]	
D obv. i 13	[...ér]im ku$_{5}$-ru-da nu-mu-na-gig-ga	
E	[...nu-m]u-un-na-gig-ga	
32a # 22	*mu diŋir-ra-na nu-mu-un-na-ka[l]-la	*(32a)* to whom the name of his god is not dear,
D obv. i 14	[...]-ra-ni nu-mu-un-kal-le	
33	*u$_{4}$ ti-la-ni si nu-sá-e	*(33)* the days when he lives will not be right.
A	u$_{4}$ ti-la-a-ni si in-nu-sa-na-˹e(?)˺	
C iii 6	u$_{4}$ til-la-˹a˺-[...]	
D obv. i 14	[...-l]a-ni si nu-sá-e	
E	[...]-˹e˺	
34 # 28		
A	˹eŋir˺-a-ni šu nu-<mu(?)-na>-ni-ib-gi$_{4}$-gi$_{4}$	*(34)* His descendants will not experience good health.
C iii 7	eŋir-ra-[...]	
35 # 29		
A	ibila-a-ni a nu-mu-un-na-de-e	*(35)* His heir will not pour water libations for him.
C omits		
D obv. i 15	[ibila]-ni si(sic!) nu-sá-e	

35a # 28		
D obv. i 16	[eŋir-ra-ni] šu-gi$_4$ nu-mu-ni-íb-sù-sù	*(35a, D only:)* His descendants will not experience long lasting health.
36		
A	lú-lú níŋ-diŋir-ra-ka nu-ub-bé-a šu IRI igi A ugu an-ni-DU(?)-e	*(36)* A man who does not respect his god, (who) has ever seen [him being successful?] ...
C iii 8	lú-ùlu níŋ-diŋir-[...]	
D obv. i 17–18	[...]-a nu-mu-[na]-dé-e / [...] x-è-a-˹ni(?)˺ ˹igi˺ [ba]-ni-im-du$_8$-a	
37		
A	[á-áŋ]-˹ŋá˺(?) diŋir-ra [...] ˹x˺ ni [...]	*(37)* These are instructions of a god.
C iii 9	á-áŋ-ŋá [...]	
D obv. i 19	[á-áŋ-ŋá diŋir-ra]-kam	

Dividing line in C. Dividing line in A may be broken.

38		
A	˹x˺ ˹gán˺-˹maḫ˺(?) a-šà ˹x˺(?) kiŋ (or tag$_4$?) mu-u[n-...-ša$_4$(?)] (additional traces: x mu)	*(38)* Huge fields and arable land ...
C iii 10	gán-maḫ a-šà ˹x˺ [...]	
39		
A	˹x˺(cannot be ki, lú possible)-˹kúr˺-šè [(x)] ˹x˺ ˹x˺-ta udu x x (like IM×X(?)-ZA?) edin-bi [...]	*(39)* At a ... place ...
C 11	ki-kúr-šè im-˹x˺ [...]	
40		
A	[sa]ŋ a-šà-ga-ke$_4$(?) gán-dur$_5$ ḫé-gub e gán-šè ˹x˺ [x]	*(40)* At the "head" of a field a wet area should be established, a ditch [should be dug close] to a field.
C 12	saŋ a-šà [...]	
41		
A	[x] ˹x˺ nam ḫé e ˹x˺(like SAL) ˹x˺-me nam-me- [(x)]	*(41ff.) (No connected translation attempted)*
C iii 13	URUDU IGI nam [...]	
42		
A	[x] ŋiš iti-saŋ$_x$(MURUB$_4$)-ta x [x x (a)]-ab-ba mu-šè-bi ku$_6$-b[i]	*(42)* ... the birds and fish of the marshes ...
C iii 14	ù ŋiš [...]	
43		
A	˹x˺ x (like IG) dug$_4$-ga-àm a-šà-ga ˹zag˺ ˹ḫé˺(or bi) (-)na-ab-BI-ši-˹x˺-˹x˺ / a-šà-ga-àm x [x]	*(43)* ... a field ... work ...
C iii 15	kiŋ(?) ˹x˺ [...]	
44		
A	a-šà-ga-àm nam-lú-lú úrdu-ni šul-a-ni ki-bi ma-ra-˹x˺-[x]	*(44)* On a field, the slaves and the young men belonging to a man [should be(?)] in place(?) (for the work to be done).
B rev. 1	[...] na-˹ám˺(?)-[...]	
C iii 16	a-šà-g[a ...]	

45		
A	a-šà kiŋ-àm zi-ba ab-ba kiŋ-àm dúr-bi-šè e-zu ama kiŋ-à[m]	*(45)* As to field work, it is good(?) that a father does work; it is to disadvantage that a mother does work on your canal.
B rev. 2	[...-à]m zi-b[u ...]	
C iii 17	a-šà ki[n- ...]	
46		
A	gán-na nam-daŋal-la kiŋ ninta ḫé-re-ša$_4$ ú-gub-ba ḫé-eb-gur$_8$-⸢re⸣-⸢e⸣	*(46)* Do not postpone(?) (the work to be done on) a field; let the males do the work for you; let *them* harvest the standing crop.
B rev. 3	[...] ⸢x⸣ ⸢x⸣ ⸢x⸣ ⸢x⸣ [...]	
C iii 18	gán na-an-⸢x⸣ [...]	
47		
A	a-šà nam-daŋal-⸢la⸣ še-zu nu-ub-gur$_8$-re	*(47)* Do not postpone(?) (the work to be done on) a field; you will not get your grain harvested.
B rev. 4–5	[...-daŋ]al-⸢x⸣-e-en še(?)-⸢zu⸣ / [...-n]a-ab-x(like gùr)-e-en	
C iii 19	a-šà nam-daŋal [...]	
48		
A	gud sa$_{10}$-šè ⸢á⸣(?)-zu ḫu-mu-ra-bad igi ḫa-ba-ab-du$_8$-en	*(48)* Toward a bought ox, let your arms(?) be "open," let your eyes see!
B	[...] ⸢x⸣-DU á-kala(?)-ga ḫu(!)-⸢x⸣-[...]	
C iii 20	gud sa$_{10}$-šè á-[...]	
49		
A	áb a-šà-ki-nam ma-ra-ù-tu-ù-tu ⸢níŋ⸣(?)-gi-na gán-na íd(?) daŋal-la	*(49)* When a cow is born for you in a field(?) ...
B rev. 7	[...]-kiŋ mà-ra(?)-ù-tu ⸢x⸣ [...] / [...] ⸢x⸣ lú AD/ZÉ [...]	
C iii 21	áb-e a-šà-gin$_7$-[nam ...]	
50		
A	šà-ŋar-zu u$_4$-ta-àm ùŋ-ta ba-ab-ba-ad gu ⸢x⸣ g[ul(?)-x]⸢x⸣ / ki-bi kal-la(-)ki-⸢x⸣ [(x)]	*(50)* Your hunger every(?) day ... from the people(?) ... that place ....
B rev. 8	[...]-ta un ⸢NU⸣(?) ba-e-KU-e-⸢dé⸣ [...] / [ki-b]i-a kal-l[a(?) ...]	
C iii 22	šà-ŋar-zu GA ⸢x⸣ [...]	
51		
A	ki-ur$_5$-ša(?)-⸢ga⸣ KA-NE-zu ḫa-<ra>-DU níŋ é dù-dù-à[m](?)	*(51)* A joyous mood ... builds houses.
B rev. 9	[...] KA-⸢na⸣(?)-zu ḫa-ra-DU níŋ ⸢é⸣ [...]	
C iii 23	ki-ur$_5$-sa$_6$(?)(copy: dug$_4$)-ga KA ⸢x⸣ [...]	
52		
A	u-buru$_{14}$ ezen-gal ^{d}en-líl-lá-ka	*(52)* At the time of the harvest, the great feast of Enlil,
B rev. 10	[...] ^{d}en-líl-lá-[...]	
C iii 24	buru$_{14}$ ezen-gal [...]	

53		
A	u-buru$_{14}$ si-iš-ta šà diŋir-ra-ne-ka	*(53)* At the time of the harvest, when cool water is libated to the heart of the gods,
B rev. 11	[...š]à diŋir-re-e-n[e ...]	
C iii 25	buru$_{14}$ a-šed$_{17}$-d[a(?) ...]	
54		
A	u-buru$_{14}$-šè ní-zu ḫa-ra-an-kal-kal-e	*(54)* At the time of the harvest you should know what is important to you,
B rev. 12	[...n]í-zu ḫa-ra-ab(!)-kal-k[al-...]	
C iii 26	u$_4$-buru$_{14}$-ke$_4$ ní-zu [...]	
55		
A	^{ŋiš}šu-kár-zu šu ḫa-ab-⸢gi⸣-né(erased)-da	*(55)* You should have your tools redied for you;
B rev. 13	[...] ⸢x⸣ (like g]ú) ḫa-ra-ab-⸢x⸣ [...]	
C iii 27	^{ŋiš}šu-kár-zu [...]	
56	*diri-šè ugu lú á-šè ḫu-mu-ra-an-ŋá-[ŋá]	*(56)* Let him (= your worker) put an effort harder than anyone else for your sake.
A	diri-šè ⸢á⸣-šè mu-re-ŋar-ŋar	
B rev. 14	[...] x x x ḫu-mu-ra-an-ŋá-[ŋá]	
C iii 28	diri-šè ugu lú [...]	
E	[S]I.A-š[è]	
57		
A	gú-e da ḫé-re-du$_8$ ⸢a⸣-⸢sì⸣-⸢ga⸣-àm a-šà-ge si-si-e-te	*(57)* ... to fill the fields with irrigation water,
B rev. 15	[...]-da-sì-ke-bi a a-šà-zu sá-sá-dè	
C iii 29	gu$_4$(?)-ba(?) da(?) ḫé-ni-[...]	
E	gud-da [...]	
58		
A	a-ia-aš-túb a-gàr ⸢x⸣ ⸢DI⸣-sá-te	*(58)* to have the early flood reach the fields,
B rev. 16	[...] x x x-e-dè	
C iii 30	a-eštub a-gàr-[...]	
E	a-eštub [...]	
59		
A	šu-ni-in-ta a-šà-zu a ḫa-ra-ab-si {aš}	*(59)* let your fields be irrigated early.
B rev. 17	[...] a ḫa-ra-ab-si	
C iii 31	šu-nim-ta a-š[à ...]	
E	šu-nim-ta [...]	
60		
A	ki e-da-ka PA(?)-zu ḫa-[r]a-ni-zu bí-ib-si	*(60)* In the irrigated places ... your ditch ...
B rev. 18	[...] pa$_5$-zu ḫa-ra-⸢x⸣ [...]	
C iii 32	ki-za dé K[A ...]	
E	ki a-dug$_4$-ga [...]	

61		
A	x su-zu(?) KU(= ba$_9$?)-na-àm ⸢še⸣-zu daḫ-ba-ab	*(61)* Do the threshing(?) in your (own) threshing floor, and add more of your grain.
B rev. 19	[…] x še-⸢zu⸣ […]	
C iii 33	⸢su$_7$⸣ […]	
E	su$_7$-za x KU $^{\text{ku-ur-⸢x⸣[(…)}}$ …]	
62		
A	šu(?) ⸢na⸣-ab-ta-⸢ta⸣ gán še-zu [tu]r-tur-e	*(62)* Do not touch(?) (the grain in untimely greediness)(?); the field will become short of grain.
C iii 34	n[am …]	
E	šu na-ab-tag-tag […]	
63	★ ur$_5$ ì-me-àm kiŋ-ŋá-àm ḫé-en-zu	*(63)* Thus it is, you(?) should know about working!
A	mu-ri me-àm kiŋ-ga-àm ḫ[é]-en-zu	
C iii 35	⸢lú⸣ […]	
E	mur ì-me-àm […]	
63a		
A *om.*		*(63a)* Thus it is, [you(?) should know about working!]
E	mur ì-me-àm […]	
64		
A	a-⸢áŋ⸣-ŋá eŋar [x x]	*(64)* (These are) instructions of a farmer.
E	á-áŋ-ŋá […]	
A	——27 mu-bi	
E	*dividing line*	
65	★lú ní-te-a-ni ki mu-un-za-za	*(65)* A man should by himself know submission.
A	l[ú] ní-ta-a-ni ki mu-un-za-⸢za⸣	
C iv 1	⸢lú⸣ […]	
E	ní-te-a-ni […]	
66	★lugal ere^{ki}-na-ka ní-te-ŋá-bi mu-un-zu	*(66)* He should know how to fear the lord of his city!
A	lugal ere^{ki}-na-ka mi-it-te-èn-bi mu-un-z[u]	
C iv 2	lugal érin […]	
E	lugal ere-na-ka […]	
67	★šu-kiŋ-dab$_5$-ba ḫé-en-zu ki-su-ub-ba ḫé-en-zu	*(67)* He should know how to bow down (in submission), he should know how to kiss the ground.
A	šu ku-un-di-ip-pa ḫé-en-zu ki-su-ba ḫé-en-⸢zu⸣	
C iv 3	šu ku-[…]	
E	šu-kiŋ-dab$_5$-ba ḫé-[…]	
68	★sun$_5$-sun$_5$-na ḫé-en-zu gub-bu ḫé-en-zu tuš-ù nu-zu-a	*(68)* He should know how to be humble, he should know how to stand in attention, he should not know how to wait (for orders)!
A	su-un-su-na ḫé-en-zu gu-bu ḫé-en-zu tuš-⸢šè⸣ nu-⸢zu⸣-⸢a⸣	
C iv 4	sun$_5$(BÚR)-sun$_5$-[na …]	
E	⸢sun$_5$-sun$_5$-na⸣ […]	

69		
A	e ni-mà-al in-tuku-šè(or túg!) un nam-bi-dul-e	*(69)* [He who is] in charge(?) should not be covered …
C iv 5	á níŋ(?) […]	
70		
A	KUŠ-ah-he ib-mu$_4$-mu$_4$ saŋ-ki na-an-áŋ(?)	*(70)* being dressed in a …, he should not …
C iv 6	KUŠ-a-[…]	
71	*lú á-áŋ-ŋá-ke$_4$ ká é-gal gú-zi-ga ḫé-en-zu	*(71)* The man who gives orders at the gate of the palace, he should know how to stir (people).
A	lú a-ŋá-ke$_4$ ká é-gal gu-zi-ga ḫé-en-zu	
C iv 7	lú […]	
A	—7 mu-bi	
A	— šu-níŋin 71 mu-bi	

Comments on Individual Lines

Lines 1–17: The structure, combining a traditional royal inscription with a literary introduction, similar to *Instr. Šuruppak*, is reasonably clear: Lines 1–4 set the time right back to the creation of the world. Lines 5–7 introduce Ur-Ninurta, whom we might expect to be the subject of what follows, although the (misunderstood) ablative -ta has been erroneously repeated in the apposition lines 6–7 from lines 1–4. With line 8 starts a final *Schachtelsatz*, erroneously introduced by si-sá-e-si instead of *si sá-e-dè, but carried on with -te (phonetic for -dè) in lines 9–11. The main sentence starts in line 12: the agent is Ninurta with appositions lines 13–14. Thereby, Ur-Ninurta turns out to be the "object" of the main verb in line 17: ŋar. Line 18 comes too late for a final infinitive construction, but this is a well-known phenomenon in royal inscriptions.

Line 1: u$_4$-ul-li-a-ta u$_4$-ub-ba is phonetic for u$_4$-ul-lí-a-ta u$_4$-ba, "days of yore": an anticipatory genitive construction typical of high style: */u$_4$-ul-li-a-ta-ak u$_4$-bi-a/, lit. "on the day of the days of yore."

The final /a/ in u$_4$-ba > /u$_4$-bi-a/ is superfluous, not required by the following verb til; *u$_4$-bi would have been sufficient. The scribe was obviously unable to account for the construction, but simply added such expressions as would imitate Sumerian high style.

The common u$_4$-ul-lí-a-ta was convincingly explained by Edzard, CANE 4, 2112, as a loanword from *ullīʾum*, "that one." The following -ta is not to be explained simply as the ablative particle -ta, meaning "since those days." In such cases -ta shifts to the noun class and becomes a nominal part of the noun phrase, followed by the genitive /-ak/. Similar constructions are well attested, such as /mu u$_4$-bi-ta(-ak)/, "the name of former days," Ukg. 4 xi 34. The genitive construction appears clearly in Ukg 6 iii 20: munus u$_4$-bi-ta-ke$_4$-ne (but strangely not in the following iii 23: munus u$_4$-da-e-ne, "the present-day women"; cf. Edzard, *Sum. Grammar*, 19). This is not the full explanation, however, because a pun on a genuine Sum. idiom may well have been intended, such as *u$_4$ ul è-a-ta, explained by van Dijk, AcOr 28 (1964) 33 as "the day when the buds came out," symbolizing primordial times. It is echoed in the similar construction in Ukg 4 iii 2–3: /u$_4$-ul-lí-a-ta(-ak) numun è-a-ta(-ak) u$_4$-bi-a/, in which the parallelism with numun, "when the seeds came up," shows that ul must denote a kind of vegetation. The expression caused difficulty in some late sources, cf. p. 306, *Chap. 3.3a–b*, comments on *The Ballade of Early Rulers* lines 3 and 14.

Line 2: gig-ri bi-ri phonetic for ŋi$_6$-ri bad-rá?

Line 4: ŋar is apparently a mistake for ùr, which is the normal expression for the flood sweeping the country.

Line 6: KA-KA remains unexplained. Mistake for *inim-ma sì-ga, or similar?

Line 7: ša-ak-šu phonetic for šà-kúš-ù.

Line 9: ḫa-la-mi-it-te = ḫa-lam-e-dè. -te is used consistently in what follows for -dè.

Line 12: A restoration of the initial signs like u_4-ba ki-sikil-la, "on that day, in the pure place (scl. Nippur)," might almost, but not quite, fit the traces.

Line 13: Restore possibly šà-pà-da, or similar.

Line 14: The first sign has a small gloss underneath (like TAR), cf. collation in *Orientalia* 60 (1991) 157. The reading ama-a-tu (= émedu) was suggested by S. Votto. This is a designation of a house-born slave, who enjoyed a privileged status compared to other slaves and, therefore, used elsewhere of the relations between a ruler and his god. Cf. the examples mentioned in *Orientalia* 60 (1991) 157; for *Urnamma's Law* line 39, see now Wilcke, in *Jacobsen MV*, 304, with n. 40. Cf. further CAD D, 199a: *dušmû*; CAD I/J, 71 s.v. *ildu* b: *ilid bīti*; *Instr. Šuruppak* 155; *Coun. Wisdom* 155.

Line 16: Nippur B: ere ul-la ..., "the old city," seems to be primary, versus A: ere ki-áŋ-ŋá-ta, "the beloved city." The ablative -ta is a late grammatical form replacing the locative. Cf. line 24.

Line 18: The reading of B follows Civil, 1997, 50, n. 8. It does not seem possible to reconcile sources A and B, but Nippur B must have been primary, something like "to let [his rule last] in Nippur, the very old city." A seems to have had a negative verb, cf. the collation in *Orientalia* 60 (1991) 157.

Line 19: lú-lú is phonetic for lú-ùlu or lú-u_{18}-lu, *awīlūtu*, here simply meaning "a man," not mankind. Cf. the similar cases in line 65 and *Couns. Wisdom* 40, etc.; cf. further the comments on *The Ballade of Early Rulers* Syr. 10; *Proverbs from Ugarit* 24–25.

Lines 19 and 30: níŋ dingir-ra, literally "the (worship of the) things of a god," i.e., religious affairs, occurs also in *Couns. Wisdom* 43; 210 and *Schooldays* 74 (cf. previously Sjöberg, *Orientalia Suecana* 23–24 [1976] 167). The phraseology is almost identical to *Couns. Wisdom* 44: lugal-ra ní-te-$ŋe_{26}$-e-bi ḫé-en-[zu].

Line 20: Civil reads A: ní-[t]a-a-ni dingir [m]u-un-da-x-r]a im-mi?-e [(x)], but either diŋir or mu- seems to be missing on the tablet. The verb sá-a is provided from a presumed parallel line 30 A (Civil, 1997, 45): nu-mu-un-da-ab-sá-e-a (cf. photo in Civil, 1997, 53, MM 478 i 12), where, however, diŋir is restored. He restores our line 20 as mu-un-da-[ab-sá-a, from E, and tentatively explains the gloss in E as *im-ḫu-u*[*r*], translating "he voluntarily [has pleased(?)] god]," scl. by means of offerings, which makes good sense in the context, but comments that the equation sá = *maḫāru* is attested only in A.i. II i 25, 30 (MSL 2, pp. 17–18), but not with a meaning suitable for our line. Relevant examples of *maḫāru* used of religious devotion are listed in CAD M, 61, *maḫāru* 2b: "to pray to a deity." The reading of A given by Alster, 1991, 145, might rather suggest: mu(?)-un-da-[ab-zu-a]-⌜ra⌝ im-mi-e-[(x)], based on line 30 in source D: [...] lú ní-te-ŋá nu-mu-un-zu-a, "he who does not acknowledge fear of god." The remaining traces in A remain unexplained.

Line 21: Alster, 1991, 145, restored [u_4-da-t]a, translating daily(?), which is not quite convincing, although it may hit the approximate meaning. Cf. the comments on *Ballade* 3 and 14; *Enlil and Namzitarra*, Emar version 25–26. Perhaps something like [u_4-šú-u]š would fit. Cf. perhaps *Akk. Couns. Wisdom*, BWL 104: 135–136 : *u_4-mi-šam-ma ìl-ka kit-rab / ni-qu-u qí-bít pi-i si-mat qut-rin-ni*, "Every day worship your god. Sacrifice and benediction are the proper accompaniment of incense." Cf. also *Counsels of a Pessimist*, BWL 107–109, lines 12: *lu-u ka-a-a-an šagigurû-ka a-na ili ba-ni-ka*, "Let your free-will offering be constant before the god who created you."

Line 22: mu = the god's "name" is the oath sworn by the god or, more generally, the invocation of the god's name. The phraseology here remarkably is reminiscent of Exodus 20: 7: "Thou shalt not take the name of the LORD thy God in vain," etc. Even in Sumerian context perjury was considered a very serious crime that, unlike other crimes, could be punished after death. Cf. Bauer, in: *Sjöberg FS*, 24–25, and Alster, AcSum 13 (1991) 1ff., n. 7.

Line 23: The gloss *dup-ru* gives the equation te-ŋá = *duppuru*, "to stay away from," already known from Aa VIII/1:191, listed in CAD D, 186 lex. (MSL 14, p. 494); also Izi E 96 ([te] restored). It seems most likely that it is the verbal infix -da/ta- in E: im-ma-da-ab-te-ŋá-a that gives te this meaning, cf. Civil, 1997, 50. Source A is apparently corrupt at this point. Cf. further line 32 for the reading te-$ŋe_{26}$. Cf. *Couns. Wisdom* 85: ní te-na-ab.

Line 24: "Cult place" is literally "the place of a god." This can be either a small altar in a private house or, in this case perhaps more likely, an official cult place. Only source E has the possessive suffix: [ki diŋir-r]a-ni-ta, a poor grammatical form for *-na(-ta), "the place of his god." The -ta suffix was convincingly explained by Civil, 1997, 50, as an Akkadianism: ta is sometimes used in older texts as a "locative of remote deixis," and in late texts simply as *ina*. Similar examples occur in A line 16; *Couns. Wisdom* 90; 184.

i-da-bé = ì-dab$_5$-bé, rather than -dib-. For si-sá-bi, "straight," cf. *Gilgameš, Enkidu, and the Netherworld* 264: é-gal si-sá-bi ba-an-ku$_4$-ku$_4$, "he goes straight to the palace."

Line 25: Instead of the signs resembling nu-KA on van Dijk's copies, one can with reasonable certainty read ugu, cf. Alster, 1991, 152. This can now be explained as phonetic for ugu <dé>, as indicated by E: [níŋ-ug]u-dé-a-ni (not as a phonetic writing for ku$_4$-ku$_4$ as suggested by Alster, 1991, 152–153).

ab-si-si(!) can now be explained by means of E: im-ma-ab-su-su as a phonetic writing for su-su, "to restore," for which see *Instr. Šuruppak* 21; also 92.

Line 27: mu-tuku-ni can be understood as "the name he has," i.e., his renown or reputation (Alster, 1991, 150) or as "year" (Civil, 1997, 50). The latter is supported by the gloss *šá-na-a-tim* and by context.

Line 28: The gloss in E gives the equation šu – gi$_{(4)}$ = *šullumu*, referring to safety and good health. This is otherwise attested in Níg-ga bil. B 139, and elsewhere, cf. Civil, 1997, 50–51. An alternative meaning, "old age," (so Alster, 1991, 153) is perhaps simply another development from the same term. This is also well attested, cf. MSL 13, p. 118: 137: šu-gi$_4$ = *šu-gu-ú-um*, and 138: šu-gi$_4$ = *ši-bu-um* (Níg-ga); AHw s.v. "Alter, Greis"; cf. further Eblaitic šu-gu (Krecher, OrAnt 22 [1983] 180). Safety and old age can, of course, be seen as two different aspects of the same notion. The variant in source D: [eŋir-ra-n]i šu-gi$_4$ bí-íb-sù-sù, "good health (or old age) will last long for his descendants," is almost identical to its negative counterpart in line 35a, only included in D. In this case, šu–gi$_4$ is constructed as a noun: "May healthy conditions last long."

Line 29: The reading ibila, "heir," is preferred here as most likely in the context, but dumu-ninta, "male child," is also possible, cf. *Instr. Šuruppak* 124 and 257.

Lines 29 and 35: The notion of pouring water libations to please someone occurs also in *Instr. Šuruppak* 161. In this case, however, the reference is most likely to be to funeral offerings after the man's death.

Lines 29a–c: These lines are included in Nippur sources B and D. The few signs from C iii 1–2 mentioned by Civil are, in my opinion, the beginnings of lines 24 and 25, and do not belong here. (They are, in fact, included twice in Civil's reconstruction, 1997, 51.) C iii 4 is doubtful, and may belong to 29b. Strangely, there is a double separating line after line 29b instead of after 29c, where it would have been expected, just before line 30.

Lines 30–35: These lines are the negative counterpart to lines 19–29.

Line 31: šu-ub-la-bi (A), and šu-wi-l[e (C), are syllabic writings for šu-íl-la, in which /i/ has been assimilated to the /u/ in šu to šu-uw$_x$-la-bi. Cf. the u-i variation in Sum. ušbar = Akk. *išpartum*.

Line 32: In A: te-ŋi$_6$-e is a phonetic rendering of te-GÁ-e, which adds another argument for reading -te-ŋe$_{26}$; cf. Civil, 1997, 51 and the literature there cited. Whereas A understood this like line 23 as "who does not keep away from swearing," the other sources had gig = *šutamruṣu*, "to whom swearing is not abominable."

Line 32a: Only in D, tentatively restored from line 22, to which it apparently is formed as an antithetic parallel. Alternatively this could be taken as a misunderstood line 34.

Line 33: The verb si sá is written phonetically si in-nu-sa-na-⌜e(?)⌝ in A. In C til is phonetic for ti(-l) = tìl.

Line 34: In view of line 28 with the variant readings in C and D, it seems that line 34 in source A is a corrupt abbreviation of: *eŋir-ra-ni šu nu-mu-na-ni-ib-gi$_4$-gi$_4$. In D (i 14), the end of the line reads] nu-mu-un-kal-le, probably best taken as line 32a. Cf. lines 22 and 31.

Line 35: Cf. the comments on line 29 above. The variant in D: [...]-ni si(sic!) nu-sá-e is either influenced by line 24, or it literally means "his heir does not walk straight to him."

Line 35a *(D only):* This is the negative counterpart to line 28, cf. var. D: n]i šu-gi$_4$ bí-íb-sù-sù.

Line 36: Lit. "who does not speak the thing of god." A: nu-ub-bé-a can perhaps be harmonized with D: nu-mu-[na]-dé-e, in which case the intended verb is dug_4/e. Lines 19 and 30, however, suggest something like * ní-te-en-bi nu-mu-un-zu-a. After that D preserves [...] x-è-a, and for what follows it is tempting to suggest a restoration such as (a-ba) ⌜igi⌝ [ba]-ni-im-du_8-a, "who has ever seen (him) being successful," or similar, which can partly be harmonized with A: ŠU-IRI a!-ba! igi(?) ... -an-ni-du-a.

Line 37: á-áŋ-ŋá diŋir-ra-kam: "(These are) instructions of a god" or simply "religious instruction," versus *á-áŋ-ŋá eŋar-ra-kam, "instructions of a farmer"; cf. line 64 and p. 222, *Chap. 2.1: Introd. to Instr. Ur-Ninurta*, referring to Civil, 1997, 49–50.

Lines 38–71: Because of the heavily phonetic character of the main source A, with few sections covered by better intelligible duplicates, no connected translation is attempted here, and the comments below are restricted to a few observations on recognizable terms.

Line 40: Reading gán-du_5, rather than gán-a or and é-dur_5/a. According to Civil, JNES 43 (1984) 286, 14, $duru_5$ means "wet from natural causes" rather than from irrigation. Cf. the comments on *Instr. Šuruppak* 272.

Line 42: (a)]-ab-ba: perhaps the marshes or the sea. mu-šè-bi: phonetic for mušen-bi.

Line 45: For a different reading, see Wilcke, ZA 68 (1978) 225, who reads A: a-šà kin àm-zi ba-ab-BA kin àm-dab_5-bé-éš e-zu UR kin àm-x-x. zi-ba tentatively interpreted as "in its throat" by Alster, 1991, 154, implying something unpleasant, but hardly convincing. B: zi-b[u may point in another direction. It could perhaps be phonetic for dùg-ga, *emesal* zé-ba, "it is to advantage that a father does the work," very doubtful, but suitable as an antithetic pair with what follows. The expression seems to be opposite to dúr-bi-šè, which approximately means "in the lowest, most miserable, place" of rank or quality, see Civil's discussion JNES 43 (1984) 285–286, and *Instr. Šuruppak* 157; 177; 220; 272. For kiŋ – $ša_4$(DU), cf. *Instr. Šuruppak* 175: kiŋ – ak, possibly to be read kiŋ – $ša_5$.

Line 46–47: daŋal here probably means "to expand" in a temporal sense, i.e., to delay the work, rather than expanding it in terms of space.

For the pair a-šà versus gán, cf. the comments on *Instr. Šuruppak*, Abū Ṣalābīkh vers. 6 = SS 15.

Line 48: It is difficult to determine what is meant by á-zu ḫu-mu-ra-bad (so A), for which B seems to have the variant á-kala-ga, "May your arm (var. strong arm) be open"; perhaps to be prepared to make the expenses needed. One may compare *Gilgameš XII* 108: *id-su pe-ta-at*, where, however, the Sumerian text (264) has á-ni ŋál bí-in-tag_4, and not á – bad (cf. AHw, 860 a s.v. *petû* 16e).

Line 50: If šà-ŋar is to be equated with *bubūtu*, "famine, hunger," then "your" is difficult. In view of the following line a word for wrath might rather be in place. If ba-ab-ba-ad = ba-ab-bad, one may tentatively translate "keeping your hunger away from the people." B does not support this, however.

Line 51: The end of the line hints at the same theme as *Instr. Šuruppak* 207–208: šà-ki-áŋa níŋ é dù-dù-dam / šà-ḫul-gig níŋ é-gul-gul-lu-dam, "a loving heart builds houses, a heart of hatred destroys houses," where é can mean a family as well as a house. Cf. the comments on the lines for further parallels.

Line 54: Lit. "You should estimate yourself highly," meaning, probably, "You should know what is important to you."

Line 56: Probably source C: ugu lú [...] can be combined with B: [...] x x x ḫu-mu-ra-an-ŋá-[ŋá] and A: diri-šè ⌜á⌝-šè mu-re-ŋar-ŋar, to form: *diri-šè ugu lú á-šè ḫu-mu-ra-an-ŋá-[ŋá]. Civil, 1997, 56, suggests: "Let him put an effort harder than anyone else." According to Civil, there are two distinct verbs: ŋar / ŋá-ŋá, "to put," versus gar / gar-gar, "to pile up." Of these only the latter can interchange with gur in gú – gur. The variant in A: ŋar-ŋar is then a late misunderstood form representing ŋá-ŋá. This distinction nicely explains such seemingly senseless phonetic complements as ^{ŋá}ŋar in Ur III texts, e.g., NG 2, 27f o. 2: igi-ni in-ŋá.ŋar-ra.

Line 57: The writing gud in C and D indicates that A: gú is phonetic for gud and does not mean "bank," as suggested by Alster, 1991, 151. Whether da here means "side" (scl. of the limitations of irrigated fields) is, therefore, doubtful, but cf. perhaps *Disputation between the Hoe and the Plow* 76: ambar-e da um-da-ak-en, "you make a 'side' to the marsh" (OECT V 34 ii 76). B:]-da-sì-ke-bi seems to be the same as is meant by A: ⌜a⌝-⌜sì⌝-⌜ga⌝-àm.

Line 58: a-is-aš-túb, reading túb in A according to Civil, 1997, 52. a-eštub, *mīlum ḫarpum*. Civil translates literally "carp-flood," and explains that this designates the time in spring when the water temperature has reached 16° C, which enables the large carps to spawn, "with spectacular splashings" (cf. Landsberger, JNES 8 [1949] 281ff. and MSL 8/2 97ff.). This may throw light on some unusual descriptions of fish, cf. Alster: "Nanše and Her Fish," in: *Klein FS*, 1–18. Civil, in his note 11, comments on the fact that the same sign, gud = eštub, is used for both "bull(-fish)" and "spring carp." This double meaning of the sign may have played a role here and in the preceding line 57.

The verb might be sá-sá, or even sá di.

Line 59: šu-nim(-ta), with the syllabic writing šu-ni-in(-ta), is equated with *qātum ḫaruptum*, "early work", MSL 13, p. 120: 193, see Civil, AOAT 25 (1976) 93, referring to *The Song of the Plowing Oxen* 63 (quoted p. 88, line 63: eŋar šu-nim-ma); there is an allusion to the same theme in SP 19 Sec. G 7 (Alster: *Proverbs* I, 249): sipa šu-nim-ma eŋar šu-nim-ma, "the early working shepherd, the early working farmer." Civil also refers to *Emeš and Enten* 180: a-gàr gal-gal gán-zi šu-nim-ta kiŋ nu-mu-ra-ab-ak-e-en (ISET II 69, Ni 4572 rev. v 10, dupl. p. 66, Ni 9724, rev. v 9), "no work is done for you on your large fields and your good fields during the early (season?)" (Summer speaking to Winter). The evidence suggests that šu-nim refers to the period of early work in the spring when the fields were irrigated. Cf. also šu-nim in Ai IV i 24–25 (MSL I 52): ab-sín šu-nim-ma ab-ŋá-ŋá = *ši-ir-a ḫ[a-ar-pa(?)] i-maḫ-[ḫ]a-aṣ*, cf. CAD s.v. *ḫarpu*, "he is to make furrows for the early sowing." Cf. also Landsberger, JNES 8 (1949) 278, n. 100, who points to ^{ŋiš}ŋišimmar šu-nim-ma = *mušaḫripu*, "early-bearing" (Ḫḫ iii 317, MSL 5, 119). Also nim alone and še-nim are equated with *ḫarpu*, cf. CAD s.v.

Line 60: A: ki e-da-ka can be explained by means of E as phonetic for ki a-dug$_4$-ga, "the irrigated places." Civil, 1997, 52, quotes further evidence for the reading /dak/ alongside with /duk/. Cf. also var. tag for dug$_4$ in *Instr. Šuruppak* 134; Civil, 1984, 194, with more examples. To these can be added SP 27.9 (Alster: *Proverbs* I, 289) var. UET 6/2 250 tag for dug$_4$.

Line 61: The translation is very tentative. Civil, 1997, 52, translates "Do ... in your threshing floor, and add more grain," but does not decide what it really means. For the verb KU = (ba$_9$(?)), Civil refers to a possible parallel in *Farmer's Instructions* 98: u$_4$ še ba$_9$-rá-zu-ne, "When you thresh ...." The gloss in E does not help, but, since both C and E support the reading su$_7$, the verb must refer to some process related to threshing. In E the first sign is explained by Civil, p. 52, as "like a NA with an indented horizontal on top, something like KU$_7$ in Neo-Assyrian."

Line 62: The reading -ta-ta in A is now certain in view of E: tag-tag. Civil, 1997, 52, translates "Do not ..., the field will be short of grain." Off-hand, šu na-ab-tag-tag would seem to mean "Do not touch (the grain) with your hands," but it seems to have more specific connotations, such as "Don't touch it too early," scl. in untimely greediness. The reading of the first tur in A: [tu]r-tur-e is somewhat doubtful.

Line 63: mu-re is phonetic for E: mur. Civil, 1997, 52, refers to Aa V/2:255 (MSL 14, p. 420, mur restored) for another, somewhat problematic, attestation of this reading, for which the reading ur$_5$ = *kīam*, "thus," would certainly have been expected. Civil, 1997, 52, translates "and so it is! he should know about working." The reference may be to the person himself to whom the text is addressed in the 2nd person (although the verb ḫé-en-zu suggests the 3rd person), or, less likely, to someone working for him. Cf. *Couns. Wisdom* 83; 94; 158; 160; 192.

Line 65: As suggested by Alster, 1991, 156, the first sign is lú and not [lu]gal; cf. Civil, 1997, 52 (versus OrNS 41 [1972] 88). I take this to mean "any man," rather than just "a man." Cf. the comments on line 19 above. The address is here in the 3rd person throughout, different from the previous composition, in which the 2nd person is intended.

ki – za-[za] = *šukênu*, "to prostrate oneself" (in prayer).

Line 66: Cf. lines 19 and 30. C: érin is phonetic for ere^{ki}-n(a). By "the lord of his city" either the city ruler or a city god can be meant, but in this case most likely it refers to an earthly ruler who can put his people to work.

Line 67: šu ku-un-di-ip-pa = šu-kiŋ-dab$_5$-ba. References in Sjöberg, ZA 65 (1975) 230. Cf. also BE 31, no. 27, obv. 6: šu(!)-kiŋ(!) àm-díb-bé-da.

A: ki-su-ba phonetic for ki-su-ub.

Both ki – za-za (l. 65) and *ki-su-ub (l. 67) are usually translated by *kamāsu*, "to bow down," but are both related to *šukênu*. Lines 66–67 "accumulate synonyms for physical expressions of submission"; cf. Civil, 1991, 52 and JCS 28 (1976) 184–187. Cf. also the similar passage in BWL 104: 139: *su-up-pu-u su-ul-lu-u u la-ban ap-pi*, "prayer, supplication, and prostration."

Line 68: The reading of C: BÚR as sun_5 appears from A; su-un-su-na. Cf. further *Couns. Wisdom* 92.

A: gu-bu is phonetic for gub-bu. The pair gub : tuš, lit. "to stand" and "to sit," occurs frequently.

Line 69: Alster, 1991, 156, very tentatively suggested "... who has something should not cover it under a garment," reading ŠÈ as túg. If this hits the approximate meaning, it would be an instruction for the one in command not to hide the signs of his authority, or those under his command not to ignore those signs. This might be the leather dress or similar mentioned in line 70, cf. below.

Line 70: I am unable to suggest any interpretation for KUŠ-aḫ-ḫe. C: KUŠ-a-[at least seems to exclude readings like *zu-uḫ-ḫe. Since what follows seems to describe some kind of dress, this may be a type of garment identifying the one who gives orders, perhaps a leather cap, or similar. The last sign is áŋ, not íl (as read by Alster, 1991, 156).

Line 71: Alster, 1991, 156 suggested: lú a-gá-ke_4 phonetic for lú á-áŋ-ŋá-ke_4 = *muwirrum*, "commander," and gu-zi-ga = gú-zi-ga. Civil, 1997, 49, suggests translating "the one who gives orders, at the gate(?) (or inside?), of the palace, should know how to 'wake up' (people)."

2.3 Counsels of Wisdom

Text Reconstruction, Translation, and Comments

Line	Source	Text	Translation
1			
	C iv 7	lú [...] / [...] (or belongs to the previous composition?)	*(1–12) (Too poorly preserved for translation)*
	D obv. ii 1'	⌜x⌝ [...]	
2			
	C iv 8	lú [...] / [...]	
	D obv. ii 2	lú [...]	
3			
	C iv 9	K[A ...]	
	D obv. ii 3	KA [...]	
4		*(D ii: omits?)*	
	C iv 10	K[A ...]	
5			
	C iv 11	níŋ mu(?)-...] / [...]	
	D ii 4	níŋ-kúr na-[...]	
6			
	C iv 12	nu-⌜x⌝ [...]	
	D ii 5	di na-an-[...]	
7			
	C iv 13	ḫu[l ...]	
	D ii 6	ù-⌜ma⌝-[ni ...]	
8			
	C iv 14	šu [...]	
	D ii 7	šu ŋál(?) [...]	
9			
	C iv 15	S[U ...]	
	D ii 8	šu ⌜x⌝ [...]	
10			
	C iv 16	KA [...]	
	D ii 9	KA ⌜x⌝ [...]	
11			
	C iv 17	nu ⌜x⌝ [...]	
	D ii 10	I[M ...]	
12			
	C iv 18	KA [...]	

13		
C iv 19	níŋ-g[i-na ...]	*(13)* Righteousness ...
14		
C iv 20	diŋir-ra ⸢x⸣(hardly i[gi) [...]	*(14)* The god ...
15		
C iv 21	é-gal lú [...]	*(15)* A "big house" (i.e., palace or prison(?)) ...
16		
C iv 22	é mu-n[a-...-dù(?)]	*(16)* A house [is built(?)] for him (cf. l. 45).
F obv. 1	[é m]u-un-n[a- (traces of at least 3 signs)]	
17		
C iv 23	saŋ ki-diri [...]	*(17)* ....
F obv. 2	saŋ ki-diri-šè mu-n[a-x]-⸢x⸣	
18		
C iv 24	u$_4$ níŋ-gi-na [...]	*(18)* On the day when justice ....
F obv. 3'	u$_4$ níŋ-gi-na ní-bi-a DU-[(x)]-⸢zu(or: da?)⸣	
19		
C iv 25	diŋir-ra [...]	*(19)* The god selects ...
F obv. 4'	diŋir-e igi-zaŋ$_x$-zag$_x$(ŠID-ŠID)-⸢e⸣-⸢zu(or: da?)⸣	
20		
C iv 26	u$_4$-bi-a l[ú ...]	*(20)* On that day the wicked man bowed down (in submission)....
F obv. 5'	u$_4$-bi-a lú-érim-ma ì-gam [...]	
21		
C iv 27	é-gal ŋiš-[búr-gim ...]	*(21)* The "big house" like a trap [arrested] the evil man.
F obv. 6'	é-gal ŋiš-búr-gim lú-ḫul-ŋál mu-n[a-...]	
22		
C iv 28	é mu-un-[...]	*(22)* A house is built for him ...
F obv. 7'	é mu-un-na-dù-e ì-gul saŋ(?)-ŋá(?)-ni [...]	
23	*(F omits)*	*(23)* ....
C iv 29	gán [...]	
24		
C iv 30	u$_4$-b[i-a ...]	*(24)* On that day, justice and righteousness [manifest(?)] themselves ....
F obv. 8'	u$_4$-bi-a níŋ-zi níŋ-gi-na ní im-ma-⸢x⸣-[...]	
I rev. i 1'	u$_4$-[...]	
25		
C iv 31	níŋ-[...]	*(25)* Wickedness is examined.
F obv. 9'	níŋ-érim-e bar im-ma-an-A[K ...]	
I rev. i 2'	níŋ-é[rim ...]	

26		
C iv 32	mìn-[…]	*(26)* For a second time the king's "heart" (= intention(?)) [becomes manifest(?)] in the river of ordeal.
F obv. 10'	mìn-kam-ma-šè šà lugal-la šà íd-lú-ru-g[ú …]	
I rev. i 3'	mìn-k[am-…]	
27		
F obv. 11'	lú níŋ-kúr-ra la-[ba-t]a-[è …]	*(27)* The hostile man does not [escape …].
I rev. i 4'	⸢lú⸣ […]	
28		
F obv. 12'	^{d}nun-gal nin-inim-gi-na ⸢x x x⸣ […]	*(28)* Nungal, the lady of the just words, …
29		
F obv. 13'	^{d}nin-é-gal-la-ke$_4$ èn-tu[kum-šè] AM[A …] / èn-tukum-šè AMA x […]	*(29)* Ninegalla, until when …, until when …
30		
F obv. 14'	[lú]-niŋ-gi-na túg im-mi-in-dul lú-ér[im …]	*(30)* The just man is covered with a cloth, the wicked man […]
31		
F obv. 15'	[é]-gal ab-sù-ra an-zag nu-⸢zu⸣ […]	*(31)* The palace(/temple?) like the wide sea knows no horizon, …,
32		
F obv. 16'	⸢x⸣ KA lugal-la NI ⸢x⸣ […]	*(32ff.) No connected translation possible.*
33		
F obv. 17'	⸢x⸣ suḫ-ù-da ⸢x⸣ […]	
34f.	*Approximately two lines missing*	
36		
F rev. 1'	[…] ŋéštu […]	
37		
F rev. 2'	[…] šà ⸢x⸣ im-[…]	
38		
F rev. 3'	[…] DU-bi lú […]	
39		
F rev. 4'	⸢lú⸣ ⸢x x x⸣ dím-e lú mu-un-[…]	
40'		
F rev. 5'	lú-ùlu lugal-bi (*erasure*?) inim-ma ba-e-[dè-gub(?)]	*(40)* The man …
41'		
F rev. 6'	níŋ-kúr níŋ-gig-zu ⸢x⸣ ḫu-mu-ra-an-ŋál é-gal […]	*(41)* "Your hostility and crime … the 'big house' …"

Line	Source	Text	Translation
42'	F rev. 7'	lugal-e níŋ-kúr ḫul ba-an-gig níŋ-šà-bi [...] / šà-ta eme DI [...]	*(42)* The king showed adversity to hostility, its inmost heart [...], from inside [...].
43'	F rev. 8'	ù-ma-ni níŋ-diŋir-za-gim lú pà-da ba-si-x-[...]	*(43)* The man [will proclaim(?)] his (= the king's(?)) triumph like the affairs of your god.
44'	F rev. 9'	lugal-ra ní-te-ŋe$_{26}$-e-bi ḫé-en-[zu]	*(44)* May he [acknowledge] fear of them before the king.
45'	F rev. 10'	é-gal ḫé-en-dù ^{ŋiš}ràb kalam-ma [...]	*(45)* Let him (= the king) build a "big house" (= prison(?)), [let it become] the "trap of the country."
46	F rev. 11'	níŋ-érim-e ba-an-zé-er šu im-ri-ri [...]	*(46)* The wicked one will glide(?) there, it will trap him.
47	F rev. 12'	kadra-ŋar-ra-bi kadra a-šed$_{10}$(MÙŠ-DI)-[da(?)]	*(47)* The gifts provided (there(?)) [are(?)] gifts of cool soothing water.
48	F rev. 13'	[x x x] ⸢x⸣-na diŋir ba-ra-è níŋ-érim n[a-...]	*(48)* He does not escape from(?) (his) god; wickedness cannot [...].
49	F rev. 14'	[x x x x] ⸢x⸣-ta(?) mu(!)-un-⸢x⸣ [...]	*(49)* ...
50		*(See commentary)*	
	F rev. 15'	[... k]adra a-šed$_{10}$	*(50)* *[The gifts provided there are(?)] gifts of cool soothing water.
	I rev. 1'	[hardly more than one sign] ⸢x⸣ KU(or ma)-ra níŋ(/ŋar) šà MÙŠ KU [...]	
51		*[lú]-zi-bi šà mu-na-[ab-ḫuŋ]	*(51)* The heart is appeased for that righteous man.
	F rev. 16'	[...] mu-na-ab-ḫ[uŋ]	
	I ii 2'	[lú]-zi-bi šà mu-na-[ab-ḫuŋ]	
52	F rev. 17'	[...] x x [...]	*(52–75)* *(Too poorly preserved for translation)*
	I rev. 3'	[... z]i-ŋál šà-bi íb(?)-⸢sig⸣ (or úr-⸢x⸣?) [...]	
53	I rev. ii 4'	[... í]b-⸢sá(could be ki)-a AN kù ⸢x⸣ (like the beginning of ri or similar) [...]	
54	I rev. ii 5'	[...] gul-gul [...]	
55	I rev. ii 6'	[...] kadra ⸢ŋiš⸣ šu ba-[x x] (cf. l. 47)	*(55)* *(Cf. l. 47)*

56		
I rev. ii 7'	[...] diŋir-re-e-[ne x]	
57		
I rev. ii 8'	[x x] in-RI (could be NUN or similar) kadra šu mu-ra-[x] (could be ti)	
58		
I rev. ii 9'	[...] AN ba-da(?)-dé(?)-en	
59		
I rev. ii 10'	[...] ⸢ba⸣(?)-⸢da⸣(?)-⸢dé⸣(?)-en nu-tuku(?) ere ki-suḫ-ḫa	*(59)* ... the city, the selected place ...
60		
I rev. ii 11'	[...] ⸢x⸣ ⸢x⸣ mu-ra-dugud	
61		
I rev. ii 12'	[...] ⸢x⸣ ⸢x⸣ ba-e-ŋá-ŋá	
62		
I rev. ii 13'	[... gu]b-bu-dè	
63		
I rev. ii 14'	[...] ⸢x⸣ ḫúb saŋ(?) kal(?)-a-na	
64		
I rev. ii 15'	[...] ⸢x⸣ áŋ(?)	

* * *

73		
G obv. 1	[... L]I ŋá ⸢x⸣ [...]	
74		
G obv. 2	[... l]ú bí-ib-gub-bé [...] (room for -en or similar)	
75		
G obv. 3	[...] ÚRU-ta ⸢lú⸣-ra bí-ib-DUB(?)-⸢x⸣ (hardly -gur?-⸢re⸣)	
76		
G obv. 4	[inim ab-ba-zu(-gim) inim diŋir-zu-gim ŋi]zzal ḫé-em-ši-ak	*(76)* May you pay attention [to the words of your father as to the words of your god].
77		
C v 1	inim ama-zu-gim inim diŋir-[zu]-gim ŋizzal ḫé-em-ši-ak	*(77)* May you pay attention to the words of your mother as to the words of your god.
G obv. 5	[...-z]u-gim ŋizzal ḫé-em-ši-ak	

78		
C v 2	á-tuku-zu-šè nam-ba-e-dib-bé	*(78)* Do not infringe on (the rights of) him who is stronger than you.
G obv. 6	[(2 signs?) -š]e(sic!) ba-e-dib-bé-en	
79		
C v 3	níŋ-šu-zu(?) šu ì-⸢ŋar⸣-[ŋa]r(?)-bi ur$_5$-ra gu$_7$(?) ḫu-mu-ra-ŋá-ŋá	*(79)* What your hands have procured, may it be (like) interest providing what you need to eat (thus C; G: *ditto*, may it be interest providing to you what your prayers are about).
G obv. 7	[... ... u]r$_5$-re šùd-dè ḫu-mu-ra-ŋá-ŋá	
80		
C v 4	šeš-gal-zu ní te-ŋe$_{26}$-e ḫu-mu-un-zu	*(80)* You should know how to fear your older brother!
G obv. 8	[... ḫ]é-en-zu	
81		
C v 5	inim šeš-gal-zu inim ab-ba-zu-gim ŋizzal ḫé-em-ši-ak	*(81)* You should pay attention to the words of your older brother as to the words of your father.
G obv. 9	[...]-⸢gim⸣ ḫé-em-ši-ak	
82		
C v 6	šà nin-gal-zu ḫul na-ab-gig-ga áš-dug$_4$ ka-bi-šè gi$_4$-bi-ib	*(82)* Let not your older sister's heart grow hateful; let the curse return to the mouth from where it came.
G obv. 10	[... š]e <gi$_4$>-bí-ib	
83		
C v 7	šeš-šeš-za [dugud(?)]-da(?)-bi ḫé-en-zu níŋ é dù-ù-dè	*(83)* You should know how to [honor] your brethren, it is edifying.
84		
C v 8	ad-gi$_4$-⸢a⸣ níŋ-érim(?) na-ab-ḫe-ḫe	*(84)* Don't mingle advice with hostility.
85		
C v 9	du$_{14}$(!) mú-[a(?)-ra(?) k]i(?)-bi-šè dug$_4$-ga-na-ab nam-tag ní te-na-ab	*(85)* Put [him who] causes a dispute in his place; stay away from guilt.
H i 1'	[ca. 4 signs -r]a(?) ⸢ki⸣-b[i-...]	
86		
C v 10	šà-ŋar-z[u x] mu-ra-ab-šub eŋir-bi-ta in-àm	*(86)* When your hunger has left you, afterward it is (only) a trifle(?).
H i 2'	[ca. 3 signs -šu]b-bé a-na ab-⸢x⸣ [...]	
87		
C v 11	siskur ⸢u$_4$-ba?⸣ nam-ba-e-dib-bé ka-ta è-a-zu diŋir íb-ta-na-an-de$_6$	*(87)* Don't overstep (the right time for your) offerings; (otherwise) the god will *distance(?) himself from what you have uttered.
H v 3'	[ca. 2 signs] ⸢x⸣-na(?) nam-bí-dib-bé ka-ta è [...]	
J obv. 5	[...] ⸢x⸣ : *ni-qá-ka* [...]	
J 6	[... k]a-ta è-(no a?)-zu / [...-ab-dé	
J 6f	: ⸢*ni*? *x* (QA over GA)⸣ *iš*? *u$_4$-mi-šú* [...]	

88
C v 12 — sa$_6$-g[a] ì-ga-an-sa$_6$ u$_4$-bi ḫa-ba-ab-gub-gub-bé-en
H i 4' — sa$_6$-ga in-ga-sa$_6$ u$_4$-bi-šè ḫa-ra-ab-[...]
J 7 — [...] ⸢x x x⸣ ḫa-ba-gub-bé-en : ⸢*da?*⸣-*mi-iq* ⸢*id-mi*⸣-[*iq/qu* ...]

(88) "It is good, it is very good, today(?) I shall be present for you (in an omen(?))," (says the god).

89
(H omits)
C v 13 — siskur u$_4$-ba na-ab-gíd-dè ki la-la-bi kaš-dé-a-zu sá-ba-ab
J 8 — [...-b]i(?) šùd-dè a-ra-an-⸢na⸣-ab-bé : *a* (*ca. 5 damaged signs*)

(89) Don't postpone the time of (your) offerings; at the place of abundance(?) make your beer serving pleasant!

90
(H and J omit)
C v 14 — gisbun-na ki-kaš-dé-a-ta

(90) At a banquet, at a drinking party,

91
C v 15 — igi gisbun-na ḫu-rí-in^{mušen}-gim lú im-ma-ab-šú-šú
H i 5' — gisbun ⸢ur$_5$(?)⸣^{mušen}-gim-ma lú im-ma-šú-[šú]
J 9 — [... ḫu-rí-in^{mu}]^{šen}-gim lú-ra in-šú-šú : ⸢*x x x*⸣ GIM *ḫ*[*u-ri-in-ni* ...]

(91) at the sight of the banquet men will come down like eagles.

92
C v 16 — tumu(IM) sa[ŋ]-šè nu-mu-e-íl-e ḫé-íb-sun$_5$-sun$_5$-na ki-bi sá-e-dè
H i 6' — tumu(IM) saŋ-šè nu-mu-un-da-íl sun$_5$-sun$_5$-na
J 10 — [... ḫ]é-sun$_5$-na : *šar* [*x*] *li-is-sa-bi* [...]

(92) The wind should not rise into your face; let it calm down in order for you to stay stable (lit., in its place).

93
C v 17 — di(!)(text KI) lú-ŋar-ra-àm inim-zu na-an-šúr-re
H i 7' — di(!)(text KI) lú-ŋar-ra-bi inim-zu šúr-[-re]
J 11 — [di nu-ŋar-ra-šè inim-zu na-a]b-sar-re-en : *ana di-in nu-ul-la-t*[*i* ...]

(93) Don't speak with irritation because of the judgment of someone unruly.

94
C v 18 — du$_{14}$-da izi-gim lú ba-an-gu$_7$-e te-en-te-en-bi ḫé-en-zu
H i 8' — du$_{14}$(!)(LÚ) izi-gim lú ba-an-gu$_7$-e te-en-te-[...]
J 12 — [...-e]n-bi ḫé-en-zu : *ṣa-al-tum* GIM ⸢*i*⸣-*ša-t*[*i* ...]

(94) A quarrel devours a man like fire; you should know how to extinguish it.

94 A
(C and J omit)
H i 9 — DI lú ki-ri-a-šè PA$_4$-LUL lú ⸢x⸣ [x x]

(94 A) (no translation)

94 B
(only J)
J 13 — [...] ⸢šed$_4$⸣-de : *a-šar ṣa-al-ti* ⸢x⸣ [...]

(94 B) At a place where there is a quarrel ...

94 C
(only J)
J 14 — [...] ⸢x x x⸣ : *ap-pa*(?)-*ra* [...]

(95 C) (no translation)

Line	Source	Text	Translation
95			
	C v 19	˹x(in(?)˺-e ḫa-ra-ab-bé šà-zu ḫé-éb-ši-dugud	*(95)* Should someone utter an insult toward you, may it weigh heavily in your heart.
	H i 10	in ḫa-ra-bé šà-˹x˺ […]	
96			
	C v 20	níŋ-kúr ḫa-ra-ab-bé gaba-ri na-an-na-ab-bé ki-bi dugud-da-àm	*(96)* Should someone utter hostility toward you, don't speak in an opposing way; that's the important thing!
	H i 11	[níŋ]-˹kúr˺ ḫa-ra-ab-bé gaba na-an-<na>-bé d[ugud …]	
97		*(H omits)*	
	C v 21	níŋ-˹x˺ KA×X nam-ba-e-sì-ge KA nam-ba-e-šub-bé	*(97–98) (no translation attempted)*
98		*(H omits)*	
	C v 22	[x (x)] ki-kúr-šè nam-ba-e-x(?) ŋál-la nam-ba-silig-ge	
99			
	C v 23	[x-z]u šà <nam>-ba-e-dib-bé šà-dib-gim NI-DUL(?)-gim u_4 ní-šè ba-ab-šú	*(99)* Don't(?) let your [anger(?)] seize your heart, like an angered(?) heart(?) … the day settles by itself.
	H i 12	[x (x) š]à nam-bí-díb-bé šà-díb-gim(!) (text ba) níŋ š[u …] ˹x x x˺	
100			
	C v 24	[x ḫ]é-a ki-bi-šè ḫa-ra-TIL	*(100–101) (no translation attempted)*
	H i 13	[x (x)]-˹šè˺ ˹ḫa˺-ra-˹an˺-[ca. 4 signs]-TIL	
101			
	C v 25	[(x) na]-ab-gíd-gíd ki(or: u_4(?))-SAR ugu-zu ḫé-in-ši-gub-bu	
	H i 14	[…]-˹x˺-bu	
102			
	C v 26	[(x) šu na-a]n-tu-lu lú im-di-ni-ib-kar-re	*(102)* Do not release [your hand toward …]; the man will flee.
	H i 15	[…]-re	
103			
	C v 27	[(x) n]a-an-dù-dù šà-ḫul-gig im-si	*(103)* Do not …; he(?) will be full of hatred.
	H i 16	[…]-gig <im>-si	
104			
	C v 28	[(x) x]-la-ra níŋ nu-mu-un-na-kal	*(104)* Nothing is precious to him.
	H i 17	[… n]a-an-kal	
105			
	C v 29	[(x) x-g]i-na é gul-gul-e	*(105)* … destroys a house.
	H i 18	[…]-e	
106		*(H omits)*	
	C v 30	[(x)] ˹x(like T]UM)˺-la-ke_4 ní ḫé-eb-ši-te-en-te-en	*(106)* … may calm down.

107		
C v 31	[(x)] ⸢x(like z]é⸣ gu$_{7}$-e nam-da-lá te-ŋe$_{26}$-e-dam	*(107)* … is not to be approached.
H i 19	[…]-⸢e⸣-dè	
108		
C v 32	[(x)-s]ì(?)-sì-ge lú-ù ba-an-ku$_{4}$-re-en	*(108)* A man does not introduce you(?) [into …].
H i 20	[…]-re	
109		
C v 33	[(x) x]-dúb-bu-e ní-zu en-nu-ùŋ-da	*(109)* … guarding yourself.
H i 21	[…]-gu$_{7}$(?)-dè	
110	*(H omits?)*	
C v 34	[(x) d]a(?) ní-zu nam-ba-šúm-mu NI-kù-gim ḫé-en-zu	*(110)* … should not give yourself; may you(?) know like a …
111		
C v 35	[(x) x]-ga ŋál-la ku$_{5}$-ru šub-bu ki-bi-a ⸢x⸣ [x]	*(111) (no translation attempted)*
H i 22	[…]-ku$_{4}$-re (belongs here?)	
112		
C v 36	[(x) x] ⸢KA×X⸣ KA-búr-ra lú saŋ-bul-e ere-bal-a ki-b[i(?)-a x (x)]	*(112)* … an angry man … a revolting town …
113		
C v 37	[…] ⸢x⸣ igi nu-mu-un-[x x x]	*(113–117, 145–146 A) (No translation attempted)*
114		
C v 38	[…] ⸢a⸣ lú ⸢ḫé(?)⸣-[x x x x]	
115		
C v 39	[…] ⸢x x⸣ […]	
116		
C v 40	[…]-bi […]	
117		
C v 41	… traces of two signs …	
* * *	*Lacuna, estimated to be ca. 20 lines*	

Following the lacuna: J: CBS 11945 rev. 1–9 too poorly preserved for reconstruction.

145		
G rev. 1	[…] ⸢x⸣ […]	
146		
G rev. 2	[…] ⸢x(like ere]⸣ ⸢x(like šè)⸣ […]	
J rev. 10'	[…]⸢x⸣ KU sa na-an-⸢x x x x⸣ bé : *ma-⸢x x⸣* […]	

146 A
J rev. 10a/11 — *(J only, belongs where?)*
[...] ⌜ḫé(?)⌝-RI : ⌜*x x*⌝ [...]

147
G rev. 3 [...] ⌜x⌝ BAD-e [x x] ⌜x⌝ [x]
J rev. *omits*

(147) [Don't] drive away a [...]

148
G rev. 4 [... n]a-an-BAD-e [x] mu-e-ši-[...]
H obv. ii 1' (traces, like ⌜a-ni⌝) [...]
J rev. *omits*

(148) Don't drive away a [...]; he will [...]

149
G rev. 5 [...] ⌜NE⌝-LABAG×U(or: ⌜x⌝ is-ḫáb(?)) šu na-an-dù-dù ID-x(or probably dè)
H ii 2' ŋuruš ⌜kar(?)⌝ [...]
J rev. *omits*

(149) Don't bind a ...

150
G rev. 6 [ŋuruš(?)...] ⌜á⌝-ni ba-ab-šúm-mu
H ii 3 ŋuruš lú(?) ḫuŋ-ŋá(?) ⌜x⌝ [...]
J rev. 12 [...] | á-ni ma-<ra>-an-šúm-ma
[e]ṭ-l[um] ⌜*x-ru*(?)⌝ *ag-[ru* ...]

(150) (If) [you pay(?) a] young man employed as a hired worker(?) well, he will lend *you(?) his (full) strength ...

151
G rev. 7 [... m]u-na-⌜x⌝-KU-UŠ(?)
H obv. ii 4 u$_4$ nam-ŋuruš-e mu-u[n-...]
J rev. 13 [...] mu-un-na-ab-⌜x⌝-⌜x⌝
: *[u$_4$-u]m* ⌜*mé-ṭe-lu-ti*⌝-*[ka* ...]

(151) Your youthful years ...

152
G rev. 8 [...] ⌜x⌝-NE(hardly = šùd-dè) ur$_5$-re ḫu-mu-ra-⌜x⌝
H obv. ii 5 u$_4$ nam-ab-ba si-si-da ⌜x x⌝ ⌜an⌝ [x x]
J 14 [...] ⌜x⌝-a(?)-ma ur$_5$-re ḫé-ni-⌜íb-x x x-e⌝ :
: *(x)* ⌜U$_4$⌝ *lit-ti-ka i-na* [...]

(152) When the years of old age are to be fulfilled, let it be ...

153
G rev. 9 [...] ḫé-sá-e-a
H obv. ii 6 ŋuruš KU (Cavigneaux áš(?))-zu ḫé-sá [...]
J 15 [...] sá bí-in-dug$_4$-ga
: *eṭ-lum ša ṣi-bu-ut-ka ú-š[ak-ša-du-ka*(?)]

(153) If you need a youth according to your needs(?) when you reach your old age,

154
G rev. 10 [...] á-ni-ta ba-ra-è-dè
H obv. ii 7 ninda šà ḫa-ra-ab-si á-ni ba-ra-⌜è(U[D.DU)⌝ [...]
J 16 [...] á-ni ma-ra-e$_{11}$-e-a
: NINDA *lu še-bi* Á-*sú [itelli*(?)]

(154) satisfy his heart with (plenty of) bread, then his strength will come out.

155		
G rev. 11	[... g]i-me-a-aš-ŋu$_{10}$ dug$_4$-ga-na-⸢ab(Cavigneaux šè(?))⸣	*(155)* Even if he is your home-born slave, say "my colleague" to him.
H obv. ii 8	émedu-zu ḫé-a gi$_4$-a-ši dug$_4$-⸢ga⸣-[na]	
J 17	[...] ši-a mu-ni-in-dug$_4$-ga šè(?)	
	: *ana* ÚRDU-*ka šu-ú ki*(!)-*na-t*[*i* ...]	
156		
G rev. 12	[...] ⸢x⸣-t[u-l]u KA×X.DI [...]	*(156)* Don't release your hand on your servants, slave girls or slaves, ...
H obv. ii 9	[saŋ]-ŋéme-úrdu-zu šu-zu na-ra-ab-tu-lu šà GUB b[a(?)-...]	
J 18	[...-r]a-ab-tu-lu KA MÙŠ gi-bí-íb	
	: *ana aš-ta-pí-ri-ka* ⸢*x x*⸣ [...]	
157		
H obv. ii 10	za-pa-⸢áŋ⸣ dugud(?) x x gig(?) x x ugu-bi ḫé(?)-ib⸣-[...]	*(157)* (*see comments*)
J 19	[... ug]u-bi-a ḫé-en-DU.DU.DU-bé	
	: ⸢x x⸣ [x x] ⸢x⸣ [x x]	
158		
H obv. ii 11	AN(?) KU(?) saŋ ur [...] ⸢x⸣ [...]	*(158–159)* (*no translation*)
J 20	[...] ḫé-en-zu [(x)]	
	: [...]	
159		
H obv. ii 12	⸢x⸣ ⸢x⸣ [...]	
J 21	[...] UD UR ba-ra-te-[(x x) : ...]	
160		
H obv. ii 13	⸢x⸣ ⸢x⸣ ⸢x⸣ ⸢x⸣ [...]	*(160)* ... you should know how to release it ...
J 22	[...] ⸢x⸣ tu-lu-bi ḫé-en-[zu ...]	
161		
H obv. ii 14	GIŠ KU IGI KU ⸢x⸣ [...]	*(161–166)* (*no translation*)
J 23	[... n]u(?)-mu-ra-ab-⸢x⸣ [... : ...]	
162		
H obv. ii 15	igi nu-mu-e-[...]	
163		
H obv. ii 16	di na-ab-[...]	
164		
H obv. ii 17	lú šà [...]	
165		
H obv. ii 18	di(?) a[b(?) ...]	

166

H rev. i 1 igi ⌜x⌝ [x] ⌜ŠE(or similar)⌝-bi-da di ab-[...]

167

H rev. i 2 nam-érim ki-lul-la lú nam-⌜tar⌝ [...]

(167) A curse in the "place of wickedness" [determines] the destiny [for(?)] a man.

168

C (r.) vi 1 di-da inim érim(!)-ŋál nu-mu-ni-íb-bé

H rev. i 3 di-da inim-érim-ŋál na-an-⌜x⌝[...]

(168) When you pronounce judgment, don't speak words of hostility.

169

C vi 2 níŋ-tuku-zu-šè ḫé-íb-kala-ga-gim níŋ-tuku níŋ daḫ-ba-ab

H rev. i 4 níŋ-tuku-zu-àm ḫé-kal-gim níŋ daḫ-ma-[ab]

(169) As to your possessions—since they are very dear to you—keep adding things to your possessions.

170

C vi 3 ur$_5$-tuku-zu-šè nam-ba-silig-ge níŋ ba-an-tur-re

H rev. i 5 ur$_5$-tuku-zu-àm nam-ba(!)-ši-li$_9$-ke bi-tur-tur-[re]

(170) Don't cause financial ruin to someone who owes you money; (because then) he will have even less (with which to pay you back).

171

C vi 4 níŋ-sì-ga ki-bi-šè ḫé-en-zu

H rev. i 6 níŋ šúm-mu-bi ki-bi ḫé-en-[zu]

(171) You(?) should know how to give something where appropriate.

172

C vi 5 lú níŋ-sì-bi(or ga(?)) mu-un-zu-àm

H rev. i 7 lú níŋ-šúm-mu-bi mu-un-zu (erasure)-[(àm)]

(172) He who knows how to give things,

173

C vi 6 níŋ mu-un-da-ab-daḫ-e DAG+KISIM$_5$×?(= kešer$_x$(?)) àm-tuku-tuku-e

H rev. i 8 níŋ mu-un-na-an-daḫ-e DAG+KISIM$_5$×?(= kešer$_x$(?)) (erasure(?)) ⌜àm(?)⌝-⌜tuku⌝-[...]

(173) he will have things added, even until it has <no> limits.

174

C vi 7 kas$_4$-tur lú-ra ŋiskim mu-un-e$_{11}$-dè ninda gu$_7$-ni-ib

H rev. i 9 DU-tur lú-ra ŋiskim(? copied like IGI.GAR) ù-mu-ni-g[u$_7$(?)-...]

(174) A "small" traveller who makes himself known to a man, give him something to eat!

175

C vi 8 tukum-bi ki-ná nu-tuku ki-ná ŋar-ì

H rev. i 10 tukum-bi ki-ná k[i-...]

(175) If he has no bed, prepare him a bed!

176

C vi 9 šu igi-ni-šè ba-e-gub-bu igi-zu-šè ì-ŋál

H rev. i 11 šu igi-zu mu-un-ni-gub igi-zu [...]

(176) His hand raised before his (own) eyes is (raised) before *your* eyes!

177		
C vi 10	šu igi-ni-šè gi$_4$-ni-ib eŋir-bi-ta in-àm	*(177)* Turn the hand backward toward his eyes, afterward it is (only) a trifle(?).
H rev. 12	šu igi-du-a-zu gi$_{16}$(?)(copy: lul)-íb(?) ⌜eŋir(?)⌝ ⌜x⌝ ⌜x⌝ [...]	
178		
C vi 11	ki-bi-šè ŋéštu bí-íb-gu-ur-ru-àm	*(178)* Where appropriate it will be kept in mind!
H rev. 13	ki-bi-šè ŋé[štu ...]	
179		
C vi 12	kas$_4$ diri-ga é im-gíd-gíd lú-kal-la ḫé-àm	*(179)* A "greater" traveller, who lingers(?) at a house, let him be (treated like) an honored man.
H rev. 14	DU diri-ga é si-sá-zu lú-kal-la ḫ[é-...]	
180		
C vi *omits*		
H rev. 15	ere-kúr-ra šu na-ab-tag-tag lú ki-bi íb-z[u-(àm)]	*(180)* Don't associate(?) with a (citizen from a) foreign city, the man is kn[own by] that place.
181		
C vi *omits*		
H rev. 16	lú kar(?) íb-tuku šeš-zu-gim ma-ra-[x x]	*(181)* A man who has a "quay" (i.e., source of income(?)) [is(?)] like a brother for you.
182		
C vi 13	é ku$_4$-ku$_4$-zu u$_4$-bi na-ab-gíd-dè igi-a nam-ba-e-gub-bu	*(182)* Don't let a man who (wants to) enter your house spend a long time (outside), let him not remain standing in front (of the house).
H rev. 17	é ku$_4$(!)(text: BU-KU)-ra-zu u$_4$ na-ab-sud igi-zu nam-[...]	
183		
C vi 14	dumu ká-gi$_4$-a šeš-zu-gin$_7$-nam íb-ak usar ká-gi$_4$-a nin-zu-gim íb-ak	*(183)* A son of your city quarter, having been treated like your brother; a female neighbor of your city quarter, having been treated you like your sister,
H rev. 18	dumu ká gi$_4$-a šeš-gin$_7$-nam!(text: zi) íb-ak usar k[á-...]	
184		
C vi 15	[e]n-na u$_4$-til-la-ta ki-kaš-dé-a-ta šu nam-ba-e-díb-bé	*(184)* as long as you live, you should not oblige(?) him (/her) at your drinking parties.
H rev. 19	⌜x(too small for en⌝-⌜na⌝ ⌜u$_4$-ti-la⌝-zu kaš d[é!(text: rather e)-⌜a-ta⌝ ⌜nam-bí-dib(!)(text: e)⌝-[bé]	
185		
C vi 16	tukum-bi šu-ni ba-lá níŋ-tuku-zu-šè níŋ-nam la-ba-e-ši-kal	*(185)* If he is bound by business connections, nothing precious (will be added) to your possessions.
H rev. 20	(illegible traces of two signs)	
186		
C vi 17	⌜ki⌝-nam-tar-ra-bi šeš nin-gim íb-ak šà-zu bí-íb-šed$_{10}$(MÙŠ)-dè	*(186)* After their status has been changed into that of a brother or sister, your heart is "soothed."

187 C vi 18	[g]ud(?) ú-naŋ(?)(copy: gu_7(?))-zu-ta ḫé-íb-ta-an-sù-ud	*(187)* (But,) no matter how far remote your cattle are from your grazing grounds and your watering places,
188 C vi 19	a-šà-ga lú-kar-zu ḫé-íb-ta-an-sù-ud	*(188)* (and,) no matter how far away your man has fled into the fields,
189 C vi 20	íd-da má-gur_8-zu ŋá-la ḫé-íb-ta-dag-ge	*(189)* (and,) no matter where your cargo ship has stopped in the river,
190 C vi 21	dumu-ká-gi_4-a šeš nin-gim íb-ak ki-za-a mu-e-tuku-tuku	*(190)* the sons of your city quarter, whom you have treated like a brother or like a sister, you (should) keep them (firmly) under you(r control)!
191 C vi 22	mìn-kam-ma-šè usar ká-gi_4-a igi-du_8-du_8-meš	*(191)* Further, the female neighbors of your city quarter who are on the look-out,
192 C vi 23	[níŋ]-tuku-zu šu im-ši-dúb-dúb-bé du_6-du_6-la ḫé-en-zu	*(192)* it they are greedy(?) toward(?) your possessions, you should know how to hide them (well).
193 C vi 24	⌜níŋ⌝-e lú-šè [...]	*(193–194)* (*Too poorly preserved for translation*)
194 C vi 25	(traces of three signs)	

* * *

D (UM 29–13–419A) rev.= ca. 204'–226' (photo).
Must overlap H = VS 10, 205 obv. ii–rev. i (= ca. 225'–246'), but uncertain where.

Ca. 204' D rev. 1'	(*Close to the upper edge*) [...] traces of one sign [...]	*(204–247)* (*Too poorly preserved for translation*)
205' D rev. 2'	[...] ⌜e(?)⌝ Í[B ...]	
206' D rev. 3'	[...] x nin-da-zu-gi[m ...]	
207' D rev. 4'	[...]-gim(?) mu-un-⌜x⌝ [...]	
208' D rev. 5'	[...]-bi(?) mu-un-da-⌜tuku⌝-tu[ku]	

209'
D rev. 6' [...]-a-bi ḫé-ši-pà-dè-a

210'
D rev. 7' [...] x x ní-diŋir(?)-ŋá ní-te-ge$_{26}$-e

211'
D rev. 8' [... a]b bar lá diŋir-ŋá ní-da x(like kam) ma x(like i)

212'
D rev. 9' [...] x x IGI ⸢li⸣ ŋá šà si-sá na-ra-sumun(BAD(?))-nam(?)

213'
D rev. 10' [...] x bi GIŠ DÙ ù SIKIL

214'
D rev. 11' [(x)(?)] šu-a x šu(?) šà-bi a-ba-a mu-un-⸢ŠUB⸣ [...]

215'
D rev. 12' [(x)] ⸢kiŋ(?)⸣-bi na ú-SAR(?)(hardly gu$_{7}$) ì-ŋál

216'
D rev. 13' ⸢ni⸣ GAM(?) šu dili(?) x x x na-an-ŋál(?)

217'
D rev. 14' x x x-zu ki-bi DI KU(?)(hardly e, but similar)-na

218'
D rev. 15' im-lu(hardly = ní-zu) ⸢x⸣-a ḫé-zé(?)-x-en-na-a

219'
D rev. 16' x du me šà UG x (ca. 4 signs)-a

220'
D rev. 17' ⸢ní⸣-⸢zu⸣ ere me ke$_{4}$(?) ib-tuku-tuku(?)

221'
D rev. 18' ⸢x⸣ ⸢ta⸣ kin-na-zu x x [x]

222'
D rev. 19' ⸢x⸣ lú-ke$_{4}$(or: like SAḪAR(?)) šu x x

223'
D rev. 20' [x x] x

224'
D rev. 21' [x] x-da lú na-gi$_{16}$-BI(?) [(x)]

225'
D rev. 22' [x] bal-e GIŠ lú(?) nu-m[u-...]

226'
D rev. 23' […] ḪUR […]

⋆ ⋆ ⋆

Connection between D and H not established.

227'
H rev. ii 1' […]-⸢dug$_4$⸣-⸢ge⸣

228'
H rev. ii 2' […] ⸢x⸣-àm

229'
H rev. ii 3 […]-bé

230'
H rev. ii 4 […]-da

231'
H rev. ii 5 […]-dè

232'
H rev. ii 6 […]-ni-ŋál

233'
H rev. ii 7 […]-ŋál

234'
H rev. ii 8 […]-e

235'
H rev. ii 9 […]-si

236'
H rev. ii 10 […]-ḫal

237'
“H rev. ii 11 [x x] ⸢x⸣-íb⸣-⸢x⸣ [ca. 5–6 signs]-ŠUB

238'
H rev. ii 12 [x (x)]-gin$_7$-nam ⸢x⸣ [ca. 5–6 signs]-la

239'
H rev. ii 13 [x (x)] ⸢x⸣-bi kù(?) KU ⸢x⸣ [ca. 5–6 signs]-ba(or zu)

240'
H rev. ii 14 [x (x)]-e-NE lú ere [ca. 5–6 signs] ⸢e⸣

241'
H rev. ii 15 [x x] sì-sì-ke-da lú B[ÚR …]⸢x⸣

242'
H rev. ii 16 [x N]E-ZU(?)-ni ÉŠ(TÚG)-GÍD lú [BÚR ca. 5–6 signs] ⌜x⌝

243'
H rev. ii 17 KA-búr-ra na-an-E+GAR Š[U ...] ⌜x⌝

244'
H rev. ii 18 KA-sun$_5$(BÚR)-na na-x(like ERIN(?))-e [½ line] ⌜x⌝

245'
H rev. ii 19 ki-gal-la [...]

246'
H ii 20 ki AB(?)-gar-ra ⌜igi⌝ [...]

247'
H ii 21 ki ⌜AB⌝ [...]

Comments on Individual Lines

Line 19: For igi-zaŋ$_x$(ŠID) = *bêru*, "to select, to chose," see Sjöberg, 1976, 175, referring to van Dijk, JCS 19 (1965) 20; CAD B, 212 *bêru* A; AHw 122.

Line 20: In F obv. 5 gam is clear on the photograph, Sjöberg, 1976, 180.

Line 21: In obv. 8, the sign read níŋ by Sjöberg, 1976, 166, is a misprint for ní. Cf. the clear IM on the photograph, p. 180. The verb may have been ní – te or similar. Cf. also the similar phraseology in lines 210–211, in broken context.

Line 26: For šà, here probably meaning "intention," or similar, cf. line 82.

Line 30: Covering the dust(?) of Nungal's "house" seems to be a theme in *Nungal Hymn* 100: saḫar(?) é-ŋá túg-tàn-tàn-na-a lú la-ba-an-si-si (Civil: "No one wears clean clothes in my dusty house"), but it does not help in restoring our line; cf. most recently Attinger, *Wilcke FS*, 34.

Line 39: In rev. 5, the signs read ⌜lú⌝ ⌜x x x⌝ dím-e by Sjöberg cannot be lú ⌜ḫul-ŋál⌝-dím-e, although this would be a tempting restoration; the traces might point to lú ⌜ÉN⌝-dím-e, but the right side has a vertical that does not really confirm it.

Line 40: There seems to be an erased sign between lugal-bi and inim-ma. For lú-ùlu, cf. the comments on *Instr. Ur-Ninurta* 19.

Line 41: In rev. 6 the sign read x by Sjöberg could nearly be SI with the lower horizontal slanted like BA; perhaps PÚ; might be gim. In line 40, and probably also 41, the verb seems to be in the second person. níŋ-gig-zu, "your crime," indicates that apparently the accused criminal is addressed.

Line 42: Apparently followed by a blank or erased line, not ruled. Line 38 apparently marks the end of the judgment scene, followed by a hymnic praise of the king's ability as judge.

For eme-di, cf. the list of similar terms in *Sag B* 233–269 (MSL SS 1, pp. 32–33), but perhaps not to be combined as one word.

Line 43: ù-ma = *irnittu*, "triumph, victory," cf. Sjöberg, 1976, 176. For níŋ-diŋir, "religious matter," cf. *Instr. Ur-Ninurta* 19 and 30. Sjöberg, ibid., refers to *Schooldays* 74: níŋ-diŋir-za-gim, and 85: níŋ-ad-da-za-gim; it also occurs in our line 210.

Line 44: The phraseology reminds of *Instr. Ur-Ninurta* 19 and 30. The reference in -bi is to níŋ-diŋir-za in line 39, "fear of the affairs of your god."

Line 45: In rev. 10 the sign read rab$_x$ by Sjöberg

is the old form of rab, which looks like LUGAL. It was read ràb by Deimel and Labat. Cf. Borger, *Ass.-bab. Zeichenliste*, p. 386 ad no. 147, who simply suggests reading rab.

The person accused of hostility is here addressed in the 2nd person. Cf. the 2nd person implied in line 43.

Line 46: níŋ-érim-e ba-an-zé-er: The verb does not accord with an ergative construction, so the interpretation remains somewhat doubtful. Cf. *Instr. Šuruppak* 171. For šu – ri-ri, see *Nungal Hymn* 61, most recently commented upon by Attinger, *Wilcke FS*, 29.

Line 47: kadra also in lines 50; 55; 57. Maybe the meaning is "no gift provided there, (even cool) water, [can appease the goddess]," or similar. Cf. line 50; also *Instr. Ur-Ninurta* 53 and *Instr. Šuruppak* 284: kadra inim-ma-bi níŋ šà-te-na m[u(?)- ...], "the gift of words [is(?)] something that soothes the heart." The "your" in "your god" apparently refers to the same person as is addressed in the 2nd person in line 41.

Line 48: The translation assumes that diŋir is the unmarked ablative (-ta) or similar. This cannot mean "the god will not let him escape," which would have required an ergative marker -e after diŋir in diŋir ba-ra-è.

Line 50: One might expect this line to read like line 47: kadra-ŋar-ra-bi kadra a-šed$_{10}$(MÙŠ-DI)-[da(?)], unless this was an antithetic counterpart to that line.

Line 51: Alster, 1991, 142, n. 5, compared this line to *Nungal Hymn* 105 (Sjöberg, AfO 24, 34): lú-ùlu-ba šà mu-un-na-ab-ḫuŋ bar mu-un-šed$_{10}$ (MÙŠ.DI)-dè, "I (Nungal) soothe that man's heart, I cool his body down," from which it is tempting to restore our line, but the spacing problems in I (ii 2) and F (rev. 16) do not support that solution. In *Nungal Hymn*, this phrase belongs to the transition to the description of the compassionate character of the goddess, who saves the man sentenced to jail by "giving birth" to him afresh. It, therefore, seems likely that a new section of our text starts with line 47, or perhaps 45 or 46, describing the positive counterpart to the evil man, who is apparently in focus in lines 27ff. It is then admittedly difficult to explain why the gift of cool water seems to come too early, in line 47. Cf. the comments on line 47.

Line 55: Cf. line 57, and the comments on line 51 above.

Line 73: A new composition probably began somewhere around the gap before line 73, or, at least, not later than line 76. Cf. *Chap. 2.1: Introd. to Instr. Ur-Ninurta, etc.*

Line 75: Apparently URU×A, or simply ùru.

Lines 76–83: It seems that these lines became separated at some early point in the transmission by an inserted section: lines 79–80 separate 76–77 from 81–83, which form a coherent unit. The sequence about the father is expected to be restored in line 76, mirrored in line 77 about the mother, then continued with the older brother in line 81, and the older sister in line 82.

Line 77: inim ama-zu-gim = *inim ama-za-gim, etc., shows that the strict rules of Sumerian grammar were no longer followed. The double -gim is perhaps best explained as an error; or the two comparisons may be seen in the light of ED Prov 4: ka-zu$_5$-gim gal$_4$-zu$_5$-gim, "like your mouth, like your vulva." Cf. Alster, 1991–92, 6, quoting "Like master, like man. Like king, like people" (ODEP, p. 426). "*Qualis dominus, talis et servus*"; "Like master, like daughter" (Ezek 16:44); "Like mother, like man. Like people, like priest" (Hos 4:9), etc. Cf. Taylor, *The Proverb*, 149, for more examples. This creates a weak anacoluth in relation to what follows, "like to the word of your mother, like to the word of your god, may you pay attention."

Line 78: G apparently uses še instead of šè. Lit. translation "Don't pass onto your strong man." Cf. the similar use of dib 184 C: šu – díb.

Line 79: I suggest ì-⌜ŋar⌝-[ŋa]r(?)-bi for the signs read by van Dijk, 1953, 103, line 3: ì-gar-a-bi, which remain doubtful. van Dijk read kú!, which undoubtedly makes sense. In C the sign could be naŋ as well as gu$_7$. Yet, in G it certainly looks like KA×ŠU = *ikribu*, "prayer," or *karābu*, "blessing," which may make sense here as the blessing of having a source of income; in this case the noun is /šude/, since /e/ in -dè hardly makes sense as the locative-terminative marker. van Dijk, p. 105, translates: "ce que tes propres mains ont produit, que cela même puisse te procurer à manger." Instead of šùd-dè = *ikribu*, one can hardly read KA×ŠÈ = ma$_5$, = *qamû*, "to grind" of flour, cf. SP 3.13. Alternatively -dè is the verbal extension morpheme /ed-e/, which would fit a verb with a non-consonant ending, such as gu_7.

If correctly read, šu ì-⌜ŋar⌝-[ŋa]r-bi is a frozen undeclined verbal form with *ḫamṭu* reduplication, tentatively "its/ their procurement." Cf. the comments on *Instr. Ur-Ninurta* 56.

ur_5-ra/re is here probably *ḫubullu*, loan, interest, rather than a demonstrative particle. Cf. line 152 and the comments on *Instr. Ur-Ninurta* 63.

Line 80: ní te-ŋá-e, "fear," ŋá is more precisely $ŋe_{26}$, cf. *Instr Ur-Ninurta* 32; Civil, 1997, 51. For ḫu-mu-un-zu, apparently a frozen 3rd person form used for the 2nd person, cf. the comments on lines 158–160.

Line 82: nin here = nin_9, "sister"; also in lines 183 and 190. Literal translation "turn back a curse to its mouth!" i.e., before it is uttered. van Dijk, 1953, 109, line 6, comments that the object of the sister's hatred is her husband, and compares *Codex Hammurapi* § 142, as well as *Ana ittišu* 7 II 49, 7 iv 1ff. (MSL 1, pp. 99 and 103). The parallelism with the following line, however, alternatively suggests that the advice may concern the relations between the one to whom the instruction is addressed and his older sister directly. šà is here rather "disposition, intention, will," cf. line 26.

Line 83: The sign tentatively read -da can be da or ama, cf. van Dijk, 1953, 109 line 7. dugud, "heavy," "to honor," would fit as a restoration here. níŋ é dù-ù-dè is reminiscent of *Instr. Šuruppak* 202: šà ki-áŋ níŋ é dù-dù-ù-dam; cf. *Instr. Ur-Ninurta* 51.

Line 84: van Dijk, 1953, 105, line 8: "dans ton conseil ne mêle pas d'inmitié." For ad – gi_4, here meant in the normal positive sense, cf. the comments on *Instr. Šuruppak* 38.

Line 85: du_{14}(!) is written as LÚ, cf. the comments on *Instr. Šuruppak* line 60.

van Dijk, 1953, 103, line 9, read du_{14}-[aka-ra??] ki?-bi-šè, etc., "A celui qui [est cause de rixe, dis-lui «à la place!» Crains le mefait." k]i(?)-bi-šè dug_4-ga-na-ab, "put him in his place," lit., "speak to him in its place." Cf. ki-bi in line 171. The English idiom "put someone in his place" unavoidably conflicts with the Sumerian non-personal construction, "in its place."

In *Instr. Ur-Ninurta* 23, ní-te is glossed *dup-ru*, "stay away from," which fits perfectly here.

Line 86: in = *pištu*, "derision." Literal translation "its outcome is (an object of) derision." The meaning here, as well as in line 177, where the same expression occurs, seems rather to be in the direction of "something worthy of derision, not worthy of mention, a trifle." Perhaps relevant *Instr. Šuruppak* 27: in-nu-uš. Cf. SP 1.80: in-na in-bi-im áš-e áš-bi-im ..., "the worst of all insults, the worst of all curses ..." (Alster, *Proverbs* I, 20, slightly differently). van Dijk, 1953, 105, line 10, translates: "ta faim qu'il t'a enlevée [maintenant], à l'issue de cela sera <de nouveau>," suggesting a restoration like u_4-ba, cf. p. 109.

Line 87: Cavigneaux, 1996, 21: "Ton sacrifice (*niqâka*) ... Ne laisse pas passer l'offrande du jour, le dieu emporte (aussi) tes paroles(?)." The final verb is DU in C, but dé in J. This suggests the reading de_6, *ḫamṭu* of túm/tùm, in C. It would then mean "(the god) will carry what came out of your mouth away," i.e., disregard it. Since there is no ergative -e following diŋir, it is nevertheless worth considering an alternative solution, that an original gub, "to stand away from," (cf. e.g., *Instr. Šuruppak* 27) may later have been misunderstood as DU = de_6, and then interpreted as dé, "to pour out," said of offerings. dib can probably be taken simply in the sense "to pass over," i.e., "to neglect." Cf. already van Dijk, 1953, 104, line 11: "A tes prières ne te fie pas, le dieu peut s'éloigner de ce que ta bouche profère." The intent of line 87 seems to be similar to that of line 89.

Line 88: Cavigneaux, 1996, 21, convincingly takes this as the statement of the god in a sort of response from him: "C'est bien, c'est parfait, aujourd'hui je serait présent (dans l'oracle?)."

Line 89: Cavigneaux, 1996, 21, translates: "Ne prolongue pas le sacrifice, fait que la beuverie soit aussi agréable" (C only), which I have accepted, assuming that sá is phonetic for sa_6. J differs: šùd-dè a-ra-an-⌜na⌝-ab-bé, which I cannot translate. van Dijk, 1953, 106 (l. 13) translates: "Ce jour-là ne prolonge pas les prières, à l'occasion de cette bienveillance <divine> prépare-moi une 'beuverie'," reading silim-ma-ab (p. 103). ki la-la-bi seems to be an Akkadianism, la-la = *lalû*, lit., "its abundant place." Cf. *Níŋ-nam Vers. B* 7.

Line 90: C: gisbun-na ki-kaš-dé-a-ta only in C.

The final -ta seems to be used as a locative. Cf. the similar form in line 184, and the comments on *Instr. Ur-Ninurta* 24. The line looks like an explicatory gloss to the following line, and then later included as part of the main text. Alternatively, but less likely, this can be taken literally as "(when coming to) a banquet from a drinking party." gisbun(KI.KAŠ.GAR) is a loanword from Akk. *kispum*, "funerary offering," normally written KI.SÌ.GA. van Dijk, 1953, 106 (l. 16), translates lines 90–91: "d'un repas ou d'une 'beuverie' à l'autre repas les hommes comme l'aigle descendent," understanding these as ordinary meals and drinking parties. ki-kaš-dé-a might be used here of the drinking libations spent at the funerary offering, but in line 184 it evidently refers to an ordinary drinking party.

Line 91: The sign tentatively read ⌜ur$_5$(?)⌝^{mušen} would, if correctly read, be phonetic for ḫu-ri-in^{mušen}; copied rather like ŠIR. Cavigneaux, p. 21, translates "Mais l''œil' de la beuverie s'abat sur l'homme comme un aigle (sur sa proi)." Could it, in fact, be taken as a reference to the spirits of the dead "men"? The situation would then be similar to the well-known episode of the Gilgameš epic, where the gods gather round the meal finally served for them after the flood. More likely, gisbun might here refer to an ordinary meal and lú to living humans. The gloss in line 92 J: *li-is-sa-bi* seems to be from *sabû*, "to draw beer" (CAD S, 5) and may point in this direction, but only if the gloss had been misplaced and, in fact, belongs to line 91; cf. Cavigneaux, p. 21, n. 10. The context is inconclusive: the preceding sequence, lines 87–88, suggests a ritual meal, but the following lines 93–94 point to relations between living persons.

Line 92: Cavigneaux, p. 21, reads: "Ne laisse pas le vent (?) te monter à la tête, il faut être mesuré, pour rester à sa place," understanding the wind as "une image pour l'ivresse?" Strictly speaking the verbal prefix nu- means simply "the wind does not rise before your head." For the gloss *li-is-sa-bi*, see the comments on line 91. sun$_5$(BÚR) = *waṣru*; cf. line 244': KA-sun$_5$(BÚR)-na; *Instr. Ur-Ninurta* 68: written phonetically su-un-su-na = sun$_5$-sun$_5$-[na]; Proto-Ea 799 (MSL 14, 61) gives su-un | sun$_5$ (BÚR). For ki-bi, cf. lines 96; 100; 111; 180; 217; for ki-bi-šè, cf. lines 85; 171; 178.

sá-e-dè might be silim-e-dè, "in order to stay healthy"; cf. *Chap. 3.4*, comments on *Prov. Ugarit* 36–39.

Line 93: Cavigneaux, 1996, 21, convincingly explained lú-ŋar-ra as phonetic for *nu-gar-ra = *nullâti*, which is visible in the Akk. col. of J; cf. *Instr. Šuruppak* 42: ù-nu-ŋar-ra = *nullâtu*; he further points out (n. 11) that the first part of the line would fit a Sum. text better reading *ki du$_{14}$ gar-ra = *a-šar ṣa-al-ti*, which actually occurs later as line 94B, but not enough is preserved to decided whether it is, in fact, the Akk. translation of our line that has been misplaced. Cavigneaux (reading súr instead of šúr) translates the second part: "ne parle pas dans l'irritation." The variant in C: sar (or šar) seems to be phonetic for šúr.

Line 94: ḫé-en-zu is best taken as the 2nd person, cf. the comments on lines 158 and 160.

Line 94 A: PAB$_4$-LUL has not be explained.

Lines 95ff.: There seems to have been space for one extra missing sign along the left edge in addition to that indicated on Zimmern's copy.

Line 95: šà-zu ḫé-éb-ši-dugud seems to mean that one should hesitate seriously before answering an insult, or, less likely, that it should weigh "heavily" on one's mind, that is, that one should, in fact, take it seriously. van Dijk, 1953, 103, reads in?? ḫa-ra-ab-bé (var. H: in clear), and translates (p. 106) "si lui, il te parle, que ton cœur médite gravement."

Line 96: van Dijk, 1953, 106, line 20, translates "s'il te dit des choses injurieuses, ne lui réponds pas de la <même> manière: cela a de l'importance!" ki-bi, lit., "its place is «heavy»."

Line 97: níŋ-⌜x⌝ KA×X nam-ba-e-sì-ge: no interpretation suggested.

Line 98: ŋál-la nam-ba-silig-ge: no interpretation suggested; cf. the comments on silig *Instr. Šuruppak* 95–96; also lines 15; 61; 259.

Line 99: C: dib, H: díb. H: š]à nam-bí-díb-bé suggests that nam- is missing in C. This apparently means "Don't let your heart be caught (by anger)," but the continuation, C: šà-dib-gim, and H: šà-dib-ba, using the same expression in the comparison, seems to suggest that an additional meaning is also involved. In C: NI-DUL-dím, "like (something) covered up"(?), remains unexplained, but something like an eclipse would fit (very tentative). It is tempting to suggest that the same expression is involved in line 110: NI-KÙ-gim, but only if one of the two has been misread. u$_4$ ní-šè ba-ab-šú seems to mean "the day settles by itself," the implication being that wrath will calm down by itself as the day ends.

Line 100: In H there is room for four missing signs, difficult to harmonize with C.

Line 101–103: These lines (or more) seem related to lines 155–156; 160, which advise one to treat domestic slaves or servants with some leniency. Perhaps the text was made up by means of two independent sources.

Line 102: The restoration [šu-zu ...] is likely in view of line 156; the first sign might then have been úrdu, "Don't release your hand toward a slave," but a more precisely specified type of relatively protected slave would fit better. For šu – tu-lu, cf. AHw 953, *ramû* III, D šu-tu-lu, "lockern, entlassen." Cf. also tu-lu in line 160. Our line might in part be restored from *Instr. Šuruppak* 155–159. There is not enough room for émedu (ama-a-tu), as ibid. line 155, or dumu-gi$_7$ as in line 156, however, although there may have been more signs missing than shown on Zimmern's copy (cf. the comments on l. 95ff. above).

Line 103: Restore perhaps [šu] – dù, "don't bind [his hands]." Cf. line 149.

Line 110: NI-KÙ-gim can hardly be the same expression as line 99: NI-DÙL-gim, unless, of course, one of the two has been misread for the other.

Line 112: There is hardly a connection to *Bird and Fish* 30: zé-za engur-ra za-pa-áŋ [(...)] nundum búr-re buluŋ$_5$-ŋá. For saŋ-bul, "he who tosses his head," cf. SP 3.88 = 18.14; UM 55-21-278 (Alster, *Proverbs* II, 305). KA-búr-ra, line 243, is apparently relevant here.

Lines 147–148: The verb BAD is reminiscent of *Instr. Šuruppak* 53; possibly also lines 63–64, reading úš, "to kill"; too little is preserved to show the extent of the parallelism.

Line 149: For šu dù, cf. perhaps line 103. If LABAG×U represents is-ḫab, this means "do not bind an ignorant person," perhaps in terms of a hiring contract, but very uncertain.

Line 150: This seems to be the beginning of a section that, apparently, deals with the services of a young man toward an elderly man. Cavigneaux, 1996, 21, translates "Un gars ... un sa[larié?] ... lui donne sa force." J must be read ma-<ra>-an-šúm-ma, 2nd person dative, or simply ma as a mistake for ba-.

Line 152: Cavigneaux, 1996, 21: "Pour avoir une belle viellesse ..." The Akkadian of J: ⌜U$_4$⌝ *lit-ti-ka*, "the day when you were born," does not correspond to H: u$_4$ nam-ab-ba si-si-da, which perhaps rather means "when the days of your elderly years are to be fulfilled." The verb attached to ur$_5$-re, perhaps "thus," is regrettably missing. Cf. line 79.

Line 153: Cavigneaux, 1996, 21, suggests reading the signs KU-zu following ŋuruš as áš(?)-zu: "Tu veux un gars qui t'aide à faire ce que tu veux? Donne-lui plein à manger et sa force s'en ira!" to fit the Akkadian translation of J: *eṭ-lum ša ṣi-bu-ut-ka ú-š[ak-ša-du-ka?]*: Cf. CAD Ṣ, 167: *ṣibûtu* A (= áš), "need, want, request"; AHw 1099, "Wunsch, Bedarf."

Line 155: For AMA-A-TU = émedu, cf. line 102; comm. on 156; *Instr. Šuruppak* 155; *Instr. Ur-Ninurta* 14. Only G has g]i-me-a-aš-ŋu$_{10}$, "my colleague"; in H and J ŋu$_{10}$ has apparently been misunderstood as -ši(-a) by some unexplained mistake.

Line 156: *ana aš-ta-pí-ri-ka*: Cf. CAD A/2, 473: sag-géme-arad = *aštapiru*, "slaves (coll.), servants"; AHw 85: = *aštapīru*, "Gesinde," possibly a Hurrian loanword; MSL 12, 228: "Hh xxv" (App. to Lu) B 13'–17': ^{lú}ama-a-tu$^{e\text{-}me\text{-}du}$ = *i-lit-ti bi-i-t[i]*; *du-uš-mu-u*; *áš-ta-pí-ri*. For šu – tu-tu, cf. line 102.

Line 157: Cavigneaux, 1996, 21, translates za-pa-⌜áŋ⌝ dugud(?) combined with H: ugu-bi and J: ug]u-bi-a: "Un bon coup de gueule ...," i.e., "a box on the ear."

Lines 158 and 160: In view of the verb ba-ra-te in line 159, ḫé-en-zu seems to be a frozen verbal form used in the 2nd person; cf. also lines 83; 94; 192: ḫu-mu-un-zu, further line 80 and *Instr. Ur-Ninurta* 63; 66–68.

Line 160: For tu-lu-bi, cf. line 102 above.

Line 167: van Dijk, 1953, 106, translates "Le serment est <cause de> la mort ...."

Lines 169–170: van Dijk, 1953, 110, suggests approximately "Quant à ton avoir, étant avare, à ta richesse en ajoute encore," which I have accepted. Line 185 seems to express a similar idea, suggesting that C: kala-ga-gim mistook kal for kalag; cf. the comments on line 185.

Line 170: In H, there seems to be a caesura between li_9 and ki, which indicates that the two signs may not belong to the same word. Cf., however, the commentary to *Instr. Šuruppak* 61, where arguments for translating ur_5-tuku as the debtor, rather than the creditor, are given, with reference to Foxvog's interpretation of the present line (Foxvog, 1976, 372). Slightly differently already van Dijk, 1953, 110, suggests "quant à intérêt, ne sois pas trop dur, réduis leur 'taux (?)'," that is, reduce the repayment rate.

Line 171: For ninda or níŋ-sì-ga, var. ninda/níŋ-šúm-mu-bi, cf. *Instr. Šuruppak* 97: ninda/níŋ ga-ra-ab-šúm-bi, which vaguely is reminiscent of our line. The reading ninda in lines 171–173 would fit the continuation, line 174, well, since this can be understood as describing the basic needs facing a traveler: food and a place to sleep. Yet, níŋ would better fit what precedes it, since accumulating wealth is in focus in line 169. ki-bi-šè, "where appropriate," lit. "at its place." Cf. line 85; 92, etc.

Line 172: Despite the -n-, ḫé-en-zu is here tentatively taken as the 2nd person, as in lines 158 and 160, etc. The 2nd person accords with the preceding lines, but the 3rd person might fit better in view of the continuation.

Line 173: DAG+KISIM5×? is tentatively interpreted as $kešer_x$(?), for which cf. kešer(GÌR.BAR) nu-tuku = *ša kišdam la išû*, cf. CAD K, 450: *kišdu*, "acquisition, assets, limit," here tentatively meaning "he will have unlimited." The same word occurs written phonetically in CT 58, no. 3 (pls. 2–3) rev. 11–12: ... ki-še-er ba-an-na-ni-in-dug_4, which seems to mean (renting her eyes, renting her face, etc.) "she exerted herself to the extreme," or similar. Cf. Civil, 1994, 69f.; Civil, JCS 20 (1960) 119–121.

Line 174: kas_4-tur lú-ra, lit. "a small traveller"; $kaš_4$ = *ubāru*. van Dijk, 1953, 106, translates "métèque" (foreigner). It seems here to denote a traveller who arrives in need of the most basic necessities, whereas kas_4 diri-ga in line 179 obviously denotes one who is be better off, tentatively meaning "a (relatively) wealthy traveller." The picture here given of good conduct toward an arriving unknown foreigner accords with that known from the Homeric epics and elsewhere: after a meal has been served he is expected to identify himself and divulge where he comes from, etc.

van Dijk, 1953, 110, compares *Instr. Šuruppak* 178: ninda-e lú kur-ra bí-in-e_{11}-dè, which he translates "descendre *pour* du pain, *pour* de l'aide."

ŋiskim – e_{11}: cf. *Curse of Agade* 215: šeš-e šeš-a-ni-ir ŋiskim na-an-ni-in-è, "his brother should not make himself known to a brother."

Lines 176–179: van Dijk, 1953, 106, somewhat differently: "«la main» qui se dresse devant lui, était devant toi, <cette>«main» rends-la-lui, à l'issue de cela il y aura <un avenir>: de ce lieu même, il se souviendra, <devenu> un métèque aisé, ... il sera à l'honneur!"

Line 176: C: igi-ni-šè, "before his (own) eyes," was misunderstood by H: igi-du-a-zu, as "before your eyes ...," but du-a? Probably influenced by IGI.DU = igi-du or palil, cf. *Chap. 3.3: Ballade of Early Rulers* 4. I do not see any problem in translating igi as "eye," as well as "face" and "in front of," since these are all covered by the Sum. igi, whereas Akk. distinguishes between *īnu* and *pānu*. Cf. line 182 and comments on *Instr. Šuruppak* 66. The point seems to be that a hand raised by a stranger in order to protect himself with little effort from others can be accepted as an appeal for help.

Line 177: šu – gi_4, cf. van Dijk, 1953, 110, who seeks to explain this as a double entendre punning on šu-diŋir-ra, šu-diŋir-x, "the hand of" = "the aid of," and šu gi_4 = *gimillu turru*, "to take revenge/return a favor." The terms šu-a gi_4 and šu gi_4 have been treated in detail by Römer, BiOr 49 (1922) 37/329.

eŋir-bi-ta in-àm: van Dijk translates "à l'issue de cela il y aura <un avenir>," which hardly is satisfactory. I suggest "in the end it is nothing but a trifle," cf. the comments on line 86, where the same expression occurs.

Line 178: For ki-bi-šè, cf. line 92, etc. ŋéštu – gu-ur-ru seems to be phonetic for ŋéštu – gur, lit., "to turn the ear to."

Line 179: é – gíd-gíd, seems to mean "to linger at (your) house," or similar. The variant in H: é si-sá-zu, seems to mean "who goes straight to your house," but we would expect é-zu si-sá(-a).

Line 180: van Dijk, 1953, 106 (12c) reading the first sign as é, translates "Un homme qui est étranger ne porte pas la main, l'homme qui [...]." The copy, however, shows clearly URU as the first sign. I take this as "(a man from) a foreign city." šu na-ab-tag-

tag, perhaps, lit., "don't embellish," i.e., "don't be too friendly, flatter, associate with"? There might be an allusion to a somewhat similar saying in SP 27.9: ere[ki] ere[ki] silim nu-ub-dug_4 lú-lú-a silim(?) ab-bé, "One town did not say hello to another town, but one man says hello to another man"; var. UET 6/2 250: ere[ki] ere[ki] silim nu-tag-ga lú-ùlu silim bí-tag-ga (Alster, *Proverbs* I, 283); here tag is probably phonetic for dug_4, cf. comm. on *Instr. Ur-Ninurta* 60.

ki-bi íb-z[u-àm], is "known by that place"; the implication seems to be that his character is unchangeable, always influenced by the manners of the city from which he came.

Line 181: The sign read kar can hardly be zu-a(!) or similar. van Dijk, 1953, 106, translates "Un homme qui est descendu au quai du porte(??)," which is dubious, although the parallelism with the preceding line might support it. The literal translation, "a man who has a quay," might rather suggest "who has a source of income," probably related to trade, or similar, since kar = *kārum* was the place where goods were exchanged. Alternatively read lú te-a íb-tuku, cf. below. van Dijk, 1953, 111, refers to *Ana ittišu* 3 iv 20 and 37 (MSL 1, p. 48), lú-kar = *arbu*, ("refugee"), which hardly is relevant here, alternatively pointing to ibid. 21: [lú-te]-a = *ṭe-ḫu-u*, "Klient"? The attitude that comes to light here and elsewhere in the text is characteristic of the private financial activities of the Isin-Larsa and OB periods, hardly older.

Line 182: For é ku_4-ku_4-zu, van Dijk, 1953, 111, points to von Soden, *Orientalia* 16 (1947) 83 and 18, 402 = *mu-uš-ta-ri-iq bi-tim*, cf. AHw 686, *muštarriqu*, (from *šarāqu*, Gtn) "der sich hereinstiehlt, Buhle." Cf. also CAD M, 287 *muštarriqu*, "secret lover." This, however, does not seem relevant here. For igi-a, "in front," cf. line 176 and the comments on *Instr. Šuruppak* 66.

Line 183: For dumu-ká-gi_4-a, cf. van Dijk, 1953, 111, referring to MSL 1, p. 148: *Ana ittišu* 6 iv 19 = "citoyen." This literally means "those of the closed city gate," suggesting that the citizens were protected by locked gates at night. van Dijk, ibid. (l. 14), comments on usar = *šettu*, "amie," (AHw 1232, *šī'ītu*, "Nachbarin; Reisefrau") that the meaning "fils resp. fille pauvre est suggéré par le contexte, sinon il n'aurait pas besoin de les traiter 'comme frère et sœur'." Treating someone like a brother or sister seems to imply including someone under one's personal protection, but whether it had precise legal implications is unknown. Line 181: šeš-zu-gim, might indicate this; cf. also lines 186 and 190–191.

Line 184: [e]n-na u_4-til-la-ta: til is here used for ti(-l) (tìl), as in *Instr. Šuruppak* 4–5 (Ur_I); *Instr. Ur-Ninurta* 1. -ta is apparently used for the locative. ki-kaš-dé-a, "drinking party," cf. line 90 above. van Dijk, 1953, 107, translates "dans la 'beuverie'' n'y jette pas la main(??)," For šu – díb, he refers to Falkenstein, ZA 49, 126. Here a meaning such as "to oblige someone to, to take advantage of his/her presence," or similar, would fit. The verb form, apparently in the 2nd person, nam-ba-e-dib-bé is difficult to explain, cf. van Dijk, p. 111 ad line 14, and perhaps the similar examples cited in the comm. to *Instr. Šuruppak* 19. Cf. the somewhat similar use of dib in line 78. It would not be possible to connect the two lines, although tempting, because šè/še is certain in line 78, whereas in line 184, šu, following -ta, cannot be a mistake for šè.

Line 185: For šu - lá, van Dijk, 1953, 111, convincingly refers to *qâpu*, *qīptu*, "Vertrauensdarlehen," *Ana ittišu* 2 i 73ff. Cf. further the comments on *Instr. Šuruppak* 13. The implication seems to be that it is not worth while to try to avail oneself of the presence of others if they are already involved in businesses elsewhere. So already van Dijk, 1953, 107: "<car> si les mains de l'un d'eux sont liées (?), à ton avoir rien de précieux ne sa'ajoutera!" A similar expression occurs in line 169, where the variant in C has kala-ga-gim, that is, kalag = *dannu*, "strong," rather than as expected kal = *waqru*, "precious." The distinction was obviously not always carefully upheld in these late sources.

Line 186: Lit. "After their place of fate has been made like a brother or like a sister (= changed into that of?), your heart is soothed." van Dijk, 1953, 107, translates "Avoir changé leur sort en celui de frère et de sœur, te soulage le cœur." Treating someone as a brother or sister seems to imply including him under one's personal protection, cf. line 183. nam-tar here as elsewhere has wider connotations than simply "fate" or destiny," rather like the "social status" to which one is entitled.

Line 187–192: van Dijk, 1953, 107, translates:

"pour loin que ton bétail se soit éloigné de ta prairie et de ton abreuvoir, pour loin que celui qui s'est évadé de chez toi, se soit éloigné sur le champs, ton GUR-bateau, en serait-il aux confins du fleuve, enfants du quartier que tu auras traités comme frère et sœur, tu les gardera soumis (?) à toi! Ensuite, si des filettes du quartier, à la vue de l'œil, vers ton avoir tendent les mains, que tu connaisses ...." I have basically accepted this translation, in particular the concessive meaning of ḫe- in lines 187–189.

Line 187: The first sign can be dug, KAŠ, ga or gud, which is the more likely reading. van Dijk, 1953, 111, reads ú-nagá (= naŋ), taking this as *ri'ītu u mašqītu*, which is convincing, although the second sign looks more like gu_7 on the copy.

Line 188: lú-kar-zu seems here to imply "your man who has fled from you,"
apparently in order to avoid working in the fields, rather than as a refugee.

Line 189: This seems to concern a boat that has stopped (ŋá-la – dag) somewhere to engage in business activities on behalf of the one to whom the advice is addressed.

Line 190: ki-za-a mu-e-tuku-tuku: It is remarkable that the verb does not have a ḫu-prefix, but is phrased as a plain indicative. van Dijk, 1953, 111, discusses the meaning of ki-za-a, which he takes as > ki-zu-a, "in your place" (= in your full control?) rather than ki-za-za = *šukênu*. For the latter, cf. the comments to *Instr. Ur-Ninurta* 67.

Line 191: For usar, lit., "female neighbor," cf. the comments on line 183 above. igi-du_8-du_8-meš seems here to be used in the sense to be "on the lookout, watching" or "to act as an informer," as in *Instr. Šuruppak* 21: igi-du_8 na-an-ak-e, "Don't give evidence against a man," rather than "good-looking, conspicuous." The use of the plural -meš is characteristic of relatively late Sumerian texts.

Line 192: van Dijk reads šu – dúb-dúb, and translates "vers ton avoir tendent les mains," which is convincing, but I know of no further parallels. For ḫé-en-zu, 2nd person, cf. the comments on line 158.

du_6-du_6-la here obviously means "hide" your valuables from the eyes of greedy persons. Cf. perhaps *Instr. Ur-Ninurta* 69.

Lines 193–247: Owing to the poor state of preservation, I refrain from attempting to interpret more of the text, noting only a few points.

Line 210: ní-diŋir-ŋá, cf. line 43 and the comments on *Instr. Ur-Ninurta* 19 and 30.

Lines 243–244: The text here apparently plays on two different readings of the sign BÚR = búr and

CHAPTER 3

The Vanity Theme in Sumerian Literature

Introduction

In *Chapter Three* some compositions related mainly to the vanity theme in Sumerian literature will be treated. These texts are unfortunately very fragmentarily preserved and extraordinarily difficult to understand. On the one hand, it is legitimate for the translator to seek inspiration from what may appear to be parallels in the well-known biblical book from which the vanity of vanities theme got its name, or from other ancient sources. On the other hand, great caution must, of course, be exercised in order to avoid reading ideas not originally intended into the fragments. Add to the difficulties that some of the texts are attested in sources that differ so widely from each other that it is questionable whether they should simply be considered variants of the same composition or as completely different texts.

Among the ideas found in these texts, one must be prepared to encounter some that may have been critical to prevalent contemporary beliefs, or even challenges them, which, of course, calls for extreme caution when drawing general conclusions with regard to the way of thinking of the ancient Mesopotamian world.

Although some of these texts are rarely attested in Sumerian sources, the fact that some of them are reflected, or even elaborated upon, in Akkadian translations from the Syro-Mesopotamian area, dating from the thirteenth century B.C., testifies to the great significance attached to them as models of Mesopotamian wisdom. The Syro-Mesopotamian Sumero-Akkadian bilinguals present many challenging difficulties for the modern interpreter. The scribes of the Syro-Mesopotamian area obviously had many difficulties in understanding the original texts, not least being when preserved only in unilingual Sumerian versions, with the result that misunderstandings and errors may have crept into the texts. Several examples are discussed in the introductions to *Chap. 3.3: The Ballade of Early Rulers*; *Chap. 3.4: Proverbs from Ugarit*; *Chap. 3.5: Enlil and Namzitarra: Emar Version.*

The very short composition *Níŋ-nam nu-kal,* (*Nothing Is of Value*) exists in at least four unilingual Sumerian versions, but is not directly attested in the Syro-Mesopotamian tradition.

In order to present the material as accurately as possible, each of the relevant sources is here, whenever possible, presented in the form of a composite reconstruction, but is also, whenever needed, transliterated separately in its entirety, with crossreferences to the composite reconstructions, in order to give a full picture of their character. Since some of the texts occur on *Sammeltafel* inscribed with sequences of compositions possibly reflecting similar themes, and sometimes in what seems to be a standardized order, care has been taken to clarify their context and position within the contents of each *Sammeltafel.*

The section below, *Chap. 3.1*, on the reconstruction of *Níŋ-nam nu-kal* versions A, B, and C, is based on a manuscript by Jeremy Black. The translations, comments, and conclusions to each of these versions were added by me. *Chap. 3.2*, on *Níŋ-nam nu-kal* version D, etc., is entirely my own.[1]

1. In the editions below, I use only the designations *Níŋ-nam A, B, C, and D,* irrespective of whether the same compositions were labelled 1–3 (Civil) or A_1 (24-line version), A_2, B_{1-3} and C (Black). My version D is not identical to what is called A_1 (24-line version) in Black's terminology below.

3.1 Nothing Is of Value
(níŋ-nam nu-kal; *Versions A, B, C*)

*Sources and text reconstruction based on a manuscript by Jeremy Black**

This short Sumerian composition, containing reflections on the vanity of mortal life, is preserved in a number of sources, but has so far not been edited in its entirety. Although Gordon, 1960, seems to have been the first to refer to the composition, identifying SLTNi 131 (Ni 3023+) as a collection of short "essays," it is easy to see why it has resisted analysis since then: the manuscript tradition is peculiarly complicated. Civil, 1972, reconstructed the tablet Ni 3023+ and proposed that the composition existed in more than one version. Alster, 1975, 85–89, gave a partial edition of Versions 1 and 2 (here A and B) with some observations on the manuscripts. Civil added further sources to the list in his unpublished *Catalogue of Sumerian Literature*, a copy of which was accessible to Black, and proposed two sub-versions of Version A (= 1) and three of Version B (= 2), outlined below (these are edited as versions A, B, C, and D below). Alster and Jeyes, 1986, published another source, BM 80184; Alster, 1990, added further details; a copy of YBC 7283 was published by Alster, 1997. Most recently Alster, 1999, clarified the sources further. Several of these are *Sammeltafel*, and as such it is clearly of interest to know what other compositions were written on the same tablets. Further discussions pertinent to this subject are found in *Chaps. 2.1: Excursus on Sammeltafel; 3.1* below; *3.2; 3.2x; 3.3: The Ballade of Early Rulers, 4: Fables*; and *5: Folktales.*[1]

Presumed Sources

BM 54699 (CT 42, 23) face B 6–13. (The correspondences are: ll. 8 = B 4; 9 = B 5; 10 = B 6; 13 = B 7; 12 = B 8); see the transliteration under Vers. B below. There is a double separating line before Face B 7, but the traces preceding it cannot be identified and may belong either to the composition *Old Man* (cf. *Chap. 5.2*) preceding it or to a version of *Níŋ-nam*. This does not end with Face B 12', but continues with at least seven more lines without a separating line. These are transliterated under *Chap. 3.2x: Sources.*

BM 80184 (CT 44, 18, *Sammeltafel*, used by Alster, 1990, 6, as source B; inscribed with hymn to *Hymn to Abī-ešuḫ B*, *Níŋ-nam*, and *Ballade*). Rev. i' 31–33 concerns *Níŋ-nam*. The correspondences are i 31 = C 1; i 32 = C 2; i 33 = C 3; see the transliteration under Vers. C below.

CBS 1208, used by Alster, 1990, 6, as source D, inscribed with *Hymn to Marduk for a King*, *Hymn to Abī-ešuḫ and Marduk*, *Níŋ-nam*, and *Ballade*. Photographs: pl. 30 (obv., by K. Danti); pl. 31 (rev. and lower edge, by E. Robson). Rev. i 10–17 concerns *Níŋ-nam*. The correspondences are ll. 10 = C 1: 11 = C 2; 12 = C 3; 13 = C 4; 14 = C 5; 15 = C 6; 16 = C 7; 17 = C 8. The remaining five lines on rev. ii concern *Ballade* 19–22.

CBS 6924 + N 3097. Photo by E. Robson pl. 34 = *Níŋ-nam Vers. D;* cf. the separate edition in *Chap. 3.2x: Sources*. The correspondences are i 2–3 = C 3/D 3 2nd part [?]; i 3= C 4; i 4 = D 4; i 5 = D 4–5; i 6 = D 5; i 7 = 8; i 8 = D 9; i 9–10 = D 10; i 11 = D 11; i 12 = D 12. Col. ii unidentified.

CBS 13777 rev. 3'–16'. Photo by E. Robson: pls. 32–33. For obv., see *Chap. 3.4: Proverbs from Ugarit*. The rev. concerns *Níŋ-nam*. The correspondences are 6' = B 1; 7' = B 2; 8' = B 4; 9' = B 5; 10' = B 6; 11' = B 7; 12' = B 8. There are remains of ll. 13'–24', of which line 18 has an indented line. Photo (by Alster): pl. 35. Obv. concerns *Proverbs*. The correspondences are: i 1'–3' = unidentified; 5' = C 1; 5' cont. = C 2; 6' = C 4; 7' = C 5; 9' = traces of one sign, identified. There is a double separating line after line 21.

* I mailed the completed manuscript of this chapter to Jeremy Black shortly before his untimely death in April 2004. His response shall therefore never be known. Since he had shortly earlier asked me how my work was progressing, there can be no doubt that he took a keen interest in it.

1. Cf. previously Alster, 1975, 125 n. 25 and 1990, 5–6.

N 3047. Fragment from a two-column tablet, rev. unidentified line. The continuation of col. i is missing. Col. ii: the beginnings of six lines, unidentified. See separate transliteration in *Chap. 3.2x: Sources.*

N 3579 + Ni 2763 ii 1'ff. (SLTNi 128); photo by Alster of N 3579: pl. 35. See separate transliteration in *Chap. 3.2x: Sources.* Obv. i contains mainly Vers. B; obv. ii contains mainly Vers. A.

Ni 2192 (ISET II 21): Lenticular school tablet inscribed on both sides, with one line on obv., and two lines on rev. = *níŋ-nam* Vers. D ca. 10–12, but different line order.

Ni 3023 (SLTNi 131) + fragments: Ni 4144 (ISET II 123), 4452 (ISET I 121), 4473 (ISET II 22), Ni 4483 (ISET I 159/101), 4484 (ISET I 125/67). See a detailed description under *Chap. 3.2x: Sources.*

Ni 9620 (ISET II 91) obv. [Civil's Ni 9624 in *Orientalia* 41 (1972) 90 is a misprint for Ni 9620]. Center fragment, apparently from a one-column tablet. The obv. seems to contain almost the complete text *Níŋ-nam* Vers. D 4(?)–18; the rev. contains about seven lines (some of which are indented) and traces of a single line after a double separating line. I have not been able to identify the reverse.

3N-T326 (IM 58427) obv. iv + 3N-T360 (A 30128). Photographs pls. 36–39. Twenty-two-line Version D, almost completely preserved, but epigraphically difficult because of partly destroyed short lines; see the edition in *Chap. 3.2: Version D.*

UM 29-16-616. Photo by E. Robson pl. 35. Fragment from the reverse of what seems to be a two-column tablet, of which the right column is entirely missing. Rev. i concerns *Níŋ-nam.* The correspondences are: i 1–2: unidentified; i 3' = A 5; i 4' = A 6; i 5' = A 8; i 6' = A 9; i 7' = A 10. Transliteration of i 1–2 in *Chap. 3.2x: Sources.*

YBC 7283 (Alster 1997, 330, copy pl. 127). Lenticular school tablet inscribed on both sides: one-line quotation from Vers. C 8.

Civil's proposal for reconstruction, outlined in his catalogue, is as follows (cited here from Black's manuscript):[2]

A_1 (24-line version):
N 3579+Ni 2763 (column two)
1 2 14 15 16 17 18 19 20 //
Ni 3023 (first version)
[...] *0 16 17 19 20 21 //*
Ni 9620
[...] fourteen lines (line eight ? = *23*)
CBS 6924+
[...] twelve lines (lines ten and eleven ? = *22 23*) [...]
N 3047
1 2 0 4 5 [...]
UM 29-16-616
0 0 16(?) *17*(?) *19 20 0 //*
Ni 2192 (lentil)
[x] *0 22 23 //*

A_2
CBS 1208
1 2 3 4 5 6 7 8 [... next column, after break: *Ballade*]
BM 80184
1 2 3 [...]

B_1 (16 lines)
CBS 13777
1 2 9 10 11 12 13 + nine more lines before ruling (unidentified)

B_2 (12+ lines)
Ni 3023 (second version)
1 2 9 10 + eight more lines [...]
N 3579+Ni 2763 (column one)
[...] *0 9 10 11 12 13* [...]

2. The italicized line numbers below have been assigned arbitrarily here to individual lines to identify them, but should not be taken as implying a definitive sequence. "0" indicates an unidentifiable line; // indicates a ruling or the end of a tablet.

B3 (14+ lines)
BM 54699
one line + 9 10 11 0 13 12 + seven more lines [...]

YBC 7283 (lentil)
13 (between rulings)

Black[3] came to the conclusion that, "strictly speaking, there are not several variants of this composition but instead three groups of extremely fluid sequences such that it is hardly appropriate to conceive of them as a single composition; however, each group begins with the same two lines. There is reasonably good evidence for these three groups. For convenience they are still referred to here as versions, but apart from the opening lines they have no other lines in common with each other. All three are attested at Nippur. Two of the Nippur sources appear to contain two of the three sequences, inscribed on the tablet one after the other: N 3579+Ni 2763 (Version B followed immediately by Version A) and Ni 3023 (Version A immediately followed by Version B). However, each of these two sources has the beginning lines 1–2 missing from one of its two sequences, so that, in fact, no lines overlap between them."

First, Black's attempt to group together the sources for these compositions is quoted; thereafter, they are presented in "score" format as versions A-C, including only the lines for which numbers have been assigned. After the first two lines, the italicized numbering of the lines is again arbitrary, with the numbers 3–8 assigned to Version C, 9–13 assigned to Version B and 14–21 assigned to Version A. However, this is not the end of the story, since individual sources continue with or include extra lines either not attested in other sources for that version or not checkable because damaged or broken. The translations and comments below are added by Alster.

Black worked from published copies and published collations of the sources, together with some photographs kindly provided by colleagues. The only source not taken into consideration by Black is 3N-T326 (IM 58427) obv. iv + 3N-T360 (= A 30218), listed by Civil, 1972: a large *Sammeltafel*. It is edited separately below by Alster in *Chap. 3.2*, as *Níŋ-nam* Version D.

Version A (*1 2 + 14–21*)
N 3579+Ni 2763 (column two)
1 2 14 15 16 17 18 19 20 //
Ni 3023 (first version)
[...] *0 16 17 19 20 21 //*
UM 29-16-616
0 0 16(?) 17(?) 19 20 21(?) //

Version B (*1 2 + 9–13*)
CBS 13777
1 2 9 10 11 12 13 + nine more lines before ruling
Ni 3023 (second version)
1 2 9 10 + eight more lines [...]
BM 54699
one line + *9 10 11 0 13 12* + seven more lines [...]
N 3579+Ni 2763 (column one)
[...] *0 9 10 11 12 13* [...]
YBC 7283 (lentil)
13 (between rulings)

Version C (*1 2 3–8*)
N 3047
1 2 0 4 5 [...]
CBS 1208
1 2 3 4 5 6 7 8 [+ up to 5 lines in next column]
BM 80184
1 2 3 [...]

The following alleged sources have now been assigned to *Níŋ-nam* Version D:

Ni 2192 (lentil)
[x] *0 22 23 //*

3. Black's description is quoted here extensively, with some additions and minor improvements that I have been able to add myself as a very useful point of departure for the discussion below, although my own conclusion differs somewhat owing to the greater attention paid to what I call Version D below.

Ni 9620
[...] fourteen lines (line eight ? = *23*)
CBS 6924+
[...] twelve lines (ten and eleven ? = *22 23*)
[...]

Composite Text of Lines 1–2

níŋ-nam nu-kal zi ku_7-ku_7-dam
me-na-àm níŋ-tuku lú la-ba-an-tuku lú níŋ-tuku ba-an-tuku

"Nothing is of value, but life itself should be sweet-tasting.
When does a man not own some piece of property and when does he own it?"

Six mss. agree on the word order of line 2, which suggests that the translation misses some emphasis of the original. It is possible that me-na-àm is used in a correlative sense, and that the translation should be "When a man does not possess any property, the man does, indeed, possess property," i.e., poverty is really riches. The translations above are those of Black, which differ slightly from mine below.

Conclusion: Four Versions of Níŋ-nam

On the basis of the evidence presented above, I have decided to present the sources as three short versions A, B, and C. These are relatively short: A about 10 lines; B about 8 lines; C about 8 lines, and reconstructed below almost as suggested by Black. However, in addition, I have added another and longer version D, based on 3N-T 326 + 360 rev. vii 9–ix 7, but duplicated in part by some of the other sources.

The three versions, A, B, and C are, in fact, very different texts, yet with a common theme to introduce them.

Version A centers on the failure of even the strongest and most powerful of mankind to achieve the unobtainable. The best thing to do is to enjoy a good and pleasant life in a good house as long as possible; in other words, this expresses the *carpe diem* theme connected with the vanity theme.

Version B centers specifically on the risks involved in relying on money gained from trade. All too often it happens that accumulated riches are lost forever. The preserved part of the text provides no clues as to what then it is advisable to rely on, but the intent may, of course, have been very similar to that of A.

Version C more specifically centers on the mortality of humankind and, apparently, the unavoidable consequences of destiny. There seems to be an allusion to a theme in *The Ballade of Ancient Rulers*: none among those living today can reach the everlasting dwelling places that apparently were allotted to those rulers, and even they failed to obtain that for ever. Since the text seems to end with a quotation from *The Ballade of Ancient Rulers*, the intent must have been similar in tone, that is, a variant of the *carpe diem* theme.

The longer D version of *Níŋ-nam* in 3N-T360 +3N-T326 goes a step further by explicitly challenging prevalent notions of the validity of religious services: religious offerings are futile, since not even smoke, the most elusive of all matter, can reach the gods in the sky—so what is the need of offerings at all?

Níŋ-nam Version A

Sources:

N 3579+Ni 2763 (column two)
Ni 3023 (first version)
UM 29-16-616

A:1 = *Line 1*	[níŋ-nam nu-kal] ⸢zi⸣ ku$_7$-ku$_7$-dam	*(1)* Nothing is of value, but life itself should be sweet-tasting.
N 3579:1	[...] ⸢zi⸣ ku$_7$-ku$_7$-dam	
A:2 = *Line 2*	[me-na-àm ní]ŋ-tuku lú la-ba-an-tuku [lú níŋ-tuku ba-an]-tuku	*(2)* Whenever a man does not own some piece of property, that man owns some property.
N 3579:2f.	[...] x-tuku lú la-ba-an-tuku / [...]-an-tuku	
A:3 = *Line 14*		
N 3579:4	[...] ⸢nam⸣-lú(?)-ùlu(?)-ka(?)	*(3)* ... of mankind ...

[*NB Continuous, or x number of lines missing?*]

A:4 = *Line 15*		
Ni 2763 ii+ 1	šà-⸢ta⸣ [...] x ra / lú nam x [...] x	*(4)* (*unintelligible*)
Ni 3023+:1	[...] x lá-e ???	
A:5 = *Line 16*	sukud-DU an-{na-}šè nu-mu-un-da-lá	*(5)* (Even) the tallest one cannot reach to the sky;
Ni 3023+:2	[...] x [...]-šè nu-mu-un-da-lá	
Ni 2763 ii 2	sukud-DU an-na-šè nu-⸢um⸣-[...]	
UM 29-16-616:3	[suku]d-da an-⸢šè⸣ [nu-mu-un-da-lá]	
A:6 = *Line 17*	⸢lú⸣ daŋal-la kur-ra la-ba-an(!)-šú-šú	*(6)* (Even) the broadest one cannot go down to the Netherworld.
Ni 3023+:3	[...] ⸢lú⸣ daŋal-la kur-ra la-ba-an(!)-šú-šú	
Ni 2763 ii 3	daŋal-la kur-ra la-ba-šú-šú	
UM 29-16-616:4	[lú-daŋa]l-e kur-re [la-ba-an-šú-šú]	
3N-T 360 ix 3	⸢kur⸣-re la(!)-⸢ba⸣-šú-šú	
A:7 = *Line 18*	kalag-ga ki-a ne nu-⸢mu(?)-un(?)⸣-[gíd-dè]	*(7)* (Even) the strongest one cannot [stretch himself] on Earth.
Ni 2763 ii 4	kalag-ga ki-a ne nu-⸢mu(?)-um(?)⸣-[gíd-dè]	
SP 17 Sec. B 2	[kal]a-ga ki-ná ní nu-mu-un-gíd-dè	
SP 22 vi 42–43	[kala-g]a ki-ná n[í n]u-mu-un-gíd-dè	
A:8 = *Line 19*		
Ni 3023+:4	⸢tìl⸣ níŋ-dùg šà-ḫúl-la šu ḫé-ni-ib-kar-kar-re	*(8)* The good life, let it be defiled in joy!
UM 29-16-616:5	[...] x šà ḫúl-la šu x [...]	
Ni 2763 ii 5	tìl níŋ-dùg šà ḫúl-[...] / šu ḫé-ni-ib-kar-[re]	
Cf. D 21	tìl níŋ-dùg(!) šà-ḫúl(?)-la / šu ⸢ḫé⸣(?)-ib-kar-kar-re	
A:9 = *Line 20*		
Ni 3023+:5	⸢ḫúb⸣-sar šà-ḫúl-la u$_4$ ḫé-ni-ib-zal-zal-e	*(9)* Let the "race" be spent in joy!
UM 29-16-616:6	[...] šà ḫúl-la u$_4$ ḫé-ni-íb-zal [...]	
Ni 2763 ii 6	ḫub-sar šà ḫúl-[...] / u$_4$ ḫé-ni-íb-⸢zal⸣-[...]	

A:10 = *Line 21*

Ni 3023+:6	[é(?)] ⸢til⸣ é-a-ni šu(!) ba-ab-te(!)-ŋá-a	*(10)* A man's good house is the house in which he has to live!
UM 29-16-616:7	[é l]ú-ùlu níŋ lú til-la é-⸢a(?)-ni(?)⸣ [...]	
D 21–22	é dùg lú-ùlu / é-a-ni ti-le-dè	(*Variant Ni 3023:* [The house in which a man] lives [is the only house] he gets. For other variants, see commentary.)

Comments

A:1 = *Line 1:* There is no easy way to interpret this; cf. the discussion above under *introduction*. This is identical to *Instr. Šuruppak* 252: níŋ-nam nu-kal zi ku_7-ku_7-da. The continuation there reads: níŋ nam-kal-kal-en níŋ-e me-kal-kal, approximately meaning "Don't attach too much value to things, (because then) you will become dependent on things evaluating you"; cf. the comments on *Instr. Šuruppak* 253, and p. 295, *Chap. 3.3: Ballade ... Attempt ... New Interpretation.*

A:2 = *Line 2:* me-na-àm = "when," is an interrogative expression that consists of the stem /men/ extended by -àm; see M.-L. Thomsen, *The Sumerian Language*, 77, § 126; cf. OBGT I col. x (MSL 4, 57ff.), lines 19–20: me-na = *ma-ti*, "when?"; me-na-àm = *a-na ma-ti*, "when is it?" Black, above, suggests a correlative sense, "When a man does not possess any property, the man does indeed possess property," i.e., poverty is really riches. Along the same lines I suggest that it means, "Whenever a man does not possess something, the man (really) possesses something." It is also possible to read this as "Whenever a man does not possess anything, the man (indeed) possesses something." The precise implication is open to various interpretations.

A:5–6 = *Lines 16–17:* This is a frequently quoted set of sayings, both in Sumerian and Akkadian, with a biblical parallel in Job 11:18: "Higher than heaven—what can you do? Deeper than *sheol*—what can you know?"; cf. the literature cited in *Chap. 3.3: Ballade ... Attempt ...*, p. 296, n. 43. Some Sumerian references are: SP 17; SP 21; *The Ballade of Early Rulers* 16–17.

A:7 = *Line 18*: Cf. SP 17 Sec. B 2 (3): [kal]a-ga ki-ná ní nu-mu-un-gíd-dè, "(Even) the strongest one cannot stretch (fully) out in bed."

A:8 = *Line 19*: Alster, 1995, 88, translated "The pleasant life, let it elapse in joy." šu – kar, perhaps approximately synonymous with kar alone = *ekēmu*, "to take away"; cf. SP 8 Sec A 4: šáḫ-gim šu ab-kar-kar-re ..., "He takes away like a pig ...," but the equation šu – kar = *ṭuppulu*, "to dirty one's reputation, to soil someone (physically)," was provided by Civil, 103 (1983) 46, n. 8. This occurs, written phonetically, also as šu – kúr = *ṭapiltu*, in *Proverbs from Ugarit* 30–31, cf. p. 325. It applies also to SP 9 Sec. A 4: šáḫ-gim šu ab-kar-kar-re, which can now be translated "he dirties himself like a pig."

A:9 = *Line 20*: ḫúb-sar = *lasāmu*, "to run," cf. AHw 539, Gtn, said of gazelles, etc. If correctly understood, "race" is here used as a metaphor of the entire human life, in a way that is unusual for Sum. literature, but would fit in with later wisdom literature.

A:10 = *Line 21*: The point seems to be that a "good house" to live in is the best obtainable good in life, possibly alluding to a similar idea in *The Ballade of Early Rulers* 22. The variant in Ni 3023 seems to mean "having received (= accepted(?)) ... his house [as the place where] he lives." It is less likely that the "good house" here is a euphemism for the grave. Note that lú-ùlu here means simply "man." The variant in UM 29-16-616 seems to mean "A man's house, that in which he lives [is what he gets as] his (only) house." Here níŋ is used as a neuter relativiser, influenced by Akkadian *ša*.

Níŋ-nam Version B

Sources:

- CBS 13777
- Ni 3023 (second version)
- BM 54699
- N 3579+Ni 2763 (column one)
- YBC 7283 (lentil)

B:1 = *Line 1*	[níŋ-nam nu-kal] ⸢zi⸣ ku$_7$-ku$_7$-dam	*(1)* Nothing is of value, but life itself should be sweet-tasting.
CBS 13777:6'	[…] ⸢ku$_7$⸣-ku$_7$-da	
Ni 3023+:7	[…] ⸢nu⸣-kal(!) zi ku$_7$-ku$_7$-da	
N 3579:1	[…] ⸢zi⸣ ku$_7$-ku$_7$-dam	
B:2 = *Line 2*	[me-na-àm ní]ŋ-tuku lú la-ba-an-tuku [lú níŋ-tuku ba-an]-tuku	*(2)* Whenever a man does not own some piece of property, that man owns some property.
CBS 13777:7'	[…]-⸢ba(?)⸣-an-tuku lú níŋ(!)-tuku ba-an-tuku	
Ni 3023+:8f.	[…] x níŋ-tuku lú la-ba-an-tuku / [lú] níŋ-tuku ba-an-tuku	
N 3579:2f.	[…] x-tuku lú la-ba-an-tuku / […]-an-tuku	
B:4 = *Line 9*	*(no complete reconstruction attempted)*	*(4)* He who hastens to …
CBS 13777:8'	[…] saŋ al-ŋá-ŋá	
Ni 3023+:10	[…] x-ru-dè saŋ íb-ŋá-ŋá	
BM 54699:8	x x x x ku$_5$-ru-dè saŋ […]	
Ni 2763 i 2	[x] x […] x […] / x […] ⸢íb-ŋá(?)⸣-ŋá-a	
B:5 = *Line 10*	*(no complete reconstruction attempted)*	*(5)* hastens to turn … into … to the detriment (of himself).
CBS 13777:9'	[…] ga x(like ÉŠ) sur(?)-ra ku$_4$-ku$_4$-dè nam-érim-šè(?) saŋ al-ŋá-ŋá	
Ni 3023+:11	[…] x-ra ku$_4$-ku$_4$-[dè]	
BM 54699:9	x x x x x sur-ra ku$_4$-ku$_4$-dè saŋ ba-x […]	
Ni 2763 i 3	dul(?) x [x] x x x sur-ra / ku$_4$-[ku$_4$]-⸢dè⸣ x x x mu-a	
B:6 = *Line 11*	umuš(?)-bi (⸢x⸣)(?) eŋir-bi im ba-e-tùm	*(6)* That plan—its outcome was carried away by the wind!
CBS 13777:10'	[…] ⸢eŋir⸣-bi im ba-an-de$_6$	
BM 54699:10	[…] x lá(?) eŋir-bi im ba-⸢na(?)⸣-[x]	
Ni 2763 i 4	umuš(?)-bi […] eŋir-bi / ⸢im⸣ ba-e-tùm	
B:7 = *Line 12*	é-bi dul-dul-da ba-šid-e a-ri-a-šè mu-un-ku$_4$	*(7)* That house was counted as a ruin, it was turned into a waste land.
CBS 13777:11'	[…] x x x ba-an-ku$_4$-re [(x)]	
BM 54699:13	é-⸢bi⸣ [x]-⸢dul⸣-da ba-an-ku$_4$ é-ri-a ba-an-[ku$_4$]	
Ni 2763 i 5	é-bi dul-dul-da ba-šid-e / a-ri-a-šè mu-un-ku$_4$	
B:8 = *Line 13*	kù-bala la-la-bi ak-da / kù íb-ba-aš ba-an-ku$_4$	*(8)* The surplus made from money transactions became lost money! (*Var.* The accumulated surplus money (lit. "silver") became lost money).
CBS 13777:12'	[…] kù im-ba-aš ba-an-ak(?) [x]	
YBC 7283:1f.	kù la-la-bi KÉŠ-da / kù im-ba-aš ba-an-ku$_4$	
BM 54699:12	⸢kù⸣ b[ala]-bi kù im-TU ba-an-[x]	
Ni 2763 i 6	kù-bal la-la-bi ak-da / kù íb-ba-aš ba-an-ku$_4$	

Comments

***B:4–5* = Lines 9–10:** saŋ ŋá-ŋá: Alster, 1975, 87, translated line 5: "The one who set his head against destiny." saŋ – ŋá may be from saŋ – ŋar = *ḫiāšu*, "to hasten."

***B:6* = Line 11:** "Went up with the wind": compare lines of the Netherworld vision in *Gilgameš, Enki and the Netherworld* 303, discussed further pp. 339–341, *Chap. 3.6*. A near parallel is *Lugalbanda-Hurrumkurra* 223: níŋ-érim-e saŋ-bi um-DU-DU eŋir-bi-šè im bí-ib-tùm, "when wickedness exerts itself, in the end it evaporates in wind." Apparently this was a proverbial expression.

***B* 7 = Line 13:** la-la-bi apparently means *lalû*, "abundance," i.e., the surplus from the sum of silver invested in trade or money to rely upon. Cf. *Chap. 2.3: Counsels of Wisdom* 89. kù im-ba-aš = *imbû*: Cf. Sjöberg, RA 60 (1966) 92.

Níŋ-nam Version C

Sources:
- N 3047
- CBS 1208
- BM 80184

C:1 = *Line 1*	[níŋ-nam nu-kal] ⸢zi⸣ ku$_{7}$-ku$_{7}$-dam	*(1)* Nothing is of value, but life itself should be sweet-tasting.
BM 80184:1	níŋ-nam nu-kal ⸢zi⸣ [...]	
N 3047:5'	[...]-⸢ku$_{7}$⸣-ku$_{7}$-dam	
CBS 1208:10	níŋ-nam nu-kal zi ku$_{7}$-ku$_{7}$-da	
C:2 = *Line 2*	me-na-àm níŋ-tuku lú la-ba-an-tuku [lú níŋ-tuku ba-an]-tuku	*(2)* Whenever a man does not own some piece of property, that man owns some property.
BM 80184:2	me-na-àm níŋ-tuku ⸢lú⸣ [...]	
N 3047:5' con't	[...] ⸢níŋ⸣-tuku ba-an-tuku	
CBS 1208:11	me-na-àm níŋ-tuku lú ⸢la-ba⸣-an-tuku lú níŋ-tuku ba-[x x]	
C:3 = *Line 3*	nam-úš-*àm(?) ⸢ḫa⸣-la lú-u$_{18}$-lu-kam	*(3)* Death is the share of man.
BM 80184:3	⸢nam-úš⸣-a x [...]	
N 3047:5' con't	[...]lú-ùlu-ka	
CBS 1208:12	nam-úš-a x ⸢ḫa⸣-la lú-u$_{18}$-lu-kam	
Cf. D 3	nam-ti-⸢x⸣-[x] nam-⸢ḫa(?)-[...] nam-lù-[ùlu-kam]	
C:4 = *Line 4*	(As CBS 1208:13)	*(4)* The consequences of his destiny, no man can escape them.
CBS 1208:13	⸢níŋ⸣-nam-a-ka-ni lú na-me ⸢la⸣-ba-an-ši-in-kar	
N 3047:6'	[... lú na-me] ⸢la⸣-ba-an-kar-re	

C:5 = *Line 5*	*an-ta é-ùr-ra-ni ki-ta é da-rí-ka-ni	*(5)* Above is his elevated house, below is his everlasting house.
CBS 1208:14	⸢an-ta⸣ é-ùr-ra-ni ki-ta é du-⸢rí(!)⸣-šè	
N 3047:7'	[an]-ta é da-rí-ka-ni	
C:6 = *Line 6*		
CBS 1208:15	[...]-bé-en lú na-me uš ḫa(?)-x	*(6)* (*unclear*)
C:7 = *Line 7*		
CBS 1208:16	⸢ú⸣ [...] ⸢diŋir⸣-re-e-ne bí-in-šúm-⸢ma(?)⸣	*(7)* (For him) who gives the ⸢food⸣ of the gods,
Cf. Ballade 21/2	⸢ú⸣(?)-gu$_{7}$-gu$_{7}$-(ra) nam-ti ì-kiŋ-kiŋ	
C:8 = *Line 8*		
CBS 1208:17	níŋ-⸢sa$_{6}$⸣-ga diŋir-re-e-ne bí-in-šúm-⸢ma(?)⸣-re	*(8)* (for him) who gives the ⸢good⸣ stuff of the gods (life is found).
Cf. Ballade 21/1	[níŋ-sa$_{6}$(?)-ga] diŋir-re-e-ne bí-in-šúm-ma-àm	

Comments

C:3 = *Line 3*: For nam-úš-a, cf. *The Ballade of Early Rulers* 19, written phonetically na-ma-uš-ta = *mūtu*.

C:4 = *Line 4*: The translation assumes that nam alone here means "destiny," instead of the expected nam-tar, or the like. nam alone is used in this sense, e.g., in *Gilgameš' Death* 35: ^{d}gilgameš nam-zu nam-lugal-šè mu-du ti-da-rí-šè nu-mu-un-du, "Gilgameš, he (= Enlil) made your destiny fitting for kingship, but he did not make it fitting for an everlasting life." In that case, ⸢níŋ⸣-nam-a-ka-ni means, lit., "his things of destiny," i.e., presumably, the consequences of the unavoidable destiny that has been decreed for him.

C:5 = *Line 5*: This is identical to *The Ballade of Early Rulers* 6, where the reference is to the everlasting dwelling places of the bygone early rulers. Cf. p. 308, *Chap. 3.3: Ballade: ... Attempt ...* with comments on line 6, where further parallels are given.

C:7–8 = *Lines 7–8*: Alster, 1990, 25, suggested níŋ-⸢sa$_{6}$⸣-ga, "the favor," as a restoration in line 8 (CBS 1208: 17), which fits the traces very well. The two lines recur in *The Ballade of Early Rulers* 21, which suggests the reading [ú-gu$_{7}$-gu$_{7}$] ⸢diŋir⸣-re-e-ne in line 7. The final -re in bí-in-šúm-⸢ma(?)⸣-re can now be explained as a misunderstood reminiscence of the final dative -ra in *Ballade* 21, which suggests that our text is quoted from there, not vice versa.

The most likely solution is that our lines 6–7 are an incomplete quotation from *Ballade* 21, with the two parts of the line in reverse order, and the point: nam-ti ì-kiŋ-kiŋ, "life is found," omitted. The dative -ra, preserved in *Ballade*, source A 21, shows that what preceded it is meant to be the dative in all sources.

References

B. Alster, *Studies in Sumerian Proverbs*. Mesopotamia 3 (Copenhagen, 1975), 86–89.

B. Alster, "The Sumerian Poem of Early Rulers and Related Poems," OLP 21 (1990) 5–25.

B. Alster, *Proverbs of Ancient Sumer* (1997).

B. Alster and U. Jeyes, "A Sumerian Poem about Early Rulers," AcSum 8 (1986) 1–11.

B. Alster, "The Vanity of Vanities Theme in Mesopotamia: Nippur Sources?" *N.A.B.U.* 1999, 88D (p. 89).

M. Civil, "Supplement to the Introduction to ISET 1," *Orientalia* 41 (1972) 83–90, appendix 2: reconstruction of SLTN 131 = pp. 89–90.

M. Civil, *Catalogue of Sumerian Literature* (n.d.).

E. Gordon, "A New Look at the Wisdom of Sumer and Akkad," BiOr 17 (1960) 122–152, esp. pp. 141 and 151.

3.2 Nothing Is of Value
(*Long Version of* níŋ-nam nu-kal; *Version D*)

The Contents of 3N-T 360 + 3N-T 326

I know 3NT 326 (+) 3N-T 360 only from casts in the University Museum, as well as from the photographs on pls. 36–39, of the same casts. Since the two parts are in Baghdad (3N-T 326 = IM 58427) and Chicago (3N-T 360 = A 30128), I have not been able to check the joins physically. 3N-T 326 obv. is the upper part of 3N-T360 obv, and, accordingly, 3N-T 326 rev. is the lower part of 3N-T360 rev. The complete tablet had ten columns (with five cols. on each side), clearly visible on 3N-T 360. The most likely solution is to connect the remains of four columns visible on the rev. of 3N-T 326 with cols. vii–x of the complete tablet. This seems to accord with Civil's description, cf. below.

Civil's description of the tablet as "complete with ten columns" (AfO 25 [1974/77] 67) refers to the physical shape of the complete tablet (otherwise it would be too optimistic). There are many damaged parts, and the precise points of contact are difficult to ascertain without the actual fragments in hand. A further difficulty is that the tablet has short lines, with two or three lines corresponding to one line of normal length, which makes it difficult to harmonize the lines with other fragmentary duplicates.

Civil's description is basic: the complete ten-column tablet included what Civil calls "the entire «Lisinna-group»." Civil identifies this as including: (a) *The Tale of Lisina* (UET 6, 144; published dupls. STVC 121, Ni 9898 [ISET I 142], SLTNi 38, TMH-NF 4, 48); (b) A short letter(?) of ca. 14 lines (cf. below); (c) *Níŋ-nam nu-kal zi ku₇-ku₇-dam* version A (but edited below as version D using my designation); (d) *Enlil and Namzitarra* (edited by Civil in AfO 25 [1974] 65–71; here included in *Chap. 3.5*); (e) A short composition of 8 or 9 lines, beginning [nam]-dub-sar-ra [x]-ta [é-g]al lugal-la-kam, very incompletely preserved. Cf. below for more details.

The Contents of Related Sammentafel

A number of these compositions occur together on *Sammeltafel*: Both Civil's A = 3N-T360+3N-T326 and F = UM 29-16-79A include the entire «Lisinna-group».[1] B = CBS 4605 (PBS 12, 31) includes (d) followed by (e). C (N 5149), D, (N 5909), and E (CBS 7917+) are exercise tablets, the obv. of which contained (d) (for the contents of the E rev. see Civil, p. 67). G (= N 3097, a small fragment) contained at least (b) and (d).

On SLTNi 131 vii (= rev. ii) there are two versions of *Níŋ-nam nu-kal* (A-B) immediately following each other. Preceding them in v–vi are: Ali *Letters*, B 12; *Nintinuga's Dog*; List of diseases (MSL 12, 197). Cf. also p. 286.

Níŋ-nam Version D: 3N-T 326+3N-T360 with dupls.

3N-T 360+ starts with Civil's composition (a) = the Lisina tale itself, and then continues with some minor compositions, including, in col. vi: apparently an unknown *edubba*-composition (referred to by Civil, p. 67, as (b): «a short letter(?) of ca. 14 lines»); one version of (c) = *Níŋ-nam nu-kal*. Col. vii: apparently, the continuation of (c). Col. viii: perhaps the continuation of the very same version of *Níŋ-nam nu-kal*, as started in col. vii. Col. ix 1–7: end of *Níŋ-nam nu-kal*. The rest of col. xi, from line 8: the beginning of (d) = *Enlil and Namzitarra*; ending, apparently, in 3N-T 326 col. ix; followed by the beginning of Civil's composition (e): 8 or 9 lines, beginning [nam]-dub-sar-ra [x]-ta [é-g]al lugal-la-kam (Civil [1974/77] 67). This is visible on 3N-T 326 ix ca. 8–9, dupl. PBS 12, 31, ca. rev. 7–8.

How do the two parts of *Níŋ-nam* relate to each other? There are two possibilities: either that these are two versions on the same tablet, with a separate composition between them, or that there is only one

1. Col. vi: Starts with 3N-T 360 rev. i (= vi), ca. 17 short lines preserved = the end of the Lisina-tale. Seems to parallel UET 6/2 144; cf.: 68: ama ᵈli₉-si₄-na dili-ni ba-da-an-[. Line 74, is reminiscent of 3N-T 360 vi 15': dili-ni ⌜x⌝ KU, but does not duplicate it.

version on this tablet, which is then considerably longer that those hitherto known. I consider the latter the more likely possibility, and designate it *Níŋ-nam Version D.* The following, at least partial, duplicates are known to me:

- CBS 6924 + N 3097, shown here on pl. 34 in E. Robson's photograph.
- Ni 2192 (ISET II 21), a lenticular school tablet inscribed with ll. 9–12 but different line order. It is a fragment from the obverse of a one-column tablet, with no edges preserved.
- Ni 9620 obv. (ISET II 91), obv. = 1(?)–17; rev. is apparently something else.

I have here combined the short lines on the main source into a composition of 22 lines of normal length. The result may be slightly arbitrary, but hardly very incorrect. It is not identical to the 24-line Version A suggested above (*Chap. 3.1: Níŋ-nam Versions A-C*) by Black.

Version D of *Níŋ-nam* apparently questions the validity of smoke offerings: not even by means of these can the tallest of humans reach the gods in heaven, so what is their validity?

Níŋ-nam Version D

Transliteration

3N-T326 rev. i (= vii) 9ff. = *Níŋ-nam nu-kal,* apparently the beginning of the same version as ends in col. ix; cf. above.

D 1		
vii 9	níŋ-nam nu-kal	*(D 1)* Nothing is of value, but life itself should be sweet-tasting.
vii 10	zi ku$_7$-ku$_7$-dam	
vii 11	me-na-àm	
D 2		
vii 12	níŋ-tuku lú la-ba-an-tuku	*(D 2)* Whenever a man does not own some piece of property, that man (nevertheless) owns something.
vii 13	lú níŋ-tuku	
vii 14	ba-tuku	
D 3		
vii 15	nam-ti-⌜x⌝-[x]	*(D 3)* Life(?) [that does not last(?)] is the sha[re] (allotted to) man-[kind](?).
vii 16	nam-⌜ḫa⌝(?)-[...]	
vii 17	nam-lú-[ùlu-kam]	
D 4		
viii	umuš nam l[ú(?) ...] |	*(D 4)* The plans(?) [...]
	na-me l[ú(?) ...]	
CBS 6924+ i 2–3'	[níŋ(?)] nam-ka-ni na-[me] / [lú] la-ba-an-kar (cf. C 4)	
Ni 9620 obv. 1'	[... -t]a-kar(?)-[x (x)] (may not belong here]	

(End of col. vii; beginning of col. viii: 3N-T 360 rev. iii. Apparently no lines missing between the two parts.)

D 5

viii 1	⸢an⸣-⸢ta⸣-⸢àm⸣	(*D* 5) Above is his elevated house;
viii 2	é-ur$_5$-ra-ka-ni	
Cf. CBS 6924+ i 4	[an-t]a-àm é-ur$_5$-ra-ka-ni (C 4)	
Ni 9620 obv. 2	[...ur$_5$]-ra-ka-[ni]	

D 6

viii 3	ki(?)-ta-àm	(*D 6*) below is his everlasting house.
viii 4	é da-rí-ka-ni	
CBS 6924 + i 5	[ki-t]a-àm é-da-ra-ka-ni	
Ni 9620 obv. 3	[...d]a-ra-k[a-ni]	

D 7

viii 5	usu(Á.TUKU) ḫé-kiŋ-kiŋ	*(D 7)* Let the strong one strive;
CBS 6924+ i 6	usu(Á-TUKU) ḫé-kiŋ-kiŋ	
Ni 9620 obv. 4	[...ḫ]é-kiŋ-kiŋ	

D 8

viii 6	šà-ga-ni	*(D 8)* Let his heart('s desires(?)) become reality;
viii 7	inim-ma	
viii 8	ḫé-em-mi-ib-sì-ge	
Ni 9620 obv. 4–5	šà-[...] | [ini]m-ma ḫé-i[m-...]	
CBS 6924+ i 7	šà-ga-ni inim-ma ḫé-im-mi-ib-sì-ge	

D 9

viii 9	lú níŋ tuku	*(D 9)* (but,) whatever a man possesses is given by his god as a gift.
viii 10	diŋir-ra-ni	
viii 11	saŋ-e-eš	
viii 12	rig$_7$-ga-a	
CBS 6924+ i 8	[saŋ ri]g-ga(?)-bi	
Ni 2192 rev. 1a	⸢saŋ⸣(copied like KA)-⸢ga⸣(possible) ... (traces)	
Ni 9620 obv. 6	[...] diŋir-ra-na saŋ-⸢x⸣-[x]	

D 10

viii 13	tukum-bi	*(D 10)* If his god has looked favorably upon him,
viii 14	diŋir-ra-ni	
viii 15	igi-zi mu-ši-in-bar	
CBS 6924+ i 9–10	[tu]kum-bi diŋir-ra-ni [igi-z]i mu-e-ši-bar	
Ni 2192 rev. 1b	igi-zi mu-un-ši-bar	
Ni 9620 obv. 7	[...tuku]m-bi diŋir-ra-na-ka(?) [...]	

D 11

viii 16	ŋéštu-KA-ni	*(D 11)* his mind (lit., ears) are opened,
viii 17	ŋál ba-an-tag$_4$	
CBS 6924+ 11	[...-n]i ŋál ba-an-tag$_4$	
Ni 2192 rev. 2	ŋéštu-<ga>-ni ŋál ba-an-tag$_4$	
Ni 9620 obv. 8	[ŋéštu]-ga-ni ŋál ba-an-t[ag$_4$]	

D 12

viii 18	⸢x⸣ ⸢AN(?)⸣ ^{d}lama ^{d}ŋuruš	*(D 12)* (and so) his personal god and his protective deities will be present in (his) body.
viii 20	diŋir-[ra]-ni	
viii 21	su ba-ŋál-[x]	
CBS 6924+	[...] ^{d}⸢lama⸣ ^{d}ŋuruš-⸢ni⸣	
Ni 2192 obv. 1	[^{d}]⸢lama⸣(not sure) ^{d}ŋuruš diŋir-ra-na	
Ni 9620 obv. 9	[...] ki ^{d}lama ^{d}ŋuruš diŋir-ra-[ni]	

D 13

viii 22	IZI-gim lá-a-ni	*(D 13)* His smoke offering(?, lit. "his thing which extends like fire/smoke") does not cease.
viii 23	nu-til-le	

D 14

viii 24	da-bi	*(D 14)* Its far end (lit. "side") at the place where he worships his god does not set a limit to his doings(?).
viii 25	ki-diŋir-ra-na-ka	
viii 26	níŋ-šu-dug$_4$(?)-ga-ni	
viii 27	nu-mu-un-til	
Ni 9620 obv. 10	[...]-ra-na níŋ šu-dug$_4$-ga-⸢ni⸣(?)	

D 15

viii 28	ní-bi-šè	*(D 15)* By itself may it increase(?).
viii 29	ḫé-su-su	
Ni 9620 obv. 11	[n]í(?)-bi zu-zu	

D 16

viii 30	šu(?) zi-ga	*(D 16)* A promise(?) shall not be effectuated(?); in his heart extispicy ...
viii 31	na-an-dug$_4$-dug$_4$	
viii 32	šà-ga-na	
viii 33	šu(?)-⸢gíd(?)⸣(perhaps SAR partly erased)⸣-SAR	
Ni 9620 obv. 11 cont.	šu-zi-⸢ga⸣	

D 17

viii 34	giš(?)-šu(?) ⸢x⸣ (like GABA×x, or two signs)	*(D 17)* ... He(?) who performs a smoke offering(?), let him serve(?) it as with a favorable heart.
viii 35	a dug$_4$-ga	
viii 36	nam-IZI-lá-e	
viii 37	šà-še-ga-gim	
viii 38	ḫé-en-dé	
UM 29-16-616 ii 2'	[...šà-še]-⸢ga⸣-gim ḫé-en-dé [...]	
Ni 9620 obv. 12	[x (x)] ŋiš SAR [S]AR-ra-gim a d[ug$_4$(?)-ga]	
Ni 9620 obv. 13	[...-b]i(or similar) a ḫé-en-[dé]	

D 18

viii 39	lú nam-IZI-lá-e	*(D 18)* (But) the man who performs a smoke(?)-extending (ritual):

D 19

40	⸢lú⸣(?)-sukud-⸢du⸣	*(D 19)* *even the tallest one cannot reach the heavens;
41	[...(?) a]n(?)-⸢šè⸣	

End of col. viii. Beginning of col. ix: 3N-T 360 rev. iv. There are probably no lines missing between the two parts.

ix 1 ⸢nu⸣-⸢mu⸣-da-[lá]
Ni 9620 obv. 14 [lú-sukud-d]u an-šè nu-m[u-da-lá]

D 20
ix 2 ⸢lú⸣-⸢daŋal⸣-la
ix 3 ⸢kur⸣-re la-ba-šú-šú

(D 20) even the broadest one cannot descend to the underworld.

D 21
ix 4 tìl níŋ-dùg(!) šà-ḫúl(?)-la /
ix 5 šu ḫé(?)-eb-kar-kar-re

(D 21) The good life, let it be defiled in joy!"

D 22
ix 6 é dùg lú-ùlu /
ix 7 é-a-ni ti-le-dè

(D 22) A man's good house is the house in which he has to live!

D 22 marks the end of the composition. It is followed by *Enlil and Nam-zitarra*; cf. the introduction above.

Comments

D 11: This seems to provide the unique information that the protective deities were thought to enter the body through the ears. The verb is a typical example of the timeless use of a perfective (*ḫamṭu*) verbal form; cf. p. 209, *Chap. 1.9: Tense- or Aspect related verbal system*.

D 13: NE-gim-lá can be read izi-gim lá, which might mean "smoke offering," lit. "(something that) extends like fire"; or, possibly, if read bí-gim, it could mean "extending like smoke." A third possibility is to read dè-gim lá, in view of na-NE, to be read na-dè = *qutrēnu*, "incense"; cf. the literature cited in the commentary on *The Goose and the Raven* 23. Either a term for smoke offering or a ritual performed to obtain an omen could be meant. Cf D 17–18: (lú) nam-IZI-lá-e.

D 14: I tentatively understand níŋ-šu-dug$_4$-ga as "his doings." For šu – dug$_4$, cf. p. 402, *Chap. 6.2: Cornell Univ. Lib. Kroch-05*, line 25 and the literature cited in the commentary there.

D 16: Cf. Gudea Cylinder A ii 13: ur-saŋ ma-a-dug$_4$ šu-zi-ga mu-ra-ab-ŋar, "hero, you have spoken, I have made a promise." Similarly, if the reading šu-gíd is trustworthy, this seems to refer to extispicy, possibly by means of liver omens. Cf. Gudea Cylinder A xii 16–17: máš-bar$_6$-bar$_6$-ra šu mu-gíd-dè máš-a šu ì-gíd máš-a-ni ì-sag$_5$.

D 17: nam-IZI-lá, etc: Probably refers to a religious office or smoke offering, or one who takes omens from smoke. Cf. D 13; D 18.

D 22: Meaning, apparently, that there is no good house other than the pleasant present one; in other words, *carpe diem*!

Sources for "Nothing Is of Value"

BM 54699 (*CT* 42, Pl. 36, no. 23)

BM 54699 is a four-sided prism. Face A contains the folktale *The Old Man and the Young Girl* (edited in *Chap. 5.2*). Face B has five unidentified lines before a separating line. After the separating line follows one unidentified line. Face B 8–13 has *Níŋ-nam* Version B 4–8 with a slightly different line order. The remaining seven lines are transliterated below. These follow without any separating line. Provided that the copy is trustworthy, this seems to be the only example of *Níŋ-nam* that did not include the three initial lines, which are otherwise found in all versions. A parallel has now been recognized, p. 287: Royal Ontario no. 506.

Face B 13ff:

1–5	*(illegible remains before the double line not transliterated)*
6	⸢x⸣ [x x (x)] ⸢x⸣
7	⸢x⸣ [x] ⸢x⸣ ⸢x⸣ ⸢x⸣
8	x x x x ku$_5$-ru-dè saŋ [...] (= B 4)
9	x x x x x sur-ra ku$_4$-ku$_4$-dè saŋ ba-x [...] (= B 5)
10	[...] x lá(?) eŋir-bi im ba-⸢na(?)⸣-[x] (= B 6)
11	⸢x⸣ [x]-bi-da i-bí-gim an-šè ba-e-⸢e$_{11}$⸣-[(x)]
12	⸢kù⸣ b[ala]-bi kù im-TU ba-an-[x] (= B 8)
13	é-⸢bi⸣ [(x)]-⸢dul⸣-da ba-an-ku$_4$ é-ri-a ba-an-[ku$_4$] (= B 7)
14	⸢KA⸣ ⸢x⸣ [(x)]-ga nu-um-sè-g[e]
15	nam-[(x)]-⸢x⸣ diŋir-ra-ni íd-da nam-t[a (x)]
16	ba-a[n]-zi-ir u$_4$ mi-ni-ib-za[l-zal-(le)]
17	r[i-ri(?)-g]a-gim ⸢nu-mu⸣-un-zu-a
18	GE [(x)] PI(= ŋéštu?)-ni ta n[u-mu-u]n-na-kal [(-kal-le)]
19	[...] ⸢x⸣(like ri) [...] ⸢x⸣ ⸢ḫa⸣ ⸢x⸣ [(x)]
20	(traces of one sign)

There seems to be a major lacune, maybe 5–10 lines, toward the end of Face B. Face C seems to start after a lacuna of a few lines:

Face C:

1'	⸢ta⸣-àm [... / ...]
2'	lú é [...]
3'	[l]ú mu ⸢x⸣(like ná) [...] / GIŠ SUR [...]
4'	[l]ú é ⸢x⸣ [...]
5'	[^{ŋiš}]gu-za im-zuḫ-zuḫ-gim ⸢x⸣ [...]

Face C 1'–7' seems to belong to a different text, followed by a double separating line. Face C from line 8 onward contains *The Fable of the Goose and the Raven* (cf. *Chap. 4.2*).

Note Face B line 11: "[The ...] with its ... went up to the sky like smoke." Cf. previously Alster, 1975, 87–88 ("Version 2").

CBS 6924 + N 3097

CBS 6924 + N 3097, shown here on pl. 34 in E. Robson's photograph, is at least a partial duplicate to *Níŋ-nam D*. It is a fragment from the obverse of a two- (or more) column tablet, with no edges preserved. There may well have been three or more columns on each side, since it seems that nothing is missing before Á in col. i 6, although there may have been room for a whole column preceding it on the tablet. The tablet is transliterated separately below and the relevant lines duplicating *Níŋ-nam* D are incorporated into the edition above.

Obv. i'

1' [...] ⸢NI⸣(?) [(x)]
2' [...] nam-ka-ni ⸢x⸣(cannot be me) [(x)] (cf. C 4)
3' [lú na-me] la-ba-an-kar-r[e] (cf. C 4)
4' [an-t]a-àm é-ur$_5$-ra-ka-ni
5' [ki-t]a-àm é-da-ra-ka-ni
6' usu(Á-TUKU) ḫé-kiŋ-kiŋ šà-ga-ni
7' inim-ma ḫé-im-mi-ib-sì-ge
8' [saŋ ri]g$_7$-ga(?)-bi
9' [tu]kum-bi diŋir-ra-ni(over erasure? hardly kam)
10' [igi-z]i mu-e-ši-bar
11' [...-n]i ŋál ba-an-tag$_4$
12' [... ^{d}la]ma ^{d}⸢ŋuruš⸣-⸢ni⸣

Continuation broken

Obv. ii'

1' ⸢nu⸣(?) ⸢en⸣ [....]
2' nam-mu [...]
3' ŋá-e(!) AN ⸢x⸣ [...]
4' a-gim ⸢x⸣ [...]
5' UD en ⸢x⸣ ⸢x⸣ [...]
6' lú [...]
7' ⸢AN⸣ ⸢x⸣ [...]

Continuation broken

CBS 1208

CBS 1208 is a four-column tablet, probably not from Nippur, photographs pl. 30–31. Rev. i 10–17 is transliterated in *Chap. 3.1*, under *Níŋ-nam* C 8. Rev. ii is *The Ballade of Early Rulers* 19–22; cf. *Chap. 3.3*.

CBS 13777

Photographs by E. Robson, pls. 23–33. The obv. contains the proverbs seemingly duplicated in Ugaritic, edited in *Chap. 3.4: Proverbs from Ugarit.* On the rev., part of the right column is preserved, probably of two, with the right edge preserved. Rev. 6'–11' corresponds to B 1–8. It is not possible to identify the traces of what went before and after that, but note that there was no separating line in either case.

Rev. i

1' *(probably one line missing, close to edge)*
2'–3' [*traces of the last signs in the lines*]
4' [...]
5' [...]-ŋá
6' [níŋ-nam nu-kal] ⸢zi⸣-⸢ku$_7$⸣-ku$_7$-da (= B 1)
7' [me-na-àm níŋ-tuku lú la]-⸢ba(?)⸣-an-tuku lú níŋ(!)-tuku ba-an-tuku (= B 2)
8' [...] saŋ al-ŋá-ŋá (= B 4)
9' [...] ga x(like ÉŠ) sur(?)-ra ku$_4$-ku$_4$-dè nam- érim-šè(?) saŋ al-ŋá-ŋá (= B 5)
10' [...] ⸢eŋir⸣-bi im ba-an-de$_6$ (= B 6)
11' [...] x x x ba-an-ku$_4$-re [(x)] (= B 7)
12' [...] kù im-ba-aš ba-an-ak(?) [x] (= B 8)
13' [...] ⸢x⸣-aš ba-an-ku$_4$ [(x)]
14' [...] ⸢x⸣ izi-lá [(x)] (cf. perhaps D 17)
15' [...]-⸢x⸣-⸢x⸣-zal-zal-⸢x⸣
16' [...]-⸢x⸣-sì-⸢ge⸣ (cf. BM 54699 Face B 14)
17' [...]-a
18' [...]-na
19' [...]-ga
20' [...] x(like ur) ⸢x⸣
21' [...] ⸢x⸣(like ba)
22' [...]-⸢x⸣(like uš)
23' *(probably traces of one last line before the end of the column)*

N 3047

Middle fragment, probably from a two-column tablet, with parts of the right and left columns preserved, and no edges preserved. Photo pl. 35. Obv. i is basically *Níŋ-nam* C 1–5, probably continued as in CBS 1208. The composition preceding it (without a clear separating line) has not been identified; neither has the composition in col. ii. Obv. i 5' cont.: [me-na-àm] níŋ-tuku ba-an-tuku has a shortened version of the main versions, omitting la-ba-an-tuku lú níŋ-tuku by haplography.

Obv. i

i 1' [...] traces of 4 signs
i 2' [...] ⸢x⸣ TUR-TUR nu nam-dub-sar-ra

---

i 3' [...] ⸢x⸣ ⸢x⸣-bi zi-ga-àm

---

i 4' [...] ⸢x⸣ lú-bi-zu-NE

---

i 5' [níŋ-nam nu-kal zi] ku$_7$-ku$_7$-dè (= C 1)
i 5' cont. [me-na-àm] níŋ-tuku ba-an-tuku (= C 2)
i 5' cont. [... ḫa(?)-la] lú-ùlu-ka (= C 3)

---

i 6' [níŋ-nam-a-ka-ni lú na-me] ⸢la⸣-ba-an-kar-re (= C 4)

---

i 7' [an-ta é-ùr-ra-ni ki-t]a ⸢é⸣ da-rí-ka-ni (= C 5)

---

i 8' [...] ⸢x⸣ [x]

Continuation of col. i broken.

Obv. ii

ii 1' TAB(?)[...]
ii 2' šà [...]
ii 3' ama [...]
ii 4' x(like BAR with an extra horizontal) [...]
ii 5' dub ⸢x⸣ [...]
ii 6' dub ⸢x⸣ [...]

Ni 2763 (SLTNi 128) joins N 3579

SLTNi 128 is a bottom fragment from a two-column tablet (unless there was an extra column in the right side), with the bottom and left edges preserved. Of these obv. i is inscribed with *Níŋ-nam*, probably C 1–5 ; obv. ii is inscribed with *Níŋ-nam* A, ca. 5–10; iii (= rev. i) is inscribed with some proverbs concerning old age, also quoted in the folktale of *The Old Man and the Young Girl* 27–31; iv (= rev. ii) has five lines of an unknown composition, followed by a double separating line, and five more lines from an unknown composition.

Ni 3579 is the top fragment from a two-column tablet, with the upper edge preserved. This may well be the missing top fragment of SLTNi 128. If so, rev. ii contains remains of three or four lines continuing SLTNi rev. ii; rev. ii is then four or five lines of a numerical excercise hardly related to what precedes them in SLTNi 128 rev. ii.

N 3579 obv. (starting from the edge)

i 1 [níŋ-nam nu-kal z]i ku_7-ku_7-dam (= C 1)
i 2 [me-na-àm níŋ]-tuku lú la-ba-an-tuku (= C 2)
i 3 [lú níŋ-tuku ba-an]-tuku (= C 2)
i 4 [...] ⸢nam⸣-lú-ùlu-ka (= C 3)
i 5 [...] ⸢x⸣ da-rí (= C 5?)
(break)

Ni 2763 (SLTNi 128) obv. i

i 1' [ki]-ta ⸢é⸣ da-rí (to be joined with N 3579 i 5?)
i 2' [x] x [...] x [...] (could perhaps be restored an-ta é-ùr-ra-ni, but we expect reverse line order)
i 2' cont. ⸢x⸣ [...] ⸢íb(or ḫé)⸣-ŋá(?)-ŋá-a (= B 4)
i 3' dul(?) ⸢x⸣ [x] ⸢x⸣ ⸢x⸣ ⸢x⸣ sur-ra / ku_4-[ku_4]- ⸢dè⸣ ⸢x⸣ ⸢x⸣ ⸢x⸣ mu-a (= B 5)
i 4' umuš(?)-bi [x] eŋir / ⸢im⸣ ba-e-tùm (= B 6)
i 5' é-bi dul-dul-da ba-šid-e / a-ri-a-šè mu-un-ku_4 (= B 7)
i 6' kù-bala la-la-bi ak-da / kù íb-ba-aš ba-an-ku_4 (= B 8)
End of col.

N 3579 obv. ii

Two lines broken at the beginning of the col.
ii 3' KA ⸢x⸣ [...]
ii 4' PA+? [...]
ii 5' lú⸣ [...]
Continuation broken.

Ni 2763 (SLTNi 128) obv. ii

(counting the break from col. i, hardly more than one or two lines are missing)
ii 1' šà-ta ⸢a⸣(?) [...] / lú nam ⸢x⸣ [...]
ii 2' sukud-du an-na-šè nu-um-[da-lá] (= A 5)
ii 3' daŋal-la kur-ra la-ba-an-šú-šú (= A 6)
ii 4' kala-ga ki-a nu-⸢mu⸣-⸢um⸣-[gíd-dè] (= A 7)
SP 17 Sec. B 2 [kal]a-ga ki-ná ní nu-mu-un-gíd-dè

SP 22 vi 42–43 [kala-g]a ki-ná n[í n]u-mu-un-gíd-dè
ii 5' ti níŋ-dùg šà-ḫúl-la [(room for two signs)] / šu ḫé-ni-ib-kar-[re] (= A 8)
ii 6' ḫub-sar šà-ḫúl [nothing missing?] /u_4 ḫé-ni-íb-zal-[zal-e] (= A 10)
End of column marked with a double line.

Ni 2763 (SLTNi 128) rev. i (= iii), continues from obv. ii 6 without break.
iii 1 nam-ŋuruš anše-kar-ra-[gim] / ḫáš(ZÍB)-ŋá ba-⸢e⸣-[tag_4]

Parallels to rev. ii 1–5 are quoted in Alster, *Proverbs* I, p. 238, sub SP 17 Sec. B 3: SP 10.9–12; SP 19 Sec. A 1; *Chap. 5.2: Old Man* 27–31.

iii 2 ḫur-saŋ-gi_6-$ŋu_{10}$ im-bar_6-bar_6 ba-an-mú
iii 3 ama-$ŋu_{10}$ tir-ta lú mu-ši-in-gi_4-⸢gi_4⸣ šu <dab_5>-ba ma-an-šúm
iii 4 ^{d}nin-kilim uzu ḫáb gu_7-gu_7-[$ŋu_{10}$] dug [...]
iii 5 ⸢x⸣ [...]

Ni 3579 rev. i (= iii), continues after at most a few missing lines:
iii 1' ⸢x⸣ [...]
iii 2' ⸢x⸣ [...] / ⸢x⸣ [...]

Ni 2763 (SLTNi 128) iv, starts from the upper edge:
iv 1' 11 iti SAL+ḪUB
iv 2' 12 iti-$ŋu_{10}$
iv 3' 13 níŋ-ba $gudu_4$-e-ne
iv 4' 14 dílim(LIŠ) má-gur_8-kù-ga
iv 5' 15 ^{d}nanna lugal-zu / an-na ši-gub-bu
iv 6' [x] ⸢x⸣ AN-ne-ne
iv 7' [x] AMAŠ ùz-da
iv 8' [x] iti ur-da
iv 9' [x] amaš áb [x]
iv 10' [x] TÚG ⸢x(like DIM) [...]
Continuation broken.

N 3579 iv: numerical.

Comments

The presence of Ni 2763 (SLTNi 128) iv 1' – 10' in this context is enigmatic. There seems not to have been enough space to carry the numerals through from 1 to 20 or more, in which case this might have been a sort of calendar. Perhaps these are entries of a literary catalogue, in which some lines are numbered. iv 4'-5' seems to mean: "14: (As) a "spoon,"(as) a pure boat, 15: Nanna, your lord, positions himself on the sky." If correctly understood, this may be taken as confirmation of a theory by M. E. Cohen, "The Sun, the Moon, and the City of Ur," in: *Religion and Politics in the Ancient Near East*, ed. by A. Berlin (Bethesda, 1996), 7–20, p. 11 n. 20, who interprets the name of the moon-god usually read Ašimbabbar as dilim-babbar, in which dilim is a phonetic writing for dílim, meaning "bowl," as a symbol of the bowl- or boat-shaped form of the moon. These lines may be taken as evidence for the moon appearing as just that, or, in my opinion perhaps rather as a spoon-like symbol. See now B. Alster, "Exit Ašimbabbar?" in: JCS 56 (2004) 1–3.

Ni 3023 (SLTNi 131) + joins

Ni 3023 is a large fragment of a tablet that had four columns on each side. The physical shape with many joins was clarified by Civil, *Orientalia* 41 (1978) 89–90. The complete tablet contained: obv. i(?) – iii 2' (including ISET I 159/101: Ni 4483; ISET II 22: Ni 4473; ISET I 125/67: Ni 4484 = A letter, unduplicated; *The Fable of the Millstone and the gul-gul-Stone*); iii 3' –1 4' = The fable of *The Lazy Slave Girl* (cf. *Chap. 4.5*); iii 15'–1 8' (continued by ISET II 121: Ni 4452 i') = according to Civil: A series of four proverbs(?) of 4, 2, 4, and 4 lines, followed by a lacuna of unknown length and contents; iii–iv (including ISET II 123: Ni 4144) = The Tummal text (see most recently Oelsner, *Wilcke FS,* 209–224), perhaps followed by something else; (rev. i =) v 1–5 = *The Ax of Nergal* (see most recently Römer, *Wilcke FS*, 237–249); v 6–1 7: Ali, *Letters B* 12, also Ali, *Sumer* 20, 66ff. (dupl. CBS 10346); v 18–23 = *Nintinugga's Dog* (see Ali, ArOr 34, 289ff.; CBS 14115 [RA 63, 180]) ; vi = A Letter or Prayer to Ninisinna or Nintiugga, including list of diseases (cf. MSL 12, 190); vii 2' –6' = *Níŋ-nam Vers. A* 2–10 (1' doubtful); v 7'–11' = *Níŋ-nam Vers. B* 1–5 (continues with about five more poorly preserved lines, probably belonging to the same composition). There are no traces shown on the copy of SLTNi 131 of col. viii, since what may look so are, in fact, the beginnings of vii 3–4 ; cf. Alster, 1975, 124, n. 13. Civil, 1978, 90, stating that there are, in fact, remains of col. viii preserved, must, therefore, refer to traces not shown on the copy.

UM 29-16-616

UM 29-16-616 is basically *Níŋ-nam* Vers. A 5–7, but remarkably it seems to be introduced by a quotation from Vers. D 17. The first line of the excerpt cannot be identified, and what else the tablet my have contained is unknown.

Rev. ii 1' [...] ⌜PA⌝ ùlu(?) dúr-ra-gim [...]
ii 2' [šà še]-⌜ga⌝-gim ḫé-en-dé [...]
D 17: ... nam-izi-lá-e nam-izi-lá-e šà-še-ga-gim ḫé-en-dé
ii 3' [suku]d-da an-šè [nu-mu-un-da-lá] (= A 5)
ii 4' [lú-daŋa]l-e kur-re [la-ba-an-šú-šú] (= A 6)
ii 5' [ḫúb(?)-sar] šà-ḫúl-la u_4 ḫé-zal-z[al-e] (= A 7)

Double line; end of excerpt; no more preserved on the tablet.

A Proverb

A tablet published by Sigrist: *Neo-Sumerian Texts from the Royal Ontario Museum*, II (Bethesda, Md., 2004) includes a proverb (text 506) inscribed on an OB lentil:

> níŋ-šu ŋál-la
> i-bí-gim
> an-šè(! copy: LAGAB) ba-è-dè

> "All he has
> will evaporate into the sky
> like smoke."

This is no clear duplicate to any of the known níŋ-nam compositions, but it is included here because of its similarity to *Níŋ-nam* B 6; D 11ff. I owe the reference to N. Veldhuis. Only in the final stage of proofreading was the parallel BM 54699 Face B 11 recognized.

3.3 The Ballade of Early Rulers

On the Syro-Mesopotamian Tradition

Already in RA 63 (1969) 179,[1] Civil observed that a text from Ugarit published by Nougayrol as *Ugaritica* 5, no. 164, is a partial duplicate to a Sumerian collection of "Counsels of Wisdom" published as CT 44, no. 18 (BM 80184). Another duplicate from the British Museum was found and published in 1986.[2] This could be combined with texts from Emar published in 1987 by Arnaud, as "La Ballade des héros du temps jadis," here titled *The Ballade of Early Rulers*. The textual history of that text is particularly interesting in that it is possible to retrieve both an "eastern" version from the traditional Babylonian area, dating from the early second millennium B.C., and a "western" Syro-Mesopotamian one from the Syrian area, dating from around 1300 B.C.

In order not to overestimate the significance of the differences between the two traditions, it is wise to keep in mind an observation by Civil,[3] who in 1989 pointed out that the title "Sagesse syrienne" used by Arnaud, strictly speaking, is a misnomer, because an OB catalogue published by M.E. Cohen,[4] lists [*še-me*]-*e mi-il-kam*, which must be *Counsels for Šūpē-amēli*, that is, one of the most significant texts from the Syro-Mesopotamian area.[5] That text is so far known only from Syro-Mesopotamian and Hittite sources, but seems accordingly to rest on an older source from Mesopotamia proper. Other texts treated in the present volume point in the same direction; even a short extension to *The Ballade of Early Rulers* in the Ugaritic version (*Ugaritica* 5, 164),[6] quoting proverbs, now appears to have a Nippur forerunner.[7]

It should further be borne in mind that the designation "Sippar" tradition should be taken *cum grano salis*. The relevant texts may well come from Babylon. Here Standard Sumerian (SS) is used instead.[8]

The Syro-Mesopotamian literary tradition has been the subject of an extensive monograph by Th. Kämmerer: *šimâ milka. Induktion und Reception der mittelbabylonischen Dichtung von Ugarit, Emār und Tell el-ᶜAmārna*.[9] Among the texts included, the following are of particular interest in our context: pp. 170–173: "Ein ungehorsamer Sohn" (Akkadian text from Ugarit, otherwise unknown); pp. 176–207: "Dialog zwischen *Šūpê-amēli* und seinem 'Vater'" (Akkadian text from Ugarit, Emar, and Boğazkale, otherwise unknown, apart from Civil's observation mentioned above); pp. 218–227: *Enlil und Namzitarra* (OB Sumerian version with mB bilingual version from Emar, including, pp. 224–227, "Der Rat eines Vaters": a ca. 35-line Akkadian fragment with no Sumerian counterpart);[10] pp. 208–213 *Ein Leben ohne Freude*, that is, our *Ballade of Early Rulers* (only the Akkadian versions from Ugarit and Emar are included in Kämmerer's volume).

The texts mentioned above can justly be regarded as "wisdom literature," because, apart from the mere purpose of scribal training, they served to promulgate new and deeper insight into the conditions of human life.[11]

1. Also JNES 28 (1969) 72, and *Orientalia* 41 (1972) 30.
2. Alster and Jeyes, "A Sumerian Poem about Early Rulers," AcSum 8 (1986) 1–11.
3. In AuOr 7 (1989) 2, commenting on no. 778.
4. RA 70 (1976) 131, line 15.
5. Last treated by Dietrich: "Dialogue zwischen Šūpê-amēli und seinem 'Vater'," UF 23 (1991) 38–65.
6. Lines 24'–39' in Dietrich's edition, 1992, 28–29; cf. also p. 12. For the Nippur duplicate, cf. Alster, in: *N.A.B.U.* 89 (1999) 88ff.
7. The text is edited here in *Chap. 3.4: Proverbs from Ugarit.*
8. "Sippar" was used because Sippar is one of the places from which many of the texts of unknown provenience in the British Museum may have come, including the range of BM numbers to which the tablets in question belongs. Using the designation "Standard Sumerian" implies that it is considered a mere coincidence that the text in question has so far not been found duplicated among the tablets that can be said with certainty to come from Nippur.
9. AOAT 251 (Münster, 1998).
10. Cf. Klein, 1990, 67, n. 26. *Enlil and Namzitarra*, including its Emar version, is here treated in *Chap. 3.5*.
11. Or with Dietrich's words, "eine neue oder tiefere, weisere Einstellung zum Leben" (UF 22, 45).

Both Kämmerer, 1998, 2, and Klein, AcSum 12 (1990) 60, emphasize the independent character of the Syro-Mesopotamian tradition. Lambert (quoted below), however, sees it as fundamentally dependent on traditional Babylonian sources. That the scribes obviously had many difficulties in coping with the Sumerian language certainly seems to point in that direction.

On the other hand, not only the links to the biblical instruction genre pointed out by Klein,[12] but also the studies by Dietrich and Kämmerer, showing that the command of Akkadian displayed by Syro-Mesopotamian sources was more advanced than sometimes thought, speak for their greater independency.

The study of *The Ballade of Early Rulers* presented below, however, leads to the inevitable conclusion, already anticipated by Nougayrol in *Ugaritica* 5, that, when occasionally we are lucky enough to have sources from both sides available, the Syro-Mesopotamian ones were so closely tied to their Babylonian forerunners that they cannot be studied successfully if the genuine Babylonian, or even unilingual Sumerian, sources are left out of consideration. This also implies that, whenever the Syro-Mesopotamian versions differ from their presumed genuine Babylonian forerunners, there may have been Babylonian models for specific additions in the Syro-Mesopotamian texts, whether "genuine" Babylonian models are presently known or not. The relative scarcity of Middle Babylonian and older literary finds from Babylonia proper must always be taken into account in such cases. A characteristic case discussed below occurs in *The Ballade of Early Rulers* 21: the ending, connecting the text with the beer-goddess, has been thought to represent a specific Syro-Mesopotamian version, but may well have come from a genuine Babylonian forerunner now lost.

Irrespective of how far advanced knowledge of Akkadian may have been in learned circles of the Syrian area in the late Bronze Age, the fact remains that the presence of Sumerian versions in that area is best explained by assuming that such texts were basically dependent on older already existing Babylonian sources, in particular since a specific format was invented for the purpose: the three-column format, in which a Sumerian version in ordinary orthography (left), a syllabic Sumerian one (middle), and an Akkadian translation (right), are included in three parallel columns arranged horizontally.[13]

Publication History

The first attempt to edit the Sumerian text was made by Alster, 1986, who, in collaboration with Ulla Jeyes, presented a preliminary edition of the Sumerian "Poem of Early Rulers," then known from two Sumerian tablets, presumably from Sippar, and two bilingual fragments from Ugarit. It came as a great surprise that new sources should appear virtually simultaneously, in the Emar volumes published by Arnaud. Another duplicate, CBS 1208, to the best of my knowledge first identified by Civil, turned up in the collections of the University Museum, Philadelphia; more recently a Neo-Assyrian duplicate, K. 6917 + 13679, identified and joined by R. Borger, has been found, cf. below. It is edited here for the first time under *Chap. 3.3c: The Neo-Assyrian Version* below, based on a copy by M.J. Geller.

In the study below the following designations are used: Alster and Jeyes, 1986;[14] Arnaud, 1987;[15] Wilcke, 1988;[16] Alster, 1990;[17] Dietrich, 1992;[18]

12. Cf. J. Klein: "The 'Bane' of Humanity: A Lifespan of One Hundred Twenty Years," AcSum 12 (1990) 57–70, in which he studied the Emar version of *Enlil and Namzitarra*, as well as his study from 2000 of *The Ballade of Early Rulers*.
13. These are, of course, no more than a variant of the true trilingual tablets. Comparable tablets, albeit with mostly two parallel columns, are otherwise considered Kassite or later. The oldest bilingual texts started as interlinear Akkadian translations of Sumerian texts.
14. Alster and Jeyes, "A Sumerian Poem about Early Rulers," AcSum 8 (1986) 1–11.
15. D. Arnaud, in: *Emar VI/4: Textes de la bibliothèque: transcriptions et traductions.* Missions Archaéologique de Meskéné-Emar, Recherches au pays d'Aštata (1987), 359–365 (copies in *Emar* VI/1–2 [1985]); cf. previously Arnaud, in: D. Beyer (ed.): *Meskéne-Emar. Dix ans de travaux 1972–1982* (Paris, 1982), 51.
16. Cl. Wilcke, in: "Die Sumerische Königsliste und erzählte Vergangenheit," in: J. von Ungern-Sternberg and H. Reinau (eds.): *Vergangenheit in mündlicher Überlieferung.* Colloquium Rauricum Band 1 (Stuttgart, 1988), 113–40.
17. B. Alster: "The Sumerian Poem of Early Rulers and

Lambert, 1995;[19] Black, [1995];[20] Kämmerer, 1998,[21] and Klein, 2000.[22]

There are important observations in every one of these contributions, but some of them were regrettably made without taking already published works into account. A new attempt, basically to re-edit the Sumerian text, therefore, seems warranted. In order to make comparisons easier, the Syro-Mesopotamian version is, however, included separately (*Chap. 3.3b: The Syro-Mesopotamian Version*). All sources are taken into account in the reconstruction of the SS version in *Chap. 3.3a*, yet with clear indication of which lines are particular to each version. The Syro-Mesopotamian sources are considered invaluable for the reconstruction of parts missing in the older sources, and vice versa.

Basic Interpretation

The text was understood by Alster and Jeyes, 1986, 2, and Arnaud, 1987, as a "wisdom" text relating to the conditions of human life, whereas Wilcke, 1988, took it as a drinking song comparable to *Gaudeamus igitur* ("ein Trinklied, frech und Zynisch. Ein Studentenlied ...").

Alster, 1990, 5, however, described the text somewhat differently as "a drinking song, in which the learned nostalgic remembrance of the happy bygone days of the rulers of the distant past is used as a pretext for enjoying the present time with the help of the beer-goddess." One could object that this description may have been too readily influenced by Wilcke's opinion, but, perhaps apart from "drinking song," it may still be a suitable description of the composition as a whole.[23] It could have been stressed more clearly, admittedly, that the mention of Siraš, the beer-goddess, gives the Syro-Mesopotamian version a special twist. Yet, since the end of the Standard Sumerian version has now been retrieved, it is clear that its intent was not very different from that of the Emar version.[24] The line mentioning Siraš may, in fact, already have been a variant in an as yet unknown Babylonian copy, and there is no reason to restrict it to the Syro-Mesopotamian version alone.

Wilcke's comparison to *Gaudeamus igitur* is certainly worth considering as a relevant aspect of the text among others. I do not regard the text as belonging to any easily definable pre-existing "genre," be it a "drinking song" or similar. One need not claim that it has ever been used as an actual drinking song or that that was its main purpose. The text is *sui generis* as a new invention that probably had no predecessor. As such it may allude to older genres in a

Related Poems" *Orientalia Lovaniensia Periodica* 21 (1990) 5–25.

18. M. Dietrich: "«Ein Leben ohne Freude». Studie über eine Weisheitskomposition aus dem Gelehrtenbibliotheken von Emar und Ugarit," UF 24 (1992) 9–29. Instead of the title, Klein, 2000, 208, n. 35, suggests as an alternative "Rejoice, O young man, in your youth" (from Eccl 11:9) since "Ein Leben ohne Freude" (quotation from l. 19) would be unfortunate if applied to the composition as a whole, because the intent is rather the opposite, that one should enjoy life with joy, by making the best out of the present situation, and enjoying as much happiness as one can, however short it may last.
19. W.G. Lambert, in: "Some New Babylonian Wisdom Literature," in: *Studies Emerton*, 37–42.
20. J. Black: "A Note on Genre and Translation," in *The Groningen workshop on genre* 1995; used here by courtesy of the author; forthcoming 2005(?).
21. Th. Kämmerer, as listed above, pp. 208–213, cf. also ibid., pp. 118–119.
22. J. Klein: "«The Ballade about Early Rulers» in Eastern and Western Tradition," *Orientalia Lovaniensia Analecta: Languages and Cultures in Contact* (2000), 203–216.
23. The problem is, ultimately, that "wisdom" is not a usable genre designation, although it may be suitable as a label that tells something about the existential attitude of a text. Or, is the problem, rather, that "wisdom" is not expected to be contained in a humorous text? By seriously arguing whether or not this was a "drinking song," one overlooks the fact that genre designations can be misleading if they do not take into consideration that in an innovative literary environment, genre designations should reflect the open-mindedness that creates something new out of something old. Black's reference (1995) to Brahms using *Gaudeamus igitur* in his *Akademische Festouverture* is a good point. It beautifully illustrates the re-use of older literary material in new settings.
24. Cf. Klein, 2000, 208, n. 35. I consider the SS version to end in a tone that approximately expresses the same idea as the Emar version, although with a different wording. Cf. *Attempt at a New Interpretation* below.

sophisticated or humorous way, even pretending to be a drinking song, but "ballade" seems to hit the mark well.[25]

It is now clear that the text ends with the assertion that life is found for "the one who gives the good things of the gods, the food provider" (l. 21), so it is obvious that it may allude to a banquet in which not only food, but also drink were served as kind of *ambrosia* and *nectar*. The decisive point is that the text exemplifies the *re-use and re-interpretation of literary motifs* in a way that would have been unthinkable without the spiritual atmosphere characteristic of the *belles lettres* of the Sumerian scribal schools of the Isin-Larsa or early Old Babylonian period. In this sense it is a worthy Mesopotamian predecessor of the Qoheleth tradition. By introducing the beer-goddess and alcohol at the end of the text, the Syro-Mesopotamian version stayed true to the original tone and intent of the Standard Sumerian version. Wilcke correctly captured its tone, perhaps overstating it slightly, but this is forgivable in view of its amalgamation of seriousness, wit, humor, and cynicism.

In 1995, Lambert accepted the text as a "wisdom" text, relating it to the *carpe diem* theme expressed in the Siduri episode of the Old Babylonian *Gilgameš Epic*. He rejected Wilcke's interpretation as a drinking song, emphasizing that the beer-goddess Siraš is mentioned only as an addition to the text in the Syro-Mesopotamian version (Syr. 23). According to him "the Emar recension and the Ugaritic copies ... obviously are based on something very like the unilingual Sumerian version and have inserted into it a second, more specific, idea of how to find happiness," i.e., by means of alcohol (ll. 21, 23, and 24). Lambert correctly saw the text as a Mesopotamian forerunner of ideas expressed in Qoheleth, often thought to be inspired under late Greek influence.[26]

Dietrich, 1992, also rejecting the "drinking song," presented a detailed edition of the Emar and Ugaritic versions, of which he saw that from Emar as the more elaborate one ("eine in sich geschloßene Komposition mit sechs Abschnitte").[27] Like Lambert, Dietrich saw the text as closely connected with the Siduri episode of the Old Babylonian *Gilgameš Epic*. He found a strophic pattern worth studying for its own literary merit, and stressed the independent literary qualities of the Syro-Mesopotamian scribal schools.[28]

While fully recognizing the merits of a more

25. I prefer the English title ballade, which seems to suggest the right associations. This belongs to a literary type among which perhaps *Sage mir wo die Blumen sind* comes most readily to mind. The most famous example is, however, François Villon's "Ballade des dames du temps jadis" ("Ballade of the Ladies of Bygone Times") to which already Arnaud referred. Among Coleridges's *Lyrical Ballads* from 1798, *The Ancient Mariner* is best known.
26. Others have already pointed to parallels between, e.g., the *Gilgameš Epic* and Qoheleth. First was H. Grimme: "Babel und Koheleth-Jo-jakin," OLZ 8 (1908) 432–438. More recent studies are Karel van der Toorn, "Did Ecclesiastes Copy Gilgamesh?" *Bible Review* (2000) 6(1): 22–30: according to him there are many parallels between Ecclesiastes and the *Gilgamesh Epic*, but he concludes that there is no direct literary relationship. Similar parallels are found also in Egyptian and Greek literature. Surprisingly he thinks that the *carpe diem* theme (Eccl 9:7–9) and the strength of the three-strand rope (Eccl 4:12) may have been mediated to Israel from Mesopotamia through Egypt, not the most obvious way. Further: C.L. Seow, "Beyond Mortal Grasp: The Usage of *hebel* in Ecclesiastes," *Australian Biblical Review* 48 (2000) 1–16. According to him, the term *hebel* (traditionally translated "vanity") indicates transience, as in the *Gilgameš Epic* that Ecclesiastes parallels. (I owe these two references to J. Sasson.); Jean de Savignac, "La sagesse du Qoheleth et l'epopée de Gilgamesh," *Vetus Testamentum* 28 (1978) 318–323. I have not had access to the studies by A. Shaffer, *Eretz Israel* 8 (1967) 246–250; 9 (1969) 159–160 (in Hebrew), mentioned by Klein, 2002, 214. R. Gordis, *Koheleth: The Man and His World*, 3rd ed. (New York: Schocken, 1968), 304, warned against drawing too rash conclusions since universal concepts are involved, also well attested in Egyptian literature. For a good critical approach to the question, see J.H. Tigay, "On Evaluating Claims of Literary Borrowing," in: *Hallo FS*, 250–256.
27. The Ugarit tablets *Ugaritica* 5, 164, 165 and 166, are "school tablets," in which repeated sections occur. No. 164 stands apart as including a group of proverbs for which at that time no duplicates had as yet been found (cf. Dietrich's description 1992, 26, and further *Chap. 3.4: Proverbs from Ugarit* below).
28. On pp. 10–11 Dietrich, commenting on the relationship between the two versions, states with regard to Wilcke's edition: "Er behielt die Zeilenfolge des Emar (-Ugarit)-Textes bei und versuchte ihn lediglich dort,

detailed discussion of the Emar and Ugaritic sources, I have refrained from discussing the strophic pattern in detail.[29]

Textual History: The Standard Sumerian Version versus the Syro-Mesopotamian Version

The basic differences between the two versions relate to the forward position of SS 16–18, which became lines 7–9 in the Syro-Mesopotamian version, following directly upon the six introductory lines.

It was undoubtedly the similar implications of SS 16–18 and 1–6, all expressing the futility of human ambitions, that caused this change. The result seemingly makes perfectly good sense, but it interrupts the meaningful sequence relating to the dwelling places of the early rulers (SS 7–9), and the climatic effect of SS 18 (= Syr. 9) is lost.

In SS 20 = Syr. 22 the verb was adjusted to a precative form with a different Sum. verb (du instead of ak) (Dietrich: "An die Stelle der herzensfreude einen ganzen Tag lang soll (ruhig) ein Kummertag von 36.000 Jahren treten"). This is detrimental to the easily understandable and straightforward intent of the original indicative SS verb, which was meant as a logical conclusion of the preceding nineteen lines. These can be paraphrased as follows: "after all the early rulers had died, etc., (remember that) «instead of one day of joy 36,000 silent year reigned» (note: the simple indicative in-ak, versus *lillika*) (so therefore): Now rejoice!" The precative of the Syro-Mesopotamian version still makes good sense as a rhetorical exaggeration, something like "let 36,000 years of silence come, (so now circumvent this by finding happiness!)."

These changes do not make the Syro-Mesopotamian version a fundamentally different text. It seems that the sources are affected by two kinds of changes: (1) such as depend upon a mB source now lost. This must have been perfectly meaningful, although the structure of the OB version had become somewhat weakened, and some of its well-intentioned additions result in confusion rather than clarity (esp. Syr. 22 = SS 20); (2) such as were caused by the failure of the Syro-Mesopotamian scribes to understand the mB source fully. In particular, the Emar source can at best be characterized as a praise-

wo er wegen seines schlechten Erhaltungszustandes nicht mehr verständlich war, mit Hilfe parallel verlaufende Zeilen aus den Sippar-Texten zu rekonstruiren." This conforms to my own position, seen vice versa from the point of view of the SS version. Dietrich, however, drew the following conclusion: "So blieb B. Alster bei seinem Versuch, die Textzeugen aus Ost und West ... synoptisch zusammenzustellen, keine andere Wahl, als die syrische Komposition in einzelsprüche zu zerlegen," echoed by Klein, 2000, 205 ("forces him to take the Emar version apart"). The following statement, p. 25: "Denn B. Alster mußte, um dies nachweisen zu können [i.e., that "ein sumerische Köningslied aus Sippar umgearbeitet wurde" scl. to serve as a model for *The Ballade of Early Rulers*], die Emar-Komposition in Einzelsprüche zerlegen," is based on the erroneous impression that I edited all the four compositions (1–4) inscribed in the same order on some *Sammeltafel* (A, B, D), in order to show that one of texts was derived from one of the others (p. 297, n. 48, *The Contents of the Sammeltafel*). This was not my intension, and the statement is opposite to my own opinion and contradictory to the conclusions that can be deducted from the chart shown in Alster, 1990, 9–10. I consider a historical synopsis a legitimate and potentially very enlightening way to approach texts that have a very complicated textual history. By no means does that approach necessarily serve to "take the text apart," as the complete editions given here in *Chaps. 3.3a* and *3.3b* will, I hope, show. The very different alternative conclusions are summarized below under *Textual History*.

29. In principle I consider translations of sententious sayings and proverbs to be successful provided that they fulfil two requirements: (1) they make good sense *when read as separate lines* alone without being dependent on any given context; (2) *simultaneously* they make *good sense in every context* in which they occur. Cf. *Chap. 1.4:* Comments on *Instr. Šuruppak* 66. If (1) has to yield to a strophic pattern required by (2) in order to make sense, I would prefer first to reconsider that pattern. I would not go so far as to let a rigorous strophic pattern take precedence over interpretations that may sometimes be suggested on the basis of the Standard Sumerian line of textual evidence, in cases where such alternative interpretations seem to make better sense, without being forced to fit a rigorous strophic pattern. A typical example is line 6 of *The Ballade of Early Rulers*. Line 3 is another very telling example that throws serious doubts on the strophic pattern. Cf. further p. 41, *Context Related Expansion of the Strophic Pattern*.

worthy attempt to make the best possible out of an imperfectly understood Babylonian source. Cf. further below: *The Relations between the Syro-Mesopotamian Sources.*

The different ending of the Emar version can simply be regarded as a rephrasing or "update"—perhaps, but not necessarily, to suit local circumstances—of the underlying intent of the SS version. The beer-goddess was not expressly mentioned there, but food and drink were, indeed (cf. *Attempt at a New Interpretation* below). Siraš is the Akkadian name for ᵈnin-ka-si, the Sumerian beer-goddess, known since Early Dynastic times (even in the ED version of *The Instructions of Šuruppak*, l. 86), as well as in ED lexical lists. That this has a Hebrew cognate (תירוש) does not necessarily imply that the name entered the text in the Syro-Mesopotamian area.

In Syr. 24 (not included in SS), a concluding line was added that seemingly gives the entire text a moral twist not previously present: ⸢e⸣-ne ŋiš-ḫur nam-u_{18}-lu gi-na = *an-nu-um ú-ṣ[u-ur-tum] ša a-mi-lu-ut-ti*, "this is the plan for righteous mankind." In view of the preceding humorous contents and in light of the persistence of similar "bits" of the composition in scribal circles, it is not unlikely that this bombastic statement should be read with a humorous glint in the eye. Only then it makes sense to say that the plan drawn for righteous men is to drink beer and enjoy a short moment of happiness. Cf. *Chap. 3.3c: The Neo-Assyrian Version*, where a humorously resigned attitude is similarly suggested.

The Relations between the Syro-Mesopotamian Sources

As to the relations between the Emar source and the Ugaritic sources, some interesting observations can be made. In some cases the Ugaritic version remarkably stayed closer to the (sometimes presumed) SS text:

Line 3: ⸢u_4-da⸣-ta im al-ŋál-la, "since time immemorial there has been wind," was at least partly understood in the Ugaritic sources, but the Emar version apparently had become so corrupted that it totally omitted the translation of the second part of the line.

In SS 14 = Syr. 17, the Sumerian expression: u_4-ul-lí-a-ta, ("those kings were the vanguards of times immemorial") was not understood in the presumed mB version (although it is well known in Sumerian literary high style; cf. *Chap. 2.2*: Comments on *The Instructions of Ur-Ninurta* l. 1). Instead it was reinterpreted as "from then till now" (Emar ii: ú-sa(?)-ŋá-ta-e-né e-še-ta (= *u_4(?)-saŋ-ŋá-ta?) = Emar iii: *ša iš-tu u_4-mi pa-na-a a-di i-na-a[n-na]*).

In Uc, line 5: a characteristic stylistic feature of a Sumerian original seems to be reflected, that is, the adding parallelism: *[e-l]i(?)-šu-nu šu-nu-ma [šarrū(?)] šu-nu ša-nu-tu-ma*, "Those (scl. kings) were above them; those [kings] were different."

In Syr. 22 = SS 20, one of the Ugaritic sources, Ua, remarkably preserved the Sum. verb as ak, although the Akk. translation conforms to DU, as, in fact, Uc and Emar have it. Ua or its model must, therefore, have been written at a time when a copy of the SS version was still available.

In conclusion, if the Emar text is said to be primary (cf. Dietrich, 1992, 27) and the Ugaritic sources derived from it, it would mean that the Ugaritic scribes had the luck to invent solutions that were considerably closer to a Sumerian original, without understanding them themselves. I would rather draw the opposite conclusion, that the Ugaritic sources were derived more directly from a Babylonian source, compared to the Emar source.

One cannot deny the possibility that the author of the Emar text may have reworked his sources deliberately in an original way and created a new literary work of his own, but I prefer first to approach it from the point of view of traditional Mesopotamian literary history, which places his result in an inferior rank compared to the original sources, as a text that has suffered considerable losses in the transmission process (for more details, cf. *Chaps. 3.3a; 3.3b* below). The types of errors committed are common and well documented in Sumerian texts transmitted in late copies. The only unexpected thing about this would have been if the opposite had been the case. In conclusion, the "western" texts can safely be regarded as basically derived from the "eastern" sources, but expanded or modified along the lines discussed by Lambert, 1995.

The Significance of the Longevity of Ancient Rulers

The *Ballade of Early Rulers* is one of the oldest texts in the world that features a theme well known from world literature: the longevity of bygone early rulers, some of which may have been considered half divine. Significant examples are the patriarchs of Genesis, who lived up to 900 years, the *Shahname* of Firdowsi, Egyptian, and Chinese kings lists.[30] The relations to the concept of longevity in *The Sumerian King List* are obvious. According to this, some of the earliest kings lived, e.g., 64,000 years. *The Sumerian King List* is now known to go back at least to King Šulgi of the Ur III period, ca. 2095–2047 B.C.[31]

A common feature is that the human life span is said slowly to decrease until it becomes shorter than a hundred years, or 120 years in biblical tradition. A similar idea is expressed in Hesiod, *Works and Days*, 130–135, according to which it took a hundred years for babies to become mature adults, but then they lived only a few unhappy and sinful years; in other words, their childhood lasted for a very long time, but was while they were not fully conscious.

Whether or not the Hesiod variant is a specifically Greek "rationalized" version of an older concept, it obviously is along the same lines as that scholarship seeking to explain the long life spans in realistic terms. A classic example is Jacobsen's edition of *The Sumerian King List*, 1939.[32]

It is possible, however, that these sources intend to connect the decreasing span of human life with the tacit exhortation to make the best out of life under the present circumstances.[33] This is the explicit implication that appears from *The Ballade of Early Rulers*, but it may well have been the implicit intent of semi-mythological king lists as well. The possibility, therefore, exists that the *carpe diem* theme rests on very old traditions genuinely at home in Sumerian literature, or that it is a "re-interpretation" deduced from them, perhaps inspired by the Siduri episode of the Akkadian *Gilgameš Epic* in its Old Babylonian form, but not exclusively bound to it.[34]

Attempt at a New Interpretation of The Ballade of Early Rulers

There is no direct reference tying it to the Siduri episode of the Old Babylonian *Gilgameš Epic*, but its *carpe diem* theme has correctly been seen as connecting the two compositions.

The whole text of *The Ballade of Early Rulers*, however, consists of intertextual references, mostly to semi-mythological figures, or to proverbial wisdom. It is the combination of these, in particular, the *vanity* theme, with the *carpe diem* attitude, that creates its characteristic tone of nostalgic humor, which may be rephrased as "Have you ever heard this before: things aren't what they used to be, and they never

30. This is reflected also in *The Sumerian King List from Lagaš*, published by E. Sollberger: "The Rulers of Lagash," JCS 21 (1967) 279–291, which apparently parodies *The Sumerian King List*. It starts with assigning 2760 years to a ruler in line 102, but has a remarkable parallel to Hesiod in that it clearly states that, after the flood, childhood lasted very long, i.e., 100 years (l. 16). There are other texts that hint at the early legendary rulers of the King List, cf., e.g., Alster: "A Dumuzi Lament in Late copies," AcSum 7 (1985) 1–9, and the literature cited there. Cf. also *The Tummal Chronicle*, last edited by J. Oelsner, in: *Wilcke FS*, 209–244.
31. Steinkeller: "An Ur III Manuscript of the Sumerian King List," in: *Wilcke FS*, 266–292.
32. G. Steiner, "Der 'reale' Kern in den 'legendären' Zahlen von Regierungsjahren der ältesten Herrscher Mesopotamiens," AcSum 10 (1988) 129–152, is a detailed attempt to find a calculation method (a factor 40) by means of which such numbers can be recalculated in terms of rational chronology. A similar approach remarkably also interested one of the fathers of modern linguistics, the Danish scholar Rasmus Rask, who in 1827 published a study *Den gamle Ægyptiske Tidsregning* (Ancient Egyptian Time Reckoning); a similar study, *Die älteste hebraische Zeitrechnung bis auf Moses*, 1828, was published in 1839 in a German translation by Gottlieb Mohnike; Engl. trans. 1863: *A Short Tractate on the Longevity Ascribed to the Patriarchs in the Book of Genesis, and Its Relations to the Hebrew Chronology*. Rask considered the unrealistically high numbers mistakes caused by transmission and counting errors.
33. Laura Feldt points out to me that the longevity of the early rulers also indicates that these were half divine, so that they bridge the semi-mythic times in which they lived with the present reality. In the present text, the point is that even these semi-mythological rulers of yore are gone, so *carpe diem*!
34. Fixing the length of the human lifetime was also a particular concern of the Emar version of *Enlil and Namzitarra*. Cf. *Chap. 3.5* for details.

were, so now, hurry up: find a way to rejoice before it's too late!"[35]

Is the Siduri episode of the Akkadian *Gilgameš Epic* the only, or most likely, source from which this is likely to have come? In view of the much increased knowledge we now have of older Sumerian literature, it is time to reconsider the matter.[36]

The SS version of *The Ballade of Early Rulers* is inscribed as the last of a sequence of four compositions, of which the preceding one is *Níŋ-nam nu-kal*, version C, to which our text alludes in line 21, or vice versa. So it might be worthwhile to consider the full wording of that title: níŋ-nam nu-kal zi ku_7-ku_7-da, "Nothing is of value (but) life is sweet" (or as Black puts it: "life should be sweet tasting"). In other words, this very title combines the two themes in an antithetical pair. The juxtaposition of two contradictory pairs (same type as *sophomore*, lit., a "wise fool") is a very characteristic feature of Sumerian proverbial wisdom, and by no means coincidental.[37] The title simply implies "All is vanity, but (nevertheless) enjoy life!"—in other words, the vanity theme is here in a nutshell combined with the *carpe diem* theme. We are fortunate enough to be able to prove that that composition, which is known in at least four versions (see *Chap 3.1: Vers. A-B; 3.2: Vers. D*), uses an older proverbial phrase as its initial line, for it occurs as line 252 of *The Instructions of Šuruppak*. The concept must, therefore, be older than the Akkadian *Gilgameš Epic*, and must have existed independently. Therefore, it is evident that the *carpe diem* theme did *not necessarily* come from the Akkadian *Gilgameš Epic*, but that it had an earlier Sumerian prehistory.

Nevertheless, it is telling that there are three references to stories related to the Gilgameš cycle: line 12 seems to refer to the Sumerian story of *Gilgameš and Huwawa*; lines 10 and 12, however, seem more directly to refer to the Old Babylonian form of the Akkadian *Gilgameš Epic*; line 12 alludes to Gilgameš' struggle with Enkidu in a way that belongs to the lesser-known themes of the Sumerian Gilgameš texts. More important is, however, line 11, comparing Gilgameš to Ziusudra, who obtained the eternal life that Gilgameš sought in vain.[38]

Therefore, the tone of the following lines (16–17) of *The Ballade of Early Rulers* is by no means coincidental. These recur later in the Akkadian so-called *Dialogue of Pessimism*, (BWL 139–149, ll. 83–84): *a-a-ú ar-ku šá a-na šamê^e e-lu-ú a-a-ú rap-šú šá erṣetim^tim ú-gam-me-ru*, "Who is so tall as to ascend to the heavens? Who is so broad as to encompass the underworld?" The tone is very similar to our text.[39] These lines are quoted also in the OB *Gilgameš Epic* III iv 3. A Sumerian form is quoted in *Gilgameš and Huwawa* 28–29, in which it refers to the futility of Gilgameš' ambitions, when he seeks to establish an eternal renown by defeating Huwawa, the guardian of the cedar forest. In other words, these were ambitions on a minor scale, but similar, to those of the Akkadian *Gilgameš Epic*.

Sumerian forms of these lines are cited also,

35. Implying perhaps, but not necessarily: "drink!" as the Syro-Mesopotamian version spells it out.
36. J.H. Tigay: "On Evaluating Claims of Literary Borrowing," in: *Hallo FS*, 250–258, points out (p. 252), quoting Gordis, 1968, 304, that the claim that the *carpe diem* passage of Eccl 9: 7–9 is inspired by the *Gilgameš Epic* is based on the order in which some elements occur, such as eating, rejoicing, fresh clothing, …, loving one's wife, which are much too general, even in Egyptian literature, to warrant the conclusion that they owe their existence to a literary borrowing.
37. For an early attempt, which could now be much refined, to deal with this, see Alster: "Paradoxical Proverbs and Satire in Sumerian Literature," JCS 27 (1975) 210–230. Cf. the *Introduction* to the present volume, n. 30, and the literature there cited. Cf. also Lambert, 1995, 32, who points to a common Sumerian personal name Mir-šà-kúšu, "Savage-relenting," attested in several Ur III sources, also discussed in the *Introduction* to this volume, above (p. 23, n. 31).
38. This seems to set a relatively late *ante quem* date for the text, maybe sometime during the Hammurapi dynasty, not later than Abī-ešuḫ, who is mentioned on the Sumerian *Sammeltafel* on which the text was inscribed. A single relatively "late" grammatical feature in the Sumerian text seems to corroborate this impression: line 19: [a]-ba-àm, "what?" non-personal, instead of *a-na-àm.
39. The interpretation of the *Akkadian Dialogue of Pessimism* is much disputed, but in view of the similarity in tone with the texts discussed here, there is every reason to appreciate it as a seriously meant humorous discussion, not simply a seriously meant pessimistic discussion. Cf. Lambert, 1995, 36, who, referring to Theophrastus' *Characters* and Thackeray's *Book of Snobs*, seems to have modified his earlier view.

though somewhat expanded, as SP 17 Sec. B 2: [suk]ud-dè an-na šu nu-um-[da-lá] [daŋa]l-e ki-a nu-um-ma-an-íl-íl [kal]a-ga ki-ná ní nu-mu-un-gíd-dè [za]-⌜e⌝-me-en u_4-gim dug_4-dug_4-ga piriŋ-gim ne ḫé-gub [š]à(?)-zu ᵍⁱˢkiri$_6$-a ḫé-eb(?)-gub lú nam-bí-ib-til-e, "even the tallest one cannot reach the heavens, even the broadest one cannot lift(?) the earth. Even the strongest one cannot stretch himself (fully) out in bed. [You(?)] are one who, when he roared like the storm, position himself like a lion. Your ...(?) was positioned in a garden! No man should bring about an end."[40] This occurs, slightly differently, also as SP 22 vi 38–48.[41] Although the details are far from clear, the ironic tone, sounding like a mock royal hymn, has already been noted.[42] It has long ago been noted that this set of proverbial phrases touches the tone of biblical wisdom.[43]

Other lines also recurring in *Nothing Is of Value* (*Níŋ-nam nu-kal*) affect the interpretation of our text in a most decisive way.

Line 6: "Above is his elevated house, below is his everlasting house," implying: "they are all dead," is remarkably included in *Níŋ-nam nu-kal*, version C line 5: ⌜an-ta⌝ é-ùr-ra-ni ki-ta é du-⌜rí(!)⌝-šè (cf. *Chap. 3.3a* for variants). Since this is inscribed on the very same *Sammeltafel* as *The Ballade of Early Rulers*, the allusion cannot be a mere coincidence. The line is included also in the long 3N-T 360 version D, lines 5–6, of *Níŋ-nam nu-kal* (col. viii 1–4): ⌜an-ta-àm⌝ é-ur$_5$-ra-ka-ni ki(?)-ta-àm é da-rí-ka-ni (cf. *Chap. 3.2*).[44]

Line 21 further quotes or hints at *Níŋ-nam*, Version C 8: níŋ-⌜x⌝(= sa$_6$?)-ga diŋir-re-e-ne bí-in-šúm-[m]a-re(?).[45] This may help considerably in understanding crucial final lines of *The Ballade of Early Rulers*. The initial signs in the second, indented, part of the line were restored as [zi-u_4-sud-r]a-ra by Alster, 1986 and 1990. This is clearly unsatisfactory,[46] but it was, nevertheless, a definite step in the right direction. We can now safely restore ⌜ú⌝-gu$_7$-gu$_7$(-ra), "for the food provider," and this is not meant as a kind of staple food, but rather as *ambrosia* and *nectar*, as indicated by a parallel in a royal hymn to Marduk inscribed on the same *Sammeltafel*.

The reason for the allusion to Ziusudra, already mentioned in line 11, is evident. It was he who obtained the eternal life that Gilgameš sought in vain. So we expect another person in Ziusudra's place who can obtain on a minor scale what Ziusudra did on the larger, mythological, scale. Who is he? A cupbearer at a joyous banquet is a good guess![47] If we combine this with what we know from the Syro-Mesopotamian version, that that person is advised to find happiness in alcohol (Syr. 23), with what we know from SS 22, that is, that this takes place in the "house of youthful men," then it is obvious that the happy days of youth are praised in a way that is reminiscent of Qoheleth. In other words, the young man might well be a bachelor of a scribal school who is advised to enjoy a good drink, although that latter point is spelled out expressly only in the Syro-Mesopotamian version.

Conclusion

This leads to the inevitable conclusion that Wilcke's "Studentenlied" might, after all, come close to the mark. One might object that a student song is

40. Alster: *Proverbs* I, 238. Slightly modified translation. The Atlas motif occurs also in SP 4.4.
41. Alster, *Proverbs* I, 266.
42. Alster, *Proverbs* II, 436, tentatively understood this as a "mock laudatory royal hymn."
43. Cf. Alster, *Proverbs* II, 436, giving references to Hallo, in: *Studies Moran*, 216, and a number of literary references, among these Job 11:18: "Higher than heaven—what can you do? Deeper than *sheol*—what can you know?" Cf. *The Ballade of Early Rulers* 17.
44. The interpretation was anticipated by Alster, 1990, 24, and later reached by means of the parallels cited here from *Níŋ-nam*, but reached independently by Klein, 2000, 211. Cf. also Eccl 12:5: for a man is on the way to his "long-lasting house," meaning, his life is approaching its end.
45. Cf. also line 6 of the same composition. This was disregarded by Klein, 2000, 210, but anticipated by Alster, 1990, 25, who correctly referred to this parallel. The reading of the two first signs is reasonably certain. The final -re seems to be a rudiment of the dative -ra, indicating an unfinished quotation; cf. photos pls. 31–32.
46. But not because of the spacing, which Klein, 2000, 212, saw as a problem.
47. See the detailed discussion in the commentary on Syr. 23 in *Chap. 3.3b*.

unlikely to deal with "wisdom," and if, indeed, it does, it should definitely not do so in humorous terms. Nevertheless, this is precisely what the text is about, the humorous play with literary allusions in a joyous academic society.

It is wise to keep in mind that if there had been no students in the Sumerian scribal schools, we would know nothing about Sumerian wisdom. That would be a shame, since it was found worthy of being echoed in Qoheleth, one of the great literary creations of the ancient world.

The conclusions that can deduced from our seemingly modest 22-line composition have amazing consequences for the literary history of the ancient Near East. It should now be clear that the spiritual atmosphere of Qoheleth was not inspired by Greek influence alone. The inspiration came, at least in part, from Sumerian texts of the early second millennium B.C. So far one would have thought that the most likely channel through which they might have passed to the biblical world is through the Syro-Mesopotamian area of the late Bronze Age (thirteenth century B.C.). We can now dismiss that possibility, because the scribes of that area evidently had so many difficulties in coping with the original sources that they were unable to understand them fully, or even seriously misunderstood crucial points. So the transmission is more likely to have happened much later, during the exile through learned circles in Babylon itself.

The Contents of the Sammeltafel

In the 1990 edition I included four compositions inscribed in the same order on two or three *Sammeltafel.*[48] These were preliminarily numbered compositions 1–4 and can now be identified as:

No. 1. Blessing of a king, now titled *Hymn to Marduk for a King.*
No. 2. Poem of Abī-ešuḫ, now titled *Hymn to Abī-ešuḫ B.*[49]
No. 3. *Níŋ-nam nu-kal*, version C, edited here in *Chap. 3.1.*
No. 4. The Poem of Early Rulers, now titled *The Ballade of Early Rulers*, edited below.

In line with the general approach in the present volume, an attempt was made to account for the contents of all relevant compositions that occur on the same *Sammeltafel.* The point that can be made in this case seems to be that ideas related to the concept of the brevity of life and the possibility of obtaining more lasting possibilities, be it for a king, whether legendary or not, or for ordinary humans, were a common concern in all these texts.

48. Dietrich, 1992, 10, cf. pp. 23 and 25, understood my 1990 edition as if I intended to provide evidence ("Beweis") that the Sumerian version of *The Ballade of Early Rulers* was part of a prayer hymn to a king, possibly Abī-ešuḫ of Babylon, or that it was a forerunner ("Vorlage") of the Emar version; also on p. 25 ("Ob diese nach B. Alster allerdings so zu verstehen ist, daß hier etwa ein sumerisches Königslied aus Sippar umgearbeitet wurde"). This was never my intention. I simply edited the texts present on the same tablets because it was an edition of those *Sammeltafel.* This had the extra advantage that it facilitated the study of their possible thematic relations, yet, without necessarily implying anything with regard to their origin. Cf. p. 226, *Chap. 2.1: Excursus on Sammeltafel.*

If one of the texts was derived from the other, it would rather have been the relatively late hymns from the first dynasty of Babylon that in this case were influenced by some notions relating to "wisdom," which may, or may not, at that time have been felt as innovative. This also applies to the ambrosia-nectar motif (present in Marduk hymn l. 21), the *Ziusudra* theme, both present in *The Ballade of Early Rulers* (l. 21), *The Sumerian King List*, and *The Instructions of Šuruppak*, possibly already in the ED versions, although the name itself does not occur there (cf. *Chap. 1.4*, commentary on ll. 5–6).

On p. 25, Dietrich discusses the relation to the Siduri-episode of the *Gilgameš Epic*, and, undoubtedly correctly, underscores the similarity with our text, but note that it is the *combination* of this existential attitude with other older themes relating to "vanity" that creates its special character.

49. *Abī-ešuḫ Hymn A* is the text published by van Dijk, "L'hymne à Marduk avec intercession pour le roi Abi'eshuh," *Mitteilungen des Instituts für Orientforschung* 12 (1966–67) 57–74 (pp. 66–74).

Sources

On the Reconstruction of the Beginning of the SS Version and Two Sets of Line Numbers

In the edition of the SS version presented below, the first six lines are tentatively restored and marked with an asterisk*. These restorations were based on the Syro-Mesopotamian sources, in as far as it could be established with a reasonable degree of certainty what Standard Sumerian text lay behind the preserved Syro-Mesopotamian version. There is no reason to assume that the SS text had a fundamentally different introduction, especially since the Syro-Mesopotamian introduction seems to rest on older Babylonian textual evidence, which evidently presented insurmountable difficulties to the Ugaritic and Emar scribes.[50]

In order to avoid unnecessary confusion, I have used two sets of line numbers, one for the Standard Sumerian version (*Chap. 3.3a*) and one for the Syro-Mesopotamian version (*Chap. 3.3b*), but with cross-references from the one to the other.

Standard Sumerian Sources:- All Sammeltafel

Only the lines belonging to *The Ballade of Early Rulers* are mentioned below. For more details about the other compositions grouped together with it, see the complete publication of the *Sammeltafel* by Alster, 1990.

A: BM 80091. Copy by Ulla Jeyes, pl. 70 (previously AcSum 8 [1986] 10–11). Fragment from a two-column tablet with a small part of the upper edge preserved. There is a double ruler line after rev. ii followed by a blank space, indicating the end of *The Ballade of Early Rulers*. The length of the columns seems to have been about 18 lines.

Rev. ii = SS 18–22.

B: BM 80184. Copy CT 44, no. 18. Fragment from the reverse of a two-column tablet with no edges preserved. There is a double ruler line after rev. ii followed by a blank space, indicating the end of *The Ballade of Early Rulers*.

The length of the columns must have been over 33 lines.

Rev. ii = SS 7–22.

D: CBS 1208 (possibly from Sippar or Babylon, not a Nippur text). Two-column tablet with parts of the upper and left edges preserved.

First published in complete transliteration in OLP 21. Photographs by K. Danti and E. Robson are provided here pls. 31–32.

The length of the columns must have been about 24 lines.

Rev. ii = SS 19–22.

Syro-Mesopotamian Sources

See the detailed description by Dietrich, 1992, 11–13.

E: *Emar* VI/4, 359–365: *Emar* VI/1–2, 316: covers (numbering in Syr. vers.): Syr. 1–24, but omits SS 21–22.

SS correspondences (SS numbers): 74123x (SS 13–13 A (= Syr. 16)) + p. 32: 74127ac + 74128x + 74136b (obv. = SS 7–12, rev. = SS 13–20) + p. 339: 74132t (= SS 9–13) + 346: 74137m (= SS 6, plus SS 16–18) + p. 385f: 74153 (= SS 1–6, plus SS 16–18) + p. 676: 74344 (= SS 7–12).

50. In the reconstruction presented in the 1990 edition, a lacuna of five lines was estimated between compositions 3:8 and 4:1. This was thought to be too short for the six-line Emar introduction that would have been required if the SS version had included approximately the same introduction. Cf. Alster, 1990, 7: "This hardly leaves room ... for the 6 line Emar introduction (4:1–6)"), and Black, [1995]. These reservations can now safely be set aside. The decisive point is that 3:8 = CBS 1208 rev. i 17 is, in fact, likely to represent the very end of version C of *Níŋ-nam nu-kal* (cf. *Chap. 3.1*), which thus was considerably shorter than hitherto assumed, and the gap, therefore, nearly as precisely as one could wish has the size that would fit the expected introduction.

E is a six-column tablet with the Sumerian text in col. i, a syllabic version of the same text in col. ii, and the Akkadian translation in col. iii. It corresponds to SS 1–6 plus SS 16–18, 7–15, 19–22.

Ua: J. Nougayrol, *Ugaritica* 5 (Paris, 1968), 164 (p. 438), R.S.25.130.

Covers (numbering in Syr. vers.): Syr. 1–3; 7–9; 15; (16 om.); 17–19; (20–21 om.); 22.

Description with SS correspondences: Ua obv. 1–17 is a bilingual version of SS 13–20. Obv. 18–23 is a bilingual version of Syr. 1–3 (= *SS 1–3). (Rev.) 24–39 is a bilingual collection of sayings (cf. J. Nougayrol, in: *Ugaritica* 5, 294–295), edited here in *Chap. 3.4: Proverbs from Ugarit*) (for further details see Dietrich, 1992, 28–29). (Rev.) 40–44 is a repetition of Syr. 1–3 (= *SS 1–3); cf. the description of Uc below.

Ub: J. Nougayrol, *Ugaritica* 5, 165 (p. 439), R.S.23. 34 (+) 23.484 + 23.363.

Covers (numbering in Syr. vers): Syr. 1–9; 18–24 (SS 21–22 omitted).

Description with SS correspondences: Ub is a two-column tablet with the Sumerian text in obv. i and rev. i, and the Akkadian text in obv. ii and rev. ii. Obv.(!) = lines [SS] 1–6; 16–18. Rev.(!) = lines 15–22, plus colophon.

Uc: J. Nougayrol, *Ugaritica* 5, 166 (p. 440), R.S.25. 24.

Covers (numbering in Syr. vers.): Syr. 2–7; 22 A; 23–24.

Uc is a fragment of a tablet similar to Ub. Only part of the Akkadian column, obv. and rev., is preserved. It is tempting to suggest that Uc is part of the same tablet as Ub. This would imply that Syr. 22 Aff. = Syr. 19 were included twice, but is not unlikely in view of the NA version, which repeats the introductory lines as a refrain; this may also explain the repetition in Ua.

Description with SS correspondences: Obv. = SS *2–6, plus SS 16. Rev. = SS 22 A, 23–24 (SS 21–22 omitted).

Neo-Assyrian Sources

Neo-Assyrian: K.6917 + 13679: Cf. Lambert, 1995, 38: identified and joined by R. Borger. Edited in *Chap. 3.3c: The Neo-Assyrian Version*, and published on pl. 16 in M.J. Geller's hand copy. The fragment comes from a carefully written tablet, see the description under *Chap. 3.3c*.

3.3a The Standard Sumerian Version

The Standard Sumerian text is marked with an asterisk⋆ when tentatively reconstructed from the Syro-Mesopotamian sources.

Note different line order in E and Ua, Ub, and Uc: 1–6 (6 lines introduction), 16, 17, 18, 7, 9, 10, 11, 12, 13, 13 A (Emar), 14, 15, 19, 19 A, 19 B, 20, 20 A, 21, 22.

⋆1 (= Syr. 1)

⋆ki ^{d}en-ki-ke$_4$ ŋiš-ḫur ḫur-ḫur-re
⋆*it-ti* ^{d}*é-a uṣ-ṣu-ra-m[a(?) u]ṣ-ṣu-ra-tum*

(1) ⋆With Enki the plans are drawn:

E	i 1	[ki ^{d}en-ki-ke$_4$ ŋiš-ḫu]r-ḫur-re
	ii	= ki [e]n-ki-ik-ki ki-iš-ḫur ḫu-re
	iii	= [*i*]*t-ti* ^{d}*é-a u*[*ṣ* - …]
Ua	18	ki ^{d}en-ki-ke$_4$ ŋiš-[ḫu]r ḫur-ḫur-re
	19	= *it-ti* ^{d}*é-a uṣ-ṣu-ra-m*[*a*(?) *u*]*ṣ-ṣu-ra-tum*
	40	ki ^{d}en-ki-ke$_4$ ŋiš-ḫur [ḫu]r-[ḫu]r-re
	41	= *it-ti* ^{d}*é-a uṣ-ṣu-r*[*a-* …]
Ub o 1		x […]
		[…] ⸢^{d}⸣*é-*[*a* …] / [*u*]*ṣ*(?)*-re-*[…]

⋆2 (= Syr. 2)

⋆ dima diŋir-re-e-ne-ke$_4$ ki nam-sur-[sur]-re
⋆ [*i*]*-na ṭè-em* DINGIR*-ma us-*<*su*>*-qa us-qé-*[*e*]*-tu*

(2) ⋆According to the decisions of the gods lots are allotted.

E	i 2	[dima diŋir-re-e-ne-k]e$_4$ ki nam-sur-sur-re
	ii	= te-em-ma ti-gi-re-e-né ki nam-sur-šu-re
	iii	= *a-na ṭe$_4$-em* DINGIR*-lim-m*[*a* …]
Ua	20	dima(KA.DÙG) diŋir-re-e-ne-ke$_4$ ki gal nam(!)-sur-[sur]-re
	21	= [*i*]*-na ṭè-em* DINGIR*-ma us-*<*su*>*-qa us-qé-*[*e*]*-tu*
	42	= dima diŋir-re-e-ne-ke$_4$ […]
	43	= *i-na ṭe-em* DINGIR*-ma* […]
Ub	o 2	te-x[…] / sur […]
		= [… *ṭ*]*e-e-i-i*[*m* …]
Uc	o 1	[… *-k*]*u-nu us-q*[*è-* …]

⋆3 (= Syr. 3)

⋆ ⸢u$_4$-da⸣-ta im al-ŋál-la
⋆ [*i*]*š-tu u$_4$-mi pa-na-*⸢*a*⸣*-ma ip-pa-á*[*š*(?) *ša-ru*]

(3) ⋆Since time immemorial there has been [wi]nd! (based on Ua)

E	i 3	[…] NI ŋál-la
	ii	= u-du i-gi-du-uṭ-ṭu i-nim NI ig-ŋál-l[a]
	iii	= [*i*]*š-tu u$_4$-mi pa-na-*⸢*a*⸣*-ma*
Ua	o 22	[u$_4$-d]a(?)-ta im al-ŋál-la
	23	= […] *x x i-ba-áš-ša-a-an-n*[*i* (*x*) *ša*]*-ru*
Ua	o 44	⸢u$_4$-da-ta⸣ im […]
Ub	o 3	ú-tu ⸢x x⸣ […]
Uc	o 2	= [*iš-tu*] *u$_4$-mi pa-na-nu ip-pa-á*[*š*(?) *ša-ru*]

***4 (= Syr. 4)**

* me-na-*àm(?) ka lú-igi-du-*ka-né ŋiš la-ba-an-tuku
* *im-m[a-t]i-me-e i-na pí-i a-l[ik pa-ni] / ul [té]š-mi*

E	i 4	[...] igi-du-a-ni / [x x]x a
	ii	= me-na-a ka lu i-gi-du-ga-an-ni / ki-iš la-ba-an-tu-ka(!?)-a
	iii	= *im-m[a-t]i-me-e i-na pí-i a-l[ik pa-ni] / ul [té]š-mi*
Ub	o 4	me-e-tum ka lu [...] / ki-iš LÀḪ-ba-an-t[u ...]
Uc	o 3	[...]*x-a i-na pí-i a-lik pa-ni-x* / ˹*x te*˺*-iš-mi* [(*x*)]

(4) *Has there ever been a time when one did not hear this from the mouth of one's predecessor?

***5 (= Syr. 5)**

* diri *e(?)-ne-ne * lugal-bi [...]
* = [*e-l*]*i-šu-nu šu-nu-ma* [*šarrū*(?)] *šu-nu ša-nu-tu-ma*

E	i 5	[x x] ˹e˺-ne ˹lu˺(?)-[gal(?)-bi] / [x x g]a-ki-e-ne
	ii	= [x] ˹a˺-ia-na-an-ni lu-gal-bi / [x]-ga-ki [x x a]n-ni [x x]
	iii	= [...]*-ši-na ši-na-m*[*a* ...] / [*x x*]*x ša-an-nu x* [*x x*]
Ub	o 5	diri-NI-in-né lu-gal-bi x [x x] / in-ni x[...]
Uc	o 4	= [*e-l*]*i-šu-nu šu-nu-ma* / [(*x*)] *šu-nu ša-nu-tu-ma*

(5) *Above them were those (scl. kings), (and above) those kings were others.

(Uc:) (They were above them, they were different.)

***6 (= Syr. 6)**

* an-ta é ùr-ra-*ke$_4$-ne-ne ki-ta é-da-rí-*ke$_4$-ne-ne
= * *elēnum bīt ašābišunu šaplānum bīt darûtišunu*

E	i 6	[an-ta] é ùr-ra-ke$_4$-e-ne / [ki-ta] ˹é˺-da-rí-ki-e-ne
	ii	= [a]n-ta e-ur-ra-ki-[...] / [ki-ta] e-da-ra-ga-an-n[i ...]
	iii	= [...] ˹a˺-ša(?)-[...] / [...] x x [...]
Ub	o 6	[a]n-ta e-ur-ra-ga-an-ni [x x]
Uc	o 5	[... g]a-an(!)-ni
		= *e-*[*l*]*e-nu* É *a-*˹*ša*˺*-bi-*[*šu-nu šaplānum* É *da-ru-ti-šu-nu*]

(6) *Above (are) the houses where they lived, [below (are)] their everlasting houses. [i.e., they are all dead!]

7 (cf. Syr. 10)

B		[...] x li-bí-in-dù-a
E	i 10	[...]
	ii	= nam-ti nam-lu-˹u$_{18}$˺-[lu] / u$_4$-da-ri-iš nu-ni-˹x˺-[...]
	iii	= [*ba-la-aṭ a-mi-l*]*u-ut-ti* [...] / [...] *ú-ul i-*[...]

(7) [The houses(?) (or similar) of those kings] were not built (scl. to last for ever).

8 (Syr. om.)

B		[...] x-àm lú-bé-ne šu bal-ak-a
E		*omits*

(8) ... those men were overthrown.

9 (Syr. 11)

B		[me-a ^{m}a-lu-lu lu]gal-e mu 3600×10-àm in-ak
E	i 11	[... -i]a-ka :
	ii	= me-e ^{m}a-lu-lu m[u ...]
	iii	= [*a-l*]*e-e* ^{m}*a-lu-lu* [...]

(9) Where is Alulu, the king who reigned 36,000 years?

10 = Syr. 12

B [me-a ⋆e-ta-na lu]gal-e lú an-šè bí-in-è-dè

E i 12 [me]-e ^{m}en-te-n[a …]-⸢e$_{11}$⸣-e-dè
ii = me-e ^{m}en-t[e …] x x
iii = *a-⸢le-e⸣ ^{m}[x] x ša* […]

(10) Where is Entena (= Etana) the king, the man who ascended to heaven?

11 = Syr. 13

B [me-a ^{m}bìl-ga-meš z]i-u$_4$-sud-rá-gim nam-ti ì-kiŋ-kiŋ

E i 13 [me]-e ^{md}ŋiš-kin(!)-m[aš …] /
[… -gi]m nam-ti-la kin-[…]
ii me-e ^{md}ki-iš-mas-su […]-ki nam-ti-la k[i(?) …]
iii = *a-le-e*(?) ^{m}*gil-[ga-meš š]a k[i-ma zi-u$_4$-sù]- /*
ud-ra na-pu-u[l-t]a [išteʾʾû]

(11) Where is Gilgameš, who, like Ziusudra, sought the (eternal) life?

12 = Syr. 14

B [me-a ^{m}ḫu-wa-wa (…) ki] ba-an-za-za dab$_5$(?)-ba(?)-ta

E i 14 [me]-e ^{m}ḫu-wa-wa […] / [x z]a-da mu-x-[…]
ii = me-e ^{m}ḫ[u-wa-wa …] / [x] x x […]
iii = ⸢*a-le-e*⸣ ^{m}*ḫu-[wa-wa* …] / [… -*t*]*i*(?) *i-na* […]

(12) Where is Huwawa, who was caught in submission?

13 = Syr. 15

B [me-a ^{m}en-ki-dù nam-kalag-ga-ni kal]am(?)-ma(?) nu(?)-dar-ra-ke$_4$

E i 15 [me-e] ^{m}en-k[i-dù …] / […]-ta mu-[…]
ii [me-e ^{m}e]n-ki-dù nam-ka-lag-[x] /
= [x x x(?) mu-u]n-na-an-te
iii = [*a*]*-le-e* ^{m}*en-ki-du / ša da-an-nu-ti i-na* KUR-*ti ú*-[…]

Ua 1' [x x] x x […]
2' = […] ^{d}*en-ki-dù š*[*a* …]

(13) Where is Enkidu, whose strength was not defeated(?) in the country?

(Akk. version:) who made (his) strength [manifest] in the country).

(Syr. 16)

E i 16 [me-e ^{m}ba-z]i me-e [^{m}z]i-[zi]
ii = me-e ^{m}ba-[z]i me-e ^{m}zi-zi
iii = *a-le-e* ^{m}*ba-zi a-le-e* ^{m}*zi-[zi]*

14 = Syr. 17

B [me-a lu]gal-e-ne dub-saŋ / u$_4$-ul-lí-a-ke$_4$-ne

E i 17 [me-e … luga]l(!) gal-e-ne / […] x-e-ne e-še-ta
ii me-e lu-gal gal-e-né / ú-sa(?)-ŋá-ta-e-né e-še-ta
iii = *a-le-e šar-ra-nu ra-ab-bu-[tum] /*
ša iš-tu u$_4$-mi pa-na-a a-di i-na-a[n-na]

Ua 3' m[e-e]n ì-tí-eš lugal gal-gal-e-[…]
4' = *a-li-šu-nu-ti* LUGAL^{meš} […]

(14) Where are those kings, the vanguards of former days?

15 = Syr. 18

B [nu-un-peš$_4$-peš$_4$]-⌜a⌝ nu-un-tu-ud-da

(15) They are no longer engendered, they are no longer born.

E i 18 [...] nu-tu-tu-men$_5$
ii = nu-peš-ša-me-en nu-da-da-am-m[e-en]
iii = *ul in-né-ru-ma ul im-m[a-al-la-du]*
Ua 5' nu-peš-peš-e-ne nu-tu-t[u- ...]
6' = *ul in-né-ru-ú* [(*x*)] *ul* [...]
Ub iv 1 [*ú*]-*ul in*(?)-[...] *ú-ul im-m*[*a-al-la-du*]

16 = Syr. 7

B [an sù-ud-da-gi]m šu-ŋu$_{10}$ sá bí-in-dug$_4$-ga

(16) Like the remote heavens, has my hand ever reached them?

NB Note that 16–18 are placed forward in E, following line 6.

E i 7 [... -u]d-da-gim(!) šu-ti n[am(?)-x x (x) :]
ii = an ša-ut-ta-ki-im šu-ti n[am- ...]
iii = [... *i*]-*ka-aš-šu-ud* (rev. 23)
Ua 7' an sù-ud-gim šu-t[i(?) x] zu AN [...]
8' = *ki-ma šamû*^{u} *ru-qu-ma* ŠU x x AB [...]
Ub i 11 [a]n šu(!)-ut-ta-k[i- ...]
Uc 6 [... *š*]*a-mu-ú ru-qu-ma x x* /
[*qa-t*]*i ma-am-ma i-kaš-ša*[*d*]

17 = Syr. 8

B [ki bùru-da-gim] na-me nu-mu-un-zu-a

(17) Like the deep underworld (lit., earth), no one knows them.

E i 8 [...]-bi me-na nu-un-[...]
ii = [...] na-me nu-un-zu-wa-a
Ua 9' ki bùru-da-gim na-me nu-zu-[...]
10' = *ki-ma šu-pu-ul er-ṣe-ti mim-ma la i-du-ú*
Ub i 12 [ki b]u-ut-ta [...]

18 = Syr. 9

A [...]-a-bi [...]
B [nam-ti-la dù-a-bi (x)] x igi-níŋin-na-kam

(18) All life is an illusion.

E i 9 [(x)] nam-t[i- ...]
E ii = [...] x -ni-ik-k[i ...]
Ua 11 nam-ti-la dù-a-bi x x igi-niŋin-na-kam
12 = *ba-la-ṭa ka-la-šu* [*b*]*a*(?)-*ri tu-ur-ti i-ni-im-ma*
Ub i 13 [... -t]i(?)-lu [...]

19 = Syr. 19

A [nam-ti n]u-zala-ga [ugu nam-úš-a-kam] /
[a]-ba-àm bí-[in-diri-ga]
B [nam-ti n]u-zala-ga] ugu nam-úš-a-kam /
[a]-ba-àm bí-in-diri-ga
D [...] x GIŠ.KA-àm

(19) Life onto which no light is shed, how can it be more valuable than death?

E	i 19	[na]m-t[i nu-za]la-ga (blank) /
		[ugu]-nam-ú[š-(a)] ta-àm me-diri
	ii	= nam-ti nu-za-la-aq-qa /
		u-ga na-ma-uš-ta ta-àm-me-d[a-ri]
	iii	= *[ba-l]a-aṭ ša la-a na-ma-ri /*
		[a-na m]u-ti me-na-a ut-ti-i[r]
Ua	12	nam-ti-la níŋ-zala-ga nu-me-a
	13	= ugu nam-úš-a a-na-àm mi-ni-diri
		= *ba-la-ṭa ša la na-ma-ri a-na mi-ti mi-na-a ut-tir*
Ub	iv 2	*ba-la-aṭ š[a ...]*

(Syr. 20)

E	i 20	[ŋuruš] diŋir-zu šu-zi-bi-šè ga-ra-an-zu
	ii	= ku-ru-uš ti-kar-zu šu-zi-peš-še ga-r[a-zu]
	iii	= *[eṭ-l]u ša il-ka ki-ni-iš l[u- ...]*
Ub	iii 3	ŋu-ru-uš [...]-še / ga-la-[...]
	iv 3	= *eṭ-lu ⸢il-ka⸣ [x] x [...]*

(Syr. 21)

E	i 21	[is]iš sí-ki-ib-ta ša-ra / [l]u-ul-bi ù-la mu-un-na-ka
	ii	= [is]iš sí-ki-ip-ta ša-ra / lu-ul-bi ù-la mu-un-na-ak-ki
	iii	= *sí-ki[p ku]-uš-ši-id [(x)]*
		ni-is-sà-a-[ti mi-iš qu-l[a-ti]
Ub	iii 4	a-li-im sí-[x x]-ti ša-ra /
		lu-ul-bi ù-[...-u]n-na-ak(?)-ke(?)
	iv 4	= *sí-ki-ip ku-uš-ši-id [(x)] / ni-is-sà-ti mi-iš qu-la-ti*

20 = Syr. 22

(20) Instead of one day of joy, 36,000 years of silence reigned!

A		[níŋ-saŋ-í]l-la u_4 šà-ḫúl-la ⸢x⸣ /
		níŋ-me-ŋar mu 3600×10-àm in-ak
B		[... -l]a u_4 šà-ḫúl-la 1-àm /
		[ní]ŋ-me-ŋar mu 3600×10-àm in-ak
D		[...] 3600×10-àm in(?)-ak
E	i 22	[...]-⸢íl(!)-⸢la⸣(!) u_4 šà-ḫúl(!)-lá /
		[lu-u]l-bi ù-šèr-šèr ḫé-en-du
	ii	= sà-an-ki-el-la ù-ša-ḫu-la-al
		lu-ul-bi ù-šar-šar ḫé-en-du
	iii	= *di-na-nu [ša ḫ]u-ud lìb-b[i] /*
		1-en u_4-m[u] 10 ša-r[u ...]
Ua	13	níŋ-saŋ-íl-la šà-ḫúl-la [u_4] ⸢diš⸣-kam u_4-im-ba-kam mu
		10 šár ḫul in-na-ak
		= *a-na di-na-an ḫu-ud lìb-bi [ša] u_4-um-ak-kal u_4-um*
		qu-li 10 ŠÁR MU.MEŠ *lil-li-ka*
Ub	iii 5	saŋ-ki-il-la [...] ḫu-ul-la /
		ú-⸢lu⸣-ul-bi [...] ḫi-in-du
	iv 5	= *a-na ⸢di⸣-na-ni u_4-mi ḫu-ud [...] /*
		1 U_4 *qú-li ⸢e⸣-še-re-et ša-a-r[u ...]*

(Syr. 22 A, and only Ub and Uc; cf. SS 19 = Syr. 19)

Ub iii 6 nam-ti nu-x[...] ⌜ZI⌝-TA TA-A / mi x ru x [...]x x
iv 6 = *ba-la-ṭu ša la-a na-ma-[ri]* / UGU *mu-ti mi-na [ut-tir]*
Uc r 1 [...] *la-a na(!)-[...]* / [...]*-ti mi-na-am ut-tir*

21 (replaced by Syr. 23)

A [níŋ-sa$_6$(?)-ga] diŋir-re-e-ne bí-in-šúm-ma-àm / [...]-⌜gu$_7$(?)⌝-ra nam-ti ì-kiŋ-kiŋ
B [níŋ-sa$_6$(?)-ga diŋir]-re-e-ne bí-in-šúm-ma-àm / [...] x(could be g]u$_7$) nam-ti ì-kiŋ-kiŋ
D [níŋ-sa$_6$(?)-ga diŋir-r]e-e-ne bí-in-šúm-ma-àm / ⌜ú⌝-⌜gu$_7$-gu$_7$⌝ nam-ti ì-kiŋ-kiŋ

(21) For him who gives [the good things of] the gods, the ⌜food⌝ provider, life is found!

Níŋ-nam Vers. C:
C:7 = *Line 7*
CBS 1208:16 ⌜ú⌝ [...] ⌜diŋir⌝-re-e-ne bí-in-šúm-⌜ma(?)⌝
C:8 = *Line 8*
CBS 1208:17 níŋ-⌜sa$_6$⌝-ga diŋir-re-e-ne bí-in-šúm-⌜ma(?)⌝-re

22 replaced by Syr. 23

A [e(?)-ne(?)] x ⌜ḫa⌝-la lú-u$_{18}$-lu-kam / [...] x ŋuruš-ke$_4$
B [e(?)-ne(?)] ḫa-la lú-u$_{18}$-lu-kam / [...] ti-a é ŋuruš-ke$_4$
D [e(?)-ne(?) ...] x ti-a é-[ŋuruš]-ke$_4$

(22) [This is] the share of men [who] live in the house of the young men!

Syr. 23

E i 23 [n]i-in-gim(?!) lu-ú tur-ra-bi / [s]í-ra-aš ḫi-li ma-an-zu
ii = ni-in-ki lu-ú-tu-ur-ra-bi / sí-ra-aš ḫi-li ma-an-zu
iii = *ki-i-ma ma-ri* [...] / *li-ri-iš-ka* [(*x*)]
Ub iii 7 ni-[i]n-gu [...] x x / ḫi-x x [...]
iv 7 = ⌜*dsí-ra*⌝*-[aš] ki-[ma* ...] / *li-ri-iš-[ka* (...)]
Uc r 3 [...] *ki-i(!)-ma ma-a-ri* / *[li-ri-i]š-ka*

Syr. 24 (Only Syr. 24)

E i 24 ⌜e⌝-ne ŋiš-ḫur / nam-u$_{18}$-lu gi-na
ii = e-en-ni ki-iš-ḫu-ur / [nam-l]u-ul-lu gi-na
iii = *an-nu-um ú-ṣ[u-ur-tum]* / *ša a-mi-lu-ut-t[i* (*x*)]
Ub iii 8 ⌜en-ni⌝ ⌜gi-eš⌝-[...] nam-u$_{18}$-lu-lu / ki-i[n-na]
iv 8 = *[an]-nu-um-ma i-ṣ[u-ur-tum]* / *š[a] a-mi-lu-ut-ti* [(*x*)]
Uc r 5 *[an-nu-u]m i-ṣu-ur-tum* / *[ša a-mi-l]u-ut-ti*

Comments on Individual Lines

The following comments include the Ugarit-Emar versions lines 1–6, because, as stated in the introduction (*Chap. 3.3: Sources*, n. 50), there are good reasons to believe that these can legitimately be used to restore the missing introductory lines in the SS version. Comments specifically relating to the Syro-Mesopotamian version are found in *Chap. 3.3b*, but many interesting variants pertaining to the reading of the Sumerian text are included here. In order to give the best overview, the full text of both versions is included here as a textual apparatus in the "score" format.

SS 1 (restored from Syr.): Many phonetic writings show that the Syrian scribes were unfamiliar with the Sum. phoneme /ŋ/, and generally intermingled the voiced and the unvoiced stops.

The writing ki-iš-ḫur (E ii 1), with the unvoiced /k/ instead of the voiced /g/, coincides with e-ur-ra-ga-an-ni (Ub o 6) for é ùr-ra-ke$_4$-e-ne (6, E i 6) (this is relevant to the discussion of the genitive suffix; cf. the comments on *Instr. Šuruppak* lines 5–7, n. 5–7f.). Similar examples are: ti-gi-re-e-né for diŋir-re-e-ne-ke$_4$ (E ii 2), ki-iš (la-) (E ii 4) for [ŋéštu(?)] (4), an ša ut-tu-ki-im (E ii 7) for [an sù-ud-da-gi]m (16), ti-kar-zu (E ii 20) for diŋir-zu (19 A), ku-ru-uš (E ii 20) for gu-ru-uš (20, Ub iii 3 = ŋuruš), šu-zi-peš-še (E ii 20) for šu-zi-bi-šè, sà-an-ki-el-la (E ii 22) and saŋ-ki-il-la (Ub iii 5) for saŋ-íl-la (20), and ki-iš-ḫur (E ii 24) for ŋiš-ḫur (24). The opposite phenomenon also occurs: nu-da-da-am-me-en (E ii 18) for nu-tu-tu-mìn (E i 18).

SS 2 (restored from Syr.): ki gal in Ua seems to be a mistake; gal is superfluous. te-em-ma in E ii is phonetic for KA.DÙG = dima.

SS 3 (restored from Syr.): E ii 3: i-gi-du-uṭ-ṭu, gives the reading igi-du for IGI-DU, rather than palil. Cf. also E i 4: igi-du-a-ni, and E ii 4: i-gi-du-ga-an-ni.

Emar confused an ill-understood presumed model *u$_4$-da(?) of line 3 with the igi-du of the following line, and wrote syllabically i-gi-du-uṭ-ṭu in line 3, which hardly makes sense in the context. It is remarkable, therefore, that the Neo-Assyrian version (*Chap. 3.3a: NA 2(= 10)*) has [x] igi-du-ta, which looks as dependent on the Emar source.

For u$_4$-da, or similar, cf. *Lugal-e* 327 (van Dijk, *Lugal-e* I, p. 92, probably to be restored [u$_4$]-da-ta), and *Inanna raubt den großen Himmel* 147: u$_4$-da-ta (cf. van Dijk, *Borger FS*; Alster, "Gudam and the Bull of Heaven," *Larsen AV*, 37). There can, thus, be no doubt that u$_4$-da-ta occurs in Standard Sumerian, meaning "since that time," or similar. Cf. also p. 331, *Chap. 3.5: Enlil and Namzitarra, Emar Vers. Interpret.*, n. 11, referring to ibid., lines 25–26: ki-u$_4$-ta-ta, which is reminiscent of an Old Sumerian subjunction ù-da, which, however, hardly is relevant here. The most likely reading to lie behind Ua: ⌜u$_4$-da-ta⌝, with its variant [u$_4$-d]a(?)-ta, may be u$_4$-*ul-ta, "since time immemorial," reflected in Uc as *iš-tu u$_4$-mi pa-na-nu* (similar in Emar). This is clear in light of line 14, source B, which suggests that a form like *u$_4$-ul(-lí-a-ta), "since time immemorial," may lie behind lines 4 and 14. This, then, was either misunderstood or reinterpreted in the Ugarit and Emar sources: Ub has phonetically ú-tu ⌜x x⌝, which points to u$_4$-da. In Uc, the Sum. text was apparently read as u$_4$-da-ta.

Dietrich, 1992, 14, reads *i-ba-á[š]-ša an-n[i]-tum* and translates "Seit frühesten Zeiten geschieht dies (so)—," followed by Klein, 2000, 206, n. 14: "From distant days it is so!" The copy in *Ugaritica* 5 438, no. 164: 23' definitely favors *ru* rather than *tum*. So, in view of Ua:]-*ru*, there are good reasons to restore *ša*]-*ru* and understand im as "wind," as already suggested by Wilcke, 1988: *i-ba-áš-ša-an-n[i ša]-ru*. This was accepted by Lambert, 1995, 38: "From days of old there has been vanity (literally 'wind')," comparing Eccl 1:2 et passim.

Lambert was obviously right in regarding line 3 as belonging to a three-line prologue, followed by Klein, but differently Dietrich, who connects it with what follows. Lambert sees it as adding a "distinctive note, which would have warmed the heart of Qohelet," to the prologue. The precise reading of the line is, thus, crucial to the history of the "vanity" theme in ancient Near Eastern literature.

Ua: im al-ŋál-la was apparently seriously misunderstood in E: i-nim NI ig-ŋál-l[a], which hardly makes sense as a phonetic writing for inim, "word." Lines 2 and 10 of the Neo-Assyrian fragment (*Chap. 3.3c*), which repeats the three-line "prologue" as a kind of refrain, however, has [(x)] igi-du-ta NE-e al-ŋál, in which NE is unexplained. Line 5 of the same fragment, however, has má-e, not IM, which I cannot explain, unless this is a misunderstood líl, which would make sense as a variant of IM (= im or tumu; cf. *Chap. 2.3: Couns. Wisdom* 92), meaning "wind," or similar. líl is well attested with the meaning "ghost"; cf. Katz, *Image*, 170, n. 146 and the literature cited there. im is also well attested with the meaning "spirit" (of the deceased), e.g., in *The Messenger and the Maiden* 48; cf. Katz, *Image*, 80; 202–204, etc. According to a suggestion by Wilcke, 1998, 254, im denotes the spirit at the time of death, whereas gidim denotes the spirit in the netherworld; cf. Katz, *Image*, 208, n. 32. From a Mesopotamian viewpoint, it is thus highly likely that it is, in fact, the image of "wind," associated with the spirit of the dead, that lies behind the biblical notion of "vanity." Both im and líl are semantically similar to the Hebrew *hebel* (הבל), which through meanings such as "Windhauch," "Hauch" lies behind the concept of vanity (cf., e.g., Gesenius-Buhl, *Hebraisches Wörterbuch* s.v.).

SS 4 (restored from Syr.): For me-na-àm, here used in an interrogative rather than a correlative sense, cf. the comments on *Níŋ-nam* A 3.

E 4 ii: i-gi-du-ga-an-ni, probably misunderstood from *igi-du-ka-né, i.e., gen. /ka lú igi-du-ak-ani-e/. The Sum. negation la- was misunderstood as LÀḪ in Ub; this was translated "wann immer etwas aus dem Mund eines 'Altworderen' vernommen wurde" by Dietrich, 1992, 14; similarly Wilcke. The translation of Lambert, 1995, 39, as a rhetorical question, "Have you ever heard from the mouth of a man of yore?" does not clearly render the la/*ul* as a negation. I understand it as "Has there ever been a time when you did not hear (this) from the mouth of a predecessor?" (similarly Klein, 2000, 206, n. 15, Syr. Vers., reading [*u*]*l te-eš-mi*, "Have you never heard from the mouth of a predecessor?"; SS Vers. p. 210, "Whenever *was it not heard* from the mouth of a predecessor").

SS 5 (restored from Syr.): E has lu-gal, phonetic for lugal. The Sum. text must, therefore, have had *lugal.

Wilcke, 1988, 138, reads [*e-li*(?)-]*ši-na* / [*e-l*]*i-šu-nu*, "überragten diese jene, und andere überragten sie"; similarly Lambert: "these kings were superior to them, and others to those."

Ub: diri-NI-in-né suggests a form like diri-ga e-ne-ne, "(they, [scl. the "predecessors" to the early kings, l. 5]) were above those (scl. early kings, l. 5)." E iii: *ši-na ši-na-ma*, points to a feminine reference, but this seems to be an error, because Uc, as expected, has the masculine *šu-nu šu-nu-ma*; cf. Dietrich's explanation quoted below. The Sum. text can be read as an example of adding parallelism, which causes the subject to be grammatically unexpressed when it first occurs. For further examples, see, e.g., *Instr. Šuruppak* 5–7; 69–72; 209–211. It may have been the failure to recognize this common Sumerian stylistic feature that caused confusion in the Emar source. In our case, it would enable us to restore a word like *[lugal-bi = *šarrū*] at the beginning of the second part of the line, which is warranted in view of Ub and E ii (phon.): lu-gal-bi.

The sources for the second part of the line cannot be fully harmonized. Uc: *ša-nu-tu-ma* was translated by Arnaud, 1987, 362: "elles [n'étaint pas] semblables, [ils étaient] autres"; this may require a Sum. verb such as *kúr-kúr. I refrain from attempting to restore the Sumerian text, however. A reconstruction in line with the translations of Wilcke and Lambert would seem more suitable.

In Uc Dietrich, 1992, 15, reads [...] || [*la*]-*a šu-nu ša-nu-tu-ma*, translating "Sie sind solche (geworden), die nicht sind—sie sind andere (geworden)," explaining, n. 16, the feminine *ši-na* "auf ein zugrundelegenes *nišū* «Menschen», o.ä., bezogen." If correct, it would reveal a grave misunderstanding or reinterpretation on the part of the Emar scribe, since the original source certainly referred to the early rulers and not to a larger and more general group of "people."

SS 6 (restored from Syr.): The implication of these lines is that even the early rulers could only hope for an everlasting home in the underworld, e.g., they are all dead. Alster, 1990, 24, was first to suggest the restoration [ki-ta] é da-rí-ke$_4$-ne, on the basis of the parallel here edited in *Chap. 3.1: Níŋ-nam* C 5, quoted below; a further parallel occurs in *Níŋ-nam Vers. D* 5–6, also quoted below; cf. *Chap. 3.2: Comm. D* 5–6; further comments in *Chap. 3.3: Ballade: Attempt at a New Interpretation*, p. 296, n. 44, referring to Eccl 12:5.

While there, thus, can be little doubt as to the general implication of the line, the sources are difficult to harmonize in detail, as the following synopsis will show:

Níŋ-nam C 5, based on CBS 1208:
⌜an-ta⌝ é-ùr-ra-ni ki-ta é du-⌜rí⌝-šè
Variant N 3047: ... [ki]-ta é da-rí-ka-ni

Níŋ-nam D 5–6, based on 3N-T 360 rev. iii:
⌜an⌝-⌜ta⌝-⌜àm⌝ é-ur$_5$-ra-ka-ni ki(?)-ta-àm é da-rí-ka-ni

variants CBS 6924:
[an-t]a-àm é-ur$_5$-ra-ka-ni [ki-t]a-àm é-da-ra-ka-ni

variants Ni 9620:
[an-ta(-àm) é ur$_5$]-ra-ka-[ni] [ki-ta(-àm) é-d]a-ra-ka-ni

Ni 2763 (SLTNi 128 i 1'):
... [ki]-ta ⌜é⌝ da-ri (cf. *Chap. 3.2x: Sources*).

Ballade 6, Emar Version
i [an-ta] é ùr-ra-ke$_4$-e-ne [ki-ta] ⌜é⌝-da-rí-ki-e-ne
ii [a]n-ta e-ur-ra-ki-[...] / [ki-ta] e-da-ra-ga-an-n[i ...]
iii = [*elēnum bīt*] ⌜*a*⌝-*ša*(?)-[*bi-šu-nu*] / [*šaplānum*] *x x* [...]

Ballade 6, Ugarit Version
Ub [a]n-ta e-ur-ra-ga-an-ni [x x]
Uc [... -g]a-an(!)-ni
= *e-*[*l*]*e-nu-um bīt a-*⌜*ša*⌝*-bi-*[*šu-nu šaplānum bīt da-ru-ti-šu-nu*]

The Sumerian sources point to two parallel compounds, both taken as genitives (the only exception is CBS 1208): */é ùr-ak/. ùr may be understood as a platform or a place where people live, or simply as *ūru*, "roof." The Syro-Mesopotamian versions probably correctly understood it as *bīt ašābišunu*, "the house where they dwelt." This is a genitive compound, "a house of dwelling," or similar, parallel to */é da-rí-ak/, "a house of eternity." /-ani/ thus in both cases refers to the entire compound: "above (is/was) his house of residence, below (is) his everlasting house." The Syro-Mesopotamian version thus stayed close to the original Sumerian text, translating the two parts as parallel units. That the Syrian scribes obviously had difficulties with the Sum. genitive construction: /é ùr-(a)-ak-ani-ene/, "their houses of dwelling," taking the pers. suffix /ani.ene/ as a plural marker to the whole noun phrase, should not mislead us into believing that the Syro-Mesopotamian version was meant to be quite different from the SS version in this case.

é-ùr is comparable to ki-ùr, which occurs in line 3 of *The Sumerian Flood Story*, as the first place where man settled after the flood. The concern about the "house in which a man lives" comes to light also in *Níŋ-nam Vers. A* 10, edited in *Chap. 3.1*.

Klein, 2002, 211, translates the SS version (reconstructed) "Above (are) those of the (transient) living homes, [below] (are) those of the lasting homes!" and the Syrian version identically, p. 206, taking both genitives as "free" genitives without a regens, but this can be ruled out by the SS parallels quoted above, and does not conform to the Akk. translations. The translations of Wilcke, 1988, 138: "Oberhalb von deren Wohnhaus lag ihr dauerhaftes Haus!"; Lambert, 1995, 39: "Their eternal home is above their ... house"; and Dietrich, 1992, 15, Syr. vers: *e-le-nu-um a-ša-bi* [*šu-nu*(?) *šaplānum ašābi šunu*], "Oberhalb der Wohngegend [sind sie(?), unterhalb der Wohngegend sind sie(?)," reflect the text as known before the SS parallels became known.

SS 7 (cf. Syr. 10): Klein, 2002, 210, reads somewhat differently, thereby connecting this more closely to Syr. 10: [lú(?) ... da(?)-r]i u$_4$(?) li-bí-in-zal(?)-a, "[*The greatest men*] *did not endure forever*!" He translates the Emar version "The [life of man does not [last] forever!" The copy definitely favors dù rather than zal. Cf. the comments on Syr. 10.

SS 8 (not in Syr.): This line is included in source B only, and omitted in the Syro-Mesopotamian version. The concept of the dynasties having been overthrown is clearly reminiscent of *The Sumerian King List*. The expression šu-bal – ak is not used there, however, but occurs with the same implication in *Lamentation over the Destruction of Sumer and Ur* 1; 3; and 103.

SS 9 = Syr. 11: Note the phonetic variant -i]a-ka for -ak, in E i 11.

^{m}a-lu-lu is probably identical to á-lu-lim, who occurs as the very first king in *The Sumerian King List*, line 3, according to which he ruled for 28,800 years in Eridu, slightly "less" than the 36,000 years assigned to him here; cf. Jacobsen, *Sumerian King List*, p. 70 n. 6.

SS 10 = Syr. 12: ^{m}en-te-n[a is here probably identical to Etana, who occurs in *The Sumerian King List*, line 16. He ruled for 1,500 years during the first dynasty of Kiš, after the flood.

SS 11 = Syr. 13: Gilgameš, according to *The Sumerian King List*, 17–20, was king of Uruk for 126 years. Ziusudra is the hero who survived the flood in *The Sumerian Flood Story*. He is not mentioned in *The Sumerian King List*, but cf. the comments p. 32, *Chap. 1.1.1: Šuruppak's Family Relations*; cf. further the comments on *Instr. Šuruppak* 6–8.

SS 12 = Syr. 14: The translation of [ki] ba-an-za-za as "bit the grass" was proposed by Alster, 1990, 23, and accepted by Klein, 2000, 211, who translates "Where is Huwawa who was captured having been prostrated?" Wilcke, 1988, however, translates "nachdem ihm gehuldigt." Klein, 2000, 207, refers to *Gilgameš and Huwawa* 136: šu ki-a bí-in-sè inim mu-na-ab-bé, which, however, requires some extra explanation to appear as a parallel (cf. below), and on p. 207, n. 23, to *Gilgameš and Huwawa* 152 d-g (Edzard, ZA 81, 219); Akk. Gilgameš Epic V 348': *Ḫuwawa maṣṣarum [in]ēršu qaqqarum*. The explanation, which also shows that Wilcke's translation "nachdem ihm gehuldigt" above is justified, can be found in B. Alster, "Court Ceremonial and Marriage in 'Gilgameš and Huwawa': TIM IX 47," *Bulletin of the School of Oriental and African Studies* 55 (1992) 1–8. The point is that Gilgameš used guile to make Huwawa approach him the polite way, as a visitor entering before a ruler, bowing down with his hand on the ground, presumably conforming to a common court ritual.

SS 13 = Syr. 15: The translation of the SS text follows Klein, 2000, 210 ("whose strength could not be crushed in the land"). The Syro-Mesopotamian version differs: the restoration *ú-[ša-pu-ú]* in E iii was suggested by Dietrich, 1992, 17, 33 ("obwohl der Platz knapp ist"). It would correspond to a broken Sumerian verb such as pa – è.

SS 14 = Syr. 17: Earlier attempts by Wilcke and Alster tried to harmonize the two versions; cf. Wilcke, "Wo sind die grossen Könige, die von früher bis jetzt?"; similarly Alster, 1990, and Dietrich, 1992. Klein, 2000, 210, translates the SS version "Where are the kings, the early ones, those of former days?" correctly explaining dub-saŋ as *maḫrû, qudmu*. In the Syro-Mesopotamian version the Sum. u_4-ul-lí-a-ta, "of former days," was apparently not understood, but reinterpreted as e-še-ta, translated in Akk. as *adi inan[na]*, "(from former days) till now"; this is reminiscent of the pair ì-ne-éš-ta ...: u_4-da-ta ..., which undoubtedly means "from now on ... every day" in *Inanna raubt den großen Himmel* 146–147 (cf. Alster, "Gudam and the Bull of Heaven," *Larsen AV*, 37). Neither was dub-saŋ correctly understood, but reinterpreted as *(šarrānu) rabûtu*. These changes may go back to a mB source transmitted in the Syro-Mesopotamian area. These translations, together with the forward position of SS lines 16–18, so as to follow directly upon SS 6, but before SS 7, are the essential features that separate the two versions; they basically represent the same text, but the effect of the rhetorical question that follows as a conclusion (SS 16 = Syr. 7; SS 19 = Syr. 19) is somewhat weakened in the Syro-Mesopotamian version. Yet, in both versions they preserve their reference to the list of early rulers (Syr. 11–16; cf. SS 9–13). Cf. the comments below, and the summary p. 292, *Chap. 3.3: Ballade: Textual History*.

SS 15 = Syr. 18: This can be translated straight away in both versions: "They are no longer engendered, they are no longer born," similar to the proposals of Wilcke, 1988, and Alster, 1990, 23. The Emar version, however, adding -men$_5$, syll. m[e-en], seems mistakenly to have thought of a subject in the first or second person. Cf. Lambert, 1995, 39: "Have they not been conceived? Have they not been born?"

Dietrich, 1992, 18, understands this differently: "(Es scheint:) Sie sind weder empfangen noch geboren worden!" This was followed by Klein, 2000, 207: "(It seems as if) they were not conceived, they were not born." It is undoubtedly the position of the line in the Syro-Mesopotamian version that led to these translations. An important notion such as "it seems as if" would, however, have been much more explicitly expressed if that had been intended. Considering that both verbs are in the plain present tense, there is no reason not to take the statements at face value, "they are not conceived/born (scl. anymore)." In both versions this very aptly concludes the list of early rulers by implying that these belonged to a different class from those conceived "now."

SS 16 = Syr. 7: The SS version, represented by B: šu-ŋu$_{10}$ sá bí-in-dug$_4$-ga, must be a rhetorical question asked by the poet in the first person, lit.: "Has my hand (ever) reached them?" The Syro-Mesopotamian versions, however, point to a forerunner or variant like *šu sá nam-bí-in-dug$_4$-ga, "a hand indeed never reached them." This point was lost in the Syro-Mesopotamian version, which simply uses the 3rd person. Lambert, 1995, 39–40, translates Syr. 7: "Like the remote heavens, my hand has not reached (it)," but SS 16, ditto, but "(them)."

Klein, 2002, 210, translates SS vers. "Like [the remote heavens], can my hand reach them?"; p. 206, Syr. vers. 7: "As heaven is remote (they are remote) —no hand can reach them." For Dietrich's translation, see the comments on Syr. 7.

The first parts of lines 16–17 belong to a set of phrases quoted elsewhere, expressing the futility of human ambitions or limits of the obtainable; cf. the examples p. 296, *Chap. 3.3: Attempt ... New Interpretation* with n. 44, where, i.a., Job 11:18 is cited. The intent is that the early rulers are as unreachable as are the heavens; the hand only comes into the picture to express this idea, and there would be no point in stressing too much whose hand is meant.

SS 17 = Syr. 8: Cf. the comments on the preceding line.

Klein, 2000, 210, translates SS 17: "Like the deep netherworld, no one knows them!" and, p. 206, Syr. 8: "Like the depth of the netherworld—nothing is known (about them)."

As in the preceding line, I see this as an expression of the limits of human comprehension, the early rulers are as unfathomable as are the depths of the underworld.

Note the interesting phonetic writing nu-un-zu-wa-a in E ii (= *nu-un-zu-a).

SS 18 = Syr. 9: The translation of igi-níŋin-na-kam, previously understood as "a twinkling of an eye," depends on the Akk. translation *tūrti inimma*; Nougayrol, 1968, 205ff. (referring to Borger, ZA 54 [1961], esp. 185–186), translates "cécité," based on *tūrti īnē*, "malédiction des yeux." Cf. also AHw 1373 *tūrtu*, "Umwendung," esp. (1) "U(mwendung) der Augen als Krankheit." A meaning such as "the whole life is blindness" would make good sense in the context, whereas an eye disease would hardly apply. Dietrich, 1992, 21, on Syr. 9 (= SS 18) translates "Das ganze Leben [betracht]et er [= man(?)] als einen Augenblick," commenting "Wörtlich: «Rückwendung des Auges», was auch eine Augenkrankheit bezeichnen kann (etwa «Schielen» oder «Blindheit»." The translation "twinkling of an eye" (as previously suggested by Alster) would suit the context well, but is a guess from the context, and considered "highly uncertain" by Sjöberg, *Wilcke FS*, 260. Yielding to this criticism, I now rather translate "illusion," understanding this more in terms of magical blindness ("Bann der Auge"), as suggested by Borger, ZA 54, 186. igi – níŋin, if understood literally as "turning the eyes," is apparently different from igi-níŋin, otherwise known in the meaning "to supervise" or the like, treated by Sjöberg, loc. cit., 259–260. Lambert, 1995, 40, translates "[All life] is but the twinkling of an eye," thus accepting the translation of igi-níŋin proposed above.

Dietrich, 1992, 16, on Syr. 9, with nn. 26–27, reads *ba*(?)*-ri*, translating "betrachtet er (Unpersöhnliches Subjekt = "man") als einen Augenblick," tentatively taking *ba*(?)*-ri* as a form (*ibri*, *bari*(?)) of *barû*. I rather understand it as non-personal, "is seen as," almost = "aspect." This probably had no correspondence in the SS version, although it may have been represented by the two missing signs.

SS 19 = Syr. 19: Note that A and B have [a]-ba-àm "who" (also clear on the original tablet of A), instead of the expected a-na-àm, "what." The distinction between personal and non-personal pronouns was clearly not upheld. Cf. the comments on Syr. 23.

Klein, 2000, 210, translates SS 19: "Life without joy, what advantage has it over death," and p. 207, Syr. 19 identically. Alster, 1990, 23: "Life onto which no light is shed, how can it be more valuable than death?" Lambert, 1995, 40: "How is [life without joy] superior to death?"

For Dietrich's translation, see the comments on Syr. 19. Dietrich, 1992, points out, p. 18, n. 38, and p. 24, n. 58, that the use of *nawāru* (= zalag), in relation to joy is well attested; cf. AHw 768–770, *nawāru*, "hell sein, leuchten, 6. v Herz, Gemüt," and CAD N/1, 219–218, "to brighten (said of one's countenance, mood), to cheer up, to become happy ...";

nummuru, "to brighten the countenance, ... to make happy," etc. Cf. *Instr. Šuruppak* 139.

Dietrich, 1992, 18, n. 39, explains *watāru* D as "vermehren, vergrößern; Vorteil haben," referring to AHw 1490f. Cf. Ua: "What advantage has it to death?"

SS 20 = Syr. 22: SS 20 is plain: it has the verb in-ak in the simple indicative, "instead of one day of joy 36,000 years of silence reigned." This makes good sense as a conclusion to the preceding lines, and a starting point for the following invitation to enjoy happiness, while it is still possible; Syr. 22 understood this differently, taking the verb as a precative, *lillika*. This resulted in a considerably different understanding of the concluding line in the Syrian-Mesopotamian version, where this refers to the future instead of the distant past. Maybe this is meant as a resigned and exaggerated rhetorical question? Cf. the comments on Syr. 22, and p. 292, *Chap. 3.3: Ballade: Textual History*, with n. 29.

Klein, 2000, 210, translates SS 20: "Instead of one day of joy, 36,000 years of gloom will surely come!" and, p. 207, Syr. 22: "Instead of one day of joy, will surely come 36,000 years of sorrowful days," commenting, p. 207, n. 30, that "*qūlu* in this context is ambiguous: 'silence' or 'stupor'." Lambert, 1995, 40, translates: "[As a substitute] for a single day's happiness, can one pass 36,000 years in days of silence." These translations do not take into consideration the essential differences between the verbs, but mingles the plain SS 20 verbal form in-ak with the Syr. 22 precative. For further details, which obscure, rather than clarify the intent of the line, see the comments on Syr. 22.

For SS ŠÀR×U, E surprisingly has the phonetic writing ù-šèr-šèr in col. i 22, where we would expect the ordinary orthography, and the seemingly regular writing ù-šar-šar in the phonetic column, ii 22. These writings do not support the expected reading šaru. The Sum. u$_4$-im-ba-kam in Ua 13 = *u$_4$-um qu-li* might be a result of a misreading of the sign LUL-ba = lib-ba, misread as im-ba, or is it meant as a translation of *ūmakkal*? Cf. the comments on Syr. 22.

SS 21 (in Syro-Mesopotamian vers. replaced by Syr. 23): The decisive initial signs are partly preserved in A, B, and D. The beginning of the line is preserved in ms. D in the parallel text of the composition preceding *The Ballade of Early Rulers* on the *Sammeltafel*, i.e., *Níŋ-nam C* 8 (cf. previously Alster, 1990, 25; the text is edited in *Chap. 3.1*), on the very lower edge, cf. the photographs on pls. 30–31, in which the reading níŋ-⸢sa$_6$⸣-⸢ga⸣ is fairly certain. In D the beginning of the indented line can be read as ⸢x⸣-⸢gu$_7$-gu$_7$⸣, with the restoration ⸢ú⸣-⸢gu$_7$-gu$_7$⸣ as an obvious possibility. The relevant signs can be read on the photograph of CBS 1208, on pl. 31, rev. ii 3'. This provides another parallel to a composition inscribed on the same *Sammeltafel*, *Hymn to Marduk with Blessing for a King*, Composition 1:21 in Alster, 1990, 12, (previously Alster and Jeyes, 1986, 3 ii 3): diŋir ú-gu$_7$-àm a-silim ⸢nam(?)⸣-ti-la u$_4$-sù-du ŋiš-šub-ba-zu ŋá-ŋá, "May it be your lot to be a god consuming the food and healthy water of long life!" (A omits a-silim). The restoration ⸢ú⸣-⸢gu$_7$-gu$_7$⸣ is strongly suggested as an allusion to UET 6/1, 2, line 57: ^{u}ug-gu$_7$-gu$_7$-ŋu$_{10}$-uš z[a-e] a-ba-a mu-ra-ab-túm, also hinted at in line 59: u$_4$-g[u$_7$-g]u$_7$ nu-dé-dé for which see the discussion by Alster, "Ninurta and the Turtle," CM ... (forthcoming). Laura Feldt, oral communication, suggests that this may be a pun on *Lugal-e* 292: ú-gug-gim ú-númun-gim mu-un-[z]é. The small unidentified fragment ISET I 202 Ni 9990, 2: ú-gu$_7$-gu$_7$ [...] unfortunately does not help.

The indented part of A starts: [...] ⸢x⸣ ⸢KA⸣-ra. This can be harmonized with B (CT 44, 18 rev. ii 18):]⸢x⸣, which may be the rest of g]u$_7$ with the two horizontals squeezed a bit too narrowly, showing that the -ra in A is, in fact, the dative marker (as already suggested by Alster and Jeyes, 1986, 6, who tentatively restored [zi-u$_4$-sud]-ra-ra, where, however, the first -ra is unjustified).

SS 22 (in Syro-Mesopotamian vers. replaced by Syr. 23): The Sum. text has the two components in reverse order; we expect: *é ŋuruš-ke$_4$ ti-a (for tìl-(l)a), "dwelling in the house of the young men." The syntax seems heavily influenced by Akkadian here.

Syr. 24: The Syro-Mesopotamian version adds an extra line, for which see the comments on Syr. 24 and p. 296, *Chap. 3.3: Ballade: Textual History*.

3.3b The "Syro-Mesopotamian" Version

The most complete treatment of the "Syrian" version was by Dietrich, 1992, 9–29. To facilitate independent reading of both versions, a separate edition of the Syro-Mesopotamian version is given below, with the Emar source as the best-preserved and most complete primary source, but including the Ugaritic sources.

For the reasons stated above (p. 292, *Chap. 3.3: Ballade: Textual History*) it is likely that the "Syrian" version originated in Babylonia proper, and was based on a bilingual mB version (now lost) that went back to a unilingual Sumerian version, edited as the SS version in *Chap. 3.3a.* In fortuitous cases the Syro-Mesopotamian sources enable us to restore "backward" when the original Sumerian text is missing. For details, see the complete composite "score" edition, with comments to the SS version, in *Chap. 3.3a.*

For the reasons stated, p. 293, *Chap. 3.3: The Relations between the Syro-Mesopotamian Sources,* I consider the Ugaritic sources to be sometimes closer to the presumed mB source than to the Emar text.

All details pertaining to the reconstruction of the texts from Ugarit and Emar can be found in Dietrich's edition, pp. 11–13.

1		ki ^{d}en-ki-ke$_4$ ŋiš-ḫur ḫur-re *it-ti* ^{d}*é-a uṣ-ra-m[a(?) u]ṣ-ṣu-ra-tum*	*(Syr. 1)* With Enki the plans are drawn.
E	i 1	[ki ^{d}en-ki-ke$_4$ ŋiš-ḫu]r ḫur-re	
	ii	| | ki [e]n-ki-ik-ki ki-iš-ḫur-ḫu-r[e]	
	iii	=[*i*]*t-ti* ^{d}*é-a u*[*ṣ*- ...]	
Ua	18	ki ^{d}en-ki-ke$_4$ ŋiš-[ḫu]r ḫur-ḫur-re	
	19	= *it-ti* ^{d}*é-a uṣ-ṣu-ra-m[a(?) u]ṣ-ṣu-ra-tum*	
	40	ki ^{d}en-ki-ke$_4$ ŋiš-ḫur [ḫu]r-[ḫu]r-re	
	41	= *it-ti* ^{d}*é-a uṣ-ṣu-r[a- ...]*	
Ub o	1	x [...] [...] ⌜^{d}⌝*é-[a ...] / [u]ṣ(?)-re-[...]*	
2		[dima diŋir-re-e-ne-k]e$_4$ ki nam-sur-sur-re *a-na ṭe$_4$-em* DINGIR-*lim-m[a]* *us-**<*su*>*-qa us-qé-[e]-tu*	*(Syr. 2)* According to the decisions of the gods lots are allotted.
E	i 2	[dima diŋir-re-e-ne-k]e$_4$ ki nam-sur-sur-re	
	ii	te-em-ma ti-gi-re-e-né ki nam sur-šu-re	
	iii	*a-na ṭe$_4$-em* DINGIR-*lim-m[a ...]*	
Ua	20	dima(KA.DÙG) diŋir-re-e-ne-ke$_4$ ki gal nam(!)-sur-[sur]-re	
	21	= [*i*]*-na ṭè-em* DINGIR-*ma us-*<*su*>*-qa us-qé-[e]-tu*	
	42	= dima diŋir-re-e-ne-ke$_4$ [...]	
	43	= *i-na ṭe-em* DINGIR-*ma* [...]	
Ub	o 2	te-x[...] / sur [...] = [... *ṭ*]*e-e-i-i[m* ...]	
Uc	o 1	[... -*k*]*u-nu us-q[è-* ...]	

3 — *⸢u$_4$-da-ta⸣ im al-ŋál-la
[iš-tu] u$_4$-mi pa-na-nu ip-pa-á[š(?) ša-ru]

E i 3 [...] NI ŋál-la
ii = u-du i-gi-du-uṭ-ṭu i-nim NI ig-ŋál-l[a]
iii =*[i]š-tu u$_4$-mi pa-na-⸢a⸣-ma*
Ua o 22 [u$_4$-d]a(?)-ta im al-ŋál-la
23 =*[...] x x i-ba-áš-ša-a-an-n[i (x) ša]-ru*
Ua o 44 ⸢u$_4$-da-ta⸣ im [...]
Ub o 3 ú-tu ⸢x x⸣ [...]
Uc o 2 =*[iš-tu] u$_4$-mi pa-na-nu ip-pa-á[š(?) ša-ru]*

(Syr. 3) Since time immemorial there has been [wi]nd!

*(Based on Ua; Akk. on Uc; Emar differs; cf. the commentary on *SS 3)*

4 — * me-na-*àm(?) ka lú-igi-du-*ka-né ŋiš la-ba-an-tuku
* *im-m[a-t]i-me-e i-na pí-i a-l[ik pa-ni] / ul [té]š-mi*

E i 4 [...] igi-du-a-ni / [x x]x a
ii = me-na-a ka lu i-gi-du-ga-an-ni / ki-iš la-ba-an-tu-ka(!?)-a
iii = *im-m[a-t]i-me-e i-na pí-i a-l[ik pa-ni] / ul [té]š-mi*
Ub o 4 me-e-tum ka lu [...] / ki-iš LÀḪ-ba-an-t[u ...]
Uc o 3 *[...]x-a i-na pí-i a-lik pa-ni-x / ⸢x te⸣-iš-mi [(x)]*

(Syr. 4) Has there ever been a time when you did not hear this from the mouth of a predecessor?

5 — * diri *e(?)-ne-ne * lugal-bi [...]
* *[e-l]i-šu-nu šu-nu-ma [šarrū(?)] šu-nu ša-nu-tu-ma*

E i 5 [x x] ⸢e⸣-ne ⸢lu⸣(?)-[gal(?)-bi] / [x x g]a-ki-e-ne
ii = [x] ⸢a⸣-ia-na-an-ni lu-gal-bi / [x]-ga-ki [x x a]n-ni [x x]
iii =*[...]-ši-na ši-na-m[a ...] / [x x] x ša-an-nu x[x x]*
Ub o 5 diri-NI-in-né lu-gal-bi x [x x] / in-ni x [...]
Uc o 4 =*[e-l]i-šu-nu šu-nu-ma / [(x)] šu-nu ša-nu-tu-ma*

(Syr. 5) Above them were those (scl. kings), (and above) those kings *were others.

(Uc:) (They were above them, they were different.)

6 — * an-ta é ùr-ra-*ke$_4$-ne-ne ki-ta é-da-rí-*ke$_4$-ne-ne
* *elēnum bīt ašābišunu šaplānum bīt darûtišunu*

E i 6 [an-ta] é ùr-ra-ke$_4$-e-ne / [ki-ta] ⸢é⸣-da-rí-ki-e-ne
ii = [a]n-ta e-ur-ra-ki-[...] / [ki-ta] e-da-ra-ga-an-n[i ...]
iii = [...] ⸢a⸣-ša(?)-[...] / [...] x x [...]
Ub o 6 [a]n-ta e-ur-ra-ga-an-ni [x x]
Uc o 5 [... g]a-an(!)-ni
= *e-[l]e-nu* É *a-⸢ša⸣-bi-[šu-nu šaplānum* É *da-ru-ti-šu-nu]*

(Syr. 6) Above (are) the houses where they lived, [below (are)] their everlasting houses.

7 (= SS 16) — [an sù-u]d-da-gim šu-ti na[m-bi-in-dug$_4$]
* *ki-ma šamû^u ru-qu-ma [qa-t]i ma-am-ma i-kaš-ša[d]*

E i 7 [... -u]d-da-gim(!) šu-ti n[am(?)-x x (x) :]
ii = an ša-ut-ta-ki-im šu-ti n[am- ...]
iii =*[... i]-ka-aš-šu-ud* (rev. 23)
Ua 7' an sù-ud-gim šu-t[i(?) x] zu AN [...]
8' = *ki-ma šamû^u ru-qu-ma* ŠU *x x* AB [...]
Ub i 11 [a]n šu(!)-ut-ta-k[i- ...]
Uc 6 *[... š]a-mu-ú ru-qu-ma x x /*
[qa-t]i ma-am-ma i-kaš-ša[d]

(Syr. 7 = SS 16) Like the remote heavens, no hand, indeed, has ever reached them.

(Akk. vers.:) [... which] hand can reach them?).

8 = SS 17 [ki bùru-da]-bi me-na nu-u[n-zu-a
ki-ma šu-pu-ul er-ṣe-ti mim-ma la i-du-ú

(Syr. 8) Like the depth of the underworld (lit., earth), one knows nothing (about it/them).

E i 8 [...]-bi me-na nu-un-[...]
ii = [...] na-me nu-un-zu-wa-a
Ua 9' ki bùru-da-gim na-me nu-zu-[...]
10' = *ki-ma šu-pu-ul er-ṣe-ti mim-ma la i-du-ú*
Ub i 12 [ki b]u-ut-ta [...]

9 = SS 18 nam-ti-la dù-a-bi x x igi-níŋin-na-kam
ba-la-ṭa ka-la-šu [b]a(?)-ri [t]u-ur-ti i-ni-im-ma

(Syr. 9) All life is an illusion.

E i 9 [(x)] nam-t[i- ...]
E ii = [...] x -ni-ik-k[i ...]
Ua 11 nam-ti-la dù-a-bi x x igi-niŋin-na-kam
12 = *ba-la-ṭa ka-la-šu [b]a(?)-ri tu-ur-ti i-ni-im-ma*
Ub i 13 [... -t]i(?)-lu [...]

10 (cf. SS 7) *nam-ti nam-lú-⸢u$_{18}$⸣-l[u] u$_{4}$-da-ri-iš nu-ni-⸢x⸣-[...]
[ba-la-aṭ a-me l]u-ut-ti [...] / ú-ul i-x-[...]

(Syr. 10) The life of mankind was not [intended to last for ever].

E i 10 [...]
ii = nam-ti nam-lu-⸢u$_{18}$⸣-[lu] / u$_{4}$-da-ri-iš nu-ni-⸢x⸣-[...]
iii =*[ba-la-aṭ a-mi-l]u-ut-ti [...] / [...] ú-ul i-[...]*

11 (= SS 9) *[me-a ^{m}a-lu-lu lu]gal-e mu 3600×10-àm in-ak
[a-l]e-e ^{m}a-lu-lu [...]

(Syr. 11) Where is Alulu, the king [who reigned 36,000 years?]

E i 11 [... -i]a-ka :
ii = me-e ^{m}a-lu-lu m[u ...]
iii =*[a-l]e-e ^{m}a-lu-lu [...]*

12 (= SS 10) *[me]-e ^{m}en-te-n[a lugal-e lú an-šè bí-in]-⸢e$_{11}$⸣-e-dè
a-le-e ^{m}[en-te-n]a ša [ana šamê ilû]

(Syr. 12) Where is Entena (= Etana) the king, the man who ascended to heaven?

E i 12 [me]-e ^{m}en-te-n[a ...]-⸢e$_{11}$⸣-e-dè
ii = me-e ^{m}en-t[e ...] x x
iii = *a-⸢le-e⸣ ^{m}[x] x ša [...]*

13 (= SS 11) [me]-e ^{md}giš-m[aš-sù / [zi-u$_{4}$-sud-rá-g]im nam-ti-la kiŋ-[kiŋ]
a-le-e ^{m}gil-[ga-meš š]a k[i-ma ^{m}zi-u$_{4}$-sù]-ud-ra na-pu-u[l-ta-š]u [iš-ta-ʾu-ú]

(Syr. 13) Where is Gilgameš, who, like Ziusudra, sought the (eternal) life?

Cf. SS B [me-a ^{m}bìl-ga-meš z]i-u$_{4}$-sud-rá-gim nam-ti ì-kiŋ-kiŋ

E i 13 [me]-e ^{md}ŋiš-kin(!)-m[aš ...] /
[... -gi]m nam-ti-la kin-[...]
ii me-e ^{md}ki-iš-mas-su [...]-ki nam-ti-la k[i(?) ...]
iii = *a-le-e(?) ^{m}gil-[ga-meš š]a k[i-ma zi-u$_{4}$-sù]- /
ud-ra na-pu-u[l-t]a [išteʾʾû]*

14 (= SS 12) [me]-e ^{m}ḫu-wa-wa [x z]a-da mu-x-[...]
⸢a-le-e⸣ ^{m}ḫu-[wa-wa ...] / [... -t]i(?) i-na [...]

(Syr. 14) Where is Huwawa, who was caught in submission?]

Cf. SS B [me-a ^{m}ḫu-wa-wa (...) ki] ba-an-za-za dab$_5$(?)-ba(?)-ta

E i 14 [me]-e ^{m}ḫu-wa-wa [...] / [x z]a-da mu-x-[...]
ii = me-e ^{m}ḫ[u-wa-wa ...] / [x] x x [...]
iii = *⸢a-le-e⸣ ^{m}ḫu-[wa-wa ...] / [... -t]i(?) i-na* [...]

15 (= SS 13) [me-e] ^{m}en-k[i-dù nam-kalag-ga]-a-ni [...]
[a]-le-e ^{m}en-ki-du / ša da-an-nu-ti i-na KUR-*ti ú-[ša-pu-ú]*

(Syr. 15) Where is Enkidu, whose strength was not defeated(?) in the country?

Cf. SS B [me-a ^{m}en-ki-dù nam-kalag-ga-ni kal]am(?)-ma(?) nu(?)-dar-ra-ke$_4$

(*Akk. version:* who [showed] (his) strength in the country).

E i 15 [me-e] ^{m}en-k[i-dù ...] / [...]-ta mu-[...]
ii [me-e ^{m}e]n-ki-dù nam-ka-lag-[x] /
= [x x x(?) mu-u]n-na-an-te
iii =*[a]-le-e ^{m}en-ki-du / ša da-an-nu-ti i-na* KUR-*ti ú*-[...]
Ua 1' [x x] x x [...]
2' =[...] *^{d}en-ki-dù š[a* ...]

16 (not in SS) [me-e ^{m}ba-z]i me-e [^{m}z]i-[zi]
a-le-e ^{m}ba-zi a-le-e ^{m}zi-[zi]

(Syr. 16) Where is Bazi, where is Zizi?

E i 16 [me-e ^{m}ba-z]i me-e [^{m}z]i-[zi]
ii = me-e ^{m}ba-[z]i me-e ^{m}zi-zi
iii = *a-le-e ^{m}ba-zi a-le-e ^{m}zi-[zi]*

17 (= SS 14) [me-e luga]l gal-e-ne / [u$_4$-saŋ(?)-ŋá-t]a-e-ne e-še-ta
a-le-e šar-ra-nu ra-ab-bu-[tum] / ša iš-tu u$_4$-mi pa-na-a a-di i-na-a[n-na]

(Syr. 17) Where are those great kings, from former days till now?

E i 17 [me-e ... luga]l(!) gal-e-ne / [...] x-e-ne e-še-ta
ii me-e lu-gal gal-e-né / ú-sa(?)-ŋá-ta-e-né e-še-ta
iii = *a-le-e šar-ra-nu ra-ab-bu-[tum]* /
ša iš-tu u$_4$-mi pa-na-a a-di i-na-a[n-na]
Ua 3' m[e-e]n ì-tí-eš lugal gal-gal-e-[...]
4' = *a-li-šu-nu-ti* LUGAL^{meš} [...]

18 (= SS 15) [nu-peš-men$_5$(MIN)] nu-tu-tu-men$_5$
ul in-né-ru-ma ul im-m[a-al-la-du]

(Syr. 18) They are no longer engendered, they are no longer born.

E i 18 [...] nu-tu-tu-men$_5$
ii = nu-peš-ša-me-en nu-da-da-am-m[e-en]
iii = *ul in-né-ru-ma ul im-m[a-al-la-du]*
Ua 5' nu-peš-peš-e-ne nu-tu-t[u- ...]
6' = *ul in-né-ru-ú [(x)] ul* [...]
Ub iv 1 *[ú]-ul in(?)-[...] ú-ul im-m[a-al-la-du]*

19 (= SS 19) [na]m-t[i nu-zala]g-ga / [ugu]-nam-ú[š-a t]a-àm me-diri
[ba-l]a-aṭ ša la-a na-ma-ri / [a-na m]u-ti mì-na-a ut-ti-i[r]

(Syr. 19) Life onto which no light is shed, how can it be more valuable than death?

E i 19 [na]m-t[i nu-za]la-ga (blank) /
[ugu]-nam-ú[š-(a)] ta-àm me-diri
ii = nam-ti nu-za-la-aq-qa /
u-ga na-ma-uš-ta ta-àm-me-d[a-ri]
iii =*[ba-l]a-aṭ ša la-a na-ma-ri* /
[a-na m]u-ti me-na-a ut-ti-i[r]
Ua 12 nam-ti-la níŋ-zala-ga nu-me-a
13 = ugu nam-úš-a a-na-àm mi-ni-diri
= *ba-la-ṭa ša la na-ma-ri a-na mi-ti mi-na-a ut-tir*
Ub iv 2 *ba-la-aṭ š[a ...]*

20 (not in SS) [ŋuruš] diŋir-zu šu-bi-šè ga-ra-an-zu
[eṭ-l]u ša il-ka ki-ni-iš l[u ...]

(Syr. 20) Young man, let me truly instruct you about your god!

E i 20 [ŋuruš] diŋir-zu šu-zi-bi-šè ga-ra-an-zu
ii = ku-ru-uš ti-kar-zu šu-zi-peš-še ga-r[a-zu]
iii = *[eṭ-l]u ša il-ka ki-ni-iš l[u- ...]*
Ub iii 3 ŋu-ru-uš [...]-še / ga-la-[...]
iv 3 = *eṭ-lu ⌜il-ka⌝ [x] x [...]*

21 (not in SS) [i]siš sí-ki-ib-ta ša-ra / [l]u-ul-bi ù-la mu-un-na-ka
(= [is]iš sí-ki-ib-ta ša-ra / lu-ul-bi ù-la mu-un-na-ak-ki)
sí-[k]i-ip ku-uš-ši-id / ni-is-sà-ti mi-iš qú-la-⌜ti⌝

(Syr. 21)

(Akk:) Get rid of, chase away grief! Spurn silence!

(Sum:) Chase away grief from depression! Spurn silence!

E i 21 [is]iš (so Alster; Dietrich: [a]-lim) sí-ki-ib-ta ša-ra /
[l]u-ul-bi ù-la mu-un-na-ka (so Alster; Dietrich: gim)
ii = [is]iš sí-ki-ip-ta ša-ra / lu-ul-bi ù-la mu-un-na-ak-ki
iii = *sí-ki[p ku]-uš-ši-id* [(*x*)]
ni-is-sà-a-[ti mi-iš] qu-l[a-ti]
Ub iii 4 a-li-im sí-[x x]-ti ša-ra /
lu-ul-bi ù-[...-u]n-na-ak(?)-ke(?)
iv 4 = *sí-ki-ip ku-uš-ši-id* [(*x*)] / *ni-is-sà-ti mi-iš qu-la-ti*

22 (= SS 20) ⋆[níŋ-saŋ-íl]-la u_4 šà ḫúl-la / ⋆[lu]l-bi ù-šar-šar ḫé-en-du
di-na-nu [ša ḫ]u-ud lìb-b[i] /1-en u_4-m[u] 10 ša-r[u lil-li-ka]

(Syr. 22) Instead of a single day's joy, let there come a long day of 36,000 years <of silence!>

(For variants, see the commentary)

E i 22 [...]-⌜íl(!)⌝-⌜la⌝(!) u_4 šà-ḫúl(!)-lá /
[lu-u]l-bi ù-šèr-šèr ḫé-en-du
ii = sà-an-ki-el-la ù-ša-ḫu-la-al
lu-ul-bi ù-šar-šar ḫé-en-du
iii = *di-na-nu [ša ḫ]u-ud lìb-b[i]* /
1-en u_4-m[u] 10 ša-r[u ...]
Ua 13 níŋ-saŋ-íl-la šà-ḫúl-la [u_4] ⌜diš⌝-kam u_4-im-ba-kam mu
10 šár ḫul in-na-ak
= *a-na di-na-an ḫu-ud lìb-bi [ša] u_4-um-ak-kal u_4-um*

		qu-li 10 ŠÁR MU.MEŠ *lil-li-ka*
Ub	iii 5	saŋ-ki-il-la [...] ḫu-ul-la /
		ú-˹lu˺-ul-bi [...] ḫi-in-du
	iv 5	= *a-na* ˹*di*˺*-na-ni* u_4*-mi ḫu-ud* [...] / 1 U_4 *qú-li* ˹*e*˺*-še-re-et ša-a-r*[*u* ...] (Dietrich: u_4*-ma-k*[*al*] instead *of 1* U_4 *qú-li*)

Syr. 22 A

Ub	iii 6	nam-ti nu-x[...] ˹ZI˺-TA TA-A / mi x ru x[...]x x
	iv 6	= *ba-la-ṭu ša la-a na-ma-*[*ri*] / UGU *mu-ti mi-na* [*ut-tir*]
Uc	r 1	[...] *la-a na*(!)*-*[...] / [...]*-ti mi-na-am ut-tir*

(Syr. 22 A, Ub and Uc only, cf. Syr. 19) Life onto which no light is shed, how can it be more valuable than death?

23 (replacing SS 21)

[ni]-in-gim lu-ú tur-ra-bi / sí-ra-aš ḫi-li ma-an-zu

= *ki-i-ma ma-ri* [^{d}*sí-ra-aš*] / *li-ri-iš-ka*

E	i 23	[n]i-in-gim(?!) lu-ú tur-ra-bi / [s]í-ra-aš ḫi-li ma-an-zu
	ii	= ni-in-ki lu-ú-tu-ur-ra-bi / sí-ra-aš ḫi-li ma-an-zu
	iii	= *ki-i-ma ma-ri* [...] / *li-ri-iš-ka* [(*x*)]
Ub	iii 7	ni-[i]n-gu [...] x x / ḫi-x x [...]
	iv 7	= ˹^{d}*sí-ra*˺*-*[*aš*] *ki-*[*ma* ...] / *li-ri-iš-*[*ka* (...)]
Uc	r 3	[...] *ki-i*(!)*-ma ma-a-ri* / [*li-ri-i*]*š-ka*

(Syr. 23) As for her little child, may Siraš rejoice over you! (Sum.: over me!)

24

E	i 24	˹e˺-ne ŋiš-ḫur / nam-u_{18}-lu gi-na
	ii	= e-en-ni ki-iš-ḫu-ur / [nam-l]u-ul-lu gi-na
	iii	= *an-nu-um ú-ṣ*[*u-ur-tum*] / *ša a-mi-lu-ut-t*[*i* (*x*)]
Ub	iii 8	˹en-ni˺ ˹gi-eš˺-[...] nam-u_{18}-lu-lu / ki-i[n-na]
	iv 8	= [*an*]*-nu-um-ma i-ṣ*[*u-ur-tum*] / *š*[*a*] *a-mi-lu-ut-ti* [(*x*)]
Uc	r 5	[*an-nu-u*]*m i-ṣu-ur-tum* / [*ša a-mi-l*]*u-ut-ti*

(Syr. 24) These are the regulations of righteous mankind!

Comments on Individual Lines

Syr. 1–3 (= SS 1–3, restored): Dietrich, 1992, 14, translates "Durch Ea sind die Geschichte (vor)ge-zeichnet, auf Geheiß desselben Gottes sind zugezeilt die Lose. Seit frühesten Zeiten geschieht dies (so)." Cf. the comments on SS 1–3.

Syr. 2 (= SS 2, restored): For te-em-ma in E ii, phonetic for KA.DÙG = dima, cf. the comments on SS 2.

Syr. 3 (= SS 3, restored): Dietrich restores the second part: *i-ba-á*[*š-ša-a an-ni*]*-*˹*i*˺*-*[*t*]*um*, from Ua; cf. comments on SS line 3.

Syr. 4–5 (= SS 4–5, restored): For Dietrich's translation, see the comments on SS 4–5.

Syr. 6: For Dietrich's translation, see the comments on SS 6.

Syr. 7–8 (= SS 16–18): Dietrich translates: "Wie der Himmel weit entfernt is (, sind sie weit)—eine Hand kann niemals hinlangen—, wie die tiefe der Unterwelt (weit entfernt ist, sind sie weit)—nichts weiß man (von ihnen)," commenting, n. 22, that Uc may mean "Ebenso wie der Himmel hoch ist, kann [sie] die Hand irgend]jemandes erreichen!"

Syr. 9 (= SS 18): For Dietrich's translation, see the comments on SS 18.

Syr. 10 (cf. SS 7): Dietrich, 1992, 16, translates Syr. 10: "Das Leben der Menschen ist nicht [ewig]," commenting, n. 29, that "die Orthographie *amēlūtu* (assyrisierend *amēluttu*) dürfte in diesem Text weniger das Abstraktum 'Menschheit' als den im Westen weit verbreitete *-utū*-Plural meinen, der im Osten vornehmlich für Adjektive steht."

Syr. 11, 12, 13, 14 (= SS 9, 10, 11, 12): Cf. Dietrich, 1992,16–17, with n. 30.

Syr. 15 (= SS 13): Dietrich restores *ú-[ša-pu-ú]*, "der Stärke im Land ver[wirklicht hat?]," which I have followed, although the space is almost too limited. Cf. the comments on SS 13.

Syr. 16 (not in SS): Bazi and Zizi are attested as rulers of Mari in the copy of *The Sumerian King List* excavated at Tell Leilan, line 215, according to which "Bazi, the leatherworker ([lú]ašgab), ruled for 30 years," while "Zizi, the fuller ([lú]ázlag), ruled for 20 years"; cf. C.-L. Vincente, "The Tell Leilan Recension of the Sumerian King List," ZA 50 (1995) 234–270. Earlier Dietrich had commented on the names, comparing Bazi to the references in H. Limet, *L'anthroponymie sumerienne* (Paris, 1968), 389f., etc. Dietrich, 1992, 26, makes the interesting comment that the absence of these two names in the Ugarit-version of *Ballade* is due to a somewhat different attitude characteristic of Ugarit toward deceased kings, in that kings in Ugarit were considered mortal when alive, but deified and counted among the gods when dead. Cf. also Klein, 2000, 207, n. 25, referring to the "Ḫamazi Letter," in which a king of Hamazi is named Zizi; cf. Hallo, 1992, 84, in: M.W. Chavalas et al. (eds.): *The Syrian Contribution to Cuneiform Literature and Learning*, Bibliotheca Mesopotamia 25 (Malibu, 1992), 69–88.

Syr. 17 (= SS 14): Dietrich: "Wo sind die Großen Könige, die seit frühesten Zeiten bis jetzt (lebten)?" noting that Ua is unusually formulated, "wo sind sie, die Könige ...?" Cf. the comments on SS 14.

Syr. 18 (= SS 15): Dietrich: "(Es scheint:) Sie sind weder empfangen noch geboren worden!" Cf. the comments on SS 15.

Syr. 19 (= SS 19): Dietrich: "Ein Leben ohne Freude – welchen Vorteil hat es gegenüber dem Tod?" For the verb *nawāru* in connection with joy, and for *watāru*, see the comments on SS 19.

Syr. 20 (not in SS): Dietrich: "Junger Mann, der ich [dir] deinen Gott in rechter Weise [...-en] will: weise ab, vertreibe die Klagen, mißachte den Kümmer!" (lit., "Stille, Schweigen"). Lambert, 1995, 39: "Man, I will truly ... let you know your god." Klein, 2002, 207: "Young man, let me truly instruct you about your god." The speaker is presumably a scribe or scholar, addressing his pupils; cf. the comments on Syr. 23 below. His advice follows in Syr. 21–23.

šu-zi-bi-šè is written phonetically šu-zi-peš-še in E ii.

Syr. 21 (not in SS): The Akk. text would make good sense as "Get rid of, chase away grief, spurn silence." *mi-iš* is an imperative from *mêšu*, "to despise." It is here equated with ù-la – ak, lit. "to make to nothing," ù-la, being a strong negation, is, to the best of my knowledge, attested here for the first time with ak. The phonetic spelling -ak-ki in E ii is noteworthy.

The Sumerian text a-li-im, in Ub iii 4, strangely written in the Sum. col., seems to be corrupted from *isiš, written [A].IGI, as Emar has, but then misread as a-lim and confused with *alû*, "where"? If Ub can be translated at all, it seems to mean: "Chase away grief from depression(? = sí-ki-ib-ta); spurn silence!" It is undoubtedly the Emar reading isiš, meaning "grief," or similar, that should apply here.

The Sumerian sí-ki-ib-ta is probably to be understood as a mistaken loanword from the noun *sikiptu*. Alster, 1990, 25, however, understood it as an "artificial" imperative from the Akkadian verb *sakāpu*, accepted by Klein, 2000, 207.

ša-ra is a phonetic writing for šar-ra = *kuššudu*.

For the equation lu-ul-bi = *qu-la-ti*, see [li-ib]LUL = *qu-la-a-tum*, JCS 13 (1959) 126 IV 4, quoted in AHw s.v. *qūlu* 5.

Syr. 22 (= SS 20): Dietrich: "An die Stelle der Herzensfreude einen ganzen Tag lang soll (ruhig) ein Kummertag von 10 Sar Jahren treten! (= 36.000 Jahre)."

Only the Akkadian text of Ua preserves the final verb as *lil-li-ka*, whereas the Sum. column of the same source clearly has the plain indicative: in-na-ak (= SS 20 in-ak). The precative *lillika*, "let there come," is a late reinterpretation of the easily understandable indicative referring to the past of the SS version. The intent may be a humorously resigned rhetorical question. In E the Sum. verb has been modified to the corresponding ḫé-en-du; Ub has phonetically ḫi-in-du; only Ua preserves the Sum. verb as in-na-ak. The latter remarkably reveals that there must have been a Babylonian source not too different from the SS version behind the Syro-Mesopotamian sources. Cf. the comments on SS 20 and pp. 292ff., *Chap. 3.3: Textual History*.

The variants show that the scribes struggled with the text. E seems to mean, "let a long day of 36,000 years <of silence> come," provided that there was room for [*ūm qūlí*], or similar, at the end of the line. The word order would then be different from Ua, which seems to mean: "instead of a long day of joy, let 36,000 years of silence come"; cf. the comments on the Sum. text below.

Ua: For *u$_4$-um-ak-kal*, see AHw 1412, *ūmakkal*, from *ūmam-kal(a)*, "ein Tag, einen ganzen Tag," and Dietrich, 1992, 19, n. 41. It is strange if *u$_4$-um-ak-kal* is here intended to equal u$_4$-im-ba-kam, because Ua: [u$_4$]-⸢diš⸣-kam already means that. So the text seems to have been expanded by the inclusion of both variants, instead of the plain SS u$_4$ šà-ḫúl-la diš-àm, "one day of joy." Although clarity undoubtedly was intended, the result rather was confusion.

Ub: "instead of a day [of joy, let] a day of 36,000 years of silence [come]." Note, however, that Dietrich reads *u$_4$-ma-k*[*al*], instead of *1* U$_4$ *qú-li*, noting, p. 19, n. 43, that there is hardly room for the expected kal-e. If this is intended as an equation of u$_4$-im-ba-kam, *ūmakkal* has apparently been misplaced; it logically belongs to the first part of the line, "a long day of joy," but it here instead refers to the years of silence. Perhaps it is a misunderstanding of mu im-ma, "last year"; cf. Lambert, BWL, 243 iii 56, partial parallel to SP 5 Sec. A 72, quoted in *Chap. 4.4*; cf. Alster, *Proverbs* II, 405; AHw 1123, *šaddadaqdi*, "voriges Jahr."

For níŋ-saŋ íl-la = *dinān*, "instead of," the phonetic variants are interesting: E: sà-an-ki-il-la; Ub: saŋ ki-il-la (/nk/ = ŋ).

The Sum. ù-šèr-šèr (phon. ù-šar-šar) is difficult. Alster, 1990, 25, points out that the standard Sum. column and the syllabic one seem to be reversed. Maybe ù-šar-šar is not meant as a writing for U×ŠÁR = ušar (36,000), but is phonetic for u$_4$-šár-šár, "tens of thousands of days?"

For lu-ul-bi cf. the comments on lu-ul-bi under line 21 above.

For further discussion of the implications of the changes that affected the Syro-Mesopotamian vers., see *Chap. 3.3: Textual History*, n. 3.

Syr. 23: Dietrich: "Wie über einen Sohn freue sich Ziraš über dich!" Klein, 1990, 207: "May Siraš rejoice over you, as over her son!" *lirīška* is here equated to ma-an-zu, in which it is tempting to suggest that ma-an stems from a misunderstood *ḫi-li ma-az = *kuzbu*; *ulṣu*; cf. Sefati, *Love Songs*, 126. It is more likely, however, that ma-an should be taken as the 1st person prefix in the dative. This would imply that the text goes back to a Sumerian original speaking in the 1st person (so already Alster, 1990, 25). The Akk. translations had the 2nd person instead, "let her rejoice over you!"

The Sum. Emar: [ni]-in-gim = phon. ni-in-ki, and Ub ni-[i]n-gu, are here simply equated with *kīma*, or this may be an adverb meaning "as if you were," apparently from *e-ne-gim. In lu-ú tur-ra-bi, ú is superfluous, and -bi is the non-personal suffix used for a person, "her." It is here equated with *māru*, presumably understood as the pupils of the scribal schools, where the text was enjoyed and transmitted. The preoccupation of the scribes with similar matters apparently also comes to light in Syr. 20, and in the Neo-Assyrian version, lines 6–7 (cf. *Chap. 3.3c*).

For Siraš, also known as Siriš, see CAD S 306, explained as a Sum. loanword, but it probably had a much more widespread history, as the Hebrew *tîrôš* (תירוש) suggests; cf. Lambert, 1995, 41. The Sumerian name for the beer-goddess was ᵈnin-ka-si; cf. *Instr. Šuruppak* 86.

Syr. 24: Dietrich: "Dies ist das Schicksal der Menschen." "Schicksal" is not a precise rendering of ŋiš-ḫur = *uṣurtum*. Klein, 2000, 207, n. 32, translates similarly "This is the fate of humanity," but correctly states that this literally means "plan, rules, regulations," which, in fact, makes better sense here. It recapitulates the beginning of the text, where Enki/Ea's world order is described. Note, however, that E here, by adding gi-na, "righteous" to [nam-l]u-lu, phonetic for nam-u$_{18}$-lu-lu, gives the text an ethical twist absent from the original Sumerian sources. Since the Akk. translation of gi-na is absent, another, but less likely possibility, is that it here represents some corrupted form of the Sum. genitive. Lambert, 1995, 41, translates "This is the true rule of mankind," which would be a violation of Sumerian grammar, but may nevertheless be intended.

3.3c The Neo-Assyrian Version

K 6917 and K 13679 were identified and joined by R. Borger. The copy provided on pl. 16 was made by M.J. Geller. It is a fragment from the obverse(?) of the middle part of a tablet that had at least two columns, of which the left contains the Sumerian text, the right the Akkadian translation. There is hardy more than a half broken sign on the left side of lines 3–5. There is a separating line after line 7, coinciding with the beginning of *The Ballade of Early Rulers.* Lines 1–7 seem to contain proverbial phrases similar to the ones in *Proverbs from Ugarit* (*Chap. 3.4*), but they do not duplicate; cf. further below.

There is no Akkadian translation of lines 8ff. This might be due to the fact that the lines were repetitions of a previous section on the same tablet; thus, the scribe found it unnecessary to repeat the translation.

General Interpretation

The Neo-Assyrian fragment is a surprising addition to the history of the vanity theme in Mesopotamian tradition of the first millennium B.C. The fragment is well written and comes from King Assurbanipal's (668–627 B.C.) library in Nineveh. It shows that a Sumerian literary type known from Syro-Mesopotamian sources from about the thirteenth century B.C. was still cherished by Neo-Assyrian scribes of the first millennium B.C.

It is questionable, however, how much of the text was "new," and how much rested on older sources. It is clear from the preserved fragment that a section of about three lines was repeated as an introductory "refrain," followed by examples of how "vanity" reveals itself. In this sense, the Neo-Assyrian version is reminiscent of the Ugaritic tablets, of which at least one (Ua) repeats the three-line introductory prologue. It further includes the section of proverbial phrases edited in *Chap. 3.4: Proverbs from Ugarit,* which seems to go back to a Sumerian forerunner. The proverbs from Ugarit are not duplicated in the preserved parts of the Neo-Assyrian fragment, but the tone is very much similar. The conclusion is that *The Ballade of Early Rulers* became part of a larger collection of sententious sayings, as the Sumerian sources (A, B, and D) already suggest (cf. *Chap. 3.3: The Contents of the Sammeltafel*), and that the Neo-Assyrian fragment is the latest known attestation of this tradition. Since line 4 seems to quote a proverb also hinted at in a Sumerian hymn of the early second millennium B.C., it is quite possible that much more of the complete tablet went back to Sumerian sources. On the other hand, it is also very likely that such quotations were intermingled with sententious sayings of more recent, partly popular, origin.

Of the preserved section, line 3', apparently implying that people of low status envy those of higher status, is a rare glimpse into social history, although not surprising. The saying, commenting on the unrealistic marriage ambitions of a low-status female weaver (line 4') is, to the best of my knowledge, unique in Mesopotamian literature.

The text leaves the same impression as the Syro-Mesopotamian sources of the *Ballade,* as well as their Sumerian forerunners, that such texts were cherished in a humorous atmosphere in the scribal schools. This implies that their "pessimism" should be read *cum grano salis,* with a glint in the eye.

	Text	Translation
		(0) [With Enki the plans are drawn.]
1'	[d]i-ma ⸢diŋir⸣-⸢re⸣-e-n[e-ke$_4$ ki nam-sur-sur-re] *Akk. broken*	*(1')* According to the decisions of the gods [lots are allotted.]
2'	[x] igi-du-ta NE-e al-ŋál-[la(?)] *Akk. broken*	*(2')* Since [time immemorial] there has been *wind(?)!
3'	lú-ḫuŋ-ŋá eŋir lú níŋ-tuku ḫé-en-⸢ŠID⸣ *ag-⸢ru(?)⸣-x x x*[...]	*(3')* A hired worker counts after the inherintance of a wealthy man.
4'	[(x)] munus-uš-bar lú-ḫuŋ-ŋá ì-(erasure)-šub *iš-par-tum ag-*[*ra* ...]	*(4')* A female weaver leaves a hired worker.
5'	šà ki in-du-kám nu-dùg-ga má(so according to Geller)-e N[E?] ⸢x⸣ *šá ana lìb-bi A*[*K*(?) ...]	*(5')* Whatever the heart('s desires(?)) are on earth, they are no good, [they evaporate(?)] in *"wind(?)."
6'	[(x)] ⸢á⸣ dumu ^{m}gašam(NUN.ME.TAG)-ke$_4$ šà-ḫúl-la nu-šúm-m[u-]x *i-di mar um-ma-⸢nu(?)⸣* [...]	*(6')* The task of a scholar's pupil does not yield a joyous heart.
7'	[l]ú-bi ki kur-ir-ra-a[š(?)] ⸢x⸣ *a-me-lu šu-ú ⸢x⸣* [...]	*(7')* (Even) that man [goes] to the grave(?) [...]
8'	[ki e]n-ki-<ke$_4$> ŋiš-ḫur ḫ[ur-(x)-re]	*(8')* With Enki the plans are [drawn].
9'	[dima] diŋir(!)-re-e-ne-ke$_4$ níŋ-⸢x(Geller: ug or nínda)⸣ [x x]	*(9')* According to the decisions of the gods [lots are allotted.]
10'	[(x) igi-du]-ta NE-e a[l(?)-ŋál-(la x)]	*(10')* Since [time immemorial] there has been *wind(?)!
11'	*traces of three + three signs.*	

Comments on Individual Lines

NA 1: [d]i-ma phonetic for dima = KA.DÙG. Cf. the comments on *Ballade* SS 2.

NA 2 and 10: These lines do not confirm the expected reading im al-ŋál-la = [*ša*]-*ru* as found in Ua 22–23, but have NE instead of im. E obviously had difficulties with the line, reading i-nim NI iŋ-ŋál-la with no Akkadian translation. Cf. the comments on *Ballade* *SS 3. Since the following -e seems to be the loc.-term. suffix, NE can hardly be izi, "fire," or dè, "smoke," in these cases.

NA 3–4: The reading ŠID for the final verb in line 3 was suggested by Geller, meaning "the hired worker counts after (the inheritance share) of the rich man." Two Sumerian proverbs mention hired workers: SP 13.11 and SP 28. 22, but they do not duplicate our text. There seems, however, to be a hint at a similar saying in *Abī-ešuḫ Hymn B* (Alster, OLP 21 [1990] 13, text 2:32): lú-ḫuŋ munus-šà-zu-gim munus-uš-bar ⸢x⸣ [...]. The context is far from clear, but the juxtaposition of the pair lú-ḫuŋ and munus-uš-bar, as well as the position of -gim, favors the translation of Alster, ibid., 22 (slightly modified):

"(You, a) hired worker, a woman according to your heart [should be a] female weaver," rather than the ETCSL, translating "...a hired worker, like a midwife, a female weaver...." Alster's translation, strictly speaking, would require munus šà-za(-ak), but since this is a relatively late text, this is not decisive. Since both the preceding and the following lines speak of prayers to deities (2:30: [Marduk], 2:33–34: Utu and Nanna) in a larger context describing the king approaching the cult place (in 2:16 read ku_4-ku_4-zu, "when you enter"), a reasonable guess is that the relations between the two types of lower-class workers are compared to the relationship between a ruler and his god. In our case the point seems to be that a female weaver fails to appreciate a man whose social position is similar to her own, in other words, she has no realistic understanding of her own social position, always dreaming of a "prince" to show up; it's all vanity!

NA 5: I am unable to explain ki-in-du-kám. A meaning like (the heart's) desires (= níŋ?) would fit the context well. The sign before e, according to Geller, is má, which I cannot explain. Another expression of "vanity" might be expected here. Cf. the comments in *Chap. 3.3a* on *Ballade* *SS 3.

NA 6: The first preserved sign looks like the right side of á. I tentatively translate *i-di* as "task" here, but compare perhaps CAD I-J, 14, quoting RA 35 2 i 19 (Mari rit.): *mārī gallābi ina i-di mārī ummênu izzazzu*, "the members of the barbers' guilds take up a position next to the artisans." In this case the point seems to be that not even the "academic" profession of the scribes suffices to secure happiness, because all men must ultimately die.

NA 7: kur-ir-ra seems here to be a designation of the netherworld, the grave, or similar. ir-ra may be phonetic for kur-ír-ra, "the land of weeping."

NA 9: This must have been a repetition of NA 1', but but the two last preserved signs, níŋ-⌜x⌝ are difficult to harmonize with *Ballade* 2, so far only preserved in the Syro-Mesopotamian version.

3.4 Proverbs from Ugarit

An Addition to The Ballade of Early Rulers in the Syro-Mesopotamian Version with a Sumerian Forerunner

Publication History

A short sequence of bilingual proverbs inscribed on R.S. 25.130, published by J. Nougayrol, in *Ugaritica* 5 (1968) 293–297, and most recently treated by Dietrich, "«Ein Leben ohne Freude». ..." UF 24 (1992) 9–29 (pp. 28–29), is duplicated by the obverse of an unilingual Sumerian fragment from Nippur, CBS 13777.[1] The reverse of the same tablet is relevant for the text edited in *Chap. 3.1* as *Níŋ-nam* B.

The proverb section follows immediately after *The Ballade of Early Rulers* (edited in *Chap. 3.3*), on the reverse of R.S. 25.130. Nougayrol's copy indicates "Tranche fruste (anépigraphic?)" on the transition on the edge. It is followed by a second quotation of *The Ballade of Early Rulers*. It is, therefore, likely that further parallels could be sought on such *Sammeltafel* as include *The Ballade of Early Rulers*, immediately after that text.

The first public mention of CBS 13777 was made in PSD A/3, 28,[2] listing the following lines of CBS 13777: [...] lu$_2$-⸢kaš$_4$-e⸣ i$_3$-⸢dib-be$_2$⸣, as an OB duplicate to *Ugaritica* 5, no. 164: 34'–35': DUMU-lu$_2$-ad$_4$-ke$_4$-e dib-ba = DUMU *ḫu-um-mu-ri* DUMU *la-si-mi i-ba-ʾ*, with the translation: "the son of the cripple catches up with the son of the runner."[3]

A set of photographs of CBS 13777 by Eleanor Robson, taken in 2002, is published here, pls. 32–33.

CBS 13777 obv. is inscribed with approximately twenty lines from the right side of the tablet, with the right edge preserved. There are two double lines, one after line 6 and one after line ca. 19. I have not been able to identify the first six lines. The ca. twelve inscribed lines between the double lines may well have contained the original sequence reflected in the Ugaritic source. Of these, at least four lines, perhaps more, contain the phrase na-me (na-an-), "nobody should," in the middle part, which suggests a sequence like lines 28'–33' of the Ugaritic source, preceding lines 34'–35'. The two lines that come after that, just before the second double line, may well have corresponded to lines 36'–39' of the Ugaritic source. It is tempting, then, to read [... lú] ⸢silim-ma-kam⸣ in line 19, but the traces fit neither silim nor ma, although -kam is rather obvious. There may be traces of glosses, but this is uncertain. Perhaps this explains the uncertain signs in line 18, where some signs seem to be placed higher up than the normal lines.

Dietrich's translation is quoted in its entirety below. The transliteration below is that of Nougayrol and Dietrich with a few minimal changes.[4]

General Interpretation

The most remarkable feature of the sequence is that the theme of the cripple catching up with the runner now appears to go back to a Sumerian proverbial saying. Dietrich suggests an "ethical" interpretation of the sequence. A slightly modified interpretation is suggested below.

In the Ugaritic text, the relevant Sum. proverb occurs within a sequence that teaches social understanding in a way that seems unique to Sumerian literature: Nobody should express contempt for someone weaker than himself (U$_5$ 30'–33'), and nobody

1. Alster, in: *N.A.B.U.* 89 (1999) 88ff.
2. It was apparently listed under an erroneous number (CBS 1377) in the manuscript of Civil's catalogue, which I saw in Philadelphia around 1989–90, which meant that the fragment was not used until it was "reidentified" some years later.
3. The Sumerian terms ad$_4$ and ba-za have caused a good deal of discussion. There can, in my opinion, be no doubt that ba-za and ad$_4$ mean "halt" and "lame," rather than "cripple" and "dwarf," respectively. Cf. Alster, "Halt or Dwarf: The Meaning of ba-za = *pessû*," *von Soden FS*, 1–6. Cf. PSD B, 22 for a different opinion, and Hallo, *Moran FS*, 207, for a concurring view. ba-za is, in fact, a loanword from *pessû*.
4. In line 28, I read na-na-zu instead of na-na-ke$_4$. ke$_4$ may, in fact, easily be mistaken for zu in mB script.

should feel entitled to find faults among others (U_5 28'–29'). Non-disabled people should bear in mind that the son of a lame person may catch up with a swift runner, and a wealthy man is advised to bear in mind that a rich man's son may (one day have to) stretch his hand out toward a poor man's son (scl. in order to ask for help), etc. This is said to be the "lot of a healthy man" (U_5 38'–39': ŋiš-šub-ba lú silim-ma = *i-si-iq šal-mi*),[5] and to be the order allotted by the gods; it is further said to be "the day's order" (U_5 26'–27': u_4-da(!) šu-dù-bi = *ṭe-em ur-ri-ša*). As a consequence nobody can "make known the work assignment of mankind" (U_5: a-dù nam-lú-u_{18}-lù-ke_4 na-me na-na-zu = *a-da a-wi-lu-ti mám-ma la ú-ʾa-ad-da*). According to Dietrich, who translates "niemand darf eine Last für Menschen bestimmen," this implies that people are not entitled to pronounce judgment upon one another. Yet, careful observation of the two decisive terms a-dù = *a-da* (ll. 28–29) and silim = *šalmu* (ll. 38–39) suggests a slightly different interpretation.

a-dù nam-lú-u_{18}-lù-ke_4 na-me na-na-zu = *a-da a-wi-lu-ti mám-ma la ú-ʾa-ad-da* was translated convincingly "Qui ne fixe aux hommes une corvée (de plus)?" by J. Nougayrol, 1968, 295. a-dù is undoubtedly phonetic for á-dù = *adû*, "work assignment,"[6] cf. CAD A/1, 135: *adû* C. Alternatively, but less likely, one may consider 131: *adû* A: "(a type of formal agreement)," which, however, is attested only in Neo-Assyrian and Neo-Babylonian.[7] The implication seems to be that nobody can predict how long each man will have to fulfil the duties allotted to him in his lifetime, presumably, but not necessarily only, in terms of religious services, ultimately because the roles played by the healthy and the disabled may at any moment be reversed by the gods.

ŋiš-šub-ba lú silim-ma = *i-si-iq šal-mi*, in fact means "the lot (allotted to a) healthy man," and this refers to a man in good, healthy physical condition, rather than to a man whose behavior is ethically untarnished ("das Los eines sich tadellos Verhalten").

That a Sumerian forerunner of the Ugaritic saying is by now known suggests that more of the Ugaritic sayings are likely to have belonged to a larger collection of sayings, perhaps all exemplifying the order instituted by the gods for human life. This feature is common to both the *Ugaritic Proverbs*, and to *The Ballade of Early Rulers*, of which a copy of its Syro-Mesopotamian version was even inscribed on the same tablet as the proverbs. The same phenomenon recurs in the Neo-Assyrian fragment of the *Ballade* (*Chap. 3.3c*), of which the preserved fragment does not contain the *Ballade* itself, but rather a sequence of sayings similar to those of the Ugaritic source, all said to be the lot decreed for mankind by the gods.

One may dare to suggest, therefore, that both the Ugaritic and the Neo-Assyrian examples are fragments of a larger collection of sayings centering on ideas common in "wisdom" circles in the ancient Near East. At least some of these may go back to Sumerian sources.[8]

The Egyptian *Instructions of Amen-em-ope* contain a similar sequence:[9] "Do not laugh at a blind man nor tease a dwarf, nor injure the affairs of the lame. Do not tease a man who is in the hand of his god (i.e., insane), nor be fierce of face against him if he errs. For a man is clay and straw, and the god is his builder. He is tearing down and building up every day. He makes a thousand poor men as he wishes." Although *The Instructions of Amen-em-ope* was long ago recognized as a partial forerunner to biblical Prov 23:17ff., there is remarkably no biblical counterpart to these lines. Yet, the intent is, in fact, less biblical than may appear at first glance, as will be evident from the discussion below.

There is no verbatim similarity between our sources and the Egyptian one, but the latter reveals an awareness of the same type of social understand-

5. *šalmu* means, firstly, "healthy," cf. AHw 1149: "unverzehrt, heil, gesund," rather than the ethically meant "tadellos," although, of course, this is a case that shows that the meaning may shift to both aspects.
6. This crucial reference is listed in PSD A/1, 52.
7. I do not know the reasons for Dietrich's translation "eine Last für Menschen."
8. There can be no doubt that our Ugaritic text rests on a good Sumerian original; cf. the beautiful anticipatory genitive in lines 26–27: u_4-da(!) šu-dù-bi = *ṭe-em ur-ri*, although it seems to have been somewhat corrupted; cf. the comments below.
9. The text is cited here from J.M. Wilson's translation in ANET, 424. This occurs in the 25th "house."

ing as the Ugaritic source. In the Egyptian text the main focus is on man's inability to understand the dispositions of the gods, a theme familiar also in Babylonian culture. The ethical aspect of the advice should, therefore, not be overestimated.

The Instructions of Amen-em-ope is difficult to date precisely, but may possibly date around the seventh to sixth centuries B.C. Since the Ugaritic text is much older and the Sumerian one at least a thousand years older, the most likely conclusion is that these sources reflect ideas that may have been common in some "wisdom movement" in Western Asia in the second and first millennia B.C. The idea seems strangely not to be reflected in the biblical Proverbs, but many features in that book, as well as in Ecclesiastes, point toward the existence of such an international "wisdom movement."

The sequence is characteristic of a traditional wisdom concept: a good man is expected to be recompensed with a prosperous health in his own lifetime. Since, of course, this did not always happen in real life, various explanations may be expected in the wisdom literature. The answer given here, that this may be due to the failure of mankind to understand the dispositions of the gods, accords well with traditional Mesopotamian thinking.

U$_5$ = RS 25.130, *Ugaritica* 5, no.164: Sumero-Akkadian bilingual
B = Nippur dupl: CBS 13777 obv.: Monolingual Sumerian

U$_5$ 24'–25'	[(nam(?)-)lú-u$_{18}$-lu níŋ(?)-aka(?)-ni ní-te-n]i nu-zu-a |
	| *⌜a⌝-[wi-l]u-tu ⌜e⌝-[pé-š]a(?) ⌜i-na?⌝ ra-ma-ni-ša la i-du-ú*
Sum./Akk	People do not by themselves know their doings.
U$_5$ 26'–27'	u$_4$-da(!) šu-dù-bi ŋi$_6$-[m]e-a-bi-[da ki] diŋir ì-in-ŋál |
	= *ṭe-em ur-ri-ša ù mu-ši-ša it-ti* DINGIR *i-ba-áš-ši*
Sum.	(corrupt, see commentary)
Akk	The plans for day and night rest with the god.
U$_5$ 28'–29'	a-dù nam-lú-u$_{18}$-lu-ke$_4$ na-me na-na-zu
	= *a-da a-wi-lu-ti mám-ma la ú-ʾa-ad-da*
Sum./Akk	—Nobody should make people's working assignment known.
U$_5$ 30'–31'	šu-kúr nam-lú-u$_{18}$-lu-ke$_4$ na-me na-an-dug$_4$-ga
	= *ṭa-píl-ti a-wi-lu-ti mám-ma <la> i-qab-bi*
Sum./Akk.	Nobody should pronounce an insult against other people.
U$_5$ 32'–33'	igi-tur-sig-ga na-me <šu na->gíd-i
	= *ši-ṭu-ut en-ši mám-ma la i-leq-qé*
B o. 16	[...] an-x-ga-⌜x⌝
Sum.	*No weak man should accept a deprecation. (With a minimal emendation, see commentary.)
Akk.	Nobody should accept the deprecation of someone weak.
U$_5$ 34'–35'	dumu lú-ad$_4$-ke$_4$ dumu-lú-kaš$_4$-e dab-ba
	= DUMU *ḫu-um-mu-ri* DUMU *la-si-mi i-ba-aʾ*

B o. 17 — [...] lú-⌜kaš$_4$-e⌝ ì-⌜dib-bé⌝
Sum./Akk. — A son of a lame man catches up with the son of a runner.

U$_5$ 36'- 37' — dumu lú-níŋ-tuku-tuku dumu lú-kur-ra-šè šu{-nu}-ba [ ]x
= DUMU *ša-ri-i a-na* DUMU *la-ap-ni qa-at-su i-tar-ra-[a]*
Sum./Akk. — A son of a wealthy man stretches his hand out toward the son of a poor man.

U$_5$ 38'- 39' — e-<ne> ŋiš-šub-ba lú-silim-ma-ke$_4$ = *an-nu-ú i-si-iq šal-m[i]*
Sum./Akk. — This is the lot of a healthy man.

Dietrich's Translation

24'–25' Die Menchheit kann das (richtige) Handeln von sich aus nicht wissen,
26'–27' die Bestimmung ihres Tages und ihrer Nacht liegt bei dem Gott,
28'–29' —niemand darf eine Last für Menschen bestimmen,
30'–31' niemand darf eine Verschmähung gegen Menschen aussprechen,
32'–33' niemand darf Mißachtung gegenüber einem Schwachen bezeigen!
34'–35' Der Sohn eines Lahmen geht (vielmehr) daher mit dem Sohn eines behende Laufenden,
36'–37' der Sohn eines Reichen hebt (vielmehr) seine Hand gegenüber dem Sohn eines Armen auf—
38'–39' dies ist das Los eines sich tadellos Verhalten.

Comments on Individual Lines

Lines 24'–25': The Sumerian text may simply have had lú, although the Akkadian translation suggests [nam-lú-u$_{18}$-lu ...], etc. *awīlūtu* here is not a designation of "mankind" in general or the status of a free man or the like, but simply means any man or "people," in terms of a collective plural constructed as a singular. Cf. CAD A/2, 57f. *amīlūtu*, also "somebody, anybody"; AHw 91, *awīlūtu*, "Menschheit," but also 3) "irdendeiner." Cf. the comments on *Ballade* Syr. 10.

Lines 26'–27': The Sum. text seems to be corrupt. Perhaps something like */u$_4$ ŋi$_6$-bi-da-ak me-bi/, "the *me* of days and nights," in which me interestingly would correspond to *ṭēmu*. Because of a failure to understand the Sumerian grammar, me was reinterpreted as the plural marker me-a, and u$_4$ was omitted by mistake.

ki] diŋir seem to represent *ki diŋir-ra(-na)-ka. diŋir is generally used of a specific deity, but seems occasionally to come close to the meaning "God," although not in a monotheistic sense. Cf. *Chap. 2.2: Instr. Ur-Ninurta* 19: níŋ-diŋir(-ra), "things of God" = "religious affairs."

Lines 28–29': For a-dù = *adû*, cf. *General interpretation* above.

Lines 30'–31': For šu-kúr = *ṭapiltu*, cf. AHw 1380, "Schmähung." Cf. p. 271, šu – kar.

Lines 32'–33': In B = CBS 13777, obv. 16, the sign read x can hardly be sig$_5$(?) or ⌜a-sì⌝, but looks rather like ⌜A⌝ DÙG. It is thus uncertain whether the line belongs here.

The Sum. text can be understood as (lú) sig-ga na-me <šu(?) na->gíd-i = *la i-leq-qé*, "a weak person should not accept (a deprecation)," but the Akk. text took this as a genitive "(nobody) should accept the deprecation of a weak man."

Lines 36'–37': lú-kur-ra is phonetic for *lú-úku-ra = *lapnu*.

The Sum. verb corresponding to *i-tar-ra-[a]* is missing or corrupt. The negation nu- has mistakenly been entered from the preceding lines. The verb could hardly have been *šu – ba = šu-bar, although the remaining ba might suggest this, but rather something like *šu – lá.

Lines 38'–39': e = *annû*, "this," seems to be mistaken for e-<ne>, cf. *Ballade of Early Rulers* Syr. 24.

3.5 Enlil and Namzitarra

Publication History

The basic text edition is "Enlil and Namzitarra," Civil, 1974, 65–71. Some interesting observations were made by Vanstiphout: "Some Notes on «Enlil and Namzitarra»," RA 74 (1980) 67–71, and Lambert: "A New Interpretation of Enlil and Namzi-tar-ra," *Orientalia* 58 (1989) 508–509. Later Klein, without taking Vanstiphout's and Lambert's contributions into account, in: "The 'Bane' of Humanity: a Lifespan of One Hundred Twenty Years," Klein, 1990, 57–70, commented on some crucial points (ll. 17–18 and 19–21), including the Emar version published by Arnaud, 1985–1987. The Emar version was also included in Kämmerer, *Śimâ milka*, 218–227.

Sources

The main sources are listed in Civil's edition; cf. also *Chap. 3.2: Níŋ-nam Version D*, where another part of the main source, A = 3N-T 326 + 360, is treated.

A: 3N-T 326 (= IM 58427) + 360 (= A 30218), col. ix, from line 8ff. (3N-T 326), ending in 3N-T 326 col. x 8 = 1–27. This contains the entire text of Civil's composition (d) = *Enlil and Namzitarra*; cf. the summary under *Chap. 3.2: Níŋ-nam, vers. D.* Photographs pls. 36–39.
B: CBS 4605 (PBS 12, 31, collated by Civil) = 1–18.
C: N 5149 obv. = 2–9.
D: N 5909 obv., copy by Alster: "A Duplicate to 'Enlil and Namzitara'," *N.A.B.U.* (1990) 82, no. 102 = 6–18. Here included on pl. 48.
E: CBS 7917 + N 4784 obv. = 10–14.
F: UM 29-16-79A iii = 19–27 + 79B (a tiny chip, courtesy Y. Sefati).
G: N 3097 = 15–18.

The Emar version is published in copies by Arnaud in *Emar* VI/1–4, nos. 771, 772, 773, 774, 592.

That the Emar fragments belong to the same tablet was first recognized by Civil, 1989. These were treated by Klein, 1990, esp. pp. 58–59, with pp. 63–65, nn. 6–17, with a concordance of the lines occurring in the two versions on p. 66, n. 23; cf. already Civil, 1989, 7, n. 7.

Interpretation

All aspects of the text have been discussed in the editions by Civil and Klein. These will not be repeated here in detail.

The "fable" of *Enlil and Namzitarra* is included in *Chap. 3* among texts relating to the vanity theme, because it clearly raises questions about the lasting values of life, material versus nonperishable, such as an office in Enlil's temple, as opposed to cattle, gold, and silver. From a strictly formal point of view, it could well be said rather to belong in *Chap. 4*, as a fable dealing with an animal and a deity. The text seems to have been included in the scribal curriculum, not so much for its folkloristic qualities as such, but because it represents an example of sophisticated use of both mythology and folktale motifs, combined with "the Sumerian scribes' fondness for puns" (Civil, p. 67; cf. below).[1] In this respect, it resembles the two "folktales" included in *Chap. 5*; these deal with legal proceedings in a humorous, or even parodying, way characteristic of scribal wit.

The protagonists are Namzitarra, who probably was a low-ranking official in Enlil's temple, and the god Enlil, who, disguised as a raven, appears before Namzitarra (ll. 1–9). When Enlil questions him about where he comes from (l. 3), Namzitarra is able to see through the disguise, immediately recognizing Enlil as the great god (ll. 10–15). Since this surprises Enlil, he asks how Namzitarra was able to recognize

1. For puns, cf. especially G. Farber, "«Daß Lied von der Hacke», ein literarischer Spaß?" CRRAI 41, 269–373; Scott B. Noegel (ed.), *Puns and Pundits* (Bethesda, 2000), with contributions by J. Klein, Y. Sefati, V.A. Hurowitz, A. Kilmer, and S.W. Greaves. Further, G. Selz, "«Babilismus» und die Gottheit ᵈNindagar," *Dietrich FS*, 647–684. Cf. also Alster, 2000, and the comments on *Instr. Šuruppak* 263.

him (l. 16). The answer that follows (ll. 17–18) shows that Enlil had succeeded a predecessor by the name of Enmešarra, to whom Enlil was related (cf. l. 18: šeš-ad-da-zu, "your uncle"). This is an allusion to a myth, according to which, apparently, Enmešarra had deprived Enlil of his "Enlilship" (l. 17) and thus for a time had claimed to be able to decree the destinies (cf. l. 18); but Enmešarra had then been taken captive and, apparently, had returned the "Enlilship" to Enlil.

The following lines (19–21) are best understood as Enlil's continued speech, warning that material wealth is perishable, and that the inevitable end of human life is approaching. But implicitly, is it not rather the scribe who speaks here, promulgating his wisdom? The point is obvious, anyway: Enlil, as a compensation, offers something more lasting than material wealth. So, when Enlil, once more emphasizing that he is the one who is now in power (l. 22), asks about Namzitarra's name (l. 23), he promises that his name, meaning "the one blessed with a good destiny" (l. 25) will match the destiny he is going to decree. Accordingly, Namzitarra is blessed with constant access to Enlil's temple for all his successors (ll. 26–27).

If Civil's suggestion (p. 67) is correct, it was a phrase spoken by Enmešarra that gave Namzitarra the clue that enabled him to recognize Enlil in the disguise of a raven (l. 18): u_4-dè en-gim nam ⌜ga-zu⌝-e-še, "«Now I shall know the fates, like a lord», he said." In my opinion, this is spoken by Enlil.[2] But, in any case, the important point is that the words were a kind of prophetic saying that contained a typical scribal pun: the words u_4 … ga-zu, which Namzitarra recognized as a pun on uga^{mušen}, interpreting them as "to know the raven."[3]

There are two main motifs. First, the ability to take advantage of the promise of a blessing, even if obtained through cunning or fraud, so abundantly illustrated in Genesis. It was clearly cunning that enabled Namzitarra to recognize Enlil, thanks to his ability to look through a difficult pun. Second, and related to it, is the motif of matching a favorable name to the destiny of its bearer, also well known from Genesis. The play on names also is reminiscent of the Aesopian type of fable, best illustrated in Sumerian literature by *The Fable of the Lion and the She-goat* (see *Chap. 4.4*). Cf. also *Instr. Šuruppak* lines 139; 254; 268.

The text is not simply a folkloristic fable, but a composition that uses a fable as its outer form, incorporating other literary references in a sophisticated manner. That Enlil appears in disguise is a feature that occurs elsewhere; in particular in *Enlil and Ninlil*, in which Enlil, consecutively disguised as a gatekeeper, a man from the river, and a boatman, seduces Ninlil and so engenders the moon-god.[4]

It is difficult to look through the allusions the text makes to earlier mythology. We do not know any complete "myth" of Enmešarra, but must be satisfied with what can be retrieved from scattered references in other texts, as well as from parallels that can be inferred, in particular from the Ninurta-Anzu mythology.[5]

The most likely solution is that Enlil himself usurped the role of the supreme ruler of the world, the "Enlilship." This, apparently, was then later taken from Enlil by Enmešarra, who, according to our text, was Enlil's uncle (l. 17), but then reconquered by Enlil (l. 18). We do not know any details relating to this episode, but may justly infer from the Anzu-Ninurta mythology that Enmešarra, like Anzu, was defeated by Enlil, who regained his power. It is remarkable that Enmešarra is not said to have been

2. As already seen by Lambert, *Orientalia* 58 (1989) 508; cf. below under comments on lines 17–18.
3. Enmešarra is elsewhere associated with a rooster and the *šuššuru*-bird, but not specifically with the raven; cf. Civil, p. 67, referring to Lambert, AnSt 20, 112: 2 and 114: 14. For connections between Enlil and the raven, see the references listed by Civil, p. 65: Lambert, AnSt 20, 112: 15; én uga^{mušen} mud-lá ^{d}en-líl-lá (Caplice, *Orientalia* 34, 112); Kutscher: YNER 6, 97: 108f. It is worthy of mention that the Nordic god Odin, whose role is here somewhat similar to Enlil's, is associated with two ravens, Hugin and Mugin.
4. Cf. Civil, p. 65. Cf. further *Chap. 4.2: CBS 438: The Fable of a Fox and Enlil as Merchant*, and Civil, JCS 28 (1976) 72–81. This is reminiscent of Odin in Old Norse mythology; cf. also Gen 6:4; 32:28, etc.
5. Cf. the discussion by Civil, p. 66, who lists earlier literature to Enmešarra in n. 5, and already mentions the possible Ninurta-Anzu parallel; cf. also Klein, p. 63, n. 3.

killed, but only taken captive (l. 17), like his counterpart, amar-anzu, in *Ninurta and the Turtle*.

That the Sumerian literates favored elaborating upon divine succession myths clearly appears from UET 6/1 2: *Ninurta and the Turtle*, in which the Anzu-bird and Ninurta both tried to conquer the symbols of world power for themselves, that is, the *me*, the ŋiš-ḫur ("plans"), as well as the dub-nam-tar-ra (the tablet of destinies), albeit in that case from Enki rather than from Enlil. That text was hardly meant as a serious theological treatise, but rather as a good-humored parody of divine ambition. So whatever theological message may have been embedded in our text, it may not have been too seriously meant. Yet, there must have been awareness of divine succession myths.

A Sumerian fragment of such a myth is UET 6/1, 30.[6] Further, *Curse of Agade* 209: ér ama-a-a ᵈen-líl-lá-ke$_4$, "the lament of Enlil's ancestors," indicates that another generation of gods preceded Enlil's reign. This accords with some god-lists and other literary texts as well.[7] Two later texts hint at Enmešarra's misadventures: KAR 307: 24–29 (Ebeling TuL 33) and CBS 16: 2 (cf. Weidner, AfO 19, 108, partly duplicated by LKU 45)[8] indicate that Enmešarra was defeated by Enlil. This can be combined with information contained in an incantation, according to which Enmešarra yielded power to An and Enlil.[9] So, in conclusion, Enmešarra seems to have been defeated and to have returned his power to Enlil, to whom it justly belonged. In this respect, his mythology is clearly comparable to the Anzu-Ninurta sequence.

A somewhat different interpretation was suggested by Vanstiphout, 1974, 67–68, according to whom Enlil may have been "disguised as a raven when he captured Enmešarra, and thus regained Enlilship." He translates lines 17–18 as follows: *(17)* "«When Enmešarra, your father's brother, was captured, *(18)* and you (again) carried off Enlilship, as on (= from?) that day, I surely know this/you!», he said."

Lambert, in *Orientalia* 58 (1989) 509, correctly pointed out that the "placing of nam.mu.tar.ra first indicates that these words contain the nub of the question," and that the question in line 16 is "not about Enlil's disguise, but about Enlil's power to decree destinies." Lambert accordingly translates lines 16–17: *(16)* "How do you know that I, Enlil, am he who decrees destinies?" *(17)* "When, from Enmešarra, your father's brother, the prisoner, *(18)* you took Enlilship, you said, 'Now like a lord I will fix destinies'" (or: 'As of now I will fix destinies.')" Lambert is thus the only commentator so far who attributes line 18 to Enlil, with which I agree.

That our protagonist was named Enmešarra, "The Lord of countless *me*," is a clue that the struggle for the *me*, that is, the power to rule the world, was similar to that described in *Ninurta and the Turtle*, and was probably intended to be taken in a humorous way.[10] After all, the story may have been told mainly for the enjoyment of how Namzitarra obtained the blessing of Enlil, not because he was particularly pious, but simply because he was able to recognize a scribal pun. The students would have enjoyed the story of how an ominous utterance in the past was used to persuade Enlil to give the best blessing imaginable, an office in Enlil's temple, to Namzitarra. And yet, even this may have been told with a humorous glint in the eye. This would fit the tone of the entire composition. A prebend at a temple of the great gods was considered attractive in Sumerian

6. Cf. UET 6/1, 31. Cf. also Vanstiphout: "Inanna/Ishtar as a Figure of Controversy," in: *Struggles of Gods. Papers of the Groningen Work Group for the Study of the History of Religions*, H.G. Kippenberg (ed.) (Amsterdam: Mouton Publishers, 1984), 225–238.
7. Cf. van Dijk, "Gott," in: RlA, 532–534, esp. p. 541; *Gilgameš' Death* 17 has: ᵈen-me-en-šár-ra as the last mentioned in a list of Enlil's forefathers, lit., "mothers and fathers of Enlil" (l. 18).
8. Both quoted by Civil, p. 66.
9. *nādin ḫaṭṭi u palê ana* ᵈ*Anu u* ᵈ*Enlil*, "who gave scepter and rod to Anu and Enlil," Borger, ZA 61 (1971) 77: 49 = ABRT II 13, 8; cf. Civil, p. 67.
10. Cf. Alster, "Ninurta and the Turtle: On Parodia Sacra in Sumerian Literature," in: CM ... (forthcoming). That deities could become parodied in Greek mythology and elsewhere is a well-known phenomenon, cf. Veyne, 1983. Cf. also the comments on *me*, in the commentary on *Instr. Šuruppak* 204.

society, as a source that provided a constant income for its holder.[11] It is no wonder, therefore, that occasionally such offices were inherited.[12] So Namzitarra could hardly have done anything better for his successors. The story of Namzitarra, who, although probably a low-ranking official, was clever enough to ensure Enlil's blessing for future generations, was undoubtedly told in the Sumerian schools as a great example of scribal wit.

The Emar Version: Interpretation

The Emar bilingual version is particularly interesting because of the unique information it provides with regard to thoughts on the decreasing length of human life, ending with one hundred and twenty years, which anticipates the same number in Gen 6:3, as has been demonstrated by Klein. See the discussion in *Chap. 3.3: The Ballade of Early Rulers: The Significance of the Longevity of Early Rulers*, and the literature there cited. The Emar version is written on the same tablet, Emar no. 771, as a unilingual father-and-son instruction fragment, which has most recently been treated by Klein, 1990, 67, n. 26, and Kämmerer, 1998, 224–227.

The Emar version, elaborating on the length of human life and the decreasing life time of human beings, is, in fact, understood best as an independent version rather than a genuine duplicate, for the following reasons.

First, the Emar version elaborates upon a theme that might have been well versed in Mesopotamian scribal tradition, suggesting alternative values to material wealth (l. 19 = Emar ll. 13'–17').[13] It is the crucial phrase "the day of mankind is always getting closer" (l. 20) that prompted the elaboration of the theme, almost in the form of a commentary or explanation, as the Emar version lines 19'–26' may perhaps best be understood. It is remarkable, however, that the explanation goes far beyond what is required in the context of *Enlil and Namzitarra*. Second, the Emar version has given the text a new twist, by restructuring it so that lines 1 and 7–8, the encounter and conversation between Enlil and Namzitarra, have been moved to the end of the text. In this way Namzitarra's words "I am on my way home" gets a new meaning, because line 27': é-šè ŋá-e-me-en = *i-na bītī-ia a-lak*, in connection with the following composition, is understood as Namzitarra preparing himself for his final destination, that is, death![14]

Where did it originate? Note that line 20 is quoted with a reading, al-GAM-na (= al-ku-na), which raises doubts as to how well the sentence was understood in the Emar source.[15] So, although the geographical proximity, as well as the similarity with ideas occurring in the Hebrew Bible, makes it natural to think of the Syrian area as the place where the Emar version originated, I would consider an alternative solution, that is, that the Emar version reflects an original source from Babylonia proper, in which the theme of the approaching "day of mankind," that is, death, was elaborated upon, perhaps, but not necessarily and not exclusively, as a comment prompted by *Enlil and Namzitarra*.

Some lexical details that show that the original text was at home in a genuinely Akkadian-speaking

11. Cf. Civil, 65, n. 1, referring to E.C. Stone, *The Social and Economic Organization of Old Babylonian Nippur* (Ph.D. diss., University of Chicago); cf. now *Nippur Surroundings* (Chicago, 1987).
12. Cf. Postgate, *Ancient Mesopotamia*, 125.
13. That the question of values other than material wealth was a widespread sapiential theme was shown by Klein, 1990, n. 22, who refers to *Dumuzi's Dream* 130–132 (loyalties!); *Inanna's Descent* 273–275; (add to these *Lugalbanda and Enmerkar* 141–158), and, most importantly, 1Kings 3:4–14, where Solomon is praised and rewarded for not seeking material wealth and longevity, but wisdom and understanding how to rule his people.
14. Cf. in particular lines 35'–36' of the Syrian Father-and-Son composition, quoted by Kämmerer, 1998, 224: *⸢e⸣-nu-ma a-li-ka mi-tù-ṭi* | *⸢ur⸣-ḫa al-li-ka a-na-ku maḫ-ru*, "when I go to the dead, I shall walk forward on the road (of those living)."
15. Cf. Klein, 1990, 63, n. 11, who suggest that al-GAM-na may stand for al-ga$_x$-na; or that it may be a miscopy or scribal error for al-ku$_5$-na. None of these suggestions brings much clarity. It is a pity that the corresponding Akkadian verb is missing here, but I would allow myself to question whether the relatively rare verb ku-nu = *qerēbu* was understood at all. Since GAM may have been better known in association with death, this may have caused the confusion.

environment, in which the Sumerian text was added as a secondary and less correct translation, support the theory of Babylonian origin. These are:

The Sumerian text in lines 20'–21' has the sequence u_4-an-na ... iti-an-na, apparently, but, hardly correctly, imitating the well-known expression mu-an-na, lit., "a year of Heaven."[16] This is strange, because the Akkadian version of these lines, as expected, has the plain *u_4-mi*, ITU, and MU, "day, month, and year." It is a question, of course, how these peculiarities came about: my guess is that the lexical peculiarities already entered the text in a Babylonian original, maybe in early Middle Babylonian times, when knowledge of the Sumerian language was still intact in scribal circles, although far from perfect.

A single detail might, however, suggest that the Emar scribe struggled with an imperfectly preserved original Babylonian tablet that had become damaged: in line 23' the Sumerian text has: mu 2 šu-ši mu-meš nam-lú-u_{18}-lu / níŋ-gig-bi ḫé-a, "One hundred and twenty years (as) the years of mankind— let it be their *bane*," which makes good sense as it stands, but it is obvious that the scribe had difficulties in translating it into Akkadian, which is strange, because the number is written in Akkadian in the Sumerian line. My guess is that he did not recognize the standard Sumerian expression ḫé-a, "let it be," but mistook it for the verb ḫi-a, "mixed," which would have been familiar to any scribe as a plural designation of cattle, etc. In this way the Akkadian text *ba-la-x* can be explained as a form of *balālu*.[17] This error may have come into being through an attempt to restore a damaged tablet, or it may have been caused by dictation.[18]

The most difficult lexical problem occurs, however, in line 25', where the Sumerian text has: ki-u_4-ta-ta nam-lú-u_{18}-lu / e(!)-na ì-in-éš ti-la-e-ni, equated with 26': *iš-tu* UD.⌜DA(?) *a-di*⌝ *i-na-an-na / a-mi-lu-ut-tù bal-ṭu*. Since the Akkadian text here makes reasonably good sense: "from that time(?) until now, when mankind has been existing," whereas the Sumerian text hardly can be understood as it stands, influenced as it obviously is by Akkadian syntax, there can be no doubt that the Sumerian translation is secondary. It is even possible to see that the scribes struggled with approximately the same problem as occurs in *The Ballade of Early Rulers* SS 14 (cf. Syr. 17), where the Sumerian expression lu]gal-e-ne dub-saŋ / u_4-ul-lí-a-ke$_4$-ne "the rulers (who were) the vanguards of those old days," was misunderstood and reinterpreted as *šar-ra-nu ra-ab-bu-[tum] / ša iš-tu u_4-mi pa-na-a a-di i-na-a[n-na]*, "the great kings from those former days until now." This shows that our *iš-tu* UD.DA was understood as *iš-tu u_4-mi <pa-na-a>*, or similar; cf. *Chap. 3.3a–b* for full documentation and discussion. This entailed the reinterpretation of the *Ballade* that appears in the sources from Ugarit and Emar, but is it necessary to draw the conclusion that they originated there? Hardly? Note that line 3 of *Ballade* has a variant: [u_4-d]a(?)-ta that is quite reminiscent of our line 25': ki-u_4-ta-ta, and both were understood similarly in the Akkadian translations as something like "since those days." It is thus clear that the Sumerian expression, whatever it precisely was, was understood as referring to the distant past, although this would not be correct in the standard Sumerian of the Isin-Larsa period.[19] A fair guess is that this understanding dates from early Middle Babylonian times, and that the

16. Cf. Klein, 1990, 63, n. 14, and the references cited there, considering mu-an-na "a poetic expression for «year» (to be translated «Himmelsjahr»)." Or would it be totally unthinkable that it simply was the similarity between the Akkadian MU *a-na* MU, etc., that mislead a scribe or copyist to "translate" backward into Sumerian by mu-an-na, etc., especially since it is clear that the Sum. lines, omitting a second u_4 and iti in ll. 20'–21', was at any rate poorly understood?

17. Cf. Klein, 64, n. 15, who already considered *balālu* as a "mistranslation of Sum ḫi-a"; none of the other suggestions mentioned by Klein is satisfactory, such as taking the verb as a form of *balāṭu*. Arnaud and Kämmere read ba-šu(!)-ša; cf. the comments on Emar 23'–24' below.

18. It is known that some Ugarit texts were written from dictation, cf. van Soldt, 1995, 188; van Soldt, 1999, 41, and the same may well have been the case at Emar. The scribes were not really bilingual, with Akkadian as a second language, but, with van Soldt's term, "biscriptal"; cf. van Soldt, 1995, 186. No wonder, therefore, if the Sumerian lines were very imperfectly understood.

19. ki-u_4-ta-ta and u_4-d]a(?)-ta rather look as if they were coined on ù-da-ta, which could reflect an old Sumerian subjunction ù-da, for which see Edzard, *Sum.*

"Syrian" version of *The Ballade of Early Rulers*, as well as the Emar version of *Enlil and Namzitarra*, originated in Babylonia proper.

A further argument supporting the theory of Babylonian origin is that the mythology that comes to light in the Emar fragment of *Enlil and Namzitarra* clearly is based in genuine Mesopotamian mythology.[20] In the *Atraḫasīs Epic*, it was the problem of threatening overpopulation that caused the gods to set a limit as to how long human beings were allowed to stay alive. They accomplished this by assigning death to mankind after the flood,[21] whereas in the Bible, it was man's sinful behavior that caused God to assign death to mankind. According to the Akkadian OB *Gilgameš Epic* X iii 3–5, death was assigned to man already on the day of his creation, which also accords with the Late version X vi 10ff.[22]

There thus was no uniform answer as to how death became an inevitable condition for all mankind, but it is clear that this was a question that occupied the attention of the scribes. Yet, the Emar version, elaborating upon the theme of death and the length of human life, certainly gives the impression of having come from another context than the Sumerian fable of *Enlil and Namzitarra*. It is true, as stated by Klein,[23] that the verbs in lines 20'–21' are assertives in the present context, but since, as already stated, they represent an addition that goes far beyond what is required within the fable of *Enlil and Namzitarra*, it is possible that they come from a different context, one in which they may certainly have been meant as precatives. The Sumerian verb in line 23', níŋ-gig-bi ḫé-a, is, indeed, best understood as "let it be their bane," since ḫé-a is a normal formula indicating the outcome of a myth.

Text Reconstruction

The text below is basically that of Civil's edition, where all details can be found, with minimal changes in lines 12–13 and 16. In a few cases, D and sources other than A seem to have better readings, although the omission of line 12 in D is suspicious.

(1) nam-zi-tar-ra ᵈen-líl mu-zal-le	*(1)* Namzitarra walked by Enlil,
(2) inim in-na-an-dug$_4$	*(2)* who said to him:
(3) me-ta-àm nam-zi-tar-ra	*(3)* "Where have you come from, Namzitarra?"
(4) é ᵈen-líl-lá-ta[1]	*(4)* "From Enlil's temple.
(5) bal-gub-ba-ŋu$_{10}$ bí-silim-ma-àm	*(5)* My turn of duty is finished.
(6) ki gudu$_4$-e-ne-ka[1] udu-bi-da[2] ì-gub-bu-nam[3]	*(6)* I serve at the place of the *gudu* priests, with their sheep.

Variants

Line 4: 1) B: -kam, "preceeded by an unidentifiable sign (erased ?)" (Civil).
Line 6: 1) ACD: -ka; B: -ke$_4$. 2) A: -dè; BC: -da. 3) A: -b]u-uš? (or: -ta); B: -⸢x⸣(= ub?)-nam; C: -bu-nam; D: -bu-[.

Grammar, 16; 162, but it is unlikely, because this would have been obsolete already in OB.

20. Cf. already Klein, 61 with p. 68, n. 37 and the literature there cited.
21. As understood in Lambert's interpretation of *Atraḫasīs* III vi 47–50; cf. Lambert in: B. Alster (ed.), *Death in Mesopotamia*, Mesopotamia 8 (1980), 53–58; cf. the new translations by Foster, *Before the Muses*, 3rd edition, 251, and Bottéro: *Lorsque les hommes*, 554.
22. Cf. Klein, 1990, 69, n. 37.
23. Klein, 1990, 63, n. 13.

(7) é-ŋu$_{10}$-šè al-du-un

(7) I am on my way home.

(8) nam-mu-un-gub-bé-en

(8) Don't stop me;

(9) ŋìri-ŋu$_{10}$ u$_4$ táb-táb

(9) I am in a hurry.

(10) ★a-ba-me-en za-e[1] lú èn mu-e-ši[2]-tar-re-en[3]

(10) Who are you who asks me questions?"

(11) ŋá-e ^{d}en-líl-me-en

(11) "I am Enlil."

(12) ^{d}en-líl-le igi-ni mu-ni-in-gi$_4$[1]

(12) But Enlil had changed his appearance:

(13) [1]uga^{mušen}-aš[2] ù-mu-ni-in[3]-ku$_4$

(13) he had turned into a raven

(14) gù al-dé-dé-e[1]

(14) (before) he spoke.

(15) uga^{mušen} nu-me-en ^{d}en-líl-me-en[1]

(15) *(Namzitarra:)* "But you are not a raven, you really are Enlil!"

(16) [1]★^{d}en-líl-[m]e-en nam mu-tar-ra ŋá-e ^{d}en-líl-me-en a-gim bí[2]-zu[3]

(16) *(Enlil:)* "Yes, I am Enlil who decrees the destinies, but how did you recognize that I am Enlil?"

(17) u$_4$ ^{d}[1]en-me-šár-ra šeš-ad-da-zu eše$_5$(LÚ#GÁN-*tenû*)[2]-da-a

(17) *(Namzitarra:)* "When your uncle Enmešarra was taken captive,

Variants

Line 10: 1) D: a-ba-me-en za-e lú èn mu-e-tar-r[e(?); since a-ba-me-en za-e is supported also by E and makes good sense; I take this as the main text; Civil takes A: a-ba-àm za-e-me-en, perhaps supported by B, as the main text; B: -àm(?) ⌜za-e⌝-me-[en] (uncertain). 2) A: -e-ši-; DE: -e-; B om. 3) A: -en; BE om.

Line 12: 1) Line included in BE; omitted in AD (Civil).

Line 13: 1) AD: ^{d}en-líl-le (before uga); BE om. (so Civil, but see the following note on ll. 12–13); 2) AB: -aš; DE om. 3) ABD: -in-; E om.

Lines 12–13: D: ^{d}en-líl-le uga^{mušen}-šè mu-ni-íb-[; I take this as lines 12–13 with igi-ni mu-ni-in-gi$_4$ omitted.

Line 14: 1) E: -e; A om.

Line 15: 1) Second half of the line in ABG; D om. (so Civil, but cf. the following note).

Line 16: 1) D: I read the first signs ★^{d}en-líl-[m]e-en, rather than ^{d}en-líl-le, as read by Civil, p. 68, note on line 16; cf. copy on pl. 48. These signs are omitted in G and seemingly A, which has no room for them. 2) A: bí-zu; D: ì-[zu. 3) The entire line is omitted in B, but included in ADG. I have included it in the form it has in D, although the text makes perfectly good sense without ^{d}en-líl-[m]e-en.

Line 17: 1) BD: ^{d}; AG om. 2) G: LÚ×ŠÈ; A: LÚ#GÁN-*tenû*. For the reading eše$_5$-da-a, cf. Vanstiphout, 1980, 67, n. 2, who bases it on the note on p. 70 in Civil's edition.

(18) nam-^{d}en-líl ba-e-de$_6$-a u$_4$-dè en-gim nam ⸢ga⸣-zu-e-še

(18) and you carried Enlil-ship away (scl. from him), (you) said: «Now I shall surely know the fates, like a lord»."

(19) kù ḫé-tuku za ḫé-tuku gud ḫé-tuku udu ḫé-tuku

(19) *(Enlil:)* "You may acquire precious metals, you may acquire precious stones, you may acquire cattle or you may acquire sheep;

(20) u$_4$ nam-lú-u$_{18}$-lu[I] al-ku-nu

(20) but the day of mankind is always getting closer,

(21) níŋ-tuku-zu me-šè[I] e-tùm-ma

(21) so where does your wealth lead?

(22) ^{d}en-líl-me-en nam mu-tar-ra

(22) Now, I am, indeed, Enlil, who decrees the fates.

(23) a-ba-àm mu-zu

(23) What is your name?"

(24) nam-zi-tar-ra mu-ŋu$_{10}$-um

(24) *(Namzitarra:)* "My name is Namzitarra (= The one blessed with a good destiny)."

(25) mu-zu-gim nam-zu ḫé-tar-re

(25) *(Enlil:)* "Your fate shall be assigned according to your name:

(26) é lugal-za-ka è-a

(26) leave the house of your master,

(27) ibila-zu é-ŋá si sá-e[I] ḫé-en-dib-dib-bé-ne

(27) and your successors shall come and go regularly in my temple."

Variants

Line 20: 1) F: ^{lu}: A om.
Line 21: 1) A: -šè; F om.
Line 27: 1) A: -e; F: om.

Comments on Individual Lines

Line 14: Civil translates "and was croaking," but there is nothing that indicates that the sound of the bird is meant, since the verb is normal for "to speak." I take lines 12–14 as an explanation preceding the conversation in lines 3–11, and translate "Enlil had changed his appearance (before) he spoke." How Enlil as a raven could speak as a human being is a question that probably should be raised in a larger context relating to the nature of fables. Cf. Vanstiphout, AcSum 10 (1988) 196–198.

Lines 17–18: Civil translates "when Enmešarra your uncle, the captive, took away Enlilship, he said «now I want to know the fates, like a lord»." The verbal form ba-e- is problematic; I prefer to take it as the 2nd person in the perfective, as suggested by Vanstiphout, quoted above under *Interpretation*. This solution seems straightforward, with no easy alternative. Cf. also Klein, 1990, 63, n. 3. I understand the captivity of Enmešarra as the result of an attempt to steal the "Enlilship" from Enlil, like Anzu in the Akk. Anzu-myth, but other interpretations are possible. If the interpretation is justified, Enlil was already in power when Enmešarra took it from him. Yet, references to Enmešarra from other texts might rather suggest that Enmešarra was in power before Enlil. This would imply that "Enlilship" (nam-^{d}en-líl) in this case is used as a general designation of the rulership of the world, even before Enlil came to power, which is highly likely in this context, since it does not in any way aim at chronological precision. The most likely explanation is, in fact, that the text simply makes allusions to generally known divine succession myths, in which the parallel to the Anzu-myth may have been drawn further than strictly warranted in "official" theology—if that ever existed. Such myths afforded great opportunities for elaborating literary themes; compare the *Kutha-Legend*, *Enuma-Eliš*, and the *Kumarbi Myth*, to mention a few examples; cf. the comments on *Ninurta and the Turtle* above under *Interpretation*.

I retain Civil's word division nam ⌈ga⌉-zu-e-še, «Now I shall surely know the fates, like a lord» he said" in line 18, although Vanstiphout's suggestion nam-ga-zu, "I surely know this/you," makes good sense. In any case, this puns on name and destiny (mu and nam); cf. Vanstiphout, p. 68.

All commentators so far—with the exception of Lambert—seem to agree that line 18 is spoken by Enmešarra, but, in fact, it makes better sense to take it as spoken by Enlil. The saying then has the character of a prophetic utterance matching the continuation. The quotation marker e-še, following the quoted speech, does not indicate any specific person, but just means "spoken," so there is no need to take this as referring to what Enmešarra said. To envisage concretely how, and when, Namzitarra overheard this is a question that should not be raised too seriously in the context of a fable. It would bring us back to time immemorial, when the gods struggled for their powers, but, as already stated, this seems merely to be of interest as a literary background for the story.

Line 19: This set of proverbial expressions occurs elsewhere, with minor variations. In addition to *Laḫar and Ašnan* 189f., cited by Civil, p. 70, note also the parallel from *Martu's Marriage*, cited by Klein, 1990, 59 60; and the love song SLTNi 90+141 + dupls., edited by Sefati, *Love Songs*, 210–217, lines 26–31, as *Dumuzi-Inanna* O. Cf. also SP 3.23 and parallels (Alster, *Proverbs* I, 84).

Line 20: Civil translates "when people come (to steal)," but cf. Klein's comment, 1990, 57–60.

Line 21: me-šè – tùm = *ajîš abālu*, cf. the references listed by Civil, p. 71. Note also that this seems to mean approximately the same as me-da tùm, "to have success(?)," which occurs in SP 1.2; cf. the comments in Alster, *Proverbs* II, 341.

Emar Version

(1'–3') x [...] / x [...] / x [...]	*(1–3 destroyed)*
(4') ^{d}e[n-líl ...]	*(4)* Enlil ...
(5') a-ni [...]	*(5)* ...
(6') ^{d}en-[líl ...]	*(6)* En[lil ...]
(7') ^{d}en-líl-me-me-[e]n nam-tar-[ra]	*(7)* *(Enlil:)* "I am Enlil who decrees the destinies."
(8') nam-zi-tar-ra ^{d}en-l[íl mu-zal-le]	*(8)* Namzitarra [passed by] En[lil].
(9') [a-b]a-àm [mu-zu]	*(9)* *(Enlil:)* "What [is your name?]
(10') [nam-z]i-tar-ra mu(!)-ŋu$_{10}$-[um] [mu-zu-gim]	*(10)* *(Namzitarra:)* "Namzitarra is my name." *(Enlil:)* ["According to your name]
(11') [nam]-zu ḫi-ib-[tar-re]	*(11)* your destiny will be [decreed]!
(12') [x] ḫé-ib-[...]	*(12)* ... let ...
(13') ⌜en⌝-na kù-babbar ḫé-tuku	*(13')* As much silver as you may have,
(14') ^{na_4}za-gìn ḫé-tuku	*(14')* (as much) lapis lazuli as you may have,
(15') gud hé-tuku	*(15')* (as many) oxen as you may have,
(16') [u]du ḫé-tuku	*(16')* (as many) sheep as you may have,
(17') kù-babbar-zu ^{na_4}za-gìn-zu gud-zu udu-zu ⌜KÙ.BABBAR-*ka* ^{na_4}ZA⌝.GÌN-*k*[*a* GUD-*ka* UDU-*ka*]	*(17')* your silver, your lapis lazuli, [your oxen, your sheep]
(18') me-šè al-tùm [*a-a-iš ib-ba-ba-lu*]	*(18')* whither do they lead?
(19') u$_4$ nam-lú-u$_{18}$-lu al-GAM-na UD^{meš} *a-mi-lu-ut-t*[*i i-ka-an-nu-šu*]	*(19')* The days of mankind [are bending forward].
(20') u$_4$-an-na ḫa-ba-lá *u$_4$-mi a-na u$_4$-mi li-im-ṭ*[*ì*]	*(20)* Day to day they decrease.
(21') itu-an-na ḫa-ba-lá ITU *a-na* ITU *li-im-ṭ*[*ì*]	*(21)* Month after month they decrease.
(22') mu mu-an-na ḫa-ba-lá MU *a-na* MU *li-im-ṭì*	*(22)* Year after year they verily decrease.

(23'–24')	mu 2 šu-ši mu-meš nam-lú-u$_{18}$-lu / níŋ-gig-bi ḫé-a *2 šu-ši* MU^{meš} *lu-ú ik-ki-⌜ib a-mi-lu⌝-ut-ti ba-la-x*	*(23–24)* One hundred and twenty years (as) the years of mankind—verily it is their misfortune;
(25'–26')	ki-u$_4$-ta-ta nam-lú-u$_{18}$-lu / e(!)-na ì-in-éš ti-la-e-ni *iš-tu* UD.⌜DA(?) *a-di*⌝ *i-na-an-na / a-mi-lu-ut-tù bal-ṭu*	*(25–26)* (This is so) from the earliest(?) times(?) until today when humanity has existed!"
(27')	é-šè ŋá-e-me-en *i-na bītī*(É-*ti*)-*ia a-lak*	*(27)* "I am on my way home,
(28')	nu-na-an-gub na-an-gub ŋìr(!)-ŋu$_{10}$(!) ub-bé	*(28)* one cannot stop me, don't stop me!"

Comments on Individual Lines

Line 8: Cf. Kämmerer, 1998, 222, n. 465, referring to Frg. 773, Msk 742381, obv.: (1) li-ma-⌜ad ra x SAĞ x⌝ [...]; cf. Civil, AuOr 7 (1989) 7: "an overrun from the reverse." (2) nam-zi(!)-tar-ra ^{d}en-líl x [...] (3) [(x)] mu-tál [(x)] (4) [é] ⌜^{d}en-líl-ta [(x)] (5) [bala-gub-b]a-ŋu$_{10}$ silim-ma-[àm] (6) [...] DU ⌜x x na⌝ [...].

Line 9: Cf. Civil, AuOr 7 (1989) 7: Frg. 774, Msk 74182a.

Line 13': Assuming that ⌜en⌝-na represents en-na = *adi*, cf. Klein, p. 63, n. 8, and Kämmerer, 1998, 222, who translates "Soviel Silber Du (auch) haben magst," etc.

Line 18: *ib-ba-ba-lu* restoration by Klein, 1990, 63, n. 10, who assumes that the Sum. al-tùm is an intrans.-passive form.

Line 19: al-GAM-na is probably as mistake for al-ku-na, apparently not understood at Emar. Kämmerer, 1998, 222, restores [*i-ka-an-nu-šu*], "Die Tage der Menschen [neigen sich]," but cf. Klein, 63, n. 11 for different solutions, restoring [*i-qé-er-ri-bu*]. Cf. the comments above under *Emar version: Interpretation.*

Line 20: *li-im-ṭì*, sing. affirm.

Lines 23'–24': The Sum. line writes the number 2×60 in the Akk. way as 2 *šu-ši*, cf. Klein, 1990, 64, n. 15, who translates the Sum. text: "One hundred and twenty years (are) the years of mankind— verily it is their *bane*," or, alternatively, for both the Sum. and Akk. columns: "(A maximum life span of) one hundred and twenty years is verily the bane of mankind," convincingly commenting that here níŋ-gig may refer to the "contempt and dislike, whereby man relates to his mortality." This applies to the Sum. text, which I understand slightly differently, as a weak anacoluth: "(That) one hundred and twenty years (were imposed on them as a limit to how long they were to live)—this is their bane"; the -bi can then refer either to humankind or, rather, as a demonstrative, to the limitations imposed on them.

Strangely this does not apply to the Akk. translation, which seems to rest on a grave misunderstanding of the Sumerian line; see the comments above under *Emar Version: Interpretation*, and the following earlier suggestions.

Arnaud, *Emar* VI/4 368, and Kämmere, 1998, 224, read line 24 somewhat differently: níŋ-gig-bi ḫé-a = *ba-šu*(!)-*š*[*a*]; the copy, in *Emar* VI/2, 74174 ii 24' shows *ba-LA-ša*, so emendation to *ba-šu*(!)-*ša* is perhaps the most likely solution. Arnaud, p. 369, translates "c'est le lot indubitable"; Kämmerer translates lines 23–26 "120 Jahre sind den (einzelnen) Menchen vorbehalten, (sind) deren Existenz. Von dem Tag (der Geburt) bis jetzt (dem Tag des Todes) leben die (einzelnen) Menchen (d.h. 120 Jahre)."

níŋ-gig-bi = *ikkibu*, is common in Sumerian

meaning "abomination" (rather than "taboo"). Cf. Klein, 1990, 64, and the literature there cited. I have accepted Klein's translation "bane," in the sense "a constant source of trouble or anxiety," in the present context. The following examples in Alster, *Proverbs* I are essential for the general meaning: SP 1.23: níŋ-gig-ga-àm; SP 3.8: níŋ-gig ^{d}utu-kam = SP 5.3; SP 3.14: am-e níŋ-gig ^{ŋiš}apin-na-kam; SP 3.118: níŋ-gig-^{d}suen-na-kam; 3.161: šu nu-luḫ-ḫa ka-e tùm-da níg-gig-ga-àm, "putting unwashed hands in one's mouth is disgusting"; SP 3.168–169 (cf. Alster, *Proverbs* II, 393); SP 3.170: níŋ-gig-^{d}suen; níŋ-gig-^{d}inanna-ka; SP 3.175: níŋ-gig-^{d}nin-urta-ke$_4$; SP 11.66 (rest.): níŋ-gig-^{d}nin-urta-kam (with parallels); SP 13.57 (rest.); SP 26 Sec. A 4–7; SP 28.20; UM 29-16-519, 19; UET 6/2 261 and 262 = SP 1.23; UET 6/274: níŋ-gig-ga, "it's a bad thing" = *Emeš and Enten* 162 (cf. Alster, *Proverbs* II, 470); MCL 618; Free Lib. Phil. (Alster, *Proverbs* I, 334). These show that níŋ-gig can mean a "nuisance," or "something disgusting, abominable," or, more specifically something sacred to, or reserved for, a spirit or god, as demonstrated by Geller, JCS 42 (1990) 105–117. The line from *Gilgameš' Death* 39 cited by Klein with references to earlier literature is translated by the ETCSL as Sec. E 17: níŋ-gig ak nam-lú-u$_{18}$-lu-ke$_4$ ne-en de$_6$-a ma-ra-dug$_4$, "You must have been told that this is what the bane of being human involves"; cf. Cavigneaux's edition. This is the earliest and closest parallel one can come to níŋ-gig-bi of our Emar source.

Lines 25'–26': Klein, translates: "(This is so) from the day that humanity exists until today!" but cf. the comments above under *Emar Version: Interpretation*, also referring to *Chap. 3.3: The Ballade of Early Rulers* 3 and 14. It would, of course, be tempting to suggest that here the reference is to some event, such as the outcome of the flood story, that caused death to become the lot for all mankind. But this would probably be unwarranted; it would at least have required another beginning of the tale than that suggested by *Enlil and Namzitarra.*

Line 26: For e(!)-na, cf. Civil, AuOr 7 (1989) 7.

Lines 27'–28': Cf. Kämmerer, 1998, 224, n. 471: "rechte Columne wirklich sumerisch? grundsätzlich handelt sich bei der rechten Columne um die babylonische Übersetzung der sumerischen Version ...," commenting on Civil, loc. cit., 7. line 28'.

These lines were moved from lines 1 and 7–8 of the Sumerian original, which entailed the restructuring of the composition discussed above.

Literature

B. Alster, "Ninurta and the Turtle: On Parodia Sacra in Sumerian Literature," in: CM ... (forthcoming).

B. Alster: "A Duplicate to 'Enlil and Namzitara'," *N.A.B.U.* 4 (1990) 82, note 102.

D. Arnaud: *Emar VI/1–4: Textes de la bibliothèque: transcriptions et traductions.* Missions Archaéologique de Meskéné-Emar, Recherches au pays d'Aštata, 1985–87, nos. 771, 772. 773, 774, 592.

A. Cavigneaux and Farouk N.H. Al-Rawi: *Gilgamesh et la Mort.* Texts de Tell Haddad VI, avec un appendice sur les textes funéraires sumériens. Cuneiform Monographs 19 (Groningen: Styx Publications, 2000).

M. Civil: "Enlil and Namzitarra," AfO 25 (1974) 65–71.

M. Civil: "The Texts from Meskéné-Emar," *Aula Orientalis* (1989) 5–25.

J. Klein: "The 'Bane' of Humanity: A Lifespan of One Hundred Twenty Years," AcSum 12 (1990) 57–70.

W.G. Lambert: "The Theology of Death," in: *Death in Mesopotamia*, ed. B. Alster, *Mesopotamia* 8, 1980, 53–58.

W.G. Lambert: "A New Interpretation of *Enlil and Namzitarra*," *Orientalia* 58 (1989) 508–509.

H. Vanstiphout: "Some Notes on 'Enlil and Namzitara'," RA 74 (1980) 67–71.

H. Vanstiphout: "The Importance of the Tale of the Fox," AcSum 10 (1988) 191–227.

3.6 The Underworld Vision of "Gilgameš, Enkidu, and the Netherworld"

The Benefit of an Early Death

The Greek concept that an early death was the best thing that could happen to a man was known to the Sumerians. This appears from a uniquely interesting passage of *Gilgameš, Enkidu, and the Netherworld*, in which it forms the very end of the underworld vision, and the very end of the text itself in its main version.[1]

Gilgameš asks Enkidu how each group of deceased are faring in the netherworld, and Enkidu provides a short answer in each case:[2]

298 nìŋin-gar tur-tur-mu ní-ba nu-zu igi bí-du$_8$-àm
299 ^{ŋiš}banšur kù-sig$_{17}$ kù-bar$_6$-bar$_6$ làl ì-nun-ta e-ne im-di-e-ne
300 lú til-àm [sa]ŋ-na[3] ì-til [igi bí-du$_8$-àm]
301 ki ŋiš-ná diŋir-re-e-na al-ná[4]
302 lú izi-lá igi bí-du$_8$-àm igi nu-mu-un-ni-du$_8$-àm
303 gidim-a-ni nu-ŋál i-bí-ta an-na e$_{11}$(!)-àm(!)

1. The netherworld description is the first example of a literary type well known from Homer, Virgil, and Dante. In the present study the designation "netherworld" is used well knowing that the physical position of the realms of the dead does not necessarily have to be under the surface of the earth. For a full discussion, see Katz, *Image*. For a short statement, see M.J. Geller: "The Landscape of the «Netherworld»," in: *Landscapes, Frontiers and Horizons in the Ancient Near East*, XLIV Rencontre Assyriologique Internationale, 1997, ed. L. Milano et al., History of the Ancient Near East, Monographs iii, 3 (Padova, 1999), who points out that the realms of the dead may have to be sought elsewhere, such as in the desert surrounding the inhabited areas or in the mountains, where Inanna disappears. The evidence of *The Ballade of Early Rulers* 6, for a "heaven" above and an "underworld" below, is overwhelming, however: *an-ta é ùr-ra-*ke$_4$-ne-ne ki-ta é-da-rí-*ke$_4$-ne-ne = **elēnum bīt ašābišunu šaplānum bīt darûtišunu* "Above (are) the houses where they lived, below (are) their everlasting houses." This was a set phrase in the wisdom literature, quoted elsewhere (all parallels are cited in *Chap. 3.3a*, comment on *SS 6*). In a case such as this, the pair an-ta : ki-ta cannot be explained simply as "in front : behind," or similar. This inevitably created some contradictions, perhaps to be explained by assuming that two different concepts existed side by side in a non-dogmatic environment. Of these, that which places the realm of the dead under the surface of the earth—as the wisdom literature, including the Hebrew Bible, evidently has it, perhaps almost as a figure of speech—was apparently a widely known "international" wisdom concept already in the early second millennium B.C.
2. Duplicates HAV 11 rev. 33–38; TMHNF III 14 iv 5–8. Cf. A. Shaffer, *Sumerian Sources of the Gilgamesh Epic* (Ph.D. diss., University of Pennsylvania, 1963), 21. Parts of the text have been treated by Falkenstein, in: *La divination en Mésopotamie ancienne* (Strasbourg, 1966), 67–68; and Kramer, *Iraq* 60 (1960) 64 and 67. The relevant lines are not covered by the texts from Meturan published by Cavigneaux and Al-Rawi, "La fin de Gilgamesh, Enkidu et les Enfers d'après les manuscrits d'Ur et de Meturan (Textes de Tell Haddad VIII)," *Iraq* 62 (1960); cf. now Cavigneaux and Al-Rawi, *Gilgamesh et la Mort*, Cuneiform Monographs 19 (Groningen: Styx Publications, 2000).
3. In line 300, the ETCSL edition has lú ug$_7$-àm(?) (x) x-na ì-úš, "the man who died, but died in his ...," which seems less meaningful; it is unlikely that two forms of the same verb would occur beside each other in the same meaning. It makes better sense to read til, phonetic for tìl, "to live," but punning on til, "to end."
4. In line 301 we expect *diŋir-re-e-ne-ka. A variant of line 301 in HAV 11 rev. 36: ki x x-ŋá-na x [...] is regrettably not clear because of its poor state of preservation. Perhaps one can restore something like ⌜saŋ⌝-ŋá-na, "in his head," i.e., "prime, best quality, top," or similar, yielding a pun like that of line 300: ⌜saŋ⌝-ŋá-na. A similar variant occurs in UET 6/1, 58, obv. 12: lú-tìl-la ⌜x⌝ [(x) x] saŋ bí-in-[til]-la / igi bí-in-du$_8$-[àm igi] i-ni-du$_8$-à[m a-n]a-gim ak / (13:)

298 (*Gilg:*) My little stillborn children who never came to consciousness, did you see them?
299 (*Enk:*) <Yes, I saw them>: They play at a table of gold and silver with honey and ghee.
300 (*G:*) The man who lived, but ended early (lit. "in his head"), did you see him?
301 (*E:*) < Yes, I saw him>: He lies on the bed of the gods.
302 (*G:*) The man who was set on fire, did you see him?
303 (*E:*) No, I did *not* see him: His ghost is not there, it went with the smoke up into heaven!

The strict progression of the sequence is decisive for the interpretation here. According to lines 298–299 the stillborn children who never came to consciousness are relatively well off in the netherworld, playing with ghee and honey. The nest step is lines 300–301, the man who lived, but died early. He is even better off, lying on the bed of the gods. The final case, lines 302–303, will be briefly discussed below. It concerns the man whose body burned away and whose "spirit," therefore, disappeared with the body, with the result that he is not present in the netherworld at all.

The decisive point is that the man who lived, but died early, is better off than the stillborn children, who, on their part, are better off than the rest of the dead, whose "life" as dead is mostly dull and not very attractive. A number of details in the description of the individual cases are undoubtedly due to the slight touch of morbid humor that characterizes the whole netherworld episode, in which many puns, audible or sensible, prevail. Yet, one cannot escape noticing that the sequence expresses an idea similar to the Greek concept that it is best not to be born, and, if born, then to die young, i.e., in one's prime.

The Greek notion is most clearly expressed by Herodotus (i 14), in the story of *Cleobis and Biton.* These two young men died very young, and very happy, because, as the story tells, they died just after having done something extraordinary: they stepped in for some oxen that came too late to draw a cart with their mother to a temple festival. Herodotus then comments, "they were granted the most happy end to their lives; and by their example the goddess gave us to understand that it is better for a man to die than to live." This can further be compared to the following passage in Sophocles' *Œdipus at Colonus* 1224–27:[5] "There is no better wish than not to be born. Second best is for you who are living to return as soon as possible to the place from where you came."

Similar ideas are expressed in Eccl 4:2–3: "I thought the dead who are already dead more fortunate than the living who are still alive. [3]Better off than either is he who has not yet been, and who has not witnessed the evil that is done under the sun." The following sentence is similar, but concerns specifically a prominent man who does not find happiness, Eccl 6:3: "... I declare that a stillborn child is better off than he."

Our final case, lines 302–303, is equally significant: the man whose body burned up is not present in the underworld at all, since his ghost disappeared with the smoke and evaporated into the sky. The point is that that man disappeared completely with the smoke and was totally annihilated, both body and soul, and so had no place in the realm of the dead at all. There is a short discussion of this uniquely interesting passage by T. Abusch, *Jacobsen MV,* 13. Abusch connects this with the ritual practice of burning witches, described in Mesopotamian magical sources, commenting "burning the body makes it impossible to give the dead person proper funeral

gidim(!)-ma-ni ˹x˺ [...] ˹ka˺, "the man who lived, but ended early (lit., in (his) "head") [...]." Perhaps the more likely reading of line 12 is, in fact, *lú-til-la s[aŋ-ŋá-na]-ka(!) bí-in-[til]-la, "who lived, but ended in «that of his head»," i.e., "in his prime," expressed through a headless genitive, which would be very suitable here. UET 6/1, 58 has weakened the structure of the text considerably, by making too many additions in unfortunate places.

5. Already quoted in this connection by Alster, RA 68 (1974) 59.

rites."[6] That disinterment could be used with the same purpose is shown by the ample examples from later Assyrian sources given by Abusch, pp. 16–18.

This should be compared to *Níŋ-nam (Nothing Is of Value)* B 6 (cf. *Chap. 3.1*): umuš-bi eŋir-bi im ba-e-tùm, "that plan—its outcome was carried away by the wind," i.e., it came to nothing.

6. Alster, RA 68 (1974) 59, n. 1, referred to Josh 7:25 as a parallel example, showing that cremation was considered the most severe of all punishments because it destroys both the body and the soul. The ban against cremation in some religions, incl. Christianity, is due to the same idea, i.e., that it would prevent the resurrection of both body and soul on the final day.

CHAPTER 4

Fables in Sumerian Literature

4.1 Introduction

In fables, animals act and speak as humans, but apart from this simple statement, there are as many different opinions and problems involved in the definition and understanding of fables as is the case with proverbs. In particular, the relations between popular literature and fables preserved in ancient written sources is a much debated question. Fables are generally thought to belong to the domain of popular literature, but in classical times "the adaption and invention of fables became a regular part of rhetorical training,"[1] and the same could probably be said of fables in the Sumerian scribal curriculum almost one-and-a-half millennia earlier. The recognition of fables in Sumerian literature has interesting implications with regard to the history of the literary type as such, which sometimes is thought to be a Greek invention.

There are no fables in the Homeric poems, but already Hesiod included a fable of a hawk and a nightingale in *Works and Days* 202–212. Two other early examples of fables are the Archilochos fragments of a tale of an eagle and a vixen, and one about a fox and a monkey, dating from the eighth or seventh century B.C. If the Mesopotamian fables had not been known, these would have been the oldest in the world.

According to Herodotus, the author of the well-known fables of Aesop was a slave from Samos who lived at the time of the Egyptian pharaoh Amasis, i.e., the middle of the sixth century B.C. The stories traditionally ascribed to him come from various sources, but at least some of them must have been commonly known in Athens from the fifth century B.C. onward, when references to Aesop were made by Aristophanes, Aristotle, Plato, Xenophon, and other writers.

The first extant Greek collection of fables was made by Babrios, a hellenized Roman, who wrote some 140 fable versions in verse, not later than the second century A.D.[2] In addition, about 350 anonymous Greek prose fables are known, and a number of fables are known through the works of Plutarch and Lucian of the first and second centuries A.D. Also Horace and other authors made frequent references to fables. The earliest Latin fable collection in verse was made by Phaedrus at the time of the emperor Augustus. Forty-two Roman fables in verse were composed by Avianus about 400 A.D., and paraphrases of Babrios and Avianus were made from the fifth century onward. The later development of the antique fable was characterized by the addition of Christian "morals" to the fables. Fable collections became popular in French and English medieval literature, culminating with the fables of Jean de la Fontaine in the seventeenth century.

In view of today's knowledge of Mesopotamian literature, the opinion that the fable as a literary type originated with the Greeks cannot be upheld. Neither the earliest known Egyptian examples nor those from India are old enough to likely be the source that

1. See, e.g, S.A. Handford, *Fables of Aesop* (Penguin Classics, 1954), xvi, for a brief but informative introduction, and, e.g., M. Nøjgaard: *La fable antique* (Copenhagen, 1964), for a thorough discussion of the subject.

2. The basic editions are B.E. Perry: *Aesopica* (Urbana: University of Illinois Press, 1952); and A. Hausrath: *Corpus Fabularum Aesopicarum* (Leipzig: Teubner, 1956–59).

inspired the invention by the Greeks.[3] The origin is thus to be sought further back in time, toward Mesopotamia. The only alternative seems to be to consider the phenomenon universal.

Fables in Babylonian and Assyrian Literature

Already in 1927, Ebeling studied some Babylonian fables and their relations to Egyptian and Greek literature.[4] The basic Akkadian texts were edited by Lambert in BWL, 150–212: "Fables or Contest Literature"; pp. 213–221: "Popular Sayings"; some entries under pp. 222–282: "Proverbs" are also relevant. Fables are thus placed under popular sayings, and what are called fables are rather dialogues or contest literature. Yet, this is a relevant way of grouping the material, since a number of hybrids between dialogues and fables exist.

The remains of collections of popular sayings and fables in Assyrian and Babylonian are of considerable interest. In a number of Mesopotamian examples one of the speakers is a god or human being rather than an animal, but obviously these were not thought of as belonging to a group different from the others.

The close connection between fables and contest literature is a feature that is also characteristic of Sumerian literature.[5]

THE WREN AND THE ELEPHANT

An Akkadian fable with relations to Greek fables, and even a possible Sumerian forerunner, is Ebeling, KAR 174 iii 50–54: "Die Müche und der Elephant," republished by Lambert, in BWL 216f. iii 50–54. Lambert translates: "A *mosquito* as it settled on an elephant, said, «Brother, did I press your side? I will make [off] at the watering-place.» «I do not care whether you get on—what is it to have you?—Nor do I care whether you get off»." On p. 339 he points to an almost exact Greek parallel in Aesop, where, however, an ox takes the place of the elephant. Borger, *Orientalia* 33 (1964) 462, points out that the Akk. *ni-ni-qu* is more likely to correspond to a bird than to a mosquito, and suggests "Zaunkönig und Elephant," reading *diq-diq-qu* instead of *ni-ni-qu*. This makes it possible to see SP 5.1 (Alster: *Proverbs* I, 121) as a Sumerian forerunner. In the main text the animals are an elephant and an an-ti-rí-gu$_7$^{mušen}-bird, whereas a variant, YBC 9886, has al-ti-ri-gu$_7$^{mušen}= *si-pi-di-qá-ar*, which is likely to be a small bird, such as a wren, rather than a mosquito. The full Sumerian and Akkadian texts are cited in *Chap. 4.4*.

THE AKKADIAN FABLE OF THE FOX

Lambert, BWL 186–209, edited the known fragments of the "Series of the Fox," which he considers to go back to not earlier than the First Dynasty

3. B.E. Perry: "Fable," *Studium Generale* 12 (1959) 17–37, on p. 26 with n. 37, recognizes the relevance of the Babylonian fables for the origin of the Greek fables.

   There is a rare example of an Egyptian fable, *The Dispute between a Man and His Ba* (Papyrus Berlin 3024) —12 Dynasty? Cf. Miriam Lichtheim: *Ancient Egyptian Literature,* Vol. I, 163–169. This is a fable of a dispute between the body and the head over bodily supremacy, known from a poorly preserved schoolboy's exercise manuscript.

   The Indian fable collections, the *Pañchatantra* and the *Hitopadeśa*, contain numerous proverbs with which they illustrate the wisdom of the fables. Their dating is disputed, but even with much optimism the original sources can hardly be assumed to be older than the second century B.C. These became known in Europe only much later. The *Hitopadeśa* was first translated into German by Max Müller (Leipzig, 1844), then by J. Hertel (Leipzig, 1894); into English by E. Arnold (London, 1861) and H. Morey (London, 1888). The *Pañchatantra* was translated into Persian, and then, in 721 A.D., by Ibn al-Muqaffaʿ into Arabic as *Khalīla wa Dimna.* These are often assumed to have been a source of inspiration for the medieval *Disciplina Clericalis* by Peter Alfonso.
4. Ebeling: "Dei babylonische Fabel und ihre Bedeutung für die Literaurgeschichte," in: *Mitteilungen der Altorientalischen Gesellschaft*, 2. Band Heft 3 (Leipzig 1927).
5. Judg 9:7–15, the contest told by Jotham about the fig tree and the vine electing a king is a biblical example reminiscent of the same type. Another fable is told by Jehoash about the impertinence of the thistle who wanted to woo the daughter of a cedar of Lebanon (2Kings 14:9). There is a "riddle-proverb" of the eagle, the cedar, and the vine in Ezek 17:1–10, and the talking ass of Balaam in Num 22:21–35 is notable.

of Babylon, while he assigns a Kassite date to the Middle Assyrian version (p. 189), of which one fragment (now lost) differs from the others by being bilingual.

Vanstiphout, "The Importance of the Tale of the Fox"[6] seeks to show that the European medieval "beast epic" *Roman de Renart* and other medieval European sources, as well, are anticipated in the Babylonian fragments, which he seeks to combine into a coherent sequence.

Possible Sumerian forerunners are edited below, *Chap. 4.2: Fables of a Fox.*

THE ETANA LEGEND

The Akkadian legend of Etana was last edited by Kinnier Wilson in 1985. There is much literature on the eagle-motive, for which folklore parallels have been found elsewhere. A study by Selz (1998)[7] traces the setting of the text in a larger context of epic literature. The literary history in classical sources has been traced by R. Williams, "The Literary History of a Mesopotamian Fable."[8]

Fables in Sumerian Literature

What is presently known of Sumerian fables is only a small glimpse of what was once a colorful variety of tales. This may be inferred from some inlaid reliefs from the royal tombs of Ur, in which animals are depicted as serving other animals at a kind of mock banquet, the full story behind which we can only guess at.

In Sumerian literature, some texts include narrative episodes that may with some right be regarded as fables. These are:

Gragg, "The Fable of the Heron and the Turtle" *AfO* 24 (1973) 51–72; this assumes the character of a contest between a heron-bird (igiru) and a turtle (níŋ-bún-na), in which Enki intercedes and, apparently, finds a solution involving the regulation of the lagoons (poorly preserved and not clear in detail).

The Disputation between Bird and Fish[9] includes a narrative section in which the fish is said to destroy the bird's nest.

Enlil and Namzitarra: This is included on some *Sammeltafel*, which contain other compositions, some of which are treated in this volume; cf. *Chap. 3.2* for details. The full text is edited in *Chap. 3.5*.

An episode involving a fox is attested as far back as the Fara-period, in the middle of the third millennium B.C. A fox acts in a myth of Enlil and Nuška, in which, apparently, the fox saves the god Nuška, who has been detained in the netherworld.[10] It is reminiscent of an episode in *Enki and Ninhursag* from the standard repertoire of the Isin-Larsa period.[11]

Some Sumerian short texts involve humans rather than animals, but seem otherwise to be of the same type: *The Fowler and His Wife*, edited as SP 21 Sec. A 5 in Alster: *Proverbs* I, 253–254; *The Lazy Slave Girl*, edited as SP 21 Sec. A 16 in Alster: *Proverbs* I, 256–257. These are both included here in *Chap. 4.5*.

An overview of fables and animal proverbs was given by Falkowitz in his contribution "Discrimination and Condensation of Sacred Categories: The Fable in Early Mesopotamian Literature."[12]

There is no known fable collection as such in Sumerian. Yet, a number of animal proverbs are included in the Sumerian proverb collections, notably Collections 5 and 8, and some of them have the character of fables. Fables also sometimes come close to a certain type of proverb, the wellerism.[13] What is needed to identify a wellerism is basically (1) a short

6. AcSum 10 (1988) 191–227.
7. AcSum 20 (1998) 135–179.
8. *The Phoenix. The Journal of the Classical Association of Canada*, 10/2 (1956) 70–77.
9. Translation: Vanstiphout, in Hallo (ed.): *Context of Scripture*, 581–584; now also available on the ETCSL site.
10. Kramer, *From the Tablets of Sumer* (Falcon Wing Press, 1956), jacket illustration and p. 106, fig. 6a; cf. Alster, JCS 41 (1989) 187.
11. Most recently edited by Attinger, ZA 74 (1984) 1–52, lines 223–225.
12. In: *Entretients sur l'antiquité classique*, Tome 25 (Vandœvres-Genève: Fondations Hardt, 1984), 1–32. Cf now Limet, 2002.
13. For a brief definition, see Alster: *Proverbs* I, xi, 21–22. Failure to recognize the wellerism as a proverbial type is the reason why Falkowitz in his contribution "Discrimination and Condensation of Sacred Categories" mistook a number of wellerisms for condensed fables, originally reflecting cosmogonic myths. Although similar notions have been raised elsewhere, and may occasionally be true, the objection raised by M. West, in the discussion following Falkowitz's article, p. 25, is

description of a situation; (2) a quoted speech uttered in that situation; (3) identification of the speaker. Wellerisms are abundantly attested in Sumerian literature; in some of these the speaker is an animal, which has led to the belief that these may in origin be condensed fables, or vice versa. The most likely explanation is that wellerisms as such are to be regarded as jokes or humorous sayings in their own right, not necessarily dependent on references to external texts.

Select Literature to Fables

B. Alster: "An Animal Proverb and the Assyrian Letter ABL 555," JCS 41 (1989) 187–193.

H.J. Blackham: *The Fables as Literature* (London, 1985).

P. Carnes: "The Fable and the Proverb: Intertext and Reception," in: W. Mieder (ed.), *Wise Words* (New York & London: Garland, 1994), 467–493 (repr. from *Proverbium* 8 [1991] 55–76).

M. Nøjgaard: *La fable antique* (København, 1964).

F. Edgerton: *The Pañchatantra Reconstructed* (New Haven, 1924), 2 vols.

R.S. Falkowitz; "Discrimination and Condensation of Sacred Categories: The Fable in Early Mesopotamian Literature," in: *Entretients sur l'antiquité classique*, Tome 25 (Vandœvres-Genève: Fondations Hardt, 1984), 1–32.

Th.J.H. Krispijn: "Dierenfabels in het oude Mesopotamia," in: Idema, E.L. et al. (eds.), *Mijn naam is haas. Dierenverhalen in verschillende culturen.* (Baarn: Ambo, 1993), 131–148 (not accessible to me).

H. Limet: "Le bestiaire des proverbes sumériens," *L'animal dans les civilisations orientales,* AcOrB 14 (2002) 29–43.

Andrea Remete and Raúl Franco: "La literatura sapiencial: Fábulas y proverbios en la antigua Mesopotamia," *Transoxiana* 5 (Dec 2002) 1–12.

I. Trencscényi-Waldappel: "Eine Aesopische Fabel und ihre orientalischen Parallelen," *Acta Scientiarum Hungarica* 7 (1959) 317–327.

B.E. Perry: *Aesopica* (Urbana: University of Illinois, 1952).

G. Selz: "Die Etana-Erzählung, Ursprung und Tradition eines der ältesten epischen Texte einer semitischen Sprache," AcSum 20 (1998) 135–179.

H. Vanstiphout: "The Importance of the Tale of the Fox," AcSum 10 (1988) 191–227.

Ronald J. Williams: "The Literary History of a Mesopotamian Fable," *The Phoenix. The Journal of the Classical Association of Canada*, 10/2 (1956) 70–77.

J.V. Kinnier Wilson: *The Legend of Etana. A New Edition* (Warminster, 1985).

very pertinent indeed: "It seems to me that a saying such as 'the fox urinated into the sea. «The whole sea is my urine» he said»' [SP 2.67] is self-contained and self-explanatory. It can be understood without reference to any cosmological myth. It could be taken out of Mesopotamian context." This conclusion can be corroborated by taking the recognition of the wellerism as a proverbial type into account, even more so because similar wellerisms are known from elsewhere; see the examples cited in Alster, *Proverbs* II, 367. Cf. also the discussion by Taylor, *The Proverb*, 200–220. Besides, allusions to mythological tales would, at any rate, be an unusual feature in proverbs.

4.2 Fables of a Fox

The Fox and Enlil as Merchant

Already Gordon, BiOr 17 (1960) 147, pointed to the existence of a Sumerian fragment, CBS 438: a tale involving a fox and a merchant. This was published by Cavigneaux, in AcSum 18 (1996) 66, as no. 9, with a copy on p. 46, and some useful comments on p. 45. He edited the text again with a translation in *Wilcke FS*, 59–60, with slightly improved readings, after he had recognized the Uruk text W 20248,4 (edited below) as a partial duplicate. The overlapping lines are quoted below marked as W.

Despite its very fragmentary state of preservation, enough of the tale is preserved to show that it was a tale of great humor: Fox tried to cheat the god Enlil, disguised as a merchant, in the first recorded story of smuggling in history. Fox, sailing downstream from Nippur, sought to pass a control point at Larsa, where Enlil was clever enough to see through Fox's intentions and so tried to stop him. Yet, Fox, making Dog an accomplice, was fast enough to take flight, swift "like a swallow," and hid in a hyena's hole. Although the fragment ends here, it requires little fantasy to imagine that the story might have continued in a lengthy sequence, in which Fox, unimpressed, played hide-and-seek with Enlil, the leading god of the Sumerian pantheon, apparently charging Dog of the crime! The following fragment, *A Fox and a Dog*, seems to belong to the continuation of the same tale, or, rather, a very free variant of it, partly duplicating it. Enlil's role as an itinerant merchant is known from elsewhere, cf. Civil, JCS 28 (1976) 72–81.

A Hyena and a Dog, below, may be related, but cf. the comments below.

Text Reconstruction

CBS 438 is the lower part of a one-column tablet with the left, right, and bottom edges preserved. Maybe half the tablet is missing on both sides. In view of the low CBS number it is doubtful whether the tablet came from Nippur, in particular since the style of script is hardly typical of Nippur. The tablet is published here in photographs, pls. 40–41.

Obv.

1' ᵈen-líl-le ⌜x⌝ ⌜x⌝ [(ca. 3 signs)] ⌜x⌝ ⌜x⌝ / igi má-gi-ke$_4$ má-šú-a ba-ni-in-šú	*(1')* Enlil ... covered the prow of the boat with a reed mat.
2' dam-gàr-ra-gim nibru[ki]-ta nam-mi-diri	*(2')* Like a merchant he left Nippur downstream.
3' kar larsa[ki] má(?) li-bí-⌜íb(?)⌝-⌜ús(?)⌝ má-bi ba-ni-⌜x⌝-⌜a⌝	*(3')* He did not moor the boat at the quay of Larsa, but [directed] that boat [onward].
4' ka$_5$-a dam-gàr-ra gù mu-un-n[a(?)-d]é-a-ta	*(4')* After Fox had spoken to the merchant:
5' dam-gàr má-me si ì-dab$_5$-bé má-zu ⌜da⌝-⌜x⌝-⌜na⌝	*(5')* "Merchant! He (i.e., a controller(?) or Enlil(?)) will seize our boat at the prow, your boat ..."
6' ka$_5$-a ⌜tur(?)⌝-⌜tur(?)⌝- ... (illegible) / ... (illegible)	*(6')* (*Enlil said:*) "Fox, ...
7' ... (traces) ... -ke$_4$ má-zu gub(?)-ba-ab	*(7')* stop your boat!(?)"

8'	[. . .] *(traces of 4 signs)*	*(8–12')* *(Too poorly preserved for translation)*
9'–11'	*(almost completely destroyed)*	
12'	[. . .] ⸢x⸣-⸢x⸣-⸢ni⸣-íb-[. . .] / [. . .] x x [. . .]	
Rev.		
13'	ka$_5$(?)-⸢a⸣ (3 signs) da (traces of four signs) / ur-gi$_7$ igi bí-in-d[u$_8$]	*(13')* Fox . . ., . . . saw a dog (and said:)
14'	dumu ere-ŋá má-zu diri-ga-ab / ⸢ki⸣ ⸢x⸣-bar(?)-zu ḫé-re-íb-gi-gi	*(14')* "Citizen (lit., Son of my city), let your boat sail downstream! Let let it return to your . . . place for your sake!"
15' W ii' 6'	si-sá-bi ḫul((?) text: IGI.IB)-le bí-in-du$_8$ ^{gi}kid-má(erased?) / níŋ mu-ra-gim níŋ-gi-na ⸢sa$_{10}$(?)⸣-a / giskim-ti mu-NE [x]-ba-a i-ib-le-e (7') [(x) e]n-⸢mu(?)⸣ ŋiš-kiŋ-ti (8') [m]u-e-TÚG	*(15')* Straight away he . . ., the reed mat like a . . ., (as) when buying(?) something just, he . . . the sign(?).
16' W ii' 11'	dam-gàr-ra AMA(?) ^{gi}kid-má-šú-a ba-x-x-a-gim GAM.GIŠ ^{gi}kid-má-[níŋin-n]a (12') ur-gi$_7$-re (13') igi bi-in-du	*(16')* As the merchant . . . [removed] the reed mat (from the boat),
17' W14–15'	ka$_5$-a bar-rim$_4$-e sim^{mušen} x(like ta) ⸢x⸣ ab-kar-re ka$_5$-a am-bar-šè sim [(x)] NE kar x kar-kar-re	*(17')* Fox (at once) took flight onto dry land (swift) like a swallow.
18' W ii' 17'	ur-gi$_7$-re eŋir-bi-a in-ús-ús-a / ur-gi$_7$-re (18') eŋir$_x$(íb)-bé im-ús-ús	*(18')* Dog followed behind it.
19' W 18'	ì-tar-tar-re-eš zi-ni ḫabrud-da KA-a / ba-ni-in-⸢x⸣(like Á) ì-tar-tar zi-bi ḫi(?)-li(?) KA (20') ku$_4$-ku$_4$-dè	*(19')* They took different paths (lit. they separated). (Fox) took refuge in a hole (belonging to) a hyena.
20' W ii 21'	KA ka$_5$-a ù-bí-in-du$_8$ èn ab-⸢tar-tar-tar⸣-re LÚ×NE(= du$_{14}$(?) (Cavigneaux: LÙ.LÙ.NE) nu-mu-un(?)-a[k(?)] . . .	*(20')* (W: (The hyena) did not protest.) Hyena, seeing Fox, asked:
21'	ka$_5$-a ugu-ŋu$_{10}$-šè nam-ŋu$_{10}$ gin-na-zu	*(21')* "Fox, what does it matter to me that you have come to me?"
22'	⸢ka$_5$⸣-⸢a⸣ ⸢igi⸣ ⸢ŠUB⸣ ⸢te⸣ lá ⸢KA⸣-⸢a⸣ ⸢èn(?)⸣ ⸢tar(?)⸣-⸢tar(?)⸣-⸢tar(?)⸣-[. . .]	*(22')* Fox . . . asked . . .

Continuation broken

Line 1: igi má ^{gi}kid: Cf. below, W 20248,4, ii' 3': [^{gi}kid-m]á-níŋin-na, etc. má-gi = má-gur$_8$.

Line 14: dumu-ere-ŋá, lit. "my citizen." Fox uses a pompous expression to impress its fellow dogs. The situation might be somewhat similar to SP 2.69.

Line 15: The details are far from clear, but it seem certain that Fox tries to hide his goods as a kind of smuggler.

Line 19: The expected expression is certainly some form of zi(-ni) – túm, "he saved his life." Note that Fox here is constructed as a person (-ni), as is frequent in the Sumerian fables.

A Fox and a Dog

A Sumerian school tablet, W 20248,4: *An Uruk Fragment of a Fable of a Fox*; was recognized by Cavigneaux, 2003, 57–58, as at least a partial duplicate to CBS 438: *The Fox and Enlil as Merchant*, edited above. W 20248,4 was first published by Cavigneaux, in: *Baghdader Mitteilungen* 13 (1982) 22, with a copy p. 24, transliteration pp. 23–27. The text had already been mentioned by Falkenstein, in: *Baghdader Mitteilungen* 2 (1963) 42, and Civil had earlier suggested that it might belong the same text as CBS 438; cf. also Alster, JCS (1991) 187.

These may have been independent tales not belonging to a larger series, but it is likely that they formed part of a series of the fox or, at least, they may have shared other features, which the preserved fragments do not allow us to judge. Cavigneaux in 1982 surmised that the Uruk fragment would turn out to be a forerunner of the Akkadian *Fable of the Fox*. In both fragments there is a "dialogue" in which the speakers are a fox and a dog.

The Uruk fragment in its more complete form may simply have been elaboration on the story of how Fox tried to escape from Enlil, fleeing into the holes of different animals. Such stories are likely to have enjoyed great popularity, and Fox's cunning and wit were by then already proverbial, most clearly expressed in a proverb that says "the fox outfoxed its mother" (lit., "made a bigger fox than its (own) mother," SP 2.60, Alster, *Proverbs* I, 57). Cf. also the Neo-Assyrian proverb treated by Alster: "An Akkadian Animal Proverb and the Assyrian Letter ABL 555," in: JCS 41 (1991) 187–193.

This makes it natural to seek to combine the two fragments with the Jena fragment published below as *A Hyena and a Dog*, but this may, in fact, have been somewhat different; cf. the comments below.

i' 1'–2' (*traces*)
i' 3' [...] TÚG(?)
i' 4' [...] ⌜x⌝-ra
i' 5' [mu-un-na-n]i-ib-gi-gi
i' 6' [...] é(?)-dù-a
i' 7' [...] ⌜x⌝ til-la
i' 8' [...] má-zu-uš
i' 9' [gi-ma-n]i-ib

———

i' 10' [... S]Ù?-ra
i' 11' [mu-un-na-ni-ib-g]i?-gi

Approximately 4 lines missing at the end of col. i and over 12 lines missing at the beginning of col. ii.

ii' 1' [... ú]s(?)-a
ii' 2' [...]-NE-DÙG
ii' 3' [^{gi}kid-m]á-nigín-na
ii' 4' [...] ⌜x⌝ LI
ii' 5' [má]-gi-na-ka
ii' 6' [a(?)]-ba-a i-ib-le-e
ii' 7' [x e]n-⌜ŋu$_{10}$(?)⌝ ⌜ŋiš-kiŋ⌝-ti
ii' 8' mu-e-TÚG
ii' 9' ⌜dam⌝-gàr gin-na dug$_4$-ge PA(?) la(?)
ii' 10' íl-íl-e(?)(rather too long for e)
ii' 11' gam ŋiš ^{gi}kid-má-[nigín-n]a
ii' 12' ur-gi$_7$-re
ii' 13' igi bí-in-du
ii' 14' ka$_5$-a am-bar-šè
ii' 15' nam-[x]-sar(?)
ii' 16' kar(?)-⌜šè(?)⌝ [x]-kar-kar-re

———

ii' 17' ur-gi$_7$-re
ii' 18' eŋir$_x$(ÍB)-bé im-⌜ús⌝-ús

———

ii' 19' ì-tar-tar zi-bi x x (Alster: ḫi-li) KA
ii' 20' ku$_4$-ku$_4$-dè
ii' 21' LÚ+NE(= du$_{14}$) (Cavigneaux: LÙ-LÙ.NE) nu-mu-⌜un⌝-⌜ak⌝
ii' 22' [x(?)] a(?)(or ⌜e⌝(?))-⌜ta⌝ ⌜ḪA⌝ UD KA [x]
ii' 23' [ku$_4$]-ku$_4$-[dè]
ii' 24' [...] ⌜ús⌝(?)

———

End of Col. ii. x number of lines missing at the beginning of col. iii.

iii' 1' [...] ⌜x⌝
iii' 2' [...] ⌜x⌝
iii' 3' [...] ⌜x⌝ ^{d}suen
iii' 4' [nam? ...]-tar-re
iii' 5' [...]-TÚG

iii' 6' [...]-na-ka
iii' 7' [...]-ir
iii' 8' [...]-ma
iii' 9' [...]ERIN(?)-bi (or: sa$_5$-ga(?), cf. iii 12)
iii' 10' [...] ⌜x⌝ lugal-la-ke$_4$
iii' 11' [x x (x) m]u-ni-in-niŋin-na
iii' 12' [x x s]a$_5$-ga
iii' 13' [x x] ⌜x⌝ ⌜x⌝ al-tuš
iii' 14' [x x] ⌜x⌝ [x] ⌜x⌝-ni-a
iii' 15' ugu-ŋu$_{10}$-šè [x] ì-gub
iii' 16' ní-zu ⌜x⌝ [x (x) m]u-ni(?)-ib(?)-ak
iii' 17' úr ⌜x⌝ ⌜x(Cavigneaux: sig?)⌝ ⌜mu-ni-in-ku$_4$-ku$_4$⌝
iii' 18' é-lugal [i]n-dab$_5$(?)
iii' 19' nar-r[e? x x) KA-a
iii' 20' ú ⌜nu(?)⌝-DIB (or síg(?)) K[A x] ⌜x⌝ ⌜x⌝
iii' 21' za-e níŋ-tur lú ⌜x⌝ ⌜x⌝ [x]
iii' 22' níŋ-gul igi-⌜zu⌝ n[a-x)
iii' 23' ní-zu sa ḫa-[...]
iii' 24' la-ba-an-⌜x⌝(Cavigneaux: ša) [...]
iii' 25' ki-tuš gi-[...]
iii' 26' lú ga ⌜x⌝ [...]
iii' 27' nam-ú-[...]
iii' 28' NI-[...]
iii' 29' šà [...]
iii' 30' ⌜x⌝ [...]

Approximately 5 lines missing at the end of col. iii'. An unknown number of lines missing at the beginning of col. iv'.

iv' 1' [...] ⌜x⌝ ⌜x⌝ ⌜x⌝
iv' 2' ⌜x⌝ ⌜x⌝ GIŠ ḪÚB(?)-re-e

---

iv' 3' ka$_5$-a di-da
iv' 4' mu-un-na-ni-ib-gi-gi

---

iv' 5' šà-tur ⌜šà(?)⌝-ga
iv' 6' šu nu-re-⌜re(?)⌝-re
iv' 7' nin-ŋu$_{10}$ gi-nam
iv' 8' E NUN-gá(?)-bi(?) sa$_6$(?)-ga
iv' 9' za-e nam-ku-li-ŋu$_{10}$-zé(?)

It is possible to retrieve connected sense only from a few lines:

ii' 11'–16': Dog saw ... the reed-boat ..., and chased(?) away Fox into the marshes(?) driving it into ...
ii' 17'–18': Dog pursued (Fox) into ...
ii' 19'–21': They separated and (Fox) saved his life entering a hyena(?)('s hole), and (Hyena) did not protest.
ii' 23'–24': (Dog) entering the ... from the watery side kept pursuing (Fox).

General: The parallels to CBS 438 are indicated as variants to the transliteration of that text, above.

ii' 6' – ii' 21' run approximately parallel to CBS 438. In iii' 3' the god Suen appears, so it seems likely that this was part of a longer story similar to the *Akkadian Fable of the Fox*. iv' 9' seems to represent the end of the text, since the continuation is a sign list.

i 6–9: The "built house" in i 6 might, of course, be a metaphor for the fox's hole, but this is very uncertain.

ii 5: If the reconstruction [má]-gi-na, "the just boat," is justified, this is reminiscent of SP 1.83: má-níŋ-gi-na, but very uncertain. Here, "just" and "unjust" very much give the impression of fair trade versus smuggling.

ii 6: Cavigneaux, 1966, 66, suggests that this is perhaps = íb-bala-e, but see now *Enlil as Merchant* 15.

ii 15': Cavigneaux reads nam [x] NE. With a minor emendation this might be sar, which would make good sense, "chased him into the marshes(?)." In line 14, am-bar seems to be phonetic for ambar.

ii' 19': KA = *būṣum*, "hyena," cf. MSL 3, 117 note ad line 254: KA = *bu-ṣu*, but uncertain.

iii' 3': It is, of course, tempting to suggest that Suen's role here is to decide the "fate" of the fox, which might then be to live forever in a foxhole, but as long as the text is so poorly preserved, this remains guesswork.

iii' 15'ff.: The impression is that here the fox's hole is compared to a royal palace and its functions (very tentative).

iii' 19': If the reading is really nar-re, "singer," rather than ka$_5$-a, "fox," this might well be an intended graphic pun on the readings of the same sign.

iv' 3–4: "The fox quarrelsomely answered." This shows that the text perhaps had the character of a contest poem, apparently between a fox and a dog.

iv' 7–8': The transliteration follows Cavigneaux, but the copy may be interpreted slightly differently. In iv' 9' it is tempting to suggest za-e nam-ku-li-mu-zé, but the final zé would be obscure. zé is hardly a mistake for ku$_4$. Could it perhaps rather stand for *za-e-me-en, but then nam(-ku-li) would be superfluous.

A Hyena and a Dog

HS 1535, previously published as TMHNF 4, 41, is a fragment from the middle of a one-column tablet with the left edge preserved. The fragment from Nippur in the Hilprecht Sammlung in Jena was first published by I. Bernhard and S.N. Kramer in 1967. It was collated by Wilcke, *Kollationen*, 1976, 73.

The text is transliterated below from an invaluable copy kindly made by M. Krebernik from the original tablet, reproduced here on pl. 71. There is a clear separating line after rev. 1', but none of the separating lines shown on the older copy seems to be warranted; cf. the photograph by J. Dahl, provided on pl. 40, which agrees with Krebernik's copy.

Little attention has so far been paid to the fragment. It is presented here as a fragment possibly belonging to the same cycle of tales as the two preceding ones. It is apparently a fragment from a larger tale, in which a dog plays the hypocritical role to be expected of a fox, appealing to the moon-god Nanna-Suen for help.

A dog seems to speak in rev. 2. Suen and Nanna are mentioned in rev. 3–4. Since a hyena seems to be involved in obv. 3, it is highly likely that this is a fragment from a story similar to the fable of *A Fox and a Dog*, treated above. If that is the case, it seems that the dog, seeking to escape into the hiding places of various animals, tried to appeal to a number of gods, among whom Nanna-Suen was one; cf. rev. 4: "Nanna, my lord …." In view of rev. 1, it may, however, rather belong to the contest-like type of fable also represented by the *The Goose and the Raven* (edited in *Chap. 4.3*). Since a sheepfold and its products seems to be mentioned in rev. 5, one may surmise that the text included a competition as to which of the two animals could bring some products from a sheepfold.

A related text might be Ni 4166 (ISET II 113).

Obv. (after a break of unknown size)

o' ⸢x⸣ […]
1' igi-ni-ta ⸢x⸣(like búr(?)) ⸢x⸣ ⸢x⸣ ⸢x⸣ […]
2' ⸢ḫabrud⸣-da-ni-ta nam-ta-⸢x⸣-[…]
3' KA ḫabrud-⸢da⸣-⸢ni⸣-ta mu-e-ši-du(?)-u[n(?) …]
4' ab(?)-ba ba-da-⸢su$_8$⸣-⸢un⸣(?)-⸢na(?)-za […]
5' ù-lu ba-da-⸢su$_8$⸣-⸢x⸣(hardly un?)-na(?) (no trace of za) ⸢KU(?)⸣-⸢KU⸣ […] (alt. suggest. Krebernik, 2nd part: ud–40!+4 […])
6' UR(? or téš/kiŋ/siki(?) hardly níŋ?) nu-⸢x(perhaps ub? erased)⸣-ne(over erasure?)-su ⸢x(like ḪAR)⸣ ⸢si⸣ […]
7' KA-ŋu$_{10}$-šè(?) ⸢ga(!)⸣-⸢ras(!)⸣-⸢sar⸣ ⸢nu⸣-[…]
8' [x x] ŋéšt[u(? = GIŠ.TÚG.PI, but a bit too long for PI, might be ŋál/gi$_4$) …]

An unknown number of lines missing

Rev.

o' ⸢x⸣(like UD or IGI) […]
1' e-dab$_5$(?)-⸢ba⸣ […] / za-e ŋá-[ra …]

2' ur-gi$_7$-re(! hardly mušen) an-ta-ni(? only if very squeezed, may be erased)-šè(?)⌝ ⌜a⌝-⌜ab⌝(?) [...] / ù-um-niŋin-ne-e[n]

3' ^{d}suen-ra dùg bí-in-gam-ma ír mu-[un-še$_8$-še$_8$]

4' ^{d}nanna lugal-ŋu$_{10}$ u$_4$-da ŋá-[e ...]

5' níŋ(?)-ul níŋ(?)-ì-dé(?)-a amaš ḫa(or ku$_6$?)-⌜re(?)⌝-[...] / ⌜níŋ⌝ ⌜GIŠ⌝ ⌜x⌝ [...]

Continuation broken

It is possible to retrieve only a few details from this fragment: In obv. 1'ff. it seems that an animal (a dog, fox, or hyena?) comes out from its hole: Obv. 1: "In front of him ...." Obv. 2: "[He (= Hyena?) came] out from his hole ...." Obv. 3: Hyena coming out from his hole went before you." In obv. 6 Hyena apparently speaks to a dog: *(6':)* "Dog! ...." Rev. 2 seems to be part of a conversation between the two. In rev. 2ff. a dog appeals to Nanna-Suen: (*(2':)* The dog ... circling ... *(3':)* It knelt on its knees before Suen, and we[pt] (saying): *(4')* "Oh Nanna, my lord, today ..."), but the nature of the appeal is not clear. In all likelihood it had been caught somewhere and wanted to escape.

Obv. 3: KA is likely to be a hyena in line 3, but perhaps rather just "mouth" in line 7.

Obv. 4–5: Seem to have the same sequence in the middle, slightly better preserved in line 5 than in line 4.

Obv. 7: Or read giri$_{17}$-ŋu$_{10}$-šè, "toward my face," or similar.

Rev. 1: Perhaps this can be restored from *The Goose and the Raven* 14ff. (cf. *Chap. 4.3*), somewhat like [an-ta-zu] e-ra-[...-gub-bé-en] za-e [ki-ta-ŋu$_{10}$ ...-gub-bé-en], "[should I stand above] you, [or should] you [stand under me?]." If this is the case, the fragment rather has the character of a literary contest.

Rev. 2: The interpretation of an-ta is decisive for the interpretation of the fragment, but the context is unfortunately too damaged to be of much help. On the one hand, an-ta can mean "above, over, in front of," as in *The Goose and the Raven* 14ff., and frequent in the Sumerian disputations. On the other hand, it can be understood as an appeal for help (= an-ta – gi, phonetic for gi$_4$), as in *The Three Ox-Drivers from Adab* 3 and 18; cf. *Chap. 5.1*. The continuation rather favors the second possibility.

Rev. 3: Perhaps went round to Suen's temples for help (= an-ta), but very uncertain.

Addendum

Only in the final stage of proofreading were the partial parallels HS 1535 and the bilingual PBS 1/2 135 recognized. The latter was treated by van Dijk in *Sagesse*, 128–134, as part of the Sumerian *Righteous Sufferer* poem, and recopied and edited by Cavigneaux, in *Limet FS*, 22–26. PBS 1/2 135, already in 3ff., alludes to animal stories and continues in 32–33, so it seems that already existing animal tales were quoted, but the precise relationship between the texts must await further investigation. Perhaps it was rather the animal tales that ironically quoted phrases normally used in prayers, cf. HS 1535, rev. 3, compared to PBS 1/2 135, 50. PBS 1/2 135, in fact, does not belong to *The Righteous Sufferer* poem, but is related to magical prayer literature, similar to PBS 1/2 122, edited by M.J. Geller, *Sjöberg FS*, 193–199, cf. Cavigneaux, p. 23, n. 13.

4.3 The Goose and the Raven

Publication History and Introduction

The Sumerian fable *The Goose and the Raven* is so far not attested in the proverb collections, but exists as an independent composition. An attempt is made here to edit it, although so far it has not been possible to reconstruct and interpret it fully.

This text was first observed by Gordon in 1960, but apart from a short connected sequence translated by Alster in: *Assyriological Miscellanies* I (1980) 45–47, there titled *The Crow and the Goose*, with a preliminarily treatment of the first 13 lines, and in Alster, 1992, 190–191, nn. 7–8, no edition has as yet been attempted. The basic sources were identified by Gordon and Civil; cf. Gordon, BiOr 17 (1960) 151.

Civil, AfO 25 (1974–75) 65 refers to this as *The Fable of the Crane and the Raven*, and discusses the identity of the *uga*-bird, for which both the raven and the crow are possible. He favors the raven, because it is the one that had "more personality" of the two, which fits better to a number of occurrences in literary texts. Landsberger, MSL 8/2 151 ad line 138, however, regarded it as the crow.

According to Civil the two words uga and buru$_4$, i.e., /gburu/, are related through metathesis of the r. He explain these as reflections of Semitic ġrV:b or ʿV:b, corresponding to Akk *(ḫ)erēbu*, but different from buru$_5$, which is related to *ʾrb*, corresponding to Akk. *er(i)bu*.[14]

The Sumerian kur-gi$_4$-a (kur-gi) bird is equated with Akk. *kurgû*, usually understood as a goose, crane or domestic hen. The translation "crane" is suggested by its Aramaic cognate *kurkjā*, Arabic *kurkī*.[15] It is obvious that the name itself imitates the sound of the bird, and in our text the kur-gi$_4$ bird is a wild animal, such as a crane or wild goose that could fly high and wide away. Since it is also well attested as a domesticated bird that could be fattened together with ducks, I consider it most likely that here it refers to a type of wild goose that could be domesticated.

The initial address by the raven evolves into a competition as to which of the two should be considered superior to the other. In other words, this is an animal tale partly structured as a contest between the two birds. It is regrettably not yet possible to retrieve the end of the story. Toward the end a fowler's wife appears, speaking to the birds. What she says remains obscure, but apparently an attempt is made to deceive the raven. A possibility is that she tried to convince the raven that something edible was hidden in the net above it, hoping that it would fly into the net and, thereby, lift it high enough to enable the goose to escape. However, for the time being, the preserved fragments do not allow any definite solution. Yet, comparison with *The Fowler and His Wife*, translated in *Chap. 4.5*, lines 6–7 and 10, might support that interpretation.

The Manuscript Tradition

At least ten sources are known. These differ so much from one another that each manuscript ideally would have to be treated separately. It was nevertheless decided to transliterate them as far as possible in a "score" under each other as ordinary duplicates, although this might in some cases give a slightly misleading impression. Also the vacillation between short lines versus long ones at times makes it difficult to decide which lines are to be connected. In particular the Ur source A differs considerably from the Nippur sources C and D[16] (cf. also E and H), in that it seems to have been considerably expanded compared to the others. It is highly likely that much better results could have been achieved had the Nippur fragments C and D been better preserved. Not unexpectedly the Uruk source seems to differ consider-

14. A short comment on the identity of the bird was made by Landsberger, WO 3 (1964–66) 246–263. Cf. further A. Salonen, *Vögel und Vogelfangst im alten Mesopotamien*, Ann. Acad. Scient. Fennicae 180, 124–131, and Veldhuis, *The Sumerian Composition Nanše and the Birds*, CM 22 (Brill, 2004).

15. Cf AHw 510: "eine Haushühnart?"; CAD K, 561–562: *kurkû*, "goose"; MSL 8/2 153, 359 (also p. 154). It must be admitted that "crane" might fit better here, since the competition is about flying high and widely. Yet, this might also be said of a wild goose. It is not unthinkable that etymologically related terms of animals shifted meaning to become designations of two different species in two languages.

16. C and D do not join, checked by Y. Sefati, Jan. 2004.

ably from the others. The manuscripts may reflect oral versions of the text, current at the time when the sources were written down, or somewhat earlier, since it is likely to have enjoyed great popularity.

Sources

These following sources have been used:[17]

A: UET 6/2 199. Nearly complete one-column tablet containing the entire composition: 38 (short) lines. Collated by M.-C. Ludwig. Provenience: Ur.

B: CT 42, no 23 (pl. 36) face C 8–17 (BM 54699), prism. Collated by M. J. Geller. Starting after a section separator: face C has the first 10 lines of the text. Face D, containing the ends of 7 lines, might, in fact, belong the first column of the prism. In that case, the remains of face D may belong to the beginning of the folktale of *The Old Man*, which is then continued on Face A, although they have not yet been precisely placed. Cf. the edition in *Chap. 5.2*. Provenience: Unknown, possibly Sippar.

C: PBS 5, 13 (correct number according to Sefati: CBS 14047, not CBS 8804). Small fragment from a two-column tablet. Remains of 7 lines on col. i(?), and 5–6 lines on col. ii(?). If this is from the obv., col. i might be from a different composition, or the remaining signs on col. i must belong before line 10 of the composition. If this is, in fact, from the rev., col. ii cannot be placed. Provenience: Nippur.

D: PBS 5, 11 (CBS 15109). Small fragment from an unidentified side of a tablet of unknown size. Probably from the rev., around lines 15–16; 20. Provenience: Nippur.

E: CBS 6564 + 8078 + N 4708 + N 5888, obv. Published here in photograph: pls. 46–47. Two-column type-2 exercise tablet, of which the left col. on the obv. contains ca. lines 1–21 of the fable of *The Goose and the Raven*. The right column is erased. The rev. is inscribed with a lexical list. Provenience: Nippur.

F: YBC 8625, from a transliteration made in 1992 with the kind permission of W.W. Hallo. Provenience: Unknown.

H: Ni 3546 (ISET II 91), identified by M. Green, BiOr 35 (1978) 180. Small fragment from the right side of a one-column tablet. Obv. has 10 lines. Rev. has 4 + 6 lines with approximately two broken lines between them. Right, top, and bottom edges preserved. Apparently this had relatively long lines. Provenience: Nippur.

I: W 20248, 3, obv., publ. by Cavigneaux, "Schultexte aus Warka," *Baghdader Mitteilungen* 13 (1982) 21–30; copy of obv. on p. 25 (copy of rev. on p. 24: *The Fox and Enlil as Merchant*, cf. *Chap. 4.2*). Remains of 5 ruled lines. Larger script than on obv. Perhaps a fragment from a type-2 tablet with the same text repeated in the right column (now missing). Cf. Cavigneaux, p. 22. Belongs approximately to lines 16–17; 29, but not placed with certainty. Provenience: Uruk-Warka.

J: UM 29-13-329. Center fragment with no edges preserved. Small, but very careful writing. A photograph of the obverse by K. Danti pl. 72. The reverse has 5 damaged lines (not photographed). Starts in obv. 12 and covers lines 1–2 plus one or two unidentified lines. The composition before line 12 is unidentified. Cf. the description under *Sources* below.

K: CBS 3907. Center fragment from the left column of a type-2 exercise tablet, of which the preserved parts of col. ii are uninscribed. Col. i has remains of 8 lines, unidentified, but similar to lines 13–14 and 20.

L: CBS 6930. Photograph pl. 72. Not placed with certainty.

M: N 3695 (not used, cf. Civil's list).

N: N 3700 (not used, cf. Civil's list).

17. According to Civil's list, the following sources are relevant: BM 54699 c 8'ff. (= B above); CBS 6564 + CBS 6559 + CBS 8078 + N 4708 + N 5888 (= E above); CBS 6930 (= L above; photograph pl. 72; no join to the other fragments, according to Sefati); CBS 15109 (= D above); H 149 + H 155 (Tell Hadad number, to be published by A. Cavigneaux); N 3695 (not used); N 3700 (not used; no join to the other fragments, according to Sefati); Ni 3546 (ISET II 91) (= H above); UET 6, 199 (= A above); UM 29-13-329 (= J above; no join, Sefati); YBC 8625 (= F above).

1
A 1 — [u$_4$ kur-gi$_4$]^{mušen} diš-àm
A 2 — ⸢NI⸣ [x é] ⸢mušen⸣-dù-ka ì-gub-bu
B ~1 — [u$_4$ kur-g]i$_4^{\text{mušen}}$ sig-ta igi-nim-šè im-ma-⸢N[I- ...]
E 1 — u$_4$ kur-gi$_4^{\text{mušen}}$ igi nim-bi-⸢šè(?)⸣
E 2 — im-ma-ra-an-e$_{11}$-⸢dè⸣
J 12 — [u$_4$ kur-gi$_4$]^{mušen} sig-ta i[gi-nim-šè]
J 13 — [im]-ma-da-ra-a[n-e$_{11}$-dè]

A 1–2 — [When a goose]—alone—[...] was standing in [the house(?)] of a fowler,
B ~1 — [When (some) gee]se [descended] (flying) from south to north,
E 1–2 — When (some) geese were descending (flying) north,
J — [When (some) geese] descended (flying) from south [to] north,

2 — (*A and F shorter*)
B ~2 — [x] kur-gi$_4^{\text{mušen}}$ sa-diš(coll. Geller) mušen-dù-ke$_4$ l[a(?)-...]
E 3 — diš-àm kur-gi$_4^{\text{mušen}}$ sa-⸢a⸣ ⸢ši⸣-⸢x⸣ / ⸢ŋá⸣-⸢x⸣-gub
F 1 — diš ⸢x⸣ [. . .]
J 14 — [diš-à]m] kur-gi$_4^{\text{mušen}}$ é (NB not sa!) [mušen-dù-ke$_4$ ...].
J 15 — [u]ga^{mušen} bàd-si-a [im-gub(?)]

B ~2 — a [lone] goose [remained standing(?)] in a fowler's house(?).
E 3 — all alone a goose was [caught] in a net, (and) ... stood ...

H obv.1–2 — (*apparently a shorter introduction to the text*):
H 1 — [...] ⸢GUB⸣ BI IS(sic? perhaps one sign, but hardly NE)
H 2 — [... u]ga-ke$_4$ al-gub

3
A 3 — [u]ga^{mušen}
A 4 — [(x)] KA bàd(? text ab, coll. Ludwig)-si-ke$_4$ me-en ì-gub
B ~3 — [ug]a^{mušen} bàd-si-a im-⸢x⸣-[...]
B ~4 — [u]ga^{mušen} kur-gi$_4^{\text{mušen}}$ gù mu-n[a-dé-e]
E 4 — [(x)] ⸢uga⸣^{mušen} ⸢x⸣ ⸢x⸣ im-e$_{11}$(?)
F 2 — uga (no mušen) bàd-[si]-e i[m- x] bí-gub
H 3 — [...]-ke$_4$ bí-gub ugu-ni za(?)-šè(?)

A 3–4 — A raven stood ... on the parapet (and said:)
B 3–4 — A raven [stood] on the parapet and spoke to the goose:
E 4 — A raven ... came down (and said:)
F 2 — A raven stood on the parapet (and said:)
H 3 — [A raven] stood on [the parapet] ... over him...(?) (and said:)

3a
E ~5 — [x] zu NI-ra
E ~6 — [u]ga^{mušen} k[ur-g]i$_4^{\text{mušen}}$
E ~7 — [x] gù m[u-na-d]é(?)-e

E 5–7 — ... The raven sp[oke to the goo]se:

4

A 5	[(x) su]kud-da-zu-ne daŋal-la-zu-ne
B ~5	[sukud-da]-zu-ne daŋal-la-zu-ne ⸢x⸣ ⸢x⸣ [x (x)]
E 8–9	[x x x] ⸢x (like KU×x)⸣ ⸢x⸣ [x x x]-⸢zu⸣-ne
F 3	[sukud]-da-zu-ne dagal-la-zu-ni(sic!)
A, B, E, F:	Since you can fly as high as you wish, since you can fly as widely about as you wish,

5

A 6	a-na-àm i-im-GUB-en ì-šè
E 10	[x x] ⸢an⸣ ⸢x⸣ [x x] / [...] (belongs where(?)]
F 4	[a-na-à]m im-gub ì-šè
A, F:	Why do you keep standing there(?)?, it said.

5a

E 10	kur-gi$_4$^{mušen} uga^{mušen} ⸢x⸣ / mu-na-ni-g[i$_4$-gi]$_4$
B ~6	[(x)] ⸢ú⸣ (coll. Geller) uga^{mušen} [...]
E 10	The goose answered the raven,

6

A 7	sa-zu ma-ná-ma
E 11	mušen-dù sa(?) ma-ná ⸢x⸣ ⸢ta⸣ ⸢la⸣ ⸢x⸣(= erasure?)
B ~7	[x]-⸢x⸣ sa ma-ná-e s[a ...]
F 5	mušen-dù-e sa ma-ná-ma
A (and B?)	(*Goose:*) A net intended for you was thrown upon me, and so:
E, F:	A fowler threw a net upon me, and so:

7

A 8	še-numun-zu ma-an-ŋar-ra-ma
F 6	[x]-ra-ta im-ma-an-šár-re ì-šè
A	the seeds that were intended for you were laid out for me, and so:
F	(*not translated*)

8

A 9	sa-zu mu-un-dib-bé ì-šè
A	it is a net set up for you that holds me, it said.

9

A 10	a-na-àm sa-zu la-ba-ra-an-gíd
E 12	a-na-aš-àm ⸢sa⸣ nu-bir$_7$-ma
F 7	[a]-na-àm igi-àm sa nu-bùr(? text: GAM)-re-⸢x⸣
A	(*Raven:*) Why don't you (just) strech the net? it said.
E	(*Raven:*) Why don't you rip the net apart, and so
F	(*Raven:*) Why don't you tear(?) the net in front apart?

10

A 11	la-ba-da-dal-dal šè
E 12 cont.	la-ba-dal e-še
F 8	[a-n]a(?)-àm dal-dal ì-šè
A, E, F	(why) don't you just fly away? it said.

11

A 12	ŋiš-búr im-ma-an-díb
E 13	⌜á⌝(?)-šu ŋ[ìri(?)-ŋ]u$_{10}$ im-ma-da(?)-ra-RI (x)]
F 9	sa (or é)-da-na ŋìri-ŋu$_{10}$ in-dab
A	(*Goose:*) A trap has caught me(!)
E 13	My wings(?) and feet are …
F	My feet are caught in the net(?) of his ….

12

A 13	la-(erasure)-ba-da-dal-dal šè
E 14	[… da]l-le [(šè)]
F 10	⌜x⌝(?)-a an-dal-dal ì-šè
A(, E and F?)	(Therefore,) I cannot (just) fly away, it said.

13

A 14	kur-gi$_4^{mušen}$ uga^{mušen}
A 15	[gù m]u-un-na-dé-e
E 15ff	(*about 2–3 lines destroyed or illegible*)
H 4	[…] kur-gi$_4^{mušen}$ / [… -n]a(?)-dé(?)-e(?)
A, H	The goose spoke to the raven:

14

A 16	[ŋá-e an-ta-z]u(coll. Ludwig) ù za-e ugu-ŋu$_{10}$-uš
F 11	⌜a⌝-⌜x⌝ igi-àm al-dab igi-ni-šè al-gub
A	[Should I(?) be over(?) you] or you over me?
F	… caught in front … stood in front of him:
E 17	[…] RI ⌜UD⌝ (or UD belongs to the preceding line?)
F 12	x (like nam) ŋéštu-šè hé-UD (neither tál, nor im)-tál-⌜x⌝-⌜x⌝
F 13	[za-e ugu]-ŋu$_{10}$ an-ta gub ŋá-e ki-ta gub
F 14	[za-e ugu]-ŋu$_{10}$ ki-ta gub ŋá-e an-ta gub
F	[Should you] stand over me, and I stand under (you)?
F	[or should you] stand under me, and I stand over (you)?

15

A 17 [...]-ŋu$_{10}$-šè ḫé-díb-bé ì-šè

A To my [...] let [...] take! it said.

D 3' [...] ⸢ì(?)⸣-íb-zé-zé(?) TAR Ḫ[U ...]
[...] á-bi muru$_{9}$(IM-DUGUD)-[gim ...] (indented) (belongs where?)
D 4' [...] igi kur-gi$_{4}$^{mušen}-šè i-im-sar-[...] (belongs where?)

D 3' [...] its wings like a thundercloud ...
D 4' [... chased away ...] in front of the goose.

16

A 18 [(x) u]ga^{mušen} kur-gi$_{4}$$^{mu[šen]}$-⸢e(?)⸣(coll. Ludwig)
A 19 [(inim) mu]-ni-ib-gi$_{4}$-gi$_{4}$
B ~8 [ug]a^{mušen} kur-gi$_{4}$^{mušen} [...]
D 5' [...] kur-gi$_{4}$^{mušen} uga[^{mušen} ...] /
[(...)] gù mu-un-na-dé-[e]
E 18 [ug]a^{mušen} kur-gi$_{4}$ mu-na-{KAL-e}-gi$_{4}$-gi$_{4}$
H 7 [... ug]a^{mušen} mu-na-ni-ib-g[i$_{4}$-g]i$_{4}$
I i 1' [u]ga[^{mušen}] [(kur-gi$_{4}$^{mušen}-ra(?))] / im-ma-⸢ni⸣-[...] (belongs here?)

A, B, D, E, H The raven answered the goose:

17

A 20 [x x n]á-zu sa ba-bar-ra-zu-ne
B ~9 [(x) x] sa kad kéšda ⸢x⸣ [...]
F 15 x (like ⸢gá⸣) (no room for e) ki-ná x (nearly = šè) nu-GAM-d[è-x]
I o i 1'.3 [...]-ni-šè š[e(?) ...]

A ..., when you break loose from the net,

18

A 21 [x x k]i-ta-zu ŋá-e im-ta-zu
F 16 a-na-àm ŋá-e in-dab-e-[x (x)]

A [should I stand] under you, or should I stand over you?
F (*No translation attempted*)

19

A 22 [x x] im-ta-zu *ŋá-e(? coll. Ludwig looks like LAG) ki-ta-zu
{# F 13 [x]-ŋu$_{10}$ an-ta gub ŋá-e ki-ta gub}
{# F 14 [x]-ŋu$_{10}$ ki-ta gub ŋá-e an-ta gub}

A [or should I stand over you, or I] under you?

20

A 23 [dam mu]šen-dù ḫar-ŋiš-⸢gan(?)⸣ im-<mi>-ni-in-tuk-tuk
D 6' [dam mušen-dù-k]e$_{4}$ ŋéštu e-tuku-[...]
E 19 [dam(? only one sign)]-e ŋéštu an-tuku
F 17 dam mušen-dù-ke$_{4}$ ŋéštu-tuku

(A), F The fowler's wife, ... listening to it, (said:)

21
A 24 ù-zu búr-mu-ra-ka
D 7' [...] ⸢x⸣-e ÉŠ-sa-kala-ga ⸢saŋ⸣ [...] (belongs where?)
E 20 ⸢sa⸣ ná-a e-zu sa-e ga-e-zu
F 18 mu ḪAR un su ra ka(?) im- x - dul ⸢x⸣
H 12 [... -n]a(?)-ab-dul
A (*unintelligible*)

D ... the strong net [covered your] head,
E, F and H (*not translated, seem to differ*)
[*For the continuation in E, see the separate transliteration below.*]

22
A 25 níŋ ba-ni-in-ŋál
D 8' [... ku]r(?)-gal ⸢x⸣ [...] (belongs where?)
F 19 TÙG x x [. . .]

A there was something put into it.

23
A 26 na-zi ba-an-ŋar

F ... put incense(?) ... (*mostly unintelligible*)

24
A 27 sa-zu ì-ná-ma

A having laid it(?) in your net,

25
A 28 še-numun-zu ŋiš(sic! read ma?)-an-ŋar-ma

A and having placed(?) the seeds intended for you (in it?), then,

26
A 29 sa-zu mu-na-díb-bé ì-šè

A you(?) will ... your net for him, it said.

27–28
A 30 kur-⸢gi$_4$^{mušen}⸣ uga^{mušen}-ra
A 31 ⸢gù⸣ mu-⸢na⸣-[an(?)]-dé-e

A The goose spoke to the raven:

29
A 32 [...] ME-àm
I o i 2'.1 [...]^{mušen}(?) (or ús?) SU-NI GAR [long break]-ŋá la-[x] (belongs here, or 2 cols.?)
I o i 2'.2 [...] AN me-š[è(?) ... (long break)] -⸢ni⸣-[x] (belongs here(?); maybe 2 cols.)

(*No translation suggested*)

30
A 33 […]-e im-ta-zu
A [Should you be over me, and I] under you?

31
A 34 […] ⸢x(not e)⸣ ki-ta-zu
A [Or should you be over me and] I under you?

32
A 35 […] en [x (x)]-⸢x⸣ ([x])

33
A 36 […] (traces of 4 signs)

34
A 37 [x]-zu níŋ íb(or perhaps ḫé)-gu$_7$-e
A Your … was(?) eaten ….

35
A 38 [x (x)]-⸢e⸣ nu-um-zu (end of text)
A […] did not know.

Sources not placed:

B Face D~1	[…] ⸢ní⸣-zu ⸢kéšda⸣ e-še	*(B~1)* "… bind(?) yourself" (he/she) said.
B Face D~2	[…] ḫé-gi$_4$-gi$_4$	*(B~2)* … answered:
B Face D~3	[…b]a-ši-in-ak	*(B~3)* … should(?) pay attention.
B Face D~4	[… ŋizzal …]-in-ak	*(B~4)* … should(?) pay attention.
B Face D~5	[… inim …]-in-gi$_4$	*(B~5)* [… answered]:
B Face D~6	[…] ga-àm-si	*(B~6)* "[…] let me fill."
B Face D~7	[…]-⸢di⸣-ni-íb-⸢x⸣-⸢x⸣	*(B~7)* …

May not belong to this text; cf. list of sources above and *Chap. 5.2: The Old Man and the Young Girl.*

Source E Separate Transliteration Lines 16ff.:

From line ca. 18 = composite text ca. lines 16ff., the Nippur source E seems to have had a shorter continuation different from the reconstruction above, which mainly is based on the Ur source A. It is highly likely that this represents the same version as C and D, as well as other Nippur sources, but since our excerpt ends after only four more lines, this cannot at the present time be verified.

16

E ca. 18	[ug]a^{mušen} kur-gi$_4$ mu-na-{KAL-e}-gi$_4$-gi$_4$

17

E ca. 19	[dam(? only one sign)]-e ŋéštu an-tuku
E ca. 20	⸢sa⸣ ná-a e-zu sa-e ga-e-zu
E ca. 21	sa sa TÚG šu bal-ak e-zu
E ca. 22	ŋiš-búr ḫar ná-a e-zu
E ca 23	⸢ŋá⸣(?)-e(?) an-ta NI-DÙ ŋá-e ⸢ki⸣-⸢ta⸣ (remains of one sign below)

End of excerpt

Separate Transliteration of Source J

J = UM 29-13-329 has 17 lines from the center of a tablet of unknown size. There are separating lines after lines 5 and 17. A photograph by K. Danti is provided on pl. 72 (obverse only; the reverse has 5 damaged lines). The tablet may have had more than one column. Since *The Goose and the Raven* begins after the separating line following line 11, the most likely solution is that the 11 lines before the separating line belong to a different composition, and that there may have been a number of other short compositions inscribed on the tablet. The same may, in fact, have been the case with some of the other fragments. Lines 12–13 indicate that the tablet used short lines, and hardly more than one sign is missing on the left side, and hardly more than two signs are missing on the right side.

Transliteration of 12–17:

Separating line

12 [u$_4$ kur-gi$_4$]^{mušen} sig-ta i[gi-nim-šè] (= l. 1)

13 [im]-ma-da-ra-a[n-e$_{11}$-dè] (= l. 1 f)

14 [diš-à]m] kur-gi$_4$^{mušen} é (NB not sa!) [mušen-dù-ke$_4$ ...].

15 [u]ga^{mušen} bàd-si-a [im-gub(?)] (= l. 3)

16 [...]-ka-na za-ra [...] (not placed)

17 [...] traces [...] (not placed)

Comments on Individual Lines

Line 1: The text is introduced by a dependent relative clause, u$_4$, lit., "when," not u$_4$-ba, "on that day," or similar, which might have been expected.

Of the initial pair sig-ta igi-nim-šè, "from south to north," in B, E strangely omits sig-ta.

The Sum. text, which does not explicitly mark the plural of non-personal nouns, permits the translation suggested above, according to which line 1 kur-gi$_4$^{mušen} refers to a flock of migratory birds, among which only one was left behind in what follows. This point has been lost in A, however, which introduces diš-àm, "one," too early.

Line 2: The negation in B: l[a-, if correctly read, seems to be mistaken. Reading B: sa-diš suggested by

Geller, who finds it possible on the tablet, but it is very doubtful, since J clearly has é; cf. the photograph on pl. 72.

Line 3: bàd-si = *sītu*, "parapet," occurs, e.g., in SP 1.186; 3.2; 10.13; *Instr. Šuruppak* 231.

Line 4: For the variant daŋal-la-zu-ni in F, indicating the reading -zu-ne, cf. p. 217, *Chap. 1.9: NI : NE variation*, and the literature there cited.

Line 5: A has the expected -gub-en, but here and elsewhere later F strangely omits the 1st or 2nd person marker -en.

Line 6: There is no introductory line indicating that now the goose is the speaker. Similarly lines 10, 11, etc.

Line 8: In A: mu-un-dib-bé, -un- is the 1st person "object" marker; cf. p. 211, *Chap. 1.9: 2nd person "object" element in pre-radical position*, and the literature there cited.

Line 9: For bir_7(ŠÀ×A) = *šarāṭum*, cf. PSD B, 160, and *Instr. Šuruppak* 136. Source E is quoted in PSD B, loc. cit., as CBS 6559+ i 11: "... sa nu-bir_7-ma (var. ba-ra-an-bu, in UET 6/2 199, 10) la-ba-dal e-še, "he said «why did you not rip the net and fly away?»." Note, however, that in the line quoted there as a variant, that is, our source A, BU/gíd is not necessarily a phonetic variant of bir_7, but simply a different verb gíd, which in the context means something different, although semantically related, "to stretch (a net to let a bird fly away)"; for this meaning, see Alster, ZA 82 (1992) 190–191 with nn. 9–10 on *The Fowler and His Wife*, also included here in *Chaps. 4.5* and *6.2*. I have transliterated the Yale source F as found in my handwritten notes from 1991: GAM-re-⌈x⌉, but a closer look is likely to show bir_7. Or, perhaps GAM is a misreading of bùr, phonetic for bir_7. Cf. line 17 below.

Line 12: Note the unusual writing ì-še in F for the quotation particle e-še. This supports the reading of ŠÈ as éše, for which see Edzard, *Sum. Grammar*, 157. In A 10 and 12 it is written šè (= éše), which is reminiscent of Gudea Cylinder A v 13: ri-ba-šè(/éše). Cf. also *Chap. 5.2: The Three Ox-Drivers from Adab* 7 with comments and references to earlier literature, etc.

Line 14: In F, an-ta and ki-ta seem to have been mistakenly reversed.

Line 17: Cf. Alster, 1992, 190, n. 9, for an attempt to explain the variant kéšda. In F the variant GAM may be a transliteration error; cf. line 9 above.

Line 18: A in lines 18, 19, and 30 writes im-ta- for an-ta, "above." In view of such a grave error, one wonders how much of the text was properly understood.

Line 20: No attempt is made here to interpret A: ḫar-ŋiš-⌈gan(?)⌉.

Line 23: For na-zi (in A), cf. perhaps Veldhuis, "The Sumerian Word na-IZI," in: CDLN 2003:002, available on the website http://cdli.ucla.edu, who understands it as na-dè = *qutrēnu*, "incense," with references to Gudea Cyl. B iv 4–5; Michalowski, *Hallo FS*, 153, etc.

4.4 "Aesopian" Fables in Sumerian

The brief animal tales translated below stand out as the first examples of the wit characteristic of the Greek fables of Aesop. The first edition was by Gordon, 1958, but a more complete edition by Alster, 1997, meant considerable progress. Many fine observations on animal proverbs and tales were made by H. Limet, 2002, and R.S. Falkowitz, 1984.

The Lion and the She-Goat

This short fable has been repeatedly translated, and most fully edited in Alster, *Proverbs* I, 128–129, with comments in *Proverbs* II, 403, as SP 5.55. As translated below, the point rests on the clever conversion of the name the she-goat gives itself: umun-mu-e-da-ak-e (l. 5), lit., "I was clever with you," which I understand as "I was cleverer than you." With a minimal grammatical change this is converted to the ironic conclusion "you were clever" (úmum mu-e-ak), with which the text ends when finally it becomes clear that the weak she-goat has cheated the strong lion. The textual evidence is admittedly not well preserved at this point, however. (The text below is based on H as the most reliable manuscript, which, however, omits "you were clever" in l. 9.) If correctly understood, this represents the oldest known and clearest example of the humorous punning on wit characteristic of the fables of Aesop.

5.55

(1) ur-maḫ-e ùz-ḫu-nu-a ù-mu-ni-in-dab$_5$	*(1)* A lion had caught a helpless she-goat (and she said):
(2) šu ba-àm u$_8$-tab-ba-ŋu$_{10}$ gur-ra ga-mu-ra-ab-šúm	*(2)* "Let me go, and I will give you my fellow ewe in return."
(3) tukum-bi šu mu-ri-bar-re mu-zu dug$_4$-ma-ab	*(3)* "If I let you go, tell me first your name!"
(4) ùz-dè ur-mah-e mu-na-ni-ib-gi$_4$-gi$_4$ za-e mu-ŋu$_{10}$ nu-e-zu	*(4)* The she-goat answered the lion: "You do not know my name?
(5) úmum mu-e-da-ak-e mu-ŋu$_{10}$-um	*(5)* 'I am cleverer than you' (úmum-mu-e-da-ak-e) is my name."
(6) u$_4$ ur-mah-e é-tùr-šè ì-gin-na	*(6)* After the lion had come to the sheepfold,
(7) mu-e-búru-e-en gù al-dé-dé-e	*(7)* he roared: "I released you."
(8) e-ne gú-ri-ta mu-un-na-ni-ib-gi$_4$-gi$_4$	*(8)* She answered from the other side:
(9) mu-e-búru-e-en úmum mu-e-ak bar-udu-ḫi-a-ka nu-dúr-ru-na e-še	*(9)* "You released me, you were clever (úmum mu-e-ak), because the sheep are not here!"

(Variants: A omits "You released me." H omits "you were clever.")

Selected Variants: Line 5, text based on H: úmum mu-e-da-ak-e mu-ŋu$_{10}$-um; A: ú]mun mu-e-du[g$_4$ ...]; UET 6/2 212: [úmun mu-e-da-ak]-⸢e⸣; CT 58, 67 A I: úmun mu-e-<ak>-en mu-ŋ[u$_{10}$-um ...]. Line 7, text based on H; A: ur-[ma]ḫ-⸢e⸣ mu-e-b[úr-e-en] gù al-dé-dé-e, "«I released you» he roared"; H: mu-e-búr-e-en gù al-dé-dé-e. Line 9, text based on H, which, however, omits úmum mu-e-ak; A omits mu-e-búru-e-en, "I released you"; CT 58, 67 A I: [...]-⸢e⸣-ak-en bar-udu-ḫi-a-ka nu-dúr-ru-un e-še.

Nine Wolves and a Fox

The text is preserved in two almost identical versions, Alster, *Proverbs* I, 133, SP 5 Vers. A 71 and B 72, with comments in *Proverbs* II, 405.

This short fable could almost have been taken from the fables of Aesop. As usual, it is Fox that appears to be cleverer than Wolf, although Wolf is the stronger of the two.

5 Vers. A 71. This is a variant of Vers. B 74.

(1) ur-bar-ra 9-bi 10-àm udu-hi-a an-[...]	*(1)* Nine wolves [caught] ten sheep.
(2) diš-àm ab-si-àm ḫa-<la>-ne nu-ḫ[a-la-a]	*(2)* One was superfluous, so they did not (know how to) divide their lots.
(3) ka$_5$-⸢a⸣ [ugu-b]i-⸢šè⸣ ù-bí-i[n-DU]	*(3)* A fox came to them,
(4) ŋ[á-e ga-m]u-e-ne-ḫa-[la]	*(4)* "Let me divide your share for you.
(5) 9 za-e-me-en-zé-en diš-à[m ...]	*(5)* You are nine, [take] one!
(6) ŋá-e dili-ŋu$_{10}$ 9 šu ga-[b]a-ab-[ti]	*(6)* I am alone, let me take nine.
(7) ne-en ḫa-la-[š]à-ŋu$_{10}$ e-[še]	*(7)* That will be my favorite share," he said.

The Always Stinking Wolf

The text is preserved as Alster, *Proverbs* I, 133, SP Vers. A 72, with comments in *Proverbs* II, 405.

The point is obvious: one cannot change one's own bad nature. Wolf reveals his ignorance by being unable to understand the reasons for his own bad smell.

5 Vers. A 72

(1) ur-bar-ra alal ùr-⌈é⌉(?)-⌈a⌉(?)-šè ù-bí-[...]	*(1)* A wolf ...
(2) mu-im-ma zé-[d]a-zu-šè ì-S[AR-]	*(2)* "Last year your stench [nauseated(?) us];
(3) DU me-en-dè ⌈mu⌉-ú-a ba-⌈SAR⌉-[...]	*(3)* come! this year we will [still be nauseated by your stench(?)].
(4) me-na zé-da-zu áš bí-bala-en-d[è-en]	*(4)* How long shall we be cursed by your stench?"
(5) DU ŋá-e šà-ŋar-tuku-a a-na ga-g[u_7 e-še]	*(5)* "Come! I am hungry, what shall I eat?" (said the wolf).

The Hypocritical Wolf (A)

The text is preserved as Alster, *Proverbs* I, 133, SP 5 Vers. B 72; cf. *Proverbs* II, 405.

The point is to describe the wolf as a hypocrite who one moment can play innocent and pretend not to be interested in hunting sheep anymore, but the next moment, it has forgotten all about its sacred vows!

5 Vers. B 72

(1) ur-b[ar]-ra / ^{ŋiš}⌈ad_x(GÚ)⌉^{ad} / ù-⌈mu⌉-mi-in-tuš (written TÚG) /	*(1)* A wolf had taken a seat in a thorny bush,
(2) ^{d}utu-ra an-na-ab-bé / i-im-ta-è-dè-en /	*(2)* and spoke to Utu, "When I come out,
(3) a-da-al-ta / $sila_4$ na-an-gu_7-e-en /	*(3)* from now on, let me eat no more sheep.
(4) u_4 šà-ŋar an-tuku / $sila_4$ šu ba-ni-in-ti-a /	*(4)* When I am hungry, the sheep I have taken,
(5) níŋ mu-e-dug_4-ga-zu / a-na na-nam /	*(5)* whatever you mentioned, what do they mean to me?
(6) mu-zi-$ŋu_{10}$-a / i-ni-dug_4-ga / DU ŋá-e a-na ga-gu_7 e-še	*(6)* I have taken a just oath! Now, what shall I eat?" he said.

The Hypocritical Wolf (B)

The text is preserved as Alster, *Proverbs* I, 133, SP 5 Vers. A 73, and Vers. B 73; cf. *Proverbs* II, 405.

This is a shorter version of the preceding fable, expressing the same idea in fewer words.

5 Vers. A 73 = B 73

ur-bar-ra ^{d}utu-ra ír ⌜ì⌝-še$_8$-še$_8$ máš-anše ba-du$_7$-du$_7$
ŋá-e dili-ŋu$_{10}$-ne-e-⌜še⌝

(1) A wolf cried before Utu:

(2) "The livestock butt, and I,

(3) I am all alone!" it said.

The Fox who Demanded Horns of Enlil

The text is preserved as SP 8 Sec. B 20 in Alster, *Proverbs* I, 169; cf. *Proverbs* II, 415.

This time it is unexpectedly Fox that makes a fool of himself: Fox demands a wild bull's horns of Enlil, the leading god of the Sumerian pantheon, but when it starts to rain, the horns prevent it from entering its hole. When Fox realizes his mistake, he responds with a pompous utterance that surely is meant to provoke laughter.

8 Sec. B 20

(1) ka$_5$-a ^{d}en-líl-le si-am-e	*(1–2)* Fox demanded a wild bull's horns of Enlil:
(2) al ù-bí-in-dug$_4$	
(3) si-am-e ba-ni-in-lá	*(3)* As he was wearing a wild bull's horns,
(4) im im-šèŋ mu-na-an-zi-zi	*(4)* it started to rain, and they rose high before him,
(5) ḫabrud-da-ni nu-mu-da-an-ku$_4$-ku$_4$	*(5)* so he could not enter his hole.
(6) ŋi$_6$-sa$_9$-bi-šè im-mir-mir	*(6)* The northwind kept blowing until midnight,
(7) muru$_9$ im-šèŋ-ŋá-[a(?)]	*(7)* and the clouds gave rain.
(8) ugu-ba i-im-til-la-⌜ta⌝	*(8)* After it had stopped (raining) upon him,
(9) ḫé-em-ta-laḫ ŋárza(PA.LU[GAL) lugal-a-<ni>-ir	*(9–10)* (he said) "It has dried up! The office has been returned to his lordship!"
(10) ba-ni-ib-gur e-še	

The Elephant and the Wren

The text exists in two versions: a Sumerian one, and an Akkadian translation of the same. Both are edited in Alster, *Proverbs* I, 121, as SP 5.1. The Akkadian version is inscribed on a small bilingual tablet in the Yale collection; cf. the comments in *Proverbs* II, 400.

The point is that all things must be evaluated according to their relative size. This is very soberly expressed in the Sumerian version, but the Akkadian version has added a slightly indecent tone, clearly intended to arouse laughter.

5.1

A i: [...] / [an-t]i-⸢ri⸣-gu$_7$^{mušen} mu-n[a-ni-gi$_4$-gi$_4$] /
[ù] ŋá-e igi-te-ŋ[u$_{10}$-šè] /
za-gin$_7$-nam al-dím-me-en ⸢e-še⸣

B o. am-si ⸢ní⸣-⸢te⸣-a-ni má[š- ...]
níŋ-ŋá-gin$_7$-nam nu-ŋál n[a- ...]
an-ti-rí-gu$_7$^{mušen}-e mu-na-[...]
ù ŋá-e igi-te-en-ŋu$_{10}$-šè z[a- ...]

YBC 9886 am-si ni-ta-na máš-anše ^{d}šakan-ka
níŋ-ŋá-gi-na-am al-sá-me-en nu-ŋál na-ab-bé-a
al-ti-ri-gu mu-na-ni-ib-gi$_4$-gi$_4$
ù ŋá-e i-gi$_4$-te-ŋu$_{10}$-uš
za-a-gi-nam al-sá-me-en e-še
um-ma pi-ru-um i-na ra-ma-ni-ša
i-na bu-ul ša-am-ka-an
ša ki-ma ia-ti-ma zu-ú ú-ul i-ba-ši
si-pi-di-qá-ar i-ip-pa-al
ù a-na-ku ki-ma ka-a-ti
a-na ma-na-ti-ia-ma zé-a-ku

An elephant spoke to himself and said: "Among the wild creatures of Šakan *(god of the wild creatures)*, there is no one comparable to me."
The *altirigu*-bird *(wren)* answered him: "And yet, I, in my own proportion, I am equal to you," it said.

Akkadian version of the same:
An elephant spoke to himself and said: "Among the wild creatures of Šakan *(god of wild creatures)*, there is no one who can defecate like me."
The *sipidiqar*-bird *(an unknown species of bird)* answered: "And yet, I, in my own proportion, I can defecate like you."

The Akkadian "The Elephant and the Wren"

The Akkadian fable of *The Elephant and the Wren* is the first Babylonian fable that attracted attention as early as 1927, when Ebeling discussed its relevance for literary history. The identity of the bird, previously understood as a mosquito, as a wren or a similar very small bird, was recognized by R. Borger, in 1964. The translation below is that of Lambert, BWL, 217–218, from "Popular Sayings" VAT 8807, rev. iii 50–51, with a minor change following Borger's suggestion; cf. p. 343, *Chap. 4.1*.

Although the point is not quite the same as the Sumerian *The Elephant and the Wren*, translated above, it testifies to the existence of the same tone of irony in Babylonian literary tradition. Someone very small should not overestimate himself, since in the eyes of someone bigger he may not even be recognized.

50 *diq-diq-qu ina m[u]ḫḫi pēri ki-i ú-š[i-bu]*
51 *um-ma ta-lim id-[k]a an-a-a-ma ina ši-qi mé*^{meš} *e-ra-[aq-ma]*
52 *pe-e-ru a-na diq-diq-qi ip-[pal]*
53 *ki-i tu-ši-bu ul i-de-e-[ma] ka-la-ka mi-[i-nu]*
54 *ki-i ta-at-bu-ú ul i-de-e-[ma]*

"A wren as it settled on an elephant, said, «Brother, did I press your side? I will make [off] at the watering-place.»
The elephant replied to the wren, «I do not care whether you get on —what is it to have you?—Nor do I care whether you get off»."

4.5 Short Stories and Morality Tales Involving Humans

There exists a limited number of Sumerian short tales not involving animals. The message is rarely directly expressed, and humor and wit play a great role.

The tales included here do not exhaust the complete number of texts that could possibly be considered relevant. Not included here are some rare examples of satires or diatribes: "«He is a Good Seed of a Dog» and «Engardu, the Fool»," edited by Sjöberg, in: JCS 24 (1972) 107–19; "The Slave and the Scoundrel" (PBS 8/1 100) edited by M. Roth, JAOS 103 (1983) 275–282; with a suggested reinterpretation by Alster, ZA 82 (1992) 195–201.

The Adulterer

This unique text is known from only three sources of unknown origin. The first of these, in the National Museum in Copenhagen, was published by Alster in 1988, but, owing to its imperfect state of preservation, its contents remained largely unintelligible until a clearly inscribed and well-preserved duplicate was identified by Alster in the Yale collection in 1991. A third duplicate, a round school tablet in the Schøyen collection in Oslo, was recognized by Alster in 2002, and is quoted here by the kind permission of the owner of the Schøyen Collection. The edition below is the first to take all these sources into account. Previous edition in Alster, *Proverbs* I, 271–272, SP 23.8; comments in *Proverbs* II, 449.

The text is the only one known to me in Sumerian that tells a straightforward morality lesson. The reason for warning someone against sleeping with another man's wife was not exclusively seen from the point of view of the woman, since clearly this might make the man unwelcome in society, and provoke heavy retaliation. The text is modelled in the form of a riddle with its solution, which was a literary type well known in the Sumerian schools; cf. Civil, 1987.

Sources

A: Copenhagen, Antiksamlingen A 10062 = SP 23.8 (Alster: *Proverbs* I, 271–272). Fragment from a two-column tablet. Copy pls. 42–43 (previously AcSum 10 [1988] 10–15), photographs pls. 44–45.

B: YBC 5828, copy Alster: *Proverbs* II, pl. 123. One-column tablet, obverse inscribed with 12 lines, complete.

C: MS Schøyen 2268/03. Round school tablet, obverse inscribed with 11 lines, complete. Photograph pl. 41.

1

A iii 13	nu-mu-un-na-du-du ŋìri mu-na-ŋá-[ŋá]	*(1)* One does not walk (openly) to him, (although) paths are directed toward him.
B	nu-mu-un-na-[d]u-du / ŋìri mu-un-na-ŋá-ŋá	
C	⸢nu⸣-mu-un-na-du-du | ŋìri mu-un-na-ŋá-ŋá	

2

A iii 14	nam-ti-la a-<ne>-gim ì-díb-bé	*(2)* (His) life passes away as he does himself.
B	nam-ti e-ne-gim / mu-ni-in-díb-bé	
C	nam-ti e-ne-gim | mu-ni-ib-díb-bé	(variant, A only: Life passes away like water).

3		
A iii 15	lú-zi nu-kal(!)-la nam-úš-ta diri	*(3)* He is not dear to any decent man, for life .... (So C; A: Ditto, how is (his life) more valuable than death); B: Ditto, he is not given life).
B	lú-zi nu-kal-la / nam-ti ⸢li⸣-bí-in-⸢šúm⸣	
C	lú-zi nu-kal-la nam-ti-šè bí-in-DU-a	
4		
A iii 16	nu-kù-gim mu-⸢un⸣-TI GAR-e nu-tar(!)-[re]	*(4)* He is thrown away like a worthless penny (lit., "a no-silver"), nobody cares about him.
B	nu-kù-gim mu-un-ni-šub / èn-na nu-⸢tar⸣-re	
C	⸢nu⸣-kù-gim mu-un-ši-šub | ⸢en(?)⸣-nun-nu-tar-re	
5		
A iii 17	túg-gim ì-mú-mú	*(5)* He is covered up as with a garment.
B	túg-gim ì-mu$_4$-mu$_4$	
C	túg-gim im-mi-im-mú	
6		
A iii 18	nam-tag dugud un-ŋar-ra	*(6)* A: heavy punishment is assigned to him. (C: An endless(?) crime of unknown ...).
B omitted		
C	nam-tag nu-til-e-dè | KA ga-ra-bi til(?) nu-zu	
7		
A iii 19	a-ba mu-ni lú dam-lú-kam ba-ná(!)	*(7)* Who is he? A man who sleeps with another man's wife.
B	a-ba-àm e-ne / lú dam-lú-ka / in-da-ná-a	
C	a-ba-àm e-ne lú dam ⸢x x x⸣	(Var. A: Who (is he): His name is: "Man who sleeps with another man's wife.").

Line 2: If the reading in A, a-gim, is taken at face value, instead of the emendation to a-<ne>-gim, it could be compared to Job 3:24, "my roarings are poured out like water."

Line 3: The A variant seems to have meant approximately the same as *The Ballade of Early Rulers* 19; cf. *Chap. 3.3a-b*. B: ⸢li⸣-bí-in-⸢šúm⸣ is hardly correct; what is expected might be nu-mu-na-šúm, or similar. C: nam-ti-šè bí-in-DU-a seems to have mistakenly omitted the negation, perhaps nam-ti-šè <li>-bí-in-túm-a, "not worthy of life," although this meaning of túm otherwise requires the locative, not the terminative -šè. Perhaps the šúm of B is, in fact, a misheard túm of C, or vise versa.

Line 4: C has an interesting case of contraction *en(-na?) nu-tar-re > en-nun-nu-tar-re.

Line 6: I cannot explain C: KA ga-ra-bi til(?) nu-zu.

The Lazy Slave Girl

The first attempts at translating the text were by van Dijk, 1953, and Alster, 1976. It exists on a number of tablets, some of which belong to proverb collections. All the known sources are edited as SP 21 Sec. A 16, in: Alster, *Proverbs* I, 256–258, where all sources and variants are quoted.

This short text may be regarded also as a morality tale, but the message is much more indirectly expressed than in *The Adulterer*. The translations "slave" and "slave girl" may not be entirely justified here, where "male and female servant" might be more fitting. The message seems clear: if those of lower rank do not do their job in a household, it will result in a disaster, ultimately to their own detriment.

Sources

The text below is that of SLTNi 131 (Ni 3023) obv. ii 13–16. This is also included in SP 21 as Sec. A 16, cf. Alster: *Proverbs* I, 256–257, where all variants are quoted; comments in *Proverbs* II, 442–444.

SLTNi 131 obv. ii 3–16

Sumerian	Translation
(1) á-še gi$_4$-in-e kiŋ(? copied as da) na-an-sa$_6$	*(1)* Now, should the work not please the slave girl;
(2) dumu gi$_4$-in-na-ke$_4$ U na-ab-sal-e	*(2)* should the slave girl's children not …;
(3) kunga-da še na-an-gu$_7$-e	*(3)* should barley not be (distributed to be) eaten by donkeys;
(4) ù-mu-un-bi húb-dar-šè na-an-zé-e	*(4)* should their owner not drive them to run;
(5) pú-lá a-zé-ba na-an-dé-e	*(5)* should fresh water not be drawn from the deep well;
(6) da-pú(!)-ba ú-šim na-an-mú-mú	*(6)* should herbs not grow at the side of the well;
(7) gùd-ùmun-na síg(? copied as pú) ba-sì-ge	*(7)* a "nest" of lice will settle in the woollen cloth(?);
(8) túg-níŋ-dára a-ì-gim ba-ab-naŋ-ŋá	*(8)* a loincloth will be used for drinking as if it were flowing water;
(9) lú ma-an-zi-le ^{kuš}súhub šu-ti-a	*(9)* he whose heels were split(?) would (have to) take on shoes;
(10) túg-èŋ-dára(? copy: ma) mu$_4$-mu$_4$ túg-èŋ-lám šu-ti-a	*(10)* he who was dressed in a loincloth would (have to) take on a woollen cloth;
(11) gi$_4$-in ù-mu-un gam ga-ša-an gam ' sila-a úr zé-zé	*(11)* you, slave girl, when the lord has succumbed; when the lady has succumbed, and you roam the streets;

(12) e-re na-áŋ ù-mu-un ir-ra ' gi_4-in-e na-áŋ ga-ša-an ir-ra	*(12)* you, slave, the fact that the lord is gone; you, slave girl, the fact that the lady is gone—
(13) èŋ-e-me-a ma-ra-ma-ma-al-la	*(13)* the state of things that used to be yours,
(14) èŋ u_4-bi-ta nu-mu-da-ab-sá-en /	*(14)* you will never compare those affairs of former days to this,
(15) nam-tar eŋir-ra-ta mu-da-ab-sá-en	*(15)* but you will have to compare the future order to this.

The Fowler and His Wife

This tale was first published by Alster, 1974, who republished it with various additions that had turned up later, in 1992 and in *Proverbs* I, 252–254, as SP 21 Sec. A 4.

The text was evidently popular, and exists, both as part of proverb collections and as a single text inscribed on small tablets, in various shortened versions, of which the latest example is published here p. 391, *Chap. 6: Examples of Proverb Collections Used as Literary Sourcebooks*. The main point remained stable in these versions, however. That the text is a double entendre in which the fowler's wife complains about her husband's potency problem was first recognized independently by two scholars, I.M. Diakonoff in 1980, and P. Michalowski, 1981, cf. Alster, 1992. A fuller attempt to interpret the allusions is made below, under the introduction to *Chap. 6*, where the relevant excerpt is discussed.

Sources

The text below is basically D = N 1237. The text is included in SP 21 Sec. A 5: *The Fowler and His Wife*; cf. Alster, *Proverbs* I, 253–254, where all sources and variants are included. This is slightly more complete than Alster, ZA 82 (1982) 187–188 (cf. a minor correction in *Proverbs* II, 442: in line 12: ambar is probably justified). The sequences of SP 21 can be improved, however, in view of the observations by Veldhuis, 2000, 394: Sec. A should really be Sec. C (as shown on the ETCSL-site). New sources are:

- Cornell University Proverb tablet 2, Kroch-05, edited in *Chap. 6.2*.
- 3N-T 168 (= A 30175). Obv. = lines 1–4; see the separate transliteration below, kindly provided by N. Veldhuis.

Another new source was published by Veldhuis: "Kassite Exercises," JCS 52 (2000) 67–94, p. 72 and fig. 5 (p. 89): UM 29-15-848, of which the obverse has a one-line extract from the *Fowler*: dam mušen-dù dam-a-n[i-ir?], "The fowler's wife spoke to her husband," in which the sentence is not even completed. For the rest of the tablet, see Veldhuis' edition.

D = N 1237

(1) [mušen-d]ù kaš in-tuku-⌜ma⌝ /	*(1)* A fowler who had some beer,
(2) [ku]-li-ni-ir gù dé-dè ì-gin /	*(2)* went to talk to his friend.
(3) ku-li-ni-ir igi nu-mu-ni-du$_8$-a /	*(3)* As he did not find his friend,
(4) e-ne lú-bar-ra im-ma-da-an-ri /	*(4)* he turned to a stranger.
(5) dam mušen-dù-ke$_4$ dam-a-ni-ir gù mu-un-na-dé-e /	*(5)* The fowler's wife spoke to her husband:
(6) e-sig^{mušen}-e sa ù-bí-in-ná buru$_4$^{mušen}-e sa ù-bí-gíd /	*(6)* "After you had cast the net upon an *esig*-bird (*an unidentified species of bird*), after you had drawn up the net upon a raven,
(7) si-si-ig ì-lù-lù /	*(7)* a whirlwind blew,
(8) ambar-tur-zu a mu-da-an-laḫ /	*(8)* and dried up the water in your little swamp,
(9) má-zu peš$_{10}$-peš$_{10}$ ab-tag-tag-ge /	*(9)* so that your boat touches the ground.
(10) mušen-dù sa-zu ḫé-gíd-i mušen ḫé-zi-zi-i	*(10)* Fowler, let your net be drawn up, let the bird rise!"
(11) dam-a-ni mu-un-na-ni-ib-gi$_4$-gi$_4$ /	*(11)* Her husband answered her,
(12) ⌜ambar⌝-gu(?)-la-zu ambar-tur-zu a ḫé-en-ta-bal-e	*(12)* "Let your big swamp pour water into(?) your little swamp,
(13) [e]me(?)-na ḫé-en-zu ní-te-a-ni ḫé-en-zi-zi-i	*(13)* Let him know his language(?), let him rise himself!"
	(Variant D instead of 3–5: His wife [spoke to him] at the entrance of the "bedroom.")

Selected variants:

3N-T 168, obv. has: *(1)* mušen-dù kaš in-tuku-ma; *(2)* ku-li-ni-ir / gù dé-dè ì-gin; *(3)* ku-li-ni-ir / igi nu-mu-ni-du$_8$-àm / *(4)* e-ne lú-bar-ra / [im-ma]-[d]a-[a]n-[r]i (break) (translit. provided by N. Veldhuis). This suggests the reading -ma as the main text instead of -⌜e⌝ in line 1, and does not support Edzard's suggested translation "A fowler was about to fetch beer" in Alster, 1992, 195. The new text in line 8 has -àm instead of -a.

Line 5: Iowa: dam-a-ni ká pa$_4$-paḫ-ka gù mu-na-dé-e, "his wife spoke to him at the entrance of the «bedroom»."

CHAPTER 5

Sumerian Folktales

5.1 *The Three Ox-Drivers from Adab*

Publication History

The Sumerian folktale *The Three Ox-Drivers from Adab* is know from two Louvre fragments, TCL 16, 80 and TCL 16, 83, shown later by Cavigneaux to belong to the same tablet. The first part of the composition was edited by Falkenstein, 1952, 114–120.[1] The first complete edition was presented by Foster, in his study of humor in cuneiform literature (Foster, [1974] 70–72).[2] The tablet had previously been collated by Kramer, and the results had been taken into account in Foster's edition. Collations were made by Cavigneaux, 1987, 51–52.[3]

A duplicate, CBS 1601, which meant considerable progress, was identified by Alster in 1991.[4] This was published with a complete edition of the text in 1993. The edition below is basically the same, but an important improvement by Lambert, 1995, has been incorporated.

The Sources

A_1: TCL 16, 80 (AO 7739). The tablet was dated by H. de Genouillac (p. 10) to Ammiṣadūqa 8, on the strength of the colophon, whose full reading is given by Cavigneaux, p. 52.[5] According to Cavigneaux, the ductus itself suggests a Kassite date.[6] The findspot is unknown. The tablet has ten line marks. According to the colophon, the complete tablet had 95 lines (cf. the comments below).[7] Obv. = 1–23, rev. = 80–95.

A_2: TCL 16, 83 (AO 8149). This is the lower part of A_1. Obv. = 19–28. Cavigneaux, 1987, 51, assigned the reverse to 69–71, and the duplicate seems to show that this is exactly right.

B: CBS 1601. Copy pl. 48 (previously JCS 43–45 [1991–93] 28, figs. 1–2). Old Babylonian. The tablet belongs to the Khazaba collection, and the findspot is unknown. It has 20 line marks. The left edge is preserved. The tablet is not ruled. Seven lines are missing on the top, and the thickest part is around line 20 of the composite text, so the complete tablet may have had approximately 80 lines. Obv. = 7–20, rev. = 69–88.

1. The first to comment on the conclusion of the text was van Dijk, 1953, 11–12.
2. An attempt to place the composition in a wider cultural context was made by Lipiński, 1985.
3. A number of Cavigneaux's readings have been confirmed by the new duplicate B published in 1993.
4. This is the first duplicate identified for the composition. Another fragment, STVC 97, has sometimes been assigned to this composition, cf. van Dijk, 1953, 11, n. 11, and Gordon, 1962, 139, n. 133, but it was identified by Alster, 1975, 90, as belonging to another folktale, *The Old Man and the Young Girl*, which shares a number of characteristics with this one; cf. the edition in *Chap. 5.2*. In both tales a problem is presented to the king, who subsequently asks a cloister woman (*sekrum*) to solve it.
5. Cf. previously Foster, 1974, 72, n. 7.
6. The possibility should be kept in mind that a later copyist could have copied an earlier tablet with its colophon without changing the date; cf. my comment to source D, which copies the date of A, of *Incantation to Utu*, AcSum 13 (1991) 34.
7. The name of the scribe was *Qīšti-êa*, the king's scribe. Cf. Hunger, *Babylonische und assyrische Kolophone*, 27, no. 19.

Text Reconstruction

I have followed the colophon of the Louvre sources and counted the lines on the reverse backward from 95, in spite of the fact that a total of 95 lines seems surprisingly high for the length of the composition, notwithstanding its extremely repetitious character (cf. below).

A good deal of instability in the sources of Sumerian literary compositions attested exclusively outside the well-established Nippur-Ur repertoire would not have been unexpected. However, in the present case, the two duplicates actually follow each other so closely that one has the impression that they came from the same site, or even that one of them was copied from the other. There is a minor discrepancy in that B has a 20 line mark in rev. 10, which corresponds to line 78 in A, where 60 or 80 would have been expected. A problematic case is the relations between lines 12 and 82. In 12, A is to be read ù-un-du-du-ru, which can easily be harmonized with B: ù-un-⸢dúr⸣-⸢dúr⸣-ru, which, however, as pointed out by Lambert, 1995, 2, is a misunderstanding from *ù-un-⸢ku-ku⸣-ru, which renders a verb different from dúr, as appears from 82 B: um-ku$_5$-ku$_5$-ru-a, meaning "to separate," or similar. Cf. the discussion below. In line 82, A: ù-un-d[u-du-ru] and line 12, B: ù-un-⸢dúr⸣-⸢dúr⸣-ru, this was mistakenly understood as the verb dúr, but glossed correctly as *ta-az-za-ba-al*, which is a 3rd fem. sing. N present form of the verb *zabālu*, meaning "will be carried off."

This suggests the reading ù-un-ku-ku-ru in B line 12. In this case, B line 82 seems to have the better text, and this may have been a general feature of the complete tablet. A feature exclusively characteristic of B is the presence of a few Akkadian glosses.

The Story

The fundamental character of the plot was clarified by Falkenstein. Three ox-drivers, one of whom was the owner of an ox, one of a cow, and one of a wagon, became thirsty. Fearing that the ox would be devoured by a lion, that the cow would disappear into the desert, or that a heavy load would be carried away from the wagon, none of them was willing to leave their possessions to go (alone) and fetch water, and so they all went together. In the meantime the ox apparently made the cow pregnant (the text is not clear here),[8] and the cow gave birth to a calf. This calf did something to the wagon (which may have entitled the owner of the wagon to think that the calf was his, but the text is not clear at this point).[9] The three men then started a quarrel about which of them should own the calf. After some deliberation they went to the king and asked him to act as arbiter. He did not solve the problem himself, but presented it to a "cloister woman." She suggested a solution, which the king then apparently conveyed to the three men. The problem clearly has the character of a riddle and its solution—and the whole story—reflects the king's traditional role as judge in ancient Near Eastern societies.[10]

The details of the story are still far from clear, however. First of all, it is difficult to imagine what

8. Line 14; Falkenstein, 1952, 115, translates: "Der Stier *bespringt* sie, *bepringt* sie." Foster, 1974, 71, translates: "The ox *mounts her* and *mates with her*" (italics are used by both authors to indicate uncertain translation). The text was understood similarly by van Dijk, 1953, 12. It should be admitted that if all of this happened while the three men were away to fetch water, there would have been no time for the cow to be pregnant and give birth to the calf so soon. While this might be acceptable in a fairy tale, it certainly makes a burlesque impression in the very realistic character of the present composition. Cf. the comments to line 14. The tentative translation suggested in this edition does not directly indicate that the ox made the cow pregnant, but I agree that this must after all somehow be implied, and that it was part of the burlesque features of the text.

9. I rather think that it just touched it with its mouth, cf. the comments to line 14 (with 29 and 84) below.

10. Both van Dijk and Foster recognized the similarity of the conclusion of the story to that of a legal case (cf. van Dijk, 1953, 12, "certain que le récit déguise un cas juridique"); Foster, 1974, 72, n. 8, "we may have here a parody on a legal case, or merely a story with a scribal legal touch at the end"). Two commentators have tentatively proposed how the story could have ended. Foster, 1974, p. 72, n. 7, suggested that "one obvious solution would have been for the king to keep the calf for himself and justify his action with a saying(?) like line 91: «remove the cause of the quarrel»." Independently, Alster, 1975, 127, suggested that the three men lost their possessions. The new duplicate rather seems to support this.

could have gone into the lacuna between lines 32 and 65. Lines 65ff. actually seem to contain the cloister woman's answer, which is expected to follow immediately upon line 32. A possible explanation might be that the lacuna contained the woman's answer to the king, and that 65ff. contain her speech repeated by the king to the three men. The missing lines 33–ca. 53 would thus have been identical to 65–85(? or 88?), but approximately 15 lines of the composition would still be missing. Yet, in view of 86, where it is said that the king was informed of her words, and 89, according to which he came from her, it is more likely that the woman is the speaker of 65–88.[11]

How exactly the problem was solved has so far remained enigmatic. The main difficulty continues to be the fragmentary state of preservation of the text. The new duplicate does bring us closer to a solution, but presents no definite answer. We can now see that the solution offered by the wise woman involves an analogy between the three men and their ox, cow, and wagon, on the one hand, and the following partly ambiguous terms: their a-šà ("field"), wife, and me (here tentatively translated "his belongings(?)," see below) on the other hand. This can be illustrated by the following:

The man of the ox: lines 7–8 = lines 22–23. Solution: lines [65–68]+69–72 (too poorly preserved for translation). The key word seems to be a-šà(-g) (l. 72, possibly to be restored in ll. 65 and 67), perhaps here meaning "his field." It is uncertain how this relates to line 90, to be read: a-šà-ga-ni or diš šà-ga-ni.[12]

The man of the cow: lines 9–10 = lines 24–25. Solution: lines 73–80. The key word is dam-a-ni, "his wife" (ll. 73, 75, 80). Summary, apparently: line 91 (dam-a-ni).

The man of the wagon: lines 11–12 = lines 26–27. Solution: lines 81–84(?). The key word is me-ni, here tentatively translated "his belongings(? = me)" (l. 83). Summary: line 92 (me-ni).

The difficulty in interpreting the crucial lines 90–92 rests on the ambiguity of the terms a-šà-ga-ni and me-ni, and little progress has been made here since van Dijk commented on the lines in 1953.[13] In view of the mention of a wife and a house (80 and 83) in the adjacent lines, a-šà in 72 (and 65 and 67, if correctly restored there), as well as in 90 (if correctly read there), is likely simply to mean "field."[14] me could perhaps mean "function" or "office," but from 83 one gets the impression that it is a concrete thing that can be placed somewhere. Alster, 1993, tentatively understood it as a reference to the cargo of the wagon, and this seems to be the best suggestion so far, although it is not clear precisely how.[15]

11. The three times repeated ga-nam, "well" (ll. 65 restored, 73, and 81) certainly indicates that these lines contain quoted speech, but it is possible that the three sequences introduced by ur-saŋ, "hero" (ll. 69–72, 77–80, 85–88) do not belong to the speech, and actually describe the carrying out of the advice contained in lines [65–68], 73–76, and 81–84. Yet, the continuation (ll. 86 and 89) rather suggests that all this was spoken to the king by the woman.
12. See the comments to line 90 below.
13. van Dijk, 1953, 12, "que je n'arrive pas à interpréter, parce que a-šà et me ont plusieurs significations."
14. One could separate a from šà-ga-ni, and understand a as "semen" and šà-ga-ni as "womb." This might be a humorous pun on the ox impregnating the cow, but it is more than doubtful. The implication would be obscure, in particular since no woman is otherwise mentioned in this part of the text. Another solution was suggested by Foster, see the comments to line 90 below.
15. Alster, 1993, translated "what befits him," which ultimately seems to refer to the load belonging to him. I here take the consequences and tentatively translate "his possessions," which suits the context well, but without attempting to explain how this might be possible in view of the usual meanings of me. For these, cf. the comments on *Instr. Šuruppak* 203, and the literature there mentioned. If me here denotes something the man has taken possession of without being entitled to do so, one could see it as a parallel to the use of me in the list of the cultural functions in *Inanna and Enki*, but here the context clearly favours a meaning like "that which he is entitled to." Occasionally me seems to denote a concrete thing, like an emblem, cf. Gudea, Cylinder B vi 23 (and parallels): me-ni-da mu-na-da-díb-e, "he introduced (the god) with his emblems before (Ningirsu)." One may here compare *Lahar and Ašnan* 98: me(= ba_{13}?)-ni u-gùn mu-un-na-ab-ak-e, "(Šakkan) adorns his (the king's) emblem (or festive clothing?) with incrustations" (cf. Alster and Vanstiphout, AcSum 9, 1987, 35). In *Inanna's Descent* the me are Inanna's jewels. me otherwise denotes "cultural functions," "divine power," and "ritual," and is equated with Akkadian *parṣu*. For the possible meanings "function," or "affairs," cf. the proverb SP 11.52: èm-é èm-gal-la-àm

From what little can be understood, it seems that the verdict was not in favor of the three men.[16] If lines [65] and 74 correctly are to be restored and interpreted in analogy with 8 and 10, the owners of the ox and the cow both lost their animals, so they were exposed to exactly that which they had feared and tried to avoid. The fear of the disappearance of the cow into the desert further materializes in the analogy of the cowherd's wife walking on the street, presumably as a prostitute. Whether the owner of the wagon was more successful is a question that cannot be answered at the present time. Depending on how the verb is to be read and restored in 84, the calf may have become his, or he might have had to give it up after he had taken possession of it.[17] In the same vein, 88 seems to suggest that his load was unloaded from the wagon and confiscated by a mighty official.

Should the latter interpretation turn out to be correct, it would represent a burlesque folktale, in which the three men are ridiculed for not considering that nothing ventured is nothing gained. More precisely, the story can be summarized as a humorous tale teaching a social lesson: social cooperation is what the three men lacked. One of them could have fetched water while the other two looked after his possessions. Instead, they all went together, while, apparently, their possessions were left unattended. This resulted in the birth of a calf, of which they could have availed themselves. Instead, they started a quarrel, with the result that they lost all they had.

Although there is a fair chance that the main outlines of the story, as described here, are correct, the details still need clarification in almost every respect. Word-plays and logical puns apparently played a decisive role in the articulation of the solution,[18] but at the present time we can do little more than start being aware of such subtleties. It is hoped that the discovery of new duplicates will soon lead to a more satisfactory understanding of the composition.

Wisdom as a Profession or: An Anti-Folktale?

The existence of a "professional" class of wise men or women in the Hebrew Bible has been recognized long ago. Those in highest esteem were royal counselors, whereas those on a lower level could make services available to men of a lesser rank. Chief among these was one with a special title "the King's Friend" (2Sam 15:37; 1Kings 4:5; cf. Gen 26:26), a title also used at the Egyptian royal courts (cf., e.g., Scott 1973, xxxii). Prov 23:23: "Buy truth, and do not sell wisdom, instruction, and understanding," seems to suggest that counsels might be bought for money.

The two folktales presented in this volume give the impression that there was a group a wise men, or, rather, women whom the kings consulted in difficult cases. Such cases were clearly seen as similar to judicial court decisions, but were obviously independent of them, depending more on the counsellor's ability to find a clever solution, like Solomon's judgment.

me-ŋu$_{10}$ me-gal-la-àm, "the affairs of the house are great affairs, my functions are great functions" (cf. the English, "Every man is nearest himself"). Here a meaning like "belonging" might actually be considered. If that is the case, I would see this as detached from all mythological and cosmological associations attached to me, but the connection with ní, "self," may be relevant. The fundamental identity of the noun me with the existential verb, me, meaning "existence," is no longer accepted by all specialists. The readings ba$_{13}$ and ma$_{6}$ would hardly help here. Yet, there is some suspicion that the writing me-ni covers a graphic pun of some undisclosed nature.

16. Yet, one cannot completely avoid the impression that 80 ends in a positive tone. We do not know exactly how it is to be restored, and the complete text could have stated that the man's wife stayed happily in his house, but, on the other hand, this is less likely given that fact that it has just been said that she will roam the streets (l. 75). Line 91 definitely suggests that the man was divorced from his wife, although the phrase may be used in a metaphorical sense (cf. Foster's comments note 11 above). Yet, line 90 does indicate a diplomatic reconciliation, provided that Foster's translation is accepted (cf. the comments to the line below).
17. The latter presupposes the reading [i]-i, but this is not unproblematic, see the comments to the line below.
18. In line 71, ur-re may play on ur-maḫ (to be restored in 66), ur-saŋ (69), and ḫur-saŋ (70). In line 77, im-a, "in the rain (or: wind)" (if correctly understood), may be meant as a joke when seen in relation to um-sur-sur-ru (76), "having dropped" (said of the birth of the calf). Cf. also the comments to line 81.

The most remarkable feature of the text presented here is that, although it has so far been described as a "folktale," it seems rather to be the opposite, almost an "anti-folktale," as pointed out in the introduction to this volume (*Introduction*, p. 29). In a characteristic folktale a "small" man prevails over his superiors, when in the end he proves to be cleverer than they. In this text, however, none of the main characters is successful in the end, but their problem creates an opportunity to present a solution that carries the marks of sophisticated literature. It is clear that the solution is expressed through puns and allusions, even to legal procedures. This may have been the main reason why the text was written down and incorporated into the scribal curriculum. The important lesson, "nothing ventured, nothing gained," is phrased in a way that may have been very characteristic in wisdom circles. If the interpretation proposed above is justified, the outcome seems rather to have been to the benefit of the king, who, ultimately, benefitted from the incompetence of the three ox-drivers. The whole setting is more like a parody of a legal case, or, as phrased by Lipiński, 1986, 142: "The burlesque character of all these 'king's judgments seems evident ... To be enjoyed these tales only require on the part of the reader the suspension of logic, and the willing acceptance of the incongruous ... These ancient tales are related to wisdom literature ..., because they express, as it seems, a wise criticism."

1	A	ku(?)-li-li eš$_5$-àm dumu adab^{ki}-ke$_4$-ne	*(1)* There were three friends, "sons" of (the city of) Adab,
2	A	di in-da-ab-tuku-uš-àm di-da ab-kiŋ-kiŋ-e	*(2)* who fell into a dispute one with the other, and sought justice.
3	A	inim íb-ta-an-šár-šár-eš-àm lugal-e an-ta ba-an-gi	*(3)* They deliberated the matter with many words, and went before the king.
4	A	lugal-me gud-da-ri ì-ak-e-dè-nam	*(4)* "Our lord, we are ox-drivers.
5	A	gud lú-diš-a-kam áb lú-diš-a-kam ^{ŋiš}mar lú-diš-a-kam	*(5)* "The ox belongs to one man, the cow belongs to one man, and the wagon belongs to one man.
6	A	énmen bí-tuku-un-da-nam a nu-mu-e-da-ŋál	*(6)* "We became thirsty and had no water.
7	A B	lú-gud-da-ra a ù-um-te-si a ga-naŋ-en-dè-en e-še ⸢lú-gud⸣-d[a- ...]	*(7)* "If one could provide the ox-driver with water, then let us drink! (we) said.
8	A B	gud-ŋu$_{10}$ ur(!)-maḫ-e ù-bí-gu$_7$(text: KA) gud-ŋu$_{10}$-ta ba-ra-è-dè-en e-še gud-ŋu$_{10}$ ur-maḫ-e ⸢ù⸣-[...]-g[u$_7$ ...]	*(8)* "What if my ox is devoured by a lion! I will not leave my ox! said (the ox-driver).
9	A B	lú-áb-ba-ra a ù-um-te-si a ga-naŋ-en-dè-en e-še lú-áb-ba-ra a ù-um-te-si a g[a- ...]	*(9)* "If one could provide the man of the cow with water, then let us drink! (they) said.
10	A B	áb-ŋu$_{10}$ edin-šè ù-ba-gin áb-ŋu$_{10}$-ta ba-ra-è-dè-en e-še áb-ŋu$_{10}$ edin-šè ù-ba-gin áb-ŋu$_{10}$-ta ba-ra-⸢è⸣(?)-[...]	*(10)* "What if my cow went out on the plain! I will not leave my cow! said (the man of the cow).

11 A lú ^{ŋiš}mar-ra-ra a ù-um-te-si a ga-naŋ-en-dè-en e-še
B lú ^{ŋiš}mar-ra-ra a ù-um-te-si a ga-naŋ-en-dè-[en e-še]

(11) "If one could provide the man of the wagon with water, then let us drink! (we) said.

12 A ^{ŋiš}mar-ŋu$_{10}$ gú(!)-un(?) ù-un-du-du-ru (mistake for *ku$_{(5)}$-ku$_{(5)}$-ru) ^{ŋiš}mar-ŋu$_{10}$-ta ba-ra-è-dè-en e-še
B ^{ŋiš}mar-ŋu$_{10}$ gú-un ù-un-⸢dúr-dúr⸣-ru (gloss: *ta-az-za-ba-al*) ^{ŋiš}mar-ŋu$_{10}$-ta [...]

(12) "What if the load is carried away from my wagon! I will not leave my wagon! said (the man of the wagon).

13 A gana ga-ni-re$_7$-en-dè-en gana ga-an-ga-àm-gi-dè-en
B gana ga-ni-re$_7$-en-dè-en gana ga-an-[...]

(13) "Come, let us (all) go, come, let us also return (together)!

14 A gud éš(?) ba-a-lá-e um(?)-lá áb a-sìla-ŋar-ra-bi um(?)-sur-sur-ru amar ^{ŋiš}mar-ra KA bí-in-túm
B gud ⸢éš⸣ ba-a-lá-a um-lá áb a-sìla-ŋar-ra-bi um-sur-sur-[...]

(14) "The ox, bound to a leash(?), "stretched" (itself); the cow dropped its young; the calf raised(?) its mouth(?) to the wagon.

15 A amar-e a-ba-kam amar-e a-ba-àm ba-an-túm
B amar-⸢e⸣ a-ab-a-kam amar-e a-ba-⸢a⸣ [...]

(15) "This calf, whose is it? Who can take the calf?"

16 A lugal-e inim nu-mu-un-ne-ši-íb-gi sé-ek-rum-šè ba-da-an-ku$_4$
B lugal-e inim nu-mu-un-ne-ši-íb-gi s[é- ...]

(16) The king did not answer them, but went to a "cloister woman."

17 A lugal-e sé-ek-rum-ta ad mu-un-di-ni-íb-gi-gi
B lugal-e sé-ek-rum-ta ad [...]

(17) The king took counsel with the cloister woman (and said):

18 A [ŋuruš eš$_5$-à]m an-ta ba-an-gi-eš-a
B ŋuruš eš$_5$-àm a[n- ...]

(18) "Three young men went before (me and said:)

19 A ⸢lugal-me⸣ gud-da-ri ì-ak-en-dè-nam
B lugal-me g[ud(?) ...]

(19) "Our lord, we are ox drivers.

20 A gud lú-diš-a-kam áb lú-diš-a-kam ^{ŋiš}mar lú-diš-a-kam
B gud lú-diš-a-kam áb lú-[...]

(20) "The ox belongs to one man, the cow belongs to one man, and the wagon belongs to one man.

21 A énmen(text: KA) bí-⸢tuku⸣-un-da-nam a nu-mu-e-da-ŋál

(21) "We became thirsty and we had no water.

22 A lú-gud-da-ra a ù-um-te-šub a ga-naŋ-en-dè-en-e-[še]

(22) "If one could provide the ox-driver with water, then let us drink! they said.

23 A gud-ŋu$_{10}$ ur-maḫ-e ù-bí-gu$_7$ gud-ŋu$_{10}$-ta ba-ra-⸢è⸣-[dè-en e-še]

(23) "What if my ox is devoured by a lion! I will not leave my ox! said (the ox-driver).

24 A lú-áb-ba-ra a ù-um-te-šub a ga-naŋ-en-dè-[en e-še]

(24) "If one could provide the man of the cow with water, then let us drink! [(they said)].

25 A áb-ŋ[u$_{10}$ edin-š]è ù-ba-gin áb-ŋu$_{10}$-ta ba-ra-è-[dè-en e-še]

(25) "What if my cow went out on the plain! I will not leave my cow! said (the man of the cow).

26	A	lú-^{ŋiš}mar-ra-r]a a ù-um-te-šub a ga-naŋ-en-dè-e[n e-še]	*(26)* "If one could provide the man of the wagon with water, then let us drink! (they) said.
27	A	[^{ŋiš}mar-ŋu$_{10}$ gú-un] ⸢ù⸣-[un-du-du-ru] ^{ŋiš}mar-ŋu$_{10}$-ta ba-ra-⸢è⸣-[dè-en e-še]	*(27)* "What if the load is carried away from my wagon! I will not leave my wagon! [said (the man of the wagon)].
28	A	[gana ga-ni-re$_7$-en-dè-en] ⸢gana⸣(?) ⸢ga⸣(?)-[an-ga-àm-gi-dè-en]	*(28)* "Come, let us (all) go, come, let [us also return (together)!]
29	A	[gud éš(?) ba-a-lá-e ab(?)-lá áb a-sìla-ŋar-ra-bi ab(?)-sur-sur-ru amar ^{ŋiš}mar-ra KA bí-in-túm]	*(29)* ["The ox, bound to a leash(?), "stretched" (itself); the cow dropped its young; the calf raised(?) its mouth(?) to the wagon.]
30	A	[amar-e a-ba-kam amar-e a-ba-àm ba-an-túm]	*(30)* ["This calf, whose is it? Who can take the calf?"]
31	A	[sé-ek-rum-e lugal-ra mu-na-ni-íb-gi$_4$-gi$_4$]	*(31)* [The cloister woman answered the king:]
32	A	[lugal-ŋu$_{10}$ ì(?)-gi$_4$-in-zu …]	*(32)* ["My lord, if …
Lacuna			*(Lacuna)*
65	A	[ga-nam lú-gud-da-ke$_4$ a-šà-ga-ni …]	*(65)* ["Well, the man of the ox, his field …]
66	A	[gud-da-ni ur-maḫ-e ù-bí-gu$_7$ …]	*(66)* ["After his ox has been eaten by a lion …]
67	A	[a-šà-ga-ni …]	*(67)* ["His field …]
68	A	[…]	*(68)* ["…]
69	A	ur-saŋ lu[gal/ḫ]é […]	*(69)* "The hero …
	B	⸢ur⸣-⸢saŋ⸣ x x x […]	
70	A	lú-[ḫur(?)]-⸢saŋ⸣(?)-⸢gim⸣(?) […]	*(70)* "Like a mountaineer …
	B	lú-ḫur-saŋ-gim AN ⸢x⸣ […]	
71	A	[x] x x […]	*(71)* "The ox-driver(?), a dog …
	B	gù-ra ur-⸢re⸣ ba-⸢x⸣-[…]	
72	B	á-tuku(? nearly: gùb!) a-šà-ga-na zag l[ú(?) …]	*(72)* "A strong man(?), on his field …
73	B	ga-nam lú-áb-ba-ke$_4$ dam-a-[ni …]	*(73)* "Well, the man of the cow, his wife …
74	B	áb-ba-ni edin-šè ù-ba-gin-na […]	*(74)* "after his cow has gone out onto the plain …
75	B	dam-a-ni tílla-a ù(!)-ba-an-ak-[…] (gloss: *im-sú-qí i-la-ak-ma*)	*(75)* "his wife will walk on the street …

76	B	áb a-sìla-ŋar-ra-bi um-sur-sur-ru [...]	*(76)* "The cow that dropped its young ...
77	B	ur-saŋ IM-a gin-na-da [...]	*(77)* "The hero, walking in the rain(?) [...]
78	B	dam-a-ni ní-te(?)-ni ri-ri-e-⸢a⸣ ⸢di⸣ ⸢x⸣ [...]	*(78)* "His wife, she herself ...
79	B	gù-ra kurum$_6$-ma-ni úr-ra-na-šè bí-in-gur-ra šà-ŋar AN-[...]	*(79)* "The ox-driver(?), his food ration which has been turned to his ..., his hunger ...
80	A	dam-a-ni é-a-⸢ni⸣(?) [...]	*(80)* "His wife, dwelling with him in his house, his desired one ...
	B	dam-a-ni é-a-na an-da-tuš(? text: TÚG)-àm šà-ge gur$_6$-⸢ni⸣ [...]	
81	A	ga-nam lú-^{ŋiš}mar-ra-ke$_4$ ⸢x⸣ [...]	*(81)* "Well, the man of the wagon, after "his belongings(? = me)" have been left on behalf of him,
	B	ga-nam lú-^{ŋiš}mar-ra-ke$_4$ me(! text: diš)-ni ugu-na um-da-šub-ba-⸢x⸣ [...]	
82	A	^{ŋiš}mar-ra-ni gú-un ù-un-d[u-du-ru] ^{ŋiš}mar-⸢ra⸣-⸢ni⸣-⸢ta⸣ ⸢ù⸣-[...]	*(82)* "and the load has been carried away from his wagon, and he has [left] his wagon,
	B	^{ŋiš}mar-ra-ni gú-un um-ku$_5$-ku$_5$-ru-a ^{ŋiš}mar-ra-ni [...]	
83	A	me é-na ù-da-an-túm é-a-ni-ta ba-ra-⸢šub⸣-[ba]	*(83)* "and after he has taken "his belongings"(? = me) into his house, they will be made to leave his house.
	B	me-ni é-a-na ù-ba-túm é-a-ni-ta [ba-ra-šub-ba]	
84	A	amar ^{ŋiš}mar-ra KA bí-in-tum$_4$-mu-⸢da⸣(?) x x é-a-na ab-ta-an-[tur(?)]-tur(?)	*(84)* "His calf that raised(?) its mouth(?) to the wagon, they will make it leave(?) his house.
	B	amar ^{ŋiš}mar-ra KA bí-in-tùm-⸢tùm⸣-a-ni é-a-[na ...]	
85	A	ur(?)-saŋ(?) á bad-du-ur(?) um-ma-ni-ti-e-a	*(85)* "Having approached the open-armed hero,
	B	ur-saŋ á-bad-du-a-⸢te⸣(?) um-ma-n[i-ti-e-a]	
86	A	lugal-e inim-inim-ma-nì ù-bí-in-⸢zu⸣ ki-šub-ba-ni-ta me-ni um-ta-an-šub-ba	*(86)* "the king, having learnt about his case, will make 'his belongings(? = me)' leave his dwelling.
	B	[lugal]-e ⸢inim⸣-[inim-ma-ni ù]-bí-in-zu ki-gub-ba-[...]	
87	A	gù-ra x é AŠ ur ke$_4$ a giš ad-bi ŋéštu-ŋá(?) ù-un-ḫal-ḫa nu-mu-da-zi-zi	*(87)* "The ox-driver(?), ... whom this advice has made to partake of my(?) wisdom, can not oppose(?) it.
	B	[...]-a šà(?)-bi ⸢ŋéštu⸣-⸢ga⸣(?) [...]	
88	A	gú-un-na-ni búr-búr-da énsi(?) gu-la an-dib-ba nu-mu-un-da-⸢gi⸣(?)-gi	*(88)* "His cargo, unloaded, taken in possession by the mighty ruler(?), will not return(?)."
	B	[...] ⸢x⸣-gu-⸢la⸣ [...]	
89	A	lugal-e sé-ek-rum-ta è-da-ni-ta	*(89)* When the king came out from the "cloister woman,"
90	A	lú diš(?) šà-ga-ni <....> diš(text: a?) šà-ga-ni ba-an-ši-íb-si	*(90)* Each(?) man <whose heart had not been satisfied(?)>, his heart was satisfied.

91	A	lú dam-a-ni ḫul an-gig-ga-àm dam-a-ni-ta ba-an-da-gin	*(91)* The man who was annoyed with his wife left his wife.
92	A	lú me-ni <...> me-ni ba-an-da-⸢šub⸣(?)	*(92)* The man <who had taken(?)> "his belongings(? = me)" left "his belongings(?)."
93	A	inim galam-galam-ma dumu adab^{ki}-ke$_4$-ne	*(93)* With the elaborate words, the sons of Adab,
94	A	inim galam-galam-ma-ta di in-dab$_5$-dab$_5$-bé	*(94)* with the elaborate words, their case was settled.
95	A	^{md}pa$_5$-nìŋin-ŋar-ra pa$_4$-šeš-ne-ne um-mi-a diŋir adab^{ki}-ke$_4$ dub-sar-bi	*(95)* Panigingarra, their sage, the scholar, the god of Adab, was clerk.

Comments to Individual Lines

Line 1: ku(?)-li-li seems to be a truncated, reduplicated form of ku-li. However, the reading of the first sign as ku is not certain. Cf. Cavigneaux, 1987, 51. On the copy it looks like ma. Line 18 rather makes us expect ŋuruš.

Line 2: The reading of the first sign as di was given by Cavigneaux, 1987, 51. Previous editors read du$_{17}$.

Line 6: énmen and ŋál conform to Kramer's collations. In lines 6 and 21 I would hesitate to take mu-e-da-ŋál as an (otherwise hardly attested) hypothetical 1st person pl. /mu-e-da/, assimilated from */mu-me-da-/ (so Edzard, *Sum. Grammar*, 106), but rather assume that a 2nd person sg. verbal form inadvertently has been carried on in the 1st person pl.

Line 7: Falkenstein, 1952, 114, understood e-še here and in the following lines as an irrealis or potentialis suffix ("Würde dem Mann mit dem Stier Wasser eingegossen, so möchten wir wohl Wasser trinken!"). Foster, 1974, 71, translates "If the ox driver would get water, then we will all drink." I see no reason for not interpreting it in its usual sense as a quotation marker. This would line up well with the common use of e-še in many proverbs and short tales, and fit the frequent shift of speakers in the lines in question. The dative constructions in lines 7, 9, and 11 = 22, 24, and 26, -ra, lit., "when water has been poured for the man of the ox," etc., undoubtedly reflects the friends' polite way to soften the imperative of the message, that they want him to go and fetch it himself.

Line 8: Falkenstein, 1952, 115, translates "Meinen Stier möchte der Löwe fressen und ich würde meinen Stier verlieren!" The verbal phrase (gud-ŋu$_{10}$-ta, etc.) ba-ra-è-dè-en was translated similarly in lines 10, 12 = 23, 25, and 27. Foster, 1974, 71, translates "A lion might devour my ox, then I would be out my ox!" I consider it much more likely that ba-ra- here denotes the 1st person vetetive, as often in promissory oaths. This would imply that, quite in line with the abrupt way in which quoted speech is often rendered in Sumerian compositions, there is an ellipsis after the first sentence of the line, lit. "When my ox has been devoured by a lion (I will lose it, so) I will not leave my ox!"

Line 10: Here and in 25 Cavigneaux, 1987, 51, gives the readings áb, edin, and gin.

Line 12: In line 82, B has the correct spelling: ku$_5$-ku$_5$-ru-a, which Lambert, 1995, 2, explains as a verb meaning "to cut" or "to separate," based on á A = *naqû*, MSL 14, pp. 345–346, which gives *batāqu, nakāsu, parāsu*. This appears as du-du-ru in A line 12, and as ⸢dúr-dúr⸣-ru in B line 12, which is a result of a misunderstanding of ku$_5$ as KU, read as dúr.

Line 14, cf. 29: For previous interpretations, see note 8. The reading éš(?) was suggested by Cavigneaux, 1987, 51. It seems probable in view of B, which has éš rather than e. In A, previous editors read the verbal prefix as ab-, but in view of B it is likely to be um-. This applies also to a number of other lines, where ab and um are difficult to distinguish.

The verbal phrase KA – túm seems lit. to mean "brought its mouth (or: teeth, nose) to the wagon." Whether this simply means that it touched the wagon with its mouth or sniffed at it, or the expression has more specific connotations, is not clear. The reading túm for DU is reasonably certain, in view of KA ... tum_4, in 84, which undoubtedly is another spelling of the same expression (so already Falkenstein, 1952, 118, comment to line 14). Foster, 1974, 72, n. 6, reads zú bí-in-gub, "to eat," suggesting that "the calf ate the cargo on the wagon, hence the carter's claim and the cloister woman's refutation(?) of it, 81–84."

Line 15: According to Kramer's collation, A has a-ba-àm.

Line 19: The reading of A follows Cavigneaux, 1987, 51.

Lines 22, 24, and 26: The copy shows um-te-šub, but according to lines 7, 9, and 11, um-te-si is expected. Cf. 86.

Line 32: The reconstruction follows *The Old Man* 19.

Lines 65ff.: It is assumed that the missing lines 65–68 plus 69–72 refer to the man of the ox, 73–80 refer to the man of the cow, and 81–88 refer to the man of the wagon.

Lines 66ff.: The prospective ù- should be translated either as referring to a past event, "when his ox has been devoured by a lion," or to a future event preceding another, "when his ox will have been devoured." Most likely, the entire sequence describes what will happen to the three men in the future, seen from the point of view of the speaker, in view of the Akkadian gloss to line 75 (see below).

Lines 69, 77, and 85: ur-saŋ, "hero" in these three cases seems to refer to each of the three men, perhaps with a stroke of irony.

Lines 71, 79, and 87: I tentatively read KA-ra as gù-ra. This could mean either lit. "the shouting one" or it would be a spelling for gud-ra. In both cases it seems to be a designation of the ox-drivers.

Line 75: The translation renders the Akkadian gloss. The Akkadian present suggests that the Sumerian prospective, ù-, here refers to a future event. The Sumerian text actually means "after she 'made the street'." I tentatively read the gloss as *im-sú-qí* = *ina sú-qí*, in spite of the fact that the assimilation of *ina* to a sibilant would be irregular.

Line 78: ri-ri could perhaps mean "taken captive."

Line 79: I hesitate to translate úr-ra-na-šè. If this means "in his lap," one would have expected úr-ra-ni-šè. It is difficult to see how this would make sense here.

Line 80: Cavigneaux, 1987, 51, reads the first sign as nin?, but dam is reasonably certain in view of B.

Line 81: diš-ni would mean "he alone," but dili-ni would rather be expected. It is tempting to emend diš-ni to me-ni. ugu-na, lit., "on top of him," may be a pun playing on the analogy between the man and the load on top of the wagon.

Line 82: For the reading of B: ku_5-ku_5-ru-a, cf. line 12 above.

Lines 82 and 86: In 82 I follow Cavigneaux, 1987, 51, who gives the reading ^{ŋiš}mar-ra-ni. This implies that the sign copied as níŋ by Genouillac, is -ni. It is also tempting to suggest the reading -ni for the corresponding sign in 86, where the reading inim-inim-ma-ni is expected. However, since neither Cavigneaux nor Kramer commented on the sign in line 86, I retain the reading inim-inim-ma-nì, as copied by Genouillac. Further collation might help here. The readings níŋ or nì, phonetic for -ni, would actually make sense in 82, where níŋ could represent -ni contracted to the following /ŋ/. Conversely, ni is used for níŋ in *Incantation to Utu* 233 (AcSum 13 [1992] 66).

Line 84: Foster reads sag!? bí-in-tùm-mu-⌜da⌝. The last sign in the sequence could equally well be uš. Cavigneaux gives the reading ab-ta-an-[tur?]-tur?. [tur]-tur, "to be/make small" would hardly make sense here. With great hesitation I suggest ab(or: um)-ta-an-[i]-i, a reduplicated, weak form of è, "he makes it go out of his house," but the reduplicated form is difficult to explain. That A has é-ni-na, "in his house," is only a minor difficulty, for the use of the locative instead of the ablative would not be unusual. Line 83 has the ablative, é-a-ni-ta, however.

Line 86: A has ki-šub-ba-ni, "his dwelling place," and B: ki-gub-ba-ni, lit., "his standing place." There is some suspicion that the sign šub in

A needs further collation; cf. lines 22, 24, 26.

Line 87: The verbal phrase, nu-mu-da-zi-zi, is difficult to understand in the context. If -da- is taken as the comitative, it would mean "he will not raise with it." It could also be taken as a spelling for the ablative -ta-, in which case one could translate "he will not raise from it." The reference could perhaps be to the load of the wagon or to the wisdom taught by the clever woman. I tentatively translate "will not oppose it," assuming that zi-zi here means to "rise," i.e., "to revolt." Cf. *Instr. Šuruppak* 188: lú zi-zi-i-dè lú ša-ba-da-an-zi-zi-i, "when men are revolting, (every) man will revolt with them."

Line 88: Cavigneaux, 1987, 52: gú-un-na-ni NAM? BÚR UŠ? AR⌜UŠ? GUR(?) gu-la AN dib-ba nu-mu-un-da-šilig?-ge. Foster, 1975, 71, read: gú-un-na-ni aš-du$_9$-du$_9$-da x x gur?-gu-la an-díb-ba nu-mu-un-da-gi-gi. The sign read -da could perhaps be uš. The copy gives PA.⌜TE⌝.GUR, but, since GUR and SI obviously are difficult to distinguish on this tablet (cf. l. 90), it is very tempting to read énsi(PA.TE.SI). If the last two signs are in fact gi-gi, they certainly represent gi$_4$-gi$_4$, "to return." Cf. the use of gi for gi$_4$ in lines 3, 13, and 17.

Line 90: Cavigneaux, 1987, 52, reads tentatively: lú DIŠ? šà-ga-ni a(DIŠ?) šà-ga-ni ba-an-ši-íb-gur?/si?. The reading DIŠ was suggested by Foster, 1974, 71, who translates "Each man's heart was satisfied." If correctly read, this would literally mean, "The man, his heart on the one side, his heart on the other side." The translation of šà si, lit., "fill the heart," "satisfy" (*šebû*), is certainly possible; cf. Foster, 1974, 72, n. 7. I have tentatively accepted this translation, but for the following reasons not without a good deal of hesitation. Genouillac's copy suggests a-šà in both places. Cavigneaux's collation virtually confirms this in the second case, and also marks the first instance of DIŠ with a question-mark. The parallelism, as discussed in the introduction to this study, suggests that this line refers to the man of the ox,[90] and it is highly likely that this resumes the same expression as a-šà-ga-na, in 72. However, I am unable to explain how the reading a-šà-ga-ni, "his field," would make sense. This might mean "The man whose field <was not irrigated> his field was irrigated," in which case there might still be an allusion to the way the calf was engendered. Cf. also note 14.

Lines 90 and 92: Unlike previous commentators I would point to the possibility that both lines 90 and 92 are incompletely transmitted,[90;92] in that the verbal phrases following the first me-ni and šà-ga-ni may be missing. This is strongly suggested by the parallelism with line 91. Line 92 can perhaps be completed as lú me-ni <é-a-na ù-da-an-túm> me-ni ba-an-da-šub, in analogy with 83. Line 90 could perhaps have been completed as analogous to 67, had it been preserved.

Line 92: Foster, 1974, 72, translates, "What was proper for the man befell him." This translation is attractive (lit., "what was proper for the man fell as that which was proper for the man"), but one is compelled to ask if it was not influenced by the connotations of the English verb "befall," to the best of my knowledge alien to the Sumerian verb šub, which simply means "fall" or "leave."

Line 95: The reading pa$_4$ is according to Kramer's collation.

Literature:

B. Alster: *Studies in Sumerian Proverbs*, Mesopotamia. Copenhagen Studies in Assyriology 3 (1975).

B. Alster: "The Sumerian Folktale of the Three Ox-drivers from Adab," JCS 43–45 (1991–93) 27–38.

A. Cavigneaux: "Notes Sumérologiques," AcSum 9 (1987) 45–66.

J.J.A. van Dijk: *La Sagessse suméro-accadienne* (Leiden, 1953).

A. Falkenstein: "Das Potentialis- und Irrealissuffix -e-še des Sumerischen," *Indogermanische Forschungen* 60 (1952) 113–130.

B. Foster: "Humor and Cuneiform Literature," *Journal of the Ancient Near Eastern Society of Columbia University* 6 (1974) 69–85.

E.I. Gordon, "A New Look at the Wisdom of Sumer and Akkad," BiOr 17 (1960) 122–152.

W.G. Lambert: "A Note on the Three Ox-Drivers from Adab," *N.A.B.U.* 1995/1, no. 2 (pp. 1–2).

E. Lipiński: "The King's Arbitration in Ancient Near Eastern Folk-Tale," in: K. Hecker and W. Sommerfeld, (eds.), *Keilschriftliche Literaturen*, Berliner Beiträge zum Vorderen Orient 8 (Berlin, 1985), 137–141.

90. Already suggested by Alster, 1975, 127, n. 22.

90, 92. Cf. already Alster, 1975, 127, n. 22.

5.2 The Old Man and the Young Girl

Publication History

In a preliminary edition in *Studies* (1975), 90–97, Alster recognized CBS 8010 as a dupl. of BM 54699, and thereby identified this as a separate composition, which had previously been understood by Gordon and van Dijk as belonging to *The Three Ox-Drivers from Adab*. In the revised edition below, collations of BM 54699 have been taken into account, but, regrettably, no new duplicates have been identified.

Sources

Apart from B, the relevant dupls. are cited under their museum numbers with no siglas assigned. The sigla B has been chosen here to conform to the sigla assigned to the same tablet in the edition of *The Goose and the Raven* in Chap. 4.3; cf. the brief description given there.

B: CT 42, 36: BM 54699, unusual four-sided prism. "Face A," almost complete with 30 lines and probably two missing lines at the end = *Old Man* 10'–42'; "Face B": 1'–6': About 8 completely lost lines plus remains of 6 almost illegible lines, representing the end of *Old Man*. "Face B" 7'-"Face C" 7': *Níŋ-nam* B + *Goose and Raven*, cf. below; "Face D": remains of 8 lines out of ca. 32 lines, of uncertain identification, cf. the discussion below.
Collated in the British Museum, March 1993.

CBS 8010: STVC 97: = i 1–6 = lines 10'–15'; iv 1'–6' = remains of 6 lines from near the end of the composition. Fragment from a four-column tablet.

Ni 4305:ISET 2, 18; Alster, *Studies*, 90 source C. Col. ii = lines 23'–31'.
Small fragment from the obverse of a tablet that had at least four columns. Col. i contains ends of ca. 9 unidentified lines, too poorly preserved for transliteration. Rev. destroyed.

N 3183: Very small fragment. Transliterated below. = lines 36' Ex a-b - 40.
Identified by Civil, cf. Kramer, JCS 18 (1964) 47, n. 94.

Description of the Sammeltafel

If the description of B given above is justified, each col. had about 32 lines. The possibility should be taken into account that "Face D" in fact may represent the first column on the prism. If our composition covers "Face D," = [32] lines, plus "Face A" = 32 lines, plus Face B 1'–6' (out of 13 lines), this would give a length of about (2 × 32) + 13 = 77 lines to the entire composition of *The Old Man*, which is rather more than expected. If "Face D" is assigned to *The Goose and the Raven*, it would give about 45 lines to *The Old Man*, which is a bit less than expected, although not impossible. Following our composition in "Face B" 7 starts a subversion of *Níŋ-nam* Version B ("Face B": 14 + "Face C": [x] + 7) = max. 21+x lines (cf. *Chap. 3.1* and the separate transliteration in *Chap. 3.2x: Sources*), ending in "Face C" 7. If the remaining lines of "Face C," 8–17, belong to *The Goose and the Raven*, it would yield about C: 17 + [15] + D: [ca. 15] + 8 + [max 9] = a total of ca. max. 49 lines to that composition, which is more than expected, since it has 37 (short) lines in source A; cf. *Chap. 4.3*. There is thus no simple solution to the assignment of source B "Face D," but, since the phraseology is most reminiscent of a dialogue or fable, it is most likely to belong to an otherwise unknown variant version of the end of *The Goose and the Raven*. To make things even more complicated, the possibility that the prism may have been inscribed with an extra composition, of which only "Face D" remains, in addition to those already identified, should be considered.

The two four-column fragments, CBS 8010 and Ni 4305, may actually also have been a *Sammeltafel*, in which case the unidentified remains may not belong to *The Old Man*.

Quotations in Other Sources

It is remarkable that this small composition occurs on at least two four-column tablets (CBS 8010 and Ni 4305). In addition, a sequence of lines are quoted in proverb tablets or similar. Cf. the comments on lines 27–31 below. A special case is SLTNi 128, which is a four-column tablet that contains *Níŋ-nam* in obv. i-ii, but *The Old Man* in iii (Rev.i), and an unidentified composition in iv. Cf. the transliterations below, and p. 284, *Chap. 3.2x: Sources.*

Conclusion

The story is the oldest known example of a theme well attested in world literature. Best known is 1Kings 1:1ff and 2:17f., in which the young girl Abishag is given to the old King David. Further, in Chaucer's *Canterbury Tales* note the Merchant's Story about January and May. The description of the man getting increasingly old may be compared to the metaphorical description in Eccl 12:1–7.

The story as presented here is surprisingly briefly formulated, at least as far as the preserved fragment allows us to judge. The problem itself, the old man's declining physical abilities, seems to be contained in only three metaphorical and mostly obscure lines, i.e., lines 15–17 (# [8–9]+10). Only the answer given by the old man upon the king's further interrogation (ll. 26–35) is phrased in detailed circumlocutions, quoting a sequence that obviously was popular in scribal circles, since some of the same phrases occur elsewhere with the same implications. The entire story may have been meant as an occasion to present just that section as an example of scribal wit, rather than as an exemplification of the king's justice. Add to this that the invention of the solution suggested by the wise woman, to give the old man a young girl in marriage, could easily have been invented without her help. The text is, therefore, best described as a burlesque invention of the scribal schools, similar to *The Three Ox-Drivers from Adab.*

B Face D may belong to *The Goose and the Raven*, cf. above. It is transliterated p. 359, *Chap. 4.3: Sources not placed.* Alternatively it may contain the first lines of our composition.

Line / Source	Transliteration	Translation
		(The old man speaking:)
9'		
(# 15)	[lú(?) diš-àm ⸢gaba⸣ mu-un-ri-ba]	*([9'])* ["(I was) a unique man, whose breast(?) was very strong.]
10'		
CBS 8010 i 1	ù-mu-un-ŋu$_{10}$ *ì al(?)-sa$_6$(?) [SA]R(?)-ŋu$_{10}$ / si-mul *ŋanba(KI(!).LAM)-ŋu$_{10}$	*(10)* My blood was fine, my «vegetables(?)» (= hair?), my «shining horn» and «marketplace»
11'		
CBS 8010 i 2	al-gùn še-sa-a-ŋu$_{10}$ diŋir la-ba-<ni>-in-tuku	*(11)* were multicolored, (but now) my «roasted barley» (= digestion?) has no success (lit. «has no god»)."
12'		
CBS 8010 i 3	lugal-e inim-ma-ni la-ba-ni-in-gi$_4$	*(12)* The king did not reply,
13'		
CBS 8010 i 4	sé-ek-ru-um-šè ba-an-ku$_4$	*(13)* but entered (the house of a) "cloistered woman,"
14'		
B Face B1'	[x x] ⸢x⸣(like é, giš, or similar) [...]	*(14)* and repeated his words to the "cloistered woman":
CBS 8010 i 5	sé-ek-ru-um-e inim šu-a ba-ni-in-gi$_4$	
15'		
B ~2	[x x]-àm gaba mu-⸢un⸣(?)-[...]	*(15)* "(I was) a unique man, whose breast(?) was very strong.
CBS 8010 i 6	lú(?) diš-àm ⸢gaba⸣ mu-un-ri-ba	

Line	Source	Transliteration	Translation
16'	B ~3	[ù]-⸢mu-un-ŋu$_{10}$⸣ al-sa$_6$ SAR-ŋu$_{10}$ si(? could nearly be kuš)-MUL(= súhub?) ŋanba(clearly: KI-LAM)-mu-[um?]	*(16)* "My blood was fine, my "vegetables" (= hair?), my "shining horn" and "marketplace"
17'	B ~4	[al]-⸢gùn⸣(possible) še-sa(tab nearly possible)-a-ŋu$_{10}$ diŋir la-ba-ni-in-tuku ur$_5$-gim ba-an-[dug$_4$(?)]	*(17)* were multicolored, (but now) my «roasted barley» (= digestion?) has no success (lit. «has no god»). Thus he [spoke]."
18'	B 5	[sé-e]k-rum-e lugal-e mu-na-ni-ib-gi$_4$-gi$_4$	*(18)* The «cloistered woman» answered the king:
19'	B 6	[lugal]-ŋu$_{10}$ i-gi$_4$-in-zu ab-ba ki-sikil-tur-ra nam-dam-šè b[a-an-tuku]	*(19)* [My lord, suppose that the old man got a young girl as wife,
20'	B 7	[x] ⸢x⸣ ⸢x⸣ ⸢x⸣-ni ba-an-sù-sù ab-ba nam-ŋuruš-na ba-an-ku$_4$	*(20)* [...] ... the old man will regain his youthful vigor,
21'	B 8	⸢x⸣ ⸢x⸣ ⸢nam⸣-um-ma ba-an-ku$_4$	*(21)* [and the young girl] will become a mature woman."
22'	B ~9	[x] ⸢x⸣ sé-ek-rum-e è-da-ni-ta	*(22)* [When the "cloistered woman" had left [the king/palace],
23'	B ~10 Ni 4305	[x] ⸢x⸣ ⸢ab⸣-ba gen-na-ab-zé-⸢en⸣ ⸢x⸣ [...]	*(23)* [(*she said:*) [... "Come!] Fetch the old man!"
24'	B ~11 Ni 4305	[luga]l-⸢e ab-ba⸣-ra gù mu-na-dé-[e] lugal-e ⸢x⸣ [...]	*(24)* The king then spoke to the old man:
25'	B ~12 Ni 4305	[a-na]-⸢aš-àm⸣ ⸢dam(?)⸣-zu a-ra-pag-pag-g[e] a-na-aš-àm [...]	*(25)* "Why has your wife(?) become shut in?"
26'	B ~13 Ni 4305	[ab]-ba ⸢lugal⸣-⸢a⸣(?)-⸢ni⸣(? or read ⸢ra⸣?) mu-na-ni-íb-gi$_4$-g[i$_4$] ab-ba lugal-ra m[u-...]	*(26)* The old man then answered the king:
27'	B ~14 Ni 4305	[ŋá-e(?) space for two signs here] ⸢šul⸣(?) diŋir-ŋu$_{10}$ usu-ŋu$_{10}$ ^{d}lama-ŋu$_{10}$ šul diŋir-ŋu$_{10}$ us[u-ŋu$_{10}$ ...]	*(27)* "I, (who was) a youth, (now) my luck (lit., god), my strength, my protective god,

Line	Source	Text	Translation
28'			
	B ~15	nam-ŋuruš-ŋu$_{10}$ anše-kar-ra-gim háš-ŋá ba-e-díb	*(28)* and my youthful vigor have left my loins like a runaway ass.
	Ni 4305	nam-ŋuruš-ŋu$_{10}$ anše-kar-[...]	
29'			
	B ~16	ḫur-saŋ ŋi$_{6}$-ŋu$_{10}$ níŋ-babbar ba-an-mú(not ku$_{4}$)	*(29)* My black mountain has produced white gypsum.
	Ni 4305	ḫur-saŋ ŋi$_{6}$-ŋu$_{10}$ im-[...]	
30'			
	B ~17	ama-ŋu$_{10}$ tir-ta lú mu-e-ši-in-gi$_{4}$ šu-dab$_{5}$-ba ba-an-šúm-m[u]	*(30)* My mother has turned a man from the woods toward me, he gave (me) paralyzed hands.
	Ni 4305	ama-ŋu$_{10}$-šè(? or: ur?)^{ŋiš}tir-[ta ...] / šu-dab$_{5}$ mu-[...]	
31'			
	B ~18	^{d}nin-kilim níŋ-háb-ba gu$_{7}$-gu$_{7}$-ŋu$_{10}$ dug(?) ì-nun-na-šè gú nu-mu-da-l[á-a]	*(31)* My mongoose that used to eat strong-smelling food does not (anymore) stretch its neck toward a jar(?) with fine oil.
	Ni 4305	^{d}nin-kilim ⌜x⌝(perhaps níŋ?) [...]	
32'			
	B ~19	zú-ŋu$_{10}$ níŋ-kala-ga ì-ur$_{5}$-ra níŋ-kala-ge nu-ur$_{5}$-re	*(32)* My teeth that used to chew strong things do not (anymore) chew strong things.
33'			
	B ~20	kàš-ŋu$_{10}$ iz-zi kala-ga ì-bùr(! U with a weak vertical through the top of the sign)-e IM-ŋu$_{10}$-ta ì-DU-zé-en	*(33)* My urine used to break forward in a strong torrent, but (now) you ....
34'			
	B ~21	dumu-ŋu$_{10}$ ì-ga-ra gu$_{7}$-gu$_{7}$-a níŋ-gu$_{7}$ nu-mu-na-šúm-mu	*(34)* My son who used to feed me with butter and fine cream does not anymore give me something to eat,
35'			
	B ~22	ù géme-tur-ŋu$_{10}$ a-ab-sa$_{10}$-e gal$_{5}$-lá-ḫul gig ba-ab-ŋar	*(35)* and my little slave girl whom I have bought (is like) an evil demon that harasses me."
36'			
	B ~23	lugal-e inim ab-ba-šè ŋizzal ḫé-em-ši-ak	*(36)* The king paid attention to the words of the old man.
36' Ex a-b			
	N 3183	kaš(sic!)-ni i[z(?)...] (belongs where?)	*(36 Ex a)* His urine [used to break forward] in a [strong tor]rent.
	N 3183	ab-ba sù-ga [...] (belongs where?)	*(36 Ex b)* The old man ...
37'			
	B ~24	lugal-e ki-sikil-e gù mu-na-dé-e	*(37)* The king spoke to the young girl:
	N 3183	lugal-e ki-sikil [...]	
38'			
	B ~25	⌜e⌝-ra-ab-šúm-mu-na-ta lú-tur-ra-gin$_{7}$-nam úr-za-a hé-ná	*(38)* "When I have given him to you, he will lie as if he were a young man in your lap.
	N 3183	e-ra-ab-šúm-mu-na-ta [...] / úr-za-a [...]	

39'		
B ~26	[gen-n]a úrdu-zu eme ḫé-da-ak-e é-zu ḫé-en-da-dul(NB: not ku$_4$)	*(39)* Come, let your servant announce(?) it, let your house be covered (for wedding festivities?)!"
N 3183	gen-na úrdu-zu [...] / ù é-[...]	
40'		
B ~27	[ki-sikil] ⸢é⸣-gal-ta è-da-ni-ta	*(40)* The girl, upon leaving the palace (said):
N 3183	ki-sikil é-gal-ta [...]	
41'		
B ~28	[gu$_4$-ud-da-an-z]é-en gu$_4$-ud-da-an-zé-en ki-sikil tur-tur-re PI-PI-en-zé-en	*(41)* "[Dance], dance, all young girls, rejoice(?)!"
42'		
B ~29	[...] ⸢re⸣(?) gi$_4$ ⸢ga⸣(or similar) ⸢re⸣(or similar) ⸢x⸣ ⸢x⸣ ba-an-ŋar	*(42)* (*Almost completely destroyed*)

(*Continuation almost completely destroyed*)

Two lines missing at the end of B "face A." B "Face B": 8 completely destroyed lines in woh CBS 8010 iv–6 (transliterated below) might belong. The end of the composition was contained in B "Face B" 1'–6', which are too poorly preserved to be transliterated.

CBS 8010 iv 1	[t]ir(?)-ra(?) a(?) inim-bi ḫa ⸢x⸣ [...]
CBS 8010 iv 2	igi lu zi [x] ⸢x⸣ ka(?) [...]
CBS 8010 iv 3	inim(?)-galam-galam igi [x x] mu [...]
CBS 8010 iv 4	ur-⸢x⸣ si [x x x] ⸢x⸣
CBS 8010 iv 5	u[r] ŋar re ⸢x⸣ [...]
CBS 8010 iv 6	[x x x] ni [...]

Comments on Individual Lines

Lines 9–11/15–17: This sequence apparently describes the physically declining health condition of the old man in metaphorical terms, but the precise connotations are mostly very elusive. The subdivision remains dubious, especially because one does not expect the verb al-gùn in lines 11 = 17 to belong to the previous line. The sequence that follows in lines 27–35 is a lot more explicit, but also very elusive.

In lines 10 = 16, ù-mu-un = *dāmu*, "blood." In 10: *ì al(?)-sa$_6$(?) is according to collation, but 16 has no ì.

SAR perhaps = nisig, *(w)arqu*, "vegetable."

si-mul could nearly be kuš-MUL, i.e., súḫub = *s/šuḫuppatu*, "boot," in line 16', but very uncertain.

The reading KI-LAM in line 16 is according to collation; cf. also Kramer's collation in JCS 23 (1970) 13. This is = ŋanba, *maḫīru*, cf. CAD M, 92–98: "market place; business transaction; tariff; purchase price." Alster, 1975, 93, translated "my yield was brilliant," but the verb gùn, in line 17, if correctly read, rather points to a concrete physical part of the body. It is of course easy to suggest that these parts are sexual metaphors, but the general impression rather is that it is the basic physical abilities, such as eating, chewing, and smelling, that troubles the old man. Cf. the remarks on this passage and lines 27–35 by Alster, in: *Mesopotamian Poetic Language*, 1966, pp. 14–15, with nn. 95–96.

Line 11: diŋir, here personal "luck," cf. the similar use in line 27. Cf. Th. Jacobsen, ZA 52 (1957) 138, n. 108, who refers to the expression *ilam rašû*. še-sa-a = *qalītu*, cf. CAD Q, 59, "parched grain"; interpreted by Alster, 1975, as "grain roasting," metaphorical for digestion.

Line 13': That ZI.IK.RU-UM is to be read sé-ek-ru-um/rum was pointed out by Lipiński, 1986, 140, n. 11, who explains this as the logogram SÉ-EK-RUM = *sekrum*, "cloister woman." Cf. CAD S, 215: svv *sekēru* A, and *sekretu*, "(a woman of high rank, possibly cloistered)." The Sumerian grammar may be influenced by Akkadian, but, nevertheless, the terminative sé-ek-ru-um-šè might point to the building in which the woman lived, rather than to the person herself. Similarly *Three Ox-Drivers* 16, and ibid., 17: sé-ek-rum-ta, "from the *sekrum*."

Line 19: i-gi$_4$-in-zu is the modal adverb i-gi$_4$-in-zu treated by Wilcke, JNES 27 (1968) 229–242; perhaps from ì-ga-an-zu < inga-zu, but far from certain; cf. Edzard, *Sum. Grammar*, 165.

Line 20: Lit., "the (elderly) man will enter his youth." In the beginning of the line, Alster, 1975, 93, translated "(In the rest of) his days—as long as they last, as long as they are," which may be approximately correct, although it is not clear precisely how to restore the line.

Line 22: Alster, 1975, 93, read [é-gal-t]a, but a reference to the king might be equally possible; cf. line 13.

Line 25: Alster, 1975, 92, read gaba(?) for the sign preceding zu, which fits the traces on the copy. However, my collation indicates ⌜dam⌝-zu, which would imply that the old man was already married, and received the young girl only as a second wife. The implication might then be that the old man had sexual problems in his relationship with his wife, which only comes to light when the king addresses him a second time, since it was remarkably not included in the first description of his problems in lines 15–17 # [9]–10. For the verb pag = *esēru*, "to shut in" (said of birds, etc., but also sickness demons, etc.), cf. CAD E, 334: *esēru* B; N "to become constricted"; AHw 249. This might, thus, mean that his wife had become inaccessible to him, but the meaning is not quite satisfactory, since what we expect is rather that *she* had refused *him*. Should the reading ⌜gaba⌝ be justified, it probably would mean that his breast has become constricted so that he breathes only with difficulty.

Line 27: diŋir, lit., "god," here translated "personal luck," cf. line 11. Cf. also *Chap. 6.2: Cornell Univ. Prov 2*, 6: šul diŋir tuku(-da).

Lines 27–31: These lines are quoted with small variations as SP 17 Sec. B 3 (2–7) (Alster, *Proverbs* I, 238; cf. the comments in *Proverbs* II, 436), SP 19 Sec. A 1 (Alster, *Proverbs* I, 243); shorter in SP 10.9–10 (Alster, *Proverbs* I, 189).

Line 29: The black mountain and the white gypsum are metaphors meaning that the old man's black hair has become white. Cf. Düringsfeld II, 342, "Schwarze Kühe geben auch weisse Milch." Also the *Rigveda* 4.39: "Obwohl sie (die Kuh) schwarz ist, strotz sie von weisser Nahrung."

Line 30: The man turning toward the old man from the woods and apparently causing him paralysis (šu-dab$_5$?) is perhaps metaphorical for the old man having to walk on crutches. The verb forms mu-e-ši- and na-an-šúm-m[u] are not in the expected 1st person, but possibly were copied from a now lost repetition of the same passage, in which they fitted.

Line 31: ^{d}nin-kilim = *šikkû*, "mongoose." Alster, 1975, 93, read the sign before ì-nun-na as kaš. It is here tentatively read as dug. The mongoose that used to eat strong-smelling food but does not (anymore) stretch its neck toward fine oil seems to be a metaphor for his nose that has lost its ability to smell.

Line 32: For this line, cf. the discussion of the various meanings of ur$_5$ of *Instr. Šuruppak* 49, referring to an earlier discussion by Civil, 1984, 295–296. Civil quotes this line and consents to the interpretation first proposed by Alster, 1975, 93.

Line 33: iz-zi probably phonetic for i-zi = *agû*, cf. Sjöberg, TCS III 106, and the discussion by Alster, "Nanše and Her Fish" (*Klein FS*, 1–18). Heimpel, RlA 9, 153–54, understands this as "swells," accepted by Alster, loc. cit. Here it is rather a strong "torrent" or similar. IM-ŋu$_{10}$-ta can mean either "from my wind" or "from myself" (ní-ŋu$_{10}$-ta), but in either case the implication is obscure. The verb ì-DU-zé-en seems to be the 2nd person plural = /-DU-enzen/.

bùr is written like U with a weak vertical stroke through the top of the sign, apparently by scribal error. U is probably bùr = *palāšu*, "to break through," typically said of burglars.

Line 35: ì-ga-ra: seems to be phonetic for ì-gára, which is the GA-*gunû* form of GA (GA+NI) = *lil/šdu*, "cream," that often appears in the inscriptions of Gudea, etc. Cf. CAD L, 215; AHw 552, and, e.g.,

Bauer, AWL, 423.

Line 39: eme – ak occurs in (1) our line; (2): SP 2.75: anše-ŋu$_{10}$ kaš$_{4}$-kar-re-dè nu-mu-un-túm eme-ak-da mu-un-túm; (3): SP 3.8: eme-ak an-bar$_{9}$ an-dùl nu-ŋá-ŋá; and (4): *Dumuzi-Inanna D* 13: dili-dili-ta eme-ak dili-dili-ta. Cf. also (5) van Dijk/Geller, *Ur III Incantations*, 48, no. 12, line 5: me ka ba-ni-ak, which Geller translates "the *lizard* of heaven and of earth licked him," taking me as phonetic for eme, and comparing SP 5.82 (Alster, *Proverbs* I, 136 [cf. II, 406]): ur-gi$_{7}$-re ^{na4}kín eme ka ak, "a dog licked a millstone." For (1–4) see Sefati, *Love Songs*, 161, who translates (2) "My donkey is not destined to run quickly, (but) he is destined 'to make tongue' (i.e., to copulate)"; and (3) "copulating at noon without covering oneself—is an abomination to Utu"; (4): "Time after time, 'making tongue,' time after time." In the latter the sexual connotations seem certain; yet, the reference may not necessarily be to sexual intercourse, but, in view of the context, rather a poetic circumlocution. Jacobsen's translation, referred to by Sefati, loc. cit., "to talk, to chat," is too vague, however. In (3) the reference to sexual activities is reasonably clear in view of the context, but not necessarily sexual intercourse; cf. Alster, *Proverbs* I, 80, who translates "... to kiss with the tongue at midday without providing shade ...." In (2) it is not necessary to see this as an implicit reference to copulating; Alster, *Proverbs* I, 61, translates "My donkey is not fit for fast running. It is fit for braying," which, although a guess from context, would fit (1), where sexual connotations seem excluded. Alster, *Proverbs* II, 368, commenting on (2), explains, lit., "working the tongue" as a reference "to the sound of an ass, and thus different from [(3)]." Cf. also Alster, *Proverbs* II, 277, and the references cited there, who explains (4) as "kissing," but (3) as possibly sexual intercourse, and (2) as the sound produced by an ass. In (1) this would fit the sound produced by the slaves to announce a joyous wedding celebration; Alster, 1975, 94, translated our line "Come, let your slave announce it," which thus seems approximately correct. PSD A/3, 81, translates our line, under 8.49, "let your servant now converse with you(?), let him enter your house," which seems less satisfactory.

For the last sign in the line, collation shows dul, not ku$_{4}$. The translation of Alster, loc. cit., "let him enter your house!" is thus dubious, although it seems to fit the context.

Line 41: For the verb PI-PI Alster, 1975, 92, read wu-wa-en-zé-en, translating the entire line "Dance, dance, all young girls, rejoice!" referring, p. 126, to SRT 5, 42 (dupl. CBS 8037): gu$_{4}$-ud-an-zé-en gu$_{4}$-ud-an-zé-en, for which see now Sefati, *Love Songs*, 135, *Dumuzi-Inanna C* lines 42 and 44. Line 43 of that text contains the divine name ^{d}ba-ba$_{6}$, but this is hardly hinted at here. One may compare the verb wu-wa – za, last treated by Black, *Wilcke FS*, 46, but since there is no za, it is uncertain whether it is relevant in this case.

Synopsis

Ll. [Lost: Probably a brief introduction setting the scene].
Ll. [?–8'–10']+11': The old man's address to the king.
Ll. 12'–14': The king addresses the "cloistered woman."
Ll. 15'–17': The king repeats the old man's words (= [8']–11').
Ll. 18–21: The "cloistered woman's" answer.
Ll. 22':–25': The king interrogates the old man again.
Ll. 26'–35': The old man describes his aging problems in detail.
Ll. 36'–39': The king addresses the young girl.
Ll. 40'–41': The young girl leaves the palace expressing her joy.
(*Continuation missing or illegible*)

Addendum

After the completion of this chapter a uniquely interesting bilingual parallel to the proverbs contained in lines 27-31 was identified in the Schøyen proverb tablet MS 3279, semi-bilingual, nos. 7–10. The relevant lines are as follows: No. 7 = *Old Man* 28: *ki-ma* ANŠE *mu-un-na-ab-tum ḫal-⸢li⸣ iz-ba-am.* No. 8 = *Old Man* 29: *ša-di-i ṣa-al-mu qa-aṣ*(?)-*ṣú*(?)-⸢*um*(?)⸣ .... No. 9. = *Old Man* 30: *a-na i-li*(?)-*it RU*(?)-*DA*-⸢*AN*⸣ ⸢*x*⸣ ... ; *ṣa-bi-it qá-tim-ma*(?) *x-mu*(?). No. 10. = *Old Man* 31: *ši-ik-ku*$_{14}$(KUN)-*um-mi-tum bi-ša i-ku-lu; a-na* DUG Ì-NUN *TAK*(?)-*ši-x*(?).

CHAPTER 6

Examples of Proverb Collections Used as Literary Source Books

The rediscovery of Sumerian literature is an ongoing process, as two tablets in the Kroch Library at Cornell University, brought to my attention by David I. Owen, illustrate. One of these tablets covers some lacunae that obstinately have resisted recovery, in *Sumerian Proverb Collection* 1, although the latest edition, by Alster, *Proverbs* I, from 1997, utilizes no less than close to a hundred sources for this collection alone. The two Cornell University tablets are characteristic products of the scribal schools, probably from a non-Nippurian site, in which the teachers were used to making their own specific choice of lines to be included from proverb collections and other literary works. They contain sententious sayings from the Nippur scribal curriculum, reflecting the needs that may have arisen during the teachers' confrontation with the pupils' varying degree of competence (cf. Veldhuis, 2000, esp. p. 384). An illustrative example is the quotation from *Gilgameš and Huwawa* 107–110 appearing in the second Cornell University tablet published below. The teachers' command of the Sumerian language was far from always impeccable, however.

A small section quoted below will illustrate the procedure. A short extract from *The Fowler and His Wife*, the full text of which is edited above p. 371, *Chap. 4.5: Short Stories ... Involving Humans*, was included on the second Cornell University tablet, and is translated below.

Excerpt from The Fowler and His Wife

(1) "The water dried up from your small swamp.
(2) A whirlwind blew,
(3) so that your boat touched the bank.
(4) Fowler, should you {not} stretch your net? let a bird rise into it!
(5) The net was "laid" upon an *esig*-bird (an unidentified species of bird),
(6) but a raven stretched your net!"

As it stands, this makes little sense, but if compared to the full text of *The Fowler and His Wife* (ll. 6–12), it is possible to see how the excerpt came about. Although some details are far from certain, such as the precise implication of the *esig*-bird, this much is clear. Our scribe included just those points that were needed for someone who already had the whole story in mind to recapitulate the essential parts. Yet, some errors, such as the erroneous negative "not" in line 4, raise some doubts as to how well he understood every detail of the full story. Since we are now lucky enough to be able to retrieve it almost completely, we can see that he alluded to the section in which the fowler's wife talks to her husband, hinting at her irritation at his poor sexual performance. By letting a raven, a less-valued bird, stretch or rip his net, thereby apparently enabling a more valuable bird (an *esig*-bird) to escape, she rather obviously intends to say that he missed a great opportunity to make love. All details, such as the fowler going to drink beer with a friend, were omitted as superfluous details once that essential point was understood, that is, that the "bird" rising by itself stood for some sexual metaphor, as did his boat touching the ground, as well as the "little swamp" and "big swamp," etc.

The extract written on the Cornell University tablet was not unique. It should be compared to the extract on the Iowa duplicate, translated separately by Alster, 1992, 189. Another extract occurs on the Kassite tablet published by Veldhuis; cf. *Chap. 4.5* for details.

The type of excerpt we encounter here strongly corroborates the impression that in the scribal schools the written excerpts and even the lexical series were accompanied by oral comments, which, of course, becomes apparent only in rare glimpses. As a result there may have been a mutual relationship between the written texts and the oral comments that accompanied them, and this even went so far that lexical series could become the basis for literary compositions, as most clearly demonstrated by Civil, 1987. This kind of literary environment, of course, left marks on the existing manuscripts, which is one of the reasons why the traditional dichotomy of "oral" versus "written" literature now seems obsolete when related to ancient manuscript traditions reflecting a similar environment of scribal education. This is true, not least, as far as ancient proverb collections go, because these would be unthinkable had they not ultimately reflected living proverbs in a spoken environment. Cf. p. 34, *Chap. 1.1.1: Theoretical Outlook on Proverbs* and ibid. *Proverbs and School Education*, further p. 42, *Chap. 1.1.2: Father-and-son Compositions from Other Linguistic Areas*, with references to Egyptian, Aramaic, Classical, Anglo-Saxon, Old Norse, and medieval sources, etc.

Literature

B. Alster: *Proverbs of Ancient Sumer*, 1997.

M. Civil: "Feeding Dumuzi's Sheep: The Lexicon as a Source of Literary Inspiration." American Oriental Series 67 [E. Reiner vol.] (1987), 37–55.

ETCSL: Oxford Electronic Text Corpus of Sumerian Literature: http://www-etcsl.orient.ox.ac.uk/catalogue/ (sub 6); (with many valuable observations on Sumerian proverbs by Jon Taylor, 2003).

N. Veldhuis: *Elementary Education at Nippur: The Lists of Trees and Wooden Objects* (Ph.D. diss., Groningen, 1997).

N. Veldhuis: "Sumerian Proverbs in Their Curricular Context," JAOS 120 (2000) 383–399.

M. Vogelzang and H. Vanstiphout (eds.): *Mesopotamian Poetic Language: Sumerian and Akkadian* (Groningen: Styx, 1996); (with many useful references pertaining to the discussion of oral/aural versus "written" literature).

6.1 Sumerian Proverbs in the Cornell University Library (Kroch-04)

This is a well-preserved, horizontally oblong, one-column tablet. The obverse is inscribed with seven entries duplicating SP 1.113 – 1.118 (l. 3 seems to be an extra line following SP 1.114, here numbered 114a). The reverse is not fully inscribed, but contains SP 1.118f – SP 1.119. No. 8 (rev.) seems to contain the continuation of SP 1.118. The variants are quoted below from Alster, *Proverbs* I, 26ff. The writing is clear with no exceptional regional characteristics; cf., however, the comments on lines 1 (ù) and 3 (TÚG) below. The provenience is unknown, but the tablet resembles proverb tablets from Ur, rather than those from Nippur.

This tablet adds considerably to the reconstruction of SP 1.113–1.119.

== indicates a double separating line on the original tablet.

Photographs on pls. 50–51.

1 = SP 1.113

Kroch-04:1 BU-ud-bar ma-ad ù(! written ŠI-KU)-sù-a

==

SP 1.113:
A: BU-ud ma-ad ù-sù-ud
B: BU-ud-bar ma(written as KU) [...]

(1 = SP 1.113) An unclean(?) ...

2 = SP 1.114

Kroch-04:2 BU-ud-bar ḫul-dím-ma

SP 1.114:
A: BU-ud-bar ḫul-dím-m[a] ˹x˺
B: BU-ud-bar ˹ḫul˺-[dím-ma]
AAA: ˹BU˺-u[d-bar...] (+ indt'd line broken)

(2 = SP 1.114) is a badly shapen unclean ... .

3 = *SP 1.114a

Kroch-04:3 TÚG-ní-ba šu è

==

(3 = SP 1.114a) Stretching a hand out toward one's own behind(?),

4 = SP 1.115

Kroch-04:4 bìd-da mí dug$_4$-dug$_4$

==

SP 1.115:
A: ˹bìd-da˺ ˹mí˺ [x] ˹x˺ [...]
B: bìd(?)-da(?) ˹x˺ dug$_4$-[...]
AAA: bìd-da ˹mí˺ [...]

(4 = SP 1.115) (means) caressing the anus.

5 = SP 1.116

Kroch-04:5 ^{ŋiš}buŋin-gi$_7$ níŋ-sila$_{11}$-ŋá nu-luḫ-ḫa

==

SP 1.116
B: ^{ŋiš}buŋin níŋ-si[la$_{11}$-ŋ]á nu-luḫ-ḫ[a]
AAA: ^{ŋiš}buŋin níŋ-[...]

(5 = SP 1.116) A «noble» kneading trough not kept clean,

6 = SP 1.117

Kroch-04:6 ŋiš-<buŋin>-kù níŋ šáḫ gu$_7$-gu$_7$ nu-luḫ-⸢ḫa⸣

═

SP 1.117

B: ŋiš buŋin šáḫ ⸢gu$_7$-gu$_7$⸣

AAA: ŋiš-kù(?) ⸢x⸣ [...]

(6 = SP 1.117) (is like) a pure <kneading> trough from which pigs eat, not kept clean.

7 = SP 1.118

Kroch-04:7 e-DÚR gu$_7$-a

SP 1.118: B: ⸢e⸣-DÚR ⸢gu$_7$-a⸣

(7–8 = SP 1.118) Feeding an «I(?) am settled» (means) feeding a «let me stay with you»(?).

8 = SP 1.118f

Kroch-04:8 (rev.) ga-ra-dúr gu$_7$-a

SP 1.118f:

B cont.: ga-ra-D[ÚR ...]

9 = SP 1.119 (0)

Kroch-04:9 dam-tag$_4$ šu è-ni-íb

SP 1.119(0): B: ⸢e⸣-DÚR šu è-ni-ib

(9 = SP 1.119.0) Reach out for «a divorce»,

10 = SP.119

Kroch-04:10 ga-ra-DÚR šu è-ni-íb

═

SP 1.119:

B cont.: d[am-tag$_4$(?) šu è-ni-ib]

No more inscribed on rev. of Kroch-04.

(10 = SP 1.119) (means:) reach out for «a let me stay with you».

(var. SP 1.119:) Reach out for an «I am settled» (means:) reach out for «a divorce»).

Comments on Individual Lines

Line 1 = SP 1.113: Lit. "A long BU-ud-bar ma-ad."

A photograph of A (obv. iv end) is available on pl. 1 in Gordon, SP, pointing to the reading given above; S.N. Kramer's copy, ibid., pl. 28, seems to point to the same reading. B: Photo in Gordon, SP pl. 3; copy, ibid., pl. 30, iv, 2nd Sec 5.

Although the new text clearly writes ŠI-KU as two separate signs, the duplicates suggest that this is a writing for ù, with extra spacing added to fill in the line.

The meaning of BU-ud-bar as "unclean person," i.e., *ḫaršum*, masc. of *ḫarištum*, has been suggested by Veldhuis, who will deal with the term in a forthcoming study. Cf. below.

Gordon, SP, p. 105, (= Gordon No. 116), read BU-ud-bar ma-ad ù-sù-ud, and translated "A planter(?) ..." as a guess based on Akk. *ḫaršum*, referring to §L 371:98, i.e., *Nabnītu* 20, 222 (MSL 16, 183): LÚ BU-ud-bar = *ḫaršum*. This is interpreted by AHw 328 as *ḫarāšu* II, "binden" (also said of a boat); CAD s.v. *ḫaršu* A interprets it as "tied up" (said of a boat), or possibly "lame." *Nabnītu* rather places this in the context of ... food, flour, bread? (cf., e.g., the preceding line, 221: ninda-ḫar-šum = MIN (*ḫa-ri-iš-tum*) *šá ḫar-šum*).

ma-ad is hardly to be connected with Ḫḫ vi 82 (MSL 6,58) ŋiš-ma-lamadla(BU) = *ma-ak-ku-u*. (84 has ŋiš-ga-zi-in-bugazinbu(BU) = *ga-ši-šú*; cf. also 86: ŋiš-MIN(ma-ad-la) madla(BU) = *ma-a*ʾ*-du-u*). A kind of food tied together on a string might fit.

ù-sù-a, var. ù-sù-ud: undoubtedly a nominalized verbal form with prefix ù, "after it has been made long."

Line 2 = SP 1.114: Lit., "A badly shapen BU-udbar."

Line 3: The first sign is here TÚG, but line 4 has KU = bìd. The same sign might be expected in both lines, however, so TÚG may simply be a minor error for KU or DÚR, meaning "backside" or similar, from a place or period when the distinction between the two signs was no longer upheld. Alternatively TÚG may be taken quite literally as "clothes." Apparently this is an extra line in Kroch-04, but since it seems indispensable for the meaning, it is here tentatively added as SP 1.118f to SP 1, which, however, is very imperfectly preserved at this point.

In all probability lines 3–4 are related to SP 9 Sec. D 3 (3): is-ḫáb ki-bìd-da šu-ša-an-ša-ša-da šu-ni bìd-da ba-ni-in-g̃íd = SP 19 Sec. E 3 = UET 6/3 464; cf. Alster, *Proverbs* I, 183, "A fool who was «overwhelmed» at his behind stuck his hand into his behind." Cf. also SP 13.29 (poorly preserved). If it is valid to connect these sayings with ours, they show that šu–è, here, as well as in lines 10–11, does not means something like "to greet" = *karābu*, but, rather, should be taken literally as "stretching a hand out to reach something with it," like the variant šu – ša-an-ša-ša(-da), or ka – ditto, which is a pseudo-loanword from Akkadian *kašāšu*; cf. the literature cited in Alster, *Proverbs* II, 420. The ETCSL, basically accepting Alster's interpretation, translates "A fool who was overwhelmed ...... by his backside stuck his hand up his backside."

Line 4 = SP 1.115: "Caressing (its/one's own) anus": The non-personal construction bìd-ní-ba might be used of the personal class if taken as a collective plural, similar to the English "one's own."

Line 5 = SP 1.116: "A noble kneading trough not made clean." The additional ÉŠ following ^{ŋiš}buŋin is probably = gi$_7$(-r). Here the meaning is somewhat like "noble," parallel to ŋiš-kù in the following line, and not something like "native." Steinkeller, "Early Political Development in Mesopotamia and the Origins of the Sargonic Empire," in: M. Liverani (ed.): *Akkad*, 110–111, n. 9, suggests the meaning "native" for gi$_7$(-r). Note that the other duplicates omit the sign.

Line 6 = SP 1.117: "A pure vessel from which pigs eat, not made clean." SP 1.117: "A trough from which pigs eat."

Note the variant *ad sensu*, B: ^{ŋiš}buŋin, "a though," versus ŋiš-kù, "a pure vessel," in A, apparently also reflected in AAA. The most likely reading is, however, simply to assume that <buŋin> has been omitted by mistake. Only the new text has the second part of the line.

Line 7–8 = SP 1.118: "Feeding an «I am settled» (means:) feeding a «let me stay with you»." e-DÚR(KU) seems to be a frozen verbal form, with e-DÚR corresponding to ga-ra-DÚR as the 1st and the 2nd person respectively. Since the new text has dam-tag$_4$, relating to a divorce, one may suggest that ga-ra-DÚR is the opposite, lit., a "let me stay with you," i.e., a person who wants to enter or remain in marriage. The verbal forms are very ambiguous, however, (How to read DÚR? tuš? Which person is involved? etc.) so any interpretation remains highly tentative. Further, the exact value of the dative -ra is uncertain here. Cf. perhaps *Instr. Šuruppak* 123: ga-ba-ra-gu$_7$, etc.

Lines 9–10 = SP 1.119: "Reach out for «a divorce», reach out for a «let me stay with you»" does not immediately seem to make much sense. The two parts of the line seem to be inverted compared to SP 1.119(0)–119, which seems to mean: "reach out for an «I am settled» (means:) reach out for «a divorce»." B, however, has e-DÚR instead of ga-ra-DÚR in the first part of the line. This might be a reminder that by provoking a divorce, one should bear in mind that it entails losing someone who is able to maintain a household.

6.2 Sumerian Proverbs in the Cornell University Library (Kroch-05)

This is a well-preserved one-column tablet with twelve inscribed entries, mostly double, on the obverse, approximately corresponding to: 1 = SP 2.2 (1–2); 2 = SP 2.67?; 3 = SP 2.19; 4 = SP 2.2; 5 = UET 6/2 368, no. 2; 6 = similar to UET 6/2 295; 7 = SP 2.54 (no. 1–2); 8 = SP 2.37; 9 = SP 2.38; 10 = SP 2.39; 11 = SP 2.50 (inverted line order); 12 = SP 2.53; 13 = one double line on the lower edge = unidentified; 14–23: rev. plus right edge has nine entries of uneven length (2 to 6 lines) (for the left edge i–iii, see below), corresponding to: 14 = unidentified; 15 = quotation from *Gilgameš and Huwawa* 107–110; 16 = excerpt from *The Fowler and His Wife*; 17 = SP 3.41; 18 = SP 1.125; 19 = SP 1.126 (first line plus two unidentified lines); 20 = SP 2.29 (different line order); 21 = unidentified, but cf. the beginning of UET 6/337; 22 = unidentified; 23 (one line on lower edge) = unidentified; 24 (left edge i) = unidentified; 25 (left edge ii (1–2) = unidentified; 26 (left edge ii (3) = SP 3.66 (first line): 27 (left edge iii) = SP 3.67. Since there are no separating lines on the edges, the division proposed here is only tentative.

The physical appearance of the tablet, as well as the relatively high number of parallels among the small proverb tablets from Ur, suggests that the tablet comes from Ur. Some phonetic writings suggest relatively poor understanding on the part of the scribe; cf., e.g., line 5: ga-ba = gaba; u_4-u_4-da = gu_4-gu_4-ud-da, etc. In line 12: diri-a = diri-ga shows that his knowledge of standard orthographic conventions was far from perfect. Line 16:3: má-za for má-zu throws doubts on his grammatical competence. Similarly line 9: šu-a for šu-ni, probably through *šu-a-ni; cf. the comments below.

Photographs on pls. 51–57.

1 1 ki gul-la-ba ki ḫé-[en-gul]
2 ki nu-gul-la-ba gú-ŋìr ḫ[é-en-ŋál]

= SP 2.2 (1–2)

(1 = SP 2.2:1–2) At the places where destruction has been caused, let a(ny) place be destroyed; at the places where destruction has not been caused, let [there be (total) submission].

2 1 x(like ki)-a-a x(like IM) a-ab-A-⌜x⌝[...]
2 ŋeštin du-a ^{ŋiš}TÙN a ab àm ([nothing missing?])

Cf. SP 2.67 — ka_5-a-a a-ab-ba-šè ŋìš-a-ni ù-bí-in-sur
a-ab-ba TÙN-bi kàš-$ŋu_{10}$-um-e-še

(2, not clearly identified) (no translation).

3 1 úku(?) niŋ šu-ti-a ur_5 ⌜ur_5(?)⌝

= SP 2.19 — úku níŋ šu-ti-a zú an-ur_5

(3 = SP 2.19) A poor man chews (whatever) bread(?) he receives.

4 1 nam-tar-$ŋu_{10}$ ga-àm-dug_4 in-àm
2 pa ga-àm-è KI.SAG.DU-àm

= SP 2.2 — pa ga-àm-è sulummar-àm (sulummar = KI.TÙN.DU or sim.)

(4 = SP 2.2) Let me tell you about my destiny; it is dishonorable; let me reveal it to you; it is a disgrace;

5 1 díb-díb-ba-ta u$_4$ ba-an-da-zal
2 u$_4$-u$_4$-da ^{d}utu ba-an-da-an-ŠÌR
3 šul-e ga-ba diri-ga u$_4$-sumun-na ba-an-šú

===

Cf. UET 6/2 368 (no. 2):
dib-dib-ba-da u$_4$ ba-da-zal
gu$_4$-gu$_4$-ud-da ^{d}utu ba-an-da-ŠÌR (gloss: *it-ta-am-ra-at nam(?)-ri*)

———

šul-e gaba diri-ga (gloss: *ša lu-še-te-er-mi*)
iti$_6$ ba-an-da-an-šúm

(5, cf. UET 6/2 368) For him who walks, the day lasts; For him who dances(?), the sun shines; for the hero whose strength is enormous, the day settles late (lit. as an old day).

(var. UET 6/2 368 moonlight is given).

6 kaš$_4$ ga-an-dug$_4$-ga ŋìri ga-kaš$_4$-kaš$_4$
šul diŋir tuku-da a-ba mu-un-dè-sá-en

===

Cf. UET 6/2 295:
ḫu-mu-un-kaš$_4$-e ḫu-mu-un-sar-re
ḫu-mu-un-ŋìr ì-íl-í[l]
bí-in-dug$_4$-ga lú diŋir in-tuku-àm
Cf also SP 19 Sec G 7:
… ⌜a⌝-ba-a [m]u-da-ab-sá-e

(6, cf. UET 6/2 295) (He who says) «Let me run, let me hurry»: who compares with him (in being a) youth having success?

7 1 dub-sar pe-e-lá lú-KA×LI-KA×LI-kam
2 nar pe-el-lá lú gi-di-da-kam

===

= SP 2.54 (1) dub-sar pe-el-lá lú-KA×LI-KA×LI-a-kam
(2) nar pe-el-lá lú gi-di-da-kam, etc.

(7 = SP 2.54) (1) A disgraced scribe becomes an incantation priest;

(2) a disgraced singer becomes flutist.

8 dub-sar-me-en mu ní-za nu-e-zu
igi ní-za sìg-ga
= SP 2.37 [du]b-sar-me-en mu ní-za
igi ní-za sìg-ga

(8 = SP 2.37) You are a scribe and you don't even know your own name; shame on you!

9 dub-sar-e mu diš-àm ḫé-en-zu
šu-a ḫé-en-sa$_6$-sa$_6$
= SP 2.38 [dub-s]ar-re mu diš-àm ḫé-en-zu(?)
[šu-n]i ḫé-sa$_6$-sa$_6$ e-ne-àm dub-sar-ra

(9 = SP 2.38?) If a scribe knows only a single line, but his(!) hand is very good (, he is indeed a scribe).

10 nar-e èn-⌜du⌝ diš-àm ḫé-en-zu
ad-DU-ba-àm ḫé-en-sa$_6$

===

= SP 2.39 nar-re èn-du diš-àm ḫé-en-zu ad-ša$_4$-àm
ḫé-en-sa$_6$ e-ne-àm nar-ra-àm

(10 = SP 2.39) If a singer knows only a single song, but his tremolo is good (, he is indeed a singer).

11 dub-sar im-ma šid-e ba-lá
dub-sar šid-e im-e ba-lá
= SP 2.50 dub-sar ŠID-ma im-ma ba-an-lá
dub-sar im-ma šid-e ba-an-lá

(11 = SP 2.50) A scribe (who is master) of clay is deficient in numbers. A scribe (who is master) of counting is deficient on clay.

12 dub-sar-tur níŋ šà-gal-la-ni-šè
a-diri-diri-a
nam-dub-sar-ra ŋéštu nu-ŋá-ŋá

=

= SP 2.53 dub-sar-tur níŋ šà-gal-la-ni-šè bí-íb-diri-diri-⸢ge⸣
nam-dub-sar-ra-šè ŋéštu nu-un-ši-ŋá-ŋá

(12 = SP 2.53) A young scribe who is too much concerned with food supply will not pay attention to scribal art.

Lower edge

13 gud-e si mu-ub-du$_{7}$ ⸢dùr⸣(ANŠE.NINTA)(or: šagub; written ⸢GÌR⸣.UŠ) ŋìri mu-ub-du$_{7}$

=

(Apparently no parallels?)

(13) An ox butts with (its) horns, but a male donkey butts with (its) feet.

Reverse

14 1 … (5 signs nearly illegible)
ŋìr tu ki
2 ŠID TU?-ba ba-ra gi íl

=

(Not yet identified)

(14 = *unidentified, no translation attempted*)

15 1 lú min-ne nu-úš-e
2 má-ta-lá nu-su-su
3 é gi-sig-ga izi nu-ub-te-en-te

=

Quotation from *Gilgameš and Huwawa* 107–110.

(15) Two men together will not perish; a raft tied together will not sink; fire in a reed house cannot be extinguished.

16 1 ambar-tur-ra a mu-da-an-laḫ
2 si-si-ig ì-si-si-ig
3 má-za peš$_{10}$ mu-tag-tag-tag
4 mušen-dù sa-zu na-an-gíd-e mušen ḫé-zi-zi
5 e-sig$_{17}$(GI)-ga^{mušen} sa bí-ná
6 buru$_{4}^{\text{mušen}}$-e sa bí-gíd

=

Quotation from *The Fowler and His Wife* (SP 21 Sec A 5ff.) with many variants and abbreviations: cf. the comments below.

(16:1) The water dried up from the small swamp;

(2) a whirlwind blew,

(3) so that your boat touched the bank.

(4) Fowler: Should you not should stretch your net?; let a bird rise into it!

(5) The net was "laid" upon an *esig*-bird,

(6) (but) a raven stretched the net! (*i.e.*, lifted it so that the *esig*-bird could escape?)

17 1 é-ta è-a sila-ta ku$_{4}$-ra
2 gi$_{4}$-in-⸢e⸣ ka-ša-an-na-na
3 gisbun ⸢x(like ra?)⸣-ma(?) bí-in-tuš

=

= SP 3.41 é-ta è sila-ta ku$_{4}$-ra gi$_{4}$-in-e
ga-ša-an-an-na-ni gisbun-ma bí-in-tuš

(17 = SP 3.41) Upon leaving the house and entering from the street,

(2) the slave girl sat down at a banquet for(?) the lady of heaven.

18 1 dam-ŋu$_{10}$ ma-dub-e dumu-ŋu$_{10}$ ma-áŋ-e
2 mu-ud-na-ŋu$_{10}$ ku$_{6}$-ta x ⸢ŋìr⸣.⸢pad⸣.[du] ⸢x⸣ ⸢x⸣
3 ma-ni-ib-ri-ri-ge
(*NB no double line here*)
= SP 1.125' dam-ŋu$_{10}$ ma-dub-bé
dumu-ŋu$_{10}$ ma-an-ág-e
[m]u-ud-na-ŋu$_{10}$ ku$_{6}$-ta ŋìr-pad-du [ḫé]-bí-ib-ri-ri-ge

(18 = SP 1.125) My husband piles up for me; my child metes out for me;

(18:2–3) my husband picks the bones from the fish for me.

19 1 ú dam-gim zé-ba edin-e nu-un-mú
2 ú dam-ŋu$_{10}$ nam-ninta(?)-zu(?) íl si a
3 munus zé dù mu x x ⸢nam⸣ BU mu ak x x

1 = SP 1.126 ú dam-gim zé-ba edin-na nu-un-mú
2 = ? (not identified)
3 = ? (not identified)

(19:1) A plant sweet like a husband does not grow in the steppe;

(19:2) a plant ...

(19:3) a woman...

20 níŋ-ú-gu-dé-a-ni nu-⸢x⸣-⸢x⸣-NE
túg-bir$_{7}$(?)-bir$_{7}$-ra-ni nu-kala-ge-dè
úku-e a-na-⸢A⸣ i-im-tur

3 = SP 2.29:4 níŋ-ú-gu-dé-a-ni nu-mu-un-kiŋ-kiŋ
2 = SP 2.29:3 túg-bir$_{7}$-ra-ni nu-kala-ge-dam
3 = SP 2.29:1 úku a-na-àm al-tur

(20:1) Nobody searches for what he has lost;

(20:2) his ripped clothes are not mended;

(20:3) how lowly is the poor man!

21 1 a-GIŠ(with U; different from UŠ below) ki-GUB-ŋu$_{10}$ nu-zu
2 má-gim šà ŋìš-ŋu$_{10}$ nu-zu
3 eri.ki-ŋu$_{10}$-uš ḫé-a ŋá-e en la x x(... edge nearly illegible)

Cf. UET 6/337
1 [(x) x]-e tur-tur-e lú nu-su-uš
2 [x] ⸢x⸣(perhaps [da]m)-tur-e ŋìš-ŋu$_{10}$ nu-su-uš
3 [x]-ŋu$_{10}$ saŋ-ŋá ^{d}dag-gìr
(8 more entries, not related)

(21:1) A ... does not know my ...;

(21:2) ... like a boat ... does not know my penis.

(21:3) (no translation suggested)

22 ere.ki (traces of 5 signs) ri
ŋìri (traces)

Lower edge
23 ⸢ra⸣(?)-ke$_{4}$ ⸢x⸣ [½ line]

(22 and 23) (too poorly preserved for translation)

Left edge: three columns of 2+3+2 lines (to be read from the upper left corner of the right edge, with the reverse of the tablet facing upward; probably simply meant as the continuation of the reverse)

i
24 1 ⸢lú⸣-ŋu$_{10}$ ŋiš-gíd-da nu-mu-un-gub
2 ⸢x(like [K]A)⸣-ak-da mu-un-gub
(unidentified)

(24) My man does not stand to the "long wood," (but he) stands to doings(?).

ii

25	1	ere-gu-la kúr-ra šu-dug$_4$-ga	*(25:1)* The big city …
	2	tur-ra SAL nu-DI-⌜DI(?)⌝	*(25:2)* A small …
26	3	dam-gàr-ra lagab ^{na4}za-gìn-na	*(26)* A merchant (…) lapis lazuli stones in blocks.

25: 1–2 unidentified
26: 3 = SP 3.66
nam-dam-gàr-ra ^{na4}lagab-za-gìn-na / na$_4$ lugal-bi-ir a-d[a …]

iii

27	1	si-ga ba-<ra>-gíd-e	*(27)* One can<not> drag out the weak; one cannot hold back the strong.
	2	kala-ga ba-ra-ab-è	

27: 1–2 = SP 3.67
si-ga ba-ra-gíd-dè kala-ga ba-ra-ab-gub

Comments on Individual Lines

1 *(SP 2.2, ll. 1–2):* Alster, *Proverbs* I, 44–45, translates, *(1)* "In those places which have been destroyed, let (more) places be destroyed. *(2)* In those places which have not been destroyed, let a breach be made there." Our lines 1–2 contain only the initial lines of the sequence SP 2.2, the full text of which has ten lines. Cf. a similar feature in no. 7 below, etc. Veldhuis, 2000, 386, describes SP 2.2 as an exercise in "grammatical opposition." In no way do I want to contest this opinion, but I would nevertheless emphasize that the kernel of the full sequence seems to rest on genuine proverbial expressions, similar to *Instr. Šuruppak* 187–188, etc.

2: Not identified with certainty, but perhaps a misunderstood version of SP 2.67. Cf. the comments in Alster, *Proverbs* II, 367.

3 *(SP 2.19):* The sign read ur$_5$ is written over a weak erasure, like the rest of š[è or similar. The sign following ur$_5$ looks like another ⌜ur$_5$⌝, apparently as a variant of zú an-ur$_5$. The following traces belong to the signs from the reverse running into the corresponding line on the obverse. For the possible readings and meanings of KA-ḪAR, cf. Civil, 1984, 295–296, and *Chap. 1.4:* comm. to *Instr. Šuruppak* 49, which provides the equation: zú-ur$_5$ = *šelû*, "to neglect"; *Instr. Šuruppak* 136: gù–mur = *qardu*, "one who shouts, is noisy"; another meaning seems to be "to tear or grind with the teeth"; cf. *Chap. 5.2: Old Man 32*: zú-ŋu$_{10}$ níŋ-kala-ga ì-ur$_5$-ra níŋ-kala-ge nu-ur$_5$-re. The latter reference suggests a meaning like "the poor man chews whatever bread he receives" for SP 2.19, indicating that he has to be satisfied with it although it is hard for him to chew. SP 2.19 was understood somewhat differently by Gordon, SP, p. 189, who translates "A poor man worries about what he has borrowed," reading KA – ḪAR as *appam quddudum*, "to frown," or, alternatively, *gunnuṣum*, "to rub the nose." Th. Jacobsen, ibid., 478, translates "The beggar, who borrows bread, is sniffed at (contemptuously)." Cf. also SP 3.69: in-dúb-dúb-bu-ra in mu-na-an-ŋar; kiri$_4$-ur$_5$-e kiri$_4$ mu-na-an-ur$_5$-r[e], "He who insults is insulted; he who sneers is sneered at."

4 *(SP 2.2):* sulummar is here written KI.SAG.DU, apparently mistaking SAG for TÙN; cf. SP 2.2, which has KI.TÙN.DU.

in-àm, lit., "it is chaff," probably implies something like "is dishonorable"; but cf. *Chap. 2.3: Couns. Wisdom* 86 and 177: eŋir-bi-ta in-àm, where the translation "afterward it is (only) a trifle(?)" is suggested.

5: *cf. UET 6/2 368 (?):* In line 2 our text has u$_4$-

u$_4$-da, a remarkable phonetic writing for UET 6/2 368 (Alster, *Proverbs* I, 324): gu$_4$-gu$_4$-ud-da; the gloss *it-ta-am-ra-at nam*(?)*-ri* to ŠÌR indicates that the verb *namāru* is intended, and this is corroborated by line 3, where UET 6/2 368 has iti$_6$, cf. below.

In line 3, our text has ga-ba diri-ga, phonetic for UET 6/2 368: gaba diri-ga. Alster, 1997, 324, translates UET 6/2 368 "For him who walks, the day lasts. For him who dances, the sun ... For the hero whose strength is enormous, moonlight is given," commenting, p. 475: "may be extolling the virtues of an active life, which will always be blessed with long days, sunlight, and even moonlight." For line 3, our text has the variant u$_4$-sumun-na ba-an-šú(?), which apparently means "settles late," lit., "(as) an old day."

6: This is similar, but not identical, to UET 6/295. For the expression šul diŋir tuku(-da), cf. *Chap. 5.2: Old Man* 27: ⸢šul⸣(?) diŋir-ŋu$_{10}$ usu-ŋu$_{10}$ ^{d}lama-ŋu$_{10}$, lit., "(I am) a young man whose god (= success) (has left him)."

7: This is only the first two lines of SP 2.54, which in its full form has seven entries. Quotation of the first lines may well have sufficed to call the entire sequence to mind. Cf. no. 1 above, etc.

***9** (SP 2.38):* SP 2.38 is here quoted in a truncated form: the final e-ne-àm dub-sar-ra, "he is indeed a scribe," has been omitted. šu-a seems to be a mistake for *šu-a-<ni>, although standard writing would have had only *šu-ni.

10: Truncated form of SP 2.39. Note the variant ad-DU-ba-àm, which does not confirm the reading ad-šà$_4$-àm in SP 2.39, but apparently the scribe thought of *ad-gub-ba-àm by mistake. For ad-ša$_4$, cf. the comments in Alster, *Proverbs* II, 363, referring to Krispijn, *Akkadica* 70 (1990) 15, etc.

11: The lines are reversed in relation to SP 2.53.

13: Probably ANŠE.NINTA(.ùr) = dùr, is meant, and hardly šagub (the precise reading is unknown), here written GÌR.UŠ = *šakanakku*. To the best of my knowledge this saying has not been found elsewhere.

14: The first line seems to read: EN.TI^{ki} x x, but very uncertain.

15: This is a quotation from *Gilgameš und Huwawa*, lines 107–110: ŋar-ra en-ki-du$_{10}$ lú min-e nu-úš-e; ^{ŋiš}má-da-lá nu-su-su; túg 3 tab-ba lú nu-kud-dè; bàd-da a lú nu-šú-šú; é gi-sig-ga izi nu-te-en-te-en; "Stop, Enkidu, two men together will not perish! A raft bound together does not sink! No one can cut through a three-ply cloth! Water cannot wash someone away from a wall! Fire in a reed house cannot be extinguished!" cf. Edzard, "Gilgameš und Huwawa A, II. Teil," ZA 81 (1991) 160–233. Our text omits line 109. ^{ŋiš}má-da-lá, for which our text offers the variant má-ta-lá, has been explained by Civil, *Wilcke FS*, 81–82, as a raft.

16: Cf. p. 371, *Chap. 4.5: Short Stories ... Involving Humans*, where the complete text of *The Fowler and His Wife* is cited; all variants are cited in Alster, *Proverbs* I, 253–254, under SP 21 Sec. A 5, but cf. the comments under *Chap. 4.5*: the sequences of SP 21 can be improved in view of the observations by Veldhuis, 2000, 394: Sec. A should really be Sec. C (as shown on the ETCSL-website). See further *Chap. 6: Introduction*, where an attempt is made to explain the nature of the excerpt. Note the following variant: line 3, má-za for má-zu, obviously mistaken.

Line 16:4: tag-tag-tag for tag-tag-ge is a rare example of triple reduplication; cf. Edzard: *Sum. Grammar*, 81, and the literature cited there. sa-zu na-an-gíd-e, variant of sa ù-bí-in-ná ù-buru$_4$^{mušen}-e sa ù-bí-gíd (l. 6 of *Fowler*) (for more variants see the edition in *Chap. 4.5*), "after you had 'laid' (= cast) the net upon an *esig*-bird, after you had stretched the net upon a raven." Also in *16:4*, the negative na-an-gíd-e, "don't stretch your net," seems to reveal some deficiency in understanding the story, which requires a positive form, but it is, in fact, possible to understand it ironically as it stands, "should you not stretch?" etc. The reading gíd instead of bu is retained here, since a variant bir$_7$ that could suggest bu does not apply, although this has been proposed; cf. the comments on line 16:6 below.

Line 16:5: e-sig$_{17}$(GI)-ga^{mušen}, var. of e-sig/sig$_{17}$^{mušen}(-Ø/e); our text marking the bird in the locative, as well as the locative-terminative variants, suggests that ná is here used as a technical term of a fowler casting a net upon a bird = **šētam nadû*; cf. Alster, 1992, 189–190, and the literature cited there. This is corroborated by *Chap. 4.3: The Goose and the Raven* 6: sa-zu ma-ná-ma, "A net intended for you was thrown upon me."

For the reading of buru$_4$, cf. Alster 1992, 188, n. 1, pointing to the variant in source E: ŠIR.búru^{mušen}, suggesting $buru_x$(ŠIR)$^{\text{búru mušen}}$. The sign is here the "square" form of the ŠIR-sign, whose outer shape resembles na; it has a broken right vertical. For the signs $buru_4$ and $buru_5$, see Veldhuis, 2000, with references to Civil, 1994, correcting the PSD, etc. Cf. also the discussion of the meaning of uga^{mušen} in the introduction to the fable of the *The Goose and the Raven* (*Chap. 4.3*).

Line 16:6: Note that *The Goose and the Raven* 8, in similar context, but not as a direct variant of BU, has: [a]-na-àm igi-àm sa nu-bir_7-re-⌜x⌝, "Why don't you rip the net in front of you into pieces?"; cf. Alster, 1992, 190 and the references cited there; bir_7 is not directly a variant of bu, unlike the impression given by PSD B, 160.

17: Our text has two signs following KI.KAŠ. GAR = ŋisbun/m. Of these, the second may be -ma, indicating the reading gisbum-ma, but the first looks like perhaps -ra, which might be a misunderstood duplication of the final consonant in GAR, not recognizing the reading gisbuN, or some other unexplained gloss. The ETCSL translates SP 3.41: "When the lady left the house and the slave girl entered from the street, away from her lady the slave girl sat at her own banquet," which basically agrees with Alster, *Proverbs* I, 88. None of these translations can explain the variant occurring in our text: ka-ša-an-na-na, which seems to indicate that an *emesal* form of */nin-an-ak/ > *ga-ša-an-an-na(-k), is intended; yet, since this would have yielded *-ka-ni with the possessive suffix, it seems that some sort of corruption is involved. Of the two parallels, SP 19 Sec. D 9 has ŋéme nin-a-ni ŋisbuN-ma-ni and SP 28.25 ŋéme nin-a-ni-ta ŋisbun-n[i ...]. It is the latter variant that suggests "away from"; cf. the comments in Alster, *Proverbs* II, 381. As quoted on the Cornell University tablet, the point seems to rest on the contrast between the trivial nature of the slave girl's doings and the august deity for whom the banquet is served, but there is no uniform way to reconcile all the duplicates.

18 = *SP 1.125:* For all parallel texts, see Alster, *Proverbs* I, 27, under SP 1.125. Our text has in line 3 ma-ni-ib-ri-ri-ge, which corresponds to SP 3.112.

19 = *SP 1.126:* The first line corresponds nicely to the first line of SP 1.126, but the following two lines have some variants that I cannot explain.

20 = *SP 2.29:* Here the first line of the sequence of four lines is placed as the last of a sequence of three, which results in a considerable weakening of the structure. The second line of SP 2.29 does not figure here. If correctly read, the verb in the third line, bir_7-bir_7 is reduplicated, whereas SP 2.29 has the unreduplicated verb. Note also a-na-⌜A⌝, for a-na-àm.

21: The first two lines seem related to UET 6/2 337 (Alster, *Proverbs* II, 321), but I am at a loss to explain them further. I can offer nothing as to the interpretation of UET 6/2 337, but note that if the parallel suggested here is valid, it shows that the inclusion of the tablet among the proverbs from Ur was justified, although Veldhuis, 2000, 394, considered "the inclusion ... in the corpus questionable." In line 2 má-gim, "like a boat," is an obvious sexual metaphor.

22–24: For ŋiš-gíd-da, cf. *Father and Son* 113, Sjöberg, JCS 25 (1973) 117 with comments p. 128, referring to earlier suggestions by Kramer ("counsels, wisdom") and I. Kaneva ("profession"). This is likely to denote a long rod or whip used for the instruction of young pupils, and then used to denote "wisdom" itself. There is no lexical attestation of such a meaning, however. Perhaps DU is here gub, "my man does not stand to 'instruction', but he stands to doings," or similar. This would then be similar to "he who will not hear must be made to feel."

25: For ere-gu-la, the "very big city," if correctly read, one may compare *Instr. Šuruppak* 181: úru tur-re lugal-bi-ir amar ši-in-ga-an-ù-tu, contrasting 182: úru maḫ-e é-dù-a ši-ḫur-re, "A small town creates calves for its master; (but) a huge city designs house buildings." The second line might then have had <ere> tur-ra, "the small city," but note that tur is more likely to correspond to maḫ than to gu-la, which is elsewhere used of a person, cf. *Instr. Šuruppak* 261: lú-gu-la. Cf. also *Instr. Šuruppak* 271: é ere-bar-ra-ke_4 ere šà-ga ši-dù-dù-e.

šu – dug_4, approximately meaning "to touch with hand" or similar, is also attested in SP 2.64: ka_5-a-a a-númun še šu bí-in-dug_4; cf. the comments in Alster, *Proverbs* II, 366–367; SP 3–170 (2): ugu ⌜túg⌝-ga gal_4-la šu-dug_4-ga, "touching the vulva on top of the clothes"; SP 4.52; SP 17 Sec. B 4 (1): úku-re dumu-na tibir-ra diš-àm šu nu-um-ma-ni-dug$_4$-g[e], cf. SP 2.23, "the poor man does not strike his son a single blow." Cf. also *Níŋ-nam* D 14 (*Chap. 4.2*).

I cannot suggest anything constructive as to the meaning of 25 (2): SAL nu-DI-DI. SAL may well be munus.

26: This is the first line of SP 3.66, the second part of which is poorly preserved. Regrettably, it cannot be restored from our text. It is, of course, easy to understand it as something like "a merchant (carries) lapis lazuli stones in blocks," but the duplicates do not really support this. Note that our text has dam-gàr instead of nam-dam-gàr, "merchantship"; cf. the comments in Alster, *Proverbs* II, 384.

27: This is SP 3.67.

Conclusion

Truncated and abbreviated quotations of proverbs that occur in fuller versions in the "standard proverb collections" are typical features of this tablet, which thus is a typical example of a "minor" proverb collection, like SP 4; SP 7; SP 9: SP 10; SP 12; SP 14; SP 15; SP 16; SP 17; SP 18; SP 19; SP 21; SP 22; SP 23; SP 24; SP 25; SP 26; SP 27; SP 28. Some of these are attested in Ur, Kish, Sippar, and Uruk, but may well be excerpts from collection that originated in Nippur. Cf. pp. 26–30, *Critical Wisdom*.

Addendum to Chap.6

More proverb tablets similar to those published here will be listed in a forthcoming study by B. Alster, "Some New Sumerian Proverbs," in E. Robson et al. (eds.), *Your Praise is Sweet. A Memorial Volume Presented to Jeremy Allen Black by Colleagues, Students, and Friends*, AOAT (forthcoming). These include from the forthcoming UET 6/3 volume no. 404, duplicating no. 26 above, as well as from Schøyen Collection, in particular MS 2108, duplicating no. 15 above, and MS 2605, duplicating no. 5 above, MS 2893, duplicating no. 17 above, etc.

Kroch-05 no. 5 is duplicated also in Schøyen MS 2625 no. 1, which among other variants substitutes ŋi$_6$ for u$_4$. This will be published in a forthcoming volume of the Sumerian proverbs in the series *Manuscripts in the Schøyen Collection*. For gu$_4$-ud, see also Civil, 1984, 92, who explains the Ebla entry gú-du-gú-du-wu-um as possibly a loanword from Sum. gu$_4$-ud-gu$_4$-ud, "one that is always jumping," i.e., a frog; cf. also Sjöberg, *Kienast FS*, 551–552, n. 39.

Addendum

Introduction

A study by Cl. Wilcke, "Konflikte und ihre Bewältigung in Elternhaus und Schule im Alten Orient," in: *Schau auf die Kleinen ... Das Kind in Religion, Kirche und Gesellschaft*, edited by Rüdiger Lux (Leipzig: Evangelische Verlagsanstallt, 2002), 1–31, came too late to be taken into account in this work. It translates some of the key texts described above as expressions of "critical wisdom," foremost *Schooldays* and *Father-and-Son*, and corroborates what is said there about critical wisdom in the Sumerian *edubba*-literature, showing that these question the validity of values traditionally taken for granted, in particular, obedience and punctuality in the school and the obedience of a son to his father.

Instructions of Šuruppak

Lines 40–41: I now consider the Akkadian translations of Akk$_2$ to be Middle Babylonian interpretations of the original Sumerian text, which presumably meant (line 40) "Don't sprinkle your hands with blood" and (line 41) "When you cut the bones, they will make you restore the ox, they will make you restore the sheep." This meaning fits the context well, warning against theft and receiving stolen goods, whereas the Akkadian translation, more connected with ritual practices, seems less appropriate in the context.

Line 204: I now consider the translations by Selz and Wilcke, quoted on p. 160, approximately correct, and now translate: "To have authority and to acquire richnesses are the faring (*Brustwehr*) of the aristocracy." I thus accept Wilcke's interpretation of nir-ŋál-e as an –ed verbal extention of nir-ŋál.

Indices

Unless otherwise stated references are to line numbers in the compositions listed below. Akkadian equivalents attested in *Instr. Šuruppak* sources Akk_1, Akk_2, and Akk_3 are given without parentheses. Equivalents damaged to such an extent that their reading relies solely on the Sumerian version are not included. Glosses are marked "glossed." Akkadian equivalents given in parentheses are meant as explanatory classifications not included in the texts cited. References to the commentaries (comm.) are only exceptionally given. The index neither includes terms discussed in the introductions to the individual compositions, nor in *Chap. 1.9: Comments on the Grammatical and Graphical Elements*, etc. The Early Dynastic sources are included when later parallels can be clearly identified. A separate index by G. Wilhelm of the Hurrian version of *Instr. Šuruppak* is provided below, pp. 419–420.

Abbreviations

Adulterer:	*The Adulterer*, see *Chap. 4.5.*
Ballade:	*The Ballade of Early Rulers*, see *Chap. 3.3a–c*, SS, Syr.-Mesop., and NA versions.
Corn. Univ. 2:	See *Chap. 6.2: Cornell Univ. Proverbs 2.*
CW:	*Counsels of Wisdom*, see *Chap. 2.3.*
Elephant Wren:	*The Elephant and the Wren*, see *Chap. 4.4.*
EnNam:	*Enlil and Namzitarra*, see *Chap. 3.5.*
Fables:	see *Chap. 4.4*, cited under their SP numbers.
Fowler:	*The Fowler and His Wife*, see *Chap. 4.5.*
Fox Merchant:	*Chap. 4.2.*
GEN:	*Gilgameš, Enkidu, and the Netherworld*, see *Chap. 3.6.*
Goose Raven:	*The Goose and the Raven*, see *Chap. 4.3.*
Hyena Dog:	*Chap. 4.2.*
IŠ:	*The Instructions of Šuruppak*, see *Chap. 1.3–1.6.*
IŠH:	*The Instructions of Šuruppak*, Hurrian version, see *Chap. 1.7.*
IU:	*The Instructions of Ur-Ninurta*, see *Chap. 2.2.*
Lazy Slave Girl:	*The Lazy Slave Girl*, see *Chap. 4.5.*
Níŋ-nam:	*Níŋ-nam nu-kal*, versions A–D, see *Chap. 3.1–2.*
Old Man:	*The Old Man and the Young Girl*, see *Chap. 5.2.*
Ox-Drivers:	*The Three Ox-Drivers from Adab*, see *Chap. 5.1.*
Prov. Ugar:	*Proverbs from Ugarit*, see *Chap. 3.4.*
SP 1:	See *Chap. 6.1: Additions to SP 1.*
SP 2:	See *Chap. 6.2: Additions to SP 2.*
::	Indicates occurs in a pair with.

Sumerian Terms

cf. áš – bal; šu-bal – ak.
bal: Fowler 12 w. a.
^{ŋiš}bala: IŠ 65 = *pi-li-ik-ki*; 227.
bala-gub-ba: EnNam 5.
^{ŋiš}banšur: GEN 299.
bar :: šà: IŠ 271 ere-bar-ra :: ere šà-ga.
bar: Goose Raven 17; cf. igi – bar; šu – bar.
bar: IŠ 134 w. dar.
bar(-ta – gub): IŠ 27.
bar .../-(ak)-a/: SP 5.55.
bar: IŠ 134; 209 bar :: šà.
bar – ak: CW 25.
bar-rim$_4$: Fox Merchant 17, var. am-bar.
bar-šu-ŋál: IŠ 219 munus-bar-šu-ŋál.
-bi versus kaš: Cf. comm. IŠ 97–99.
*^{m}bìl-ga-meš: Ballade Syr 13 ^{md}ŋiš-kin(!)-m[aš = ^{md}ki-iš-mas-su = ^{m}*gil-*[*ga-meš*].
bir$_7$-(bir$_7$) (*šarāṭum*): IŠ 136, phon. var. bi-ir-bi-re, w. túg; Goose Raven 9 bir$_7$ w. sa, var. gíd; Corn. Univ. 2.20.
BU: IŠ 97 ED var. mistake for -ka/kam$_4$?
bu-bu$_7$(KU): 235 ED var. of ù-bu-bu-ul.
bu(-r) (= *nasāḫum*): IŠ 105 ì-bu-re var. e-búr-re.
BU-ud-bar (= *ḫaršum* "unclean person"?): SP 1.113, cf. comm.; 114.
bulug: IŠ 16 = **pu-<-lu-uk>-ku*?.
^{ŋiš}buŋin: SP 1.116.
búr(u): SP 5.55; Ox-Drivers 88.
búr: IŠ 43 ED, cf. ŋiš-búr/pàr.
bùr: IŠ 29 w. é = *bītam palāšu*; Old Man 33(?).
bùru: Ballade 17 = Syr 8 ki bùru-da-gim, phon. var. b]u-ut-ta = *kīma šupul erṣetim*.
buru$_4$: Fowler 6.
buru$_{14}$: IŠ 131: u$_4$-buru$_{14}$-šè; 221 ED var. gu[ru$_7$]; IU 52–54.

D

da "side": IŠ 47 da-bé-eš = *a-na a-di-šu* (mistake for *i-di-šu*? cf. comm.); IŠ 222 da nu-sá, cf. comm.; 230 (uncertain); Níŋ-nam D 14.
da(-b): phon. for dab$_5$/dib: IU 24.
da(-k): phon. for dug$_4$: IU 60.
da(-ga): IŠ 58 = *rikištu/kiṣru*, ED var. da]g-ga, cf. comm.
da-pú: Lazy Slave Girl 6.
da-rí: IU 17 var.; Níŋ-nam C 5, var. du-rí.
da-ru-šè: IU 17 phon. for da-rí-šè.
dab: Prov. Ugar. 34–35: dab-ba = *i-ba-a*?.
dab: Goose Raven 14.
dab$_5$/dib: IŠ 30; IU 24 phon. da(-b).
dab$_5$ w. na-ri: IŠ 11 = *ašīrti ṣa-bat*; Fox Merchant 5; SP 5.55; Ox-Drivers 94 w. di; Old Man 30 šu-dab$_5$-ba.
dag (= daggan): IŠ 34 = *dakkannu*.
daḫ w. u$_4$: IU 26; 61 w. še.
dal-dal: IŠ 222 nim-gim ... dal-dal; Goose Raven 10; 12.
dam: IŠ 33 w. tuku = *šá mu-ti aḫzu*; 118; 185–186 dam tuku : dam nu-tuku; 208 w. du$_{12}$-du$_{12}$, cf. comm.; 258–259 w. kar, cf. comm.; Goose Raven 20 dam mušen-dù; Adulterer 7; Fowler 5; Ox-Driver 80; Old Man 25; Corn. Univ. 2.18; 19.
dam-gàr: Fox Merchant 2; 4; 5; 16; Corn. Univ. 2.26.
dam – tag$_4$: SP 1.119.
daŋal: IU 46–47 "to expand" in a temporal sense?; 49; Níŋ-nam A 6 (lú-)daŋal-la; Goose Raven 4.
dar: IŠ 134; 201; Ballade 13(?).
dé: IŠ 111–112: ú-gu – dé; 116 lú úr-šè – dé.; 161 a ... dé; IU 29; 35 phon. de; Níŋ-nam D 17; Lazy Slave Girl 5; cf. gù – dé.
de$_6$(DU): CW 87 (var. dé, phon. for TÚM, *ḫamṭu*, w. -ta-,: "to carry away"); EnNam 18.
di (from dug$_4$/di/e): IŠ 95 sá nu-di-dam, cf. sá – di.
DI: IŠ 142: DI-da, cf. comm; cf. Corn. Univ. 2.25 SAL – DI-DI.
di w. dab$_5$: Ox-Drivers 94.
di w. e: IŠ 126.
di w. kiŋ: Ox-Drivers 2.
di w. tuku: Ox-Drivers 2.
di-ma: Ballade NA 1, phon. for di-ma.
dib: EnNam 27; Ox-Drivers 88(?).
dib: CW 78, "to infringe"; "to overstep (time)"; CW 87.
díb(dab$_5$): IŠ 266 of inim word, cf. comm.; IU 24, phon. var. i-da-bé; Goose Raven 11; 15; 26; Adulterer 2; Old Man 28; Corn. Univ. 2. 5.
dili: IŠ 69–70 dili-ni = *e-diš-šu*; 166 dili-zu-ne; SP 5 A 71; SP 5.73.
dilmun^{ki}: IŠ 275.
dím: SP 1.114 ḫul-dím.
dìm: IŠ 118 dam dìm-e, cf. comm. for various meanings.
dim$_4$: IŠ 46 ED var.
dima(KA.DÙG): Ballade 1 = *ṭēmu*, phon. var te-x[.
diŋir: IŠ 266 inim diŋir-za; 269; 278 diŋir-kur-ra; IU 22 mu diŋir-ra w. kal; 29a; 32a; 35; 37 á-áŋ-ŋá diŋir-ra (rest.); CW 19; Níŋ-nam C 7; 8; D 9; 10; 12 (personal god); BM 54699 B 15 (Chap. 3.2x); Ballade 2, phon. var. ti-gi-re-e-né; Syr. 19 diŋir-zu;, phon. var. ti-kar-zu; 21 = Syr. 23; Ballade NA 1: Prov. Ugar. 26–27 ki] diŋir ì-in-ŋál = *itti* DINGIR *i-ba-áš-ši*: GEN 301 ki-ŋiš-ná diŋir-re-e-na; Ox-Drivers 95 diŋir adab^{ki}; Old Man 27; cf. ki-diŋir-ra; níŋ-diŋir(-ak).
diŋir – tuku: Old Man 17; Corn. Univ 2.6.
diri: IŠ 138 inim-diri; 235; 265; IU 56 diri-šè; šà-ḫúl-la i-im-diri-ge; Adulterer 3; Corn. Univ. 2.5 *gaba diri, glossed *ša lu-še-te-er-mi*; 12.
diri: CW 17 saŋ ki-diri-šè; Ballade 5 diri-NI-in-né = [*e-l*]*i-šu-nu*.
diri(-g) "to sail downstream": Fox Merchant 2; 14.
diš: IŠ 200 á-diš; Goose Raven 1 diš-àm; 2; SP 5 A 71; Ox-Drivers 5; Old Man 15; Corn. Univ. 2.10.
du: IŠ 47 = *alākum*; 55 du-dè "walking," but trans. *ṣâlu*, cf. comm.; 56 = *ina* IGI *alka*; 161 igi-zu-šè ḫé-du; 162–163 é-ni-šè etc.; 177 é dúr-bi-šè mu-un-du; Ballade 20 = Syr. 22, var of -ak, = *lillika*, cf. comm.; EnNam 7 al-du-un; Old Man 33.
DU "come": SP A 72.
du: IŠ 107 phon. var. for dug$_4$; cf. comm.; du for dù 109 var.
du-du: Adulterer 1.
du-ru-du-ru: Ox-Drivers 12, mistake for ku$_{(5)}$-ku$_{(5)}$-ru.
dù: IŠ 202 w. é; cf. é-dù-a; 243; 271, 279 w. é and ere; cf. šu – dù.
dù: IŠ 17 w. pú = *burtam ḫerû*.
dù: IŠ 49 phon for dug$_4$.
dù: IŠ 104 ka-dù-dù-e; 109 kuš-dù-dù-e.
dù-a-bi: Ballade 18 = Syr 9 *ka-la-šu*.
du$_7$(-du$_7$): IŠ 183 á šu im-du$_7$-du$_7$; 185; cf. si – du$_7$.
du$_7$(-n): IŠ 20 ED w. ní-zu.
du$_7$(-du$_7$): IŠ 94; SP 5, 73: Corn. Univ. 2.13 w. ŋìri.
du$_8$: IŠ 58 = *paṭāru*.
du$_8$: Fox Merchant 15; 20 (= igi du$_8$).
du$_8$: IŠ 220 var. of (é dúr-bi-šè ...) du.
du$_{12}$(-du$_{12}$) (tuku): IŠ 204, var. du$_8$-du$_8$, ED var. du$_{10}$-du$_{10}$; 208 dam – du$_{12}$-du$_{12}$; 235 šà-hul-gig du$_{12}$-du$_{12}$, ED var. du$_8$-du$_8$.
du$_{14}$(-d): IŠ 22 = *ṣaltu*; 24 w. ní-zu ... zu; 25 w. ak; 27, phon. du$_7$;

hind," var. ÍB.
ere (= iri, uru): IŠ 56 vars. ere^{ki}, ki-tuš, ere-tuš; IŠ 64 ere-ta – gur = *u[l-tu âli] puḫḫuru*; 163 ere nu-tuku; 181 ere tur-re, var. úru; 191; 271 ere-bar-ra :: ere šà-ga: 279; Fox Merchant 14 dumu ere-ŋá; Corn. Univ. 2.25 ere-gu-la (uncert.).
ere ul-la: IU 16 "the old city" epithet of Nippur.
érim: IŠ 137 níŋ-érim; CW 20 lú-érim-ma; Níŋ-nam B 5(?).
érin: IŠ 14 (= *ṣimittu*, "yoke"?); IU 66 phon. for ere^{ki}-n(a).
éš "rope": Goose Raven 21 éš-sa-kala-ga; Ox-Drivers 14 w. lá.
èš (eš)-kam-ma-šè: IŠ 146.
eš$_5$ (3): Ox-Drivers 1.
eše$_5$(LÚ#GÁN-*tenû*)(-d): EnNam 17.
eštub, cf. a-eštub.
ezem: IŠ 208 ezem-ma-ka.
ezen-gal ^{d}en-líl-lá: IU 52.

G

ga: IŠ 225 ga w. gu$_7$; 264 ga-arḫuš-a-ke$_4$, alt. reading ga-ama$_5$-a-ke$_4$, cf. comm.
ga-ba: Corn. Univ. 2.5, phon. for gaba, cf. comm.
ga-nam: Ox-Drivers 81.
ga-ra-bi: Adulterer 6 KA ga-ra-bi (uncert. meaning).
ga-ras^{sar}: Hyena Dog 7.
ga-ša-an (*emesal* for nin): Lazy Slave Girl 11: 12.
ga-ti(-la) "ex voto": IŠ 114, cf. comm.
*gaba w. diri(-g): Corn. Univ. 2.5 wr. phon. ga-ba, cf. comm.
gaba-kur-ra: IŠ 277.
gaba-ŋál: IŠ 204.
gaba – ri(-b): Old Man 15.
gada: IŠ 211(?).
gal: Cf. dub-gal-gal.
gal-gal-di (*mukabbirum*): IŠ 107.
gal$_5$-lá-ḫul: Old Man 35.
galam: IŠ 4–5; 262 galam-ma, cf. comm.; Ox-Drivers 93 inim galam-galam-ma.
gam: IŠ 261; CW 20; Hyena Dog rev. 3 dùg – gam; Lazy Slave Girl 11.
gana "come!": Ox-Drivers 13.
gán: IŠ 15 = *mērešu* (var. gam). Cf. aša$_5$. IŠ 17; 215 gán-zi; 272 gán dur$_5$ šè-ŋ[ál-la]; IU 40 gán dur$_5$; 46; 62; CW 23.
gán-maḫ: IU 38.
^{m}gašam(NUN-ME.TAG): Ballade NA 6 dumu-^{m}gašam = *mār ummānu*.

géme: IŠ 30; 49; 132; 133: 154 [kar-k]id, ED géme kar-kíd; 157 géme é-gal-la; 193; 245; Old Man 35 géme-tur.
gi: Ox-Drivers 13, phon. for gi$_4$.
gi: cf. ŋiš-gi.
gi: IŠ 226 KA×LI gi-gi-dè, phon. for gi$_4$-gi$_4$; gú ... gi-gi-dè, phon. for gíd-gíd.
GI = sig$_{17}$: e-sig^{mušen}: Fowler 6, var. Corn. Univ. 16 e-sig$_{17}$(GI).
gi(-n): IU 11 gi-ne-te; 49(?).
gi-na: Ballade 24 Syr nam-<lú>u$_{18}$-lu gi-na, cf. comm.
gi-sig(-ga): IŠ 58 = *ki[kkišu]*? var. gi-sì-ga, cf. da(-g) = *rikis/štu* or *kiṣru*? cf. comm.; Corn. Univ. 2. 15.
gi$_4$: EnNam 12 w. igi "to change appearance"; Old Man 30.
gi$_4$(-gi$_4$): IŠ 281 udu gi$_4$-gi$_4$; IU 10 ki-bi gi$_4$-gi$_4$.
gi$_4$(-gi$_4$): IŠ 38 ad – gi$_4$(-gi$_4$).
gi$_4$-gi$_4$ (= inim gi$_4$-gi$_4$): Goose Raven 5a; 15; SP 5.55; Fowler 11.
gi$_4$-in: IŠ 55 *emesal* for géme "slave girl"?, but perhaps trans. *ina mi-iṣ-ri* (l. 54) cf. comm.: Lazy Slave Girl 1; 2; 11; 12; Corn. Univ. 2.17.
gi$_7$(-r): IŠ 156 dumu-gi$_7$; SP 1.116 ^{ŋiš}buŋin-gi$_7$; cf. ur-gi$_7$.
gíd: Níŋ-nam A 7 w. NE, phon. for ní; Fowler 6 w. ná; Corn. Univ. 2.27.
gíd: Goose Raven 9 w. sa, var. bir$_7$.
gidim: GEN 303.
gig (verb): IU 32, but cf. 23 var. -te-ŋi$_6$-e, cf. comm. Cf. ḫul-gig.
gig: IŠ 138: ú-libiš-gig; 155.
gig: IŠ 184 gig-šè im-ŋar, ED var. àš-gig(-)šè(-)ŋar, cf. comm.; 247 nam-gig.
gig: IU 2 phon. for ŋi$_6$.
gig – ŋar: Old Man 35.
gin: Fox Merchant 21 gin-na-zu; SP 5.55 ì-gin-na; Fowler 2; Ox-Drivers 10; 91; Old Man 23 gan-na-ab-zé-en; 39 gen-na.
gin, phon for gi(-n): IU 9.
gín: IŠ 275 gín-dilmun^{ki}-na.
GÍR: IŠ 276 ED var. of ḫul, unexplained.
gisbun: CW 90: 91; Corn. Univ. 2.17.
giskim-ti (or ŋiskim?): Fox Merchant 15 w. NE/TÚG, phon. var. ŋiš-kiŋ-ti.
gu-bu: IU 68 phon. for gub(-bu).
gu(-l): IŠ 191 lú-gu-la; 261; Ox-Drivers 88(?); Corn. Univ. 2.25 ere-gu-la.
^{ŋiš}gu-za: BM 54699 B 15 (Chap. 3.2x).

gu-zi-ga, phon. for *gú zi-ga, IŠ 71.
gú: IŠ 36 (cf. saŋ-gú – sal-sal); 189; 243.
gú: IŠ 258 phon. for gù in gú KA – ŋá-ŋá; 260 a ŋìri a gú.
gú: IU 57, var. gud.
gú – ak: IŠ 13 = *qâpu* Ntn, var. gú-zi ... ; 82A (rest.); 153A.
gú – gi(-gi): IŠ 229, phon. for gíd-gíd.
gú – lá: Old Man 31.
gú – ŋál: IŠ 205, cf. comm. Cf. 13 var. gú-zu – ŋál.
gú-ŋìr – ŋál: Corn. Univ. 2.1
gú-ri-ta "from the other side": SP 5.55.
gú-tar – lá: IŠ 218.
gú-un: Ox-Drivers 12.
gù(-ra): Ox-Drivers 87, phon. for gud(?).
gù – dé: EnNam 14; Fox Merchant 4; Goose Raven 16 var.; SP 5.55 Fowler 2; Old Man 24; Old Man 37.
gù-di: IŠ 14 = *na-gi-ga*.
gù KA – ŋá-ŋá: IŠ 258 gù (var. gú) KA – ŋá-ŋá.
gù-mur (= *qardu*): IŠ 136, phon. var. gu-mu-ru, cf. comm.
gu$_4$-ud: IŠ 68 šu – gu$_4$-ud = *mup-pišāta* (D of *epēšu*), cf. comm.; Old Man 41.
gu$_7$: IŠ 39; IŠ 60 = *šutākulum* (*akālum* Št); 120; 123; 127 šà-zu w. gu$_7$; 132–133; 199; 217; 225 w. ga; 278 lú gu$_7$-gu$_7$; CW 79; Goose Raven 34; SP 5 A 72; SP 5 B 72; Ox-Drivers 8; Old Man 31 gu$_7$-gu$_7$; 34; SP 1.117; 1.118.
gub: IŠ 22: 27; IŠ 66 igi-a ... gub = *ina pāni izuzum*; ^{d}utu-da gub-bu-dè = *[a-na]* ^{d}*šamaš i-ziz*, cf. comm.; 117 u$_6$-e ba-gub; é-gal-la ba-gub; IU 29b; 40; EnNam 5: bala-gub-ba; 6 ("serve"); 8; Emar 28, cf. comm.; Goose Raven 1 (of birds); 2; 3; 5; 14 :: an-ta ... ki-ta w. gub; 18; Corn. Univ. 24 w. ŋiš-gíd-da & [K]A-ak-da.
gub :: tuš: IU 68.
gud: IŠ 41 = *alpum* (GUD); 45; 94; 189 gud maḫ; 213; 214 gud lul-la; IU 48; 57; EnNam 19; Ox-Drivers 4ff.; 79 phon. gù(-ra). Cf. also eštub; Corn. Univ. 2.13.
gud-da-ri – ak: Ox-Drivers 7.
gùd: Lazy Slave Girl 7 gùd-ùmun-na.
gudu$_4$: EnNam 6 ki gudu$_4$-e-ne(-k).
gul: IŠ 63 *abātum*, but var. trans. *sak-kul-šu la tu-qa-ba-ar*, cf. comm.; 182; 203 w. é; 214 w. é-tùr; CW

(or read inim?); 199B; cf. gù KA – ŋá-ŋá; cf. 266 inim ka-šè – díb/dab$_5$; Ballade 4 ka lu (phon. for lú) i-gi-du-ga-an-ni = *ina pî* ....; Hyena Dog 7 KA-ŋu$_{10}$-šè.
KA (= KA-A *būṣum* "hyena"): Hyena Dog 3, cf. 7.
KA-A (*būṣum* "hyena"): Fox Merchant 19, cf. Uruk vers. ii 19 comm.; 20 KA.
ka(-bi-šè gi$_4$): CW 82.
ka-dù-dù (= *pûm waštum*): IŠ 104.
KA.DÙG: See dima.
KA-ḪAR: See zú-ur$_5$ and gù-mur, comm. ll. 49; 136.
KA-KA unexplained: IU 6.
ka-làl: IŠ 105.
ka-ŋìr(-k): IŠ 16.
ka-sa$_6$-sa$_6$(-g): IŠ 103.
ka-sù-ga (= *riqātum*): IŠ 108 var. ka-su-ga.
ka-ša-an-an-na: Corn. Univ. 2.17 = ga-ša-an, cf. comm.
ka-ta è-a: CW 87.
ka – tar (or read inim – tar?): IŠ 37 = *muštālu*; 67 = *tuš-tar-ra-ah* (*šarāḫum* Dt).
ka-tuku: IŠ 106.
KA – túm: Ox-Drivers 14.
KA×LI: IŠ 226 KA×LI gi-gi-dè, phon. for gi$_4$-gi$_4$.
ká: IŠ 26; Fowler 5 var. ká-pa$_4$-paḫ-ka.
ka$_5$-a: Fox Merchant 4; 6; 13; 17; 20; 21; 22; SP 5 A 71; B 20.
kad: Goose Raven 17 sa kad kéšda.
kadra: IŠ 284; 284 kadra inim-ma-bi; 285a CW 47; 50; 55; 57.
kal: IŠ 252 níŋ-nam nu-kal; 253; Níŋ-nam A B, C, D 1; Adulterer 3.
kal: IU 22 w. mu diŋir-ra; (glossed *šu-qú-ru-šu*); 32a. Cf. níŋ-kal IŠ 13; 153A.
kal: IŠ 128 ki kal-kal-la-àm; 131 u$_4$ kal-kal-la-šè.
kal: IU 31; 54 with ní-zu.
kala(-g): Corn. Univ. 2.20; 27 kala-ga w. è.
kalag: Níŋ-nam 7; nam-kalag: Ballade 13 = Syr 15, phon. var nam-ka-lag = *šá da-an-nu-ti*; Goose Raven 21 ÉŠ-sa-kala-ga; Old Man 33.
kalam(-ma ti-la): IŠ 4–5.
kalam: IŠ 142 ŋizzal-kalam-ma; IU 8; 18.
kar: Níŋ-nam C 4.
kar: IŠ 258–259 w. dam, cf. comm.; CW 101; Fox Merchant 17; Old Man 28 anše-kar-ra; cf. šu – kar.
kar "quay": CW 181; 188.
kar-kid: IŠ 154 [kar-k]id, ED géme kar-kíd(AK), cf. comm.
kaskal: IŠ 15; 46; 47 = *ḫarrānum*; 166 w. du; 277.
kaš: IŠ 67, cf. é-kaš(-k); 83, 84; 98 prob. read -bi, see comm. 97–99; 126 kaš naŋ-a-zu-ne; 221 kaš kúrun; Fowler 1.
kàš: Old Man 33.
kaš$_4$: Prov. Ugar. 34–35 lú-kaš$_4$-e = *lāsimu*.
kaš$_4$ – dug$_4$: Corn. Univ. 26; ibid. ŋiri kaš$_4$-kaš$_4$.
KÉŠ-da: IŠ 18; Goose Raven 17 sa kad kéšda.
ki: IŠ 61 w. ús, trans. *uq-qú-rak ma-tum ma-ʾ-da*, cf. comm.; 128 ki kal-kal-la-àm; 233; 241 ki-a naŋ-e; 259 ki dam kar-re; IU 10 ki-bi gi$_4$-gi$_4$; Níŋ-nam A 7; Ballade 1 ki ^{d}en-ki-ke$_4$ = *itti* ^{d}*ea*; 17 = Syr 8 ki bùru-da-gim = *kīma šupul erṣetim*: Prov. Ugar. 26–27 ki] diŋir ì-in-ŋál = *itti* DINGIR *i-ba-áš-ši*; EnNam 6 ki gudu$_4$-e-ne(-k).
ki(-bi-šè dug$_4$): WC 85.
ki(-du$_{14}$-da-(k)): IŠ 22 = *ašar ṣa-al-*[*te*]; 232.
ki-áŋ: IŠ 202 šà-ki-áŋ.
ki-diŋir-ra "cultplace": IU 24; Níŋ-nam D 12.
ki-diri: CW 17.
ki-dur$_5$: IŠ 198, cf. comm.
ki-gub: Corn. Univ. 21.
ki – gul: SP 2.1.
ki(-)in-in-du(-kám): Ballade NA 5 [níŋ] šà ki(-)in-in-du-kám = *šá ana libbi*.
ki-inim-ma: IŠ 23.
ki-kur-ir-ra: Ballade NA 7.
ki-kúr: IU 39.
ki-nam-ninta(-k): IŠ 68 = *ašar zikāri*.
ki-nu-zu: IŠ 159 lú ki-nu-zu-a-ni-ta; 280 ki-<nu>-zu-a.
ki-ŋiš-ná: GEN 301.
KI.SAG.DU: Corn. Univ. 2.4, mistake for KI.TÙN.DU = sulummar.
ki-sikil "girl": IŠ 33 = *ardatum*; 290 of Nisaba; Old Man 37; 41 ki-sikil-tur.
ki-sikil "pure place": (epithet of Nippur): IU 9.
ki-su-ba phon. for ki-su-ub: IU 67.
ki – sur: Ballade 2: ki nam-sur-sur-re = *us-*<*su*>*-qa usqētu*; Ballade NA 1.
ki-ta: Níŋ-nam C 5; D 5; Ballade 6 = *šaplānum*; Goose Raven 14 :: an-ta, w. gub; 18; 31.
ki-u$_4$-ta-ta: EnNam Emar 25–26 = *ištu* UD.DA *adi inanna*, cf. comm.
ki-ur$_5$-sa$_6$(?)-ga, var. ki-ur$_5$-ša(?)-⌜ga⌝: IU 51.
ki-^{d}utu-è-a: IŠ 160; 165.
ki – za-[za]: IU 65.
^{ŋiš}kid: Fox Merchant 15.
^{ŋiš}kid-má-šú-a: Fox Merchant 16, var. GAM.GIŠ ^{ŋiš}kid-má-[níŋin-n]a.
kiŋ: IŠ 44 nu-kiŋ-ŋá = *lā šite'û*, ED nu-ḪUL(= kiŋ$_x$?).
kiŋ: IU 38; 45; 63; 67 šu-kiŋ-dab$_5$-ba.
kiŋ – ak: IŠ 175.
kiŋ-kiŋ: IŠ 281; Níŋ-nam D 7; Ballade 11 – Syr 13 ì-kiŋ-kiŋ = [*išteʾʾû*]; Ballade 21; Ox-Drivers 2 w. di; Corn. Univ. 2.20 (rest.).
kiŋ – sa$_6$: Lazy Slave Girl 1 (uncert.).
kiŋ – ša$_4$(DU): IU 46.
kiri$_4$ (or read giri$_{17}$) "nose": IŠ 113 kiri$_4$ šu – ŋál.
^{ŋiš}kiri$_6$: IŠ 58 = *ki-ri-i*.
kiri$_{11}$: IŠ 256.
kisal: IŠ 62 phon. gis-sal = *puḫrum*.
kišib w. íl: IŠ 104.
KU = ba$_9$ "to thresh"?: IU 61, cf. comm.
KU(-KU) = dab$_5$-dab$_5$?: IŠ 118.
ku(-n) (*qerēbum*): IŠ 97 ku-nu-a var. gùn-a; EnNam 20 al-ku-nu, Emar var. al-GAM-na = [*i-ka-an-nu-šu*], cf. comm.
ku-li: Fowler 1; Ox-Drivers 1 ku-li-li cf. comm.
kù: IŠ 210; EnNam 19.
kù-bala: Níŋ-nam B 8.
kù-bar$_6$-bar$_6$: GEN 299.
kù íb-ba-aš (= *imbû*): Níŋ-nam B 8, var. kù im-TU.
kù-sig$_{17}$: GEN 299.
ku$_4$(-r): IŠ 285; Níŋ-nam B 7; 8; SP 5 B 20; Corn. Univ. 2.17.
ku$_4$(-r): EnNam 13 w. -šè "to turn into."
ku$_4$(-ku$_4$): IŠ 22; 163 B; 228 é-é-a ku$_4$-ku$_4$-ku$_4$; Níŋ-nam B 5; Fox Merchant W 18.
ku$_5$(-r): IU 23; 32 w. nam-érim.
ku$_5$-ku$_5$(-ru-a): Ox-Drivers 82, var. d[u-du-ru, cf. line 12 and comm.
ku$_6$: Corn. Univ. 2.18.
ku$_7$: IŠ 252 zi ku$_7$-ku$_7$-da; Níŋ-nam A B, C, D 1.
^{ŋiš}kun$_5$: IŠ 222.
kunga: Lazy Slave Girl 3.
kur: IŠ 130 kur-kur-re; 158 saŋ-kur-ra kur-bi-ta ... e$_{11}$; 163 A (rest.); 169 kur-ra kur ... dub; 178; 277 gaba-kur-ra; 278 diŋir-kur-ra; Níŋ-nam A 6 w. šú-šú; D 20.
kur: Prov. Ugar. 36–37 dumu lú-kur-ra (= *kúr-ra, cf. comm) = DUMU *la-ap-ni*.

mu-ud-na: Corn. Univ. 2.18.
mú(-mú): IŠ 35 (rest.); 248; Lazy Slave Girl 6; Old Man 29 im-babbar – mú, var. níŋ-babbar; Corn. Univ. 2.19; cf. du_{14} – mú.
mu_4: Adulterer 5 túg-gim mu_4-mu_4 var. mú-mú; 10.
mu_4-mu_4: IU 70.
mud_5: IŠ 274 ED var. of níŋ-meŋar.
mul: IŠ 285a; 286.
MUL = súḫub?: Old Man 16.
MUNŠUB: IŠ 28 ED = úš?; 213 ED var.
munus: IŠ 213 munus-zi; Corn. Univ. 2.19.
munus-bar-šu-ŋál: IŠ 220.
munus-šu-ḫa: IŠ 222.
munus-uš-bar: Ballade 4 = *išpartum*.
munus-zú-ur_5-ak: IŠ 226.
$muru_9$(IM.DUGUD): Goose Raven 15; SP 5 B 20.
mušen: Fowler 10.
mušen-dù: Goose Raven 1; 2; 20; Fowler 1.

N

na – ri(-g): IŠ 6ff.; IŠ 9ff., 73ff = *ašāru*; 73 na-šè – ri, cf. comm. line 6; 143ff.
na-áŋ: Lazy Slave Girl 12.
na-me nu-: Ballade 17 = Syr 8 na-me nu-mu-un-zu-a = *mim-ma la idū*; Prov. Ugar. 28–29 na-me na-na-zu = *mamma lā ú-ʾa-ad-da*.
na-nam: IŠ 30; 69; 70; 93; 117; 172, ED na-nám.
na-ŋá-aḫ: IŠ 142 na-ŋá-aḫ DI-da.
na-ri (= na-de_5): IŠ 9 na-ri .... dab_5 = *a-ši]-ir-ti ṣa-bat*; 137, vars. na-ri; 151ff.; 270 na-ri ab-ba; 287; 288.
na-zi: Goose Raven 23.
ná: IŠ 186, ED var. DU; Adulterer 186; Old Man 38.
ná: Goose Raven 6 w. sa; 17; 24; Fowler 6; Corn. Univ. 21.
nam: Abbrev. for nam-tar "fate" Níŋ-nam A 3 nam lú-ùlu(?)-ka; D 3; Níŋ-nam C 4 níŋ-nam-a-ka-ni; EnNam 18.
nam-dub-sar: Corn. Univ. 2.12.
nam-[d]en-líl: EnNam 18 "Enlilship."
nam-érim: IU 23; 32 w. ku_5(-d), "swearing"; Níŋ-nam B 5(?).
nam-gig: IŠ 247.
nam-IZI-lá: Níŋ-nam D 17; 18.
nam-kalag: Ballade 13 = Syr 15 = *šá da-an-nu-ti*.
nam-lu-u_{18}-lu: Ballade Syr 10 nam-ti nam-lu-u_{18}-[lu] = [*ba-la-aṭ a-mi-l*]*u-ut-ti*; Ballade 24 Syr nam-lu-u_{18}-lu gi-na, phon. vars. nam-u_{18}-lu-lu ki-na, [nam-l]u-ul-la = *ša amīlutti*, cf. comm.; Prov. Ugar. 24–25; 28–29: 30–31 = *awīlūti*, cf. comm.; EnNam 20 u_4-nam-lú-u_{18}-lu.
nam-lú-lú: IU 44.
nam-ninta: IŠ 67, cf. ki-nam-ninta(-k).
nam-nun: IŠ 204 me nam-nun-na-ka.
nam-ŋu_{10} "what is to me?": Fox Merchant 21.
nam-ŋuruš: Old Man 28.
nam-silig: IŠ 15; 259.
nam-silig – ak: IŠ 61 = [*šagap*]*urūtum epēšum*.
nam-sipa: IU 11 said of kingdom (rest.).
nam-tag: CW 85; Adulterer 6 w. dugud, var. nu-til-e-dè.
nam-tar "fate, destiny": IŠ 118; 170, cf. comm.; Lazy Slave Girl 15 nam-tar eŋir-ra-ta; Corn. Univ. 2.4.
nam – tar: IŠ 115; 264; EnNam 16; 22; 25.
nam-ti: Ballade Syr 10 nam-ti nam-lu-u_{18}-[lu] = [*ba-la-aṭ a-mi-l*]*u-ut-ti*; 11 = Syr. 13 nam-ti = *na-pu-u*[*l-t*]*a*; 18 = Syr 9 nam-ti-la = *balāṭu*; 19 = Syr. 9 nam-ti dù-a-bi = *balāṭa kalašu*; Adulterer 1 w. díb; 3 var.
nam-úš: Níŋ-nam C 3; Ballade 19 = Syr. 19 nam-úš-a-kam = *ana m*]*u-ti*, var. *mi-ti*, phon. na-ma-uš-ta; Adulterer 3, var. nam-ti.
nam-zi-tar-ra: EnNam 1.
[d]nanna: IŠ 263, phonetic for na-an-na-, cf. comm.; Hyena Dog rev. 4.
naŋ: IŠ 83, 84 w. kaš; 126 w. kaš: 221 kaš-kúrun naŋ-naŋ; Lazy Slave Girl 8.
nar: Corn. Univ. 2.10.
NE: Níŋ-nam A 7 w. gíd, phon. for ní – gíd.
NE: Ballade NA 2 NE-e al-ŋál-[[la], cf. comm.; 10.
ne-en "this": SP 5 A 71.
ni-in-gim(?): Ballade Syr 23, phon. var. ni-in-gu = *kīma*.
NI.LAK 134 = i-ni? IŠ 27 ED.
ní w. lá: IŠ 206 ní-zu ḫé-en-ne-ši-lá.
ní(-ba): SP 1.114a.
ní(-bi-a): CW 18; Níŋ-nam D 15 ní-bi-šè; GEN 298 ní-ba – zu.
ní(-zu): IŠ 20 ED "yourself"; 24; 28 (= *ramanka*); 31; 32; 35; 92 lú ní-zu(-k); 109 kuš-ní var. of kuš-ni.
ní – gíd: See NE – gíd.
⌜ní⌝-[it]-⌜te⌝-èn-bi: IU 19 phon. for *ní-te(-a-ni/-bi), "spontaneously"; 20; 30.
ní – ŋál: IŠ 213.
ní-te: IU 20 written ní-ta-a-ni "voluntarily." CW 85.
ní-te(-a-ni), var. ní-ta-a-ni: IU 65 "spontaneously"; Prov. Ugar. 24–25 [ní-te-n]i = *ina ramāniša*; Fowler 13; Ox-Drivers 78.
ní – te-en-te-en: CW 170. Cf. phon. ní-it-te-èn(-bi): IU 30.
ní-zuḫ: IŠ 30 = ED nu-zuḫ = *šarrāqu*.
nibru[ki]: IU 12; 16; Fox Merchant 2.
nim: IŠ 222 nim-gim ... dal-dal.
nin: IŠ 289 nin dub-gal-gal-la.
nin-gal: CW 82 = nin_9-gal "older sister."
[d]nin-ka-si: IŠ 85.
[d]nin-kilim: Old Man 31.
[d]nin-urta: IU 14.
nin_9-gal: IŠ 172 šeš-gal :: nin_9-gal.
ninda: IŠ 97, 100; 178.
ninta (nitaḫ, UŠ): IŠ 32.
$ninta_x$(SAL+NINTA): IŠ 32 ED.
níŋ: IŠ 28 w. zuḫ = *šarāqu*; 52 níŋ-e w. šub, unclear; 96, 102; 111–112 w. ú-gu – dé; 252; 253; Goose Raven 22; 34; SP 5 B 72; SP 1.117; Corn. Univ. 2.2 níŋ-šu-ti-a.
níŋ – ra: IŠ 153; Fox Merchant 15(?).
[níŋ-ak]: Prov. Ugar. 24 (rest.).
níŋ-gu_7: Old Man 34.
níŋ-saŋ-íl-la: Ballade 20 = Syr. 22 = *di-na-nu*.
níŋ-šu: Royal Ontario prov 1 (Chap. 3.2x).
níŋ-šu-dug_4-ga: Níŋ-nam D 14.
níŋ-tuku: IŠ 184 lú níŋ-tuku, lú-níŋ nu-tuku; cf. IŠ 204 níŋ-du_{12}(du_{12}); Níŋ-nam A B, C, D 2; A 10; D 9; Prov Ugar 36–37 dumu lú-níŋ-tuku = DUMU *ša-ri-i*; EnNam 21.
níŋ w. é dù: IŠ 202; IU 51.
níŋ: IŠ 203 w. é gul.
níŋ w. lu(-lu): IŠ 129: IŠ 176.
níŋ-á-sì-ga: IŠ 101.
níŋ-babbar (UD): Old Man 29, var. im-babbar.
níŋ-diŋir-ra "religious affairs": IU 19; 21; 30; 36.
níŋ-dùg: Níŋ-nam A 8.
níŋ-è: IŠ 96, cf. comm.
níŋ-érim: IŠ 137; IU 8 with ḫa-lam; CW 25 w. bar – ak; CW 46 w. zé-er.
níŋ-gi-na: IU 9, also with gin phon. for gi(-n); CW 13; Fox Merchant 15.

ŋ

P

R

S

sa "net": Goose Raven 2; 6 w. ná; 8; 9 w. gíd or bir$_7$; Goose Raven 17 sa kad kéšda; 21 ÉŠ-sa-kala-ga; 24; 26; Fowler 6 w. ná and gíd.
sa-gaz – ak: IŠ 31 = *ḫabbatūtam epēšum*.
sá: IŠ 47 ED phon. var. of sa$_6$(-g)?.
sá (= *maḫārum*, said of offering?): Cf. comm. on UI 20 (rest.) and 30A; 30 has zu.
sá w. com. infix -da-: IŠ 102: 212; 222 da nu-sá, cf. comm. IU 20; Lazy Slave Girl 14; 15; Corn. Univ. 2.6.
sá – di (from sá – dug$_4$/di/e): IŠ 95, cf. comm 95–96.
sá – dug$_4$ (*kašādum*): IŠ 106 vars. sá – du; Ballade 16 sá bí-in-dug$_4$-ga = Syr 7 = *ikaššad*.
sá-sá: IU 57 phon. var. si-si.
sa$_4$: IŠ 49, var. šà, phon. for ša$_5$(= AK).
sa$_6$(-g): IŠ 47 = *damqu*; 103; 195; 196; 198; 199A. Cf. ka-sa$_6$-sa$_6$(-g); CW 88; 219 zag-si mu-un-sa$_6$-sa$_6$; Níŋ-nam C 8 níŋ-⸢sa$_6$⸣-ga; Lazy Slave Girl 1; Corn. Univ. 2.10.
sa$_9$: SP 5 B 20 ŋi$_6$-sa$_9$ "midnight."
sa$_{10}$-(sa$_{10}$): IŠ 14; 48 = *šâmu*; IŠ 154; 155; 156; 157; 213; 214; 216; 275; IU 48.
SAḪAR (= šùš or kuš$_7$ = *kizû*): var. SS 5–6, cf. comm.
sal: Lazy Slave Girl 2.
saŋ: Goose Raven 21.
saŋ: IŠ 91 w. dúr(?)(-dúr); CW 22(?).
saŋ "slave": IŠ 30; 167 saŋ šu-bal – ak.
saŋ: CW 17.
saŋ: GEN 300 [sa]ŋ-na "in his prime time," cf. comm.
saŋ(-e-eš) – rig$_7$: Níŋ-nam D 9.
saŋ-a-šà: IU 40.
saŋ-du nu-tuku: IŠ 115; 168 saŋ-du.
saŋ – e: IŠ 44 = *nasāḫu*, ED ság – KA.
saŋ-gú (var. kù, KU) – sal: IŠ 36 = *qaqqadu qa[lālu]*.
saŋ – íl: Ballade 20 = Syr. 22 níŋ-saŋ-íl-la = *di-na-nu*.
saŋ-ki – áŋ: IU 71(?).
saŋ-kur-ra: IŠ 158.
saŋ – ŋá-ŋá: Niŋ-nam B 4.
saŋ-ŋiš – ra: IŠ 135.
saŋ – sal: IŠ 20.
sal(-sal): IŠ 36 w. saŋ(-gú).
SAL – DI-DI: Corn. Univ. 2.25.
SAL.ŠAḪ: IŠ 225.
sar: Níŋ-nam A 9, cf. ḫúb-sar.
SAR "vegetables"(?): Old Man 16.
sé-ek-rum: Ox-Drivers 17; Old Man 22.
si "to fill": Ox-Drivers 7ff.
si: IU 59 w. a; SP 5 A 71 "to be enough."
si "prow" of a boat: Fox Merchant 5.
si "horn": SP 5 B 20 si-am.
si(-il): IŠ 14 = *sapāḫu* D.
si – du$_7$: Corn. Univ. 2.13.
si-ga: Prov. Ugar 32–33 sig-ga = *enšu*, cf. comm.; Corn. Univ. 2.27 w. gíd.
si-iš-ta: IU 53, phon. for a-šed$_{17}$-da.
si-mul: Old Man 16.
si – sá: IU 8; 33; EnNam 27.
si-sá-bi "straight": IU 24; Fox Merchant 15.
si-si: IU 57, var. sá-sá, "to fill."
si-si-ig: Fowler 7 w. lù-lù, var. Corn. Univ. 16 w. ì-si-si-ig.
sí-ki-ib-ta: Ballade Syr 21 = *sí-ki-ip*, cf. comm.
sì(-g): IŠ 45 nu-sì-ga = *lā búr-ru-tú* (unexplained); 168 mu-mu-a sì-ga; Lazy Slave Girl 7.
sì(-g): IŠ 46 = *damqu*, phon. for sa$_6$(-g)/sig$_7$ or mistake for sì(-g) = ★*šutamḫurum*? cf. comm.
sì(-ke-bi): IU 57 var. ⸢a⸣-⸢sì⸣-⸢ga⸣-àm, of water.
sig: see á-sig IŠ 51.
sig(-ta): Goose Raven 1 "from south."
síg: Lazy Slave Girl 7 (uncert.).
sig$_{17}$ = GI: e-sig^{mušen}: Fowler 6, var. Corn. Univ. 16 e-sig$_{17}$(GI).
sila: IŠ 224; 225; Lazy Slave Girl 11; Corn. Univ. 2.17.
sila-daŋal(-la): IŠ 18.
sila-kúr: IŠ 27.
sìla: Ox-Drivers 14 a-sìla-ŋar-ra.
sila$_4$: SP 5 B 72.
sila$_{11}$-ŋá: SP 1.116 níŋ-sila$_{11}$-ŋá.
silig: IŠ 15; 61 cf. nam-silig; 259; 95 nu-silig-ge-dam, cf. comm.
silim: Prov. Ugar. 38–39 lú-silim-ma = *šalmu*, cf. comm; EnNam 5 (to complete a duty).
silim-dug$_4$: (cf. *muštarriḫum*) IŠ 108 var. ṣilim-di.
sim^{mušen}: Fox Merchant 17.
sipa(-d): IŠ 281; IU 11.
sir$_5$(-sir$_5$): IŠ 65 said of the movements of a spindle = *namāšu*, *târu*, cf. comm.
siskur (*naqû*): CW 87 (glossed *ni-qá-ka*); IU 27 w. ŋá-ŋá.
su: IU 61, phon. var. of su$_7$.
su (*ṭebû*): IŠ 200 má ḫé-en-da-su; IŠ 221 buru$_{14}$ im-su-su-su, ED var. LAGAB-LAGAB; Corn. Univ. 2.15 má-ta-lá nu-su-su.
su "body": Níŋ-nam D 12.
su(-g): IŠ 41 = *râbum* (SS reinterpretation? cf. comm.); 59 = *riābum*; 92; IU 25, phon. var. su-su.
su(-su): IŠ 21 ED var. sù; 40 w. úš = *rušâ babālum*.
su(-su): Níŋ-nam D 15.
su-ga: IŠ 108 var.of sù-ga.
su-un-su-na: IU 68 phon. for sun$_5$-sun$_5$-na.
sù: IŠ ED var. of su(-su).
sù: SP 1.113.
sù(-g): IŠ 107 "empty," 108 ka sù-ga var. ka su-ga; 262 dumu in-sù-ge tu-da, cf. comm.; 275 ★sù-ga?; Old Man 36 Ex b.
sù(-ud): IŠ 128, cf. 1, 3; IU 35a; Ballade 16 an sù-ud-gim, phon. var šu(!)-ut-ta-k[i = Syr 7 an sù-ud-da = *šamû rūqu*.
su$_7$ "threshing floor": IU 61, phon. var. su.
sud(-r/d): IŠ 1; IU 2 mu-sù-da.
^{d}suen: IU 13 (rest.); Hyena Dog rev. 3.
suḫ: IU 29c; CW 33; 59.
^{kuš}súḫub: Lazy Slave Girl 9.
suḫuš: IU 11 w. gi(-n).
sukud: Níŋ-nam A 5; D 19; Goose Raven 4.
sulummar: Corn. Univ. 2.4.
sun$_5$(BÚR)(-sun$_5$): IU 68: CW 242.
sun$_7$ (*ṣaltu*): IŠ 54; 164 la-ba-e-da-sun$_7$-e, var. sun$_7$-na.
sur: Níŋ-nam B 5(?); Ox-Drivers 14.
sur(-sur): Ballade 1, see ki – sur, phon. var. sur-šu-re.

Š

ša-ak-šu: IU 7 phon. for šà-kúš-ù.
ša-ra: Ballade Syr. 21, phon. for ★šar-ra = *ku-uš-ši-id*.
šà: IŠ 47 = *libbu*; 66, cf. kúr(-kúr); 93; 94; 127 šà-zu w. gu$_7$; IU 53; CW 26; 82; 141 šà-ge im-šed$_4$-e; 195; 196; 198; 202; 203; 209 :: bar; Níŋ-nam A 4 šà-ta; D 8 šà-ga-ni inim-ma – sì(-g); Ballade NA 5 *šá ana libbi*; SP 5 A 71 ḫa-la šà-ŋu$_{10}$ "my favorite share"; Corn. Univ.2.21 šà-ŋiš –zu.
šà: IŠ 20 ED mistake for za-e or ur?.
šà: IŠ 49 phon. var. of ★ša$_5$(= AK).
šà-gal(-la): Corn. Univ. 2.12.
šà-ḫul-gig: IŠ 235.
šà-ḫúl-la: IŠ 251; Ballade 20 = Syr. 22 šà-ḫúl-la: (*ḫūd libbi*, cf. comm.), phon. var. ù-ša-ḫu-la-al; Níŋ-nam A 8; 9; 21; Ballade NA 6.

TÚG: SP 1.124a mistake for bìd?, cf. comm.
túg-èŋ-lám: Lazy Slave Girl 10.
túg-níŋ-dára: Lazy Slave Girl 8; cf. 10 túg-èŋ-dára(?).
tuku: IŠ 33; 115 saŋ-du nu-tuku; 110 usu-tuku; 116 téš nu-tuku; 184 lú níŋ-tuku, lú níŋ nu-tuku; 185–186 lú dam tuku dam nu-tuku. Cf. du$_{12}$(-du$_{12}$); Níŋ-nam A B, C, D 2 EnNam 19; SP 5 A 72; Fowler 1; Ox-Drivers 1 w. di; cf diŋir – tuku.
tukum-bi: Níŋ-nam D 10; SP 5.55.
túm (= de$_6$): IŠ 107; 159 ù-mu-e-túm var. tùm; 193 ši-im-ta-an-tùm … ši-im-ta-an-túm; Ox-Drivers 14 KA – túm; 83.
tùm: IŠ 110 var. túm; IŠ 193, antithetic parr. w. túm; Níŋ-nam B 6, var. túm(de$_6$): EnNam 21 me-šè – tùm.
tùm: Ox-Drivers 84, var. tum$_4$.
TÙN: Corn. Univ. 2.2.
tur: IŠ 181; Old Man 35 géme-tur; ki-sikil-tur; corn. Univ. 2.25.
tur(-tur): IU 62 "to be too little"; Corn. Univ. 2.20.
tùr: IŠ 214, cf. é-tùr.
tùr: IŠ 272 tùr-šè ŋ[ál, var. of dúr-bi-šè ŋ[ál-la].
tuš: IU 68 tuš-šè, var. tuš-ù; SP 5 B 72; Ox-Drivers 80 written TÚG; Corn. Univ. 2.17.

U

u-buru$_{14}$: IU 52–54 phon. for u$_4$-buru$_{14}$.
U – sal: Lazy Slave Girl 2.
ú: IŠ 44 = *šammu* "grazing ground"; cf. 93 máš-ú.
ú: Corn. Univ. 2.19.
ú-a: Cf. mu-ú-a.
ú-gu – dé: IŠ 111–112; 274; Corn. Univ. 2.20.
ú-làl: IŠ 105.
ú-libiš-gig: IŠ 138, cf. comm.; 155.
ú-rum: IŠ 101.
ú-šim: Lazy Slave Girl 6.
ù: Old Man 39.
ù-bu-bu-ul: IŠ 138, cf. comm.
ù-la – ak: Ballade Syr. 21 = *mêšu* "to despise" (hapax).
ù-ma: IU 7.
ù-mu-un (*dāmu* blood): Old Man 10.
ù-mu-un (*emesal* for en): Lazy Slave Girl 4.
ù-nu-ŋar-ra: IŠ 42 = *nullâtu.*
ù-sá: IŠ 112 (or read u$_6$-di? cf. comm.).
ù-sar: IŠ 154, vars., cf. comm.
ù-tu: IŠ 181 ši-in-ga-an-ù-tu; 256–257 dumu-munus … dumu-ninta in-ù-tu-un; 267 lú mu-un-ù-tu; IU 12; 49.
u$_4$(-d): IŠ 48 u$_4$ da-bé-eš = *ši-tam-ma a-na a-di-šu a-lik*, cf. comm.; 131; 244; IU 26 w. daḫ; 18; CW 89 w. gíd; Prov. Ugar. 26–27 u$_4$-da šu-dù-bi = *ṭe-em ur-ri-ša*, cf. comm.
u$_4$(-d): EnNam 17 "when"; Goose Raven 1.
u$_4$-an-na: EnNam Emar, cf. comm.
u$_4$-bad-rá: IŠ 1ff.
u$_4$-bi-ta(-ak): Lazy Slave Girl 14.
u$_4$-buru$_{14}$(-k): IŠ 131; 216.
u$_4$-da-ri-iš: Ballade Syr 10.
u$_4$-da-ta: Ballade 3 = *ištu ūmi panāma*, phon. vars. ú-tu …, -d]a-ta, cf. comm.
u$_4$-dè: EnNam 18 "today."
u$_4$-nam-lú-u$_{18}$-lu: EnNam 20.
u$_4$-ri-a: IŠ 1ff.
u$_4$-sù-šè: IU 15.
u$_4$-sud-rá ri-a: IŠ 1.
u$_4$-sumun-na: Corn. Univ. 2.5 w. šú.
u$_4$-šà-ḫúl-la: Ballade 20 = Syr. 22 (*ḫūd libbi*, cf. comm.).
u$_4$-ti-la: IU 33 phon. var. u$_4$-til-la.
u$_4$-ub-ba: IU 1 phon. for u$_4$(-bi-a)?
u$_4$-ul-lí-a(-ke$_4$-ne): Ballade 14, Syr 17 differs: *ša ištu u$_4$-mi pa-na-a a-di i-na-a[n-na]*, cf. comm.
u$_4$-ul-li-a-ta: IU 1, cf. comm.; Ballade SS 14.
u$_4$-u$_4$-da: Corn. Univ. 5, var. gu$_4$-gu$_4$-ud-da, cf. comm.
u$_4$ – zal: Níŋ-nam A 9; Corn. Univ. 2.5.
u$_6$: IŠ 117 u$_6$-e ba-gub.
u$_6$-di: Cf. IŠ 112 var. of ù-sá.
u$_8$: SP 5.55.
ubar-tu-tu: IŠ 7 ff.; 143ff.; 285b; 287–288.
udu: IŠ 41 – *immerum*; EnNam 6. (UDU.NINTA); 44 = *būlum*; 281; EnNam 19; SP 5 A 71.
ug$_5$: IŠ 263.
uga^{mušen}: EnNam 13; 15; Goose Raven 2; 3; 5a; 16.
ugu: IU 25 phon. for ú-gu (dé); 36; 56; Ballade 19 ugu – diri(-g) = *ana … uttir.*
ugu "over": Fox Merchant 21 ugu-ŋu$_{10}$-šè "to me"; Goose Raven 3; 14; SP 5 B 20; Ox-Drivers 81.
úku (úŋu?): Corn. Univ. 2.3; 20.
um-mi-a: Ox-Drivers 95.
ummeda: IŠ 264.
^{kuš}ùmmu(-d) (A.EDIN.LÁ): IŠ 201, ED var. ^{kuš}A.EDIN, cf. comm., w. dar.
úmum – ak: SP 5.55.
ùmun: Lazy Slave Girl 7 gùd-ùmun-na.
umuš: Níŋ-nam B 6; D 4.
ùŋ: IŠ 17; IU 10; 17; 50.
ur: IŠ 20 ED var. of za-e, pronoun? cf. Comm. Adab vers. Segm. 2.3.
ur: IŠ 60 = *aḫû* "foreigner."
ur "dog": IŠ 276 ur nu-zu.
ur-bar-ra: SP 5 A 71: B 72; B 73.
ur-gi$_7$(-r): Fox Merchant 13; 18; Hyena Dog rev. 2.
ur-maḫ: SP 5.55; Ox-Drivers 8.
ur-^{d}nin-urta: IŠ 11.
ur-saŋ: IŠ 69 & 71 = *qarrādu*; Ox-Drivers 69.
úr "lap": IŠ 116 úr-šè w. dé; Ox-Drivers 79; Old Man 38.
úr – zé-zé: Lazy Slave Girl 11.
ÚR.AŠ (ED name of Ziusudra): IŠ Adab version of SS 5–6 and parallels, cf. comm. SS ll. 5–6.
ùr: IŠ 86, 87, 88, cf. comm. 86 for the ED form.
ùr (*ūru*) "roof": IŠ 230; SP 5 A 72.
ùr(-ùr): IŠ 60 var. úr, w. du$_{14}$, cf. comm.
ur$_5$: IU 63 phon. mu-re (mistake?).
ur$_5$: IŠ 133 ur$_5$ ḫé-en-na-nam-ma-àm.
ur$_5$ "to chew": Old Man 32; Corn. Univ. 2.3, var zú – ur$_5$.
ur$_5$(-re): IŠ 41 w. su-su = *esēqum* "to draw lot," prob. SS reinterpretation, cf. comm.
ur$_5$(-re) (demonstrative?): IŠ 91 ur$_5$-re ḫé-em-me-re-a-e$_{11}$-dè, cf. comm.
ur$_5$-gim: Old Man 17.
ur$_5$-ra: IŠ 227 ^{ŋiš}bala ur$_5$-ra, cf. comm.
ur$_5$-ra/re (*ḫubullu*): IŠ 199 é-níŋ-gur$_{11}$-ra ur$_5$-re la-ba-an-gu$_7$-e, cf. comm.; CW 79.
ur$_5$-tuku: IŠ 53 = *[be-el ḫu-bul-l]i-ka*, cf. comm.
úrdu(-d): IU 44; Old Man 39.
úru: IŠ 21 (= "city"?), ED var. URU×A, uru$_5$ cf. comm.; 181 var. ere tur-e, úru maḫ.
uru$_5$: IŠ 21 ED = úru.
URU×A: IŠ 21, ED var. = úru.
ús: IŠ 163 A šu – ús.
ús: IŠ 99.
ús: Fox Merchant 3 w. má.
ús: IŠ 61 lú ki w. ús, cf. comm.; 156 zag é-ŋar$_8$-e ús-sa; Fox Merchant 18 w. eŋir "behind."
usu: Níŋ-nam D 7 w. kiŋ-kiŋ; Old Man 27.
usu-tuku: IŠ 110.

Akkadian Terms

Only a few points of special interest are included below, mostly from the Akkadian translations of *Instr. Šuruppak*, which has a number of unexpected or unusual equivalents, as well as a few hitherto unexplained ones. All Akkadian equivalents included in the same sources are listed in the Sum. index above.

Hurrian Terms

by Gernot Wilhelm

I§H: *The Instructions of Šuruppak*, Hurrian version, line number.
Line numbers and "comm" refer to the commentary in *Chap. 1.7: The Hurrian Version.*

AḪ-*(a-)aš-te-tap*	IŠH 63 (comm, fn)
AḪ-*a-aš-te-et-u*	IŠH 63 (comm, fn)
alad- "buy"	IŠH 14 (comm, fn)
aladumma epēšu "buy, pay"	IŠH 14 (comm, fn)
Am-ma-ri-ik-e	IŠH 63 (comm, fn)
Am-ma-ri-ik-ki	IŠH 63 (comm, fn)
am-me-e-et-a	IŠH 63 (comm, fn)
*a-ri-*BA$^{?}$[	IŠH 12
ašḫ=i=a=šše "sacrificer"	IŠH 65 (comm)
ašk- "to demand compensation"	IŠH 11, 13 (comm)
ašk=ir-	IŠH 11, 13 (comm)
at-ki	IŠH 63, 63 (comm)
avari "field"	IŠH 15, 16 (comm)
av/b(i)=ī=da	IŠH 66 (comm)
az-k[i-ir(-) (= na-ri = *ašertu* "instruction"?)	IŠH 11, 11 (comm)
az-ki-ir[(-) (= na-ri = *ašertu* "instruction"?)	IŠH 13, 13 (comm)
da/ta-aḫ-e	IŠH 63 (comm)
da-aḫ-e	IŠH 63 (comm, fn)
e-x[...] (= gán = *mērešu*, a-šà = *eqlu* "field"??)	IŠH 16, 16 (comm)
e-ba-[...] (gán = *mērešu*, a-šà = *eqlu* "field"??)	IŠH 15, 15 (comm)
eban(i)=n(a)=až=a-	IŠH 15, 16 (comm)
ebāni	IŠH 15, 16 (comm)
e-ba-ni-we-	IŠH 15, 16 (comm, fn)
eġelli	IŠH 63 (comm, fn)
e-ḫé-el-e	IŠH 63 (comm, fn)
e-ḫé-el-e-na	IŠH 63 (comm, fn)
e-ḫe-el-li	IŠH 63 (comm, fn)
fur(i)=ī=da "with regard to"	IŠH 66 (comm)
futt=ož=a "he begot him"	IŠH 65 (comm)
ḫa- "to take away"	IŠH 14 (comm)
ḫa-i-...	IŠH 14, 14 (comm)
ḫa-i-x[ ] (= *ú-sà-pa-ḫa* "it will scatter"?)	IŠH 14, 14 (comm)
ḫam(a)z=i=a=šše "oppressor"(?)	IŠH 65 (comm, fn)
ḫa-at-ḫé-e-et-a	IŠH 63 (comm, fn)
ḫa-wa-al-e	IŠH 63 (comm, fn)
Ḫa-wa-al-im^{ki}	IŠH 63 (comm, fn)
ḫi-ra[(...)]	IŠH 62, 62 (comm)
id- "to beat"	IŠH 63 (comm)
I-ki-in-kal-iš	IŠH 63 (comm, fn)
ir-[	IŠH 11
itki (= Akk. *urṣu* "mortar")	IŠH 63 (comm)
ki-iḫ-e-né-eš	IŠH 63 (comm, fn)
ki-ip-e	IŠH 63 (comm, fn)
ku-la-aḫ-e-na	IŠH 63 (comm, fn)
ku-la-aḫ-ḫe-na "die genannten"	IŠH 63 (comm, fn)
ma-aḫ-a-ar-(r)a	IŠH 63 (comm, fn)
pin=i=a=šše "s.o. who raises (a child)"	IŠH 65 (comm)
pud-	IŠH 65 (comm)

Urartian Terms

by Gernot Wilhelm

Cuneiform Tablets

The following list includes all the cuneiform tablets that have been used in this volume, whether published here for the first time or published previously.

A 649 and 645: OIP 14, 55–56: IŠ.
AbS-T 323: OIP 99,323 (+) AbS-T 393: OIP 99,256: IŠ.
AO 7739: TCL 16, 80 (+) AO 8149: TCL 16, 83: Ox-Drivers.
AO 8899: TCL 16, no. 93: IŠ.
Ashmolean Museum Nr 1932.156 b: OECT 5, 33: IŠ.
BM 50522 + 52767 + 52946 + 77468 + ?: IŠ.
BM 54699 (CT 42, 23): Níŋ-nam; Goose Raven; Old Man.
BM 80184 (CT 44, 18: Níŋ-nam, etc.
BM 82952: IŠ.
CBS 438: AcSum 18 (1996) 66, No. 9: Fox Merchant.
CBS 1208: Níŋ-nam, etc.
CBS 1601: Ox-Drivers.
CBS 2203: IŠ.
CBS 3907: Goose Raven.
CBS 4611: PBS 10/1 4: IŠ.
CBS 4605: PBS 12, 31: EnNam.
CBS 6564 + 8078 + N 4708 + N 5888: Goose Raven.
CBS 6924 + N 3097: Níŋ-nam, etc.
CBS 6930: Goose Raven.
CBS 7917 + N 4784: EnNam.
CBS 8001: IŠ.
CBS 8010: STVC 97: Old Man.
CBS 10320: IŠ.
CBS 11945: Couns. Wis.
CBS 13107 + CBS 2203: IŠ.
CBS 13777: Níŋ-nam; Prov. Ugar.
CBS 14047 (not CBS 8804): PBS 5, 13: Goose Raven.
CBS 15109: PBS 5, 11: Goose Raven.
Copenhagen National Museum Antiksamlingen 10062: Alster, *Proverbs* I, 271–272: The Adulterer.
Copenhagen National Museum, Antiksamlingen A 10054: IŠ.
Cornell University Kroch-04: Ch. 6; SP 1.
Cornell University Kroch-05: Ch. 6; SP 2; Fowler.
Emar VI/4, 359–365; *Emar* VI/1–2, p. 316: 74123x + p. 32: 74127ac + 74128x + 74136b + p. 339: 74132t + 346: 74137m + p. 385f: 74153 + p. 676: 74344: Ballade Syr.
Emar VI/1–4, 771, 772, 773, 774, 592: EnNam Emar vers.
Hermitage, St. Petersburg 15339 (previously GE 45445): IŠ.
HS 1535, previously published as TMHNF 4, 41: Hyena Dog.
IM 55403: TIM 9.1: IU.
K. 6917 + 13679: Ballade NA.
K. 13942 (not a Kuyundjik text): IŠ.
KAR 174 iii 50–54: BWL 216f iii 50–54: Elephant Wren.
Krebernik bilingual unnumbered: ZA 86 (1996) 170–176: IŠ.
MDP 27, 109: IŠ.
MDP 27, 186: IŠ.
MDP 27, 260: IŠ.
MM 487b: IU; Couns. Wis.
MM 477: IŠ.
N 901: IŠ.
N 1237: Fowler.
N 2715: IŠ.
N 3047: Níŋ-nam.
N 3097: EnNam.
N 3183.. Old Man.
N 3260: IŠ.
N 3298: IŠ.
N 3432: IŠ.
N 3579 + Ni 2763 ii 1'ff. (SLTNi 128): Níŋ-nam, etc.
N 3643: IŠ.
N 3695: Gooose Raven; not used.
N 3700: Goose Raven; not used.
N 3707: IŠ.
N 3708: IŠ.
N 3757: IŠ.
N 3774: IŠ.
N 4148: IŠ.
N 5149: EnNam.
N 5909: EnNam.
N 7047: IŠ.
Ni 2192 (ISET II 21): Níŋ-nam, etc.
Ni 2763 ii 1'ff. (SLTNi 128): Níŋ-nam, etc.: See N 3579.
Ni 3023 (SLTNi 131) + fragments: Ni 4144 (ISET II 123), 4452 (ISET I 121), 4473 (ISET II 22), Ni 4483 (ISET I 159/101), 4484 (ISET I 125/67): Níŋ-nam; Lazy Slave Girl.
Ni 3546: ISET II 91: Goose Raven.
Ni 4001: ISET II 92: IŠ.
Ni 4035: SLTNi 137: IU.
Ni 4152: ISET I 134: IŠ.
Ni 4193: ISET I 78: Couns. Wis.
Ni 4271: ISET I 138: IŠ.
Ni 4305: ISET 2, 18: Old Man.
Ni 4543: ISET I 125: IŠ.
Ni 9558 (courtesy Kramer): IŠ.
Ni 9559: ISET I 187: IŠ.
Ni 9612: ISET II 92: IŠ.
Ni 9620 (ISET II 91): Níŋ-nam, etc.
Ni 9731: ISET I 181: IŠ.
Ni 9778: ISET I 183: IŠ.
Ni 9793: ISET II 55: IŠ.
Ni 9820: ISET I 188 (also copied by Kramer as Ni 3820 in ISET II 34): IŠ.
Ni 9884: ISET I 193: IŠ.
Ni 9917: ISET I 201: IŠ.
Ni 9928: ISET I 203: IŠ.
Ni 9989: ISET I 202: IŠ.
PRAK II B 20: IŠ.
Royal Ontario Museum prov.: Sigrist, *Neo-Sumerian Texts from the Royal Ontario Museum* II: See Chap. 2.2x.
R.S. 23.34 (+) 23.484 + 23.363: Ugaritica 5, l65: Ballade Syr.
R.S. 25.130: *Ugaritica* 5 (1968) 293–297: Prov. Ugar.
R.S. 25.424: *Ugaritica* 5 (1968), 166: Ballade Syr.
Sb 12355 (Susa): IŠ.
Schøyen MS 2040: IŠ.
Schøyen MS 2268/03: The Adulterer.
Schøyen MS 2291: IŠ.
Schøyen MS 2788: IŠ.
Schøyen MS 3352: IŠ.
Schøyen MS 3366: IŠ.
UET 6/2 169: IŠ.
UET 6/2 170: IŠ.
UET 6/2 171: IŠ.

Plates

List of linedrawings and photographs

Unless otherwise stated the photographs and copies are by the author.

Šuruppak UM_2.

Pl. 20 UM 29-16-240, rev. = Instructions of Šuruppak. UM_2.
UM 29-13-326, rev. = Instructions of Šuruppak UM_2.

Pl. 21 3N-T 917,397, obv. = Instructions of Šuruppak T_1.
3N-T 917,397, rev. Instructions of Šuruppak T_1.
UM 29-13-326, right edge. = Instructions of Šuruppak UM_2.

Pl. 22 CBS 4611, obv. = Instructions of Šuruppak C_1.
CBS 4611, rev. = Instructions of Šuruppak C_1.
UM 55-21-345 = 3N-T 549, obv. = Instructions of Šuruppak UM_3.
UM 55-21-345 = 3N-T 549, rev. = Instructions of Šuruppak UM_3.

Pl. 23 CBS 8001, obv. = Instructions of Šuruppak C_2.
CBS 8001, rev. = Instructions of Šuruppak C_2.
CBS 2203 + 13107, obv. = Instructions of Šuruppak C_3.
CBS 2203 + 13107, rev. = Instructions of Šuruppak C_3.

Pl. 24 10054, obv. Photograph by courtesy of the National Museum of Denmark, Department of Classical and Near Eastern Antiquities, no. 10054. = Instructions of Šuruppak Cop.

Pl. 25 10054, rev. Photograph by courtesy of the National Museum of Denmark, Department of Classical and Near Eastern Antiquities, no. 10054. = Instructions of Šuruppak Cop.

Pl. 26 AbS-T 323, obv. Photograph by courtesy of R.D. Biggs and the Oriental Institue, Chicago, Abs T neg. 332, obv. and rev. Cf. Chap. 1.5: The Abū Ṣalābṣkh Version.

Pl. 27 AbS-T 323, rev. Photograph by courtesy of R.D. Biggs and the Oriental Institue, Chicago. Cf. Chap. 1.5: The Abū Ṣalābṣkh Version.

Pl. 28 OIP 14, 55-56. Photograph by courtesy of the Oriental Institute, Chicago. Cf. Chap. 1.6: The Adab Version.

Pl. 29 Akkado-Hurrian bilingual fragment of Instructions of Šuruppak, unnumbered. Copy by M. Krebernik, ZA 86 (1986) 172. Cf. Chap. 1.7.

Pl. 30 CBS 1208, obv. Photograph by K. Danti. Cf. Chap. 3.3: Ballade of Early Rulers D.

Pl. 31 CBS 1208, rev. Photograph by E. Robson. = Chap. 3.1: Níŋ-nam Vers. C; Chap. 3.3: Ballade of Early Rulers D.
CBS 1208 lower edge. Photograph by E. Robson. = Chap. 3.1: Níŋ-nam Vers. C.

Pl. 32 CBS 13777 obv. Photograph by E. Robson. = Chap. 3.4: Proverbs from Ugarit.
CBS 13777 right edge. Photograph by E. Robson. = Chap. 3.1; Chap. 3.2x: Níŋ-nam (Vers. B).

Pl. 33 CBS 13777 rev. Photograph by E. Robson. = Chap. 3.1; Chap. 3.2.x: Níŋ-nam (Vers. B).

Pl. 34 CBS 6924+N3097 obv. Photograph by E. Robson. = Chap. 3.2x: Níŋ-nam Vers. D.

Pl. 35 N 3047 obv. Photograph by Alster. = Chap. 3.1: Níŋ-nam.

Pl. 35 UM 29-16-616 obv. Photograph by E. Robson. = Chap. 3.1: Níŋ-nam Vers. A.
N 3579 obv. and rev. Photograph by Alster = Chap. 3.1 Níŋ-nam (Vers. A).

Pl. 36 3N-T326 obv. (cast). = Chap. 3.2: Níŋ-nam Vers. D, etc.

Pl. 37 3N-T 360 obv. (cast). Chap. 3.2: Níŋ-nam Vers. D, etc.

Pl. 38 3N-T 360 rev. (cast). Chap. 3.2: Níŋ-nam Vers. D, etc.

Pl. 39 3N-T 326 rev. (cast). Chap. 3.2: Níŋ-nam Vers. D, etc.

Pl. 40 HS 1535 obv. and rev. Photograph by J. Dahl. = Chap. 4.2: Fable of Hyena and a Dog. Cf. Pl. 71.

Pl. 41 Schøyen MS 2268/03. Photograph by courtesy of the Schøyen collection, Oslo. = Chap. 4.5: The Adulterer.

Pl. 42 10062 obv. Copy by B. Alster (AcSum 10, p. 13) = SP 23.

Pl. 43 10062 rev. Copy by B. Alster (AcSum 10, 14) = SP 23, rev. including Chap. 4.5: The Adulterer.

Pl. 44 10062 obv. Sum. Proverb Collection 23. Photograph by courtesy of the National Museum of Denmark, Department of Classical and Near Eastern Antiquities, photo no. 10062. = SP 23.

Pl. 45 10062 rev. Sum. Proverb Collection 23, including Chap. 4.5: The Adulterer. Photograph by courtesy of the National Museum of Denmark, Department of Classical and Near Eastern Antiquities.

Pl. 46 CBS 6559 + 8078 + N 4708 obv. Obv. = Chap. 4.3: Goose and Raven D.

Pl. 47 CBS 6559 + 8078 + N 4708 rev. Lexical.

Pl. 48 CBS 1601 obv. and rev. (Alster, JCS 43–45, 28) = Chap. 5.1: Three Ox-Drivers of Adab B.

Pl. 48 N 5909 (Alster, *N.A.B.U.*990/3, 82, no. 102) = Chap. 3.5: Enlil and Namzitarra D.

Pl. 49 Cornell University Kroch-04 obv. Photograph by D.I. Owen. = Chap. 6.1: Addition to SP 1.

Pl. 50 Cornell University Kroch-04 rev. Photograph by D.I. Owen. = Chap. 6.1: Addition to SP 1.

Pl. 50 Cornell University Kroch-04 right edge. Photograph by D.I. Owen. = Chap. 6.1: Addition to SP 1.

Pl. 51 Cornell University Kroch-05 obv., upper part. Photograph by D.I. Owen. = Chap. 6.2: Addition to SP 2, etc.

Pl. 52 Cornell University Kroch-05 obv., right side of upper part. Photograph by D.I. Owen. = Chap. 6.2: Addition to SP 2, etc.

Pl. 52 Cornell University Kroch-05 obv., right edge. Photograph by D.I. Owen. = Chap. 6.2: Addition to SP 2, etc.

Pl. 53 Cornell University Kroch-05 obv., lower part. Photograph by D.I. Owen. = Chap. 6.2: Addition to SP 2, etc.

Pl. 54 Cornell University Kroch-05 rev., upper part. Photograph by D.I. Owen. = Chap. 6.2: Addition to SP 2, etc.

Pl. 55 Cornell University Kroch-05 rev., lower part. Photograph by D.I. Owen. = Chap. 6.2: Addition to SP 2, etc.

Pl. 56 Cornell University Kroch-05 rev., right edge of the lower part. Photograph by D.I. Owen. = Chap. 6.2: Addition to SP 2, etc.

Pl. 57a Cornell University Kroch-05, right part of left edge. Photograph by D.I. Owen. = Chap. 6.2: Addition to SP 2, etc.

Pl. 57b Cornell University Kroch-05, left part of left edge. Photograph by D.I. Owen. = Chap. 6.2: Addition to SP 2, etc.

Pl. 57c Cornell University Kroch-05, bottom edge. Photograph by D.I. Owen. = Chap. 6.2: Addition to SP 2, etc.

Pl. 57d Cornell University Kroch-05, rev., bottom edge. Photograph by D.I. Owen. = Chap. 6.2: Addition to SP 2, etc.

Pl. 58 CBS 438 obv., left part. Chap. 4.2: The Fox and Enlil as Merchant.

Pl. 58 CBS 438 obv., right part. Chap. 4.2: The Fox and Enlil as Merchant.

Pl. 59 CBS 438 rev., left part. Chap. 4.2: The Fox and Enlil as Merchant.

Pl. 59 CBS 438 rev., centre part. Chap. 4.2: The Fox and Enlil as Merchant.

Pls. 60–65: Photographs by courtesy of the Schøyen collection, Oslo.

(Pls. 64–67 by Renee Kovacs)

Pl. 60 Schøyen 2.2788 obv.
Schøyen 2.2788 right edge.
Schøyen 2.2788 bottom edge.

Pl. 61 Schøyen 2.2788 rev.
Schøyen 2.2788 left edge.

Pl. 62 Schøyen 9.3352 obv.
Schøyen 9.3352 left edge.

Pl. 63 Schøyen 9.3352 rev.
Schøyen 9.3352 right edge.

Pl. 64 Schøyen 3366 obv.

Pl. 65 Schøyen 3366 rev.

Pl. 66 Schøyen 3366 obv left; rev. left.

Pl. 67 Schøyen 3366 rev. right.

Pl. 68 Schøyen 0.2291, obv., rev., left, right, top and bottom edges.

Pl. 69 Schøyen 0.2040, obv., rev., left, right, top and bottom edges.

Pls. 70–72: Additional copies to Chaps. 3 and 4

Pl. 70 BM 80091, obv. and rev. Copy by Ulla Jeyes (Alster and Jeyes, AcSum 8 (1986) 10–11) = Chap. 3.3: Ballade of Early Rulers A.

Pl. 71 HS 1535, obv. and rev. Copy by Manfred Krebernik. Cf. Chap. 4.2: Fable of a Hyena and a Dog). Cf. pl. 40.

Pl. 72a CBS 6930, obv. Photograph by K. Danti. Cf. Chap. 4.3: Goose Raven L.

Pl. 72b UM 29-13-329, obv. Photograph by K. Danti. Cf. Chap. 4.3: Goose Raven J.

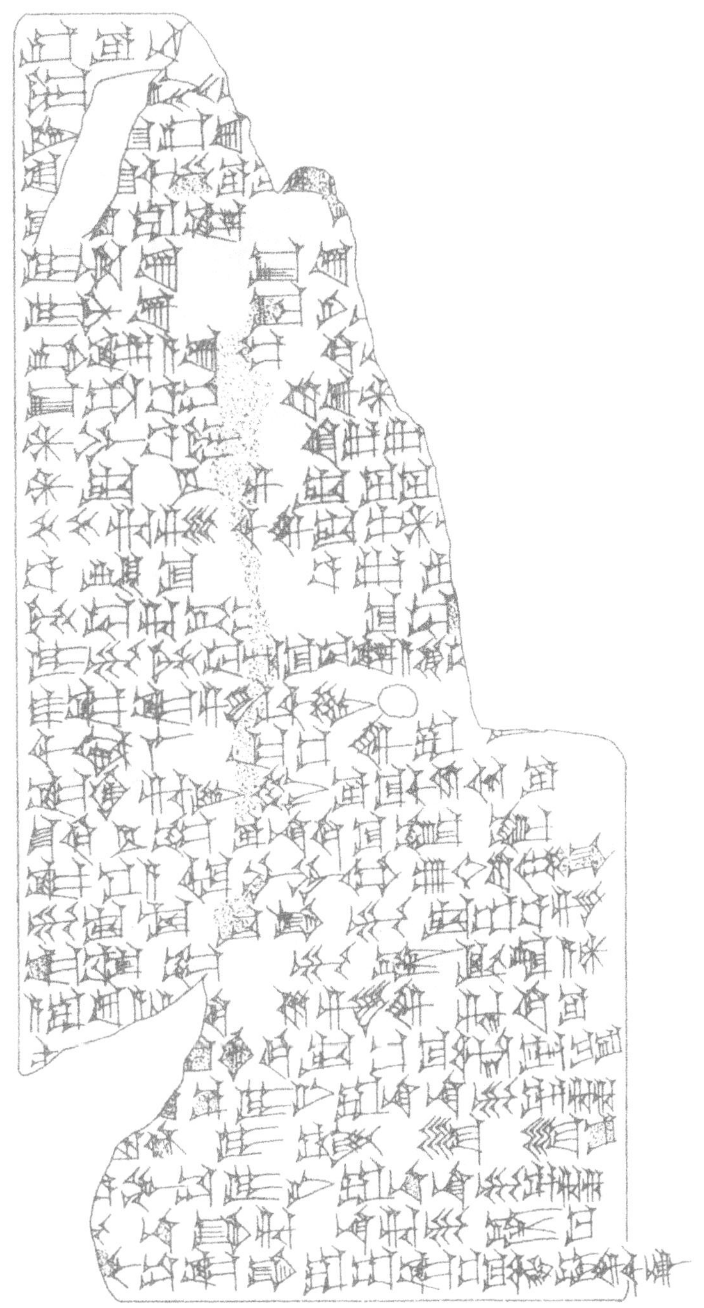

UM 29-16-9, obv.

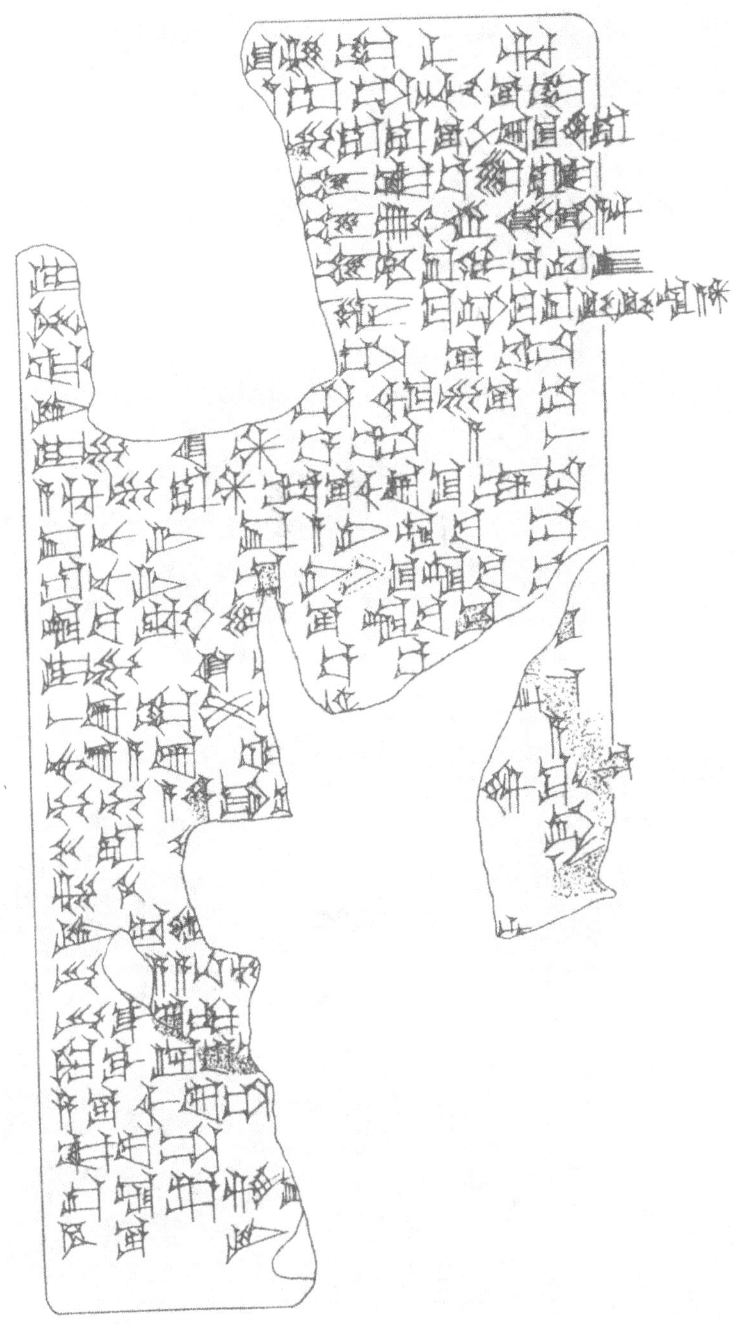

UM 29-16-9, rev.

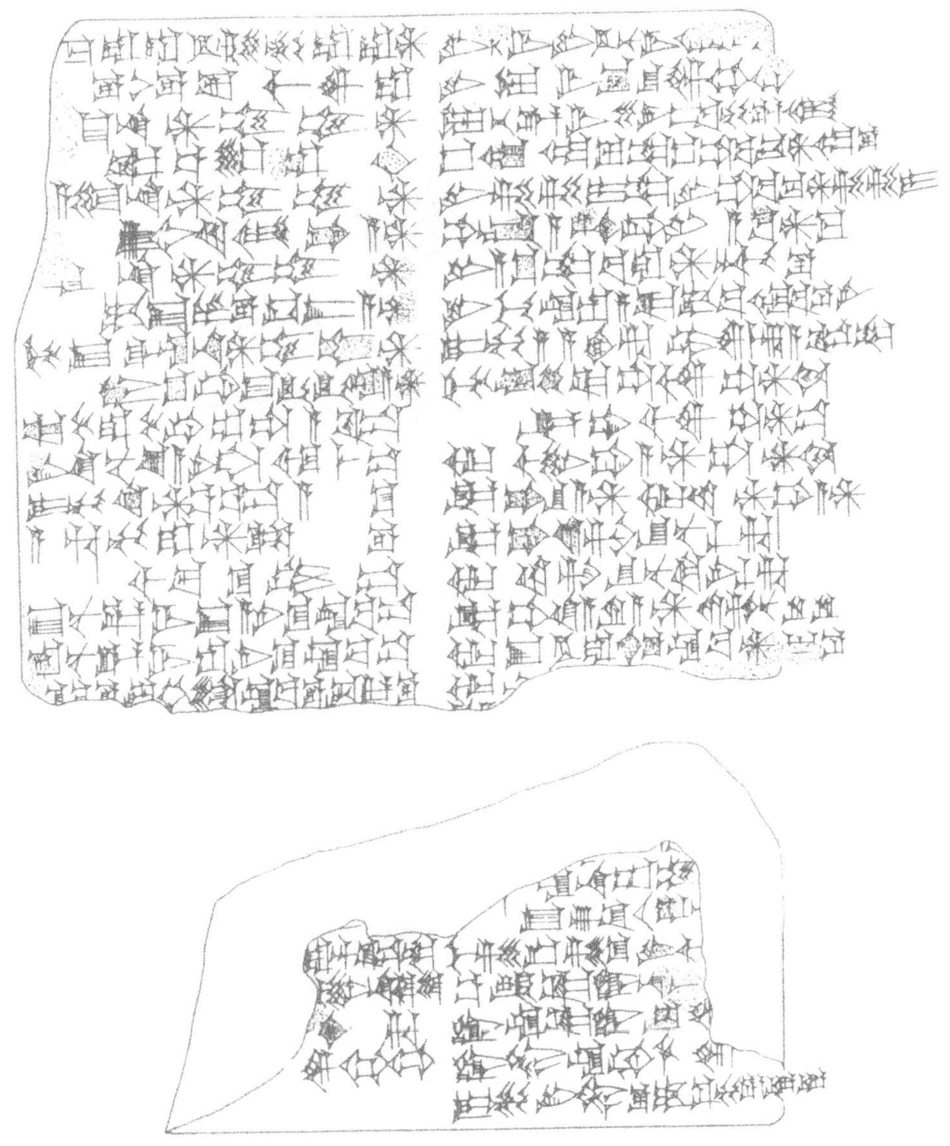

UM 29-13-326 (above) (+) UM 29-16-240 (below)

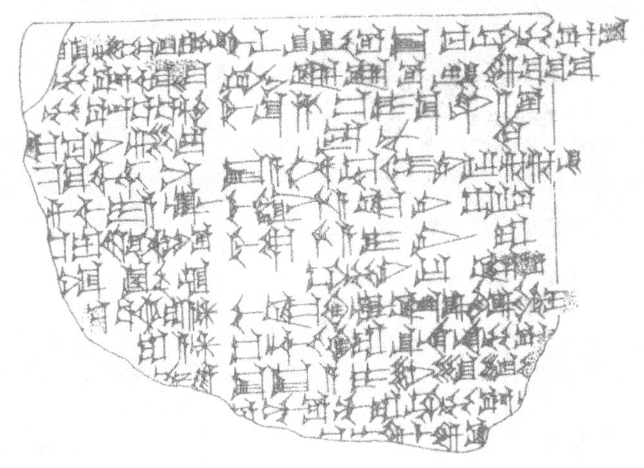

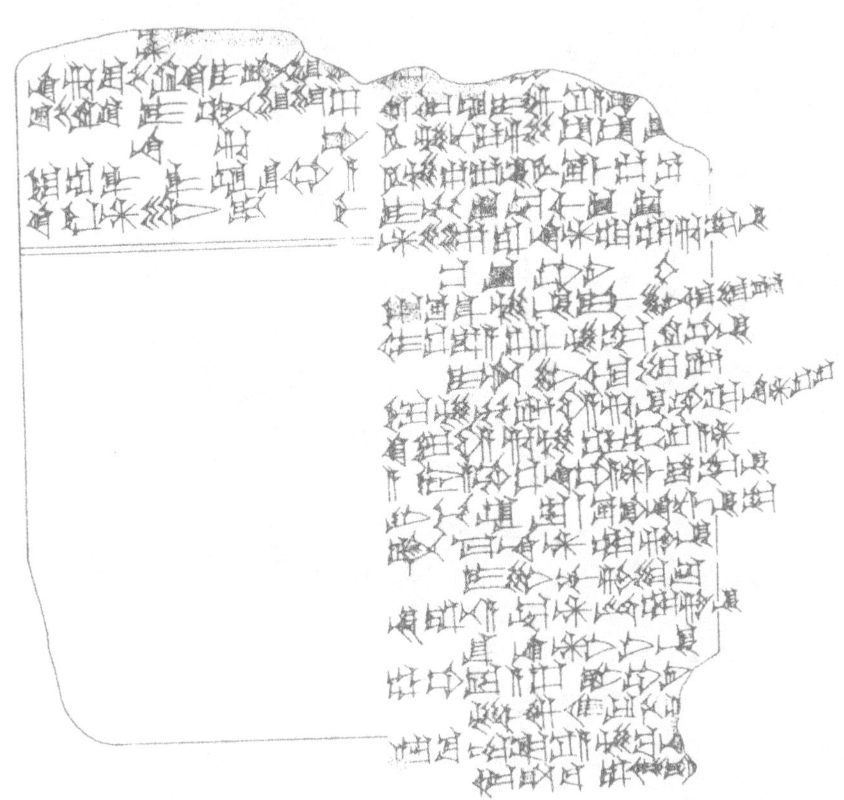

UM 29-13-326 (below) (+) UM 29-16-240 (above)

Plate 5

UM 55-21-345

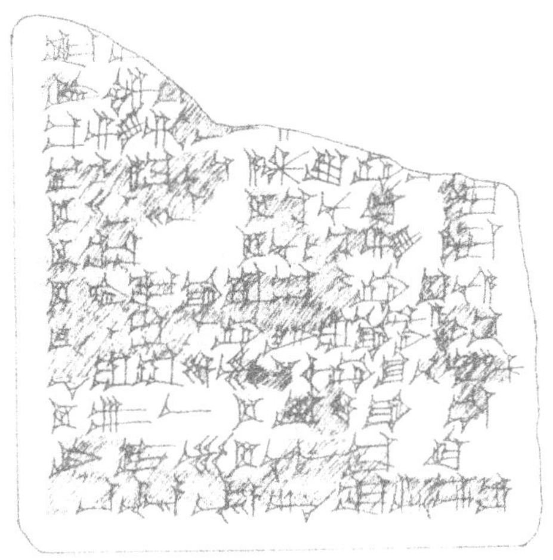

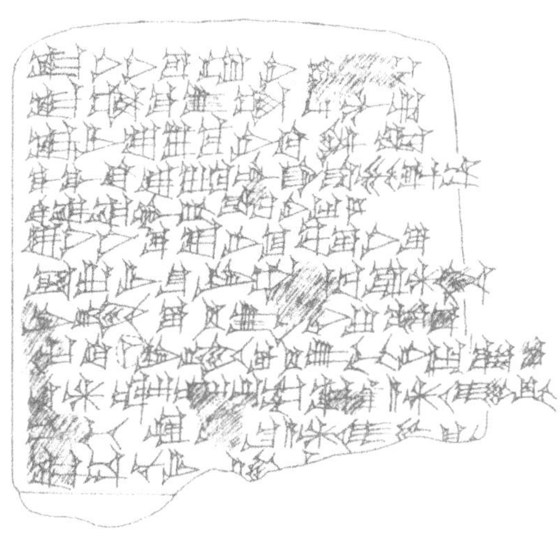

UM 55-21-334

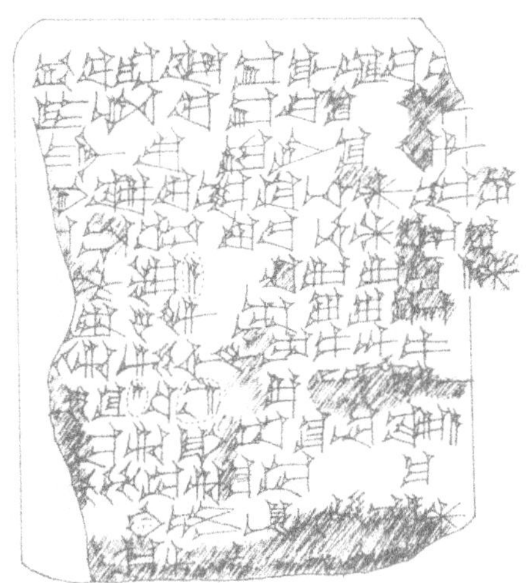

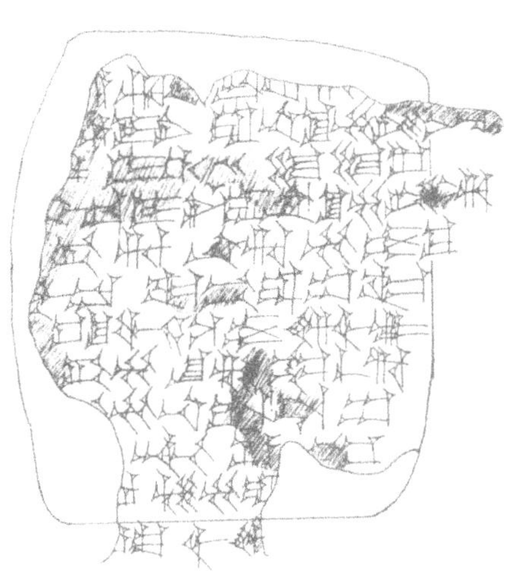

CBS 13107 + CBS 2203

Plate 6

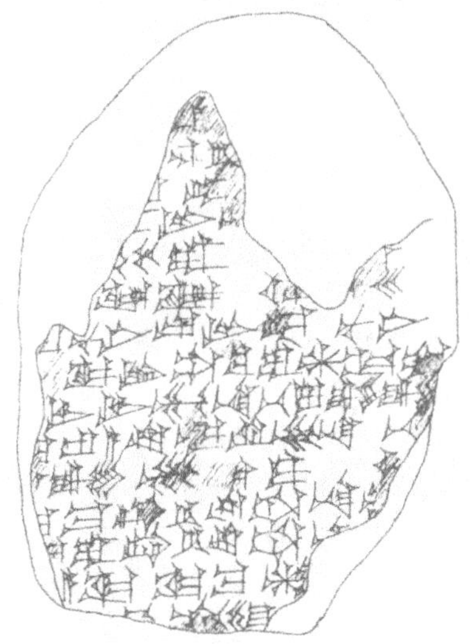

CBS 8001

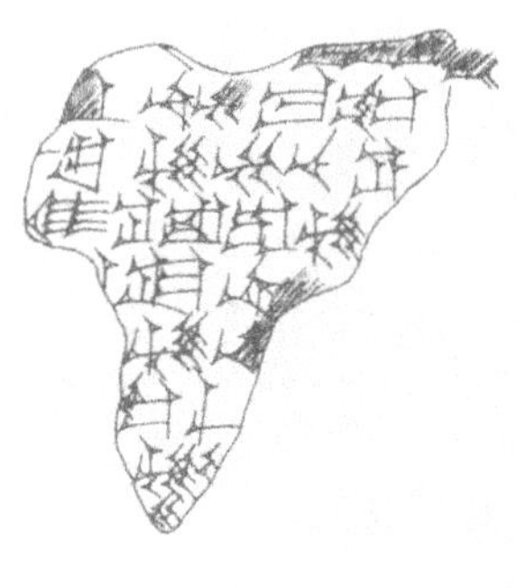

3N-T 917,397

3N-T 543, obv.(?)

Plate 7

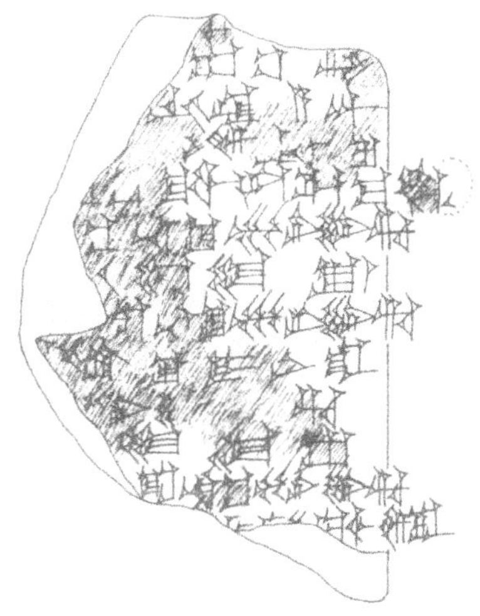

3N-T 537

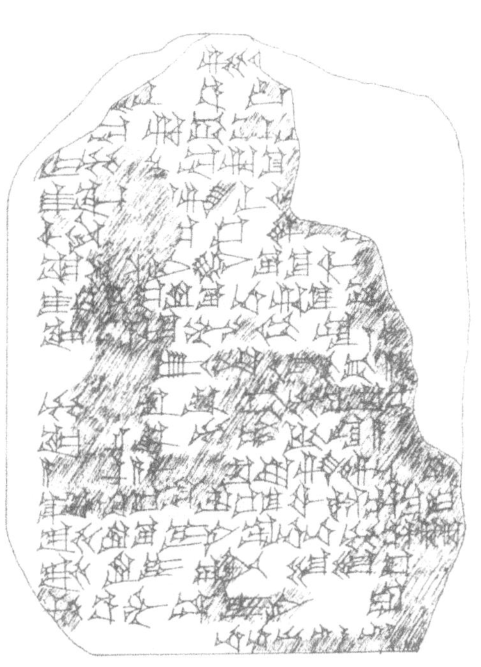

3N-T 722

Plate 8

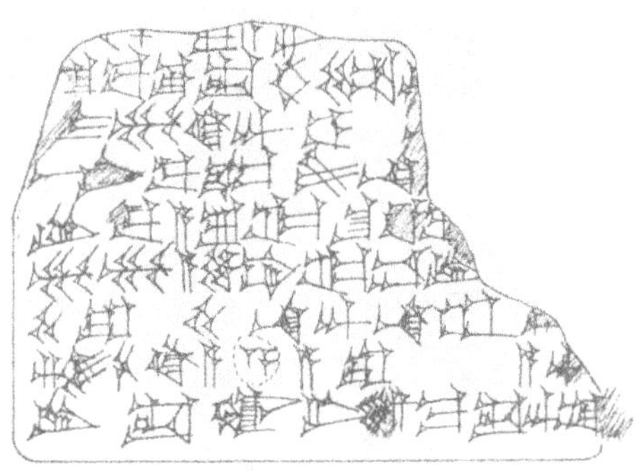

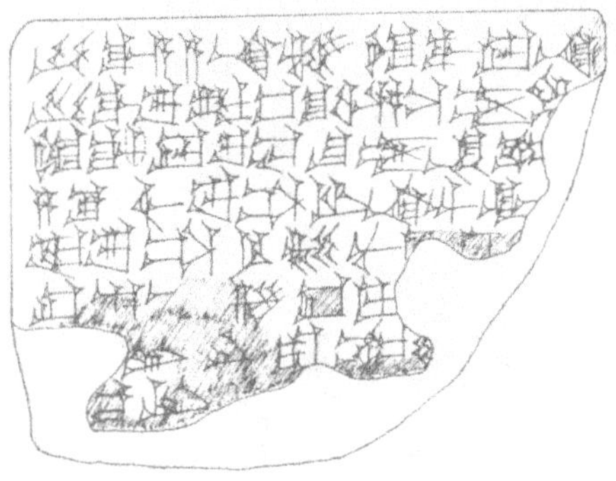

3N-T 460

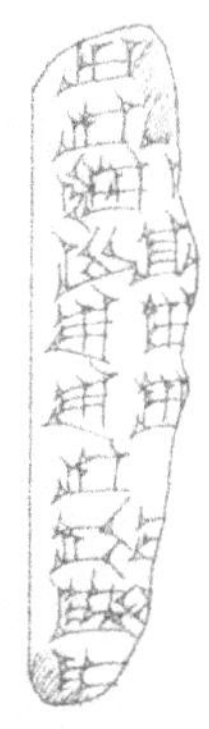

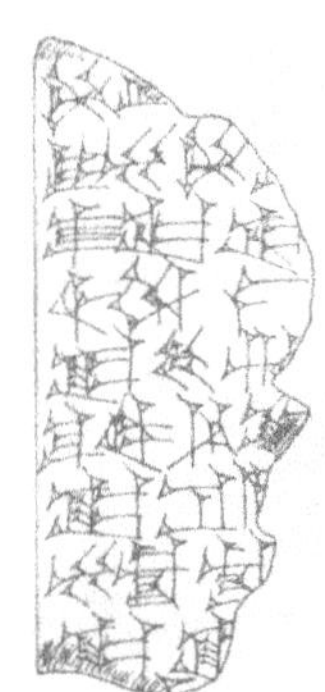

N 901

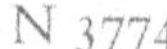

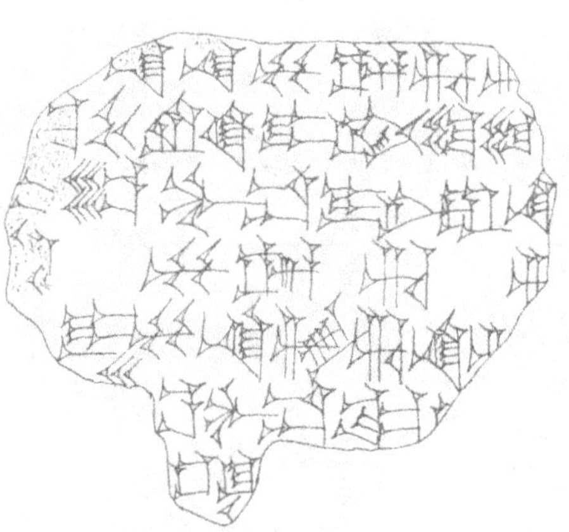

N 3774

N 3708

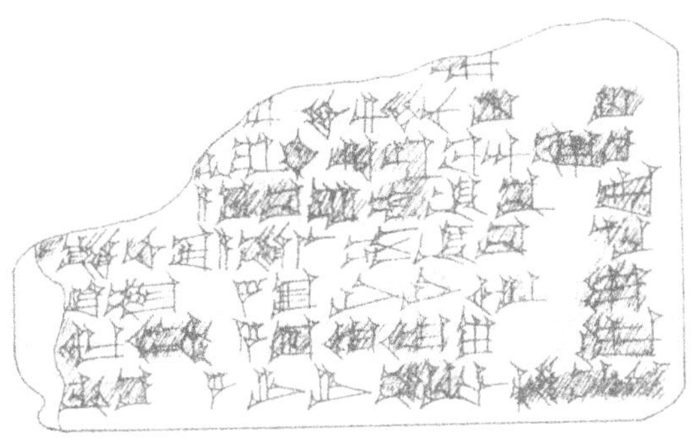

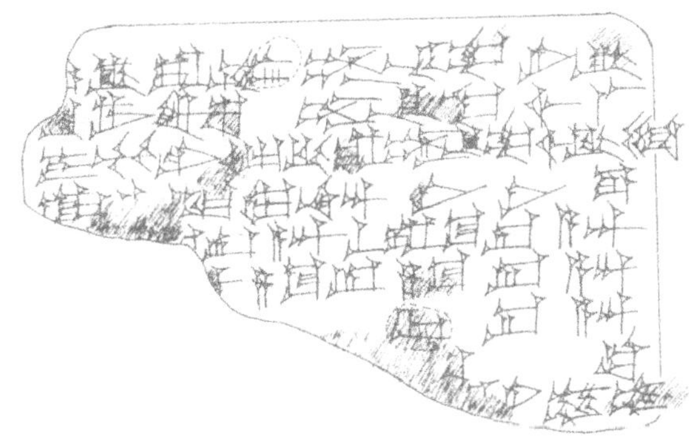

N 3298

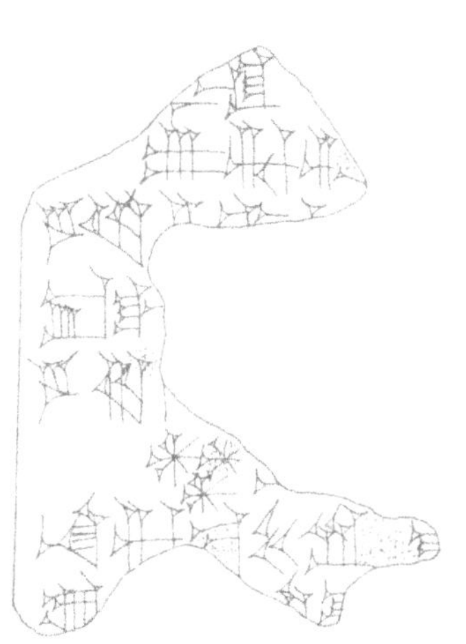

N 3757

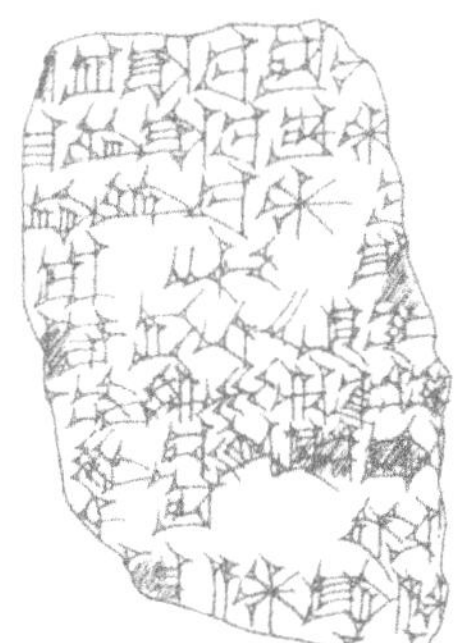

N 3432 obv.

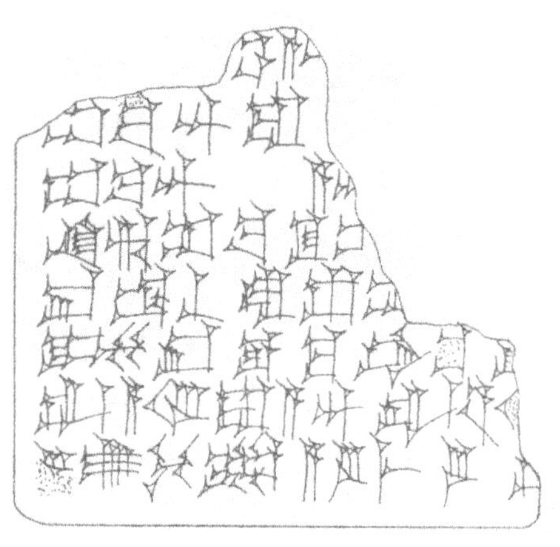

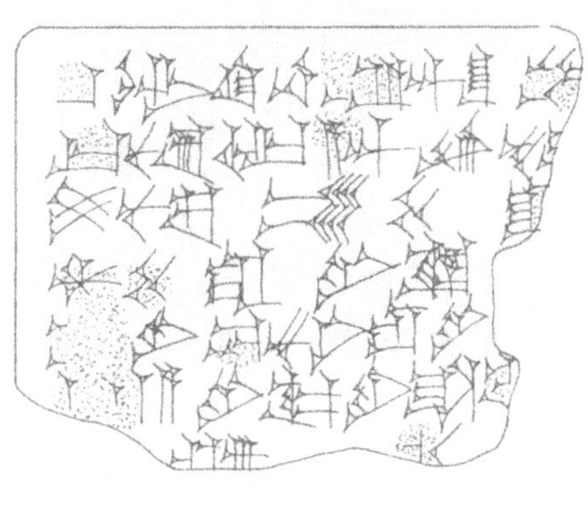

3N-T 918,422

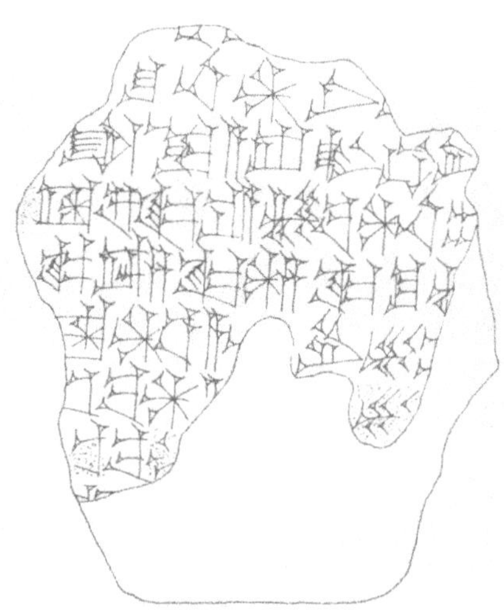

N 4148, obv.(?)

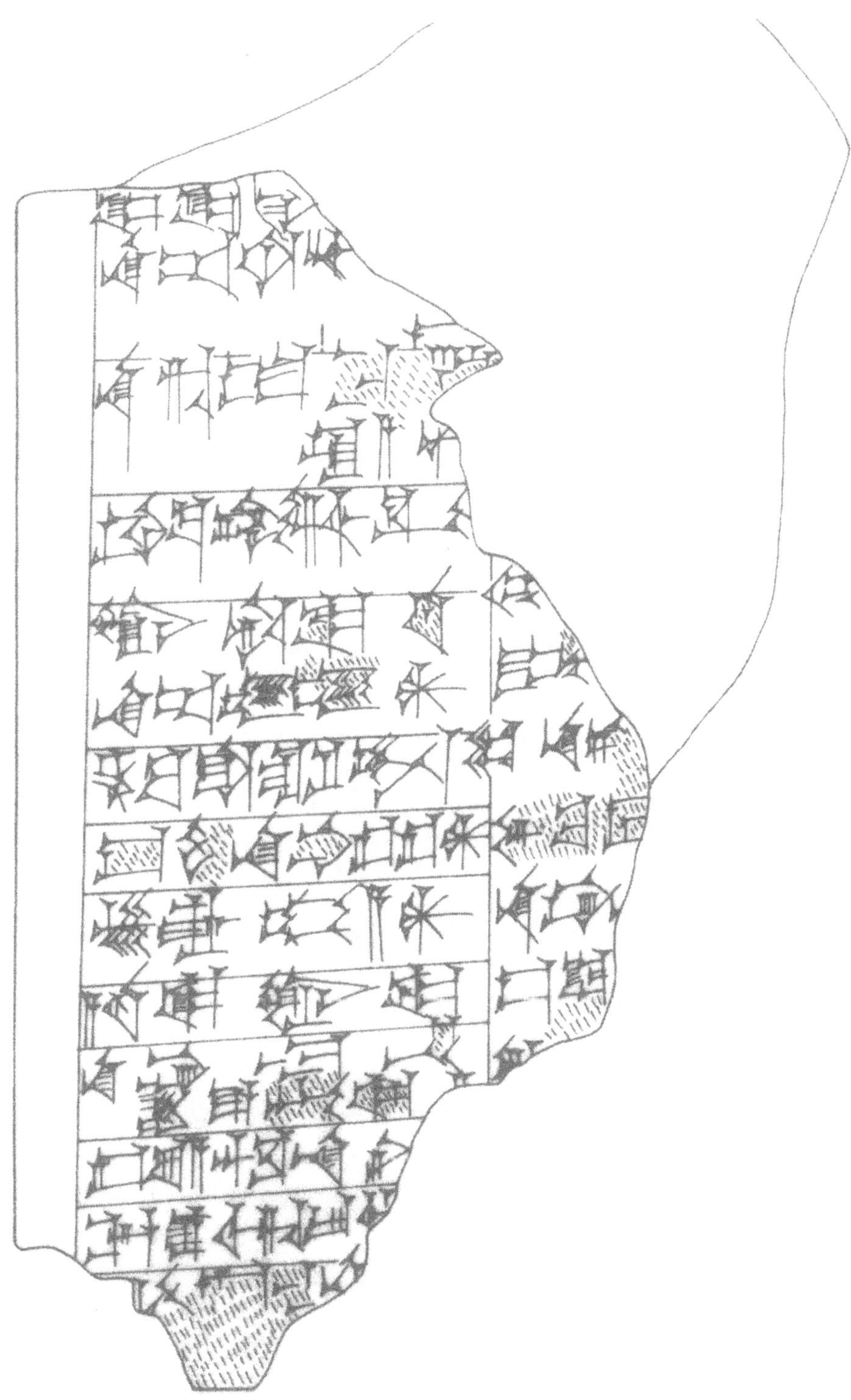

UET 6/3 429, obv.

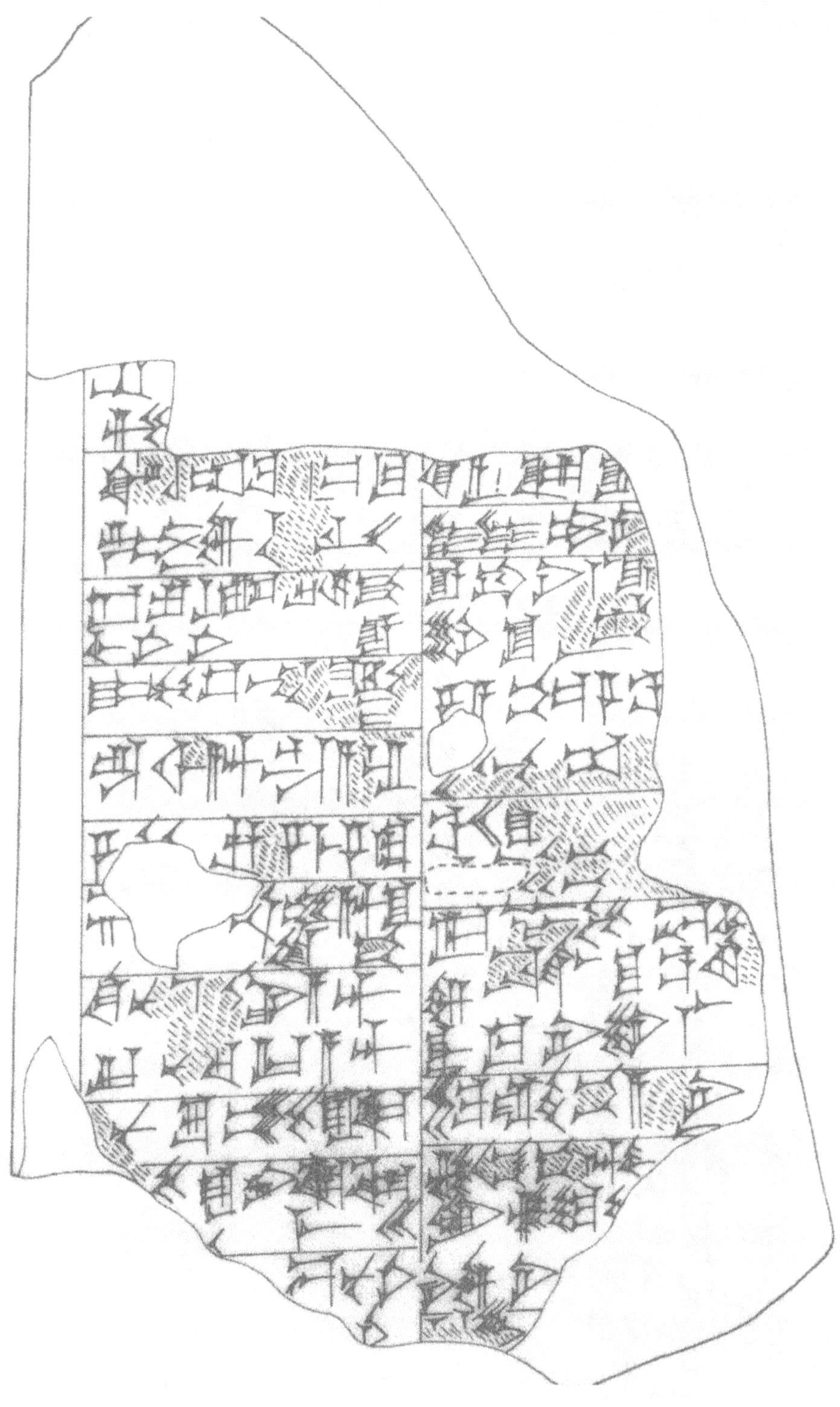

UET 6/3 429, rev.

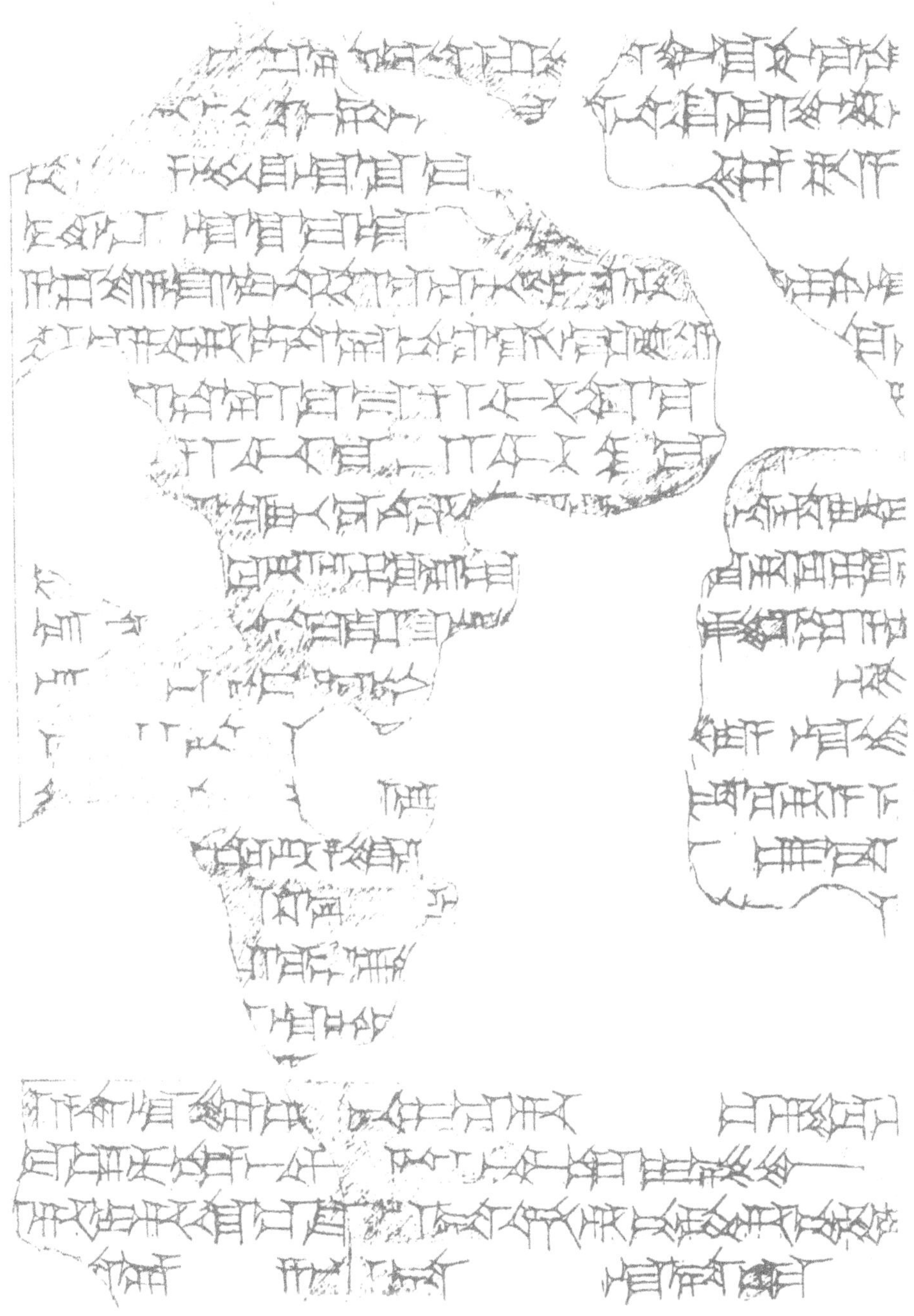

BM 56522+ obv.

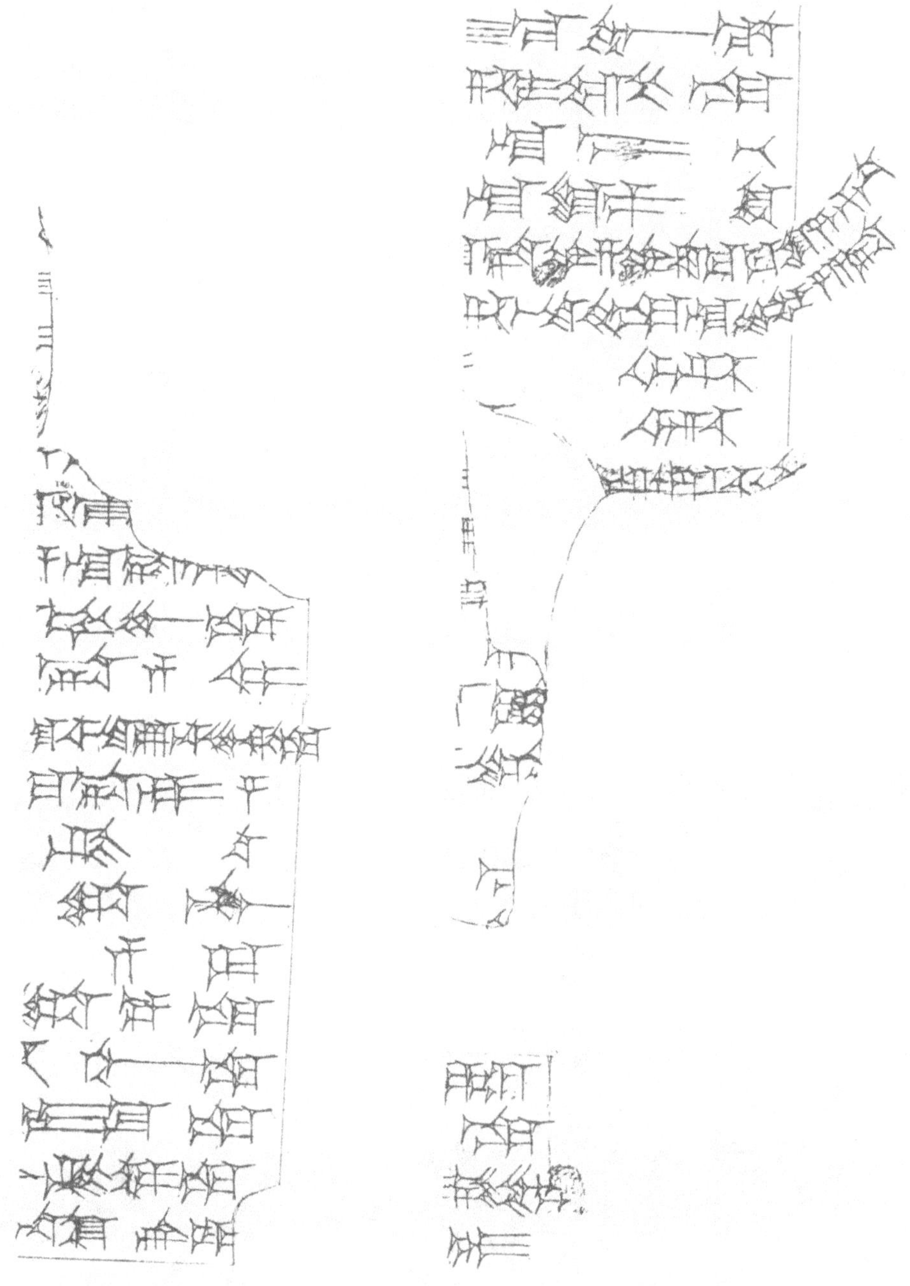

BM 56522+, edges

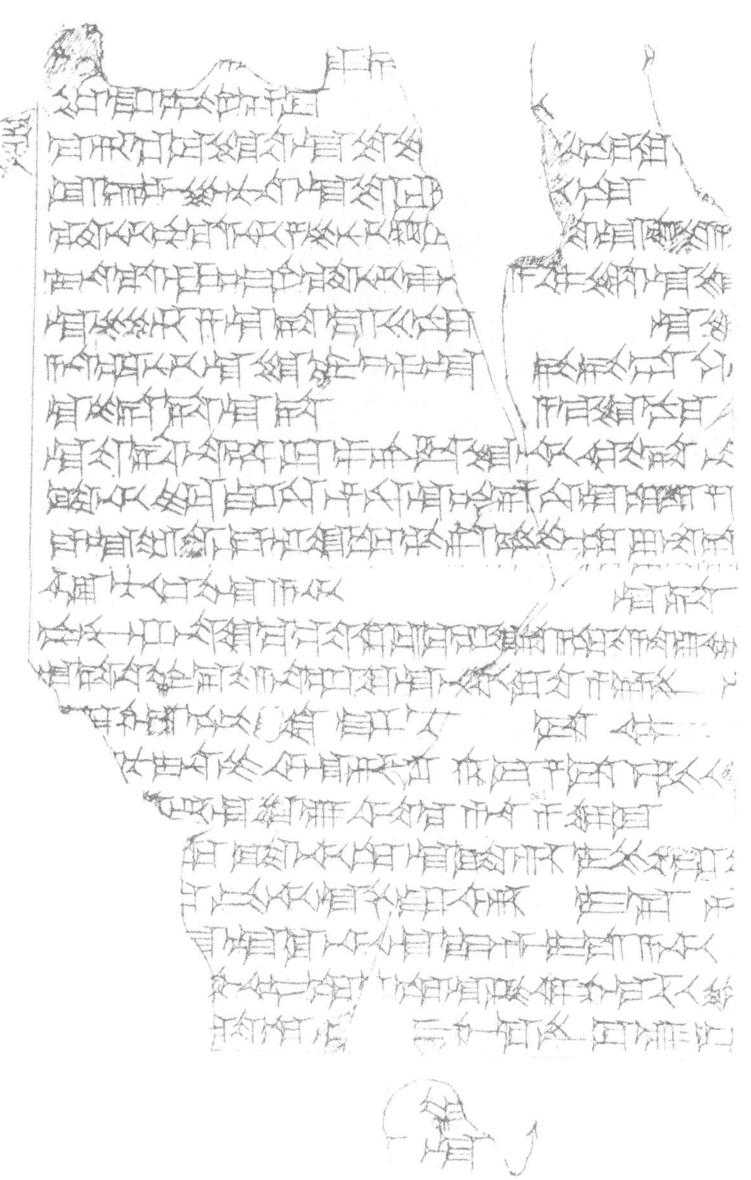

BM 56522+ rev.

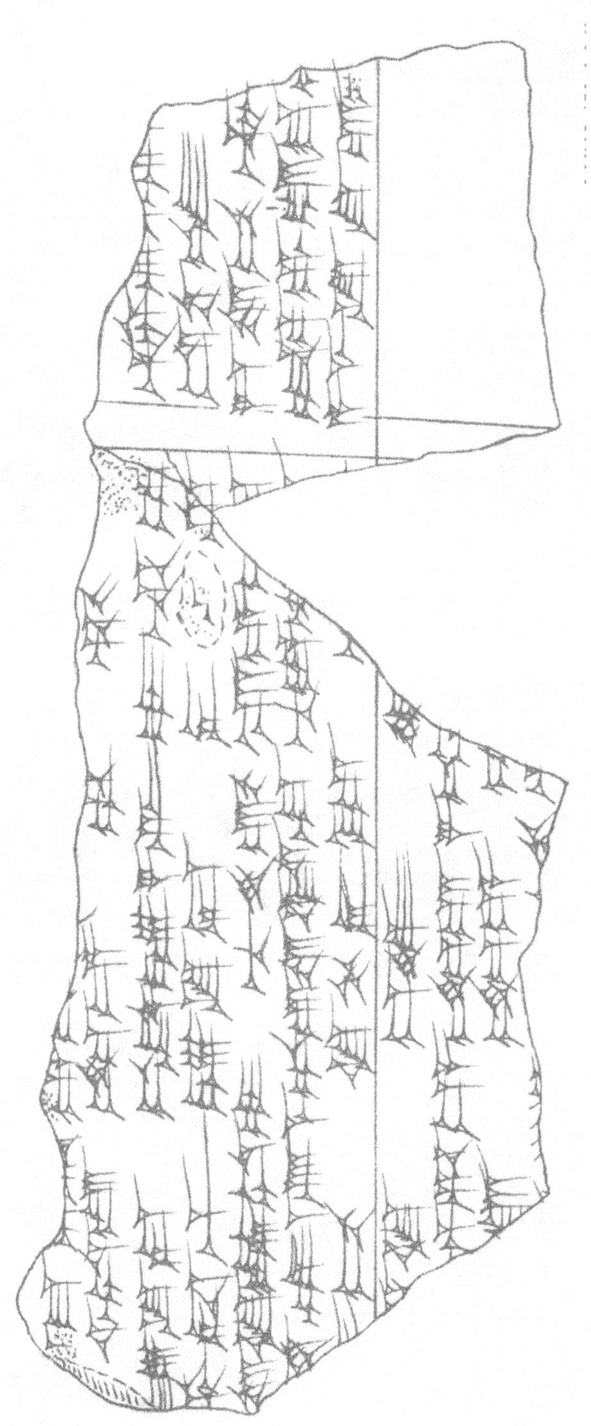

K 6917 + K 13679

UM 29-16-9, obv.

Plate 18

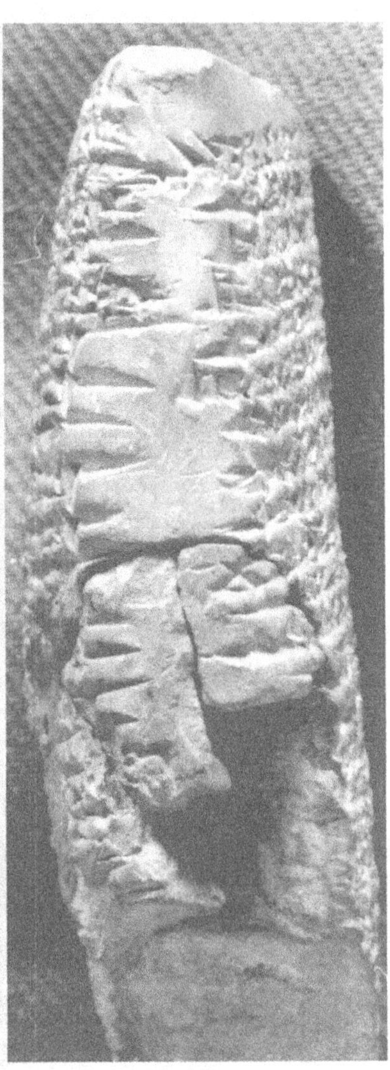

UM 29-16-9, rev. and right edge

UM 29-16-326, obv.

UM 29-16-240, obv.

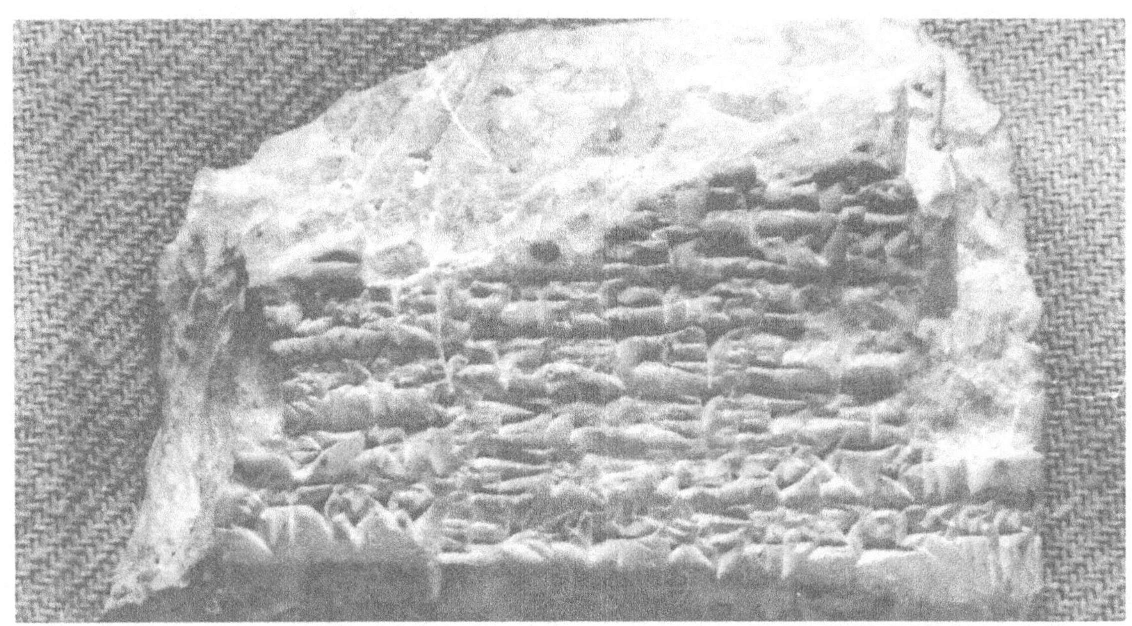

UM 29-16-240, rev.

UM 29-13-326, rev.

3N-T 917,397

UM 29-13-326, right edge

CBS 4611

UM 55-21-345

Plate 23

CBS 2203 + 13107

CBS 8001

Plate 24

10054, obv.

10054, rev.

AbS-T 323, obv.

AbS-T 323, rev.

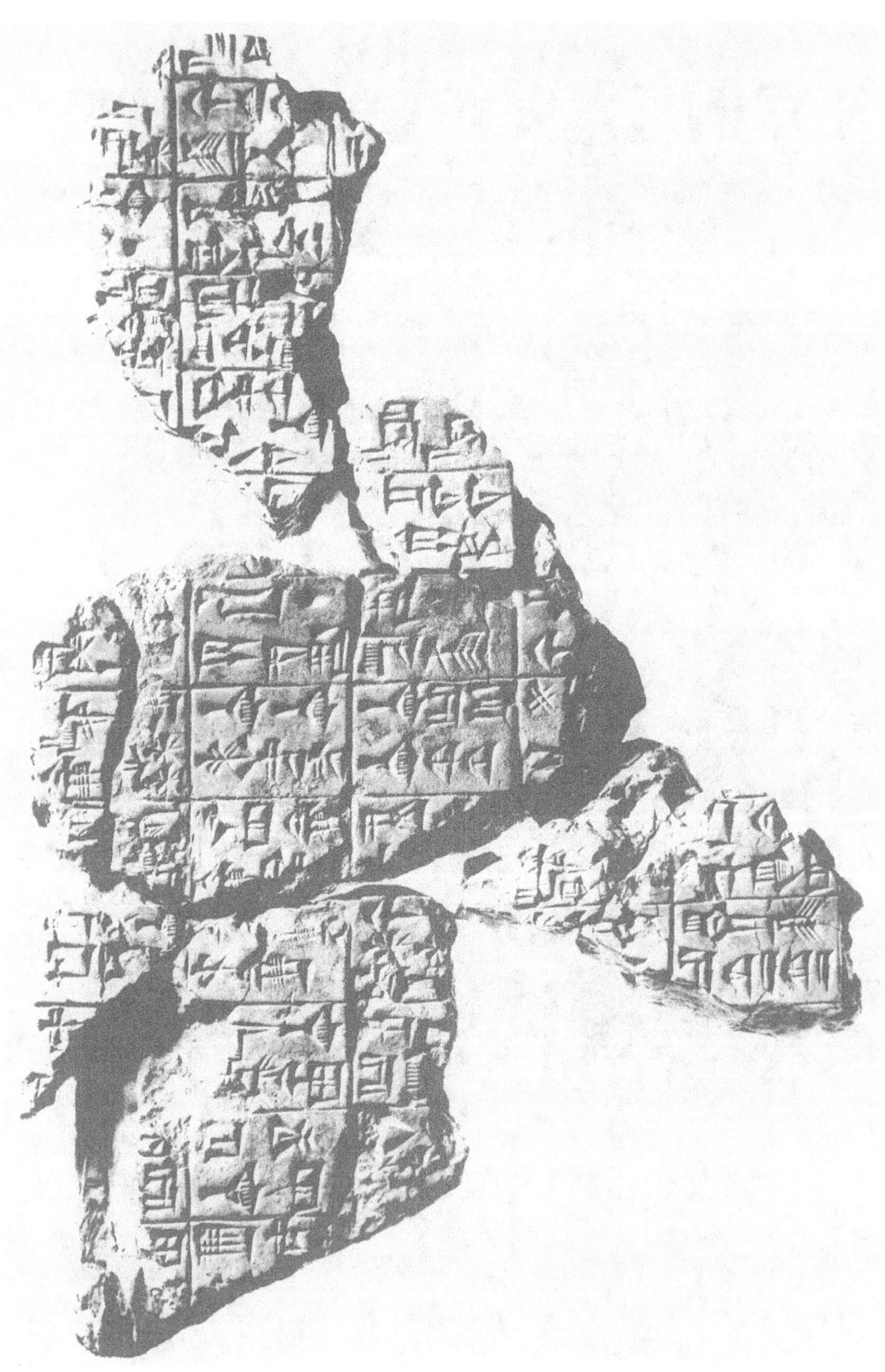

OIP 14, 55-56.

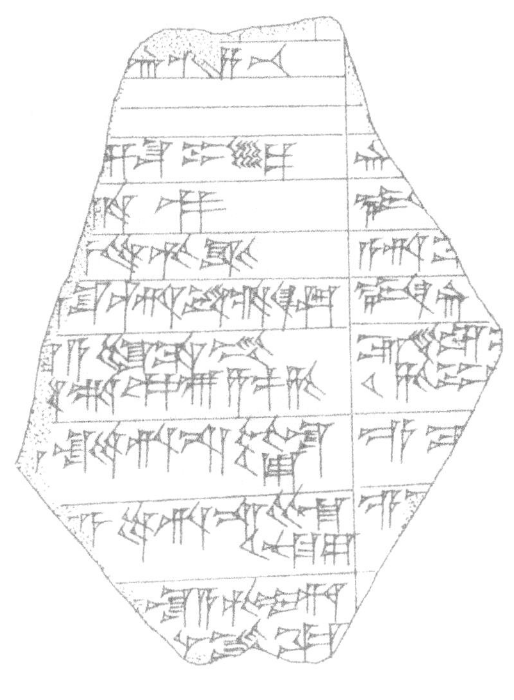

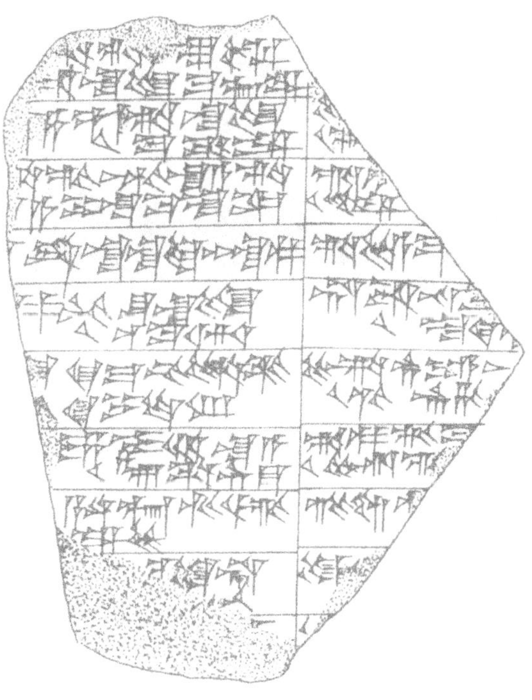

Akkado-Hurrian bilingual fragment

CBS 1208, obv.

Plate 31

CBS 1208, rev. and lower edge

CBS 13777 obv.

Plate 33

CBS 13777 rev. and edge

CBS 6924+N3097 obv.

N 3047 obv.

UM 29-16-616 obv.

N 3579

3N-T326 obv. (cast).

3N-T 360 obv. (cast)

3N-T 360 rev. (cast)

3N-T 326 rev. (cast)

HS 1535

Plate 41

Schøyen MS 2268/03

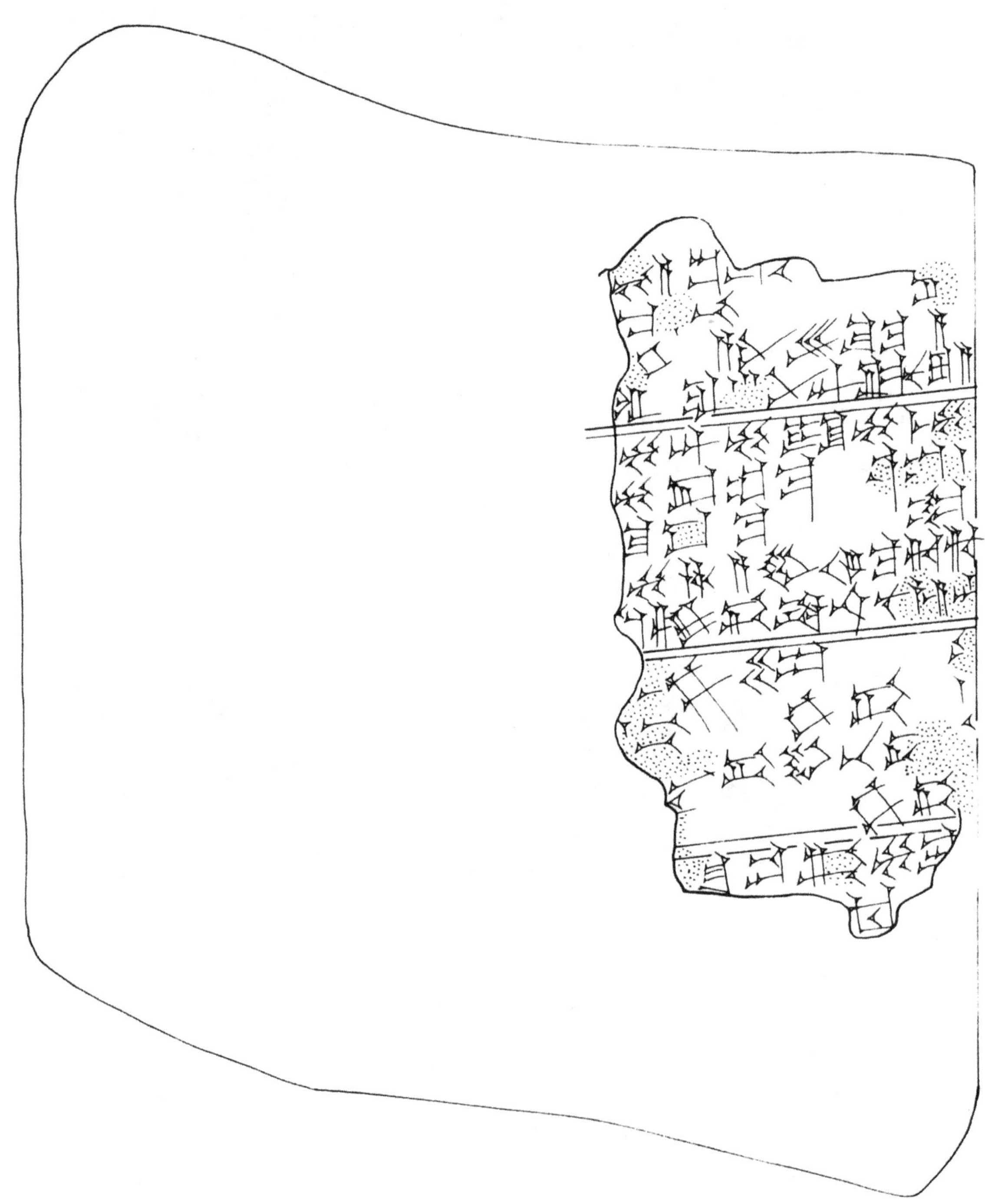

10062 obv.

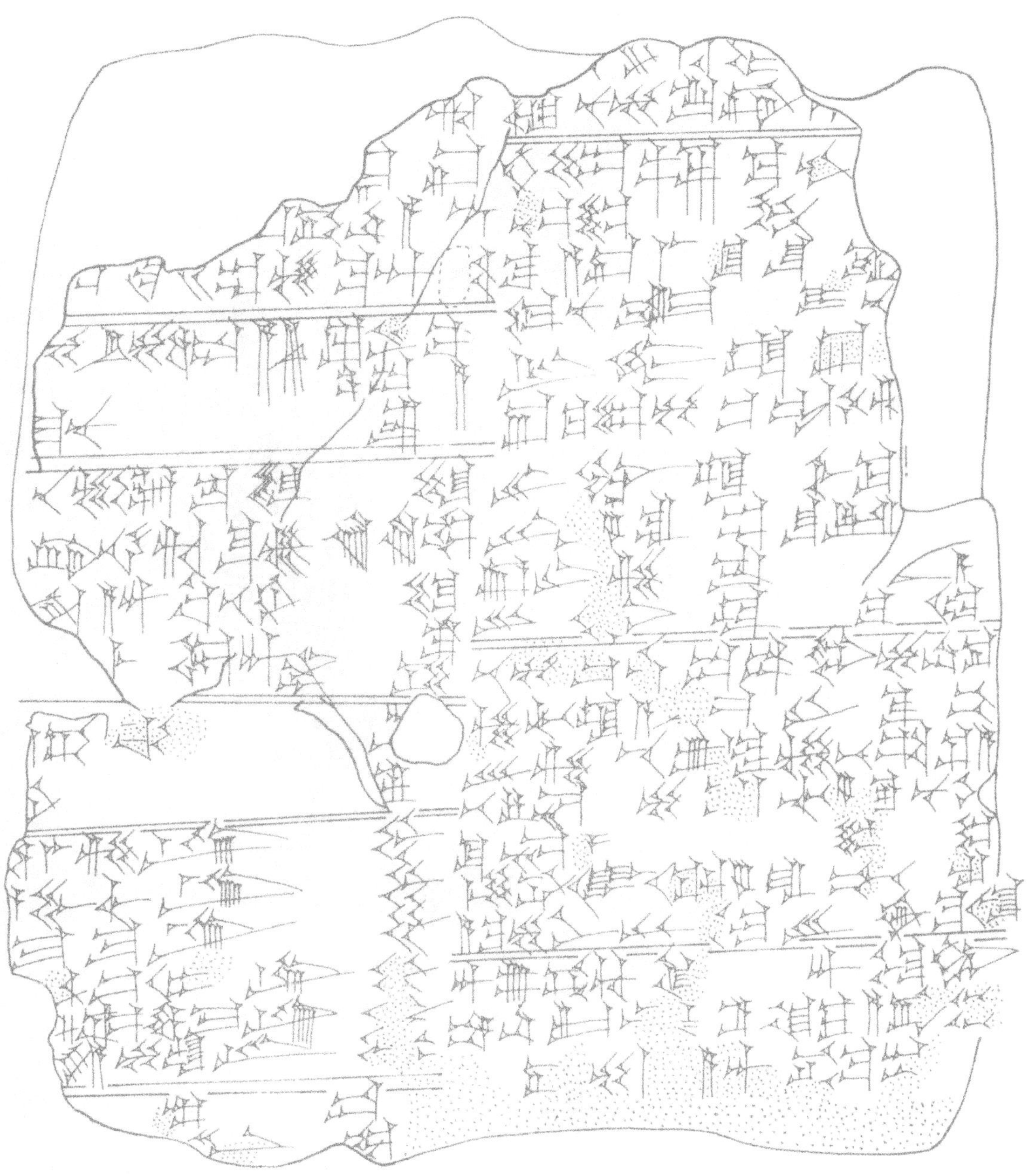

10062 rev.

10062 obv.

10062 rev.

Plate 46

CBS 6559 + 8078 + N 4708 obv.

CBS 6559 + 8078 + N 4708 rev.

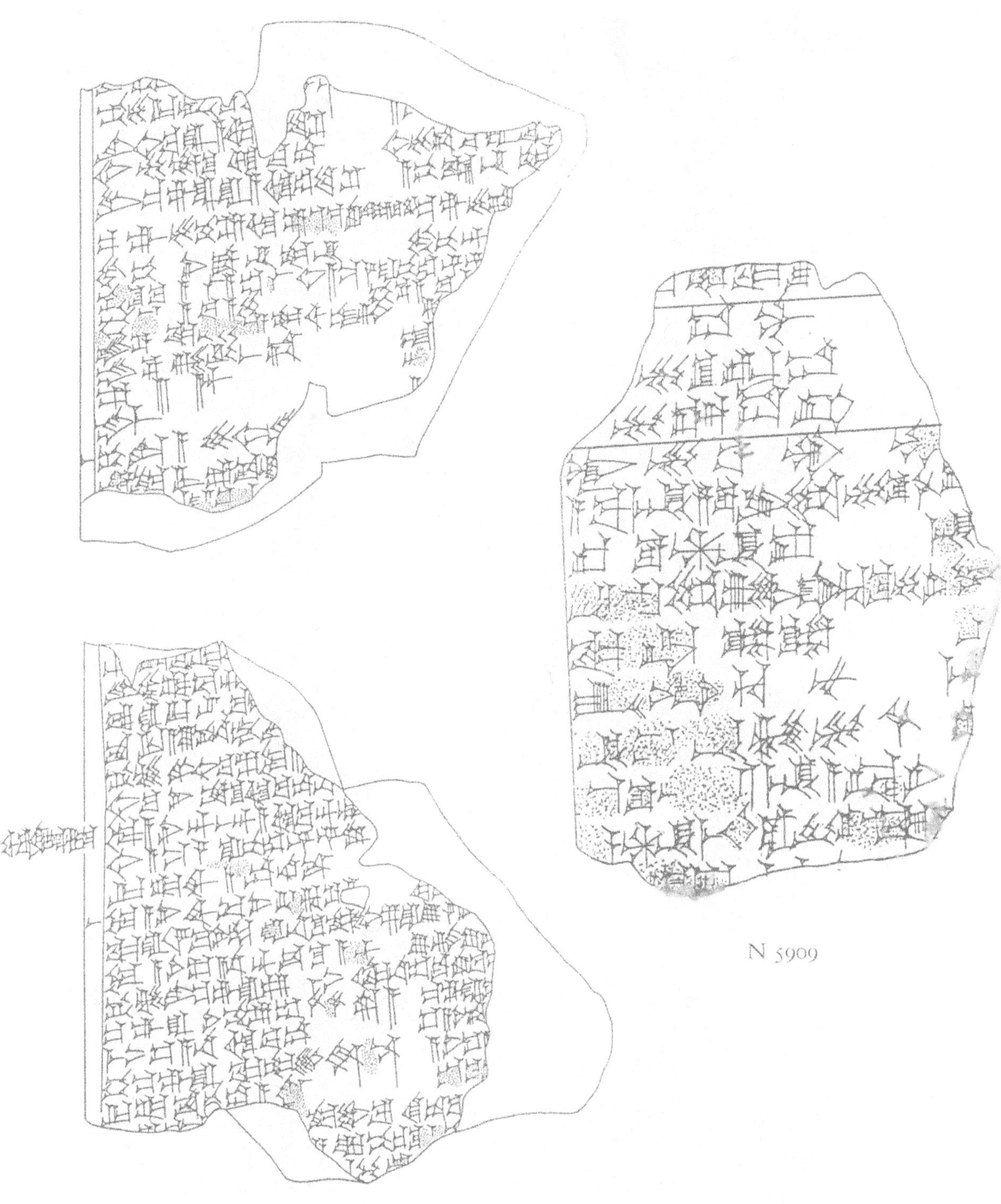

N 5909

CBS 1601 obv. and rev.

Cornell University Lib04 obv.

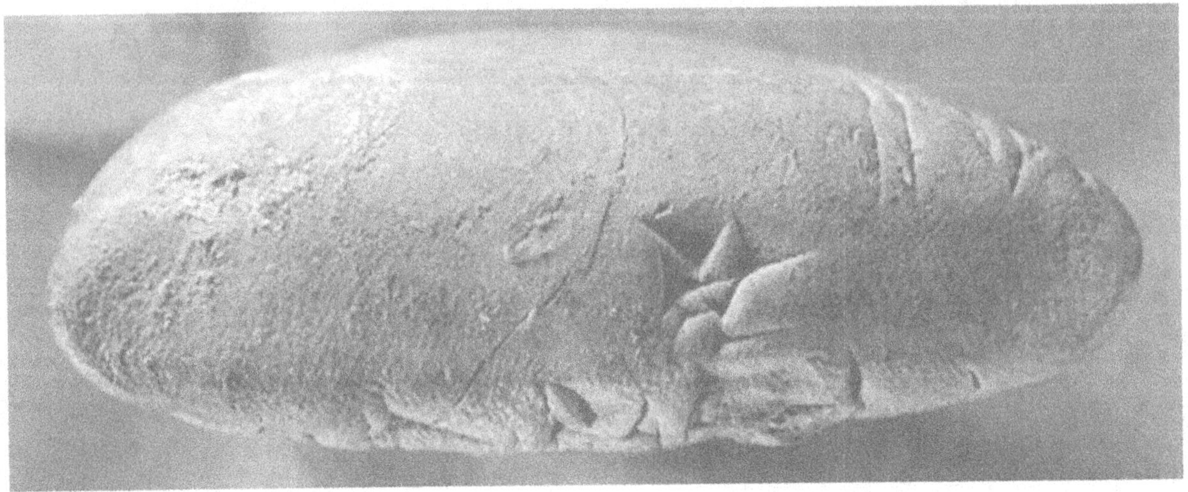

Cornell University Lib04 rev. and right edge

CBS 13777 obv.Cornell University Lib05 obv., upper part.

Cornell University Lib05 obv., right edge.

Cornell University Lib05 obv., lower part.

Cornell University Lib05 rev., upper part.

Cornell University Lib05 rev., lower part.

Cornell University Lib05 rev., right edge of the lower part.

Cornell University Lib05, left part of left edge.

Cornell University Lib05, right part of left edge.

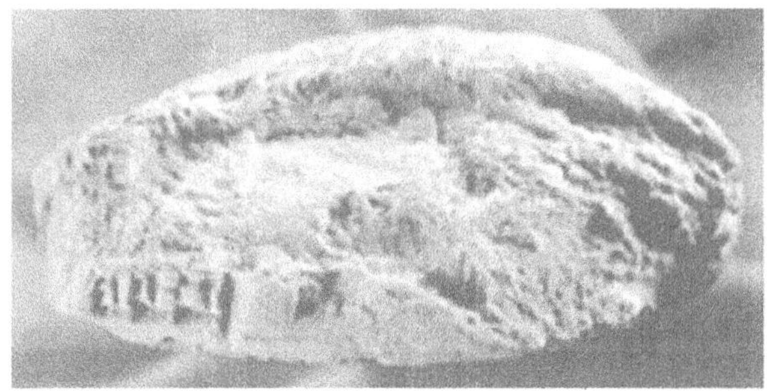

Cornell University Lib05, bottom edge.

Cornell University Lib05, rev., bottom edge.

CBS 438 obv.

CBS 438 rev.

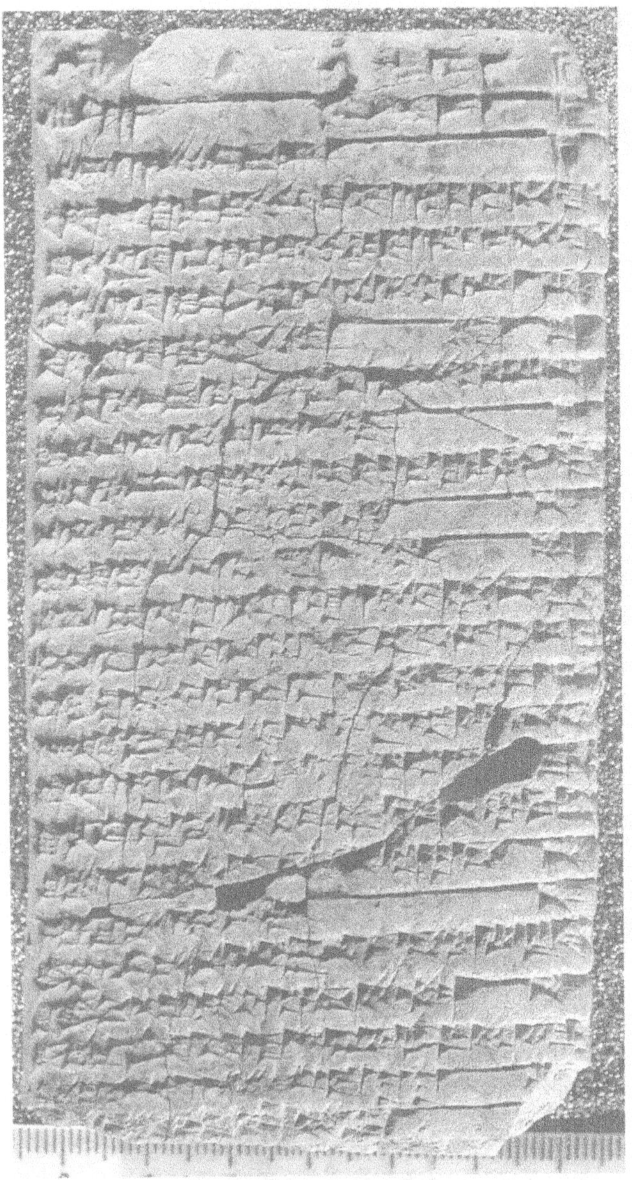

Schøyen 2.2788 obv.

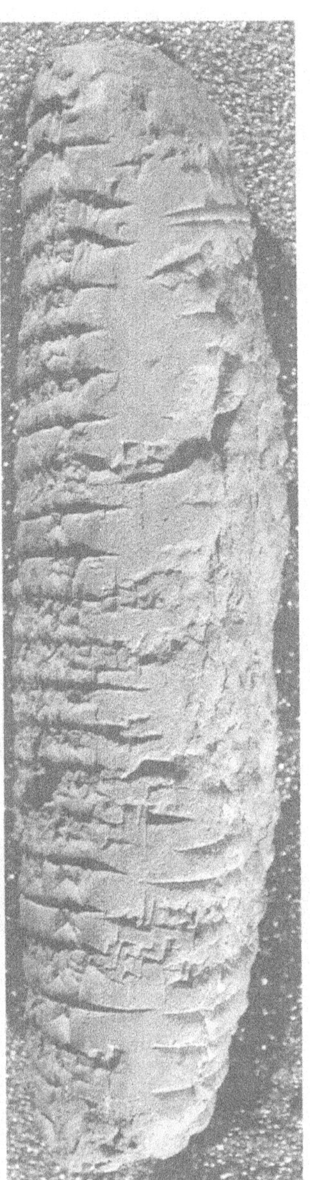

Schøyen 2.2788 right edge

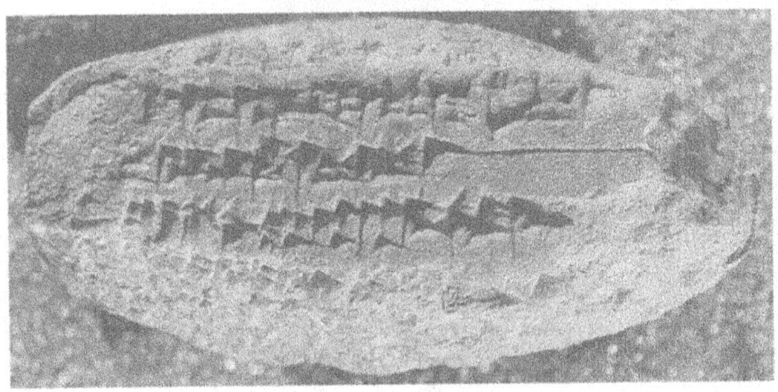

Schøyen 2.2788 bottom edge

Plate 61

Schøyen 2.2788 rev.

Schøyen 2.2788 left edge

Schøyen 9.3352 left edge

Schøyen 9.3352 obv.

❦ Plate 63 ❦

Schøyen 9.3352 rev.

Schøyen 9.3352 right edge

Schøyen 3366 obv.

Schøyen 3366 rev.

Schøyen 3366 obv left; rev. left

Schøyen 3366 rev. right

Plate 68

Schøyen 0.2291, obv., rev., left, right, top and bottom edges

Schøyen 0.2040, obv., rev., left, right, top and bottom edges

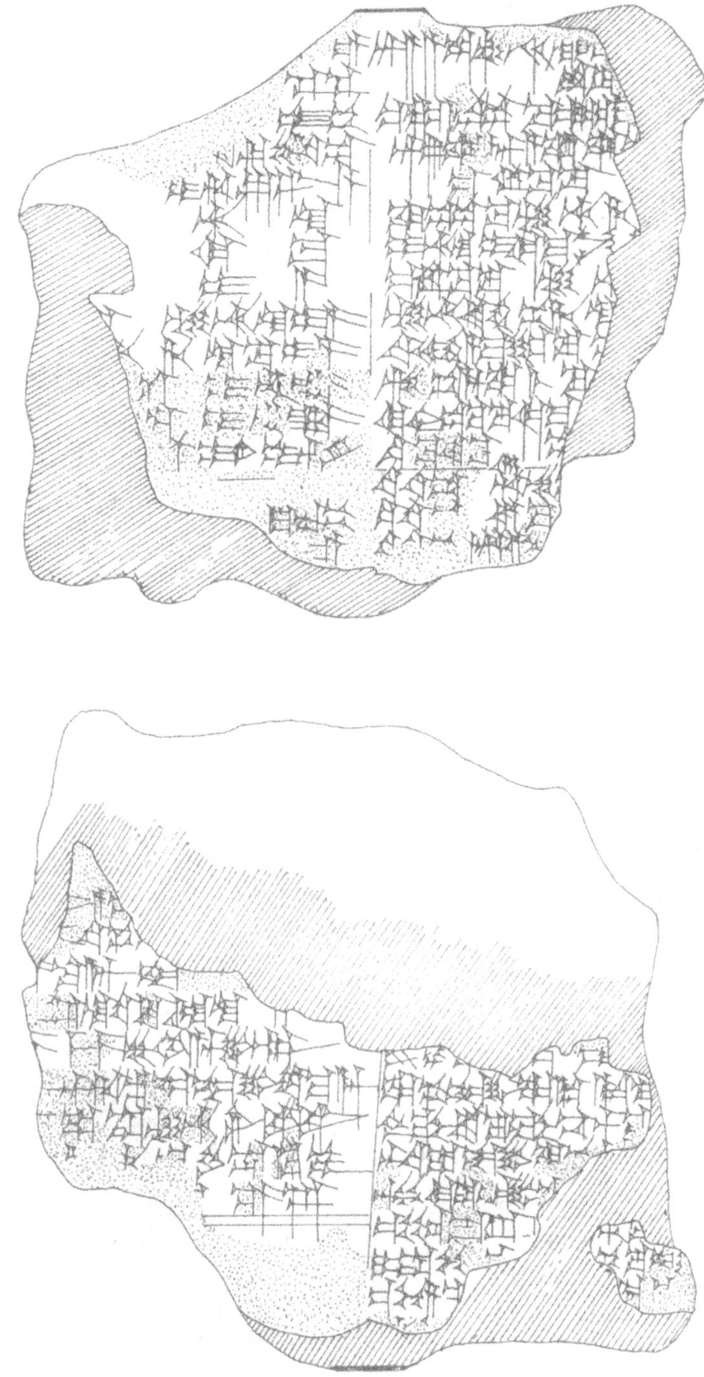

BM 80091

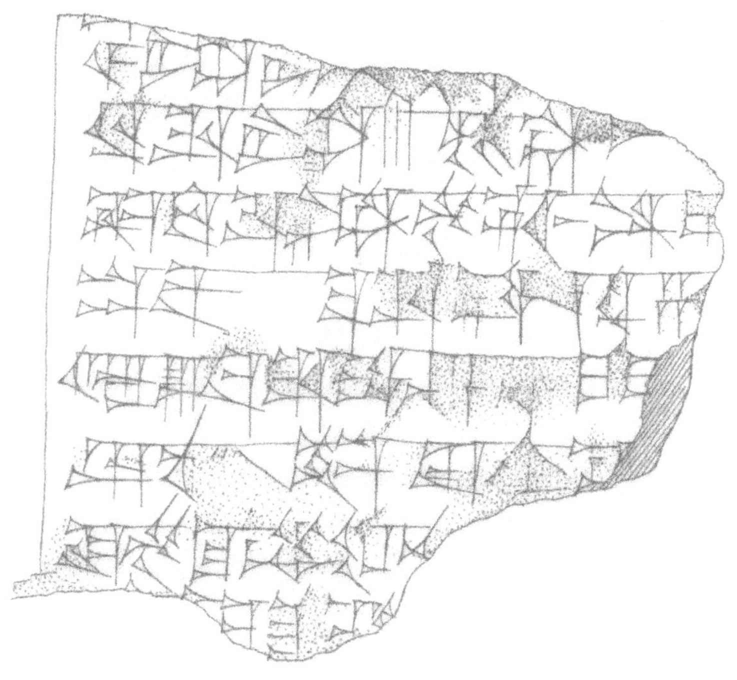

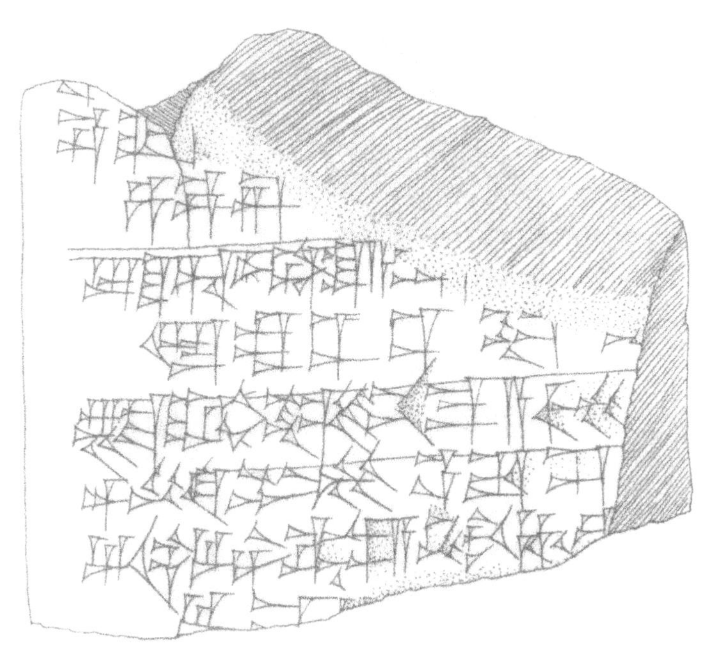

HS 1535

Plate 72

CBS 6930, obv.

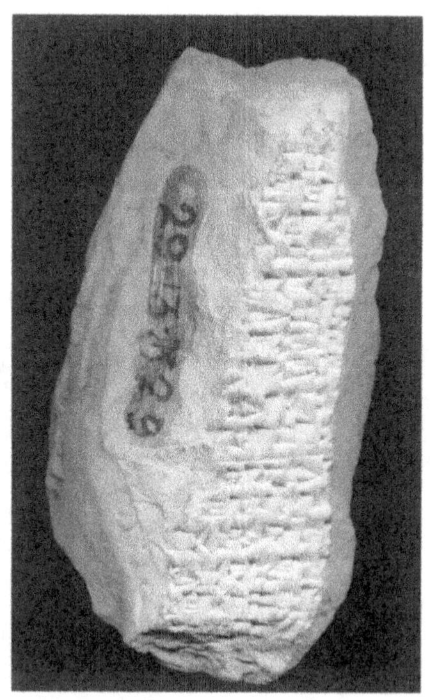

UM 29-13-329, obv.

www.ingramcontent.com/pod-product-compliance
Lightning Source LLC
Chambersburg PA
CBHW081141300726
48982CB00006B/1026
9781883053925